Research Handbook on Torture

Legal and Medical Perspectives on Prohibition and Prevention

Edited by

Malcolm D. Evans

Professor, University of Bristol Law School, UK

Jens Modvig

Director, Health department, DIGNITY – Danish Institute against Torture, Denmark

RESEARCH HANDBOOKS IN HUMAN RIGHTS

 Edward Elgar
PUBLISHING

Cheltenham, UK • Northampton, MA, USA

Published by
Edward Elgar Publishing Limited
The Lypiatts
15 Lansdown Road
Cheltenham
Glos GL50 2JA
UK

Edward Elgar Publishing, Inc.
William Pratt House
9 Dewey Court
Northampton
Massachusetts 01060
USA

A catalogue record for this book
is available from the British Library

Library of Congress Control Number: 2020948594

This book is available electronically in the **Elgar**online
Law subject collection
http://dx.doi.org/10.4337/9781788113960

ISBN 978 1 78811 395 3 (cased)
ISBN 978 1 78811 396 0 (eBook)

Printed and bound in Great Britain by TJ Books Limited, Padstow, Cornwall

Contents

List of contributors

Kirstine Amris, The Parker Institute, Copenhagen University Hospital, Denmark

Barbara Bernath, Secretary General, Association for the Prevention of Torture, Geneva, Switzerland

Christine Bicknell, Senior Lecturer in Law, University of Exeter, UK

Moritz Birk, Advocacy and Research Director, Amnesty International Austria

Richard Carver, Reader in Human Rights and Governance, Oxford Brookes University, UK

Robert Cryer, Professor of International and Criminal Law, University of Birmingham, UK and Extraordinary Professor of Law, University of the Free State, South Africa

Malcolm D. Evans, Professor of Public International Law, University of Bristol, UK

Michelle Farrell, Reader in Law, University of Liverpool, UK

Carla Ferstman, Senior Lecturer, University of Essex, UK

Felice Gaer, Director, Jacob Blaustein Institute for Human Rights, New York, USA

Yuval Ginbar, Legal Advisor, Amnesty International, UK

Claudio Grossman, Professor of Law and Dean Emeritus, American University Washington College of Law, USA

Lisa Handley, Visiting Researcher, Oxford Brookes University, UK

Christof Heyns, Professor of Human Rights Law, University of Pretoria, South Africa

Vincent Iacopino, Adjunct Professor of Medicine, Minnesota Medical School, USA

Steffen Jensen, Professor, Department of Politics and Society, Aalborg University, Denmark

Lester E Jones, Senior Lecturer, Singapore Institute of Technology

Tobias Kelly, Personal Chair of Political and Legal Anthropology, University of Edinburgh, UK

Morten Koch Andersen, Researcher, Center for Global Criminology, University of Copenhagen, Denmark

Juan E. Méndez, Professor of Human Rights Law in Residence, American University Washington College of Law, USA

Jens Modvig, Director, Health department, DIGNITY – Danish Institute against Torture, Denmark

Lorna McGregor, Professor of International Human Rights Law, University of Essex, UK

Lawrence Murugu Mute, Lecturer, School of Law, University of Nairobi and Member, United Nations Fund for Victims of Torture

Vivienne Nathanson, Member, UN Voluntary Fund for Victims of Torture, Switzerland

Andra Nicolescu, Advocacy and Legal Advisor, Association for the Prevention of Torture, Geneva, Switzerland

Manfred Nowak, Secretary General, Global Campus of Human Rights, Venice, Italy and Professor of International Human Rights, University of Vienna, Austria

Lutz Oette, Reader in International Law, SOAS, University of London, UK

Nimisha Patel, Professor of Psychology, University of East London, UK

Pau Pérez-Sales, Director, Postgraduate degree on Mental Health in Political Violence and Catastrophes, Complutense University of Madrid, Spain

Daniel du Plessis, University of Pretoria, South Africa

Matt Pollard, Senior Legal Advisor, International Commission of Jurists, Geneva, Switzerland

Tom Porteous, Deputy Programme Director, Human Rights Watch, Washington DC, USA

José Quiroga, Co-founder, Program for Victims of Torture, Los Angeles, USA

Diego Rodríguez-Pinzón, Professorial Lecturer in Residence, American University Washington College of Law, USA

Carmen Rueda, Human Rights Specialist, OHCHR, Geneva, Switzerland

Nora Sveaass, Professor of Psychology, University of Oslo, Norway

Amanda Williams, Clinical Reader, University College London, UK

Editors' preface

There are many works on the prohibition of torture, written from many different perspectives. It would be impossible to reflect all those perspectives in a single work and so, as explained in more detail in the introductory chapter, we have chosen to focus on the legal and medical dimensions of that prohibition. During the time of its writing, we have served as Chairs of the UN Committee against Torture and the UN Subcommittee for Prevention of Torture and so the collection inevitably has a particular focus on international action through the United Nations, but by no means exclusively so. A positive consequence of this is that those contributing to this work come from a broad range of countries as well as a wide array range of disciplines. This adds greatly to the breadth of perspectives offered and, rather than impose unnecessary and constraining uniformity, we have been happy to permit contributors to conform to their respective academic writing styles and conventions. All, however, conform to the common tradition of rigour and of insightful commentary and analysis – for which we are grateful.

We are also grateful to the authors for their patience with a project which has taken longer to come to fulfilment than they, in their initial enthusiasm, had intended. It would have taken much longer again but for the outstanding assistance and support which we received from Una Marquard-Busk, to whom we are immensely indebted. We are also very grateful indeed for the patience of the publisher – and can only hope that authors, publisher and readers will agree that the product has been worth the waiting. We believe it to be so.

Malcolm Evans and Jens Modvig
October 2020

1. Addressing torture: an introduction

Malcolm D Evans and Jens Modvig

Torture is a difficult word. Whilst casually used by some to describe things they do not like or do not enjoy, for others it recalls the extremes of human suffering and of indescribable pain, both mental and physical.[1] For some, that pain has been their own, whilst for others that pain has been the focus of their attention in many different ways, for example, as medical practitioners seeking to address the needs of victims through various means or as lawyers seeking to secure redress and hold those responsible to account. Civil society has been heavily engaged in shedding light upon the continued practice of torture, and the international community has been mobilised, through regional and international organisations – as well as through bilateral and other multilateral channels – to address the continuing evil of torture in the contemporary world.

There remains, however, a deep-seated ambiguity concerning responses to torture. The moral opprobrium which attaches to torture – sometimes described as the 'special stigma'[2] – is such as to seemingly mark it out as amongst the most forbidden of practices. The 1984 United Nations Convention against Torture makes it clear that 'No exceptional circumstances whatsoever, whether a state of war or a threat of war, internal political instability or any other public emergency, may be invoked as a justification of torture'.[3] Indeed, in the language of the international lawyer, the prohibition of torture is recognised as being a norm of 'ius cogens'[4] – a prohibition which overrides any other legal obligations which a state might have. Yet the reality is that torture remains widely practised, and, even if not always condoned, is all too often the subject of justification by those who have resort to it. The second chapter in this collection, by Michelle Farrell, explores the arguments of those who suggest that terrible times can justify the commission of terrible crimes, and in particular the torture of those who might be in possession of information which, if discovered, might save the lives of others. The enduring appeal of this argument, despite the evidence that it is fundamentally misconceived, requires that it be addressed at the outset.

If the appeal to necessity is shown to be false, it becomes necessary to consider whether it is possible to take steps to combat the continued prevalence of torture. In many ways, this is the leitmotif of this Handbook, as it seeks to explore various dimensions of contemporary responses to torture. Can this ever be successful? Clearly, attending to the medical, psychological and social needs of victims can yield its own successes (though the impacts of torture on its victims are often enduring – indeed, lifelong); likewise, the prosecution and punishment

---

[1]   See generally Scarry, E (1985) *The Body in Pain* (Oxford University Press).
[2]   See, for example, *Ireland v the United Kingdom*, 18 January 1978, Series A no 25, para 167; *Selmouni v France* [GC], no 25803/94, ECHR 1999-V, para 96 and many others.
[3]   Convention against Torture and Other Cruel, Inhuman or Degrading Treatment or Punishment (adopted 10 December 1984, entered into force 26 June 1987) 1465 UNTS 85, Article 2(2).
[4]   *Jurisdictional Immunities of the State (Germany v Italy: Greece Intervening), Judgment of 3 February 2012, ICJ Reports 2012*, p 99, para 99.

of perpetrators. But is it possible to stop torture from happening in the first place? The third chapter of this book, by Richard Carver and Lisa Handley, drawing on the fruits of the most extensive research yet conducted into the efficacy of preventive methodologies, seeks to show that it is. The challenge, then, is to bring this about. Before doing so, however, the third chapter offers a timely reminder that there is a great deal more to the practice of torture than its use in extreme situations, or, indeed, in routine detention. Tobias Kelly, Steffen Jensen and Morten Koch Andersen cause us to reflect on other factors which feed the prevalence of torture, and which concern the vulnerability of marginal communities and the inequalities and corruptions which characterise so many countries and so many systems and places of detention.

As these chapters demonstrate, there are many dimensions to, and perspectives on, the question of addressing torture, both substantively and methodologically. No one approach, or combination of approaches, can make any valid claim for priority, let alone exclusivity. This permits a Handbook of this nature to surmount what might otherwise have been a near-insuperable problem: how to tackle the subject, and with what focuses? The only 'right' answer to this conundrum is to accept that no single work can satisfactorily engage with the issues which torture presents. Rather than seek to justify its approach in the face of competing alternatives, this Handbook simply embraces its potential to contribute towards an understanding of the responses to torture in the 21st century. It claims to be neither comprehensive nor definitive.

It does, however, claim to draw on the experiences of the editors and authors of this introduction, who at the time of writing occupy the positions of Chair of the UN Committee against Torture (Jens Modvig), established by the UN Convention against Torture,[5] and Chair of the UN Subcommittee on Prevention of Torture (Malcolm Evans), established by the Optional Protocol to the UN Convention against Torture.[6] This unique collaboration between the Chairs of the two bodies established by the global community by means of internationally legally binding treaties immediately defines its approach and frame of reference, and does so unashamedly. It is an approach founded on the prohibition of torture and cruel, inhuman and degrading treatment and punishment as a matter of international human rights law, and reflects the authors' personal expertise, which they bring to its realisation, in the fields of medicine and of international law.

Against this background, the logic of this Handbook becomes self-evident. A first set of chapters explore aspects of the protections from torture established through international law, followed by a second set of chapters which explore both the phenomenon of torture and responses to it from a medical perspective. Chapter 5, by Moritz Birk and Manfred Nowak (a former UN Special Rapporteur on Torture) present a 'tour de horizon' of the prohibition of torture in its many dimensions, both procedural and substantive. This is followed by a series of chapters which look in further detail at the work of bodies established within the UN system which have a particular focus on torture. Chapter 6, by Christof Heyns, Carmen Rueda and Daniel du Plessis, looks at the work of the UN Human Rights Committee (of which Christof Heyns is a member) concerning Articles 7 and 10 of the International Covenant on Civil and

---

[5] Convention against Torture and Other Cruel, Inhuman or Degrading Treatment or Punishment (n 3 above).

[6] Optional Protocol to the Convention against Torture and Other Cruel, Inhuman or Degrading Treatment or Punishment (adopted 18 December 2002, entered into force 22 June 2006) 2375 UNTS 237.

Political Rights[7] which set out the prohibition of torture and ill-treatment within the framework of the 'UN Bill of Rights'. This is followed in Chapter 7 by a detailed examination of the work of the UN Committee against Torture by Felice Gear, who was a member of this body for 20 years. This is a particularly interesting as well as important Committee, combining as it does the tools of both international human rights protection, through the use of reporting, communication and inquiry procedures, with the oversight of Convention obligations concerning the establishment of torture as a transnational crime open to domestic prosecution by any state party.

Of course, treaties only bind states parties – and although today there are approaching 170 states parties to the Convention against Torture, it was not always thus, and there are a considerable number of states who are still outside of its system. However, they are not beyond the reach of UN mechanisms, and Chapter 8 looks in detail at the mandate of the UN Special Rapporteur on Torture, one of the oldest of the Special Procedures of the UN Human Rights Council (and of the Commission on Human Rights before it). This is written by Juan Mendez – a former Special Rapporteur himself – and Andra Nicolescu, who amply demonstrate both the power and the reach, but also the limitations, of that mandate and how it sits alongside those other bodies within the UN system which have previously been considered.

Of course, international legal prohibitions on torture do not exist only at the level of the UN: each of the principal regional systems for human rights protection also have mechanisms whose work needs to be explored. To this end, Chapter 9, by Christine Bicknell, gives an overview of various mechanisms operating within the European space which address questions of torture, and of torture prevention. Whilst this naturally includes the various bodies and mechanisms established under the auspices of the Council of Europe, and in particular the European Convention on Human Rights[8] and the European Convention for the Prevention of Torture,[9] it also looks at the work of the European Union and touches on that of the Organisation on Security and Cooperation in Europe too. Chapter 10 pursues the regional approach, with Diego Rodríguez-Pinzón, currently a member of the UN Committee against Torture, introducing the architecture and jurisprudence of the system of protection established by the Organization of American States, through both its Charter[10] and the Inter-American Convention on Human Rights.[11] Particular attention is paid to the innovative jurisprudence developed within the system concerning awards of interim measures, which can play a vital role in both protecting potential victims, staying abusive practices and bringing those responsible to justice. This set of chapters focusing on regional approaches is completed by a chapter looking at the African Charter on Human and Peoples' Rights,[12] and other bodies working within the framework of

---

[7]   International Covenant on Civil and Political Rights (adopted 16 December 1966, entered into force 23 March 1976) 999 UNTS 171.

[8]   European Convention for the Protection of Human Rights and Fundamental Freedoms (ECHR) (adopted 4 November 1950, entered into force 3 September 1953) ETS no 5.

[9]   European Convention for the Prevention of Torture and Inhuman or Degrading Treatment or Punishment (adopted 26 November 1987, entered into force 1 February 1989) ETS no 126.

[10]   Charter of the Organization of American States (1948), Treaty no A-41, OAS Treaty Series nos 1C and 61, Article 53.

[11]   American Convention on Human Rights (adopted 22 November 1969, entered into force 16 July 1978), Treaty no B-32, OAS Treaty Series no 36.

[12]   African Charter on Human and Peoples' Rights (adopted 27 June 1981, entered into force 21 October 1986), OAU Doc CAB/LEG/67/3 rev. 5.

the African Union, by Lawrence Mute, himself a former member of the African Commission on Human and Peoples' Rights and Chair of the Committee for the Prevention of Torture in Africa. Once again, this chapter highlights distinctive aspects of the regional protective system, including its focus on promotional work, and the distinctive manner in which its jurisprudence is developing.

The primary focus of all of these chapters has been on the work of these various bodies established by international and regional treaties and organisations to help ensure that states comply with their obligation under international human rights law that 'no one shall be subjected to torture or to cruel, inhuman or degrading treatment or punishment'.[13] Commonly referred to as reflecting the 'prohibition' of torture, this wording in fact goes further: it requires that not only should such actions be 'prohibited', in the sense that they are to be forbidden, but that 'no one shall be subjected' to such actions. This underlines the often-overlooked point that it is not enough that those responsible for torture be held to account, and victims supported: the obligation is that such actions should not occur at all.

From the point of view of the individual perpetrator, the prohibition means that their actions are wrongful and must be the subject of punishment. For the 'perpetrator state' (which cannot be held criminally responsible or 'punished' in the same manner as an individual), it means that they can be held to have been in breach of their obligations and must provide redress (in its several dimensions). From the point of view of the victim, however, the 'prohibition' of torture takes on a very different hue: the obligation of states is that 'no one shall be subjected' to such ill-treatment – and this requires that protections be in placed which seek to ensure that this is so. Whilst there is truth in the old adage that 'prevention is better than cure', from a victim perspective it should not be a question of 'choice': if the obligation is properly realised then there should be nothing to 'cure', since the ill-treatment will not have happened. This leads us to the 'preventive' dimension of the international response to torture. Article 2 of the UN Convention against Torture expressly requires states to take steps to prevent torture and ill-treatment from occurring,[14] and the Committee against Torture has spelt out the implications of this at some length in its General Comment on the subject.[15]

In their own ways, all the work surveyed in the chapters of this book contribute to the prevention of torture and the realisation of its prohibition. However, just as distinct methodologies have emerged for scrutinising the compliance of states with their international obligations (for example, through reporting processes), of challenging the conduct of states, their agents and those for whom they are responsible through international processes for their actions in specific cases, and of holding individuals personally to account at a national level through the application of criminal civil law processes, so also have specific methodologies of prevention emerged. In Chapter 12 Malcolm Evans explores the emergence of preventive visiting as a discrete preventive methodology and looks at the work of the European Committee for the Prevention of Torture,[16] of the UN Subcommittee for Prevention of Torture[17] (of which he is

---

[13]   Universal Declaration of Human Rights, UNGA Res 217A (III) (adopted 10 December 1948), Article 5.
[14]   Article 2(1) provides that 'Each State Party shall take effective legislative, administrative, judicial or other measures to prevent acts of torture in any territory under its jurisdiction'.
[15]   UN Committee Against Torture, General Comment no 2, Implementation of Article 2 by States parties, UN Doc CAT/C/GC/2 (24 January 2008).
[16]   Established by the European Convention for the Prevention of Torture (n 9 above).
[17]   Established by the Optional Protocol to the UN Convention against Torture (n 6 above).

currently Chair) and of the domestic-level 'National Preventive Mechanisms'[18] which have been established to undertake preventive work based on visits to closed institutions.

Having looked at the 'preventive' response to torture, the next set of chapters move to aspects of the criminal law responses – which, as has been seen, are expressly called for by the UN Convention against Torture. Chapter 13, by Robert Cryer, sets out the parameters of the criminal law response by the international community. Whilst the UN Convention calls on states to make torture a criminal offence in domestic legal systems, he points to the fact that it has not yet been rendered an international crime as such. Rather, torture is recognised as an element of other international crimes, such as war crimes, crimes against humanity and genocide. Because of the way in which it 'sits' within these more generally framed international crimes, what 'amounts' to torture may vary from case to case – and it is certainly true that much of what is torture for the purposes of international human rights law falls beyond the scope of international criminal law itself. As a result, one must look to domestic jurisdictions to take up the burden of holding many perpetrators to account.

Domestic systems have other responsibilities which flow from the UN Convention in addition to that of prosecuting those suspected of torture. A first concerns the use of evidence. Article 15 of the UN Convention prohibits the use of statements made as a result of torture being used in criminal proceedings.[19] By removing what is often thought to be a key 'incentive' to torture (particularly in legal systems which place a strong emphasis on confession-based evidence), this forms a vital element of the architecture of both prevention and of ensuring the integrity of the criminal justice system. The contours of the Article 15 prohibition are, however, opaque – and in Chapter 14, Matt Pollard explores its parameters in order to better understand its meaning and practical application. Another key element of the preventive architecture of the Convention is Article 3(1), which prohibits the return of a person to a state where they might face the risk of torture[20] and this is explored by Carla Ferstman in Chapter 15. This has proven to be one of the most fertile areas of activity for the Committee against Torture, which receives many claims concerning individuals who are challenging their removal,[21] and domestic courts are playing an increasingly important role in ensuring that individuals are not placed in situations of risk.

But despite such safeguards, torture still takes place and perpetrators must be held to account. Since torture is so often undertaken by state officials, or is tolerated by them, there is often a reluctance to bring criminal charges against those responsible, despite the clear obligations in the UN Convention to do so. However, and as was emphasised in Chapter 13,

---

[18] Designated as such in accordance with the Optional Protocol to the UN Convention against Torture (n 6 above), Articles 17–23.

[19] Article 15 provides that 'Each State Party shall ensure that any statement which is established to have been made as a result of torture shall not be invoked as evidence in any proceedings, except against a person accused of torture as evidence that the statement was made'.

[20] Article 3(1) provides that 'No State Party shall expel, return ("refouler") or extradite a person to another State where there are substantial grounds for believing that he would be in danger of being subjected to torture'.

[21] The Committee Against Torture has also issued two General Comments concerning Article 3. See UN Committee Against Torture, General Comment no 1: Implementation of article 3 of the Convention in the context of article 22, UN Doc A/53/44 Annex IX, 16 September 1998; UN Committee Against Torture, General Comment no 4 (2017) on the Implementation of article 3 of the Convention in the context of article 22, UN Doc CAT/C/GC/4, 4 September 2018.

doing so has been greatly assisted by the recognition that torture, even if it is not an 'international' crime, is a 'transnational crime' over which a multiplicity of domestic jurisdictions might exercise jurisdiction. Indeed, through the UN Convention against Torture, it has become generally accepted that states may extend their domestic jurisdiction so that anyone who commits an act of torture – anywhere, and against anyone – can be prosecuted before their courts, thus rendering torture one of the most 'transnational' of crimes and attracting universal jurisdiction,[22] the most expansive form of jurisdiction which domestic courts can exercise, and reserved for the most heinous of crimes. This is explored by Lutz Oette in Chapter 16, who also highlights the many practical hurdles which still stand in the way of effectively using extraterritorial jurisdiction more generally, as well as universal jurisdiction in particular. Such practical barriers further support the need for complementary means of redress. Indeed, there may be many reasons why a criminal prosecution may fail, but that does not mean there is not sufficient evidence to ground a civil prosecution. This chapter therefore also examines the rise – and some might argue, fall – of transnational civil claims, in particular under the US Alien Tort Claims Act,[23] which, for a period, appeared to offer a powerful route through which to provide recognition and redress for victims.

A final topic in this area, which is considered by Lorna McGregor in Chapter 17, again concerns barriers to redress, in this case, that of the immunity that attracts to states and state agents from proceedings before domestic courts. Given that under Article 1 of the UN Convention, torture is by definition an act of, or an act committed with the toleration or acquiescence of, a public official,[24] immunity presents a powerful hurdle to the exercise of both criminal and civil jurisdiction, should it be asserted. This is a complex area of law – not made any easier by the assertion by the International Court of Justice that 'immunity' does not imply 'impunity'.[25] Whilst doubtless true in theory, in practice immunity often does indeed result in impunity – and the promise held out by the prohibition of torture is, as a result, stunted or thwarted.

In combination, these chapters demonstrate both the power of the international condemnation of torture and of its reflection in law. They also show the strengths – and weaknesses – of the multifarious and multi-faceted legal and political instruments, bodies and processes which have been established at international, regional and domestic levels to address it. They also highlight the opportunities for further positive development, as well as charting some regrettable weakening of protections. Taken as a whole, they aim to give a realistic 'feel' for how the international community has sought to tackle torture through the mechanisms of international law. They do not, however, claim to be comprehensive, nor do they seek to support a claim

---

[22]   As recognised by the International Court of Justice in *Jurisdictional Immunities of the State (Germany v Italy: Greece Intervening), Judgment of 3 February 2012* (n 4 above), para 74.

[23]   Alien Tort Statute, 28 USC § 1350 of 1789 and see also the Torture Victim Protection Act of 1991, 28 USC § 1350.

[24]   Article 1(1) provides that 'For the purposes of this Convention, the term "torture" means any act by which severe pain or suffering, whether physical or mental, is intentionally inflicted on a person for such purposes as obtaining from him or a third person information or a confession, punishing him for an act he or a third person has committed or is suspected of having committed, or intimidating or coercing him or a third person, or for any reason based on discrimination of any kind, when such pain or suffering is inflicted by or at the instigation of or with the consent or acquiescence of a public official or other person acting in an official capacity. It does not include pain or suffering arising only from, inherent in or incidental to lawful sanctions.'

[25]   See *Arrest Warrant of 11 April 2000 (Democratic Republic of Congo v Belgium), Preliminary Objections and Merits, Judgment, ICJ Reports 2002*, p 3, para 60.

that the law – and the lawyers – hold the keys to an understanding of torture, and how it is to be addressed. That becomes even clearer as the collection turns to a second tranche of contributions, which explore medical perspectives and approaches to torture.

Chapter 18, by Vivienne Nathanson (and currently Chair of the UN Voluntary Fund for Victims of Torture) explores the ethical implications of the prohibition of torture, charting the increasing number of declarations by the World Medical Association and others developed in the light of the evolving understandings of the role of the medical profession. This is followed by José Quiroga and Jens Modvig (currently Chair of the UN Committee against Torture) considering in Chapter 19 the various ways in which torture can be categorised, and, using a typology based upon the mechanisms for the infliction of pain or suffering, they set out various methods of torture which remain prevalent today. In addition to describing such methods, this chapter carefully considers their various health impacts, emphasising not only the extent of the harm which torture can cause, but also the range of harms which need to be identified and addressed. Indeed, the inter-relatedness of the various forms of harm which might result from different kinds of torture lies at the heart of Chapter 20, in which Pau Pérez-Sales examines in detail the concept of psychological torture. The chapter highlights how physical pain can be harnessed as an element of mental trauma, thus breaking down what for some is a 'hard' distinction between torture as the imposition of bodily pain and torture understood in terms of mental suffering.

The theme of interconnectedness also lies at the heart of Chapter 21, by Vincent Iacopino, though in a rather different way. It reaches across the primary disciplinary focuses of this Handbook by considering the seminal document, the Istanbul Protocol.[26] First adopted in 1999 and recently updated and in part revised, the Istanbul Protocol addresses the documentation of torture. This is a very important topic, not only because it is vital to ensure the proper identification of the forms of torture from which a person has suffered in order to ensure they are most effectively treated and helped, but also to provide the evidence necessary to support the prosecution of those responsible for that torture. The timely and effective documentation of torture is vital if investigative and criminal law processes are to be effective means of holding perpetrators to account and, through this, to contribute to the realisation of the legal prohibition.

If Chapter 21 shows how the work of medical practitioners can contribute to the effectiveness of legal responses to torture, then Chapter 22 shows how the outputs of the legal mechanisms can assist the medical professionals in their work by looking at how Article 14 of the UN Convention against Torture has been understood and interpreted to further the rehabilitation of torture victims. Appropriately enough, it is written by three former members of the Committee against Torture who were instrumental in the drafting of its General Comment no 3,[27] Nora Sveaass (who is currently a member of the UN Subcommittee for Prevention of Torture), Felice Gaer and Claudio Grossman, whose areas of expertise – again, appropriately enough – span both the legal and medical spheres. This exemplifies the constructive manner in which insights gained from one disciplinary perspective can be harnessed in order to enhance

---

[26]   *Istanbul Protocol: Manual on the Effective Investigation and Documentation of Torture and Other Cruel, Inhuman or Degrading Treatment or Punishment*, UN Doc HR/P/PT/8/Rev.1, (2004).

[27]   UN Committee Against Torture, General Comment no 3: Implementation of article 14 by States parties, UN Doc CAT/C/GC/3 (19 November 2012).

the contribution that can be made to the fight against torture by others: true complementarity, rather than competition.

Implicit in this is the need for different disciplinary perspectives to be challenged by the insights and understandings of others, in order to allow them to consider whether, and how, they might best respond. In that spirit, Chapter 23, by Nimisha Patel, broadens the horizon concerning the impact of torture and its 'ripples of harm', considering not only 'traditional' therapeutic interventions by clinicians focused on the medical needs of the victim or survivor, but also the broader social dimensions of the impact of torture. These include impacts not only on the victims or survivors themselves but also on their families and broader communities. The chapter highlights the roles which can be played by those broader networks in the structuring and delivery of psychological care – which in turn sheds light on the significance of the innovative approach to remedies developed particularly within the Inter-American human rights system and which focus on community recognition and reconciliation. Again, there is much here which explains the practical potency of what to a more traditionally oriented legal mind might appear somewhat unorthodox. Above all, however, the chapter highlights the need to pay more attention to what victims and survivors want, rather than what others (both the medically and legally trained) might believe that they need.

The necessity for further understanding is also a feature of Chapter 24, by Kirstine Amris, Lester E Jones and Amanda Williams, which considers what for many remains a central question in the treatment of torture survivors – the alleviation of pain in the aftermath of torture. Enough has been said already to make it clear that this is a multi-dimensional topic, one that is not limited to 'healing' in a purely physical sense, but which encompasses the restoration of the person as a whole. As a result, the complexities regarding how pain is experienced need to be understood if it is to be properly alleviated over time – which again challenges some traditional ideas concerning legal 'remedies' and what counts as 'reparation'. Above all, the subjective nature of the experience of pain is highlighted – which once again serves to put the individual at the heart of the response.

Of course, for the victim, torture is a personal, subjective experience. But it is also a matter of societal concern, at all levels of society. Once again, it is not a question of 'either'/'or'; of a victim-centred approach or a societal response to wrongs to the person. It is about drawing these, and other, perspectives together in order to address torture in all its dimensions and complexities. Torture is not only a 'lived' reality for its victims: its very presence becomes a reality for the systems, structures and societies in which it exists, and which must also find their own responses to that reality. You do not need to be a torture victim to live under the threat, or the shadow, of torture – although, perhaps, in some ways that very threat, or shadow, may make one a form of victim in itself. It is, then, appropriate for the book to conclude with a series of short chapters comprising reflections by authors drawing on their experiences when working for NGOs concerning the reality of torture in the world today, in all its complexities. In Chapter 25, Yuval Ginbar sets out the experiences of three torture victims, in very different contexts but united by the enduring truths that underpin their suffering. In Chapter 26 Tom Porteus reflects on the propensity of so many states to continue to resort to torture, despite its absolute prohibition. This is a disquieting reality which is met by the final reflections of Barbara Bernath in Chapter 27 on the need for vigilance in pursuit of prevention, and highlighting the continuing need to challenge the positive portrayals of torture which are all too often to be found in populist culture, literature and media.

Taken together, these reflections serve to remind us why – after so many years of official opprobrium – there is a need to intensity efforts to make the prohibition of torture what it should be – absolute.[28]

---

[28]   Mirroring the words of Sir Nigel Rodley, former UN Special Rapporteur on Torture and member of the UN Human Rights Committee in the title of his article 'The Prohibition of Torture: Absolute Means Absolute' (2006) 34 Denver Journal of International Law and Policy 145–160.

2. The ticking bomb scenario: evaluating torture as an interrogation method

Michelle Farrell[1]

INTRODUCTION

> '... all these prisoners who have been tied up and "interrogated"...'[2]

Whilst there are numerous adaptations of the ticking bomb scenario,[3] the construct generally refers to a hypothetical situation in which an individual has been detained and the authorities believe, or are certain, that the individual has the information to prevent an impending attack which will kill or injure many people. The individual is unwilling to disclose the information in interrogation. The authorities believe that the information can be obtained through torture. The hypothetical asks, in such a scenario, is it justifiable to torture the individual in order to save lives?[4]

Revived by the events of 11 September, the ticking bomb scenario and the related question of torture as a method of interrogation have become ubiquitous in public and academic debate.[5] These debates should not be treated lightly. This discussion ought to give rise to considerable unease. My sense of unease is twofold. First, writing about this issue at all is unsettling. Why are we giving so much attention to the ticking bomb scenario whilst others are undertaking the urgent task of thinking about how to enforce the prohibition on torture, or of working to prevent torture, and to protect and treat victims? It is also a troubling prospect that engaging in this debate breathes life into a topic that should be left to smoulder and be smothered in the ruins of the 'war on terror'.

This uneasiness is accompanied by a background anxiety about the impossibility of foreclosing arguments, thereby preventing them from being exploited by those ready for a 'debate', or worse, by those who advocate for torture. Rodley, in this regard, recognised the pitfalls in defining torture very narrowly or prescriptively, thus playing into the hands of states

---

[1] I would like to thank Robert Knox, Thomas Beaumont, Kathleen Cavanaugh, Elvira Dominguez-Redondo, Mike Gordon and Helen Stalford for extremely useful, thoughtful and provocative comments on drafts of this chapter. I also owe special thanks to the editors of this collection for their support. In particular, I would like to thank Malcolm Evans for extensive and productive comments as the work progressed.

[2] Césaire, A (Joan Pinkham trans), *Discourse on Colonialism* (Monthly Review Press, 2000), 35.

[3] For a collection of the various ticking bomb scenarios which have been proffered in the literature, see Ginbar, Y, *Why Not Torture Terrorists? Moral, Practical, and Legal Aspects of the 'Ticking Bomb' Justification for Torture* (Oxford University Press, 2008), 379–386.

[4] Farrell, M, The Prohibition on Torture in Exceptional Circumstances (Cambridge University Press, 2013), 7.

[5] The geography of this debate is important. Sometimes described as a global debate, it is more accurate to describe it as quite geographically limited, particularly to the United States, and, to a lesser extent, to so-called Western countries including the United Kingdom, Germany, Australia and Israel.

and torturers eager to evade the ban. 'It is obvious', he argued, 'that a juridical definition cannot depend upon a catalogue of horrific practices; for it to do so would simply provide a challenge to the ingenuity of the torturers, not a viable legal prohibition'.[6] The euphemism of the Bush administration – 'enhanced interrogation' – and the 'ingenuity' of those who manipulated legal discussion of practices of torture and inhuman and degrading treatment, gave very concrete expression to Rodley's concern.[7]

Shue provides an even more approximate expression of my own worry in the opening paragraph of his 1978 article *Torture*:

> Whatever one may have to say about torture, there appear to be moral reasons for not saying it. Obviously, I am not persuaded by these reasons but they deserve some mention. Mostly they add up to a sort of Pandora's box objection. If practically everyone is opposed to all torture, why bring it up, start people thinking about it, and risk weakening the inhibitions against what is clearly a terrible business.[8]

Shue was right to recognise that Pandora's box was already open. In 2006, however, he readdressed some of his own earlier arguments about interrogational torture in 'rarefied situations'.[9] He reaffirmed his position that 'artificial cases make bad ethics'[10] but then emphasised how the ticking bomb scenario misleads through 'idealisation and abstraction'.[11] The timing of his 2006 article no doubt reflected the fact that abstract musings on torture had proved attractive (his own and the abundant writing of others); advocates were relying all too heavily on the ticking bomb scenario and ignoring his clear direction that the hypothetical 'assumed untenable circumstances and background conditions'.[12] It also seems likely, though, that he must have lamented how the residual ambiguity of his own examination of interrogational torture – his sense of 'the permissibility of torture in a [ticking bomb scenario] *just like this*' –[13] had been interpreted and had fed in to debates since 1978.[14] His two articles caution against

---

[6] Rodley, NS, *The Treatment of Prisoners under International Law* 2nd edn (Oxford University Press, 1999).

[7] This is particularly the case as the Bush administration's so-called 'torture memos', which gave birth to the enhanced interrogation programme, relied in part on an assessment which compared and contrasted its methods with the 'five techniques' that were central to the infamous 1978 European Court of Human Rights case of *Ireland v United Kingdom*. See, Jay S Bybee, Memorandum for Alberto R. Gonzales, 'Standards of Conduct for Interrogation under 18 U.S.C. §§ 2340–2340A, 1 August 2002, cited in Greenberg, K and Dratel, J (eds), *The Torture Papers: The Road to Abu Ghraib* (Cambridge University Press, 2004), 172, 173, 196–198; Waldron, J, *Torture, Terror and Trade-Offs: Philosophy for the White House* (Oxford University Press, 2010), 209–210; Farrell, M, 'Transatlantic Torture and the Regrettable Role of the European Court of Human Rights', *The Liverpool View* (12 December 2014) available at https://news.liverpool.ac.uk/2014/12/12/liverpool-view-transatlantic-torture-regrettable-role -european-court-human-rights/

[8] Shue, H, 'Torture' (1978) *Philosophy and Public Affairs* 124.

[9] *Ibid*, 143.

[10] *Ibid*, 141.

[11] Shue, S, 'Torture in Dreamland: Disposing of the Ticking Bomb' (2006) 37 *Case Western Reserve Journal of International Law* 231.

[12] Farrell (n 4 above), 106.

[13] Shue (n 8 above), 141

[14] Shue (n 11 above), 231.

discussing and debating torture in hypothetical scenarios as though those scenarios correlate with, or represent, the realities of the practice of torture.[15]

Torture was then, and is now, practised widely. It continues to be concealed and denied; in some cases, it is justified publicly with reference to necessity, ticking bombs or an equivalent defence. Whatever the academic value of debate, legal, moral or philosophical rubberstamping is a questionable response to the practice of torture; the provision of legal, ethical or philosophical firepower to states who need no help hypocritically upholding their normative commitment to the ban whilst denying or justifying their practice of torture may indeed be moral reason not to say 'whatever one may have to say about torture'.[16] The lesson is to try to understand torture in practice, not to accept the justifications of states and perpetrators and not to engage in abstract hypothesising.

It is frustrating that so much attention is given to the category of so-called 'interrogational torture' and to the hypothetical scenarios that underpin this category. We remain far from understanding torture. In recent years, the field has been conditioned by the appeal of Hollywood, the heroic, life-saving, remorseful, good guy who had no choice but to strong arm the bad guy.[17] Beyond the screen, and the ivory tower, the histories of torture are piled up, packed with reality. As Wolcher so neatly put it, the ticking bomb scenario 'threatens to lead us into a sort of bad infinity where we keep on overlooking instances of actual torture in order to take notice of the sort of "torture" that only occurs inside works of fiction'.[18]

The waning of the post-11 September torture debate stymied, though certainly did not stop,[19] the production of interventions on the ticking bomb scenario,[20] facilitating, perhaps,

---

[15] Farrell (n 4 above), 24 citing Rejali, D, *Torture and Democracy* (Princeton University Press, 2007), 547.

[16] See Shue (n 8 above).

[17] For a discussion of the representation of torture in the aftermath of 11 September 2001, see Buescher, B, 'Exceptional Torture: Torture Imagery as Neocolonial Rhetoric' in Schwartz-DuPré, RL (ed), *Communicating Colonialism: Readings on Postcolonial Theory(s) and Communications* (Peter Lang, 2014), 128.

[18] Wolcher, L, 'Foreword' in Farrell (n 4 above), xi.

[19] Proving the point that the ticking bomb torture debate is metastatic, the Human Rights Law Review has hosted a number of articles discussing the absolute nature of the prohibition against torture, precipitated by Greer's reading of the European Court of Human Rights case of *Gäfgen v Germany* as demonstrating the 'virtually' absolute nature of the prohibition, except in the 'rarest circumstances'. Greer, S, 'Should Police Threats to Torture Suspects Always be Severely Punished? Reflections on the Gäfgen Case' (2011) 11 *Human Rights Law Review* 67; Greer, S, 'Is the Prohibition against Torture, Cruel, Inhuman and Degrading Treatment Really "Absolute" in International Human Rights Law?' (2015) 15 *Human Rights Law Review* 101. These articles have generated thoughtful responses. In particular, Mavronicola rebuts the fictive idea that there is a rights conflict, manifested, as Greer attempts to argue, in cases such as *Gäfgen*, where, he argues, a kidnap victim's rights should trump those of an unforthcoming suspect. Mavronicola, N, 'Is the Prohibition against Torture and Cruel, Inhuman and Degrading Treatment Absolute in International Human Rights Law: A Reply to Steven Greer' (2017) 17 *Human Rights Law Review* 479. See also, Mavronicola, N, 'Torture and Othering' in Goold, B and Lazarus, L (eds), *Security and Human Rights*, 2nd edn (Hart Publishing, 2019), 27, 31 where she shows that Greer has 'miscast the issue and glossed over important aspects' in confusing the legal reality of rights in conflict. See also, Graffin, N, '*Gäfgen v. Germany*, the Use of Threats and the Punishment of those who Ill-treat during Police Interrogation: A Reply to Steven Greer' (2017) 17 *Human Rights Law Review* 681.

[20] It is difficult to gauge how the shift away from this particular debate impacts the practice of torture. The practice, to be clear, continues. It is certainly true, though, that the US practice and justi-

a turn to a different kind of sustained and enlightening scholarly engagement with the study of torture.[21] There are reasons to be cautious though in assessing the Bush administration era of torture. The 'war on terror' did not end, those truly responsible in the Bush administration have faced little sanction,[22] and the torture debate was never really 'won' or put to bed. The Findings and Conclusions and Executive Summary of the Senate Intelligence Committee Report on Torture made an enormous splash when first published.[23] The product of around five years of work and of the analysis of 'more than six million pages of CIA materials', the declassified executive summary determined, amongst other damning findings:

> #1: The CIA's use of its enhanced interrogation techniques was not an effective means of acquiring intelligence or gaining cooperation from detainees;
> #2: The CIA's justification for the use of its enhanced interrogation techniques rested on inaccurate claims of their effectiveness;
> #3: The interrogations of CIA detainees were brutal and far worse than the CIA represented to policymakers and others.[24]

There has, however, been no real effort to prosecute those most responsible within the CIA for executing and delivering the enhanced interrogation programme or to seek out any mechanism of accountability.[25] Whilst criminal accountability was never really the objective of the Senate Select Intelligence Committee in pursuing its inquiry and in preparing the report, nothing significant has, to date, resulted from its publication.[26] The focus of the Committee on the CIA also allowed those responsible within the Bush administration to fly below the radar. Obama, who fought his first campaign on a decisively anti-torture stance, left office having never let go of his compulsion to move forward rather than spending time 'laying blame for the

---

fication of torture and ill-treatment, as well as the ticking bomb rationale, have been used to license or legitimate torture around the world. See UNHRC, 'Report of the Special Rapporteur, Manfred Novak' A/HRC/13/39/Add. 5, para. 44. It may also be the case that the turn of public attention away from torture impacts the scrutiny of extensive ongoing practices.

[21]　There are already a few examples. For an excellent study of the collaboration between France and Argentina through French military 'assistance' in training torturers, see Collard, M, *Torture as State Crime: A Criminological Analysis of the Transnational Institutional Torturer* (Routledge, 2018). For an important study of the effectiveness of torture prevention, see Carver, R and Handley, L, *Does Torture Prevention Work?* (Liverpool University Press, 2016).

[22]　For an account of the construction of the legal advice that led to the use of torture in interrogation and for a discussion of the responsibility of the lawyers, see Sands, P, *Torture Team: Deception, Cruelty and the Compromise of Law* (Allen Lane, 2008).

[23]　Senate Select Committee on Intelligence, 'The Senate Intelligence Committee Report on Torture: Committee Study of the Central Intelligence Agency's Detention and Interrogation Program' (Melville House, 2014).

[24]　*Ibid*, 5.

[25]　Vladeck, S, 'The Torture Report and the Accountability Gap' (2015) Summer/Fall *Georgetown Journal of International Affairs* 174.

[26]　It could be argued that the appointment of Gina Haspel as CIA Director actually shows that the opposite is the case. See Serwer, A, 'Obama's Legacy of Impunity for Torture', *The Atlantic* (14 March 2018)　https://www.theatlantic.com/politics/archive/2018/03/obamas-legacy-of-impunity-for-torture/555578/; Hajjar, L, 'Why Gina Haspel, the Queen of Torture, was able to rise to the top of the CIA', *The Nation* (16 March 2018) available at https://www.thenation.com/article/why-gina-haspel-the-queen-of-torture-was-able-to-rise-to-the-top-of-the-cia/

past'.[27] Moreover, the report's findings and the underpinning inquiry were, at any rate, deemed partisan, an exercise in cherry-picking.[28] Trump then entered office having fought a campaign promising to waterboard and worse,[29] fully convinced, despite everything, of his own 'feelings' on the matter: 'absolutely, I feel it works'.[30] His defence of torture sounded particularly preposterous. But the only real difference between Trump and his torture defending predecessors was in his more frank choice of words. Bush and his administration used euphemisms for torture and were less likely to parse their convictions in the indeterminacy of feelings: enhanced interrogation methods work … are necessary … have thwarted attacks or led to finding Osama Bin Laden … do not constitute torture; these were, and still are for many, the assertions of the Bush administration and CIA torture programme architects.[31] As O'Mara so aptly remarks, however, on this conviction around efficacy or necessity, Bush administration 'policy seems to have been based on some combination of political preference and intuitive belief about human nature'.[32] The mask slipped with Trump.

The ticking bomb scenario has, in all that time, been popularised and debated, in classrooms, newspapers and newsrooms, in TV shows and films and across the academy. It lies around like a torture device.[33] Moreover, the ticking bomb scenario continues to underpin, with Supreme Court approval, the policy of 'special interrogation methods' against Palestinians in Israel.[34]

Despite the unease and the despair with this infatuation with the ticking bomb scenario, there is value in examining why the idea of torture as a method of interrogation is so prevalent and in understanding how and why so many have been seduced by the ticking bomb scenario. The hypothetical also has some value when treated – merely – as the site from which to pursue an archaeology of torture – sifting through rhetoric, ideology and histories of torture can help us to understand the contemporary practice of torture.

This chapter shows how the ticking bomb hypothetical inhibits understanding of the practice of torture and how it operates to neutralise the ideology of torture. The acceptance of the ticking bomb discourse as a legitimate starting point, simultaneously and paradoxically, facilitates the practice – torture is greeted as exceptional rather than understood as a continuous practice of violence. By exposing the ideology, this chapter reveals the way in which the ticking bomb scenario serves as a proxy for domination and control, that is, for the erasure of

---

[27]   The White House, Office of the Press Secretary, 'Statement of Barack Obama on Release of OLC Memos', 16 April 2009.

[28]   Pythian, M, 'An INS Special Forum: The US Senate Select Committee Report on the CIA's Detention and Interrogation Program' (2016) 31 *Intelligence and National Security* 8, 9.

[29]   Mavronicola, 'Torture and Othering' (n 19 above), 32–33.

[30]   Weaver, M and Ackerman, S, 'Trump Claims Torture Works but Experts Warn of its "Potentially Existential" Costs' *The Guardian* (26 January 2017) interview and analysis available at https://www.theguardian.com/us-news/2017/jan/26/donald-trump-torture-absolutely-works-says-us-president-in-first-television-interview

[31]   See, for example, Rizzo, J, *Company Man* (Scribe, 2014), 186, 233, 297–302; Rodriguez, JA, *Hard Measures: How Aggressive C.I.A Actions after 9/11 Saved American Lives* (Threshold Editions, 2012), 66, 69; Rumsfeld, D, *Known and Unknown: A Memoir* (Sentinel, 2012), xii, 570–572, 582, 601–609.

[32]   O'Mara, S, *Why Torture Doesn't Work: The Neuroscience of Interrogation* (Harvard University Press, 2015), 12.

[33]   Wolcher (n 18 above), x.

[34]   Ben-Natan, S, 'Revise your Syllabi: Israeli Supreme Court Upholds Authorisation for Torture and Ill-Treatment' (2019) 10 *Journal of International Humanitarian Legal Studies* 41.

'political subjectivity',[35] and the creation of new political subjectivities, whether in the 'war on terror', the Empire or in the metropole. Torture, I argue, is not about information and is not a method of interrogation. Torture is about the subjugation, pacification or correction of those constructed as not fully human, barbarians or sinners.

In this chapter, I will, first, critique how we talk about torture. I will argue that many of the most common ways in which torture and the ticking bomb scenario are discussed reinforce an ideology of torture. The discussion of torture's efficacy, efforts to question the plausibility of the ticking bomb scenario and examinations, through ethical argument, of torture in the ticking bomb scenario should all be treated with caution as these approaches inadvertently advance the ideology. Unpacking these overtures to the ticking bomb scenario is essential, first, for uncovering the ideology and, second, for reaching an understanding of torture as a civilising process.

Secondly, I critique the approach of categorising torture as interrogational. The tendency to discuss torture according to its purported purpose of obtaining information in interrogation manufactures an understanding of torture at serious odds with reality or history. This understanding of torture is, perhaps, inevitable, reified as it is by the definition of torture under international law where 'torture means any act by which severe pain or suffering, whether physical or mental, is intentionally inflicted on a person *for such purposes ... as obtaining ... information*'.[36] Whilst a *prohibited* purpose, this definition reinforces the idea that torture has such a purpose, that torture is a method of interrogation. Torture is not a 'method of interrogation'; its aim is to destroy subjectivity. The words 'purpose' and 'method', however, condition a comprehension of torture as a means to an end (though most accept it to be a morally and legally prohibited means). That interrogation is merely the context for a form of violence, which aims at destroying subjectivity, is hard to grasp in the face of such rationalising language, law and learned intuition. Separating torture from interrogation in this way is a further essential step in reaching an understanding of torture as a civilising process.

Finally, I will show that the ticking bomb scenario is an imperial concept which remains, today, an instrument of the civilising mission. The ticking bomb scenario emerged out of a colonial context – expressly Algeria, although, equivalent constructions were used elsewhere.[37] It was a rationale that solved the equation between 'their' use of terrorism and 'our' use of torture (of course, the word torture is always avoided). The priority of thwarting terrorism provided a more palatable substitute to the reality of torture as an exercise of power to

---

[35]   Sturken, M, 'Comfort, Irony and Trivialisation: The Mediation of Torture' (2011) 14 *International Journal of Cultural Studies* 423, 424.

[36]   UN Convention against Torture and Other Cruel, Inhuman and Degrading Treatment or Punishment (adopted 10 December 1984, entered into force 26 June 1987), 1465 UNTS 85, 113, Art 1(1) (emphasis added).

[37]   The British government justified their brutality and the so-called five techniques in Northern Ireland on the grounds of saving the lives of civilians and members of the security forces: 'information must be sought while it is still fresh so that it may be used as quickly as possible to effect the capture of persons, arms and explosives, and thereby save the lives of members of the security forces and of the civil population'. See, Her Majesty's Stationery Office, 'Report of the enquiry into allegations against the Security Forces of physical brutality in Northern Ireland arising out of events on the 9th August, 1971' (1971). In Kenya, where the British were responsible for widespread and systematic torture in the context of the Mau Mau rebellion, they used 'euphemisms, technical jargon, and a sanitized vocabulary of abuse'. See Pringle, Y, 'Humanitarianism, Race and Denial: The International Committee of the Red Cross and Kenya's Mau Mau Rebellion, 1952–60' (2017) 84 *History Workshop Journal* 89, 97.

subdue the 'savage' for the preservation, and extension, of 'our' values, 'our' civilisation.[38] The ticking bomb scenario is the conceptual or political mechanism by which the colonised, the terrorist, or the deviant, more generally, can be excluded from the universal prohibition on torture.[39]

DEBATING TORTURE

There are important points of departure to avoid – or, at a minimum, to take great care with – in the discussion of torture and the ticking bomb scenario.[40] These points of departure are: first, the question of torture's efficacy, second, the plausibility of the ticking bomb hypothetical, and, third, taking part in the debate by promoting a moral or ethical normative perspective in response to the ticking bomb scenario. Even the most rigorous and well-intentioned discussant seems unable to avoid the traps of this 'torture in the ticking bomb scenario' debate and, though they may not notice it or admit, they may find themselves reinforcing the torturer's justificatory perspective. These points of departure snare commentators in an escapist, circuitous, subservient debate that is entirely detached from the lived reality of torture. By examining how commentators have engaged in this debate, I illuminate just how this ticking bomb debate is rigged.

The Efficacy Debate

The efficacy of torture is a treacherous point of departure. The most watertight study will still be met with the incredulous, 'but what about x', or the dogged refrain, 'it might work in y'. As such, the debate is intractable. It also concedes too much. If torture is proved always inefficacious, then we can stop debating efficacy and concentrate on why it is practised, and we can criticise states for torturing 'superfluously'. The dark side of the coin, however, is in the submission, however unintentionally, first, to the idea that efficacy matters – that torture, argued to be efficacious, is up for debate, and, second, to the suggestion that states would not practise torture if they understood its inefficacy.

There may be exceptions in the literature to the otherwise seemingly unavoidable problem of reifying the efficacy of torture through debate. In *Why Torture Doesn't Work: The Neuroscience of Interrogation*, O'Mara provides a rigorous, meticulous and persuasive evidence-based argument demonstrating the inefficacy of torture. He also undertakes his study with integrity, grounding the examination in an attentive rebuttal of any case for the use of torture, whatever the science. His discussion of how the Bush administration's torture policy architects 'consulted their consciousness' in defining and authorising torture and of their bad faith in picking and choosing the law and the science is scathing and grounds his thesis in an informed political context.

---

[38]   See generally Maran, R, *Torture: The Role of Ideology in the French Algerian War* (Praeger, 1989) and for a concrete discussion of this point see 81–84 and 95–97 in particular.
[39]   Anghie, A, 'The War on Terror and Iraq in Historical Perspective', (2005) 43 *Osgoode Hall Law Journal* 44, 52.
[40]   Farrell (n 4 above), 14–17.

His central argument holds that torture has the completely contrary effect to the torturer's claim, to the folk or common-sense myth and to that which is portrayed in fiction. Torture, 'a profound and extreme stressor that causes widespread and enduring alterations to the very fabric of the brain', inhibits memory.[41] The stress and pain of torture – techniques such as those used by the Bush administration, including sleep deprivation, drowning, environment and diet manipulation and physical violence – suppress cognitive ability: '... when one is experiencing threat, especially predator threat, which profoundly threatens one's bodily integrity and which is associated with pain, conscious regions are to a very large extent overridden'.[42] O'Mara makes a plea for scientific, empirically grounded examination of the efficacy question, although he is wholly aware that the myth of efficacy is deeply embedded, intuitively and socially.

For many, the practice of torture is evidence of efficacy. Levinson maintained, at one point: 'If, after all, there were no genuine lure of the sirens, Ulysses would scarcely have needed to tie himself to the mast'.[43] In other words, the prohibition is needed because the practice exists and that practice shows torture's efficacy. Because he explains and then destroys this kind of (il)logic – those 'insights' that are rooted in common-sense simplicity – O'Mara's book is an inestimable contribution.

O'Mara's argument and conclusions are, however, not without issue. Despite apprehending the political context, O'Mara leaves the, perhaps inadvertent, impression that a science or evidence-based understanding might prevent torture or have prevented the Bush policy, or that this evidence basis disproving efficacy could abolish the practice of torture. There are two important issues here. First, evidence matters, he says; in so doing, however, he also suggests that efficacy matters. It is not far-fetched to claim that a state, the US for example, acting in bad faith, wishing to torture, will find alternative evidence, a scientific study that yields to their needs. Indeed, the CIA has done it before.[44] Evidence is not infallible. Second, though, and more importantly, O'Mara takes the torturing state or the torturer at their word. The attention given to this purported purpose of extracting information maintains the transubstantiation of justification into fact or truth (albeit a fact/truth he sets out to disprove). By examining the use of torture for information – obtaining information being the only rationale or justification that contemporary states tend to provide when forced – O'Mara assumes that perpetrators torture in a *mistaken* belief in the reliability of torture. He gives too much credibility to, what Luban described fittingly as, the 'liberal ideology of torture':

---

[41] O'Mara (n 32 above), 8.

[42] *Ibid*, 144. As well as this more general examination of the effect of stress and pain on the brain, O'Mara examines in detail the specific effects on the brain of sleep deprivation and of drowning, cooling, heating and starving the brain.

[43] Levinson, S, '"Precommitment" and "Postcommitment": The Ban on Torture in the Wake of September 11' (2003) 81 *Texas Law Review* 2013, 2030.

[44] Shue, S, 'Book Review: Why Torture Doesn't Work: The Neuroscience of Interrogation: By Shane O'Mara' (2016) 37 *Political Psychology* 753, 756. See, in particular on this point, Klein, N, *The Shock Doctrine* (Penguin, 2007) 25–46, describing CIA funding, and manipulation, of psychological research carried out at McGill University in the 1950s. See also, generally, McCoy, AW, *A Question of Torture: CIA Interrogation, From the Cold War to the War on Terror* (Metropolitan Books, 2006); Harbury, J, *Truth, Torture and the American Way: The History and Consequences of US Involvement in Torture* (Beacon Press, 2005).

The liberal ideology insists that the sole purpose of torture must be intelligence gathering to prevent the catastrophe; that torturing is the exception, not the rule so that it has nothing to do with state tyranny; that those who inflict the torture are motivated solely by the looming catastrophe, with no tincture of cruelty ...[45]

In order to really get to grips with torture, its history in various contexts and its future, it is, of course, important to destabilise the folk myth about efficacy and obtaining information because the ignorance can nourish the political context or environment in which torture is practised and feed the impunity of the perpetrators. But it is more important to redirect focus completely to why states practise torture. In order to understand why, it is essential to come to terms with the reality that claims about obtaining urgent information may disguise an individual's underlying motivations but, more importantly, such claims certainly conceal the underlying policy context,[46] and, crucially, ideology. Simply put, we cannot take states at their word; a deeply deconstructive, sceptical approach is warranted.

The treacherous question – 'does torture work?' – is a good starting point for a healthy dose of scepticism. It is rare for either the questioner or the respondent to define what they mean by 'work' and just as rare to see the question itself placed under scrutiny. There is merit in doing so. Agency – the perpetrator's and the victim's – is neutralised in the question – torture is doing the torturing and the 'working'. This is pure abstraction. But, more importantly, what is meant by the verb 'work' is generally left to the imagination. In Algeria, torture was geared at liquidating the leadership of the National Liberation Front (*Fronte de libération nationale* or FLN) and breaking the organisation completely.[47] Torture 'worked' because, by arresting and torturing thousands of people (many to death), the French shattered the resistance and terrorised and repressed the population – they broke their enemy.[48]

Central to the question – does torture work – is, of course, the assumptions that the torture is 'interrogational' and applied for a worthy, or good, purpose, as well as the presupposition of identification with whoever is doing the torturing. In this framing, intimidation and dominance over the suspect or victim are by-products of the urgency of obtaining the information, not central features of torture. The question is loaded and circuitous, and, it seems, it is perfect fodder for the fearful, the retributive, and the opinionated, roused by anecdote.[49]

---

[45]   Luban, D, 'Liberalism, Torture and the Ticking Bomb' (2005) 91 *Virginia Law Review* 1425, 1439.

[46]   Kelman, HC, 'The Policy Context of Torture: A Social-Psychological Analysis' (2005) 87 *International Review of the Red Cross* 123.

[47]   Evans, M, *Algeria: France's Undeclared War* (Oxford University Press, 2012), 206.

[48]   By the end of the Battle of Algiers, 24,000 individuals had been arrested: most were tortured – 80% of the men + 66% of the women; 3,024 were disappeared, following summary execution or death in interrogation. Branche, R, *La torture et l'armée pendant la guerre d'Algérie* (Gallimard, 2001), cited in Rejali (n 15 above), 482. See also, generally, Branche, R, 'Torture of Terrorists? Use of Torture in a "War Against Terrorism": Justification, Methods and Effects: The Case of France in Algeria, 1954–1962' (2007) 89 *International Review of the Red Cross* 543.

[49]   O'Mara (n 32 above), 2–3. O'Mara makes a couple of neat assertions that have inspired my point here. He remarks, '... the protorture and procoercian case is almost always made with an ad hoc mixture of anecdote, cherry-picked stories, and entirely counterfactual stories that the authors usually find convincing – like the ticking bomb scenario'. He also says, correctly, '... it also seems to me, having read many of these protorture cases, that at least some authors are motivated by a barely uttered desire to engage in torture ... for retributive or punitive reasons'.

The Plausibility of the Ticking Bomb Scenario

As torture became a matter of public debate in the years following the attacks of 11 September, it became common for commentators to rest their arguments against the use of torture on the implausibility of that scenario ever materialising.

For example, in its guidance on the appropriate response to the ticking bomb scenario, the Swiss-based non-profit Association for the Prevention of Torture (APT) attempted to formulate a scheme for discrediting the scenario whilst reiterating the legal and ethical value of the torture prohibition.[50] The detailed response to the scenario, as the report explains, exposes the hidden assumptions of the ticking bomb scenario and debunks those assumptions. For the APT, the problematic assumptions included supposed certainty about: the existence of the attack and its imminence; having the right person in custody, with the information, only available through torture; and the existence of a torturer motivated only by stopping the attack, and only in this particular case.[51] The report also warned of the risk of the descent down the slippery slope – allowing for torture in the exceptional case would open the floodgates to widespread and systematic torture.[52] The APT aimed to equip the public, human rights advocates, academics and government officials with central arguments to rebut the ticking bomb exception to the prohibition. Their task, as for others in this debate, was Sisyphean. The ticking bomb hypothetical aims to elicit one's intuition about the use of torture in an exceptional circumstance; in so doing, it constructs, or reinforces, a particular account or understanding of torture. Rebutting the hypothetical without challenging this learned and constructed understanding of torture misses the very deception of the hypothetical – the hypothetical renders reality in a way that edits out apprehension or understanding of torture.[53]

In his 2006 essay, Shue argued that imaginary examples like the ticking bomb hypothetical are misleading because they both idealise and abstract: 'Idealisation adds sparkle, abstraction removes dirt.'[54] So, for Shue, the ticking bomb scenario idealises by adding positive features that make them more concrete than is likely under real circumstances: 'The right man' *is* in custody and he *will* promptly and accurately disclose information under torture. And torture will *only* be used in this 'rare, isolated case'.[55] The ticking bomb scenario abstracts from reality by removing negative features: the hypothetical erases the reality that torture requires institutional competence – proper administration, thus, trained torturers.[56] We know, though, that Shue is unable to disregard fully catastrophic logic, and, as such, he winds up reproducing the state's excuse: 'If the perfect time for torture comes, and we are not prepared to prevent a terroristic catastrophe, we will at least know that we have not sold our souls and we have not brutalized the civilization.'[57]

---

[50]   Association for the Prevention of Torture, *Defusing the Ticking Bomb Scenario: Why We Must Say No To Torture, Always* (Association for the Prevention of Torture, 2007).

[51]   *Ibid*, 4–11.

[52]   *Ibid*, 13–14.

[53]   Farrell (n 4 above), 25; Thaler, M, *Naming Violence: A Critical Theory of Genocide, Torture, and Terrorism* (Columbia University Press, 2018), 105.

[54]   Shue (n 11 above), 231.

[55]   *Ibid*, 233.

[56]   *Ibid*, 237.

[57]   *Ibid*, 239.

According to Brecher, 'to use a hypothetical example as though it were a real case without first considering very carefully its plausibility in the real world is intellectually and politically irresponsible'.[58] Brecher echoes Scheppele who dismissed the hypothetical as 'irresponsible' because of its presentation of the 'purity of the extreme'.[59] Like Scheppele, Brecher set about undermining the scenario with the goal of showing it to be a fantasy and, thus, no basis for public policy. Brecher focused his attention on the problems with the internal logic of the scenario by querying assumptions around capacity to torture, its effectiveness, within the necessary time, perpetrated on the person who knows, in a situation of necessity. Like so many others, Brecher is also wary of the 'slippery slope', allowing torture in the ticking bomb scenario would 'lead to its spread', 'normalizing the practice'.[60] Brecher is not just concerned with the ticking bomb scenario. He goes deeper to recognise that 'interrogational torture' itself – that is, torture as a method applied to obtain information in interrogation – is a fantasy and that torture is inherently wrong. Brecher is particularly self-conscious, attentive to the intellectual poverty of the approach that he has had to take by engaging in such an engrossed deconstruction of ticking bomb logic: 'My excuse … and I hope a justification, is that I had to get my hands intellectually dirty if I was to offer arguments that stood a chance of being listened to', he remarks.[61] Brecher, like O'Mara, is persuasive but the examination has limits. He closes off so many of the arguments of the apologists and demonstrates the moral bankruptcy at the heart of the ticking bomb debate. However, he is unable to fully avoid the traps of the scenario and, like Shue, he reproduces the logic of the state – that the use of torture could avoid the catastrophe: 'The very occasional catastrophe', he writes, 'is the price we have to pay to avoid creating a torturous society'.[62]

Debating the plausibility of the materialisation of a ticking bomb scenario, in these ways, is – like efficacy – treacherous. Arguments advocating a moral standpoint do not stand a chance in a debate characterised by moral contestation, submerged in ideology. Implausibility arguments, moreover, are a gift to those imaginative or ill-intentioned enough to mould what they think is the ever more conceivable or realisable scenario. To those who are primed to think with the ticking bomb, ticking bombs become omnipresent – kidnapping cases, hostage scenarios all earn ticking bomb logic.

Some commentators have recognised, and taken seriously, the treachery of the ticking bomb scenario.[63] For Luban, the ticking bomb 'cheats its way around … [the] difficulties by stipulating that the bomb is there, ticking away, and that officials know it and know they have the man who planted it'.[64] These exact circumstances will, he argues, seldom be met. Whilst even opening this 'seldom' space risks concession, Luban's uneasiness with the ticking bomb

---

[58]   Brecher, B, *Torture and the Ticking Bomb* (Blackwell Publishing, 2007), 9.

[59]   Scheppele, KL, 'Hypothetical Torture in the War on Terrorism' (2005) 1 *Journal of National Security Law and Policy* 285. Scheppele mounts a sociological attack on the gap between the hypothetical and real-life and cautions against consequentialist analyses of the ticking bomb scenario.

[60]   Brecher (n 58 above), 75.

[61]   *Ibid*, 88.

[62]   *Ibid*.

[63]   See, for example, Scarry, E, 'Five Errors in the Reasoning of Alan Dershowitz' in Levinson, S (ed), *Torture: A Collection* (Oxford University Press, 2004), 281. Understandably, like Brecher, Scarry did find it necessary to counteract the arguments advocating torture in ticking bomb situations because they had become so common not just in academic writing but also in policy-making.

[64]   Luban (n 45 above), 1442.

scenario goes, at any rate, far beyond it having these obvious deceptions and impracticalities. Luban dismisses the ticking bomb scenario as intellectual fraud, and because he views it as signposting a liberal ideology of torture whilst ignoring the actual practice of torture,[65] he maintains that 'any responsible discussion of torture must address the practice of torture, not the ticking-bomb hypothetical'.[66] It is on Bush administration policy and practices, and not the ticking bomb scenario, that his analysis concludes. It is crucial to resist engaging in the ticking bomb discussion because, as I will now show, the ticking bomb scenario operates to neutralise an ideology of torture.

Shaping reality: the ticking bomb as ideology
First, approaching the hypothetical as mere fantasy, or as a thought-experiment that can be dismantled conclusively, leaves the impression that the root of this discussion or issue is practical – *but those exact circumstances could never happen in that way!* – rather than ideological. The ticking bomb scenario and the understanding of torture it creates is an ideological construct precisely because it is a concept which shapes reality – that is, which shapes a reality of torture.

The meaning of ideology is not easily rendered. It has a complex history,[67] and multiple meanings,[68] but the concept is constructive. In general terms, and in Freeden's words, ideology can be understood as referring to a 'specific way of interpreting and decoding political reality, to construing political practices as expressions of, and constitutive of, political ideas, with the ultimate goal of formulating a legitimated public policy'.[69] Freeden's account of ideology implies neither a negative or positive reading. It is, for him, an important way of understanding the political tradition at work.[70] But even this quite neutral definition of ideology can help to understand how the act of torture, often spoken of as beyond the pale, as medieval, as dictatorial or tyrannical, indeed, as evil, can, using the ideological construct of the ticking bomb scenario, be translated into, or construed as, something necessary, acceptable and legitimate, and, thus, made policy.

A more critical or analytical examination of the ideology of the ticking bomb scenario is revealing of the myriad ways in which this ideology is sustained through its discussion and deconstruction as well as through its deployment in a policy context. To sharpen the examination, a critical, penetrative understanding of ideology is needed. Thompson, informed primarily by Marx's use of the term,[71] says, 'to study ideology is to study the ways in which meaning

---

[65]   *Ibid*, 1439; Farrell (n 4 above), 130.

[66]   Luban (n 45 above), 1445.

[67]   Thompson, JB, *Ideology and Modern Culture: Critical Social Theory in the Era of Mass Communication* (Polity Press, 1990), 29.

[68]   Eagleton, T, *Ideology: An Introduction* (Verso, 1991, 2007 edn), 1–2.

[69]   Freeden, M, *Ideologies and Political Theory: A Conceptual Approach* (Oxford University Press, 1996), 553.

[70]   Marks, M, 'Big Brother is Bleeping Us – With the Message that Ideology Doesn't Matter' (2001) 12 *European Journal of International Law* 109, 111.

[71]   Whilst Thompson finds no single conception of ideology in Marx's writings, he is primarily informed by Karl Marx and Frederick Engels, *The German Ideology, part 1*, ed. CJ Arthur (Lawrence & Wishart, 1970); Marx, K, 'Preface to A Contribution to the Critique of Political Economy', in Marx K and Engels F, *Selected Works in One Volume* (Lawrence & Wishart, 1968); Marx, K and Engels, F, 'Manifesto of the Communist Party', in *Selected Works in One Volume* (Lawrence & Wishart, 1968). Thompson departs from Marx on points. See Thompson (n 67 above) 33–44.

serves to establish and sustain relations of domination'.[72] Marks, drawing on Thompson, understands ideology as 'the mystifications through which ideas help to establish and maintain' domination in asymmetrical power relations.[73] Marks isolates insightfully the distinction between being ideological and perpetuating ideology through one's actions, however unintentionally. This insight is crucial in helping to explain how the ticking bomb discussion is handled, by voices on all sides and why this discussion is part of the problem. She remarks:

> ... the mystification lies not in unawareness of social reality, but in unawareness of, or at any rate inattention to, the extent to which actions and words, and the ideas expressed through them, serve to shape social reality ... the mystification lies in a failure adequately to consider the *reflexivity* of social life—the way social practices are continually re-examined and reformed *in the light of what is said about them*.[74]

The ideology at stake in the ticking bomb debate starts to crystallise under this observation. Ideology is not only (or even importantly) about what you or I, Shue or Brecher think of the practice of torture or of the ticking bomb scenario. The ideology is contained within the scenario itself and in the conception of torture that it provokes. It is no good being against torture, *even* in the catastrophic case, or being sceptical of the catastrophic case itself, whilst engaging it, arguing its merits, pros and cons, because this engagement and argument perpetuates an ideology of torture. Eagleton provides the elegant framework for this understanding. He says:

> Ideology ... [is] not just a matter of what I think about a situation. It is somehow inscribed in the situation itself. It is no good my reminding myself that I am opposed to racism as I sit down on a park bench marked 'Whites Only': by the action of sitting on it, I have supported and perpetuated racist ideology. The ideology, so to speak, is in the bench, not in my head.[75]

It is not easy to explain the practice of torture. However, by investigating and exposing the ideological architecture of the ticking bomb construct, it is possible to reach an authoritative comprehension of torture on terms that simultaneously eschew and explain those that have been set by the state. In this respect, Luban and Rejali are very useful to my analysis of the ideology of the ticking bomb scenario and to my argument that the ticking bomb scenario is an imperial construct.

Luban examines torture's complicated relationship with liberalism as embodied in the ticking bomb scenario. He views the ticking bomb scenario as rhetorically valuable, first, as a mechanism to unravel the prohibitionist's absolute moral stance against torture: 'Dialectically, getting the prohibitionist to address the ticking bomb is like getting the vegetarian to eat just one little oyster because it has no nervous system. Once she does that – gotcha!'[76] He disregards this kind of utilitarian or cost-benefit approach as a way of thinking about torture.[77] Second, he views it as a mechanism for placating liberal aversion to cruelty by portraying the torturer 'in a different light': 'The torturer is ... a conscientious public servant,

---

[72]   Thompson (n 67 above), 56.
[73]   Marks (n 70 above), 109 and 111.
[74]   *Ibid*, 113 (emphasis added).
[75]   *Ibid*, citing Eagleton (n 68 above), 40.
[76]   Luban (n 45 above), 1427.
[77]   Luban, D and Engel, MJ, 'Intersections of Torture and Power: An Interview with David Luban' (2014) 15 *Georgetown Journal of International Affairs* 110.

heroic …, willing to do desperate things only because the plight is so desperate and so many innocent lives are weighing on the public servant's conscience. The time bomb clinches the great divorce between torture and cruelty'.[78] The ticking bomb scenario, for Luban, is principally a way of making a barbarous practice liberally palatable. Luban is reluctant to get into the mechanics of the ticking bomb scenarios.

Rejali opens up the space to consider the complex gender norms that underpin torture and the ticking bomb scenario. Drawing particularly on the Algerian context, on Fanon, Sartre, and Lartéguy's novel *Les Centurions*, he situates the ticking bomb scenario within the context of hegemonic gender norms,[79] fears of fading masculinity, and of democracy corrupting masculinity. 'Torture generates a kind of manly strength' for those who 'worry that we have become sissies and our enemies know it'.[80] The ticking bomb scenario, he observes, provokes 'a long-felt, common anxiety that democracy has made us weak and there are no real men anymore'.[81] Torture is employed then in defence of civilisation, a civilisation that, to defeat its enemies, must 'man-up'. His analysis augments an understanding of torture that is otherwise stunted by the ticking bomb framing. His point is not to simplify or caricature torture perpetrators as male (though the ticking bomb hypothetical does invite a gendered reading). Rather, Rejali found that 'manhood and democracy' were 'very much at issue in discussions of torture during the Algerian War', where ticking bomb logic was pervasive, and he finds these same discussions underpinning the rise of the ticking bomb and the use of torture in the post-11 September United States context. Rejali taps into important gendered configurations which structure social practice and, as such, his work invites a deeper reading of torture.

The state is a masculine institution.[82] The US military is 'a masculinist and heterosexist environment'.[83] Crucially, in this setting, gender and race interlock: the reclamation or defence of masculinity, observable in the aftermath of 11 September, meshed with 'white fears' of the violence of the racialised other.[84] The torture memos, and the masculinist ideology that inspired them,[85] could take root easily in such a fertile environment. Torture is 'not a simple dyadic relationship' as the ticking bomb scenario would have it; rather torture occurs in complex organisational contexts that are intersected by constructions of masculinity, gender and race.[86] Hyper 'masculine socialisation' is at play in armed conflict and counterinsurgency.[87] The interaction of gender, race and class in armed conflict and in imperial and counterinsurgency contexts is essential to understanding torture.[88]

---

[78] Luban (n 45 above), 1441.
[79] In particular, Rejali highlights 'hegemonic masculinity' whereby a particular masculinity dominates. See Connell, RW, *Masculinities*, 2nd edn (Polity Press, 2005), 77.
[80] Rejali, D, 'Torture Makes the Man' (2007) 24 *South Central Review* 151, 151 and 169.
[81] Rejali (n 15 above), 548.
[82] Connell (n 79 above), 75.
[83] Caldwell, RA, *Fallgirls: Gender and the Framing of Torture at Abu Ghraib* (Ashgate, 2012), 44.
[84] Paul Hoch cited in Connell (n 79 above), 75.
[85] See, for example, Hersh, SM, 'The Gray Zone: How a Secret Pentagon Program came to Abu Ghraib', *The New Yorker* (16 May 2014) discussing the neo-con view of Iraq, Arabs and violence in the lead up to the invasion.
[86] Rejali (n 80 above), 163.
[87] Zurbriggen, EL, 'Sexualised Torture and Abuse at Abu Ghraib Prison: Feminist Psychological Analysis' (2008) 18 *Feminism and Psychology* 301.
[88] Khalili, L, 'Gendered Practices of Counterinsurgency' (2011) 37 *Review of International Studies* 1471, 1482.

This interaction was represented in the Abu Ghraib photographs and the scandal of, as Khalili puts it, the 'transgressive women' torturers.[89] The mainstream and media monstering of the female soldiers at Abu Ghraib 'trafficked in gendered stereotypes'.[90] In so doing, they missed how gender roles were being performed, in what Kaufman-Osborn has called a 'logic of emasculation': the aim of the disciplinary techniques was 'to strip prisoners of their masculine gender identity and turn them into caricatures of terrified and often infantilized femininity'.[91] The emasculating and homoerotic approach to torture at Abu Ghraib[92] was underpinned by racism at the highest levels, where the intentional exploitation of 'the Arab mind' was part of the enhanced interrogation narrative.[93] The prominence of sexual violence and sexual humiliation at Abu Ghraib reflected the long-standing Orientalist interpretation of the Muslim or Arab world as sexually repressed and homophobic. Torture at Abu Ghraib aimed at exploiting this construction of the victims, but this torture was played out through 'a cultural code of masculinity',[94] where, as Caldwell shows, power and control were exerted over the male body,[95] and their feminization through torture and sexual humiliation served 'to humiliate and mock cultural constructions of masculinity itself'.[96] Torture enacted a kind of liberation of the repressed Muslim or Arab victim whilst simultaneously enacting the United States 'as a place free of such sexual constraints'.[97] The misogyny, homophobia and racism that drove the torture at Abu Ghraib are hard to miss.

Yet, Abu Ghraib has been read as an unfortunate exception and as chaotic, the result of the deviance of a few bad apples.[98] The ticking bomb scenario is positioned in contrast to Abu Ghraib: it is the necessary exception to an otherwise commendable rule; in the ticking bomb scenario, only what is necessary is done, mechanistically, by a cool, poised and professional public official. In reality, however, the ticking bomb hypothetical and torture at Abu Ghraib are manifestations of the same ideological codes of masculinity. Moreover, torture at Abu Ghraib was the product of the ticking bomb exception. That 'exception' was negotiated by the Bush administration and was operationalised by the CIA and by the United States military, including at Abu Ghraib.

For his part, in coming to terms with the ideology of the ticking bomb scenario, Hannah has drawn out the symbiosis between torture and terrorism as characterised by the hypothetical. He argues that the ticking bomb scenario is used to represent the geographical extent of, and the unacceptably severe extent of, the threat posed by terrorism. Widespread, imminent

---

[89]   *Ibid.*

[90]   Kaufman-Osborn, T, 'Gender Trouble at Abu Ghraib?' (2005) 1 *Politics & Gender* 597, 605.

[91]   *Ibid*, 606.

[92]   Caldwell (n 83 above), 66.

[93]   Hersh (n 85 above) cited and discussed in Puar, J, *Terrorist Assemblages: Homonationalism in Queer Times* (Duke University Press, 2017), 83–84.

[94]   Caldwell (n 83 above), 47.

[95]   The photos and the publicity around Abu Ghraib have mainly concerned male victims. Women were tortured and women were raped, though this has been vastly underreported. See Puar (n 93 above) 98; see also Harding, L, 'The Other Prisoners', *The Guardian* (20 May 2004).

[96]   Caldwell (n 83 above), 16.

[97]   Puar (n 93 above), 92.

[98]   Caldwell (n 83 above), 1, 44. Rumsfeld says of Abu Ghraib: 'These acts could not conceivably have been authorised by anyone in the chain of command, nor could they have been any part of an intelligence-gathering or interrogation effort. Rather, they were the senseless crimes of a small group of prison guards who ran amok in the absence of adequate supervision' (Rumsfeld (n 31 above), 545).

terrorism makes torture seem like a reasonable response: 'the ticking-bomb scenario prompts a reimagining of the landscape of everyday life as suffused with an unacceptably high level of risk'.[99] But Hannah fails to fully grasp the ideology of the construct. Where Hannah could have developed his analysis to show how the ticking bomb scenario is characterised by fear tactics, he falls back into the troubling investigation of the motives of perpetrators and, ultimately, he gives the scenario 'an objective value ... he disbands responsibility by presenting the ticking bomb scenario back to the authorities as justification for its actions'.[100] He remarks, rather trustingly: 'High officials in the Bush administration appear not only to have taken the premises of the ticking-bomb scenario seriously but also to have drawn the same permissive conclusions regarding torture as have many ethicists'.[101] It is important to grasp the significance of this. Being awake to the ideology of the ticking bomb scenario reduces the likelihood of slipping into a narrative that winds up accepting the state's rationalisation.

Whilst there have then been many well-argued efforts to diffuse,[102] dispose of,[103] and otherwise dismiss the ticking bomb, such dismantling will only convince those who had not really thought about the impracticalities. Even the most benevolent and well-prepared disputant can fall into traps when arguing against the ticking bomb scenario on the basis of implausibility. Exposing the fallacies of the scenario is unlikely to eliminate its appeal either to those convinced by the rare case, or to those who are ideologically committed – consciously or unconsciously – to torturing enemies and who have internalised the ticking bomb as their rationale. As well as perpetuating a particular ideology of torture, it is also the case, at times, that the exclamation that such a scenario would never arise can imply that plausibility is the problem rather than torture. In order, then, to understand torture, it is necessary to investigate the ideology that founds the ticking bomb scenario to show the ideologically constructed connection between torture and interrogation and torture and information.

Shaping torture: the ticking bomb and the purpose of interrogation

The second reason to resist debating the plausibility of a ticking bomb scenario is deeply related to this failure to recognise ideology at work. Debating plausibility may, and, more often than not, in my reading, does, signal acceptance of the premise that torture *is* a purposeful method of interrogation. By way of illustration, many commentators raise a point about competence through the question, 'who will torture?'[104] Brecher, in asking this question, makes a significant point:

> The first reason why the ticking bomb scenario remains a fantasy, and not a description of a rare but realistic possibility, is that it fails to distinguish between what you or I *might* do in that imagined case and what you or I *could* do in an actual case. It fails to distinguish between individuals' possible visceral response and any proper basis of public policy.[105]

---

[99] Hannah, M, 'Torture and the Ticking Bomb: The War on Terrorism as a Geographical Imagination of Power/Knowledge' (2006) 96 *Annals of the Association of American Geographers* 622, 623.

[100] Farrell (n 4 above), 132–133.

[101] Hannah (n 99 above), 624.

[102] Association for the Prevention of Torture (n 50 above).

[103] Shue (n 11 above).

[104] Brecher (n 58 above), 21. See also Shue (n 11 above), 236–237.

[105] Brecher (n 58 above), 22.

This is significant because the ticking bomb scenario is a poor thought experiment.[106] It aims to elicit an intuitive response to whether torture is necessary, to whether 'you' would torture;[107] the layperson debating this scenario is, however, incompetent to answer. As such, the ticking bomb scenario is presented to persuade the listener rather than to get them thinking.

However, and more importantly, raising the issue of incompetence is not an ethical strategy of dismissal. Consider Shue's incompetence-based rebuttal: '... it is simply dreamy to think that all of a sudden we are simply going to stumble upon someone who happens to have the skills to make a man who planted a ticking bomb reverse the direction of his life and assist us in defusing his bomb.'[108] The abstraction here is quite startling. Arguing against the plausibility of the ticking bomb scenario on the basis that only trained torturers could torture concretises the idea of a profession of *interrogational* torture and simultaneously imagines away the reality that torturers do exist, fully trained and otherwise. Dreaming up a torturer-free world of deficient proficiency as an argument to counteract the ticking bomb scenario is, at best, misrepresentative, at worst, perverse.

Ginbar undertakes a similarly problematic discussion[109] of the 'institutionalisation trap', as part of his more general examination of the slippery slope and other dangers of states resorting to torture in ticking bomb situations.[110] Apparently to demonstrate the bureaucratisation that would be required in a world where torture would be lawful or permissible – and seemingly effective or successful – in ticking bomb scenarios, Ginbar depicts institutionalisation in great detail:

> I would therefore submit that, in a state facing terrorism, the pro-torture reasoning inevitably calls for sending in professionals: for example, martial arts experts (perhaps assisted by neurologists) would teach interrogators where and how to hit a detainee in order to achieve the desired effect. And for such interrogations to be truly efficient, other physicians must be attached to our crack interrogation unit, as people are not physiologically uniform, and minute-by-minute monitoring is required, to ensure that the right (or exact) amount of pain is administered. Similarly, psychologists or psychiatrists must be on the scene, to advise interrogators as to the methods that would be most efficient against the particular individual, and monitor the effect of the methods used on the terrorist's willpower, endurance and sanity. Where the use of methods ... such as rape, electric shocks, and so on, is deemed unavoidable, properly trained and equipped staff should similarly be available. The same is true ... of methods such as loud music, white noise, extreme heat and cold—and even 'stress positions' and sleep deprivation.[111]

---

[106]   For a useful discussion of thought experiments in political theory, an argument in favour of distinguishing between relevant and irrelevant hypotheticals and a careful consideration of the ticking bomb thought experiment, see Thaler, M, 'Unhinged Frames: Assessing Thought Experiments in Normative Political Theory', (2018) 48 *British Journal of Political Science* 1119.

[107]   Farrell (n 4 above), 8.

[108]   Shue may make this point somewhat tongue in cheek – at any rate, by 'assist us in defusing his bomb' he almost certainly means 'assist us in providing information' (Shue (n 11 above), 237).

[109]   Ginbar's examination of torture is thorough in so far as he does not examine the ticking bomb scenario in the abstract *only*. He examines the practice of a number of states where the ticking bomb scenario has been used. He is convinced by some state justifications for using the ticking bomb scenario: 'Neither Israel nor the USA have succeeded in limiting torture to ticking bomb situations ... Both states claim, probably rightly in some specific cases, that torturing (not so named) has thwarted terrorist attacks and saved lives ...' But he is critical of the way in which that scenario has been used to justify expansive use of torture and he favours overall the absolute prohibition against torture (Ginbar (n 3 above), 264).

[110]   Ginbar (n 3 above), 112, 133–134.

[111]   Ginbar (n 3 above), 134.

It may seem surprising that the quoted passage was written as part of Ginbar's defence of a minimal absolutist prohibition against torture. In constructing that position, Ginbar may have felt it necessary to paint for his readers, and the pro-torture commentators, just what it is that they are supporting when they advocate for the use of torture in catastrophic cases. In so doing, however, he concretises the idea that torture is for the purpose of retrieving information, that it requires a professional skill set.

There should be an adage in these debates about straying onto the 'slippery slopes' and winding up as the torturer's accomplice. The ticking bomb scenario in these debates is a thought experiment, a hypothetical, but torture is not. Torture is practised and there are torturers. Beyond the debates, the ticking bomb scenario is, therefore, more than a thought experiment. It is an ideology that is invoked by states to justify practices and policies of torture.[112]

Shaping justification: the ticking bomb, policy and the state

Finally, then, and intimately connected to the previous point, dismissing the ticking bomb scenario as implausible ignores the extent to which it is the touchstone in practice for states and perpetrators to justify their use of torture. In the sense that states do employ ticking bomb justifications, there is something very real about the scenario.

States may invoke the ticking bomb scenario directly, as the Landau Commission of Inquiry famously did in Israel in 1987.[113] Ticking bomb logic underpinned the Landau Commission's decision, as part of that inquiry, to authorise the General Security Services to use 'moderate physical pressure' during the interrogation of Palestinians suspected of engagement in acts of terrorism.[114] The ticking bomb continues to provide the basis for the application of the necessity defence, following the use of torture (or supposed 'special interrogation methods') in Israeli Security Agency interrogations.[115] For its part, the Bush administration did not directly quote the kind of catastrophic case imagined in the ticking bomb scenario but it did couch its policy in the impending threat of terrorism, in an environment in which the ticking bomb was omnipresent. The ticking bomb scenario supplied 'the imagery' for Bush and his administration.[116] Bybee's infamous 2002 memo reflects the imagery: 'If a government defendant were to harm an enemy combatant during an interrogation in a manner that might arguably violate Section 2340A, he would be doing so in order to prevent further attacks on the United States by the al Qaeda terrorist network'.[117] The doctrine of necessity, according to the memo, allowed supersession of the prohibition on torture.[118]

The practice in Israel provides a striking contemporary illustration of the use of the ticking bomb scenario both as a blanket justification for the practice of torture and as a backstop for

---

[112]   Farrell (n 4 above), 8; Hannah (n 99 above), 623.

[113]   'Excerpts of the Report of the Commission of Inquiry into the Methods of Investigation of the General Security Service Regarding Hostile Terrorist Activity' (1989) 23 *Israel Law Review* 146.

[114]   Farrell (n 4 above), 109.

[115]   Elena Chakho, '*Tabish v Attorney General* and the Legal Framework Governing Physical Coercion in ISA Interrogations', *Lawfare* (6 December 2018) available at https://www.lawfareblog.com/tabish-v-attorney-general-and-legal-framework-governing-physical-coercion-isa-interrogations

[116]   Hannah (n 99 above), 624.

[117]   Jay S Bybee, Memorandum for Alberto R Gonzales, 'Standards of Conduct for Interrogation under 18' U.S.C. §§ 2340–2340A, 1 August 2002, cited in Greenberg and Dratel (n 7 above), 213.

[118]   Scharf, MP, and Williams, PR, *Shaping Foreign Policy in Times of Crisis* (Cambridge University Press, 2010), 188.

political or legal scrutiny of that use of torture.[119] The Landau Commission authorised the use of 'moderate physical pressure' in interrogations, in their reasoning, to prevent impending acts of terrorism. The Commission opined that the use of 'moderate physical pressure' would be justified, *ex ante*, under the necessity defence, for the purpose of obtaining any information that could contribute to foiling potential acts of terrorism:

> ... the information which an interrogator can obtain from the suspect, about caches of explosive materials in the possession or the knowledge of the suspect, about acts of terrorism which are about to be perpetrated, about the members of a terrorist group to which he belongs, about the headquarters of terrorist organizations inside the country or abroad, and about terrorist training camps – any such information can prevent mass killing and individual terrorist acts which are about to be carried out.[120]

The Commission explained what it meant by a ticking bomb situation: 'And indeed, when the clock wired to the explosive charge is already ticking, what difference does it make, in terms of the necessity to act, whether the charge is certain to be detonated in five minutes or in five days?'[121] As such, the Landau Commission reasoned that physical pressure could escalate in time with the detonator – but the act itself rather than danger or time was the important point of imminence.

This authorisation of the use of 'moderate physical pressure' was the subject of a famous decision before the Israeli Supreme Court, sitting as the High Court of Justice, in 1999. In that decision, the Court determined that methods employed by the General Security Services surpassed the requirements of a reasonable investigation and that the general advance authorisation of techniques of interrogation, so-called 'moderate physical pressure', under the necessity defence was incompatible with Israeli law.[122] However, the Court also allowed that the necessity defence, which precludes criminal liability, might be available to an interrogator *ex post facto* in 'appropriate circumstances' of immediate need, as provided for in Israeli penal law:

> ... we are prepared to accept ... that the 'necessity defense' can arise in instances of 'ticking bombs,' and that the phrase 'immediate need' in the statute refers to the imminent nature of the act rather than that of the danger. Hence, the imminence criteria is satisfied even if the bomb is set to explode in a few days, or perhaps even after a few weeks, provided the danger is certain to materialize and there is no alternative means of preventing its materialization.[123]

The Court left it to the Attorney General to determine the fallout of this ambiguous reasoning.[124] The Attorney General reacted by issuing a document outlining the guidelines according

---

[119]   For a discussion (that reads as quite cavalier given the subject matter) of the ticking bomb scenario in national news, see Bob, YJ, 'Shin Bet Enhanced Interrogations to Stop Ticking Bombs – Legal or Torture?', *The Jerusalem Post* (21 October 2017) available at https://www.jpost.com/International/Ticking-bomb-507917. For his discussion of the outcome of that case, see Bob, YJ, 'High Court: Enhanced Interrogations was Legal to Stop "Ticking Bomb"', *The Jerusalem Post* (20 June 2018) available at https://www.jpost.com/Israel-News/High-Court-Enhanced-interrogation-was-legal-to-stop-ticking-bomb-517905
[120]   'Excerpts' (n 113 above), 172.
[121]   *Ibid*, 174.
[122]   *The Public Committee against Torture in Israel et al. v Government of Israel et al.*, HCJ 5100/94 (6 September 1999), paras 32, 33, 35.
[123]   *Ibid*, para 34.
[124]   *Ibid*, para 38.

to which he would instruct himself in such cases – the so-called internal guidelines.[125] Rather than outlawing torture, this decision simply reoriented the way in which torture was managed. As Mann has written, the decision, whilst lauded for its rejection of torture and defence of human dignity, entrenched abusive interrogation methods.[126]

Ticking bomb logic continues to underpin the Israeli security forces' use of torture.[127] That logic has been endorsed in two recent high-profile cases before the Supreme Court, sitting as the High Court of Justice.[128] Most recently, the Court, in *Tbeish*,[129] dismissed the applicant's challenge to the lawfulness of the Israel Security Agency's (ISA) internal guidelines on special interrogation methods. The applicant also challenged the Attorney General's failure to order a criminal investigation into his allegations of torture in interrogation. The security services had applied so-called 'special interrogation techniques' to the applicant during interrogation. He was suspected of involvement in 'a plot to collect and conceal a large quantity of dangerous weapons, with the intention of using them for the perpetration of terrorist activity'.[130] The Court held:

> Under these circumstances, in which the danger that led to the use of the special means in the interrogation was certainly real; the attack that the interrogation sought to prevent was serious harm to human life; the ISA interrogators had no other means for obtaining the information about the weapons stockpile hidden in a storage unit, and of the plans to perpetrate terrorist attacks; and the special means employed in the interrogation were … proportionate relative to the serious threat that their use was intended to frustrate – I am of the opinion that the finding of the Director that 'employing the special means of interrogation under the circumstances, falls within the purview of the necessity defense' is well founded.[131]

Agreeing with Justice Elron, Justice I. Amit held:

> The case before us is not one of a classic 'ticking bomb' that may explode any minute, but … the immediacy requirement in … the Penal Law … concerns the immediacy of the act and not the immediacy of the danger. In the present case, the combination of the seriousness the nearly-certain danger [sic], if not the certainty of the realization of the danger, and the inability to act in an alternative manner in the concrete situation that faced the security authorities (the necessity condition) in order to obtain information that would very probably thwart a real danger of life-threatening terrorist activity – all lead to the conclusion that the proportionate act adopted by the ISA interrogators falls under the aegis of the necessity defense.[132]

---

[125] Kremnitzer, M and Segev, R, 'The Legality of Interrogational Torture: A Question of Proper Authorization or a Substantive Moral Issue?' (2000) 34 *Israel Law Review* 509, 541; Mann, I and Shatz, O, 'The Necessity Procedure: Laws of Torture in Israel and Beyond, 1987–2009' (2010) 6 *Unbound: Harvard Journal of the Legal Left* 59, 72.

[126] Mann, I, 'The Law behind Torture', *Boston Review* (15 December 2014) available at http://bostonreview.net/blog/itamar-mann-torture-necessity-legal-israel-united-states/?utm_source=Sprout&utm_medium=Social&utm_campaign=Twitter; see also Mann and Shatz (n 125 above), 72.

[127] Berger, Y, 'Israeli High Court Ruling may make it Easier for Interrogators to Use Violence', Haaretz (30 November 2018) available at https://www.haaretz.com/israel-news/.premium-israeli-high-court-ruling-may-make-it-easier-for-interrogators-to-use-violence-1.6701416

[128] *Tbeish v Attorney General et al.* HCJ 9018/17 (26 November 2018); *As'ad Abu Gosh et al. v Attorney General et al.* HCJ 5722/12 (12 December 2017).

[129] *Tbeish v Attorney General et al.* HCJ 9018/17 (26 November 2018). See Ben-Natan (n 34 above).

[130] *Tbeish v Attorney General et al.* HCJ 9018/17 (26 November 2018), para 59.

[131] *Ibid*, para 59.

[132] *Ibid*, Justice Amit, para 2.

The ticking bomb is the basis for a policy of torture – euphemised as special interrogation techniques – in Israel. The construct provides the imagery, the rationale and the justification for the use of torture. The judiciary, to date, has simply consolidated a ticking bomb-based ideology of torture.

The extensive commentary challenging the plausibility of the ticking bomb scenario and deconstructing ticking bomb logic might greet a decision like this with exasperation, arguing that this is not a real ticking bomb scenario or that this is evidence of the problem of the slippery slope. That approach mistakes an ideology of torture for some kind of wayward fuzzy logic. Torture by the state of Israel demonstrates fully the way in which the ticking bomb scenario is operationalised to neutralise the ideology of torture.

Adopting a Stance: 'Gotcha!'[133]

The final point of departure, in the torture and ticking bomb debate, which merits cautious handling is the participation through an 'in my view' moral or ethical argumentative approach. Whilst the prospect of engaging in the debate on torture and the ticking bomb scenario by presenting moral or even legal arguments on one side or the other is alluring (and can generate very thoughtful work),[134] it is often a debate that gets nowhere.[135] One moral proposition or legal innovation trumps another and, along the way, the few who defend torture earn too many concessions from those who condemn it. In this respect, taking a position risks accepting a ticking bomb scenario as a legitimate starting point; even the most committed deontologist by, in any way, engaging with the ins and outs of the ticking bomb scenario has already had to make a compromise. More specifically, by entering 'slippery slope' territory, consequentialists against torture concede the starting point – what happens on the slippery slope is portrayed as the problem.[136]

In respect to the all too common approach of ethical inquiry into the purported moral dilemma of torturing in ticking bomb circumstances, abstraction is the governing frame of analysis. The ticking bomb 'equivocates on what is relevant for consideration' and erases awkward realities.[137] The commentator's application of an ethical inquiry in this context doubly abstracts because the ethical analysis is rooted in moral intuitionism or a judgement call about torture and about the ticking bomb; moral intuitionism and judgement calls about torture are necessarily subjective and learned, often from fictional depiction;[138] reflection on

---

[133]   Luban (n 45 above), 1427. See also Waldron's point that the hypothetical is designed 'deliberately to undermine the integrity of certain moral positions': Waldron, J, 'Torture and Positive Law: Jurisprudence for the White House' (2005) 105 *Columbia Law Review* 1681, 1715.

[134]   For an interesting account of what is morally wrong with torture, for example, see Sussman, D, 'What's Wrong with Torture' (2005) 33 *Philosophy and Public Affairs* 1.

[135]   Kahn, PW, *Sacred Violence: Torture, Terror, and Sovereignty* (University of Michigan Press, 2008), 175.

[136]   See, for example, Twiss, SB, 'Torture, Justification and Human Rights: Toward an Absolute Proscription' (2007) 29 *Human Rights Quarterly* 346, 360; Strauss, M, 'Torture' (2004) 48 *New York Law School Law Review* 201, 267.

[137]   Farrell (n 4 above), 242.

[138]   For a discussion of how public perception is informed by popular depiction of torture, see Delahunty, C and Kearns, E, 'Wait, There's Torture in Zootopia? Examining the Prevalence of Torture in Popular Movies', February 2019 available at https://papers.ssrn.com/sol3/papers.cfm?abstract_id=3342908.

the ticking bomb is necessarily informed by the extent to which the topic of, and the threat of, terrorism has dominated both the international and national agendas and media coverage in recent years,[139] and the extent to which the idea of a ticking bomb suddenly exploding exploits 'our greatest fears'.[140] Moral intuitionism on the use of torture in ticking bomb scenarios is, as such, ideologically primed, unconnected to reality and history.

'INTERROGATIONAL TORTURE': MISCONSTRUING CONTEXT AS METHOD

The very idea that torture may be understood as a method of interrogation, or categorised as 'interrogational torture', assumes there are different categories of torture according to the purpose for which it is being applied; it also suggests that these categories are distinct – they derive somehow from the character of the torturer – the professional interrogator, the sadist, the monster. In debates about the efficacy of torture and about the ticking bomb scenario, it is assumed that torture is a method of interrogation, and its success as a method is implied or assumed. This compartmentalisation of torture according to its purpose is, more often than not, taken for granted by those who debate torture in ticking bomb scenarios and 'is accepted by both absolutists and apologists'.[141] The categorisation is pervasive in the literature;[142] commentators have developed a kind of taxonomy of torture: amongst the categories are interrogational torture, terroristic torture, judicial torture, punitive torture, sadistic torture and deterrent torture. Interrogational torture, then, is not to be conflated with terroristic or sadistic torture.

Shue was misled by this approach in 1978. He distinguished 'terroristic torture' from 'interrogational torture'. The former involved the always unjustifiable 'goal of the intimidation of people other than the victim'.[143] Interrogational torture, 'for the purpose of extracting information', could, in a pure case, 'satisfy the constraint of possible compliance, since it offers an escape, in the form of providing the information wanted by the torturers, which affords some

---

[139]   On this point, see Zedner, L, 'Securing Liberty in the Face of Terror: Reflections from Criminal Justice' (2005) 32 *Journal of Law and Society* 507, 511.

[140]   Zedner, L, 'The Concept of Security: An Agenda for Comparative Analysis' (2003) 23 *Legal Studies* 153, 156. Zedner's work on the concept of security is eye opening. For our purposes, she is particularly adept at thinking through how security mediates the gulf between risk and our subjective feelings.

[141]   Matthews, R, 'An Empirical Critique of "Interrogational Torture"' (2012) 43 *Journal of Social Philosophy* 459.

[142]   For an example of the way in which torture is often categorised, see Wisnewski, JJ, *Understanding Torture* (Edinburgh University Press, 2010), 7–8. His taxonomy of the types of torture lists: judicial, punitive, interrogational, dehumanizing, terroristic/deterrent and sadistic torture. For some examples of the use of the distinct category of 'interrogational torture', see, Gross, O, 'The Prohibition on Torture and the Limits of the Law' in Levinson, S (ed), *Torture: A Collection* (Oxford University Press, 2004), 229, 232, using the term 'preventive interrogational torture'; Kershnar, S, 'For Interrogational Torture' (2005) 19 *International Journal of Applied Philosophy* 223; Kremnitzer and Segev (n 125 above), 509; Lee, P, 'Interrogational Torture' (2006) 51 *American Journal of Jurisprudence* 131; Sussman (n 134 above), 4; Tindale, C, 'The Logic of Torture: A Critical Examination' (1996) 22 *Social Theory and Practice* 349, 350–351, categorising torture into 'interrogational torture', 'deterrent torture' and 'dehumanising torture'.

[143]   Shue (n 8 above), 131.

protection against further assault'.[144] Shue was sceptical of the ability of the victim to bring the torture to an end through compliance. Significantly, he also recognised that 'very few instances of torture are likely to fall entirely within the category of interrogational torture'.[145] In making the latter point, Shue almost grasped a crucial, yet subtle, difference between interrogation as the context, or setting, for torture and torture as a method of interrogation. His observations were, however, overshadowed by his presentation of the possibility of pure interrogational torture in that rare, isolated case. In failing to fully let go of the 'rare case', he was precluded from differentiating between interrogation as the context for torture and interrogation as a justification for torture. Understanding this difference is essential to cracking the 'enigmas of denial and bad faith encoded within the language we use to converse with ourselves' about torture.[146] Indeed, given the interrogation room's ubiquity as the setting for torture, a lot of torture happens in an interrogational setting – but this environmental context is generally, and dangerously, substituted for method, purpose and motive. The decision of the Bush administration policy-makers to rename torture 'enhanced interrogation techniques' was parasitic on this rationalisation of torture. What better way to represent and repackage torture than to use the language of enhanced *interrogation* – interrogation for information to stop a bomb.

Whilst much has been written about the objective of torture and about torture's efficacy, few have really considered the way in which the rhetoric around torture creates an understanding of torture.[147] Words matter. Torture is widely considered to be a method of interrogation because we call it a method of interrogation. Because they do not suit the narrative, are less intuitive and more difficult to grasp, accounts which complicate and disrupt this reproduction of torture simply do not prevail. It is easier – more intuitive – to accept the categories.

Crelinsten, however, writing in a pre-11 September environment, did manage to articulate the complexity of torture. He saw that torture was understood to revolve around interrogation, but, he argued, 'it is more complex than this'.[148] Whilst perpetrators usually excuse their use of torture on the basis of the need to get information or a confession, Crelinsten identified in these excuses that there was more at stake than 'making them talk'. Crelinsten saw that this excuse of '"making them talk" is also about power, about imposing one's will on another'.[149] Crelinsten advocated against the simplification of torture into categories and torturers into typologies. Crelinsten's grasp of the complexity both of torture and of the torturer's purposes means that he was able to decipher the debates about torture's acceptability, in the post-11 September environment, for what they were – an important element of the construction of a reality in which torture can be seen as acceptable: 'To enable torture to be practised systematically and routinely, to be taken for granted and even to be celebrated, not only do torturers have to be trained and prepared, but wider elements of society must also be prepared and, in a sense, trained to accept that such things go on.'[150] So torturers needed to be trained – in the

---

[144]   *Ibid*, 134.
[145]   *Ibid*.
[146]   Cohen, S, *States of Denial: Knowing about Atrocities and Suffering* (Polity Press, 2001), 116.
[147]   See, however, *ibid*.
[148]   Crelinsten, RD, 'In Their Own Words: The World of the Torturer' in Crelinsten, RD and Schmid, AP (eds), *The Politics of Pain: Torturers and their Masters* (Westview Press, 1995), 35, 37.
[149]   *Ibid*, 37.
[150]   Crelinsten does not mean training in the sense of learning techniques. He employs training more widely to denote the construction of a new social reality. Crelinsten, R, 'How to Make a Torturer' (2005) *Index on Censorship* 72.

sense that they need to be conditioned to accept a new reality and made morally malleable to the dehumanisation of the enemy – and persuaded of the need for torture, in order that they can serve the interests of the state. Simultaneously, the public or society needs to be made amenable to torture. The production of torture as interrogational – purposeful and necessary in ticking bomb situations – is part of this ideological landscaping.

On the purposes or goals of torture, Asad has said:

> Critics sometimes claim that 'the extraction of information' is not the real goal of torture, but rather torture's justification. But I suggest that there is no such thing as 'the *real* goal of torture.' The motives (conscious and unconscious) of someone who carries out specific acts of torture are usually varied and mixed. The idea that specific acts of torture should be understood by the agent's motivation is either circular or based on the sentimental (and false) belief that only peculiar psychosocial types are capable of great cruelty.[151]

In making this point about the absence of a true goal of torture, Asad does seem to somewhat underestimate the significance of understanding information extraction as the justification for torture, rather than its purpose. This distinction between justification and purpose is essential to grasping the ideology of modern torture. It should not be assumed, though, that, by pursuing the exposure of ideology, there is an inevitable next step of pursuing, or discovering, truth; that is to say, by exposing the ideology we do not simply reveal the true goal of torture.[152] However, on the whole, Asad's observation is critical, and his decisive contribution is in his de-rationalisation of torture. The dominant rationalisation for torture today is on the basis of its supposed interrogational purpose – the assumption that torture is or can be a method of interrogation. But Asad topples the myth of the good torturer pursuing a particular goal. Our intuitions are primed to view the torture of a member of the political resistance in a dictatorial regime as entirely distinguishable from the torture of a 'ticking bomb' terrorist or a kidnapper in a liberal democracy. The distinguishing feature between these tortures, however, is our standpoint. The idea of interrogational torture as distinguishable from terroristic, sadistic, communicative or punitive torture is not sustainable under historical and contextual examination.

Klein, more sharply than many other thinkers, has grasped the function of torture. In attempting to convince a potential interviewee to speak to her – an interviewee who had experienced devastating psychological experimentation at the hands of researchers at McGill University in the 1950s – Klein explained her research interest in the interviewee as follows: 'I recently travelled to Iraq, and I am trying to understand the role torture is playing there. We are told it's about getting information, but I think it's more than that – I think it may also have to do with trying to build a model country, about erasing people and then trying to remake them from scratch.'[153] Through her study of how the CIA used psychological experimental research (research which, in part, aimed at breaking down and rebuilding individuals who had mental health problems) in its development of an interrogation programme in the 1950s, and her observations on torture in Iraq and in the 'war on terror', Klein has understood torture as about unmaking bodies and minds, so that they can be remade or rebuilt. Klein's under-

---

[151]   Asad, T, *Formations of the Secular: Christianity, Islam, Modernity* (Stanford University Press, 2003), 104.
[152]   Eagleton (n 68 above), 11.
[153]   Klein (n 44 above), 26.

standing evokes the civilising mission: civilising the uncivilised, by breaking and remaking, through torture.

TORTURE AND THE CIVILISING MISSION

This link between torture in Iraq and the civilising mission maps on to the wider reading of the 2004 invasion of Iraq, the underpinning Bush doctrine, and, indeed, the wider 'war on terror', as imperial in character, as 'yet another version of the civilising mission'.[154] For Anghie, the identification of Iraq as a 'rogue state', ripe for liberation and transformation, the expansionist arguments around the use of force, encapsulated in the Bush doctrine's policy of pre-emption, and the strategic engagement of rights arguments to justify the invasion, all demonstrate, and replicate, the old imperial order.[155] The imperial nature of the Bush doctrine, which included this expansionist interpretation of the rules on the use of force, and self-defence, is evidenced in the Third World's exclusion from use of the doctrine whilst being subject to its application and elaboration.[156] The legal manoeuvres through which the 'war on terror' was established – including the Bush doctrine of self-defence, the reinterpretation of the 'laws of armed conflict', the rhetoric around 'unlawful combatants',[157] and the necessity exception to the laws prohibiting torture – were an exercise in legitimating war against an 'uncivilised' other.[158]

This understanding of the 'war on terror' and the Iraq war echoes, and continues, the European conquest, and 'civilisation', of the 'uncivilised' world.[159] That conquest was legitimated through the civilising mission – the colonised were excluded from the universal, civilised norms or values of the colonial state, whilst being subject to their application and elaboration. As Anghie writes, the civilizing mission 'has justified colonialism as a means of redeeming the backward, aberrant, violent, oppressed, undeveloped people of the non-European world by incorporating them into the universal civilization of Europe'.[160] International law was both complicit in, and shaped by, the colonial encounter. It was used to legitimate colonialism and exploitation and colonial practices fed back into its normative architecture.

A French concept,[161] civilisation connotes the opposite to barbarianism; to civilise means to bring out of barbarism or savagery. The civilising mission is a French imperial doctrine. As France extended its colonial empire in the latter part of the 19th century, 'French publicists, and subsequently politicians, declared that their government alone among the Western states had a special mission to civilise the indigenous peoples now coming under its control – what

---

[154]   Anghie (n 39 above), 61.

[155]   *Ibid*, 61, 63, 65.

[156]   *Ibid*, 52.

[157]   Mégret, F, 'From Savages to "Unlawful Combatants": A Postcolonial Look at International Humanitarian Law's "other"', in Orford, A (ed), *International Law and its Others* (Cambridge University Press, 2006).

[158]   Anghie, A, *Imperialism, Sovereignty and the Making of International Law* (Cambridge University Press, 2012), 298.

[159]   *Ibid*, 4.

[160]   *Ibid*, 3.

[161]   Conklin, AL, *A Mission to Civilise: The Republican Idea of Empire in France and West Africa, 1895–1930* (Stanford University Press, 1997), 1.

the French called their *mission civilisatrice*', Conklin explains.[162] For those who supported the French empire and who were immersed in the idea of bettering 'dependent peoples', this was an enunciated creed.[163] But the French were not alone in this ideology. Other imperial powers shared this claim of bringing civilisation to the colonies.[164] As Fanon reveals, their claims rested on the 'systematic negation of the other person and a furious determination to deny the other person all attributes of humanity'.[165]

The civilising mission dovetailed with international law in Empire's favour. Kiernan describes 'the colonial scene, where no international law obtained'.[166] For the colonists, international law was unavailable to the colonial subject.[167] In international legal terms, the colony lacked legal personality and sovereignty, was incapable of partaking in international law, and, accordingly, imperial powers were free from the 'legal constraints on the use of violence (to subjugate and pacify native populations) that bound them in their relationships with one another and their own metropolitan populations'.[168] International law was not absent. Colonial conquest was justified through international legal language. As such, international law was both universalised and shaped in a racialised context.[169] As the Third World Approaches to International Law scholarship has shown, the hierarchies and biases formalised in the colonies persist in international law and institutions.[170]

The torture prohibition and the ticking bomb scenario are part of this history. The abolition of judicial torture in Europe was almost complete by the end of the 18th century.[171] This history of abolition has been translated into two fairy-tales, which, combined, have aided the construction of torture as aberrational, a violation of the norm. The first fairy-tale presents abolition as driven by enlightenment humanitarianism; the second fairy-tale has the happiest of endings – the near complete abolition of torture. In reality, *judicial* torture was abandoned as it was no longer required by the law of proof.[172] Torture continued, not least in the colonies.

In the era of decolonisation – and the overlapping era of human rights, the laws of armed conflict, and media and civil society scrutiny – it was difficult to justify torture on the basis of the necessity to civilise or pacify the racially inferior or savage colonial subject. It was certainly not possible to justify torture on the basis of the imperial need to create political subjects amenable to the retention of the colony. As such, the ticking bomb – the 'interrogation' of the lawless terrorist – became the face of the civilising mission. The ticking bomb justification for

---

[162]   *Ibid.*

[163]   Thomas, M, *Fight or Flight: Britain, France and their Roads from Empire* (Oxford University Press, 2014), 22.

[164]   Conklin (n 161 above), 1. On Kenya, torture and the civilising mission, see generally, Elkins, C, *Imperial Reckoning: The Untold Story of Britian's Gulag in Kenya* (Owl Books, 2005).

[165]   Fanon, F, *The Wretched of the Earth* (Macgibbon and Kee, 1965), 203.

[166]   Kiernan, VG, *European Empires from Conquest to Collapse, 1815–1960* (Leicester University Press, 1982), 154.

[167]   Colby, E, 'How to Fight Savage Tribes' (1927) 21 *American Journal of International Law* 279; see also Kiernan (n 166 above), 146–166; Mégret (n 157 above).

[168]   Reynolds, J, *Empire, Emergency and International Law* (Cambridge University Press, 2017), 66.

[169]   Chimni, BS, 'The Past, Present and Future of International Law: A Critical Third World Approach' (2007) 8 *Melbourne Journal of International Law* 499, 501.

[170]   See Mutua, M and Anghie, A, 'What is TWAIL?' (2000) 94 *ASIL Proceedings* 31.

[171]   Langbein, JH, *Torture and the Law of Proof: Europe and England in the Ancien Régime* (University of Chicago Press, 2006 edn), 10.

[172]   *Ibid*, 10–12.

the use of torture crystallised in the colony. Torture at Abu Ghraib exposed this dark under-belly. But the state has a way of arguing away torture, burying its realities in the rotten apples and necessity exceptions. As with the practice of torture in the French-Algerian war, the state's narrative on Abu Ghraib predominated.

Translating the Civilising Mission into Ticking Bomb: The French Algerian War

The practice of torture in Algeria is particularly useful both for understanding the infatuation with the ticking bomb scenario and for pouring cold water on that infatuation. However, despite the wealth of stellar research on torture during the French Algerian War and the Battle of Algiers, in particular, the torturer's perspective has prevailed. There are a couple of broad illustrations to support that claim.

First, the ticking bomb justification, which is so ubiquitous today, has its roots in the French Algerian war – it was during that war that this justification was most explicitly internalised and wielded.[173] In the aftermath of the war, the justification was truly conceptualised. Today, the ticking bomb scenario is a globalised construct. Less ubiquitous in contemporary debates is awareness of the systematic practice of torture, and the reasons for that brutal practice, by the French during the war.

Second, the sheer power of the French state both to censor voices and to amnesty crimes means that it was able to shape the discourse.[174] French torturers have been given numerous platforms to air their version of events. Following Algerian independence and the end of the war, military personnel took the opportunity to impart their experience, and knowledge, of perpetrating torture. French torturers gave advice and instruction in the United States,[175]

---

[173]   Of course, the practice of torture was extensive throughout the colonies.

[174]   As part of the Evian accords, signed in 1962, by French and Algerian representatives, amnesties were agreed for both sides; torture was not specifically mentioned in the accords. In 1968, the French parliament introduced a further law granting amnesty for all offences committed in connection with the war. See Beigbeder, Y, *Judging War Crimes and Torture: French Justice and International Tribunals and Commissions* (1940–2005) (Martinus Nijhof Publishers, 2006) 95–96; Lazreg, M, *Torture and the Twilight of Empire: From Algiers to Baghdad* (Princeton University Press, 2007) 1.

[175]   Paul Aussaresses, renowned torturer and torture advocate, as well as General and Chief of Military Intelligence during the Battle of Algiers, was an instructor on counterinsurgency methods at Fort Bragg Army Training Centre in the United States in the early 1960s. See, Beigbeder (n 174 above) 124; Harcourt, B, *The Counterrevolution: How Our Government Went to War Against its Own Citizens* (Basic Books, 2018) 45. Aussarrasses showed up again in the United States, in 2002, on CBS's 60 Minutes, alongside Alan Dershowitz, advocating for the use of torture, specifically against Zacarias Moussaaoui. See the publisher's foreword in General Paul Aussaresses, *The Battle of the Casbah: Terrorism and Counter-Terrorism in Algeria 1955–1957* (Enigma Books, 2002) iii. The segment is no longer available on YouTube, likely because in 2002 the General was convicted in the French courts of complicity in justifying war crimes, following the publication of what became in the English translation, *The Battle of the Casbah*: Paul Aussaresses, *Services Spéciaux: Algérie 1955–1957* (Perrin, 2001). See Löytömäki, S, 'Legalisation of the Memory of the Algerian War in France' (2005) 7 *Journal of the History of International Law* 157.

Argentina[176] and other countries.[177] Victims, on the other hand, were silenced both during the war[178] and in their subsequent efforts to secure any kind of accountability.[179] Public opinion in France turned against the war, in part, because of the outcry at the use of torture; however, the outrage, arguably, failed to fill the public memory.

From the outset, the French state repressed the fresh memory of its activities in Algeria. The fact that torture in Algeria was both structural and approved by the highest authorities[180] has only recently begun to be acknowledged.[181] Official discourse mediated the history of torture – only when it had to – as aberrant, the work of individuals acting alone;[182] subsequent leaders failed to condemn the systematic practice of torture. Individual military personnel were, though, given spaces and opportunities to explain and justify their use of torture. All the while, public and popular discourse facilitated legitimation through the image of the good torturer and the ticking bomb.[183] Historical amnesia in France has been accompanied by what Lazreg describes as the exercise of 'monopoly over meaning', enabling the empire 'to reproduce itself, by deconstructing itself with one hand, and recomposing itself with the other'.[184]

Towards torture: strategy, law, ideology
The use of torture by the French was underpinned by strategies of 'revolutionary warfare', advocated in particular by figures such as Trinquier, who Maran describes as having provided the French army with the 'theoretical' justifications for the use of torture. In Algeria, as elsewhere, euphemisms for the word torture were, unsurprisingly, employed.[185] Revolutionary warfare established that the violence of terrorism countenanced an equivalently violent

---

[176] Chelala, C, 'The French Connection in the Export of Torture', *International Herald Tribune* (22 June 2001) available at https://www.nytimes.com/2001/06/22/opinion/IHT-meanwhile-the-french -connection-in-the-export-of-torture.html. See also Collard (n 21 above).

[177] Aussaresses was also an advisor in Brazil in the early 1970s. French military personnel also served as advisors in Chile. See Beigbeder (n 174 above) 124; Dobie, M, '"The Battle of Algiers" at 50: From 1960s Radicalism to the Classes at Westpoint', *Los Angeles Review of Books* (25 September 2016) available at https://lareviewofbooks.org/article/battle-algiers-50-1960s-radicalism-classrooms-west-point/

[178] *La Question*, Henri Alleg's celebrated account of his torture at the hands of the French military, published in 1958, had the dubious honour of being the first book banned by the French government since the 18th century, Alleg, H, *The Question* (John Calder, 1958) xiv. Similarly, *Gangrene*, a collection of testimonies of Algerian torture victims, published in 1959, was banned and suppressed in France. See *Gangrene* (John Calder, 1959). French censorship was not successful at the time; it really only added to public interest, as Maran explains. Maran (n 38 above) 171.

[179] As one high-profile example, Josette Audin spent 61 years demanding that the French state accept responsibility for the death in custody in 1957, through torture, of her husband, Maurice Audin. In September 2018, to media shock, Emmanuel Macron sent a letter to the Audin family, apologising on behalf of the French state. 'Déclaration du Président de la République sur la mort de Maurice Audin' 13 September 2018 available at https://www.elysee.fr/emmanuel-macron/2018/09/13/declaration-du -president-de-la-republique-sur-la-mort-de-maurice-audin.

[180] Branche, 'Torture of Terrorists?' (n 48 above), 547.

[181] Chrisafis, A, 'France Admits Systematic Torture during Algeria War for the First Time', *The Guardian* (13 September 2018) available at https://www.theguardian.com/world/2018/sep/13/france -state-responsible-for-1957-death-of-dissident-maurice-audin-in-algeria-says-macron

[182] Löytömäki (n 175 above), 171.

[183] For example, Lartéguy, J, *Les Centurions* (Presses de la Cité, 1960).

[184] Lazreg (n 174 above), 2.

[185] Maran (n 38 above), 82. It is worth noting that France had, at this stage, been heavily involved in the drafting of the European Convention on Human Rights, which contains the Article 3 prohibition on

response and that information about the terrorist's next move was essential to thwart the random attacks, justifying coercion.[186] French theories of revolutionary warfare later migrated to the United States.[187]

In his memoirs, *La Vraie Bataille,* Massu, commander of French forces in Algeria during the Battle of Algiers, acknowledged the use of torture, though he disputed both its severity and the extent to which it was used; he went to great lengths, however, to justify its use in reference to the necessity of gaining 'urgent operational information'.[188] His men tortured thousands.[189] Unambiguously referencing revolutionary warfare, he saw the savagery of the enemy as having compelled their ferocious response. Massu's outlook signifies and continues a deep history, exposed by Mégret, of anthropologising the savage as '*incapable of showing restraint in warfare*'.[190] In an about turn, in 2000, in an interview in *Le Monde*, Massu expressed his regret at the use of torture in Algeria, admitting that it had been not been useful or necessary and acknowledging that things could have been done differently.[191]

Aussaresses illustrates how justificatory logic circulated within the police and intelligence forces. He narrates a conversation in Philippeville, in which a police officer confronted him with a ticking bomb-like dilemma, as the turning point in his own attitude towards the necessity of torture.[192] Although Ausseresses resolutely defended his actions, on the basis of urgency and necessity, until the end of his life, his own memoirs depict torture in Algeria as a routine method of 'intelligence-gathering' and the necessity justification as a defence mechanism internalised by a brutal, remorseless, torturer.

So-called revolutionary warfare was facilitated within a legal regime characterised by emergency powers, providing 'the executive with an almost totalitarian mandate to introduce by administrative order any form of repressive measures it saw fit'.[193] Although 'the army was in charge', by 1957, when police powers were transferred by Lacoste to the military, under Massu,[194] the 'conflict' was, nevertheless, treated by France as an internal affair – an insurrection or revolution; the opposition were cast as terrorists or outlaws.[195] Absent sovereignty, and

---

torture. France signed the treaty on the day that it opened for signature, 4 November 1950, but it did not ratify the treaty until 3 May 1974.

[186]   *Ibid,* 82.

[187]   Harcourt (n 175 above), 45.

[188]   Maran (n 38 above), 101–102.

[189]   Evans, M, *Algeria: France's Undeclared War* (Oxford University Press, 2012), 206.

[190]   Mégret (n 157 above), 289 (original emphasis).

[191]   Planchais, J and Beaugé, F, 'Jacques Massu, Le géneral repenti', *Le Monde* (22 May 2008) available at https://www.lemonde.fr/le-monde-2/article/2008/05/22/jacques-massu-le-general-repenti _1048161_1004868.html; see also Farrell (n 4 above), 100.

[192]   Aussaresses, *Services Spéciaux* (n 175 above), 31. He writes: "Imagine a situation in which you are opposed in principle to the use of torture and you have arrested an individual who is clearly involved in the preparation of an attack. The suspect refuses to talk. You do nothing. As a result, a particularly deadly attack ensues. What would you say to the parents of the victims, for example, to the parents of a child mutilated by the bomb to justify the fact that you failed to do whatever possible to make the suspect talk?" (author's translation).

[193]   MacMaster, N, 'Torture: From Algiers to Abu Ghraib' (2004) 46 *Race & Class* 1, 6. For a detailed explanation of the legal framework in place as well as the use, and effect, of emergency powers in Algeria during the war, see Farrell (n 4 above), 84–95.

[194]   Farrell (n 4 above), 7.

[195]   Van Cleef Greenberg, E, 'Law and the Conduct of the Algerian Revolution' (1970) 11 *Harvard International Law Journal* 37, 44.

incapable anyway of obeying it, according to French thinking, the Algerians did not benefit from international humanitarian law. Combatant status simply did not apply.

Revolutionary warfare and emergency powers were deadly bedfellows. It was the civilising mission, however, that provided the ideological pillar in the violent trilogy that allowed systematic torture against the Algerians. Revolutionary warfare encouraged justificatory thinking and emergency powers permitted the French forces to place the FLN and other detainees outside of any protective legal order. But the civilising mission drove French policy.

For the French, Algeria was the 'lynchpin of the French empire', its jewel, its most intimate colonial conquest. Algeria was France.[196] The government and military claimed that, in Algeria, the French were upholding the 'highest principles of the French republican tradition';[197] French civilisation, in short. Their mission, as they saw it, was to establish peace in Algeria, to bring social and economic reform, to liberate the Algerians.[198] It may seem contradictory to suggest that the civilising mission drove French torture, especially given the centrality of *les droits de l'homme* and the French Declaration to 'French civilisation'. To understand the civilising mission, it is necessary to come to terms with the dehumanising logic of colonialism and with the intersection of colonialism and rights. Torture was necessary in defence of France, of civilisation, of Christian values. Maran, in her outstanding examination of the civilising mission in the discourse of French government and military personnel, concluded: 'The shared understanding was that France's presence in Algeria was philanthropic, bringing civilisation to Algerians ... not least through notions of rights. When this process was disrupted by the Algerian revolution, the government acting through its military ... took the position that unusual means were justified to restore order.'[199] Within a racialised settler hierarchy,[200] for most, torture was also permissible, necessary even, because the adversary, long constructed as, non-equal, was not yet fully civilised, not yet fully human. Asad's evocative words connect the dots between torture and the colonised subject: 'Pain endured in the movement toward becoming "fully human," ... was necessary, in the sense that there were social or moral reasons why it had to be suffered'.[201] Torture was part of the process of creating new human subjects.

Ticking bomb-like thinking and rationalising became rife in the French Algerian war. Such logic was pressed into service as part of the civilising mission. French torture was systematic, widespread and brutal. That the ticking bomb scenario is the thriving memento of that history of torture is a damning indictment of our failure to come to terms either with why torture was practised in Algeria and elsewhere or with the colonial encounter, its remnants, transnationalism and the 'boomerang effect'.[202]

---

[196] Sessions, JE, *By Sword and by Plow: France and the Conquest of Algeria* (Cornell University Press, 2011) 2, 8, 9.

[197] Evans (n 189 above), 206.

[198] *Ibid*, 155–159, 193.

[199] Maran (n 38 above), 188.

[200] Keller, RC, *Colonial Madness: Psychiatry in French North Africa* (University of Chicago Press, 2007), 4.

[201] Asad (n 151 above), 113.

[202] On the imperial boomerang effect, see Reynolds (n 168 above), 31; Césaire (n 2 above).

CONCLUSION

The many histories of torture overwhelmingly elucidate it as a practice that looks nothing like the apologetic portrayal du jour.[203] Yet it is the slick assembly of a worthy professional, doing only what is necessary, with managed violence, to the reticent terrorist, to stop the bomb which has come to dominate our understanding; that is to say, this is the understanding of torture as perpetrated by the United States, France, Israel and other 'Western' states – the practice of torture by dictatorships is viewed differently, through a more medieval lens.

Rejali, reflecting on the erasure of the histories and the realities of torture, wondered how the ticking bomb scenario is able to bend all argument – and history – to its narrative.[204] We can continue to reach answers to Rejali's urgent question by exploring the complex interplay of Empire and ideology. Just as – through the act of torture – the victim is broken and remade, civilised, in the eyes of the torturer, so too the history of torture is erased and rebuilt, civilised, in the eyes of its authors. The remnants of the colonial encounter are visible everywhere, in practices of torture, in discussions on torture and in the law prohibiting torture.

In the recent history of US torture, parallels and links to the French Algerian war abound. There were similarities in strategy – warfare, characterised by pre-emptive force necessitated by the novelty of the threat;[205] in law – the use of emergency powers and the removal of legal protection and status, placing the 'terrorists' beyond the law; and in ideology – the logic of interventionism to liberate and to bring democracy, to defend and extend 'civilisation'.[206] The Bush administration worked hard to construe their actions as within the bounds of legality, through definitional gymnastics, and reliance on necessity. That history of torture has, nevertheless, been examined through the lens of ticking bombs and justificatory or necessity logic. Far less attention has been given to the racialised, civilising nature of American conduct.

The same can be said of the academic and popular attention given to the ticking bomb scenario. There has been much frenzied typing about this so-called dilemma. Many have accepted the construct at face value, failing to grasp the civilising ideology that it conceals. There are interlocking reasons for the lethargy in understanding torture. Torture is misunderstood today as being for the purpose of obtaining information; there is an utter failure to understand this as its justification. Part of the problem lies in the way that the internationally accepted definition of torture has reified this justification in law.[207] We are also living in a culture of denial.[208] As Cohen has argued in respect of our ability to ignore atrocities and suffering, 'a culture of

---

[203] There are many excellent histories and genealogies of torture. There is insufficient space to list the more specific country- and case-based studies. For a more general account, however, there is no better work than Peters, E, *Torture* (University of Pennsylvania Press, 1999). The history of torture in the Middle Ages cannot be understood without recourse to Langbein. For a short introduction see, Langbein, JH, 'The Legal History of Torture' in Levinson, S (ed), *Torture: A Collection* (Oxford University Press, 2004). Rejali has produced an unparalleled history of modern torture, see Rejali (n 15 above).

[204] Rejali (n 15 above), 547.

[205] Knox, R, 'Civilising Interventions: Race, War and International Law' (2013) 26 *Cambridge Review of International Affairs* 111, 113.

[206] Kumar, D, 'Framing Islam: The Resurgence of Orientalism during the Bush Era II' (2010) 34 *Journal of Communication Inquiry* 254, 259–260.

[207] UN Convention against Torture and Other Cruel, Inhuman and Degrading Treatment or Punishment (n 36 above), Art 1(1).

[208] Cohen (n 146 above), 115.

denial is in place'. [209] Justifications for torture, like the ticking bomb, are part of this denial; they 'have been offered and accepted long enough to be part of the moral fabric'.[210] The ticking bomb scenario provides a simple and persuasive construct. The construct allows apologists to substitute deeply held ideologically beliefs for more acceptable theories of necessity. It allows the quieter majority an alternative to subjecting their governments, their values, their civilisation to the relentless critique they require.

It was really only in the closing stages of the French Algerian war that the ticking bomb scenario was fully formalised in its contemporary, beguiling, urgent construct. Suitably, the construct was first set out in a work of fiction,[211] Lartéguy's *Les Centurions*. Inspired by events in the French Algerian war, *Les Centurions* erases the intimate connection between the ticking bomb and the civilising mission. It was far easier to memorialise torture in Algeria, as the novel attempts to, through the lens of the good guy, stopping bombs, conscientiously.

The ticking bomb scenario conceals the civilising mission, an ideology underpinned by racial hatred and dehumanisation. When asked, then, what would you do in a ticking bomb situation, it may be best to remember, before wading in, that you are being asked to perpetuate an ideology of torture.

---

[209] *Ibid.*
[210] *Ibid.*
[211] Rejali (n 15 above), 546.

3.   Effective torture prevention

Richard Carver and Lisa Handley

INTRODUCTION

The prohibition of torture is not only one of the strongest principles of international human rights law, it also has the most detailed underpinning in treaty law, reinforced by the jurisprudence of regional and national courts, and treaty bodies. If a state is genuinely committed to eradicating torture, there is little doubt as to what international law requires it to do. The question, rather, is whether any of these things actually work. The requirements of international human rights law tend to be a combination of broad principle and common sense. They are not usually formulated in response to detailed empirical inquiry, so the detailed prescriptions of the Convention Against Torture (UNCAT)[1] and its Optional Protocol (OPCAT)[2] (not to mention the various dicta of the treaty bodies and special procedures) are based on a set of educated guesses.

The findings reported in this chapter are the outcome of a four-year multi-country study conducted by a team of more than 20 researchers, funded by the Association for Prevention of Torture (APT), a Geneva-based international non-governmental organization. Our research addressed a very specific question: does torture prevention work?[3] We were not seeking to uncover the root causes of torture or the political, economic or social factors associated with its increase or decline. Instead, we focused solely on the effectiveness of preventive measures in reducing the incidence of torture. Much thought and practical effort has been expended – by international experts, civil society activists, legislators, and others – in determining what steps governments should take to prevent torture. The outcome of this thought and effort is to be found in the international instruments themselves, primarily the UNCAT and the OPCAT, as well as in the reports and recommendations of international, regional and national bodies. Yet no one had actually studied whether the various legal obligations and practical steps actually had any effect in reducing the risk of torture. The APT, which devotes its time and money to promoting these preventive measures, sought an honest answer to this question and funded us to lead an entirely independent scholarly project to give an answer.

Previous academic approaches to the issue of torture prevention fell broadly into three categories. Much of it is legal/normative and the very best of this has been produced by scholars who have also been prominent in implementing these norms through the international system. Secondly, there are a number of country case studies, usually qualitative in approach. These

---

[1]   Convention against Torture and Other Cruel, Inhuman or Degrading Treatment or Punishment (adopted 10 December 1984, entered into force 26 June 1987) 1465 UNTS 85.

[2]   Optional Protocol to the Convention against Torture and Other Cruel, Inhuman or Degrading Treatment or Punishment (adopted 18 December 2002, entered into force 22 June 2006) 2375 UNTS 237.

[3]   We focused solely on torture or purposive ill-treatment. Other forms of ill-treatment fell beyond the scope of our study.

are often helpful in understanding the specific dynamics behind successful torture prevention in a given context and were useful to us in identifying variables to test in our own research. But they cannot offer generalizable conclusions. Thirdly, political scientists have conducted some large-n quantitative studies, but these have generally focused on questions adjacent to our own research. For example, several scholars have looked at the relationship between ratification of human rights treaties such as the UNCAT and improved respect for human rights (often concluding that treaty ratification has no positive effect). For us, this was the wrong question. We were not interested in the impact of ratification in itself; rather we wanted to know whether practical implementation of the obligations in the UNCAT, for example, would contribute to reducing the risk of torture.

We used two distinct methodological approaches to answer the question "does torture prevention work?". First, in-country research teams carried out detailed qualitative case studies of torture prevention efforts and their impact in 16 countries over a 30-year period (1985–2014). Secondly, we quantified much of the information collected in order to conduct a statistical analysis to determine if there were any discernible patterns across the 16 countries. We were specifically interested in ascertaining which preventive measures, if any, were most likely to be associated with a decrease in the incidence of torture. Once this analysis was completed, we drew on our country examples to illustrate the patterns our examination uncovered.

The results of our analysis indicated that torture prevention does indeed work. The introduction of some specific preventive measures undoubtedly reduced the incidence of torture in the countries we studied. We also found that some of the preventive steps we looked at were more effective at reducing torture than others across these countries.

Of the four clusters of preventive measures we considered, clearly the most important were the safeguards in place in the first hours and days after arrest, particularly promptly notifying the family of the arrest, informing the detainee of the right to a lawyer (which the detainee then exercises), and providing a medical examination shortly after detention. The second most important set of measures were those related to the prosecution of torturers, especially that torture complaints are lodged and investigated, that conviction rates for torture are comparable to those of other serious crimes, and that no amnesties or pardons are granted to torturers. Also important were measures related to monitoring, particularly that detainees are interviewed and that sanctions are not brought against monitors or those who cooperate with them. The least effective set of preventive measures we examined were those related to complaints bodies, with the caveat that complaints bodies that feed directly into an investigative or prosecutorial authority are more effective in reducing torture than those that do not.

Our analysis uncovered another important finding: practice is far more important than law at reducing the incidence of torture. As we began to collect information, it became quite evident there is often a gap between practice and law – that is, there is often a failure to fully implement and enforce legislation that has been enacted. We felt it was important to note both the state of the law and the degree to which it was being enforced in any given year for each country. Our analysis confirmed the gap, and indicated that the size of the gap varies depending on the specific set of preventive measures, with it being the widest between prosecution law and practice (ie, although torture is illegal in all of the countries included in our research, torturers are rarely tried or, when tried, seldom convicted in these countries).

HOW DO WE KNOW THIS?

As noted above, our study encompassed 16 countries over a 30-year period. The countries were selected to provide geopolitical diversity. Given that a 30-year time span was covered, most countries had a variety of different experiences of both the prevalence of torture and the existence of preventive mechanisms or measures. Additional pragmatic selection criteria included the availability of experience and high-quality researchers, as well as safe access. One country had to be replaced at an early stage because of risks to the researcher. The final list of countries was: Argentina, Chile, Ethiopia, Georgia, Hungary, India, Indonesia, Israel, Kyrgyzstan, Norway, Peru, Philippines, South Africa, Tunisia, Turkey, and the United Kingdom. In addition to producing qualitative case studies for most of these countries, we also generated a quantitative database. We identified 66 possible preventive mechanisms and for each country, for each year, we coded whether the mechanism was fully present, partially present, or absent. We then constructed eight indices, two for each of the four clusters of preventive mechanisms studied: detention law and practice; prosecution law and practice; complaints law and practice; and monitoring law and practice. The higher a country scored on an index, the more preventive mechanisms were in place.

Our independent variables were drawn from the broad array of legal standards, binding and non-binding, and recommendations from human rights bodies.

The first cluster of preventive measures was derived from the UNCAT and primarily directed at criminalizing torture and holding its perpetrators accountable through criminal law. Article 2(1) of the Convention makes it clear that the overarching purpose of the treaty is prevention. That is, the criminalization and effective investigation of acts of torture, and the prosecution or extradition of alleged torturers are aimed at preventing the further incidence of torture.

Secondly, the OPCAT exemplifies the role of monitoring bodies in preventing torture, with its requirement that states parties establish their own national preventive mechanism (NPM) to work in concert with the UN Subcommittee on Prevention of Torture (SPT), both of which enjoy powers to visit places of deprivation of liberty. An external visiting body has existed in Europe for nearly three decades, under the European Convention on the Prevention of Torture,[4] while many countries already have domestic bodies empowered to conduct such visits.

Thirdly, complaints bodies are seen by many as another important preventive mechanism.[5] Independent complaints mechanisms in this sense are usually understood to be something distinct from prosecutorial bodies that investigate complaints of torture. They are normally no-cost, semi-formal bodies such as ombudsman offices or national human rights institutions.

Finally, campaigners against torture have often argued for the significance of safeguards on arrest and during police detention, when the risk of ill-treatment is likely to be greatest. While there is some overlap with the fair trial protections to be found, for example, in Articles 9 and

---

[4]   European Convention for the Prevention of Torture and Inhuman or Degrading Treatment or Punishment (adopted 26 November 1987, entered into force 1 February 1989) ETS no 126.

[5]   European Committee for the Prevention of Torture and Inhuman or Degrading Treatment or Punishment, *CPT Standards*, CPT/Inf/E (2002) 1 – Rev 2015.

14 of the International Covenant on Civil and Political Rights,[6] these mechanisms tend to be less well protected in international law.

In addition to creating a coding scheme for the presence or absence of preventive mechanisms, we had to adopt a scheme for measuring the incidence of torture. Although countries vary in the both their legal and colloquial definitions of torture, we needed to employ a uniform measure across all 16 countries over the entire 30-year scope of the study. We devised the Carver-Handley Torture Score (CHATS) for this purpose. The CHATS was compiled using a variety of primary and secondary sources.[7] It is composed of three elements:

- *Frequency*, scored on a scale of 0 to 3, which measures the degree to which torture within the custodial system is routine and pervasive. Answers range from never (no case of torture) to very likely (torture is systematic, pervasive or routine).
- *Geographical spread*, scored from 0 to 2, which measures whether torture occurs across the entire jurisdiction of the state ('2') or only in particular regions or areas ('1').
- *Severity*, scored from 0 to 2, which measures how severe the treatment is after it has been established that ill-treatment is sufficiently severe to qualify as torture. The CHATS distinguishes torture ('1') from more severe torture ('2'). To be clear, when we consider the issue of torture methods, it is important to underline that we are not distinguishing between those that are more or less detectable. Nor are we passing judgment on the scale of pain and suffering endured by any particular victim of torture. Rather, this measure seeks to capture the intent of the state agents who commit torture. Severity is assessed partly in terms of the torture techniques commonly used, but also considers combinations of method, and duration and repetition.

The overall CHATS score combines the three measures on a scale of 0 to 5. Because CHATS automatically registers a minimum score of '3' if torture is present (since there must be a score of at least '1' on each of the three measures), we have corrected for this by assigning a point for severity or geographical spread only when these scores reach more than 1.

The first step in the statistical analysis was to produce bivariate correlations of each of the eight indices with CHATS to determine which of the eight indices were most strongly associated with the incidence of torture. The results are listed in Table 3.1. All the correlations are statistically significant, and the signs are all in the expected direction. The higher the correlation (that is, the closer it is to 1.0), the stronger the relationship between the two variables. The correlations in Table 3.1 indicate that, first, practice is a better predictor of the incidence of torture than law (none of the law indices correlates very strongly with CHATS), and secondly, of all the indices, detention practice, with a correlation of -.763, is the best predictor of the incidence of torture. This is followed by prosecution practice (-.558), and monitoring practice (-.457). Complaints law (-.352) and complaints practice (-.312) have similar correlation coef-

---

6   International Covenant on Civil and Political Rights (adopted 16 December 1966, entered into force 23 March 1976) 999 UNTS 171.
7   We used as a starting point the annual reports put out by the US State Department (Human Rights Country Reports) and Amnesty International (Annual Reports) because they are contemporaneous and use the year as their unit of reporting. We supplemented this information with numerous other sources, including contemporaneous reports by different international and domestic human rights organizations, official and unofficial statistics, and extensive interviews with primary sources.

Table 3.1   Correlation of law and practice indices with CHATS

Law and Practice Prevention Indices	Correlation Coefficient
Detention law	-.227**
Prosecution law	-.198**
Complaints law	-.352**
Monitoring law	-.276**
Detention practice	-.763**
Prosecution practice	-.558**
Complaints practice	-.312**
Monitoring practice	-.457**

Note: Pearson's r correlation coefficients, * $p < .05$, ** $p < .01$.

ficients, and come fourth and fifth in order of strength. Prosecution law (-.198) has the lowest correlation with CHATS.

The high correlations between CHATS and several of the indices indicate that at least some sets of potential preventive mechanisms are associated with reducing the incidence of torture. To further explore this, and determine which sets are particularly effective relative to the others, a multivariate statistical analysis is required.

Our database of 480 data points (16 countries times 30 years produced a database with 480 country-years) allows us to test the effectiveness of our eight indices both over time and across countries simultaneously. We also included a set of control variables in our multivariate models to isolate the effects of the preventive mechanisms we are interested in from other broad factors we know from previous research may be related to the level of torture. These control variables included how democratic the country was, whether the country was engaged in international and civil conflict, the level of economic development, and the size of the population at a given time. The results of one of our multivariate analyses are found in Table 3.2.

This multivariate regression model indicates that detention practice is the only statistically significant preventive factor, with a coefficient of -.182.[8] Two control variables are also statistically significant: democracy, with a coefficient of -.064 (the more democratic the country, the less likely it is to torture), and population, with a coefficient of .429 (the larger the country, the more likely it is to torture). All the regression models that we used underlined the centrality of detention safeguards in practice as the most effective group of preventive measures.[9] However, for statistical reasons, the multivariate analysis only considers the relative importance of different groups of preventive measures – detention, prosecution, monitoring and complaints, in both law and practice. The bivariate correlations elucidate by demonstrating the strength of the relations between the risk of torture and each specific prevention measure within these groups.

---

[8]   Although we report the results of one statistical model here, we actually employed a number of different statistical approaches to measure the relative weight of the various preventive indices. Regardless of the approach adopted, detention practice emerged as the single most important set of preventive measures in explaining the incidence of torture. It was consistently statistically significant, the sign of the coefficient was always in the expected direction, and the correlation between detention practice and CHATS was consistently stronger than CHATS and any other index. Clearly good detention practices are key to reducing the incidence of torture.

[9]   A full discussion of the multivariate regression models and findings can be found in Carver, R and Handley, L (eds), *Does Torture Prevention Work?* (Liverpool University Press, 2016), 57–66.

Table 3.2   *Effects of preventive mechanisms on incidence of torture*

Explanatory Variables	Coefficient	(Std. Error)	p-value
Detention law	.016	(0.038)	0.681
Prosecution law	-.006	(0.036)	0.862
Complaints law	.088	(0.046)	0.059
Monitoring law	-.011	(0.017)	0.523
Detention practice	-.182	(0.031)	0.000
Prosecution practice	-.024	(0.034)	0.465
Complaints practice	-.018	(0.039)	0.643
Monitoring practice	-.004	(0.015)	0.769
Democracy	-.064	(0.028)	0.021
Conflict	.036	(0.027)	0.188
GDP_{ln}	.080	(0.121)	0.508
$Population_{ln}$	.429	(0.132)	0.001

WHAT DOES THIS MEAN FOR PREVENTING TORTURE?

The European Committee for the Prevention of Torture (CPT) describes third-party noti-fication, access to a lawyer, and an independent medical examination as the "trinity" of anti-torture safeguards.[10] While we would avoid the faintly religious terminology, our findings completely concur. Taken together, these three safeguards address an observation of Sir Nigel Rodley's that sums up the collective experience of many anti-torture activists: "torture is a crime and, like many other crimes, is a crime of opportunity." Recalling his work at Amnesty International in the 1970s and 1980s he stated:

> We were aware that torture happened to people when they were held at the sole mercy of their captors and interrogators (incommunicado detention). The longer they were denied access to and from the outside world (i.e., to families, lawyers, doctors, courts) the more they were vulnerable to abuse by those wishing to obtain information or confessions from them.[11]

The first element of this protection against incommunicado detention is that someone in the world outside has knowledge that the individual is in custody. The argument for not making such a notification is usually framed in terms of not alerting accomplices or facilitating the destruction of evidence. Yet it is perfectly possible to frame an exception where the right may be overridden, for a limited period, to prevent interference with the investigation; in the United Kingdom, Section 56(2) of the Police and Criminal Evidence Act (PACE)[12] provides just such an exception.

In most of the 16 countries we studied, there has been significant improvement in third-party notification in recent years, not only because of strengthened legal requirements, but also because of technological developments – the widespread use of cellular phones – that make contact much easier.

---

[10]   European Committee for the Prevention of Torture and Inhuman or Degrading Treatment or Punishment, *CPT Standards*, Strasbourg 2015, CPT/Inf/E (2002) 1 – Rev. 2015.
[11]   Rodley, NS, 'Reflections on Working for the Prevention of Torture' (2009) 6 *Essex Human Rights Review* 15.
[12]   Police and Criminal Evidence Act 1984 (PACE) (1984 c. 60).

The right to notify a third party may be framed in one of two ways. Sometimes it is a direct obligation on the arresting authority to contact a family member or friend (for example, Kyrgyzstan, South Africa). Otherwise it is a right of the arrested person that they may choose whether or not to exercise (United Kingdom, Norway). The reasoning behind this is that a person may sometimes *not* want friends or family to know they have been arrested. Yet the second framing is problematic. The Inter-American Court of Human Rights considered the celebrated case of Walter Bulacio from Argentina – where the right to notify is framed as one to be exercised by the suspect, not the police. Bulacio was beaten to death with no opportunity to notify.[13]

The second element is the right of access to a lawyer. As with third-party notification, the argument against this right is that legal access will impede the investigation. Unlike third-party notification, however, this has been elevated to the status of a positive principle in many legal systems, most obviously French criminal procedure (until very recently) with its *garde à vue* detention. It is this positive exclusion of lawyers in the early stages of detention that has impeded the affirmation of the right to legal counsel as hard international law. Matters are also confused by the fact that where the right to counsel does exist in international law it is as an element of the right to a fair trial rather than the right not to be tortured. While there is clearly an overlap between the two, often the importance of the right to a lawyer may be more to do with physical presence than legal advice. Access to a lawyer as part of the right to a fair trial does not necessarily provide protection at the time of greatest risk in the first hours after arrest. We learned that one of the most effective measures in reducing torture and ill-treatment in England and Wales was the duty solicitor scheme that was introduced pursuant to the Police and Criminal Evidence Act (PACE). It was the constant presence of lawyers in and around police custody suites that had the impact, not the legal advice provided.[14] Similarly, groups of lawyers in Chile organize visits to police stations in the aftermath of social unrest in order to identify and interview those held in detention.[15]

The general pattern in countries we studied was one of increased access to lawyers at an early stage of detention over the past three decades. The problem is often that broadly defined exceptions are provided in law. In the United Kingdom, exceptions under PACE are determined on a case-by-case basis, but in countries like India and Turkey emergency provisions may deny or delay legal access for whole categories of detainee. Under Israel's Criminal Procedure Code, arrested persons are guaranteed immediate access to a lawyer; in the Occupied Palestinian Territories, security detainees may have their access to a lawyer delayed for up to 30 days.[16]

The obstacles to realizing this right are considerable and not confined to legally defined exceptions. Deliberate official obstruction is clearly one factor, with one of the most effective methods being not informing an arrested person of their right to a lawyer. We found that as soon as suspects were told of their right to see a lawyer, they were highly likely to exercise it and the incidence of torture was reduced. Authorities can then impede effective exercise of the right in various ways. In Hungary, for example, while lists of lawyers are drawn up by

---

[13] IACt.HR, *Bulacio v Argentina*, Judgment of September 18, 2003, Merits, Reparations and Costs, Series C no 100.

[14] Carver, R, 'United Kingdom' in Carver and Handley (n 9 above), 105.

[15] Fernández Neira, K and Engstrom, P, 'Chile' in Carver and Handley (n 9 above), 143.

[16] Ballas, I, 'Israel' in Carver and Handley (n 9 above), 273.

regional bar associations, the actual choice in any given case is made by the police. There is also a tendency to notify lawyers at the last minute – often literally – so that the formal box has been ticked but it is impossible in practice for the lawyer to attend the interview.[17]

In many countries that we studied there were simply not enough lawyers. In Kyrgyzstan, for example, this meant that suspects would often end up being visited by pro-police lawyers unsympathetic to their complaints. In South Africa, this often means that they have no lawyer at all. In many places there is no system of free legal representation, with the result that poor detainees are simply unrepresented.

Our finding that an independent medical examination is an important protection against torture has been well understood for a long time. No doubt this is partly because of the leading role played by the medical profession in the global struggle against torture, resulting in the development of the Istanbul Protocol as a set of sophisticated guidelines for the assessment of medical evidence of torture.[18] The importance of medical examinations in torture prevention is self-evident, whether these are routine examinations at pre-determined moments (such as entry into custody or transfer between facilities) or exams triggered by a particular event, such as a request from the detainee. The knowledge that a detainee will be routinely examined can act as a deterrent to deliberate ill-treatment, while an examination also offers the possibility of identifying medical evidence of torture or other ill-treatment in a timely manner. However, there are several obstacles to effective and independent examinations. Obstruction by the detaining authority is clearly one. In many countries we heard of police preventing proper medical examinations, remaining in the room while the examination took place and demanding to see the medical report, which should of course remain confidential. Although these practices are widespread, they may not be the greatest problem.

In many instances, the only available medical personnel are employees of the detaining authority who cannot be relied upon to act independently. Public healthcare systems are not necessarily a problem. In the UK National Health Service personnel are rightly regarded as independent in the police or prison context. By contrast, the position of the district surgeons in South Africa is a well-documented example of the conflicts that result.[19]

A further problem is a lack of the specific skills required to identify the signs and symptoms of torture, which are not part of the normal competence of medical personnel. In Turkey, for example, where the medical profession plays a particularly important role in campaigning against torture, there has been a major effort to train personnel in the standards contained in the Istanbul Protocol. Yet it is an uphill struggle, since most of those trained soon end up in other branches of medicine.[20]

A final problem, which has possibly been neglected, is that medical personnel may simply be unsympathetic to torture victims. This was the finding of a survey from India, which discovered that more than half of doctors thought that coercive methods could be justified.[21]

---

[17] Ivany, B, Kádár, A and Nemes, A, 'Hungary' in Carver and Handley (n 9 above), 183.
[18] *Manual on the Effective Investigation and Documentation of Torture and Other Cruel, Inhuman or Degrading Treatment or Punishment* (United Nations, New York and Geneva 2004), HR/P/PT/8/Rev.1.
[19] Gready, P and Gruchy, JD, 'District Surgeons in Apartheid South Africa: A Case Study of Dual Obligations' (2003) 7 *Health and Human Rights* 112.
[20] Altiparmak, K, Carver, R and Handley, L, 'Turkey' in Carver and Handley (n 9 above), 439.
[21] Lokaneeta, J and Jesani, A, 'India' in Carver and Handley (n 9 above), 501.

The idea that a person should only be held in a lawfully designated place of detention is obviously fundamental. At the extreme, secret prisons are associated with enforced or involuntary disappearances and are almost inevitably associated with the ill-treatment of those held in them, at the very least. A number of such instances could be found in the countries that we studied, including Argentina, Chile, Ethiopia, Indonesia, Peru and the Philippines. Unfortunately, unlawful detention may also be a consequence of well-intended but poorly-implemented efforts to protect detainees. Kyrgyzstan, for example, has seen a pro-liferation of secret detention places because of a police backlash against new rules protecting criminal suspects.[22] Even lawful exercise of police powers, such as random identity checks, can constitute a form of effective "custody" whereby a person never actually enters into a lawful place of detention. For example, in Argentina the police round up urban youth in *razzias*, while Turkish police conduct ID checks and British police enjoy "stop and search" powers. These can often be the site of ill-treatment, or even torture.

Other Detention Safeguards

Another safeguard we found to be of importance is the electronic recording of police interviews with the suspect. The purpose of this is primarily to establish that the interview is conducted in a non-coercive manner. It is essential for this purpose that the entire interview be recorded and, in systems that use this procedure, strict protocols are established governing the conduct of the interview and the storage of the tape or digital file. In our study, the only country that uses electronic interview recording comprehensively is the United Kingdom. Its introduction in the 1980s was prompted by a series of miscarriages of justice involving false confessions, some of them induced by torture. Other countries that we studied only used the recording of interviews selectively, which largely undermines their purpose. In Argentina, for example, a judge can order the recording of interrogations in complex cases, but to assist in assessing the evidence, not to protect the suspect. Another problem with how recorded interviews have often worked in practice is the non-availability of electronic records when they are needed – and the same thing applies to closed-circuit video recording of police stations, detention centres and prisons. In almost every country that we studied, video recording, storage and retrieval systems have a quite uncanny failure rate, precisely when they are required to document allegations of abuse. In other words, this only works as a safeguard if there are serious protocols ensuring that recordings will be made and preserved free of interference.

The issue of the electronic recording of interviews is closely related to another question, namely the reliance of investigators and prosecutors on confession evidence. This can be seen as a practical cognate of the principle of non-admissibility of evidence derived from torture, as enunciated in Article 15 of the UNCAT. We found a clear and strong relationship between reduced reliance on confessions and a decline in the incidence of torture. The purpose of torture is very often to secure a confession or other statement. If this avenue is blocked, or if other alternatives are available, torture will be significantly reduced. Qualitative support for this claim comes in an inverted form from the two post-Soviet countries in our study. With the collapse of the Soviet Union in 1991, Georgia and Kyrgyzstan overnight lost almost all their trained and experienced police investigators. The consequence was a rapid increase in the use

---

[22]   Baijumanova, A, Birk, M and Ismailova, L, 'Kyrgyzstan' in Carver and Handley (n 9 above), 549.

disadvantageous, since evidence already held by the police is not disclosed and the interviewee does not know what she needs to explain in order to establish innocence. In his final report to the UN General Assembly, the former Special Rapporteur on Torture, Juan Méndez, made a detailed call for an international protocol on investigative interviewing as an essential tool in torture prevention.[28] The aim is something equivalent to the Istanbul Protocol on medical evidence of torture or the Minnesota Protocol on autopsies, which are widely perceived as setting the most advanced standards. Méndez's call precisely corresponds to our findings about the most effective protections for suspects in police custody.

INVESTIGATION AND PROSECUTION

The criminalization of torture, and the prosecution of those who commit the crime, has been the cornerstone of the international strategy for torture prevention for decades. The 1975 Declaration Against Torture,[29] expanded and hardened into the 1984 Convention, made criminalization, investigation and prosecution the overriding priority. While the Convention does include other elements, such as the absolute prohibition on refoulement where there is a risk of torture, the rule excluding evidence obtained under torture, and the need for training and unspecified rules and procedures to prevent torture, it is, in the main, structured as a crime prevention treaty.

It has long been held as axiomatic by anti-torture campaigners that the "cycle of impunity" is one of the main reasons for the persistence of torture, although there has never previously been a strong cross-country empirical underpinning for this belief. Some scholars have even associated ratification of the Convention with an increase in the incidence of torture. Our finding, to the contrary, was that ratification was weakly associated with a reduction in torture. (We found a similar weak negative correlation between incidence of torture and ratification of the Optional Protocol to the Convention.) We assume it is not the ratification itself that reduces torture, but ratification may be evidence of the necessary political will to translate abstract commitments. Whether or not this assumption is correct, we note that those who argue that treaty ratification correlates with increased torture may be falling foul of a particular measurement fallacy, whereby the reporting obligations and increased scrutiny inherent in the treaty regime gives the impression of increased torture at a time when it is in fact decreasing.[30]

Our overall conclusion is that, when the Convention's requirements are actually implemented in practice, the long-standing view about the need to end impunity is precisely correct. As might be expected, the gap between law and practice is greatest in this area; almost all countries explicitly criminalize torture, yet the actual investigation, prosecution, conviction and punishment of torturers falls far short of the practice in relation to equivalent acts commit-

---

[28]   Interim report of the Special Rapporteur on torture and other cruel, inhuman or degrading treatment or punishment, 5 August 2016, UN Doc A/71/298.
[29]   Declaration on the Protection of All Persons from Being Subjected to Torture and Other Cruel, Inhuman or Degrading Treatment or Punishment, UNGA Res 3452 (XXX), 9 December 1975.
[30]   Clark, AM and Sikkink, K, 'Information Effects and Human Rights Data: Is the Good News about Increased Human Rights Information Bad News for Human Rights Measures?' (2013) 35 *Human Rights Quarterly* 539.

ted in a normal criminal context. The sad truth is that even the countries with best practice fall short of what the Convention requires.

As with detention safeguards, none of the legal provisions that we looked at had any significant impact in reducing torture incidence merely by its presence in the statute book. However, several practice variables were of particular importance. Most relevant of all was simply whether complaints of torture were filed with the courts or the prosecuting authority in the first place, which goes to the overall credibility of the justice system. In many countries where there is serious torture, victims simply do not report this to prosecutors or investigators because they have no confidence in the impartiality and competence of the system. Another important factor is the likelihood of conviction. We considered whether those accused of torture had a chance of being convicted comparable to those accused of serious offences against the person in an ordinary criminal context. Equally important is whether the state granted amnesties or pardons for torturers, short-circuiting the whole process. When complaints are filed; when they are properly and independently investigated; when torturers are convicted; and when those convicted serve a full sentence without amnesty or pardon – then, the prosecution of torturers is a particularly effective way of preventing torture in the future.

MONITORING PLACES OF DEPRIVATION OF LIBERTY

The monitoring of places where there may be a risk of torture has increasingly been seen as the central strategy for preventing torture. Indeed, it is sometimes seen as being synonymous with torture prevention, which is somewhat misleading, since safeguards that remove the opportunity to torture – such as ending incommunicado detention – seem more purely preventive.[31] Nevertheless, the adoption of the Optional Protocol to the Torture Convention (OPCAT), and in particular the creation of national preventive mechanisms, have indeed brought monitoring centre stage.

The origins of the strategy of "preventive monitoring" lie with the International Committee of the Red Cross (ICRC). Central to the ICRC's protective role have been monitoring visits to prisoners in wartime and, in some circumstances, also to security detainees outside conflict situations. Formed in the 1970s by Geneva businessman Jean-Jacques Gautier, the Swiss Committee Against Torture advocated using the ICRC approach as a general strategy to prevent torture. In the course of the campaign for a UN convention against torture, it argued for an international monitoring body with the power to inspect places of detention and imprisonment. This was a step too far in the 1980s, but the proposal was picked up by the Council of Europe in its regional anti-torture convention, which led to the creation of the European Committee for the Prevention of Torture (CPT), whose primary function has been preventive monitoring. A decade or so later, debate on a proposed optional protocol to the UN Convention took an interesting turn. A number of countries from the global South took exception to the proposal for a global monitoring body and proposed instead that states parties should establish their own domestic monitoring bodies. The somewhat bizarre compromise adopted was to include *both* mechanisms in the OPCAT: a Sub-Committee on Prevention of Torture as

---

[31] Rodley (n 11 above).

a treaty body and national preventive mechanisms (NPMs) as domestic monitors.[32] In practice, the inclusion of NPMs has preserved the relevance of the OPCAT. Even though the SPT is the largest of UN human rights treaty bodies and the parties to the Optional Protocol remain relatively low in number – around 90 at the time of writing – the international body is scarcely able to fulfil its monitoring role.

In our study we not only looked at national preventive mechanisms or at international monitoring bodies established by treaty. The OPCAT is a relatively recent phenomenon, and one that still does not include the majority of states globally. However, across the entire three decades that we researched there were many other bodies with responsibility for inspecting or monitoring places where people were deprived of their liberty. Such bodies have sometimes been specialized – focusing only on prisons, for example – and may not have been endowed with the full legal powers that an OPCAT-compliant NPM would now enjoy. These features were accounted for in our coding scheme and allowed us to make a much broader assessment of the effectiveness of monitoring as a preventive measure.

As might be expected, the gap between law and practice scores was considerably less for monitoring than for either detention or prosecution. However, in the later years covered in our study a gap did appear. In the earlier years, a body tasked with monitoring would more or less fulfil its legal mandate. Later, perhaps, paradoxically, because of the OPCAT and the external pressure to establish monitoring mechanisms, the institutions that existed were on average less compliant with their legal obligations than in earlier years.

Again as might be expected, the most effective operational practice of monitoring mechanisms is that they actually conduct individual interviews with persons deprived of their liberty in the course of their visits; this might appear elementary, but some of the bodies that we studied did not do this. More surprisingly, legal immunity for monitors seemed to have no particular relationship to the effectiveness of a monitoring body. However, whether *in practice* monitors were able to go about their work without threat or interference emerged as the most important predictor of a body's effectiveness. Or conversely, threats, attacks or legal sanctions against monitors are an extremely effective and dangerous way of undermining the positive impact of a monitoring mechanism.

Our finding was that monitoring mechanisms clearly correlated with a reduction in the incidence of torture in the countries that we studied. However, the relationship was not as strong as either detention safeguards or prosecution of torturers. This conclusion does have to be qualified somewhat. First, we looked only at the impact of preventive measures on the incidence of torture, not on other forms of ill-treatment. It might be that if our focus had been broader, we would have reached a different conclusion. Secondly, there is clearly a close relationship between the role of monitoring bodies and the implementation of legal safeguards to protect detainees. If done properly, monitoring is not merely inspection of facilities but a serious probe into procedures and practices. Reports of the European CPT, for example, have generally been very effective in identifying systemic legal and practical failings. Hence monitoring is likely to remain an important element in a coordinated torture prevention strategy.

A common weakness of monitoring in the countries that we studied is that it tended to be focused overwhelmingly on the prison or penitentiary system rather than on those held in

---

[32]   Evans, MD and Haenni-Dale, C, 'Preventing Torture? The Development of the Optional Protocol to the UN Convention against Torture' (2004) 4 *Human Rights Law Review* 19.

police custody. Yet torture is overwhelmingly more likely to take place in the latter setting – which is why detention safeguards were found to be so important.

INDEPENDENT COMPLAINTS MECHANISMS

Independent, semi-formal complaints mechanisms have proliferated since the early 1990s. Their original model was the ombudsman institutions of Scandinavia and some Commonwealth countries, although these bodies were directed towards rectifying relatively minor cases of maladministration rather than serious violations of human rights. Since the 1980s there have emerged dozens of national human rights institutions with a specific mandate to examine complaints of violations without immediate recourse to either the criminal or civil justice systems. Most often these are human rights ombudsman institutions (primarily in central and eastern Europe and in Latin America) or national human rights commissions (in the Asia-Pacific region and Africa). These complaints mechanisms usually cover the full range of human rights issues, although some focus on specific institutional frameworks such as the prison system. In our study, we understood complaints mechanisms to refer to all these types of body, whether general ombudsman or national human rights institutions, or specific police or prisons ombudsman bodies. We did not understand it in this context to refer to complaints to the court or prosecutor.

It is argued that complaints mechanisms are an important part of the system that prevents torture. Our research found little evidence to support this contention.

Why might complaints mechanisms not be a particularly effective means of preventing torture? It seemed to us that ombudsman-style complaints procedures have all the disadvantages of the prosecutorial system when it comes to investigating torture allegations and none of the advantages. The principal disadvantage, from the perspective of the torture victim, is that the act of making a complaint creates further jeopardy for the complainant. As we have seen, the whole prosecution mechanism most often falls at the first hurdle, with victims declining even to lodge a complaint of torture. However, if a victim perceives some possibility that a complaint will result in further action against the perpetrators, then he or she may be willing to take this risk. In the case of a semi-formal, ombudsman-style complaints mechanism, which has no binding power to secure a prosecution even if it finds in the complainant's favour, then lodging a complaint looks like a very poor gamble.

This interpretation is made more likely by a parallel finding of ours. Several of the complaints mechanisms in our study are organically linked to the prosecutorial process. Bodies such as the Northern Ireland Police Ombudsman, the Independent Office for Police Conduct in England and Wales, and the Independent Police Investigative Directorate in South Africa are essentially a much more accessible route into the prosecutorial system, with the complaints bodies *required* to refer any finding of torture to the prosecutors. In these instances, we found that such mechanisms do appear to be associated with a reduced incidence of torture.

LAW AND PRACTICE

A common thread through our country case studies, as well as in the quantitative findings, is the significant gap between law and practice. There is not a single legal mechanism that is strongly correlated with a decrease in torture. It is only when laws are put into practice that they have their effect in reducing torture. This seemed to us a commonsensical finding although some (usually lawyers!) have disagreed. Of course, legal reform is important because it usually, although not invariably, precedes improvement in practice.

The gap between law and practice, as we have indicated, is greatest in relation to the investigation and prosecution of torturers, in regard to which no country has a particularly impressive record, even though all criminalize torture to some extent. The gap is smallest in relation to complaints and monitoring where institutions established in law usually do a reasonable job of executing their functions. Most importantly, there remain significant gaps between the legal safeguards for detainees or suspects and the actual protection that they enjoy in custody.

The precise reasons for these gaps will vary. There may well be a general disinclination on the part of police to comply with rules that they see as unduly favouring suspects, and their readiness to do so will be determined by levels of corruption, discipline and professionalism. But there are other contextual factors that are not necessarily the fault of the detaining authority. We have indicated that many countries lack the professional personnel – such as lawyers or doctors – to make these safeguards a reality.

Training is a potentially important way of bridging the gap between law and practice. We measured the impact of training in relation to investigative and custodial personnel, as well as for judges, prosecutors, monitors and complaints handlers. Training clearly does have a positive effect, according to our findings. In addition, our finding about reducing the reliance on confession evidence needs to be understood in conjunction with this. Training that enhances the professional capacities of the police can play a very important part in reducing the risk of torture.

THREE CASE STUDIES

As further illustration of our findings, below we discuss three of our country case studies in further detail.[33] Both the United Kingdom and Turkey are strong examples of the positive impact of improved detention practice, which followed positive legal reforms in criminal procedure. The difference is that in Turkey a collapse of political will (and the persistence of impunity) has resulted in the serious recurrence of torture. Argentina also saw a substantial decrease in torture after the fall of its military dictatorship, but improved detention safeguards were never translated into practice. Police indiscipline and impunity have allowed torture to persist.

United Kingdom[34]

The United Kingdom presented the clearest example in our study of a state that had effected a major and sustained reduction in the incidence of torture. Economically developed democracies are generally less disposed towards the use of torture than either poor countries or autocracies, but it is easy to forget that in the 1970s, before the start of our study period, the UK

---

[33] All three of these countries were included in the pilot stage of the research, which meant that the authors of this chapter were directly involved in the field research.

[34] A full discussion of the UK case study is to be found in Carver (n 14 above).

had a serious torture problem. This was most famously associated with counter-insurgency policies in Northern Ireland, where British treatment of prisoners was the subject of an inter-state complaint at the European Court of Human Rights.[35] Equally famously, the Court found that the sensory deprivation techniques used on Irish nationalist prisoners amounted "only" to inhuman or degrading treatment – a decision most unlikely to find favour today. Torture was endemic in the behaviour of the security forces in Northern Ireland up until the 1990s, although never again quite reaching the same pitch of atrocity as the 1970s. However, the problem was not confined to these political cases. Many of Britain's decentralized police forces regularly resorted to threats, coercion and worse in their treatment of criminal suspects. While human rights campaigners warned of how police in mainland Britain might acquire repressive techniques from their Northern Ireland counterparts, the arrow often pointed in the other direction. One of the great *causes célèbres* for the civil liberties campaigners of the period was the case of the Birmingham Six – Irish residents of the Midlands city wrongfully convicted of planting a bomb in a bar, killing 21 people. This was one of a number of serious miscarriages of justice in this period. The case was investigated by a unit called the West Midlands Serious Crimes Squad, which tortured confessions out of some of the Six. Yet, while there was no doubt a particular anti-Irish animus in this case, this was actually the way that this unit regularly handled cases.[36] They often inflicted beatings and near suffocation with plastic bags, resisting reforms until the unit had to be wound up in 1989. Twenty-five years after the squad's dissolution, the courts were still handling the aftermath of its torturous practices.[37]

The main response to the slew of miscarriages of justice and consequent public disquiet was a radical review of criminal procedure. Given that this was initiated by the Conservative government of Margaret Thatcher, it was greeted with great scepticism by civil libertarians. Yet, in retrospect, it is clear that the Police and Criminal Evidence Act 1984 (PACE) has resulted in dramatic improvements to the safety of people taken into police custody.[38] As discussed above, arguably the most important of the PACE innovations was the creation of a state-funded duty solicitor scheme. This ensured that criminal suspects had permanent 24-hour access to a defence lawyer in private practice. The scheme is such that, even if an individual decides not to avail themselves of the right to a lawyer, there will most likely be other lawyers present at the police station, at least at busy stations and at busy times.

Many of the PACE safeguards, such as the right to prompt consultation with a lawyer, already existed under the common law, but their codification in statute law proved very important. There are PACE Codes that give practical and detailed guidance to police officers on issues such as notification of family or friends, presentation before a judge, and medical examinations. PACE also provided new rules on the conduct of interviews with suspects, making audio (and later video) recording mandatory. This triggered a more widespread review of interviewing, with an increased focus since the early 1990s on investigative interviewing,

---

[35]   *Ireland v the United Kingdom*, 18 January 1978, Series A no 25.
[36]   Kaye, T, *Unsafe and Unsatisfactory? The Report of the Independent Inquiry into the Working Practices of the West Midlands Serious Crime Squad* (Civil Liberties Trust, 1991).
[37]   *R v The Director of Public Prosecutions ex parte Treadaway* [1997] EWHC Admin 741; *R v Keith Twitchell* [2000] 1 Cr.App.R. 373; *R v Foran* [2014] EWCA Crim 2047.
[38]   Versions of the same legislation were enacted in the distinct jurisdictions of Northern Ireland and Scotland in 1989 and 1994 respectively.

with the purpose of fact-finding rather than securing confessions, as noted previously.[39] This fits with our overall observation that a reduced reliance on confession evidence leads to a lower incidence of torture.

PACE is not perfect; one of its continuing weaknesses is that certain guarantees are weakened or suspended in cases involving terrorist offences. Detention conditions for terrorist suspects undoubtedly remain much more oppressive than for ordinary criminals. However, the intense public scrutiny of such cases has, at least since the end of the Northern Ireland conflict, provided some protection.

The treatment of prisoners in Northern Ireland, where the worst torture took place, was improved in part by the application of the PACE standards. The decisive change, however, came with the political settlement leading to the 1998 Belfast (or Good Friday) Agreement. Among the outcomes was the creation of a completely new Police Service of Northern Ireland to replace the Royal Ulster Constabulary, which had been deeply implicated in the torture and ill-treatment of political prisoners. Equally important was the creation of new civilian oversight bodies: a Northern Ireland Policing Board that, among other things, has a statutory responsibility to ensure police compliance with the Human Rights Act; and a Police Ombudsman that investigates complaints against the police. The Police Ombudsman is extremely well resourced, has access to an independent forensic service, and can investigate criminal cases against the police and refer them directly to the prosecutorial authorities.

The effectiveness of police reform in Northern Ireland contrasts with the experience of most of the countries we studied. Out of the 16, almost all had experienced some sort of political transition over the 30-year period covered by our study, whether from conflict to peace or from authoritarianism to democracy. Yet only one country, Georgia, undertook radical police reform of the type implemented in Northern Ireland. Demilitarization of the police in Indonesia may have played an important part in the reduction of torture, but countries like South Africa had only imperfect or incomplete reform, while Argentina (see below) scarcely addressed the issue at all.

Turkey[40]

It is a commonplace that political will is necessary to tackle the problem of torture. Turkey provides a very clear example of what political will can achieve – and what happens when that will evaporates. It also is an interesting case study in how the requisite political will achieves its objectives through preventive mechanisms.

In the 1980s and 1990s the incidence of torture in Turkey was at critically high levels. Torture occurred both in the context of a brutal counter-insurgency campaign in the Kurdish areas of the country and as part of the regular functioning of the criminal justice system. There was no significant attempt to address this problem until the very end of the 1990s. Four developments contributed to generating the political will to do something about torture. First, there was a change of government, with a left-leaning coalition led by Bülent Ecevit more inclined to address the problem. Secondly, Turkey formally applied for membership of the European Union, which comes with heavy human rights conditionality. Thirdly, the Parliamentary

---

[39]   Shawyer, A, Milne, B and Bull, R, 'Investigative Interviewing in the UK' in Williamson, T, Milne, B and Savage, SP (eds), *International Developments in Investigative Interviewing* (Routledge, 2009).
[40]   Full details of the Turkey case study are in Altiparmak and others (n 20 above).

Human Rights Commission was very active in exposing torture and poor detention practices, with frequent unannounced visits to prisons and places of detention – an interesting example of the potential impact of monitoring on other preventive measures. Fourthly, the 1999 capture of the Kurdish insurgent leader Abdullah Öcalan led to a distinct winding down of the armed conflict and a gradual lifting of emergency powers.

Our research suggested that by the time Ecevit handed over the premiership to Abdullah Gül of the newly elected Justice and Development Party (AKP), in 2002, there had been a discernible decline in the incidence of torture. Where torture continued, it appeared to be less severe than previously. This improvement continued throughout the first decade of the century.

The principal reason behind the decline in incidence of torture appears to have been substantial and successive improvements in detention safeguards to bring them into line with European standards. One of the consequences of the highly centralized and disciplined Turkish state system was that legal improvements were rapidly translated into practice. This was reinforced by clear public statements condemning torture on the part of successive governments.

The effort to reduce torture was also helped by the acquisition of alternative techniques of criminal investigation. These included extensive electronic surveillance powers that raise their own human rights issues. This problem notwithstanding, it is clear that, in the words of one civil society monitor: "Previously the police would reach evidence through the accused; now they reach the accused through evidence."[41]

The aggressive monitoring conducted by the Parliamentary Commission in the late 1990s proved to be an exception. The Commission's chairperson during this period was even threatened with suspension of parliamentary immunity to force her to reveal the names of those who alleged torture. Thereafter this parliamentary body became less independent and was seriously weakened. A network of official Human Rights Boards, created in 2001, proved notably ineffective in either monitoring or complaints-handling. The later creation of a national human rights institution and an ombudsman office has barely improved matters when it comes to questions of ill-treatment or torture.

Equally, the investigation and prosecution of the crime of torture was almost non-existent. Although there were various legal reforms from 1999 onwards – increasing and later abolishing the statute of limitations for torture, repealing obsolete laws protecting public officials from investigation – the actual investigation of torture cases has been limited, convictions extremely rare, and penalties derisory.

Turkey provides a case study that illustrates very clearly our contention that detention safeguards constitute the most effective preventive mechanism – for the simple reason that none of the other mechanisms even existed to a significant degree. Sadly, the Turkish case also demonstrates how political will is a highly changeable factor. By the end of our study period, the increase in popular protest against the AKP government was being met with an increase in police violence and ill-treatment. An alleged coup attempt in 2016 resulted in a full-blown return to the 1990s. National security overrides that had never been fully abolished came into effect and there was mass torture of so-called Gülenists – essentially a broad spectrum of the government's political opponents.

---

[41]   *Ibid.*

Argentina[42]

Argentina is often held up as a positive example. Specifically, it is claimed that "transitional justice" has contributed to the consolidation of democracy and a more solid protection of human rights.[43] Our research in Argentina suggests a much more complex picture, at least in relation to torture. While torture and other gross human rights violations are not remotely comparable to the situation under the military dictatorship that ended in 1983, neither has torture disappeared. In the 35 years since the end of the dictatorship, justice against military human right violators has been pursued unevenly, but nevertheless on a scale that is relatively unusual. Yet this appears not to have deterred present-day torturers because they are different actors – police, not military – inflicting ill-treatment on different victims – poor urban youth, not middle-class political dissenters.[44] To the extent that torture in Argentina has reduced, this has been primarily the consequence of improved safeguards at the time of arrest. To the extent that it continues, this is because of the police sidestepping the safeguards, and doing so with impunity.

The fall of the military dictatorship led to an immediate decline in the incidence of torture because the new democratic administration was not repressing its political opponents. The first post-dictatorship government, led by Raúl Alfonsín, introduced reforms to protect suspects in the early hours and days after arrest, most importantly reducing the limit for incommunicado detention from 30 to three days. Further proposed reforms did not win sufficient congressional support and it was not until 1991, under Alfonsín's successor, Carlos Menem, that a rather weaker package of laws was enacted. These included immediate notification of family or friends for anyone arrested without a warrant and a provision that suspects could only be directly interrogated by a judge, not by the police.

The problem was that, although the legal reforms undoubtedly pointed in the right direction, the police effectively operated as a law unto themselves. Partly this was simply a consequence of decentralization. Argentina is a federal state with 24 police forces – 23 provincial and one federal. The contrast to Turkey, with twice the population but a single police chain of command, is striking. Even more importantly, the police were subject to no systematic reform after the fall of the military dictatorship. The military had been primarily responsible for human rights abuses under the junta and were hence the priority for reform. Alfonsín's attempts to initiate reform in the 1980s – to restructure the police, restrain corruption and create external accountability – came to nothing. By the 1990s, politicians were competing to advocate "iron fist" responses to crime. Most bizarrely, the police even fabricated crimes in order to get the credit for solving them[45] – yet still there has been no effective move to hold them accountable.

The public dramatization of the threat of crime has allowed the police to get away with corruption and torture, as in other countries in our study such as South Africa. The paradox, of course, is that non-corrupt police that used proper investigative methods, rather than beating

---

[42]   The Argentina case study was not included in *Does Torture Prevention Work?* although the data gathered was included in our quantitative analysis.

[43]   See, for example Sikkink, K and Walling, CB, 'The Impact of Human Rights Trials in Latin America' (2007) 44 *Journal of Peace Research* 427; Sikkink, K, *The Justice Cascade: How Human Rights Prosecutions Are Changing World Politics* (WW Norton, 2011).

[44]   Lessa, F, 'Beyond Transitional Justice: Exploring Continuities in Human Rights Abuse in Argentina between 1976 and 2010' (2011) 3 *Journal of Human Rights Practice* 25.

[45]   Interview with Judge Daniel Rafecas, Buenos Aires, June 2013.

confessions out of suspects, would deal with crime much more effectively. Nevertheless, these attitudes have allowed the police to get away with ignoring detention safeguards. They have also exploited legal loopholes, such as the fact that a person may be detained for up to 10 hours for the purposes of identification, without triggering the right to a lawyer. Buenos Aires police conduct round-ups of poor youth, ostensibly for the purposes of identification but in reality to commit acts of violence against them.

Despite the picture of Argentina as a country where human rights violators are held criminally accountable, in reality the police enjoy almost total impunity for torture and ill-treatment. Victims are in fear and extremely reluctant to lodge complaints. Even when complaints are filed, these are not systematically investigated. And cases that do finally make it to court are frequently reclassified as lesser offences (a phenomenon we observed in many countries).

None of this is mitigated by effective monitoring or complaints mechanisms. Again, the federal structure is a large problem, with a patchwork of national and provincial mechanisms creating some overlaps and many gaps. In some instances, activists at the provincial level have been able to turn federalism to their advantage and create reasonably effective "provincial preventive mechanisms," but this is the exception rather than the rule. In any event, it is difficult to see what monitors or complaints-handlers would bring to a situation where the problem has been clearly diagnosed in many reports by national, regional and international bodies: a continuing culture of impunity and police lawlessness.

CONCLUSION

Our study found a gradual decline in torture over 30 years in the 16 countries that we examined, attributable at least in part to the impact of preventive mechanisms and especially to the practical observance of detention safeguards.

Discussion of the problem of torture tends to focus too much on political cases, in particular counter-terrorism and thought experiments such as the "ticking-bomb" scenario. Yet, these discussions are largely irrelevant since such cases represent a tiny fraction of the global incidence of torture. Most instances of torture occur in the context of dysfunctional criminal justice systems. Police are undereducated, undertrained, underpaid and corrupt. They lack the skills to investigate crime and yet are under political and public pressure to deliver results. (In one country that we studied torture tended to increase towards the end of the month when prosecutors struggled to deliver their quota of indictments.) Provisions to provide legal representation or medical examinations do not work because there is no one to deliver these services. Complaints of torture are not properly investigated, either because there is no independent body to conduct the investigation or because there is no will to do so, or both. Detention safeguards will achieve the desired effect of dramatically reducing torture, but only if fully implemented in practice. This in turn requires both resources and political will. Argentina and Turkey are both examples of how political will can very rapidly dissipate.

If the overall conclusion is that torture prevention measures do work, the paradox is that those that work most effectively are those that are least strongly supported in international law. Prosecution of torturers and monitoring mechanisms are both important in preventing torture and are underpinned by global (and regional) treaties. At a global level, detention safeguards only exist in hard law to the extent that they overlap with fair trial provisions. The UN Body of of torture since police knew no way of investigating a case other than beating a confession out of someone. Both countries have made some progress in climbing out of that particular hole, with Georgia having undergone a wholesale reform of the police after 2004, with the aim of improving professional standards and rooting out corruption.[23]

In our study, only two countries, the United Kingdom and Norway, have made a deliberate decision to end sole reliance on confessions, requiring that they be corroborated by other types of evidence. It is presumably not coincidental that these are also the two most economically developed countries that we looked at, with greater resources to allocate to other avenues of investigation, such as forensic science. However, most of the countries in our study exhibited some shift away from a sole reliance on confession evidence since the 1980s. Usually this appears to have been through the use of electronic surveillance evidence. A South African judge rather theatrically took his cell phone from his pocket to illustrate that most criminals these days now carry a GPS tracking device on their person (although sadly this does not stop the police from torturing anyway).[24] Government officials in Turkey were proud of the purported benefits of large-scale surveillance of citizens.[25] These types of evidence are clearly problematic in their own way, but they do appear to have contributed to an understanding that confessions are not the only or the most effective route to criminal convictions.

The move away from the confession as the goal of criminal investigation is intimately bound up with a change in the way that the suspect is questioned by police, away from the interrogation towards the investigative interview. The United Kingdom and Norway have both made this shift in recent years, encouraging interviewing based upon building rapport rather than conflict. Scholars have effectively demonstrated that such an approach is more effective not only in protecting the suspect from physical abuse but also in gathering accurate and useable evidence for the investigators. This applies not only in regular criminal cases, but also in the counter-terrorism investigations that are so often used to argue in favour of "enhanced interrogation."[26] A clear example in the countries we studied was the case of Anders Behring Breivik, the far-right terrorist who killed 77 people in Norway in 2011. On arrest, Breivik claimed that other "units" were still active but refused to provide the police with information – precisely the "ticking bomb" scenario often used to justify torture. The Norwegian authorities gave command of the investigation to Asbjorn Rachlew, a police superintendent with a doctorate in psychology who was a leading advocate of the new techniques of investigative interviewing. It was quickly established, without resort to torture or ill-treatment, that there were no more terrorists at large.

Rachlew has become one of the principal advocates of investigative interviewing, which he describes as "an operationalization of the presumption of innocence."[27] In other words, rather than seeking to prove or falsify one particular hypothesis about responsibility for a crime, the purpose is to test a variety of alternative hypotheses. This benefits the suspect, in so far as it is premised upon innocence and precludes coercion, but for the guilty suspect it may be

---

[23]   *Ibid.*
[24]   Interview with Judge Vincent Saldanha, Cape Town, 23 July 2014.
[25]   Interview with officials of the Ministry of the Interior, Ankara, 16 January 2013.
[26]   Alison, L, Giles, L and McGuire, G, 'Blood from a Stone: Why Rapport Works and Torture Doesn't in "Enhanced" Interrogations' (2015) 7(2) *Investigative Interviewing: Research and Practice* 5.
[27]   Rachlew, A, 'From Interrogating to Interviewing Suspects of Terror: Towards a New Mindset' (Prison Reform International, 14 March 2017), https://www.penalreform.org/blog/interrogating -interviewing-suspects-terror-towards-new-mindset

Principles for the Protection of All Persons under Any Form of Detention or Imprisonment[46] provides more extensive protections, for example in relation to notification of a third party on arrest and the right to a medical examination. But even here, in this soft law instrument, the right to a lawyer is framed weakly and sometimes negatively: it may not be "suspended or restricted save in exceptional circumstances." There is no mention that this right should be available promptly upon arrest.[47] The reason, of course, is that many national legal systems – particularly those based upon the French and Spanish codes – make exclusion of legal counsel a positive feature of the early days of the investigation. While regional bodies such as the European Court of Human Rights are increasingly addressing this problem, the global diffusion of these legal norms will take a much longer effort to unravel.

---

[46]   Body of Principles for the Protection of All Persons under Any Form of Detention or Imprisonment, UNGA Res 43/173, 9 December 1988.

[47]   Rodley, NS, and Pollard, M, *The Treatment of Prisoners under International Law*, 3rd edn (Oxford University Press, 2009).

4. Fragility, states and torture

Tobias Kelly, Steffen Jensen and Morten Koch Andersen

INTRODUCTION

The prohibition of torture, as established in the Universal Declaration of Human Rights and numerous other global and regional general human rights instruments, is couched in absolute and universal terms. These instruments set out sophisticated systems for oversight that seek to set up monitoring mechanisms and to criminalize torture at both the international and domestic level, as well as mapping out a route towards democratic states marked by the rule of law. But how do these procedures and assumptions play out in contexts where the state has either limited or disparate reach; where violence, threats and coercion by state and non-state actors and exploitive leadership(s) might be a routine part of everyday life, and where legal institutions are under-resourced or under-prioritized in the political and economic landscape? And what can we learn for the wider fight against torture from such situations?

Seemingly weak and violent states have often been understood through the concept of state 'fragility'. This chapter uses the concept of fragility cautiously to provide a critical reflection on some of the key conceptual and research issues associated with the prevention of torture. It does so from the perspective of social science rather than law, and focuses on the institutions, actors, procedures and assumptions that make torture possible. The meanings and implications of the concept of state fragility are widely contested, not least for being based on a particularly narrow set of normative assumptions about how states should behave.[1] While we agree with many of the critiques, we suggest that examining state fragility can also open up new ways of thinking about torture, and not only in situations of skewed institutional capacity, disparate levels of legitimacy and entrenched forms of violence. Many of the challenges of eradicating torture in seemingly 'fragile' states can also be found in states with apparently greater respect for the rule of law and well established forms of institutional stability. Looking at these challenges through the lens created by the idea of state fragility can open up new perspectives and approaches. In particular, it can help us pay attention to the role of informal processes and inequality in the infliction of torture, and help us push back against a simplistic assumption that the eradication of torture is straightforwardly linked to the growth of democracy and the rule of law. By paying attention to different histories of violence, we can avoid thinking about the eradication of torture as part of a unilinear model of development.

Crucially, pointing out that torture might have diverse causes and forms in different places is not to make a culturally or morally relativist point. We are not suggesting that standards around torture should be lower in fragile states or situations, for example. Torture is prohibited by international law irrespective of its particular causes. Instead, the chapter pays close atten-

---

[1] Grimm, S, Lemay-Hébert, N and Nay, O, '"Fragile States": Introducing a Political Concept' (2014) 35 *Third World Quarterly* 2, 197; Roitman, J, 'Productivity in the Margins: The Reconstitution of State Power in the Chad Basin' in Das, V and Poole, D (eds), *Anthropology in the Margins of the State* (Duke University Press, 2004), 191–224.

tion to the potential narrowness of approaches to combating torture, and uses these different histories to reflect back on the ways in which we approach torture more generally. In doing so, it does not draw a simple line between 'fragile' and 'stable' states, or between the global North and the global South. Rather, it looks at multiple points of convergence and interdependence. This involves contextualizing approaches to torture that might have their roots in specific times and places, and therefore carry particular, and limiting sets of assumptions. Reflecting on the experience of so-called fragile states in the global South and elsewhere can help us see new things about torture in other parts of the world. We invite the reader to consider where in the world – how many places, nations or states – the rule of law and access to justice for all citizens exists, and where torture, threats and coercion are considered to be a rare exception?

The chapter is set out as follows. In the next section, we begin by looking at the history of the anti-torture movement and the challenges faced when confronting torture in so-called fragile states. We then move on to critically examine how approaching torture through the lens of fragility – despite the problems of the concept – allows us to open up questions around the eradication of torture. The chapter then considers how these issues play out in the particular examples of public authority, corruption and extra-custodial violence. We focus on these three areas as they pose particular challenges for the eradication of torture. In conclusion, we examine the implications for policy and practice and highlight possible areas of research.

HISTORIES OF TORTURE

The fight against torture has historically been anchored in a very particular set of assumptions about the relationship between democracy, the rule of law and knowledge. In particular, the implicit assumption of much of the historiography of the anti-torture movement is that the fight against torture was significantly influenced by the European Enlightenment.[2] There is not the space to go into details here, save to point out some general implications of this history. For Enlightenment liberals, the fight against torture took place in the contexts of attempts at political and legal reform.[3] Indeed, the abolition of torture was often used to mark opposition to the *ancien régime*.[4] In this context the concept of torture has often – problematically – been used as marker of civilizational difference.[5] As the decades of the War on Terror have taught us, liberal democracies are not immune from torture, and we should not assume that simply becoming a liberal democracy is an antidote to acts of torture. Darius Rejali has argued, for example, that liberal democracies can have their own particular styles of torture, which

---

[2]   Evans, MD, and Morgan, R, *Preventing Torture: A Study of the European Convention for the Prevention of Torture and Inhuman or Degrading Treatment of Punishment* (Oxford University Press, 1998).

[3]   Beccaria, C, *On Crimes and Punishment* (first published 1778, Create Space, 2009).

[4]   Peters, E, *Torture* (University of Pennsylvania Press, 1996), 75.

[5]   Rejali, D, *Torture and Modernity: Self, Society and State in Modern Iran* (Princeton University Press, 1994). Even for scholars as critical as Michel Foucault, the use of torture marked a form of anti- or pre-modern politics and violence. See Kelly, T, *This Side of Silence: Human Rights, Torture and the Recognition of Cruelty* (University of Pennsylvania Press, 2012); Foucault, M, *Discipline and Punish: The Birth of the Prison* (Penguin, 1991).

combine outsourcing with techniques that leave few physical marks.[6] In a point we shall return to below, we therefore need to avoid thinking about violence and torture as being a legacy of a not fully modernized state.

For the reformers of Enlightenment liberalism, the eradication of torture was also often seen as an issue of specifically legal – as opposed to economic or political – change. This took place in a context where judicial torture – as a formal, explicit and public-sanctioned process of evidence gathering – was widespread across early modern Europe.[7] Attempts to eradicate torture therefore focused on the processes through which evidence was gathered, and the regulation of interrogation in particular. As such, approaches to the eradication of torture have often been closely associated with forms of police investigation, prison cells and other places of detention. It took a long period of campaigning for parts of the international human rights community to recognize the other places, such as immigration detention and hospitals, where torture might take place. It is also only very recently that human rights practitioners have begun to think through what might count as a place of detention (schools, care homes, hospitals, etc.), and the forms of torture that might take place outside spaces of detention (e.g. the home, the street, the police van, the camp, etc.).[8] As we shall also see below, this can have important implications in so-called fragile states, where criminal investigations and places of detention might take hybrid forms, with many actors involved other than police and prosecutors in their formal capacities.

The second half of the twentieth century has been widely understood as marking a new stage in the fight against torture – building on, but extending previous developments. This new stage was arguably marked by three key foci. The first was establishing legal norms against torture – most obviously in the 1984 UN Convention Against Torture. The assumption was that if torture was the product of a legal regime, then the legal regime needed to be changed, and changed through the development of new legal norms.[9] As part of this, impunity was seen a major cause of torture, and therefore torture had to be comprehensively criminalized. The question remains though as to how such an approach applies in contexts where judicial procedures are themselves frail, or the law itself has limited legitimacy. If laws are simply ignored, or cannot be enforced, what difference does producing new national, regional and international legal norms around the prohibition of torture make?

The second focus of the renewed campaign against torture was on human rights monitoring. This can take either a form that prioritizes critical dialogue, best seen in parts of the practice of the International Committee of the Red Cross (ICRC), the UN Sub-Committee for the Prevention of Torture, and the European Committee for the Prevention of Torture, or other more accusatory forms of shaming, perhaps most obviously seen in human rights campaigns by Amnesty International or Human Rights Watch. Although monitoring can take many forms,

---

[6]   Rejali, D, *Torture and Democracy* (Princeton University Press, 2007). For a more popular account, see for instance Cobain, I, *Cruel Britannia: A Secret History of Torture* (Portobello Books, 2012).

[7]   Langbein, JH, *Torture and the Law of Proof* (Chicago University Press, 1977); Peters (n 4 above).

[8]   See, for example, Special Rapporteur on torture and other cruel, inhuman or degrading treatment or punishment, Report to the General Assembly, Extra-custodial use of force and the prohibition of torture and other cruel, inhuman or degrading treatment or punishment, 2017, UN Doc A/72/178.

[9]   Celermajer, D, *International Legal Frameworks and Existing Approaches to Preventing Torture* (2015) http://sydney.edu.au/arts/research/ehrp/downloads/EHRP_Issues_Paper_1.pdf; Nowak, M, 'On the Prevention of Torture' in Dunér, B (ed), *An End to Torture: Strategies for its Eradication* (Zed Books, 1998).

the implicit assumption is that torture is a problem of knowledge, and that torture takes place because the right people at the right time do not know about it, or know that what they are doing is wrong.[10] It is important to ask though, what happens in contexts where people might know about torture and do not care that it is taking place – and perhaps even endorse its use on particular groups, such as alleged criminals – or know about it, but due to factors outside their control are unable to prevent it taking place? The Assad regime in Syria, or Guantanamo might be examples of the former, whilst governments such as those in Somalia might be an example of the latter. Furthermore, we might also ask what happens when survivors, for multiple possible reasons, do not want their experiences to be known?[11] In some situations survivors can be too scared to come forward, or see little practical purpose in exposing what they have been through. Rather than having a light shone on their experiences, they might want to hide away, fearful of possible stigma or repercussions, lacking confidence that the legal system or even human rights actors can offer them the type of practical support or forms of justice they might be after.[12]

The third focus has been a partial emphasis on political detainees. Historically, this was especially the case in the context of human rights responses to the dictatorships in Latin America. Anti-torture campaigns, partly for strategic reasons, focused on relatively high profile political prisoners. In this process, torture victims were presented, often with good cause, as heroic survivors.[13] However, in contexts where the threat of torture and ill-treatment is an endemic part of many interactions between public officials and citizens, there is a danger that the less dramatic, and seemingly more routine forms of torture, and the less obviously virtuous victims, are not given attention.[14] Many survivors of torture do not necessarily fit a heroic ideal, but still need to be protected. Furthermore, the experience of the human rights organizations suggests that most victims of torture are not high profile political figures, but rather are relatively anonymous victims of public officials' negligence and misconduct, and an under-resourced and under-prioritized criminal justice system.[15]

None of this is to say that the above assumptions are misplaced in the right context. Torture is clearly linked to interrogation and impunity. Normative legal change clearly has played a central part of the process of reducing torture. And political detainees have been significant victims of torture. But if we understand torture in the sense of the UNCAT definition and its broad requirements of severe pain or suffering, intention, and the direct or indirect involvement of public officials, focusing largely on places detention, legal change and political prisoners can limit the ways we understand the causes and consequences, and we might overlook major groups of victims and their needs. In the next section, we discuss how the category of state fragility might therefore open up alternative ways of thinking about torture.

---

[10]   Celermajer (n 9 above); Alston, P and Knuckey, S (eds), *The Transformation of Human Rights Fact-Finding* (Oxford University Press, 2016).

[11]   Jensen, J, Kelly, T, Andersen, MK, Christiansen, C and Sharma, JS, 'Torture and Ill-Treatment Under Perceived: Human Rights Documentation and the Poor' (2017) 39 *Human Rights Quarterly* 2, 393.

[12]   Andersen, MK, 'Filtering Information: Human Rights Documentation in Bangladesh' (2019) 11 *Journal of Human Rights Practice* 1, 81.

[13]   Fassin, D and Rechtman, R, *The Empire of Trauma: An Inquiry into the Condition of Victimhood* (Princeton University Press, 2009).

[14]   Jensen and others (n 11 above), 393.

[15]   *Ibid.*

FRAGILE STATES AND TORTURE

If the fight against torture has often been marked by a focus on building strong states bound by the rule of law, focusing on state fragility can help throw this history and its associated assumptions into stark relief. If state fragility is linked to violence, we might understand many acts of torture as the product of weakness, as a regime with limited institutional capacity and democractic accountability lashes out against its citizens. The term 'fragility' is used by important parts of the international development community to refer to countries with limited institutional capacity, leaving citizens vulnerable to shocks, crisis and violence.[16] The OECD for instance defines fragile states as those that 'lack political will and/or capacity to provide the basic functions needed for poverty reduction, development and to safeguard the security and human rights of their populations'.[17] In this context, fragile states are associated with cycles of violence, of which torture can be a significant part.[18]

The concept of state fragility has been criticized for being overly normative, containing Eurocentric assumptions about how states should behave and what strong states look like. As Janet Roitman argues, this rests on a number of ideals largely derived from a modular notion of the state, that very few, if any countries fulfill in practice, even if they want to.[19] Critics have also pointed out that we should not assume that what on the surface looks like the same form of fragility has the same causes and consequences in all places.[20] As such, we should not assume that the institutional practices associated with a minority of high-income liberal democracies can simply be transferred to the world's poorest countries. The implications of this general line of argument is that whilst the prohibition of torture itself might be a near universal aspiration, the institutional arrangements and political relationship that provide the conditions both for torture and its prevention are not the same all over the world. There is a burgeoning realization of this. For instance, the National Prevention Mechanisms, established in relation to the Optional Protocol to the Convention against Torture (OPCAT), are not created on the basis of a narrow template but allow for different institutional arrangements that resonate with national histories.

Perhaps the biggest issue with the concept of 'fragility' in relation to torture is that we should not assume that the resort to violence is inherently a product of state weakness. Torture

---

[16]   ARD, Measuring Fragility: Indicators and Methods for Rating State Performance (ARD, 2005); Bertoli, S and Ticci, E, 'A Fragile Guideline to Development Assistance' (2012) 30 *Development Policy* 2, 211–230; Besley, T and Persson, T, 'Fragile States and Development Policy' (2011) 9 *Journal of the European Economic Association* 3, 371; Cammack, D, Mcleod, D, Menocal, AR and Christiansen, K, *Donors and the 'Fragile States' Agenda: A Survey of Current Thinking and Practice* (ODI, 2006). The World Bank defines fragile states according to their ranking in the Country Policy and Institutional Assessment (CPIA) that includes 16 criteria grouped in four clusters: economic management, structural policies, policies for social inclusion and equity, and public sector management and institutions. The result is published every year in the 'Harmonized List of Fragile Situations'. Fragile Situations include countries or territories with (i) a harmonized CPIA country rating of 3.2 or less, and/or (ii) the presence of a UN and/or regional peacekeeping or political/peace-building mission during the last three years.

[17]   OECD/DAC, *Principles for Good International Engagement in Fragile States and Situations* (OECD, 2007) 2.

[18]   World Bank, *Conflict, Security and Development* (World Bank, 2011).

[19]   Roitman, J, *Fiscal Disobedience: An Anthropology of Economic Regulation in Central Africa* (Princeton University Press, 2004), 193.

[20]   Grimm and others (n 1 above), 197.

can be linked to a strong state, and might, historically speaking, be central to the ways in which a strong state is built, however problematic that might be at a normative level. As John Langbein has argued, for example, the growth of judicial torture in medieval Europe was not simply the product of an arbitrary and a capricious politics but rather a desire to create legally reliable evidence.[21] In a different context, Janet Roitman argues that the apparently fragile states of the African Sahel region have been quite capable of crushing rebellion through violence and savvy political maneuvering, and therefore have a particular type of strength.[22] The Philippines might be another example here where the state, often seen as institutionally limited, has emerged victorious almost every time through a century of insurgency and warfare.[23] Its latest campaign against drugs, leading to thousands of deaths and incidents of ill-treatment is yet another example. It is therefore useful to think about the resort to torture as a product of particular politically directed state priorities, enabling the full potential of institutional control, coercion and violence.

We need to be careful to avoid a binary distinction between 'fragility' and 'stability', ignoring the ways that relative fragility and stability can often exist in the same institutions and social spaces. There are complex links between torture and its eradication that can cross over the borders of states. As Darius Rejali has shown for example, virtually all the techniques of torture found in the late twentieth and early twenty-first century in Iraq, Afghanistan and Vietnam began their development in the prisons and police cells of France, Britain and the US.[24] Equally importantly, since the War on Terror at least, but also well before this period, liberal democracies have outsourced torture to keep their 'hands clean'.[25] One could ask, if the relative absence of torture in some states should be seen as the direct result of torture taking place in other places?[26] We therefore need to avoid assuming an end position of state development, where all states are eventually moving in the same direction, and fragility, and therefore implicitly torture, has been eradicated. States can move in and out of violence, in and out of torture, and the absence of torture in one place can be linked to the presence of torture elsewhere. This means going beyond an approach which sees the existence of torture as simply the product of an absence of the correct laws or culture, to looking at the multiple relational factors that drive torture in particular times and places.

However, notwithstanding the above criticism, an awareness of relative fragility can still in itself help open up new questions around torture. For example, it can help us to pay attention to the multiple relationships and pressures in which public officials find themselves enmeshed. In the absence of strong forms of institutional and bureaucratic capacity and accountability, states can be fragmented and divided. Even if one part of the state, however formally important, wants to stop torture, this does not mean we should assume it has control over, or even a relationship with other parts of that same state. We need to recognize that states might be

---

[21]   Langbein (n 7 above); Peters (n 4 above).

[22]   Roitman (n 19 above).

[23]   Quimpo, NG, 'The Philippines: Predatory Regime, Growing Authoritarian Features' (2009) 22 *The Pacific Review* 3, 335; McCoy, AW, *Policing America's Empire: The United States, the Philippines, and the Rise of the Surveillance State* (University of Wisconsin Press, 2009).

[24]   Rejali (n 6 above).

[25]   Pugliese, J, *State Violence and the Execution of Law: Biopolitical Caesurae of Torture, Black Sites, Drones* (Routledge, 2013).

[26]   See for instance Sadat, LN, 'Ghost Prisoners and Black Sites: Extraordinary Rendition under International Law' (2005) *Case W Res. Int'l L.*, 37(15), 309.

too dysfunctional and/or under-resourced to eradicate torture. Chains of command and bureaucratic accountability might be too fragmented, dispersed and overtly complicated, or slow, non-transparent and conflicted to ensure that the prohibition of torture is followed through, despite political willingness and leadership support. We also need to pay attention to ways in which states are not unified entities and to the fact that state actors, from politicians to police, can have multiple affiliations and obligations as well as interests and demands, which do not necessarily support the prohibition and prevention of torture.

The actions of public officials are not simply governed by formal legal rules and relationships, but also by a host of relatively more informal processes and interests.[27] This is arguably the case in all states, but especially so in apparently fragile states. Torture does not necessarily take place because of the absence or presence of particular formal rules, but can also be carried out as a result of multiple, more diffuse and often informal aspirations, norms and assumptions and multiple institutional rationalities. As Andrew Jefferson shows, for example, the behavior of Nigerian prison guards is influenced as much by their families' expectations, as it is by formal prison regulations.[28] The implication for the fight against torture is that it is not much use to focus simply on technical reforms of public institutions and laws, if those laws and institutions themselves have limited legitimacy or influence, or are systematically bent and bypassed without state sanction and with political impunity. We need to be careful to take other norms, expectations and relationships into account.

It is not just norms and affiliations though that can influence the behavior of public officials, but also the structural conditions under which they work. Jensen and Jefferson argue that the actions of state officials are "circumscribed by structures and arrangements ... partially beyond their control".[29] In states marked by fragility, the limited resources available to public officials can put real pressures on them as they go about their work. As Evans and Morgan argue, acts of torture can be driven by a host of factors, which can include issues linked to such factors as 'pay, social status and working conditions'.[30] We should not give public officials, at all levels, too much agency, and assume once they know something they will be able to act upon it. One possible policy response to recognizing the limitations under which public officials work is, as Celermajer has pointed out, a pragmatic approach to torture prevention that seeks to understand the conditions within which people work and provide new skills and incentives, whilst keeping a broader eye on systemic issues.[31] Focusing on judicial issues alone, for example, might fail to acknowledge these practical constraints and structural problems.

Finally, and in a related point, a focus on state fragility can also bring our attention to situations of poverty and inequality. Although it is also important to note that poverty and fragility are not inherently linked, many states categorized as fragile are also marked by relatively high levels of poverty and inequality. By paying attention to the relationship between state fragility, poverty and violence we can begin to understand the ways that torture, like other forms of violence, is rooted in social relations and differences in power, rather than simply rooted

[27] Punch, M, *Police Corruption: Exploring Police Deviance and Crime* (Routledge, 2009).
[28] Jefferson, A, 'On Hangings and the Dubious Embodiment of Statehood in Nigerian Prisons' in Jefferson, A and Jensen, S (eds), *State Violence and Human Rights: State Officials in the South* (Routledge, 2009).
[29] Jefferson and Jensen (n 28 above), 11.
[30] Evans and Morgan (n 2 above), 25–26.
[31] Celermajer (n 9 above).

in cultural norms or individual pathology. The poor, for example are often highly vulnerable to torture by law enforcement agents and their proxies.[32] This vulnerability to torture is both a symptom of poverty and one of the reasons why political and economic participation can be so problematic. Importantly, it is not just the poverty in and of itself that is an issue, but relative forms of poverty in particular, and the inequalities that these can produce – a subject we will return to in relation to corruption specifically. Not only can the poor be stigmatized, but they can also lack the social, political and economic capital necessary to seek redress or to mobilize support. As the former UN Special Rapporteur on Torture noted, 'most of the victims of arbitrary detention, torture and inhuman conditions of detention are usually ordinary people who belong to the poorest and most disadvantaged sectors of society'.[33]

At the same time, human rights organizations, including the anti-torture movement, can also face challenges in confronting the forms of torture experienced by people living in poverty. As the UN Special Rapporteur on Extreme Poverty has noted in relation to people living in poverty: 'their civil and political rights are often completely ignored, explicitly excluded from the analysis or mentioned only in passing'.[34] Elsewhere, we have argued that many human rights organizations can systematically under-perceive the extent and nature of torture amongst the poor.[35] Limitations in institutional capacities mean that, for example, human rights organizations are often geographically and socially distant from low-income neighborhoods. A predisposition towards prosecution and reparations can also sometimes run in tension with a situation where, in everyday practice, if not in aspiration, many people living in poverty prioritize safety and protection above accountability.

In the next three sections we will examine how situations of relative fragility – marked by institutional fragmentation and resource limitations, and low levels of state legitimacy and accountability – play out in relation to public officials, extra-custodial violence and corruption. Thinking through these specific issues can widen the ways we think about perpetrators and victims of torture, where torture might take place and why it happens.

PUBLIC AUTHORITY

One of the key things that looking at torture through the lens of relative state fragility can do is to call attention to the complex nature of public authority. The direct or indirect involvement, consent or acquiescence of a public official is a central part in the human rights definition of torture, but what counts as a public official and the ways they act should not be taken for granted. Alongside the propensity for violence and low levels of legitimacy, two factors in particular are important here for the ways in which we think about fragile states, public authority and torture. The first is that a defining feature of state fragility can be states' failure (willing

---

[32]   Dissel, A, Jensen, S and Roberts, A, *Torture in South Africa: Exploring Torture and Cruel, Inhumane, Degrading and Treatment Through Media* (Centre for the Study of Violence and Reconciliation, 2009), http://www.csvr.org.za/publications/1755-torture-in-south-africa-exploring-torture-and-cruel-inhuman -and-degrading-treatment-or-punishment-through-the-media

[33]   Special Rapporteur on Torture and Other Cruel, Inhuman or Degrading Treatment or Punishment, Report to the UN General Assembly, 2009, UN Doc A/64/215, para 40.

[34]   Special Rapporteur on Extreme Poverty and Human Rights, Report to the UN General Assembly, 2017, UN Doc A/72/502.

[35]   Jensen and others (n 11 above), 393.

or otherwise) to exercise a monopoly over the use of legitimate force. It is not just that fragile states can resort to violence, but there might also be many other actors that do so. This means that it is not only the state that inflicts and sanctions violence on its citizens, and indeed state actors might have a relatively limited presence on the ground, in all corners of state territory. What counts, in practice, as a public figure, in a context where militias, gangs, or political groups can carry out many of the functions usually associated with the state, not least in relation to violence, policing and justice, can therefore be complex.

There has been a move in human rights jurisprudence away from focusing on the specific acts of identifiable public officials, towards a more normative focus on acts for which the state can 'legitimately be held responsible.'[36] Acts carried out by public officials in a 'private capacity' though are usually seen to fall outside the definition. The UN Committee Against Torture has indicated, for example, that acts carried out by 'non-government entities without consent or acquiescence of government' generally fall outside the definition of torture. However, where state authority is lacking, non-state actors can be seen as 'acting in an official capacity' and their action can therefore be seen to count as torture.[37] Immediately, we can see that there are important questions as to when and where a state becomes weak (or fragile), as well as what counts as acting in a private capacity? As a vast amount of social science has shown, the structure and meanings of public authority are historically and contextually specific.[38] Public authority can be embedded in very different political, economic and cultural processes that create different forms of legitimacy, different boundaries between the private and the public, and different relationships with the deployment of violence, amongst other things. What counts as a public official can therefore never be taken for granted, either normatively or empirically. Public authority is not a yes/no binary distinction, but a spectrum, with ebbs and flows of intensity and meaning over both time and space.

To give an example, the authors of this chapter have carried out research on the prevalence and distribution of torture in low-income neighborhoods in Nairobi, Kathmandu and Dhaka. The practice of public authority had very different structures and textures in each place. In all three places though there were dense webs of relationships and organizations involved in the provision of what might be thought of as public goods such as water, schooling and housing, or exercising public authority, for example through arbitration and policing. In Bangladesh, there is a complex relationship between the formal structures of the state, political parties, and criminal gangs.[39] In some cases, the same actors might be involved in all three sets of activities. In Kenya, public authority is caught up in wider political networks linked to political parties,

---

[36] Barrett, J, 'The Prohibition of Torture Under International Law, Part 2: The Normative Content' (2001) 5 *International Journal of Human Rights* 1; Evans, MD, 'Getting to Grips with Torture' (2002) 51 *International and Comparative Law Quarterly* 365; Sivakumaran, S, 'Torture in International Human Rights and International Humanitarian Law: The Actor and the Ad Hoc Tribunals' (2005) 18 *Leiden Journal of International Law* 541.

[37] For elaboration see, Nowak, M, Binz, M and Monina, G, *The United Nations Convention Against Torture – A Commentary* (Oxford University Press, 2019).

[38] Lund, C, 'Twilight Institutions: An Introduction' (2006) 37 *Development and Change* 673; Hansen, TB and Stepputat, F (eds), *Sovereign Bodies: Citizens, Migrants and States in the Postcolonial World* (Princeton University Press, 2005).

[39] Islam, MM, 'The Toxic Politics of Bangladesh: A Bipolar Competitive Neopatrimonial State?' (2013) 21 *Asian Journal of Political Science* 148; Andersen, MK, 'Time-Use, Activism and the Making of Future' (2016) 39 *South Asia: Journal of South Asian Studies* 415; Osman, AF, 'Bangladesh Politics: Confrontation, Monopoly and Crisis in Governance' (2010) 18 *Asian Journal of Political Science* 310.

ethnic affiliations, and local government structures built on 'chiefly authority.'[40] The result is an often blurred line between an action done in public and private capacities. In Nepal, political parties, development agencies, and ethnically based networks play out across a terrain where the state itself is often unable or unwilling to provide basic services.[41]

The dispersal of public authority can be seen particularly in the area of law and order, where the formal state might struggle to hold the monopoly on the legitimate means of violence. In Kenya, for example, alongside the Kenyan Police, private security firms, *nyumba kumi* (community based policing) and *mungiki* (ethnically based militia) have all sought to enforce particular visions of law and order. In Bangladesh, the Police, the semi-autonomous Rapid Action Battalion, *mastaans* (criminal kingpins), and political parties have all attempted to impose their visions of order, at times colliding and at other times colluding. In Nepal, the Police and municipal officials have stood alongside political parties (often Maoist), and private security firms, amongst others. In all three countries therefore, the de facto 'legitimate' and 'illegitimate' deployment of force in the name of the public good has been dispersed across a range of actors, often loosely tied to the formal state.

Importantly, the blurring of the line between public and private officials is not simply and necessarily a product of state fragility. In some cases, it can also be the result of deliberate state policy. Practices such as outsourcing, decentralization and privatization can create new conditions of the public and the private. As numerous studies have shown, state agencies can encourage and rely on private security companies, for example, to provide and enforce particular types of order.[42] And the promotion of community-based policing can blur the line between state and non-state actors.[43]

The implicit assumption of some human rights practice is that the key public officials involved in torture are prison officers, police officers, soldiers and security officials. There are at least two possible limitations to this approach however. First of all, singling out police or prison officers does not capture all possible public officials, their relationships and varied levels of involvement, across time and space. According to the human rights definition, any public official could be involved – from teachers to medical staff. To focus on the police is to *a priori* decide who carries out torture. This implicitly defines torture as a momentary act of inflicting pain and injury, not a process with a pre- and post-history involving multiple actors with interests and conflicts.[44] We therefore need to take into account the different ways in which the state (and public authority) is manifested and the implications that this can have for how we think about torture, its causes and possible prevention. It also means that we need to

[40]   Rasmussen, J, 'Outwitting the Professor of Politics? Mungiki Narratives of Political Deception and their Role in Kenyan Politics' (2010) 4 *Journal of Eastern African Studies* 435; Anderson, DM, 'Vigilantes, Violence and the Politics of Public Order in Kenya' (2002) 101 *African Affairs* 531.

[41]   Gellner, D and Hachhetu, K, *Local Democracy in South Asia: Microprocesses of Democractization in Nepal and its Neighbours* (Sage, 2008).

[42]   Leander, A and Van Munster, R, 'Private Security Contractors in the Debate about Darfur: Reflecting and Reinforcing Neo-Liberal Governmentality' (2007) 21 *International Relations* 2, 201; Abrahamsen, R and Williams, MC, *Security Beyond the State: Private Security in International Politics* (Cambridge University Press, 2010).

[43]   Albrecht, P and Kyed, HM (eds), *Policing and the Politics of Order-Making* (Routledge, 2014).

[44]   Andersen, MK, 'Accidental Victimhood and Citizenship: Violent Exchanges in Dhaka' in Jensen, S and Andersen, MK (eds) *Violent Exchanges* (Aalborg University Press, 2017); Andersen, MK, 'Why Corruption Matters in Human Rights' (2018) 10 *Journal of Human Rights Practice* 179.

expand the sites where we think torture is likely to take place. It is to this issue that the chapter will now turn.

EXTRA-CUSTODIAL TORTURE

Anti-torture activities have historically focused on places of detention in many states marked by limited institutional capacity and resources. This focus on detention has been further entrenched with the OPCAT whose centerpiece is the monitoring of places of detention, although there has been an increasing expansion of the definition of what counts as a place of detention. However, we should still be careful when focusing all our attention here. The use of extra-custodial force is a widespread phenomenon across a range of contexts that includes a variety of practices including extra-judicial punishment, intimidation, corruption and crowd control. In many circumstances being taken into custody is a relative privilege. And in some low-income countries, detention facilities are severely limited and under-resourced, meaning that much policing takes place elsewhere.[45] Rather than focus on whether a particular activity qualifies as custodial or not, it is probably more productive to focus on the ways in which people are actually treated and by whom.

Widespread evidence suggests that the use of apparently extra-custodial force is a significant issue in many countries around the world. In 2016, DIGNITY and the University of Edinburgh carried out surveys amongst the residents of informal settlements in Kenya, Nepal, and Bangladesh. The surveys showed that violence, or the threat of violence, was the dominant experience of many poor citizens in their interactions with the police and security forces.[46] A survey carried out by the authors in Nairobi showed police were responsible for 26 percent of incidents of violence experienced by the respondents. This suggested that almost 10 percent of the population in the sample had experienced state violence within the previous year.[47] The survey also showed 18 percent of respondents felt that the police were the main perpetrators of violence in their area. A further survey carried out by the Independent Medical Legal Unit amongst informal traders in Nairobi revealed that 9 percent claimed to have been beaten in the previous year by public officials, and over 50 percent knew of another trader who had been beaten in the same period.[48] In Bangladesh, police harassment and extortion is an everyday fact of life for many, and the police are viewed by much of the population as "predators rather than protectors". In Nepal, acts of torture and ill-treatment also often appear to be associated with

---

[45]   Jefferson and Jensen (n 28 above).
[46]   Sharma, JR, Sijapati, B, Baniya, J, Bhandari, A, Pathak, D, Bhattarai, A, Kelly, T and Jensen, S, *Torture and Ill-Treatment: Perceptions, Experiences and Justice-Seeking in Kathmandu's Squatter Communities* (Social Science Baha, 2016), available at http://soscbaha.org/book/index.php/fbook/extract/101; Choudhoury, Z, Durrat, F, Hussain, M, Alam, MS and Andersen MK, *Poverty and Violent Conflict in Korail Slum in Dhaka* (University of Dhaka, 2016), available at https://torturedocumentationproject.files.wordpress.com/2014/05/poverty-and-violence-in-korail-slum-in-dhaka.pdf; Kiama, P, Christiansen, C, Jensen, S, Kelly, T, 'Violence Amongst the Urban Poor in Nairobi' (IMLU, 2016), available at http://www.imlu.org/index.php/shortcode/key-features/typgraphy/summary/3-reports/43-violence-among-urban-poor-in-nairobi
[47]   Kiama and others (n 46 above).
[48]   Independent Medico-Legal Unit, *A Cry for Justice: Torture and Ill-Treatment of Hawkers and Small Scale Traders in Nairobi City County* (IMLU, 2014).

relatively mundane accusations of criminal activities, and the police are perceived as the main source of violence. In our survey, the police were involved as perpetrators in nearly 55 percent of all reported violent incidents.[49]

Police brutality often routinely takes place outside of places of detention. According to the surveys that we carried out in Dhaka, Kathmandu and Nairobi, the residents of informal settlements commonly experienced violations at the hand of state officials in their own neighborhoods and homes. In Kenya, people were often not formally detained, but beaten and extorted 'off the book'. Similarly, in our Nepal survey, respondents reported that less than 5 percent of the identified acts of torture and ill-treatment had occurred in a place of detention.[50] Our Dhaka survey showed that victims are often not detained, but beaten up in public or in their homes.[51] Another survey, carried out by the human rights organization DIGNITY in Bangladesh, showed that 46 percent of incidents of torture and ill-treatment took place in the victim's home.[52] In Kenya, similarly to the Philippines, legitimized police brutality has left thousands dead on the streets in the war on drugs and crime.[53]

In contexts where legal systems are inefficient, unresponsive or unable to bring alleged perpetrators of crime to account, the police can try to short-circuit the criminal justice system through the use of extra-judicial punishment. Instead of detaining people, the police resort to summary forms of justice, often in an open and public manner. This is a form of violence that has links to extra-judicial killings and disappearance, except that it is often deliberately carried out in public in order to intimidate wider populations. Moreover, this violence can also have the support of parts of the wider population, who do not trust the criminal justice system.[54] Minorities and marginal groups are the main victims of such violence, which in a discriminatory manner further enforces their marginalization.

Evidence from South Africa, for example, suggests that police violence is often an attempt at immediate, tangible and visible forms of punishment, which might be supported by sections of the public.[55] Alleged criminals are often never charged or taken to police stations, but kept in the back of police vans or beaten in public. Similarly, evidence from Brazil suggests that police violence in the favelas can often be a deliberately public show of force.[56] Evidence from South Africa, as well as in many other countries around the world, furthermore suggests that support by sections of the community lead police to consent to and even promote non-state

---

[49]   Sharma and others (n 46 above).

[50]   *Ibid.*

[51]   Choudhoury and others (n 46 above).

[52]   Wang, SJ, Modvig, J and Montgomery, E, 'Household Exposure to Violence and Human Rights Violations in Western Bangladesh (I): Prevalence, Risk Factors and Consequences' (2009) 9 *BMC Int'l Health H. Rts* 29.

[53]   Warburg, AB and Jensen, S, 'Policing the War on Drugs and the Transformation of Urban Space in Manila' (2020) 38 *Environment and Planning D: Society and Space* 3, 399–416; Reyes, DA, 'The Spectacle of Violence in Duterte's "War On Drugs"' (2016) 35 *Journal of Current Southeast Asian Affairs* 3, 111; van Stapele, N, '"We Are Not Kenyans": Extra-Judicial Killings, Manhood And Citizenship in Mathare, A Nairobi Ghetto' (2016) 16 *Conflict, Security & Development* 4, 301.

[54]   Wacquant, L, 'Toward a Dictatorship Over the Poor' (2003) *Punishment & Society* 2, 197.

[55]   Hornberger, H, 'From General to Commissioner to General – on the Popular State of Policing in South Africa' (2013) 38 *Law & Social Inquiry* 3, 547.

[56]   Larkins, ER, 'Performances of Police Legitimacy in Rio's Hyper Favela' (2013) 38 *Law and Social Inquiry* 3, 553.

forms of policing that is inherently brutal, intentional and purposeful.[57] Police may for instance be present at violent vigilante disciplining or hand over suspects to vigilante groups. Both practices are of course clearly covered by the Convention Against Torture.[58]

CORRUPTION

In this final section, we will examine the multi-dimensional relationship between torture and corruption. Although corruption is by no means limited to fragile states, it can be a crucial feature of the lack of will or the capacity of states to provide fairly and equitably for their citizens, which often takes more dramatic and public forms in fragile situations and where the possible negative impact on society and implications for individuals are greater. In the context of low salaries and limited state resources, corruption might also be a key way in which public officials provide for themselves, their dependents, or the institutions within which they work. As such, corruption can involve coercion or exploitation of other citizens for personal ends or on behalf of political and economic (elite) interests. State fragility, corruption and torture are therefore linked in complex ways. Torture and corruption though have long been addressed in both academia and policy circles as two separate domains of knowledge and practice – as examples of gross human rights violations or bad governance respectively, which can explain an implementation gap between human rights and rights based approaches, and anti-corruption efforts.[59] Yet, not only can corruption and torture proliferate in the same spaces, but corruption can also lead to torture, and vice versa. There is a growing focus on and recognition of this relationship at the UN, especially since the Seventh Annual Report of the Subcommittee on Prevention of Torture and Other Cruel, Inhuman or Degrading Treatment or Punishment on 20 March 2014.[60] This was followed by Human Rights Council Resolution of 19 March 2018 on the negative impact of corruption on the right to be free from torture and other cruel, inhuman or degrading treatment or punishment.[61] In 2019, this was followed by the United

---

[57] Jensen, S, 'Above the Law: Practices of Sovereignty in Surrey Estate, Cape Town' in Hansen, T and Stepputat, F (eds), *Sovereign Bodies: Citizens, Migrants and States in the Postcolonial World* (Princeton University Press, 2005), 218–238.

[58] Buur, L, 'The Sovereign Outsourced: Justice and Violence in Port Elizabeth' in Hansen and Stepputat (n 57 above), 190–201; Jensen, S, 'Vision of the State: Audiences, Enchantments and Policing in South Africa' in Jefferson and Jensen (n 28 above).

[59] Peters, A, 'Corruption as a Violation of International Human Rights' (2018) 29 *European Journal of International Law* 1251; Rose, C, 'The Limitations of a Human Rights Approach to Corruption' (2016) 65 *International & Comparative Law Quarterly* 405; Boersma, M, *Corruption: A Violation of Human Rights and a Crime under International Law?* (Intersentia, 2013); Bicknell, C, 'A Hydra in Detention Settings: A Context-Based Inquiry of Corruption's Many Heads' (2017) 17 *Human Rights Law Review* 1; Jensen, S and Andersen, MK (eds), *Violent Exchanges* (Aalborg University Press, 2017); Andersen, MK, 'Why Corruption Matters in Human Rights' (2018) 10 *Journal of Human Rights Practice* 179.

[60] Seventh Annual Report of the Subcommittee on Prevention of Torture and Other Cruel, Inhuman or Degrading Treatment or Punishment, 2014, UN Doc, CAT/C/52/2, paras 72–100.

[61] UN Doc A/HRC/RES/37/19.

Nations Special Rapporteur on Torture's thematic report on the relation between corruption and torture.[62]

Importantly, the meanings and implications of the term 'corruption' are far from self-evident. Indeed, there is no universally comprehensive and accepted definition of corruption. The World Bank, for example, defines corruption as 'abuse of public office for private gain',[63] whereas the Asian Development Bank defines it as officials 'misusing the position in which they are placed'.[64] In practice, such formal definitions can fail to capture the multiple forms that corruption takes. What these definitions do share though is a sense that corruption – like torture – is inherently about the abuse of public office in situations of inequality.[65] As Rose-Ackerman states, widespread corruption is a sign that something has gone wrong in the relationship between the state and society.[66] As with fragile states more generally, the evidence suggests that there are many different forms that public authority, and therefore corruption, can take. The literature on formal and informal forms of policing, for example, suggests that there are multiple groups that seek to extract resources, mixing notions of public interest and private gain.[67]

A significant part of the social science research on corruption has attempted to move beyond narrow legal definitions to explore the different behaviors that people categorize as corrupt and to 'identify the frameworks in which they make these judgments', in order to grasp the drivers of such actions.[68] As such, approaches that see corruption as a problem of individual pathology have been criticized for failing to take into account institutional, economic, political or cultural context.[69] At the same time, approaches that focus on the institutional cultures of particular public offices – such as police departments – have also been criticized for failing

---

[62]   Report of the Special Rapporteur on Torture and Other Cruel, Inhuman or Degrading Treatment or Punishment, 2019, UN Doc A/HRC/40/59. The Special Rapporteur usefully identified a number of ways that corruption and torture are linked. These comprise: demanding 'undue advantages' that per se amount to torture or ill-treatment; instrumentalizing torture or ill-treatment for 'undue advantages'; instrumentalizing 'undue advantages' for torture or ill-treatment; exploiting exposure to torture or ill-treatment for 'undue advantages'; torture or ill-treatment as a foreseeable 'side effect' of corruption; and torture or ill-treatment and corruption as foreseeable 'side effects' of other policies and practices.

[63]   World Bank, *Helping Countries Combat Corruption* (World Bank, 1997), 8.

[64]   Asian Development Bank, *Anticorruption Policy* (ADB, 2004), 9.

[65]   Klitgaard, R, *Controlling Corruption* (UCP, 1988); Klitgaard, R, Maclean-Abaroa, R and Parris, HL, *Corrupt Cities: A Practical Guide to Cure and Prevention* (World Bank, 2000); Rose-Ackerman, S and Palifka, BJ, *Corruption and Government: Causes, Consequences and Reform* (Cambridge University Press, 2016).

[66]   Rose-Ackerman, S, 'The Political Economy of Corruption' in Elliot, K (ed), *Corruption and the Global Economy* (PIIE, 1997), 34.

[67]   Kyed, HM, and Albrectsen, P (eds), *Policing and the Politics of Order Making* (Routledge, 2014); Buur, L and Jensen, J, 'Introduction: Vigilantism and the Policing of Everyday Life in South Africa' (2004) 63 *African Studies* 139; Baker, B, 'Living With Non-State Policing in South Africa: The Issues and Dilemmas' (2002) 40 *Journal of Modern African Studies* 29.

[68]   Philp, M, 'The Definition of Political Corruption' in Heywood, PM (ed), *Routledge Handbook of Political Corruption* (Routledge, 2015), 20, 24; Olivier de Sardan, J-P, 'A Moral Economy of Corruption in Africa' (1999) 37 *Journal of Modern African Studies* 25.

[69]   Agbiboa, DE, 'Protectors Or Predators? The Embedded Problem of Police Corruption and Deviance in Nigeria' (2015) 47 *Administration and Society* 244; Justice Tankebe, 'Public Confidence in the Police: Testing the Effects of Public Experiences of Police Corruption in Ghana' (2010) 50 *British Journal of Criminology* 296; Scully, J, 'Rotten Apple or Rotten Barrel? The Role of Civil Rights Lawyers in Ending the Culture of Police Violence' (2009) 21 *National Black Law Journal* 137.

to take into account that not all officials are corrupt.[70] To understand the causes of corruption we therefore need to understand the diverse and often contradictory allegiances, obligations and normative registers within which people operate, which can extend far beyond the formal institutional realm.

Although not all corruption leads to torture, and not all torture is linked to corruption, paying attention to the relationship between the two can help us understand how torture is produced in the context of unequal and overlapping social relations, as the Special Rapporteur on Torture also noted in his 2019 report.[71] Corruption and torture can be seen as part of the same social dynamic. Much corruption can be understood as 'extortive', that is rooted in compulsion or force, with money or favors paid in order to 'fend off some form of harm or impediment being inflicted on the giver or on individuals close to him/her.'[72] The classic example is a police officer 'asking' for a bribe in return for not imprisoning or violating someone. The threat of violence is embedded in such encounters, and can then be used as a form of punishment for not paying up. Whilst many anti-torture interventions can focus on the act of the infliction of violence, it is also important therefore to take into account the social relations – what we elsewhere have called 'violent exchanges' – that might lead up to acts of violence, and these are social relations that have a broader scope than criminal justice interventions.[73]

We can see corruption as the background to many acts of torture. Importantly, in fragile states in particular, the processes of corruption, and its linked forms of torture, do not necessarily take place in formal judicial institutions. They are just as, if not more, likely to take place in extra-custodial and pre-detention settings. At one level, as has been argued in the previous section, the routine harassment of street traders, sex workers and other marginal people, for example, is often accompanied by requests for bribes and threats of violence. This often takes place on the street or in the back of a van, rather than in the police station, and therefore never enters the formal judicial register.[74] At another level, in contexts where the formal judicial process is deeply inefficient or violent, there is a strong incentive for potential detainees to stay out of its clutches. Paying a bribe to a police officer to avoid arrest can be an effective way to avoid being tortured. For police officers, who themselves might have little faith in the criminal justice system, demanding a bribe and resorting to extra-judicial forms of violence, might, in their eyes at least, be the best way to work the system, do their job and obtain some form of justice, the latter often with the support of the general public.

While the threat of violence is what propels people to pay, this is often couched in languages of 'help'. The Philippines provides illustrative evidence of this. Police officers in the Philippines will sometimes be paid to assist in mediating between, for instance, a husband and wife in cases of domestic violence where the woman wants the beating to stop but does not want the household breadwinner in jail. Other examples are attempts by people to stay out of

---

[70] Punch (n 27 above), 11.

[71] Report of the Special Rapporteur on Torture and Other Cruel, Inhuman or Degrading Treatment or Punishment, 2019, A/HRC/40/59.

[72] Alatas, SH, *Corruption: Its Nature, Causes and Consequences* (Avebury, 1990).

[73] Jensen, S and Andersen, MK (eds), *Corruption and Torture: Violent Exchange and the Everyday Policing of the Poor* (Aalborg University Press, 2017); Andersen (n 59 above).

[74] See for instance Dragsted, B, 'Crackdown Economics: Policing of Hawkers in Nairobi as Violent Inclusion' (2019) 102 *Geoforum* 69–75.

prison where police officers might exclaim, 'I wish I could help you'.[75] The war on drugs has radicalized the need to avoid prison – both because of the violence associated with the war but also because it has led to extreme congestion within the jails. This is not only so in the Philippines. In contexts where prisoners awaiting trial wait for long periods, sometimes years, in horrible conditions, staying out of jail is imperative. This suggests that corruption is often part of complex social relations between public officials and those caught up in the system, and the system itself within which they work. Demands and targets for arrest and solving crime in under-resourced and under-prioritized criminal justice systems, can be seen to result in the use of extra-legal force and measures in arrest, detention and interrogation. Furthermore, when public authorities and citizens know the criminal justice system and legal institutions are arbitrary, can be swayed by private and economic interests and are overtly bureaucratic and slow, the immediate solution of paying to escape, avoid or fend off the attention of the law becomes a viable resolution of the present conflict and future problems, for many people. The relations between torture and corruption do not just link public authorities and citizens in new complex ways, but also highlight that wider solutions to the problems of violence, torture and ill-treatment cannot be isolated within the language of legally enforced prohibition and prevention. Furthermore, solutions might appear outside the increasingly technicalized and mechanicalized realm of conventions and standards, examinations, oversight and monitoring.

CONCLUSION

A large part of the long history of the struggle against torture has been rooted in states with relatively strong institutional capacities. However, as many human rights practitioners recognize, we also need to think carefully about the limitations and potentials of the assumptions and tools that come out of this history when applied to places with skewed and limited institutional capacity, histories of entrenched violence, and limited state legitimacy and accountability. Importantly, state fragility does not automatically lead to torture. We also need to be careful not to think about fragility in ways that assume a unilinear direction in the struggle against state violence. There are many apparently extremely weak states where torture remains relatively rare. Strong states – or states that have a capable and powerful security sector – can in fact be more likely in many cases to resort to acts of violence and use torture as a calculated act of intimidation and control. Many of the issues discussed here, corruption in particular, are just as pertinent to all states, but looking at torture through the lens of fragility can put issues of inequality, informality and history into particularly sharp relief. A *focus* on fragility can help alert us to the complex and contextual nature of torture and the methods we might use to fight it, expanding the places we look for torture, the types of victims and perpetrators we think might be involved, and the ways in which we understand the drivers and motivations. Doing so enables us not only to ask questions about fragile states but also to think about the causes and forms of torture elsewhere.

One key issue is that although anti-torture activities sometimes focus on the specific encounter between public authorities and individuals, we should also be attentive to the wider political, economic and cultural context within which violence takes place. Narrow legal

---

[75]   Hapal, K and Jensen, S, 'The Morality of Corruption: A View from the Police in Philippines' in Jensen and Andersen (n 73 above), 39–68.

interventions will have particular limits. As an increasing amount of evidence suggests that an emphasis solely on formal state institutional structures obscures the ways in which and why torture takes places. Hence, we also need to address political and economic issues. As many human rights practitioners acknowledge, an overly technical approach that focuses on legal reform and training alone, or that focuses on particular actors – such as the police, prosecutors and judges – needs also to take into account the wider social relations within which torture takes place.

The challenge of combating torture requires further research on the multiple possible actors involved in acts of torture and how torture is practiced in and across different state institutional systems, political situations and socio-economic contexts. Furthermore, if we are to widen the places where we think that torture takes place, we also need more research on the dynamics of torture outside custodial settings. And finally, this means widening what we think of as the conditions, motivations and drivers of torture. An emphasis on criminal justice related processes should not necessarily come at the expense of understanding the multiple relationships and obligations within which public officials are embedded, and the ways in which these can lead to acts of violence. Such an understanding may lead to new and surprising ways to combat torture and ill-treatment that complement a legal approach.

ACKNOWLEDGMENT

The research and analysis upon which this chapter is based was funded by an ESRC/DfID Poverty Alleviation [grant no. ESRC ES/L005395/1], 1 May 2014 to 30 August 2016; and British Academy GCRF Sustainable Development Grant SDP2/100029.

5.   An overview of international protection

Moritz Birk and Manfred Nowak[1]

INTRODUCTION

There are many different mechanisms providing international protection from torture and other forms of ill-treatment. They stem from the United Nations Charter as well as international and regional treaties, most of which contain an explicit prohibition of these practices. The prohibition has been interpreted broadly to include positive state obligations to provide protection from and prevent torture and other forms of ill-treatment. The explicit prohibition is complemented by numerous other human rights obligations that are key to protection, such as the right to personal integrity and human dignity, the right to liberty, fair trail guarantees and the right to an effective remedy. General human rights and specialised anti-torture bodies established by international organisations and treaties provide protection through different means. They monitor country situations and the implementation of human rights obligations, through the examination of reports, dialogues with state representatives and other stakeholders or even through fact-finding missions to the countries concerned. Such fact-finding can include far-reaching powers to carry out unannounced visits to places of detention opening up the most closed and secret places to international scrutiny. Moreover, victims of torture are provided with different avenues through which to file individual complaints, formally to Courts and Committees or less formally through urgent appeals and allegation letters. These powers are complemented by promotional and advisory roles that have significantly raised awareness of the situation concerning torture and ill-treatment in the world and strengthened domestic mechanisms to develop effective strategies to fight these practices.

The following chapter will provide a broad overview of the existing protection framework, illustrating the mandate and role of the different bodies in the global fight against torture and ill-treatment. Almost all the systems and mechanisms of protection which are introduced in this chapter will be considered in greater detail in the chapters which follow within this volume. For reasons of space the focus is on the system as it is today, rather than its historical development.[2] Moreover, the chapter limits itself to the mechanisms specifically dedicated to the protection from torture and ill-treatment. However, torture and ill-treatment are a highly complex phenomenon and its prevalence 'is influenced by a broad range of factors, including the general level of enjoyment of human rights and the rule of law, levels of poverty, social exclusion, corruption, discrimination, etc'.[3] Consequently, there are many more relevant mechanisms than are illustrated in this chapter, and they are difficult to delimit. This chapter

---

[1]   The authors would like to thank Andreas Sauermoser, Arwa Hleilel and Pia Jacobs for their research support.
[2]   For a historical account see Rodley, NS, and Pollard, M, *The Treatment of Prisoners under International Law*, 3rd edn (Oxford University Press, 2009), 195.
[3]   'The approach of the Subcommittee on Prevention of Torture to the concept of prevention of torture and other cruel, inhuman or degrading treatment or punishment under the Optional Protocol to the

focuses on the mechanisms of international protection. This is not to ignore the fact that it is essentially the national system that needs to ensure protection from torture and ill-treatment. An effective law enforcement, judiciary, security, health sector, etc, and a vibrant and free civil society cooperating and coordinating their efforts are the prerequisite to ensure a holistic system to protect human dignity and personal integrity.

THE UN SYSTEM OF PROTECTION

The United Nations (UN) provides for a broad system of protection and promotion of human rights. Human rights were first defined in the Universal Declaration of Human Rights (UDHR) of 1948[4] – recognised by all member states of the UN. The UDHR includes the absolute prohibition of torture and ill-treatment in Article 5. It does not define these acts and the non-binding document provides no explicit monitoring mechanism but it provides the basis for the UN charter mechanisms to address the problem of torture and ill-treatment and develop detailed treaties to advance human rights protection. The UN system of human rights protection is divided into the charter mechanisms – based on the UN Charter (UNC) – and treaty mechanisms – based on international treaties. These are complemented by numerous UN offices and agencies that play an important role in the promotion and protection of human rights.

Charter-Based Protection

The different UN Charter bodies can offer protection from torture and ill-treatment, albeit in a more indirect manner, such as: the Security Council condemning and urging states to take measures against the use of torture and ill-treatment in wartime and establishing international tribunals to deal with crimes against humanity including torture;[5] the General Assembly denouncing the situation of torture in a country and adopting treaties and soft law standards relevant to providing protection from torture and ill-treatment;[6] the Economic and Social Council initiating relevant studies and reports, calling international conferences and coordinating the activities of specialised agencies;[7] and the International Court of Justice (ICJ) settling disputes between states – including addressing violations of the UN Convention against Torture (UNCAT)[8] – and giving advisory opinions.

Convention against Torture and Other Cruel, Inhuman or Degrading Treatment or Punishment', CAT/OP/12/6 (2010), para 5(a).

   [4]   Universal Declaration of Human Rights, UNGA Res 217A (III) (adopted 10 December 1948).

   [5]   See e.g., International Criminal Tribunal for the former Yugoslavia (ICTY), International Criminal Tribunal for Rwanda (ICTR), Extraordinary Chambers in the Courts of Cambodia (ECCC), The Special Court for Sierra Leone (SCSL).

   [6]   Such as the UN Convention against Torture, considered further below and in Chapter 7 of this volume. For an overview of relevant soft law standards, see e.g., https://www.unodc.org/documents/justice-and-prison-reform/compendium/English_book.pdf; https://www.apt.ch/en/international-level/

   [7]   Such as including the United Nations Development Programme (UNDP), UN Women, the Commission on the Status of Women (CSW) and the Commission on Crime Prevention and Criminal Justice (CCPCJ). For further details on the ECOSOC's functions and powers see Articles 62–66 of the UN Charter.

   [8]   See *Questions relating to the Obligation to Prosecute or Extradite* (*Belgium v. Senegal*), *Judgment, ICJ Reports 2012*, p 442 where the ICJ decided that Senegal had violated Article 6(2) and Article 7(1) of

Human Rights Council

The Human Rights Council (HRC) is the main UN political body focusing on human rights issues. It was created in 2006 to replace the UN Commission on Human Rights which had been criticised for excessive politicisation and selectivity in dealing with country situations. It was 'upgraded' from a subsidiary body of the ECOSOC to a subsidiary body of the General Assembly (GA), the system for the election of members was changed and measures were taken to significantly enhance its effectiveness. It has a broad mandate, being '[r]esponsible for promoting universal respect for the protection of all human rights and fundamental freedoms for all'.[9] The HRC is composed of 47 member states, elected by the General Assembly for three year terms in accordance with the 'equitable geographical distribution' principle. It holds three regular sessions each year to discuss the situation of human rights in the world.[10] Special sessions may be called by one third of the members in response to urgent situations related to its mandate, to be held within five days of the request.

As of April 2020, the HRC has held 43 regular sessions in which it has frequently addressed torture and ill-treatment in country-specific as well as in thematic resolutions and recommendations. Thematic resolutions have included *inter alia* safeguards to prevent torture during police custody and pre-trial detention, the role of medical and other health personnel, judges, prosecutors and lawyers, the rehabilitation of torture victims, the death penalty, human rights while countering terrorism, arbitrary detention, enforced and involuntary disappearances and corruption. Moreover, the HRC annually adopts a general resolution on human rights in the administration of justice, including juvenile justice.[11] It also regularly addresses the issue of torture and ill-treatment in its country-specific resolutions. As of July 2019, the HRC has furthermore held 28 special sessions, mainly in regard to country situations, and often condemning acts of torture and ill-treatment.[12]

The Council's most innovative mechanism is the Universal Periodic Review (UPR). This involves a review of the human rights record of all UN member states, based on reports which each state presents every four to five years on the situation in the country and measures taken to improve human rights. The state report is complemented by a report collecting information from independent UN experts (such as Special Procedures and treaty bodies – see below) and by another collecting information from civil society organisations and national human rights institutions. The review of all three reports is conducted by a UPR working group open to all UN member states and led by three states (the 'Troika') during an interactive discussion with the member state concerned. All UN member states (but not civil society organisations) can pose questions during the dialogue, after which the Troika prepares an outcome report summarising the discussion and which includes recommendations which are then accepted or just 'noted' by the reviewed state. Torture and ill-treatment rank among the issues most

---

the UNCAT by refusing to extradite the former president of Chad, Hissène Habré, to Belgium despite an international arrest warrant.

[9]   UN Doc A/60/251 (2006), para 2.

[10]   The Agenda of the HRC is determined in accordance with the HRC Institution Building Resolution, UN Doc A/HRC/RES/5/1 (2007).

[11]   See UN Doc A/HRC/RES/24/L.28 (2013).

[12]   For an overview of the HRC resolutions visit the HRC's website (https://www.ohchr.org/en/hrbodies/hrc/pages/sessions.aspx), the OHCHR's Universal Human Rights Index (https://uhri.ohchr.org) or the external databases: www.universal-rights.org; www.right-docs.org; www.atlas-of-torture.org

frequently addressed in the UPR process, with a total of 4,933 respective recommendations.[13] As the review is entirely state-driven, bilateral relations play a key role in determining the content of recommendations, as countries tend to deliver more lenient recommendations to states with which they wish to maintain good diplomatic relations. While this at times damages the credibility of the UPR – showing that some countries receive better treatment than they deserve – this political element also has the positive effect of turning accepted recommendations into political commitments, which states tend to implement for fear of losing face with their allies.[14]

Since they address all human rights issues, UPR country reports are not as detailed as the reports of Special Procedures or specialised treaty bodies. However, their findings and recommendations are important and are often drawn on by national actors. Furthermore, in many countries, the UPR creates a valuable process of national mobilisation, with civil society organisations coordinating and cooperating to prepare their input.

The HRC has also retained the complaint procedure from the former Commission (known as the 1503 procedure), this being the only procedure enabling individuals and organisations to bring confidential complaints 'to address consistent patterns of gross and reliably attested violations of all human rights and all fundamental freedoms occurring in any part of the world and under any circumstances'.[15] Complaints are processed by a Working Group on Communications and another Working Group on Situations in a confidential manner. Confidentiality is only lifted in exceptional cases, such as where the state does not reply or cooperate. The procedure is thus not the best way to seek redress or address a country-specific situation.

The HRC also continued and even extended the practice of the Commission to mandate Special Procedures 'to report and advise on human rights from a thematic or country-specific perspective', covering civil and political as well as economic, social and cultural rights.[16] Their appointment and functions are defined in a Code of Conduct adopted in 2007.[17] Special Procedures comprise independent experts selected according to expertise, experience in the field of the mandate, independence, impartiality, personal integrity and objectivity, giving due consideration to gender balance and equitable geographic representation and usually appointed for a period of three years (but no longer than six years). Depending on their mandate, they examine complaints, carry out fact-finding missions upon invitation by states, conduct research and report annually to the HRC and sometimes also to the GA.

Currently there are 44 thematic and 12 country mandates.[18] Country-mandate holders can address the situation of torture and ill-treatment and there is a specific Special Rapporteur on Torture and numerous other thematic mandates relevant to the prevention of torture and ill-treatment, notably: the Working Group on Enforced Disappearance; the Working Group on Arbitrary Detention; the Special Rapporteur on the promotion and protection of human

---

[13] Torture and ill-treatment are ranked at place 4, making up 7.69 per cent of all recommendations (in April 2020). See https://www.upr-info.org/database/statistics/

[14] Carraro, V, 'The United Nations Treaty Bodies and Universal Periodic Review: Advancing Human Rights by Preventing Politicization?' (2017) 39 *HRQ* 943, 965–969.

[15] UN Doc A/HRC/RES/5/1 (2007), para 85.

[16] See http://www.ohchr.org/EN/HRBodies/SP/Pages/Introduction.aspx

[17] UN Doc A/HRC/RES/5/2 (2007).

[18] For an overview, see https://www.ohchr.org/EN/HRBodies/HRC/Pages/SpecialProcedures.aspx

rights and fundamental freedoms while countering terrorism; and the Special Rapporteur on extrajudicial, summary or arbitrary executions.

The Special Procedures have been called the 'crown jewel' of the international human rights system[19] and are the 'eyes and ears' of the HRC due to their independence and broad mandate to investigate the situation of human rights on the ground. Their specific advantage over treaty mechanisms is that they can investigate the human rights situation anywhere in the world, irrespective of whether the country in question has ratified a human rights treaty. Country and thematic procedures have not only brought to light the situation of torture and ill-treatment and their root causes worldwide but have also played an important role in standard-setting. The challenge to and weakness of Special Procedures are their very limited resources. The mandate holders occupy part-time, unpaid positions and receive only limited support from the UN, making it difficult for them to adequately fulfil their mandate. In consequence, mandate holders are not able to conduct regular visits to countries worldwide and often struggle to promptly and adequately respond to the many complaints received. Further, they greatly depend on the cooperation of states, especially as regards fact-finding missions. They can only visit a country if invited and several country-specific mandates – particularly regarding countries where systematic torture is reported – are unable to do so. Moreover, mandate holders have repeatedly reported State interference during fact-finding missions and have been increasingly subject to forms of attempted censorship, notably through the development of the 'Code of Conduct'.[20] While such interference makes their work even more difficult it also illustrates the importance and impact of their work, and how seriously this is taken by member states.

While the reform of the UN Commission on Human Rights and the establishment of the HRC has not solved the problem of politicisation, Special Sessions have allowed better reactivity and UPR has been a useful tool through which to examine all States and to engage civil society. The HRC remains a political body and thus some polarisation and group-thinking will not go away. However, it is important to recognise the HRC's political power to advance protection against torture and ill-treatment and to consider the important work of its independent experts when making a holistic evaluation of the contribution of the HRC to the combatting of torture.

The Special Rapporteur on Torture
The Special Rapporteur on Torture (SRT) was created in 1985 and has developed into one of the most prominent and important international mechanisms to fight torture and other forms of ill-treatment.[21] The core mandate of the SRT is to analyse the situation of torture in the world, alert the international community, issue recommendations, support survivors and victims, foster cooperation and undertake follow-up.[22] The SRT receives urgent appeals (where there is an imminent risk of torture or ill-treatment) and allegation letters (where violations have already occurred) without the need for the procedural requirements of individual complaints

---

[19]   Subedi, SP, 'Protection of Human Rights through the Mechanism of UN Special Rapporteurs' (2011) 33 *HRQ* 201.

[20]   Nowak, M, 'An Introduction to the UN Human Rights System' in Nowak, M, Januczewski, K and Hofstätter, T (eds), *All Human Rights for All – Vienna Manual on Human Rights* (NWV, 2012), 82.

[21]   The mandate of the Special Rapporteur is considered in more detail in Chapter 8 of this volume.

[22]   Manual of Operations of the Special Procedures of the Human Rights Council, see https://www.ohchr.org/Documents/HRBodies/SP/Manual_Operations2008.pdf

procedures, including the exhaustion of domestic remedies and acceptance of the relevant complaints procedure by the state in question. It aims at urging states to respond promptly and adequately, by clarifying the circumstances, initiating an appropriate investigation and providing redress. The SRT issues observations in about 200 communications each year and publishes these in an annual 'Observations Report'. Complaints and the governments' reactions are made public three times a year in the Special Procedures joint communications report.[23] Government action following a communication from the SRT are however rare. Nevertheless, they can be a useful advocacy tool for human rights defenders. The SRT has also participated in joint communications with other mandate holders, drawing attention to particularly critical situations and empowering national anti-torture advocates in their work.

The main tool of the SRT is fact-finding missions, allowing them to get a picture of the practical reality by conducting unannounced visits to places of detention, without restrictions, and carrying out interviews with detainees and detention staff in private, accessing all relevant documents and engaging with representatives from the state, civil society and media. However, invitations to country missions are not always made in good faith and without restrictions. On several occasions, invitations have been withdrawn at the last minute, Terms of Reference have been objected to, the visits obstructed or findings rejected.[24] Nevertheless, such visits and the ensuing public reports presented to the HRC and brought to the attention of the GA have generally generated very broad national and international attention, strengthened anti-torture advocates and often led to significant changes, including legal and institutional reforms, ratification of human rights treaties and the establishment of monitoring mechanisms.

The SRT's Annual Reports to the HRC and GA are also of great importance as they address a broad range of thematic issues and have involved consulting experts and practitioners worldwide on issues such as the root causes of torture and ill-treatment; the protection of specific groups, including women, children or persons with disabilities; independent and effective investigations; forensic expert examination; solitary confinement; protection of women and gender aspects; domestic violence; female genital mutilation; abuses in healthcare settings; excessive use of force in non-custodial settings; the use of evidence obtained under torture; investigative interviewing and the implementation of key procedural safeguards by law enforcement officials; as well as corporal and capital punishment.[25] The Annual Reports have had an important impact on the development of legal opinion[26] and the SRT has also developed General Recommendations[27] and a Global Study on the Phenomena of Torture and Ill-treatment,[28] as well as contributing to the review of UN Standard Minimum Rules for the Treatment of Prisoners ('Nelson Mandela Rules'),[29] the Manual for the Effective Investigation

---

[23] See https://www.ohchr.org/EN/HRBodies/SP/Pages/CommunicationsreportsSP.aspx

[24] For an overview of 'States' Methods to Impede Objective Investigations', see Nowak, M, *Torture – An Expert's Confrontation with an Everyday Evil* (University of Pennsylvania Press, 2018), 16–23.

[25] For an overview of the issues addressed see the webpage of the SRT, https://www.ohchr.org/en/issues/torture/srtorture/pages/srtortureindex.aspx or www.atlas-of-torture.org; http://antitorture.org

[26] See e.g., in regard to the consideration of the death penalty as torture or other form of ill-treatment (UN Doc A/67/279), influencing the Human Rights Committee's General Comment 36 to the right to life (UN Doc CCPR/C/GC/36), or the prohibition of indefinite or prolonged solitary confinement in excess of 15 days, which was taken up in the Nelson Mandela Rules 43 and 44 (UN Doc A/RES/70/175).

[27] See https://www.ohchr.org/Documents/Issues/SRTorture/recommendations.pdf

[28] UN Doc A/HRC/13/39/Add.5 (2010).

[29] See UN Doc A/64/215 (2009); UN Doc A/68/295 (2013).

and Documentation of Torture and Other Cruel, Inhuman or Degrading Treatment or Punishment (Istanbul Protocol) and the development of a Universal Protocol for Investigative Interviewing.[30] The SRT also regularly participates in conferences and workshops, issues media statements, offers technical assistance and advice to states and civil society organisations, develops research and policy papers, and much more besides.

The SRT – like other Special Procedures – suffers from a well-known lack of resources and the lack of follow-up by the HRC to the reports and recommendations. Consequently, the effectiveness of the SRT's mandate is therefore largely reliant on the commitment and expertise of the mandate holders, as well as teams of assistants outside of, as well as within, the Office of the High Commissioner for Human Rights (OHCHR).[31]

Voluntary Fund for Victims of Torture

The UN Voluntary Fund for Victims of Torture, established in 1981,[32] 'supports projects implemented by civil society actors and other channels of assistance aimed at providing rehabilitation, redress and empowerment of, as well as access to remedies to victims of torture and their family members through direct assistance'.[33] It receives voluntary contributions, mainly from states but also from NGOs, the private businesses and individuals. Under the management of the Secretary-General, through the OHCHR and with the advice of a Board of Trustees of five independent experts, it awards grants and finances activities and has become a knowledge platform for health professionals, social workers and lawyers. Since its establishment, the Fund has awarded more than 620 organisations and rehabilitation centres worldwide reaching out to over 50,000 victims every year.[34]

Treaty-Based Protection

The key international protection from torture and ill-treatment emanates from the different binding human treaties adopted following the UDHR, namely the International Covenant on Civil and Political Rights (ICCPR), the Convention against Torture (UNCAT) and its Optional Protocol (OPCAT) but also other specialised treaties such as the Convention of the Rights of the Child (CRC), the Convention on the Rights of Persons with Disabilities (CRPD) and the Convention on the Protection of the Rights of all Migrant Workers and Members of their Families (CMW).

All treaties are monitored by Committees, quasi-judicial bodies whose decisions, unlike courts', are not binding in the strict legal sense. With the exception of the UN Subcommittee for the Prevention of Torture (SPT), treaty bodies have three key mechanisms through which to monitor the implementation of treaty obligations. Firstly, they require state parties to submit

---

[30]   See UN Doc A/69/387 (2014).
[31]   Manfred Nowak's mandate (2004–2010) was, for example, supported by a team of up to five assistants at the Ludwig Boltzmann Institute of Human Rights. At this point it is also worth mentioning that the past mandate holders Manfred Nowak and Juan Mendez have continued to follow up their work after the expiration for the mandate. See: https://bim.lbg.ac.at/en/human-dignity-and-public-security; www.atlas-of-torture.org; http://antitorture.org. See also Chapter 8 in this volume.
[32]   UN Doc A/36/151 (1981).
[33]   Mission Statement Adopted by the Board of Trustees of the UN Voluntary Fund for Victims of Torture (2014), see https://www.ohchr.org/Documents/Issues/Torture/UNVFVT/MissionStatement.pdf
[34]   See https://www.ohchr.org/en/issues/torture/unvft/pages/index.aspx

regular reports, which are examined by the relevant Committee and subsequently discussed in an oral dialogue, following which the Committees adopt Concluding Observations. These assess the status of implementation (commending or expressing concerns whilst not explicitly declaring violations) and provide recommendations on how to improve the situation. Secondly, Committees can draw up General Comments or Recommendations which are general interpretations of convention obligations. Thirdly, the Committees provide for an individual complaints procedure that states can choose to accept by declaration or ratification of an optional protocol. Individual complaints, generally known as 'communications', are submitted by (or on behalf of) individuals who have been directly affected, have exhausted domestic remedies and have not availed themselves of another international complaints procedure.[35] The Committees examine the complaint, considering also inputs from the state concerned and then adopt 'views' on whether the rights in question have been violated. These quasi-judicial decisions closely resemble judgments although the argumentation is usually shorter. Finally, the Committees also provide for an inter-state complaints procedure that is however very rarely used.

The International Covenant on Civil and Political Rights (ICCPR) contains an absolute prohibition of torture and ill-treatment (Article 7) and a right for detainees to be treated with humanity and dignity (Article 10). Moreover, the right to security in Article 9 is considered as a self-standing right that 'protects individuals against intentional infliction of bodily or mental injury'.[36] In addition, there are numerous other obligations relevant to the protection from torture and ill-treatment, namely the right to liberty (Article 9), prohibiting arbitrary detention and providing for numerous procedural safeguards key to the prevention of torture and ill-treatment, the right to a fair trial (Article 14) and the right to an effective remedy (Article 2(3)). The Human Rights Committee monitors the ICCPR and is arguably the most prominent international human rights treaty body. The Committee issues Concluding Observations to approximately 20 states per year and the issue of torture and ill-treatment is nearly always addressed. It has, moreover, adopted a specific General Comment (GC) 20 on the prohibition of torture, which although dating from 1992 provides useful guidance on the negative and positive duties of states.[37] Moreover, the Committee considers individual communications of member states that have accepted the first Optional Protocol, the majority of which deal with torture and ill-treatment, and in particular the prohibition of refoulement and inhuman conditions of detention, excessive use of force, etc.

The Convention on the Rights of the Child (CRC) – the most widely ratified international human rights treaty – contains a specific prohibition of torture and ill-treatment and a duty to treat children deprived of liberty with humanity and dignity in Article 37(a) and (c), mirroring

---

[35] For general guidance on the complaints procedure of Human Rights Treaty Bodies, see https://www.ohchr.org/en/hrbodies/tbpetitions/Pages/IndividualCommunications.aspx

[36] UN Human Rights Committee, General Comment no 35, Article 9, Liberty and security of person, UN Doc CCPR/C/GC/35 (2014), para 9. The ICCPR and the work of the Human Rights Committee is considered in more detail in Chapter 6 of this volume.

[37] UN Human Rights Committee, 'General Comment no 20 on Article 7', 10 March 1992, UN Doc HRI/GEN/1/Rev.9 (Vol. I). Other GCs also deal with the protection from torture and ill-treatment, such as GC 21 to Article 10, GC 35 to Article 9, and the most recent GC 36 concerning the right to life (Article 6).

Articles 7 and 10 ICCPR.[38] It further obliges states to promote recovery from torture and ill-treatment (Article 39) and contains other relevant obligations such as the rights to liberty, to a fair trial and to a remedy and rehabilitation. The issue is commonly addressed by the Committee on the Rights of the Child in Concluding Observations and views on individual complaints. Moreover, the Committee has also addressed the issue in a General Comment on the 'protection from corporal punishment and other cruel or degrading forms of punishment', on 'freedom from all forms of violence' and in the most recently revised General Comment on 'Children's rights in juvenile justice'.

The Convention on the Rights of Persons with Disabilities (CRPD) also contains an explicit prohibition of and a duty to prevent torture and ill-treatment (Article 15), as well as a duty to protect persons with disabilities from violence and abuse (Article 16) and other obligations relevant for the protection from torture and ill-treatment. While the Committee on the Rights of Persons with Disabilities has not passed a specific General Comment dealing with these articles, in its 'Guidelines on article 14 (the right to liberty and security)', it has 'called on States parties to protect the security and personal integrity of persons with disabilities who are deprived of their liberty, including by eliminating the use of forced treatment, seclusion and various methods of restraint in medical facilities, including physical, chemical and mechanical restraints' and has 'found that these practices are not consistent with the prohibition of torture and other cruel, inhumane or degrading treatment or punishment.'[39]

The Convention on the Protection of the Rights of all Migrant Workers and Members of their Families (CMW) absolutely prohibits torture and ill-treatment (Article 10) and contains the right to respect for the physical and mental integrity of this group on an equal basis with others (Article 17). An entire section of its General Comment 2 on the rights of migrant workers in an irregular situation and members of their families, concerns 'Protection against inhumane treatment' detailing the obligations stemming from Article 17 as well as including an explicit reference to the principle of non-refoulement.[40] The CMW has however only been ratified by 54 states so far, and mainly by countries of origin of migrants.

While the Convention on the Elimination of All Forms of Discrimination against Women (CEDAW) does not explicitly prohibit torture and ill-treatment, the Committee makes explicit reference to it in its General Recommendation 19 on Violence against Women.[41] It has explicitly stated that it can address torture and ill-treatment since 'such gender-based violence impaired or nullified the enjoyment by women of a number of human rights and fundamental freedoms'.[42]

Although the Convention for the Protection of All Persons from Enforced Disappearance does not explicitly prohibit torture and ill-treatment, it provides an elaborate catalogue of

---

[38]   Torture and cruel, inhuman and degrading treatment or punishment is defined rather broadly for the purposes of the CRC. The Committee on the Rights of the Child in its General Comment no 13 (2011): The right of the child to freedom from all forms of violence, 18 April 2011, CRC/C/GC/13, notes that 'violence in all its forms against children' is to be included under the heading of torture and inhuman or degrading treatment or punishment. The implied prohibition against corporal punishment is made explicit in paragraph 22 of the General Comment.

[39]   UN Doc A/72/55 (2015), 16.

[40]   General comment no 2 on the rights of migrant workers in an irregular situation and members of their families, 28 August 2013, UN Doc CMW/C/GC/2.

[41]   General Recommendation no 19: Violence against women, 1992, para 7.

[42]   *M.N.N. v. Denmark*, CEDAW/C/55/D/33/2011, (2013), para 8.7.

measures – modelled after the Convention against Torture – to protect against enforced disappearance, which is in itself considered to be a form of torture and ill-treatment.[43]

Most states are parties to several of these treaties. Therefore, information on and protection from torture and ill-treatment can be sought from multiple treaty mechanisms. However, this has also led to duplication and inefficiency.[44] Individuals are faced with many different options, concerning bodies with different focuses and working methods and consequently diverging chances of success. Moreover, the work of treaty bodies is not sufficiently well known, and many victims and survivors are not aware of the possibility of seeking their protection. Additionally, the strict criteria for admissibility obliges individuals to exhaust domestic remedies and to approach only one of the treaty mechanisms (principle non-duplication). The treaty bodies also suffer from a lack of resources and have had difficulties with a growing backlog of work, including examining state reports, individual communications and urgent actions. Many states do not comply with their reporting obligations, either submitting their reports late or even missing entire reporting cycles. For these reasons, the UN has launched a process to strengthen the treaty bodies, with a focus on the alignment of working methods and procedures.[45] Others have proposed more ambitious reforms, such as the creation of a World Court on Human Rights.[46]

The Convention and Committee against Torture
The main treaty concerning protection from torture and ill-treatment is the UN Convention against Torture (UNCAT) adopted by the UN General Assembly in December 1984 and entered into force on 26 June 1987, today known as the International Day for the Commemoration of Torture Victims. The UNCAT does not contain a prohibition of torture and ill-treatment but a broad catalogue of obligations for states to adhere to in order to fight torture and ill-treatment.[47]

It starts with a definition of torture in Article 1 and a general all-encompassing obligation to 'take effective legislative, administrative, judicial or other measures to prevent acts of torture in any territory under its jurisdiction' (Article 2). This is mirrored for other forms of ill-treatment in Article 16. There are numerous specific preventive obligations such as the prohibition of refoulement (Article 3), a duty to train personnel (Article 10), to review interrogation and detention rules (Article 11) and a rule of non-admissibility of evidence extracted under torture (Article 15). A large part of the Convention is dedicated to the criminalisation of torture and bringing torturers to justice through the use of universal jurisdiction (Articles

---

43 *Guerrero Larez v. Venezuela*, CAT/C/54/D/456/2011, (2015).

44 Egan, S, 'Strengthening the United Nations Human Rights Treaty Body System' (2013) 13 *HRLR* 209; Tistounet, E, 'The Problem of Overlapping Among Different Treaty Bodies' in Alston, P and Crawford, J, *The Future of UN Human Rights Treaty Monitoring* (Cambridge University Press, 2009), 383–402; Krommendijk, J, 'The (in)Effectiveness of UN Human Rights Treaty Body Recommendations' (2014) 33 *NQHR* 194.

45 UN Doc UNGA Res 68/268 (2014); see also https://www.ohchr.org/EN/HRBodies/HRTD/Pages/TBStrengthening.aspx

46 Nowak, M, 'It's Time for a World Court of Human Rights' in Bassiouni, MC and Schabas, WA (eds), *New Challenges to the UN Human Rights Machinery – What Future for the UN Treaty Body System and the Human Rights Council Procedures?* (Intersentia, 2012), 17–34.

47 For a detailed commentary on the content of the provisions, see Nowak, M, Birk, M and Monina, G, *The Convention against Torture and Ill-Treatment – A Commentary*, 2nd edn (Oxford University Press, 2019). The Convention against torture is considered in greater detail in Chapter 7 of this volume.

4 to 9).[48] Moreover, states have a duty to establish independent investigation and complaints mechanisms and provide victims with adequate redress and rehabilitation (Articles 12, 13, 14). While the UNCAT contains a strong catalogue of obligations which if properly implemented would significantly reduce torture and ill-treatment, procedural safeguards – proven to be the most effective preventive measure[49] – are not explicitly enumerated but must be read into the general preventive duty (Articles 2 and 16).

The Committee against Torture (CAT) is established in Part II of the Convention (Articles 17 to 24) and is composed of 10 elected experts from all regions of the world who, unlike the HRC which is dominated by lawyers, usually have different backgrounds, including medical and psychological experts.

States parties must submit reports every four years (if not otherwise requested, Article 19 UNCAT). Similar to other treaty bodies, the CAT rarely receives state reports on time, with more than a fifth of the reports submitted more than five years late.[50] The quality of state reports varies greatly, depending on commitment, capacities and influences from National Human Rights Institutions (NHRI), NGOs or other states. Too often the reports are a positive description of reforms and activities rather than a serious and self-critical assessment of the situation of torture and ill-treatment in the country. Therefore, the 'parallel/shadow reports' submitted by civil society organisations and national monitoring bodies are of vital importance in providing a counterweight to the picture drawn by the state. The CAT also invites NGOs as well as national monitoring bodies, NHRIs, and National Preventive Mechanisms (NPMs) to coordinate on the implementation of the treaty obligations. The 'constructive dialogue' with the state party takes place with a delegation of government representatives for six hours over two days where they are asked questions, often based on a 'list of issues' provided by the Committee beforehand. The review ends with Concluding Observations by the Committee specifying positive measures taken and concerns, and making recommendations to the state party. The Concluding Observations do not contain explicit judgments on whether a state is in violation of the UNCAT but rather provide an assessment and advice on the measures to be taken. After the review, the Committee asks states to provide information on the measures taken within one year, and to draw up a full implementation plan which is scrutinised by an assigned Rapporteur for follow-up. In most cases such information is provided, but often in an insufficient manner. The lack of follow-up and implementation of the CAT's recommendations have been a serious issue which prompted the Rapporteur on follow-up to propose a reform of procedures, including the possibility of conducting in-country follow-up visits.[51] The challenge remains that the Committee's recommendations are not binding and no enforcement mechanism exists. Thus, the follow-up largely rests with national actors for whom the CAT's findings provide a very useful source for advocacy.

Although provided for in Article 21 CAT, the inter-state complaints procedure has never been used. The individual complaints procedure provided for in UNCAT Article 22 – currently accepted by 68 of the 165 state parties – has, however, been used extensively. The Committee

---

[48]   This is examined in greater detail in Chapter 16 of this volume.
[49]   Carver, R and Handley, L, *Does Torture Prevention Work?* (Liverpool University Press, 2016). See also Chapter 3 of this volume.
[50]   Creamer, CD and Simmons, BA, 'Ratification, Reporting and Rights: Quality of Participation in the Convention against Torture' (2015) 37 *HRQ* 579–608.
[51]   UN Doc A/69/44 (2014), 71–99.

will consider an individual complaint if it is admissible, that is, if it is: not anonymous, not an abuse of the right of submission, compatible with the Convention's provisions, not already examined under another international procedure and all domestic remedies available have been exhausted.[52] The Committee also has a significant backlog of cases due to a lack of resources. Where violations are found, remedies include terminating expulsion proceedings, legislative changes or financial compensation. It has been reported that only half of all decisions have been implemented to the Committee's satisfaction.

Compared to other treaty bodies, the CAT has issued relatively few General Comments. Its four General Comments deal with the general duty to adopt effective preventive measures (GC 2 (2007) concerning Article 2),[53] the prohibition of refoulement (GC 1 (1997) and GC 4 (2017) concerning Article 3)[54] and the right to redress and rehabilitation (GC 3 (2012) concerning Article 14).[55]

The CAT can also undertake a confidential inquiry when it 'receives reliable information which appears to it to contain well-founded indications that torture is being systematically practised', including the possibility of conducting a country mission and of publishing an inquiry report. The inquiry procedure has only been used 10 times in 30 years, involving nine countries and eight country missions. In all but two cases the use of torture has been found to be systematic. It is therefore a much under-used mechanism and has hitherto received relatively little attention.[56]

The OPCAT: SPT and NPMs

The Optional Protocol to the CAT (OPCAT) was adopted in December 2002 and entered into force in 2006. Its objective is 'to establish a system of regular visits undertaken by independent international and national bodies to places where people are deprived of their liberty, in order to prevent torture and other cruel, inhuman or degrading treatment or punishment'. Based on the experiences of the International Committee of the Red Cross (ICRC), and the European Committee for the Prevention of Torture (CPT – see below), its purpose was to open up places of detention to external scrutiny and to support states in the prevention of torture and ill-treatment. This is done by establishing an international treaty body – the Subcommittee on Prevention of Torture – and obliging states to establish domestic monitoring bodies, so-called National Preventive Mechanisms.[57]

The Subcommittee for the Prevention of Torture (SPT) is composed of 25 independent experts with a specific preventive mandate 'focused on an innovative, sustained and proactive

---

[52] See CAT, 'Rules of Procedure' UN Doc CAT/C/3/Rev.6 (2014).

[53] General Comment no 2, Implementation of Article 2 by States parties, UN Doc CAT/C/GC/2 (24 January 2008).

[54] UN Committee Against Torture, General Comment no 1: Implementation of article 3 of the Convention in the context of article 22, UN Doc A/53/44 Annex IX, 16 September 1998; UN Committee Against Torture, General Comment no 4 (2017) on the Implementation of article 3 of the Convention in the context of article 22, UN Doc CAT/C/GC/4, 4 September 2018.

[55] General Comment no 3: Implementation of article 14 by States parties, UN Doc CAT/C/GC/3 (19 November 2012). See also Chapter 22 in this volume.

[56] See Chapter 7 of this volume, which examines the work of the CAT in relation to inquiries in detail.

[57] The work of the CPT, SPT and NPMs is considered in more detail in Chapter 12 of this volume.

approach to the prevention of torture and ill treatment'.[58] The work of the SPT is based on three pillars: visits to states parties; work with NPMs; and cooperation with other UN and international bodies.[59] The OPCAT grants the SPT broad visiting powers, including unrestricted access to places of detention and relevant information and the ability to hold private interviews with anyone deemed relevant to its mandate (Article 14). The visits are followed by the submission of a report and recommendations to the state party, but this report is confidential and can only be published with the consent of the state party. The visits are based on a forward-looking, preventive concept, seeking to combine the identification of problems with an exploration of good practices.[60] However, the reports do not greatly differ from those of the SRT and due to the limited length of visits and the resources available they do not provide the concrete, practical guidance some had expected or hoped for. Moreover, although the SPT advocates for a broad concept of prevention, it has channelled its own preventive work primarily through visits.[61] The SPT also plays an important role in regard to NPMs, by advising states on their establishment and the NPMs on their operation. After five years of functioning, the SPT introduced NPM advisory visits as a practical tool to assist NPMs and state parties through technical advice and assistance.[62] This was an important advance designed to deliver on the promise to advance the prevention of torture and ill-treatment 'on the ground'.[63] Moreover the SPT has provided concrete guidance through its annual reports, information and guidelines on NPMs, a practical guide on the role of NPMs, a NPM self-assessment tool and matrix, a compilation of SPT advices to NPMs as well as a checklist on health-care issues relating to the monitoring of places of detention.[64] The SPT suffers from a notorious lack of resources and a lack of capacity to engage in effective follow-up to its country visits. However, it plays an increasingly important role in advancing national protection mechanisms through strengthening and advising NPMs.

NPMs are domestic mechanisms based on the OPCAT and drawing on international norms and standards for the prevention of torture and ill-treatment as a basis for their assessments and advice. It is their domestic nature which has made them so effective. NPMs have the same broad visiting mandate as the SPT. However, since they are able to visit places of detention more regularly than an international mechanism, as well as being grounded in the national context, they are able to go deeper in their analysis of root causes and issue more concrete recommendations. Moreover, their establishment has significantly raised awareness of the issue of torture and ill-treatment. There are a variety of models of NPMs and, while they are

---

[58]   https://www.ohchr.org/EN/HRBodies/OPCAT/Pages/OPCATIndex.aspx

[59]   See Murray, R, Steinerte, E, Evans, M and Hallo de Wolf, A, *The Optional Protocol to the UN Convention against Torture* (Oxford, 2011), 90–114.

[60]   'The approach of the Subcommittee on Prevention of Torture to the concept of prevention of torture and other cruel, inhuman or degrading treatment or punishment under the Optional Protocol to the Convention against Torture and Other Cruel, Inhuman or Degrading Treatment or Punishment' (n 3 above).

[61]   Murray, Steinerte, Evans, Hallo de Wolf (n 59 above), 104, 105.

[62]   SPT, Outline of SPT advisory visits to NPMs: https://www.ohchr.org/EN/HRBodies/OPCAT/Pages/NoteSPTAdvisoryvisitstoNPMS.aspx

[63]   Steinerte, E, 'The Changing Nature of the Relationship between the United Nations Subcommittee on Prevention of Torture and National Preventive Mechanisms: In Search for Equilibrium' (2013) 31 *NQHR* 129.

[64]   All accessible on the SPT website: https://www.ohchr.org/EN/HRBodies/OPCAT/Pages/OPCATIndex.aspx

not mandated to receive complaints, some that are attached to ombuds institutions do. The effectiveness of NPMs depends on different factors, most notably their full independence as required by the OPCAT and sufficient resources to carry out their ambitious mandate. Despite their obvious advantages when compared to international bodies, the follow-up and implementation of NPM recommendations still often remains a challenge.[65]

To assist implementation, the OPCAT provides for the establishment of the OPCAT Special Fund in 2011. This fund aims to provide direct support 'to help finance the implementation of the recommendations made by the Subcommittee on Prevention after a visit to a State Party, as well as education programmes of the national preventive mechanisms' (Article 26). While it has the possibility of being a major new resource for torture prevention,[66] it has only been utilised by a small number of institutions in relatively few countries worldwide and has been hampered by a lack of contributions.[67]

UN Offices and Agencies

There are numerous other UN organisations and entities[68] which also play a role in the protection from torture and ill-treatment.

The Office of the High Commissioner for Human Rights (OHCHR) is the main office responsible for the promotion and protection of human rights, for example by supporting standard-setting and monitoring, and promoting implementation on the ground through regional and country offices. The High Commissioner – currently Michelle Bachelet, herself a survivor of torture – as the highest-ranking human rights official in the UN, regularly speaks out against torture and ill-treatment in the world.

The UN Office on Drugs and Crime (UNODC) supports states to advance crime prevention and criminal justice reform, including the fight against torture and ill-treatment. It has played a key role in developing relevant standards and norms, such as the UN Nelson Mandela Rules (Revised UN Standard Minimum Rules on the Treatment of Prisoners) and the UN Model Strategies and Practical Measures on the Elimination of Violence against Children in the Field of Crime Prevention and Criminal Justice. UNODC moreover plays a significant role in advancing criminal justice reforms through research, technical assistance to states and providing guidance materials.[69]

The UN High Commissioner for Refugees' (UNHCR) work is grounded in the UN Convention Relating to the Status of Refugees (CSR, 1951) and its Protocol (1967), which contain an explicit prohibition on refoulement (Article 33 CSR). The High Commissioner and the UNHCR's Executive's Committee regularly comment on the importance of protecting ref-

---

[65] Birk, M, Zach, G, Long, D, Murray, R and Suntinger, W, *Enhancing Impact of National Preventive Mechanisms. Strengthening the Follow-up on NPM Recommendations in the EU: Strategic Development, Current Practices and the Way Forward* (Ludwig Boltzmann Institute of Human Rights/Bristol University, 2015).

[66] Ploton, V, 'The OPCAT Special Fund: A New Resource for Torture Prevention?' (2015) 7 *JHRP* 153.

[67] https://www.ohchr.org/EN/HRBodies/OPCAT/Fund/Pages/SpecialFund.aspx

[68] For an overall list, see https://www.unsystem.org/alpha; https://www.un.org/en/sections/about-un/funds-programmes-specialized-agencies-and-others/

[69] See www.unodc.org

ugees from torture and ill-treatment and developed a significant amount of relevant guidance materials.

International Criminal Court

The Statute of the International Criminal Court (ICC) was adopted in 1998 and entered into force in 2002. Currently 122 states are a party to the Statute. The ICC has jurisdiction over core international crimes which the international community have recognised as a threat to peace, security and the well-being of the international community as a whole.[70]

It has jurisdiction over individuals for genocide, crimes against humanity, war crimes and the crime of aggression (Article 5). Under Article 12, the ICC jurisdiction extends only to offences committed on the territory of, or by nationals of, a Member State. However, the United Nations Security Council (UNSC) may refer any situation to the ICC prosecutor, irrespective of whether the state of nationality is a party to the Statute. The ICC may investigate and prosecute acts of torture and ill-treatment if they form part of a crime against humanity, war crime or genocide. Torture is explicitly mentioned as a crime against humanity in Article 7(1)(f). Compared to the definition of the UNCAT, the scope of Article 7(1)(f) is much broader, as it does not require the involvement or participation of a person acting in an official capacity or that there be any specific purpose.[71]

The ICC cannot act autonomously, and situations must be brought to its attention. The Rome Statute provides three 'trigger mechanisms' which initiate preliminary investigations, and which authorise the prosecutor to take action. A situation may be referred to the Prosecutor by a state or by a resolution of the UN Security Council.[72] In addition, an investigation may be initiated by the prosecutor on the basis of requests (so-called *communications*) received from individuals and organisations.[73]

The ICC is a tribunal of last resort and, as the Preamble of the Rome Statute states, it is 'the duty of every state [...] to exercise its criminal jurisdiction over those responsible for international crimes'. Consequently, it has no jurisdiction, or it may not exercise it, if a state initiates criminal proceedings relating to the relevant matter at the national level. The only exception is where a state is unwilling or unable to conduct criminal proceedings itself. Moreover, the Court only initiates investigations against those who are at the very top of the political and military hierarchy.[74] The ICC Statute allows for broad participation and protection of victims.

---

[70] See Rome Statute of the International Criminal Court, 2187 UNTS 3, Preamble, para 4.

[71] The existing case law does not determine which absolute threshold of severe pain or suffering has to be reached. The ICC jurisprudence in *Prosecutor v. Bemba Gombo* (Judgment, ICC-01/05-01/08-T, 21 March 2016) interpreted 'severe pain' in accordance with the jurisprudence of the European Court of Human Rights, and the Inter-American Court of Human Rights and stated that 'although there is no definition of the severity threshold as a legal requirement of the crime of torture, it is constantly accepted in applicable treaties and jurisprudence that an important degree of pain and suffering has to be reached in order for a criminal act to amount to an act of torture'. See also the discussions of torture and international criminal law in Chapter 13 of this volume.

[72] The Security Council has referred two cases to the Court: the situation in Darfur, Sudan in March 2005 and the situation in Libya in February 2011. Neither country is a state party to the Rome Statute.

[73] Information on how to file a communication to the ICC Prosecutor can be found at http://coalitionfortheicc.org/how-file-communication-icc-prosecutor.

[74] See ICC, *Prosecutor v. Lubanga*, ICC-01/04-01/06-8, Judgment, 24 February 2006, para 50: 'the Court initiates cases only against the most senior leaders suspected of being the most responsible for the crimes within the jurisdiction of the court'.

REGIONAL SYSTEMS OF PROTECTION

In Europe, the Americas and in Africa regional human rights systems have developed and today offer a great deal of protection from human rights abuses through separate treaties and soft-law standards. All three regions have established courts that can hand down binding judgments and order just reparation. While not institutionally connected, they still refer to and draw from each other's experiences and findings, as well as that of UN experts. Such systems do not cover Asia or the Middle East however, meaning that many people cannot access regional protection mechanisms. The following section provides a brief description of the three regional human rights systems and the protection they provide from torture and ill-treatment.

Europe

Europe is the region with the highest level of integration and has the most sophisticated human rights protection system.[75] The Council of Europe (47 member states) is at its centre and is complemented by the European Union (currently 27 member states) and the Organization for Security and Co-operation in Europe (57 participating states), which expands beyond Europe to embrace North America and Central Asia.

The Council of Europe
The Council of Europe (CoE) is the leading human rights organisation in Europe and was founded in 1949. Its key achievement is the adoption in 1950 of the European Convention on Human Rights (ECHR),[76] complemented by 16 additional protocols and many soft-law standards, including the European Prison Rules (EPRs).[77] The EPRs – currently under revision – contain a catalogue of rights of detainees and good practices for the management of detention facilities similar to the UN Nelson Mandela Rules.

The ECHR contains similar provisions to the ICCPR, including an explicit prohibition of torture and other forms of ill-treatment (Article 3) and numerous other obligations relevant to its prevention. The European Court of Human Rights (ECtHR) established by the ECHR is the pre-eminent human rights body in Europe and the most used human rights mechanism in the world. All individuals living in a CoE member state can lodge an individual complaint directly to the ECtHR, after having exhausted domestic remedies. The Court passes legally binding judgments and can award just satisfaction (Article 41, ECHR).

The ECHR is a 'living instrument […] which must be interpreted in the light of present-day conditions'.[78] The Court interprets Article 3 flexibly, in the light of the circumstances of each case, recognising that '[c]ertain acts which were classified in the past as 'inhuman and degrading treatment' as opposed to 'torture' could be classified differently in the future.'[79] Torture and ill-treatment cases figure among the most frequently dealt with issues. A considerable

---

[75] For further examination see Chapter 8 in this volume.
[76] European Convention for the Protection of Human Rights and Fundamental Freedoms (ECHR) (adopted 4 November 1950, entered into force 3 September 1953 ETS no 5).
[77] Rec (2006) 2 of the Committee of Ministers to member states on the European Prison Rules (11 January 2006).
[78] See *Tyrer v. the United Kingdom*, 25 April 1978, Series A no 26, para 31.
[79] *Selmouni v. France* [GC], no 25803/94, ECHR 1999-V.

amount of its case law on Article 3 deals with inhuman conditions of detention[80] but it has expressed itself on very different matters and handed down interim measures (Rule 39 of the Rules of Court), where there is an imminent risk of irreparable harm, something which it has often done to prevent an expulsion or extradition.[81]

The key challenge for the ECtHR is its massive case load and the lack of prompt and effective execution of judgments. It has sought to enhance the implementation process (see Protocols 14 and 16 to the ECHR), expanded the use of remedial powers and has introduced a 'pilot judgment procedure' to address recurring situations.[82] Consequently the ECtHR is no longer just handing down judgments but 'setting legal binding standards for the prevention of torture and ill-treatment'.[83]

In 1987 the CoE adopted the European Convention for the Prevention of Torture and Inhuman or Degrading Treatment or Punishment, leading to the establishment of the European Committee for the Prevention of Torture (CPT) when it entered into force in 1989.[84] The purpose of the CPT is 'by means of visits, [to] examine the treatment of persons deprived of their liberty with a view to strengthening, if necessary, the protection of such persons from torture and from inhuman or degrading treatment or punishment'. This was a 'revolutionary step' which opened up places of detention within sovereign states to international scrutiny.[85] The CPT, which preceded and is very similar to the SPT – is a preventive body and composed of one independent expert per CoE member state. Its main function is to conduct country missions, visiting places of detention, conducting private interviews with detainees and staff and holding meetings with state and non-state stakeholders. It conducts periodic country missions (every three to six years) as well as 'ad hoc visits' to monitor a particularly serious situation, the timings of which are unannounced. Each mission results in a detailed report and recommendations submitted to the authorities. The CPT operates under the principle of confidentiality and cooperation, aiming to assist governments fulfil their obligations through continuous dialogue.[86] CPT reports are only made public with the consent of the state concerned which is granted in the great majority of cases, albeit sometimes with considerable delay. Under exceptional circumstances when a state 'fails to co-operate or refuses to improve the situation' the CPT can make a public statement (Article 10(2), ECPT), but it has done this very rarely. The CPT also has had a very important role in setting standards for the prevention of torture and ill-treatment ('CPT-Standards'). These have become a key source for national monitoring bodies and are frequently referenced by the ECtHR as well as by other regional institutions and agencies.

---

[80]   See e.g., *Peers v. Greece*, no 28524/95, ECHR 2001-III; *Kalashnikov v. Russia*, no 47095/99, ECHR 2002-VI.

[81]   See https://www.echr.coe.int/Documents/FS_Interim_measures_ENG.pdf

[82]   See https://www.echr.coe.int/Documents/Pilot_judgment_procedure_ENG.pdf; see also Open Society Justice Initiative, *From Judgment to Justice: Implementing International and Regional Human Rights Decisions* (OSF 2010) 41 et seq., https://www.justiceinitiative.org/uploads/62da1d98-699f-407e-86ac-75294725a539/from-judgment-to-justice-20101122.pdf

[83]   Birk, M and Zach, G, 'Torture Prevention in the EU – Many Actors, Few Outcomes?' (2015) EYHR 179.

[84]   European Convention for the Prevention of Torture and Inhuman or Degrading Treatment or Punishment (adopted 26 November 1987, entered into force 1 February 1989) ETS no 126.

[85]   See 1st General Report on the CPT's Activities (1990), CPT/Inf (91) 3, 97.

[86]   *Ibid*, 50.

Thirty years after its establishment, the CPT has developed into a key mechanism for the protection from torture and ill-treatment within Europe and as a role model beyond. However, the lack of implementation of recommendations remains a key challenge and has led to a certain degree of 'fatigue' by member states as regards cooperation with the CPT.[87] The CPT does not have an adequate system in place to monitor and follow up its recommendations and the infrequency of missions make continuous dialogue difficult.[88] At the same time, the findings of the CPT are a very important resource for advocacy by national actors and have led to significant legal and practical changes in numerous countries.[89]

The European Union
The European Union (EU), originally established as an internal single market, has developed into a political union with an increasingly important role in the protection of human rights. The absolute prohibition of torture and ill-treatment is enshrined in Article 4 of the Charter of Fundamental Rights of the European Union (CFREU) of 2000 that entered into force with the Treaty of Lisbon (TFEU) in 2009 and is applicable to EU institutions and member states alike. The CFREU is largely based on the ECHR and thus contains numerous obligations relevant to the protection from torture and ill-treatment. It is monitored by the Court of Justice of the European Union (CJEU), the EU's 'supreme court'. The CJEU can only be directly accessed by an individual if the EU violates the CFREU in a manner which 'is of direct and individual concern to them, and against a regulatory act which is of direct concern to them and does not entail implementing measures' (Article 263 TFEU). Therefore, in practice, it is very difficult for an individual to complain about EU legislation because it usually applies to everyone, or to large groups of people, rather than to a distinct individual. Individuals therefore tend to turn to national courts if it is claimed that the EU or a member state when implementing EU law is violating the CFREU. If national courts have doubts about the interpretation of the CFREU, they must refer these questions to the CJEU. As regards torture and ill-treatment this has happened in cases where a national court has asked the CJEU whether extradition under the European Arrest Warrant is permissible if there are strong indications that detention conditions in the country to which the person would be extradited might violate the prohibition of ill-treatment. The Court has found that national authorities must determine whether there are substantial grounds that an extradition may lead to a real risk of ill-treatment in violation of Article 4 CFREU, notwithstanding the principles of mutual recognition of judicial decisions and of mutual trust that EU member states respect human rights.[90]

The CJEU can also institute 'infringement procedures' upon the initiative of the EU Commission (Articles 258–260) should an EU member state fail to implement EU legislation

---

[87] Kicker, R, 'The European Committee for the Prevention of Torture and Inhuman or Degrading Treatment or Punishment (the CPT)' in de Beco, G (ed), *Human Rights Monitoring Mechanisms of the Council of Europe* (Routledge, 2011), 52.

[88] Birk and Zach (n 83 above), 178.

[89] Bicknell, C, Evans, M and Morgan, R, *Preventing Torture in Europe* (Council of Europe, 2018).

[90] Joined cases C-404/15, *Aranyosi* and C-659/15 PPU, *Caldararu* (ECJ 5 April 2016) 104; see also Tomkin, J, Zach, G, Crittin, T and Birk, M, *The Future of Mutual Trust and the Prevention of Ill-treatment – Judicial cooperation and the Engagement of NPMs* (Ludwig Boltzmann Institute of Human Rights/Academy of European Law, 2017).

or implements it in a manner that conflicts with the CFREU (Article 51(1)). This could become a powerful tool to protect victims from ill-treatment by the state.[91]

The European Commission, the executive branch of the EU, is responsible for proposing legislation and implementing decisions and plays an increasing role in the protection from torture and ill-treatment, notably in the development of legislation in the area of migration control and criminal justice. For example, the 'Directive on common standards and procedures in Member States for returning illegally staying third-country nationals (Return Directive)' establishes common standards for detention conditions (Articles 16 and 17) whilst a whole 'procedural rights package' has, in effect, been established by a series of directives concerning the protection of the rights of suspects and the accused.[92] These have significantly strengthened the procedural rights in the EU, with greater impact and leading to more reforms than the jurisprudence of the ECtHR and CPT findings. The EU has moreover adopted Guidelines on EU Policy Towards Third Countries on Torture[93] and a Regulation concerning trade in certain goods which could be used for capital punishment, torture or other cruel, inhuman or degrading treatment or punishment.[94]

The EU established a Fundamental Rights Agency (FRA) in 2007 to collect, record, analyse and disseminate information and data, carry out scientific research and formulate and publish conclusions and opinions on specific thematic topics.[95] The FRA has issued numerous publications relevant to the protection from torture and ill-treatment, ranging from criminal detention and alternatives to it, rights of suspects and accused, including child-friendly justice, border security, rehabilitation of torture victims, migration and non-refoulement, involuntary placement and treatment of persons with disabilities, violence against women and LGBTIQ persons.[96] Moreover, it has initiated a process to create a comparative tool on detention conditions, aimed at supporting EU member states when making extradition decisions in order to prevent torture and ill-treatment.[97]

The Organization for Security and Co-operation in Europe

The Organization for Security and Co-operation in Europe (OSCE) was created as a security organisation which includes a 'human dimension' based on respect for human rights and fundamental freedoms.[98] It has established a large set of human rights 'commitments', including the absolute prohibition of torture and ill-treatment and the punishment and prevention of such

---

[91]   De Schutter, O, *Infringement Proceedings as a Tool for the Enforcement of Fundamental Rights in EU* (Open Society Foundations, 2017).

[92]   See https://ec.europa.eu/info/policies/justice-and-fundamental-rights/criminal-justice/rights-suspects-and-accused_en

[93]   Guidelines on EU Policy Towards Third Countries on Torture and Other Cruel, Inhuman or Degrading Treatment or Punishment – 2019 Revision of the Guidelines, 12107/19 (2019).

[94]   REGULATION (EU) 2019/125 concerning trade in certain goods which could be used for capital punishment, torture or other cruel, inhuman or degrading treatment or punishment (2019) L 30/1.

[95]   Council Regulation (EC) No 168/2007 establishing a European Union Agency for Fundamental Rights (2007) Article 4(1).

[96]   See https://fra.europa.eu/en/charterpedia/article/4-prohibition-torture-and-inhuman-or-degrading-treatment-or-punishment

[97]   See https://fra.europa.eu/en/news/2017/national-preventive-mechanisms-discuss-building-comparative-tool-detention-conditions-0; https://fra.europa.eu/en/event/2017/european-network-improve-monitoring-criminal-detention

[98]   Conference on Security and Cooperation in Europe, Final Act Helsinki (1975).

practices.[99] The OSCE discusses its human dimension in a variety of settings (e.g. the Human Dimension Committee and Human Dimension Implementation Meeting) and has established institutions to promote human rights, including the Office for Democratic Institutions and Human Rights (ODIHR), the High Commissioner on National Minorities, the Representative on Freedom of the Media, and the Special Representative and Co-ordinator for Combating Trafficking in Human Beings. With the chairmanship of Switzerland in 2014, torture prevention was placed high on the OSCE's agenda and has since been continuously addressed in the different forums. The ODIHR, the principal institution dealing with the 'human dimension', works closely with its partners to strengthen efforts to eradicate torture and ill-treatment within the OSCE region. To this end, ODIHR has cooperated over the past years with countries from across the OSCE region as well as with international and regional institutions and civil society organisations, including providing support for independent monitoring in prisons and other places of detention. Since 2015 the ODIHR has had an Adviser on Torture Prevention who coordinates the work of the OSCE/ODIHR on that issue, and several practical tools have been developed to support the fight against torture and ill-treatment.[100]

The Americas

The human rights system in the Americas is based on the Organization of American States (OAS) and has been much concerned with the issue of torture and ill-treatment due to the history of repressive and violent military dictatorships in the region. The OAS was founded on 30 April 1948 and is currently comprised of 35 member states.

As well as creating the OAS and adopting the OAS Charter, American states also adopted the American Declaration of the Rights and Duties of Man (effective 2 May 1948), which was the first general human rights document in the world. It does not expressly prohibit torture and ill-treatment but contains numerous human rights relevant to its protection.[101]

The American Convention on Human Rights (ACHR) was adopted in 1969 and entered into force in 1978 and was ratified by 25 of the 35 OAS member states.[102] It expressly and absolutely prohibits torture and ill-treatment in Article 5 and provides additional guarantees for persons deprived of liberty. Like the ICCPR and ECHR, it contains numerous other obligations which are relevant to the protection from torture and ill-treatment. There is also an Inter-American Convention to Prevent and Punish Torture (IACPPT) that was established in parallel with the UNCAT and contains similar specific obligations. It also contains a definition of torture

---

99   For an overview of the commitments see OSCE, *Human Dimension Commitments: Volume 1, Thematic Compilation*, 3rd edn, https://www.osce.org/odihr/76894; *OSCE Human Dimension Commitments: Volume 2, Chronological Compilation*, 3rd edn, https://www.osce.org/odihr/elections/76895

100   OSCE/PRI, *Guidance Document on the Nelson Mandela Rules: Implementing the United Nations Revised Standard Minimum Rules for the Treatment of Prisoners* (2018), see https://www.osce.org/odihr/389912?download=true; CTI/OSCE, *Providing Rehabilitation to Victims of Torture and Other Ill-Treatment* (2018) https://cti2024.org/content/images/CTI-Rehabilitation_Tool5-ENG-final.pdf

101   See e.g., Articles 1, 25 and 26.

102   American Convention on Human Rights (1969), Treaty no B-32, OAS Treaty Series no 36. The Inter-American system is considered in detail in Chapter 10 of this volume.

(Article 2) but this differs from that found in the UNCAT.[103] Moreover, the Inter-American Convention on the Prevention, Punishment and Eradication of Violence against Women and the Inter-American Convention on Protecting the Human Rights of Older Persons contain explicit prohibitions of torture and ill-treatment. The Inter-American Convention on Forced Disappearance of Persons also directly relates to torture and ill-treatment.

The key human rights mechanisms in the Americas are the Inter-American Commission on Human Rights and Inter-American Court of Human Rights. The Commission (IAComHR) was founded in 1959 and has a broad quasi-judicial mandate, 'to promote the observance and protection of human rights and to serve as a consultative organ' of the OAS (Article 106). As a charter-based body, it monitors all OAS states on the basis of the 1948 Declaration. In addition, it has functions under the ACHR and other treaties irrespective of whether states accept the jurisdiction of the Court. The IAComHR can consider individual cases and issues provisional measures where there is an imminent risk of irreparable harm to individuals or groups of people. It raises awareness by developing reports on thematic issues (including on the Human Rights of Persons Deprived of Liberty),[104] advises states, requests information, conducts on-site visits and can appear before and request advisory opinions and provisional measures from the Court.[105]

The Commission has developed a system of thematic rapporteurs and in 2004 established a Rapporteur on the rights of persons deprived of liberty in the Americas.[106] The Rapporteur has a broad mandate to monitor the situation of persons deprived of liberty in OAS member states by obtaining information from governments and civil society organisations and by conducting visits to places of detention, the results of which are published in annual, country and thematic reports, including recommendations.[107] Thematic reports have been issued by the Rapporteur, for example on the Human Rights of Persons Deprived of Liberty[108] and on the Use of Pre-trial Detention.[109] The Rapporteur also issues urgent actions where necessary; promotes the adoption of legislative, judicial and administrative measures, and raises awareness of the rights of persons deprived of their liberty. The Rapporteur – together with a variety of stakeholders and experts – developed the 'Principles and Best Practices on the Protection of

---

[103]   Inter-American Convention to Prevent and Punish Torture (1985), Treaty no A-51, OAS Treaty Series no 67, Article 2 provides that 'Torture shall be understood to be any act intentionally performed whereby physical or mental pain or suffering is inflicted on a person for purposes of criminal investigation, as a means of intimidation, as personal punishment, as a preventive measure, as a penalty, or for any other purpose. Torture shall also be understood to be the use of methods upon a person intended to obliterate the personality of the victim or to diminish his physical or mental capacities, even if they do not cause physical pain or mental anguish.'

[104]   http://www.oas.org/en/iachr/pdl/docs/pdf/PPL2011eng.pdf

[105]   See Statute of the Inter-American Commission on Human Rights (1979), http://www.oas.org/en/iachr/mandate/Basics/statuteiachr.asp

[106]   See http://www.oas.org/en/iachr/pdl/mandate/mandate.asp

[107]   See IAComm.HR, Rapporteurship on the Rights of Persons Deprived of Liberty and to Prevent Torture, http://www.oas.org/en/iachr/pdl/default.asp

[108]   OAS/IACHR, Report on the Human Rights of Persons Deprived of Liberty in the Americas, OEA/Ser.L/V/II. Doc 64 (2011).

[109]   OAS/IACHR, Report on the Use of Pretrial Detention in the Americas, OEA/Ser.L/V/II. Doc.46/13 (2013).

Persons Deprived of Liberty in the Americas', which was adopted by the Commission.[110] This contains key soft-law standards concerning protection from torture and ill-treatment, as well as ensuring adequate detention conditions and due process guarantees.

The Inter-American Court of Human Rights (IACtHR) was established under the ACHR in 1979 as a judicial supervisory body. The Court, unlike the ECtHR, does not directly accept complaints by individuals. Only the IAComHR and member states that have accepted its jurisdiction may submit cases to the Court, which can hand down binding judgments, including orders of just satisfaction. It can also make orders of provisional measures in cases of extreme gravity and urgency when necessary to avoid irreparable damage to persons. Moreover, all parties to the ACHR and OAS can request advisory opinions from the Court.[111]

Like the UN treaty bodies and the ECtHR, the IACtHR and IAComHR have taken a broad approach to what comprises torture and ill-treatment. Notably, the Commission and Court have repeatedly found that the inadequate state response to disappearances and summary executions (that has been a serious concern in the Americas) may amount to ill-treatment of the family members.[112] Moreover, both bodies make regular use of their right to issue provisional measures, a tool that has been crucial in the protection from torture and ill-treatment.

The IACtHR has been particularly innovative as regards the use of its power to order reparations under Article 63(1). It seeks to restore as much as possible to the situation that would have prevailed had the violation not occurred, setting out in detail how its judgments should be implemented. It has developed the concept of a 'life plan' as an element of reparations, which 'is akin to the concept of personal fulfilment, which in turn is based on the options that an individual may have for leading his life and achieving the goal that he sets for himself.'[113] This may include an education scholarship to restore the 'life plan' and provide an opportunity to learn a profession.[114] It has also ordered states to organise official public acts to acknowledge its international liability and to apologise to the relatives of victims, prepare audiovisual presentations for schools illustrating the risks of compulsory military service, and the naming of a street after a victim.[115] The IACtHR has also been noted for its strong opposition to amnesty laws in the region, determining them to be without effect[116] and prohibiting domestic courts from applying laws which it considers to be in violation of the ACHR.[117] It thus asserts 'supra-

---

[110] IAComm.HR, Rapporteurship on the Rights of Persons Deprived of Liberty, Principles and Best Practices, http://www.oas.org/en/iachr/pdl/activities/principles.asp

[111] ACHR, Section 2 – Jurisdiction and Functions, Articles 61–64.

[112] *Alcides Torres Arias, Angel David Quintero et al.*, Report no 101/17, Case 12.414 (IACommHR, 5 September 2017); *Nelson Carvajal Carvajal and Others v. Colombia*, Report No. 54/04, Case 559/02 (IACtHR 13 March 2018).

[113] *Loayza Tamayo v. Peru*, Reparations and Costs, Judgment of November 27 1998, Series C no 42, para 148.

[114] *Cantoral Benavides v. Peru*, Judgment of August 18, 2000, Merits, Series C no 69, para 88.

[115] *Vargas Areco v. Paraguay*, Judgment of 26 September 2006, Merits, Reparations and Costs, Series C no 155, para 136(d).

[116] *Barrios Altos v. Peru*, Judgment of 14 March 2001, Merits, Series C no 83; *La Cantuta v. Peru*, Judgment of 29 November 2006, Merits, Reparations and Costs, Series C no 162.

[117] *Almonacid-Arellano v. Chile*, Judgment of 26 September 2006, Preliminary Objections, Merits, Reparations and Costs, Series C no 154.

national force' to its judgments, seeing itself as akin to a constitutional court and demanding that national courts also assume the role of guardians of the ACHR.[118]

The African System

The African system of human rights protection has also developed into an important one despite the constant financial struggles and dependency on the support of external donors.

The African Charter on Human and Peoples' Rights (ACHPR) adopted on 27 June 1981 by the Organisation of African Unity (OAU – now the African Union), and entered into force in 1986, explicitly prohibits torture and other forms of ill-treatment in Article 5, together with other acts violating the dignity of a person.[119] It does not define torture but its open-ended formulation ('all forms of exploitation and degradation') suggest that it also extends to non-state actors.[120] The ACHPR, like the other general international and regional human rights treaties, contains numerous other obligations relevant for the protection from torture and ill-treatment. It is complemented by special treaties that prohibit and oblige states to offer protection from torture and other forms of ill-treatment, such as the African Charter on the Rights and Welfare of the Child, the Protocol to the African Charter on Human and Peoples' Rights on the Rights of Women, the African Youth Charter, the Convention for the Protection and Assistance of Internally Displaced Persons in Africa, and the Protocol to the African Charter on Human and Peoples' Rights on the Rights of Persons with Disabilities in Africa. The Protocol to the African Charter on Human and Peoples' Rights on the Rights of Older Persons in Africa does not explicitly mention torture and ill-treatment but prohibits practices that could affect life and dignity (Articles 8, 9). Unlike in Europe and the Americas there is no specific African anti-torture treaty.

The African Commission on Human and Peoples' Rights (ACHPR, established by Articles 30 et seq.) has a promotional mandate to collect documents, undertake research, organise events and make recommendations to states, formulate principles and rules and give advisory opinions upon requests of member states (Article 45), as well as a protective mandate including emergency procedures to inform the AU of serious and massive HR violations, urgent appeals and protection missions. It accepts inter-state complaints (Articles 47–54) and, although not explicitly mentioned, it also accepts individual complaints (this being implicit in Articles 55–57). While there are also admissibility criteria (Article 56), the individual complaints procedure is more accessible than that of the other international mechanisms. It does not need to be expressly accepted by a state party, complaints may also be received from NGOs or individuals on behalf of the victims, and there is also considerable flexibility in regard to the exhaustion of domestic remedies. The Commission suffers from a chronic lack of resources

---

[118]   Binder, T, 'The Inter-American Human Rights System' in Nowak, Januczewski and Hofstätter (n 20 above), 244–245.

[119]   *African Charter on Human and Peoples' Rights*, adopted by the OAU Assembly on 27 June 1981, OAU Doc CAB/LEG/67/3 rev. 5. Article 5 provides that 'Every individual shall have the right to the respect of the dignity inherent in a human being and to the recognition of his legal status. All forms of exploitation and degradation of man, particularly slavery, slave trade, torture, cruel, inhuman or degrading punishment and treatment shall be prohibited'. The African system is considered in detail in Chapter 11 of this volume.

[120]   Viljoen, F and Odinkalu, C, *The Prohibition of Torture and Ill-Treatment in the African Human Rights System: A Handbook for Victims and their Advocates* (OMCT, 2006), 36.

which results in long delays in decision-taking. Moreover, decisions are not binding and are often not followed by the member states. As with the American bodies, the Commission has also found that failure to inform the families of the detainees' whereabouts, may amount to inhuman treatment of both the detainees and their families.[121]

The Commission examines bi-annual reports submitted by member states in order to assess their implementation of the ACHPR and of the Protocols. Following an interactive dialogue, the Commission issues concluding observations and recommendations, though follow-up and implementation remain a challenge. The Commission has carried out several fact-finding missions, called 'protection missions' to investigate reports of widespread human rights violations in a state party, both on its own initiative and at the request of an AU organ,[122] although often with significant delay due to a lack of cooperation by the state concerned. It also carries out promotion missions to collect relevant information, raise awareness and engage in dialogue with member states on implementation.[123]

The Commission also has an important standard-setting role. It has issued a General Comment on the Right to Redress for Victims of Torture and Ill-treatment,[124] passed numerous thematic and country-specific resolutions addressing issues relevant to the protection from torture and ill-treatment and adopted key normative standards, notably the Robben Island Guidelines for the prohibition and prevention of torture (2002)[125] – mirroring the key international standards – and the Luanda Guidelines on arrest, police custody and pre-trial detention (2014).[126]

The Commission has established 17 special mechanisms dealing with particular human rights challenges, including the Committee for the Prevention of Torture in Africa (2002) to disseminate, promote and facilitate the implementation of the Robben Island Guidelines through newsletters, press statements, regular and thematic reports, advocacy and technical assistance activities. It appears that this Committee has not been very successful, largely due to a lack of financial resources and states' unwillingness to cooperate. Another special mechanism of the Commission is the Special Rapporteur on prisons, conditions of detention and policing in Africa, established in 1996. The mandate of the individual expert is to examine the situation of persons deprived of their liberty within the territories of states parties to the African Charter. Similar to the UN SRT, the Special Rapporteur can undertake missions to countries, issue 'urgent actions' and provide assistance to the African Commission when it is considering communications relevant to the mandate, as well as prepare thematic reports which support the development of standards.

---

[121] Communication nos 48/90, 50/91, 52/91, 89/93, *Amnesty International, Comité Loosli Bachelard, Lawyers' Committee for Human Rights, Association of Members of the Episcopal Conference of East Africa v. Sudan* (ACHPR, 5 November 1999), 54; Communication no 151/96, *Civil Liberties Organisation v. Nigeria* (ACHPR 15 November 1999), 27.

[122] See African Charter of Human and Peoples' Rights, Article 46 and Rules of Procedure of the African Commission on Human and Peoples' Rights, Rules 81–82.

[123] Rules of Procedure of the African Commission on Human and Peoples' Rights, Rule 70.

[124] General Comment No 4: The Right to Redress for Victims of Torture and Other Cruel, Inhuman or Degrading Punishment or Treatment – Article 5 (2017).

[125] Adopted by the African Commission at its 32nd Ordinary Session, 17–23 October 2002.

[126] Resolution 228 on the need to develop guidelines on conditions of police custody and pre-trial detention in Africa, ACHPR/Res.228(LII)2012.

The African Court on Human and Peoples' Rights was established in 2004, on the basis of the Optional Protocol to the ACHPR to complement the human rights protection mandate of the African Commission. It can examine individual complaints if states make an explicit declaration in that regard and pass final, binding judgments (compliance with which is to be supervised by the Executive Council of the AU). It can moreover issue advisory opinions at the request of an AU member state, organ of the AU or non-governmental organisations with observer status to the AU. It has the jurisdiction to examine violations not only of the ACHPR and its Protocols but of all international human rights treaties to which the concerned state is a party. However, access to the Court is limited to states parties and African inter-governmental organisations. Individuals and CSOs can only file a complaint if the State Party in question has accepted the procedure. However, those able to bring a complaint do not have to show that they have been directly affected by a violation. The Court is a relatively new regional human rights body and is gradually developing its jurisprudence but it has the potential to be an important additional body to consider allegations of torture and other ill-treatment.

Finally, there have been a number of sub-regional courts within Africa which have competence to hear human rights cases submitted by individuals. Perhaps the best known is the Community Court of Justice for the Economic Community of West African States (ECOWAS), established in 2005, which has issued a number of rulings on torture. Unlike the African Commission and Court, there is no requirement that individuals exhaust domestic remedies before bringing a case before the ECOWAS Court.

CONCLUSION

There is an impressive number of mechanisms that can offer protection from torture and ill-treatment. Most states are bound by treaties which absolutely prohibit torture and ill-treatment, and this prohibition is also binding on all states through customary law. The obligation is interpreted broadly to include far-reaching positive obligations, as reflected in specialised treaties and soft-law standards. In addition to the Universal Periodic Review by the HRC, the implementation of these obligations is being monitored by international committees and commissions composed of independent experts through a variety of means, including periodic reviews and dialogues, visits and the consideration of complaints.

Most mechanisms foresee individual complaint procedures for victims, although accessing them can be difficult due to institutional obstacles or strict admissibility criteria, including the requirement to exhaust domestic remedies. The principle of non-duplication can also pose a problem since it forces victims to carefully consider which mechanism to utilise. Although international and regional mechanisms increasingly exchange information and refer to each other's work, the level of protection which they offer is not necessarily the same and it is difficult to expect non-experts to make a reasoned choice concerning which of the mechanisms open to them is most likely to afford the best protection. Besides, all human rights mechanisms complain of a serious lack of resources, resulting in significant backlogs of cases and consequently the prospect of very lengthy proceedings for the victims.

The last decades have seen the rise of new treaty bodies with a specific preventive mandate focusing on a constructive dialogue rather than 'naming and shaming'. The system created by the OPCAT is promising, establishing complementarity between international and national mechanisms. However, the continuous international dialogue envisaged by all the treaties is compromised by the scarcity of resources, whilst the national mechanisms depend on the willingness of the state parties to genuinely open up their places of detention and effectively prevent torture and other forms of ill-treatment.

Regrettably, follow-up and implementation are the key challenges for the international system of protection. The views of UN mechanisms are not formally legally binding and even the judgments of regional courts are not followed up by efficient international enforcement mechanisms that can force states to comply with the absolute prohibition of torture and ill-treatment. Therefore, the situation in practice depends on the attitudes of the governments in power, and in many countries positive developments have been followed by serious back-lashes with negative consequences for protection from torture and ill-treatment.

All in all, the net of international protection has clearly become denser. But although exchange and cooperation between the different mechanisms has increased, even at the UN level one cannot say there is a coherent sub-system of protection from torture and ill-treatment. Differences in working methods, duplication and overlaps are not only issues of efficiency but can become seriously problematic where they hamper the access of victims to protection or lead to conflicting standards. For these reasons some experts have proposed the establishment of a World Court of Human Rights, an ambitious and promising idea that has, however, been stuck given the global 'human rights crisis' and negative attitudes towards international human rights protection from both governments and public opinion in an increasing number of states.

Torture and ill-treatment is a highly complex phenomenon. There is an unambiguous and absolute prohibition and a great wealth of obligations and standards for protection. Efforts need to be stepped up, so the call for the eradication of torture does not remain an empty promise. The key lies in better cooperation and coordination between the various international mechanisms in order to raise awareness of the global crisis of torture and ill-treatment which still exists, counter toxic narratives which seek to justify such practices, and hold states accountable for violations of their legal commitments. Above all, the international system cannot fall into complacency and lose sight of what really counts: the implementation of protection and prevention measures needs to happen nationally. Therefore, the ultimate aim of international protection always needs to be the strengthening of domestic protection mechanisms in order to create real change.

6. Torture and ill treatment: the United Nations Human Rights Committee

Christof Heyns, Carmen Rueda and Daniel du Plessis

INTRODUCTION

The international human rights system was established just over 70 years ago, in order to define the extent to which individuals can, as a matter of right, demand that states to whose power they are subjected will protect their basic interests – including, at the most basic level, their personal security. This may relate to threats to their lives but also threats of harm to their physical or mental well-being, even if it does not necessarily result in death. This conduct is generally considered today as torture or cruel, inhuman or degrading treatment or punishment. The emblematic example of torture occurs when a state official beats a detainee to obtain evidence or a confession, but international human rights law protects people against a much wider range of maltreatment. Various United Nations treaty bodies play a central role in countering such conduct.

The Universal Declaration of Human Rights of 1948 provides in Article 5 that 'No one shall be subjected to torture or to cruel, inhuman or degrading treatment or punishment'. While this was an important first step, much would still be needed to develop the tools necessary to allow the pursuit of the effective enforcement of the right. In the first place, the Declaration used very general and non-defined terms to proscribe the conduct in question. Moreover, it did not provide that states would be legally bound by the norm against torture and cruel, inhuman or degrading treatment or punishment, and it did not create enforcement mechanisms for the right to be enforced.

Article 7 of the 1966 Covenant on Civil and Political Rights (ICCPR) took the matter further. In addition to providing an explicit legal basis for the binding nature of the protection against torture and cruel, inhuman or degrading treatment or punishment in respect of states that are party to the Covenant (currently there are 172 states parties), the inclusion of this norm in the Covenant also meant that compliance would be subjected to monitoring by the treaty body established to perform this function in respect of all the rights in the Covenant, namely the UN Human Rights Committee (HRCttee).

Article 7 does not define what is covered by the norm, or circumscribe its scope of application. It repeats the language of Article 5 of the Declaration, adding a further sentence dealing specifically with medical experimentation, and reads as follows: 'No one shall be subjected to torture or to cruel, inhuman or degrading treatment or punishment. In particular, no one shall be subjected without his free consent to medical or scientific experimentation.' The definition and scope of the application of Article 7 would be left to the HRCttee to develop. In what follows the term ill treatment will be used as short-hand for 'cruel, inhuman or degrading treatment or punishment'.

The Committee fulfils its monitoring function through three mechanisms. In the first place, it requires states parties to submit regular written reports to the Committee on their compliance with the rights recognised in the Covenant, typically every four years. The Committee then engages in an oral dialogue with the state concerned and issues 'concluding observations', setting out its views on the extent to which the rights in question are given effect by the state party and recommending actions to remedy unlawful or potentially unlawful conduct. These concluding observations serve as one source of its jurisprudence, including on Article 7. Currently the Committee issues concluding observations on around 20 states per year, and in recent years it has expressed itself on compliance with Article 7 in nearly all those states.

Second, with respect to states that have ratified not only the ICCPR but also the first Optional Protocol to the Covenant (currently there are 116 state parties to this Protocol), the Committee can examine complaints, also known as 'communications', submitted by individuals who have exhausted the domestic remedies available to them, but to no avail. After having considered the inputs from the author of the complaint as well as the state in question, the Committee adopts 'views' setting out whether there has indeed been a violation of the Covenant's rights and why. These views serve as a further source of the jurisprudence of the Committee. Currently the Committee issues views in around 60 cases per year, and in recent years findings on claims related to Article 7 have formed part of the majority of those cases.

Third, the Committee elaborates 'general comments', which constitute a detailed interpretation of the substantive as well as the procedural provisions of the Covenant. In doing this, the Committee also provides a restatement of the approach it has taken to the Covenant's rights in its concluding observations and views. The Committee has adopted a total of 36 such general comments to date. In 1992, the Committee adopted General Comment 20, dealing specifically with Article 7. While this is the most relevant General Comment for our current purposes, it is also obviously quite dated. The Committee has developed a rich body of jurisprudence subsequent to its adoption, and references to the Comment in what follows will be supplemented with references to these more recent views and concluding observations. General Comment 36 of 2018, on the right to life under Article 6, also deals to some extent with torture and ill treatment under Article 7 and will thus be quoted below where relevant.

In addition to Article 6, other provisions of the Covenant are also of relevance to Article 7. Of particular importance is Article 2, which sets out the obligations on states imposed by the Covenant, and Article 10, which deals with prison conditions. Both articles will be discussed in more detail below. Other relevant provisions include Article 9 (personal security and arbitrary detention); Article 12 (freedom of movement); Article 13 (procedural rights concerning expulsion); Article 14(3)(g) (protecting people against being compelled to testify against themselves) and Article 17 (privacy). Space does not permit an elaboration on the role of these rights.

As is the case with some of the other rights recognised in the Covenant, subsequent UN instruments were developed over time to give clearer contents and more detailed protection to the right protected in Article 7 of the Covenant. Pride of place in the case of Article 7 should go to the Convention Against Torture and Other Cruel, Inhuman and Degrading Treatment or Punishment of 1984 (UNCAT) which provides its own, detailed definition of the right that it protects, and elaborates upon the obligations that it imposes. It also creates its own monitoring body, the Committee against Torture (CAT). Like the HRCttee, the CAT has developed its jurisprudence through concluding observations, views and general comments. Moreover, in 2002, the Optional Protocol to the Convention (OPCAT) was adopted, entering into force in 2006, which established new mechanisms focusing on preventing torture and ill treatment.

In addition to the ICCPR and CAT, other UN instruments contain provisions on torture and ill treatment, although they will not be covered in any detail here.[1] For instance, Article 37(a) of the Convention on the Rights of the Child (CRC) includes an explicit prohibition of torture or other cruel, inhuman or degrading treatment or punishment of children;[2] and Article 39 makes explicit provision for measure to be taken in order to promote recovery and social reintegration of child victims of such practices.

Although the Convention on the Elimination of All Forms of Discrimination against Women (CEDAW) contains no explicit prohibition on torture and cruel, inhuman or degrading treatment or punishment, the CEDAW Committee has made use of the jurisprudence of bodies such as CAT and HRCttee to determine that state parties have a general duty against, for instance, *refoulement* of women where there is a risk of their being tortured.[3] More generally, the Committee has expressed its determination that gender-based violence, including torture or other forms of cruel, inhuman or degrading treatment or punishment, represents an instance of 'discrimination against women', as defined in Article 1 of CEDAW.[4]

This chapter addresses the question of how the jurisprudence of the Human Rights Committee defines torture and ill treatment, and the obligations it places on states in respect of such conduct. The application of Article 7 in specific contexts is then investigated. Various 'soft law' instruments also play a role in the context of Article 7 of the ICCPR, and in what follows these instruments will be introduced in the contexts where they are most relevant.

THE SCOPE OF THE RIGHT: THE DEFINITION OF TORTURE AND ILL TREATMENT

In establishing the scope of the right against torture and ill treatment, much turns on the use of definitions, and as will be clear from what follows, the approaches of the HRCttee and CAT are not always identical. The first question is what exactly is being defined (and thus being condemned). Is it 'torture' on its own; is it 'other forms of ill treatment'; or is it a broader category of abuse which covers both torture and ill treatment? There is no doubt that affixing the specific label 'torture' to conduct signifies a special stigma, calling for a strong response, but even if less intrusive abuse does not ring the same alarms, the international community has an interest in condemning such conduct as well. At the same time, it is often hard to draw a fixed and certain line between these different levels of mistreatment, especially for an international body with limited insight into the situation on the ground.

---

[1]   Convention on the Rights of the Child (CRC), Articles 37, 39; International Convention on the Protection of the Rights of all Migrant Workers and Members of their Families, Article 37; Convention on the Rights of Persons with Disabilities, Article 25. International Convention on the Elimination of All Forms of Racial Discrimination, Article 5 and the Committee on the Elimination of Discrimination against Women, General Recommendation 19, para 7.

[2]   Torture and cruel, inhuman and degrading treatment or punishment is, for the purposes of the CRC, defined rather broadly. The Committee on the Rights of the Child includes torture and ill treatment within its General Comment no 13 concerning 'Violence in all its forms against Children' in which an implied prohibition of corporal punishment is made explicit (CRC/C/GC/13 (2011) para 22).

[3]   *M.N.N. v. Denmark* (CEDAW/C/55/D/33/2011).

[4]   See CEDAW General Recommendation no 19, Violence against Women (1992), para 1.

One option is to use the term 'torture or ill treatment' collectively, as a label for conduct that meets the threshold set for either. Going that route has the advantage of casting the net more widely than covering just the most extreme cases, but it may also dilute the sense of outrage that the term 'torture' rightfully evokes. The ICCPR and the UNCAT systems have responded in different ways to this dilemma, probably reflecting their respective general and specialised roles.

The HRCttee, following *Giri v. Nepal*,[5] has on occasion identified particularly egregious conduct falling under Article 7 specifically as 'torture'.[6] However, in line with the more general description of the right in Article 7, the Committee routinely refers to acts of torture or ill treatment collectively as 'violations of Article 7', without further specification. Where it does refer to conduct as 'torture', this is often to express special indignation or to provide a basis for a requirement of special remedies such as a request for rehabilitation services.[7]

Our focus in what follows is primarily on the HRCttee, but some reference will also be made to the approach under CAT where a distinction needs to be made.

Since Article 7 of the Covenant does not contain a definition of the conduct that it prescribes, as is the case in CAT, the understanding by the HRCttee of the scope of the right must be established by piecing together its jurisprudence and practice.

General Comment 20 does not try to define torture or ill treatment either. However, it does state that the aim of Article 7 is 'to protect both the dignity and the physical and mental integrity of the individual',[8] and that the prohibition in Article 7 'relates not only to physical pain but also to acts that cause mental suffering to the victim'.[9] It appears that the problem that the recognition of the right seeks to address is the unwarranted infliction of pain or suffering which meets a certain threshold of severity through conduct that violates domestic or international law.

The HRCttee's approach may usefully be contrasted with that followed under CAT. UNCAT recognises 'torture' as a separate category of proscribed conduct and provides a detailed definition of the term in its Article 1(1).[10] Severe pain or suffering must have been intentionally inflicted at the instigation of, or with the consent or acquiescence of, a public official for a specific purpose such as obtaining evidence, to qualify as 'torture'. In addition to torture, Article 16(1) of UNCAT also recognises as a separate category 'other acts of cruel, inhuman or degrading treatment or punishment which do not amount to torture as defined in Article 1'. The threshold for conduct to qualify as 'torture' under the UNCAT regime is set high, and special obligations are imposed on states to avoid or address such a situation.

The question arises whether any of the UNCAT requirements described above, namely official capacity, specific purpose, intent and severity are posed by the HRCttee in order to find a violation of Article 7. We will now consider them in turn.

The HRCttee does not pose the requirement that the act was performed by someone in an *official capacity*. Instead, its approach is that 'it is the duty of the State party to afford everyone

---

[5]   *Giri v. Nepal* (CCPR/C/101/D/1761/2008).
[6]   See also e.g. *Bhandari v. Nepal* (CCPR/C/112/D/2031/2011); *Basnet v. Nepal* (CCPR/C/112/D/2051/2011); *El Hagog Jumaa v. Libya* (CCPR/C/104/D/1755/2008/Rev1).
[7]   See e.g. *Purna Maya v. Nepal* (CCPR/C/119/D/ 2245/2013), paras 12.2, 12.3 and 14.
[8]   CCPR General Comment no 20, Article 7, Prohibition of Torture, or Other Cruel, Inhuman or Degrading Treatment or Punishment (1992), UN Doc A/47/40 pp 193–195 (10 March 1992), para 1.
[9]   *Ibid.*
[10]   See Chapter 7 of this volume.

protection ... against the acts prohibited by Article 7, whether inflicted by people acting in their official capacity, outside their official capacity or in a private capacity'.[11]

While this distinction has to be recognised, its practical implications should not be overestimated, as the CAT takes a broad view of what constitutes acquiescence. Thus, its General Comment 2 indicates that:

> the failure of the State to exercise due diligence to intervene to stop, sanction and provide remedies to victims of torture facilitates and enables non-State actors to commit acts impermissible under the Convention with impunity, the State's indifference or inaction provides a form of encouragement and/or de facto permission. The Committee has applied this principle to States parties' failure to prevent and protect victims from gender-based violence, such as rape, domestic violence, female genital mutilation, and trafficking.[12]

The latter acts are also covered by Article 7.

UNCAT furthermore requires conduct to be performed for a *specific purpose*, such as the extraction of information or a confession, to punish, to intimidate, or to discriminate, in order to be described as torture. The HRCttee generally does not pose such a requirement for Article 7 violations. However, the practical consequences are once again not as far-reaching as it may appear at first sight. The list of purposes provided by UNCAT is merely illustrative, and in any event covers the motivation of the vast majority of perpetrators in cases where Article 7 violations have been found by the HRCttee.

UNCAT also requires the presence of intention for a finding of torture to be made. While 'purpose' relates to motivation, 'intent' relates to the question whether the perpetrator in fact wished to bring about – or was at least reckless about bringing about – the pain and suffering caused by his or her actions. The HRCttee rarely focuses expressly on the element of *intent,* but it seems from its jurisprudence that intent to inflict the pain or suffering is normally as a matter of fact present where explicit findings of torture are made.[13] The fact that this requirement has been met is probably in most such cases assumed by the HRCttee.

As set forth in Article 1 of the Convention, UNCAT requires the intensity of the pain inflicted to reach the level of being 'severe' to be branded as torture. The HRCttee in practice also requires a certain level of severity to have been reached,[14] though like CAT it makes such assessments on a case-by-case basis.[15]

According to UNCAT, 'legitimate sanctions', or actions such as self-defence, are not covered by the right against torture, provided in both cases that the domestic law meets the applicable international standards.[16] Article 7 does not explicitly exclude actions taken in

---

[11]   General Comment no 20 (n 8 above), para 2.
[12]   CAT General Comment no 2, Implementation of Article 2 by States Parties, (2008), CAT/C/GC/2, para 18.
[13]   See e.g. *Giri v. Nepal* (n 5 above).
[14]   General Comment no 20 (n 8 above), para 4; *Giri v. Nepal* (n 5 above), para 7.5.
[15]   General Comment no 20 (n 8 above), para 4.
[16]   See e.g. *Vuolanne v. Finland* (CCPR/C/35/D/265/1987). Severing limbs as a form of punishment provided for under domestic law violates Article 7 because this form of punishment is in conflict with international standards. See Concluding Observations on Iraq (1997) CCPR/C/79/Add.84 para 12.

accordance with domestic law, such as imprisonment, from the scope of the right, but it can generally be assumed that they are not covered.[17]

Most human rights are not absolute and may be limited, subject to stringent conditions. It is important to note in this respect that the right contained in Article 7 of the ICCPR is absolute and may thus not be limited in any way.[18]

In deciding whether rights have been legitimately limited, the HRCttee often follows a two-stage procedure. First, the scope of the right is determined, and then the question is asked whether an infringement is justified, with reference to concepts such as necessity and proportionality. However, given the absolute nature of Article 7, limitations have no role to play in this context. Neither proportionality nor necessity can be used to *justify* the actual infringement of its contents. They do, however, play an important role in determining whether a violation has taken place – in other words, in *defining* the scope of the right.

It seems fair to say that in practice, where an individual communication concerns the use of force by the police outside the custodial context which does not meet the high threshold of 'torture', the process to establish whether a violation of Article 7 has occurred often resembles a two-stage procedure. The working assumption in such cases is that once it has been established that force was used, the onus is on the State to justify the use of force, using notions such as necessity and proportionality.

In *Chernev v. Russian Federation*, concerning the treatment inflicted upon the victim while being apprehended, the Committee held that 'the use of force by the police, which can be justified in certain circumstances, may be viewed as contrary to Article 7 under circumstances in which the force used is deemed excessive'.[19] In *V.S. v. Russian Federation*[20] the Committee declared a communication inadmissible based on the arguments advanced by the State to 'justify' the degree of force used during arrest. In *Abromchik v. Belarus*[21] the Committee found that the State had failed to provide such justification and found that a violation had occurred.

In *Cabal and Pasini v. Australia*, the authors complained about their treatment in preventive detention, including the fact that they were shackled when travelling to and from prison and subjected to cavity searches after each visit to court. Australia provided justification for the treatment in question based on safety and security concerns, and the Committee concluded that, in its assessment, there had been no violation of Article 7.[22]

Derogation of Article 7 in times of emergency is not possible under the ICCPR. Given the formulation of Article 7, this applies to both torture and other forms of ill treatment.[23]

---

[17]   The question of the compatibility of the death penalty and corporal punishment with Article 7 is considered below.

[18]   General Comment no 20 (n 8 above), para 3.

[19]   *Chernev v. Russian Federation* (CCPR/C/125/D 2322/2013), para 12.2.

[20]   *V.P. v. Russian Federation* (CCPR/C/104/D/1627/2007), para 8.4.

[21]   *Abromchik v. Belarus* (CCPR/C/122/D/2228/2012).

[22]   *Cabal and Pasini v. Australia* (CCPR/C/78/D/1020/2001), para 8.2.

[23]   For the HRCttee's jurisprudence in this respect, see Joseph, S and Castan, M, *The International Covenant on Civil and Political Rights: Cases, Materials, and Commentary* 3rd edn (Oxford University Press, 2013), 216. See also CCPR General Comment no 29, Article 4: Derogations during a State of Emergency (2001), CCPR/C/21/Rev.1/Add.11; General Comment no 20 (n 8 above), para 3.

THE OBLIGATIONS THAT ARTICLE 7 PLACES ON STATES

Article 2 of the ICCPR sets out the general obligations that the rights in the Covenant impose on states.

Article 2 (1) provides that states parties must 'respect and ensure' the rights in the Covenant. As is the case with the other rights, Article 7 thus imposes upon states the obligation to perform essentially negative as well as positive duties, and to respect as well as to protect the bearers of the rights. The negative duty to respect the right in question represents the quintessential obligation on states as far as torture and ill treatment is concerned: States must ensure that their officials do not engage in torture or ill treatment. It is not, however, confined to that. For example, states must also exercise due diligence to protect individuals from violations by other individuals, as may be the case for instance with domestic violence.

There appears to be little sense in trying to draw a bright line between negative and positive duties in such contexts, or to identify the exact position that each obligation takes in the broader spectrum. For example, the obligation on states to act against transgressions by members of its police force requires the state acting through its agents to refrain from engaging in prohibited conduct, in other words it imposes a negative duty; but it also requires the state to act to engage in actions such as setting up a legal framework regulating the use of force, and to ensure accountability for violations. In many cases negative and positive obligations are intermixed. Clearly no state can prevent all mistreatment which could potentially constitute a violation of Article 7 from taking place, but the legal and administrative framework must pursue this goal, and accountability where violations occur must be ensured.

Reference should be made in this context to an increased emphasis by the HRCttee in recent years on the positive obligation of precaution in the context of the right to life. States must take all feasible precautions to prevent a situation from arising where deadly force may have to be used.[24] This must clearly also apply to the excessive use of force even if it does not have fatal consequences.[25] As will be argued below, this obligation underlies the duty on states to provide access to less lethal weapons to public order policing officials.

Article 7 has a special, though not exclusive, importance for detainees, as they are particularly vulnerable to the misuse of power by state officials. The United Nations have developed a range of soft-law instruments in order to guide states on measures to be taken to comply with their positive obligation to ensure the security of detainees.

The outer boundaries of the positive obligation on states to prevent acts of torture and ill treatment committed by non-state actors are not well delimited in the Covenant or the UNCAT. The obligation on the state, as developed in the jurisprudence, is to exercise due diligence, which is an obligation of means, not of result. Thus, the CAT held the state accountable in a case where the police failed to intervene in a pogrom against a group of Roma by other members of the community, following threats of which the police were well aware.[26]

Article 2(2) of the Covenant requires states to 'adopt such laws or other measures as may be necessary to give effect to the rights recognized in the present Covenant.' The requirement to

---

[24]   See, for instance, Concluding Observations on Israel (2003) CCPR/CO/78/ISR, para 15.

[25]   See, for instance Concluding Observations on Israel (2014) CCPR/C/ISR/CO/4, para 13; Concluding Observations on South Africa (2016) CCPR/C/ZAF/CO/1, para 27; and Concluding Observations on France (2015) CCPR/C/FRA/CO/5, para 15.

[26]   *Dzemajl and Others v. Yugoslavia* (Communication no CAT/C/29/D/161/2000).

put into place a protective legal and administrative framework to prevent acts of ill treatment in all its forms from occurring applies to detention but also extends to other areas in which potential violations occur, for example, laws concerning human trafficking and domestic violence.[27]

Are states required to recognise torture and ill treatment *as crimes* in its domestic law? Article 4 of UNCAT sets up this obligation explicitly only with respect to acts of torture. Furthermore, the CAT considers that states should codify an independent crime of torture in their domestic law based on the definition of torture in Article 1 of the Convention.[28]

In the case of the ICCPR, General Comment 20 specifies that when presenting their reports states should indicate the provisions of their criminal law which penalize torture and cruel, inhuman and degrading treatment or punishment.[29] In its concluding observations the HRCttee has often requested states to incorporate into legislation the crime of torture, in conformity with Article 7.

The concluding observations by the Committee on matters covered by Article 7 in recent years often use language like the following, which comes from the Committee's 2018 concluding observations for the Lao People's Democratic Republic:

> The State party should take vigorous measures to eradicate torture and ill-treatment and more specifically, inter alia, to: (a) Bring the definition of torture, including in the draft Penal Code currently under consideration, into conformity with article 7 of the Covenant and other international standards, preferably by codifying it as an independent crime that is not subject to a statute of limitations and that stipulates sanctions commensurate with the gravity of the crime …[30]

As for the requirement of Article 2(3) that states must ensure an effective remedy to victims of violations of all Covenant rights, it implies that where there is reason to believe that a violation of Article 7 may have occurred, the state has to ensure that this will be investigated according to acceptable standards.[31] Not to do so constitutes a violation of Article 7, read in conjunction with Article 2(3).[32] The soft-law instrument most often referenced by the HRCttee and other international bodies as setting out the standards for investigations of torture is the Istanbul Protocol.[33] Following investigation, victims must also have access to effective remedial action, such as, for instance, compensation.[34]

A failure by the authorities to conduct a proper investigation of allegations of crimes against the person may also result in the re-victimisation of the person affected, a fact which can on its own also constitute a violation of Article 7, even if the state carries no responsibility for

---

[27]   *Ng v. Canada* (Communication no CCPR/C/49/D/469/1991). Compare also CCPR General Comment no 28, Article 3 The Equality of Rights Between Men and Women (2000), CCPR/C/21/Rev.1/Add.10, para 11.

[28]   CAT General Comment no 2 (n 12 above), para. 11.

[29]   CCPR General Comment no 20 (n 8 above), paras 8, 13.

[30]   Concluding Observations on Lao People's Democratic Republic (2018) CCPR/C/LAO/CO/1, para 24.

[31]   See CCPR General Comment no 20 (n 8 above), para 14.

[32]   See, for instance, HRCttee, *Askarov v. Kyrgyzstan* (CCPR/C/116/D/2231/2012), para 8.3; *Zheikov v. Russian Federation* (CCPR/C/86/D/889/1999).

[33]   Manual on the Effective Investigation and Documentation of Torture and Other Cruel, Inhuman or Degrading Treatment or Punishment (*Istanbul Protocol*), 2004.

[34]   CCPR General Comment no 20 (n 8 above), para 16.

the initial crime.[35] As noted below under the heading 'impact on third parties', a failure to investigate some crimes, for example disappearances, may also constitute ill treatment of the family members of the author.

CAT not only allows but requires states to exercise universal jurisdiction over acts of torture (though not other ill treatment). As a result, the state must prosecute alleged offenders present on its territory or extradite such a person for prosecution.[36] The ICCPR does not place such an obligation on states for violations of Article 7, though it certainly does not prohibit prosecutions either.

States have a general duty to disseminate 'relevant information' concerning the contents of Article 7.[37] This information is not only to be distributed amongst personnel employed by the state, or who are at risk of potentially violating the provision, either by conduct or a failure to act, but also to the populace as a whole. The aim is to create a culture where torture and ill treatment does not have a place.

APPLICATION OF ARTICLE 7 IN SPECIFIC CONTEXTS

Conduct that falls within the scope of Article 7, and that can thus trigger the obligations outlined above, often occurs in well-established contexts. It is worth enquiring to what extent the HRCttee has developed specific practices in these contexts.

Detained Persons: The Role of Article 10

As alluded to earlier, persons in custody are especially vulnerable to the risk of torture and ill treatment. Detention, by its very nature, reflects a highly unequal and often adversarial power relationship, manifested in concrete physical and psychological terms, far from the searchlight of public scrutiny. States are responsible for the security of all persons held in detention. In addition to Article 7, Article 10 of the Covenant also tries to address the abuses that may emanate from these conditions.

Article 10(1) of the Covenant provides as follows: 'All persons deprived of their liberty shall be treated with humanity and with respect for the inherent dignity of the human person.' The implications of this article have been further elaborated upon by the HRCttee in General Comment 21, which provides that Article 10(1) 'applies to everyone deprived of liberty under the laws and authority of the state who is held in prisons, hospitals – particularly psychiatric hospitals – detention camps or correctional institutions or elsewhere'.[38]

The interplay of Articles 7 and 10
There is clearly at least a partial overlap between Article 10, which deals only with people deprived of their liberty, and Article 7, which often but not always relates to people deprived

---

[35]   See, for instance, *L.N.P. v. Argentina* (CCPR/C/102/D/1610/2007).
[36]   *Questions relating to the Obligation to Prosecute or Extradite (Belgium v. Senegal)*, ICJ Reports 2012, 99.
[37]   CCPR General Comment no 20 (n 8 above), para 10.
[38]   CCPR General Comment no 21, Article 10, Humane Treatment of Persons Deprived of Their Liberty (1992), para 2.

of their liberty. In this respect, Article 10 complements the prohibition against torture and ill treatment contained in Article 7. What are the respective roles assigned to these two rights by the HRCttee?

While the jurisprudence is not always consistent, in general it can be said that in addition to the fact that Article 10 applies only in a detention setting, the threshold of the severity of the pain inflicted for an Article 10 violation is lower than it is for an Article 7 violation. Article 10 is in practice typically used to apply to what is called the 'general conditions of detention' (though this phrase is not used in Article 10) in which the author of the complaint is held. Even if these conditions are the same for fellow detainees, it may be beyond a certain point of what can be considered acceptable.[39] Article 7, in the detention setting, is brought to bear specifically on those cases where the individual is subjected to direct physical or mental attacks on his or her body by the wardens or other inmates or similar abuse.[40] However, there are cases where the conditions in which the person is held are so appalling that they (also) qualify as a violation of Article 7 in their own right, even where there is no direct physical or mental attack.[41]

Does a violation of Article 7 in a detention setting automatically also constitute a violation of Article 10? The HRCttee has said that this could be argued,[42] and this seems to be a logical conclusion, but in practice the Committee often simply does not deal with Article 10 once it has found a violation of Article 7 for the same facts, which is generally considered to be more serious.[43]

Simultaneous but separate violations of both rights may of course occur in the same case, as happened in *Kennedy v. Trinidad and Tobago*,[44]where the prison was overcrowded, solitary confinement was used for those on death row, and the author was in addition also singled out for beatings.

The HRCttee has set out aspects of its understanding of the general conditions in which detainees are to be held in General Comment 20.[45] In this context the Committee also often

---

[39]   In this respect, the HRCttee has expressed its preference for a number of United Nations standards. State parties are invited to indicate in their reports to what extent they are applying the relevant United Nations standards applicable to the treatment of prisoners: the Standard Minimum Rules for the Treatment of Prisoners (1957), the Body of Principles for the Protection of All Persons under Any Form of Detention or Imprisonment (1988), the Code of Conduct for Law Enforcement Officials (1978) and the Principles of Medical Ethics relevant to the Role of Health Personnel, particularly Physicians, in the Protection of Prisoners and Detainees against Torture and Other Cruel, Inhuman or Degrading Treatment or Punishment (1982).

[40]   In *Pinto v. Trinidad and Tobago* (CCPR/C/57/D/512/1992), para 8.3, the author failed to prove such a distinction. In *Mukong v. Cameroon* (CCPR/C/51/D/458/1991) the author succeeded in showing that he had been singled out and a violation of Article 7 was found.

[41]   See, for example, *Portorreal v. Dominican Republic* (CCPR/C/31/D/188/1984).

[42]   See *Linton v. Jamaica* (CCPR/C/46/D/ 255/1987), para 8.5.

[43]   Note, for instance, the decision in *McCallum v South Africa* (CCPR/C/100/D/1818/2008) and the implicit distinction between the different categories of prohibited conduct as proscribed by Articles 7 and 10 respectively. See also *Wilson v. Philippines* (CCPR/C/76/D/868/1999) and *Edwards v. Jamaica* (CCPR/C/55/D/529/1993).

[44]   *Kennedy v. Trinidad and Tobago* (CCPR/C/67/D/845/1999).

[45]   For example, CCPR General Comment no 20 (n 8 above), para 11 stipulates that 'provision should be made for detainees to be held in places officially recognised as places of detention', that 'the time and place of all interrogations should be recorded, together with the names of those present', and that 'All places of detention must be free of equipment liable to be used for inflicting torture or ill-treatment'. General Comment no 20, para. 11. See also CCPR General Comment no 21 (n 38 above), para 5.

refers to other international guidelines, such as the United Nations Standard Minimum Rules for the Treatment of Prisoners (Mandela Rules).[46] It is the cumulative effect of violations of these standards, not necessarily the transgression of any one of them seen in isolation, which informs the decision on whether the level of severity required to find a violation of Article 10 (and exceptionally Article 7) has been met. The determination of whether this level has been reached is made with reference to the 'nature and context of the treatment, its duration, [and] its physical and mental effects …'.[47]

Not surprisingly, states often argue that conditions of detention depend on the resources available to them, and should be compared not to what is internationally acceptable, but to the living conditions in the country as a whole. The Committee, however, sees Article 10 as posing minimum standards that are applicable globally: 'Treating all persons deprived of their liberty with humanity and respect for their dignity is a fundamental and universally applicable rule. Consequently, the application of this rule, as a minimum, cannot be dependent on the material resources available in a state party.'[48]

Solitary confinement
While the Committee has expressed strong misgivings about the practice of solitary confinement, it has not completely ruled out its use as a form of punishment for those in detention, in appropriate cases and subject to strict restrictions.[49] Where these bounds are transgressed, however, it may constitute a violation of Article 10.[50] In its Concluding Observations of 2000 on the report of Denmark, the HRCttee said that 'the use of solitary confinement other than in exceptional circumstances and for limited periods' is inconsistent with Article 10(1).[51] In its General Comment 20 it has indicated that, in extreme cases it may also violate Article 7.[52]

Incommunicado detention and enforced disappearance
While solitary confinement refers to the separation of someone who has been detained from other detainees, the term 'incommunicado detention' refers to the prevention of contact by a detainee with the outside world. The latter practice is especially closely linked, and is indeed often a euphemism for, enforced disappearance, which in turn can in extreme cases be a smokescreen for other violations, including violations of the right to life. There is often no telling which is which, because of the cloak of secrecy that hangs over places of detention. General Comment 20 thus urges states to adopt provisions against incommunicado detention, and requires safeguards such as the keeping of accessible registers.[53]

---

[46]   United Nations Standard Minimum Rules for the Treatment of Prisoners (2015). See Concluding Observations on the fifth periodic report of Romania (2017) CCPR/C/ROU/CO/5 para 32; Concluding Observations on the fifth periodic report of Cameroon (2017) CCPR/C/CMR/CO/5 para 29; Concluding Observations on the fourth periodic report of the Democratic Republic of the Congo (2017) CCPR/C/COD/CO/4, para 34. See also *Suleimenov v. Kazakhstan* (CCPR/C/119/D/ 2146/2012), para 8.7 on the treatment of a disabled prisoner.

[47]   *Brough v. Australia* (CCPR/C/86/D/1184/2003), para 9.2.

[48]   CCPR General Comment no 21 (n 38 above), para 4.

[49]   See, for example, *Vuolanne v. Finland* (n 16 above).

[50]   See for instance *Aminov v. Turkmenistan* (CCPR/C/117/D/2220/2012), para 9.3.

[51]   Concluding Observations on the periodic report of Denmark CCPR/CO/70/DNK, para 12.

[52]   CCPR General Comment no 20 (n 8 above), para. 6. See also, for instance, *Matyakubov v. Turkmenistan* (CCPR/C/117/D/ 2224/2012), para 7.2.

[53]   CCPR General Comment no 20 (n 8 above), para 11.

While constant communication with the outside world is not required, any severance of such ties may not be prolonged. In *MacCallum v. South Africa* the HRCttee found that even one month of incommunicado detention was enough to breach Article 7,[54] though longer periods were not met with the same consequences in other cases.[55]

Incommunicado detention and enforced disappearance *per se* have in specific cases been held to constitute violations of the Article 7 rights of the victims themselves, because of 'the degree of suffering involved in being held indefinitely without contact with the outside world'[56] and of the Article 7 rights of their loved ones because of the anguish it causes.[57]

Extra-Custodial Use of Force by Law Enforcement Officials

While cases where the use of force by law enforcement officials constitutes a violation of Article 7 often occur in places of detention, that is not always the case. The HRCttee has, for example, found in a number of cases that the excessive use of force by law enforcement in the context of public order policing and arrest has violated Article 7. In *Alzery v. Sweden*, for instance, the HRCttee was willing to rule that the treatment suffered by the author of the communication at the airport during expulsion proceedings 'was disproportionate to any legitimate law enforcement purpose' and, accordingly, in violation of Article 7.[58]

While the excessive use of force by law enforcement agents may arguably also be categorised as a violation of personal security under Article 9 of the Covenant, the practice has been established by the HRCttee that Article 7 is to be used for these purposes. The Committee has, where death occurred under similar circumstances, not followed a practice of requiring proof of intent to find a violation of Article 6,[59] and it seems logical to argue that the same approach should be followed where a violation of Article 7, which is less intrusive, is at stake. Certainly, the fact that the police did not intend to shoot the specific individuals concerned should not exonerate the state from responsibility for an Article 6 or 7 violation when they nevertheless fired indiscriminately into a crowd.[60]

The point of reference of the Committee on when force (and which type of force) may be used is typically the UN Basic Principles on the use of force and firearms of 1990.[61] The Basic Principles impose a strict regime on the use of force generally,[62] and on the use of firearms in

---

[54]   *McCallum v. South Africa* (n 43 above).
[55]   See e.g. *Boimurodov v. Tajikistan* (CCPR/C/85/D/1042/2001).
[56]   *Nakarmi v. Nepal* (CCPR/C/119/D/2184/2012) para 11.7; *Boathi v. Algeria* (CCPR/C/119/D/2259/2013), para 7.6.
[57]   See e.g. *Grioua v. Algeria* (CCPR/C/90/D/1327/2004); *Nakarmi v. Nepal* (CCPR/C/119/D/2184/2012), para 11.8.
[58]   *Alzery v. Sweden* (CCPR/C/88/D/1416/2005), para.11.6.
[59]   See e.g. *Burrell v. Jamaica* (CCPR/C/53/D/546/1993), para 9.5.
[60]   See *Umetaliev v. Kyrgyzstan* (CCPR/C/94/D/1275/2004).
[61]   See e.g. CCPR General Comment no 36 Article 6, the right to life, (2018), CCPR/C/GC/36, para 13.
[62]   See, for instance, the duty that vests in law enforcement officials to apply non-violent means before the use of force, wherever possible. *Basic Principles on the Use of Force and Firearms by Law Enforcement Officials*, 1990, Principle 4.

particular.[63] It also requires internal reporting when firearms have been used and investigations into subsequent deaths.[64]

This brings us to a dilemma. The requirements on the use of force by law enforcement are generally understood to include elements of necessity and proportionality, and, as a result, some kind of weighing process between the interests that are protected and those that are affected is required. In the case of the right to life under Article 6, for example, the intentional deadly use of force may be justified if it is the only way to counter an imminent threat to life. This is because the right to life is not absolute, and limitations are permissible if there is a good justification, involving necessity and proportionality.[65] As was pointed out above, the approach of the Committee is to let such considerations play a role as far as the scope of the right is concerned.

In line with international trends, the HRCttee places emphasis on the need to make less lethal weapons available to law enforcement officials, in line with the human rights duty of precaution.[66] However, the Committee has also emphasised that these weapons should be used with great caution and moderation, as they can be abused and indeed be fatal, and should be used only within certain parameters.[67]

The HRCttee is currently in the process of developing a General Comment on the right of peaceful assembly, which will also deal with the use of force during demonstrations and other ways to properly manage an assembly, including pre-emptive steps to avoid the necessity of using force in the first instance.[68] The newly developed *Guidance on the Use of Less-Lethal Weapons in Law Enforcement* (2020) of the Office of the UN High Commissioner for Human Rights will probably also play a role, especially as far as public order policing is concerned.[69]

Other Article 7 Violations that Do Not Take Place in Custodial Settings

Article 7 has also been held to have been violated in other contexts. Many of the Article 7 cases that currently reach the HRCttee deal with the return of foreigners to countries where they risk being subjected to torture. If the Committee considers that such risk exists, it will find a violation of Article 7 should the state concerned proceed to return the person.

As indicated above, violations can also be found in cases involving private parties in the role of the abuser. Thus, some practices threaten specific categories of people and individuals in particular, and because of their special vulnerability there is a heightened duty on the state when exercising due diligence to protect them.[70] In this regard the HRCttee has often focused on abuses aimed at women and girls and has required states to take particular measures to

---

[63]   *Ibid*, Principle 9.
[64]   *Ibid*, Principles 6 and 22.
[65]   CCPR General Comment no 36 (n 61 above), para 10.
[66]   *Ibid*.
[67]   See, e.g., Concluding Observations on the United States of America (2006) (CCPR/C/USA/3), para 30.
[68]   https://www.ohchr.org/EN/HRBodies/CCPR/Pages/GCArticle21.aspx
[69]   https://www.ohchr.org/Documents/HRBodies/CCPR/LLW_Guidance.pdf
[70]   See, e.g., Concluding Observations on Germany (2009) CCPR/C/DEU/CO/6, para 9.

prevent female genital mutilation,[71] and domestic violence.[72] States are, in addition, obliged to take appropriate legislative measures to ensure that criminal prosecution will follow domestic violence and marital rape[73] and that women are given adequate access to reproductive health services.

The state is also obliged to be mindful of the fact that foreigners on its soil may need additional protection, particularly where social pressures may be inflamed due to public sentiment. This principle applies, likewise, to endemic violence against ethnic and religious minorities.[74]

Punishment

Are the death penalty and corporal punishment, if provided for by domestic laws which comply with international standards, legitimate sanctions, which as a result fall outside the scope of what is covered by Article 7? The HRCttee appears to be leaning strongly in the direction of saying that the death penalty as such is a violation or Article 7, and holds the firm position that corporal punishment, at least if imposed by the courts, is also incompatible with that provision.

The death penalty
The HRCttee has not made a conclusive finding that the death penalty as such, in all its manifestations, constitutes a violation of Article 7. However, in 2018 the Committee published General Comment 36 on the right to life, which consolidates and carries forward the general opposition of the HRCttee to this form of punishment and requires states, at a minimum, to progressively abolish the death penalty. Although the General Comment focuses primarily on the right to life, it also engages in some detail with the Article 7 implications of the death penalty.

In the General Comment the HRCttee stops just short of saying the death penalty as such violates Article 7, but it makes its strong opposition to this form of punishment clear. According to the Committee 'considerable progress may have been made towards establishing an agreement among the States parties to consider the death penalty as a cruel, inhuman or degrading form of punishment. Such a legal development is consistent with the pro-abolitionist spirit of the Covenant.'[75]

Even in the limited number of instances where the death penalty may still be imposed by states in accordance with Article 6, it must be done in conformity with strict rules in order not to fall foul of various provisions of the ICCPR, including Article 7. General Comment 36 summarises the approach of the Committee as follows:

> States parties that have not abolished the death penalty must respect article 7 of the Covenant, which bars certain methods of execution. Failure to respect article 7 would inevitably render the execution

---

[71]   Concluding Observations on Cameroon (2017) CCPR/C/CMR/CO/5, para 19.

[72]   *Ibid*; Concluding Observations on the Democratic Republic of the Congo (2017) CRC/C/OPSC/COD/CO/1, para 17.

[73]   Concluding Observations on Cameroon (2017) CCPR/C/CMR/CO/5, para 19; Concluding Observations on the Democratic Republic of the Congo (2017) CRC/C/OPSC/COD/CO/1, para 17.

[74]   *Choudhary v. Canada* (CCPR/C/108/D/1898/2009); S.A.H. *v. Denmark* (Communication CCPR/C/121/D2419/2014).

[75]   General Comment no. 36 (2018) on Article 6 of the International Covenant on Civil and Political Rights, on the right to life, para 51.

arbitrary in nature and thus also in violation of article 6. The Committee has already opined that stoning, injection of untested lethal drugs, gas chambers, burning and burying alive, and public executions, are contrary to article 7. ... Failure to provide individuals on death row with timely notification about the date of their execution constitutes, as a rule, a form of ill-treatment, which renders the subsequent execution contrary to articles 7 of the Covenant. Extreme delays in the implementation of a death penalty sentence, which exceed any reasonable period of time necessary to exhaust all legal remedies, may also entail the violation of article 7 of the Covenant ...[76]

It is sometimes argued that, seen within the larger ICCPR context, there will always be a foothold for the retention of the death penalty, even if that foothold is narrow, because Article 6(2) provides as follows: 'In countries which have not abolished the death penalty, sentence of death may be imposed only for the most serious crimes ...' This implies that the death penalty may be used for the 'most serious crimes'. However, it should also be noted that Article 6(6) provides that 'Nothing in this Article shall be invoked to delay or prevent the abolition of the death penalty ...'. As a result, we would argue, a finding by the HRCttee that the death penalty as such violates Article 7 will mean that the Article 6(2) exception cannot save the death penalty, even for the most serious crimes.[77]

Corporal punishment
In General Comment 20, the HRCttee has stated that the prohibition in Article 7 extends to 'corporal punishment, including excessive chastisement ordered as punishment for a crime or as an educative or disciplinary measure'; and that in this regard 'Article 7 protects, in particular, children, pupils and patients in teaching and medical institutions'.[78] In *Higginson v. Jamaica* the HRCttee confirmed that the imposition of corporal punishment by the judicial process constitutes cruel, inhuman and degrading treatment or punishment contrary to Article 7.[79]

Given its approach not to require direct official involvement in a violation of Article 7, the question arises whether corporal punishment is also proscribed in the private, family sphere. The Committee has not pronounced itself firmly on this, but in 2007 it stated in concluding observations on Zambia that the state was required to 'prohibit all forms of violence against children wherever it occurs'.[80] Similarly, in its 2011 concluding observations on Iran the Committee expressed concern 'that corporal punishment of children is lawful in the home' and requested the state party to explicitly prohibit the use of corporal punishment in child rearing.[81]

---

[76]   *Ibid*, para 40.
[77]   See Heyns, C and Probert, T, 'Casting Fresh Light on the Supreme Right: The African Commission's General Comment no. 3 on the Right to Life' in Maluma, T, Du Plessis, M and Tladi, D, *The Pursuit of a Brave New World in International Law* (Brill Nijhoff, 2017).
[78]   CCPR General Comment no 20 (n 8 above), para 5.
[79]   *Higginson v. Jamaica* (CCPR/C74//D/792/1998), para 4.6.
[80]   Concluding Observations on Zambia (2007) CCPR/C/ZMB/CO/3, para 22.
[81]   Concluding Observations – on the Islamic Republic of Iran (2011) CCPR/C/IRN/CO/3, para 16. See also Concluding Observations on Mauritius (2017) CCPR/C/MUS/CO/5, para 23; Concluding Observations on Jamaica (2011) CCPR/C/JAM/CO/4, para 20.

The Impact of Article 7 Violations on Third Parties

Family members and others close to the victims of violence (e.g. torture or murder) may also be subjected to what may be termed secondary mental distress and suffering because of their exposure to the suffering of the victim, and thus be the victims of Article 7 violations in their own right. To this should be added the fact that a lack of investigations into allegations of harm done to a loved one, as outlined above, may also result in an Article 7 violation in respect of family members and others close to the victim. The same set of facts may underlie both kinds of violations.

In *Quinteros v. Uruguay*, for instance, the HRCttee found that the author was also the victim of an Article 7 violation in view of the anguish and distress caused by the disappearance and torture of her daughter, and the continuing uncertainty concerning her fate and whereabouts.[82]

According to the Committee's General Comment 36:

> The arbitrary deprivation of life of an individual may cause his or her relatives mental suffering, which could amount to a violation of their own rights under article 7 of the Covenant. Furthermore, even when the deprivation of life is not arbitrary, failure to provide relatives with information on the circumstances of the death of an individual may violate their rights under article 7, as could failure to inform them of the location of the body, and, where the death penalty is applied, of the date in which the carrying out of the death penalty is anticipated.[83]

In *Zakharenko v. Belarus*[84] the Committee found that the stress and emotional suffering caused by a failure to properly investigate the enforced disappearance of a family member violated Article 7. In this instance, the state had not only made no progress in the investigation but was also unable or unwilling to inform the relatives on the status of said investigation.

Removal to Another Country

The HRCttee, in General Comment 31, dealing with the general legal obligations placed on states by the Covenant, stated that Article 2 requires states

> not to extradite, deport, expel or otherwise remove a person from their territory, where there are substantial grounds for believing that there is a real risk of irreparable harm, such as contemplated by articles 6 and 7 of the Covenant, either in the country to which removal is to be effected or in any country to which the person may subsequently be removed.[85]

The threat may emanate from official sources or, under certain conditions, from members of the public where the state is unwilling or unable to protect the person concerned from such threat. Like the other obligations on states not to subject people to torture, this obligation is absolute and may not be balanced against other state interests such as national security.[86]

---

[82] *Quinteros v. Uruguay* (CCPR/C/19/D107/1981), para 14. See also, for instance, *Sharma et al. v. Nepal* (CCPR/C/122/D/2364/2014), para 9.11.

[83] CCPR General Comment no 31, The Nature of the General Legal Obligation Imposed on States Parties to the Covenant, (2004), CCPR/C/21/Rev.1/Add.13, para 51.

[84] *Zakharenko v. Belarus* (CCPR/C/119/D/2586/2015), para 7.4.

[85] CCPR General Comment no 31 (n 83 above) para 12.

[86] See e.g. *Israil v. Kazakhstan* (CCPR/C103/103/D/2024/2011), para 9.4.

In its General Comment 20, focusing on Article 7, the HRCttee stated that states parties 'must not expose individuals to the danger of torture or cruel, inhuman or degrading treatment or punishment upon return to another country by way of their extradition, expulsion or *refoulement*.'[87]

The question as far as Article 7 is concerned is not whether there are grounds to remove the person in question, but whether doing so, even if there are grounds, will amount to exposing the person to levels of ill treatment that will violate Article 7.

The agenda of the HRCttee, as far as communications concerning possible violations of Article 7 is concerned, is these days largely occupied by cases dealing with removals which may fall into this category. While under Article 3(1) of UNCAT the prohibition on such expulsions relates only to the risk of torture, the threshold for the ICCPR prohibition may be lower and cover the risk of other forms of ill treatment.[88]

The obligation on states not to remove people from their territory is subject to specific limits. The threat to those who are about to be transferred, as stated above, must rise to the level of being 'a real risk of irreparable harm' for a violation of Article 7 to occur. The HRCttee has stated that 'all relevant facts and circumstances must be considered, including the general human rights situation in the author's country of origin', and that 'there is a high threshold for providing substantial grounds to establish that a real risk of irreparable harm exists'. Moreover, the risk must be 'personal'.[89]

In general, membership of a particular group which is at risk in the country concerned is not enough.[90] However, the Committee did find a violation of Article 7 in *M.K.H. v. Denmark* as the author had demonstrated the risk he would be exposed to in Bangladesh due to his homosexuality.[91] It also found a violation of Article 7 in *Kaba v. Canada*, as it considered that a 15-year-old girl risked being subjected to female genital mutilation if deported to Guinea, given, among others, the particular circumstances regarding this practice in her own family and ethnic group.[92]

In cases where the person about to be removed faces crimes for which the death penalty may be imposed, the Committee has allowed such removal to happen based on diplomatic assurances that such a sentence will not be imposed. This is relatively easy to monitor, but the same does not apply to cases where there is a risk of torture and ill treatment. Monitoring is harder to do in such cases and the facts may be subject to contestation. As a result, the HRCttee tends not to place much weight on such assurances, requiring 'utmost care' in doing so, and pointing out that the more systematic the practice of torture and ill treatment is in a particular state, the less reliance can be placed on assurances.[93]

In *Maksudov et al v. Kyrgyzstan*, for instance, the Committee held that the procurement of assurances from the Uzbek General Prosecutor's Office, which, moreover, contained no

---

[87]   CCPR General Comment no 20 (n 8 above).
[88]   See, e.g., *Chitat Ng v. Canada* (CCPR/C/49/D/469/1991), para 16.4; *C. v. Australia* (CCPR/C/76/D/900/1999), para 8.5.
[89]   See, e.g. *S. v. Denmark* (CCPR/C/122/D/2642/2015).
[90]   See, e.g. *W.K. v. Canada* (CCPR/C/122/D/2292/2013); *A. and B. v Denmark* (CCPR/C/117/D/2291/2013); and *A. and B. v. Canada* (CCPR/C/117/D/2387/2014).
[91]   *M.K.H. v. Denmark* (CCPR/C/117/D2462/2014).
[92]   *Kaba v. Canada* (CCPR/C/92/D/1465/2006), para 10.2.
[93]   Concluding Observations of the Human Rights Committee: United States of America (2006) CCPR/C/USA/3 para 16. See also *Alzery v. Sweden* (n 58 above), para 11.5.

concrete mechanism for their enforcement, was insufficient to protect the authors against the risk of torture; and 'that at the very minimum, the assurances procured should contain such a monitoring mechanism and be safeguarded by arrangements made outside the text of the assurances themselves which would provide for their effective implementation'.[94]

Many of the cases involving extradition and *refoulement* currently reaching the Committee involve the so-called *Dublin Regulation*, currently in its third iteration,[95] the cornerstone in the European Union's common refugee agenda. In terms of this set of regulations, European states are permitted remove a foreign national from within their borders to the state deemed responsible for that person by virtue of having been the first state where the person sought asylum. In a range of cases, however, the Committee has held that such a transfer was not permitted because the person concerned would be likely to face a violation of Article 7 in that state.

In *Jasin v. Denmark*, for instance, the author was a single mother of three minor children, with health problems, who faced deportation to Italy as first country of asylum. She was dependent on medical support and claimed to have, in the past, faced extreme poverty, deprivation and a lack of medical care in Italy. The HRCttee held that Denmark had

> failed to devote sufficient analysis to the author's personal experience and to the foreseeable consequences of forcibly returning her to Italy. It [has] also failed to seek proper assurance from the Italian authorities that the author and her three minor children would be received in conditions compatible with their status as asylum seekers entitled to temporary protection and the guarantees under article 7 of the Covenant.[96]

The Committee often uses the *Jasin* case in its deliberations and views as a benchmark of how far it is willing to go in extending the protection of Article 7. In *YAA v. Denmark*, for instance, the Committee held that the deportation of the authors and their four very young children to Italy, where they had earlier faced serious hardship, would without assurances to the contrary amount to a violation of Article 7.[97]

However, the precedent of *Jasin* did not, for instance, extend far enough to cover a married couple with four children about to be returned to Bulgaria. The Committee held that:

> the fact that they may possibly be confronted with serious difficulties upon return ..., by itself does not necessarily mean that they would be in a special situation of vulnerability – and in a situation significantly different to many other refugee families – such as to conclude that their return to Bulgaria would constitute a violation of the State party's obligations under Article 7.'[98]

---

[94]   *Maksudov v. Kyrgyzstan* (CCPR/C/93/D/1461).
[95]   Regulation (EU) No 604/2013 of the European Parliament and of the Council of 26 June 2013 establishing the criteria and mechanisms for determining the Member State responsible for examining an application for international protection lodged in one of the Member States by a third-country national or a stateless person.
[96]   *Jasin v. Denmark* (CCPR/C114//D/2360/2014), para 8.9.
[97]   See *Y.A.A. v. Denmark* (CCPR/C/119/D/2681/2015), para 7.9; *A.A.I. and A.H.A. v. Denmark* (CCPR/C116//D/2402/2014) (inadmissibility); *Hashi v. Denmark* (CCPR/C/120/D/2470/2014 (no violation); *O.A. v. Denmark* (CCPR/C/121/D/2770/2016) (violation); *Hussein v. Denmark* (Communication no CCPR/C/124/D/2734/2016) (no violation).
[98]   *M.A.S. v. Denmark* (CCPR/C/121/D/2585/2015), para 8.12.

The Extraterritorial Application of Article 7

The quintessential example of the extraterritorial application of the prohibition on torture on states – holding them responsible even though such torture occurs outside their borders – is where the state has a detention facility abroad, for example during an armed conflict, and a detainee is mistreated. According to CAT, this is because the detainee is under the effective control of the state.[99]

There appears to be no direct case law on the point in the HRCttee. However, in *Hicks v. Australia* the Committee found that, because Australia did not have effective control over the author while he was detained in Guantanamo Bay by the United States of America, it precluded a finding that Australia had violated Article 7.[100] This implies that if there is such control, a violation could occur.

Medical Experimentation

The inclusion of the sentence covering medical experimentation in Article 7 was motivated by the general abhorrence of the atrocities committed during the Second World War by people such as Dr Mengele. While its relevance to the modern-day situation remains, the HRCttee has not often dealt with this issue.

The HRCttee has expressed disquiet on occasion in respect of medical experimentation carried out on minors and other persons with impaired capacity.[101] It has also expressed caution in respect of consent obtained from persons who, though not lacking in capacity, are generally vulnerable to coercion, such as incarcerated persons and the economically disadvantaged.[102]

Termination of Pregnancy

The HRCttee has determined that restrictive provisions relating to abortions may under certain circumstances constitute a violation of Article 7.[103] This principle applies *mutatis mutandis* in the case of forced abortions,[104] which have a similar effect upon the mother's physical and mental integrity.

In the 2016 landmark case of *Mellet v. Ireland*[105] the Committee dealt with a case where the author was informed by public medical authorities that the foetus had congenital defects and would die in utero or shortly after birth. Because of the prohibition on abortion in Ireland also under such circumstances her only option apart from carrying to term was to have a voluntary termination of pregnancy performed in a foreign country. She chose the latter option which turned out to be a traumatic experience, inter alia because this was done outside her support structures. The Committee found that this among other rights violated Article 7.

---

[99] CAT General Comment no 2 (n 12 above), para 16.
[100] *Hicks v. Australia* (CCPR/C/115/D/2005/2010), para 4.5.
[101] Concluding Observations of the Human Rights Committee Netherlands (2001) CCPR/CO/72/NET, para 7.
[102] Concluding Observations on the United States of America (2014) CCPR/C/USA/CO/4, para 31.
[103] Concluding Observations on Peru (2000) CCPR/CO/70/PER, para 20.
[104] See e.g. Concluding Observations on Jordan (2017) CCPR/C/JOR/CO/5, para 21.
[105] *Mellet v. Ireland* (CCPR/C/116/D/ 2324/2013). See also *Llantoy Huamán v. Peru* (CCPR/C/85/D/1153/2003), para 6.3.

The HRCttee has subsequently set out its position on the termination of pregnancy in a comprehensive way in General Comment 36. Paragraph 8 provides as follows:

> Although States parties may adopt measures designed to regulate voluntary terminations of pregnancy, such measures must not result in violation of the right to life of a pregnant woman or girl, or her other rights under the Covenant. Thus, restrictions on the ability of women or girls to seek abortion must not, inter alia, jeopardize their lives, subject them to physical or mental pain or suffering which violates article 7, discriminate against them or arbitrarily interfere with their privacy.

Exclusion of Evidence

Since torture and other ill treatment is often aimed at obtaining confessions or information to be used to support criminal proceedings, a powerful way of countering such practices is to prohibit the use of such information in a court of law. Hence, in General Comment 20 the HRCttee recognises that 'It is important for the discouragement of violations under Article 7 that the law must prohibit the use or admissibility in judicial proceedings of statements or confessions obtained through torture or other prohibited treatment.'[106] The Committee has endorsed and applied this approach in a number of views and concluding observations.[107]

PROVING TORTURE AND ILL TREATMENT IN THE HUMAN RIGHTS COMMITTEE

The success or failure of many communications to the HRCttee as far as violations of Article 7 are concerned, turn on an assessment of the facts, not the law. States will rarely defend torture, but they often deny that what is alleged had occurred, or that they are the responsible parties. Moreover, an alleged act of torture or ill treatment invariably takes place behind closed doors. As a result, it becomes important to take note of how the Committee deals with evidentiary matters, and who it believes when there is uncertainty about the facts.

Burden of Proof

It would seem that the HRCttee does not impose any technical or strict rules with regard to the burden of proof in the cases involving individual communications brought before it. In general, there is the requirement that whoever alleges must prove it, and the standard of proof is a balance of probabilities.

At the same time, it is clear that the state is responsible for the security of all persons held in detention, and that, in Article 7 cases, it often has superior access to evidence about what transpired in places of custody, and is expected to make that evidence available, and carries at least part of the burden of proof.[108] The HRCttee regularly quotes its own statement in *Bleier v. Uruguay* in this context:

---

[106] CCPR General Comment no 20 (n 8 above), para 12.
[107] See, for instance *Bazarov v. Uzbekistan* (CCPR/C/87/D/959/2000).
[108] *M.T. v. Uzbekistan* (CCPR/C/114/D/2234/2013), paras 7.3 and 7.4.

With regard to the burden of proof, this cannot rest alone on the author of the communication, especially considering that the author and the State party do not always have equal access to the evidence and that frequently the State party alone has access to relevant information. It is implicit in article 4(2) of the Optional Protocol that the State party has the duty to investigate in good faith all allegations of violation of the Covenant made against it and its authorities, especially when such allegations are corroborated by evidence submitted by the author of the communication, and to furnish to the Committee the information available to it. In cases where the author has submitted to the Committee allegations supported by substantial witness testimony, as in this case, and where further clarification of the case depends on information exclusively in the hands of the State party, the Committee may consider such allegations as substantiated in the absence of satisfactory evidence and explanations to the contrary submitted by the State party.[109]

Such a situation may arise where the state is unwilling to present the relevant evidence, but also where it is unable to do so, because it failed to keep proper records at the time when the author of a communication was detained.

The HRCttee is often confronted with cases where state parties fail to respond during the process before the Committee to allegations of torture or ill treatment, or to accusations of a lack of investigations into such allegations. This may be because the states are unwilling to present evidence to rebut these allegations, but also because they simply do not have the information because the necessary investigations had not been done at the time. In both instances the consequences are the same – an adverse finding against the state. Depending on the facts alleged by the author, such an approach may result in a finding of a violation of Article 7 on its own, or of Article 7 as read with Article 2(3), or both.

What is to be done if the author of a communication does not make specific allegations about having been subjected to prison conditions which violate Article 10, but merely states in general terms that the conditions of detention were unacceptable, and in support refers to NGO or other reports? In *Bailey v. Jamaica*[110] the majority found that the author who simply cited external reports in his communication had failed to substantiate his claim. Given the fact that what is at stake is an individual complaint, not a state report, this is probably the right approach.

Deference to State Authorities on the Assessment of Facts

In addition to the issue of the burden of proof, as discussed above, there is the question of which institution's understanding of the facts should be given preference – that of the local courts or similar institutions, or the HRCttee. The HRCttee generally follows the approach that it will not substitute its own judgement on the facts for that of domestic procedures, because it is not well placed to make such assessments.[111] Only where the proceedings were arbitrary or manifestly unreasonable or amounted to a denial of justice will the Committee depart from

---

[109]   *Bleier v. Uruguay* (CCPR/C/15/D/30/1978), para 13.3. See also *Mukong v. Cameroon* (n 40 above), para 9; *Al Khazmi v. Libya* (CCPR/C/108/D/1832/2008), para 8.2.

[110]   *Staselovich v. Belarus* (CCPR/C/77/D/887/1999).

[111]   See, for instance, the HRCttee's reluctance to overrule a finding by a domestic court in *Singh v. Canada* (CCPR/C/86/D1315/2004). Also see *Pillai et al. v. Canada* (CCPR/C/101/D/1763/2008), para. 11.4; and *Lin v. Australia* (CCPR/C/107/D/1957/2010), para 9.3.

it.[112] The Committee – like other international bodies – does not see itself as 'a fourth instance, competent to re-evaluate findings of fact'.[113]

The Committee has in a number of deportation cases for example found that the local authorities had a proper system in place to make risk assessments, that the author has not demonstrated a denial of justice, and hence there was no violation.[114] While the test is consistently recognised, on occasion Committee members disagree on whether they are in fact serving as a 'fourth instance'.[115]

It seems particularly important that the Committee will continue not to substitute too easily its own judgement for that of the bodies closer to the ground. The Committee, meeting in Geneva, with only limited exposure to the evidence, is not well placed to make the final call on that front and to assume such responsibility.

CONCLUSION

The Human Rights Committee has developed a rich and coherent jurisprudence about torture and cruel, inhuman or degrading treatment or punishment. It serves an important role in countering such conduct. At the same time, it should be recognised that the Committee is only one of a wide range of role players who deal with this issue, and a full understanding of its work can only be gleaned when it is seen within this broader context.

The Committee serves and will continue to serve an important function especially as far as norm determination is concerned. It is well placed to do this, and to determine what the legal standards are in a way that sets the tone worldwide, in a time when global norms change, when the authority of the international human rights system is under pressure and new technologies present new challenges. Where the Committee is not as well placed is to determine what the facts are.

The Committee generally takes a careful approach in determining that conduct should be branded as torture or other ill treatment. This is to be welcomed. Only serious cases, about which the facts are established with a high degree of certainty, should be placed in the first category. As has been said, if everything is torture, nothing is torture. But where the Committee finds that conduct falls within the category of torture or ill treatment, the message must go out that a serious violation has occurred.

---

[112] *Omo-Amenaghawon v. Denmark* (CCPR/C/114/D/2288/2013).
[113] *Arenz v. Germany* (CCPR/D/80/D/1138/2002), para 8.6.
[114] See e.g. *M.A. v. Denmark* (CCPR/C/119/D/2240/2013), para 7.7 and *Contreras v. Canada* (CCPR/C/119/D/2613/2015).
[115] See e.g. *M.S. v. Denmark* (CCPR/C/120/D/2601/2015).

7. The Committee Against Torture: implementing the prohibition against torture

Felice Gaer

INTRODUCTION: A COMMITTEE TO MONITOR HOW STATES PREVENT TORTURE AND ILL-TREATMENT

The 1984 Convention against Torture and other cruel, inhuman or degrading treatment or punishment (hereafter "the Convention" or "UNCAT") sets out a number of obligations of States parties to achieve the Convention's aims. Recognizing that torture was already prohibited in international law, the Convention calls upon States parties to "take effective legislative, administrative, judicial or other measures to prevent" acts of torture and other forms of ill-treatment.[1] Key drafters of the Convention recall that "The principal aim of the Convention is to strengthen the existing prohibition of [torture and ill-treatment] … by a number of supportive measures." Many such measures are set out in articles 2–16 of the Convention but many are not specified in this way. However, a key element of the Convention is its emphasis on the absolute prohibition against torture. It is the grave nature of the crime of torture that has itself led to a special, separate human rights treaty to be established in the first place.

To maintain some scrutiny over whether the undertakings to prevent and punish torture as set forth in the Convention were being implemented by States parties, the Convention mandates the establishment of an entity named "The Committee Against Torture" (hereafter "CAT" or "the Committee"), a 10-person body of "experts of high moral standing and recognized competence in the field of human rights, who shall serve in their personal capacity." The Committee is called upon to "carry out the functions" set forth in the treaty to implement the substantive provisions of the Convention.[2] This mechanism resembles those of other UN human rights treaty monitoring bodies, except the CAT committee is smaller. Neither in the Convention nor other deliberations did the States parties that drafted and adopted the Convention define what threshold would amount to "effective" measures.

In its 30 years of activity, the reporting procedure specified in article 19 of the Convention has been actively used because there are a growing number – presently 168 – of States parties to the Convention, all of whom are required to submit an initial report and subsequent periodic reports.[3] During these years, the Committee, which is authorized by article 18 of the

---

[1] Convention against Torture and Other Cruel, Inhuman or Degrading Treatment or Punishment (adopted 10 December 1984, entered into force 26 June 1987) 1465 UNTS 85, Article 2. See also Burgers, JH and Danelius, H, *The United Nations Convention against Torture: A Handbook on the Convention against Torture and Other Cruel, Inhuman or Degrading Treatment or Punishment* (Martinus Nijhoff, 1988), 1.

[2] Convention against Torture (n 1 above), article 17.

[3] Report of the Committee against Torture, UN Doc A/74/44, para 1. The report covers activities until May 17, 2019. By the end of September 2019 there were two additional States parties to the Convention, Kiribati and Grenada.

Convention to "establish its own rules of procedure,"[4] has developed, revised and refined the rules as it learns what States parties are doing to prevent acts of torture and ill-treatment. In its concluding observations, the Committee articulates its understanding of what constitutes effective measures.[5]

While the Committee against Torture was provided with more authority and tools to bring about compliance with the prohibition against torture than other UN human rights treaty bodies at the time it was established, it was not always obvious that the Convention would be more than hortative. Moreover, it was not clear initially that any new implementation body would be established at all. The first requests of the UN General Assembly (UNGA) to the Commission on Human Rights to draft a treaty against torture did not make "any reference to the possibility that the Convention might incorporate measures of implementation."[6] This changed, however, when UNGA responded positively to the language added to a resolution adopted at the 6th UN Congress on Crime Prevention which specifically requested UNGA to ask the Commission on Human Rights to "examine all the proposals that would ensure the effective application of the convention against torture."[7] UNGA thus began a drafting process calling for "provisions for the effective implementation of the future convention."[8]

At issue was the question of what kind of implementation mechanisms might, in fact, advance the Convention's aims. When the Working Group charged with drafting the Convention against Torture convened (under the auspices of the Commission on Human Rights) after being prodded by UNGA to include an implementation proposal, several suggestions were made. Three types of issues arose in these deliberations: first, if there was to be "effective application" of the Convention, what kinds of assessment of compliance or violations of the Convention should take place; secondly, who should carry out monitoring compliance and offering technical advice, and under whose authorization; and finally, whether the procedure(s) established would be required of every State party or only those that opt in voluntarily.

Though many issues were considered, in the end, the primary implementation mechanism that was proposed for the Convention was the submission of State party reports on the measures taken to prevent and punish torture and ill-treatment. As with other human rights treaties, there were also proposals to permit complaints from State parties about other states; and complaints from individuals about violations of the Convention domestically.

To these familiar mechanisms, the drafters also added a new implementation procedure: a special "inquiry" into allegations of "systematic torture" to be conducted through on-site visits by members of the Committee to a country, based on confidential interaction with officials from the State party concerned about the findings of those visits. The inquiry consists of a mixture of fact-finding and technical assistance, taking place through discussions with the State party concerned, and occasional deliberations by the members of the Committee.

---

[4]   Convention against Torture (n 1 above), article 18(2).
[5]   See UN Doc CAT/C/GC/2, 24 January 2008, General Comment 2: Implementation of article 2 by States parties, para 12.
[6]   Rodley, NS, *The Treatment of Prisoners under International Law*, 2nd edn (Oxford University Press, 1999), 150.
[7]   See A/CONF.87/14/Rev.1, Sixth United Nations Congress on the Prevention of Crime and the Treatment of Offenders, Caracas, Venezuela, 25 August–5 September 1980, Resolution 11, para 3.
[8]   UNGA Res 35/178 cited in Rodley (n 6 above), 150.

All four – periodic reports, an inquiry procedure, individual complaints, and state-to-state complaints – were thus included in the final text of the Convention.

The review of periodic reports today not only provides for concluding observations to be issued following a dialogue in which Committee members and representatives of the State party engage in a dialogue about each report, but also establishes a follow-up procedure. Through it, the Committee identifies a few recommendations in its concluding observations for scrutiny after one year, and offers an optional "simplified reporting procedure." Use of a "List of Issues Prior to Reporting" (LOIPR) to States parties aims to focus the topics to be included, and reviewed, in the next periodic report.

Observers ask whether these reports and procedures result in compliance with the Convention. To date, academic studies on impact have been inconclusive, although scholars and advocates have presented a variety of examples of direct impacts from the reporting procedure and recommendations. These studies also raise questions about the effectiveness of the treaty body system as a whole.[9] They ask, in various ways, whether the Convention and the Committee which monitors it have eradicated – or prevented – torture and ensured that its perpetrators are punished. While academic observers, Hathaway and Vreeland, are quite skeptical about the results of the CAT treaty, others like Creamer and Simmons, as well as Goodman and Jinks, have been able to identify patterns of learning and action that they consider effective and able to produce positive results.

This chapter explores ways in which the Committee has advanced efforts to combat torture and ill-treatment, noting that it has conveyed the urgency of preventing torture to government officials, but not the actual eradication of abusive practices. After reviewing each of the bureaucratic mechanisms created for oversight of State compliance with the Convention, the chapter points out the serious limitations placed by States parties on the Committee's capacity to prevent torture and hold responsible actors to account, including through both the review of periodic reports and its new inquiry procedure. The chapter discusses an example of how both a State party under scrutiny and the Committee have changed in their approaches to assessing compliance, and then considers measures the Committee has identified as "effective" and how its understanding of these has been changed by experience.

EARLY PROPOSALS AND ARGUMENTS ABOUT MONITORING COMPLIANCE

There were several proposals about who would review and decide on how to assess compliance with these four mechanisms: one idea was to assign responsibility to an already existing treaty monitoring mechanism (the Human Rights Committee), whereas others proposed creating a new expert treaty body. Still others wanted to assign responsibility to a political

---

   9   See e.g., Inglese, C, "The Committee Against Torture: One Step Forward, One Step Back" (2000) 18 *Netherlands Quarterly of Human Rights* 307; Vreeland, JR, "Political Institutions and Human Rights: Why Dictatorships Enter into the UN Convention against Torture" (2008) 62 *International Organization* 65; Kelly, T, "The UN Committee Against Torture: Human Rights Monitoring and the Legal Recognition of Cruelty" (2009) 31 *Human Rights Quarterly* 777; Hathaway, O, Nowlan, A and Spiegel, J, "Tortured Reasoning: The Intent to Torture under International and Domestic Law" (2011) 52 *Va. J. Intl. L* 791; Creamer, CD and Simmons, BA, "Do Self-Reporting Regimes Matter? Evidence from the Convention against Torture" (2019) 63 *International Studies Quarterly* 1051.

body like the Commission on Human Rights. Initially, the Swedish delegation proposed that State parties should submit periodic reports on compliance, entrusting review of the reports to the Human Rights Committee which reviewed reports under the International Covenant on Civil and Political Rights (ICCPR).[10] Because of a proliferation of human rights treaties and monitoring mechanisms, there was concern that the new treaty would create yet another such entity. Assigning implementation of the new treaty to the Human Rights Committee could possibly avoid further proliferation of monitoring bodies, different interpretations of the treaty provisions and unnecessary costs. The Swedes also proposed establishing two complaint procedures, involving petitions by individuals or by states.[11]

Dutch representatives proposed that an entirely new monitoring committee should be created and, noting Costa Rica's separate proposal to create a visiting committee, suggested that the new treaty's expert committee be authorized to conduct fact-finding visits to places of detention on a confidential basis.[12]

As these alternatives were being studied, the UN's Legal Counsel cautioned that the "legal validity" of the plan to ask the Human Rights Committee to monitor the new Convention could be challenged because it would modify the terms of the ICCPR which had established the Human Rights Committee.[13] States parties argued over whether a new body should be created at all,[14] but a preference emerged to establish a new international body of experts.[15] Although small, it would be responsible for the four distinct procedures provided for in the Convention.

The authority conferred by the Convention against Torture, in article 17 and thereafter, does not provide any actual assurances of enforcement. The Convention itself merely creates an expert committee with the authority to review or monitor reports, to request new reports, and to implement or monitor certain optional procedures, including inquiries into systematic torture and individual complaints.[16] Thus, the authority provided to the Committee against Torture is for oversight, but not necessarily for corrective measures to be introduced or for accountability for violations of the Convention's obligations. The challenge faced by the Committee, therefore, is to be effective in preventing torture without having any real executive capacity to implement its views. As a result, much depends upon the knowledge and skill of the individual members of the Committee to probe effectively into what each State party has done regarding specific laws, policies and individual cases, and upon the information provided by States parties in their reports, as well as the willingness of each State Party to take effective measures to eradicate torture and ill-treatment, including the measures recommended by the Committee. In practice, the Committee members benefit greatly from information provided by non-governmental organizations, as well as that developed by national human rights

---

[10]   Burgers and Danelius (n 1 above), 74–77.
[11]   *Ibid.*
[12]   *Ibid,* 75. The visiting committee idea was later enshrined in the Optional Protocol to the CAT.
[13]   *Ibid,* 76.
[14]   *Ibid,* 76–77.
[15]   *Ibid,* 86–89.
[16]   The Convention references "communications" in Articles 21 and 22, but the Committee has adopted the term "complaint" for such documents. It uses this term in its Rules of Procedure (UN Doc CAT/C/3/Rev 6), e.g., in rules 103–104, 109–113. At one point the Committee also referred to these communications as "petitions" in accordance with the terminology of the Office of the High Commissioner for Human Rights.

mechanisms and other UN and regional human rights bodies with overlapping jurisdictions and mandates.

MEMBERSHIP OF THE COMMITTEE

The Convention provides that 10 members be elected to the Committee for a four-year term,[17] and that consideration be given to "equitable geographic distribution" and "the participation of some persons having legal experience."[18] From 1988 to the present, experts have been elected to serve on the Committee – but they have come from just 30 different countries.[19] There has been representation from all geographic regions[20] – with two exceptions, in 1992, when there was no Asian member elected, and 2009, when no East European member was elected. Generally, there has been a low proportion of representatives from Asian states and a high representation of experts from the Western European and Other States Group (WEOG) countries. Initially, this seemed to reflect the higher proportion of ratifying states from the WEOG region, but today, with 168 States parties, there is no longer such an imbalance. It is noteworthy that experts have largely come from the same prominent States – for example, Senegalese experts have served more often than other Africans, and, similarly, China, Chile, Russia, and Denmark have served more often on the CAT from their regional groups than experts from other countries in each of the UN regional groups during the past 30 years.

Lawyers and jurists have most commonly been elected as Committee members; a fair number of Committee members were/are serving or former diplomats. Because of special provisions in the Convention about redress and reparation to victims of torture, as well as the need to understand the dimensions of both physical and psychological torture, having medical expertise on the Committee alongside lawyers and judges was recognized by States parties as important. The repeated election of medically trained professionals with experience in treating torture victims (physicians from Denmark, and a clinical psychologist from Norway) made this a reality.

The Convention is silent on the issue of gender balance, but the trends merit note: Until 2005, there was an overwhelming preponderance of male members of CAT (male to female proportions being 8–2, 10–0, and 9–1 until 2005). There were no female members at all during 1992–94 and 1998–2000. In 2005, the Committee membership was seven males and three females; in 2007, six males and four females. The Committee has maintained three or four

---

[17]   Convention against Torture (n 1 above), article 17(5).
[18]   *Ibid*, article 17(1).
[19]   If one considers the USSR as distinct from its successor state, the Russian Federation, there have been experts elected since 1988 to 2019 from 31 States parties. These States include, by region, Africa (Cameroon, Egypt, Mauritius, Morocco, Senegal, Tunisia); Asia (China, Cyprus, Nepal, Philippines); Eastern Europe (Bulgaria, Georgia, Moldova, Slovenia, USSR/Russian Federation); Latin America (Argentina, Chile, Ecuador, Mexico, Uruguay) and Western Europe and Others (Canada, Denmark, France, Greece, Italy, Norway, Portugal, Spain, Switzerland, United States).
[20]   The United Nations has established five regional groups of States, for electoral and other purposes. See https://www.un.org/depts/DGACM/RegionalGroups.shtml

female members ever since.[21] The Committee's attention to gender-based violence amounting to a violation of the Convention expanded with the increase in gender diversity.

Achievements of an oversight committee like CAT depend in large measure on the skills and actions of the members of the Committee itself. Their expertise and their independence from the States that have nominated and elected them to the Committee are key determinants of the impact of their actions. In recent years, non-governmental organizations have begun to submit questionnaires to the candidates for election to the CAT Committee, which are then posted on a public website. While only States parties can nominate or vote in elections of the Committee members, this public airing of the visions and skills of the candidates is a promising development in working to ensure election of the most qualified candidates.

ASSESSING COMPLIANCE: STATE REPORTS

Article 19 of the Convention requires all State parties to submit periodic reports on compliance for review by the Committee, and article 22 permits States parties to opt into procedures for examining complaints from individuals (and, if article 21 is ever used, from other States parties) alleging failure to carry out the undertakings in the Convention. However, the drafters of the Convention also added two new provisions: the first, in article 20, permits the Committee to initiate an inquiry into alleged "systematic" torture which could involve an investigative visit to the country concerned, unless a State party opts out of this procedure,[22] which is aimed at addressing the most severe violations of the Convention. The second provision, set out in article 19, specifically authorizes the CAT to make such "general comments on the [periodic] report" as it deemed necessary, which encouraged the Committee to offer individualized assessments and recommendations about each State party's report. The authority to make such country-specific observations and recommendations was not explicit nor agreed to in the other treaty bodies existing at that time.

Article 19 requires all States parties to submit periodic reports "on the measures they have taken to give effect to their undertakings under this Convention." The reports are due one year after the Convention comes into force and then again every four years or when the Committee requests.[23]

Most of the Committee's official meeting time in fact has been devoted to the review and assessment of such reports from State parties. From 1989 until 17 May 2019, the Committee had received 448 reports from State parties and completed the review of 426 following a series of "constructive dialogues."[24] Non-reporting and late reporting have been common. According

---

[21]   The author considers that this change in gender composition can be correlated with the Committee's enhanced attention to abuses affecting women in detention, gender-based violence and related issues. See for example, Gaer, F, "Rape as a Form of Torture: The Experience of the Committee against Torture" (2012) 15 *CUNY Law Review* 1111. For more on the composition and election of the Committee members, see Byrnes, A, "The Committee Against Torture", in Alston, P, *The United Nations and Human Rights: A Critical Appraisal* (Oxford University Press, 1992), 511 and Carraro, V, "Electing the Experts: Expertise and Independence in the UN Human Rights Treaty Bodies" (2019) 25 *European Journal of International Relations* 826.

[22]   Convention against Torture (n 1 above), article 20.

[23]   *Ibid*, article 19.

[24]   UN Doc A/74/44, para 22.

to one scholarly analysis, as of 2012, only 6 percent of reports have been submitted on or before their due dates (deadlines), and as many as 20.8 percent were submitted more than five years late.[25] European states reportedly have the highest reporting rates, and African and South Asian states the poorest.[26]

According to CAT's Secretariat, as of September 2019, 25 of the Convention's 166 State parties had never submitted any periodic report.[27] Moreover, there were 12 overdue initial reports that were more than 10 years late in their presentation,[28] only two of which are from countries located outside the African continent.[29] There is no penalty for late submission of a report, nor for non-submission of an initial report, other than that the Committee will publicly "note" a report's lateness in its concluding comments after it has publicly reviewed it. The Committee has begun to review countries that have grossly overdue first reports by conducting a review with or without the State party being present.[30]

Scholars have confirmed what Committee members have experienced: that the quality and timeliness of reports submitted to CAT is heavily influenced by the degree of human rights commitment of the State party concerned (with more committed and active states submitting more complete reports in a more timely manner), the institutional capacity of the State party and, significantly, whether it has a national human rights institution and active non-governmental organizations on the treaty topics. Practices of neighboring countries are also influential.[31]

The Committee itself has recognized in practice that non-governmental organizations (NGOs) and independent national institutions provide important data and insights into the issue of implementation of the Convention.[32] It therefore invites NGOs, in advance of the interactive exchange with the representatives of the State party, to submit documentation and to meet privately with Committee members in advance of each review. It also invites representatives of national human rights institutions, as well as persons from national preventive mechanisms created under the Optional Protocol to the Convention, to separate in-session private discussions with the Committee.

---

[25] Creamer, CD, and Simmons, BA, "Ratification, Reporting and Rights: Quality of Participation in the Convention against Torture" (2015) 37 *Human Rights Quarterly* 579, 586.

[26] *Ibid.*

[27] Status of reports as at 13 September 2019, provided by CAT Secretariat to author. Also see earlier data tables in UN Doc HRI/MC/2018/2, 23 March 2018, para 11. There are currently 168 State parties.

[28] *Ibid.* See also UN Doc HRI/MC/2018/2, 23 March 2018, Table 7, which had identified 16 States with reports overdue by 10 years or more, suggesting some progress is being made.

[29] As of Sept 13, 2019, initial reports are overdue from St. Vincent (due 2002) and San Marino (due 2007); the others that are overdue are from the following States parties in Africa: Somalia (due 1991), Malawi (1997), Côte d'Ivoire (1997), Mali (2000), Botswana (2001), Lesotho (2002), Nigeria (2002), Equatorial Guinea (2003), Liberia (2005), and Eswatini (2005).

[30] So far, fewer than a handful of such states have been reviewed in the absence of a report – Cape Verde, Antigua and Barbuda. While Seychelles was scheduled for such a review, it submitted a report two days before the scheduled dialogue. Seychelles then arranged for its delegation to participate by video link. This was the Committee's first experience with such a virtual dialogue. Bangladesh, scheduled for a review without a report on July 30, 2019, submitted its report just a week before the actual review, and sent a large delegation to Geneva headed by its Minister of Law.

[31] Creamer and Simmons (n 25 above), 607–608.

[32] For more on this, see Gaer, FD, "Implementing International Human Rights Norms: UN Human Rights Treaty Bodies and NGOs" (2003) 2 *Journal of Human Rights* 339.

The actual review of a State party's report has consisted of the State party's representatives traveling to Geneva to discuss the report in person with Committee members in what is called a "constructive dialogue." Two Committee members are given a leading role in the questioning to serve as "co-rapporteurs." In a six-hour procedure over two days, officials are subjected to a barrage of questions – often hundreds of them – about their reports. State party representatives present answers and Committee members seek additional clarifications as needed, and as time permits.

As explained already, when a second or subsequent report is submitted (called a periodic report), the Committee attempts to focus the review further by preparing either a "List of Issues" to guide discussion of the report submitted, or, in an optional procedure called the "simplified reporting procedure," composing a "List of Issues Prior to Reporting," the replies to which serve as the State party's report.

After the "constructive dialogue" between government representatives and members of the Committee ends, Committee members review and adopt "Concluding Observations" – essentially a balance sheet that sets out positive measures along with Committee concerns, and recommendations to the State party under review. These constitute "general comments on the report ..." as set out in article 19. As noted earlier, CAT was the first and only treaty body assigned this specific responsibility when the treaty was adopted; today all the treaty bodies prepare concluding observations.[33]

These conclusions and recommendations are themselves the principal means through which the Committee advises States parties on the "effective legislative, judicial, administrative and other measures"[34] needed to prevent torture and ill-treatment, and to bring their laws and practice into compliance with the obligations of the Convention.[35]

In practice, in its review of initial reports and subsequent submissions, the Committee often dwells on whether a State party has defined torture in accordance with the Convention, and whether it is a separate crime in the State party as article 4 of the Convention requires. This is aimed at "alerting everyone, including perpetrators, victims and the public, to the special gravity of the crime of torture."[36] Such codification itself can facilitate other "effective" measures, such as the need for appropriate punishment, the need to strengthen the deterrent effect of the Convention, and ways to enhance the ability of responsible officials to monitor

---

[33]   When CAT began, it initially published summaries of the questions raised and the government replies in its annual report; however, after 1993 it began to issue conclusions as stand-alone decisions consisting of a page or two of positive measures, concerns and recommendations. Initially, these were read out in a public meeting 48 hours after the review with the State's representatives present. Later, CAT began to issue all the concluding observations together at the very end of the session (the time saved was used to hear from NGOs prior to country reports). The observations adopted since 1993 have tended to be much longer and more detailed regarding CAT's specific concerns and the actions it urged the State party to implement to respect the Convention's obligations than those contained in the earlier conclusions which largely used summary language from the Convention itself.

[34]   Convention against Torture, articles 2(1) and 16.

[35]   At its first review of country reports, CAT members asked questions, article by article, of seven states and commended some of them for "model" reports (Sweden, Mexico) and pressed others (Egypt, Philippines) for answers they either did not provide or on which they needed to take specific ameliorative action (see UN Doc A/44/46). This practice of reviewing initial and periodic reports by posing questions and awaiting further answers has continued, with some refinement, in the hundreds of reports received and examined since.

[36]   CAT General Comment No 2 (n 5 above) para 11.

and prosecute torture. A well-crafted law criminalizing torture can also enable the public to monitor and challenge State action or inaction in violation of the Convention.[37]

Many countries argue that crimes with different definitions than that specified in article 1 are adequate for meeting their obligations under the Convention; by and large, the Committee does not accept such argumentation, because discrepancies in the definition can "create actual or potential loopholes for impunity."[38] CAT routinely presses for codification of the crime of torture in conformity with all of the elements of the definition in article 1. Similarly, it routinely calls on States parties to uphold their obligations to implement the undertakings in the other articles of the Convention as well. Concluding comments which were 2–3 pages in length in the Committee's first decade now can run as long as 15–20 pages, depending on the Committee's findings. A compilation of the Committee's conclusions and recommendations for 58 States parties reporting to it between 1993 and 1998 reveals the brevity and generality of the concerns expressed: 52 of the 85 reports received during that period were cited for between two and five concerns; only four had nine or more concerns cited, with 11 being the maximum.[39] By comparison, at the 67th session of CAT in 2019, four countries were reviewed, with between 16 and 21 concerns cited in the Conclusions of each country.[40] The Committee reviews about 16 periodic reports annually at present.

SPECIAL REPORTS

States are also required by article 19 to submit "such other reports as the Committee may request." The Committee has used this power sparingly. In April 1990, because there were so many inadequacies in China's report – submitted within six months of the Tiananmen Square crackdown – the Committee asked for a "supplementary report," which China provided in October 1992.[41] A few years later, in November 1996, the Committee requested a "special report" from Israel and in February 1997 Israel's government submitted its report responding to concerns about decisions of Israel's Supreme Court.[42]

In November 2011 the Committee again requested a special report – this time from Syria about widespread violations of the Convention that followed the Committee's concluding observations after Syria's initial report to the Committee.[43] Syria challenged the Committee's authority to request this, claiming it amounted to a double standard. Although the Committee clarified the basis of its authority and persuasively outlined extensive allegations concerning torture and ill-treatment that prompted it, Syrian officials refused to participate in a public dis-

---

[37]   *Ibid.*
[38]   *Ibid*, para 9.
[39]   Holmstrom, L (ed), *Conclusions and Recommendations of the UN Committee against Torture* (Martinus Nijhoff, 2000).
[40]   See CAT website https://tbinternet.ohchr.org/_layouts/15/treatybodyexternal/SessionDetails1 .aspx?SessionID=1293&Lang=en
[41]   Report of the Committee against Torture, UN Doc A/45/44 (June 21, 2990), paras 471–502; see also UN Doc CAT/C/SR.51, paras 49, 51; and UN Doc. CAT/C/7/Add.14 (18 January 1993); and Gaer, FD, "International Human Rights Scrutiny of China's Treatment of Human Rights Lawyers and Defenders: The Committee against Torture" (2018) 41 *Fordham International Law Journal* 1169.
[42]   CAT/C/SR.297/Add.1 4 September 1997, para 2.
[43]   CAT/C/SYR/CO/1.

cussion of the requested report[44] or to send a special report, or to respond to the Committee's demand that Syria "cease its clear breach of the obligations of the Convention."[45] Both in a public meeting and in correspondence posted on its website, the Committee aired concern over the grave situation, raising public awareness of the problems, and drawing attention to its severity, using its authority under article 19 and the follow-up procedure. But despite the severity of the abuses reported about Syria at that time, the CAT Committee did not obtain any answers from the Syrian government nor an end to the widespread abuses that prompted its request for the special report. This exercise reveals starkly the lack of enforcement powers of the Committee in the face of a State party engaged in extensive violations of the Convention and unwilling to cooperate with the international oversight body. It sharply reveals the limitations CAT faces in calling for compliance when its only formal action is to send letters of reminder to States parties that simply refuse to cooperate.

Subsequent requests for an additional report from Turkey following a crackdown accompanied by extensive reports of torture and ill-treatment in response to a failed *coup d'état* just weeks after the CAT review of Turkey's periodic report, initially produced some information together with promises of more details which were not provided. Again, the Committee tried to be more active in response to a reportedly grave situation, but the result it obtained was meager. This too reveals how little capacity the Committee possesses to enforce the norms it is supposed to guard.

FOLLOW-UP REPORTING

The lack of responsiveness – and effectiveness – regarding a special report from Syria was hardly the first frustrating encounter by the Committee. In 2003, after almost 15 years of reviewing State party reports, and 10 years of issuing formal conclusions, CAT Committee members were increasingly asking one another what has been the result of all these reviews? Concern over the slow pace of reviews and the apparent lack of implementation of their recommendations led CAT members to establish a formal follow-up procedure for article 19 reports, using its authority to seek "other reports" and to determine its own rules of procedure. At the simplest level, the follow-up procedure offers another means of seeking added information, especially when a crisis situation is reported. It facilitates more active engagement with each State party to the Convention as well. Through its follow-up procedure, which has been modified a number of times since 2003, the Committee has evaluated and often rigorously questioned information submitted by governments, with the goal of seeing genuine and prompt implementation of at least three of its recommendations for each State party.

At the end of the Committee's review of each State party report under article 19, several recommendations are identified for follow-up to prevent acts of torture and/or ill-treatment. States parties are asked to provide, within one year, information on the measures taken to give effect to those recommendations. Items selected must meet three criteria: be serious, be protective

---

[44]   See UN Doc CAT/C/SR.1072, 22 May 2012.
[45]   Letter from Rapporteur on Follow-up to country conclusions, 21 December 2012, available at https://tbinternet.ohchr.org/Treaties/CAT/Shared%20Documents/SYR/INT_CAT_FUL_SYR_13124_E .pdf

and be achievable within one year. The Committee also asks the State for an implementation plan for the recommendations made.[46]

The Committee appoints a rapporteur for the follow-up to concluding observations, who consults with country rapporteurs, assesses the responses of States parties, and communicates with the government's representatives. The Committee's experience with follow-up measures taken by States parties is discussed at each Committee session and in its annual reports, addressing substantive trends and procedural modifications.

At issue, first, is the question of whether the procedure is effective in eliciting necessary informational responses. From May 2003 through May 2019, the Committee reported that it had reviewed 247 periodic reports for which it identified follow-up recommendations. Of the 225 follow-up reports that had been due by 17 May 2019, 166 had been received by the Committee, for a 74 percent overall response rate.[47] By and large, these responses suggest that States parties that submit periodic reports regularly also provide follow-up responses, but that those countries that have reported only after long delays are unlikely to provide requested follow-up information.

Secondly, as to the effectiveness of the follow-up procedure in eliciting specific actions recommended by the Committee, the picture is more mixed.

Although there had been a number of discussions on strengthening and focusing the follow-up procedure, it was only in May 2014, after the first rapporteur on follow-up[48] reported her ongoing concerns about the overall effectiveness of the procedure, that the Committee agreed to try a follow-up procedure that explicitly assigns a grade to each State's compliance with follow-up.

The Committee's rapporteur on follow-up noted that the procedure had helped maintain direct contact between the Committee and States parties following adoption of concluding observations on a State party report and before submission of its next periodic report. Follow-up also helped foster transparency about the Convention's implementation. However, many concerns were not addressed effectively through the procedure. Precision was absent on how officials instruct on the right of detainees to obtain prompt access to an independent doctor, a lawyer and a family member. Despite questions being asked directly to them, States parties rarely clarified why they did not create separate, independent and impartial bodies to examine complaints of torture and ill-treatment, especially to conduct unannounced prison visits. The follow-up procedure revealed inadequate statistics on various topics including offences, charges and convictions, particularly complaints of police misconduct, and information on victims of sexual violence and abuse.

The rapporteur on follow-up concluded that the procedure should receive greater attention in Committee sessions and be better sequenced with the preparation of the List of Issues Prior to Reporting (LOIPR), so that States parties were not confused by multiple communications from the Committee within the same calendar year. To date, the Committee has not developed a procedure for updating these LOIPRs when a State does not respond within the expected two-year period. For those submitting reports late, this will be necessary to make the LOIPR procedure and the periodic reporting itself address the most relevant issues in each State party.

---

[46]   See CAT website for a description, at http://tbinternet.ohchr.org/_layouts/TreatyBodyExternal/FollowUp.aspx?Treaty=CAT&Lang=en

[47]   UN Doc A/74/44, para 42.

[48]   The author was the first rapporteur on follow up, from 2003 to 2013.

CAT's first rapporteur on follow-up also encouraged consideration of a new approach to monitoring compliance – in-country follow-up visits by a team consisting of the rapporteur for follow-up, the country co-rapporteurs and a Secretariat member. At the 52nd session of the Committee this proposal evoked considerable interest among Committee members and remains a subject of consideration.[49] Similarly, Committee members discussed whether they might be more successful and efficient if there was a fixed questionnaire for such follow-up visits.

In 2014, considering the recommendations stemming from the UN General Assembly's treaty strengthening process,[50] a CAT working group considered and endorsed a revised procedure to evaluate and enhance follow up.[51] A new rapporteur on follow up identified two overarching concerns: how to strengthen compliance with the Convention and how to measure the extent of that compliance. In May 2015, the rapporteur proposed reforms to employ an assessment grading system to evaluate compliance and to use quantitative indicators to assist with the assessment of implementation. He also proposed inviting State parties to meet with the Committee on follow-up, and highlighted the role of civil society organizations in the follow-up procedure. The Committee endorsed the new changes promptly.[52]

Guidelines on follow-up were adopted at the Committee's 55th session, in August 2015.[53] Previously (in sessions 51–54), the Committee reviewed 33 State reports and received follow-up reports from 23 of them, for a reporting compliance rate of 69 percent. The rapporteur told the Committee that he had assessed information relating to 87 recommendations in the 23 follow-up reports and found that thorough and extensive information had been provided on the recommendations in 52 percent of cases; 38 percent had addressed the recommendations to some degree; but the remaining 10 percent failed to relate to the recommendations. He concluded that 6 percent had fully implemented the recommendations; 24 percent had taken "substantive steps;" 33 percent had begun "initial steps" and 29 percent had no implementation. Insufficient information for assessment was found in the remaining 8 percent.[54] This information enabled the Committee to consider the results of its efforts more rigorously, and to begin a new phase of evaluation of compliance with its recommendations.

SIMPLIFIED REPORTING PROCEDURE

In 2007, CAT initiated an innovative proposal related to article 19 periodic reporting by preparing a "List of Issues Prior to Reporting" (LOIPR) in advance of the submission of periodic reports by States parties. Called the "Simplified Reporting Procedure" in the UN

---

[49]   UN Doc A/69/44, May 2014, paras 71–99. For an elaboration of this concept, as adopted by the Committee in the context of the treaty strengthening process, see A/74/44, Annex II, paras 13–15.
[50]   See UN Doc A/RES/68/268, "Strengthening and enhancing the effective functioning of the treaty body system", April 14, 2014.
[51]   Its members consisted of the new rapporteur on follow-up, Mr Modvig, his predecessor, Ms Gaer, and a third Committee member, Ms Praham-Malla. Mr Hani became the third follow-up rapporteur in 2017.
[52]   UN Doc A/70/44.
[53]   UN Doc CAT/C/55/3.
[54]   UN Doc A/71/44, esp. paras 52–53.

High Commissioner's report on Treaty Strengthening,[55] the process aims to focus the dialogue with representatives of States parties. According to UNGA Resolution 68/268 (para 5), the simplified procedure "… creates an opportunity … to significantly streamline and enhance the reporting procedure …" and has the aim of "making the dialogue more effective, maximizing the use of the time available and allowing for a more interactive and productive dialogue with States parties".[56]

The simplified reporting procedure requires the Committee to prepare and submit to States parties a list of specific questions (these are presented in the LOIPR); the answers to the questions submitted to the Committee become the country's periodic report. As of 17 May 2019, 97 States parties have agreed to an invitation from the Committee to accept this procedure; only four States parties (China, Algeria, Uzbekistan, Sri Lanka) have rejected it; another 37 have not answered the Committee's invitation or have not yet been invited.[57]

A preliminary study of the LOIPRs[58] submitted by the author to the members of CAT suggests that the LOIPR reduces the workload for the State party, but does not yet reduce the number of questions asked in the dialogue. It did not shorten the length of time involved in submitting reports.[59] However, this study involved only a small selection of countries that had gone through both LOI and LOIPR processes as of that time.[60] CAT has emphasized that while the LOIPR has "facilitated the States parties' reporting obligations," the procedure of drafting LOIPRs "has increased its workload substantially, as their preparation requires more work" than LOIs. For a small committee, CAT considers this "particularly significant". [61] Despite this, the Committee has decided to extend the opportunity to receive a LOIPR to States parties with long overdue initial reports outstanding. Cote d'Ivoire, Malawi, Somalia, Dominican Republic, and Lesotho have each accepted this approach.[62] However, it remains to be seen if this will produce an actual reply from any of those States parties.

INQUIRIES

The submission of periodic reports as required in article 19 are a routine requirement – the only one required of all States parties. But what happens when there is evidence of a gross pattern of torture and/or a sudden and sustained decline in meeting the obligations of the Convention? Through article 20, the Committee was given the authority to undertake an inquiry when "reliable information" with "well-founded indications that torture is being systematically

[55] Pillay, N, *Strengthening the United Nations Human Rights Treaty Body System: A Report by the United Nations High Commissioner for Human Rights*, June 2012, 48. Available at: http://www2.ohchr .org/english/bodies/HRTD/docs/HCReportTBStrengthening.pdf

[56] UNGA Resolution 68/268, para 5.

[57] UN Doc A/74/44, para 29.

[58] The study examined five states reviewed by CAT at different times, first with a List of Issues (an "LOI" prepared after the submission of an ordinary periodic report) and then with an LOIPR.

[59] Initial Assessment of the CAT's LOIPR procedure, 2015: submitted by Felice Gaer to the Committee against Torture.

[60] A similarly-designed 2018 study by the Human Rights Committee (CCPR-C-123-3) involving 17 States parties to the ICCPR found the overall workload was decreased because of using the LOIPR and the quality of the dialogue process was improved.

[61] UN Doc A/73/44, para 26.

[62] UN Doc A/74/44, para 29.

practiced" is received concerning such practices in a State party. When this new procedure was established (in 1984), there were hopes that the ability to conduct inquiries, including visits to the country and its detention facilities, would give the Committee greater capacity to act effectively to expose and help end such practices, as well as to promote the accountability of those responsible.[63]

The Convention specifies for article 20 inquiries that a series of measures – all on a confidential basis – should take place to seek "cooperation" with the State concerned. This includes the possibility of a visit to the country. The Convention specifies that at the end of an inquiry, the Committee may decide to publish a summary account of the inquiry in its annual report.

Although CAT's inquiry procedure marked an important addition to the mechanisms used by UN treaty monitoring bodies, and represents the most labor-intensive and fact-specific examinations of allegations of torture undertaken by the Committee, it has been little used by the Committee (there have been a total of only 10 inquiries in the Committee's 30-year history) and has received relatively scant attention from academics and NGOs.[64]

While the results or impact of the inquiry procedures already conducted by CAT have not been subjected to academic scrutiny, there has been some academic discussion about the procedure itself and how to ensure an "effective visit." An article by Alessio Bruni who was the UN staff member "responsible for the first four inquiries" of CAT in the UN Secretariat sets out some of the early preparations made for inquiries.[65] "Key issues" regarding the procedure were later discussed at a workshop on the inquiry procedures, convened by OHCHR and the Geneva Academy.[66] Prior to the first CAT inquiry visit to places of detention, according to Bruni, the Committee met with the European Committee for the Prevention of Torture "in order to learn from it methods for visiting places of detention"[67] – a practice which continued for several inquiries but which has now lapsed. There were joint meetings with the International Committee of the Red Cross prior to the initial CAT inquiries as well. Although there are now manuals and new visiting committees (most notably, the Subcommittee on Prevention of Torture created under the Optional Protocol to the Convention against Torture), Bruni concludes that "nothing replaces the exchange of views, experiences, lessons learned, and new approaches among mandate holders." Key to successful inquiry visits have been collecting the maximum amount of information possible about the detention centers themselves, reaching a clear agreement on cooperation with national authorities regarding the visits, and selecting key places of detention to be visited – especially places "managed by security forces specialized in anti-terrorism" and "places where interrogations take place." [68] Bruni cautions

---

[63] Although CAT's inquiry procedure was the first to be set up, five other treaty bodies have also established inquiry-related procedures to deal with allegations of grave or systematic violations of their respective Conventions: CEDAW, CRC, CRPD, and CESCR (through optional protocols to the respective conventions) and CED (through the Convention itself). UN Doc HRI/MC/2018/ CRP.1, para 2.

[64] While States parties have an option upon signature or ratification of the Convention to make a declaration that they opt out of article 20, only 14 countries have done so out of the 165 States parties to the Convention.

[65] Remarks of Alessio Bruni, "Panel 3: Collaboration to Increase the Impact of Detention Visits" (2011, Special Edition) 18 *Human Rights Brief* 42.

[66] UN Doc HRI/MC/2018/CRP.1, available on the OHCHR website at https://tbinternet.ohchr.org/_layouts/treatybodyexternal/TBSearch.aspx?Lang=en&TreatyID=20&DocTypeID=62&ctl00_PlaceHolderMain_radResultsGridChangePage=1_20

[67] Bruni (n 65 above), 43.

[68] *Ibid.*

that "a major challenge experienced by the Committee is guaranteeing the protection of persons who are in contact with the visiting experts for the purpose of the inquiry ...."[69] For this, CAT has subsequently created a follow-up mechanism, especially focused on reprisals against persons providing information to or otherwise cooperating with the Committee.[70]

It had been expected that the inquiry procedure would improve the effectiveness of CAT in efforts to prevent torture as it would now be able to do much more than mere conference room diplomacy and exchanges of correspondence. But, as noted, in 30 years, CAT has only undertaken 10 inquiries,[71] involving nine countries, with only eight visits to the countries concerned.[72] In two cases, CAT found no systematic torture (Sri Lanka;[73] Serbia and Montenegro[74]), but it did confirm the systematicity of torture in eight other situations examined (Turkey;[75] Egypt 1994;[76] Peru;[77] Mexico;[78] Brazil;[79] Nepal;[80] Lebanon;[81] and Egypt 2017[82]). In nine cases, the inquiries were triggered by information separately submitted by NGOs; in one (Nepal), it began at the Committee's own initiative at a session that followed an article 19 review. There has been little follow-up on these inquiry proceedings as evidenced by the fact that we could only find four references to the article 20 procedure itself in concluding observations to subsequent periodic reports by the countries studied (Egypt; Peru; Mexico; Lebanon).[83]

---

[69]   *Ibid*, 45.
[70]   The OHCHR's "Workshop on the inquiries procedure" explored operational issues for inquiries, including the methodology for the engagement of key stakeholders, maintaining the confidentiality of the inquiry proceedings, establishing thresholds for what constitutes grave or systematic violations that trigger an inquiry procedure, the means of protecting persons cooperating with a treaty body inquiry, as well as elements of visit planning, writing reports and making recommendations. UN Doc HRI/ MC/2018/ CRP.1, 21 March 2018.
[71]   Turkey 1992, Egypt 1994, Peru 1999, Sri Lanka 2002, Mexico 2003, Serbia and Montenegro 2004, Brazil 2008, Nepal 2012, Lebanon 2014, and Egypt 2017. See CAT website, Inquiries procedure at https://www.ohchr.org/EN/HRBodies/CAT/Pages/InquiryProcedure.aspx
[72]   No on-site visits were made to Egypt or Nepal.
[73]   UN Doc A/57/44(SUPP), paras 117–195.
[74]   UN Doc A/59/44(SUPP), paras 156–240.
[75]   UN Doc A/48/44/Add.1, 15 November 1993.
[76]   UN Doc A/51/44(SUPP), paras 180–222.
[77]   UN Doc A/56/44(SUPP), paras 144–193.
[78]   UN Doc A/58/44 (SUPP), paras 147–153.
[79]   UN Doc A/63/44, paras 64–72.
[80]   UN Doc A/67/44, paras 88–100.
[81]   UN Doc A/69/44, paras 100–115 and Annex XIII.
[82]   UN Doc A/72/44, paras 58–71. The Committee encountered a problem about making its summary account public: this was an unanticipated result of the UN General Assembly's resolution A/Res/68/268 which specified an upper length limit for treaty body documents. The Convention specifies that at the end of an inquiry, the Committee may decide to publish a summary account of the confidential inquiry in its annual report. Because of the decision on length of annual reports in A/Res/68/268, the entire annual report (which used to run hundreds of pages and include all kinds of information including supplements with lengthy summaries of the inquiry findings) was limited to about 20 pages. Hence the published summary of the very detailed Egypt inquiry was only about three pages long.
[83]   See CAT website for the following: Egypt, 2002 Concluding Observations, para 7; Peru, May 2006 Concluding Observations, para 19; Mexico, 2006 Concluding Observations, para 14; and Lebanon, 2017 Concluding Observations, para 9.

Observers may ask why the CAT inquiry procedure has received so little use, and had so little academic or practical attention. It is all the more surprising since relatively few States parties opted out of the article 20 process. It may be that other treaty bodies have adopted inquiry procedures in new protocols and amendments precisely because CAT utilized it so rarely – but there is no hard evidence of this. A review of the 10 inquiries leads to the following possible reasons.

First, there was widespread dissatisfaction by NGOs with the CAT inquiry procedure as a result of the conclusions of the Sri Lanka report. The Committee's Sri Lanka inquiry took place during the period April 1999–May 2002 and was published in October 2002. It found widespread torture but claimed that it was not "systematic."[84] After the publication of its conclusion, Amnesty International sent a letter to the Committee expressing its disappointment and disagreement with the findings, indicating that it and other NGOs which had previously submitted materials to the Committee on article 20 cases might no longer do so. Amnesty had sent CAT well-documented article 20 complaints on Turkey and Egypt which were the basis for the first two inquiries of the Committee.

Indeed, in the initial CAT inquiries, the process was triggered by material submitted specifically to the Committee by NGOs and mainly from international NGOs: allegations concerning Turkey and Egypt came from Amnesty International; a dossier on Peru was submitted by Human Rights Watch. The documentation on Sri Lankan did not come from Amnesty, but from five UK-based NGOs (British Refugee Council, Medical Foundation for the Care of Victims of Torture, Refugee Legal Center, International Law Practitioners, and the Refugee Legal Group). In contrast, national NGOs played a role in the documentation of the next inquiries: the complaint on Mexico emanated from HR Center Miguel Augustin pro-Juarez known as PRODH; for Serbia and Montenegro, the inquiry was initiated a Yugoslav NGO, the Humanitarian Law Centre. For Brazil, the source of information was the international NGO, World Organization against Torture (OMCT) explicitly basing itself on reports from six Brazilian NGOs. The Nepal inquiry was initiated by the Committee itself after an article 19 periodic report was reviewed, with attention to information published by the Special Rapporteur on Torture, the Human Rights Committee, and NGO submissions to CAT (from the Human Rights Treaty Monitoring and Coordinating Committee, as well as Amnesty International and the Asian Legal Resource Center).[85] The inquiries on Lebanon and Egypt were launched by submissions from a non-governmental organization working primarily on Middle Eastern countries, al-Karama.

A second reason that there was a lack of activity around the article 20 inquiry procedure may be the standards employed by the Committee itself. The Committee's definition of "systematic" torture has been presented in its first inquiry on Turkey and that definition has remained the standard for the Committee ever since:

> ...Torture is practiced systematically when it is apparent that the torture cases reported have not occurred fortuitously in a particular place or at a particular time, but are seen to be habitual, wide-

---

[84] UN Doc A/57/44(SUPP), paras 117–195. See para 181 for the conclusion that torture was not "systematic."

[85] UN Doc CAT/C/37/2, paras 28–30.

spread and deliberate in at least a considerable part of the territory of the country in question. Torture may in fact be of a systematic character without resulting from the direct intention of a Government.[86]

But in some subsequent inquiries, the Committee seemed to shift its analysis about the role and attitude of the government as an entity working to eradicate torture or using it.

Regarding Turkey, CAT's first inquiry report[87] the Committee confirmed the "systematic" practice of torture in that country[88] by arguing that there was no compelling countervailing evidence: CAT stated that "the copious testimony gathered is so consistent in its description of torture techniques and the places and circumstances in which torture is perpetrated that the existence of systematic torture in Turkey cannot be denied."[89] While the report congratulated Turkish government authorities for measures "to improve the human rights situation," it concluded "nevertheless, the Committee remains concerned at the number and substance of the allegations of torture received, which confirm the existence and systematic character of the practice of torture" in Turkey.[90]

CAT's second inquiry considered allegations about Egypt,[91] citing information received as "well-founded."[92] Its report emphasizes that:

> the Committee is forced to conclude that torture is systematically practiced by the security forces in Egypt, in particular by State Security Intelligence, since in spite of the denials of the Government, the allegations of torture submitted by reliable non-governmental organizations consistently indicate that reported cases of torture are seen to be habitual, widespread and deliberate in at least a considerable part of the country.[93]

The inquiry on Peru[94] concluded that "the large number of complaints of torture, which have not been refuted by the information provided by the authorities, and the similarity of the cases, in particular the circumstances under which persons are subjected to torture and its objectives and methods, indicate that torture is not an occasional occurrence but has been systematically used as a method of investigation."[95]

---

[86]   *Ibid* para 39. It adds that "Torture may in fact be of a systematic character without resulting from the direct intention of a Government. It may be the consequence of factors which the Government has difficulty in controlling, and its existence may indicate a discrepancy between policy as determined by the central Government and its implementation by the local administration. Inadequate legislation which in practice allows room for the use of torture may also add to the systematic nature of this practice."

[87]   UN Doc A/48/44/Add.1, 15 November 1993. The Committee began the inquiry on Turkey in April 1990, concluded it in November 1992 and published it in November 1993.

[88]   *Ibid*, para 58.

[89]   *Ibid*, para 38.

[90]   *Ibid*, paras 57–58.

[91]   UN Doc. A/51/44(SUPP), paras 180–222. The Egypt inquiry began in November 1991, concluded in November 1994, and was published in 1996.

[92]   *Ibid*, para 199.

[93]   *Ibid*, para 220.

[94]   UN Doc A/56/44(SUPP), paras 144–193. The Peru inquiry began in 1995, ended in 1999, and was published in 2001.

[95]   *Ibid*, para 163.

The Committee's inquiry on Mexico[96] cited a decline during the inquiry process in complaints of torture,[97] but concluded that various factors (e.g., "the information collected had not been refuted by the Government..."; the "similarity of circumstances in which the cases occurred," the similarity of methods employed; and the "methods were widespread") convinced the Committee that torture was "systematic" since "these were not exceptional situations or occasional violations committed by a few police officers. On the contrary, the police commonly used torture and resorted to it on a systematic basis as a method of criminal investigation ...."[98]

But in the case of Sri Lanka, the Committee's reasoning seems to have shifted. The Committee's summary account stated that, while torture was frequent in connection with the internal conflict by the police, army, and paramilitaries, the "majority of suspects are not tortured" – arguing for the first time that such a threshold had to be reached to constitute a "systematic" practice and finding that "The Government does not condone torture and is employing various means to prevent it. It appears that instructions to that effect are not always obeyed, and there was no appropriate follow-up to ensure compliance."[99] Yet several of the earlier inquiries also stated that the government concerned did not condone torture, although another element in the society might be employing it regularly or ignoring instructions to end the practice. In those cases, the Committee concluded there was systematic torture, but in Sri Lanka it argued the opposite. In contrast to the Committee's previous approach, the inaction of the Sri Lankan government (regarding follow-up) was not considered evidence of "systematic" behavior, although it was considered to constitute such evidence in the case of several other countries.

In its Brazil inquiry,

> the Committee noted that the Government of Brazil fully cooperated ... [and] constantly expressed its awareness and concern with the seriousness of the existing problems, as well as its political will to improve. However, ... tens of thousands of persons were still held in *delegacias* and elsewhere in the penitentiary system where torture and similar ill-treatment continued to be meted out on a widespread and systematic basis.[100]

Despite the government's full cooperation, and political will to improve the situation, the Committee determined that the abuse in Brazilian jails was systematic and amounted to torture.

The Committee's analysis in the Nepal study[101] was more detailed, relying heavily on the reasoning set forth in the Committee's General Comment 2 on the application of effective measures to prevent torture. Following a detailed review of the measures taken and *not* taken by the Government of Nepal, the Committee concluded that torture "remained systematic in Nepal, mainly in police custody." It further stated that "Actions and omissions of Nepal therefore amount to more than a casual failure to act. It demonstrates that the authorities not only

---

[96]   UN Doc A/58/44 (SUPP), paras 147–153. The Mexico inquiry began in May 1999, ended in May 2002 and was published in full as well as summary form in 2003.

[97]   The full report on Mexico is in UN Doc CAT/C/75, 26 May 2003, consisting of 83 pages, including a reply from the Mexican government beginning on p 49.

[98]   *Ibid*, para 151.

[99]   UN Doc A/57/44(SUPP), para 178.

[100]   UN Doc A/63/44, paras 64–72, esp. 70 for the conclusion.

[101]   UN Doc A/67/44, paras 88–100.

fail to refute well-founded allegations but appear to acquiesce in the policy that shields and further encourages these actions, in contravention to the requirements of the Convention."[102]

On Lebanon[103] the Committee found that "Torture in Lebanon is a pervasive practice that is routinely used by the armed forces and law enforcement agencies ...." The report identified "a clear pattern of widespread torture and ill-treatment of suspects in custody, including individuals arrested for State security crimes."[104] In addition, "[u]nlawful arrests and torture by non-State actors, such as militias affiliated to Hizbullah and other armed militias, and the subsequent handover of the victims to the Lebanese security agencies"[105] helped lead to the conclusion that "torture is, and has been, systematically practiced in Lebanon."[106]

CAT's second inquiry into Egypt[107] found that "Torture appears to occur particularly frequently following arbitrary arrests and is often carried out to obtain a confession or to punish and threaten political dissenters. Torture occurs in police stations, prisons, State security facilities, and Central Security Forces facilities." Citing impunity, the Committee concluded that "prosecutors, judges and prison officials also facilitate torture by failing to curb practices of torture, arbitrary detention and ill-treatment or to act on complaints."[108] For the second time CAT did not succeed in visiting Egypt; however, it reached the "inescapable conclusion that torture is a systematic practice in Egypt."[109]

A third reason for the lack of attention to the CAT inquiry procedures might be the rise of competing mechanisms, particularly the Subcommittee to Prevent Torture (SPT) under the Optional Protocol to the Convention (OPCAT), which itself undertakes country visits on a confidential basis as a matter of course. An enthusiastic NGO campaign has been directed towards the SPT, including both for its development of national preventive mechanisms to eradicate torture and for publicizing its own country visits and reports. These visits, also confidential in accordance with the OPCAT, have increasingly obtained cooperation of the State parties concerned who have adopted the practice of openly publishing the SPT reports in full. This has expanded the reliable information available, informing the reviews of State party periodic reports by the CAT itself. In the case of Lebanon, SPT had already conducted a preventive visit before CAT began its inquiry into allegations of systematic torture.

It seems obvious that the inquiry procedure has not achieved its potential – it is used rarely and even the most exacting report and recommendations are not carried forward (for example in the periodic reports) once the article 20 inquiry concludes. As illustrated by CAT in its decision to launch an inquiry on Nepal, it is not necessary to receive a dossier from an NGO or other entity in order to begin an inquiry. Yet neither NGOs, nor other UN mechanisms, nor the Committee itself have employed this procedure often. The Committee should consider ways for it to be more active in identifying cases for new article 20 inquiries.

---

[102]   *Ibid*, para 104.
[103]   UN Doc A/69/44, paras 100–115 and Annex XIII.
[104]   *Ibid*, Annex XIII, para 29.
[105]   *Ibid*, Annex XIII, para 31.
[106]   *Ibid*, Annex XIII, para 37.
[107]   UN Doc A/72/44, paras 58–71. The inquiry on Egypt was initiated in March 2012 by submissions from the non-governmental organization al-Karama, concluded in 2015, and published only in a summary in CAT's much-abbreviated 2017 annual report.
[108]   UN Doc. A/72/44, paras 58–71 and esp. 69.
[109]   *Ibid*, esp. 69–71 for the conclusion cited above in the Committee's 2017 report.

INDIVIDUAL COMPLAINTS[110]

Another form of oversight that the Committee carries out, as specified in Article 22 of the Convention, is an optional procedure authorizing the Committee to "receive and consider communications." For persons from countries that have explicitly opted in to the procedure, it permits individuals who claim to be victims of a violation of the Convention by a State party to approach the Committee for its consideration of their claims, as long as the complaint is not anonymous, nor an abuse of the right of submission or incompatible with the Convention's provisions. (In those cases, the Committee "shall consider" the communication inadmissible.) Before the Committee can consider such communications, it has to ascertain that the same matter has not been examined under another international procedure and that the individual has exhausted all domestic remedies. According to the Convention, the consideration of such complaints takes place in "closed meetings."

Despite all the provisions to make the procedure fair and even favorable to the State party concerned, as of August 2019 only 68 of the 168 States parties to the Convention (40 percent) had accepted this procedure.

From 1988 through May 2019, a total of 932 complaints had been registered concerning 39 States parties, according to the latest CAT annual report. Of those, 279 were discontinued; and 108 were found inadmissible. Of another 383 on which there were decisions on the merits, CAT had found violations of the Convention in 150 cases (about 39 percent[111]). In the autumn of 2018, CAT's Chairperson told the UN General Assembly that "considering the fact that individual communications submitted to CAT are all about alleged very grave human rights violations, CAT's finding of a violation rate of 39 percent is rather modest."[112] Indeed, it is considerably lower than the rates found in other UN human rights treaty bodies with individual complaint procedures. An overwhelming proportion of the decisions dealt with violations of article 3 of the Convention.

Deciding about these communications consumes a substantial portion of CAT's meeting time.[113] Yet despite an increased CAT effort to resolve more complaints annually, according to the UN secretariat, there was a backlog of 178 individual communications to CAT as of 19 May 2019, a number that is continuing to increase.[114] According to CAT Chairperson Modvig's oral remarks to the UN General Assembly a few months earlier, there were 160

---

[110]   There is also a procedure under Article 21 of the Convention that provides for the possibility of state-to-state complaints. This procedure has never been used by CAT; in 2018 the first state-to-state human rights treaty-based complaints were lodged with the CERD Committee.

[111]   UN Doc A/74/44, para 56.

[112]   Statement by Mr Jens Modvig, Chairperson Committee against Torture, at the 73rd session of the General Assembly, 15 October 2018, https://www.ohchr.org/EN/NewsEvents/Pages/DisplayNews.aspx?NewsID=23725&LangID=E

[113]   About 89 percent of all individual communications are sent either to the Human Rights Committee which monitors the ICCPR, or to CAT. Roughly 80 percent go to the Human Rights Committee and 9 percent to CAT. See UN Doc A/71/118, 18 July 2016, para 36.

[114]   *Ibid.* The backlog of communications for CAT was: 2012: 48; 2013: 45; 2014: 68 and 2015: 76. This number has grown even though the number of cases decided by CAT had increased substantially. According to UN Doc A/71/118, Annex VII: 32 cases were decided in 2013 and 65 in 2015. The reason for this is said to be an overall increase in cases registered with the Committee (A/71/118, para 31). Figures for 2019 can be found in UN Doc A/74/44, para 56, which shows an increase over the 160-case backlog reported in October 2018 by the Chairperson to UNGA.

complaints pending consideration in October 2018 despite the Committee giving priority to reviewing communications that were ready for decision. He warned that there is a staffing problem: "If the Secretariat cannot provide the necessary assistance in preparing cases, the Committee will not be able to eliminate the backlog." Indeed, the Petitions Unit remains very small, which hampers the processing of the views of the State party and the complainants and inhibits the Committee's capacity to decide cases. This is ironic since the Committee has actually increased the number of cases it decides, and has established a new working group to "rationalize its workload by considering the draft discontinuances and inadmissibility decisions" in advance of the session and reporting on its deliberations in order to speed the Committee's overall review of such cases.[115]

In cases where a violation has been found (or in article 3 cases, a potential violation), CAT routinely seeks a remedy. Most often it has simply asked the State party to inform it in 90 days of the measures taken to remedy the violation. According to a recent study of "satisfactory" outcomes of individual communications that found violations, the most common remedies carried out by States parties are compensation, legislative changes, and symbolic reparation.[116] For individual communications to CAT, former Human Rights Committee Secretary Kate Fox Principi found that for most article 3 cases where a violation was found, the remedy was to avoid removal or deportation of the individual: 46 CAT cases cited in an appendix were satisfactorily resolved through action to avoid removal, either by issuing a temporary or permanent residence permit, granting refugee status, or some similar action.[117] In the prominent CAT case of *Guengueng et al. v. Senegal*, involving a former head of a neighboring state, an amendment was made to legislation and the Constitution in Senegal removing technical impediments to trying Hissene Habre regarding alleged torture;[118] and in the case of *Gerasimov v. Kazakhstan*, involving failure to investigate alleged torture, compensation was paid (although the State party took no other remedies such as a new impartial investigation of torture claims).[119] In another case (*Dar v. Norway*), a complainant who had been removed was returned to the State party.[120]

The particular nature of article 3 violations may be responsible for the relatively high number of cases categorized as resolved satisfactorily through the communication procedure. Article 3 complaints most commonly address a decision to expel a person which has not yet been carried out. Furthermore, the States parties against whom complaints are brought are among the 68 that have agreed to the article 22 procedure, and generally have agreed to delay a person's forced return until the Committee reaches a determination on whether there is a violation. (According to the UN website, the highest number of complaints have been submitted against Canada, Switzerland, Sweden, Australia, Denmark, France and the Netherlands.) Thus it is relatively easy to avoid sending the person back and, hence, to comply with the Committee's decision and remedy the violation. Unlike recommendations regarding violations

---

[115] UN Doc A/73/44, para 68.
[116] Fox Principi, K, "Implementation of Decisions under UN Treaty Body Complaint Procedures – How do States Comply?" (2017) 37 *Human Rights Law Journal* 1.
[117] *Ibid*, Annex D 15–18.
[118] *Ibid*, 7, 21.
[119] *Ibid*, 25.
[120] *Ibid*, 29.

of other articles of the Convention, this is surely easier than conducting investigations and prosecutions, or even than paying compensation.

ASSESSING COMPLIANCE

The members of the CAT Committee have struggled with the question of whether their dialogues with representatives of States parties, and the conclusions and recommendations adopted, are in fact having the impact desired – to promote compliance with the undertakings set forth in the Convention. This can be difficult to ascertain. If the Committee's comments and recommendations on each periodic review (called "concluding observations") are well drafted and specific, then assessment of their implementation can be made more easily.

Such assessment necessarily requires a case-by-case examination of each State party's experience. For example, in one study, I examined the approach taken by the Committee against Torture regarding the role of lawyers, and of human rights defense lawyers in particular, over a 25-year period during which China's compliance with the Convention came before the Committee. I found a number of specific legal changes which could be directly attributable to the Committee reviews. I also found that the Committee itself changed its approach: it moved from asking general questions about the legal entitlement to have access to a lawyer to a more rigorous examination of specific concerns – and individual cases – about whether this right is provided in practice for criminal suspects and others in custody, and whether it has been violated by threats, reprisals and other attacks – physical or legal – against lawyers and human rights defenders. The article concluded that China's approach to the Committee also changed over time: Chinese authorities began by being willing to discuss access and legal provisions affecting lawyers when it was presented in the abstract. However, they became increasingly unwilling to respond specifically to the Committee's questions when it involved discussion of specific alleged cases of harassment of defense lawyers and human rights defenders. Chinese representatives also displayed hostility towards the use by the Committee of sources of information other than that provided by the government of China, and were particularly critical about allegations made by non-governmental human rights organizations.[121] It would be valuable to conduct other similar studies of State parties that have engaged in periodic reviews with CAT in order to gain clearer accounts of compliance and effectiveness.

In the years prior to 1993, UN human rights treaty bodies (including CAT) commonly included in their annual reports a summary of the "constructive dialogue" and recommendations made orally by members to the State party representative. Some of the treaty bodies consolidated their interpretation of certain of the treaty's requirements by preparing "general comments" that reflect the general views expressed by committee members of each monitoring committee reached following examination of numerous State reports.[122] Human rights treaties

---

[121] Gaer (n 41 above).

[122] "A General Comment can focus each State party on the inadequacies and lacunae and recurring violations of the treaty as found in the reports submitted ... or through the interactive dialogue ...; inform States parties of the experiences gained by the members of the treaty body which can assist them in strengthening the treaty; guide States parties in their general implementation of the treaty and possible improved reporting procedures ...; and identify future preventive measures that the States parties can take to realize the rights in the ... treaty." See Report on the Working Methods of the Human Rights Treaty Bodies relating to the State Party reporting Process, UN Doc HRI/MC/2006/4, para 105 and UN

such as the Covenants, adopted well before 1984, provided for such "general comments," and some of their members insisted that was the only outcome or conclusion that could be attributed to the monitoring body, which they sought to keep rather weak. However, the Convention against Torture (adopted in 1984 but which came into force in 1988) stated in Article 19(3) that, after consideration of a state party's periodic report, the Committee "may make such general comments on the report as it may consider appropriate." The Committee adopted individual comments on reports beginning in 1993. This was clearly an advance insofar as implementation measures were concerned, since it permitted country-specific conclusions to be formulated about a specific report of a specific State party after it had been reviewed.

At CAT, such assessments of State party reports were initially very brief, amounting to 1–3 pages, and general. However, these assessments have evolved over time into lengthy statements of concerns and recommendations, amounting to as much as 15–20 single-spaced pages of evaluation of a State party's compliance with the Convention. Some of these are then examined in a follow-up process which has had mixed results – not least because many States parties simply do not respond. Results of the follow-up procedure are now noted prominently in a lead paragraph in the conclusions adopted by CAT after each periodic review takes place. In this way, the Committee's assessment of compliance has become more precise and clear than it was in earlier years, setting out concerns about laws and practices, and the gravity of the crime of torture and what must be done to prevent and punish it, in ways that all States parties can clearly understand.

Another outcome of the review of State party reports is what Creamer and Simmons have called "elite socialization" – that is, informing State officials what is expected of them in order to be in compliance with the Convention. This kind of "socialization" has also been aided by the decision of the CAT Committee to make "general comments" that consolidate its interpretation of some of the articles of the Convention, similar to those made by other human rights treaty bodies.[123]

From 2004 to 2007, Committee members expressed a heightened sense of frustration with the reporting process as a means of advancing the prevention of torture. After establishing a follow-up procedure in 2003, the Committee adopted General Comment 2 in 2007,[124] which sets forth and elaborates on what effective measures to prevent acts of torture each State party must take to exercise its obligations under article 2 of the Convention. Key to the preparation of the General Comment was an analysis and consolidation of the Committee's concerns and

---

Doc HRI/MC/2010 and Chatham House, "The Treatment of Torture Victims: What are a Government's Obligations?", International Law Discussion Group Meeting Summary, 21 January 2013.

[123]   To date, these have addressed articles 2, 3 and 14 of the Convention, aiming to advise States parties on ways to most effectively implement the Convention. Such comments were not questioned until the USA offered its views on General Comment No 2 in December 2008; since then one or two other countries have raised questions about the authority of CAT to make general comments. See https://www.state.gov/documents/organization/138853.pdf (para 31) in which the USA states: "the United States notes that, unlike other treaty bodies that issue general comments or recommendations for consideration by all States Parties, the Convention authorizes the Committee to issue "general comments" only with respect to the report of a State Party." However, according to key participants in the drafting process, there was no intention by the drafters of the Convention to prohibit the Committee from addressing all States parties collectively based on their examination of reports (Burgers and Danelius (n 1 above), 159). In this connection, it is noteworthy that when CAT adopted General Comment 1 (on article 3) in 1996, neither the USA nor any other State party raised objections.

[124]   CAT General Comment No 2 (n 5 above).

recommendations to States parties during the review of periodic reports.[125] By carrying out this analysis and setting forth the Committee's expectations about "effective measures," General Comment 2 has advanced awareness and understanding by the representatives and officials of each State party as to what the Committee actually expects them to be doing. This guidance reminds States parties that the Convention prohibits any justification of torture on grounds of "exceptional circumstances" or superior orders.

The Committee has reminded States parties that they are obligated to adopt effective measures "to prevent public authorities and other persons acting in an official capacity from directly committing, instigating, inciting, encouraging, acquiescing in or otherwise participating or being complicit in acts of torture as defined by the Convention."[126] When they fail to fulfil their obligations under the Convention, the Committee considers States to be in violation of the Convention.

Through its now extended procedure for scrutinizing State actions through the periodic reporting procedure (consisting of voluntary reports, CAT conclusions and follow-up, a focused LOIPR, to which replies constitute a new report), as described earlier in this chapter, the Committee has created an interactive process for the reporting and oversight of the measures taken that enable States parties to prevent torture that is focused and linked to past reporting. The "dialogue" process, which is now webcast and archived officially on the UN webcast page, has not only exposed the crimes of torture and ill-treatment, but enables domestic and international actors worldwide to be engaged in the effort to eradicate it.

The Committee has reminded all States parties and stakeholders of the Convention's applicability to all persons under the State's control or custody, and emphasizes how broadly the word "all" extends by referring explicitly to an array of institutions, locations, and actors – in listing contexts of custody or control (prisons, hospitals, schools, institutions that care for children, the aged, the mentally ill or disabled, and military institutions, etc.). It has also reminded states that they have obligations regarding acts of State agents, private contractors, and others acting in an official capacity or on behalf of the State or under its direction or control. It also explicitly emphasized "contexts where the failure of the state to intervene encourages and enhances the danger of privately inflicted harm," and the need for protection of individuals and groups made vulnerable by discrimination – a group that explicitly includes women and victims of gender-based violence.

The Committee's review of periodic reports and conduct of inquiry procedures require State parties themselves to closely monitor its officials and those acting on its behalf, as well as to report to the Committee on any incidents prohibited by the Convention, as well as on measures taken to investigate, punish and prevent further incidents.

Our review of the Committee's concluding comments and recommendations clearly demonstrates that "experience … has enhanced the Committee's understanding of the scope and nature of the prohibition against torture, … as well as of evolving effective measures to prevent it in different contexts."[127] As the Committee stated, article 2 "provides authority to build upon the remaining articles and to expand the scope of measures required to prevent torture."[128] For

---

[125] The author of this chapter served as rapporteur for the drafting and adoption of CAT General Comment No 2 (n 5 above).

[126] CAT General Comment No 2 (n 5 above), para 17.

[127] *Ibid*, para 14.

[128] *Ibid*.

example, the Committee identified video surveillance as a preventive measure earlier than many others; it also has cited preventing ill-treatment as a means to prevent torture.[129]

Significantly, the Committee has identified certain fundamental legal safeguards that apply to all people deprived of their liberty, and it asks about and cites these safeguards in virtually all its reviews of periodic reports. These include the right to access a lawyer, a medical examination, and to notify a family member from the outset of detention, as well as the right to be informed of the reasons for one's detention, and the right to have one's detention recorded in a central register which is accessible to one's lawyer and family.[130] Such safeguards aim to limit the opportunities for abuse of persons under the control of the State's officials, and to ensure as much transparency as possible for the detainees as well as a fair process.

Former UN Special Rapporteur on Torture, Theo van Boven, welcomed the Committee's adoption of General Comment No 2 at a time when States were increasingly citing reasons to ignore or reinterpret the Convention's prohibition against torture. By so doing, he felt the Committee clearly affirmed "its authority by providing guidance to States parties and all other organs of national and international society as to the meaning and implications of the Convention as an instrument of international law."[131]

The Committee has recognized that States parties may carry responsibility for acts of torture or ill-treatment committed by non-state officials or private actors if State authorities fail to exercise due diligence to prevent such acts and protect individuals from violence – especially gender-based violence. Vulnerable individuals in particular or groups at risk of torture or ill-treatment require the States parties to take positive measures of prevention or protection, according to the CAT Committee's victim-oriented approach. In General Comment 2, the Committee outlined a long list of categories of such vulnerable persons that go well beyond usual UN categorizations, including in particular explicit references to sexual orientation and transgender identity long before other such bodies did so.[132]

A review of the Committee's ongoing assessment of periodic reports and article 20 reviews shows that it considers that preventive measures must be effective, and that evaluation and reporting are themselves preventive measures.[133] State responsibility for violence against women and other abuses by private actors has been identified by the Committee on many occasions. It was the subject of a seminar with leading experts conducted in May 2019.[134] The Committee has also adopted interpretive general comments on articles 14 and 3 which offer State parties' authorities a way to understand their obligations under the Convention but which will not be discussed here due to space limitations.[135]

---

[129]   *Ibid*, para 3.

[130]   *Ibid*, para 13. See also Concluding observations of States parties.

[131]   van Boven, T, "Remarks on the Convention against Torture's General Comment No. 2" (2008) 11 *N.Y. City L. Review* 217.

[132]   *Ibid*, 218 and Gaer, FD, "Opening Remarks: General Comment No. 2" (2008), 11 *N.Y. City L. Rev.* 187. These and other articles in the same volume are from a Symposium in 2008 focused on the General Comment entitled "Preventing Torture: Implications of General Comment 2".

[133]   Gaer (n 132 above).

[134]   "Violence Against Women by Private Actors: Is there State Responsibility under the Convention Against Torture?", 12 March 2015, OMCT blog. Also see Gaer (n 21 above).

[135]   CAT General Comment No 3 on article 14 (2012) UN Doc CAT/C/GC/3. See Broecker, C, "United Nations Committee against Torture Adopts new General Comment on Right to Redress" (2012) available at http://www.intlawgrrls.com/2012/11/united-nations-committee-against.html; CAT General Comment No 4 on implementation of Article 3 in the context of Article 22 (2018) UN Doc CAT/C/

Since the adoption of General Comment 2, the Committee has reminded States parties about many conclusions articulated in it. This takes place not only in the dialogue with representatives of the State party, but also by incorporating these concerns in the Lists of Issues Prior to Reporting, in the Conclusions and Recommendations adopted after the dialogue, and in the follow-up process. The Committee thus tries to ensure that the examination of periodic reports is not a mere bureaucratic process, but one that enhances the understanding and actions of State authorities to actually prevent torture and ill-treatment. In addition, by making public all proceedings under article 19, the Committee strives to ensure that domestic audiences are aware of and can invoke the Committee's findings in proceedings within their country.

The CAT Committee's review of periodic reports clearly has worked to inform States parties of the gravity of the crime of torture and of States parties' obligations under the Convention and ways to implement them. Because States parties' cooperate voluntarily with the Committee, whether for the article 19 review of periodic reports or article 20 inquiries, or the implementation of decisions on article 22 cases, there are questions about whether the CAT is – or can be – effective in demanding implementation of all of the Convention's obligations. But as we look at the web of responsibilities and obligations that are highlighted by CAT in its reviews, it becomes clear that it has done a great deal to advance implementation of the Convention obligations, and to raise awareness and advocate action to promote effectiveness. This is no small accomplishment for a committee of experts facing 168 States parties that have granted it only limited power to conduct oversight of compliance and who repeatedly insist that its decisions are merely advisory.

GC4. See Cali, C and Cunningham, S, "Part 1: A Few Steps Forward, a Few Steps Sideways and a Few Steps Backwards: The CAT's Revised and Updated GC on Non-Refoulement" (2018) EJILTalk at https://www.ejiltalk.org/part-1-a-few-steps-forward-a-few-steps-sideways-and-a-few-steps-backwards -the-cats-revised-and-updated-gc-on-non-refoulement/; see also Part 2 (2018) at https://www.ejiltalk .org/part-2-a-few-steps-forward-a-few-steps-sideways-and-a-few-steps-backwards-the-cats-revised-and -updated-gc-on-non-refoulement/

8. The mandate of the Special Rapporteur on torture: role, contributions, and impact

Juan E. Méndez and Andra Nicolescu

INTRODUCTION

The 'Special Procedures' of the United Nations Human Rights Council (UNHRC) are recognized as occupying a foremost role in the international human rights architecture and playing a pivotal role in the protection of human rights around the world by 'shaping the content of international norms, shedding light on how states comply with such norms, and influencing how governments behave, to the benefit of millions of people'.[1] The Special Procedures are independent human rights experts, in the form of individuals or working groups, with mandates 'to report and advise on human rights from a thematic or country-specific perspective', covering civil and political as well as social, economic, and cultural rights.[2] Operating under the principles of transparency, cooperation, and accountability, the Special Procedures are currently divided into 44 thematic and 12 country mandates.[3] Of these, the thematic mandate of the Special Rapporteur on torture and other cruel, inhuman or degrading treatment or punishment ('SRT' or 'SRT mandate') was created in 1985 to 'examine questions relevant to torture'.[4]

This chapter will provide an overview of the role, contributions, and impact of the SRT mandate, beginning with a brief discussion of the history and accomplishments of, and challenges faced by, the Special Procedures of the UNHRC – the bedrock within which the SRT mandate is embedded. The role, working methods, and activities of the SRT will then be addressed, with particular emphasis on the flexible nature of the mandate and the intersectional broadening in its scope in recent years, which have enabled the SRT to emerge as a stalwart and progressive defender of human rights and dignity. Some specific examples of the SRT's thematic and country-specific work in recent years will be provided in this context. The importance of cooperation with a multitude of other mechanisms and actors, from high-level government representatives to grassroots activists, as well as the need for dedicated, consistent, and well-coordinated follow-up, will be emphasized. The chapter will conclude with some reflections on opportunities for assessing and measuring impact, and a look ahead to new opportunities and challenges facing the mandate in the continued quest to end and prevent torture around the world.

---

[1] Piccone, T, *Catalyst for Rights: The Unique Contribution of the UN's Independent Experts on Human Rights* (Brookings, October 2010), ix, https://www.brookings.edu/wp-content/uploads/2016/06/10_human_rights_piccone.pdf

[2] United Nations Office of the High Commissioner for Human Rights, *Special Procedures of the Human Rights Council*, http://www.ohchr.org/EN/HRBodies/SP/Pages/Introduction.aspx

[3] *Ibid.*

[4] United Nations Commission on Human Rights, *Special Rapporteur on Torture and other Cruel, Inhuman or Degrading Treatment or Punishment*, UN Doc A/HRC/RES/1985/33.

THE SPECIAL PROCEDURES: HISTORY

The Special Procedures have been identified as the 'crown jewel' of the international human rights system,[5] in view of their unique mandate to undertake independent, periodic, on-the-ground scrutiny of States' human rights records.[6] Academic studies have traced the origins of the modern Special Procedures mandates to the critical efforts of a 'small group of Africa, Asian, and Caribbean states [of the UN] that, between 1966 and 1967, took a determined decision to act against human rights violations associated with colonialism, racism, and apartheid … sen[ding] a clear message to the world that, when faced with serious human rights abuses, the UN did indeed have "the power to act"'.[7] The group successfully advocated for the creation of an Ad Hoc Working Group of Experts on South Africa and a Special Rapporteur on Apartheid by the Commission on Human Rights (which was replaced by the UNHRC in 2006) in 1967, pursuant to United Nations Economic and Social Council (ECOSOC) resolutions emphasizing the need to devise tools designed to improve 'the capacity of the UN to put a stop to violations of human rights wherever they may occur'.[8] In terms of a precursor to the Special Procedures' unique working methods, a 1963 UN mission to examine violations of human rights in South Viet-Nam, which sought to 'seek factual evidence … collect information, conduct on-the-spot investigations, receive petitions and hear witnesses and thereafter report back to the General Assembly', has been identified as pioneering the pillars in their 'toolkit'.[9]

In this context, it is emblematic that the Special Procedures developed out of an imperative, in the words of Judge Thomas Buergenthal, to 'pierce the veil of national sovereignty' and contest the principle of non-interference in domestic affairs in response to serious cases of human rights violations.[10] During the 1970s and 1980s, Special Procedure mandates continued to emerge in what has been described as an 'accidental' manner, or by means of a process of 'auto-development', 'individual innovations', and organic growth whereby both thematic and country-specific mandates responding to specific human rights concerns – such as the Special Rapporteur on Chile (1979), the Working Group on enforced disappearances (1980), and the Special Rapporteur on extrajudicial, summary and arbitrary executions (1982) – were created and proceeded to 'develop and apply a flexible interpretation of their mandate (often in the face of state opposition), which afterwards the Commission [on Human Rights] would endorse' and the ECOSOC would approve.[11]

The systematization of the Special Procedures mandates and working groups into a coherent mechanism – what has become recognized as the Special Procedures system/branch – transpired gradually. Recognizing that the individual mandates had largely similar roles and working methods and increasingly projected themselves collectively, the 1993 Vienna Declaration and Programme of Action encouraged the Special Procedures to 'harmonize

---

5   Subedi, SP, 'Protection of Human Rights through the Mechanism of UN Special Rapporteurs' (2011) 33 *Human Rights Quarterly* 201.

6   Piccone (n 1 above), 5.

7   Nifosi, I, *The UN Special Procedures in the Field of Human Rights* (Intersentia, 2006), 12.

8   *Ibid.*

9   Limon, M and Power, H, *History of the United Nations Special Procedures Mechanism: Origins, Evolution and Reform* (Universal Rights Group, 2014), 5.

10   Buergenthal, T, 'New Customary Law: Taking Human Rights Seriously?' (1993) 87 *Am. Soc. Int. L. Proc.* 230, 231.

11   Piccone (n 1 above), 7.

and rationalize their work through periodic meetings'.[12] This led to the emergence of annual meetings that systematized and professionalized the mechanism, culminating in the adoption of a Manual of Operations in 1999 (which was updated in 2008) and the creation of a Coordination Committee in 2005.[13] Finally, with the establishment of the UNHRC in 2006, the Special Procedures became formally systematized in their present form, pursuant to the Resolution mandating the UNHRC to 'assume, review and, where necessary, improve and rationalize all mandates, mechanisms, functions and responsibilities of the Commission on Human Rights in order to maintain a system of special procedures, expert advice and a complaint procedure'.[14]

THEMATIC SPECIAL PROCEDURES MANDATES: PRESENT SITUATION

The mandate of thematic Special Procedures, such as the SRT, is to investigate the situation of human rights in all parts of the world, irrespective of whether a State is a party to the relevant human rights treaty – such as the UN Convention against Torture in the case of the mandate under discussion here. This broad mandate 'requires them to take the measures necessary to monitor and respond quickly to allegations of human rights violations against individuals or groups, either globally or in a specific country or territory, and report on their activities'.[15]

While an in-depth discussion of the present-day strengths and weaknesses of the Special Procedures, as well as of the challenges they face, is beyond the scope of the present chapter, the issue has received increasing attention in recent years. For the purposes of examining the work of the Special Rapporteur on Torture more specifically, it is important to highlight that Special Procedures are recognized as having played a critical role in norm setting, identifying key issues and best practices, uncovering and exposing material facts, issuing reports and recommendations, and exerting influence in monitoring and protecting human rights.

As will become clear from the discussion of the SRT's work below, mandate holders are continuously challenged and prompted to adopt innovative working methods and approaches in response to the specific political, legal, and resource-related contexts in which they operate. Despite such challenges and frequently cited shortcomings, regular attacks by States, and financial and human resource constraints, the Special Procedures continue to play a fundamental role in the architecture of international human rights law. Their expansion into one of the principal human rights mechanisms of the UN system has not been unrecognized, with the Special Procedures increasingly being 'the subject of significant state, civil society, and academic expectations, resulting in sometimes harsh public criticism'.[16]

At the same time, and in spite of the progress made in terms of harmonizing and streamlining the working methods of the Special Procedures, their *ad hoc* development has nevertheless

---

[12]   United Nations Office of the High Commissioner for Human Rights, *Vienna Declaration and Programme of Action* (25 June 1993).
[13]   United Nations Office of the High Commissioner for Human Rights, *Manual of Operations of the Special Procedures of the Human Rights Council* (2008).
[14]   UN Doc A/RES/60/251, para 6 (3 April 2006).
[15]   *Manual of Operations of the Special Procedures of the Human Rights Council* (n 13 above), 5.
[16]   Nolan, A, Freedman R, and Murphy, M, 'Introduction' in *The United Nations Special Procedures System* (Martinus Nijhoff, 2017).

been said to have given rise to 'significant problems in terms of conceptualization and effective functioning', and the system is in some ways 'a victim of its own success' as the proliferation of mandates has exerted pressure in terms of logistics on the resources of the OHCHR, compromising its efficiency and effectiveness.[17] Indeed, the source of the Special Procedures' successes has at the same time constituted a source of weakness, and one that leaves them open to political attacks in bad faith by member States. As explained by one author:

> the lack of foresight in the creation of [the mandates] is a fundamental factor in explaining the evolution of methods of work developed by different mandate holders ... The 'soft' legal basis and geo-political factors surrounding the creation and renewal of mandates explains the freedom and flexibility they have enjoyed in establishing innovative monitoring activities that are more intrusive upon state sovereignty than any other UN human rights mechanism. As the significance of the Special Procedures' work has grown, attempts to curtail their autonomy and impact have increased accordingly, facilitated precisely by what has been seen as, until recently, their major strength: the lack of a strong institutional and coherent legal framework regulating their activities.[18]

Likewise, as others have explained,

> [w]hile the legitimacy of the system, which relies on States' consent, rests on its universal application, state-driven political processes are central to the way the system operates in practice. Indeed the part played by States in creating, terminating, and providing support to mandates, in engaging and cooperating (or not) with S[pecial] P[rocedures], has resulted in concerns about politicization of the system, not least because of efforts recently to control mandate holders' independence.[19]

Indeed, as States have begun to understand the relevance of the Special Procedures mandates in recent years, some attempts have been made to weaken their mandates and make it more difficult for mandate holders to carry out their duties, for instance in seeking those mandates via a code of conduct regulating their work,[20] and by influencing the appointment process.[21] At the same time, the growing effectiveness and profile of the work of some of the mandates have resulted in greater support, often for specific mandates, from some States. Other challenges for the Special Procedures – some of which will be highlighted below in the case of the SRT

---

[17]   *Ibid.*
[18]   Dominguez-Redondo, E, 'History of The Special Procedures: A "Learning-by-Doing" Approach to Human Rights Implementation' in Nolan, Freedman and Murphy (n 16 above), 9.
[19]   Nolan, Freedman and Murphy (above n 16), 6.
[20]   Former Special Rapporteur on Torture Sir Nigel S Rodley explained that 'the discussions in the Human Rights Council of a code of conduct [for Special Rapporteurs] were originally motivated by an attempt to make it harder for the Special Rapporteurs to discharge their traditional role. This was particularly so in light of the fact that there was already a code of conduct for experts on mission, the content of which had reflected the concerns of the special procedures. However, in fact there was little in the code as it eventually emerged that did not conform to responsible functioning of Special Rapporteurs. The main setback had been the restriction of communications with governments through "diplomatic channels", thus undermining the practice of sending urgent appeals directly to the capitals of member states'. Centre for International Governance, Law School University of Leeds, *Report of the International Workshop: 'The Role of the Special Rapporteurs of the Human Rights Council in the development and promotion of international human rights norms'* (7 June 2010).
[21]   For some examples of how Member States have politicized and attempted to influence the appointment processes of Special Rapporteurs in certain cases, see International Service for Human Rights, *Reform of Selection Process Needed to Strengthen Special Procedures* (May 20, 2016).

– include issues of regional and gender representation, particularly as pertaining to specific mandates, a lack of public information about the system, and difficulties in coordination with other UN agencies.

THE MANDATE OF THE SPECIAL RAPPORTEUR ON TORTURE: AN OVERVIEW

The mandate of the SRT was created in 1985, following a determination by the Commission that the phenomenon of torture was 'in need of a fact-finding mechanism of its own'.[22] The establishment of the mandate was largely regarded as filling a gap in the architecture of human rights protection against torture and other ill-treatment, particularly at a time when the UN Convention against Torture (UNCAT) had not yet entered into force.[23] More specifically, the creation of the Rapporteurship responded to the concerns identified by the 1975 UN Declaration on the Protection of All Persons from Being Subjected to Torture and Other Cruel, Inhuman or Degrading Treatment or Punishment, which identified the phenomenon of torture as being on the rise, noting that in view of 'the increase in the number of alarming reports on torture, further and sustained efforts are necessary to protect under all circumstances the basic human right to be free from torture and other [ill-treatment]'.[24]

Aside from setting the stage for the creation of the Special Rapporteurship on Torture, the 1975 Declaration also paved the way for the development of the Convention against Torture. The first concrete step towards the creation of the Convention came in the form of a specific request by the General Assembly in 1977, which called upon the Commission to draw up a draft torture convention. The request led to the creation of successive working groups by the Commission for several years, which were tasked with drafting the text. The Convention was formally adopted by the General Assembly in December 1984 in its Resolution 39/46, and entered into force on 26 June 1987 after being ratified by 20 states.[25] The Committee against Torture (CAT), the treaty body in charge of monitoring the implementation of the Convention, was concomitantly set up and began its work when the convention entered into force.[26]

The dynamic development of the UN's anti-torture architecture continued through the 1990s and into the early 2000s, with the Optional Protocol to the Torture Convention (OPCAT) being adopted by the UN General Assembly in December 2002 and entering into force in June 2006. The Optional Protocol has created a system of regular visits by international and domestic bodies to places of deprivation of liberty with a view to preventing the occurrence of torture or other ill-treatment in order to prevent torture and other cruel, inhuman or degrading treatment or punishment, including the establishment of the Subcommittee on Prevention of Torture

[22]   Rodley, NS and Pollard, M, *The Treatment of Prisoners Under International Law*, 3rd edn (Oxford University Press, 2009), 202–203.
[23]   Evans, MD, 'The UN Special Rapporteur on Torture in the Developing Architecture of UN Torture Protection', in Nolan, Freedman and Murphy (n 16 above), 351.
[24]   UN Doc A/RES/3453 (9 December 1975).
[25]   Burgers, JH and Danelius, H, *The United Nations Convention against Torture: A Handbook on the Convention against Torture and Other Cruel, Inhuman or Degrading Treatment or Punishment* (Martinus Nijhoff, 1988).
[26]   United Nations Office of the High Commissioner for Human Rights, *Fact Sheet No.17: The Committee Against Torture*.

and Other Cruel, Inhuman or Degrading Treatment or Punishment (SPT), which is mandated to carry out such visits and support States parties and national institutions in performing the relevant functions domestically.[27]

The SRT's Defining Characteristics and Place in the UN Anti-Torture Architecture

Presently, the mandate co-exists with and complements the work of the CAT and the SPT, the treaty bodies tasked with monitoring the implementation of the UNCAT and its Optional Protocol, respectively.[28] Together with the UN United Nations Voluntary Fund for Victims of Torture, these mechanisms comprise one of the strongest human rights architectures of the UN, reflecting torture's unique status under international law (along with that of enforced disappearances), which mandates that even a single episode of torture gives rise to the solemn obligation to investigate, prosecute, and punish the perpetrators, as well as to provide redress to the victims – including compensation, reparation, and as full a rehabilitation as possible – and to adopt measures of non-repetition.

The SRT is expressly mandated to cooperate with the CAT and the SPT, as well as with other relevant UN mechanisms and bodies, regional organizations and mechanisms, governmental authorities and institutions at the domestic level, such as national human rights institutions and national preventive mechanisms, as well as civil society, including non-governmental organizations.[29] While examples of specific instances of cooperation between the SRT and regional- and domestic-level actors will be provided below, some elaboration on the distinctions and interrelation between the SRT and the Treaty Bodies, with a view to highlighting the former's unique mandate, is warranted first.

Significantly, unlike the CAT, the SRT is not a judicial or quasi-judicial complaint mechanism operating under a constituent human rights treaty. While the SRT is empowered to examine and issue decisions on individual complaints, as will be described below, its main task is to promote measures by which States can better promote human rights by combating and preventing torture and other ill-treatment in their domestic jurisdiction. To this end, and as outlined in the UNHRC's *Manual of Operations of the Special Procedures of the Human Rights Council*, the principal functions of the SRT are to:

- analyze relevant thematic and country-specific issues and situations pertaining to the prohibition of torture and other ill-treatment;
- advise and issue recommendations on measures that States and other relevant stakeholders ought to take to address the problem of torture and other ill-treatment;

---

[27]   For information on the OPCAT see its home page at United Nations Office of the High Commissioner for Human Rights, *Optional Protocol to the Convention Against Torture*, http://www.ohchr.org/EN/HRBodies/OPCAT/Pages/OPCATIntro.aspx

[28]   For further information see United Nations Office of the High Commissioner for Human Rights, Committee against Torture, http://www.ohchr.org/en/hrbodies/cat/pages/catindex.aspx; Optional Protocol to the Convention against Torture (OPCAT) Subcommittee on the Prevention of Torture, http://www.ohchr.org/EN/HRBodies/OPCAT/Pages/OPCATIndex.aspx. See also Chapters 7 and 12 in this volume.

[29]   UN Doc A/HRC/Res/25/13 (2014) para 1.

- alert the international community to specific situations and issues requiring attention, with a view to providing early warning and encouraging the prevention of troubling and escalating situations;
- advocate on behalf of survivors and victims and encourage the provision of adequate redress and rehabilitation;
- mobilize and foster collaboration between the international community and regional and domestic actors, as well as civil society and grassroots advocates; and
- undertake effective follow-up.[30]

The broad-ranging mandate of the SRT is partly due to the fact that its functioning, unlike that of the treaty bodies, is not dependent on any given State's ratification of an international human rights treaty. While the SRT applies the standards enacted in human rights treaties related to the prohibition of torture if and when ratified by any given State, it is additionally able to address situations and cases where a Government has not become a party to the specific treaty, by relying on the *jus cogens* nature of the prohibition against torture and other cruel, inhuman, and degrading treatment and punishment, and on other State obligations derived from this prohibition that are generally recognized as binding as a matter of customary international law. The SRT mandate as such is not bound by any particular treaty and applies to all member States of the UN. Additionally, the SRT and most Special Procedures are not bound by the same procedural requirements for receiving complaints and other functions as are the treaty-based UN mechanisms, thereby allowing it flexibility to react quickly to cases of human rights abuse, to cover a broad scope of issues and to work with a wide range of international and domestic entities. Due to the flexibility and the complementary nature of their mandates, the Special Rapporteurs are able to coordinate and collaborate with a number of treaty-based mechanisms, as well as with other regional entities such as the Inter-American Commission on Human Rights, the African Commission on Human and People's Rights, and their respective Rapporteurships.

The SRT mandate furthermore applies various 'soft law' instruments that are widely authoritative, such as the Nelson Mandela Rules (the Standard Minimum Rules for the Treatment of Prisoners), the Istanbul Protocol (the Manual on the Effective Investigation and Documentation of Torture and Other Cruel, Inhuman or Degrading Treatment or Punishment), and the UN General Assembly and HRC resolutions, which are widely considered authoritative. Additionally, unlike the treaty bodies, the mandate does not require the exhaustion of domestic remedies. The Special Rapporteur's competence to review individual complaint does not have to be expressly recognized by the State concerned, nor does the mandate holder have to abstain if the case has been examined by another procedure of international investigation.

Although a full examination of the relationship between the SRT mandate, the CAT, and the SPT, is beyond the scope of this article, it is important to note that the three bodies work as a complementary set of anti-torture mechanisms, by means of coordinating visits and other country-specific activities; providing mutual support to one another; and developing and adopting coherent positions in relation to thematic issues. Nevertheless, and despite instances of such cooperation on specific matters,[31] they cannot yet be said to be operating

---

30 *Manual of Operations of the Special Procedures of the Human Rights Council* (n 13 above).
31 See, e.g. United Nations Office of the High Commissioner on Human Rights, Targeted and Tortured: UN Experts Urge Greater Protection for LGBTI People in Detention, a joint statement was

as a 'functional subsystem' of anti-torture mechanisms due to extant 'powerful legal and practical barriers'.[32] Nevertheless, certain regular practices, such as the Special Rapporteur's recent attendance of yearly joint CAT-SPT sessions, have been identified as symbolizing 'the desire of the three bodies to develop and deepen their working relationships in order to present a coherent, connected and common front to combat torture'.[33]

Mandate Holders

Like the other mandate holders appointed by the UNHRC as Special Rapporteurs, the SRT serves in his or her personal capacity, is independent of governments, and carries out the mandate on a voluntary, non-remunerated, basis. A term limit of six years (two three-year terms) is attached to each appointment. The selection and appointment of Special Rapporteurs is done pursuant to a competitive process within the UNHRC, which involves candidates submitting applications either upon nomination by entitles such as Governments, international or non-government organizations, other human rights bodies, or individuals.[34]

The resolution laying out the considerations and procedures for the selection of the Special Rapporteurs sets out the criteria of expertise; experience in the field of the mandate; independence; impartiality; personal integrity; and objectivity. According to a 2014 study, 56 percent of mandate holders were employed in academic or research capacities for the duration of their mandates, with another 23 percent coming from NGOs, grassroots organizations, and national human rights institutions.[35] Within these, a fair number of mandate holders do have legal backgrounds or prior experience working with the UN, as is the case with the torture mandate holders.

In addition, the resolution mandates that 'due consideration should be given to gender balance and equitable geographic representation, as well as to an appropriate representation of different legal systems'.[36] There have been six SRT mandate holders from 1985 to the

---

issued by the UN Subcommittee on Prevention of Torture, the UN Committee against Torture, the UN Special Rapporteur on Torture and other cruel, inhuman or degrading treatment or punishment, and the Board of Trustees of the UN Voluntary Fund for Victims of Torture (23 June 2016), available at http://www.ohchr.org/EN/NewsEvents/Pages/DisplayNews.aspx?NewsID=20165&LangID=E. Other instances of cooperation during the term of former SRT Juan Méndez include exchanges of views and commentary regarding the CAT's General Comment No 3 on rehabilitation, and the SPT's paper detailing its approach to the rights of persons institutionalized and medically treated without informed consent. Similarly, the SRT regularly consulted with members of the CAT and SPT on both thematic and country-specific aspects of his work.

[32] Evans (above n 23), 383.

[33] *Ibid*, 384.

[34] After written applications are made in response to calls by the UNHRC Secretariat, candidates are interviewed by a specially constituted Consultative Group composed of ambassadors from each of the UN's five regional groups. The Consultative Group recommends the selected candidate to the President of the UNHRC, which must approve the nomination. See *Institution-Building of the United Nations Human Rights Council*, UN Doc A/HRC/RES/5/1 (18 June 2007), para 40.

[35] Limon, M and Piccone, T, *Human Rights Special Procedures: Determinants of Influence: Understanding and Strengthening the Effectiveness of the UN's Independent Human Rights Experts*, Policy Report, Brookings Institution, 14 (March 2014).

[36] *Institution-Building of the United Nations Human Rights Council* (n 34 above), para 40.

present, five from Western Europe and one from Latin America, and all have been males.[37] The geographical and gender balance of the SRTs has therefore been less diverse than that of other Special Procedures, which, as of January 2018, are comprised of 56 percent males and 44 percent females, with individual experts representing the following geographic divide: 32.50 percent from the Western Europe and Other States group, 20 percent from the Latin American and Caribbean group, 11.25 percent from the Eastern European group; 13.75 percent from the Asia-Pacific group; and 22.5 percent from the African group.[38] It is the hope of the authors that future appointments of torture mandate holders will adequately represent the gender and geographical balance sought by the resolution and that increasingly characterizes the Special Procedures as a whole.

Key Areas and Methods of Work

The SRT's methods of work are varied and involve cooperation with a broad range of actors at the international, regional, and national levels. The three main areas of work, namely allegation letters and urgent appeals; country visits; and thematic reports and contributions to normative developments, are complemented by other activities carried out on an *ad hoc* basis, which can range from support for strategic litigation and for civil society advocacy activities to participation in conferences and panels, issuing press releases and media interviews, and designated follow-up activities. This section will discuss allegation letters and urgent appeals, country visits, and additional complementary areas of work. The SRT's role in producing thematic reports and contributing to normative developments will be discussed in the next section, which will also overview evolving standards for torture under international law and the broadening scope of the SRT's mandate.

Allegation letters and urgent appeals
A major component of the SRT's work involves the transmission of urgent appeals and allegation letters to States.[39] Such communications procedures or petitions, as they are sometimes referred to, are among the few, if not 'the only direct link between the victims of human rights violations and the international human rights protection system', and thus constitute a vital component of that system.[40]

Urgent appeals are submitted where individuals or groups are facing an imminent risk of torture or mistreatment in a particular place, or where pending legislation or policies threaten to undercut the prohibition of torture. Allegation letters, on the other hand, are submitted when abuses have already occurred, or where a pattern of past violations has been detected. The purpose of these communications is to give the States an opportunity to clarify the cir-

---

[37]   Peter Kooijmans (Netherlands, 1985–1993); Sir Nigel S Rodley (United Kingdom, 1993–2001); Theo van Boven (Netherlands, 2001–2004); Manfred Nowak (Austria, 2004–2010), Juan Méndez (Argentina, 2010–2016), and Nils Melzer (Switzerland, 2016–present).

[38]   United Nations Office of the High Commissioner for Human Rights, *Nomination, Selection and Appointment of Mandate Holders*, http://www.ohchr.org/EN/HRBodies/HRC/SP/Pages/Nominations .aspx

[39]   United Nations Office of the High Commissioner for Human Rights, *Seventeen Frequently Asked Questions about United Nations Special Rapporteurs*, http://www.ohchr.org/Documents/Publications/ FactSheet27en.pdf

[40]   Piccone (n 1 above), 49.

cumstances surrounding the allegations, to call on the Government to investigate them and to prosecute and punish all perpetrators of torture or other ill-treatment, to provide adequate redress for victims, and to prevent the future recurrence of such acts.

In transmitting allegation letters and urgent appeals, the SRT acts upon information provided by the victims or their representatives. While the communication process with the governments is confidential, the complaint, as well as the Governments' responses – or lack thereof – are later on made public three times a year in Special Procedures joint communications report. It is instructive that because the SRT has been operating for longer than most other currently existing mandates and covers a very broad range of issues – torture and mistreatment in interrogation, inhumane conditions of detention in prisons as well as in mental health hospitals, and even mistreatment by non-State actors in circumstances in which the State fails to protect the victim – it is one of the mandates that receives the most communications from the public each year. On average, the SRT mandate issues observations in two hundred communications every year, covering a wide range of issues. Additionally, the Special Rapporteur may choose to publish his or her conclusions regarding each case addressed in a letter or appeal and the government's responses in an annual 'Observations Report' presented to UNHRC sessions in March. Indeed, the SRT has been one of the few mandates that have chosen to publish such reports, which serve as an important advocacy tool in support of specific cases or with regard to specific country contexts, and provide a useful glimpse into the challenges facing the prohibition and prevention of torture in most countries.[41]

To evaluate whether a victim or representative of the victim has adequately presented an allegation, the SRT makes an initial examination to determine if there are 'reasonable grounds' to assess that there exists an identifiable risk of torture or other ill-treatment or it is likely that torture or other ill-treatment have taken place. In other words, contrary to national and international courts, the SRT does not require hard evidence, but can act and request the Government to provide further information, related court decisions, forensic documentation and information related to national investigations. Nevertheless, the SRT examines the credibility of the allegations seriously and acts only on those that are *prima facie* reliable.

With regard to the reliability of the source and the allegations made, the SRT may consider a number of factors, such as the consistency of the information received with the general situation in the concerned country, or information received on other cases from the same region and findings of other national or international bodies (such as National Human Rights Institutions or the UNCAT's Concluding Observations), in support of the mandate's own findings and conclusions. More specifically, the SRT may take into consideration factors such as accounts by witnesses of the person's physical condition while in detention; the fact that a person is kept in conditions conducive to torture and cruel, inhuman, or degrading treatment (CIDT), such as incommunicado detention, solitary confinement, or prolonged death row detention; cases of overreliance on confession by the prosecution and the judiciary in the absence of corroborative evidence, in particular those confessions obtained without the presence of a lawyer.

Research reveals that of 8,921 communications sent by all mandates between the years 2008 and 2014, just over half received responses from the Government concerned. Of these, 23

---

[41]   The SRT's annual Observations Reports are compiled on the website of the United Nations Office of the High Commissioner for Human Rights, *Reports of the Special Rapporteur on torture and other cruel, inhuman or degrading treatment or punishment – Addendum – Observations on communications transmitted to Governments and replies received*, http://ap.ohchr.org/documents/dpage_e.aspx?m=103

percent of responses were immaterial and 24 percent rejected the allegations without substantiation, while 39 percent were deemed to be responsive though incomplete. Only 8 percent of allegations' responses indicated that steps were taken to address the violations.[42] Nevertheless, allegation letters and urgent appeals constitute an important tool for advocacy for civil society and grassroots activists, for instance by providing an opportunity for them to refer to the conclusions in domestic litigation. These interventions can be even more effective when several Special Procedures mandates and independent experts join together in issuing an appeal, as they usually do if the communication alleges violations that fall under several mandates.

In a number of instances, communications have helped to bring attention to pressing situations and, often in combination with the efforts of civil society and grassroots activism, led to Government and other actions designed to address the allegations. The Special Rapporteur's communication regarding the use of electric shock 'aversive therapy' in treating children with disabilities at the Judge Rotenberg Center in Massachusetts, US, for instance, drew global media attention to this practice and intensified efforts to bring an end to it.[43] While the US Government, in response to the communication, provided examples of subsequent measures and proposed reforms aimed at limiting the use of such treatment, the mandate urged the Government to conduct further investigations into the continuing abuses, and to enact a blanket prohibition against all such practices at the national and state levels. Similarly, the Special Rapporteur's communications regarding the dangerous and violent conditions in the immigration detention facility run by Australia in Manus Island, Papua New Guinea, and particularly the detention and treatment of migrant children, led to increased international attention on the issue, including an intemperate reaction by a former Prime Minister of Australia.[44] While the Manus Island detention center was officially closed down in 2017, refugees and asylum seekers have remained, and continue to be sent to 'transit centers' on the island, in conditions tantamount to detention and which do not meet basic standards; reports of deaths, including suicides, have continued in the years 2018 and 2019.[45]

Joint communications by mandate holders regarding the indefinite detention and mistreatment of detainees at Guantanamo Bay,[46] as well as cases involving the arbitrary detention of

[42]   Limon and Piccone (n 35 above), 29–30.
[43]   Pilkington, E, 'UN Calls for Investigation of US School's Shock Treatments of Autistic Children', *The Guardian* (June 2, 2012), https://www.theguardian.com/society/2012/jun/02/un-investigation-shock-treatments-autism
[44]   Kozaki, D, 'Abbott Says Australians "Sick of being Lectured to by UN" after Scathing Report on Asylum Policies, *ABC News* (March 9, 2015), http://www.abc.net.au/news/2015-03-09/tony-abbott-hits-out-united-nations-asylum-report/6289892
[45]   Refugee Council of Australia & Amnesty International, *Until When? The Forgotten Men on Manus Island* (November 2019), https://www.amnesty.nl/content/uploads/2018/11/Until-When-The-forgotten-men-on-Manus-Island.pdf?x68103; Human Rights Watch, *World Report: Australia* (2019), https://www.hrw.org/world-report/2019/country-chapters/australia
[46]   Inter-American Commission on Human Rights, *UN Working Group on Arbitrary Detention, UN Rapporteur on Torture, UN Rapporteur on Human Rights and Counter-Terrorism, and UN Rapporteur on Health Reiterate Need to End the Indefinite Detention of Individuals at Guantánamo Naval Base in Light of Current Human Rights Crisis* (May 1, 2013), http://www.oas.org/en/iachr/media_center/preleases/2013/029.asp

human rights defenders and journalists,[47] and cases on the death penalty,[48] have also brought much-needed attention to critical situations on the ground and empowered civil society, grassroots activists, and other national human rights actors to more effectively pursue human rights campaigns and accountability and remedies in individual cases. While the direct impact of most communications procedures is difficult to measure in quantitative terms, there is no doubt that they play an important role in some individual cases, and bolster the efforts of civil society and others working on the ground in support of human rights every day. While a discussion of the need for reform of the communications procedures is beyond the scope of this chapter, it should be noted that the system should be reformed with a view to ensuring that it is made more visible, understandable, accessible, and user-friendly for activists on the ground. At the same time, there have been calls to strengthen the system by providing greater financial and human resource allocations, as well as by making it more responsive to the needs and situations of victims.[49]

Country visits
The second main activity of the mandate is to conduct country visits. These fact-finding missions are initiated upon the invitation of a Government. They are aimed at directly assessing the situation in that State regarding the prohibition of torture and cruel, inhuman, and degrading treatment, and to issue recommendations to the State. As has been noted, country visits have perhaps the greatest role in actualizing the Special Rapporteurs' status as the 'eyes and ears' of the UN human rights system, by allowing them to 'assess real-world conditions' and directly observe and evaluate situations, practices, and even specific complaints relevant to their mandates.[50] As explained by former mandate holder Sir Nigel Rodley, the specific added value of country visits is that they 'make possible substantive uncovering of those aspects of the reality that governments prefer to conceal and which, indeed, may be unknown to important higher level decision makers, whether by preference or inadvertence'.[51]

Aside from shedding light on the situation of torture and other ill-treatment in a specific jurisdiction, country visits are also an important way of mobilizing and empowering civil society in that State, and provide an opportunity for victims and their families to meet with and submit complaints to the Special Rapporteur. Additionally, a key role of country visits is to provide effective assistance to the State in question, in terms of pursuing reforms, which

---

[47] See, e.g., United Nations Office of the High Commissioner for Human Rights, *UN Rights Expert Raises Alarm over Saudi Arabia's Growing Clamp Down on Freedom of Expression* (December 16, 2015) http://www.ohchr.org/en/NewsEvents/Pages/DisplayNews.aspx?NewsID=16892&LangID=E; *Iran: UN Rights Expert Calls for the Immediate Release of Dual Nationals* (October 7, 2016) http://www.ohchr.org/EN/NewsEvents/Pages/DisplayNews.aspx?NewsID=20653
[48] See, e.g., United Nations Office of the High Commissioner for Human Rights, *Pakistan: UN Rights Experts Urge Pakistan Authorities to Halt Execution of a Person with Disabilities* (September 27, 2016) http://www.ohchr.org/EN/NewsEvents/Pages/DisplayNews.aspx?NewsID=20593
[49] Piccone (n 1 above), 49.
[50] Gaer, F, 'Picking and Choosing? Country Visits by Thematic Special Procedures' in Nolan, Freedman and Murphy (n 16 above), 88.
[51] Rodley, NS, 'United Nations Human Rights Treaty Bodies and Special Procedures of the Commission on Human Rights: Complementarity or Competition?' (2003) 25 *Human Rights Quarterly* 882.

must be premised on a 'thorough and objective fact-finding and assessment of the respective needs for reform'.[52]

In inviting the SRT to conduct a country visit, the State commits to ensuring free and unrestricted access to all places of deprivation of liberty, including the ability to conduct interviews with detainees, torture victims, and their families without governmental presence, and to meet freely with government authorities at all levels and civil society representatives.[53] Indeed, the terms of reference for fact-finding missions by Special Rapporteurs require Governments to guarantee mandate holders' freedom of movement throughout the whole country, and in particular to restricted areas, contacts with the media and any private institutions and persons, as well as full access to all documentary materials relevant to the mandate.[54] The information collected on these fact-finding missions, as well as the SRT's final conclusions and recommendations are communicated to the State initially on a confidential basis. The final report, together with the State's response, are presented before the Human Rights Council and brought to the attention of the General Assembly, and thus they become an official UN document that is widely distributed and made available to the public.

Because Special Rapporteurs can only conduct visits at the invitation of – meaning with the agreement of – the Government, it is implicit that goodwill and cooperation on the part of the State is essential for the success of the visit. In practice, this means that countries that receive visits by the SRT are very likely to be in the process of, or at least intend to begin, undertaking reforms or to step up efforts to combat and prevent torture and other ill-treatment. Nevertheless, it can be the case that a country will invite the SRT to visit 'for other reasons, such as earlier pledges to the Human Rights Council in order to be elected and a general political desire to show to the international community that they actively cooperate with special procedures'.[55] In such a situation, the SRT's task will be more difficult, as he or she may encounter obstruction on the ground, for instance in obtaining access to prisons or police custody centers, as was the case in the SRT's visit to The Gambia.[56]

Additionally, it is important for the SRT to ensure that visits are only undertaken on terms that comply with the OHCHR's terms of reference, and which do not compromise the independence of the mandate or set a damaging precedent for future visits. For these reasons, former SRT Juan Méndez declined the invitation to visit the US detention facility at Guantanamo Bay, which carried terms that he could not accept, namely a prohibition from interviewing detainees in private and restricted access to certain parts of the detention facility.[57] Similar unacceptable restrictions were attached to invitations to visit the Russian Federation and mainland United

---

[52]   Gaer (n 50 above), 89.

[53]   Nowak, M, 'Fact-Finding on Torture and Ill-Treatment and Conditions of Detention' (2009) 1 *Journal of Human Rights Practice* 101.

[54]   United Nations Office of the High Commissioner for Human Rights, *Revised Terms of Reference for Country Visits by Special Procedures Mandate Holders Of the United Nationals Human Rights Council* (June 2016) http://www.ohchr.org/Documents/HRBodies/SP/ToRs2016.pdf

[55]   Gaer (n 50 above).

[56]   *Report of the Special Rapporteur on Torture and Other Cruel, Inhuman or Degrading Treatment or Punishment: Mission to Gambia* A/HRC/28/68/Add.4 (March 16, 2015), para 4.

[57]   'UN Torture Expert Refused Access to Guantánamo Bay and US Federal Prisons', *The Guardian* (March 11, 2015) https://www.theguardian.com/us-news/2015/mar/11/un-torture-expert-refused-access -guantanamo-bay-us-prisons; 'UN Investigator Rejects Conditions of Guantanamo Invite', *Aljazeera* (March 11, 2015) https://www.aljazeera.com/news/2015/03/torture-investigator-guantanamo-invite -150311220052454.html

States, which the former SRT declined. In other cases, States have invited the SRT to visit but cancelled the trip at the last minute. This was the case in Bahrain, whose authorities repeatedly 'postponed' the SRT's visit, without providing for alternative dates – thus effectively amounting to a cancelation; in this case, the Government continues to act in bad faith, by falsely claiming that the SRT had 'put off' the visit.[58] In other instances, a State may invite the SRT for a visit, but fail to assist the SRT in making proper preparations for it – for instance in setting up meetings with the authorities and making security arrangements – as was the case with Iraq.

The task of interviewing detainees during visits to prisons, pretrial detention centers, and other places of deprivation of liberty, such as police custody cells, is a particularly critical one that requires special attention. As excellently outlined in a paper by former SRT Manfred Nowak, such considerations range from the need to adequately identify detainees for interviews, to ensuring that the SRT's role and the purpose of the interview is properly explained, that interviews take place with full informed consent and in a situation of complete confidentiality and privacy, and that the greatest possible measures are taken to ensure that there will be no reprisals against detainees who speak with the SRT.[59] In all places that SRT Juan Méndez visited (other than The Gambia), including Mauritania, Ghana, Brazil, Mexico, Georgia, Tajikistan, Tunisia, Uruguay, Morocco and Western Sahara, Sri Lanka, and Kyrgyzstan, he obtained the full cooperation of the authorities and unobstructed access to places of deprivation of liberty, and was able to speak to detainees and hold other interviews in private. This state of affairs is not surprising in view of the fact that Special Rapporteurs can only make country visits with the consent of the Government.

Aside from visiting places of deprivation of liberty and assessing the state of torture and other ill-treatment within the prison system, in police custody, and in other institutional settings, during country visits the SRT and his team also conduct meetings with State authorities, with a view to holding frank discussions about the Government's efforts to combat and prevent torture, and to offer assistance in these efforts – both during and after country visits via continued engagement and follow-up – and the provision of technical assistance, as will be explained below. In addition, the SRT's contacts with other stakeholders, ranging from civil society organizations, lawyers, victims and their families, and professionals who may play a role relevant to the prevention of torture and other ill-treatment in certain circumstances, such as physicians and police officers, for instance, are also very important. Such a range of actors is particularly important in assisting the SRT to uncover and understand situations.

In the experience of former SRT Méndez, States that he visited typically received his post-visit findings in good faith, and authorities engaged in constructive efforts to undertake meaningful changes in accordance with his recommendations (and often those of other international and regional human rights mechanisms). In this vein, the SRT's recommendations following country visits have contributed to the elaboration of national plans of action on torture and the implementation of reforms strengthening procedural safeguards in criminal

---

[58] United Nations News, 'UN Independent Expert 'Deeply Disappointed' over Bahraini Postponements of Visit' (April 24, 2013), https://news.un.org/en/story/2013/04/437932-un-independent-expert-deeply-disappointed-over-bahraini-postponements-visit#.V07XZucgugQ

[59] Nowak (n 53 above).

procedure codes, as was the case in Kyrgyzstan;[60] the ratification of the OPCAT and the establishment of a National Preventive Mechanism in Tunisia;[61] the adoption of federal anti-torture legislation in Mexico;[62] and the establishment of the Mental Health Authority Board in Ghana, which seeks to end the chaining of persons with psychosocial and other disabilities in so-called 'prayer camps'.[63] In some, but rare, cases, the SRT's conclusions and recommendations have drawn sharp disputes and criticism from the authorities, as was notably the case following SRT Méndez's visit to Mexico, during which he found that torture in Mexico was 'generalized'.[64] Regrettably, authorities' unwillingness to constructively engage in dialogue in such cases can significantly damage prospects for effective cooperation in support of meaningful changes on the ground.

Thematic reports and normative developments: the broadening scope of the mandate
The third main activity within the mandate is the production of thematic reports, which are presented twice annually to the Human Rights Council and the General Assembly. These thematic reports cover a wide range of issues relating to the prohibition of torture and other cruel, inhuman and degrading treatment. In producing thematic reports, the mandate undertakes research on the different global trends and practices pertaining to the selected issue and how they impact the prohibition of torture, attempts to draw conclusions about emerging human rights norms, and issues recommendations to prevent such future treatment.

As with country reports, civil society, practitioners in a diverse array of fields, and academics play an important role in assisting the SRT in identifying issues and in the research, drafting, and publication process of thematic reports. The drafting of comprehensive and nuanced thematic reports requires collaboration with organizations and experts from a wide range of fields in the form of private consultations and promotional and advocacy initiatives. To this end, former SRT Juan Méndez established a practice of holding specific expert consultations designed to inform the drafting of thematic reports, which include the leading international experts and NGO representatives in the relevant field. This methodology enables the SRT to base his or her research, conclusions, and recommendations to States on the solid knowledge and experiences of civil society organizations and lawyers and other experts who have been working on the specialized issues under discussion for many years.

As the authors have previously emphasized, over the past several decades the scope of the torture and other ill-treatment framework has evolved to cover acts and situations extending beyond its traditional spheres, which were largely limited to examining instances of mistreat-

---

[60]   World Intellectual Property Organization, Kyrgyzstan, Criminal Procedure Code of the Kyrgyz Republic No. 62 of June 30, 1999 (as amended up to Law No. 162 of July 28, 2017).

[61]   Association for the Prevention of Torture, Tunisia: OPCAT Ratification, https://apt.ch/en/opcat_pages/opcat-ratification-64/

[62]   Amnesty International, *Mexico: New Torture Law, Glimmer of Hope that must Translate into Justice* (April 26, 2017), https://www.amnesty.org/en/latest/news/2017/04/mexico-la-nueva-ley-contra-la-tortura-un-atisbo-de-esperanza-que-debe-traducirse-en-justicia/

[63]   See, e.g., Walker, GH, 'Ghana Mental Health Act 846 2012: A Qualitative Study of the Challenges and Priorities for Implementation' (2015) 49 *Ghana Medical Journal* 266.

[64]   Wilks, A, *Mexico's Torture Problem*, Oxford Human Rights Hub (22 April 2015), http://ohrh.law.ox.ac.uk/mexicos-torture-problem/

ment in the context of detention settings and/or interrogation.[65] Initially, the mandate of the SRT was placed by the UN under the agenda item pertaining to the 'question of the human rights of all persons subjected to any form of detention or imprisonment'.[66] However, this understanding has evolved in view of growing authoritative consensus that the prohibition of torture and other ill-treatment necessarily encompasses the obligation of States to adopt positive measures to prevent torture and inhuman treatment, and to investigate, prosecute, and punish these crimes. Moreover, those obligations apply when they are committed not only by State agents but also by private individuals, under circumstances where the State knows or ought to know of the risk faced by vulnerable victims and fails to protect them. The standard extends to torture and ill-treatment in prisons or police custody but also in situations extending beyond detention settings, such as excessive use of force in repressing demonstrations and in other non-custodial settings.[67] This has led to an expansion in the thematic issues tackled by the SRT mandate. In this context, issues like domestic violence, female genital mutilation (FGM), and abuses in healthcare settings have increasingly been incorporated into the discourse on the prohibition of torture.[68]

The boundaries of the normative framework pertaining to the prohibition of torture and other ill-treatment are constantly evolving to encompass an ever-greater range of practices and circumstances. The SRT mandate has an important role to play in exploring those boundaries, tackling intersectional issues that require further analysis and elaboration, and offering sound and progressive legal interpretations in ever-changing contexts. As such, in his thematic reports former SRT Juan Méndez tackled a diverse range of issues, including conditions of detention that can amount to torture or cruel, inhuman and degrading treatment, such as solitary confinement; violence against women and LGBTI persons; the mistreatment of children deprived of liberty; torture and inhuman treatment in healthcare settings; the role of the exclusionary rule and the use of torture-tainted evidence in courts; the role of forensic sciences in detecting and investigating torture and other ill-treatment; investigative interviewing and the implementation of key procedural safeguards by law enforcement officials; and the death penalty.

The SRT's thematic work has led to significant breakthroughs in the analysis and conceptualization of key practices and circumstances requiring attention from the perspective of the prohibition of torture and other ill-treatment. Aside from assisting States, policy-makers, and lawyers in this regard, the SRT's thematic reports also play a role in fostering further dialogue and debates among diverse stakeholders on key issues, and contributing to advocacy efforts by civil society. For instance, the SRT's 2011 report on the death penalty as it relates to the prohibition of torture, concluded that although it may still be considered that capital punishment does not constitute a violation *per se* of the prohibition of torture, international standards and state practice are in fact moving in that direction and the ability of states to impose the

---

[65]   Méndez, JE and Nicolescu, A, 'Evolving Standards for Torture in International Law' in Başoğlu, M (ed), *Torture and its Definitions in International Law* (Oxford University Press, 2017).

[66]   *Question of the human rights of all persons subjected to any form of detention or imprisonment*, UN Doc E/CN.4/RES/1985/16 (11 March 1985).

[67]   *Report of the Special Rapporteur on Torture and Other Cruel, Inhuman or Degrading Treatment or Punishment*, UN Doc A/HRC/34/54 (14 February 2017).

[68]   Méndez and Nicolescu (n 65 above).

death penalty without violating the prohibition of torture is becoming increasingly restricted, contributing significantly to the growing global trend towards abolition.[69]

Similarly, in his report on torture in healthcare settings, the SRT provided important clarification on the nexus between certain practices occurring in medical settings and the prohibition of torture and other ill-treatment, concluding that forced sterilizations, denial of abortions in certain cases, involuntary detention, and other intrusive 'therapeutic' measures taken in the name of treatment and under the guise of medical 'necessity', could rise to the level of torture or cruel, inhuman and degrading treatment. Recognizing that grey areas certainly remain where healthcare and prohibited infliction of pain collide, often controversially, the report and subsequent analysis clarified that there is an increasing consensus that torture and ill-treatment in healthcare settings can and frequently do occur in the form of reproductive rights violations, the denial of pain treatment, the mistreatment of persons who use drugs, LGBTI persons, and persons with physical and psychosocial disabilities.[70]

The SRT's 2016 report on gender perspectives on torture made similar progress in characterizing abuses experienced by women, girls, and LGBTI persons as crossing the threshold into torture and other ill-treatment. For instance, the report elaborated on the denial of abortion in some cases, highlighting that the social stigma that surrounds abortion in many societies is such that – even where abortion is legally available in certain circumstances – women have to suffer humiliating treatment by doctors, hospital administrators, prosecutors, and other officials, only for seeking what the law allows them to have. In such cases, the SRT elaborated, the State is responsible for finding ways to protect women from humiliation, since humiliation is the very definition of degrading treatment. The SRT also spoke out against non-consensual and medically unnecessary so-called 'genital normalizing' surgeries in children born with atypical sex characteristics, who are often subject to such surgeries, irreversible sex assignment, and involuntary sterilization, leaving them with permanent, irreversible infertility and causing severe mental suffering.[71] In his report on children deprived of liberty, the SRT spoke to the unique vulnerability and heightened needs of children deprived of liberty, assessing that the deprivation of liberty of children is inextricably linked – in fact if not in law – with ill-treatment. The SRT's analysis of various practices and the recommendations issued, ranging from clear calls that children should never be subjected to life sentences without parole, solitary confinement, the use of restraints or corporal punishment, and immigration detention, proved important to advocacy efforts around the world.[72]

At the same time, the SRT continues to play an important role in supporting and advancing relevant normative developments, often in more 'traditional' areas of the mandate, such as with regard to the revision of the UN Standard Minimum Rules for the Treatment of Prisoners (SMR), now known as the Nelson Mandela Rules, and recent efforts to drive forward the development of a Universal Protocol on the topic of non-coercive interviews, sometimes referred to as investigative interviewing, and attendant procedural safeguards. The SRT's rec-

---

[69]   *Interim Report of the Special Rapporteur on Torture and Other Cruel, Inhuman or Degrading Treatment or Punishment, UN Doc* A/67/279 (9 August 2012), para 26.

[70]   *Report of the Special Rapporteur on Torture and Other Cruel, Inhuman or Degrading Treatment or Punishment,* UN Doc A/HRC/22/53 (1 February 2013).

[71]   *Report of the Special Rapporteur on Torture and Other Cruel, Inhuman or Degrading Treatment or Punishment,* UN Doc A/HRC/31/57 (5 January 2016), para 50.

[72]   *Report of the Special Rapporteur on Torture and Other Cruel, Inhuman or Degrading Treatment or Punishment,* UN Doc A/HRC/28/68 (5 March 2015).

ommendations and interventions during the SMR revision process in particular had an appreciable impact in fostering consensus on several key provisions of the updated standards. These changes constituted important improvements and additions to the Rules, from the perspective of the prohibition of torture and ill-treatment in international law. One such major achievement is the prohibition of indefinite or prolonged solitary confinement (as well as its definition as solitary confinement in excess of 15 days), which is now contained in Rules 43 and 44.[73] Other enhancements include the prohibition of certain types of restraints and/or stricter regulation of their use, and more progressive standards with regard to searches, prison conditions, and the duties of medical professionals.

The mandate of the SRT has also played an important role in initiating and fostering support for the advancement of normative developments, by proposing and – together with partners – guiding the development of standard-setting processes. This has been the case with former SRT Juan Méndez's call for the development of a Universal Protocol on Non-Coercive Interviewing and Legal Safeguards in his last thematic report.[74] The former SRT's call for the development of such a non-binding set of guidelines was enthusiastically welcomed by an array of stakeholders – including States, civil society organizations, professionals including law enforcement officials and psychologists, and international and regional organizations[75] – and has led to the creation of an expert-driven Steering Committee, which will oversee the development of the guidelines. The former SRT was also instrumental in initiating discussions concerning the need to update the Istanbul Protocol (following his thematic report on the role of forensic and medical science in the prevention of torture),[76] leading to a multi-stakeholder process to produce an updated Istanbul Protocol, which came into being in 2020.

Follow-up initiatives and complementary methods of work
The main areas of the SRT's work are complemented by additional methods of work that he or she may choose to undertake on a discretionary basis. In this sense, it is worth noting that all mandate holders are appointed as independent experts and discharge their mandate without instructions or censorship from any United Nations agency or authority; they are expected, nonetheless, to report to the Human Rights Council, to comport themselves within the limits of each one's specific mandate and to observe the Code of Conduct prescribed by the HRC.[77]

---

[73]   United Nations General Assembly, *United Nations Standard Minimum Rules for the Treatment of Prisoners (the Nelson Mandela Rules)* A/RES/70/175 (8 January 2016).

[74]   United Nations Office of the High Commissioner for Human Rights, Set universal standards for interviewing detainees without coercion, UN anti-torture expert urges States (October 18, 2016), http://www.ohchr.org/EN/NewsEvents/Pages/DisplayNews.aspx?NewsID=20722&LangID=E. *Report of the Special Rapporteur on Torture and Other Cruel, Inhuman or Degrading Treatment or Punishment*, UN Doc A/HRC/71/298 (5 August 2016).

[75]   See, for instance, the high-level event on this issue, which took place on the side-lines of the United Nations General Assembly in New York City in September 2016. UN Web TV, *Torture during Interrogations: Illegal, Immoral, and Ineffective* (22 September 2016), http://webtv.un.org/search/torture-during-interrogations-illegal-immoral-and-ineffective/5584494563001/?term=torture&sort=date&page=2

[76]   *Interim Report of the Special Rapporteur on Torture and other Cruel, Inhuman or Degrading Treatment or Punishment*, UN Doc A/69/387 (23 September 2014).

[77]   United Nations Office of the High Commissioner for Human Rights, *Code of Conduct for Special Procedures Mandate-Holders of the Human Rights Council*, http://www.ohchr.org/Documents/HRBodies/SP/CodeOfConduct.pdf

The SRT's mandate as an independent expert provides a unique opportunity for engagement in other methods of work, either as a means to explore new issues – whether thematic or country-specific – that may not otherwise be addressed in the principal areas of work, or as a way to complement, deepen, and follow-up on the mandate's principal areas of work.

Due to the limited resources received by the SRT mandate from the OHCHR, which often do not permit mandate holders to sustain in-depth engagement and consistent follow-up on key areas of work, mandate holders may seek to obtain external support for their activities, both in terms of financial and human resources. To this end, former SRT Juan Méndez created the Anti-Torture Initiative (ATI), a project of the Center for Human Rights & Humanitarian Law at the American University Washington College of Law, with the aim of assisting the SRT in conducting follow-up in key thematic areas and in selected jurisdictions.

The ATI, which was launched in 2011, provided essential support for the mandate, with the specific aim of conducting meaningful follow-up and broadening and deepening the impact of the SRT's work. More specifically, the ATI developed a coherent follow-up model that transformed the landscape of follow-up by the mandate in both country-specific and thematic areas, and inspired the development of activities and new methods of outreach and engagement with anti-torture advocates and activists, as well as other stakeholders at the international, regional, national, and local levels. The financial and human resources that the ATI was able to provide to these ends enabled the SRT to pursue complementary methods of work in key thematic and country-specific priority areas, including the following.

Follow-up country visits and reports
Between 2011 and 2016, the SRT mandate conducted follow-up visits with the aim of evaluating the State's implementation of the SRT's initial recommendations, issuing additional recommendations when necessary, and facilitating collaboration between Government and civil society in strengthening protections and reforms against torture and other ill-treatment. Follow-up visits were undertaken to Uruguay, Ghana, Tunisia, and Tajikistan, and the resulting follow-up reports were published by the Human Rights Council. A follow-up report was also produced for Mexico in the absence of a follow-up visit, on the basis of a questionnaire, wide-ranging discussions with authorities, national and state human rights institutions, and civil society, and in-depth analysis of the situation on the ground.[78]

In-country activities and technical assistance
The SRT's main activities can be very effectively complemented by the conduct of in-country activities and technical assistance outside of official country or follow-up visits. Examples of such activities undertaken during SRT Juan Méndez's mandate include the conduct of training on the Istanbul Protocol with the National Preventive Mechanism and networks of medical and legal professionals in Brazil; the provision of input into anti-torture bills and other relevant legislation, for instance in Mexico; advice to legislatures on efforts to reform solitary confinement practices, as was the case in a number of US states, including Connecticut and New York; and the facilitation of the development of innovations on key topics in select jurisdictions, such as the elaboration of the National Action Plan against Torture in Kyrgyzstan, through meetings,

---

[78]   *Report of the Special Rapporteur on Torture and Other Cruel, Inhuman or Degrading Treatment or Punishment, Juan E. Méndez: Mission to Mexico*, UN Doc A/HRC/28/68/Add.3 (29 December 2014).

roundtables, and other activities; and briefings and submissions to policy-makers.[79] Strong local partnerships and the cooperation of national actors are essential to such undertakings, which go a long way in bringing the impact of the SRT's work to bear on practical changes on the ground.

Publications on specific thematic and country-specific topics and associated research efforts
The SRT has spearheaded the development of important publications on key issues relevant to the eradication and prevention of torture and other ill-treatment. Such publications include edited volumes published by the ATI on the topics of torture in healthcare settings, the torture of children deprived of liberty, and gender perspectives on torture,[80] which feature articles exploring and expanding upon key issues addressed in the SRT's biannual thematic reports on the same subjects. Given the necessarily limited scope – in length – of the SRT's thematic reports, such publications constitute an essential platform for exploring thematic topics in depth and from interdisciplinary perspectives, and fostering discussions amongst stakeholders at the normative, policy, and practical levels. Such volumes can also be used to address particular issues in priority countries, such as a volume on the reform of the penitentiary system in Uruguay.[81] Likewise, the SRT has worked with diverse partners to undertake discreet research efforts on key thematic issues, such as a study and comparative analysis of solitary confinement laws, policies, regulations, and practices in 36 jurisdictions.[82] Such endeavors broaden and deepen the impact of the SRT's reach, by providing an opportunity to delve into relevant topics in-depth and across a wide geographical scope.

---

[79]   *Report of the Special Rapporteur on Torture and Other Cruel, Inhuman or Degrading Treatment or Punishment, Juan E. Méndez: Mission to Kyrgyzstan*, UN Doc A/HRC/19/61/Add.2 (29 December 2014).

[80]   American University Washington College of Law, Center for Human Rights & Humanitarian Law, Anti-Torture Initiative, *Protecting Children against Torture in Detention: Global Solutions for a Global Problem* (2017), http://antitorture.org/wp-content/uploads/2017/03/Protecting_Children_From _Torture_in_Detention.pdf; *Torture in Healthcare Settings: Reflections on the Special Rapporteur on Torture's 2013 Thematic Report* (2016), http://antitorture.org/wp-content/uploads/2014/03/PDF _Torture_in_Healthcare_Publication.pdf; Gender Perspectives on Torture: Law and Practice (2018), https://www.wcl.american.edu/impact/initiatives-programs/center/documents/gender-perspectives-on -torture/

[81]   American University Washington College of Law, Center for Human Rights & Humanitarian Law, Anti-Torture Initiative, *Próximos Pasos Hacia Una Política Penitenciaria de Derechos Humanos en Uruguay: Ensayos de seguimiento a las recomendaciones de 2009 y 2013 de la Relatoría de Naciones Unidas contra la tortura* (2014), http://antitorture.org/wp-content/uploads/2014/08/Uruguay.pdf

[82]   American University Washington College of Law, Center for Human Rights & Humanitarian Law, Anti-Torture Initiative, Cyrus R. Vance Center for International Justice, and Weil, Gotshal & Manges, LLP, *Seeing into Solitary: A Review of the Laws and Policies of Certain Nations Regarding Solitary Confinement Detainees* (2016), https://www.weil.com/~/media/files/pdfs/2016/un_special _report_solitary_confinement.pdf. The study addresses practices in Argentina, Austria, Brazil, China, the Czech Republic, England and Wales, Ethiopia, Finland, France, Germany, Guatemala, Hungary, Japan, Kenya, Kyrgyzstan, Mexico, New Zealand, Norway, Poland, Russia, South Africa, Turkey, Uganda, Uruguay, Venezuela, and the United States. With respect to the United States, both the federal prison and the federal immigration system were surveyed, as well as the states of California, Colorado, Florida, Illinois, Maine, New York, Pennsylvania, and Texas.

Support for strategic litigation efforts
The SRT can also play an important role in supporting strategic litigation initiatives in priority thematic areas and in specific countries. For instance, former SRT Juan Méndez submitted a number of briefs *amicus curiae* and presented expert testimonies, particularly on the issue of solitary confinement, in cases across the United States and Canada, which produced demonstrable results in terms of curtailing the practice. One such result occurred in the case of *Ashker v. Governor of California*, which resulted in a landmark settlement between the petitioners and the US state of California, which will effectively lead to the end of indeterminate, long-term solitary confinement in all California state prisons.[83] Likewise, the SRT intervened in the case of *BCCLA and JHSC v. Attorney General of Canada*, which led to a decision by the Supreme Court of British Columbia ruling that prolonged and indefinite solitary confinement is unconstitutional.[84] Former SRT Méndez has also testified as expert witness in three cases in the United Kingdom involving extradition and the *non-refoulement* rule. Interventions in strategic litigation involve close collaboration between the SRT, lawyers, courts, prosecutors, and civil society actors.

Advocacy, awareness-raising, public statements, participation in events, and social media activities
The SRT also has an important role to play in conducting advocacy and awareness-raising on topics related to torture and ill-treatment around the world, by a variety of means. Primary among these are frequent public statements[85] on developments and issues of concern around the world, often in collaboration with other mandate holders or with other regional and international bodies such as the Inter-American Commission on Human Rights and the OSCE;[86] participation in public events, including lectures, conferences, panels, side-events, and expert meetings, as well as press interviews and media appearances; meetings with victims and survivors and their families; and social media campaigns, such as the SRT and the ATI's 2015 and

---

[83]   *Ashker v. Governor of California*, 2014 U.S. Dist. LEXIS 75347 (N.D. Cal. 2 June 2014).

[84]   Kassam, A, 'Canada's Use of Lengthy Solitary Confinement in Jails is Unconstitutional', *The Guardian* (17 January 2018) https://www.theguardian.com/world/2018/jan/18/canadas-use-of-lengthy-solitary-confinement-in-jails-is-unconstitutional-judge?CMP=Share_AndroidApp_Email. Additionally, the SRT's report was mentioned in the dissenting opinion of Justice Breyer in in the US Supreme Court case of *Glossip et al. v. Gross et al.* (2015), decided on 29 June 2015, which cited the report in arguing that use of the death penalty in the State of Oklahoma violates the Eight Amendment, due to the fact that a majority of death row inmates are kept in isolation for 22 or more hours per day, in contravention of the SRT's global call for a ban on solitary confinement in excess of 15 days. The report was also cited in the UK Supreme Court case of *Shahid v. Scottish Ministers* in support of the finding that solitary confinement, as applied to the defendant, was illegal.

[85]   United Nations Office of the High Commissioner for Human Rights, Latest News, http://www.ohchr.org/en/NewsEvents/Pages/NewsSearch.aspx?MID=SR_Torture

[86]   See, e.g., the case of the 'Angola Three', Albert Woodfox, Herman Wallace, and Robert King, United Nations Office of the High Commissioner for Human Rights, US: 'Four Decades in Solitary Confinement Can Only be Described as Torture' – UN rights expert (October 7, 2013), http://newsarchive.ohchr.org/EN/NewsEvents/Pages/DisplayNews.aspx?NewsID=13832&LangID=E. Organization of American States, Inter-American Commission on Human Rights, 'IACHR, UN Working Group on Arbitrary Detention, UN Rapporteur on Torture, UN Rapporteur on Human Rights and Counter-Terrorism, and UN Rapporteur on Health Reiterate Need to End the Indefinite Detention of Individuals at Guantánamo Naval Base in Light of Current Human Rights Crisis' (May 1, 2013), http://www.oas.org/en/iachr/media_center/preleases/2013/029.asp

2016 #TortureFreeWorld campaign on the occasion of June 26, International Day in Support of Victims of Torture. The ATI has also assisted the mandate of the SRT in providing a clearinghouse and platform for outreach and engagement with anti-torture stakeholders via its online presence, helping to raise the profile of the mandate and disseminate its work widely.[87]

In all its endeavors, the SRT works closely with a wide range of local and international civil society organizations in a number of different capacities. These groups play an important role in the work of the SRT and the Special Procedures particularly in the key areas of work described above, by producing submissions regarding human rights abuses, providing background information for the preparation and assessment of fact-finding missions, providing resources and consultation for thematic and country reports, and collaborating on public engagement and advocacy initiatives. In recent years, the SRT has undertaken a number of initiatives aimed at strengthening relationships with civil society, including the SRT's recent collaboration with ATI and in the areas of follow-up. This is a critical way in which the mandate can ensure that it is well informed, supported, and impactful.

REFLECTIONS: CHALLENGES AND OPPORTUNITIES LOOKING AHEAD

The Special Procedures of the United Nations face a daunting task with very limited resources. Indeed, those resources seem to be dwindling at an alarming rate, as they suffer the general budgetary shortfalls of the United Nations and also the need to spread those fewer resources among a growing number of mandates and other human rights-related tasks of the Office of the High Commissioner for Human Rights.

On the other hand, experience shows that the opportunities that mandates enjoy to make an important difference on the ground are enormous. Those opportunities are bolstered by the prestige of the United Nations and of the very system of protection that has been perfected over the years. To be sure, the impact is uneven. There are societies that are so closed that even the United Nations flag makes little difference to the victims of torture, and those countries are among the worst offenders in terms of the prohibition of torture and cruel, inhuman or degrading treatment or punishment. The impact is also somewhat diminished in countries that feel so powerful in the international arena that they can afford to ignore the pronouncements of United Nations representatives and get away with the continuation of unlawful practices.

The impact of the Special Procedures is greatest where there is a vibrant civil society and a free press that can multiply the voice of the SRT and insist on reform with creative solutions of their own. It helps also if the authorities (of all branches) acknowledge that they have a problem with torture and are willing to look for ways to curb it. Despite this uneven impact, there are always opportunities to appeal to the moral, legal and pragmatic arguments for the prohibition of torture and the related State obligations that form the well-established normative framework in this area.

The mandate is tremendously helped by the fact that the international community has developed a detailed and sophisticated normative framework that can assist decision-makers in promoting public policies and taking preventive measures to eradicate torture in our time.

---

[87]   Torture Free World, https://torturefreeworld.org

Although that objective continues to seem elusive, the office of the Special Rapporteur on Torture is still a powerful tool to that end. In this regard, the authors offer several recommendations to future SRT mandate holders:

- Capitalize on often solid existing legal frameworks, at the international, regional, and local levels, in assisting domestic authorities to bridge the gap between law and practices.
- Employ diverse methodologies of work, with a view to responding to specific challenges, needs, and opportunities, and tailor interventions creatively and strategically, looking beyond the traditional scope of duties associated with Special Procedures mandates.
- Work with a wide array of partners at all levels, including governmental authorities, civil society organizations, other international and regional mechanisms and agencies, professional networks, grassroots activists, and victims and their families, in seeking to affect change in a concerted and meaningful way. This will require striking a delicate balance between exposing violations and engaging in advocacy, and working constructively with State authorities and other actors seeking to affect change in good faith, often in precarious environments.
- Keep up to date with the latest normative developments in international law, and particularly in intersectional areas, with a view to encouraging normative developments in emerging areas of the law, and with regard to practices and situations to which the torture and other ill-treatment framework was not applied.
- Engage in concerted and carefully designed follow-up efforts in both country-specific and thematic areas, with a view to maximizing the mandate's reach and impact. Seeking additional resources (beyond those made available to the mandate by the OHCHR), whether human or financial, and strategic partnerships will likely be important in this regard.
- Foster greater cooperation with other UN independent experts and mechanisms, with a view to enhancing collective impact.
- Pay particular attention to the status of persons in situations of vulnerability, marginalized groups, and to the root causes of torture and other ill-treatment, such as discrimination, corruption, and even poverty.
- Maintain a victim-centered approach at the forefront of the mandate's work, whilst prioritizing a holistic, preventive approach to the fight against torture and other ill-treatment.

9.   The Council of Europe and the European system

Christine Bicknell

INTRODUCTION

Within Europe there are three principal regional organizations which play a role in the protection and promotion of human rights: the Council of Europe (CoE); the European Union (EU); and the Organization for Security and Cooperation in Europe (OSCE). The geographic coverage, institutional and legal arrangements, and relative approaches of each to addressing and eradicating torture and other ill-treatment mean that, whilst distinct, there are some considerable areas of overlap between them. In what follows, the relevant legal and institutional frameworks and the work of these three systems to address the prohibition of torture and inhuman and degrading treatment or punishment are introduced. A very brief contextual overview of the three systems within which normative and institutional means of addressing torture and ill-treatment have been developed is followed by sections focusing on the CoE and EU and their legal frameworks and principal institutions and mechanisms. This is followed by a more detailed overview of how torture and ill-treatment is addressed by the European Convention on Human Rights (ECHR), in particular through the jurisprudence of the European Court of Human Rights (ECtHR). Areas of complementarity and of tension in approaches to torture across the European systems and institutions are highlighted and examined in the following discussion as they arise.

CONTEXT

Within Europe, the CoE, EU and OSCE all have mandated institutions whose work relates to the prohibition of torture and ill-treatment. Helpfully, albeit incidentally, all Member States of the EU are also Members of the CoE, and likewise all CoE states are 'participants' in the OSCE. With 57 participating states, the OSCE embraces the largest area, including the USA and Canada. The CoE has a membership of 47 states, and the EU (post-Brexit) 27. It is beyond the scope of this overview to set out the structure or workings of these organizations more generally, the focus being on their work relevant to the prohibition of torture and ill-treatment. That said, the historical foundation and underlying philosophy of each helps to explain their respective approaches and levels of engagement with both torture and ill-treatment, and human rights more broadly.

The key reason for the creation of each organization concerned the desire to foster peace and stability in the region. Following the Second World War, thinking pulled in two competing directions. On one side a supranational system, a 'United States of Europe', marked by deep economic integration and overarching political structures was advocated. On the other, an intergovernmental model was favoured which would retain more fully the individual sovereignty of its Member States but nevertheless foster cooperation between them, including institutions for the promotion and protection of democracy, the rule of law and human rights. The history is covered capably elsewhere,[1] but the net outcome was that Europe developed both. In the organizations known to us today, the supranational, integrationist preference gave rise ultimately to the European Economic Community (EEC) in 1957 which, in 1993, became the EU.[2] The intergovernmental path was reflected in the establishment of the CoE in 1949.

Whilst the EEC was centred on economics, the CoE made 'the maintenance and further realisation of human rights and fundamental freedoms'[3] central to its work from the outset. One of its key treaties, concluded in 1950, is the European Convention on Human Rights and Fundamental Freedoms (ECHR) which sets out the (mainly civil and political) rights to be protected and created the European Court of Human Rights (ECtHR).[4] The CoE's most notable contribution in respect of torture and ill-treatment specifically is the European Convention for the Prevention of Torture and Inhuman and Degrading Treatment or Punishment, which entered into force in 1989, and the European Committee for the Prevention of Torture that it creates.[5] Additionally, in 1999 the CoE established the office of Council of Europe Commissioner for Human Rights[6] which works for the promotion and protection of human rights in Europe.

Conversely, the EU developed its interest in human rights protection much later. This was marked particularly by the adoption of its Charter of Fundamental Rights in 2000, though it was not until the Treaty of Lisbon in 2009 that the Charter gained full legal status, making it binding on EU institutions and states. In 2007, the EU created the European Union Fundamental Rights Agency[7] some of whose work has been relevant to the fight against torture. The EU has also produced Guidelines on Torture and other Cruel, Inhuman and Degrading Treatment or Punishment, their most recent iteration in September 2019.[8]

Regarding the relationship between the EU and the ECHR, the Lisbon Treaty states that the EU 'shall accede' to the ECHR.[9] However, a 2014 decision from the Court of Justice of the

---

[1]   Greer, S, Gerrards, J and Slowe, R, *Human Rights in the Council of Europe and the European Union* (Cambridge University Press, 2018).

[2]   Treaty on European Union (Consolidated Version), Treaty of Maastricht (OJ C 325/5, 7 December 1992).

[3]   Statute of the Council of Europe, 5th May 1949, ETS no 001, Article 1(b).

[4]   European Convention for the Protection of Human Rights and Fundamental Freedoms (ECHR) (adopted 4 November 1950, entered into force 3 September 1953 ETS no 5) (hereafter, 'ECHR').

[5]   European Convention for the Prevention of Torture and Inhuman or Degrading Treatment or Punishment (adopted 26 November 1987, entered into force 1 February 1989) ETS no 126 (hereafter 'ECPT'). See further below and Chapter 13 of this volume.

[6]   Resolution 99(50) on the Council of Europe Commissioner for Human Rights (adopted by the Committee of Ministers on 7 May 1999 at its 104th Session).

[7]   Council Regulation (EC) no 168/2007 of 15 February 2007 establishing a European Union Agency for Fundamental Rights.

[8]   Guidelines to EU policy towards third countries on torture, and other cruel, inhuman or degrading treatment or punishment – 2019 Revision of the Guidelines, adopted by the Council at its 3712th meeting held on 16 September 2019.

[9]   Treaty of Lisbon amending the Treaty on European Union and the Treaty establishing the European Community (OJ 2007/C 306/01, 17 December 2007), Article 6(2).

European Union (CJEU) rendered this all but impossible in practice.[10] It has not happened and it is unlikely that it ever will.

The OSCE came into being much later in 1975 as the 'Conference on Security and Cooperation in Europe' with the adoption of the Helsinki Final Act. It was created against the backdrop of the Cold War 'as a security organisation … aimed at creating a comprehensive framework for peace and stability in Europe'.[11] The legal status of the OSCE as an international organization remains a matter of some debate: it has avoided the creation of treaties, including its founding documents; it has 'participating states' rather than Member States; and commitments made by those states are always made unanimously but are binding only politically.[12] Nevertheless, the OSCE's 'comprehensive' approach to regional security is built on three thematic pillars: politico-military; economic; and human 'dimensions' of security, each of which is considered equally important.[13] In the human dimension, the OSCE recognizes 'respect for human rights and fundamental freedoms' as one of its 10 guiding principles and participating states have made and confirmed specific commitments, including directly on torture and other ill-treatment.[14] The main OSCE institution responsible for the human dimension is the Office for Democratic Institutions and Human Rights (ODIHR). It was created by the 1990 Charter of Paris, and 'provides support, assistance and expertise to participating states and civil society to promote democracy, rule of law, human rights and tolerance and non-discrimination'.[15] The ODIHR thus plays a significant role, mainly in capacity building and technical support. It is beyond the scope of this chapter to explore its work in greater detail, but for completeness, it should be noted.[16] The institutional context in Europe is, therefore, complex to say the least. It offers a range of norms, institutions and approaches which engage with the prohibition of torture and ill-treatment. In what follows the relevant structures and work in the CoE and EU are explored in greater detail.

---

[10]   *Opinion 2/13 on EU Accession to the ECHR*, 18 December 2014, ECLI:EU:C:2014:4:2454. See Greer, Gerrards and Slowe (n 1 above), 37–38.

[11]   Zannier, L, 'Human Rights and the OSCE's Comprehensive Security Concept' in *Vienna Manual on Human Rights*' (OSCE, 2012), available at: https://www.osce.org/sg/103964?download=true

[12]   Steinbrock, M, Moser, M and Peters, A (eds), *The Legal Framework of the OSCE* (Cambridge University Press, 2019); Froehly, JP, 'The OSCE 40 Years after Helsinki: Fall Back or Reset?' (2016) 25 *Polish Quarterly of International Affairs* 7–21.

[13]   Strohal, C, 'Consolidation and New Challenges: The ODIHR in the OSCE's 30th Anniversary Year', *OSCE Yearbook* (Baden-Baden, 2006).

[14]   These are compiled in OSCE Human Dimension Commitments, Volume 1, Thematic Compilation, 3rd edn (ODIHR, 2012).

[15]   https://www.osce.org/odihr

[16]   Notable work includes a handbook for practitioners outlining the OSCE's experience of prevention work, best practice and strategies: OSCE, *The Fight Against Torture: The OSCE Experience* (ODIHR, 2009), available at https://www.osce.org/odihr/37968?download=true. A recent example of the OSCE's technical support is advising Poland on its torture legislation, particularly on the definition of torture see OSCE/ODIHR, *Opinion on Definition of Torture and its Absolute Prohibition in Polish Legislation* (ODIHR, 2018) available at: https://www.osce.org/odihr/388763

LEGAL FRAMEWORK

Council of Europe

Article 3 ECHR
Article 3 of the ECHR comprises a single sentence:

> No one shall be subjected to torture or to inhuman or degrading treatment or punishment.

Whilst this is an elegant formulation, it is not particularly illuminating regarding what it means in detail and in practice. The definition of the respective terms and the scope of the prohibition, for example the extent to which it applies extra-territorially, have necessarily been developed by the jurisprudence of the ECtHR and, before its abolition in 1998, the European Commission on Human Rights. This is examined more closely in a later section, but two key observations on the text can be made at this point. Firstly, unlike other instruments such as the CAT and the ICCPR, the wording of the prohibition in the ECHR does not refer directly to 'cruel' treatment. This should not be seen, and is not seen, as meaning that the ECHR prohibition is a weaker prohibition than its comparators elsewhere which do include this term. Instead, since torture and any other deliberately inflicted ill-treatment meeting the threshold of inhuman is also evidently cruel, a European interpretation would tend to see cruelty as being implicit in the prohibition.

Secondly, and more crucially, Article 3 provides an absolute prohibition. The text is clear that 'no one' shall be subjected to torture or ill-treatment, and this does not allow for any circumstances in which an exception might arise. The absolute nature of the prohibition is confirmed by Article 15(2) ECHR which is explicit that even in 'time of emergency threatening the life of the nation' there can be no derogation from Article 3. Neither is Article 3 subject to any other restriction, qualification or balancing with competing rights claims or interests.[17] This however, is as far as the text of Article 3 takes us – and the force of an absolute prohibition is compromised if there is a lack of clarity over either its content or its scope. It is the ECtHR, over many years, which has thrashed out this detail, returned to below the penultimate section.

---

[17]   It has been observed that the notion of absolute rights is nebulous, not being precisely defined in the case law and including assessment of subjective factors: Addo, MK, and Grief, N 'Does Article 3 of the European Convention on Human Rights Enshrine Absolute Rights?' (1998) 9 *European Journal of International Law* 510–524. It has elsewhere been argued that Article 3 cannot be fully absolute. This is based on the argument that in (rare) situations where absolute rights clash – such as one person's right to life with another's Article 3 right – a moral assessment should cause one person's right to yield to another's: Greer, S, 'Is the Prohibition Against Torture, Cruel, Inhuman and Degrading Treatment or Punishment really "Absolute" in International Human Rights Law?' (2015) 15 *Human Rights Law Review* 101–137. For replies to this: Mavronicola, N, 'Is the Prohibition Against Torture and Cruel, Inhuman and Degrading Treatment Absolute in International Human Rights Law? A Reply to Steven Greer' (2017) 15 *Human Rights Law Review* 479–498; Graffin, N, '*Gäfgen v Germany*, the Use of Threats and the Punishment of Those Who Ill-Treat During Police Questioning: A Reply to Steven Greer' (2017) 15 *Human Rights Law Review* 681–699. Both were responded to by Greer in the same journal in 2018.

European Convention for the Prevention of Torture
The European Convention for the Prevention of Torture and Inhuman or Degrading Treatment or Punishment (ECPT) entered into force on 1 February 1989. It established the European Committee for the Prevention of Torture (CPT), a non-judicial, preventive body, and introduced an approach to dealing with torture and ill-treatment that was nothing short of revolutionary at the time. It establishes a system of regular visits by the CPT, a regional inter-disciplinary group of independent experts, to places of detention within the Member States. Based on those visits, and subsequent CPT reports and recommendations, an on-going relationship of dialogue between the CPT and states is developed as a means of combatting torture and ill-treatment, and more generally to improve the treatment and situation of people detained by the state.

In addition to regular visits and on-going dialogue, the system's central features are confidentiality[18] and cooperation.[19] It is not and was never designed to be adversarial. With its focus on prevention, it is forward-looking: to 'strengthen ... protection' and improve the situation of detainees. In ratifying the treaty, states grant the CPT permission to visit 'any place within its jurisdiction where persons are deprived of their liberty by a public authority'.[20] Article 3 ECPT obligates the CPT and 'the competent national authorities' of Member States to co-operate', whilst Article 11 ECPT protects the confidentiality of 'information gathered by the Committee in relation to a visit, its report and its consultations with the Party concerned'. Though almost all states publish the CPT's reports as a matter of course (albeit it often with some considerable delay), the principle of confidentiality within the treaty affords space for open and honest discussion between the parties.

The CPT has never put forward definitions of torture or of inhuman or degrading treatment, the very things the CPT is mandated to prevent. As a non-judicial body, it is not within the CPT's mandate to do so (see below) and it has always been cautious not to stray into this area which rightly belongs to the ECtHR. Normatively, what the CPT has done is to offer a more concrete conception of preventive standards. Through its long experience of preventive visiting the CPT has developed such standards on numerous themes relating to the treatment of people in detention and the conditions in which they are held. This began with the CPT publishing thematic standards in its Annual Reports, but later the CPT published a repository of these standards both in copy and on its website.[21] In reality, the standards are generally reformulations of recommendations made frequently to states, but they are nevertheless helpful in setting out the CPT's expectations and approach. More recently, the CPT has produced several 'Factsheets' on women in prison, immigration detention, and the transport of detainees. It has also published 'Checklists' for evaluation of, for example, psychiatric hospitals.[22]

---

18 ECPT, Article 11.
19 ECPT, Article 3.
20 ECPT, Article 2.
21 https://www.coe.int/en/web/cpt/standards
22 *Ibid.*

European Prison Rules

The most prominent and impactful CoE soft law instrument relevant to Article 3 ECHR is the 2006 European Prison Rules (EPR).[23] Now in its third iteration, it has developed significantly since the first. That 1973 version, the (European) Standard Minimum Rules for the Treatment of Prisoners, very closely mapped onto the 1953 version of the UN Standard Minimum Rules, with very little value added.[24] The Rules were revised in 1987, made more European, and renamed becoming the EPR. By more than one account, neither of these earlier versions was 'as influential as its authors may have hoped', partly because the CPT's reports gave greater detail[25] and also because they were barely ever referred to in the ECHR jurisprudence. That said, in 2006 the CPT commented positively that previous versions had been influential.[26] Reference to the EPR by the ECtHR and the CPT cannot be taken fully as evidence of their impact or importance, but is at least illustrative and the EPR are frequently referred to by both bodies. In 2016, 2017 and 2018 the EPR were referred to in respectively 13, six and six ECtHR Article 3 cases,[27] in many of which extracts from CPT reports had referred to the EPR.

The 2006 EPR updated the previous version to reflect the ECHR, ECtHR jurisprudence and the CPT's work, particularly its standards.[28] It is thus considered the 'most comprehensive modern European formulation' of state policy that should govern the administration of prison systems[29] and 'represent[s] a synthesis of many of the trends that preceded it'.[30] With the purpose of ensuring respect for the human rights and dignity of prisoners,[31] the EPR provides a high level of detail for a general document. It is organized thematically and opens by setting out some basic principles. In particular, '[a]ll persons deprived of their liberty shall be treated with respect for their human rights' (Rule 1); they retain all rights that have not been removed 'lawfully' (Rule 2); and any restrictions must be the 'minimum necessary and proportionate to the legitimate objective' (Rule 3). Moreover, lack of resources cannot justify conditions that 'infringe prisoners' human rights' (Rule 4).

Following the (nine) basic principles, the EPR addresses a number of core issues: conditions of imprisonment; health; good order; management and staff; inspection and monitoring; untried prisoners; and regime for sentenced prisoners. Each issue is divided into sub-themes: for example, Part II, concerning conditions of imprisonment, has various subsections including on the needs of specific groups: women, children and infants.

Part II also has a subsection on 'admissions', which can be used to illustrate both the level of detail included in the EPR and their correlation with CPT (preventive) standards. The Rules outline what must be 'immediately' recorded 'at admission', including 'any visible injuries

[23] Rec (2006) 2 of the Committee of Ministers to member states on the European Prison Rules (11 January 2006).
[24] Reynaud, A, *Human Rights in Prisons* (Council of Europe, 1983) cited in van Zyl Smit, D and Snacken, S, *Principles of European Prison Law and Policy: Penology and Human Rights* (Oxford University Press, 2009).
[25] Van Zyl Smit and Snacken (n 24 above), 23.
[26] 15th General Report on the CPT's Activities, CPT/Inf (2005) 17, para 49.
[27] Based on a search of the ECtHR HUDOC search database.
[28] EPR, Preamble.
[29] Van Zyl Smit and Snacken (n 24 above), 87.
[30] *Ibid*, 36.
[31] EPR Preamble. (The 1987 draft refers to 'dignity', whereas the adopted version refers to 'human rights').

and complaints about prior ill-treatment'.[32] Also 'at admission', the detainee should be given information including on their rights.[33] 'Immediately after admission' a third party should be informed,[34] and 'as soon as possible' the prisoner should be examined by a medical practitioner.[35] These safeguards accord strongly with CPT standards, which present them as three of four fundamental rights that should be present from the outset of deprivation of liberty. Whilst the EPR does not in this subsection refer to the fourth of the CPT's fundamental safeguards, access to a lawyer, this is addressed in Rule 23 concerning the provision of legal advice. Unlike CPT standards, Rule 23 does not indicate a timeframe for access to a lawyer, but the difference is contextual. The EPR apply to convicted prisoners or those remanded in custody by a judicial authority, that is, people in prisons. The CPT comparison drawn here is generally applied from the time of apprehension by the police. Indisputably, 'there is a high degree of consonance between the revised EPR and the principles and recommendations contained in CPT visit reports as well as in the Committee's General Reports'.[36]

European Union

Charter of Fundamental Rights
The Charter of Fundamental Rights of the European Union (CFR),[37] adopted 1999 and adapted in 2007, was originally a soft law instrument. It became legally binding only with the entry into force of the Treaty of Lisbon (TEU) in 2009.[38] Article 6(1) TEU accords the CFR the 'same legal value' as the EU Treaties, meaning its content is both binding on EU states and institutions and justiciable. The CJEU can therefore hear human rights cases. Article 6(2) obligates the EU to accede to the ECHR, and Article 6(3) states:

> Fundamental rights, as guaranteed by the European Convention for the Protection of Human Rights and Fundamental Freedoms [i.e. the ECHR] and as they result from the constitutional traditions common to the Member States, shall constitute general principles of the Union's law.

This is now especially important given the EU is unlikely to accede to the ECHR. There is a clear intention that there be coherence between the two systems. Notably, the CFR's content is primarily 'addressed to the institutions and bodies' of the EU and binds Member States 'only when they are implementing Union law'.[39] Hence, although the CFR covers a wider spectrum of rights than the ECHR, its impact governing the conduct of EU states is more limited. Consequently, emphasis remains with the CoE and ECHR for rights common to both systems, and overlap regarding which treaty applies and which court has competence is mostly avoided.

The danger of differing interpretations, scope and definitions being given to rights under the two respective frameworks is also mitigated by Article 52(3) CFR. Where rights under the CFR correspond with rights under the ECHR, 'the meaning and scope of those rights

---

[32] Rule 15.1
[33] Rule 15.2 with Rule 30.
[34] Rule 15.3 with Rule 24.9.
[35] Rule 16(a) with Rule 42.1.
[36] 15th General Report on the CPT's Activities, CPT/Inf (2005) 17, para 50.
[37] Charter of Fundamental Rights of the European Union (2000/C 364/01), Nice, 7 December 2000.
[38] Treaty of Lisbon (n 9 above).
[39] CFR (n 37 above), Article 51.

shall be the same as those laid down by' the ECHR. The prohibition of torture and inhuman or degrading treatment or punishment is one such right, and the corresponding Article 4 CFR and Article 3 ECHR have identical wording. Article 52(3) CFR adds that Union law may still provide 'more extensive protection', and indeed, the EU's position on the death penalty, considered never to be lawful, is an example. Nevertheless, it is the ECtHR which has through its extensive jurisprudence developed definitions and clarified the scope of the prohibition of torture and inhuman or degrading treatment or punishment in Europe.

EU Legislation

The EU's approach to the prohibition of torture through legislation and soft law has been outward looking: directed towards the EU's interactions with third (non-EU) states, far more than looking inward on itself. This can be largely explained by measures having been taken under the EU's Common Foreign and Security Policy, and by the CFR's limited scope regarding EU states noted above. The key legislation is Regulation (EU) 2019/125 *concerning trade in certain goods which could be used for capital punishment, torture or other cruel, inhuman or degrading treatment or punishment.*[40] This codifies a previous 2005 Council Regulation,[41] itself referred to as 'the Anti-Torture Regulation',[42] and amendments to it, and is binding on all EU states. Regulation (EU) 2019/125 not only 'lays down Union rules governing trade' of such goods with third countries. It also sets 'rules governing the supply of brokering services, technical assistance, training and advertising related to such goods'.[43]

An interesting feature of this Regulation is it that, unlike the CFR (and of course the ECHR), it provides definitions. Although these definitions were intended to apply only narrowly to the Regulation, they are worth highlighting. Torture is defined by wording identical to Article 1 of the UNCAT, with a single line addition at the end. Whereas the UNCAT definition ends by noting that torture 'does not include pain or suffering arising only from, inherent in or incidental to lawful sanctions', the EU Regulation adds that 'Capital punishment is not deemed a lawful penalty under any circumstances'.[44] This puts a particularly European stamp on the definition of torture, and certainly makes clear the EU's stance as regards its relationship to the death penalty. This stance, it should be added, is consistent with that across the CoE: all 47 states having abolished the death penalty in peacetime, most at all times.[45] In 1989 the ECtHR indicated that the 'death row phenomenon' 'could give rise to' an Article 3 ECHR violation,[46] but strengthened its position in 2010, finding that the mental suffering caused by fear of execution constitutes inhuman treatment, and hence the death penalty violates Article 3.[47]

---

[40]   Regulation (EU) 2019/125 of the European Parliament and of the Council of 16 January 2019 concerning trade in certain goods which could be used for capital punishment, torture or other cruel, inhuman or degrading treatment or punishment (codification).

[41]   Council Regulation (EC) No 1236/2005 of 27 June 2005 concerning trade in certain goods which could be used for capital punishment, torture or other cruel, inhuman or degrading treatment or punishment.

[42]   EU Commission: https://ec.europa.eu/fpi/what-we-do/anti-torture-measures_en

[43]   Regulation (EU) 2019/125 (n 40 above), Article 1.

[44]   *Ibid*, Article 2(a).

[45]   ECHR, Protocols 6 and 13. Armenia, Azerbaijan and Russia are the only states not to have ratified Protocol 13 which completely abolishes the death penalty and allows no derogation.

[46]   *Soering v. The United Kingdom*, 7 July 1989, Series A no 161, para 111.

[47]   *Al-Saadoon and Mufdhi v. The United Kingdom*, no 61498/08, ECHR 2010.

Perhaps surprisingly, Regulation (EU) 2019/125 also defines 'other cruel, inhuman or degrading treatment or punishment'. This is unusual, not least because neither the UNCAT, the ECHR nor the CFR define these types of ill-treatment. The definition given however is somewhat underwhelming and not especially helpful. It states:

> other cruel, inhuman or degrading treatment or punishment' means any act by which pain or suffering attaining a minimum level of severity, whether physical or mental, is inflicted on a person, when such pain or suffering is inflicted either by or at the instigation of, or with the consent or acquiescence of, a public official or other person acting in an official capacity. It does not, however, include pain or suffering arising only from, inherent in or incidental to, lawful penalties. Capital punishment is not deemed a lawful penalty under any circumstances.[48]

There is clearly no attempt to distinguish 'cruel', 'inhuman' or 'degrading' or to explain what, if anything, might set them apart. All this definition really says is these other forms of ill-treatment must cause sufficiently severe pain or suffering to fall within *their* scope, and impliedly not be sufficiently severe to be considered as torture.[49] This EU definition differs from the definition of torture also for its silence on the purposive element which under the UNCAT is required for there to be an act of torture. It could therefore be assumed for the Regulation's purposes that there need not be a purpose at all for this *less severe, but 'severe enough'* ill-treatment. However, this reading is potentially problematic since the definition indicates that ill-treatment is to be 'inflicted', which may suggest intention, though it is possible that there can be intention without purpose. The key point is that this inclusion does not suggest an especially developed or sophisticated understanding of what might be termed together 'other ill-treatment', yet claims to be a definition.

Although this definition is included for the purposes of the Regulation itself, it has the potential to mislead. For example, it is uncontested (and recognized also in the EU Guidelines, discussed below), that detention conditions are capable of amounting to inhuman and degrading treatment, but the Regulation is silent on this. Given the Regulation's specific focus on torture, it might probably have been better not to seek to define other forms of ill-treatment at all.

EU Guidelines on torture and other cruel treatment

In September 2019, the EU adopted new 'Guidelines to EU Policy towards third state countries on torture and other cruel, inhuman or degrading treatment or punishment'[50] (the Guidelines), revised from earlier versions in 2001, 2008 and 2012. This comprehensive and authoritative soft law document sets out the EU's approach to eradicating torture and ill-treatment globally. Its purpose is to 'provide practical guidance to EU institutions and Member States, that can be used in their engagement with third countries as well as in multilateral human rights fora, to support ongoing efforts' to that end.[51] The UNCAT, OPCAT and the relevant ECtHR jurisprudence 'form the basis of the EU's policy against torture and other ill-treatment',[52] and the

---

[48]   Regulation (EU) 2019/125 (n 40 above), Article 2(b).
[49]   Arguably this same approach is seen in UNCAT Article 16, but that provision does not purport to be a definition as such.
[50]   EU Guidelines (n 8 above).
[51]   *Ibid*, para 6.
[52]   *Ibid*, para 10.

Guidelines are consistent with these, drawing also from international and regional standards and from the work of relevant bodies. Helpfully the Guidelines also clarify the EU's use of terminology, confirming its adoption of the UNCAT definition of torture, and that the definition of 'other cruel, inhuman or degrading treatment … should be in line with' ECtHR case-law and can include sub-standard detention conditions.[53]

The Guidelines set out action to be taken by the EU towards the goal of eradicating torture and other ill-treatment and include a statement of the EU's policy approach. The EU's objective is 'to engage with third countries to take effective measures against torture and other ill-treatment to ensure that their absolute prohibition is enforced and that victims have access to rehabilitation services, legal support and other forms of reparation'.[54] This is 'an integral part of [the EU's] human rights policy'. The EU takes a 'holistic and proactive approach' to the 'global eradication' of torture, 'including awareness-raising, education and training, prevention, monitoring and accountability, protection and redress, including rehabilitation for the victims of torture and other ill-treatment'.[55] 'EU Member States are determined to comply fully with international obligations prohibiting torture and other ill-treatment'.[56] 'The EU encourages third countries to mainstream safeguards against torture and other ill-treatment'.[57] It also 'promotes and supports' the work of National Human Rights Institutions and National Preventive Mechanisms under OPCAT.[58]

After stating EU policy, the Guidelines give an overview of its practical support – 'political and financial tools' – towards its objective. This includes political dialogue; monitoring, assessing and reporting; making statements; and even observing trials where it is believed the defendant or witnesses have been subjected to torture or ill-treatment. It is a highly detailed statement of action with decisive undertakings that, variously, the 'EU', 'EU Delegations' and 'EU Heads of Mission', etc. 'will' take.

The EU's approach is 'comprehensive' and 'encompasses all essential elements to eradicate torture: prohibition, prevention, accountability and redress'.[59] The 'operational section' of the Guidelines are arranged by these four themes and identify measures, 'important safeguards' the EU will 'urge and support third [non-EU] countries to take'. In this section also, the Guidelines offer an impressive level of detail. Not only are they consonant with other international and regional standards, they both reinforce and are bolstered by references to treaties, soft law and reports. Space does not permit detailed engagement with these measures, suffice to say the 2019 revision is a significant reworking of the previous version and arranged under the following themes: prohibit torture and other ill-treatment in law; reaffirm the absolute prohibition of torture and other ill-treatment in policy; comply with safeguards and procedures relating to detention; provide efficient and safe complaints mechanisms; allow efficient detention monitoring and oversight mechanisms; combat impunity; and provide redress for victims. It is authoritative, relevant and an invaluable tool towards the eradication of torture.

---

[53]   *Ibid*, para 9.
[54]   *Ibid*, para 16.
[55]   *Ibid*, para 17.
[56]   *Ibid*, para 18.
[57]   *Ibid*, para 18.
[58]   *Ibid*, para 18.
[59]   *Ibid*, para 4.

Some Comments on the Legal Framework

The main thrust of EU law regarding the prohibition of torture is directed towards third states. Apart from the CFR itself, which is only binding on EU states when they are implementing EU law, there is little which looks to the practice of EU states themselves. There is no document for example, setting out expectations on EU states to meet their obligations under Article 4 CFR. It would require no leap of the imagination for this to be understood as including those set out in the Guidelines, but it is unlikely that all EU states would choose to do so unless expressly required. EU states have been responsible for a considerable number of violation findings under Article 3 ECHR, including 27 findings for torture in the years 1959–2018.[60] In the same period, Romania and Greece have been in held in violation for (substantively) inhuman and degrading treatment in 263 and 115 cases respectively. Moreover, the Guidelines call for third states to criminalize torture, whilst it is well known that Italy only did so in July 2017, and this through legislation that many have deemed inadequate.[61] It is also notable that not all EU states are prepared to extradite suspects to other EU states. For example, certain states routinely refuse to extradite to Greece and Romania because of the detention conditions in those states.[62] Following a decision in its Supreme Court, Denmark has refused to extradite suspects to Romania on this basis.[63] In May 2019, the Netherlands refused to return a prisoner to the UK considering the prison conditions where he would likely end up 'inhumane'.[64]

It is absolutely correct, indeed necessary, that the EU puts pressure on third states to eradicate torture and ill-treatment using such tools as the Guidelines and Regulation (EU) 2019/125. At the same time, more needs to be done by the EU and by EU states to get their own houses in order. Currently, this is addressed neither by soft law nor legislation by the EU. It is, however, clear from the manner in which the EU has striven for compatibility with the ECHR that the main source of normative guidance for the EU and Member States regarding the prohibition and prevention of torture will in practice derive from the CoE, from which it will have difficulty in departing.

PRINCIPAL INSTITUTIONS

This section introduces the principal institutions in Europe whose work is relevant to the prohibition of torture and other ill-treatment. The intention is to give a flavour of what each does and the contribution they make. It is beyond the scope of this chapter to explain and examine all aspects of each institution in detail. The intention is to show, through its various institutions,

---

[60]   Violator states: Austria (1); Belgium (1); Bulgaria (1); France (2); Greece (1); Italy (9); Netherlands (1); Poland (2); Romania (2); Slovak Republic (1); Sweden (1); United Kingdom (2). For a statistical breakdown of violations see: https://www.echr.coe.int/Documents/Stats_violation_1959 _2018_ENG.pdf

[61]   https://www.hrw.org/news/2017/07/11/italys-new-law-torture-fails-meet-international-standards

[62]   Statistics on European Arrest Warrants, including their refusal, are available at: https://e-justice .europa.eu/content_european_arrest_warrant-90--maximize-en.do

[63]   Council of the European Union, Replies to questionnaire on quantitative information on the practical operation of the European arrest warrant – Year 2017, 11804/19, Brussels, 30 August 2019, 44.

[64]   https://www.theguardian.com/world/2019/may/10/dutch-court-blocks-extradition-of-man-to -inhumane-uk-prisons

how the European region is equipped to address the prohibition. Institutional responses are not only reactive but also proactive, including directly through preventive visiting and financial and technical assistance. In the drive to eradicate torture and ill-treatment in Europe, two institutions are key: the ECtHR and the CPT.

Council of Europe

European Court of Human Rights
The ECtHR's role extends beyond determining accountability for Article 3 violations. Its jurisprudence (for which see the following section) is instrumental in determining the scope and content of the prohibition not only for the purposes of the ECHR, but also the CFR.

The ECtHR derives its mandate from the ECHR, as amended by Protocols 11 and 14, and has jurisdiction to 'consider all matters concerning the interpretation and application' of the ECHR and its protocols.[65] It may receive inter-state applications, these being a claim by a state party that another has acted in breach of its Convention obligations.[66] It may also receive individual applications 'from any person, non-governmental organisation or group of individuals claiming to be the victim of a violation' by an ECHR state.[67] Inter-state applications are relatively rare, though they are becoming less so.[68] As regards Article 3, however, the foundations of the ECHR's approach are rooted in two early inter-state applications, the *Greek case*[69] and *Ireland v. UK*,[70] discussed below. Individual applications form the overwhelming majority of cases considered by the ECtHR.[71] Most applications are rejected on preliminary grounds, but cases considered on the merits are usually decided by a Chamber of seven judges, but exceptionally, although not infrequently, might be considered by a 'Grand Chamber' composed of 17 judges.

The ECtHR has a very high case load and many of the applications are 'repetitive cases'[72] deriving from 'a common dysfunction at the national level'. To address this, the ECtHR has developed a 'pilot judgment procedure',[73] by which, when there are several applications with the same root cause, it may select one or more to prioritise. The ECtHR will then decide the immediate case before it and at the same time identify the underlying structural issues giving rise to repeat cases, and indicate to the state in question 'the type of remedial measures needed

---

[65] ECHR, Article 32.
[66] ECHR, Article 33.
[67] ECHR, Article 34.
[68] There have been 24 inter-state applications since 1953. Of these, eight applications were made since 2014 (three in 2018). A further three applications were made between 2007 and 2009: https://www.echr.coe.int/Documents/InterState_applications_ENG.pdf. See also: Ulfstein, G and Risini, I, 'Inter-state Applications under the European Convention on Human Rights: Strengths and Challenges', *EJILTalk*, 24 January 2020: https://www.ejiltalk.org/author/gulfstein/
[69] *Netherlands v. Greece*, Report of 18 November 1969, 1969 12 Yearbook 1 (the *Greek case*).
[70] *Ireland v. The United Kingdom*, 18 January 1978, Series A no 25.
[71] On 31 December 2019 the ECtHR had 59,800 pending cases, almost all individual applications. ECtHR Statistics: https://www.echr.coe.int/Pages/home.aspx?p=reports&c=
[72] In January 2019 there were 57,250 such cases, Court Pilot Judgment Factsheet, January 2019: https://www.echr.coe.int/Documents/FS_Pilot_judgments_ENG.pdf
[73] See generally: Leach, P, Hardman, H, Stephenson, S and Blitz, B, *Responding to Systemic Human Rights Violations: An Analysis of "Pilot Judgment" of the European Court of Human Rights and their Impact at National Level* (Intersentia, 2010).

to resolve it'.[74] The ECtHR can then choose to adjourn ('freeze') similar pending cases (it may also reinstate them if not satisfied by the State's response) and so reduce its caseload. This means that, in effect if not in by design, the ECtHR now has a preventive dimension to its work.

To date, there have been five pilot judgments concerning Article 3 ECHR, all in respect of inhuman or degrading treatment. Four of these have related to structural problems within the respective states – Russia, Italy, Bulgaria and Hungary – causing inadequate detention conditions in prisons,[75] the fifth, to structural inadequacies in the Belgian psychiatric detention system.[76] Of the prison cases, the Court has decided at present not to adjourn similar cases from its pending list concerning Russia, Bulgaria or Hungary until appropriate measures are fully implemented. The potential benefits of the pilot judgment approach are illustrated by *Torreggiani v. Italy*, concerning severe overcrowding due to 'chronic dysfunction' in the prison system, a situation which had resulted in 'several hundred' similar pending applications. The ECtHR directed Italy to put in place effective and appropriate measures to address prison overcrowding within one year of its decision becoming final, during which time it adjourned similar pending cases. In response, Italy made legislative changes and introduced a compensation scheme. The ECtHR has since indicated its view that, in principle, these measures should afford appropriate relief.[77]

Two further aspects of the ECtHR's general approach to Article 3 ECHR should be noted. First, the ECtHR distinguishes between 'substantive' and 'procedural' dimensions of the prohibition, distinguishing between the question of whether (substantively) there has been torture or ill-treatment, or whether (procedurally) there has been a failure to fully investigate allegations or to safeguard. This maps onto the second point. The ECtHR is more than willing to make 'strong inferences' of fact and to reverse the burden of proof,[78] and it frequently does so. The ECtHR is not a court of first instance and in most of the cases it hears the facts are already fully established. However, torture and ill-treatment, which can include disappearances, are invariably strongly contested by the respondent state to the point that state denial can be considered a defining aspect of them.[79] Rightly or wrongly, the ECtHR applies the high 'beyond reasonable doubt' standard of proof.[80] However, while it may already be possible for the ECtHR to find a violation on the procedural grounds that, for example, the state has not adequately investigated allegations of ill-treatment, the application need not necessarily fail

---

[74]   Pilot Judgment Factsheet (n 72 above).

[75]   *Ananyev and Others v. Russia*, nos 42525/07 and 60800/08, 10 January 2012; *Torreggiani and Others v. Italy*, nos 43517/09 and six others, 8 January 2013; *Neshkov and Others v. Bulgaria*, nos 36925/10 and five others, 27 January 2015; *Varga and Others v. Hungary*, nos 14097/12 and five others, 10 March 2015.

[76]   *W.D. v. Belgium*, no 73548/13, 6 September 2016.

[77]   Pilot Judgment Factsheet (n 72 above).

[78]   *Ireland v. United Kingdom* (n 70 above).

[79]   Keller, H and Heri, C, 'Enforced Disappearance and the European Court of Human Rights: A "Wall of Silence": Fact-Finding Difficulties and States as "Subversive Objectors"' (2014) 12 *Journal of International Criminal Justice* 735.

[80]   This may be compared to the Human Rights Committee which applies the balance of probabilities. See Chapter 6 of this volume.

on the substantive question because of a lack of evidence due to the possibility of reversing the burden of proof in appropriate cases.[81]

Committee for the Prevention of Torture

The CPT and its work were briefly introduced above.[82] This section provides an overview of the CPT's general approach to its mandate and its use of key terminology.

The CPT's function, as its full name suggests, is preventive. It is an independent, non-judicial and multi-disciplinary body of experts mandated 'by means of visits, [to] examine the treatment of persons deprived of their liberty with a view to strengthening, if necessary, the protection of such persons from torture and from inhuman or degrading treatment or punishment'.[83]

Preventive visiting is thus central to the CPT's mandate. By ratifying the ECPT, all CoE Member States agree to allow and accommodate the CPT's visits, which may be announced or unannounced. This means allowing the CPT to enter the country and to have unrestricted and immediate access to, and circulation within, any place of detention in the state, including the ability to speak privately with detainees and others who consent, and being provided with any information it requests which is relevant to the exercise of its mandate. Visits are regular, and the CPT aims to make an announced ('periodic') visit to every Member State roughly once every four to five years, although in reality there is some variation from this, in part because of the differing size of the countries and of the detained populations. Periodic visits are generally for two weeks, during which the CPT visits a range of detention types including police custody, remand centres and prisons in the criminal justice sector, as well as immigration detention, psychiatric and social care facilities. Unannounced ('ad hoc') visits are shorter in duration but focused on a particular problem area identified in the state.

The CPT's country visits form the basis of an on-going dialogue between the Committee and the state. During a visit, and even during its preparation phase, the CPT is attentive to legal and other safeguards against torture and other ill-treatment, the treatment of detainees, detention conditions and the regime in the state in question. A visit usually begins with the delegation meeting with high-level officials and separately with civil society organizations before the main part of the visit: going into institutions, meeting and talking with detainees, staff and other interested parties, especially in confidential interviews, looking at registers and records and generally building a picture of the practical experience of detention within the facility in question. On completion of a visit, the CPT adopts and transmits a report to the state authorities, including its recommendations to improve the situation of detained people. States are expected to take positive steps in the light of the CPT's findings and recommendations. Frequently, visit reports include 'immediate observations', which are points the CPT highlights as high priority, often giving the state a short time-frame within which to address or at least to reply to them. Article 10(2) ECPT also allows the CPT to issue a 'Public Statement' where the state is not cooperating. The CPT has only eight times made such statements, and they should be considered the end point of a process, but which can by themselves be suffi-

---

[81] Bicknell, C, 'Uncertain Certainty? Making Sense of the European Court of Human Rights' Standard of Proof' (2019) 8 *International Human Rights Law Review* 1.

[82] For a detailed study of the CPT see Bicknell, C, Evans, M and Morgan, R, *Preventing Torture in Europe* (Council of Europe, 2018).

[83] ECPT, Article 1.

cient to cause a state to adjust its behaviour. In accordance with the ECPT, the reports and all relevant discussion between the CPT and the state are confidential. Most states do, however, authorize the CPT to publish its visit reports and their responses to them,[84] albeit often with some considerable delay.

Because of its specific mandate, the CPT does not work with fixed definitions of torture or inhuman or degrading treatment and avoids applying these labels to situations: it is a non-judicial body and that is the ECtHR's domain. The CPT is also categorically not a fact-finding arm of the ECtHR. Its role – through visits and cooperative dialogue with states to prevent torture and ill-treatment – would be undermined were that the case, whilst the preventive dimension of its work means it is not oriented towards accountability through the ECtHR. This said, as both are CoE bodies with Article 3 ECHR as their common reference point, their work inevitably intersects and relationships have matured to a point at which they now work synergistically, with one often referring to and reinforcing the findings or work of the other.[85]

The CPT has developed a 'non-judicial approach to labelling'[86] in order to distance itself somewhat from the language of Article 3 ECHR. Firstly, the CPT always refers to 'allegations'. Whilst it often qualifies allegations as being credible or consistent with recorded injuries, it never reports ill-treatment as an established fact. Secondly, instead of using the terms 'torture', 'inhuman' or 'degrading, to describe reported mistreatment, the CPT usually refers to 'ill-treatment', an overarching term a step removed from the language of the ECHR. The CPT will again usually qualify this with some indication of the severity or intentionality of the ill-treatment, for example 'severe', 'deliberate' or 'serious'. Finally, when the CPT does use the terms 'torture', 'inhuman' or 'degrading' it again introduces a form of qualified distancing, most commonly the formulations that 'x' treatment 'could be considered to be' or 'could be considered as amounting to' torture, etc. It is probable that in such cases the CPT has formed its own view of the nature of the treatment it is describing. It nevertheless approaches the wording cautiously in its reports and accompanies it with detailed factual accounts of the basis of its impression.

Commissioner for Human Rights

The office of Commissioner for Human Rights was established in 1999 by a Resolution of the CoE Committee of Ministers.[87] The Commissioner is an impartial and independent[88] non-judicial institution with a mandate to 'promote education in, awareness of and respect for human rights' in CoE states.[89] This includes promoting 'the effective observance and full enjoyment' of human rights; facilitating the activities of national human rights institutions; giving advice and information on human rights protection and prevention; and identifying shortcomings in Member States.[90] Whenever the Commissioner deems it appropriate, she may

---

[84] See https://www.coe.int/en/web/cpt/home
[85] Bicknell, Evans and Morgan (n 82 above).
[86] *Ibid*, 73–78.
[87] Resolution (99) 50 on the Council of Europe Commissioner for Human Rights (adopted by the Committee of Ministers on 7 May 1999 at its 104th Session).
[88] *Ibid*, Article 2.
[89] *Ibid*, Article 1 and 3(a).
[90] *Ibid*, Article 3.

address a report to the Committee of Ministers or also to the Parliamentary Assembly.[91] The Commissioner must cooperate with international institutions for the promotion and protection of human rights while avoiding unnecessary duplication of activities.[92] In its awareness raising and thematic work the office cooperates with other CoE bodies and with 'a broad range' of international institutions including specialized UN offices, the EU and the OSCE. The Commissioner cooperates also with national human rights institutions, NGOs, universities and think-tanks.[93]

As a non-judicial office, the Commissioner does not decide individual complaints, though it is her office's role to be informed and to build a better understanding of human rights issues within CoE countries as well as issues of thematic concern. Accordingly, the 'Commissioner *may* act on any relevant information' which might come from governments, national parliaments, national ombudsmen, individuals or organizations,[94] and the Commissioner can issue recommendations, opinions and reports.[95]

The Commissioner's work is divided into three main areas: country visits, including dialogue with state authorities and civil society; thematic reporting and advising on human rights implementation; and awareness-raising. Although the office has not yet published thematic work specifically concerning torture and ill-treatment, many of the themes explored have a bearing upon it, such as children's rights; counter-terrorism; LGBTI; migration; and persons with disabilities.[96]

Issues concerning Article 3 are also a prominent feature of the Commissioner's country-specific work, which includes publishing relevant 'issue papers' (reports), acting as third party intervenor in ECtHR cases, country visits, issuing statements and written letters to heads of government that the situation is being monitored and urging specific action. For example, the mass influx of migrants to Europe fleeing persecution and war has created a crisis in Europe and placed acute pressure particularly on first port of entry states. The Commissioner undertook a country visit to Greece in October 2019 following which she made a statement that the situation had 'dramatically worsened' over the previous year and called on Greece to urgently transfer asylum seekers from the Aegean islands and improve living conditions in reception centres.[97] When Italy introduced legislation affecting the rights of refugees, asylum seekers and migrants, the Commissioner wrote a letter to the Italian Prime Minister expressing concern, including over measures 'hampering and criminalising the work of NGOs who play a crucial role in saving lives at sea, banning disembarkation in Italian ports, and relinquishing responsibility for search and rescue operations to authorities which appear unwilling or unable

---

[91] *Ibid*, Article f.
[92] *Ibid*, Article 3(i).
[93] https://www.coe.int/en/web/commissioner/mandate
[94] Resolution (n 87 above) Article 5.
[95] *Ibid*, Article 8.
[96] For example, the Commissioner has published papers on the corporal punishment of children: *Children and Corporal Punishment: 'The Right Not to Be Hit, Also a Children's Right'* CommDH/IssuePaper(2006)1; juvenile justice: *Children and Juvenile Justice: Proposals for Improvements* CommDH/IssuePaper(2009)1; and the right to family reunification for refugees: *Realising the Right to Family Reunification for Refugees in Europe* (COE 2017).
[97] https://www.coe.int/en/web/commissioner/-/greece-must-urgently-transfer-asylum-seekers-from -the-aegean-islands-and-improve-living-conditions-in-reception-facilities

to protect rescued migrants from torture or inhuman or degrading treatment'.[98] Following up on a letter sent to Bosnia and Herzegovina in May 2018,[99] the Commissioner issued a statement calling for the urgent relocation of migrants who were being held in overcrowded, 'deplorable' conditions in an improvised camp without running water or electricity and poor sanitation.[100]

This is just a snapshot of the Commissioner's work in one thematic area which demonstrates some of the tools used to promote respect for Article 3 ECHR in the CoE.

European Union

Court of Justice of the EU

The Court of Justice of the EU (CJEU) has jurisdiction to hear claims invoking the CFR. The CJEU case law relating to the prohibition of torture and inhuman or degrading treatment or punishment (Article 4 CFR) is far more limited than the ECtHR's (on corresponding Article 3 ECHR) for at least three reasons. Firstly, the CFR binds EU states 'only when they are implementing Union law'. Secondly, the CFR has only been legally binding since 2009. Thirdly, since the ECtHR is exclusively focused on human rights and very well established it is the main point of reference for litigants. There have, nevertheless, been more Article 4 cases than might first be expected, particularly in respect of non-refoulement for asylum seekers and under the European Arrest Warrant (EAW) scheme, of which the latter is the most revelatory.

Recently, in *Dumitru-Tudor Dorobantu v. Geralstaatsanwaltschaft Hamburg*,[101] the CJEU's Grand Chamber made a preliminary ruling on the interpretation of Article 4 CFR and legislation applicable to the EAW,[102] which, on the face of it, conflict. In summary, the EAW is a mechanism by which suspects connected with significant crimes may be arrested and subsequently extradited from one EU state (the 'executing state') to another (the 'issuing state'). It is based on EU principles of 'mutual trust' and 'mutual recognition', meaning that, 'save in exceptional circumstances, EU states must consider all the other Member States to be complying with EU law and particularly with the fundamental rights recognised by EU law'.[103] Additionally, 'save in exceptional cases', they may not check whether another EU state has 'actually, in a specific case, observed the fundamental rights guaranteed by the European Union'.[104] At the same time, Article 4 CFR must be interpreted as having 'the same meaning and scope' as Article 3 ECHR,[105] which provision will not allow extradition or return to a receiving state where there is a 'real risk' of torture or inhuman or degrading treatment or punishment. Herein lies the

---

[98]   https://rm.coe.int/native/0900001680921853
[99]   https://rm.coe.int/commdh-2018-12-letter-to-the-authorities-regarding-the-migration-situa/1680870e4d
[100]   https://www.coe.int/en/web/commissioner/-/commissioner-calls-for-urgent-relocation-of-migrants-from-vucjak-in-bosnia-and-herzegovina
[101]   *Dumitru-Tudor Dorobantu v. Geralstaatsanwaltschaft Hamburg*, Case C-128/18, Judgment of the Court (Grand Chamber), 15 October 2019.
[102]   Namely, Council Framework Decision 2002/584/JHA of 13 June 2002 on the European arrest warrant and the surrender procedures between Member States (OJ 2002 L 190, p 1), as amended by Council Framework Decision 2009/299/JHA of 26 February 2009 (OJ 2009 L 81, p 24) ('Framework Decision 2002/584').
[103]   *Dumitru-Tudor Dorobantu v. Geralstaatsanwaltschaft Hamburg* (n 101 above), para 46.
[104]   *Ibid*, para 47.
[105]   *Ibid*, para 47.

problem, which has been known for quite some time[106] but not fully resolved: not all EU states are compliant and a 'real risk' may exist. Indeed, it was noted above that extraditions including to Greece, Romania and the UK have been refused on this basis.

The same difficulty arose when Romania issued a request to Germany, which led to the German Courts seeking a preliminary ruling from the CJEU. *Dumitru-Tudor Dorobantu* shines real light on the relationship between the ECHR and EU law. Although divided into a series of specific sub-questions, Germany asked two overarching questions, which put broadly were: (a) under Framework Decision 2002/584 (i.e. the EAW) what are the minimum standards for custodial conditions required by Article 4 CFR, including whether there is an 'absolute' minimum cell size requirement and whether and how cell size can be mitigated; and (b) what standards are to be used to assess whether conditions comply with fundamental rights, including how comprehensive an assessment of custodial conditions in the issuing state (Romania) is permitted, namely were the German courts in this case limited to an 'examination as to manifest errors'?

The judgment considers these questions together and the CJEU expressly confirmed that Article 4 CFR corresponds with Article 3 ECHR, including the 'meaning and scope' of the right as determined by ECtHR case law as well as the text.[107] The CJEU's examination of personal space is notable for its fidelity to the ECtHR position, particularly that set out in *Muršić v. Croatia*.[108] Regarding the extent and scope of the review of custodial conditions in the issuing state, the absolute nature of the prohibition of torture and ill-treatment means that more is required than a superficial assessment limited to 'obvious inadequacies'.[109] The review is to 'determine, specifically and precisely' whether there is a real risk to the person whose extradition has been sought,[110] hence authorities in the executing state are 'solely required to assess' prisons (and temporary facilities) where that individual would, according to the issuing state, be detained.[111] However, and perhaps controversially,

> when the assurance that the person concerned will not suffer inhuman or degrading treatment on account of the actual and precise conditions of his detention, irrespective of the prison in which he is detained in the issuing Member State, has been given, ... the executing judicial authority must rely on that assurance, at least in the absence of any specific indications that the detention conditions in a particular detention centre are in breach of Article 4 of the Charter.[112]

Accordingly, the CJEU anticipates that 'only in exceptional circumstances' will there be a 'real risk' and a request be refused. This approach seeks to maintain as far as possible the mutual recognition principle and harmony between EU states, whilst ensuring against 'pockets of impunity' within the EU. However, since some EU states do not necessarily meet an acceptable ECHR/CFR-compliant baseline, whilst this approach may well protect the particular individual in question, its overall impact is limited. It would be far bolder and send a much

---

[106]   For example: Justice, *European Arrest Warrants: Ensuring an effective defence* (Justice, 2012).

[107]   *Ibid*, para 58.

[108]   *Muršić v. Croatia* [GC], no. 7334/13, 20 October 2016. See also Bicknell, Evans and Morgan (n 82 above), 35–36.

[109]   *Dumitru-Tudor Dorobantu v. Geralstaatsanwaltschaft Hamburg* (n 101 above), para 62.

[110]   *Ibid*, para 63.

[111]   *Ibid*, para 66.

[112]   *Ibid*, para 68.

stronger message politically and preventively to block extradition where detention conditions are more generally unacceptable.

Fundamental Rights Agency

The Fundamental Rights Agency (FRA) was created in 2007 and has produced important work helping to embed a rights-based culture across the EU. Similar to the CoE's Commissioner for Human Rights, the FRA works on themes, many of which intersect with Article 4 CFR, including asylum, migration and borders; LGBTI; hate crime; racism; rights of the child; Roma; and people with disabilities. It engages in research to identify and understand issues as well as best practices to resolve them. It assists EU institutions and states and offers significant practical guidance. Examples of relevant work produced by the FRA include: a manual for fundamental rights-based police training;[113] continuously reporting, reminding and keeping pressure on EU states about the extent of human suffering at immigration reception centres;[114] and participating in expert meetings convened for example on the theme of responding to violence against children.

ECtHR JURISPRUDENCE: DEFINITIONS AND SCOPE OF ARTICLE 3 ECHR

The ECtHR's jurisprudence plays a fundamental defining role through which the scope and content of the Article 3 ECHR prohibition of torture and inhuman or degrading treatment or punishment are clarified as well as implemented. This is important for the CoE and equally for the EU, particularly its institutions which are not already bound by the ECHR, since Article 4 CFR corresponds to Article 3 ECHR and the EU has, to date, readily adopted the ECtHR's interpretation. Therefore, the ECtHR Article 3 jurisprudence carries significant authoritative weight across both systems.

The ECHR is recognized as a 'living instrument which must be interpreted in the light of present-day conditions', meaning:

> certain acts which were classified in the past as 'inhuman and degrading treatment' as opposed to 'torture' could be classified differently in future. It [the ECtHR] takes the view that the increasingly high standard being required in the area of the protection of human rights and fundamental liberties correspondingly and inevitably requires greater firmness in assessing breaches of the fundamental values of democratic societies.[115]

Consequently, the ECtHR's understanding of acts prohibited under Article 3 have changed over time and will almost certainly continue to do so. Additional uncertainties mean that even when the facts are established it can often be difficult to predict whether the ECtHR will find

---

[113] https://fra.europa.eu/en/publication/2013/fundamental-rights-based-police-training-manual-police-trainers
[114] https://fra.europa.eu/en/news/2019/migrants-continue-suffer-reception-centres-remain-overcrowded-and-violence-against
[115] *Selmouni v France* [GC], no 25803/94, ECHR 1999-V, para 101.

that the acts, circumstances or conditions in question violate Article 3, or how they will be classified.[116] The case law nevertheless provides some clear guidance.

Key Terminology

Torture

Perhaps surprisingly, it was not until the case of *Aksoy v. Turkey* in 1996 that the ECtHR first determined that an act of torture had taken place.[117] The general approach to torture and ill-treatment under Article 3 had, however, been set out in two earlier cases which considered what sets 'torture' apart from 'inhuman' and/or 'degrading' treatment or punishment. Since *Aksoy*, findings of torture have become far more frequent as the ECtHR has matured and grown in confidence. Its approach to the terms is something of a blend between its two earlier positions and subsequent development and now appears to be very much more aligned with the UNCAT definition which emphasizes the relevance of the *purpose* as well as the *severity* of deliberately inflicted ill-treatment.

Article 3 was first considered in the *Greek case*, where the Commission[118] attempted to differentiate the prohibition's key elements.

> It is plain that there may be treatment to which all these descriptions apply, for all torture must be inhuman and degrading treatment, and all inhuman treatment also degrading. The notion of inhuman treatment covers at least such treatment as deliberately causes severe suffering, mental or physical, which in the particular situation is unjustifiable. The word 'torture' is often used to describe inhuman treatment which has a purpose such as the obtaining of information or confessions, or the infliction of punishment, and it is generally an aggravated form of inhuman or degrading treatment. Treatment or punishment of an individual may be said to be degrading if it grossly humiliates him before others or drives him to act against his will or conscience.[119]

The statement became discredited because of the unfortunate implicit suggestion that the deliberate infliction of severe mental or physical suffering might in some situations be justifiable. Categorically, it cannot be, and the ECtHR's case law has since stated the absolute nature of the prohibition in no uncertain terms.[120] This false start aside,[121] the basic approach remains one in which torture is 'often' inhuman treatment which is inflicted for a purpose, and 'generally' an 'aggravated' form of inhuman treatment. It remains true that the ECtHR has always looked for an aggravating factor which, in the *Greek case* was the presence of purpose.[122]

In *Ireland v. UK*[123] the ECtHR again recognized the importance of purpose,[124] but took the position that because a 'special stigma' attaches to torture it must attain a greater level of

---

[116] Bicknell, Evans and Morgan (n 82 above) 63.
[117] *Aksoy v. Turkey*, 18 December 1996, Reports of Judgments and Decisions 1996-VI.
[118] Now defunct.
[119] The *Greek case* (n 69 above).
[120] *Gäfgen v. Germany* [GC], no 22978/05, ECHR 2010, para 107. This is not withstanding nuanced arguments in the literature noted above (n 17).
[121] The Commission itself did so in *Ireland v. The United Kingdom* (Report, paras 388–390) in 1976. See also Rodley, NS, 'The Definition(s) of Torture in International Law' (2002) 55 *Current Legal Problems* 467–493.
[122] Bicknell, Evans and Morgan (n 82 above), 64–67.
[123] *Ireland v. United Kingdom* (n 70 above).
[124] *Ibid*, para 167.

severity than other ill-treatment. In consequence, *torture*, *inhuman* and *degrading* treatment have long been understood as comprising a sliding scale, with the level of severity determining how the ill-treatment should be categorized. The severity was also contingent on the characteristics of the victim, including sex, age, and state of health. Severity, however, is no longer quite so central. Indeed, *Aksoy* itself indicated the relevance of both severity and purpose to a finding of torture, and more recent cases tend to take both elements together as determinants of categorization.[125] Context also increasingly plays a role in the ECtHR's assessment of what labels to apply. But, it is argued, particularly based on the *Greek case*, that purpose itself is capable of being the aggravating factor which can turn what would otherwise be inhuman treatment into an act of torture without the need for it to be 'more' severe.[126]

Inhuman treatment and/or degrading treatment

The 'scale of severity' approach based on where along a continuum of severity particular ill-treatment fits is perceptible in the jurisprudence.[127] The ECtHR frequently refers to 'inhuman and degrading' together without differentiating between them, as if this were a single category in its own right. However, there has relatively recently been a shift in approach, with the ECtHR considering degrading treatment alone, linking it with human dignity and introducing a subjective dimension. According to the Grand Chamber in *Kudła v. Poland* degrading treatment is 'such as to arouse in the victims feelings of fear, anguish and inferiority capable of humiliating and debasing them'.[128]

The Grand Chamber in *Bouyid v. Belgium* emphasized that human dignity lies at the core of the Article 3 prohibition, a 'particularly strong' link with degrading treatment.[129] The judgment illustrates the ECtHR's broad approach. Firstly, whether ill-treatment is degrading includes objective and subjective elements. All ill-treatment must be of a minimum level of severity to engage Article 3, and this, *Bouyid* confirms, 'usually involves actual bodily injury or intense physical or mental suffering'. Even without it,

> where treatment humiliates or debases an individual, showing a lack of respect for or diminishing his or her human dignity, or arouses feelings of fear, anguish or inferiority capable of breaking an individual's moral and physical resistance, it may be characterised as degrading and also fall within the prohibition set forth in Article 3.[130]

What distinguishes this from inhuman treatment or torture in this case is the severity of suffering, which must be 'serious physical or mental suffering' in these latter categories. Hence, torture and inhuman treatment may be distinguished from each other based on severity and the presence or absence of purpose, whilst degrading treatment is distinguishable based on severity.

---

[125] See for example *Ateşoğlu v. Turkey*, no 53645/10, 20 January 2015, para 20; also *Süreyya Eren v. Turkey*, no 36617/07, 20 October 2015, para 35.

[126] Bicknell, Evans and Morgan (n 82 above), 64–67.

[127] E.g. *Costello-Roberts v. the United Kingdom*, 25 March 1993, Series A no 247-C.

[128] *Kudła v. Poland* [GC], no 30210/96, ECHR 2000-XI, para 92.

[129] *Bouyid v. Belgium* [GC], no 23380/09, ECHR 2015, paras 81 and 90.

[130] *Ibid*, para 87.

Positive Obligations

Article 3 imposes a negative duty that states must not commit acts of torture or ill-treatment, and also imposes positive obligations on ECHR Member States.[131] In particular, there is the duty to undertake an effective investigation for alleged violations, for which failure results in a procedural violation even where a substantive violation cannot be established. Investigations need to be 'conducted independently, promptly and with reasonable expedition'. When appropriate (and it is not always possible, e.g. disappearance cases), the 'victim should be able to participate effectively'. In principle, the investigation should be 'capable of leading to the establishment of the facts of the case and to the identification and punishment of those responsible'.[132] There are many cases in which such procedural failings are found.

Positive obligations under Article 3 are not exclusively procedural. The state may have a duty to protect against the acts of private individuals. If ill-treatment by private parties is with the 'acquiescence or connivance' of the state authorities this 'may engage the State's responsibility under the Convention'.[133] Even without acquiescence safeguards need to be in place. For example, in *O'Keeffe v. Ireland*, concerning the sexual abuse of a child in a non-state primary school, the Grand Chamber made clear 'the content of the positive obligation to protect' connotes 'effective measures of deterrence against [such] grave acts' and 'can only be achieved by the existence of effective criminal-law provisions backed up by law-enforcement machinery'.[134] Safeguards in this case needed to include

> at a minimum … effective mechanisms for the detection and reporting of any ill-treatment by and to a State-controlled body, such procedures being fundamental to the enforcement of the criminal laws, to the prevention of such ill-treatment and, more generally therefore, to the fulfilment of the positive protective obligation of the State.[135]

Non-Refoulement

As under other systems, the ECHR prohibition of torture and ill-treatment includes the principle of *non-refoulement*: that a person may not be extradited or otherwise returned to a third state if, once there, they might be ill-treated.[136] Under Article 3 ECHR the principle applies when there are 'substantial grounds' for believing there is a 'real risk' to the individual if returned.[137] This principle has already been discussed in respect of the EAW above, and applies equally to irregular migrants and/or failed asylum seekers, and indeed to anyone else being extradited or deported. The burden of proving the risk falls to the applicant. However,

---

[131] For a detailed study of positive obligations see Lavrysen, L, *Human Rights in a Positive State* (Intersentia, 2016).

[132] *O'Keeffe v. Ireland* [GC], no 35810/09, ECHR 2014 (extracts), para 172.

[133] *Ilaşcu and Others v. Moldova and Russia* [GC], no 48787/99, ECHR 2004-VII, para 318, referring to *Cyprus v. Turkey* [GC], no 25781/94, ECHR 2001-IV, para 81.

[134] *O'Keeffe v. Ireland* (n 132 above), para 148.

[135] *Ibid*, para 162.

[136] For insight into the ECtHR's views see *Non-refoulement as a principle of international law and the role of the judiciary in its implementation* (Council of Europe, 2017): https://www.echr.coe.int/Documents/Dialogue_2017_ENG.pdf

[137] *Soering v. United Kingdom* (n 46 above); *Chahal v. The United Kingdom*, 15 November 1996, *Reports of Judgments and Decisions* 1996-V.

the ECtHR recognizes the difficulty this presents for asylum seekers and *J.K. v. Sweden* sets out very clearly its approach.[138]

First, 'real risk' is objectively evaluated, and must be 'assessed primarily with reference to those facts which were known or ought to have been known to the Contracting State at the time of expulsion'.[139] Second, the risk need not be of ill-treatment perpetrated by the state: the 'absolute character' of the prohibition[140] dictates that Article 3 protects also against non-state actors in this context. Third, the burden of proof is on the applicant, but for asylum seekers it is 'frequently necessary to give them the benefit of the doubt when assessing the credibility' of statements and documents.

> As a general rule, an asylum-seeker cannot be seen as having discharged the burden of proof until he or she provides a substantiated account of an individual, and thus a real, risk of ill-treatment upon deportation that is capable of distinguishing his or her situation from the general perils in the country of destination.[141]

Additionally, individual factors which on their own might not suggest a real risk must be considered cumulatively and, taken together, may meet the threshold.[142] Finally, although not decisive, past ill-treatment 'may be relevant for assessing the level of risk of future ill-treatment'. *J.K. v. Sweden* notably shows synergy with the EU Qualification Directive and UNCHR documents in making this point, citing Article 4(4) of the Directive directly:

> [t]he fact that an applicant has already been subject to persecution or serious harm, or direct threats of such persecution or such harm, is a serious indication of the applicant's well-founded fear of persecution or real risk of suffering serious harm, unless there are good reasons to consider that such persecution or serious harm will not be repeated.[143]

Extra-Territoriality

Under Article 1 ECHR states parties must 'secure to everyone within their jurisdiction' the rights and freedoms sets out in the Convention. This is uncomplicated if applied, for example, to a psychiatric hospital in mainland France. '[A]cts of the Contracting States performed, or producing effects, outside their territories can constitute an exercise of jurisdiction within the meaning of Article 1 only in exceptional cases',[144] to be determined in each case on its facts.[145] The Grand Chamber in *Al-Skeini v. UK* set out circumstances in which exceptions have applied. Most, albeit not all, examples in the case law concern overseas military operations. Broadly, jurisdiction applies where the ECHR state exercises effective control over either a person or persons; or a territory.

---

[138] *J.K. and Others v. Sweden* [GC], no. 59166/12, 23 August 2016.
[139] *Ibid*, para 87.
[140] *Ibid*, para 80.
[141] *Ibid*, para 94.
[142] *Ibid*, para 95.
[143] *Ibid*, para 99.
[144] *Al-Skeini and Others v. The United Kingdom* [GC], no 55721/07, ECHR 2011, para 131.
[145] *Ibid*, para 132.

'State agent authority and control' means that acts of diplomatic and consular agents 'may amount to an exercise of jurisdiction when [they] exert authority and control over others'.[146] It may equally apply when, 'through the consent, invitation or acquiescence of the Government of that territory, it exercises all or some of the public powers normally to be exercised by that Government'.[147] Also, where the use of force by a state's agents who are not in their own territory bring an individual under their control, jurisdiction may apply.[148]

Control giving rise to extra-territorial effect may be territorial, such as when an ECHR state party exercises 'effective control of a territory' not its own, by consequence of (lawful or unlawful) military action. Whether a state has effective control over a territory is a question of fact decided with reference to such indicators as 'the extent to which its military, economic and political support for the local subordinate administration provides it with influence and control over the region'.[149] The ECtHR has not accepted the argument that during 'active hostilities' in international armed conflict, international humanitarian law rather than human rights law is applicable.[150] The ECHR and international humanitarian law apply concurrently. Moreover, *Jaloud v. the Netherlands* confirmed that in joint military operations, the fact that the UK had operational control did not divest the Netherlands of its jurisdiction and thus its responsibility.[151] On the high seas, a vessel is subject to the exclusive jurisdiction of the state whose flag it is flying.[152]

Torture Committed by Non-ECHR States Parties

European standards regarding how people are treated have a reach far beyond the CoE area. As noted above, the EU regulates the behaviour of third states through trade regulation and soft power. Non-refoulement means that extradition requests from third states necessarily require an assessment of risk to the individual against ECHR standards.

In several cases the ECtHR has made incontrovertible findings of torture and ill-treatment perpetrated by the United States' Central Intelligence Agency (CIA) in the context of extraordinary rendition. Whilst the ECtHR has no jurisdiction to hear cases brought directly against the United States, its findings were relevant to cases brought against Poland,[153] Romania[154] and the Former Yugoslav Republic of Macedonia (FYROM)[155] for complicity. In order to

---

[146]   *Ibid*, para 134.
[147]   *Ibid*, para 135.
[148]   *Ibid*, para 136.
[149]   *Ibid*, para 139.
[150]   *Hassan v. The United Kingdom* [GC], no 29750/09, ECHR 2014, paras 76–77.
[151]   *Mozer v. the Republic of Moldova and Russia* [GC], no 11138/10, 23 February 2016 which concerned the Moldovan breakaway territory of Transdniestria over which Moldova has no control and which is supported by Russia, shows again that jurisdiction may apply concurrently for more than one state. Although Russia had effective control (and was found in violation), Moldova still had positive obligations under the ECHR.
[152]   *Hirsi Jamaa and Others v. Italy* [GC], no 27765/09, ECHR 2012.
[153]   *Al Nashiri v. Poland*, no 28761/11, 24 July 2014; *Husayn (Abu Zubaydah) v. Poland*, no 7511/13, 24 July 2014. See also Jorgensen, NHB, 'Complicity in Torture in a Time of Terror: Interpreting the European Court of Human Rights Extraordinary Rendition Cases' (2017) 16 *Chinese Journal of International Law* 11.
[154]   *Al Nashiri v. Romania*, no 33234/12, 31 May 2018.
[155]   *El-Masri v. The Former Yugoslav Republic of Macedonia* [GC], no 39630/09, ECHR 2012.

establish these states' involvement, the CIA's activity inevitably had first to be established. Al Nashiri and Abu Zubaydah were both subjected to extraordinary rendition and held in CIA-run 'black sites' in Poland, where they were tortured by the CIA. Al Nashiri was subsequently transferred to Romania where he was held by the CIA in conditions and under a regime that cumulatively amounted to inhuman treatment. El-Masri, a German national, was arrested by the Macedonian authorities and detained for 23 days without being permitted to contact the German authorities. The circumstances of this amounted to inhuman and degrading treatment.[156] The Macedonian authorities then handed him to the CIA whose treatment of him at Skopje airport amounted to torture. FYROM was found 'directly responsible' for this 'since its agents actively facilitated the treatment and then failed to take any measures that might have been necessary in the circumstances of the case to prevent it from occurring'.[157] El-Masri was then transferred by air to Afghanistan where he was held for five months, in violation of FYROM's non-refoulement obligation.

These cases are significant. Both the CoE and EU made important contributions to uncovering the truth about rendition by commissioning reports to investigate the involvement of European states. These are known respectively as the Marty[158] and Fava Reports,[159] and both provide an extraordinary level of detail, naming victims, flight numbers, destinations and times. They provided important, but not exclusive, evidence for the ECtHR. The particular significance of these cases, however, is that they represent definitive findings by an international Court that a third state, operating outside both its jurisdiction and that of the Court, has committed acts of torture. The United States is a state party to the ICCPR and UNCAT but does not accept the individual communications procedures of either, nor that of the Inter-American Convention on Human Rights. El-Masri's case had also collapsed before the US Courts, due to the government invoking the 'state secrets privilege' to withhold vital supporting evidence.[160] Although the ECtHR could not award reparation or just satisfaction against the United States, this case provided a degree of justice and complete impunity was avoided.

CONCLUSION

The prohibition and prevention of torture and other ill-treatment in Europe is not covered by a single institution or set of norms. With three principal organizations playing a role in the protection and promotion of human rights across the region, Europe is complex, offering *systems* rather than a system. The focus of this chapter is on the CoE and EU laws and institutions relevant to the prohibition of torture. Space has not permitted more on the OSCE, but its

[156] *Ibid*, para 204.
[157] *Ibid*, paras 205–211.
[158] *Alleged secret detentions and unlawful inter-State transfers of detainees involving Council of Europe member States*, Doc. 10957, 12 June 2006 ('the 2006 Marty Report').
[159] European Parliament: the Fava Inquiry, CIA Activities in Europe: http://www.europarl.europa.eu/sides/getDoc.do?type=IM-PRESS&reference=20070209IPR02947&language=EN accessed 30 August 2019.
[160] *El-Masri v. Tenet* 437 F.Supp. 2d (E.D.Va. 2006); *El-Masri v. United States* 479 F. 3d (4 Cir. 2007). See also: Vedaschi, A, 'Globalization of Human Rights and Mutual Influence between Courts: The Innovative Reverse Path of the Right to the Truth' in Shetreet, S (ed), *The Culture of Judicial Independence, Rule of Law, and World Peace* (Martinus Nijhoff, 2014).

contribution particularly through capacity building and technical support, is not insignificant. As outlined above, all Members of the EU are also Members of the CoE and respectively through Article 4 CFR and Article 3 ECHR, both organizations have binding law prohibiting absolutely torture and other ill-treatment. Moreover, within both, the death penalty is understood as violating the prohibition. There is intentionally a great deal of coherence and synergy between the EU and CoE regarding torture. Article 6(3) TEU makes clear that the ECHR rights are 'general principles' of EU law, whilst Article 52(3) CFR indicates that the same 'meaning and scope' should be given to Article 4 CFR as under Article 3 ECHR. This provision, and the fact the ECtHR jurisprudence is so rich in setting out the content and scope of Article 3, pushes a great deal of emphasis for understanding the prohibition onto the CoE. As regards accountability, the CFR is rather more limited than the ECHR, binding EU states only when they are implementing EU law. A key problem faced by the EU is marrying its 'mutual recognition' requirement of states with the non-refoulement requirement under Article 4 CFR. This has been addressed by the CJEU in the context of EAWs, but not necessarily in the strongest terms that would advance prevention. Indeed, the EU's focus on protection from torture is outward looking, addressed to third, non-EU states. It is erroneous to assume EU states do not have detention conditions amounting to inhuman treatment, or even commit acts of torture, and the EU would do well to create additional guidelines directing the conduct of its own states in this regard. The CoE has a much more advanced system for prevention, provided by the CPT which is now in its 30th year of preventive visiting and also (albeit to a lesser extent and incidentally) by the pilot judgment system of the ECtHR.

10. The prohibition of torture and cruel, inhuman or degrading treatment or punishment in the Inter-American Human Rights System: systems, methods and recent trends

Diego Rodríguez-Pinzón[1]

The Inter-American Human Rights System is rooted in the Organization of American States (OAS). The System has evolved to comprise a quite sophisticated set of standards and monitoring mechanisms and techniques. The tragic history of the Americas has unfortunately made the issue of torture and cruel, inhuman and degrading treatment one of the core concerns of the Inter-American Human Rights System, and the practice of its human rights organs has been robust.[2]

NORMATIVE FRAMEWORK

The legal framework of the Inter-American System is comprised of several regional treaties. The core treaty is the American Convention on Human Rights (hereinafter 'American Convention'), that recognizes in Article 5 the prohibition of torture and cruel, inhuman or

---

[1]   With thanks to Silja Aabersold for her research support.
[2]   For information concerning the Inter-American System more generally see: Grossman, D, del Campo, A and Trudeau, MA, *International Law and Reparations: The Inter-American System* (Clarity Press, 2018); Antkowiak, TM and Gonza, A, *The American Convention on Human Rights* (Oxford University Press, 2017); Burgorgue-Larsen, L, et al., *Derechos Humanos en Contesto en América Latina* (Tirantnt lo Blanch, 2016); Rodríguez-Pinzón, D and Martin, C, *The Prohibition of Torture and Ill-Treatment in the Inter-American Human Rights System: A Handbook for Victims and their Advocates, Vol 2*, 2nd edn (OMCT, 2014); Goldman, RK, 'History and Action: The Inter-American Human Rights System and the Role of the Inter-American Commission on Human Rights' (2009) 31 *Human Rights Quarterly* 856; Buergenthal, T, *International Human Rights in a Nutshell*, 4th edn (West Publishing, 2009); Krsticevic, V and Tojo, L (eds), *La Implementación de las Decisiones del Sistema Interamericano de Derechos Humanos* (Cejil, 2007); Quiroga, CM, *La Convención Americana: teoría y jurisprudenci: Vida, integridad personal, libertad personal, debido proceso y recurso judicial* (Centro de Derechos Humanos de la Facultad de Derecho de la Universidad de Chile, 2005); Ledezma, HF, *El Sistema Interamericano de Protección de Derechos Humanos: Aspectos Institucionales y Procesales* (IIDH, 2004); O'Donnell, D, *Derecho Internacional de los Derechos Humanos, Normativa, Jurisprudencia y Doctrina de los Sistemas Universal e Interamericano* (Oficina en Colombia del Alto Comisionado de las Naciones Unidas para los Derechos Humanos, 2004); Ramírez, SG, *La Jurisdicción Interamericana y los Derechos Humanos* (Universidad Nacional Autónoma de México, 2002); Harris DJ and Livingstone, S (eds) *The Inter-American System of Human Rights* (Oxford University Press, 1998); Buergenthal, T and Shelton, D, *Protecting Human Rights in the Americas: Cases and Materials* (N.P. Engel, 1995); Medina, C, *The Battle for Human Rights: Gross, Systematic Violations of Human Rights and the Inter-American System* (Martinus Nijhoff, 1988).

degrading treatment or punishment.[3] The Inter-American Convention to Prevent and Punish Torture (hereinafter 'I/A Torture Convention') establishes the specific obligation of States parties to prevent and punish torture.[4] The Inter-American Convention on the Prevention, Punishment and Eradication of Violence against Women (hereinafter 'Belém do Pará Convention') reaffirms the right of women not to be subject to torture or other physical, mental and moral ill-treatment.[5]

The American Declaration on the Rights and Duties of Man (hereinafter 'American Declaration') also prohibits any conduct that constitutes torture or other cruel, inhuman or degrading treatment or punishment. Article I guarantees the right to life, liberty and personal security, but does not contain a specific provision against torture or ill treatment. However, the Inter-American Commission on Human Rights (hereinafter 'Commission' or 'Inter-American Commission' or 'IAComm.HR') considers that the right to personal security includes the right to humane treatment and personal integrity.[6] The American Declaration also recognizes the right of every person in custody to humane treatment.[7] Furthermore, it provides for the right 'not to receive a cruel, infamous or unusual punishment' for having committed a criminal offense.[8] It is important to note that every Member State of the Organization of American States (OAS) is subject to the normative dimension of the American Declaration and is bound by the supervisory powers granted to the Inter-American Commission by the OAS Charter.

Other regional treaties are also closely related to the subject matter of torture and ill treatment. For example, the Inter-American Convention on Forced Disappearance of Persons (hereinafter 'Forced Disappearance Convention') considers in its Preamble that such a practice violates 'numerous non-derogable and essential human rights,'[9] which includes torture and ill treatment. On the other hand, the Inter-American Convention on Protecting the Human Rights of Older Persons (hereinafter 'Older Persons Convention') expressly recognizes in Article 10 the right of older persons not to be subjected to torture or cruel, inhuman, or degrading treatment or punishment. It also provides that the 'States Parties shall take all necessary measures of a legislative, administrative, judicial, or other nature to prevent, investigate, punish and eradicate all forms of torture or cruel, inhuman, or degrading treatment or punishment of older persons.'[10]

SUPERVISORY FRAMEWORK

The broad quasi-judicial mandate of the Inter-American Commission on Human Rights is complemented by the judicial mandate of the Inter-American Court of Human Rights (here-

---

[3]   American Convention on Human Rights (1969), Treaty no B-32, OAS Treaty Series no 36.
[4]   Inter-American Convention to Prevent and Punish Torture (1985), Treaty no A-51, OAS Treaty Series no 67.
[5]   Inter-American Convention on the Prevention, Punishment and Eradication of Violence against Women (1984), Treaty no A-61, Articles 4(b), (d), (e).
[6]   See e.g. *Ovelario Tames v. Brazil*, Case 11.516, Report No 60/99, para 39.
[7]   American Declaration on the Rights and Duties of Man (1948), Article XXV.
[8]   *Ibid*, Article XXVI.
[9]   Inter-American Convention on Forced Disappearance of Persons (1994), Treaty no A-60.
[10] Inter-American Convention on Protecting the Human Rights of Older Persons (2015), Treaty no A-70.

inafter 'Court' or 'Inter-American Court' or 'IACt.HR'). These two international bodies have gained considerable legitimacy in national contexts and their impact in national legal systems has grown significantly. It is important to note that the Inter-American Court is the only hemispheric international tribunal available to all States in the American continent.

The Inter-American Commission

Article 53 of the Charter of the Organization of American States (hereinafter 'Charter') recognizes the Inter-American Commission as one of the main organs of the OAS.[11] The principal function of the Commission is 'to promote the observance and protection of human rights and to serve as a consultative organ' of the OAS.[12] It was originally considered as an 'autonomous entity' of the OAS, with a promotional mandate, and its 1960 Statute indicated (and remains the same in its current Statute) that 'for the purpose of this Statute, human rights are understood to be those set forth in the American Declaration.'[13] Subsequently, the Protocol of Buenos Aires that amended the OAS Charter elevated the Commission to 'principal organ' of the OAS, significantly strengthening its institutional authority and legitimacy.

The Commission is comprised of seven members elected in their personal capacity by the OAS General Assembly, from candidates presented by Member States.[14] The members are elected for a term of four years and may be re-elected only once.[15] Candidates must be 'persons of high moral standing and recognized competence in the field of human rights.'[16] The Inter-American Commission is based in the OAS headquarters in Washington, D.C.

The authority of the Commission has a dual nature: it is a principal organ of the OAS under the Charter with a statutory mandate based on the American Declaration, and it is also a supervisory body of the American Convention. The powers and functions of the Commission regarding each OAS Member State varies depending on whether the State has ratified the Convention and accepted the contentious jurisdiction of the Court.

The Inter-American Commission has a broad mandate and a wide array of powers that allow it to undertake diplomatic-political activities as well as adopt quasi-judicial measures. This broad mandate of the Commission extends to the substantive provisions of all of the regional human rights treaties previously mentioned. The Commission can make recommendations to States regarding the adoption of measures for the promotion and protection of human rights, develop awareness of human rights, provide advisory services to States, prepare studies and reports, request information from States, conduct on-site visits, recommend measures in favour of human rights, submit Annual Reports to the OAS General Assembly, and examine communications, request information and make recommendations.[17] The Commission may also request advisory opinions from the Inter-American Court, act on petitions and other communications, file applications and appear before the Inter-American Court, request provisional

---

[11]   Charter of the Organization of American States (1948), Treaty no A-41, OAS Treaty Series nos 1C and 61, Article 53.

[12]   *Ibid*, Article 106.

[13]   Statute of the Inter-American Commission on Human Rights (1979), Article 1(2)(b).

[14]   *Ibid*, Article 3.

[15]   *Ibid*, Article 4; American Convention (n 3 above), Article 37.

[16]   Commission Statute (n 13 above), Article 2; American Convention (n 3 above), Article 34.

[17]   Commission Statute (n 13 above), Article 18.

measures of the Inter-American Court, and submit additional draft protocols to the American Convention and propose amendments to the American Convention.[18]

The Inter-American Court

The Inter-American Court is the judicial supervisory body established by the American Convention and it has both a contentious jurisdiction and an advisory jurisdiction. The Inter-American Commission and those Convention State parties that have accepted the Court's contentious jurisdiction may file cases before the Court. States parties to the Convention as well as OAS Member States and organs of the OAS may request advisory opinions.[19]

The Inter-American Court is the only judicial organ of the Inter-American System. It is 'an autonomous judicial institution' of the OAS mandated with 'the application and interpretation of the American Convention.'[20] It is comprised of seven judges who serve in their individual capacity and are elected by States parties to the American Convention, from candidates nominated by those States.[21] Candidates must be jurists of the highest moral authority and recognized competence in the field of human rights.[22] The judges of the Court are elected for a period of six years and may be re-elected once.[23] The Inter-American Court of Human Rights is located in San José, Costa Rica.

TORTURE AND CRUEL, INHUMAN OR DEGRADING TREATMENT OR PUNISHMENT IN THE INTER-AMERICAN SYSTEM

The American Convention sets forth the right to humane treatment and recognizes the right to physical, mental and moral integrity.[24] Article 5(2) prohibits torture and cruel, inhuman or degrading treatment and punishment and states that persons deprived of their liberty shall be treated with respect for the inherent dignity of the human person.[25] The Inter-American Court has defined the scope of this right as having 'several gradations and embraces treatment ranging from torture to other types of humiliation or cruel, inhuman or degrading treatment with varying degrees of physical and psychological effects caused by endogenous and exogenous factors which must be proven in each specific situation.'[26] Articles 5(3) to 5(6) provide additional protections for persons deprived of their liberty as a result of a pending criminal proceeding or a conviction.[27] Moreover, Article 27 of the American Convention regulates the

---

[18]   *Ibid*, Articles 18, 19 and 20; American Convention (n 3 above), Article 41.
[19]   American Convention (n 3 above), Articles 62, 64.
[20]   Statute of the Inter-American Court of Human Rights (1979), Article 1. The Court may exercise jurisdiction over other Inter-American Conventions if they so provide.
[21]   *Ibid*, Article 6–7; American Convention (n 3 above), Articles 52–53.
[22]   American Convention (n 3 above), Article 52(1).
[23]   Court Statute (n 20 above), Article 5; American Convention (n 3 above), Article 54.
[24]   American Convention (n 3 above), Article 5(1).
[25]   *Ibid*, Article 5(2).
[26]   IACt.HR, *Loayza Tamayo v. Peru*, Merits, Judgment of September 17, 1997, Series C no 33, para 57.
[27]   American Convention (n 3 above), Article 5(3), (4), (5), (6).

suspension of rights in times of war, public danger or other emergency that poses a threat to the independence or security of a State. This provision provides that the right to humane treatment guaranteed in Article 5 is non-derogable.[28] And the Court has indicated that both the prohibition of torture and that of cruel, inhuman or degrading treatment and punishment are non-derogable.[29]

General Scope of Torture and Cruel, Inhuman and Degrading Treatment and Punishment

Torture is expressly prohibited in Inter-American human rights law.[30] Article 2 of the Inter-American Torture Convention defines torture,[31] stating that:

> torture shall be understood to be any act intentionally performed whereby physical or mental pain or suffering is inflicted on a person for purposes of criminal investigation, as a means of intimidation, as personal punishment, as a preventive measure, as a penalty, or for any other purpose. Torture shall also be understood to be the use of methods upon a person intended to obliterate the personality of the victim or to diminish his physical or mental capacities, even if they do not cause physical pain or mental anguish.

The definition does not include pain or suffering that is inherent in or which is solely the consequence of lawful measures. The Inter-American Court[32] and Commission[33] have relied on the Article 2 definition to interpret Article 5 of the American Convention. In some instances, the Court has also relied on Article 1 of the United Nations Convention against Torture and Other Cruel, Inhuman or Degrading Treatment or Punishment to aid the interpretation of this provision.[34]

Accordingly, the following three elements must be present in order to establish that an act or omission constitutes torture:[35] (1) a deliberate or intentional act; (2) severe physical or mental pain or anguish suffered by the victim; and (3) that is undertaken for one of the purposes listed. The regional definition does not require that the act be inflicted or instigated by public

---

[28]   *Ibid*, Article 27.

[29]   IACt.HR, *Lori Berenson-Mejía v. Peru*, Judgment of November 25, 2004, Merits, Reparations and Costs, Series C no 119, para 100; IACt.HR, *Caesar v. Trinidad and Tobago*, Judgment of March 11, 2005, Merits, Reparations and Costs, Series C no 123, para 70.

[30]   For a detailed description of the scope of torture and cruel, inhuman, or degrading treatment and punishment in the Inter-American System, *see* Rodríguez-Pinzón and Martin (n 2 above).

[31]   Inter-American Torture Convention (n 4 above).

[32]   IACt.HR, *Tibi v. Ecuador*, Judgment of September 7, 2004, Preliminary Objection, Merits, Reparations and Costs, Series C no 114, para 145; IACt.HR, *Gómez-Paquiyauri Brothers v. Peru*, Judgment of July 8, 2004, Merits, Reparations and Costs, Series C no 110, para 105.

[33]   IAComm.HR, *Raquel Martín de Mejía v. Peru*, Case 10.970, Report no 5/96, OEA/Ser.L/V/II.91 Doc 7 at 157 (1996), p. 185.

[34]   IACt.HR, *Maritza Urrutia v. Guatemala*, Judgment of November 27, 2003, Merits, Reparations and Costs, Series C no 103, para 90; IACt.HR, *Bámaca Velásquez v. Guatemala*, Judgment of November 25, 2000, Merits, Series C no 70, para 156; IACt.HR, *Cantoral Benavides v. Peru*, Judgment of August 18, 2000, Merits, Series C no 69, para 183.

[35]   IACt.HR, *Ruano Torres et al. v. El Salvador*, Judgment of October 5, 2015, Merits, Reparations and Costs, Series C no 303, para 121; IACt.HR, *J. v. Peru*, Preliminary Objection, Judgment of November 27, 2013, Merits, Reparations and Costs, Series C no 275, para 364.

officials or with their consent or acquiescence (which is a requirement under the UN Torture Convention definition). Additionally, the Inter-American instruments do not define cruel, inhuman and degrading treatment and punishment. However, the Court has concluded that the essential criterion for distinguishing torture from other cruel, inhuman or degrading treatment or punishment is the intensity of the suffering.[36]

Specific Acts and Situations

The Inter-American Court has also determined that certain situations can be qualified as torture or cruel, inhuman or degrading treatment because of their very nature. For example, it has dealt with cases concerning corporal punishment as a tool of discipline, concluding that this could violate Article 5 of the American Convention since its use is not strictly necessary to ensure a prisoner's proper behavior: in the *Caesar v. Trinidad and Tobago* the Court ruled that corporal punishment is *per se* incompatible with Article 5(1) and (2) of the American Convention because of its inherently cruel, inhuman and degrading nature.[37] Additionally, the Inter-American system has also considered excessive use of force as a violation of Article 5.[38] Moreover, the mere threat of an act prohibited by Article 5 of the American Convention may in itself constitute a violation of that provision when that threat is sufficiently real and imminent.[39]

The Inter-American System has also found that violence against women, including rape, is a violation of Article 5 of the American Convention. The Court has found such violations in several cases, in the context of violence from public officials or from private actors,[40] following the Commission's 1996 landmark decision in the *Martín de Mejía* case,[41] where it stated that 'rape is considered to be a method of psychological torture because its objective, in many cases, is not just to humiliate the victim but also her family or community.'[42] The Commission also found in the *Martin de Mejía case* that rape would also constitute torture under the Inter-American Torture Convention definition.[43]

---

[36] *Caesar v. Trinidad and Tobago* (n 29 above), para 50.

[37] *Ibid*, para 70.

[38] *Loayza-Tamayo v. Peru* (n 26 above), para 57; *Cantoral-Benavides v. Peru* (n 34 above) para 96; IACt.HR, *Castillo-Petruzzi et al. v. Peru*, Judgment of May 30, 1999, Merits, Reparations and Costs, Series C no 59, para 197; IACt.HR, *Durand and Ugarte v. Peru*, Judgment of August 16, 2000, Merits, Series C no 68, para 78; IACt.HR, *Neira Alegría et al. v. Peru*, Judgment of January 19, 1995, Merits, Series C no 20, para 86.

[39] IACt.HR, 19 *Merchants v. Colombia*, Judgment of July 5, 2004, Merits, Reparations and Costs, Series C no 109, para 149; *Cantoral-Benavides* (n 34 above), para 102; IACt.HR, *'Street Children' (Villagrán Morales et al.) v. Guatemala*, Judgment of November 19, 1999, Merits, Series C no 63, para 165.

[40] IACt.HR, *López Soto et al. v. Venezuela*, Judgment of September 26, 2018, Merits, Reparations and Costs, Series C no 362; IACt.HR, *Velásquez Paiz et al. v. Guatemala*, Judgment of November 19, 2015, Preliminary Objections, Merits, Reparations and Costs, Series C no 307; IACt.HR, *Rosendo Cantú et al. v. Mexico*, Judgment of August 31, 2010, Preliminary Objection, Merits, Reparations, and Costs, Series C no 216; IACt.HR, *González et al. ('Cotton Field') v. Mexico*, Judgment of November 16, 2009, Preliminary Objection, Merits, Reparations and Costs, Series C no 205; IACt.HR, *Miguel Castro Castro Prison v. Peru*, Judgment of November 25, 2006, Merits, Reparations and Costs, Series C no 160.

[41] *Raquel Martín de Mejía v. Peru* (n 33 above), p 157.

[42] *Ibid*, p 186.

[43] *Ibid*, p 185.

The Court and the Commission consider forced disappearance to be a multiple and continuing violation of several of rights protected by the Convention.[44] This is not only because forced disappearance arbitrarily deprives the victim of liberty, but also because it endangers her or his personal integrity, safety and life.[45] These organs have also found torture or ill-treatment in cases of extrajudicial execution where it is established that victims were illegally detained by State agents and where the conditions in which their remains were found indicate severe mistreatment.[46] The Court has also consistently ruled that relatives of victims who have disappeared and of those who have been executed extra-judicially experience torture or ill-treatment as a direct consequence of the treatment of their loved ones.[47]

Regarding conditions of detention, Article 5(2) indicates that any person deprived of his or her liberty has the right to be detained in conditions that are respectful of his or her personal dignity. The State is the guarantor of the rights of those held in detention facilities.[48] Therefore, the act of imprisonment carries with it a specific and material commitment to protect the prisoner's human dignity which includes, inter alia, protecting detainees from situations that could imperil their life, health and personal integrity.[49] In this context, States must take into account the heightened vulnerability of certain categories of detained persons, such as minors or those with mental disabilities.[50] The Court has also ruled that a lack of appropriate and regular medical and psychological treatment could entail a violation of the right to humane treatment.[51]

Articles 5(4), 5(5) and 5(6) of the American Convention provide for additional State obligations regarding the treatment of persons deprived of liberty.[52] Article 5(4) requires the separation of accused and convicted persons and that they receive treatment appropriate

---

[44]   *See Bámaca-Velásquez v. Guatemala* (n 34 above), para 128; see also, IACt.HR, *Blake v. Guatemala*, Judgment of January 24, 1998, Merits, Series C no 36, para 65; IACt.HR, *Velásquez Rodríguez v. Honduras*, Judgment of July 29, 1988, Merits, Series C no 4, paras 155, 158; IAComm.HR, *Ileana del Rosario Solares Castillo et al. v. Guatemala*, Case 9111, Report no 60/01, para 31.

[45]   *Bámaca-Velásquez v. Guatemala* (n 34 above), para 128.

[46]   *'Street Children' (Villagrán Morales et al.) v. Guatemala* (n 39 above), paras 157–160, 166, 168.

[47]   *Bámaca-Velásquez v. Guatemala* (n 34 above), para 129; *Blake* (n 44 above), Separate Opinion of Judge Trindade, paras 37–38; IAComm.HR, *Remigio Domingo Morales and Rafael Sánchez, Pedro Tau Cac, José María Ixcaya Pixtay et al., Catalino Chochoy et al., Juan Galicia Hernández et al. and Antulio Delgado v. Guatemala*, Cases 10.626, 10.627, 11.198(A), 10.799, 10.751, 10.901, Report no 59/01, para 6. Also, the duty to ensure and guarantee the personal integrity of persons, as well as to prevent and punish torture (investigate and prosecute perpetrators and provide effective remedies for the abuses), may constitute a continuous violation of the Convention (IA Ct.HR, *Garcia Lucero et al v. Chile*, Judgment of Aug 28. 2013, Preliminary Objection, Merits and Reparation, Series C no 267, paras 38, 39 and 40).

[48]   See IACt.HR, *Hilaire, Constantine and Benjamin et al. v. Trinidad and Tobago*, Judgment of June 21, 2002, Merits, Reparations and Costs, Series C no 94, para 165; *see also Cantoral-Benavides* (n 34 above), para 87; *Neira Alegría et al. v. Peru* (n 38 above), para 60.

[49]   IAComm.HR, *Minors in Detention v. Honduras*, Case 11.491, Report non 41/99, para 135.

[50]   IACt.HR, *Bulacio v. Argentina*, Judgment of September 18, 2003, Merits, Reparations and Costs, Series C no 100, para 126; IAComm.HR, *Víctor Rosario Congo v. Ecuador*, Case 11.427, Report no 63/99, paras 53–54.

[51]   *Tibi v. Ecuador* (n 32 above), para 157; IACt.HR, *'Juvenile Reeducation Institute' v. Paraguay*, Judgment of September 2, 2004, Preliminary Objections, Merits, Reparations and Costs, Series C no 112, para 166.

[52]   American Convention (n 3 above), Articles 5(4)–(6).

to their status.[53] Article 5(5) mandates that minors must be held separately from adults and that they must be treated in accordance with their status as minors.[54] Article 5(6) states that 'punishments consisting of deprivation of liberty shall have as an essential aim the reform and social readaptation of the prisoners.'[55]

The case law of the Inter-American System provides that, under certain circumstances, incommunicado detention can constitute a form of cruel, inhuman and degrading treatment in violation of Article 5(2) of the American Convention.[56] The Court has stated that incommunicado detention is only permissible in exceptional circumstances when it may be necessary to ensure there can be an effective investigation.[57] The Inter-American case law has also considered that solitary confinement can constitute torture or cruel inhuman and degrading treatment, depending on the circumstances.[58]

The Inter-American Court considers that even though the American Convention does not prohibit the death penalty as such, its related provisions 'should be interpreted as "imposing restrictions designed to delimit strictly its application and scope, in order to reduce the application of the death penalty to bring about its gradual disappearance."'[59] Situations associated with the death penalty have been found to violate the right to humane treatment, such as prolonged periods of detention while awaiting execution,[60] and mandatory death sentences which contravene Article 5(1) for failing to respect the victim's physical, mental and moral integrity.[61]

The Inter-American System also recognizes two fundamental prohibitions necessary for effective protection from torture and other cruel, inhuman or degrading treatment: the prin-

---

[53]   *Ibid*, Article 5(4).
[54]   *Ibid*, Article 5(5).
[55]   *Ibid*, Article 5(6).
[56]   See IACt.HR, *De La Cruz Flores v. Peru*, Judgment of November 18, 2004, Merits, Reparations and Costs, Series C no 115, para 130; *Cantoral-Benavides v. Peru* (n 34 above) para 89; IACt.HR, *Suárez Rosero v. Ecuador*, Judgment of November 12, 1997, Merits, Series C no 35, para 91; *Loayza-Tamayo v. Peru* (n 26 above), para 58.
[57]   *Suárez Rosero v. Ecuador* (n 56 above), para 89; *Bulacio v. Argentina* (n 50 above), para 127; *Castillo-Petruzzi v. Peru* (n 38 above), para 195.
[58]   IACt.HR, *García Asto and Ramírez Rojas v. Peru*, Judgment of November 25, 2005, Preliminary Objection, Merits, Reparations and Costs, Series C no 137, para 97; *Lori Berenson-Mejía* (n 29 above), paras 103–109; *Castillo-Petruzzi v. Peru* (n 38 above), paras 194–199; *Víctor Rosario Congo v. Ecuador* (n 50 above), para 59.
[59]   *Hilaire v. Trinidad and Tobago* (n 48 above), para 99 (citing IACt.HR, *Restrictions to the Death Penalty (Arts. 4.2 and 4.4 American Convention on Human Rights)*, Advisory Opinion OC-3/83, September 8, 1983, Series A no 3, para 57).
[60]   *Ibid*, para 167 (citing the judgment of the European Court of Human Rights in *Soering v. United Kingdom*, Judgment of 7 July 1989, Ser A, no 161).
[61]   IAComm.HR, *Denton Aitken v. Jamaica*, Case 12.275, Report no 58/02, para 111; IAComm.HR, *Donnason Knights v. Grenada*, Case 12.028, Report no 47/01, paras 81, 82.

ciple of *non-refoulement* in the context of deportation,[62] extradition or expulsion, and the *exclusionary rule* with respect to evidence obtained through torture.[63]

THE COMMISSION'S RAPPORTEURSHIP ON THE RIGHTS OF PERSONS DEPRIVED OF LIBERTY

The Inter-American Commission has developed a system of rapporteurships to focus its work on human rights issues of specific concern in the hemisphere. The Commission currently has 10 thematic rapporteurships, eight of which are assigned to the Commissioners themselves and two to external experts.[64]

The Rapporteurship on the Rights of Persons Deprived of Liberty in the Americas ('Rapporteurship') was created by the Inter-American Commission of Human Rights in 2004.[65] The Rapporteur monitors the situation of persons subjected to different forms of deprivation of liberty in OAS member states.[66] It collects information about such persons by conducting country visits, gathering data from governmental authorities, and visiting juvenile detention centers.[67] The Rapporteurship also carries out interviews with detainees and their relatives, with detention facility staff, and civil society organizations. It further produces reports on the situation of persons deprived of liberty in detention facilities, in specific countries or at a regional level. The Rapporteurship may issue recommendations for OAS Member States urging them to remedy particularly serious situations and coordinating with national human rights bodies to oversee detention conditions in such states.

Reporting Activities

Since its establishment, the Rapporteurship has contributed to several reports, including annual, country and thematic reports as well as questionnaires. All available Annual Reports of the Commission from 2004 to 2014 contain an overview of the Rapporteurship's promotional activities, country visits, and press releases of the specific year. Moreover, the Rapporteurship

---

[62]   Article 13 of the Inter-American Torture Convention requires that a person not be extradited or returned to a country 'when there are grounds to believe that his life is in danger, that he will be subjected to torture or to cruel, inhuman or degrading treatment, or that he will be tried by special or ad hoc courts in the requesting State'. Also, Article 22(8) of the American Convention enshrines the right not to be deported or returned to a country where a person is in danger of being subjected to a violation of the right to life or personal freedom because of her or his race, nationality, religion, social status or political opinion.

[63]   Article 10 of the Inter-American Torture Convention prohibits the use of any statement obtained through torture as evidence in a legal proceeding. Article 8(3) of the American Convention forbids the use of confessions in legal proceedings if it is established that the statement was obtained through coercion of any kind.

[64]   Those assigned to external experts are the Special Rapporteurship for Freedom of Expression and the Special Rapporteurship on Economic, Social, Cultural, and Environmental Rights.

[65]   For details see IAComm.HR, Rapporteurship on the Rights of Persons Deprived of Liberty, Rights of Persons Deprived of Liberty, http://www.oas.org/en/iachr/pdl/default.asp

[66]   *Ibid.*

[67]   For details see IAComm.HR, Rapporteurship on the Rights of Persons Deprived of Liberty, Mandate and Functions, http://www.oas.org/en/iachr/pdl/mandate/mandate.asp

has contributed to the sections of the Commission's Annual Reports concerning human rights developments in the region, highlighting the conditions of detention of certain groups of detainees in specific countries, particularly prisoners of conscience and children. These reports have repeatedly stressed the precarious conditions of detention facilities in Cuba,[68] Ecuador,[69] Venezuela,[70] Haiti,[71] Colombia[72] and Honduras,[73] determining that such situations can be characterized as amounting to ill treatment and torture. The Rapporteurship has also contributed to the follow-up of recommendations issued by the Commission in country or thematic reports concerning torture and inhumane treatment in prisons and police stations in Venezuela,[74] unlawful detentions and overpopulated prison cells in Jamaica,[75] and investigations into cases of enforced disappearances, discrimination against LGBTQ persons deprived of liberty, and prison overcrowding in Colombia.[76]

The Rapporteurship has also contributed to the sections concerning detention facilities and conditions in special country reports concerning Haiti,[77] Bolivia, Venezuela, Honduras and

---

[68] E.g., IAComm.HR, Rapporteurship on the Rights of Persons Deprived of Liberty, Annual Reports, Annual Report 2004, http://www.cidh.oas.org/annualrep/2004eng/chap.4a.htm#CD paras 59–66; Annual Report 2006, http://www.cidh.oas.org/annualrep/2006eng/Chap.4b.htm#B, paras 65–70; Annual Report 2007, http://www.cidh.oas.org/annualrep/2007eng/Chap.4b.htm#IV, paras 102–121; Annual Report 2010, paras 249–265 (discussing Case 12,476 (*Oscar Elías Biscet et al. v. Cuba*) in which the IAComm. HR condemned Cuba for violating the prohibition of ill treatment and torture with respect to 78 political prisoners detained in 2003); Annual Report 2011, paras 178–187; Annual Report 2012, paras 71–77 (also mentioning arrests of dissident journalists and artists).

[69] IAComm.HR, Rapporteurship on the Rights of Persons Deprived of Liberty, Annual Reports, Annual Report 2005, http://www.cidh.oas.org/annualrep/2005eng/chap.4b.htm#HT, paras 183–186 (mentioning excessive use of physical and psychological force in prisons and police stations).

[70] E.g., IAComm.HR, Rapporteurship on the Rights of Persons Deprived of Liberty, Annual Reports, Annual Report 2009, http://www.cidh.oas.org/annualrep/2009eng/Chap.IV.f.eng.htm#510, paras 510–512 (acts of violence and forced disappearance in prisons); Annual Report 2013, paras 535–549; Annual Report 2014, paras 606–614 (describing Venezuela's detention conditions some 'of the worst on the continent' (para 606) due to criminal activities and high levels of violence inside the prisons, overcrowding and lack of health services).

[71] E.g., IAComm.HR, Rapporteurship on the Rights of Persons Deprived of Liberty, Annual Reports, Annual Report 2006, http://www.cidh.oas.org/annualrep/2006eng/Chap.4d.htm#129, para 129 (children being detained with adults); Annual Report 2008, http://www.cidh.oas.org/annualrep/2008eng/Chap4.e .eng.htm#304, paras 304–308 (precarious detention conditions of children).

[72] IAComm.HR, Rapporteurship on the Rights of Persons Deprived of Liberty, Annual Reports, Annual Report 2011, paras 136–142.

[73] E.g., IAComm.HR, Rapporteurship on the Rights of Persons Deprived of Liberty, Annual Reports, Annual Report 2013, http://www.oas.org/en/iachr/docs/annual/2013/docs-en/AnnualReport -Chap4-Honduras.pdf, paras 381–390 (mentioning structural problems in Honduras' prison facilities, such as overpopulation and food shortages).

[74] IAComm.HR, Rapporteurship on the Rights of Persons Deprived of Liberty, Annual Reports, Annual Report 2004, http://www.cidh.oas.org/annualrep/2004eng/chap.5c.htm#V, para 264.

[75] IAComm.HR, Rapporteurship on the Rights of Persons Deprived of Liberty, Annual Reports, Annual Report 2014, http://www.oas.org/en/iachr/docs/annual/2014/docs-en/Annual2014-chap5 -Jamaica.pdf, paras 76–87.

[76] IAComm.HR, Rapporteurship on the Rights of Persons Deprived of Liberty, Annual Reports, Annual Report 2014, http://www.oas.org/en/iachr/docs/annual/2014/docs-en/Annual2014-chap5 -Colombia.pdf, paras 31, 317, 330.

[77] IAComm.HR, Rapporteurship on the Rights of Persons Deprived of Liberty, Country Reports, Haiti: Failed Justice or the Rule of Law? Challenges Ahead for Haiti and the International Community (2005), http://www.cidh.oas.org/countryrep/HAITI%20ENGLISH7X10%20FINAL.pdf, paras 197–219

Colombia.[78] The Rapporteurship has issued a comprehensive country report on the situation of persons deprived of liberty in Honduras, highlighting the main structural challenges facing the country's prison system, including the lack of adequate policies to administer prisons, violence inside the prisons, overpopulation of detention facilities, and a shortage of professional prison staff.[79] Regarding Bolivia, the Rapporteurship described detention conditions as amounting to inhumane treatment, and drawing attention to the failure to segregate accused from convicted prisoners.[80] The follow-up report also draws attention to excessive use of preventive detention, which contributes to prison overcrowding and which is one of the major problems in the country.[81] In Venezuela, the Rapporteurship described incidents of physical torture and ill treatment which had taken place during detention in police and military facilities.[82]

The Rapporteurship has produced several thematic reports, including the 'Report on the Human Rights of Persons Deprived of Liberty in the Americas' in 2011 and the 'Report on the Use of Pretrial Detention in the Americas' in 2013.[83] The first report contained recommendations concerning structural issues such as lack of public policies on detention administration and overcrowding of cells.[84] The 'Report on the Use of Pretrial Detention in Americas' notes the excessive use of pretrial detention throughout the region and describes best practices to uphold the human rights of detainees and administration of detention facilities.[85]

(stating prolonged pre-trail detention, security in the prisons, and treatment of Haitians deported back to the country and children in detention as particular concerns); Observations of the Inter-American Commission on Human Rights upon Conclusion of its April 2007 visit to Haiti (2008), http://www.cidh .oas.org/Haiti07informe.eng.htm#31, paras 31–38 (mentioning that the detention conditions in Haiti had exacerbated since the Rapporteur's last visit in 2005).

[78]   IAComm.HR, Rapporteurship on the Rights of Persons Deprived of Liberty, Country Reports, Truth, Justice and Reparation – Report on the Situation of Human Rights in Colombia, http://www.oas .org/en/iachr/reports/pdfs/Colombia-Truth-Justice-Reparation.pdf, paras 1031–1131.

[79]   IAComm.HR, Rapporteurship on the Rights of Persons Deprived of Liberty, Country Reports, Report of the Inter-American Commission on Human Rights on the Situation of Persons Deprived of Liberty in Honduras (2013), http://www.oas.org/en/iachr/pdl/docs/pdf/HONDURAS-PPL-2013ENG .pdf

[80]   IAComm.HR, Rapporteurship on the Rights of Persons Deprived of Liberty, Country Reports, Access to Justice and Social Inclusion: The Road towards Strengthening Democracy in Bolivia (2007), http://cidh.org/countryrep/Bolivia2007eng/Bolivia07cap3.eng.htm#_ftn8, para 179.

[81]   IAComm.HR, Rapporteurship on the Rights of Persons Deprived of Liberty, Country Reports, Follow-Up Report – Access to Justice and Social Inclusion: The Road towards Strengthening Democracy in Bolivia, http://www.cidh.oas.org/annualrep/2009eng/Chap.V.2.htm, paras 103–132.

[82]   IAComm.HR, Rapporteurship on the Rights of Persons Deprived of Liberty, Country Reports, Democracy and Human Rights in Venezuela (2009), http://www.cidh.oas.org/countryrep/ Venezuela2009eng/VE09CHAPVIENG.htm, para 754.

[83]   Other thematic reports are the Report of the Inter-American Commission on Human Rights on the Situation of Persons Deprived of Liberty in Honduras described above and the Guantanamo report of 2015, which is described in more detail below.

[84]   IAComm.HR, Rapporteurship on the Rights of Persons Deprived of Liberty, Thematic Reports/ Studies, Report on the Human Rights of Persons Deprived of Liberty in the Americas (2011), http://www .oas.org/en/iachr/pdl/docs/pdf/PPL2011eng.pdf

[85]   IAComm.HR, Rapporteurship on the Rights of Persons Deprived of Liberty, Thematic Reports/ Studies, Report on the Use of Pretrial Detention in Americas (2013), http://www.oas.org/en/iachr/pdl/ reports/pdfs/Report-PD-2013-en.pdf

Country Visits

The Rapporteurship has conducted numerous country visits since its creation in 2004.[86] The first country visit was to Guatemala in 2004, and resulted in the adoption of precautionary measures to protect minors in detention facilities, particularly those associated with gangs, who were subject to inhumane treatment.[87] In 2006, the Rapporteurship visited two specific detention facilities in Brazil in order to monitor the state's compliance with precautionary measures previously adopted by the Commission.[88] This resulted in the issuance of further precautionary measures aimed at improving sanitary conditions and mitigating overcrowding.[89] It is interesting to note that in the visit to Chile in 2008, the Rapporteurship indicated that it observed good practices in privately run prisons when compared to the state-run detention centers, which were characterized by overcrowding and unhygienic conditions, whilst noting the excessive use of force in both private and state-run detention facilities.[90]

In June 2011, the Rapporteurship conducted the first visit to detention facilities in Suriname by an international delegation.[91] It observed that both the accommodation and internal security were good, but there was a lack of rehabilitation programs, use of solitary confinement and insufficient quantity and quality of food and medical services.[92]

The Commission also carried out a country visit to the United States in 2014. The Rapporteurship collected information on juvenile detention centers,[93] noting that minors were incarcerated as if they were adults, in contravention of the state's international obligations.[94] Similarly, in September 2015, the Rapporteurship visiting both state and federal detention centers,[95] noting that were was 'overcrowding, corruption, improper medical care, lack of privacy, lack of real opportunities for reintegration into society, mistreatment by prison staff

---

[86]   For an overview see, IAComm.HR, Rapporteurship on the Rights of Persons Deprived of Liberty, Country Visits, http://www.oas.org/en/iachr/pdl/activities/countries.asp

[87]   IAComm.HR, Rapporteurship on the Rights of Persons Deprived of Liberty, Country Visits, Guatemala, November 2004, http://www.oas.org/en/iachr/pdl/activities/countries.asp; see also IAComm. HR, Rapporteurship on the Rights of Persons Deprived of Liberty, Press Release no 26/04, http://www .cidh.org/Comunicados/English/2004/26.04.htm

[88]   IAComm.HR, Rapporteurship on the Rights of Persons Deprived of Liberty, Country Visits, Brazil, September 2006, http://www.oas.org/en/iachr/pdl/activities/countries.asp

[89]   See, http://www.corteidh.or.cr/docs/medidas/araraquara_se_02_ing.pdf

[90]   IACHR, Rapporteurship on the Rights of Persons Deprived of Liberty, Country Visits, Chile, August 2008, http://www.oas.org/en/iachr/pdl/activities/countries.asp; IAComm.HR, Rapporteurship on the Rights of Persons Deprived of Liberty, Press Release No. 39/08, http://www.cidh.oas.org/ Comunicados/English/2008/39.08eng.htm

[91]   IAComm.HR, Rapporteurship on the Rights of Persons Deprived of Liberty, Country Visits, Suriname, June 2011, http://www.oas.org/en/iachr/pdl/activities/countries.asp

[92]   IAComm.HR, Rapporteurship on the Rights of Persons Deprived of Liberty, Press Release no 56/11, http://www.oas.org/en/iachr/media_center/PReleases/2011/056.asp

[93]   IAComm.HR, Rapporteurship on the Rights of Persons Deprived of Liberty, Country Visits, New York, United States, June 2014, http://www.oas.org/en/iachr/pdl/activities/countries.asp

[94]   IAComm.HR, Rapporteurship on the Rights of Persons Deprived of Liberty, Press Release no 44/14, http://www.oas.org/en/iachr/media_center/PReleases/2014/044.asp

[95]   IAComm.HR, Rapporteurship on the Rights of Persons Deprived of Liberty, Country Visits, Mexico, September 22 to 24, 2015 http://www.oas.org/en/iachr/pdl/activities/countries.asp

responsible for the custody of inmates, and the inability of inmates to lodge complaints with an independent agency.'[96]

Guantanamo

The situation of detainees at the US Naval Base at Guantanamo Bay has been also subject to special scrutiny by the Rapporteurship. The Rapporteur requested permission to visit the detention facilities in 2007 and again in 2011.[97] On both occasions, the United States granted the request under the condition that the delegation could not communicate with detainees. The Rapporteurship declined to perform the visit on this basis.

The Rapporteurship has repeatedly urged the United States to close Guantanamo. In its July 2006 press release, the Inter-American Commission requested the US to implement the precautionary measures that the Commission had previously issued, to close Guantanamo prison and remove all detainees, to investigate any act of torture or ill treatment, and to examine the situation of prisoners at risk of torture or ill treatment after their removal from the naval base.[98] The Commission restated these measures after the release of official documents confirming the use of torture and ill treatment against detainees in Guantanamo in April 2011.[99] In August 2011, it adopted a resolution on the closure of Guantanamo[100] and, in 2012, reiterated its demand to close the detention center.[101] In 2014, six detainees from Guantanamo were resettled in Uruguay, a step which the Commission welcomed.[102]

In 2015, the Commission released its report 'Toward the Closure of Guantanamo'.[103] The report assessed the situation of the detainees in Guantanamo, focusing on (1) the detainees' right to personal liberty, including the use of torture and prison conditions; (2) their right to access to justice; and (3) legal aspects surrounding the closure of Guantanamo. It issued recommendations to the US that it close the detention center and to other OAS Member States that they receive those formerly held there.

The Commission has carried out several other actions regarding the situation in Guantanamo, including hearings, cases and resolutions in favor of the Guantanamo detainees.[104]

---

[96]   IAComm.HR, Rapporteurship on the Rights of Persons Deprived of Liberty, Press Release no 116/15, http://www.oas.org/en/iachr/media_center/PReleases/2015/116.asp

[97]   IAComm.HR, Rapporteurship on the Rights of Persons Deprived of Liberty, Decisions Regarding the US Detention Center in Guantanamo, http://www.oas.org/en/iachr/pdl/decisions/Guantanamo.asp

[98]   IAComm.HR, Rapporteurship on the Rights of Persons Deprived of Liberty, Press Release no 27/06, http://www.cidh.oas.org/Comunicados/English/2006/27.06eng.htm

[99]   IAComm.HR, Rapporteurship on the Rights of Persons Deprived of Liberty, Press Release no 37/11, http://www.oas.org/en/iachr/media_center/PReleases/2011/037.asp

[100]   IAComm.HR, Rapporteurship on the Rights of Persons Deprived of Liberty, Press Release no 086/11, http://www.oas.org/en/iachr/media_center/PReleases/2011/086.asp

[101]   IAComm.HR, Rapporteurship on the Rights of Persons Deprived of Liberty, Press Release no 3/12, http://www.oas.org/en/iachr/media_center/PReleases/2012/003.asp

[102]   IAComm.HR, Rapporteurship on the Rights of Persons Deprived of Liberty, Press Release no 147/14, http://www.oas.org/en/iachr/media_center/PReleases/2014/147.asp

[103]   IAComm.HR, Rapporteurship on the Rights of Persons Deprived of Liberty, Towards the Closure of Guantanamo, http://www.oas.org/en/iachr/reports/pdfs/Towards-Closure-Guantanamo.pdf

[104]   IAComm.HR, Rapporteurship on the Rights of Persons Deprived of Liberty, Decisions Regarding the US Detention Center in Guantanamo, http://www.oas.org/en/iachr/pdl/decisions/Guantanamo.asp

Other Activities

Other activities of the Rapporteurship include the adoption of 'Principles and Best Practices on the Protection of Persons Deprived of Liberty in the Americas.' The drafting process commenced in 2005 with consultations with different stakeholders, including governments, civil society organizations and legal experts.[105] The Principles and Best Practices report was finally adopted by the Commission in 2008 by Resolution 01/08. The document contains best practices regarding general detention principles, such as the prohibition of inhumane treatment and due process guarantees, and provisions concerning detention conditions and the management and administration of detention centers.[106]

The Rapporteurship has also organized and participated in a vast range of promotional and other activities, including video conferences, seminars, workshops, academic exchanges and side events at the UN.[107] For instance, in 2014, it participated in the Regional Forum on the Optional Protocol to the UN Convention against Torture aimed at fostering the establishment of national torture prevention mechanisms, increasing collaboration between relevant actors, and enhancing the application of the Optional Protocol.[108]

CASE LAW CONCERNING TORTURE AND ILL TREATMENT

This section will provide an overview of the case law concerning torture and ill-treatment developed within the Inter-American System. The first subsections will consider the use of precautionary measures by the Commission and provisional measures by the Court. This will then be followed by sections looking at the merits decisions of both the Commission and the Court.

Precautionary Measures of the Commission

The 'precautionary measures' of the Inter-American Commission have evolved into a crucial tool to prevent serious human rights violations. Such measures can be issued in serious situations of gravity, irreparability and urgency. They can be requested as soon as the threat of torture or ill-treatment arises, without having to file an individual complaint under Article 44 of the American Convention.

In its recent practice, the Commission has adopted numerous precautionary measures to protect the right to integrity and humane treatment, and the prohibition of torture in cases involving a broad range of circumstances. Most precautionary measures concern detention conditions, indigenous peoples and human rights defenders. Other issues include threats against journalists, trade unionists and members of the judiciary, deportations and lack of

---

[105]   IAComm.HR, Rapporteurship on the Rights of Persons Deprived of Liberty, Principles and Best Practices, http://www.oas.org/en/iachr/pdl/activities/principles.asp

[106]   IAComm.HR, Basic Documents in the Inter-American System, Principles and Best Practices on the Protection of Persons Deprived of Liberty in the Americas, http://www.oas.org/en/iachr/mandate/Basics/principlesdeprived.asp

[107]   IAComm.HR, Rapporteurship on the Rights of Persons Deprived of Liberty, Promotion and Other Activities, http://www.oas.org/en/iachr/pdl/activities/activities.asp

[108]   *Ibid.*

medical treatment. While the measures adopted vary depending on the circumstances of the case, the Commission always orders that the state concerned coordinates with the beneficiaries of the measures to be implemented, as the examples provided below will show.

Conditions of detention

Precautionary measures addressing precarious detention conditions have frequently dealt with, inter alia, overcrowded prison cells, violent acts in the detention centers, prolonged solitary confinement and lack of medical treatment. For instance, the Commission adopted precautionary measures concerning juvenile detention conditions in Ceara, Brazil, stating that inmates' lives and physical integrity were at risk because of the 'poor conditions of the detentions, that allegedly include overpopulation, excessive use of force by instructors, torture, use of isolationism for long periods of time, sexual abuses, and lack of medical assistance.'[109] It ordered Brazil to reduce overcrowding and improve material conditions, food quality and medical treatment.[110] The Commission also observed precarious detention conditions, including physical and psychological violence, in Nicaragua following the student protests of April 2018.[111] It further adopted precautionary measures concerning Punta Coco, Panama, a detention facility located on a deserted island, both because of the detention conditions themselves and the harassment of the detainees' defense attorneys.[112] It noted that the facility's remote location limited the ability of detainees to have access to their lawyers and families and it ordered the State to end such isolated detention and to protect the life and integrity of the defense attorneys. In other cases, the Commission has ordered States to take the measures necessary to ensure the adequate medical treatment of prisoners.[113] For example, it held that the United States should guarantee adequate detention facilities and access to medical care for Mustafa Adam Al-Hawsawi, who was detained in Guantanamo.[114]

Human rights defenders

The Commission has adopted numerous precautionary measures to protect the lives and personal integrity of human rights and environmental rights defenders from threats, violence

---

[109] IAComm.HR, Precautionary Measures no 60/15, *Adolescents Deprived of Freedom in Facilities of Juvenile Detention Reform for Men in the State of Ceará, Brazil*, December 31, 2015.

[110] See similar cases: IAComm.HR, Precautionary Measures no 35/14, *Almafuerte and San Felipe Prison Complexes, Argentina*, May 14, 2015; IAComm.HR, Precautionary Measures no 302/15, *Adolescents Deprived of Liberty at the Center for Socio-Educational Services for Adolescents (CASA), Brazil*, July 21, 2016; IAComm.HR, Precautionary Measures no 496/14 and No. 37/15, *Persons Deprived of Liberty in Six Police Stations in Lomas de Zamora and La Matanza, Argentina*, May 12, 2016; IAComm.HR, Precautionary Measures no 475/15, *Members of the Voluntad Popular Political Party, Venezuela*, January 14, 2017; IAComm.HR, Precautionary Measures no 335/14, *Leopoldo Lopez and Daniel Ceballos, Venezuela*, October 12, 2015; IAComm.HR, Precautionary Measures no 260/16, *Police Coordination Center José Francisco Bermúdez, Venezuela*, April 26, 2016.

[111] IAComm.HR, Precautionary Measures no 1133/18, *Amaya Eva Coppens Zamora and others (Deprived of their Liberty at the Penitentiary Center 'La Esperanza'), Nicaragua*, November 11, 2018.

[112] IAComm.HR, Precautionary Measures no 393/15, *Persons Deprived of Liberty in 'Punta Coco', Panama*, February 25, 2016; extension on March 22, 2017.

[113] IAComm.HR, Precautionary Measures no 750/16, *Braulio Jatar, Venezuela*, December 22, 2016; IAComm.HR, Precautionary Measures no 84/19, *Ruth Esther Matute Valdivia, Nicaragua*, January 31, 2019.

[114] IAComm.HR, Precautionary Measures no 422/14, *Matter of Mustafa Adam Al-Hawsawi, United States*, July 7, 2015.

and harassment by state agents and private actors.[115] For instance, on March 5, 2016, in the case concerning the murdered Honduran activist Berta Cáceres, the Commission granted precautionary measures in respect of Gustavo Castro, a relative who had witnessed her murder, and several members of Cáceres' civil society organization, all of whom had received threats and suffered violent acts for their work to protect natural resources and human rights.[116] It ordered Honduras to guarantee Mr Castro's safety while he prepared to leave the country, and to adopt measures to ensure that the activists could continue their activities as human rights defenders. On March 23, 2016, the Commission extended these protection measures to include three other people who were representing Cáceres' relatives in the investigations into her murder. Similarly, in another case, the Commission afforded precautionary measures to family members of a murdered social justice worker who were at risk because of their demands for an investigation into the murder.[117]

The Commission has also issued precautionary measures in the case of an Ecuadorian environmental rights defender protesting against the mining industry.[118] It ordered Ecuador to ensure the right to life and personal integrity of the beneficiary and to take culturally appropriate measures ensuring that the human rights defender was able to pursue his work in a safe environment.

The Commission also adopted several precautionary measures to protect human rights defenders in Nicaragua who had received threats and suffered harassment and violence for their work following the nationwide protests that started in April 2018.[119] For instance, in September 2018, it ordered Nicaragua to protect the lives and personal integrity of 17 human rights defenders and their families, requesting the State to ensure that its agents respect their human rights.[120] In October 2018, the Commission issued similar precautionary measures to the human rights defenders Medardo Mairena Sequeira and Mario Lener Fonseca Díaz

---

[115] E.g., IAComm.HR, Precautionary Measures o 382/12, *Members of the Community Action Board of the Village of Rubiales, Colombia*, December 17, 2016; IAComm.HR, Precautionary Measures no 438/15, *Marino Alvarado, Venezuela*, October 14, 2015; IAComm.HR, Precautionary Measures no 416/15, *Members of the Ensemble des Citoyens Compétents a la Recherche l'Egalité des Droits de l'Homme, Haiti*, September 1, 2015; IAComm.HR, Precautionary Measures no 705/16, *Esteban Hermelindo Cux Choc and his Family, Guatemala*, December 6, 2016; IAComm.HR, Precautionary Measures no 121/16, *Carlos Humberto Bonilla Alfaro and others, Nicaragua*, March 24, 2016; IAComm.HR, Precautionary Measures no 209/17, *Francisco Javier Barraza Gómez, Mexico*, August 15, 2017; IAComm.HR, Precautionary Measures no 359/16, *Américo de Grazia, Venezuela*, July 21, 2016; IAComm.HR, Precautionary Measures no 331/17, *Francisca Ramírez and Family Members, Nicaragua*, August 22, 2017; IAComm.HR, Precautionary Measures no 1165/18, *Sergio López Cantera, Mexico*, October 18, 2018.

[116] IAComm.HR, Precautionary Measures no 112/16, *Members of COPINH, Berta Cáceres' relatives and other, Honduras*, March 5, 2016.

[117] IAComm.HR, Precautionary Measures no 68/18, *Marbeli Vivani González López and Family Members of Yaneth González López, Mexico*, September 6, 2018.

[118] IAComm.HR, Precautionary Measures no 807/18, *Yaku Pérez Guartambel, Ecuador*, August 27, 2018.

[119] E.g., IAComm.HR, Precautionary Measures no 847-18, 738-18, 737-18 and 736-18, *Adelaida Sánchez Mercado et al., Nicaragua*, August 8, 2018; IAComm.HR, Precautionary Measures no 893/18, *María Nelly Rivas Blanco and family, Nicaragua*, July 25, 2018.

[120] IAComm.HR, Precautionary Measures no 939/18 and 1067/18, *Yerling Marina Aguilera Espinoza and 17 other human rights defenders, Nicaragua*, September 17, 2018.

and their families. It added that the state should ensure adequate detention conditions for Mr Mairena Sequeira, including medical care, access to legal representation and family visits.[121]

Other cases
The Commission has also adopted precautionary measures to protect individuals who have received threats and suffered violence for undertaking their professional role, including journalists, trade unionists, and members of the judiciary. For instance, in the case of Miguel Henrique Otero and other journalists, the beneficiaries were subject to stigmatization, threats and violence, as well as limitations on their freedom of movement by being barred from leaving the country.[122] The Commission requested that Venezuela ensured that they could exercise their basic rights. The Commission ordered Honduras to determine the whereabouts of the president of a trade union who had disappeared and to investigate the disappearance.[123] In several cases where members of the judiciary have been subject to violence and harassment the Commission has ordered Guatemala, Honduras and Venezuela to take precautionary measures to protect the lives and personal integrity of both them and their families.[124]

Other cases have related to asylum and immigration, including deportation and the US 'Zero Tolerance' policy which has resulted in the separation of families. The Commission has ordered the US to halt the imminent deportations of Salvadoran asylum seekers fearing violence in their home country where there had been due process violations in the US asylum procedure.[125] In the case of *M.B.B.P.*, the Commission ordered the suspension of the deportation of a Venezuelan citizen living in Panama who was HIV positive, until the health risk of returning her to Venezuela has been assessed.[126]

As regards the US 'Zero Tolerance' policy the Commission granted precautionary measures in two cases due to the serious risk that separating the families could cause irreparable harm to the children.[127]

---

[121] IAComm.HR, Precautionary Measures no 1172/18, *Medardo Mairena Sequeira and Mario Lener Fonseca Díaz and their families, Nicaragua*, October 15, 2018.

[122] IAComm.HR, Precautionary Measures no 179/15, *Miguel Henrique Otero et al., Venezuela*, November 9, 2015. Other precautionary measures in favor of journalists include: IAComm.HR, Precautionary Measures no 573/15, *X et al., Mexico*, November 16, 2015; IACHR, Precautionary Measures no 5/15, *José Moisés Sánchez Cerezo, Mexico*, January 26, 2015.

[123] IAComm.HR, Precautionary Measures no 147/15, *Donatilo Jiménez Euceda, Honduras*, May 27, 2015.

[124] E.g., IAComm.HR, Precautionary Measures no 431/17, *Gloria Patricia Porras Escobar and Family, Guatemala*, August 29, 2017; IAComm.HR, Precautionary Measures no 449/17, *Luisa Ortega Díaz and Family, Venezuela*, August 3, 2017; Precautionary Measures no 52/16, *María Dolores López Godoy, Nelly Lizeth Martínez Martínez, and their families, Honduras*, December 6, 2016.

[125] In the case of *E.G.S. and A.E.S.G.* the Commission indicated that the State should suspend the deportation procedure until the Commission had reviewed a petition filed before it regarding the deportation. See IAComm.HR, Precautionary Measures no 297/16, *E.G.S. and A.E.S.G., United States of America*, May 11, 2016. See also IAComm.HR, Precautionary Measures no 152/16, *D.S., United States of America*, April 9, 2016.

[126] IAComm.HR, Precautionary Measures no 490/18, *M.B.B.P., Panama*, October 15, 2018.

[127] IAComm.HR, Precautionary Measures no 731-18, *Migrant Children affected by the 'Zero Tolerance' Policy regarding the United States of America*, August 16, 2018; IAComm.HR, Precautionary Measures no 505-18, *Vilma Aracely López Juc de Coc and others regarding the United States of America*, August 16, 2018. The measures requested included the free communication between children and parents, reunification in the best interest of the child, consular services, medical and psychological

In recent years, the Commission has also repeatedly adopted precautionary measures ensuring access to adequate medical treatment for serious illnesses or injuries.[128] For instance, it requested Colombia to protect the life and personal integrity of a six-year old boy suffering from a severe disease who had not received adequate medical treatment despite a court order.[129]

The Commission has also adopted precautionary measures to prevent the imminent execution of prisoners on death row in the US[130] and to protect girls suffering health problems after being sexual abused in Paraguay.[131]

Provisional Measures of the Inter-American Court

Turning to the Court, it has adopted numerous provisional measures and extended existing provisional measures in order to protect the personal integrity of the applicants.

Persons deprived of liberty in Brazil

The Court has adopted several resolutions on provisional measures protecting the lives and personal integrity of persons in Brazil. The Court granted provisional measures in respect of all detainees at the Curadi detention center in March 2014.[132] The measures have subsequently been extended and amplified to include protection measures for two legal representatives of the detainees.[133]

The Court also adopted provisional measures relating to those held in the Pedrinhas detention center in 2014 and requested further information about the conditions of detention in February 2017.[134] As a result, in March 2018, the Court ordered the State to adopt com-

---

assistance, and adoption of international cooperation measures to ensure that children and parents who have been deported separately are reunited. One of the requests was filed by national human rights institutions from several Central American States, and the beneficiaries included all 'migrant children that had been detained and separated from their families in the United States as a result of the implementation of the "Zero Tolerance" policy' (Migrant Children affected by the 'Zero Tolerance' Policy regarding the United States of America, Precautionary Measures No. 731-18, *ibid*, para 1). The other request was filed by four parents and their children.

[128] E.g., IAComm.HR, Precautionary Measures no 445/14, *Jessica Liliana Ramírez Gaviria, Colombia*, November 4, 2015; IAComm.HR, Precautionary Measures no 215/15, *Alejandro and Others, Mexico*, June 30, 2015.

[129] IAComm.HR, Precautionary Measures no 747/16, *Luis, Colombia*, December 22, 2016. See also: IAComm.HR, Precautionary Measures no 283/18, *T.S.G.T., Colombia*, November 5, 2018.

[130] E.g., IAComm.HR, Precautionary Measures no 82/18, *Ramiro Ibarra Rubi, United States*, October 1, 2018; IAComm.HR, Precautionary Measures no 156/17, *William Charles Morva, United States*, March 16, 2017.

[131] E.g., IAComm.HR, Precautionary Measures no 178/15, *Mainumby, Paraguay*, June 8, 2015; IAComm.HR, Precautionary Measures no 68/17, *The Adolescent Panambi, Paraguay*, March 2, 2017.

[132] IACt.HR, Order of October 7, 2015 on the *Penitentiary Complex of Curado, Brazil*, para 1. The Court ordered the Brazilian authorities to adopt an emergency plan for medical care, urgently reduce the overcrowding, remove weapons, ensure the safety of and respect for the lives and personal integrity of all within the detention center, including visitors and staff, and end humiliating practices toward visitors.

[133] *Ibid*; IACt.HR, Order of November 15, 2015 on the *Penitentiary Complex of Curado, Brazil*; IACt.HR, Order of November 23, 2016 on the *Penitentiary Complex of Curado, Brazil*; IACt.HR, Resolution of November 15, 2017 on the *Penitentiary Complex of Curado, Brazil*; IACt.HR, Resolution of November 28, 2018 on the *Penitentiary Complex of Curado, Brazil*.

[134] IACt.HR, Order of February 13, 2017 on the *Socio-Educational Internment Unit, Detention Facility of Curado, Detention Facility of Pedrinhas, and Criminal Institute of Plácido de Sá Carvalho, Brazil*.

prehensive provisional measures to protect the lives and personal integrity of all detainees, personnel and visitors.[135] In particular, it required the State and certain State agencies to submit information on structural prison reform, measures to reduce overcrowding, and statistical data on the deaths in custody.

In 2011 the Court also adopted provisional measures to protect the lives and personal, physical and moral integrity of children and adolescents deprived of liberty at the Socio-Educational Internment Unit ('Unit') in Brazil. It extended these measures in June 2015, adding that disciplinary rules should comply with the relevant international standards and the State should allow for the participation of the children's representatives when adopting measures to protect their lives and personal integrity.[136] In November 2017, these measures were again extended.[137]

The Court first adopted provisional measures in respect of the Criminal Institute of Plácido de Sá Carvalho in February 2017, concerning the high number of deaths resulting from overcrowding and insanitary conditions.[138] It requested that Brazil take all necessary measures to protect the lives and personal integrity of all detainees. The Court confirmed these provisional measures in resolutions of August 2017 and November 2018,[139] the latter resolution adding that no further detainees be sent to the prison.

Human rights defenders
Similar to the Commission, the Court has adopted provisional measures to protect the life and personal integrity of human rights defenders. For instance, the Court decided to maintain provisional measures concerning Almanza Suarez in Colombia as a result of specific threats against her and because of a general climate of fear concerning human rights defenders.[140] The Court has also repeatedly maintained provisional measures for human rights defenders in Mexico who continue to suffer violence and harassment for their involvement in indigenous rights organizations.[141]

Other cases
The Court has also adopted provisional measures on a variety of other topics. For instance, in *Alvarado Reyes and Others*, the Court granted provisional measures because of the impact which Mexico's failure to investigate cases of enforced disappearances was having on the personal integrity of those affected.[142] In another case, provisional measures were granted to

---

[135] IACt.HR, Order of March 14, 2018 on the *Socio-Educational Internment Unit, Detention Facility of Curado, Detention Facility of Pedrinhas, and Criminal Institute of Plácido de Sá Carvalho, Brazil*.

[136] IACt.HR, Order of June 23, 2015 on the *Socio-Educational Internment Unit, Brazil*.

[137] IACt.HR, Order of November 15, 2017 on the *Socio-Educational Internment Unit, Brazil*.

[138] IACt.HR, Order of February 13, 2017 on the *Criminal Institute of Plácido de Sá Carvalho, Brazil*.

[139] IACt.HR, Order of August 31, 2017 on the *Criminal Institute of Plácido de Sá Carvalho, Brazil*; Court, Order of November 22, 2018 on the *Criminal Institute of Plácido de Sá Carvalho, Brazil*.

[140] IACt.HR, Order of November 15, 2017 on *Almanza Suarez, Colombia*; see also IACt.HR, Order of November 14, 2017 on *Danilo Rueda, Colombia*.

[141] IACt.HR, Order of February 23, 2016 on *Fernandez Ortega and Others, Mexico*; IACt.HR, Order of February 7, 2017 on *Fernandez Ortega and Others, Mexico*; see also IACt.HR, Order of November 14, 2017 on *Castro Rodriguez, Mexico*; IACt.HR, Resolution of November 13, 2015, on *Specific Detention Centers of Venezuela, Humberto Prado, and Marianela Sanchez Ortiz and Family, Venezuela*.

[142] IACt.HR, Order of June 23, 2015 on *Alvarado Reyes and Others, Mexico*; IACt.HR, Order of November 14, 2017 on *Alvarado Reyes and Others, Mexico*.

protect a rural community in Colombia from the activities of illegal armed groups.[143] Finally, the Court has addressed the need to protect personal integrity in the context of irregular judicial procedures. For instance, in *Torres*, the Court granted provisional measures to a person who was an important witness of a criminal case in Peru.[144]

Cases on the Merits Determined by the Commission

In the last five years the Commission has published several reports on the merits in cases involving torture or ill treatment. For example, it decided two cases against the United States (*Felix Rocha Diaz v. US* and *Victor Saldaño v. US*) involving claims related to the imposition of the death penalty.[145] In both cases, the Commission ruled that the United States had violated, *inter alia*, the petitioners' rights to humane treatment and not to receive cruel, infamous and unusual punishment because of their being held in prolonged solitary confinement while on death row. In these decisions the Commission referred to statements of the UN Committee against Torture and the case law of the European Court of Human Rights and UN Human Rights Committee.

In four other cases, the Commission has found relatives of deceased persons to have been victims of violations of the right to humane treatment. The case of *Aristeu Guida da Silva (Brazil)* concerned a journalist who was killed for reasons related to his profession. The Commission held that Brazil had violated the right to humane treatment 'as a consequence of the lack of due diligence in the official investigative proceedings into the murder of Guida da Silva and because of the threats received by the victim's relatives during the investigation and the respective criminal cases.'[146] Similarly, in *Gilberto Jimenez Hernandez et al. (La Grandeza)*, Mexico was found to have infringed the integrity of Mr Jimenez' relatives by failing to conduct an effective and thorough criminal investigation into his death.[147] In *Jose Rusbel Lara et al.*, the Commission ruled that the lack of an investigation and a failure to provide protection to the next of kin which resulted in their subsequent displacement caused sufficient anxiety as to violate their right to personal integrity.[148] In *Alcides Torres Arias, Angel David Quintero et al.*, the Commission found there to have been an enforced disappearance which infringed their right to personal integrity.[149] It also held that Colombia had violated

---

[143]   IACt.HR, Order of June 26, 2017 on the *Matter of Peace Community of San José de Apartadó, Colombia*; IACtHR, Order of February 5, 2018 on the *Matter of Peace Community of San José de Apartadó, Colombia*.

[144]   IACt.HR, Order of December 17, 2017 on *Durand and Ugarte, Peru*; IACt.HR, Order of February 8, 2018 on *Durand and Ugarte, Peru*.

[145]   IAComm.HR, Report no 11/15, Case 12.833 (Merits), *Felix Rocha Diaz (United States)*, OEA/Ser.L/V/II.154, Doc 5 (March 23, 2015); IAComm.HR, Report no 24/17, Case 12.254 (Merits), *Victor Saldaño (United States)*, OEA/Ser.L/V/161 Doc 31 (March 18, 2017).

[146]   IAComm.HR, Report no 7/16, Case 12.213 (Merits), *Aristeu Guida da Silva and Family (Brazil)*, OEA/Ser.L/V/II.157, Doc 11 (April 13, 2016).

[147]   IAComm.HR, Report no 51/16, Case 11.564 (Admissibility and Merits), *Gilberto Jimenez Hernandez et al. (La Grandeza) (Mexico)*, OEA/Ser.L/V/II.159, Doc 60 (November 30, 2016).

[148]   IAComm.HR, Report no 35/17, Case 12.713 (Merits), *Jose Rusbel Lara et al. (Colombia)*, OEA/Ser.L/V/II.161, Doc 42 (March 21, 2017).

[149]   IAComm.HR, Report no 101/17, Case 12.414 (Merits), *Alcides Torres Arias, Angel David Quintero et al. (Colombia)*, OEA/Ser.L/V/II.164 Doc 119 (September 5, 2017).

the right to personal integrity because not knowing the whereabouts of Mr Torres Arias and Mr Quintero and the truth about their disappearance caused intense suffering to the next of kin.

Cases on the Merits Determined by the Court

Most cases on the merits decided in recent years by the Inter-American Court involved a violation of the right to personal integrity and the prohibition of torture and ill treatment. The following provides an overall view of the current trends in its work.

Enforced disappearance

The Court has decided on numerous occasions that enforced disappearance constitutes a continuous violation of fundamental human rights, including the right to personal integrity.[150] Recent examples include *Alvarado Espinoza et al. v. Mexico* where it was held that the State was responsible for the disappearance of three people at the hands of the army in the State of Chihuahua.[151] Since 2006, the Mexican army has been conducting operations to reestablish law and order and combat organized crimes, assuming the public security functions of the police. The Court held that the State had violated its international human rights obligation by disappearing three persons and placing the investigation into their whereabouts under the jurisdiction of military tribunals. In *Terrones Silva et al. v. Peru*, the Court ruled that Peru had violated, among others, the right to personal integrity of five individuals who were disappeared during the internal armed conflict, and of their next of kin.[152] In *Members of the Village of Chichupac and Neighboring Communities of the Municipality of Rabinal v. Guatemala*, the Court addressed the enforced disappearance of 81 people during Guatemala's armed conflict, 59 of whom were later found dead.[153] It found the State responsible for the enforced disappearance of 22 individuals and for violating the prohibition of ill treatment because of their prolonged isolation from their family members.

Detention, ill treatment and torture

The Court has repeatedly held States responsible for acts of torture, failure to investigate torture, and cruel and inhumane treatment in detention centers.[154] For instance, in *Villamizar*

---

[150]   Recent cases include IACt.HR, *Isaza Uribe and Others v. Colombia*, Judgment of November 20, 2018, Merits, Reparations, and Costs, Series C no 363; IACt.HR, *Munarriz Escobar and Others v. Peru*, Judgment of August 20, 2018, Preliminary Objection, Merits, Reparations, and Costs, Series C no 355; IACt.HR, *Vereda la Esperanza and Others v. Colombia*, Judgment of August 31, 2017, Preliminary Objection, Merits, Reparations, and Costs, Series C no 341.

[151]   IACt.HR, *Alvarado Espinoza v. Mexico*, Judgment of November 28, 2018, Merits, Reparations, and Costs, Series A no 370.

[152]   IACt.HR, *Terrones Silva et al. v. Peru*, Judgment of September 26, 2018, Preliminary Objection, Merits, Reparations, and Costs, Series C no 360.

[153]   IACt.HR, *Members of the Village of Chichupac and Neighboring Communities of the Municipality of Rabinal v. Guatemala*, Judgment of November 30, 2016, Preliminary Objection, Merits, Reparations, and Costs, Series C no 328.

[154]   E.g., IACt.HR, *Omeara Carrascal and Others v. Colombia*, Judgment of November 21, 2018, Merits, Reparations, and Costs, Series C no 368; IACt.HR, *Villamizar Durán et al. v. Colombia*, Judgment of November 20, 2018, Preliminary Objection, Merits, Reparations, and Costs, Series C no 364; IACt.HR, *Herrera Espinoza and Others v. Ecuador*, Judgment of September 1, 2016, Preliminary Objections, Merits, Reparations, and Costs, Series C no 316; IACt.HR, *Ruano Torres* (n 35 above); IACt.

Durán and others v. Colombia, the Court held the State liable for the extrajudicial execution of six civilians, whose deaths were falsely justified as killings of guerrilla fighters.[155] It established a violation of the right to personal integrity both because of the executions themselves and the stigmatizing statements of State agents concerning the victims' presumed status as guerrilla fighters. In another case, the Court held the Peruvian State responsible for cruel and inhumane treatment of soldiers who voluntarily joined the military service.[156] In the *Chinchilla Sandoval case*, Guatemala was found to have violated the right to personal integrity of a detainee with diabetes and other health problems by denying them medical treatment.[157] In *Women Victims of Sexual Torture in Atenco v. Mexico*, the Court held that the State committed acts of torture against, and violated the personal integrity of, a group of female detainees by sexually abusing them and discriminating against them based on their gender.[158]

Lack of medical treatment

On several occasions, the Court has held states liable for failing to provide adequate health care to citizens, even if they were not under State control. In the leading case of *Gonzales Lluy v. Ecuador*, which addresses the rights of a girl infected with HIV as a result of a failed medical treatment, the Court held that the right to personal integrity was directly linked to the right to health. It ruled that failure to provide adequate health services and effectively supervise and monitor private health providers can result in a violation of the right to personal integrity.[159] Similar cases include *Cuscul Pivaral and others v. Guatemala*,[160] *Poblete Vilchez and others v. Chile*[161] and *I.V. v. Bolivia*.[162]

Suffering of next of kin

The Court has repeatedly stated that the death of a person may cause suffering to family members, amounting to cruel and inhumane treatment. For instance, in *Carvajal Carvajal and others v. Colombia*, the next of kin of a killed journalist suffered a violation of their right to personal integrity because of the impact of the death, the State's failure to investigate and harassments they experienced after the killing.[163] In *Favela Nova Brasilia v. Brazil*, the Court

---

HR, *Humberto Maldonado Vargas v. Chile*, Judgment of September 2, 2015, Merits, Reparations, and Costs, Series C no 300.

[155] *Villamizar Durán at al. v. Colombia* (n 154 above).

[156] IACt.HR, *Quispialya Vilcapoma v. Peru*, Judgment of November 23, 2015, Preliminary Objection, Merits, Reparations, and Costs, Series C no 308.

[157] IACt.HR, *Chinchila Sandoval v. Guatemala*, February 29, 2016, Preliminary Objection, Merits, Reparations, and Costs, Series C no 312.

[158] IACt.HR, *Women Victims of Sexual Torture in Atenco v. Mexico*, Judgment of November 28, 2018, Preliminary Objection, Merits, Reparations, and Costs, Series C no 371. See also *López Soto et al.* (n 40 above).

[159] IACt.HR, *Gonzales Lluy and Others v. Ecuador*, Judgment of September 1, 2015, Preliminary Objections, Merits, Reparations, and Costs, Series C no 298.

[160] IACt.HR, *Cuscul Pivaral and Others v. Guatemala*, Judgment of August 23, 2018, Preliminary Objection, Merits, Reparations, and Costs, Series C no 359.

[161] IACt.HR, *Poblete Vilches and Others v. Chile*, Judgment of March 8, 2018, Merits, Reparations, and Costs, Series C no 349.

[162] IACt.HR, *I.V. v. Bolivia*, Judgment of November 30, 2016, Preliminary Objections, Merits, Reparations, and Costs, Series C no 329.

[163] IACt.HR, *Carvajal Carvajal and Others v. Colombia*, Judgment of March 13, 2018, Merits, Reparations, and Costs, Series C no 365. Similarly: IACt.HR, *Herzog and Others v. Brazil*, Judgment of March 15, 2018, Preliminary Objections, Merits, Reparations, and Costs, Series C no 353.

held that the relatives of 26 victims who were extra-judicially executed in the context of police operations, experienced intense suffering as a result of the killings and acts of torture that some of the victims were subject to before their death.[164]

Other cases

In other recent cases, the Court has addressed other situations that have violated the right to personal integrity, including the harassment of human rights defenders. In *Yarce and others v. Colombia*, the Court ruled that the assassination of a human rights defender, and the harassment, detention and displacement of others constituted a violation of the right to personal integrity of the activists and their relatives.[165] In particular, the State agents' derogatory statements and stigmatization of the victims as 'guerrilla fighters' infringed upon their honor and dignity. In *Hacienda Brazil Verde Workers v. Brazil*, regarding 85 forced laborers in that country, the Court held that the fact that the victims were subject to forced labor and that slavery infringed upon their right to personal integrity.[166]

FINAL COMMENTS

The Inter-American System's human rights supervisory organs have used a wide variety of monitoring tools at their disposal to promote and protect human rights. This has allowed the Inter-American System to increasingly develop and strengthen its human rights law standards using country and thematic reports, cases and interim measures, among other supervisory mechanisms. The prohibition of torture and ill-treatment is one of the substantive areas in which the Commission and the Court continue to make a difference in the lives of many people in a hemisphere where these heinous violations still exist.

Notable aspects of the Inter-American system's obligations include a broad definition of torture and ill-treatment that is not limited to actions inflicted or instigated by public officials or with their consent or acquiescence. This broad definition is reflected in decisions on torture ranging from abuses perpetrated by private armed groups, to violence against women in private or domestic settings. The Inter-American System has also been proactively interpreting this prohibition to cover sexual violence, which allowed the Commission in 1996 to be the first international human rights body to qualify rape as torture. Furthermore, it recognized that the practice of forced disappearance of persons *per se* violates the right to personal integrity.

However, the system still faces serious challenges due to the limited political and financial support it has received from countries of the Americas. For example, the Inter-American System lacks an enforcement mechanism comparable to the Committee of Ministers of the European Human Rights System. Furthermore, there are several States in the OAS that have not yet ratified the American Convention on Human Rights, which leaves the Commission with partial supervisory authority over such States and the Court with a contentious jurisdic-

---

[164] IACt.HR, *Favela Nova Brasilia v. Brazil*, Judgment of February 16, 2017, Preliminary Objections, Merits, Reparations, and Costs, Series C no 333.

[165] IACt.HR, *Yarce and Others v. Colombia*, Judgment of November 22, 2016, Preliminary Objections, Merits, Reparations, and Costs, Series C no 325.

[166] IACt.HR, *Hacienda Brasil Verde Workers v. Brazil*, Judgment of October 20, 2016, Preliminary Objections, Merits, Reparations, and Costs.

tion limited to 23 of the 35 OAS Member States. Additionally, the financial and administrative constraints of these organs have limited their ability to appropriately react to an increasing amount of work and to adequately respond to the expectations that victims and other stakeholders have of the System. In this sense, the System could be a victim of its own success.

An important aspect of the impact of this regional human rights system is the process of constitutionalizing human rights law in several countries of the region. The so-called 'block of constitutionality' has allowed the provisions of the Convention to acquire constitutional status in those States and has further propelled the authority of the work of the Commission and the Court at the national level. This reflects a trend in the hemisphere in which the Commission and the Court are slowly gaining legitimacy in certain domestic legal and political constituencies. But there still is resistance to the expanding role of the Inter-American System's organs under a sovereignty banner that appears to be stemming from the populist-nationalist movements that have been gaining political traction around the world. All those sectors of society that benefit from the Inter-American system – including government institutions, human rights defenders, lawyers, and many others – will be the ones called to protect the achievements and integrity of this international machinery and preserve the evolution of this still embryonic international human rights regime.

11. Ensuring freedom from torture under the African Human Rights System

Lawrence Murugu Mute

INTRODUCTION

The human rights institutional architecture in Africa is constituted of the African Commission on Human and Peoples' Rights, the African Court on Human and Peoples' Rights and the African Committee on the Rights and Welfare of the Child. The African Union Commission (AUC) as well as organs of the African Union (AU) such as the Permanent Representatives Committee, the Executive Council and the Assembly of Heads of State and Government also have administrative or policy mandates which impact the Continent's exercise of human rights.

This chapter explains and reflects on the normative framing of the prohibition of torture in Africa. It reviews the strategies which relevant human rights institutions have deployed towards the prohibition of torture.

The questions which this chapter addresses include: how the prohibition of torture is couched in Africa's normative instruments; the extent to which Africa's human rights institutions have sought to ensure the prohibition of torture; the value of the soft-law instruments developed to elaborate on the prohibition of torture; the extent to which normative and institutional measures cover the protection of victims of torture; and the impact of continental norms and practice in national contexts of protection from torture.

The chapter attests to the growth of a significant set of norms, standards and institutions for anchoring the prohibition of torture, as well as the development of an increasingly rich vein of supporting jurisprudence both at the continental and domestic levels. The utmost continuing and frustrating challenge revolves around limitations of implementation.

As shall be illustrated, the use of torture by state and non-state actors alike continues to mar the lives of individuals and communities, and Africans continue to be tortured for expressing non-conformist political or social views or as part of anti-terrorism initiatives or indeed for other less apparent reasons such as extracting confessions from detainees.[1] While it may be easy to rhetorise the anti-torture prohibition mantra, far more work is necessary to deal with existing or arising implementation dilemmas.

---

[1]   For example, see Amnesty International, *Welcome to Hell Fire: Torture and Other Ill-Treatment in Nigeria*, 2014, https://www.amnesty.org/en/documents/AFR44/011/2014/en/

CONTEXT

The African Charter on Human and Peoples' Rights ('African Charter' or 'Charter')[2] was adopted on 27 June 1981 by the Organisation of African Unity (OAU), the continental body constituted in 1963 by independent African states. The African Charter was adopted following extensive advocacy and negotiations which sought the establishment of a continent-wide instrument informed by an African legal philosophy[3] on which human rights could be anchored. Prior to the adoption of the African Charter, the only significant normative allusion to human rights was to be found in the OAU Charter which reaffirmed the adherence of African states to the principles established in the United Nations (UN) Charter and the Universal Declaration of Human Rights (UDHR),[4] and identified the promotion of international cooperation having due regard to the UN Charter and the UDHR as one of its purposes.[5]

It has, however, been pointed out that the OAU Charter focused far more on protecting states as opposed to protecting the individual. Its critical considerations were the dominant concerns of the time such as non-interference with internal affairs, state sovereignty, fighting neo-colonialism, self-determination and peaceful conflict-settlement.[6]

Prior to the adoption of the African Charter, the normative basis for ensuring human rights in Africa was derived from international human rights sources, principally the International Bill of Rights which comprises the 1948 UDHR, and the 1966 International Covenant on Civil and Political Rights and the International Covenant on Economic, Social and Cultural Rights. The International Bill of Rights established human dignity as the fundamental premise on which states would anchor relations with individuals and communities, and the independence constitutions of many African states reflected this dynamic by requiring that no person shall be subjected to torture or to inhuman or degrading punishment or treatment.[7] Yet, the advantages which these international human rights instruments portended also tended to be negated by a multiplicity of factors. Cold-War East-West politics pressured African states to align themselves in bipolar formations either of civil and political rights or of economic, social and cultural rights.[8]

Key features of the African Charter, therefore, were designed to deflect from the negative aspects of the International Bill of Rights. Hence, the African Charter deals with all human rights as universal, indivisible and interrelated, including civil, political, economic, social and cultural rights. It has an inclusive equality and non-discrimination clause, and recognises not only the rights of individuals but also the rights of peoples. The Charter establishes specific

---

[2]　*African Charter on Human and Peoples' Rights*, adopted by the OAU Assembly on 27 June 1981, OAU Doc CAB/LEG/67/3 rev. 5, 21 I.L.M. 58 (1982), entered into force 21 October 1986. As of January 2019, only one of Africa's 55 states (Morocco) was not a party to the Charter.

[3]　Ibhawoh, B, *Human Rights in Africa* (Cambridge University Press, 2018), 217.

[4]　*Universal Declaration of Human Rights*, Preamble.

[5]　*Organisation of African Unity Charter*, adopted on 25 May 1963, Article 2(e).

[6]　Murray, R, *Human Rights in Africa: From the OAU to the African Union* (Cambridge University Press, 2004), 7.

[7]　See Sec 18 of Kenya's Independence Constitution (1963); Sec 21 of Uganda's Independence Constitution (1962); and Sec 7 of the Constitution of Botswana (1966).

[8]　Mutua, M, 'The African Human Rights System: A Critical Evaluation', Human Development Occasional Papers (1992–2007) HDOCPA-2000-15, Human Development Report Office (HDRO), United Nations Development Programme (UNDP), http://hdr.undp.org/sites/default/files/mutua.pdf

third-generation or collective rights such as the right to development, the right to a satisfactory environment, the right to peace and the right of people to freely dispose of their wealth and natural resources. It not only establishes rights, it also sets out individuals' duties to others, their families and society, as well as the duties which the state has to individuals. The African Charter, however, also includes features such as claw-back clauses which have had the potential of limiting the rights of individuals.[9]

Significantly for the discussion on the prohibition of torture, by adopting the African Charter, states were making the commitment to abandon their previous insistence on the principle of non-interference with their domestic affairs. The African Charter's implementation would necessarily entail the monitoring and investigation of internal state actions by non-domestic institutions. Specifically, the African Union Constitutive Act,[10] which replaced the OAU Charter, includes far more forthright provisions aimed at the protection of human rights. As such, the AU's objectives include the promotion and protection of human and peoples' rights in accordance with the African Charter and other relevant human rights instruments,[11] and the principles that guide the Union's functioning include its right to intervene in a Member State in respect of war crimes, genocide and crimes against humanity;[12] respect for democratic principles, human rights, the rule of law and good governance;[13] and respect for the sanctity of human life, together with condemnation and rejection of impunity and political assassination, acts of terrorism and subversive activities.[14]

THE NORMATIVE AND INSTITUTIONAL ANTI-TORTURE FRAMEWORK

Normative framework

The African Charter
Article 5 of the African Charter provides that:

> Every individual shall have the right to the respect of the dignity inherent in a human being and to the recognition of his legal status. All forms of exploitation and degradation of man, particularly slavery, slave trade, torture, cruel, inhuman or degrading punishment and treatment shall be prohibited.

By this provision, the Charter recognises that the right to respect for every individual is predicated on the dignity inherent in a human being. It prohibits all forms of exploitation and degradation which it lists to include slavery, slave trade, torture, cruel, inhuman or degrading

---

[9]   Ibhawoh (n 3 above), 218–219. For a critical analysis of the Charter, see Mutua (n 8 above). As a matter of fact, the African Commission has determined that limitations established in national legislation may not be framed so as to erode the substance of a right established in the African Charter to the extent it becomes illusory. See Communication nos 140/94–141/94, 145/9, *Constitutional Rights Project, Civil Liberties Organization and Media Rights Agenda v. Nigeria*, 5 November 1999, para 40.

[10]   *Constitutive Act of the African Union*, adopted by the 36th Ordinary Session of the Assembly of Heads of State and Government, 11 July 2000; entered into force on 26 May 2001.

[11]   *Ibid*, Article 3 (H).

[12]   *Ibid*, Article 4 (H).

[13]   *Ibid*, Article 4 (N).

[14]   *Ibid*, Article 4 (O).

punishment and treatment. The use of the phrase 'all forms' anticipates the prohibition of both state and non-state conduct.[15] The quite credible argument therefore may be made that the Charter's understanding of the meaning of torture extends to non-state actors, unlike the more state-centric meaning of torture established in Article 1 of the Convention against Torture and other Cruel, Inhuman or Degrading Treatment or Punishment ('Convention against Torture' or 'CAT').[16]

Other instruments

Other African human rights instruments have been influenced by the human dignity mantra in the African Charter in their prohibition of torture. The African Charter on the Rights and Welfare of the Child (Children's Rights Charter) requires state parties to take measures to protect the child from all forms of torture and ill-treatment, including through the establishment of special monitoring units, and the prevention, identification and investigation of child abuse and neglect.[17] The Protocol to the African Charter on Human and Peoples' Rights on the Rights of Women in Africa (Maputo Protocol) infuses gender dimensions of torture into the continent's normative rubric, notably providing that every woman shall be entitled to respect for her life and the integrity and security of her person, before restating the prohibition of all forms of exploitation, cruel, inhuman or degrading punishment or treatment.[18] The African Youth Charter requires state parties to ensure that detained or imprisoned youth or those in rehabilitation centres are not subjected to torture, inhumane or degrading treatment or punishment.[19] The African Union Convention for the Protection and Assistance of Internally Displaced Persons in Africa (Kampala Convention) requires state parties to protect the rights of internally displaced persons regardless of the cause of displacement by refraining from and preventing arbitrary killing, summary execution, arbitrary detention, abduction, enforced disappearance or torture and other forms of cruel, inhuman or degrading treatment or punishment.[20] The Protocol to the African Charter on Human and Peoples' Rights on the Rights of Older Persons in Africa requires state parties to prohibit and criminalise harmful traditional practices targeting older persons, including those that affect their life and dignity, including

---

[15]   Viljoen, F and Odinkalu, C, *The Prohibition of Torture and Ill-Treatment in the African Human Rights System: A Handbook for Victims and their Advocates* (World Organisation against Torture, 2006), 36.

[16]   *Convention against Torture and Other Cruel, Inhuman or Degrading Treatment or Punishment*, adopted by UN General Assembly Res 39/46 of 10 December 1984, entered into force on 26 June 1987.

[17]   Article 16 of the *African Charter on the Rights and Welfare of the Child*, adopted by the 26th Ordinary session of the Assembly of Heads of State and Government of the OAU, July 1990, entered into force on 29 November 1999, OAU Doc CAB/LEG/24.9/49 (1990). As of May 2019, 49 States are party to the Children's Charter.

[18]   Articles 3 and 4 of the Protocol to the *African Charter on Human and Peoples' Rights on the Rights of Women in Africa*, adopted by the 2nd Ordinary Session of the Assembly of Heads of State and Government, 11 July 2003; entered into force on 25 November 2005. As of May 2019, 41 states were party to the Maputo Protocol.

[19]   Article 18(2)(a) of the *African Youth Charter*, adopted by the 7th Ordinary Session of the Assembly of Heads of State and Government of the AU on 2 July 2006, entered into force on 8 August 2009. As of January 2019, 39 states were party to the Youth Charter.

[20]   Article 9 of the *African Union Convention for the Protection and Assistance of Internally Displaced Persons in Africa*, adopted by the Special Summit of the Union on 23 October 2009, entered into force 6 December 2012. As of January 2019, 28 states were party to the Kampala Convention.

older women who should be protected from violence, sexual abuse and discrimination based on gender.[21] Finally, the Protocol to the African Charter on Human and Peoples' Rights on the Rights of Persons with Disabilities in Africa guarantees persons with disabilities' the right to the respect of their inherent dignity and freedom from torture or ill-treatment. State parties are required to ensure that persons with disabilities, on the basis of equality, are not subjected to torture or ill-treatment, or that they are not subjected without their free, prior and informed consent to medical or scientific experimentation or intervention, that they are not subjected to sterilisation or other invasive procedure without their free and informed consent, and that they are protected from all forms of exploitation, violence and abuse.[22]

These continent-established provisions retain an essential link with international human rights norms by dint of Article 61 of the African Charter which requires Africa's judicial and quasi-judicial institutions to:

> ... take into consideration, as subsidiary measures to determine the principles of law, other general or special international conventions, laying down rules expressly recognised by Member States of the Organisation of African Unity, African practices consistent with international norms on Human and Peoples' Rights, customs generally accepted as law, general principles of law recognised by African States as well as legal precedents and doctrine.

Although the case has been made for a specific African treaty prohibiting torture,[23] an adequate normative basis for ensuring protection from torture does in fact exist in Africa. This is particularly the case in light of a number of soft-law instruments which the Commission has adopted[24] to provide further guidance on the meaning and purport of Article 5 of the African Charter.

---

[21] Articles 8 and 9 of *Protocol to the African Charter on Human and Peoples' Rights on the Rights of Older Persons in Africa*, adopted by the 26th Ordinary Assembly of the Union, 31 January 2016. As of January 2019, only one state was party to the Older Persons Protocol and it had not come into force.

[22] Article 10 of *Protocol to the African Charter on Human and Peoples' Rights on the Rights of Persons with Disabilities in Africa*, adopted by the 30th Ordinary Session of the Assembly, 29 January 2018. As of January 2019, no state had become party to the Persons with Disabilities Protocol.

[23] For example, see Mujuzi, JD, 'An Analysis of the Approach to the Right to Freedom from Torture Adopted by the African Commission on Human and Peoples' Rights' (2006) 6 *African Human Rights Law Journal* 423.

[24] The African Commission has developed a number of soft-law instruments to affirm, clarify and enhance human rights norms by elaborating provisions of the African Charter as well as the obligations of states. They include at least five general comments, 11 guidelines, one model law, two studies and six declarations. Reference to 'soft-law instruments' by the African Commission distinguishes between legal instruments (charters or protocols) which bind states that have signed and ratified or acceded to them ('hard law') on one hand, and legal instruments adopted by the African Commission which derive content from regionally or internationally accepted principles and standards and which at the least are of persuasive value but some of whose provisions may bind states fully depending on their other legal commitments ('soft laws'). Discourses on this subject can clearly be far more complex. See Murray, J and Long, D, *The Implementation of the Findings of the African Commission on Human and Peoples' Rights* (Cambridge University Press, 2015).

Guidelines and Measures for the Prohibition and Prevention of Torture, Cruel, Inhuman or Degrading Treatment or Punishment in Africa

The Guidelines and Measures for the Prohibition and Prevention of Torture, Cruel, Inhuman or Degrading Treatment or Punishment in Africa ('Robben Island Guidelines' or 'RIG')[25] elaborate on the prohibition of torture and ill-treatment established in Article 5 of the African Charter. They seek to reaffirm relevant normative standards and to reinforce the promotion of the prohibition of torture.[26] The RIG comprises three parts covering the prohibition of torture, the prevention of torture and responding to the needs of victims.

The RIG require states to ratify regional and international human rights instruments relevant to the prohibition of torture.[27] States should promote and support cooperation with regional and international human rights mechanisms including the African Commission and relevant special mechanisms.[28] They should anchor the definition of torture in Article 1 of the Convention against Torture.[29] States should pay particular attention to the prohibition and prevention of gender-related forms of torture and ill-treatment and the torture and ill-treatment of young persons.[30] Domestic courts have universal jurisdiction in relation to crimes of torture,[31] and torture is an extraditable offence.[32] Apart from affirming the Convention against Torture's edict that no exceptional circumstances or justifications may be invoked for acts of torture,[33] the Guidelines also provide that notions such as 'necessity', 'national emergency', 'public order' and 'order public' shall not be invoked as a justification for torture or cruel, inhuman or degrading treatment or punishment.[34] A person may not be punished for disobeying an order requiring them to commit torture.[35] States should prohibit and prevent the use, production and trading of equipment or substances designed to inflict torture or ill-treatment and the abuse of any other equipment or substance to these ends.[36] A person may not be expelled or extradited to a country where he or she is at risk of being tortured.[37] Combatting impunity calls for torture suspects not to be immune from prosecution, and a range of criminal, civil or administrative actions against perpetrators of torture should be made available.[38] Complaints and investigation procedures should be readily accessible and independent,[39] and investigations should be initiated and conducted promptly, impartially and effectively.[40]

---

[25]   Adopted by the African Commission at its 32nd Ordinary Session, 17–23 October 2002.
[26]   Long, D and Murray, R, 'Ten Years of the Robben Island Guidelines and Prevention of Torture in Africa: For What Purpose?' (2012) *African Human Rights Law Journal* 327.
[27]   Guideline 1.
[28]   Guidelines 2–3.
[29]   Guideline 4.
[30]   Guideline 5. In this respect, the Guidelines provide more explicit acknowledgement on the vulnerabilities of individuals from specific groups than may be found in the Convention against Torture.
[31]   Guideline 6.
[32]   Guideline 7.
[33]   Article 2 of UNCAT which corresponds to Guidelines 9 and 11.
[34]   Guideline 10.
[35]   Guideline 13.
[36]   Guideline 14.
[37]   Guideline 15. This is consonant with Article 3 of the Convention against Torture.
[38]   Guideline 16.
[39]   Guideline 17.
[40]   Guidelines 18–19.

Provisions covering the prevention of torture deal with basic procedural safeguards for those deprived of their liberty, safeguards during the pre-trial process, conditions of detention, oversight mechanisms, and training and empowerment.[41]

The final part of the RIG focuses on responding to the needs of victims, and covers the safety of alleged victims of torture, the state obligation to offer reparations, and the affirmation that families and communities affected by torture are also considered victims.[42]

General Comment No. 4 on the African Charter on Human and Peoples' Rights: The Right to Redress for Victims of Torture and Other Cruel, Inhuman or Degrading Punishment or Treatment

The above provisions on ensuring redress for victims of torture have been further elaborated by General Comment No. 4 on the African Charter on Human and Peoples' Rights: The Right to Redress for Victims of Torture and Other Cruel, Inhuman or Degrading Punishment or Treatment,[43] which provides authoritative interpretation on the scope and content of the right to redress for victims of torture and other ill-treatment in specific African contexts. The General Comment acknowledges that survivors of torture have for far too long been unable to obtain redress because of the lack of comprehensive anti-torture legislation, the existence of laws which legalise or permit torture and other ill-treatment, and the absence of effective policies, programmes, administrative measures and institutional arrangements designed to give effect to the right. The General Comment provides guidance on the victim's place in the redress process; the meaning of prompt, full and effective access to redress; protection of victims from intimidation, retaliation and reprisals; available forms of reparations; the relationship between individual harm and collective harm; the understanding of redress for acts of sexual and gender-based violence; redress and armed conflict; the question of transitional justice; and the role of non-state actors.

The Guidelines on the Conditions of Arrest, Police Custody and Pre-trial Detention in Africa

The Guidelines on the Conditions of Arrest, Police Custody and Pre-trial Detention in Africa (Luanda Guidelines),[44] inter alia, provide guidance on how states should ensure prohibition of torture in the course of arrest, custody and pre-trial detention. The Guidelines reaffirm that a person shall not be subjected to torture while in detention, and torture may not be used to obtain confessions. Where torture is alleged, investigations must take place promptly, and victims of torture must obtain effective redress. The Guidelines provide interventions specific to vulnerable groups such as women, children and persons with disabilities.[45]

While an adequate corpus of anti-torture norms is therefore in place, the challenge facing Africa's states and institutions is the extent to which these norms are being applied in fact to protect individuals and peoples against torture.

---

[41]   Guidelines 20–48.
[42]   Guidelines 49–50.
[43]   Adopted at the 21st Extra-Ordinary Session of the African Commission, 23 February–4 March 2017.
[44]   Adopted by the African Commission at its 55th Ordinary Session, 28 April–12 May 2014.
[45]   For example, in relation to protecting persons with disabilities in pre-trial detention, see APCOF and NGEC, *Pre-trial Detention for Persons with Disabilities in Correctional Institutions* (2017).

Institutional Framework

The African Commission on Human and Peoples' Rights ('African Commission' or 'Commission') was established in 1987 after the African Charter had come into force in 1986.[46] The functions of the African Commission include the protection of human and peoples' rights and the interpretation of the Charter. A further function of the Commission is the promotion of human rights, particularly by:

1. Collecting documents, undertaking studies and researches on African problems in the field of human and peoples' rights, organising seminars, symposia and conferences, disseminating information, encouraging national and local institutions concerned with human and peoples' rights, and giving its views or making recommendations to Governments;
2. Formulating and laying down principles and rules aimed at solving legal problems relating to human and peoples' rights and fundamental freedoms upon which African Governments may base their legislation; and
3. Cooperating with other African and international institutions concerned with the promotion and protection of human and peoples' rights.[47]

The African Court on Human and Peoples' Rights ('African Court' or 'Court') was established in 2006 pursuant to the Protocol to the African Charter on Human and Peoples' Rights on the Establishment of an African Court on Human and Peoples' Rights (Court Protocol)[48] to complement the human rights protective mandate of the African Commission.[49] The African Court determines cases and disputes covering the interpretation and application of the African Charter.[50]

The African Committee of Experts on the Rights and Welfare of the Child (Children's Rights Committee) was established in 2001 to protect and promote the rights and welfare of the child in terms of the African Charter on the Rights and Welfare of the Child.[51] The mandate of the Committee is to promote and protect children's rights as well as to interpret the Children's Charter.[52]

In addition, a number of sub-regional bodies also exercise protective human rights mandates, notably the Economic Community of West African States (ECOWAS) Community Court of Justice.[53]

---

[46]   For an assessment of the early years of the African Commission, see Murray, R, *The African Commission on Human and Peoples' Rights and International Law* (Hart Publishing, 2000).

[47]   See *African Charter* (n 2 above), Articles 30 and 45.

[48]   *Protocol to the African Charter on Human and Peoples' Rights on the Establishment of an African Court on Human and Peoples' Rights*, adopted by the OAU on 10 June 1998, entered into force on 25 January 2004. As of January 2019, 30 states were party to the Court Protocol, including nine states which have made the declaration under Article 34 (6) of the Protocol enabling individuals to have direct standing before the Court.

[49]   *Ibid*, Article 2.

[50]   *Ibid*, Article 3.

[51]   *African Charter on the Rights and Welfare of the Child* (n 17 above), Article 32.

[52]   *Ibid*, Article 42.

[53]   The ECOWAS Community Court of Justice was established by Articles 6 and 15 of the *Revised Treaty of the Economic Community of West African States* (ECOWAS), 1993.

THE ANTI-TORTURE MANDATES OF AFRICAN HUMAN RIGHTS BODIES

The African Commission fulfils its functions through multiple strategies, including the communications procedure, undertaking protection missions, establishing and using subsidiary mechanisms, undertaking promotion missions, supporting and participating in the development of new binding normative standards and developing new soft-law norms, and the use of resolutions. The African Court and the Children's Rights Committee similarly employ some of the above strategies. The bulk of this section though will focus on assessing the African Commission's relevant strategies since the latter two far newer human rights institutions have undertaken limited substantive anti-torture work.[54]

Determination of Communications on Torture

The African Charter legislates for two types of communications: interstate communications[55] and other communications (filed against states by individuals or organisations).[56] An interstate communication may be filed by a state(s) which has good reasons to believe that another state(s) is violating provisions of the African Charter. The Commission may also receive and determine communications on the violation of human and peoples' rights filed by individuals or organisations against states. Filed communications are considered on the merits only if they comply with seven admissibility criteria established under Article 56 of the Charter.[57]

By 2018, of the 649 communications which it had received since its establishment, the African Commission had determined 418 communications, including 141 communications concluded on the merits.[58] The Commission had also issued numerous provisional measures calling on state parties to take measures preventing irreparable damage being done to victims litigating before it on alleged human rights violations.

---

[54]   For example, while pleadings on violation of the right to be free from torture have been filed before the Children's Rights Committee, the Committee has declined to make findings in that regard. See ACERWC Communication no 1/2005, *Michelo Hunsungule and Others v. Uganda*, 19 April 2013. Similarly, the Court was unable to make substantive findings in respect of alleged violations of Article 5 of the Charter. For example, see ACtHPR Application no 005/2015, *Thobias Mang'ara Mango and Shukurani Masegenya Mango v. United Republic of Tanzania*, 11 May 2018.

[55]   *African Charter* (n 2 above), Articles 47–54.

[56]   *Ibid*, Articles 55–57.

[57]   Pursuant to Article 56 of the African Charter, for a communication to be admitted for consideration on the merits, it must:

1. Indicate its authors even if the latter requests anonymity;
2. Be compatible with the OAU Charter or the ACHPR;
3. Not be written in disparaging or insulting language directed against the state concerned and its institutions or to the AU;
4. Not be based exclusively on news disseminated through the mass media;
5. Be sent after exhausting local remedies unless it is obvious that this procedure is unduly prolonged;
6. Be submitted within a reasonable period from the time local remedies are exhausted or from the date the Commission is seized with the matter; and
7. Not deal with a case settled by another international or regional judicial institution with jurisdiction.

[58]   Inter-Session Report on the Status of Communications (May–October 2018), presented at the 63rd Ordinary Session of the African Commission on Human and Peoples' Rights (on file with author).

From fairly modest beginnings characterised by holdings framed in quite imprecise and laconic terms,[59] the Commission now delivers far more comprehensive decisions which set out the parties' cases before detailing its analysis and determinations.[60]

The African Commission has over time developed a significant vein of anti-torture jurisprudence from its determinations on communications. Much of that jurisprudence has focused on how group or theme-specific issues intersect with torture.

Understanding of torture and cruel, inhuman or degrading punishment or treatment

During its early years, the Commission's determinations on Article 5 violations tended not to make any or clear enough distinctions between findings of torture on one hand and findings of cruel, inhuman or degrading punishment or treatment on the other. In a communication against Nigeria, the Commission remarked that Article 5 prohibits torture but also cruel, inhuman or degrading treatment, which includes not only actions that cause serious physical or psychological suffering but also those that humiliate the individual or force him or her to act against his will or conscience. Yet its finding that Nigeria was in violation of Article 5 for its treatment of Ken Saro-Wiwa did not specify whether the finding related to torture or to cruel, inhuman or degrading treatment.[61]

In due course, though, the Commission has explained that its understanding of the meaning of torture is derived from Article 1 of the Convention against Torture. Noting that Article 5 of the African Charter aims to protect both the dignity of the human person and the physical and mental integrity of the individual, the Commission has cited the definition of torture in Article 1 of CAT to explain its understanding of the term. In this regard, the Commission notes as follows:

> Torture … constitutes the intentional and systematic infliction of physical or psychological pain and suffering in order to punish, intimidate or gather information. It is a tool for discriminatory treatment of persons or groups of persons who are subjected to the torture by the State or non-state actors at the time of exercising control over such person or persons. The purpose of torture is to control populations by destroying individuals, their leaders and frightening entire communities.[62]

---

[59]   For example, in Communication nos 25/89, 47/90, 56/91 and 100/93, *Free Legal Assistance Group, Lawyers' Committee for Human Rights, Union Interafricaine des Droits de l'Homme, Les Témoins de Jehovah v. DRC*, para 41 the Commission simply recorded that the alleged torture of 15 persons by a military unit in Kinsuka, having not been contested by the state, constituted a violation of Article 5 of the Charter. See also Communication no 74/92, *Commission nationale des droits de l'Homme et des libertés v. Chad*; Communication no 97/93, *John K. Modise v. Botswana*; Communication nos 137/94, 139/94, 154/96 and 161/97, *International PEN, Constitutional Rights Project, Civil Liberties Organisation and Interights (on behalf of Ken Saro-Wiwa Jnr.) v. Nigeria*; Communication nos 140/94, 141/9 and 145/95, *Constitutional Rights Project, Civil Liberties Organisation and Media Rights Agenda v. Nigeria*; Communication nos 143/95 and 150/96, *Constitutional Rights Project and Civil Liberties Organisation v. Nigeria*.

[60]   For an instructive exposition on the Commission's early jurisprudence on Article 5 of the African Charter, see Manby, B, 'Civil and Political Rights in the African Charter on Human and Peoples' Rights, Articles 1–7' in Evans, M and Murray R (eds), *The African Charter on Human and Peoples' Rights: The System in Practice* (Cambridge University Press, 2002) 149–51.

[61]   Communication nos 137/94, 139/94,154/96 and 161/97, *International PEN, Constitutional Rights Project, Civil Liberties Organisation and Interights (on behalf of Ken Saro-Wiwa Jnr.) v. Nigeria*.

[62]   Communication nos 279/03 and 296/05, *Sudan Human Rights Organisation & Centre on Housing Rights and Evictions (COHRE) v. Sudan*, para 156.

This summation is consonant with Article 1 of the Convention against Torture which identifies four necessary elements for an act to constitute torture: the severity of the pain or suffering caused by the act; the intent behind the act; the act's purpose; and the involvement or acquiescence of a state official. In a Communication against Sudan,[63] the Commission noted that while in the detention of the National Intelligence and Security Service, the victims were subjected to acts characterised by severe beatings, credible threats and sleep deprivation which resulted in severe physical and mental pain and suffering. These acts were intentionally inflicted by public officials with the purpose of punishing the victims so as to obtain information about their laptops and bags.[64]

The African Commission has distinguished between torture and other forms of ill-treatment to determine communications where one or more of the elements constituting torture remain unproved. Its understanding is that the term 'cruel, inhuman or degrading treatment or punishment': '… is to be interpreted so as to extend to the widest possible protection against abuses, whether physical or mental'.[65] Inhuman and degrading treatment includes physical and psychological suffering as well as acts that humiliate the individual or force him or her to act against his will or conscience. Such acts can be interpreted to extend to the widest possible protection against abuses, whether physical or mental.[66] Further, refusing detainees contact with their families and not informing the families of the detainees' whereabouts may amount to inhuman treatment of both the detainees and their families.[67]

Conditions of detention which may amount to torture (when all the elements constituting torture are proved) or ill-treatment include: denial of food; chaining and confinement in overcrowded cells; denial of medical care; use of electric shock and hanging of weights on genitalia; simulated drowning; and the smearing of pepper on eyes.[68]

Absolute prohibition of torture

Torture is prohibited absolutely under all circumstances and Article 5 of the Charter permits no restrictions or limitations on the right to be free from torture. In *Article 19 v. Eritrea*, the Commission determined that Eritrea could not be excused from its Charter obligations for holding detainees incommunicado on the basis of the apparently difficult political situation

---

[63] Communication no 379/09, *Monim Elgak, Osman Hummeida and Amir Suliman (represented by FIDH and OMCT) v. Sudan*.

[64] *Ibid*, para 99; also see Communication no 368/09, *Abdel Hadi Ali Radi and Others v. Sudan*, paras 69–73.

[65] Communication no 224/98, *Media Rights Agenda v. Nigeria*, para 71.

[66] Communication no 323/06, *Egyptian Initiative for Personal Rights and Inter-Rights v. Egypt*, paras 187, 196.

[67] Communication nos 48/90, 50/91, 52/91 and 89/93, *Amnesty International, Comité Loosli Bachelard, Lawyers' Committee for Human Rights, Association of Members of the Episcopal Conference of East Africa v. Sudan*, para 54; also see Communication no 151/96, *Civil Liberties Organisation v. Nigeria*, para 27.

[68] Communication nos 54/91, 61/91, 96/93, 98/93, 164/97, 196/97 and 210/98, *Malawi African Association, Amnesty International, Ms Sarriop, Union interafricaine des droits de l'Homme and RADDHO, Collectif des veuves et ayants-Droit, Association mauritanienne des droits de l'Homme v. Mauritania*, paras 133–135; see also Communication nos 64/92, 68/92 and 78/92, *AR Krishna Achuthan (on behalf of Aleke Banda), Amnesty International (on behalf of Orton and Vera Chirwa), Amnesty International (on behalf of Orton and Vera Chirwa) v. Malawi*, para 7.

in the country.[69] Similarly, the African Court has determined that an anal search performed by agents of Tanzania on the applicant in the presence of his children amounted to a violation of his right to human dignity. The Court noted that the prohibition of indignity established in Article 5 of the African Charter is absolute and extends to the widest possible protection against abuse, whether physical or mental. Furthermore, indignity could take various forms, and assessment will depend on the circumstances of each case.[70]

The African Commission has similarly determined that individuals' rights have to be protected even in times of armed conflict. The African Charter, unlike other key human rights instruments, does not include a derogations clause, and, excepting Article 27(2) of the Charter which stipulates that the exercise of rights and freedoms have regard for the rights of others, collective morality and common interest, limitation of Charter rights therefore may not be justified by emergencies or special circumstances.[71] The Commission noted that forced eviction of the civilian population could not be considered permissible under Article 27(2) of the African Charter, and asked:

> Could the Respondent State legitimately argue that it forcefully evicted the Darfur civilian population from their homes, villages and other places of habitual residence, on grounds of collective security, or any other such grounds or justification, if any? For such reasons to be justifiable, the Darfurian population should have benefited from the collective security envisage[d] under Article 27(2). To the contrary, the complaint has demonstrated that after eviction, the security of the IDP [internally displaced persons] camps was not guaranteed. The deployment of peacekeeping forces from outside the country is proof that the Respondent State failed in its obligation to guarantee security to the IDPs and the civilian population in Darfur.[72]

Sudan was therefore found to be in violation of its obligation to protect its citizens from cruel and inhuman treatment when the state and its agents, the Janjaweed militia, actively participated in the forced eviction of the civilian population from their homes and villages, and when it failed to protect the victims against the said violations.[73]

Positive state obligations for victims under custody

The state has multiple positive obligations covering victims of torture under its custody. In a communication regarding victims who were allegedly held incommunicado and denied medical and legal attention as well as access to their families, the African Commission reaffirmed the principle that injuries sustained by a victim while in the custody of state agents are presumed to arise from torture, and the burden of proof shifts to the state to provide a plausible explanation about how the injuries were caused. In the absence of such explanation, the Commission concluded that the marks on the victims evidencing the use of torture could only have been inflicted by Egypt.[74] The ECOWAS Community Court of Justice followed the same

---

[69]   Communication no 275/03, *Article 19 v. Eritrea*, para 102.

[70]   ACtHPR, Application no 000927, *Lucien Ikili Rashidi v. United Republic of Tanzania*, 28 March 2019.

[71]   Communication nos 279/03 and 296/05, *Sudan Human Rights Organisation & Centre on Housing Rights and Evictions (COHRE) v. Sudan*.

[72]   *Ibid*, para 166.

[73]   *Ibid*, para 168.

[74]   Communication no 334/06, *Egyptian Initiative for Personal Rights and Inter-Rights v. Egypt*, paras 168–171.

approach when it found that The Gambia had not controverted the victim's evidence and as such the victim had been tortured while in the custody of its security agents.[75] Conversely, the African Commission was not able to find a violation of Article 5 against Uganda in a communication where the victim failed to support his allegations of torture with relevant corroborative material such as details of the allegations or refutations of respondent's rebuttals.[76]

The communication against Egypt also discoursed on the questions of access by victims of torture to medical care and legal representation. Noting that the victims were not examined by a doctor during their pre-trial detention despite alleging torture and that their first medical examination occurred over six months following their alleged torture, the Commission concluded that the victims' rights to prompt medical services while under custody were violated by Egypt's failure to provide them with prompt medical services.[77] The Commission has also noted that despite extensive medical evidence indicative of torture, Zimbabwe had not taken any steps to investigate and document allegations that the victim was tortured.[78] Measures taken to effect this obligation had to be commensurate with the magnitude of the violations. Apart from seeking to punish specific crimes, the state had also to take positive preventive measures such as stopping incommunicado detentions and providing effective remedies.[79] The state was also obligated to provide victims with legal counsel during their detention, including their interrogation, since prompt access to legal counsel constituted an effective measure to protect against torture.[80] Furthermore, the state was obligated to bring an accused promptly before a judicial authority as an essential safeguard against torture where charges against them could be examined promptly and impartially and where they could challenge the legality of their detention or treatment.[81]

Enforced disappearances

The Commission has interpreted Article 5 of the African Charter to cover enforced disappearances. The disappearance of persons suspected or accused of plotting against the authorities in Burkina Faso, including arrests carried out by the Presidential Guard and the subsequent disappearance in May 1990 of Guillaume Sessouma and a medical student, Dabo Boukary, constituted a violation of Article 5 of the Charter.[82] The Commission has also confirmed that:

> every enforced disappearance violates a range of human rights, including the right to security and dignity of person, the right not to be subjected to torture or other cruel, inhuman or degrading treat-

---

[75] ECW/CCJ/JUD/08/10, *Musa Saidykhan v. The Gambia*, para 38.

[76] Communication no 431/12, *Thomas Kwoyelo v. Uganda*, paras 208–212. See also ACtHPR Application No. 006/2015, *Nguza Viking (Babu Seya) and Johnson Nguza (Papi Kocha) v. United Republic of Tanzania*, 23 March 2018, paras 73–74.

[77] Communication no 334/06, *Egyptian Initiative for Personal Rights and Inter-Rights v. Egypt*, paras 172–177.

[78] Communication no 288/04, *Gabriel Shumba v. Zimbabwe*, para. 154.

[79] Communication nos 48/90-50/91 and 52/91-89/93, *Amnesty International, Comité Loosli Bachelard, Lawyers' Committee for Human Rights, Association of Members of the Episcopal Conference of East Africa v. Sudan*, para 56.

[80] Communication no 334/06, *Egyptian Initiative for Personal Rights and Inter-Rights v. Egypt*, paras 178–183.

[81] *Ibid*, para 184.

[82] Communication no 204/97, *Movement burkinabé des droits de l'Homme et des peuples v. Burkina Faso*, para 44.

ment or punishment, the right to humane conditions of detention, the right to a legal personality, the right to a fair trial, the right to a family life and, when the disappeared person is killed, the right to life.[83]

In the case of a continuing act, the violation occurs and continues over a period of time until the violation ceases. In the case of an instantaneous act, the violation itself does not continue over time, although the completion of such an act might take some time.[84]

Judicial corporal punishment

Judicial corporal punishment is incompatible with Article 5 of the African Charter. In a communication where eight students of Ahlia University were sentenced inter alia to between 25 and 40 lashes which were carried out on their bare backs with a wire and plastic whip, Sudan argued that those lashings were justified because the sentenced had committed acts found to be criminal according to the laws in force in the country. The Commission's view however was that while its role was not to interpret the Islamic Shariâ law obtaining in Sudan, its concern related to the application of the African Charter in the country. Allowing Sudan to apply physical violence to individuals for offences would be tantamount to sanctioning state-sponsored torture under the African Charter.[85]

The death penalty

The African Commission has also clarified its understanding on whether and when imposition of the death penalty may be a violation of Article 5 of the Charter. In a communication against Botswana, the Commission stated that prohibition of torture or ill-treatment includes '… actions which cause serious physical or psychological suffering or which humiliate the individual or force him or her to act against his or her will or conscience'.[86] The death penalty should be imposed after full consideration of not only the circumstances of the individual offence, but also the circumstances of the individual offender.[87] The carrying out of a death sentence using a particular method of execution may amount to ill-treatment if the suffering caused in execution of the sentence is excessive and goes beyond that which is strictly necessary to accomplish the sentence.[88] The Commission concluded by stating its belief that:

> the execution of a death sentence by hanging may not be compatible with respect for the inherent dignity of the individual and the duty to minimize unnecessary suffering, because it is a notoriously slow and painful means of execution if carried out without appropriate attention to the weight of the person condemned because hanging can result either in slow and painful strangulation, because the neck is not immediately broken by the drop, or, at the other extreme, in the separation of the head from the body.[89]

---

[83] Communication no 361/08, *J.E. Zitha & P. J. L. Zitha v. Mozambique*, para 81.
[84] *Ibid*, paras 85–94.
[85] Communication no 236/00, *Curtis Francis Doebbler v. Sudan*.
[86] Communication no 277/03, *Spilg and Mack and Ditshwanelo (on behalf of Lehlohonolo Bernard Kobedi) v. Botswana*, para 163.
[87] *Ibid*, para 164.
[88] *Ibid*, para 167.
[89] *Ibid*, para 169.

In the instant case, though, the complainants had not adduced material evidence to enable the Commission to make a finding in their favour. However, in a later communication against Botswana, the African Commission made the definitive finding that hanging as a method of execution causes excessive suffering and that it constitutes a violation of Article 5 of the African Charter.[90]

The Commission also addressed the question of whether prolonged delay in implementing the death sentence, thereby engendering in the victim fear of the sentence for a decade, constituted cruel or degrading treatment or punishment. The computation of time for purposes of assessing any delays in execution of the sentence would begin to run once the victim had finalised the judicial process including any appeals.[91] The Commission agreed with the complainants' submission that Botswana's failure to publish the unsuccessful outcome of the clemency petition and its failure to give notice of the date and time of execution amounted to inhuman treatment since it deprived the convict and his family of the important opportunity to have closure with dignity by making their last farewells. The failure to give notice of the date and time of execution of the victim amounted to cruel, inhuman and degrading punishment and treatment and therefore a violation of Article 5 of the African Charter.

In another communication, while the Commission for want of evidence declined to find Botswana in violation of Article 5 for not giving adequate notice to family members before the execution of a convict, it stated thus:

> In the circumstances it would be fundamentally unfair to the Respondent State to deal with the substance of this issue save to observe that a justice system must have a human face in matters of execution of death sentences by affording a condemned person an opportunity to 'arrange his affairs, to be visited by members of his intimate family before he dies, and to receive spiritual advice and comfort to enable him to compose himself as best he can, to face his ultimate ordeal'.[92]

Slavery

In determining its understanding of the prohibition of slavery in Article 5 of the Charter, the African Commission decided that Mauritania had the positive responsibility of ensuring the effective application of Edict N 81-234 of 9 November 1981 which had abolished slavery. Practices analogous to slavery persisted in Mauritania and these amounted to a violation of Article 5 of the Charter. It is interesting though that the Commission was at pains to stress that the evidence before it did not enable it to conclude that slavery existed in the country.[93]

---

[90]   Communication no 319/06, *Interights and Ditshwanelo v. Botswana*, para 87.

[91]   Communication no 277/03, *Spilg and Mack and Ditshwanelo (on behalf of Lehlohonolo Bernard Kobedi) v. Botswana*, para 173.

[92]   Communication no 240/01, *Interights et al. (on behalf of Mariette Sonjaleen Bosch) v. Botswana*, para 178. See also Communication no 277/03, *Spilg and Mack and Ditshwanelo (on behalf of Lehlohonolo Bernard Kobedi) v. Botswana*, para 96.

[93]   Communication nos 54/91, 61/91, 96/93, 98/93, 164/97, 196/97 and 210/98, *Malawi African Association, Amnesty International, Ms Sarriop, Union interafricaine des droits de l'Homme and RADDHO, Collectif des veuves et ayants-Droit, Association mauritanienne des droits de l'Homme v. Mauritania*, para 116.

Group-specific issues

The African Commission has also developed jurisprudence on how group-specific issues intersect with torture. Article 5 of the Charter is violated where women, children and the aged are held in conditions of detention that violate their physical and psychological integrity.[94]

Regarding how torture intersects with the rights of persons with disabilities, the African Commission has determined that branding persons with mental illness as lunatics and idiots dehumanises and denies them any form of dignity in contravention of Article 5 of the Charter, noting that:

> ... mentally disabled persons would like to share the same hopes, dreams and goals and have the same rights to pursue those hopes, dreams and goals just like any other human being. ... mentally disabled persons or persons suffering from mental illnesses have a right to enjoy a decent life, as normal and full as possible, a right which lies at the heart of the right to human dignity. This right should be zealously guarded and forcefully protected by all States PARTY to the African Charter in accordance with the well-established principle that all human beings are born free and equal in dignity and rights.[95]

Provisional measures

The African Commission issues provisional measures under the communications procedure, making specific requests of a respondent state to prevent irreparable harm arising from serious and imminent threat against a victim during the pendency of a communication. The bulk of provisional measures issued by the Commission however tend not to be implemented by respondent states, yet the Commission's only subsequent recourse has been to express its regret and make findings of violation against states that fail to heed such provisional measures. These responses have been particularly underwhelming considering that irreparable harm suffered by victims has included loss of life by the execution of victims with pending cases.[96]

Use of Subsidiary Mechanisms – the Committee for the Prevention of Torture in Africa

When it adopted the Robben Island Guidelines in October 2002, the African Commission also established a committee to follow up on the Guidelines' implementation.[97] The mandate of the

---

[94]   Communication nos 27/89, 46/91–49/91 and 99/93, *Organisation mondiale contre la torture, Association Internationale des jurists démocrates, Commission internationale des juristes, Union inter-africaine des droits de l'Homme v. Rwanda*, para 27.

[95]   Communication no 241/01, *Purohibt and Moore v. Gambia*, para 62. Also see Mute, L and Kalekye, E, 'An Appraisal of the Draft Protocol to the African Charter on Human and Peoples' Rights on the Rights of Persons with Disabilities in Africa' (2016/2017) *East African Law Journal, Special Issue on Disability Rights* 68–90.

[96]   See Communication nos 137/94, 139/94, 154/96 and 161/97, *International Pen, Constitutional Rights Project, Civil Liberties Organisation & Interights on behalf of Ken Saro-Wiwa Jnr v. Nigeria* (where a number of victims were executed despite the Commission's provisional measures against the executions); Communication no 319/06, *Interights and Ditshwanelo v Botswana* (where the victim was executed before the provisional measures could be transmitted); and Communication no 334/06, *Egyptian Initiative for Personal Rights and Interights v. Arab Republic of Egypt*.

[97]   See Long, D and Muntingh, L, 'The Special Rapporteur on Prisons and Conditions of Detention in Africa and the Committee for the Prevention of Torture in Africa: The Potential for Synergy or Inertia?' (2010) 13 *International Journal on Human Rights* 99.

Follow-Up Committee, which was renamed the Committee for the Prevention of Torture in Africa (CPTA) in November 2009, was to:

1. Organise seminars to disseminate the Robben Island Guidelines to national and regional stakeholders;
2. Develop and propose to the African Commission strategies to promote and implement the Robben Island Guidelines at the national and regional levels;
3. Promote and facilitate the implementation of the Robben Island Guidelines within states; and
4. Make a progress report to the African Commission at each ordinary session.[98]

The CPTA comprises Commissioners and Expert Members. It implements its mandates using operational strategies which it updates from time to time. In the period 2014–2018, the Committee focused on four strategic areas of intervention: raising public awareness on the Robben Island Guidelines and the prohibition and prevention of torture; advocating and providing advice and technical support to relevant actors for the effective implementation of the Robben Island Guidelines at the national level; strengthening capacities of relevant actors for the effective implementation of the Robben Island Guidelines; and providing technical tools and making recommendations to African states and other relevant actors on the effective prohibition and prevention of torture and on responding to the needs of victims.[99]

The challenges facing the Committee's mandate implementation include: limited financial resources (approximately 25,000 dollars derived annually from AU financing); human resource limitations; and operational difficulties in working with key potential interlocutors such as states, national preventive mechanisms and national human rights institutions.[100] A 2012 study indeed found that the CPTA and its predecessor, the Follow-Up Committee, largely failed '… to use the RIG within its various procedures to develop a coherent message on the prevention of torture and other ill-treatment, and … to implement its mandate'.[101] The study found that states and indeed the African Commission itself used the RIG under the state reporting procedure, during protection and promotion missions and in communications.[102]

While the Committee continues to face numerous challenges, it has undertaken significant activities to realise its objectives. It has prepared and disseminated publicity materials such as its annual Africa Torture Watch Newsletter;[103] issued press statements on key dates such as the International Day in Support of Victims of Torture (June 26);[104] prepared the annual situation of torture in Africa reports as well as thematic reports on various aspects of Article 5 of the

---

[98] Adopted by Resolution 61, *Resolution on Guidelines and Measures for the Prohibition and Prevention of Torture, Cruel, Inhuman or Degrading Treatment or Punishment in Africa adopted by The African Commission on Human and Peoples' Rights at its 32nd Ordinary Session*, 17–23 October 2002.

[99] Annex to Inter-Session Activity Report (May 2017–November 2017) of the Chairperson of the Committee for the Prevention of Torture in Africa, Detailed Activity Report of the Period 2014–2017, para 5.

[100] *Ibid*, para 80.

[101] Long and Murray (n 26 above), 339.

[102] *Ibid.*

[103] For example see Africa Torture Watch No.8 April 2019, https://www.achpr.org/newsletter/viewdetail?id=26

[104] For example see the CPTA's press statement on the situation of African migrants and refugees at risk of torture, https://www.achpr.org/pressrelease/detail?id=424

Charter, including on judicial corporal punishment; torture in respect of women with disabilities, the denial of abortion and post-abortion care as torture; and the situation of African migrants and refugees at risk of torture and ill-treatment. It has also established protocols for dialoguing with states under the periodic reporting procedure on issues of torture.[105] The Committee also spearheaded preparation of General Comment No. 4 on the African Charter on Human and Peoples' Rights: The Right to Redress for Victims of Torture and other Cruel, Inhuman or Degrading Punishment or Treatment (Article 5).

Protection Missions

The African Commission has over time developed and entrenched the use of protection missions as a strategy for ensuring human and peoples' rights.[106] Protection missions, also referred to as fact-finding missions, are undertaken to investigate reports of widespread human rights violations in a state party.[107]

Some protection missions are undertaken on the Commission's initiative while others are requested by various organs of the African Union, including the Peace and Security Council and the African Union Commission. Although states are required to provide the Commission with open invitations to undertake protection missions and they should respond promptly to authorisation requests to undertake such missions,[108] the reality is starkly different. Far too often, the Commission has been unable to undertake missions in a timely manner for want of permission or owing to the absence of administrative facilitation by states.[109]

The Commission has over time undertaken at least ten protection missions, including in Mauritania (June 1996), Zimbabwe (June 2002), Sudan (July 2004), Togo (December 2005), Botswana (August 2008), Sahrawi Arab Democratic Republic (September 2012), Mali (June 2013), Central African Republic (September 2014) and Burundi (December 2015).

While protection missions have, more likely than not, investigated violations or abuses amounting to torture, some missions did not make explicit acknowledgement of the Article 5 normative framework prohibiting torture. This was the case in the Commission's fact-finding mission to Sudan in the Darfur Region, which while not using the Article 5 framework found that violations amounting to crimes against humanity and war crimes had been perpetrated on

---

[105]   See *Indicative Questions to State Parties in Respect of Article 5 of the African Charter on Human and Peoples' Rights*, https://www.achpr.org/news/viewdetail?id=76

[106]   Pursuant to Article 46 of the African Charter and Rules 81–82 of the *Rules of Procedure of the African Commission on Human and Peoples' Rights*, 2010, http://www.achpr.org/instruments/rules-of-procedure-2010/

[107]   *Guidelines on the Format of Promotion and Protection Mission Reports of the African Commission on Human and Peoples' Rights*, adopted at the 23rd Extra-Ordinary Session of the African Commission on Human and Peoples' Rights, held from 15 to 22 February 2018, para 4.

[108]   *Rules of Procedure of the African Commission on Human and Peoples' Rights* (n 106 above), Rule 81(2).

[109]   Most recently, despite being requested by the Chairperson of the AUC to undertake a protection mission to investigate the alleged trafficking of African migrants in Libya, the African Commission had one year later not undertaken the mission due to security and administrative hurdles. See 46th Activity Report of the African Commission on Human and Peoples' Rights submitted to the Policy Organs of the African Union, November 2018–May 2019.

the civilian population of Darfur by state security forces and Janjaweed militia.[110] Similarly, when the Commission undertook a fact-finding mission to the Sahrawi Arab Democratic Republic, on the request of the Executive Council of the AU,[111] between 24 and 28 September 2012, it heard testimonies of torture and humiliating treatment of Sahrawi victims perpetrated in Moroccan jails.[112] Yet that mission did not come to any conclusions focusing on Article 5 violations. The Commission's fact-finding mission in Zimbabwe of 24–28 June 2002 found evidence of victims who were tortured while in police custody, including lawyers, journalists and opposition politicians. The Commission recommended that the government should implement the Robben Island Guidelines.[113]

A more typical investigation whose terms of reference included torture was the protection mission undertaken by the Commission in Burundi in 2015. This mission was carried out by the African Commission following the request of the Peace and Security Council of the AU which sought an in-depth investigation into the violation of human rights and other abuses of the civilian population in Burundi.[114] The mission concluded inter alia that hundreds of violations of the right to freedom from torture had been perpetrated by security agencies on individuals in detention or custody, manifested by beatings, use of electric shock, use of acid to burn bodies and the weighting of genitalia with heavy objects.[115] The mission called on the Commission's relevant special mechanisms to continue to monitor and investigate various human rights issues including extrajudicial killings, arbitrary arrests, acts of torture and the arbitrary ban or restriction of freedom of expression and freedom of association.[116] Despite presenting its conclusions and recommendations to the Peace and Security Council, and as highlighted in the next sections of the chapter, the human rights situation in Burundi remains very dire.

The Commission has also undertaken protection missions addressing some of the more esoteric themes covered by Article 5 of the African Charter. The protection mission undertaken by the Commission in Mauritania in the period 19–27 June 1996 was prompted by four communications lodged with the Commission,[117] which, in the Commission's words,

---

[110] *Report of the African Commission on Human and Peoples' Rights' Fact-Finding Mission to the Republic of Sudan in the Darfur Region*, 8–18 July 2004, adopted by the African Commission on Human and Peoples' Rights at the 41st Ordinary Session, 16–30 May 2017, paras 108–109.

[111] Executive Council Decision EX.CL/Dec. 689 (XX) requested the African Commission: '... to carry out a mission to the occupied territory of the Sahrawi Arab Democratic Republic, with a view to investigating human rights violations and report to the next Ordinary Session of the Executive Council in January 2013'.

[112] *Report of Fact-Finding Mission to the Sahrawi Arab Democratic Republic, 24–28 September 2012*, para 37.

[113] *Report of Fact-Finding Mission to Zimbabwe, June 2002*, adopted by the African Commission on Human and Peoples' Rights at its 34th Ordinary Session, 6–20 November 2003.

[114] Communiqué IV, PSC/PR/COMM.(DLI).

[115] *Report of the Delegation of the African Commission on Human and Peoples' Rights on its Fact-Finding Mission to Burundi, 7–13 December 2015*, paragraphs 124–126.

[116] *Ibid*, para 170.

[117] These communications were filed, respectively, on 16 July 1991 by the Malawi African Association, on 21 August 1991 by Amnesty International, on 12 March 1993 by Madame Sarr Diop, on 30 March 1993 by the Rencontre Africaine pour la Defence des Droits de l'Homme, the Inter-African Union of Human Rights and the Mauritanian League for Human Rights.

'... revealed disturbing violations of human rights in Mauritania ...',[118] including the issue of slavery, which is prohibited in Article 5 of the African Charter. The aim of the mission was to find amicable resolutions to the violations.[119]

On the question of slavery, the Commission analysed the bipolar positions which contend on one hand that slavery continued to be practised in Mauritania while, on the other hand, it was argued that only remnants of slavery continued to exist in the country. The Commission indeed found that vestiges of slavery continue to exist, but the executive and judiciary could not reasonably be accused of not acting in conformity with the letter and spirit of the 1981 abolition law. The Commission found that inheritance disputes between the descendants of former masters and former slaves were now being determined by the judiciary and that wrong judicial decisions were being rectified while errant judicial officials were being disciplined. The executive was taking appropriate measures which however should be deepened, including the participation of former slaves in the exercise of high political, administrative, military and trade union activities; raising the consciousness of former slaves through priority schooling of children in their dialects, and literacy for adults; and agrarian reform.

Responding to Emergency Human Rights Situations

The African Commission has over time developed protocols for responding to credible allegations of human rights violations requiring urgent interventions. Urgent appeals or letters of appeal are addressed to a head of state or government by a special mechanism of the Commission, commissioner rapporteur of a country or the Chairperson of the Commission. When the Commission receives reliable information that an individual or group or community in a country are likely to face or are facing violations of human rights that may cause irreparable harm, it issues an urgent appeal calling on the concerned state to take measures to prevent the said harm and provide the African Commission with relevant information.[120] The Commission may also issue letters of commendation and press statements.

During the period 2011–2017, the African Commission, under the spearhead of the Committee for the Prevention of Torture in Africa, issued multiple torture-specific letters of appeal or commendation – on allegations of violence, torture and unlawful arrests during election campaigns (Sudan in December 2009); the sentencing of a woman to corporal punishment and hanging for apostasy and adultery (Sudan in May 2014); on human rights violations following an attempted coup (Gambia in 2014); on the alleged mass rape of women (Sudan in March 2015); on the alleged illegal detention of individuals (Congo in July 2015 and Lesotho in September 2015); and on the alleged torture of demonstrators or protesters (Burundi in October 2015 and Ethiopia in August 2016).[121] Again, far too often, states do not make substantive responses to the Commission's appeals. Yet, this procedure provides a sound basis

---

[118]   *Report of the Mission to Mauritania of the African Commission on Human and Peoples' Rights, 19–27 June 1996*, adopted by The African Commission on Human and Peoples' Rights at its 20th Ordinary Session, 21–31 October 1996.

[119]   The Commission located its fact-finding mandate in this instance under Article 46 of the African Charter which gives it the power to resort to any appropriate method of investigation.

[120]   In accordance with Article 46 of the African Charter and Rule 80(2) of its Rules of Procedure.

[121]   See intersession activity reports of the Chairperson of the Committee for the Prevention of Torture in Africa for various relevant years at https://www.achpr.org/

for further engagements with errant states when the Commission presents its activity reports before the policy organs of the African Union.

State Periodic Reporting under Article 62 of the African Charter

The African Charter requires each state party to submit on a biennial basis a report on the legislative or other measures taken to give effect to the rights and freedoms recognised and guaranteed in the Charter.[122] Such a report should indicate the challenges affecting the implementation of the African Charter and its relevant protocols.[123] The African Commission uses these reports as an opportunity to have interactive and candid dialogues with states on progress towards implementation of their obligations. The Commission then issues concluding observations and recommendations acknowledging areas of progress and raising concerns of note, and making recommendations for the better implementation of Charter rights.[124]

During the interactive dialogues, on the theme of torture, the African Commission has commended positive normative developments such as accession to international and regional human rights instruments, notably the Convention against Torture, and the Optional Protocol to the Convention against Torture and Other Cruel, Inhuman or Degrading Treatment or Punishment (OPCAT). It has also raised concerns where it has noted gaps in practice or in the normative and institutional framework for ensuring freedom from torture. Typically, the Commission then has recommended measures for ensuring the better exercise of the freedom from torture, including:

1. The accession to human rights instruments such as OPCAT and the criminalisation of torture (Gabon[125] and Sudan[126]);
2. The establishment of a national preventive mechanism in consonance with OPCAT (Cameroon[127]); and
3. Compilation of statistical data relevant to the prohibition of torture and ill-treatment, including data on complaints, investigations, prosecutions and convictions in cases of

---

[122] *African Charter* (n 2 above), Article 62. Similar requirements are legislated in other human rights instruments whose monitoring is overseen by the African Commission, including the Maputo Protocol, Article 26 and the Kampala Convention, Article 15.

[123] *Rules of Procedure of the African Commission* (n 106 above), Rule 73(1).

[124] As of the 63rd Ordinary Session of the African Commission, in October 2018, 12 states had submitted all reports in terms of the Article 62 reporting procedure, while 14 states had one overdue report. Five and three states respectively had two and three overdue reports, and 15 states had more than three overdue reports. Five states had never submitted a report to the Commission. See *45th Activity Report of the African Commission on Human and Peoples' Rights*, presented to the Heads of State and Government of the African Union in accordance with Article 54 of the African Charter.

[125] *Concluding Observations and Recommendations on the Initial and Combined Report of the Gabonese Republic on the Implementation of the African Charter on Human and Peoples' Rights (1986–2012)*, adopted by the African Commission on Human and Peoples' Rights at the 15th Extra-Ordinary Session, 7–14 March 2014.

[126] *Concluding Observations and Recommendations on the 4th and 5th Periodic Report of the Republic of Sudan*, adopted at the 12th Extra-Ordinary Session of the African Commission on Human and Peoples' Rights, 29 July–4 August 2012.

[127] *Concluding Observations and Recommendations on the 3rd Periodic Report of the Cameroon on the Implementation of the African Charter on Human and Peoples' Rights*, adopted by the African Commission on Human and Peoples' Rights at the 15th Extra-Ordinary Session, 7–14 March 2014.

torture and ill-treatment, as well as on means of redress provided to victims, including compensation and rehabilitation (Liberia[128]).

The Commission's interactive dialogues with various states have elicited mixed results. Its recommendations to Ethiopia in two reporting cycles reiterated, with limited success, similar issues which the Commission urged Ethiopia to put in place to ensure freedom from torture. Its initial concluding observations and recommendations to Ethiopia urged it to: sensitize law enforcement officers about the Robben Island Guidelines; ratify the OPCAT; provide information on conditions of prisons and places of detention, and ensure that prisoners were held in humane conditions; provide information regarding political prisoners; and bring to justice those responsible for the death of protesters during the 2005 post-election violence.[129] In its most recent concluding observations and recommendations to that state, while commending it for incorporating the right to human dignity and the prohibition against torture in the curricula of police and prisons officers, the Commission noted that Ethiopia had failed to take steps to bring to justice perpetrators of the 2005 post-election violence killings. The state had also not become party to the OPCAT nor provided information on whether it held political prisoners. Furthermore, torture was not fully criminalised in its domestic laws.[130] In this latter report, the Commission's torture-specific recommendation was quite laconic – that Ethiopia should ensure that investigations of allegations of torture and ill-treatment with respect to detainees were conducted and perpetrators brought to justice.[131]

A more sanguine note may be sounded in respect of Uganda's interactions with the Commission during a number of reporting cycles. The Commission had, following its interactions with Uganda in 2009, recommended that it should implement the Robben Island Guidelines and in particular that it should criminalise torture.[132] During the Commission's next engagement with Uganda in 2011, the Commission urged it to expedite enactment of the Anti-Torture Bill which was pending in Parliament.[133] In Uganda's 2015 engagements with the Commission, the Commission commended it for enacting the Prevention and Prohibition of Torture Act of 2012. Yet, the Commission still recommended that the relevant regulations for enabling the Act should be put in place, and it also raised concerns about the high number of torture cases in the country and the dearth of disaggregated data in relation to torture.[134]

---

[128] *Concluding Observations and Recommendations on the Initial Periodic Report of the Republic of Liberia on the Implementation of the African Charter on Human and Peoples' Rights*, adopted by the African Commission on Human and Peoples' Rights at the 17th Extra-Ordinary Session, 19–28 February 2015.

[129] *Concluding Observations and Recommendations on the Initial, 1st, 2nd, 3rd and 4th Periodic Report of the Federal Democratic Republic of Ethiopia*, adopted at the 47th Ordinary Session of the African Commission on Human and Peoples' Rights, 12–26 May 2010.

[130] *Concluding Observations and Recommendations on the 5th and 6th Periodic Report of the Federal Democratic Republic of Ethiopia*, adopted by the African Commission on Human and Peoples' Rights at its 18th Extra-Ordinary Session, 29 July–7 August 2015.

[131] *Ibid.*

[132] *Concluding Observations of the African Commission on the 3rd Periodic Report of the Republic of Uganda*, adopted during the 45th Ordinary Session of the African Commission, 13–27 May 2009.

[133] *Concluding Observations of the African Commission on the 4th Periodic Report of the Republic of Uganda*, adopted by the African Commission at the 49th Ordinary Session, 28 April–12 May 2011.

[134] *Concluding Observations and Recommendations on the 5th Periodic State Report of the Republic of Uganda (2010–2012)*, adopted at the 57th Ordinary Session of the African Commission, 4–18 November 2015.

Promotion Missions and the Eradication of Torture

Promotion missions are undertaken by members of the Commission, individually or jointly, in their capacity as country rapporteurs or mandate-holders of special mechanisms, in order to receive information on the legislative and other measures put in place to give effect to the rights and freedoms enshrined in the African Charter, sensitise state parties on various human rights aspects, and follow up on implementation of the Commission's decisions and recommendations.[135]

Following the undertaking of a promotion mission, the Commission adopts a report which notes positive aspects and areas of concern and makes appropriate recommendations.[136] Promotion mission reports make recommendations on the ratification of relevant human rights instruments and the establishment or strengthening of relevant institutions. This was the case with the Commission's promotion mission to Gabon which recommended the establishment of a national preventive mechanism, the institution of a continuous training and education policy to prohibit torture and the dissemination of the Robben Island Guidelines.[137] A promotion mission to Lesotho recommended the criminalisation of torture,[138] as did a promotion mission to The Gambia.[139] The Commission's promotion mission to Namibia heard accusations that the trial court in the Kaprivi high treason trial had not ruled against evidence obtained allegedly through torture. The Commission urged Namibia to expedite the trial and to investigate the alleged torture of the accused.[140] A promotion mission in Uganda found endemic torture in prisons perpetrated on inmates by warders as well as by inmates who were given positions of responsibility, and also perpetrated on remandees by police officers seeking confessions. Degrading treatment included corporal punishment, being forced to wash toilets with bare hands, collective punishment and psychological torture occasioned by long stints on death-row.[141] A later promotion mission to Uganda raised concerns about the prevalence of torture and the backlog of torture-related compensations. The mission recommended that Uganda should pass regulations to make its anti-torture law operational, and that it should become party to OPCAT. It should also establish a victims' compensation fund to expedite compensating victims of torture.[142] A promotion mission to Sudan urged it to expressly crim-

---

[135] *Guidelines on the Format of Promotion and Protection Mission Reports of the African Commission*, adopted at the 23rd Extra-Ordinary Session of the African Commission, 15–22 February 2018, para 3. See also *Rules of Procedure of the African Commission* (n 106 above), Rule 70.

[136] For a list of the Commission's mission reports, see http://www.achpr.org/search/?t=834&sort = date

[137] *Report of the Human Rights Promotion Mission to the Gabonese Republic* (13–18 January 2014), adopted at the 54th Ordinary Session of the African Commission, 22 October–5 November 2013.

[138] *Mission Report of the Joint Promotion Mission to the Kingdom of Lesotho (3–7 September 2012)*, adopted by the African Commission at the 54th Ordinary Session, 22 October–5 November 2013.

[139] *Report of the Human Rights Promotion Mission to the Republic of The Gambia (19–24 April 2017)*.

[140] *Promotion Mission Report to the Republic of Namibia (24–27 August 2009)*, adopted by the African Commission on Human and Peoples' Rights at the 47th Ordinary Session, 12–26 May 2010.

[141] *Report of the Promotion Mission by the Special Rapporteur on Prisons and Places of Detention in Africa to the Republic of Uganda (11–22 March 2001)*, adopted by the African Commission at the 33rd Ordinary Session, 15–29 May 2003.

[142] *Report of the Joint Mission Undertaken in the Republic of Uganda by the African Commission (25–30 August 2013)*, adopted by the African Commission at the 55th Ordinary Session, 28 April–12 May 2014.

inalise torture and ill-treatment and establish a National Preventive Mechanism, as well as stopping the use of torture or ill-treatment at Kober Prison.[143]

Promotion missions also provide the Commission and states with opportunities to engage on more exceptional yet important human rights subjects. A promotion mission to Botswana heard allegations of torture committed on members of the Basarwa indigenous community when they were being relocated from the Central Kalahari Game Reserve. Members of the community alleged they had been tortured by park officials who whipped them all over their bodies.[144] Indeed, the mission concluded that physical force as well as intimidation[145] were used to relocate the Basarwa from the Game Reserve. The mission did not however make a finding on whether these acts amounted to torture or ill-treatment, perhaps possibly because this was a promotion rather than protection mission and since the main focus of the mission was constructive engagement on policy change on Botswana's dealings with its indigenous communities.

Furthermore, a promotion mission by the Committee for the Prevention of Torture in Africa to Mauritania offered the Commission another opportunity to deal with the sensitive subject of slavery in the country. The mission found that while Mauritania's 2012 Constitution had declared slavery a crime against humanity and enacted an anti-slavery law, and while former slaves were being empowered to assume their liberty fully, the government's continuing denial that slavery existed and the minimal practical application of the anti-slavery law undermined overall efforts to prohibit slavery.[146]

Resolutions

Resolutions were one of the earliest means by which the African Commission expressed its formal opinions on theme-specific, country-specific or administrative issues. Resolutions issued by the Commission have sought to clarify Charter provisions or offer new interpretations of particular normative aspects of the Charter, while other resolutions have expressed the Commission's concerns on and exhortations about particular human rights violations or abuses on the continent or in specific countries. Still others have established administrative measures to ensure the better realisation of the Charter.[147]

---

[143] *Report of the Joint Promotion Mission to the Republic of the Sudan (22–28 May 2015)*, adopted by the African Commission, 22 August 2016.

[144] *Report of the African Commission's Working Group on Indigenous Populations/Communities Mission to the Republic of Botswana (15–23 June 2005)*, adopted by the African Commission during its 38th Ordinary Session, 21 November–5 December 2005.

[145] This was manifested by the separation of spouses and children, the dismantling and ferrying of huts in the absence of their owners and the destruction of water pumps.

[146] *Report of the Promotion Mission of the Committee for the Prevention of Torture in Africa to the Islamic Republic of Mauritania (26 March–1 April 2012)*, adopted by the African Commission at the 12th Extra-Ordinary Session, 30 July–4 August 2012.

[147] As of October 2018, the Commission had adopted 412 thematic, country specific and administrative resolutions.

Resolutions on the theme of torture have adopted, or initiated the development of, normative standards such as the Robben Island Guidelines[148] and the Luanda Guidelines.[149] They have also sought to protect specified groups such as human rights defenders,[150] journalists,[151] migrants,[152] women and children in armed conflict,[153] persons with psychosocial disabilities,[154] sexual minorities,[155] and persons with albinism.[156] They have also addressed themes such as rehabilitation for victims of torture,[157] involuntary sterilisation,[158] the right to peaceful demonstrations,[159] police and human rights,[160] prisons[161] and terrorism.[162]

Country-specific resolutions on torture have addressed the human rights situation in specific states where the Commission's concerns have included the use of torture. Illustratively, Resolution 309 responded to the civil strife in Burundi around the 2015 elections by condemning its use of torture against peaceful protesters, and calling on the government to investigate those violations and prosecute their perpetrators.[163] This resolution illustrates one of the down-

---

[148] Resolution 61, *Resolution on Guidelines and Measures for the Prohibition and Prevention of Torture, Cruel, Inhuman or Degrading Treatment or Punishment in Africa*, adopted by the African Commission at its 32nd Ordinary Session, held from 17th to 23rd October 2002.

[149] Resolution 228, *Resolution on the need to develop guidelines on conditions of police custody and pre-trial detention in Africa*, adopted by the African Commission at its 52nd Ordinary Session, held from 9 to 22 October 2012.

[150] For example, see Resolution 376, *Resolution on the Situation of Human Rights Defenders in Africa*, adopted by the African Commission at its 60th Ordinary Session, held from 8 to 22 May 2017.

[151] Resolution 99, *Resolution on the Situation of Freedom of Expression in Africa*, adopted by the African Commission at its 40th Ordinary Session, held from 15 to 29 November 2006.

[152] Resolution 333, *Resolution on the Situation of Migrants in Africa*, adopted by the African Commission at its 19th Extra-Ordinary Session, held from 16 to 25 February 2016.

[153] Resolution 283, *Resolution on the Situation of Women and Children in Armed Conflict*, adopted by the African Commission at its 55th Ordinary Session, held from 28 April to 12 May 2014.

[154] Resolution 343, *Resolution on the Right to Dignity and Freedom from Torture or Ill-Treatment of Persons with Psychosocial Disabilities in Africa*, adopted by the African Commission at its 58th Ordinary Session, held from 6 to 20 April 2016.

[155] Resolution 275, *Resolution on Protection against Violence and other Human Rights Violations against Persons on the basis of their real or imputed Sexual Orientation or Gender Identity*, adopted by the African Commission at its 55th Ordinary Session, held from 28 April to 12 May 2014.

[156] Resolution 373 (LX) 2017, *Resolution on the Regional Action Plan on Albinism in Africa (2017–2021)*, adopted during the 60th Ordinary Session of the African Commission, held in Niamey, Niger, from 8 to 22 May 2017.

[157] Resolution 303, *Resolution on the Right to Rehabilitation for Victims of Torture*, adopted by the African Commission at its 56th Ordinary Session, held from 21 April to 7 May 2015.

[158] Resolution 260, *Resolution on Involuntary Sterilisation and the Protection of Human Rights in Access to HIV Services*, adopted by the African Commission at its 54th Ordinary Session, held from 22 October to 5 November 2013.

[159] Resolution 281, *Resolution on the Right to Peaceful Demonstrations*, adopted by the African Commission at its 55th Ordinary Session, held from 28 April to 12 May 2014.

[160] Resolution 259, *Resolution on Police and Human Rights in Africa*, adopted by the African Commission at its 54th Ordinary Session, held from 22 October to 5 November 2013.

[161] Resolution 19, *Resolution on Prisons in Africa*, adopted by the African Commission at its 17th Ordinary Session, held from 13 to 22 March 1995.

[162] Resolution 88, *Resolution on the Protection of Human Rights and the Rule of Law in the Fight against Terrorism*, adopted by the African Commission at its 37th Ordinary Session, held from 21 November to 5 December 2005.

[163] Resolution 309, *Resolution on the Human Rights Situation in Burundi*, adopted by the African Commission at its 18th Extra-Ordinary Session, held from 29 July to 7 August 2015.

sides of resolutions. In fact, the Commission has issued multiple resolutions on the human rights situation in Burundi without noticeable acknowledgement or response from the state.[164] Indeed, the 63rd Ordinary Session of the African Commission issued one more resolution on Burundi, urging it to investigate and prosecute alleged perpetrators or accomplices of extrajudicial killings and torture.[165] The Commission has also issued a number of resolutions calling on Egypt to conduct impartial and transparent investigations into cases alleging the torture of peaceful protestors, and that perpetrators be brought to justice.[166]

Other torture-specific country resolutions have: called for the protection of human rights defenders from torture;[167] called for independent monitors to have access to prisons and other places of detention in institutions such as Ethiopia's Federal Police Crime Investigation and Forensic Department of Maikelawi in Addis Ababa;[168] requested permission to undertake promotion or investigation missions;[169] condemned enforced disappearances and summary executions;[170] and asked for the release of named or unnamed individuals from unlawful detention, such as in the instance of the Commission's resolution on The Gambia where the resolution was based on a determination of the unlawful detention of Chief Ibrima Manneh by the ECOWAS Community Court of Justice.[171]

Administrative resolutions on torture have dwelt on the establishment of pertinent institutions such as the CPTA and the appointment or renewal of its members' mandates.[172]

---

[164]   Resolution 357, *Resolution on the Human Rights Situation in the Republic of Burundi*, adopted by the African Commission at its 59th Ordinary Session, held from 21 October to 4 November 2016.

[165]   Resolution 412, *Resolution on the Human Rights Situation in Burundi*, adopted by the African Commission at its 63rd Ordinary Session of the African Commission, held from 24 October to 13 November 2018.

[166]   Resolution 240, *Resolution on the Human Rights Situation in the Arab Republic of Egypt*, adopted by the African Commission at its 14th Extra-Ordinary Session, held from 20 to 24 July 2013.

[167]   Resolution 109, *Resolution on the Situation in Somalia*, adopted by the African Commission at its 41st Ordinary Session, held from 16 to 30 May 2007.

[168]   Resolution 218, *Resolution on the Human Rights Situation in the Democratic Republic of Ethiopia*, adopted by the African Commission at its 51st Ordinary Session, held from 18 April to 2 May 2012.

[169]   Resolution 356, *Resolution on the Human Rights Situation in the Federal Democratic Republic of Ethiopia*, adopted by the African Commission at its 59th Ordinary Session, held from 21 October to 4 November 2016.

[170]   Resolution 258, *Resolution on Summary Execution and Enforced Disappearance in Mali*, adopted by the African Commission at its 54th Ordinary Session, held from 22 October to 5 November 2013.

[171]   Resolution 134, *Resolution on the Human Rights Situation in the Republic of The Gambia*, adopted by the African Commission at its 44th Ordinary Session, held from 10 to 24 November 2008.

[172]   For example, see Resolution 120, *Resolution on the Renewal of Mandate and Appointment of the Chairperson and Members of the Follow-up Committee on the Implementation of the Robben Island Guidelines*, adopted by the African Commission at its 42nd Ordinary Session, held from 15 to 28 November 2007; Resolution 158, *Resolution on the Change of Name of the Robben Island Guidelines Follow-Up Committee to the Committee for the Prevention of Torture in Africa and the Reappointment of the Chairperson and Members of the Committee*, adopted by the African Commission at its 46th Ordinary Session, held from 11 to 25 November 2009; Resolution 254, *Resolution on the Appointment of the Chairperson and Renewal of the Mandate of the Members of the Committee for the Prevention of Torture in Africa*, adopted by the African Commission at its 54th Ordinary Session, held from 22 October to 5 November 2013; Resolution 322, *Resolution on the Renewal of the Mandate and Reconstitution of the Committee for the Prevention of Torture in Africa*, adopted at the 57th Ordinary Session of the African Commission, held from 4 to 18 November 2015; Resolution 387, *Resolution on the Appointment of the Chairperson, Renewal of the Mandate and Reconstitution of the Committee for the Prevention of*

IMPLEMENTATION OF DECISIONS OR RECOMMENDATIONS COVERING THE PROHIBITION OF TORTURE

The Quandaries of Implementation

Africa's interventions against torture are complemented by a corpus of international norms and institutions, including the Convention against Torture and its Committee, whose strengths and weaknesses in many respects mirror their regional counterparts. Hence, assessing the extent to which the continent's human rights system is realising the prohibition of torture faces the conceptual and practical quandaries of what successful prohibition might look like. This indeed is a question which confronts advocates who seek to prevent human rights violations of any nature globally: the essential difficulties of implementation faced by Africa's human rights system are not particularly peculiar to the continent. All human rights treaty bodies operate in supra-national spaces devoid of classic law-enforcement instruments more properly located within the competence of each nation-state.

In recent years, a number of initiatives have sought to assess the extent to which states implement decisions or recommendations made by Africa's human rights institutions. These initiatives have identified implementation challenges such as limited political commitment by states, financial and institutional constraints, limited communication and visibility, limited monitoring mechanisms, and functional constraints occasioned by legal limitations such as insufficient clarity in the African Charter on the types of remedies that may be granted or on the enforcement of decisions at the municipal level by the Commission.[173]

THE BINDING VERSUS NON-BINDING CONUNDRUM

Much of the preceding discussion on the prohibition of torture has drawn from the work of the African Commission since other continental human rights organs have as yet not made notable contributions on the subject. Yet the Commission's decisions do not carry the binding force of decisions from a court of law, rather having persuasive authority akin to the opinions of treaty bodies such as the Human Rights Committee established under the International Covenant on Civil and Political Rights.[174] Implementation provisions in the Charter are rather unspecific, simply, in the case of an inter-state communication requiring the Commission to submit a report on its findings to the Assembly of Heads of State and Government, having the option of making '... such recommendations as it deems useful'.[175] More generally, only communications relating to apparent special cases '... which reveal the existence of a series of serious or massive violations of human and peoples' rights ...'[176] may be drawn to the attention

Torture in Africa, adopted by the African Commission at its 61st Ordinary Session, held from 1 to 15 November 2017.

[173] For example, see *Report of the Second Regional Seminar on the Implementation of Decisions of the African Commission on Human and Peoples' Rights*, 4–6 September 2018, Zanzibar, Tanzania.

[174] Viljoen and Odinkalu (n 15 above), 27.

[175] *African Charter* (n 2 above), Article 53. See also Articles 48 and 52.

[176] *Ibid*, Article 58(1).

of the Assembly of Heads of State and Government.[177] Rather, the Commission's decisions on individual communications are notified to the Assembly as part of the Commission's Activity Report prior to its publication.[178]

In the case of the African Court, more elaborate implementation provisions are enunciated pursuant to which a judgement of the Court is notified not only to the parties to the case but also to the Council of Ministers, which is required to monitor its execution on behalf of the Assembly of the African Union.[179] A state party commits to comply with and guarantee execution of a judgement of the Court,[180] and the Court's annual report to the Assembly includes cases where a state has failed to comply with the Court's judgement.[181]

While the argument seeking to distinguish between the quasi-judicial decisions of the Commission and the judicial decisions of the Court is, therefore, supported by legal text, in fact, this distinction may amount to a red herring since in practice neither the Court nor the Commission can implement their decisions independently without recourse to the policy organs of the African Union. Those organs, and indeed the Committee, have to seek the intervention of policy organs for implementation of decisions by states which decline to do so. Illustratively, the Court has reported to the policy organs that only Burkina Faso has complied fully with its judgements, and that other states are either in part-compliance or, in respect of Côte d'Ivoire, Kenya, Libya, Mali and Rwanda, have not complied at all.[182]

Dichotomy between 'Soft Law' and 'Hard Law'

Related to the above discussion, it should also be stressed that reference to soft-law instruments such as the Robben Island Guidelines or General Comment No. 4 connote the reality that states are not party to those instruments through ratification or accession. The 'soft-law' character of the instruments is derived from the fact that the African Commission is empowered to prepare such instruments under the Charter to which states are party. The 'hard law' versus 'soft law' dichotomy should not be conflated with whether the Commission's decisions are binding or non-binding. The bottom line is that states should be obligated to enforce determinations made by an institution established by an instrument to which they are party. In this sense, the Commission's decisions or recommendations, however framed, should be binding to states parties to the Charter, whether these are communications, resolutions or indeed concluding observations.

State as Primary Actor and the Roles of Other Actors

It should, of course, be stressed that each state that is party to a treaty, pursuant to its Charter commitments, is the primary actor in the implementation of decisions and recommendations

---

[177]   Unfortunately, on the quite limited occasions when the Commission has employed this Article 58 procedure, the Assembly has not acted to any notable effect.

[178]   *African Charter* (n 2 above), Article 59.

[179]   *African Charter on Human and Peoples' Rights on the Establishment of an African Court on Human and Peoples' Rights* (n 48 above), Article 29.

[180]   *Ibid,* Article 30.

[181]   *Ibid,* Article 31.

[182]   *Activity Report of the African Court on Human and Peoples' Rights,* 1 January–31 December 2018, EX.CL/1126(XXXIV), para 49.

made by the Commission, the Court or the Committee. It may indeed be argued that the principal demand that litigants and stakeholders should make of continental judicial or quasi-judicial bodies is the delivery of competent and timely judgements,[183] subsequent to which litigants and other stakeholders should lobby states both at the national and continental levels. But, either way, the question of the implementation of the decisions or recommendations of these continental organs remains ever-present.

It is then incumbent on other stakeholders to institute mechanisms for chivvying and encouraging Member States to adhere to their treaty commitments.

Pursuant to Article 54 of the African Charter which requires the African Commission to submit to each Ordinary Session of the Assembly of Heads of State and Government a report on its activities, the Commission submits biennial activity reports to the Union's policy organs. These reports invariably include mention of states that have failed to comply with decisions of the Commission; yet despite being invited severally to do so, the policy organs invariably decline to take due action against errant states.

Civil society organisations as well as national human rights institutions also should use their statutory mandates or good offices to support national implementation. In the instance of national human rights institutions, the Commission, in at least one communication, urged the Uganda Human Rights Commission to use its statutory powers under Section 52(1)(h) of the Constitution of Uganda to monitor Uganda's compliance with the decision.[184, 185]

National Legislative and Judicial Responses

The question of implementation should be understood at two levels: first, as already discussed, ensuring redress for litigant victims of torture; and, second, the broader medium to long-term benefits derived by national laws and jurisprudence. On this second score, the long-term viability of continental interventions against torture should be understood by assessing national legislative and judicial responses. Some African countries have heeded the obligation to prohibit torture by enacting specific legislation to criminalise torture. Indeed, the enactment of Nigeria's Anti-Torture Act of 2017[186] and Kenya's Prevention of Torture Act of 2017[187] was supported by determined recommendations and urgings from the African Commission.[188] In the instance of South Africa, it legislated the Prevention and Combatting of Torture of Persons Act of 2013, thereby escalating torture from the common law crime of common assault or assault with intent to commit grievous harm.[189] Some laws have even departed from the

---

[183]   Mute, L, 'Innovations and Counter Measures to Ensure Protection against Torture and Ill-Treatment in Africa', Keynote Address at *Article 5 Initiative Regional Seminar on Preventing and Eradicating Torture in Africa*, Johannesburg, South Africa, 1–3 September 2014 (on file with the author).

[184]   Communication no 431/12, *Thomas Kwoyelo v. Uganda*, paras 208–212.

[185]   Also see NANHRI, *National Human Rights Institutions and African Regional Mechanisms: Guidelines on the Role of NHRIs in Monitoring Implementation of Recommendations of the African Commission on Human and Peoples' Rights and Judgements of the African Court on Human and Peoples' Rights*, 2016.

[186]   Anti-Torture Act, 2017.

[187]   Prevention of Torture Act No 12, 2017.

[188]   See *Technical Commentary on the Anti-Torture Framework in Nigeria* (Redress, 2017).

[189]   See Fernandez, L and Lukas Muntingh, L, 'The Criminalisation of Torture in South Africa' (2016) 60 *Journal of African Law* 83.

minimum anti-torture normative standards perhaps in a bid to ensure the full prohibition of torture.[190] However, even on this score, far too many states still do not have proper anti-torture legislative frameworks covering the prohibition, prevention, investigation and prosecution of torture.[191] Finally, though, another positive note is that some National judiciaries have drawn heavily from global and regional norms and precedents to ensure justice for victims of torture.

Expanding the Meaning of Torture

The definition of torture as enunciated in the Convention against Torture has on its face often been assumed as establishing a limited and exclusive rather than flexible and expansive standard. Writing about the 1986–2006 civil conflict in Northern Uganda, Chris Dolan has argued that the definition of torture in CAT is in fact a broad and wide-reaching one. He notes that while the definition emphasises the intentionality of perpetrators and identifies them seemingly narrowly to encompass public officials or their agents, the objectives of torture overreach the ones listed in Article 1 of the Convention. He explains that the phrase 'for such purposes as' suggests that while obtaining information, punishment, intimidation and coercion are major objectives of torture, they are not exclusive. The inclusion of suffering 'for any reason based on discrimination of any kind' makes the possibilities even broader.[192] While definitions of torture in municipal laws do not coincide with Dolan's bold thesis that torture should be understood to include what he refers to as 'social torture', some exceptional national laws do indeed initiate more expansive definitions of torture. Uganda's Prevention and Prohibition of Torture Act expressly includes in its definition of torture acts committed by non-state actors.[193] This broadened definition should be welcome so long as it does not undermine the minimum standard set by CAT. In this regard, Uganda's law unfortunately fails to specifically include discrimination as a possible purpose.[194]

CONCLUSION

This chapter has established the presence of a solid normative and institutional basis for ensuring protection against torture in Africa. The chapter has, however, also illustrated a significant implementation gap and dearth of contingent remedial strategies for dealing with torture.

While assessing structural indicators (such as the number of treaty ratifications/accessions) and process indicators (such as the number of laws criminalizing torture) must not be dismissed, providing succor to victims of torture demands even more single-minded focus on outcome indicators. Africa's human rights bodies must not abdicate the legal or moral task of continually affirming the prevention of torture as a peremptory norm which may not be derogated from under any circumstances.[195]

---

[190] See Uganda Prevention and Prohibition of Torture Act, 2012, Sec 3.
[191] For a study on anti-torture legal frameworks in five African countries, see Redress, *Legal Frameworks to Prevent Torture in Africa: Best Practices, Shortcomings and Options Going Forward* (Redress, 2016).
[192] Dolan, D, *Social Torture: The Case of Northern Uganda 1986–2006* (Berghahn Books, 2011).
[193] Prevention and Prohibition of Torture Act, 2012, Sec 3.
[194] See Redress (n 191 above), 17.
[195] Mute (n 183 above).

To this end, first, human rights leaders must bear the torch for guiding society away from parochialism and inhumanity.[196] Second, counterarguments must not be dismissed without careful consideration and responses, and arguments that encourage the condoning of torture such as ticking time-bomb scenarios must be engaged with robustly and not be simply dismissed out-of-hand.[197] Third, there needs to be better discoursing around and appreciation of success stories of redress, even though these may relate to historically distant rather than more current events.[198] Fourth, while it is easier to make overall assessment statements (of progression but usually regression) relating to a whole state apparatus, islands of achievement within states should be identified, ring-fenced, given plaudits and showcased as success stories. Fifth, when it comes to the crunch, it must not be forgotten that torture happens in the most far-distant nooks and crannies, the deep dungeons where Africa's articulate middle-classes remain in blissful, unheeding ignorance. Human rights work, therefore, must not be simply professionalised and globalised; it must be communalised and localised. Organic community anti-torture cells involving paralegal, paramedical and other elements must be supported with capacities to use social media and other means to intervene and document. Finally, perhaps the most important strand of anti-torture work should be rehabilitating and providing reparation for the victim. The victim, each victim, should not be made to wait until tomorrow.

---

[196] That is why abolishing capital punishment is an important mission even in countries where the majority prefer its retention.

[197] Present realities in many African countries are such that civilians are quite likely to be persuaded about the need for extra-legal actions for instance against those perceived as terrorists.

[198] Notable redress in recent years has tended to focus on historic rather than current violations: Kenyan courts have been quite happy to declare as torture acts that took place two decades ago. For example, see *A Case Digest on the Struggle for Justice by Survivors of Torture in Kenya* (Kenya Human Rights Commission, 2009).

12. The prevention of torture

Malcolm D Evans

INTRODUCTION

In the seminal work that laid the foundations of the modern era of international human rights protection, Hersch Lauterpacht observed that:

> ... we can trace two strains in modern international law. One has been concerned with the relations between States as such: with the law of treaties, with the jurisdictional immunities of diplomatic representatives and of foreign states generally, with acquisition of territory, and with the rules governing the conduct of war. The other has used international law to promote and protect, through international co-operation and institutions, the interests and the welfare of the individual.[1]

Lauterpacht distinguishes here the role of international law as law between states from its role in establishing inter-state systems and structures through which states could work to promote and protect individuals. Naturally, such systems of promotion and protection could – and in Lauterpacht's view should – include legally binding obligations upon states: and the title of his book *An International Bill of Rights* has become the name by which the Universal Declaration of Human Rights (UDHR),[2] the International Covenant on Civil and Political Rights (ICCPR)[3] and the International Covenant on Economic, Social and Cultural Rights (CESCR)[4] have collectively come to be known.

At the same time, he also observed that 'no system of protection of the rights of man can be satisfactory if the international machinery is called upon to act only after a violation of the law has occurred or is about to occur'.[5] In so saying, Lauterpacht identified a truth which has long been known – that prevention is better than cure. He highlights that mechanisms are needed which not only address violations, but which seek to ensure that violations do not occur in the first place.

The early human rights instruments addressed torture and ill-treatment in the language of prohibition: that 'thou shalt not' torture.[6] This focus on prohibition easily lends itself to an approach which focuses upon determining whether violations have in fact occurred, of holding those responsible to account and the provision of redress and rehabilitation for victims. Whilst

---

[1] Lauterpacht, H, *An International Bill of Rights of Man* (Oxford University Press, 1945, republished 2013 (Sands, P (ed)), 47.

[2] Universal Declaration of Human Rights, UNGA Res 217A (III) (adopted 10 December 1948).

[3] International Covenant on Civil and Political Rights (adopted 16 December 1966, entered into force 23 March 1976) 999 UNTS 171.

[4] International Covenant on Economic, Social and Cultural Rights (adopted 16 December 1966, entered into force 3 January 1976) 993 UNTS 3.

[5] Lauterpacht (n 1 above), 173.

[6] UDHR (n 2 above), Article 5; ICCPR (n 3 above), Article 7; European Convention for the Protection of Human Rights and Fundamental Freedoms (ECHR) (adopted 4 November 1950, entered into force 3 September 1953 ETS no 5), Article 3.

it does not preclude approaches which are more focussed on preventing violations from occurring, there has been a tendency to see prevention as being the result of the enforcement of the prohibition: as Sir Nigel Rodley, the former UN Special Rapporteur on Torture once said, 'in the case of torture prevention is not better than cure. Prevention is protection by another name. It is remedial, rather than prophylactic'.[7]

Sir Nigel's reluctance to embrace prevention as a discrete method of addressing torture is well attested and was founded on concerns (which have not been borne out in practice) that doing so might undermine the efficacy of other tools of protection (and hence of prevention).[8] The objection was not to the idea of prevention as such. Indeed, the 1984 UN Convention against Torture (UNCAT)[9] is itself largely grounded in preventive methodologies: having noted the prohibition of torture and ill-treatment in the UDHR and the ICCPR, the Preamble indicates that the purpose of the Convention is to 'make *more effective* the struggle against torture …'.[10] To that end, it introduced an obligation to render torture a criminal offence under domestic law, and to extend the principle of *aut dedere aut judicare* to that offence.[11] Crucially for the purposes of this chapter, UNCAT Article 2(1) also provides that 'Each State Party shall take effective legislative, administrative, judicial or other measures *to prevent* acts of torture in any territory under its jurisdiction' (emphasis added). For the first time, there was a clear, unambiguous treaty-based obligation within the UN framework directly related to the prevention of torture,[12] the wide-ranging nature of which has since been elaborated upon by the Committee against Torture (CAT) in its General Comment no 2.[13]

The existence of a preventive obligation in relation to torture is now well attested. As long ago as 1988, in the *Velásquez Rodríguez* case the Inter-American Court stressed that states

---

[7]   Rodley, NS, 'Reflections on Working for the Prevention of Torture' (2009) 6 *Essex Human Rights Law Review* 21, 29.

[8]   *Ibid*, 25. For a similarly downbeat assessment of its prospects see also Rodley, NS and Pollard, M, *The Treatment of Prisoners under International Law*, 3rd edn (Oxford University Press, 2009), 245.

[9]   Convention against Torture and Other Cruel, Inhuman or Degrading Treatment or Punishment (adopted 10 December 1984, entered into force 26 June 1987) 1465 UNTS 85.

[10]   *Ibid*, Preamble, para 6 (emphasis added).

[11]   *Ibid*, Articles 1 and 4–6. It is beyond the scope of this chapter to consider these provisions in detail. See Gaer in this volume and, more generally, Kittichaisaree, K, *The Obligation to Extradite or Prosecute* (Oxford University Press, 2018).

[12]   It should be noted that the obligation is not 'to prevent' acts of torture from occurring, but to take measures which are of a preventive nature. Evidence that torture has occurred does not therefore necessarily give rise to a breach of Article 2(1). But a breach of Article 2(1) may occur in the absence of evidence of torture if there has been a failure to take steps which are of a preventive nature.

[13]   UN Committee Against Torture, General Comment no 2, Implementation of Article 2 by States parties, UN Doc CAT/C/GC/2 (24 January 2008), para 3. The breadth of prevention is shown by its saying that preventive measures include activities such as the training and education of law enforcement personnel, for example. Borrowing from the language of the UNCAT, in 1992 the Human Rights Committee said that states parties 'should inform the Committee of the legislative, administrative, judicial and other measures they take to prevent and punish acts of torture and cruel, inhuman and degrading treatment in any territory under their jurisdiction', with examples of such measures including 'keeping under systematic review interrogation rules, instructions, methods and practices as well as arrangements for the custody and treatment of persons subjected to any form of arrest, detention or imprisonment …'. See Human Rights Committee, General Comment no 20 (Forty-fourth session, 1992): Article 7: Replaces General Comment 7 Concerning Prohibition of Torture and Cruel Treatment or Punishment, UN Doc. A/47/40 (1992) 193, paras 8, 11.

have a legal duty to take reasonable steps to prevent human rights violations.[14] Early on in its work the International Criminal Tribunal for the former Yugoslavia said that:

> States are obliged not only to prohibit and punish torture, but also to forestall its occurrence: it is insufficient merely to intervene after the infliction of torture, when the physical or moral integrity of human beings has already been irremediably harmed. Consequently, States are bound to put in place all those measures that may pre-empt the perpetration of torture.[15]

The International Court of Justice has also recognised that the UNCAT has established an obligation to prevent, noting that 'the content of the duty to prevent varies from one instrument to another, according to the wording of the relevant provisions, and depending on the nature of the acts to be prevented'.[16] The CAT has also recognised that the content of the preventive obligation is not static over time, but evolves in the light of changed understandings of what measures can have a preventive impact.[17]

As a result, when the UN Subcommittee for the Prevention of Torture (SPT), the body established under the Optional Protocol to the Convention against Torture (OPCAT)[18] whose work will be considered in more detail below, set out its approach to the concept of prevention, it concluded that 'it is not possible to devise a comprehensive statement of what the obligation to prevent torture and ill-treatment entails *in abstracto*'.[19] As a result, the SPT has taken the view that:

> … there is more to the prevention of torture and ill-treatment than compliance with legal commitments. In this sense, the prevention of torture and ill-treatment embraces – or should embrace – as many as possible of those things which in a given situation can contribute towards the lessening of the likelihood or risk of torture or ill-treatment occurring. Such an approach requires not only that there be compliance with relevant international obligations and standards in both form and substance but that attention also be paid to the whole range of other factors relevant to the experience and treatment of persons deprived of their liberty and which by their very nature will be context specific.[20]

It then argues that:

> It is for this reason that the Optional Protocol seeks to strengthen the protection of persons deprived of their liberty, not by setting out additional substantive preventive obligations but in contributing to the

[14] *Velásquez Rodríguez v. Honduras*, Merits, Judgment of July 29, 1988, Series C no 4, para 174.

[15] ICTFY, *The Prosecutor v. Anton Furundzija*, Case No IT-95-17/1-T, Judgment of 10 December 1998, para 148.

[16] *Application of the Convention on the Prevention and Punishment of the Crime of Genocide (Bosnia and Herzegovina v. Serbia and Montenegro)*, Merits, Judgment of 26 February 2007, para 429.

[17] See CAT General Comment no 2 (n 13 above), paras 1 and 4, where it is observed that preventive measures are 'not limited to those measures contained in the subsequent articles 3 to 16' of the Convention since 'the Committee's understanding of and recommendations in respect of effective measures are in a process of continual evolution'.

[18] Optional Protocol to the Convention Against Torture and Other Cruel, Inhuman or Degrading Treatment or Punishment (adopted 18 December 2002, in force 22 June 2006) 2375 UNTS 237.

[19] 'The approach of the Subcommittee on Prevention of Torture to the concept of prevention of torture and other cruel, inhuman or degrading treatment or punishment under the Optional Protocol to the Convention against Torture and Other Cruel, Inhuman or Degrading Treatment or Punishment', CAT/OP/12/6 (2010), para 3.

[20] *Ibid.*

prevention of torture by establishing, at both the international and national levels, a preventive system of regular visits and the drawing up of reports and recommendations based thereon.[21]

It is the indeterminate, open-ended and context-specific nature of prevention which, according to the SPT, means that there is indeed a distinct role for preventive mechanisms operating in accordance with preventive methodologies which sit alongside other tools of protection, and it is to those methodologies of prevention that this chapter will now turn.

THE MECHANISMS OF PREVENTION

The origins of the current methodologies of torture prevention stem from the ideas put forward by the Swiss banker, Jean-Jacques Gautier in the mid 1970s.[22] Inspired by the work of the International Committee of the Red Cross (ICRC) in visiting those detained in the course of armed conflict, he argued that a similar system should be established, allowing visits to all places of detention in order to better protect detainees from torture or ill-treatment. The ICRC model suggested that such work would be of a more humanitarian than investigatory nature, and that it would also be confidential. Indeed, this was considered essential if the agreement of states (which would be required) was to be had for so wide-ranging a mandate. The underlying assumption was that opening up closed places to scrutiny by independent visitors would reduce the likelihood of torture or ill-treatment occurring, and that their observations and recommendations would help bring about better protection against the risk of ill-treatment.

Some critics thought that the establishment of such a system might be used by unscrupulous states to prevent the ICRC going about its work, on the grounds that it was no longer needed. This, however, could be – and ultimately was – addressed by making it clear that the work of such bodies should not overlap with each other.[23] Others queried the very premise of such work being conducted confidentially: whilst this might have been a necessary price to pay for the establishment of such work in situations of armed conflict, it seemed to some to be too high a price to pay and failed to respect human rights approaches founded on transparency and accountability. Gautier himself said that the essence of the approach was that 'instead of a state being found guilty of a violation, stress will be laid on prevention'.[24] In response to which Rodley rather scathingly remarked many years later, 'So here we have it: prevention means that we save the state's face, in return for which we hope to get more effective action than would be achieved by exposure'.[25] That there is a potential tension between prosecution and prevention cannot be denied[26] – the real question, however, is how to hold these approaches in a positive creative tension, rather than to view them as opposing binary alternatives.

---

[21]   *Ibid*, para 4.
[22]   For the background generally see Haenni, C, *20 Ans Consacrés à la realisation d'une Idée* (Association for the Prevention of Torture, 1997); Evans, MD and Morgan, R, *Preventing Torture: A Study of the European Convention for the Prevention of Torture and Inhuman or Degrading Treatment of Punishment* (Oxford University Press, 1998), Chapter 1.
[23]   See ECPT, Article 17(3); OPCAT, Article 32.
[24]   Gautier, J-J, *Torture: How to Make the International Convention Effective* (ICJ/SCAT, 1980), 35.
[25]   Rodley (n 7 above), 28.
[26]   See, for example, Evans, M and Morgan, R, 'Torture: Prevention versus Punishment?' in Scott, C (ed), *Torture as Tort* (Hart Publishing, 2001), 135.

Indeed, this was the approach from the outset. Gautier's ideas coincided with discussions concerning the adoption of the UNCAT, and it was originally thought that such a visiting scheme might be incorporated within it. It was quickly decided that this would be too ambitious and so it was suggested that this be provided for in an Optional Protocol to be adopted at the same time as the Convention itself. This also proved too ambitious and although a draft was tabled by Costa Rica in 1980, it was on the basis that it would not be pursued at that time at the global level. Rather, this was used as a springboard for the project to be transferred to the regional level, and to the Council of Europe, which in 1981 endorsed the project,[27] taking the view that '… the countries of Europe might set an example and institute such a system among themselves in the framework of the Council of Europe, without waiting for the proposal to be implemented at the world level'.[28] That work proceeded swiftly, resulting in the European Convention for the Prevention of Torture and Inhuman or Degrading Treatment or Punishment (ECPT), which was adopted in 1987 and entered into force in 1989.[29]

With the ECPT adopted and in force, attention returned to the global stage, and in 1991 Costa Rica tabled a new draft of an Optional Protocol to the UNCAT which was considered by an open-ended working group of the UN Commission on Human Rights annually for two weeks each year from 1992 until 2002.[30] Though in many ways closely modelled on the ECPT, the OPCAT differs in that it establishes what has become known as a 'twin pillar' system, combining an international with a national preventive visiting system. The reason for this had less to do with principle than with the politics of negotiation. The idea of a body of independent international experts having a mandate to visit places of detention in states parties in the manner provided for under the ECPT remained very controversial at the UN level. In order to break the deadlock, Mexico presented a radically different proposal (the 'Mexican Draft') on behalf of the Group of Latin American and Caribbean states (the GRULAC).[31] This draft, dated 13 February 2001, refocused the Optional Protocol on national, rather than international, visiting mechanisms, proposing that States establish a national system of preventive visits, which would be supplemented by visits from an international body should this prove necessary. It was in this way that the idea of National Preventive Mechanisms (NPMs) was introduced into the OPCAT framework. Although this provoked hostile responses from some

---

[27]   Council of Europe, Parliamentary Assembly Recommendation 909 (1981) on the International Convention against Torture, adopted 26 Jan 1981.

[28]   Berrier Report, Council of Europe Doc AS/Jur (33) 18 of 9 September 1981, para 13, adopted by Council of Europe, Parliamentary Assembly Recommendation 971 (1983).

[29]   European Convention for the Prevention of Torture and Inhuman or Degrading Treatment or Punishment (adopted 26 November 1987, entered into force 1 February 1989) ETS no 126.

[30]   For the drafting of the OPCAT see Evans, M and Haenni-Dale, C, 'Preventing Torture? The Development of the Optional protocol to the UN Convention against Torture' (2004) 4 *Human Rights Law Review* 19; Murray, R, Steinerte, E, Evans, M and Hallo de Wolf, A, *The Optional Protocol to the UN Convention against Torture* (Oxford, 2011) Chapters 2 and 3; Nowak, M, Binz, M and Monina, G, *The United Nations Convention Against Torture and Its Optional Protocol: A Commentary*, 2nd edn (Oxford University Press, 2019), 700 ff.

[31]   The 'Alternative preliminary draft optional protocol to the Convention against Torture and Other Cruel, Inhuman or Degrading Treatment or Punishment submitted by the delegation of Mexico with the support of the Latin American Group (GRULAC)', E/CN.4/2001/67, Annex I.

NGOs[32] and state representatives, it opened up the way for a compromise which allowed for the adoption of the OPCAT by the UN General Assembly the following year.[33]

The idea that national mechanisms have a role to play in protecting human rights was hardly controversial in the field of torture prevention at the time.[34] The novelty was to require States to utilise such mechanisms in combating torture as a matter of international legal obligation. Although the inclusion of NPMs into the draft of the Optional Protocol was in some ways merely a tactic by which to diminish either the case for, or opposition to, an international visiting mechanism, it quickly became apparent that there was an important role for both. As with the tension between confidentiality and transparency, and protection and prevention, the question becomes how best to utilise the various opportunities that the burgeoning array of mechanisms to combat torture present. The remainder of this section will outline the work of the three forms of mechanism established by these two ground-breaking international instruments.

The CPT

The ECPT entered into force in 1989.[35] When the European Committee for the Prevention of Torture and Inhuman or Degrading Treatment or Punishment (CPT) undertook its first visit, to Austria in 1990, only eight of the then 23 member states of the Council of Europe were parties to the ECPT, though by the end of 1990 this figure had grown to 20 out of the then 25 member states. Around this time the Council of Europe underwent a dramatic transformation as the former communist countries of Central and Eastern Europe became members, with the expectation that they would become parties to its major human rights instruments, including the ECPT. Within a relatively short period participation increased dramatically and by 2006 all 47 member states of the Council of Europe were parties to the ECPT, nearly 25 per cent of all of states in the world. This could hardly have been foreseen by the drafters, and a system that was originally intended to operate principally among the democratic systems of Western Europe was swiftly transposed to others with fledgling systems of human rights protection. Since members – who are to be independent and have relevant expertise – are elected in respect of each state party, the CPT is a large body.[36]

The ECPT is a relatively simple text. Article 1 provides that 'The Committee shall, by means of visits, examine the treatment of persons deprived of their liberty with a view to strengthening, if necessary, the protection of such persons from torture and from inhuman or

---

[32]   The approach was strongly supported by the APT, International Federation of ACAT (FiACAT) and the International Rehabilitation Council for Torture (IRCT), but other leading NGOs, including Amnesty International and Human Rights Watch, had significant reservations.

[33]   See UNGA A/RES/57/199 (adopted 18 December 2002).

[34]   See, for example, Interim Report of the UN Special Rapporteur on Torture to the General Assembly, UN Doc A/57/173, paras 36–45, and the Joint Declaration (appended as an annex to that Report) issued on 26 June 2002 by the Special Rapporteur, the Committee against Torture, the Board of Trustees of the UN Voluntary Fund for the Victims of Torture and the UN High Commissioner for Human Rights, urging support for the adoption of the Optional Protocol and endorsing its twin-pillar approach.

[35]   For a recent examination of the work and practice of the CPT see Bicknell, C, Evans, M and Morgan, R, *Preventing Torture in Europe* (Council of Europe, 2018).

[36]   See ECPT, Article 4. Members are elected for periods of four years, and are eligible for re-election twice, meaning a maximum period of 12 years in office.

degrading treatment or punishment'. According to Article 2 'Each Party shall permit visits, in accordance with this Convention, to any place within its jurisdiction where persons are deprived of their liberty by a public authority'. The Convention envisages that visits will be of various natures: according to Article 7(1), 'The Committee shall organise visits to places referred to in Article 2. Apart from periodic visits, the Committee may organise such other visits as appear to it to be required in the circumstances.'

In its early years the CPT undertook three forms of visits – a 'regular' (periodic) visit, which typically lasted for up to two weeks, 'ad hoc' visits, which typically lasted four or five days, and 'follow-up visits', which, as the name suggests, were designed to build on previous visits and determine progress and which were of various lengths.[37] The latter form of visit has long been abandoned since recommendations arising out of reports can be followed up in numerous ways, including in subsequent 'regular' or 'ad hoc' visits. In addition, however, the CPT has increasingly had resort to what are termed 'High Level Talks', these being relatively short visits to discuss progress at a senior level without undertaking visits to places of detention – in reality, a follow-up discussion.[38] Visits are undertaken by delegations comprised of varying numbers of members, supported by the CPT's secretariat: periodic visits may have up to six members, whereas 'ad hoc' visits may have as few as two. The Convention also permits delegations to be accompanied by experts, and whilst this is still routine, they are perhaps less relied on today than was previously the case.

Following each visit, the CPT is to

> draw up a report on the facts found during the visit, taking account of any observations which may have been submitted by the Party concerned. It shall transmit to the latter its report containing any recommendations it considers necessary. The Committee may consult with the Party with a view to suggesting, if necessary, improvements in the protection of persons deprived of their liberty.[39]

What this means in practice is that following each visit the CPT sends a report to the state and requests a written response. On the basis of this exchange, the CPT continues to engage in dialogue concerning the implementation of its recommendations, which will of course also be followed up during the next regular or ad hoc visit.

Crucially, Article 11(1) provides that such reports are confidential. Equally crucially, Article 11(2) provides that such reports can be made public at the request of the state. As has been mentioned, the confidential nature of visit reports was widely seen as potentially problematic and antithetical to transparency and accountability. In practise, it has been otherwise: by the end of 2017 some 392 of the 428 reports then transmitted had been published,[40] and today most states routinely authorise the publication of visit reports alongside their replies as

---

[37]   For an overview of the visiting process see Bicknell, Evans and Morgan (n 35 above), 44–51.

[38]   *Ibid*, 54, 56. A section concerning 'High Level Talks' outside of the formal visiting programme was first included in the 19th General Report on the CPT's Activities (2008–2009), CPT/Inf (2009) 27, paras 30–35 and has routinely done so since.

[39]   ECPT, Article 10(1).

[40]   28th General Report on the CPT's Activities (2018), CPT/Inf (2019) 9, para 25.

a matter of course, and 10 states have given prior authorisation for this to occur.[41] The only state party which still has a significant number of unpublished reports is Russia.[42]

The CPT does, however, have the power to comment outside the framework of its visit reports. Article 8(5) provides that 'If necessary, the Committee may immediately communicate observations to the competent authorities of the Party concerned'. In practice, this means that at the end of each visit the CPT may make immediate observations, and request that immediate actions be taken, which subsequently can be referenced in the formal visit report, if appropriate. In addition, Article 11(2) provides that 'If the Party fails to co-operate or refuses to improve the situation in the light of the Committee's recommendations, the Committee may decide, after the Party has had an opportunity to make known its views, by a majority of two-thirds of its members to make a public statement on the matter'. In its 30 years of operational practice the CPT has issued public statements only nine times, in respect of Turkey (in 1992 and 1996); the Russian Federation (in 2001, 2003, 2007 and 2019); Greece (in 2011); Bulgaria (in 2015) and Belgium (2017).[43] This is intentional, the CPT taking the view that such statements are a 'last resort', since 'it much prefers that other ways and means be used to bring about the necessary changes'.[44]

The ECPT speaks of 'periodic' visits, but without indicating what that periodicity should be. In practice, this is a decision for the CPT itself and whilst some countries are visited relatively frequently (either through periodic or 'ad hoc' visits), others are not.[45] This may be for various reasons – size and the intensity of the issues is obviously relevant, but so might the nature of the dialogue, the attitude of the state and the progress being made in responding to CPT recommendations. Allowing the CPT to exercise a degree of discretion rather than its working to a mechanical formula is obviously desirable. Initially, the main focus of the CPT's work was undertaking its periodic visiting programme, typically in the region of 10 per year, supplemented by a relatively small number of 'ad hoc' visits. In recent times the focus has shifted, with more emphasis being placed on 'ad hoc' visits which are targeted on specific, and sometimes very immediate, causes of concern. In the course of 2018 it decided to shift that balance decisively in favour of 'ad hoc' visits, with only eight of its 18 visits being of a 'periodic' nature.[46] Moreover, the difference between these forms of visits has become increasingly reduced: the average length of a periodic visit in 2018 being 10 days and that of an ad hoc visit eight days.[47]

---

[41]   These being Austria, Bulgaria, Denmark, Finland, Luxembourg, the Republic of Moldova, Monaco, Norway, Sweden and Ukraine. See *ibid*, para 27.

[42]   The Russian Federation has only agreed to the publication of three of the 24 reports which it has received from the CPT (*ibid*, Annex 6). Azerbaijan was also in this category until 2018 when it agreed to the publication of seven yet to be published reports (*ibid*, para 26).

[43]   For full details, including the texts, see https://www.coe.int/en/web/cpt/public-statements

[44]   25th General Report on the CPT's Activities (2015), CPT/Inf (2016) 10, para 7.

[45]   Some disparities are easily explained – such as Monaco having only received two visits and Andorra and Liechtenstein only four. Others seem less obviously explicable: Austria, the first country to be visited by the CPT, and Ireland have received six visits, whilst Luxembourg has received five. France and Germany have, perhaps surprisingly, only received 13 visits, the same number as Albania. The most visited countries are Turkey (30 visits), Russia (28 visits) and the UK (21 visits). For details see the 28th CPT General Report (2018) (n 40 above), Annex VI.

[46]   *Ibid*, para 1.

[47]   *Ibid*.

As a result, the main practical difference between the two forms of visit concerns focus and advance notification. ECPT Article 8(1) provides that 'The Committee shall notify the Government of the Party concerned of its intention to carry out a visit. After such notification, it may at any time visit any place referred to in Article 2.' This reflects the idea that whilst a state party should be notified that it is to be visited, it is not told which places of detention are to be visited. But the Convention is also silent on the question of *how* much notice is to be given. It has – doubtless for good planning purposes – been the longstanding practice of the CPT to determine an annual programme of periodic visits which is now typically determined in the spring and announced in the summer of the preceding year: for such visits, then, a country is potentially 'on notice' that a visit may occur for anything up to about 18 months. The precise dates are usually transmitted about three months in advance, which allows sufficient time to arrange meetings with state authorities, civil society representatives and others. The position regarding 'ad hoc' visits is very different, the state being notified usually only a matter of weeks (sometimes days) before a visit is to be undertaken.[48] The net result is that the system as a whole is progressively pivoting towards a more 'responsive' approach, focusing in on areas of pressing concern or non-compliance, rather than on more routine matters of observation and comment.

Key to the success of the CPT is its having unrestricted access to all places of deprivation of liberty and to be able to visit them without notice. But this alone is not enough, and the ECPT also provides that the CPT 'may interview in private persons deprived of their liberty' and 'communicate freely with any person whom it believes can supply relevant information'.[49] It also requires states to provide the CPT with 'other information available to the Party which is necessary for the Committee to carry out its task'.[50] In combination, this means that the CPT has (or should have) unfettered access to, and within, any place of deprivation of liberty, to any person and to any materials which it wishes to see to assist it in its task.

Whilst there is, then, much said about what the CPT may do operationally, the ECPT itself has surprisingly little to say about the nature of the tasks which the CPT is to undertake. The Preamble expresses the conviction that 'the protection of persons deprived of their liberty against torture and inhuman or degrading treatment or punishment could be strengthened by non-judicial means of a preventive character based on visits',[51] and this is repeated in Article 1 of the text. But there are few other indications in the Convention itself concerning what 'non-judicial means of a preventive character' actually are, other than that there are to be visits, confidential reports and recommendations. The task of determining what amounted to a preventive visit, and what prevention was to mean in the context of such visiting, was largely left for the CPT itself to determine.

A typical visit[52] will commence with private meetings with NGOs or individuals, followed by formal meetings with ministers, senior officials and senior managers responsible for places of deprivation of liberty within the country. Thereafter, members commence their visits to

---

[48]   See Bicknell, Evans and Morgan (n 35 above), 44–49.
[49]   ECPT, Articles 8(3)–(4).
[50]   *Ibid*, Article 8(2)(d).
[51]   *Ibid*, Preamble, para 4.
[52]   For a more detailed overview of the visiting process see Bicknell, Evans and Morgan (n 35 above), 49–51. For an interesting account of the practical dimensions of CPT visiting in its early foundational years see the account written by the first President of the CPT, Cassese, A, *Inhuman States: Imprisonment, Detention and Torture in Europe Today* (Polity Press, 1996).

places of custody, inspecting records and facilities and talking to those in custody in a wide range of settings, including (but not limited to) police stations, prisons, youth detention facilities, closed psychiatric hospitals, immigration detention centres, welfare institutions for the mentally dependent, and so on. The work of the CPT is now so widely known that it rarely encounters resistance to the operation of its mandate, although this inevitably occurs from time to time. A periodic visit might include inspections of several police stations, two or three prisons, perhaps a psychiatric hospital, a youth or immigration detention centre, or a social care home. In larger countries the delegation will usually divide and work in teams before meeting together to prepare for meetings with officials at the end of the visit.

Information is gathered from a variety of sources with a view to locating and focusing on problematical practices occurring in identifiable places. Premises will be visited and conditions observed. During confidential interviews detainees will be asked, in effect, to recount their own experiences of detention and the members will follow-up issues that arise from these as appropriate. Delegations will usually include medical experts who, if consent is given, may medically examine those claiming to, or suspected of having been, subjected to ill-treatment. The delegation therefore engages in a hybrid process of observation, examination and investigation which informs their conclusions and recommendations.

But the process is not entirely driven by what is found during the visit. The CPT has a well-developed concept of prevention based on the existence of safeguards which are to be enjoyed from the outset of detention, coupled with expectations concerning the manner in which those detained will be treated by those with responsibility for them. For example, very early on in its work the CPT set out a series of 'fundamental' preventive safeguards for those taken into police custody (or its equivalent) which, though subject to refinement, has remained basically unchanged for nearly 30 years.[53] This involves having access to a lawyer and to an independent medical examination, to be able to ensure that a third party is informed of the detention (so as to avoid situations of incommunicado detention) and to be notified of such rights. Virtually all CPT reports probe the extent to which these fundamental preventive safeguards are recognised by law and are operable in practice. Building on this approach, the CPT has developed standards applicable to most areas of detention practice and routinely draws on these whilst undertaking its visiting work.[54] It is beyond the scope of this chapter to explore the content and nature of these standards in detail,[55] though the question of standards will be touched on in a little more detail below. The point which needs to be stressed is that the CPT's approach is informed both by its commitment to fundamental safeguards and to its understanding of how these operate in practice. Its work is a meeting point of theory and practice, now informed by over 400 country visits over a 30-year time span, thousands of visits to detention facilities and tens of thousands of confidential exchanges with detainees. It is a powerful pool of knowledge and expertise.

---

[53] 2nd General Report on the CPT's Activities (1991), CPT/Inf (92) 3, paras 35–43.

[54] See this chapter, below. Full details of the CPT's statements of standards can be found on their website at https://www.coe.int/en/web/cpt/standards and a printed compilation is produced from time to time, the latest being the European Committee for the Prevention of Torture and Inhuman or Degrading Treatment or Punishment, *CPT Standards*, CPT/Inf/E (2002) 1 – Rev 2015.

[55] The most recent and comprehensive analysis is to be found in Bicknell, Evans and Morgan (n 35 above), Chapters 4–7.

The SPT

The background to the adoption of the OPCAT by the UN General Assembly (UNGA) in 2002 has already been described. The Convention entered into force in 2006 once it had garnered 25 ratifications and the members of the SPT, elected by state parties later that year, met for the first time in 2007. Initially the SPT comprised only 10 members but, in accordance with OPCAT Article 5(1), this expanded to 25 members following the 50th ratification, which occurred in 2010. As a result, the SPT is now the largest of the 10 human rights treaty bodies established by UN Conventions, though its status as such is rather masked by its being somewhat inappropriately labelled by the OPCAT as a 'Subcommittee', when it is clear that it is a wholly independent expert body.[56]

Given the historical connection between the processes which led to their adoption, it is hardly surprising that the text of the OPCAT is informed by the practical experience of the work of the CPT.[57] The visiting mandate of the SPT is, in most regards, the same as that of the CPT, although this is set out in greater detail in the OPCAT than in the ECPT.

As with the CPT, the SPT is empowered by OPCAT Article 4(1) to undertake visits '… to any place under its jurisdiction and control where persons are or may be deprived of their liberty, either by virtue of an order given by a public authority or at its instigation or with its consent or acquiescence (hereinafter referred to as places of detention)'.[58] However, OPCAT Article 1 provides that 'The objective of the present Protocol is to establish a system of *regular* visits undertaken by independent international and national bodies to places where people are deprived of their liberty, in order to prevent torture and other cruel, inhuman or degrading treatment or punishment' (emphasis added). Article 13(1) then mandates the SPT to 'establish, at first by lot, a programme of *regular* visits to the States Parties in order to fulfil its mandate as established in article 11' (emphasis added). As a result, it is generally asserted that the SPT, unlike the CPT, does not have the power to undertake 'ad hoc' visits but is limited to undertaking 'regular visits' within the context of a 'regular' programme.

This understanding certainly reflects the discussions at the time of its adoption, when the question of whether the SPT would be able to undertake such 'ad hoc' visits was keenly discussed and the failure to expressly provide for them in the text has generally been seen as a grave weakness.[59] But for that background, however, it is not at all obvious that such visits would be considered to have been precluded by the OPCAT, even as a matter of textual interpretation. OPCAT Article 11(1)(a) provides that the SPT is to '[v]isit the places *referred to in article 4* and make recommendations to States Parties concerning the protection of persons deprived of their liberty against torture and other cruel, inhuman or degrading treatment or punishment' (emphasis added). The reference in Article 13(1) to the SPT establishing a programme of regular visits in fulfilment of its mandate under Article 11 does not rule out the

---

[56] This is a legacy of an early suggestion that the function of preventive visiting under the OPCAT be vested in a sub-group of the CAT itself. This idea was abandoned during the drafting process, but the term 'subcommittee' was not altered to reflect this before the OPCAT was adopted. There are also a small number of other matters which the text of the OPCAT requires be referred to CAT by the SPT. Again, this is more a historical legacy and a practical anomaly than an indication of the nature of the relationship.

[57] See Murray et al. (n 30 above), 18–21.

[58] OPCAT, Article 4(1).

[59] See, for example, Rodley and Pollard (n 8 above), 242; Murray et al. (n 30 above), 49–51.

possibility of its also undertaking other forms of visit in order to fulfil its mandate as set out in Article 4(1). Equally, and like the ECPT, the OPCAT does not spell out what a 'regular' visit, or a programme of regular visits, should look like. In practice, the SPT has, over time, developed a variety of forms of visits which reflect some of the special features of its mandate.[60] The real constraints are not the text, but the practical (and financial) limitations under which it has to operate.

Whilst the ECPT vests the CPT with one primary task, the OPCAT vests the SPT with several. This is because the OPCAT not only requires states parties to permit visits by the SPT but it also requires them to establish, within one year of ratification, a 'National Preventive Mechanism' (NPM).[61] NPMs will be looked at in more detail in the following section, but what needs to be noted here is that the SPT is entrusted with a variety of functions relating to the establishment and operation of NPMs by the OPCAT. Its work, then, has several dimensions – exercising its own visiting mandate,[62] similar to that of the CPT, and also in regard to the national preventive mechanisms to:[63]

(i)   Advise and assist States Parties, when necessary, in their establishment;
(ii) Maintain direct, and if necessary confidential, contact with the national preventive mechanisms and offer them training and technical assistance with a view to strengthening their capacities;
(iii) Advise and assist them in the evaluation of the needs and the means necessary to strengthen the protection of persons deprived of their liberty against torture and other cruel, inhuman or degrading treatment or punishment;
(iv) Make recommendations and observations to the States Parties with a view to strengthening the capacity and the mandate of the national preventive mechanisms for the prevention of torture and other cruel, inhuman or degrading treatment or punishment.

There is little in the OPCAT to suggest how the SPT is to undertake these various functions. In 2010 it issued 'Guidelines on National Preventive Mechanisms' and in 2016 an 'Analytical assessment tool for national preventive mechanisms', accompanied by a self-assessment matrix.[64] It has also produced specialised guidance for NPMs when visiting medical facilities.[65] These provide further guidance for states and NPMs and are designed to assist them as they undertake their work. It has also collaborated with the Office of the High Commissioner to produce an extensive Practical Guide for NPMs in the OHCHR Professional Training Series.[66]

Beyond the production of general guidance, the SPT has developed a number of means of engaging with both states parties and with NPMs. During parts of its plenary sessions in Geneva (and, most recently, online), the SPT meets as four 'Regional Teams', focusing

---

[60]   For an excellent overview see Nowak, Binz and Monina (n 30 above), 843–847.
[61]   OPCAT, Article 17.
[62]   OPCAT, Article 11(a).
[63]   OPCAT, Article 11(b). There is also a third, general, tasking in Article 11(c), this being to 'Cooperate, for the prevention of torture in general, with the relevant United Nations organs and mechanisms as well as with the international, regional and national institutions or organizations working towards the strengthening of the protection of all persons against torture and other cruel, inhuman or degrading treatment or punishment'.
[64]   See CAT/OP/12/5 and CAT/OP/1/Rev.1 (2016).
[65]   See 'National preventive mechanism checklist on health-care issues relating to the monitoring of places of detention', adopted November 2017, CAT/OP/7.
[66]   *PREVENTING TORTURE Professional Training Series No 21: The Role of National Preventive Mechanisms* (OHCHR, 2018).

on Africa, the Americas, Asia/Pacific and Europe, with SPT members acting as Country Rapporteur for a number of countries in each. Issues concerning the establishment and operation of NPMs are considered within the teams, which report back to the Plenary which decides on any actions which need to be taken. At most sessions, each regional team will be in contact, usually through video conferencing but occasionally in person, with a variety of states parties concerning progress on establishing NPMs as well as with NPMs themselves. NPMs frequently ask the SPT for guidance on a number of specific questions which have arisen in the course of their work, and some of these have been posted on the SPT website for more general guidance.[67] The SPT has also developed various means of working on matters related to NPMs during its country visits, which over time have taken on something of a hybrid nature.

Initially, SPT country visits were very similar to those of the CPT – and in many ways they remain so today.[68] However, they also provide an opportunity to consider matters concerning the establishment of NPMs too. In its early years the SPT was only able to undertake approximately three regular country visits each year which meant that it had limited opportunities for direct discussions with states and NPMs in the context of visits. As a result, the SPT experimented with a shorter form of visit, focusing only on the work of the NPM. If an NPM had not yet been established, this could be a very short visit meeting only with the national authorities to discuss progress. Only one such visit – known as an NPM Advisory Visit[69] – was ever conducted since it was concluded that there were other ways in which its objectives could have been fulfilled.

A different form of visit – known simply as an NPM visit – proved much more useful.[70] Such visits commenced with meetings with state officials, to highlight the work of the NPM and raise any general questions concerning its legal structure, mandate, financing or operational capacity that the SPT might have. The bulk of the visit, however, was spent with the NPM itself, exploring similar issues but also spending time learning how it went about its work in practice. This usually included accompanying the NPM on one (or more) of its visits so that the SPT could see for itself how it was able to function. The aim was not to 'evaluate' the NPM but to better understand its work and to make recommendations to both the state and to the NPM as appropriate.[71]

Over time, and following some improvements to the resourcing of the SPT, it became possible for it to undertake around 10 visits each year. Given the enhanced means of engagement with NPMs and others through the system of regional teams, and through other informal contacts, the SPT decided that it was no longer necessary to formally distinguish between

---

[67]   Details of Regional Teams and Country Rapporteurs are posted on the SPT website at https://www.ohchr.org/EN/HRBodies/OPCAT/Pages/ContactRegionalTeams.aspx. Published advice to NPMS is to be found at https://www.ohchr.org/EN/HRBodies/OPCAT/Pages/AdvicesToNPMS.aspx. SPT Annual Reports provide information of meetings held with NPMs during Plenary Sessions of the SPT.

[68]   An outline of a typical 'regular' visit is given at https://www.ohchr.org/EN/HRBodies/OPCAT/Pages/Outline.aspx

[69]   This was a three-day visit to Nigeria in April 2014. The report arising from this visit remains confidential.

[70]   The first such visit took place in 2012 to Honduras. Following such visits reports were submitted to both the state party and the NPM. The report to the NPM arising out of this visit has been published. See UN Doc CAT/OP/HND/3 (17 September 2012).

[71]   An outline of a typical 'NPM visit' (rather confusingly referred to as an NPM Advisory visit) is given at https://www.ohchr.org/EN/HRBodies/OPCAT/Pages/NoteSPTAdvisoryvisitstoNPMS.aspx

'NPM' visits and what had colloquially become known as 'Full' visits. As a result, since the start of 2016 the SPT only undertakes 'visits' – and all visits include a period focusing on the work of the NPM (in those countries where an NPM has been established).[72] At the same time, in practice the SPT continues to differentiate between visits which are longer and shorter in duration. Perhaps paradoxically, those which are shorter tend to have an enhanced focus on the NPM. The reason for this is that in those countries with an established NPM there is arguably less need for the SPT to be exercising its own visiting mandate and it is preferable to focus on building relationships with, and the capacity of, the NPM instead. As a result, the SPT now tends to undertake relatively short visits to countries with established and functioning NPMs, and somewhat longer visits to those without. In all visits, however, the SPT will spend some time visiting places of detention in pursuance of its autonomous visiting mandate. In effect, all SPT visits are now means of fulfilling its mandate under both Article 11(a) and Article 11(b) of the OPCAT.

As with the CPT, the reports written following an SPT visit remain confidential unless the state gives consent to their publication. Although the SPT encourages publication, by the end of 2019 only 53 of the 87 visit reports transmitted to states parties and NPMs had been.[73] Nevertheless, this is a significant percentage, and suggests that criticisms that the confidential nature of the process would allow states to avoid public scrutiny were, to a degree, misplaced. As with the CPT, reports are intended to be a prologue to a discussion with the state concerned regarding the implementation of SPT recommendations. States are usually asked to respond in writing within six months of receiving a report, and this is then followed up through a variety of means: further written correspondence, meetings during sessions with representatives of permanent missions, video conferencing both during and outside of sessions with those responsible for actioning recommendations, face-to-face meetings when appropriate and feasible and, of course, on future visits.

It is notable that the idea of a 'regular' programme of visits has not been interpreted as meaning that all states need to be visited before a state may be returned too. Rather, the SPT has adopted a flexible approach which takes account of the broad range of options at its disposal for engaging with states: in effect, a 'visit' is merely one 'tool in the toolbox', and the absence of a visit does not mean that there is an absence of engagement. To that extent, it is true to say that the SPT, through the OPCAT framework, is actively engaging with most of its states parties most of the time – though naturally the intensity of that engagement will vary and will be at its most intense when a visit is being conducted and in its immediate aftermath. It also means that whilst some states have been officially visited twice, a considerable number of states parties (largely in Europe) have not been visited at all.[74]

---

[72] 9th Annual Report of the Subcommittee on Prevention of Torture and Other Cruel, Inhuman or Degrading Treatment or Punishment, 2015, UN Doc, CAT/C/57/4, para 40.

[73] 13th Annual Report of the Subcommittee on Prevention of Torture and Other Cruel, Inhuman or Degrading Treatment or Punishment, 2019, UN Doc, CAT/C/69/3, paras 19–20.

[74] Of the 74 visits undertaken by the end of 2019, 12 were to previously visited countries. These being Benin (2008, 2016), Bolivia (2010, 2017), Brazil (2011, 2017), Cambodia (2009, 2013), Honduras (2009, 2012), Kyrgyzstan (2012, 2018), Liberia (2010, 2018), Maldives (2007, 2014), Mexico (2008, 2016), Paraguay (2009, 2010), Senegal (2012, 2019) and Ukraine (2011, 2016). As can be seen, the period between visits tends to be around seven years, though in some cases is notably shorter. This means that over 25 states parties are yet to be visited.

Unlike the CPT, the SPT no longer announces an 'annual programme' of regular visits.[75] Instead, at the end of each session it announces the next 'tranche' of countries which it plans to visit – usually adding between two and four new states to the list each time. A state to be visited is usually informed of the precise dates approximately three months in advance (though it can be considerably less) and it will usually have been aware that it might be visited for three or four months before that. The net result is that the SPT is able to exercise a considerable degree of flexibility in the design and execution of its visiting programme, and whilst its visits are not 'ad hoc' as such, to the extent that they are determined on the basis of an assessment of need and the likelihood of potential impact, they are more akin to 'ad hoc' visits than to a programme of 'regular' visits determined on the basis of periodicity alone. Given the recent shift in the practice of the CPT, there is an increasing similarity in how they determine and organise their work.

The NPMs

At the time of its drafting, the inclusion of national level oversight was considered by some to be a fatal flaw in the OPCAT system, potentially allowing states to avoid international scrutiny.[76] The original version of this proposal was that there would be an 'either/or' system, with the international mechanism only able to undertake visits if the national mechanism was not established, or manifestly failing in its task.[77] This indeed would have been a weakness, but in the final text of the OPCAT the SPT and the NPMs are complementary and are to work together as part of a common system – a blending of international and national systems within an international treaty framework.[78] This innovative model has proven highly effective in practice and has since become seen as the 'jewel in the crown' of the OPCAT system.[79] Moreover, it is essential – since with some 90 states parties, and with the capacity to undertake no more than 10 official visits per year, it is obvious that the SPT cannot itself be a continual presence within a country. Ongoing national-level scrutiny and oversight, backed by the force of international law and international mechanisms, is likely to be far more potent – and so it has proved.

The OPCAT Article 3 requires states parties to 'set up, designate or maintain at the domestic level one or several visiting bodies for the prevention of torture and other cruel, inhuman or degrading treatment or punishment (hereinafter referred to as the national preventive mechanism)'. This is amplified in Part IV of the OPCAT, concerning NPMs, Article 17 of which provides that:

---

[75] The SPT changed its policy on this in 2016. See the 10th Annual Report of the Subcommittee on Prevention of Torture and Other Cruel, Inhuman or Degrading Treatment or Punishment, 2016, UN Doc, CAT/C/60/3, para 64.

[76] See Evans and Haenni-Dale (n 30 above), 41–42.

[77] This being the proposal in the so-called Mexican Draft. See *ibid*, 38–41.

[78] As the Preamble to the OPCAT puts it, 'Recognizing that ... strengthening the protection of people deprived of their liberty and the full respect for their human rights is a common responsibility shared by all and that international implementing bodies complement and strengthen national measures'.

[79] Steinerte, E, 'The Jewel in the Crown and its Three Guardians: Independence of National Preventive Mechanisms under the Optional Protocol to the IM Convention against Torture' (2014) 14 *Human Rights Law Review* 1.

Each State Party shall maintain, designate or establish, at the latest one year after the entry into force of the present Protocol or of its ratification or accession, one or several independent national preventive mechanisms for the prevention of torture at the domestic level. Mechanisms established by decentralized units may be designated as national preventive mechanisms for the purposes of the present Protocol if they are in conformity with its provisions.

Article 24 permits states parties, at the time of ratification, to delay the implementation of this obligation for up to three years, which in practice grants them a total of four years in which to establish the mechanism.[80]

It is fair to say that the SPT has taken a tolerant approach to states who are tardy in establishing the national mechanism, recognising that this can be an onerous process involving complex legislation. What is important for the SPT is that there is a clear commitment to establishing an OPCAT-compliant NPM in an expeditious time frame, preferably with advice and input from the SPT. However, there are limits to tolerance, and in 2016 the SPT made public a list of states parties 'whose compliance with obligations set out in Article 17 of the Optional Protocol to the Convention against Torture and other Cruel, Inhuman and Degrading Treatment or Punishment (OPCAT) is substantially overdue'.[81] 'Substantially overdue' is understood as meaning at least three years from the date on which the NPM was due to be established, which – unless a state has made a declaration under Article 24 delaying the obligation – means four years from the date of entry into force. Experience suggests that placing states on the list can have a galvanising effect and a number of states which had not designated an NPM have been prompted to do so, and have thus been removed from it.[82] At the time of writing, the list comprises 15 countries, including some which being more than ten years overdue are 'egregiously' so.[83] Whilst this is problematic, it is equally important to bear in mind that 65 states have designated an NPM – over 70 per cent of all states parties. This, in UN terms, is a relatively high rate of compliance with a human rights commitment of this nature.

One reason why compliance is relatively high is that the OPCAT is not prescriptive as regards the type of body which may be designated as an NPM. What is important is that the body or bodies designated be independent and have the mandate and capacity to undertake the functions which they are to fulfil as set out in the OPCAT. These, essentially, are the same as that of the SPT: to be able to undertake visits to places where persons are deprived of their liberty at a time of their choosing and to have unfettered access to all detainees and to all relevant materials, to be able to interview in private and confidentially and to make recommen-

---

[80] A further extension of up to two years may be granted – oddly – with the permission of the CAT. This is a legacy of the older idea of the SPT being a 'real' subcommittee of the CAT. Only one country – Romania – has ever made such a request, which was granted.

[81] See 10th Annual Report of the Subcommittee on Prevention of Torture and Other Cruel, Inhuman or Degrading Treatment or Punishment, 2016 (n 75 above), paras 57–58. The list which is updated at the end of each SPT plenary session is to be found at https://www.ohchr.org/EN/HRBodies/OPCAT/Pages/Article17.aspx

[82] Examples include Cambodia and Lebanon, which had been OPCAT state parties from its early years and which had already been visited by the SPT. Their inclusion on the Article 17 list was an important factor in their making progress towards designation. Other states have taken accelerated action in order to avoid being included in the public listing.

[83] 13th Annual Report of the Subcommittee on Prevention of Torture and Other Cruel, Inhuman or Degrading Treatment or Punishment, 2019 (n 73 above), para 40, these being Benin, Bosnia and Herzegovina, Chile, Liberia and Nigeria.

dations to those in authority concerning both the places visited and concerning matters relating to detention and preventive safeguards more generally.[84] This requires the NPM to have appropriate expertise at its disposal, as well as sufficient funding and operational autonomy.

As every state is different, and will have its own systems of independent oversight, it makes sense to allow states to determine how this is to be achieved.[85] In practice, there are a variety of dominant approaches.[86] In many countries the NPM function is given to an existing (or newly established) National Human Rights Institution. Other countries with well-established Ombudsman's Offices have utilised these, often by extending their mandates in various ways (sometimes referred to as an 'Ombudsman plus' model). Yet other countries already have a plethora of existing sectoral inspectorates and have designated these collectively as comprising the NPM, often with a central co-ordinating body identified or created for the purpose. Further complexities arise in federal countries where different bodies may exist at state and at federal level.[87] All of these very different approaches are in principle acceptable if they deliver the core operational functionality required by the OPCAT.

The OPCAT is clear that it is for the state to designate the NPM, and that the role of the SPT is to offer it advice and assistance.[88] Beyond the generic written advice referred to above, this can take the form of in-depth discussions of various options which are being considered, offering advice on the wording of draft legislation or other relevant documents, and much else besides. Although the SPT does not advocate for a particular model of an NPM, it frequently points out the problems which others have run into when adopting certain models and is happy to give robust advice on what it thinks might work best in the country concerned. The experience of the SPT is that what might work well in one context does not necessarily work well in another. Hence the SPT does not see itself as an 'accreditation' body.[89] It accepts the designation of whatever body the state ultimately chooses to designate, but will then work with both the designated body and the State to ensure that it is able to properly fulfil its OPCAT functions – something that might well necessitate changes, and sometimes quite fundamental changes, to the designated body, its manner of working or to its resourcing.

The reality is that there remains much to be done in order to ensure that NPMs are established, including with an appropriate mandate, and have the requisite capacity to undertake their work. For example, the NPM function is sometimes given to an Ombudsman's office or to an established National Human Rights Institution (NHRI) but without additional resourcing

---

[84]   See generally OPCAT, Articles 18–20 and see Murray et al. (n 30 above), 117–119.

[85]   This has been well understood from the outset. See Murray, R, 'National Preventive Mechanisms under the OPCAT: One Size Does Not Fit All' (2008) 26 *Netherlands Quarterly of Human Rights* 485.

[86]   The Association for the Prevention of Torture maintains an excellent NPM database with interactive links to relevant legislation, as well as descriptive overviews of various forms of NPMs. See https://apt.ch/en/opcat-database/

[87]   See, for example, the NPMs of Argentina, Brazil and Germany, amongst others. There are other complex models – as, for example, in Switzerland where the NPM is based on a Cantonal model, and in the UK where a multiplicity of sectorial bodies comprise the NPM, drawn from the differing jurisdictions of England and Wales, Scotland, Northern Ireland and the Isle of Man.

[88]   The SPT website contains a list of officially designated NPMs at https://www.ohchr.org/EN/HRBodies/OPCAT/Pages/NationalPreventiveMechanisms.aspx

[89]   See SPT Guidelines on National Preventive Mechanisms (n 64 above), para 2: 'Whilst the SPT does not, nor does it intend to formally assess the extent to which NPMs conform to OPCAT requirements, it does consider it a vital part of its role to advise and assist States and NPMs fulfil their obligations under the Optional Protocol'.

being provided to allow it to undertake its additional responsibilities. In such circumstances, NPM-focused activities rarely happen, or rarely happen well. Where the role is devolved to existing inspectoral bodies, the adage 'business as usual' often applies and the fulfilment of the NPM function is little more than an exercise in relabelling existing activities. In some countries, relatively successful NPMs have been weakened by budget cuts or other forms of inappropriate interference. Even where NPMs are operating successfully, there is often a failure by the authorities to take proper account of the recommendations which they make. Against this litany of problems, has the NPM experiment really been a success?

The answer is a resounding yes.[90] Even in those countries where the NPMs are weak, the very fact of their existence involves a recognition of the need for effective independent oversight and the implementation of preventive safeguards. It also means that the SPT, and the international community more generally, can press for the development and enhancement of the mechanism.[91] Peer-to-peer networks of NPMs are also increasingly important in building support and capacity for those in need of assistance.[92] In short, it is a beginning. Equally, there are a considerable number of NPMs which are now very well established, are routinely visiting and are making a real difference to the lives and experiences of detainees. Other bodies have been able to use their designation to further enhance their role and the impact of their recommendations. Perhaps above all, however, is the power of the partnership between the national and the international in changing the nature of the discussion concerning the implementation of human rights obligations. The role accorded to national mechanisms within the OPCAT system has changed the dynamic of prevention by locating the primary engine of oversight at the domestic level, powerfully supported by international machinery. This brings the day-to-day work of internationally mandated oversight closer to the rights holders than ever before, and makes for a more informed understanding of the situations encountered and what needs to be done in response to them. Overall, this marks a major development in thinking about what constitutes effective human rights protection, and where and how 'international' protection of human rights should be undertaken.

WORKING PREVENTATIVELY

It is one thing to establish workable systems of preventive mechanisms. It is another for them to work preventively. As has been acknowledged above, many things contribute to prevention – including holding those responsible to account, providing redress and rehabilitation for torture victims, ensuring that legal systems and structure accord with international obligations, and so forth. These, and much more besides, contribute to the preventive endeavour, or form

---

[90]   See, for example, the conclusions to an extensive quantitative and qualitative study in Carver, R and Handley, L, *Does Torture Prevention Work?* (Liverpool University Press, 2016) and the chapter by the authors of that study in this volume.

[91]   For example, within the UN system issues concerning the establishment and functioning of NPMS are now routinely raised by other human rights bodies and within the Universal Periodic Review process.

[92]   See, for example, the European NPM newsletter, an outgrowth of a Council of Europe and European Union project to support and build capacity for NPMs, available at https://www.coe.int/t/democracy/migration/ressources/npm_newsletter_en.asp

parts of what has been described as the 'preventive package'.[93] As is apparent from this chapter, and indeed this volume, there are a bewildering multiplicity of mechanisms which engage with torture and ill-treatment in very many ways. The previous section has focused on what is distinctive about the methodology of prevention – based on visits – which has been established through the ECPT and the OPCAT. There is no purpose in having a system with a distinctive methodology, however, if in practice it operates as any of the other bodies with relevant competence: having a distinctive methodology needs to be matched with a distinctive approach. This section explores what 'working preventively' means in practice.

The Nature of Preventive Visiting

There is a surprising disparity in the language used to describe preventive visiting which at times reflects a lack of clarity concerning the nature of the exercise. In some ways this is understandable; preventive work draws on many different techniques and is undertaken by various bodies whose work has been shaped by various contexts or mandates which are not necessarily focused on prevention per se. Nevertheless, this can result in practical problems within NPMs comprised of multiple bodies, whose various components may not be working in the same way. It can also mean that some NPMs, whilst carrying out important work, are not necessarily putting prevention at the heart of their work. This is best explored by considering how preventive visiting differs from some other means of oversight with which it is often confused.

A first confusion is to see preventive visiting as a form of investigation. Naturally, preventive visits have 'investigatory' elements: the visiting body will be asking questions, looking at documentation, following up on information, etc. But this does not mean that the purpose of the visit is to conduct an investigation, since doing so would be counter to the ethos of prevention. This is a particular problem in those countries which have designated Ombudsman's offices, and in some countries NHRIs, as their NPM since such institutions often see themselves primarily as 'complaints' mechanisms which investigate allegations of institutional failure or abuse. At its most extreme, this can mean that some NPMs do indeed work as if they were complaints investigators and consider it necessary to be in receipt of complaints before they undertake their work.[94] Preventive visiting then becomes little more than an opportunity to 'drum up' formal complaints. More typically, such NPMs do not consider they need a 'complaint' to trigger their work, but will focus on individual cases during their visits, seeking to resolve them as if they were investigating a complaint. Equally importantly, detainees tend to understand the role of such NPMS as being complaints investigation bodies, and so relate to them in that fashion. For all these reasons, the SPT tends to recommend that where a body with a complaints investigation mandate is designated as the NPM, the NPM function is located in

---

[93]   11th Annual Report of the Subcommittee on Prevention of Torture and Other Cruel, Inhuman or Degrading Treatment or Punishment, 2017, UN Doc, CAT/C/63/4, paras 52–54, concerning the 'Capacity of national preventive mechanisms to work effectively in a preventive manner and the "preventive package"'.

[94]   For example, the author has observed situations in which those undertaking preventive visiting have told detainees with whom they have spoken that they need to lodge complaints before the NPM in question could 'investigate' the matter and report to the authorities.

a separate unit with operational autonomy so that it can develop its own working practices, ethos and identity.[95] Preventive visiting is not the same as complaints-based work.

A second area of confusion is with inspectoral work. Preventive bodies are often described as undertaking 'inspections', and once again, in a general sense they are. But the inspectorial function, properly understood, is subtly but significantly different from preventive visiting. Inspectors generally inspect to standards, the purpose being to determine whether those standards, or expectations, are being complied with. At the end of an inspection the institution will normally be given feedback on the extent to which those standards are being met. It will then be for the institution, or the authorities responsible for them, to seek to address the failings identified. The other side of the 'inspectoral coin' is that those standards will be known in advance and so the institution should know what is expected of it. The result is that the inspection visit is about compliance with standards. Built into this is the assumption that compliance makes for a positive outcome. It is not the place of those undertaking an inspection to challenge the standards which have been set by others – let alone to establish applicable standards themselves. Preventive visiting goes beyond this, allowing those undertaking visits to think creatively about what ought to be done in the light of the circumstances which they encounter and to make recommendations accordingly.

A final point of comparison is with monitoring, and it is common to refer to preventive visiting – indeed any form of human rights oversight – as a 'monitoring' exercise.[96] Yet this too falls short of what is involved. Monitoring implies a degree of passivity – it is the observation of what is occurring and the reporting of this to others who make judgments on the basis of the information received.[97] It also can imply observation over time – something which few NPMs are truly able to do, and which the international preventive visiting mechanisms certainly cannot.[98] Monitoring will often form a part of inspection, feeding into an inspectoral assessment. It is rarely the role of the monitors to respond proactively to what they observe, in the sense of formulating and leading an operational or policy response to the concerns which had arisen from their observations.

These brief comparisons are not intended to suggest that the work of investigators, inspectors or monitors is in any sense deficient or unimportant. Each plays an important role, including in the prevention of torture and ill-treatment in places of deprivation of liberty.[99] The point is that none of these fully captures the essence of preventive visiting, which is in some senses an amalgam of elements of these roles but with an added element of autonomy. Preventive

---

[95] SPT Guidelines on National Preventive Mechanisms (n 64 above), para 32: 'Where the body designated as the NPM performs other functions in addition to those under the Optional Protocol, its NPM functions should be located within a separate unit or department, with its own staff and budget'.

[96] See, by way of example, Kicker, R, *Standard Setting through Monitoring? The Role of Council of Europe Expert Bodies in the Development of Human Rights* (Council of Europe Press, 2012).

[97] An excellent example being election monitoring, which is also routinely described as election observation.

[98] For example, rarely does the SPT spend more than a single day in a place of detention and can often visit several small facilities in the course of a day. The CPT, whose visits are longer, can devote more time to larger facilities. The practice of NPMs varies considerably, but few spend more than a few days in any one place of detention. Of course, their ability to return in a relatively short time frame does allow them to monitor 'over time', though in a somewhat different manner.

[99] For an interesting analysis, drawing on the interplay between international and national oversight mechanisms see Daems, T and Robert, L, *Europe in Prisons: Assessing the Impact of European Institutions on National Prison Systems* (Palgrave, 2017).

visiting is, simply put, the process of exploring, through visit, discussion and examination, the practical experiences of those in detention in order to inform the making of recommendations by the visiting body on how best to reduce the likelihood of torture or ill-treatment. It is what the methodology is designed to deliver – and it ought not to be shackled by preconceived concepts of the nature of preventive working.

The Question of Standards

As the discussion concerning the nature of prevention makes clear, one of the difficulties concerning preventive work concerns the use of standards. As has already been observed, the SPT has taken the view that

> ... there is more to the prevention of torture and ill-treatment than compliance with legal commitments. In this sense, the prevention of torture and ill-treatment embraces – or should embrace – as many as possible of those things which in a given situation can contribute towards the lessening of the likelihood or risk of torture or ill-treatment occurring.[100]

Standards, of course, are not necessarily legal commitments, in the sense that a failure to comply with them amount to a breach of a legal obligation or give rise to legal responsibility. A failure to do so might however give rise to other forms of regulatory intervention by relevant national authorities. The question here concerns the role which standards play in the context of preventive visiting. There are two dimensions to this.

The role of standards
The first dimension concerns the roles that standards play in the context of preventive visiting. From the outset, the CPT took the view that its work had to be informed by standards which set out the expectations of the Committee in key areas. Its website has a section entitled 'Standards and Tools' which sets out an extensive array of 29 statements, fact sheets or checklists grouped into eight discrete subject areas – Police/Law enforcement, Prisons, Immigration detention, Psychiatric establishments/Social Care institutions, Juveniles, Women, Accountability/ Complaints mechanisms and Transport.[101] These have developed over time and vary in focus, from the overarching and general, such as women in prisons,[102] to the focused and granular, such as electrical discharge weapons.[103] Some of these standards are essentially normative and set out what the CPT considers to be fundamental rights and safeguards. Others are described as 'tools' which are largely procedural, describing appropriate methodologies for undertaking preventive work.[104] Lying between these two poles are those standards – in practice, the major-

---

[100] 'The approach of the Subcommittee on Prevention of Torture to the concept of prevention of torture and other cruel, inhuman or degrading treatment or punishment under the Optional Protocol to the Convention against Torture and Other Cruel, Inhuman or Degrading Treatment or Punishment' (n 19 above), para 3.

[101] https://www.coe.int/en/web/cpt/standards

[102] 10th General Report on the CPT's Activities (2000), CPT/Inf (2000) 13, paras 21–33.

[103] 20th General Report on the CPT's Activities (2010), CPT/Inf (2010) 28, paras 65–84.

[104] These are generally referred to as checklists, are not included in the General Reports and carry the names of authors. See, for example, 'Checklist for the evaluation of a psychiatric hospital', CPT (2009) 56 Rev; 'Checklist for visits to social care institutions where persons may be deprived of their liberty', CPT/Inf (2015) 23; 'Inspection of a prison medical service by a CPT doctor', CPT/Inf (2017)/20.

ity – which are considered desirable since they support and reinforce the prohibition of torture and ill-treatment, but the application of which may be more context specific. Taken overall, these statements of standards inform the work of the CPT when making specific recommendations and provide a basis upon which to make overall evaluative judgments, but how they do so differs.

The SPT has followed a somewhat different path. Rather than set out clearly articulated standards, in several of its Annual Reports it has offered reflections on the approach to prevention in a variety of contexts or in relation to a variety of concerns. Some, such as its document on the approach to pre-trial detention[105] and women[106] are not dissimilar from some of the more discursive CPT statements which seek to elaborate on the more formally couched sets of standards which the CPT had previously issued. Others tackle thematic topics which the CPT has not commented on in a similar way – examples include the SPT's papers on torture and corruption,[107] informed consent to medical treatment,[108] and torture and LGBTI persons.[109] Published SPT reports suggest that its approach it largely similar to that of the CPT in most areas of their common work, even if it has not issued statements setting out fundamental standards in the same way. Like the CPT, however, the SPT has recently moved in the direction of offering procedural guidance.[110]

The lack of more clearly articulated standards by the SPT is partly moderated by the references in the OPCAT itself to its being guided by 'the norms of the United Nations concerning the treatment of persons deprived of their liberty'.[111] NPMs likewise are to make recommendations 'taking into consideration the relevant norms of the United Nations'.[112] Whilst there is no definitive list of such norms, it is clear that well-attested and formally adopted documents such as the Nelson Mandela Rules (the updated UN Standard Minimum Rules for the Treatment of Prisoners) would be embraced by this.[113] Whilst, then, there is room for debate at the margins concerning what standards are to be drawn on by preventive visiting bodies, and whilst there may be some areas in which opinions differ, it seems clear that there is quite enough guidance to allow such bodies to exercise their preventive mandates in an informed fashion.

---

[105] 'Pretrial detention and the prevention of torture and other ill-treatment', 8th Annual Report of the Subcommittee on Prevention of Torture and Other Cruel, Inhuman or Degrading Treatment or Punishment, 2014, UN Doc CAT/C/54/2, paras 73–96.

[106] 'Prevention of torture and ill-treatment of women deprived of their liberty', adopted November 2015, UN Doc CAT/OP/27/1.

[107] 'Corruption and prevention of torture and other ill-treatment', 7th Annual Report of the Subcommittee on Prevention of Torture and Other Cruel, Inhuman or Degrading Treatment or Punishment, 2013, UN Doc CAT/C/52/2, paras 72–100.

[108] 'Approach of the Subcommittee on Prevention of Torture and Other Cruel, Inhuman or Degrading Treatment or Punishment regarding the rights of persons institutionalized and treated medically without informed consent', adopted November 2015, UN Doc CAT/OP/27/2.

[109] 'Prevention of torture and other cruel, inhuman or degrading treatment or punishment of lesbian, gay, bisexual, transgender and intersex persons', 9th Annual Report of the Subcommittee on Prevention of Torture and Other Cruel, Inhuman or Degrading Treatment or Punishment (n 72 above), paras 48–82.

[110] See 'National preventive mechanism checklist on health-care issues relating to the monitoring of places of detention', adopted November 2017 (n 65 above). Though couched as advice to NPMs, it is of general application and doubtless informs the practical work of the SPT too.

[111] OPCAT, Article 2(2).

[112] *Ibid*, Article 19(b).

[113] United Nations Standard Minimum Rules for the Treatment of Prisoners (the Nelson Mandela Rules), UN Doc A/RES/70/175 (17 December 2015).

The application of standards

This conclusion is buttressed by the second dimension which concerns the application of standards. It is axiomatic that it is not the role of preventive bodies to determine whether a state, or an institution, has or has not violated a legal obligation or a regulatory standard. Whilst it is true that the reports of such bodies may well recount factual evidence which means that in its view such a breach has occurred – and it may well say so – this has no formal status as a finding, other than its being the view of the body concerned.[114] The significance of a preventive visiting body drawing such a conclusion lies in the force which it adds to the weight of its preventive recommendations. Additionally, the failure of a state to respond positively to preventive recommendations made in the light of clear evidence that torture has occurred is likely to influence the attitude of others towards the state in question. Nevertheless, the primary purpose of a visit, and of a visit report, is to be preventive. Given that reports of the international visiting bodies are in principle confidential, they are a poor medium for condemnation and their purpose is to present constructive recommendations aimed at improving the protections of those deprived of their liberty. Honesty is one thing, confrontation is another. Beyond this, however, lie a number of difficult questions concerning the application of standards in visit reports and what has been sometimes termed 'variable geometry'.

Visiting bodies are not inspectors tasked with ensuring that certain standards are met in practice. Does this mean that they are entitled to have different expectations in different contexts? It is clearly the case that the different legal, social, cultural and political systems in the countries of the world mean that different approaches may need to be taken.[115] This does not mean that it can be acceptable to torture or ill-treat persons in one country but not in another. It does, however, mean that what might amount to degrading treatment might vary from one context to another. For example, in some parts of the world large multiple occupancy prison cells are the norm, whereas in others they are very much frowned upon. It is doubtful whether it is sensible to insist that a given model is preferable from a preventive point of view: what matters is that within the relevant model preventive approaches are maximised.[116]

Beyond this lies the question of whether it is appropriate to take account of the practical capacity of the state to bring about change. There may be practical factors which make a particular desired course of action all but impossible to achieve: for example, the SPT asks that NPMs be established through or be underpinned by legislation. In some countries this is just not possible, or wholly impractical. Under such circumstances, it is futile to insist on what cannot be done when an entirely practical alternative is available. But how far does one take this? To what extent can the geography of a country justify the departure from safeguards con-

---

[114] See, for example, the discussion above concerning the relationship between the CPT and the ECtHR.

[115] A point acknowledged in the Nelson Mandela Rules (n 113 above), Preliminary Observation 2 of which notes that 'In view of the great variety of legal, social, economic and geographical conditions in the world, it is evident that not all of the rules are capable of application in all places and at all times. They should, however, serve to stimulate a constant endeavour to overcome practical difficulties in the way of their application, in the knowledge that they represent, as a whole, the minimum conditions which are accepted as suitable by the United Nations'.

[116] Other examples might include practices which are innocuous in some contexts but which due to culture or religious factors are contentious in others.

cerning the length of time one can be held in detention before being brought before a judicial authority[117] – or can what this means in practice be modulated to take account of such factors?

Finally, there is an even more delicate question, concerning the extent to which the nature of the dialogue between the visiting body and the state, or institution, in question can influence the nature of the recommendations made: might it recommend 'baby steps' which, even if achieved, would fall far short of what is considered appropriate in order to help build a preventive culture? Should it 'tone down' any criticisms in its reports in order to encourage a more positive response? Or should it tone down criticisms in recognition of positive steps taken? In short, should the visiting body see its reports and recommendations as a tool within a broader strategic approach? The problem in doing that is, if made public and shorn of this context, such recommendations might appear to be applying 'double standards' when compared with other, similar situations.[118]

In practice, visiting bodies make such assessments all the time, sometimes consciously, sometimes not. Preventive visiting is context driven and that context includes how the report may be responded to by the national authorities. Visiting bodies must inevitably take this into account if their work is to be effective, something often overlooked by those who criticise preventive bodies for inconsistency in the application of their preventive standards. Too much ought not to be read into slight differences in the way some standards are presented from report to report. There may be good reasons for doing so, and it may not mean that there is a significant change in the underlying approach to the issue in question.

Relationships with Other Bodies

The distinct nature of preventive working inevitably means that the relationships between preventive visiting bodies and other human rights mechanisms working in the field of torture prevention can at times be strained. Healthy tensions are to be welcomed. Experience suggests, however, that the starting point has all too often been one of mild (or more) suspicion and that it is only over time that more constructive relationships have developed.

The ECPT and the ECHR

The ECPT Preamble stresses that its purpose is to strengthen the protection of persons deprived of their liberty 'by non-judicial means of a preventive nature', words which are repeated verbatim in the Preamble to the OPCAT. The origins of this lie in concerns of the European Court of Human Rights that the CPT should not usurp its judicial function.[119] This is underlined by the Explanatory Report to the ECPT, which rather bluntly says that 'The Committee should not seek to interfere in the interpretation and application of Article 3 [of the ECHR]'.[120] As a result, the CPT scrupulously avoids making 'determinations' of whether there has been a breach of the ECHR and stresses that 'the role of the Committee is not to condemn

---

[117] See, for example, *Medvedyev and Others v. France* [GC], no 3394/03, ECHR 2010, where it was accepted that the requirement of being brought before a judicial authority 'promptly' needed to take account of the context of the arrest having taken place at sea.

[118] See discussion in Bicknell, Evans and Morgan (n 35 above), 51–57 and the case studies on the relationship between the CPT and individual states *passim*.

[119] See Evans and Morgan, *Preventing Torture* (n 22 above), 118–122.

[120] Explanatory Report, para 27. For an early analysis of the relationship, stressing the scope for difference in their respective approaches see Peukert, W, 'The ECPT and the ECHR' in Morgan, R and

States, but rather to assist them to prevent the ill-treatment of persons deprived of their liberty'.[121] Nevertheless, its work has had a profound effect on the interpretation and application of Article 3, and the Court now draws heavily on the CPT's factual findings and evaluations in its decision-making.[122]

The nature of the relationship was set out by the Grand Chamber in *Muršić v. Croatia*,[123] when it said that the Court 'performs a conceptually different role to the one assigned to the CPT', this being 'pre-emptive action aimed at prevention, which, by its very nature, aims at a degree of protection that is greater than that upheld by the Court when deciding cases concerning conditions of detention'.[124] Indeed, this suggests that the standards applied by the CPT ought to be somewhat more stringent than those applied by the Court if they are to be preventive in nature. This reflects the idea that the CPT patrols the 'cordon sanitaire' around the treatment of detainees, and that not all that falls within the parameters of prevention necessarily violates the prohibition. By determining what amounts to a breach of Article 3, it is the Court that determines what is to be prevented. At the same time, the Court 'remains attentive to the standards developed by the CPT and, notwithstanding their different positions, it gives careful scrutiny to cases where the particular conditions of detention fall below the CPT's standard'.[125] Therefore, the work of the CPT acts as a source of challenge to the Court's thinking concerning what may amount to a breach. This is particularly important, since in recent years the Court's work has itself developed in what might be called a 'preventive' direction through the development of 'pilot judgments', which may well be as effective in bringing about systemic change as the CPT's own recommendations on which these judgments draw.[126]

The CPT has said that 'The work of the CPT is designed to be an integrated part of the Council of Europe system for the protection of human rights, placing a proactive non-judicial mechanism alongside the existing reactive judicial mechanism of the European Court of Human Rights'.[127] In truth, 'proactive' and 'reactive' measures are not so easily distinguished: a reaction to one situation may be an act of prevention in relation to another. Similarly, the 'bright line' between the judicial and non-judicial approaches is also difficult to maintain in practice. The progressive blurring of the boundaries between the work of the CPT and the

---

Evans, M, *Preventing Torture: The Standards of the European Committee for the Prevention of Torture in Context* (Oxford University Press, 1999), 89–92.

[121]   This is routinely set out in the sections of its General Reports concerning 'The CPT's mandate and modus operandi'. See, for example, 28th General Report on the CPT's Activities (2018) (n 40 above), 41.

[122]   For an overview of early practice see Murdoch, J, *The Treatment of Prisoners: European Standards* (Council of Europe Press, 2006), 46–52.

[123]   *Muršić v. Croatia* [GC], no 7334/13, 20 October 2016.

[124]   *Ibid*, para 113.

[125]   *Ibid.*

[126]   Key examples of cases in which the ECtHR has in effect set out standards to be generally applied within the country to which they are addressed include *Ananyev and Others v. Russia*, nos 42525/07 and 60800/08, 10 January 2012; *Torreggiani and Others v. Italy*, nos 43517/09 and 6 others, 8 January 2013; *Neshkov and Others v. Bulgaria*, nos 36925/10 and 5 others, 27 January 2015; *Varga and Others v. Hungary*, nos 14097/12 and 5 others, 10 March 2015; *W.D. v. Belgium*, no 73548/13, 6 September 2016. For background see Leach, P, Hardman, H, Stephenson, S and Blitz, B, *Responding to Systemic Human Rights Violations: An Analysis of 'Pilot Judgments' of the European Court of Human Rights and Their Impact at National Level* (Intersentia, 2010). See also the ECtHR Pilot Judgment Fact sheet (January 2020) at https://www.echr.coe.int/Documents/FS_Pilot_judgments_ENG.pdf

[127]   See 'The CPT's mandate and modus operandi' (n 121 above).

Court – despite occasional attempts to maintain a respectful distance between themselves – is likely to continue. What is clear is that the suspicion of the early years is long gone and there is now a positive and symbiotic relationship.

The CPT and the SPT
When the ECPT was drafted no other international body had a preventive visiting mandate, other than the ICRC.[128] When the OPCAT was drafted the situation was very different, and its role in relation to ECPT state parties was questioned. As a result, OPCAT Article 31 provides that:

> The provisions of this present Protocol shall not affect the obligations of States Parties under any regional convention instituting a system of visits to places of detention. The Subcommittee on Prevention and the bodies established under such regional conventions are encouraged to consult and cooperate with a view to avoiding duplication and promoting effectively the objectives of the present Protocol.[129]

Initial reports of meetings suggested a keen desire for a close relationship[130] and at a major conference convened by the CPT in Strasbourg in 2009, shortly after the SPT had commenced its work, the conveners observed:

> With more actors on the stage, there is a greater need for coordination and to share information about what each body is doing, how they are going about their tasks and what they are finding. It is also important that preventive bodies do not develop contradictory and diverging standards but instead ensure a degree of coherence.[131]

Nevertheless, there was, initially, something of a sense that this was 'one-way traffic', with the SPT being expected to fall into line with CPT practice and approaches.[132]

As regards standards, in practice the SPT has gone a long way to mitigate the risk of contradiction or divergence by deciding not to issue formal statements of standards as such and to

---

[128] Indeed, ECPT, Article 17(3) limits the ability of the CPT to visit places regularly visited by the ICRC, but this does not appear to have hampered its work in practice. See Evans and Morgan (n 22 above), 128.

[129] This is further supported by OPCAT Article 11(c), which mandates the SPT to 'Co-operate, for the prevention of torture in general, with the relevant United Nations organs and mechanisms as well as with the international, regional and national institutions or organisations working towards the strengthening of the protection of all persons against torture and other cruel, inhuman or degrading treatment or punishment'. This, again, clearly embraces the ECPT and the CPT. The 1991 Costa Rica draft text went further, suggesting that the international body should only undertake visits in exceptional circumstances if there was a regional mechanism. See generally Nowak, Binz and Monina (n 30 above), 1001–1006.

[130] See, for example, 17th General Report on the CPT's Activities (2006–07), CPT/Inf(2007)39, para 18; 18th General Report on the CPT's Activities (2007–08), CPT/Inf(2008)25, para 22. This no doubt reflecting the fact that the first Chair of the SPT, Silvia Casale, had previously been a long-serving member and President of the CPT.

[131] See the Conference Proceedings published as *New Partnerships for Torture Prevention in Europe* (Council of Europe/APT, 2010), 7–8.

[132] Something of a low point in relations occurred in 2012 when the CPT addressed 'Relationships between the CPT and NPMs' (and also matters concerning its relationship with the SPT) in its General Report without any prior notification, let alone consultation with the SPT. See 22nd General Report on the CPT's Activities (2011–12), CPT/Inf (2012)25, paras 27–52.

focus instead on the crafting of recommendations relevant to the particular situation in hand, drawing on the many sets of standards that already existed. This means that there is, at least for the time being, no real cause for concern that the SPT might propagate 'rival' standards to that of the CPT. Nevertheless, the CPT ought to be alert to the nature and focus of SPT recommendations as these will certainly convey a flavour of its thinking as regards what it believes to be of significance.

As regards operational issues, coordination was initially largely informal, this facilitated by a considerable number of SPT members having been, or being, CPT members. In its early years the SPT tended not to visit ECPT states parties, but this changed over time and as it did so the need for more effective forms of coordination became clear. To that end, in July 2018 the CPT and SPT had an 'exchange of letters' which sought to enhance cooperation and coordination through better information sharing. It also encouraged a 'strategic division of labour' by which the SPT would place primary emphasis on the work of the NPMs during its visits (this clearly falling within the mandate of the SPT under the OPCAT) rather than on visiting places of detention which could be visited by the CPT, thus freeing up time and resources for the SPT to undertake visiting work in other parts of the world where such regional mechanism did not exist.[133] It is too soon to tell how this works out in practice but given the financial and resourcing pressures which both bodies work under (in differing degrees) the sense of taking such an approach is obvious.

The SPT and the CAT

The SPT is the creation of an Optional Protocol to the UNCAT and so, whilst it is a wholly autonomous body, there are quite properly strong institutional bonds between them. Some of these are formal and provided for in the text of the OPCAT itself. The most significant of these is that public statements can be made by the CAT at the request of the SPT concerning situations in which states parties have not cooperated with the SPT, or taken steps to improve the situation in the light of its recommendations.[134] The precise implications of this are not entirely obvious. It does not, and has not, prevented the SPT from issuing statements which make it clear that states have not cooperated with the SPT – notably when it has suspended or terminated visits on the ground of non-cooperation.[135] Moreover, the CAT is yet to issue such a statement at the request of the SPT, and it seems safe to conclude that, in practice, this process is something of a dead letter.[136]

Rather than this being a mark of a poor relationship, it should be considered the opposite. The OPCAT provides that their sessions should be held simultaneously at least once each

---

[133]   12th Annual Report of the Subcommittee on Prevention of Torture and Other Cruel, Inhuman or Degrading Treatment or Punishment, 2017, UN Doc CAT/C/66/2, para 48.

[134]   OPCAT, Article 16(4).

[135]   Visits to Azerbaijan (2014) and Ukraine (2016) were suspended and later resumed. The visit to Rwanda (2017) was suspended and later terminated on grounds of non-cooperation. Press notices were released at each stage of these processes by the SPT and are available on the SPT website.

[136]   The only documented instance of its use being contemplated is recorded in the 11th Annual Report of the Subcommittee on Prevention of Torture and Other Cruel, Inhuman or Degrading Treatment or Punishment, 2017 (n 93 above), paras 56–58, where it is noted that a situation was referred by the SPT to the CAT but was resolved rendering further consideration of it unnecessary.

year.[137] As a result, their sessions overlap in November of each year and a joint session (usually lasting up to three hours) routinely takes place. In its early years this tended to be a rather awkward and stilted affair, with members of the CAT often asking questions of the SPT as if they were reporting to it and making demands for information. Over time, this has shifted towards jointly organised meetings at which both bodies meet with others and, as reported in the latest SPT Annual Report, there is now discussion of 'the implementation of the obligations of the Convention and of the Optional Protocol thereto in a range of States of current mutual interest', suggesting a heightened degree of substantive exchange.[138] The Report also records other ways in which relationships have developed positively over time, including the SPT 'transmitting to the Committee against Torture suggestions for it to consider concerning States parties to the Optional Protocol, the reports of which are to be considered at forthcoming sessions of the Committee, and issues for it to consider raising with State parties under the simplified reporting procedure'.[139]

It is still the case that the reports produced by the SPT remain confidential and are not available to the CAT, just as activities undertaken within the framework of the CAT's confidential inquiry procedure remain beyond the knowledge of the SPT.[140] For some, this may seem surprising given their close familial relationship within the UN treaty body system. However, this does not appear to pose practical problems. What has become apparent over time are the benefits to be gained by supporting each other's work; with the SPT raising issues concerning the implementation of states' obligations under the UNCAT and the implementation of recommendations in the Concluding Observations of the CAT, and the CAT increasingly raising questions through the Reporting process concerning the establishment and effective working of NPMs. Once again, over time there has been a transition from suspicion to mutual support.[141]

The NPMS and their interlocutors
The position regarding NPMs has taken a different trajectory to those considered in the preceding sections. Since the NPMs are creatures of the OPCAT (even if many NPMs have long and distinguished histories of preventive work predating their designation), they have from the outset tended to look to the SPT and others within the international framework for guidance and support in fulfilling their OPCAT mandates. The various ways in which the SPT has responded to this, through Guidelines and guidance, has been discussed previously. The SPT has faced a very real problem in meeting the needs of NPMs for more practical training and support and this has led to other international NGOs and organisations taking initiatives

---

[137] OPCAT, Article 10(3). It does not say that the purpose is to facilitate meetings. The original purpose of this was probably to prevent a person being a member of both the CAT and the SPT at the same time.

[138] 13th Annual Report of the Subcommittee on Prevention of Torture and Other Cruel, Inhuman or Degrading Treatment or Punishment, 2019 (n 73 above), para 34.

[139] *Ibid.*

[140] UNCAT, Article 20. For a detailed examination of the inquiry procedure under Article 20 see Gaer in this volume.

[141] For an extended exploration of the interaction between the SPT and CAT and the UN Special Rapporteur on Torture see Evans, M, 'The Special Rapporteur on Torture in the Developing Architecture of UN Torture Protection' in Nolan, A, Freedman, R and Murphy, T, *The United Nations Special Procedures System* (Brill/Nijhoff, 2017), 351.

in support of them. Prominent among these have been the Association for the Prevention of Torture, the Council of Europe, the European Union and the Organisation for Security and Co-operation in Europe, though this by no means exhausts the list. The CPT has issued guidance concerning NPMs, and many regional organisations have sponsored and supported NPM-related activities. There is, then, no shortage of international support for their work.

Equally importantly, there has been a growth in networking between NPMs themselves. Whereas in the early years of the OPCAT system it took the 'convening power' of international organisations to bring NPMs together, those that have become better established in their operational function and institutional security have been able to focus on sharing their own experiences and practices and lending each other mutual support. This is particularly important given the increasing prevalence of cross-border issues relating to migration detention, detention at sea and forced returns, as well as more general questions concerning non-refoulment. The interplay between NPMs holds out the prospect of the emergence of a 'meso' tier of prevention, operating at what might be termed the transnational, rather than the national or international level. Transnational prevention is a new field which merits careful exploration in the years ahead.

For now, however, the principle challenge facing most NPMs is how to ensure that their recommendations are responded to appropriately by their national interlocutors. There is no shortage of preventive recommendations being generated, but too often these provoke negative responses rather than positive engagement. Indeed, a recurring concern for the SPT is the extent to which NPMS may be subject to forms of 'reprisals' for the work that they do – something which is expressly forbidden by the OPCAT and which the SPT invariably takes up on their behalf where there is evidence of its having occurred, or a credible risk that it may occur.[142] It is already the case that the NPMs take up the recommendations found in the published reports of the CPT and SPT – indeed, in the case of the SPT the NPMS can take up the recommendations made in unpublished reports since the OPCAT permits these to be released in confidence to the NPM for the state in question.[143] Rather than focusing on the development and capacity building of NPMs, it may be that the next phase in building an effective system of torture prevention should concentrate on enhanced implementation of NPMs' recommendations, with international – and regional – preventive mechanisms working more closely with NPMs to assist in this.

CONCLUSION

The chapter has focused on the mechanisms of prevention and on the preventive approach towards combatting torture and ill-treatment. It is premised on the belief that whilst all forms of intervention have preventive effects, a distinctive preventive methodology based on visits has now come into being which needs to be properly understood, supported and engaged with.

---

[142]   See OPCAT, Article 21, this being the clearest source of legal obligation against sanctions found in any of the UN human rights treaties. The SPT adopted a formal policy on reprisals in 2016. See 'Policy of the Subcommittee on Prevention of Torture and Other Cruel, Inhuman or Degrading Treatment or Punishment on reprisals in relation to its visiting mandate', UN Doc CAT/OP/6/Rev.1.

[143]   OPCAT, Article 16(1).

It is merely an *additional* tool, though a very powerful one. As the SPT itself has indicated,[144] there is nothing exclusive about the preventive endeavour and there ought to be no sense of competition between those working in different ways and from different starting points towards the common goal of ensuring that no one is subjected to torture or cruel or inhuman treatment or punishment. The prohibition of torture requires the prevention of torture, but it should never become a debate between means. The key lies in seeking to develop and utilise effectively all those means which can play a part in addressing the prevalence and impact of torture.

There is no doubt that the preventive mechanisms described in this chapter have mandates of the utmost potency: to be able, as of right, to enter into any place where persons are suspected of being deprived of liberty, and having unfettered access to all parts of such places and all documentation within such places as well as confidential access to all persons within such places marks them out within the panoply of international rights protection. This is powerfully reinforced by the obligation to establish such mechanisms at the national level and for the national and international to work alongside each other in close mutual support. There is much to be learnt from this model for human rights protection more generally.

But it also remains the case that the international mechanisms lack the capacity they need to be able to exercise their mandates as they ought (let alone as they would wish). It is also the case that too many states have either failed to establish NPMs at all or have established NPMs which are not in accordance with the requirements of the OPCAT or are not in practice able to exercise their mandates as the OPCAT requires, or they have failed to pay sufficient attention to the work of the NPMS which they have established. Globally, it also remains the case that over 70 states parties to the UNCAT are yet to ratify the OPCAT at all. There is, then, much to be done before the full potential of the preventive mechanisms which have been imagined and established by the international community is fully realised.

---

[144] For example, as regards NPMS, it has said that they 'should complement rather than replace existing systems of oversight and [their] establishment should not preclude the creation or operation of other such complementary systems' (SPT Guidelines on National Preventive Mechanisms (n 64 above), para 5).

13. International law, crime and torture

Robert Cryer

INTRODUCTION

Torture raises many issues for international law, some of which are related to international crimes in the core sense, to transnational law, as well as human rights law and domestic law. Here the criminal law aspects, especially the definitional aspects of the crime(s) will be covered. The chapter will begin by distinguishing two ways in which international law relates to criminalisation in general before discussing the definitions of torture found in the 1984 UN Convention Against Torture (UNCAT) and in the law of genocide, crimes against humanity and war crimes.

INTERNATIONAL CRIMES AND TRANSNATIONAL CRIMES

It is necessary to differentiate two different bodies of criminal law, international crimes in the narrow sense and what are often called 'transnational crimes'.[1] Despite the fact that the two are different, they are sometimes dealt with together, under the general rubric of 'international crimes'. It is true that they are 'fuzzy sets', i.e. the boundaries between the two sets of crimes are not impermeable, and there are disagreements about whether certain crimes fall within one category or the other. Indeed there is considerable debate about what amounts to an international crime, and the criteria that must be applied to identify one.[2] Some, not without justification, argue that no standard definition of an international crime exists.[3] However, it is a distinction that States seem to draw themselves and whilst logic may dictate differentially, States are the primary creators of international law. Their decisions can and ought to be critiqued, but those critiques are best understood as examples of what Jeremy Bentham would have described as censorial, rather than descriptive jurisprudence.[4]

It must also be noted that there can be conduct which falls under both categories. Torture, for example, can be a war crime or a crime against humanity, and is subject to the treaty-regime

---

[1]   Two useful discussions are Broomhall, B, *International Justice and the International Criminal Court: Between Sovereignty and the Rule of Law* (Oxford University Press, 2003), 10–23 and Boister, N, 'Transnational Criminal Law?' (2003) 14 *European Journal of International Law* 953.

[2]   For recent contributions see, e.g. Heller, KJ, 'What is an International Crime? (A Revisionist History)' (2017) 58 *Harvard International Law Journal* 353; Greenawalt, AKA, 'What is an International Crime? in Heller, KJ, Mégret, F, Nouwven, SMH, Ohlin JD and Robinson D (eds), *The Oxford Companion to International Criminal Justice* (Oxford University Press, 2120), 293; Chechtman, A, 'A Theory of International Crimes: Conceptual and Normative Issues' in *ibid*, 317; Hathaway, O et al., 'What is a War Crime?' (2019) 44 *Yale Journal of International Law* 53.

[3]   O'Keefe, R, *International Criminal Law* (Oxford University Press, 2015), 47.

[4]   That is, on the basis of *lex ferenda* rather than *lex lata*, see Schwazenberger, G, 'The Eichmann Judgment: An Essay in Censorial Jurisprudence' (1962) 15 *Current Legal Problems* 248.

of the UNCAT.[5] But, as will be seen, there are specific consequences which follow from how such conduct is categorised, so care ought to be taken to determine accurately which classification best describes a particular prohibition regime.

International Crimes

What we often call international crimes[6] are traditionally seen as those which have been tried before international criminal tribunals, i.e. aggression, crimes against humanity, genocide and war crimes. The most important thing about these crimes, as explained by the famous dictum of the Nuremberg International Military Tribunal, is that:

> Crimes against international law are committed by men, not abstract entities, and only by punishing individuals who commit such crimes can the provisions of international law be enforced ... individuals have international duties which transcend the national obligations of obedience imposed by the individual state.[7]

Hence, the fundamental point to understand about these crimes is that the locus of the criminal prohibition is not the domestic legal order, but the international one. In other words, States have decided that international law, in exceptional circumstances, ought to bypass the domestic legal order and criminalise behaviour directly. The consequences of this will be returned to later.

Transnational Crimes

Transnational crimes cover a broad range of conduct. Examples of such crimes range from cutting submarine cables[8] to engaging in the slave trade[9] and hijacking.[10] Transnational crimes often have little in common, other than the fact States have decided that some form of international legal action ought to be taken to mutually suppress such behaviour.

The fundamental nature of such crimes is well explained by Neil Boister:

> under I[nternational] C[riminal] L[aw], T[ransnational] C[riminal] L[aw] does not create direct penal responsibility under international law. T[ransnational] C[riminal] L[aw] is an indirect system of inter-state obligations generating national penal laws. The suppression conventions impose obligations on state parties to enact and enforce certain municipal offences.[11]

---

[5]   Convention against Torture and Other Cruel, Inhuman or Degrading Treatment or Punishment (adopted 10 December 1984, entered into force 26 June 1987) 1465 UNTS 85.

[6]   In general, see Schwarzenberger, G, 'The Problem of an International Criminal Law' (1950) 3 *Current Legal Problems* 263.

[7]   'Nuremberg IMT: Judgment and Sentence' (1947) 41 *American Journal of International Law* 172, 221.

[8]   United Nations Convention on the Law of the Sea (adopted 10 December 1982, entered into force 16 November 1994) 1833 UNTS 3, Articles 112–115.

[9]   E.g. International Convention for the Suppression of the Traffic in Women and Children (adopted 30 September 1921, entered into force 15 June 1922) 9 LNTS 415.

[10]   E.g. Hague Convention for the Suppression of Unlawful Acts Against the Safety of Civil Aviation 975 UNTS 177.

[11]   Boister (n 1 above), 962.

In other words, these treaties (and where they reflect custom, obligations under that law)[12] oblige States to use their own criminal laws to place obligations on people subject to their jurisdiction. The fundamental point is that the international legal obligations are on States, rather than individuals. This can be shown by reference to one of the treaties which falls under this category; the International Convention for the Suppression of Acts of Nuclear Terrorism.[13] The Convention follows the tradition of such conventions by setting out an offence (in Article 2), and then creating an obligation on states 'to establish as criminal offences under its national law the offences set forth in article 2 …'.[14] The Convention at times engages in quite remarkable verbal gymnastics to avoid the implication that such offences are directly criminalised by international law. For example, Article 6 of the convention provides that:

> Each State Party shall adopt such measures as may be necessary, including, where appropriate, domestic legislation, to ensure that *criminal acts within the scope of this convention* … are under no circumstances justifiable by considerations of a political, philosophical, ideological racial, ethnic, religious or other similar nature …[15]

As Boister notes, language of a similar nature in earlier treaties stands in considerable contrast to that of, for example, the Nuremberg IMT Charter and the Genocide Convention.[16] The differences are not accidental.

Does it matter?

Particularly given the debate about what an international (or transnational crime) is, it might be thought that its classification does not matter, and is solely a matter of hair-splitting disputation amongst specialists. But it does matter – and the answer to such scepticism is best shown by exploring the consequences of something being declared an international crime in the narrow sense.

First, international crimes can be directly prosecuted by purely international tribunals. International tribunals are based on international law and apply international law.[17] In part because of the *nullum crimen sine lege* principle, an international tribunal could not prosecute a transnational crime unless it had been given jurisdiction over some form of domestic law, as was the suggestion, for example, regarding the putative 1937 International Criminal Court in relation to terrorism.[18]

The other reason is because unless the crime in question was a crime under international law, there would be nothing for an international tribunal to base liability on. Although recently

---

[12]   In relation to torture, at least parts of the CAT have reached that status; *Prosecutor v. Furundžija*, Judgment, IT-95-17/1-T, 10 December 1998, para 149. See also *A and Others v. Secretary of State for the Home Department* [2005] UKHL 71, paras 33–34.

[13]   *International Convention for the Suppression of Acts of Nuclear Terrorism* (adopted 13 April 2005, entered into force 7 July 2007) 2445 UNTS 89.

[14]   *Ibid*, Article 5.

[15]   Emphasis added.

[16]   Boister (n 1 above), 962–963. Note that Article 8 of the Nuclear Terrorist Convention does, however, refer to 'preventing offences under this Convention …'.

[17]   Romano, CPR, 'The Proliferation of International Judicial Bodies: The Pieces of the Puzzle' (1999) 31 *New York University Journal of International Law and Politics* 709, 713–714.

[18]   See, *inter alia*, Chadwick, E, 'A Tale of Two Courts: The "Creation" of a Jurisdiction' (2004) 9 *Journal of Conflict and Security Law* 71.

there have been some developments, in particular in relation to internationalised tribunals such as the Special Court for Sierra Leone,[19] and the Special Tribunal for Lebanon, which is directed to use Lebanese definitions of terrorism to prosecute those responsible for the assassination of Rafiq Hariri, a fully international tribunal[20] must apply international, not domestic law. Requiring a notionally international tribunal to apply domestic law would render its status as such perilous.

In addition, the default assumption in relation to such crimes is that the general principles of liability and defences in international law apply to international crimes. If a crime can be prosecuted directly based on international law, the ambit of criminality must be fully defined by that law. Otherwise, a purportedly international tribunal would have to have recourse to domestic law in order to determine liability, which, as previously mentioned, imperils its status as an international tribunal. It is notable that the Statutes of the International Criminal Tribunal for the former Yugoslavia (ICTY) and the International Criminal Tribunal for Rwanda (ICTR) do not differentiate between the various crimes within their jurisdiction as regards general principles of liability.[21] The Rome Statute of the International Criminal Court (ICC) also treats these principles as being basically the same, except as regards the crime of aggression for which they were altered to reflect the definition of aggression created for the ICC in the Kampala amendments.[22] These principles of international liability do not apply to transnational crimes, since the treaties which create transnational offences largely leave principles of liability to domestic criminal law.

The next substantive conclusion which follows from something being a direct liability international crime is that, if a state legislates at the domestic level after the fact to enable a prosecution to take place, it would not violate the *nullum crimen sine lege* principle, so long as the domestic legislation was retrospective only within the period in which the crime existed in international law. This is because those now made subject to domestic criminalisation were already subject to the criminal proscription arising directly from international law. This was the view taken in the UK during the passing of the War Crimes Act 1991[23] and the 2009 Coroners and Justice Act.[24]

---

[19] On these see Romano, CPR, Nollkaemper A and Kleffner, JK (eds), *Internationalized Criminal Courts: Sierra Leone, East Timor and Cambodia* (Oxford University Press, 2004).

[20] To which certain normative effects are said to attach, see *Arrest Warrant of 11 April 2000 (Democratic Republic of Congo v. Belgium), Preliminary Objections and Merits, Judgment, ICJ Reports 2002*, p 3, para 60; *Prosecutor v. al-Bashir*, Judgment in the Jordan Referral re al-Bashir Appeal, ICC-02/05-01/09, 6 May 2019 paras 109–119. See also *Prosecutor v. Taylor*, Decision on Immunity from Jurisdiction, SCSL-2003-1-I, 31 May 2004, paras 37–42. For critique see Deen-Racsmány, Z, '*Prosecutor v. Taylor*: The Status of the Special Court for Sierra Leone and Its Implications for Immunity' (2005) 18 *Leiden Journal of International Law* 299.

[21] When dealing with the issue of general principles of liability (or defences) the ICTY has used cases applying across the different crimes to prove a general rule, rather than separate them off. See *Prosecutor v. Tadić*, Judgment, IT-94-1-A, 15 July 1999, paras 172–234.

[22] Rome Statute of the International Criminal Court, 2187 UNTS 3, Articles 8*bis* and 25(3)*bis* (as amended).

[23] See Turns, D, 'Prosecution Violations of International Humanitarian Law: The Legal Position in the United Kingdom' (1999) 4 *Journal of Armed Conflict Law* 1, 21–23; Greenwood, C, 'The War Crimes Act 1991' in Fox, H and Meyer, MA (eds), *Armed Conflict and the New Law: Effecting Compliance* (BIICL, 1993), 215.

[24] See Cryer, R and Mora, PD, 'The Coroners and Justice Act (2009): Backing into the Future?' (2010) 58 *International and Comparative Law Quarterly* 803.

Similarly, a domestic law amnesty will not remove criminal liability from those who have committed violations of international law. This is, again, a simple derivation from the fact that individual liability arises directly from international law, not domestic law. This is perhaps the best explanation of the way in which Article 10 of the Statute of the Special Court for Sierra Leone (SCSL) has been applied to the 'Lomé Amnesty', as depriving the Special Court of jurisdiction over crimes set out in Article 5 of its Statute, which were domestic Sierra Leonean crimes, but not over the crimes set out in Articles 2–4 of its Statute, which were international crimes.[25]

Finally, in monist, or incorporationist States, it may also be possible to directly prosecute international crimes at the domestic level.[26] This would not be the case for transnational crimes, even if the relevant suppression treaties, which contain the bulk of transnational crimes, were considered to be customary international law.[27] This is for the very simple reason that since the international rules involved address States rather than individuals it would not be possible to prosecute individuals directly on the basis of such international legal obligations, irrespective of the status of international law in the domestic legal order.

TORTURE AS A TRANSNATIONAL CRIME

Individual conduct in peacetime amounting to torture falls, for the most part, under the UNCAT.[28] In view of the taxonomy adopted above, it seems clear that the UNCAT creates a transnational crime, rather than a direct liability international crime. As such, and contrary to the views of some,[29] the Torture Convention does not create an international crime in the narrow sense in which it is being used here. The UNCAT was the outcome of careful and controversial debate about both the definition and nature of the prohibition which the States parties were looking to agree upon. It is fairly clear that they did not wish conduct amounting to torture by individuals in peacetime to be given the hallowed status of a fully-fledged international crime. To show this, it is worthwhile comparing the Genocide Convention (which is generally taken as constitutive of an international crime) and the UNCAT.

Article 1 of the Genocide Convention states that 'The Contracting Parties confirm that genocide, whether committed in time of peace or in time of war, *is a crime under international law*

---

[25]   Admittedly, the Special Court justified this result on slightly different grounds, that universal jurisdiction existed over war crimes and crimes against humanity, and thus a domestic amnesty could not prevent any other State or an international tribunal exercising jurisdiction over such an offence, see *Prosecutor v. Kallon and Kamara* Decision on challenge to jurisdiction: Lomé Accord Amnesty SCSL-2004-15-AR 72(E) 13 March 2004, paras 67–71. The extent to which this diverges from the reasoning above depends on the extent to which international tribunals exercise delegated jurisdiction from States. The ICC does, but it is less clear whether the ICTY, ICTR and SCSL do.

[26]   In the UK see, although somewhat ambivalently, *R v. Jones et al.* [2006] UKHL 16, paras 22–23.

[27]   See Kolb, R, 'The Exercise of Criminal Jurisdiction Over International Terrorists' in Bianchi, A (ed), *Enforcing International Legal Norms Against Terrorism* (Hart Publishing, 2004), 227.

[28]   For a comprehensive treatment see Nowak, M, Birk, M and Monina, G (eds), *The United Nations Convention Against Torture and its Optional Protocol: A Commentary*, 2nd edn (Oxford University Press, 2019). For a drafters' view see Burgers, JH and Danelius, H, *The United Nations Convention against Torture: A Handbook on the Convention against Torture and Other Cruel, Inhuman or Degrading Treatment or Punishment* (Martinus Nijhoff, 1988).

[29]   See below, pp. 311–312.

which they undertake to prevent and to punish' (emphasis added). This is generally taken as language that creates direct individual criminal liability for genocide under international law. The UNCAT, on the other hand, only gets to the issue in Article 4(1), which simply states that 'Each State Party shall ensure that all acts of torture are offences under its criminal law.' The difference was not accidental.

The initial draft of the Torture Convention, drafted by non-Governmental actors under the auspices of the International Association of Penal Law included a provision that was, *mutatis mutandis*, the same as Article 1 of the Genocide Convention. This would have elevated individual peacetime acts of torture to the category of core international crimes. However, as soon as this draft was submitted to States, this was deleted.[30] This shows that States took the distinction seriously, and the deletion was intentional and normative.

The 1984 UNCAT Definition

The cynosure of the criminal law prohibition of torture is the 1984 UN Convention Against Torture, although it does not in itself create a crime. Rather it creates an obligation on States to make torture, as defined in Article 1 of the Convention, a crime in domestic law.[31] In many ways the UNCAT follows the traditional transnational crime model, relying on domestic legal systems to ensure its enforcement.

Article 1 of the UNCAT defines torture as follows:

1. For the purposes of this Convention, the term 'torture' means any act by which severe pain or suffering, whether physical or mental, is intentionally inflicted on a person for such purposes as obtaining from him or a third person information or a confession, punishing him for an act he or a third person has committed or is suspected of having committed, or intimidating or coercing him or a third person, or for any reason based on discrimination of any kind, when such pain or suffering is inflicted by or at the instigation of or with the consent or acquiescence of a public official or other person acting in an official capacity ...

The ICTY has pronounced the definition as reflecting customary international law, but only for the purpose of State obligations under the UNCAT. The ICTY was coy, however, about the question of what obligations may arise under customary law more generally,[32] although it did engage in a rather speculative set of *obiter* observations that it deduced from the *jus cogens* status of the prohibition.[33] It is notable that although the International Court of Justice (ICJ)

---

[30] Draft Convention for the Prevention and Suppression of Torture, Submitted by the International Association of Penal Law, UN Doc E/CN.4/NGO/213, Article 1; Draft Convention Against Torture and Other Cruel, Inhuman and Degrading Treatment or Punishment (Sweden), UN Doc E/CN/4/1285.

[31] UNCAT Articles 2 and 4–7. The scope of the obligations in Articles 6 and 7 is elaborated upon in *Questions relating to the Obligation to Prosecute or Extradite* (*Belgium v. Senegal*), Judgment, *ICJ Reports 2012*, p. 442, (the '*Habré*' case*),* paras 71–117. For a discussion of more of the obligations see Rodley, NS and Pollard, M, 'Criminalisation of Torture: State Obligations under the United Nations Convention against Torture and Other Cruel, Inhuman and Degrading Treatment or Punishment' (2006) 2 *European Human Rights Law Review* 115; Nowak, Birk and Monina (n 28 above), 176–291.

[32] *Prosecutor v. Kunarac et al.*, Judgment, IT-96-/32 and 23/1-A, 12 June 2002, paras 146, 147 (and the other cases there cited); and *Prosecutor v. Kvočka et al.*, Judgment, IT-96-30/1-A, 28 February 2002, para. 284.

[33] For further discussion of this see Cryer, R, 'International Crimes and *Jus Cogens*: What does the Latter Add?' in Kaliq U and Hartmann, J (eds), *The Achievements of International Law: Essays in Honour of Robin Churchill* (Hart Publishing, 2021, Chapter 13).

declared the prohibition of torture to be a *jus cogens* norm, it largely demurred from discussing the impact of this, speaking instead (perhaps for reasons of judicial economy) of obligations *erga omnes partes* (i.e. those applicable *inter se* between parties to the CAT) rather than more generally.[34]

The definition in Article 1 of the UNCAT entails three separate 'pillars', usefully summarised by Sir Nigel Rodley as being:

1. the relative intensity of pain or suffering inflicted: it must not only be severe, it must also be an aggravated form of already prohibited (albeit undefined) cruel, inhuman or degrading treatment or punishment;
2. the purposive element: obtaining information, confession, etc.;
3. the status of the perpetrator: a public official must inflict or instigate the infliction of the pain or suffering.[35]

The Material Element

Looking to the first material aspect, the UNCAT requires that there be physical, or mental pain or suffering, that is 'severe'.[36] What amounts to 'severe' is the operative criterion that distinguishes torture from cruel, inhuman and degrading treatment. This can be a difficult line to draw, as the jurisprudence of human rights bodies has shown.[37] Indeed the findings of the Committee Against Torture (CAT) on this point are notable by their paucity of reasoning.[38] This is largely because setting out a strict test would be ill-advised, given the malicious imagination of torturers,[39] but also given its relative nature.

For example, the European Court of Human Rights (ECtHR) (the European Commission on Human Rights having previously found differently) determined that the notorious 'five techniques' employed by the UK with respect to those suspected of being members of the Irish Republican Army (IRA) did not amount to torture in the context of Article 3 of the European Convention on Human Rights (ECHR), as the measures were not severe enough.[40] This, though, was all but overturned by the ECtHR in the case of *Selmouni v. France*, in which it asserted that:

> Certain acts which were classified in the past as 'inhuman and degrading' as opposed to 'torture' could be classified differently in the future. [The Court] takes the view that the increasingly high standard being required in the area of the protection of human rights and fundamental liberties correspondingly and inevitably requires greater firmness in assessing breaches of the fundamental values of democratic societies.[41]

---

[34]   *Habré* case (n 31 above), paras 68–69.

[35]   Rodley, NS, 'The Definition(s) of Torture in International Law' (2002) 55 *Current Legal Problems* 467, 468.

[36]   *Ibid*, 470–481.

[37]   See Rodley, NS and Pollard, M, *The Treatment of Prisoners under International Law*, 3rd edn (Oxford University Press, 2009), Chapter 3.

[38]   Nowak, Birk and Monina (n 28 above), 48.

[39]   For this reason, this chapter will also not seek to identify specifics of conduct, but for examples see *ibid*, 49–62.

[40]   *Ireland v. The United Kingdom*, 18 January 1978, Series A no 25, para 167.

[41]   *Selmouni v. France* [GC], no 25803/94, ECHR 1999-V, para 101.

Similarly, the ECtHR has noted that the test for severity is subjective, thus decision makers sometimes need to take into account the 'sex, age and state of health of the victim'.[42] Treatment also must be considered cumulatively, it is not acceptable to take each form of treatment the victim has endured separately.[43] These seem useful guidelines, although they do not provide self-applying standards in any one individual case.

Even though it is difficult, if not impossible, to set an absolute standard, that said, the concept of 'severe' certainly has certain lower limits, as shown by the rejection of the 'Bybee' Memorandum, discussed below in relation to crimes against humanity. Its interpretation that the pain in question had to be 'similar to organ failure' or death has been roundly rejected.[44]

The Purposive Element

In addition to the requirement of the 'intentional'[45] infliction of severe pain or suffering, Article 1 of the UNCAT requires that it be inflicted with a purpose in mind. It might be thought that these requirements operate as a considerable brake on the ability of decision makers to characterise conduct as torture. There are reasons to doubt this. The first is that the list in Article 1 is non-exhaustive, as is clear from the use of the term 'such as' prior to the list, so other purposes can be applied on a case-by-case basis. Even amongst those listed there, the purpose of intimidating or coercing the victim or a third party will not be difficult to infer when the conduct in question is intentional.

Official Capacity

The requirement that the conduct is either undertaken, or acquiesced in by a State or other public official applies to torture by the express terms of Article 1. The inclusion of State official is, for the most part, tolerably clear,[46] but that of 'other public official', which was introduced to broaden the category of those covered,[47] is not.

Historically, the Committee Against Torture has taken the view that such persons must be very similar to a State official if they are not actually a State official,[48] but in their more recent jurisprudence they have relaxed this somewhat. So, for example in *Elmi v. Australia* it found that since at the relevant time there was no central government in Somalia, those acting in a 'quasi-governmental' fashion could be considered public officials.[49]

---

[42] *Ireland v. UK* (n 40 above), para 162.

[43] *Ibid*, para 167. This further shows the ill-advisability of setting out specific forms of treatment *in abstracto*.

[44] See further below, p. 303.

[45] The term is not defined in CAT, so presumably it falls to be determined by the domestic law on intention. It would be surprising, though if, given the purpose requirement, reckless infliction of harm would suffice. For comment on the *travaux* see Nowak, Birk and Monina (n 28 above), 32.

[46] But see the discussion below, pp. 295–296.

[47] Nowak, Birk and Monina (n 28 above), 34.

[48] *G.R.B. v. Sweden*, UN Doc CAT/C/20/D/83/1997, 15 May 1998.

[49] *Elmi v. Australia*, UN Doc CAT/C/22/D/120/1988, 14 May 1999. A review of the decisions of the CAT is provided in Sivakumaran, S, 'Torture in International Human Rights an International Humanitarian Law: The Actor and the Ad Hoc Tribunals' (2005) 18 *Leiden Journal of International Law* 541, 549–553.

The matter has come before UK courts in the two major prosecutions for torture pursuant to the UK's implementation of Article 1 of the UNCAT in section 134 of the Criminal Justice Act 1988.[50] The first of these was the *Zardad* case in 2004.[51] Zardad was an Afghan warlord who was fighting the embattled Rabani regime. His defence claimed that he as was not a member of a recognised government and the fact that he opposed the Rabani regime meant that he could not be considered a public official. Rejecting this contention, Treacy J asserted that 'those people who are acting for an entity which has acquired de facto effective control over an area of a country and is exercising governmental or quasi-governmental functions in that area' fell under the rubric of 'public official.[52] The finding was not uncontroversial, but was not appealed.

More recently, the matter was considered by the UK Supreme Court in the case of *R v. TRA*, concerning Agnes Reeves-Taylor, Charles Taylor's ex-wife.[53] Reeves-Taylor was indicted for conduct amounting to torture during 1990, when she and her then husband, as members and leaders of the National Patriotic Front of Liberia (NPFL), were fighting to overthrow the President of Liberia (Samuel Doe). Since the Doe regime was the government of Liberia, Reeves-Taylor argued, like Zardad, that she could not be a 'public official' for the purposes of section 134. The Supreme Court (by a majority of 4-1) largely adopted *Zardad* (whilst disagreeing in part). Noting their agreement with Treacy J in that case, and having reviewed the language of Article 1 and decisions of the CAT, the Court concluded that those exercising de facto governmental functions could be considered to be public officials within the meaning of the UNCAT. However, the Court distinguished this from exercising 'mere' military control, which was not considered enough.[54]

The distinction is far from unassailable,[55] but the idea of non-State actors being caught by Article 1 in any circumstances was too much for Lord Reed, who, in dissent argued that the majority's approach was contrary to the *nullum crimen sine lege* principle.[56] This is questionable,[57] and shows that the matter is not beyond controversy. However, it must be said that the majority position, which keeps alive the possibility of non-State actors being included as potential torturers within the scope of the UNCAT, is more in keeping with trends in this area. Whether the case proves to be catalytic or it will be ignored or forgotten by other Courts and decision makers remains to be seen.

---

[50]   There has been one other prosecution, of Colonel Lama; however, as he was a high-ranking member of the Nepalese Armed Forces, this issue did not arise.

[51]   *R v. Zardad* [2007] EWCA Crim 279. The defendant was convicted of conspiracy to torture (and conspiracy to take hostages). This was appealed (unsuccessfully), but on evidential grounds.

[52]   *R v. Zardad*, Case No T2203 7676, 7 April 2004, ILDC 95 (UK 2004), para 38.

[53]   *R v. TRA* [2019] UKSC 51. For comment see Robert Cryer, '*R v. TRA*' [2020] *Criminal Law Review* 553.

[54]   *R v. TRA, ibid.,* paras 25, 81.

[55]   Cryer (n 53 above), 556.

[56]   *R v. TRA* (n 53 above), para 97.

[57]   Cryer (n 53 above), 557.

TORTURE AS AN INTERNATIONAL CRIME IN THE NARROW SENSE

As mentioned above, there are four crimes that undoubtedly fall within the ambit of international crimes in their narrow sense: aggression, genocide, crimes against humanity, and war crimes. More may be added to this pantheon in the future, and could include those which were listed as 'treaty crimes' in the Rome negotiations, but were ultimately excluded. There is no conceptual reason why there may not be more international crimes, but such a conclusion ought not to be easily drawn. What is required is that States determine that they wish particular conduct to be considered to rise to such a status.

We will not concentrate on the crime of aggression here, as it is not salient. In common parlance, aggressive war may be torture but, as defined in international criminal law (most recently in the Kampala Amendments to the Rome Statute of the International Criminal Court), the two concepts do not overlap in any real way.[58] So we will focus on the other three.

Torture as Genocide[59]

The prohibition of genocide is undoubtedly an example of, if not the paradigmatic example of, a *jus cogens* norm.[60] It received its classic definition in Article II of the 1948 Genocide Convention, which is now considered the standard one. It explains that Genocide is:

> any of the following acts committed with the intent to destroy, in whole or in part, a national, ethnical, racial or religious group, as such:
>
> (a) Killing members of the group;
> (b) Causing serious bodily or mental harm to members of the group;
> (c) Deliberately inflicting on the group conditions of life calculated to bring about its physical destruction in whole or in part;
> (d) Imposing measures intended to prevent births within the group;
> (e) Forcibly transferring children of the group to another group.

External element
It will be immediately obvious that the Genocide Convention does not speak directly of torture. However, it should be similarly clear that several of the acts can constitute the external aspect of genocide overlap with torture.[61]

---

[58] For comprehensive analysis see Kreß, C and Barriga, S (eds), *The Crime of Aggression: A Commentary* (Cambridge University Press, 2017), especially Pobjie, E, 'Victims of the Crime of Aggression' in *ibid*, 816.

[59] The standard reference work on this subject is Schabas, WA, *Genocide in International Law: The Crime of Crimes*, 2nd edn (Cambridge University Press, 2009).

[60] *Armed Activities on the Territory of the Congo (New Application: 2002) (Democratic Republic of the Congo v. Rwanda), Jurisdiction and Admissibility, Judgment, ICJ Reports 2006*, p 6, para 64, but see above note 33 for scepticism about what that adds normatively in this context.

[61] On such conduct see Mettraux, G, *International Crimes: Law and Practice. Volume I: Genocide* (Oxford University Press, 2019), Chapter 10.

Killing is not really an area of overlap, as the idea of torture in the UNCAT is not meant to embrace killings. Whilst there may be torture prior to the killing of a person, the UNCAT only covers the former, and the killing *per se* does not fall within its purview.

Probably the closest analogue in the UNCAT is the causing of serious bodily or mental harm which is proscribed both by the UNCAT and by Article 2(b) of the Genocide Convention. This was made express in the first conviction entered for genocide before an international tribunal. In the *Akayesu* case before the ICTR it was said that harm (as under the UNCAT) has to be 'serious' but '[c]ausing serious bodily or mental harm to members of the group does not necessarily mean that the harm is permanent and irremediable'.[62] There is no closed list of acts that may suffice for serious bodily or mental harm;[63] what it is required is that it must cause 'a grave and long-term disadvantage to a person's ability to lead a normal and constructive life'.[64]

Torture falling within the UNCAT definition would almost certainly fulfil these criteria. Indeed, in the *Akayesu* case it was said that 'the Chamber takes serious bodily or mental harm, without limiting itself thereto, to mean acts of torture, be they bodily or mental, inhumane or degrading treatment, persecution'.[65] This position has not been resiled from in the plethora of cases that have followed it.[66] The inclusion of torture can further be supported by the Elements of Crimes that were drafted to assist the ICC in interpreting the Rome Statute of the International Criminal Court.[67] Footnote 1 to the Elements to Article 6(b) expressly states that: 'conduct may include, but is not necessarily limited to acts of torture ...'.

The ICC has not had cause to make any major pronouncements on the interpretation of this aspect of its Statute and its Elements, but it seems unlikely that it will fly far from the interpretation given by the *ad hoc* Tribunals. There is a passing reference to torture fulfilling the requirements for serious bodily or mental harm in the *al-Bashir* Arrest Warrant Decision, but little elaboration.[68]

Given the above, it is not necessary to spend too much time looking at the other types of conduct that may suffice for genocide. Inflicting conditions, or measures intended to prevent births within the group, could intersect with torture in the general sense, although it is unlikely that in its broader dimensions it would fall into what would be generally considered torture.

---

[62]   *Prosecutor v. Akayesu*, Judgment, ICTR-95-2, 2 September 1998, para 502. Although the ICTR in the *Kayishema* case did say that the harm had to be that which 'seriously injures health, causes disfigurement or causes any serious injury to the external, internal organs or senses': *Prosecutor v. Kayishema and Ruzindana*, Judgment, ICTR-95-1-T, 21 May 1999, para 10, but it seems doubtful that they were intentionally departing from *Akayesu* on the specific point.

[63]   Sexual offences are now clearly within this, see *Akayesu, ibid*, para 731.

[64]   *Prosecutor v. Blagoević and Jokić*, Judgment, IT-02-60-T, 17 January 2005, para 645. What falls under the definition was also said (consistent with the CAT and other human rights jurisprudence canvassed) to be evaluated with respect to the specific situation of the victim. *Kayishema* (n 62 above), para 110.

[65]   *Akayesu* (n 62 above), para 504; Mettraux (n 61 above), 261 seems to agree.

[66]   See Mettraux (n 61 above), 260–263.

[67]   Albeit not bind it. See von Hebel, H, 'The Making of the Elements of Crimes' in Lee, RS et al. (eds), *The International Criminal Court: Elements of Crimes and Rules of Procedure and Evidence* (Transnational, 2001), 7–9.

[68]   *Prosecutor v. Al-Bashir*, Second Decision on the Prosecutor's Request for a Warrant of Arrest, ICC-02/05-01/09, 12 June 2010, para 30.

Perhaps this can be shown by the *Akayesu* Trial Chamber's discussion of that crime where they said that:

> In patriarchal societies, where membership of a group is determined by the identity of the father, an example of a measure intended to prevent births within a group is the case where, during rape, a woman of the said group is deliberately impregnated by a man of another group, with the intent to have her give birth to a child who will consequently not belong to its mother's group. Furthermore, the Chamber notes that measures intended to prevent births within the group may be physical, but can also be mental.[69]

This must be read against the backdrop of their entirely reasonable statement that rape necessarily involves serious bodily and mental harm.[70] It is thus not overbroad.

Contextual elements and the mental element

The first thing to note in this regard is that Article I criminalises genocide 'whether committed in war or peace', making it abundantly clear that it can occur in either situation[71] (although the application of the law of armed conflict may be relevant for the interpretation of aspects of the definition).[72] Next, with regard to the status of the perpetrator, there is nothing in the Genocide Convention, or any other authority, that requires that Genocide be committed by a person acting in an official capacity (or purporting to do so), hence the difficult debates in relation to the UNCAT definition simply do not arise. The Genocide Convention reinforces the point in Article 4, which renders official capacity irrelevant.[73] Thus in principle a lone individual could commit genocide by virtue of an act that would amount to torture and become a *génocidaire*.[74] This has raised some academic ire,[75] but the position seems relatively settled.[76]

There are those who strongly argue for the existence of a policy requirement that the commission of genocide entail some kind of official, or quasi-official activity and at least a link to it.[77] This could be supported by, for example, the Elements of Crimes for the ICC. These provide that '[t]he conduct took place in the context of a manifest pattern of similar conduct directed against that group or was conduct that could itself effect such destruction'.[78] Note, though that in spite of views to the contrary[79] this does not require either a genocidal policy or that the person be an official in any way. Furthermore, even if it did, the Element was only

---

[69]   *Ibid*, paras 507–508.
[70]   *Akayesu* (n 62 above), para 731.
[71]   As does the UNCAT.
[72]   Mettraux (n 61 above), 16–17.
[73]   See Mettraux, *ibid*, 26–27.
[74]   *Prosecutor v. Jelesić*, Judgment, IT-95-10-T, 14 December 1999, para 100.
[75]   See Schabas, WA 'The Jelesić case and the *Mens Rea* of the Crime of Genocide' (2001) 14 *Leiden Journal of International Law* 125, *contra* Triffterer, O, 'Genocide: Its Particular Intent to Destroy in Whole or in Part the Group as Such' (2001) 14 *Leiden Journal of International Law* 399.
[76]   Mettraux (n 61 above), 27.
[77]   Schabas, WA, 'State Policy as an Element of International Crimes' (2007–2008) 98 *Journal of Criminal Law and Criminology* 953; Vest, H, 'A Structure-based Concept of Genocidal Intent' (2007) 5 *Journal of International Criminal Justice* 781.
[78]   See Oosterveld, V and Garraway, C, 'The Elements of Genocide' in Lee et al. (n 67 above), 41 at 44, 45.
[79]   Vest (n 77 above).

included to limit what the Court ought to trouble itself with, rather than limit the general law on point. Its customary status has been expressly rejected by the ICTY, for example.[80]

Another major difference to the UNCAT (and other international crimes) is that, when looking at victims, the Genocide Convention requires that they be (or be perceived to be) a member of a national, ethnic, racial or religious group. This has caused very serious difficulty in practice, as group membership is far from simple.[81]

Unlike the UNCAT, the Genocide Convention does not require there to be a specific purpose behind the conduct of the accused, but this is more than counterbalanced by the very high mental element required for a charge of genocide to succeed. The mental element is provided for Article II and requires that the defendant intends to destroy, in whole or in part, one of the protected groups. Here is not the place to engage in a detailed discussion of that requirement, but suffice it to say, it is an eliminationist intention, which goes beyond the purposes elaborated upon in the UNCAT, not least as it looks beyond the individual victim and relates to the destruction of the group which the perpetrator wishes to consign to oblivion.[82]

The Tribunals have taken a very narrow approach to this, requiring that the perpetrator wanted this to happen, rather than merely have knowledge that their conduct would have that result.[83] This does not create an element of motive but it requires direct, rather than oblique, intent. This is an exacting standard, and one that characterises the offence for the Tribunals.

It is also difficult to prove.[84] The ICTY has struggled here, and has only infrequently found there to be such an intent.[85] The ICTR has had fewer problems in the regard, but there were very special circumstances, including that the Rwandan genocide was so notorious[86] and that early in the life of that Tribunal the ex-prime minister of Rwanda, Jean Kambanda, in his guilty plea, admitted that there had been a plan to exterminate the Tutsi population of Rwanda.[87] Such an admission is rare and, although not a requirement, its evidential weight is very strong. Otherwise proof is extremely difficult.

Because of this, it might be questioned whether it would be worth a prosecutor bringing conduct amounting to torture to a court under the rubric of a charge of genocide. There are two reasons why this might be the case, one practical, another more principled. The practical one is that the general principles of liability applicable to genocide include some that are not found in all domestic systems.[88] These include two fully inchoate crimes, incitement and conspiracy, both of which are provided for in both in Article III of the Genocide Convention, as well as (for incitement only) in Article 25(3)(e) of the Rome Statute.

---

[80]   *Prosecutor v Krstić*, Judgment IT-98-33-T, 2 August 2001, para 682.
[81]   For a brief overview see Cryer, R, Robinson, D and Vasiliev, S, *An Introduction to International Criminal Law and Procedure*, 4th edn (Cambridge University Press, 2019), 210–214.
[82]   *Ibid*, 219–226.
[83]   See generally Mettraux (n 61 above), Chapter 8.
[84]   *Ibid*, Chapter 9.
[85]   Cryer, Robinson and Vasiliev (n 81 above), 221.
[86]   Even William Schabas, who is well known for taking a very restrictive view on what amounts to genocide, considers the Rwandan genocide to be one of the undoubted genocides of the 20th century. See Schabas (n 59 above), 9.
[87]   *Prosecutor v. Kambanda*, Judgment, ICTR-97-23, 4 September 1998.
[88]   For the most part, transnational criminal law treaties leave general principles to the discretion of the domestic law of the State party (the exclusion of superior orders in Article 2(3) of the UNCAT is an exception here).

The second, more principled reason is related to the principle of fair labelling. This evaluative principle of criminal law more generally relates to the communicative function of criminal law and requires that a court call something by its correct name, so that the message concerning what has really happened is brought home both to the defendant/convicted person and to society more generally.[89] This was the approach adopted by the ICTY in the *Krstić* case, where they made clear that where genocide had occurred, it needed to be described as such:

> The Appeals Chamber states unequivocally that the law condemns, in appropriate terms, the deep and lasting injury inflicted, and calls the massacre at Srebrenica by its proper name: genocide. Those responsible will bear this stigma, and it will serve as a warning to those who may in future contemplate the commission of such a heinous act.[90]

Given these considerations, it may be worth domestic prosecutors charging, in appropriate cases, torture in and of itself, and torture as a means of committing genocide in the alternative.

Torture as a Crime against Humanity[91]

Crimes against humanity are a staple of modern international criminal law.[92] They were first codified in the Charter of the Nuremberg IMT. That said, their precise definition has been, and remains to this day, the subject of considerable controversy.[93] This has led to the International Law Commission (ILC) taking up the matter, and it has proposed draft articles for a multilateral treaty on point.[94]

Owing to the previous definitional diffusion and the fact that the ILC's proposed definitions trace those in the Rome Statute, it is best to focus on the definition contained in the Rome Statute, which is the first definition of crimes against humanity in a multilateral treaty. It is thus a creature of negotiation, and equally must be interpreted in the shadow of what went

---

[89]   Ashworth, A, 'The Elasticity of Mens Rea' in Tapper, C (ed), *Crime, Proof and Punishment: Essays in Memory of Sir Rupert Cross* (Butterworth, 1981), 45. See also Williams, G, 'Convictions and Fair Labelling' (1983) 42 *Cambridge Law Journal* 85.

[90]   *Prosecutor* v *Krstić*, Judgment, IT-98-33-A, 1 July 2003, para 37. See further Amann, DM, 'Group Mentality, Expressivism and Genocide' (2002) 2 *International Criminal Law Review* 93 and Luban, D, 'Calling Genocide by its Rightful Name: Lemkin's Word, and the UN Report' (2006) 7 *Chicago Journal of International Law* 303.

[91]   The standard monograph here is Bassiouni, MC, *Crimes Against Humanity: Historical Evolution and Contemporary Application* (Cambridge University Press, 2011). See also Mettraux, G, *International Crimes: Volume II: Crimes Against Humanity* (Oxford University Press, 2020, especially Chapter 6.7).

[92]   See Sadat, LN, 'Crimes Against Humanity in the Modern Era' (2013) 97 *American Journal of International Law* 334.

[93]   For an expression of frustration on this point in the 1990s see Bassiouni, MC, 'Crimes Against Humanity: The Need for a Specialized Convention' (1993–1994) 31 *Columbia Journal of Transnational Law* 457. See now Sadat, LN (ed), *Forging a Convention on Crimes Against Humanity*, 2nd edn (Cambridge University Press, 2013).

[94]   *Report of the International Law Commission on the Work of its 72nd Session*, UN Doc. A/72/10 (2017), para 45. See also Report of the Special Rapporteur on Crimes Against Humanity, UN Doc. A/CN.4/725 (18 February 2019), para 20.

before, and of the savings clause in Article 10 of the Rome Statute that provides that the definitions it contains shall not prejudice existing or developing customary international law.[95]

The Rome Statute addresses crimes against humanity in Article 7, which reads in relevant part:

> For the purpose of this Statute, 'crime against humanity' means any of the following acts when committed as part of a widespread or systematic attack directed against any civilian population, with knowledge of the attack:
>
> ...
> (c) Enslavement;
>
> ...
> (f) Torture;
> (g) Rape, sexual slavery, enforced prostitution, forced pregnancy, enforced sterilization, or any other form of sexual violence of comparable gravity;
>
> ...
> (i)   Enforced disappearance of persons;
> (j)   The crime of apartheid;
> (k) Other inhumane acts of a similar character intentionally causing great suffering, or serious injury to body or to mental or physical health.

Although this chapter will only focus on the crime of torture, as it is specifically mentioned, it also ought to be noted that this overlaps with other aspects of the definition of crimes against humanity (enslavement, sexual offences, enforced disappearances, apartheid, and other inhumane acts). Its inclusion as a crime against humanity was not in any way controversial, given that torture had been included as such in previous documents, for example Control Council Law 10, and the ITCY and ICTR Statutes.[96] This chapter will also refer to the contextual elements, which form a major part of the definitions of all crimes against humanity.[97]

The definitions in Article 7(1) of the Rome Statute are supplemented by interpretations in Article 7(2), which, as part of the Statute, are also, pursuant to Article 21 of the Rome Statute, the primary source of law for the ICC.[98] For the crime that is most pertinent here is Article 7(2)(e) which provides:

> 'Torture' means the intentional infliction of severe pain or suffering, whether physical or mental, upon a person in the custody or under the control of the accused; except that torture shall not include pain or suffering arising only from, inherent in or incidental to, lawful sanctions;

---

[95]   See Schabas, WA, *The International Criminal Court: A Commentary on the Rome Statute* (OUP, 2nd ed. 2016) 334.

[96]   See e.g. ILC, *Report of the Special Rapporteur on Crimes Against Humanity*, UN Doc. A/CN.4/680, 17 February 2015, para 159.

[97]   It ought to be noted at this stage that this part is not intended as a comprehensive treatise on the entire law on point, but to highlight the most important issues. For a useful primer on the background to the Rome Statute Definition see Robinson, D, 'Drafting Crimes Against Humanity and the Rome Conference' (1999) 93 *American Journal of International Law* 43. For a detailed overview see Cryer, Robinson and Vasiliev (n 81 above), Chapter 11 (for clarity, this chapter was written by Professor Robinson).

[98]   On this see, e.g., Grover, L, *Interpreting Crimes in the Rome Statute of the International Criminal Court* (Cambridge University Press, 2014).

It is also important in this regard that the Elements of Crimes adopted by the parties to the Rome Statute add only a little to the definition of torture in Article 7 *per se*, these either largely repeating the Statute, or being obviously derived from it. Where they do give further detail though, this will be discussed in what follows.

Material element

The definition of torture in Article 7 of the Rome Statute draws upon, but is not identical to, that in Article 1 of the UNCAT. Nor it is identical to the prohibition of torturous crimes against humanity as elaborated upon by the ICTY in its case law (the definition in Article 5 of the ICTY Statute being limited to the word 'torture' itself).[99] It ought to be said that the ICC has, so far, engaged in little discussion of the ambit of the conduct element of torture, probably as the conduct that has been come before it has not pushed the boundaries of the concept. As a result, it has not judicially elaborated upon Article 7.[100] What is clear across all of the Tribunals and the ICC, however, is that the harm must be severe.[101] As discussed in relation to genocide, this is a contextual judgment but it certainly includes sexual offences and mutilation. However, it extends further than those offences, and the ICTY in particular, did not wish to provide too many specific examples for fear of setting 'a trap for the innocent and signpost for the guilty'.[102]

One thing that is consistent in the case law, though, is that the threshold is one of 'severe' pain or suffering, defined in the ICTY as being 'the infliction, by act or omission, of severe pain or suffering, whether physical or mental'.[103] No more or less is required. In one case, defence counsel sought to dilute this standard, by reference to the infamous 'Yoo/Bybee' memoranda in the US,[104] which defined the severity of pain and suffering, on the basis of irrelevant US legislation (that related to healthcare), as requiring that suffering be extreme, such that it 'must be equivalent in intensity to the pain accompanying serious physical injury, such as organ failure, impairment of bodily function, or even death'. In the *Brđanin* case the ICTY took little time in rejecting this as representing the customary standard for the degree of suffering, reiterating that whilst there is no absolute standard for severity,

> 'severe pain or suffering' is not synonymous with 'extreme pain or suffering', and ... the latter is a more intense level of pain and suffering – one that might come closer to 'pain ... equivalent in inten-

---

[99] For a very useful elaboration of the ICTY's Jurisprudence on this issue see Burchard, C, 'Torture in the Jurisprudence of the *ad hoc* Tribunals' (2008) 6 *Journal of International Criminal Justice* 159.

[100] See e.g., *Prosecutor v. Ag Mahmoud*, Rectificatif à la Décision relative à la confirmation des charges portées contre Al Hassan Ag Abdoul Aziz Ag Mohamed Ag Mahmoud, ICC-01/12-01/18, 13 November 2019, para 790. Little can be derived from other cases prior to this.

[101] This is made express in Article 7(2), and in the settled jurisprudence of the ICTY, see e.g. *Prosecutor v. Brđanin*, Judgment, ICI-99-36-A, 3 April 2007, para 242. See also Mettraux (n 91 above), pp. 523–526.

[102] As quoted in Koskenniemi, M, 'A Trap for the Innocent ...' in Kreß and Barriga (n 58 above), 1359.

[103] *Brđanin* (n 101 above), paras 242, 247.

[104] Colloquially known as the Torture Memoranda. For a full elaboration of the documentation see Greenberg, K and Dratel, J (eds), *The Torture Papers* (Cambridge University Press 2005). Amongst the voluminous literature, one of the very best books is Luban, D, *Torture, Power and Law* (Cambridge University Press, 2014).

sity to the pain accompanying serious physical injury, such as organ failure, impairment of bodily function, or even death' – not required by the Convention against Torture …
No matter how powerful or influential a country is, its practice does not automatically become customary international law …[105]

The ICTY has also noted that omissions may suffice for commission of torture, nor is it required that the harm be permanent.[106]

Mental element
As regards the mental element for the underlying offence, it is evident from Article 7(2) of the Rome Statute that the conduct must be intentional, i.e. that (*pace* Article 30 of the Rome Statute) 'the defendant must seek the serious harm, or be aware that it will occur in the ordinary course of events'.[107] This is a consistent theme throughout all of the forms of liability for UNCAT-based torture and for an international crime.
There is, however, divergence between the UNCAT and the Rome Statute, and between the Rome Statute and the jurisprudence of the ICTY as regards the question of purpose. As we saw, the UNCAT definition includes a purposive requirement. There is, however, no such textual requirement in the Rome Statute, and the Elements of Crimes for torture as a crime against humanity explain that 'it is understood that … no purpose need be proved for this crime'.[108]

The ICTY, on the other hand, relying quite heavily on the UNCAT definition,[109] has determined that a purpose requirement is required. At trial level, the Court determined that '[t]he act or omission must aim at obtaining information or a confession, or at punishing, intimidating or coercing the victim or a third person, or at discriminating, on any ground, against the victim or a third person'[110]

It might be wondered why there is a distinction. Various reasons have been suggested, the most convincing of which is that Article 7(2)(e) of the Rome Statute requires that the victim be 'in the custody or under the control of the accused'. In the circumstances of crimes against humanity, especially the general contextual element of them occurring against the backdrop of 'a widespread or systematic attack on the civilian population', requiring purpose as an additional element seems redundant. Indeed, it must be said that, like the UNCAT, the ICTY included 'intimidating or coercing the victim or a third person' as purposes. This, as mentioned above in the context of torturous conduct, does not seem a high threshold, so outcomes would be unlikely to be different irrespective of whether the Rome Statute or customary law as identified by the ICTY was at issue.

---

[105] Which they took on point as being declaratory of customary law, para 249; the quotes come from paras 249 and 247.
[106] See Burchard, C, 'Torture in the Jurisprudence of the ad hoc Tribunals: A Critical Assessment' (2008) 6 *Journal of International Criminal Justice* 159, 164–165 and the cases cited therein.
[107] The ICTY has, to all intents and purposes adopted the same standard (using 'normal' instead of 'ordinary'). See e.g. *Kunarac* (n 32 above), para 152.
[108] Elements of Crimes Against Humanity, footnote 14.
[109] Albeit not entirely, see *Kunarac* (n 32 above), paras 465–496.
[110] *Ibid*, para 485.

Contextual element

It is now settled that a key element of crimes against humanity is that they have a nexus to a widespread or systematic attack on the civilian population. The precise ambit of the nexus requirement is not always transparent, but this does not mean it has not been the subject of a great deal of judicial, diplomatic and academic inquiry and comment.

Although the criterion of such attacks being 'widespread' or 'systematic' was only expressly introduced in Article 3 of the ICTR Statute, the ICTY interpreted this as being implicit in the condition (found in Article 5 of its Statute) that the attack occurs against the backdrop of an attack on the civilian *population*.[111] The most authoritative judicial pronouncement on the meaning of this condition came from the ICTY in the *Kunarac* case, where the Appeals Chamber opined that '[w]idespread refers to the large-scale nature of the attack and the number of victims, while the phrase 'systematic' refers to the organized nature of the acts of violence and the improbability of their random occurrence'.[112] The ICC has not disagreed.

The matter of whether or not the test was disjunctive or conjunctive (i.e. 'widespread and systematic' or 'widespread or systematic') was a matter of considerable dispute at the Rome conference. The ICTY had set out its views, but some States wished to raise the bar concerning the understanding of an attack. As a result, a compromise was reached between the two positions. This came about by adopting in Article 7(1) the disjunctive test, but in Article 7(2) defining 'attack' as meaning 'a course of conduct involving the multiple commission of acts referred to in paragraph 1 against any civilian population, pursuant to or in furtherance of a State or organisational policy to commit such an attack'. This was intended to find a *via media* between the two positions, the idea being that proof of 'widespread' would then need a small level of 'systematicity', and vice versa. Whether this achieved the right balance is a matter of debate,[113] but it is undoubtedly the law that the ICC needs to apply.

Article 7(2) thus undoubtedly requires some form of policy. This is an element that, in spite of previous wavering in the ICTY, had finally been rejected in a rather terse piece of reasoning in the *Kunarac* Appeal,[114] although this was far from uncontroversial.[115] There have been attempts to reconcile the two positions,[116] although they may be seen as valiant attempts to square the circle, or to show that the practical difference is likely to be small.

For those jurisdictions using the policy requirement, the question will immediately arise; the policy of whom? The Rome Statute provides that it is a 'State or organizational' policy. Whilst the former is tolerably (although not entirely) clear,[117] the latter has been subject of much academic debate.[118] The matter has been discussed in detail by the ICC in one case, the *Situation*

---

[111]   *Prosecutor v. Tadić*, Judgment, IT 94-1-T, 9 May 1997, paras 649–654.

[112]   *Kunarac* (n 32 above), para 94. For the ICC see *al-Bashir* Arrest Warrant (n 68 above), para 81.

[113]   See Cryer, Robinson and Vasiliev (n 81 above), 233.

[114]   *Kunarac* (n 32 above), para 94.

[115]   For a strongly made argument against, see Schabas, WA, 'State Policy as an Element of International Crimes' (2008) 98 *Journal of Criminal Law and Criminology* 953. For a powerful argument in favour of *Kunarac*, see Mettraux, G, 'The Definition of Crimes Against Humanity and the Question of a "Policy Element"' in Leila Sadat (ed) (n 93 above), 142.

[116]   Especially Robinson, D, 'Crimes Against Humanity: A Better Policy on "Policy"' in Stahn, C (ed), *The Law and Practice of the International Criminal Court* (Oxford University Press, 2015), Chapter 28.

[117]   The question of unrecognised entities may cause difficulties, but would probably be covered, if needs be, by 'organizational'.

[118]   For a brief, but assertive piece in this regard see Schabas, WA, 'Is Terrorism a Crime Against Humanity?' (2002) 8 *Yearbook of International Peace Operations* 255.

in Kenya Decision before a Pre-Trial Chamber. The Chamber split 2-1, with the majority taking a functional approach, largely saying that where a group is organised enough to have 'the capability to engage in conduct, it can be considered an organisation for this purpose', and providing a set of indicia to assist in determining it.[119] In dissent, Judge Kaul preferred a set of criteria that rendered the organisation state-like.[120] In spite of some academic support,[121] his approach has not been adopted elsewhere in the ICC.[122]

Whether or not a policy requirement is required, the status of the defendant is irrelevant. The UNCAT requirement that the defendant be a public official was deliberately omitted in the Rome Statute and was expressly rejected by the ICTY in the *Kunarac* case.[123] This is probably because the UNCAT is focused on individual acts of torture in peacetime. For crimes against humanity (and war crimes) a more functional approach was adopted, since in modern situations of turmoil non-State actors can act in a manner similar to States, something which is now accepted in relation to UNCAT too.[124]

The ICC's Elements of Crimes only require that the perpetrator knew that the conduct 'was part of or intended the conduct to be part of a widespread or systematic attack on the civilian population'.[125] This is consistent with ICTY jurisprudence, such as in the *Tadić* trial judgment.[126] The Appeals Chamber also noted, on the basis of post-World-War-II trials where private individuals had denounced their neighbours and others to the Nazi regime, that crimes against humanity could be committed for solely private reasons, so long as it was the defendant's intention to link their conduct to the attack.[127]

As is evident, in the right circumstances torture undoubtedly falls into the category of crimes against humanity, although the precise contextual contours vary between different courts and tribunals. This is made more complex by the interplay between the definitions of the conduct element of crimes against humanity and their contextual elements, which need to be read together. That said, crimes against humanity form the bulk of prosecutions at the international level[128] and are thus an important part of the overall proscription of torture.

---

[119]   *Situation in Kenya*, Decision on the Prosecutor's Application Under Article 15 of the Rome Statute on the Authorization of an Investigation into the Situation in the Republic of Kenya, ICC-01/09-19, 1 March 2010, para 93. These indicia included whether the group was under responsible command, had sufficient means to carry out the attack, controlled territory, and was part of a larger group.

[120]   *Ibid*, dissenting opinion of Judge Kaul, para 51.

[121]   Kreβ, C, 'On the Outer Limits of Crimes Against Humanity: The Concept of Organization Within the Policy Requirement: Some Reflections on the March 2010 ICC Kenya Decision' (2010) 23 *Leiden Journal of International Law* 855.

[122]   See Cryer, Robinson and Vasiliev (n 81 above), 238, and the case law cited therein.

[123]   *Kunarac* (n 32 above), para 496, 'the definition of torture under international humanitarian law does not comprise the same elements as the definition of torture generally applied under human rights law. In particular, the Trial Chamber is of the view that the presence of a state official or of any other authority-wielding person in the torture process is not necessary for the offence to be regarded as torture under international humanitarian law'.

[124]   See *R v. TRA* (n 53 above and accompanying text above p. 291).

[125]   E.g. Elements for Article 7(1)(a), Element 3.

[126]   *Prosecutor v. Tadić* (n 111 above), para 657.

[127]   *Tadić* Appeal (n 21 above), paras 255–272.

[128]   Sadat, LN, 'Crimes Against Humanity in the Modern Age' (2013) 107 *American Journal of International Law* 334.

Torture as a War Crime

The final context in which torture undoubtedly amounts to an international crime is that of war crimes. War crimes are criminalised violations of the Law of Armed Conflict (Humanitarian Law).[129] The precise relationship between the two is somewhat contentious, and what transforms a violation of the Law of Armed Conflict into a war crime is the subject of considerable academic debate.[130] Happily, that debate need not concern us presently; for at least the last century, torture has been considered a war crime. For example, the 1919 Commission on the Responsibility of the Authors of the War directly referred to torture as such.[131] There were more than enough prosecutions for torture in the aftermath of the Second Word War to vindicate this view.[132]

As the law of war crimes traces the Law of Armed Conflict, it adopts the distinction drawn in that law between international and non-international armed conflict.[133] This will be considered in this part of the chapter but, rather like the distinction between 'mere' violations of the Law of Armed Conflict and war crimes, it need not be too troubling. This is because the prohibitions are, *mutatis mutandis*, largely the same.

International armed conflicts

Material element
The war crime of torture was expressly identified as a 'Grave Breach' of the Geneva Conventions in 1949.[134] This was reflected in Article 8(2)(a) of the Rome Statute which grants the ICC jurisdiction over 'Grave Breaches' in the following terms:

> any of the following acts against persons or property protected under the provisions of the relevant Geneva Convention: …
>
> (ii)   Torture or inhuman treatment, including biological experiments.

The pertinent parts of the Elements of Crimes for this offence are that

1. The perpetrator inflicted severe physical or mental pain or suffering upon one or more persons.

---

[129]   See generally Bothe, M, 'War Crimes', in Cassese, A, Jones, JRWD and Gaeta, P (eds), *The Rome Statute of the International Criminal Court* (Oxford University Press, 2002), 381.

[130]   Hathaway et al. (n 2 above); Cryer, R, 'Individual Responsibility for Violations of the Law of Armed Conflict' in McCormack, TLH and Livoja, R (eds), *Research Handbook on the Law of Armed Conflict* (Routledge, 2016), 536.

[131]   'Commission on the Responsibility of the Authors of the War and Enforcement of Penalties: Report', reprinted in (1920) 14 *American Journal of International Law* 95 114.

[132]   See, for example, the cases digested in The Law Reports Trials of War Criminals (UNQWCC, 1948), pp. 78, 96, 114, 116, 120 ,121, 200.

[133]   For detailed discussion of this see Akande, D, 'Classification of Armed Conflicts: Relevant Legal Concepts' in Wilmshurst, E (ed), *Classification of Conflict* (Oxford University Press), 32.

[134]   On which see Fischer, H, 'Grave Breaches of the 1949 Geneva Conventions' in Kirk-McDonald, G and Swaak-Goldman, O (eds), *Substantive and Procedural Aspects of International Criminal Law* (Kluwer, 2000), 65.

2. The perpetrator inflicted the pain or suffering for such purposes as: obtaining information or a confession, punishment, intimidation or coercion or for any reason based on discrimination of any kind.
3. Such person or persons were protected under one or more of the Geneva Conventions of 1949 ...

The first is relatively uncontroversial, in so far as there is no reason to believe that the standards for severity are other than those in the UNCAT, or as regards genocide or crimes against humanity. Hence we may pass over them fairly briefly. The second Element, however, differs from the Elements for crimes against humanity in two ways. There is no requirement that the victim be in custody. This can be explained as an accident, or, perhaps more convincingly, by its referring to 'protected' people – these being those 'protected' by the Four 1949 Geneva Conventions, who are in the hands of an enemy power, and in a position of vulnerability.

Perhaps as *quid pro quo* for the deletion of the custody requirement, or maybe to reflect the consistent findings by the *ad hoc* Tribunals, the Elements do include a purposive element like that in the UNCAT. It ought to be said (again) that since this is a non-exhaustive list and includes intimidation and coercion, this should not prove a significant hurdle to overcome, given that it would likely only exclude purely sadistic acts, which may also fall under the rubric of intimidation anyway.

The categories of protected persons are, broadly speaking the wounded, sick, shipwrecked, prisoners of war and civilians who are interned/detained or in occupied territory.[135] The definitions of protected persons were expanded in Additional Protocol I,[136] but Element 3's reference to protection by the 1949 Conventions seems to make it clear that the drafters of the Elements did not wish to adopt the innovations contained therein. Most of those developments are uncontroversial but some (such as those relating to prisoner of war status in Articles 43–44) are provisions that have led to deep, and bitter divisions amongst States and commentators.[137] It is likely for this reason that they were not included.

Those who fall outside those definitions in the 1949 Conventions retain some protection. Anyone who is in the hands of a party to an international armed conflict (including their own) is entitled to protection by virtue of Article 75 of Additional Protocol I, which prohibits torture.[138] This is generally accepted as representing customary international law.[139] Furthermore, the ICTY has determined that the customary prohibition of torture exists more generally in armed conflicts (and for the purposes of crimes against humanity), and its elements are as follows:

(i)   The infliction, by act or omission, of severe pain or suffering, whether physical or mental.

---

[135] Geneva Conventions I–IV, See generally Geiss, R and Paulussen, C, 'Specifically Protected Persons and Objects' in Saul, B and Akande, D, *The Oxford Guide to International Humanitarian Law* (Oxford University Press, 2020), 175.

[136] See e.g. Sassòli, M, *International Humanitarian* Law (Edward Elgar, 2019), 232–233.

[137] E.g. Dinstein, Y, *The Conduct of Hostilities Under the Law of International Armed Conflict* (Cambridge University Press, 2004), 44–47.

[138] Additional Protocol I to the Geneva Conventions of August 1949, 1125 UNTS 3, Article 75(2)(a) (ii).

[139] *Hamdan v. Rumsfeld* (2006) 548 US 557, at 70 (note this was the plurality opinion, Justice Kennedy expressed no view and the dissentients dissented).

(ii)   The act or omission must be intentional.

(iii) The act or omission must aim at obtaining information or a confession, or at punishing, intimidating or coercing the victim or a third person, or at discriminating, on any ground, against the victim or a third person.

The overlap between these and the Elements of Crimes is clear (although they were more inspired by the UNCAT than those Elements). It is genuinely unfortunate that outside of Article 8(2)(a), and despite the certainty of the ICTY on this point, and Article 75 of Additional Protocol I, there is no further direct provision for a war crime of torture in international armed conflicts in Article 8(2)(b), although certain forms thereof would certainly fall under the proscriptions of subjecting persons who are in the power of an adverse party to physical mutilation and of committing outrages upon personal dignity, in particular humiliating and degrading treatment, which are prohibited by Articles 8(2)(b)(x) and (xxi) respectively. The elements of these crimes do not provide for status-based limitations on victims, other than that in the case of the former they be in the power of the adverse party.[140]

Contextual element

It is important to remember that Article 8(a) of the Rome Statute and the duties that pertain to Grave Breaches[141] only apply in international armed conflicts.[142] The customary position is confirmed by the ICC's Elements of Crimes.[143] There have been arguments that under customary law these duties have now become expanded to non-international armed conflicts,[144] but these have fallen on stony ground.

The requirement that there is some form of nexus to the armed conflict is found in customary law and is quite clearly sensible, since even during armed conflicts 'common or garden' criminality still occurs. This is expressed in the Elements of Crimes of all of the war crimes in the Rome Statute as being that the conduct occurred 'in the context of and related to' the armed conflict, and in the ICTY as a 'nexus' requirement.

The ICTY described the nexus as being that a war crime:

> is shaped by or dependent upon the environment – the armed conflict – in which it is committed. It need not have been planned or supported by some form of policy. The armed conflict need not have been causal to the commission of the crime, but the existence of an armed conflict must, at a minimum, have played a substantial part in the perpetrator's ability to commit it, his decision to commit it, the manner in which it was committed or the purpose for which it was committed. Hence, if it can be established ... that the perpetrator acted in furtherance of or under the guise of the armed conflict, it would be sufficient to conclude that his acts were closely related to the armed conflict.[145]

---

[140]   See Elements of Crimes Article 8(2)(b)(x) Element 4. Space prevents further discussion of these prohibitions.

[141]   The primary one of which is to criminalise them on the basis of universal jurisdiction domestically, and to search for perpetrators (see e.g. Geneva Convention I, Article 49). For elaboration on this see *Commentary on Geneva Convention I on the Protection of Wounded and Sick Members of Armed Forces in the Field* (ICRC, 2016) paras 2818–2905.

[142]   *Prosecutor v. Tadić*, Decision on the Defence Interlocutory Appeal on Jurisdiction, IT-94-1-AR72, 2 October 1995, paras 79–84.

[143]   Elements of Crimes, Article 8(a)(ii) Element 5.

[144]   Separate Opinion of Judge Abi-Saab in *Tadić* (n 142 above).

[145]   *Kunarac* (n 32 above), para 58.

The Chamber also set out some of the criteria that may be taken into account when determining the nexus. These are:

> the fact that the perpetrator is a combatant; the fact that the victim is a non-combatant; the fact that the victim is a member of the opposing party; the fact that the act may be said to serve the ultimate goal of a military campaign; and the fact that the crime is committed as part of or in the context of the perpetrator's official duties.[146]

Although not expressly adopted by the Elements of Crimes, there seems to be no reason not to treat this as the relevant definition, and this is the position adopted by the ICC.[147] It provides a useful definition, and the indicia the ICTY set out (in a non-exhaustive way) are helpful. It is notable that there is nothing in the Elements of any of the war crimes, or in the nexus, that requires that the crimes be committed by a public official. It was established at the very least by the end of World War II that this was the case.[148]

Non-international armed conflicts

Non-international armed conflicts, although they represent the majority of modern armed conflicts, are the subject of comparatively brief regulation when compared to international armed conflicts. However, when it comes to torture, the position is very similar, and so not a great deal needs to be said. Common Article 3 to the Geneva Conventions, as encapsulated in Article 8(2)(c) of the Rome Statute, provides the relevant treaty (and customary)[149] law here, granting the ICC jurisdiction over:

> In the case of an armed conflict not of an international character, serious violations of article 3 common to the four Geneva Conventions of 12 August 1949, namely, any of the following acts committed against persons taking no active part in the hostilities, including members of armed forces who have laid down their arms and those placed *hors de combat* by sickness, wounds, detention or any other cause:
>
> (i)   Violence to life and person, in particular murder of all kinds, mutilation, cruel treatment and torture;

It is, perhaps, astonishing that the Elements of Crimes for the ICC do not include a separate set of Elements for torture under this provision. The likelihood is that the definitions of the offence, in terms of severity, purpose and nexus are the same as for international armed conflict. Similarly, it seems unlikely that the involvement of a State official is required.[150] When it comes to the status of the victim, this is provided for in the *chapeau* to Common Article 3 (and Article 8(2)(c)), this being, broadly speaking, those who are not active fighters. The remainder of the Elements can be assumed to be those identified by the ICTY in *Kunarac*, which thought

---

[146]   *Ibid*, para 59.
[147]   *Prosecutor v. Bemba Gombo*, Judgment, ICC-01/05-01/08-T, 21 March 2016, para 142.
[148]   *Tesch 'The Zyklon B case'*, 1 LRTWC 93.
[149]   See, e.g. Sivakumaran, S, *The Law of Non-International Armed Conflict* (Oxford University Press, 2012), 56–57.
[150]   The ICTY has not required one, and in other contexts neither have the Elements of Crimes. For a detailed review of the case law see Sivakumaran (n 49 above).

they were the same in both types of armed conflict. In the absence of any further guidance, the better approach would be to use this indication of the relevant Elements as a lodestar.

CONCLUSION

Having discussed the definitions of torture in transnational and international criminal law, it is time to sum up. Despite these being different categories and there being varying definitions of the various international and transitional crimes, there are considerable connections and synergies between them.

The basic elements of the different definitions do not vary significantly, other than as regards the purpose requirement, which has not proved to be problematic in practice. It is their contexts which differ: for individual acts of torture to fall within the UNCAT definition requires the involvement of a public official; for war crimes, there has to be an armed conflict; for crimes against humanity, there has to be an attack on a civilian population; for genocide there has to be special genocidal intent. In many ways it is these circumstances – these contexts – which raises what would otherwise be domestic crimes to matters of international concern.

As Neil Boister said in his definitive piece on transnational law, much will depend on the level of international concern that an offence arouses. The greater the level of concern (as defined, in the end, by States) the more likely they are to be accorded a higher status. So, purely domestic crimes such as theft are not considered to fall within the purview of international law whereas those on which there is a high degree of consensus regarding their offensiveness may, if States wish, become the subject of a treaty regime. Only when there is a practical consensus on the necessity for direct liability for an offence does conduct reach the threshold for international criminalisation in the narrow sense.[151]

Boister considers torture to be in the medium category. As he says,

> Torture may not yet shock the conscience of international society sufficiently for it to take the step of classifying torture as an international crime *stricto sensu*, but it does undoubtedly shock the conscience of sufficient citizens in influential states for a treaty to be adopted to protect the citizens of other states from torture.[152]

This is the position adopted in this chapter. The appalling nature of torture has not yet persuaded States to accept the intrusion on their sovereignty that would result from accepting that torture committed by an individual in peacetime is a 'core' international crime.[153]

This position has not gone unchallenged. The two most prominent advocates of the existence of an international crime of private peacetime individual torture are Antonio Cassese and, more recently, Kevin Jon Heller. To treat them chronologically, Cassese's position is only made briefly and not always clearly. Early in his treatise on international criminal law he asserts that the creation of an international crime depends on the following cumulative criteria: (a) a violation of treaty or custom; (b) the rule being designed to protect values of the

---

[151] Boister (n 1 above), 958–962.

[152] *Ibid*, 967.

[153] This is why there is no individual section on a separate international crime of torture not referable to the definition of the accepted 'core' international crimes.

international community; (c) the existence of a universal interest in prosecuting such offences; and (d) the perpetrator acting as a *de facto or de jure* State official.[154]

On this basis, Cassese declares that peacetime torture is an international crime.[155] Later in the work, Cassese argues this on the basis of the large number of ratifications of the UNCAT, and *dicta* of the ICTY, which are read very broadly.[156] Although Cassese's humane instincts in proposing this are beyond doubt, it must be said that this is a thin basis upon which to make such a bold claim.[157]

Heller, in many ways, takes a similar approach to Cassese as regards what amounts to an international crime,[158] whilst placing heavy weight on a universal duty to domestically prosecute and punish.[159] Applying his approach to torture, he argues that the widespread condemnation of the practice, such as the high level of ratification of the UNCAT and repeated General Assembly Resolutions denouncing torture, means that it has achieved that status. It is a carefully made case, and probably does makes the case for torture being a separate international crime in his sense of the term. That, however, is not the one that is adopted here, or which is used by States.[160]

In the end, both approaches fall victim to a category error. The UNCAT, as we saw, rejected the idea of torture being an international crime in the manner of the Genocide Convention. Therefore, even if the obligation in Article 2 of the UNCAT is customary, and with it the *aut dedere aut judicare* obligation in Article 7, this would not create an international crime but a customary obligation on States to criminalise and take action against torture.

Creating a 'pure' international crime requires a decision to create direct liability and States have chosen not to take this step. They had a chance to do so in 1984, as discussed above, and had an opportunity to take a second 'bite of the cherry' in Rome in 1998. Both times they refused to exercise their discretion to 'upgrade' individual peacetime torture to the status of an international crime.

Whilst these conceptual distinctions are important, the various forms the prohibition takes ought not to be hermetically sealed from one another. They, if the lyricism may be forgiven, are not stars on their own, but part of a constellation that constitutes the overall prohibition of torture. This also includes the provisions of human rights law concerning the prohibition of torture, which is covered elsewhere throughout this volume.

The overlaps between the various, mutually supporting areas of law can be shown by the extent of inter-judicial dialogue between the various courts, committees and tribunals that have had to deal with torture.[161] For the most part this is a very good thing, the various written provi-

---

[154] Cassese, A, Gaeta, P et al., *Cassese's International Criminal Law*, 3rd edn (Oxford University Press, 2013), 20. This is not the place to consider how this would explain all the extant international crimes.

[155] *Ibid*, 21.

[156] *Ibid*, 132–54.

[157] See also the discussion relating to Heller, below.

[158] Heller (n 2 above).

[159] *Ibid*, 407–408.

[160] To be fair, Heller rejects the approach adopted here, but space prohibits further doctrinal discussion on this.

[161] On the matter more generally see McCrudden, C, 'A Common Law of Human Rights? Transnational Judicial Conversations on Constitutional Rights' (2000) 20 *Oxford Journal of Legal Studies* 499.

sions often leave many matters for interpretation, and the more high-quality primary materials available the better. That said, they must be used with an awareness of context and nuanced decision makers must work within the frameworks and definitions they are mandated to apply. If this is borne in mind, there seems no reason not to make use of that which has gone before.

To finish on a broader note, the focus of this chapter is the interplay of criminal law and torture. Criminal law, though, is not, and should never be, the first port of call when responding to harms. Law, in Keith Hawkins' felicitous formulation, ought to be a last resort.[162] Such a consideration relates both to the appropriate bounds of criminalisation (although few would disagree about torture being within this), but also to the fact that criminal law is reactive. Far better to head off such behaviour at the proverbial pass than respond when it has already come to be. Here is where the obligations relating to prevention, contained in Article 2 of the UNCAT and in the Optional Protocol to the Convention against Torture, and to dissemination and training contained, *inter alia*, in Articles 10 and 11 of the UNCAT (all discussed elsewhere in this volume) come into their own. Beyond that, and where torture has occurred, the training of medical and mental health practitioners and others involved in the treatment of survivors has at least an equal claim upon our attention. A toolbox needs more than just hammers.

---

[162] Hawkins, K, *Law as Last Resort* (Oxford University Press, 2003).

14. The use of information obtained by torture or other ill-treatment

Matt Pollard

OVERVIEW OF THE EXCLUSIONARY RULE

First among the purposes of torture to be listed in the definition in Article 1 of the UN Convention against Torture is 'obtaining from [the victim] or a third person information or a confession'. If perpetrators of torture are often seeking information, it is presumably with the ultimate aim of making use of it. Ensuring that potential torturers know that any information they obtain will not be capable of being used should therefore make an important contribution to the prevention of torture. This potential for deterrence, coupled with concern for the fairness of any proceeding that would be tainted by evidence obtained by torture, particularly given its inherent unreliability, and by the need to avoid courts or other State actors being seen to condone torture (the 'integrity' rationale), has led to the development of an 'exclusionary rule'.[1]

To these ends – deterrence, fairness, integrity – the UN Declaration against Torture, adopted by the UN General Assembly in 1975 as the first major international instrument specifically addressed to preventing and responding to torture, included the following provision:

> Any statement which is established to have been made as a result of torture or other cruel, inhuman or degrading treatment or punishment may not be invoked as evidence against the person concerned or against any other person in any proceedings.[2]

---

[1]   See Rodley, NS and Pollard, M, *The Treatment of Prisoners under International Law*, 3rd edn (Oxford University Press, 2009), 162–166; Burgers, J and Danelius, H, *The United Nations Convention against Torture: A Handbook* (Martinus Nijhoff, 1988), 148; Pollard, M, 'Rotten Fruit: State Solicitation, Acceptance, and Use of Information Obtained Through Torture by Another State' (2005) 23 *NQHR* 349; Evans, MD, '"All the Perfumes of Arabia": The House of Lords and "Foreign Torture Evidence"' (2006) 19 *Leiden Journal of International Law* 1125; Nowak, M and McArthur, E, *The United Nations Convention against Torture: A Commentary* (Oxford University Press, 2008), 503–537; UN Special Rapporteur on Torture (Manfred Nowak), *Report on Non-Admissibility of Evidence Extracted by Torture*, UN Doc A/61/259 (14 August 2006) ('SR Torture Report 2006'); Special Rapporteur on Torture (Juan E. Méndez), *Report on Use of Information Obtained by Torture and the Exclusionary Rule*, UN Doc A/HRC/25/60 (10 April 2014) ('SR Torture Report 2014'); European Court of Human Rights (ECtHR), *Othman (Abu Qatada) v. The United Kingdom*, no 8139/09, ECHR 2012 (extracts), paras 264–265. For detailed discussion of relevant legal theory, see Ernst, A, *The Transnational Use of Torture Evidence* (Herbert Utz Verlag, 2015), 68–106. For a comparative study of national laws and practices in 17 countries, see *Tainted by Torture: Examining the Use of Torture Evidence* (Fair Trials/Redress, May 2018).

[2]   *Declaration on the Protection of All Persons from Being Subjected to Torture and Other Cruel, Inhuman or Degrading Treatment or Punishment*, adopted by UN General Assembly Resolution 3452 (XXX) of 9 December 1975, Article 12.

A similar rule appears in Article 15 of the UN Convention against Torture:

> Each State Party shall ensure that any statement which is established to have been made as a result of torture shall not be invoked as evidence in any proceedings, except against a person accused of torture as evidence that the statement was made.[3]

The International Covenant on Civil and Political Rights (ICCPR) has been interpreted and applied by the Human Rights Committee to similar effect. The Committee has long held that, as part of a State's obligations in relation to torture and other cruel, inhuman or degrading treatment under Article 7 of the Covenant: '... the law must prohibit the use [or] admissibility in judicial proceedings of statements or confessions obtained through torture or other prohibited treatment'.[4] The Committee has also affirmed the relevance of the exclusionary rule in relation to Article 14 of the Covenant, on fair trial guarantees:

> Domestic law must ensure that statements or confessions obtained in violation of Article 7 of the Covenant are excluded from the evidence, except if such material is used as evidence that torture or other treatment prohibited by this provision occurred, and that in such cases the burden is on the State to prove that statements made by the accused have been given of their own free will.[5]

Furthermore, the right to life will be violated where a person is executed on the basis of a conviction in which evidence obtained by torture or other ill-treatment was relied upon,[6] and the right to liberty will be violated where a person is detained or imprisoned on the basis of such evidence.[7]

International standards on the rule of law and administration of justice also address the issue. The UN Guidelines on the Role of Prosecutors, for instance,[8] state:

---

[3]   Convention against Torture and Other Cruel, Inhuman or Degrading Treatment or Punishment (adopted 10 December 1984, entered into force 26 June 1987) 1465 UNTS 85, ('UNCAT'), Article 15.

[4]   Human Rights Committee ('HRC'), General Comment no 20: Article 7 (Prohibition of torture, or other cruel, inhuman or degrading treatment or punishment), UN Doc A/47/40(SUPP) pp 193–195 (10 March 1992) ('HRC General Comment 20'), para 12. General Comment no 20 replaced the 1982 General Comment no 7, which had stated, 'it follows from Article 7, read together with Article 2 of the Covenant, that States must ensure an effective protection through some machinery of control. ... Among the safeguards which may make control effective are ... provisions making confessions or other evidence obtained through torture or other treatment contrary to Article 7 inadmissible in court' (para 1).

[5]   HRC, General Comment no 32: Article 14 (Right to equality before courts and tribunals and to a fair trial), UN Doc CCPR/C/GC/32 (23 August 2007) ('HRC General Comment 32'), para 41. See also HRC, *Singarasa v. Sri Lanka*, UN Doc CCPR/C/81/D/1033/2001 (21 July 2004), para 7.4, and many subsequent decisions. In describing the 'effective remedy' required under Article 2(3)(a) of the Covenant in relation to violations of Article 14, the Committee has in some cases specifically held that the State is required to review whether the verdict in the case would stand if the impugned confessions were excluded (HRC, *Tyan v. Kazakhstan*, UN Doc CCPR/C/119/D/2125/2011 (16 March 2017), para 11) or to quash the conviction and if necessary conduct a new, fair, trial (e.g. HRC, *Bazarov v. Kyrgyzstan*, UN Doc CCPR/C/118/D/2187/2012 (21 October 2016), para 8).

[6]   E.g. HRC, *Deolall v. Guyana*, UN Doc CCPR/C/82/D/912/2000 (1 November 2004), paras 5.1–5.3; HRC, *Grishkovtsov v. Belarus*, UN Doc CCPR/C/113/D/2013/2010 (1 April 2015), para 8.6; HRC, *Selyun v. Belarus*, UN Doc CCPR/C/115/D/2289/2013 (6 November 2015), para 7.7.

[7]   E.g. Working Group on Arbitrary Detention, *Juan García Cruz and Santiago Sánchez Silvestre v. Mexico*, UN Doc A/HRC/WGAD/2013/21 (1 April 2014), paras 35 and 39.

[8]   Guidelines on the Role of Prosecutors, welcomed by UNGA Res 45/166 (1990). See also Body of Principles for the Protection of All Persons under Any Form of Detention or Imprisonment, UNGA

When prosecutors come into possession of evidence against suspects that they know or believe on reasonable grounds was obtained through recourse to unlawful methods, which constitute a grave violation of the suspect's human rights, especially involving torture or cruel, inhuman or degrading treatment or punishment, or other abuses of human rights, they shall refuse to use such evidence against anyone other than those who used such methods, or inform the Court accordingly, and shall take all necessary steps to ensure that those responsible for using such methods are brought to justice.[9]

The instruments governing international criminal tribunals include a more general exclusionary rule.[10] Article 69 of the Rome Statute of the International Criminal Court (ICC), for instance, provides:

69(7). Evidence obtained by means of a violation of this Statute or internationally recognized human rights shall not be admissible if:
(a) The violation casts substantial doubt on the reliability of the evidence; or
(b) The admission of the evidence would be antithetical to and would seriously damage the integrity of the proceedings.

While the ICC's general approach to the rule is one of judicial discretion and balancing, several authors have concluded that evidence obtained by torture could never be admitted under the Rule.[11]

Similar provisions appear in rule 95 of the Rules of Procedure and Evidence of the International Criminal Tribunal for the former Yugoslavia (ICTY) and International Criminal Tribunal for Rwanda (ICTR). These do not appear to have been applied specifically in relation to evidence obtained by torture.[12] However, the ICTY has several times affirmed that statements obtained by oppressive conduct cannot be admitted.[13]

The constituent instruments for the Extraordinary Chambers in the Courts of Cambodia (ECCC), a 'hybrid' national-international tribunal, do not include a specific exclusionary rule.

Res 43/173, annex (9 December 1988), Principle 27: 'Non-compliance with these principles in obtaining evidence shall be taken into account in determining the admissibility of such evidence against a detained or imprisoned person.'
9   Guidelines on the Role of Prosecutors (n 8 above), Article 16. Indeed, for the exclusionary rule to be effective in practice, prosecutors, lawyers and judges must have the necessary individual and institutional capacity and independence. See e.g. Committee against Torture ('CAT'), Concluding Observations on Chile, UN Doc CAT/C/CHL/CO/6 (29 August 2018), para 21; Basic Principles on the Independence of the Judiciary, endorsed by UNGA Res 40/32 and 40/146 (1985); Basic Principles on the Role of Lawyers, welcomed by UNGA Res 45/166 (1990).
10   See also Ambos, K, 'The Transnational Use of Torture Evidence' (2009) 42 *Israel Law Review* 362, 367–377.
11   Viebig, P, *Illicitly Obtained Evidence at the International Criminal Court* (TMC Asser Press, 2016), 107–108, 149–150, 172–179.
12   International Criminal Tribunal for Rwanda ('ICTR'), *Prosecutor v. Karemera et al., Decision on the Prosecution Motion for Admission into Evidence of Post-Arrest Interviews with Joseph Nzirorera and Mathieu Ngirumpatse*, ICTR-98-44-T (2 November 2007), where an allegation of duress was rejected by the Chamber on the basis that 'the Defence did not attempt to substantiate the allegation that the interview took place under circumstances that would amount to threats or coercion and that the transcripts show no sign thereof' (para 43).
13   International Criminal Tribunal for the former Yugoslavia ('ICTY'), *Prosecutor v. Mucić et al., Decision on Zdravko Mucic's Motion for the Exclusion of Evidence*, IT-96-21-A (2 September 1997), para 41; ICTY, *Prosecutor v. Stakić, Provisional Order on the Standards Governing the Admission of Evidence and Identification*, IT-97-24-PT (25 February 2002), Annex, para 8.

The ECCC has nevertheless excluded or limited the use of torture evidence, citing relevant provisions of Cambodian law and Article 15 of the UNCAT.[14] However, as will be explained later, the way in which the ECCC has interpreted and applied certain aspects of the exclusionary rule may raise concerns.[15]

As regards international humanitarian law, applicable in situations of armed conflict, the 1949 Geneva Conventions and 1977 Protocols each contain general provisions for the fairness of trials.[16] Indeed, 'Wilfully depriving a protected person of the rights of fair and regular trial' is expressly listed as a 'grave breach' giving rise to individual criminal responsibility as a war crime.[17]

More specifically, the 1960 International Committee of the Red Cross (ICRC) Commentary on the Third Geneva Convention highlights that Article 99 (which provides that in judicial proceedings for penal and disciplinary sanctions, 'No moral or physical coercion may be exerted on a prisoner of war in order to induce him to admit himself guilty of the act of which he is accused') is underpinned by concern with the impacts on justice and on the proceedings that result from use of evidence obtained by torture and other unreliable or otherwise unacceptable methods of questioning.[18]

---

[14] Extraordinary Chambers in the Courts of Cambodia ('ECCC') Supreme Court Chamber, *Case no 002/19-09-2007-ECCC/SC (Nuon Chea and Khieu Samphan), Decision on Objections to Document Lists – Full Reasons*, (31 December 2015); ECCC Trial Chamber, *Case no 002/19-09-2007-ECCC/TC (Nuon Chea and Khieu Samphan), Decision on Evidence Obtained Through Torture* (5 February 2016); ECCC Pre-Trial Chamber, *Case No 003/07-09-2009-ECCC/OCIJ (PTC33), Decision on Request for Annulment of D114/164, D114/167, D114/170, and D114/71* (13 December 2017).

[15] The ECCC considers itself bound only by Article 15 UNCAT and Cambodian law and tends to disregard or discount the legal weight of other relevant sources. It has on several occasions implied that the fact that the accused were facing charges of responsibility for torture should influence its interpretation or application of the exclusionary rule (e.g. Trial Chamber, *Nuon Chea and Khieu Samphan, Decision on Evidence Obtained Through Torture* (n 14 above), paras 74 to 78; *Decision on Request for Annulment of D114/164, D114/167, D114/170, and D114/71* (n 14 above), paras 33 and 38). Such suggestions echo Scharf, MP, 'Tainted Provenance: When, If Ever, Should Torture Evidence Be Admissible?' (2008) 65 *Wash. & Lee L. Rev.* 129, which was in turn strongly criticized in Ambos (n 10 above), e.g. at 380–381. While the ECCC has on balance mainly upheld the exclusionary rule against frontal challenges by the prosecutors and the defence, as discussed below some aspects remain of concern.

[16] Geneva Convention (I) for the Amelioration of the Condition of the Wounded and Sick in Armed Forces in the Field 1949, 75 UNTS 31, entered into force 21 October 1950, Articles 3(1)(d) and 49, fourth paragraph; Geneva Convention (II) on Wounded, Sick and Shipwrecked of Armed Forces at Sea 1949, 75 UNTS 85, entered into force 21 October 1950, Articles 3(1)(d) and 50, fourth paragraph; Geneva Convention (III) relative to the Treatment of Prisoners of War 1949, 75 UNTS 135, entered into force 21 October 1950, Articles 3(1)(d), 99, 102–108; Geneva Convention (IV) relative to the Protection of Civilian Persons in Time of War 1949, 75 UNTS 287, entered into force 21 October 1950, Articles 3(1) (d), 5 and 66–75; Protocol (I) Additional to the Geneva Conventions of 12 August 1949, and Relating to the Protection of Victims of International Armed Conflicts 1977, 1125 UNTS 3, entered into force 7 December 1978, Article 75(4); Protocol (II) Additional to the Geneva Conventions of 12 August 1949, and Relating to the Protection of Victims of Non-International Armed Conflicts 1977, 1125 UNTS 609, entered into force 7 December 1978, Article 6(2). See also Pejic, J, 'The Protective Scope of Common Article 3: More than Meets the Eye' (2011) 93 *International Review of the Red Cross* 189, 211–214.

[17] Geneva Convention III, Article 130; Geneva Convention IV, Article 147; Protocol I, Article 85(4) (e); and see Rome Statute of the International Criminal Court 1998, 2187 UNTS 90, entered into force 1 July 2002 ('ICC Statute'), Article 8(2)(a)(vi).

[18] de Preux, J, *Commentary: III Geneva Convention relative to the treatment of prisoners of war, published under the general editorship of Jean S. Pictet* (ICRC, Geneva 1960), 471–472.

The 1977 Geneva Protocols I and II include a non-exhaustive list of 'generally recognized principles of regular judicial procedure', which includes the stipulation that 'no one shall be compelled to testify against himself or to confess guilt',[19] in relation to which the 1987 ICRC Commentaries state:

> The majority of national judiciary systems contain provisions of this nature, but it took many centuries before the legality of torturing defendants to obtain confessions and information on their accomplices was abandoned. However, it was appropriate to include here a reminder of this legal guarantee, which is recognized today, as all too often the police or examining magistrates tend to use questionable means to extract a confession which they consider to be the 'final proof'.[20]

Recently updated ICRC commentaries to the 1949 Conventions also hold the prohibition on compelled confessions to be an essential element of the more general fair trial provisions of all the Conventions.[21]

The ICRC study of customary international law concluded that the rule that, 'No one may be convicted or sentenced, except pursuant to a fair trial affording all essential judicial guarantees' is applicable to all international and non-international armed conflicts as a matter of customary international law. The study commented that this general requirement encompasses the exclusionary rule in relation to torture and other statements obtained by compulsion.[22]

It also seems likely that the exclusionary rule forms part of general customary international law, whether on the basis that it is an inherent aspect of the prohibition of torture (itself universally accepted as a rule of customary international law), or that it is a stand-alone rule.[23]

At the regional level, the Organization of American States has also adopted an explicit exclusionary rule, in the 1985 Inter-American Convention to Prevent and Punish Torture, which provides:

> No statement that is verified as having been obtained through torture shall be admissible as evidence in a legal proceeding, except in a legal action taken against a person or persons accused of having elicited it through acts of torture, and only as evidence that the accused obtained such statement by such means.[24]

---

[19]   Protocol I, Article 75(4)(f); Protocol II, Article 6(2)(f).

[20]   Pilloud, C and others, *Commentary on the Additional Protocols of 8 June 1977 to the Geneva Conventions of 12 August 1949* (ICRC/Martinus Nijhoff, 1987), 883.

[21]   See for example, the ICRC *Commentary on the First Geneva Convention: Convention (I) for the Amelioration of the Condition of the Wounded and Sick in Armed Forces in the Field*, 2nd edn (ICRC, 2016), paras 685 and 2902. For additional commentary, not from the ICRC, see Doswald-Beck, L, 'Judicial Guarantees under Common Article 3' in Clapham, A, Gaeta, P and Sassòli, M (eds), *The 1949 Geneva Conventions: A Commentary* (Oxford University Press, 2015), 482; Akhavan, P, 'Judicial Guarantees [Geneva Convention IV]' in Clapham, Gaeta and Sassòli (eds), *ibid*, 1230.

[22]   Henckaerts, J-M, and Doswald-Beck, L, *Customary International Humanitarian Law: Volume I, Rules* (ICRC/Cambridge University Press, 2005), Rule 100 and commentary.

[23]   Special Rapporteur on Torture (Juan E. Méndez), SR Torture Report 2014 (n 1 above), paras 17, 22. See also Thienel, T, 'The Admissibility of Evidence Obtained by Torture under International Law' (2006) 17 *EJIL* 349, 365; Ernst (n 1 above), 47–56 and Viebig (n 11 above), 175–176.

[24]   Inter-American Convention to Prevent and Punish Torture 1985, OAS Treaty Series no 67, entered into force 28 February 1987, Article 10. Article 8(3) of the American Convention on Human Rights 1969, 1144 UNTS 123, entered into force 18 July 1978, also provides: 'A confession of guilt by the accused shall be valid only if it is made without coercion of any kind.'

The Inter-American Court of Human Rights and Inter-American Commission on Human Rights have found admission of evidence obtained by torture or other ill-treatment to violate this specific rule, as well as the more general provisions on torture and fair trial under the American Convention on Human Rights.[25]

Although the European Convention on Human Rights does not include an explicit exclusionary rule, the European Court of Human Rights has in numerous cases held the prohibition of torture and other ill-treatment (Article 3) and fair trial rights (Article 6) to have been violated where evidence obtained by torture or other abuse was admitted into proceedings.[26]

The African Commission on Human and Peoples' Rights has adopted a number of relevant standards invoking the prohibition of torture and other ill-treatment under Article 5, and the right to fair trial under Article 7, of the African Charter on Human and Peoples' Rights. The 2002 Robben Island Guidelines for the Prohibition and Prevention of Torture in Africa, for instance, provide that States should ensure:

> that any statement obtained through the use of torture, cruel, inhuman or degrading treatment or punishment shall not be admissible as evidence in any proceedings except against persons accused of torture as evidence that the statement was made.[27]

Most recently, in the 2015 Principles and Guidelines on Human and Peoples' Rights while Countering Terrorism in Africa, the rule was formulated as follows:

> Statements, confessions, or other evidence obtained by any form of coercion or force, in particular, through torture and cruel, inhuman, and degrading treatment or punishment, incommunicado detention, disappearance, the absence of basic procedural guarantees, or other serious violations of internationally protected human rights shall not be used as evidence in any proceedings, except when used as evidence against an individual accused of those above abuses. Such evidence may also not be considered as probative of any fact in a proceeding, including in sentencing.[28]

---

[25]   E.g. Inter-American Court of Human Rights ('IACtHR'), *Cabrera Garcia and Montiel Flores v. Mexico*, Series C no 220 (26 November 2010); Inter-American Commission on Human Rights ('IACommHR'), *Manuel Manríquez v. Mexico* Decision 2/99 (23 February 1999); IACommHR, *Alfonso Martin del Campo Dodd* Decision 117/09 (19 November 2009); IACommHR, *Rubén Luis Godoy v. Argentina (Merits)* Decision 66/12 (29 March 2012); IACommHR, *Omar Maldonado Vargas, Alvaro Yánez del Villar, Mario Antonio Cornejo, et al. v. Chile* Decision 119/13 (8 November 2013).

[26]   E.g. *Jalloh v. Germany* [GC], no 54810/00, ECHR 2006-IX; *Harutyunyan v. Armenia*, no 36549/03, ECHR 2007-III; *Gäfgen v. Germany* [GC], no 22978/05, ECHR 2010; *Othman (Abu Qatada) v. The United Kingdom* (n 1 above), paras 266–267; *El Haski v. Belgium*, no 649/08, 25 September 2012.

[27]   African Commission on Human and Peoples' Rights ('ACHPR'), *Guidelines and Measures for the Prohibition and the Prevention of Torture, Cruel, Inhuman or Degrading Treatment or Punishment in Africa* (2002), Article 29. See also ACHPR, *Principles and Guidelines on the Right to a Fair Trial and Legal Assistance in Africa*, DOC/OS(XXX)247 (2001), Article N.6(d)(i): 'Any confession or other evidence obtained by any form of coercion or force may not be admitted as evidence or considered as probative of any fact at trial or in sentencing. Any confession or admission obtained during incommunicado detention shall be considered to have been obtained by coercion.'

[28]   ACHPR, *Principles and Guidelines on Human and Peoples' Rights while Countering Terrorism in Africa*, 56th Ordinary Session (21 April to 7 May 2015), Principle 4(c)(i). See also ACHPR, *Guidelines on the conditions of arrest, police custody and pre-trial detention in Africa*, 55th Ordinary Session (28 April to 12 May 2014), Article 9(d).

The African Commission has also found, in its decisions on individual complaints, that reliance on information obtained by torture or other ill-treatment has violated the African Charter.[29]

While the Arab Charter on Human Rights does not explicitly include an exclusionary rule, it has been argued that the right under Article 16(6) of the Charter not to incriminate oneself means 'that any confession obtained through torture or the threat to use torture will not be admissible in evidence'.[30]

It may be noted from the language of most of the provisions cited above, and confirmed in related jurisprudence, that while the rule against self-incrimination as a specific fair trial guarantee in criminal proceedings applies only to the extraction of evidence from the accused,[31] the broader rule against reliance on evidence obtained through torture or other ill-treatment applies with equal force to evidence extracted from witnesses or other 'third parties'.[32]

If the exclusionary rule appears firmly embedded in international law, debate remains regarding a number of aspects:[33]

- its application to evidence obtained by forms of cruel, inhuman or degrading treatment other than torture;
- the standard and burden of proof;
- the existence and scope of exceptions to the rule;
- its application to physical and other forms of derivative evidence;
- the use of information outside of the context of judicial or other formal proceedings;
- situations where the abuse was perpetrated by a State other than the State seeking to use the information, or by non-State actors.

---

[29]   E.g. ACHPR, *Malawi African Association and Others v. Mauritania*, Nos 54/91 and others, 13th Activity Report (11 May 2000), para 95; ACHPR, *Egyptian Initiative for Personal Rights and Interights v. Arab Republic of Egypt*, No 334/06, 9th Extra-Ordinary Session (23 February to 3 March 2011). See also Mujuzi, JD, 'The African Commission on Human and Peoples' Rights and the admissibility of evidence obtained as a result of torture, cruel, inhuman and degrading treatment: *Egyptian Initiative for Personal Rights and Interights v. Arab Republic of Egypt*' (2013) 17 *International Journal of Evidence and Proof* 284.
[30]   Mujuzi, JD, 'The Protection of the Right to Freedom from Torture in the Arab League States and under the Arab Charter on Human Rights' (2010) 2 *City University of Hong Kong Law Review* 247, 257.
[31]   Nowak, M, *U.N. Covenant on Civil and Political Rights: CCPR Commentary*, 2nd edn (N.P. Engel, 2005) 345.
[32]   See Special Rapporteur on Torture (Juan E. Méndez), SR Torture Report 2014 (n 1 above), para 28; and e.g. CAT, *Ktiti v. Morocco*, UN Doc CAT/C/46/D/419/2010 (26 May 2011); *Othman (Abu Qatada) v. the United Kingdom* (n 1 above), paras 263, 266 and 267; *El Haski v Belgium* (n 26 above), para 85.
[33]   See also, generally, Nowak and McArthur (n 1 above), 503–537; Ernst (n 1 above). Another issue, rarely addressed and not further developed here, is what consequences should flow for judges or other officials who fail to apply the exclusionary rule despite credible allegations of torture: see CAT, Concluding observations on Lebanon, UN Doc CAT/C/LBN/CO/1 (30 May 2017) ('CAT Lebanon 2017'), para 32; Concluding observations on Rwanda, UN Doc CAT/C/RWA/CO/2 (21 December 2017) ('CAT Rwanda 2017'), para 21(d). See also generally, International Commission of Jurists, *Practitioners Guide no 13 on Judicial Accountability* (2016).

OTHER CRUEL, INHUMAN OR DEGRADING TREATMENT

Article 15 of the UNCAT refers only to statements obtained by torture, whereas Article 12 of the UN Declaration refers as well to other cruel, inhuman or degrading treatment or punishment. The Human Rights Committee has interpreted the ICCPR as more broadly precluding evidence obtained by any breach of Article 7, therefore including other forms of cruel, inhuman or degrading treatment that may not constitute torture *per se*.[34]

The UN Special Rapporteur on Torture has concluded that international law requires that domestic laws provide for 'the exclusion of any and all evidence obtained in violation of safeguards designed to protect against torture and other ill-treatment'.[35]

In its general comment on Article 2 of the Convention against Torture, the Committee against Torture stated that, 'The Committee considers that Articles 3 to 15 are likewise obligatory as applied to both torture and ill-treatment.'[36] This has been interpreted by many (including the UN Special Rapporteur) as confirming that the Committee considered Article 15 to encompass statements obtained by ill-treatment (possibly as an aspect of Article 16).[37] The Committee itself has sometimes taken the approach of citing both Articles 15 and 16 and referring to the exclusion of all information obtained through torture or other ill-treatment.[38]

In at least one case, however, the Committee insisted on a strict interpretation of Article 15 as applying only to torture, without referring to its earlier pronouncement in General Comment no 2.[39] It did however find a distinct violation of Article 16 in the case, citing a failure to provide 'redress and fair and adequate compensation' for the ill-treatment, referring to the merely 'symbolic' amount of monetary compensation provided, and the fact that the civil court

---

[34]   See HRC General Comment 20 (n 4 above), para 12 and HRC General Comment 32 (n 5 above), paras 6, 41 and 60.

[35]   Special Rapporteur on Torture (Juan E. Méndez), SR Torture Report 2014 (n 1 above), para 68 (and see paras 26 and 82(c)), referring also to Principle 27 of the UN Body of Principles for the Protection of All Persons under Any Form of Detention or Imprisonment (n 8 above).

[36]   CAT, General Comment No 2: Implementation of Article 2 by States Parties, UN Doc CAT/C/CG/2 (24 January 2008) ('CAT General Comment 2'), para 6.

[37]   See e.g. Special Rapporteur on Torture (Juan E. Méndez), SR Torture Report 2014 (n 1 above), para 26. Article 15 is not included in the enumerated list of Articles to which Article 16 (on other cruel, inhuman and degrading treatment) applies, but most observers interpret that list as non-exhaustive. As is explained below, the CAT itself interprets Article 16 as requiring redress and compensation parallel to that required for torture under Article 14, despite Article 14 not being included in the list in Article 16, and there seems little reason to treat Article 15 differently in this regard.

[38]   E.g. CAT, Concluding Observations on Kazakhstan, UN Doc CAT/C/KAZ/CO/3 (12 December 2014), para 23; Concluding Observations on Bahrain, UN Doc CAT/C/BHR/CO/2-3 (29 May 2017), para 17; Concluding Observations on Chile, UN Doc CAT/C/CHL/CO/6 (29 August 2018), para 21.

[39]   CAT, *Kirsanov v. Russian Federation*, UN Doc CAT/C/52/D/478/2011 (14 May 2014), para 11.4. See also Ernst (n 1 above). Her conclusion, at 130 and 189, that the exclusionary rule does not as a matter of international law generally apply to ill-treatment other than torture seems to be based on: her decision to focus mainly on Article 15 UNCAT; the limited scope of Article 14(3)(g) of the Covenant (which while clearly covering non-torture ill-treatment, only applies to statements *by the accused* in a *criminal* trial); and her rejection of the position, held by the Human Rights Committee, Special Rapporteur on Torture, and others, that the exclusionary rule is implicit in the broader prohibition of torture and other ill-treatment under Article 7, fair trial provisions, and international law more generally. Her conclusion in this regard therefore depends on rejecting a substantial body of opinion held by expert bodies expressly charged by treaties and international instruments with responsibility for interpreting and applying the relevant provisions.

awarding the compensation could not impose any measures on the individuals responsible. It did not directly address in the decision whether exclusion of a statement obtained as a result of cruel, inhuman or degrading treatment would constitute a form of 'redress' required by Article 16, but this would seem to flow as a consequence of the Committee's interpretation of 'redress' as encompassing elements of 'effective remedy' and 'restitution'.[40] It is difficult to see how a victim of cruel, inhuman or degrading treatment could be said to have received an effective remedy or restitution so long as he or she suffers negative consequences as a result of a statement obtained by the abuse having been used against them.[41]

Courts and commissions at the regional level, applying the general prohibitions of torture and other ill-treatment and the requirements of fair trial, have held the exclusionary rule to apply in relation not only to torture but other forms of ill-treatment as well.[42] As will be discussed in more detail below, this includes the European Court, though it applies the rule somewhat differently when it comes to *physical* evidence obtained as the indirect result of forms of ill-treatment other than torture.

The ECCC has taken the position that there is no 'universally-accepted international standard which would extend the exclusion of torture-tainted evidence to all evidence obtained through cruel, inhuman and degrading treatment', and consequently the ECCC 'does not consider that Article 15 of the CAT extends to evidence obtained by ill-treatment'.[43] This position seems driven by the fact that the ECCC more generally considers itself only to be bound only by Article 15 as literally interpreted and not the other sources cited above, and insists on a general preference to admit evidence unless specifically prohibited from doing so by Article 15 or Cambodian law.

STANDARD AND BURDEN OF PROOF

Article 15 of the UNCAT refers to statements that are 'established' to have been made as a result of torture. This language gives little clarity as to the particular standard and burden of

---

[40] CAT, General Comment no 3: Implementation of Article 14 by States parties, UN Doc CAT/C/GC/3 (19 November 2012), para 2. At para 7 the Committee notes that, 'Restitution is a form of redress to re-establish the victim in his or her situation before the violation of the Convention was committed, taking into consideration the specificities of each case.'

[41] Even if this particular line of reasoning would only apply to use of such information against the victim of the ill-treatment, this would not preclude the Committee from applying a third-party exclusionary rule for 'other' ill-treatment as a part of the 'prevention' aspect of Article 16, as it had seemed ready to do in its General Comment 2 and, subsequent to the decision in *Kirsanov v. Russian Federation* (n 39 above), in its 2014 Concluding Observations on Kazakhstan (n 38 above), para 23 and its 2017 Concluding Observations on Bahrain (n 38 above), para 17.

[42] E.g. *Cabrera Garcia and Montiel Flores v. Mexico* (n 25 above), paras 136, 165–167, 176–177; *Egyptian Initiative for Personal Rights and Interights v. Arab Republic of Egypt* (n 29 above), paras 212–219. The ECtHR has clearly held that statements obtained by other ill-treatment may never be admitted (*Gäfgen v. Germany* (n 26 above), para 166 and *El Haski v Belgium* (n 26 above), para 85), although admission of physical evidence obtained by other ill-treatment is not necessarily prohibited unless it had a bearing on the outcome of the proceedings, i.e. 'had an impact on his or her conviction or sentence' (*Gäfgen v Germany* (n 26 above), para 178; *El Haski v Belgium* (n 26 above), para 85).

[43] *Nuon Chea and Khieu Samphan, Decision on Evidence Obtained Through Torture* (n 14 above), para 61.

proof applicable to the exclusionary rule, whether under Article 15 of the UNCAT or other provisions.[44]

The longstanding position of the UN Special Rapporteur on Torture was recently reaffirmed as follows:

> ... the defendant must only advance a plausible reason as to why the evidence may have been procured by torture or other ill-treatment. Thereafter the burden of proof must shift to the State and the courts must inquire as to whether there is a real risk that the evidence has been obtained by unlawful means. If there is a real risk, the evidence must not be admitted.[45]

The Committee against Torture has also repeatedly called on States to ensure that where there is an allegation that a statement was made under torture, the burden of proof lies not with the victim or defendant, but with the State.[46] The Human Rights Committee has similarly held that States should ensure that 'the burden of proving that a confession has not been obtained under torture or other ill-treatment rests with the prosecution in proceedings against the alleged victim'.[47]

---

[44]   See detailed analysis in Ernst (n 1 above), 140–190, 286. Ernst concludes that in judicial proceedings the presentation by a defendant of *prima facie* evidence of a credible allegation shifts the burden of proof to the State, and suggests that the particular standard of proof the State must then meet may depend on the type of proceeding (criminal versus administrative for instance, which seems a reasonable distinction) and possibly whether it is the State in question or a third State that is alleged to have perpetrated the torture (a distinction that seems less justified).

[45]   Special Rapporteur on Torture (Juan E. Méndez), SR Torture Report 2014 (n 1 above), para 67, see also paras 31–33 and 82(f). See similarly: Special Rapporteur on Torture (Manfred Nowak), UN Doc A/61/259 (14 August 2006), paras 44–65; Special Rapporteur on Torture (Theo Van Boven), UN Doc E/CN.4/2003/68 (2002), para 26(k); Special Rapporteur on Torture (Nigel Rodley), UN Doc A/56/156 (2001), para 39(j), and Report on Visit to Turkey, E/CN.4/1999/61/Add.1 (1999), para 113(e).

[46]   E.g. CAT, Concluding Observations on the United Kingdom, UN Doc CAT/C/GBR/CO/5 (24 June 2013) ('CAT UK 2013'), para 25; CAT Lebanon 2017 (n 33 above), para 32; CAT Rwanda 2017 (n 33 above), para 21(a). See similarly *Ktiti v. Morocco* (n 32 above), para 8.8; *Evloev v. Kazakhstan*, UN Doc CAT/C/51/D/441/2010 (5 November 2013), para 9.8; *Bairamov v. Kazakhstan*, UN Doc CAT/ C/52/D/497/2012 (14 May 2014), para 8.10; *Niyonzima v. Burundi*, UN Doc CAT/C/53/D/514/2012 (21 November 2014), para 8.7; *Kabura v. Burundi*, UN Doc CAT/C/59/D/549/2013 (11 November 2016), para 7.7; *Asfari v. Morocco*, UN Doc CAT/C/59/D/606/2014 (15 November 2016), para 13.8; see also *Jaïdane v. Tunisia*, UN Doc CAT/61/D/654/2015 (11 August 2017). This current approach of the CAT is more harmonious with that of the Special Rapporteur, than were its earlier decisions in *P.E. v. France*, UN Doc CAT/C/29/D/193/2001 (21 November 2002), paras 6.3 to 6.6 and *G.K. v. Switzerland*, UN Doc CAT/C/30/D/219/2002 (7 May 2003), paras 6.10 to 6.12, where the Committee declined to find a violation of Article 15 on the basis that it was for the complainant to establish that the statement of a third party used against her was obtained by torture and she had failed to do so. (However, in the somewhat atypical later decision in *Sodupe v. Spain*, UN Doc CAT/C/48/D/453/2011 (23 May 2012), para 7.4, the Committee again declined to find a violation on the basis that the complainant had not provided sufficient evidence to show that the statement 'was in all probability a result of torture.' See also *Sarobe v. France*, UN Doc CAT/C/62/D/675/2015 (10 November 2017), discussed below.) Nowak and McArthur (n 1 above), 517–519, criticize the earlier approach of the Committee in *P.E.* and *G.K.* And see Thienel (n 23 above), 354–355, arguing that such decisions reflect only the general burden of proof regarding allegations applied by the Committee under its procedures for deciding complaints before it, which is unrelated to the burden that would apply in the actual national proceedings seeking that the national court exclude the evidence from a proceeding.

[47]   HRC, *Samathanam v. Sri Lanka*, UN Doc CCPR/C/118/D/2412/2014 (28 October 2016), para 8. See also HRC General Comment 32 (n 5 above), para 41; *Singarasa v Sri Lanka* (n 5 above), para 7.4;

The African Commission on Human and Peoples' Rights and the Inter-American Court of Human Rights have likewise held that once a credible allegation has been raised that evidence was obtained through torture or other-treatment, it should be excluded unless the State establishes that it was not established through such abuse.[48] The European Court of Human Rights has taken a similar approach in several cases where the defendant alleged that information before a court in criminal proceedings was obtained by torture or other ill-treatment in another State (particularly one where such allegations are generally not properly investigated or addressed); the European Court held that the defendant need only show that there is a 'real risk' that the evidence was so obtained in order to trigger application of the exclusionary rule, at which point the information cannot be admitted unless the court in question were satisfied, following further arguments or information, that no such risk exists.[49] The Court has however left open the question whether a similar approach would apply in proceedings other than criminal proceedings, or where the allegation of abuse is made against a State whose institutions usually operate appropriately in relation to such allegations.[50]

The International Criminal Tribunal for the Former Yugoslavia has taken the position that, 'If there is *prima facie* indicia that there was such an oppressive conduct, the burden is on the prosecuting party to prove beyond a reasonable doubt that the statement was voluntary and not obtained by oppressive conduct.'[51]

The ECCC has decided that where there is a 'real risk' that statements were obtained by torture they are to be excluded on the presumption that they were been so obtained, but that the presumption could potentially be rebutted if it were proved on the balance of probabilities

---

Chiti v. Zambia, UN Doc CCPR/C/105/D/1303/2004 (26 July 2012), para 12.6. Indeed, even in a case where the Committee found that the complainant had failed to establish that a confession was obtained by ill-treatment, or that the confession was in fact relied upon in convicting him, the Committee found a violation of Article 14(3)(g) on the basis that the court had essentially ignored the complainant's allegations rather than attempting to ascertain whether they were justified: *Kouidis v. Greece*, UN Doc CCPR/C/86/D/1070/2002 (28 March 2006) paras 2.6, 7.3–7.6. There, the Committee stated, 'it is immaterial whether or not a confession is actually relied upon, as the obligation refers to all aspects of the judicial process of determination' (para. 7.5). See, similarly *Tyan v. Kazakhstan* (n 5 above), paras 9.2 and 9.4, where the Committee did not make any finding as to whether torture or other ill-treatment had actually occurred, but found violations of Article 2(3) on effective remedy and 14(1) and (3)(g) on fair trial because the court had failed to consider the allegations (and had indeed prevented the author from speaking about them in front of the jury). In one atypical later case, *Chelakh v. Kazakhstan*, UN Doc CCPR/C/121/D/2645/2015 (7 November 2017), the Committee ruled a claim of violation of Article 14(3)(g) inadmissible on the basis that the complainant's allegations were 'very general and inconsistent and that he does not provide specific information on the kind of pressure to which he was allegedly subjected' (para 8.9). In the same paragraph the Committee also noted that the conviction was based 'on several pieces of evidence and not just on the author's confession'; however, by the Committee's own reasoning in earlier cases, this should not in any event have been relevant to its consideration of whether the specific prohibition on compelled self-incrimination in Article 14(3)(g) in itself was violated.

[48] E.g. *Egyptian Initiative for Personal Rights and Interights v. Arab Republic of Egypt* (n 29 above), paras 216–218; *Guidelines on the conditions of arrest, police custody and pre-trial detention in Africa* (n 28 above), Article 9(d); *Cabrera Garcia and Montiel Flores v. Mexico* (n 25 above), paras 136, 176–177.

[49] *Othman (Abu Qatada) v. The United Kingdom* (n 1 above), paras 272–280; *El Haski v. Belgium* (n 26 above), paras 85–89.

[50] See *Othman (Abu Qatada) v. The United Kingdom* (n 1 above), paras 274 and 276; *El Haski v. Belgium* (n 26 above), paras 86–88.

[51] *Prosecutor v. Stakić* (n 13 above), Annex para 8. See also ICTY, *Prosecutor v. Mucić et al.* (n 13 above), para 42.

that a particular statement had not been obtained by torture.[52] It is difficult to reconcile this approach which the virtually uniform approach in other international criminal proceedings that, as the prosecution must prove its case beyond reasonable doubt, it must also prove beyond reasonable doubt that any statement it relies upon was not obtained by torture (or, in the case of confessions, was voluntary). The suggestion by the ECCC that such a lower standard was warranted by the fact that the prosecutors were not themselves involved in the torture, and that automatic exclusion would be inconsistent with the search for the truth, does not provide a convincing explanation for the departure from the international standard.

EXCEPTIONS

The UN Special Rapporteur on Torture, the Committee against Torture and the Human Rights Committee have noted the absolute and non-derogable character of the prohibition of torture, of which they consider the exclusionary rule to be one aspect, and have each emphasised that the exclusionary rule is itself absolute and non-derogable.[53]

Article 15 of the UNCAT allows only one 'exception' to the exclusionary rule: statements may be used 'against a person accused of torture as evidence that the statement was made'. The Human Rights Committee has interpreted the ICCPR to similar effect.[54]

The ECCC has rejected attempts by both the prosecution and the accused to rely on statements obtained by torture, for purposes beyond the exception specified in Article 15 of the UNCAT. While some documents potentially containing evidence obtained by torture have been admitted into evidence, the ECCC has described this as being restricted to uses such as establishing the identity and number of the victims (i.e. the relevance of the documents was the fact that the statement was made).[55] It has rejected arguments that the fair trial rights of the accused can justify an exception to the exclusionary rule, or that the rule applies only to proof of the truth of the contents of the statements and does not prevent prosecutors from using the statements to prove other facts.[56] It has confirmed that such statements may not be used in

---

[52] *Nuon Chea and Khieu Samphan, Decision on Objections to Document Lists* (n 14 above), paras 50–59; *Nuon Chea and Khieu Samphan, Decision on Evidence Obtained Through Torture* (n 14 above), paras 33–38.

[53] Special Rapporteur on Torture (Juan E. Méndez), SR Torture Report 2014 (n 1 above), paras 22, 82(a); CAT General Comment 2 (n 36 above), para 6; HRC General Comment 32 (n 5 above), para 6. See similarly *Cabrera Garcia and Montiel Flores v Mexico* (n 25 above), para 165.

[54] HRC General Comment 32 (n 5 above), paragraph 6.

[55] *Nuon Chea and Khieu Samphan, Decision on Evidence Obtained Through Torture* (n 14 above), para 30.

[56] *Nuon Chea and Khieu Samphan, Decision on Objections to Document List* (n 14 above), paras 28–29, 40–47; and *Case no 002/19-09-2007-ECCC/SC (Nuon Chea and Khieu Samphan) Appeal Judgment,* 23 November 2016), paras 361–365. Ernst (n 1 above) also seems to suggest (109–113) that fair trial concerns could in some circumstances override the exclusionary rule where it is a defendant who wishes to rely on the contents of the statement. See similarly, Pattenden, R, 'Admissibility in Criminal Proceedings of Third Party and Real Evidence Obtained by Methods Prohibited by UNCAT' (2006) 10 *International Journal of Evidence and Proof* 1, 11–12 and 36–41. Ambos (n 10 above), 384, rejects that position. Indeed, to set aside the exclusionary rule on grounds of fair trial rights would contradict the wording and purposes of the exclusionary rule, one of which is to deem such statements to be inherently unreliable by reason that the means of extracting them makes it impossible to know whether the statement is true or has been made only to stop abuse, and that such statements cannot have evidentiary value.

any way that would even 'imply that it might be true, for instance by confronting a witness with it'.[57] While the ECCC Supreme Court Chamber has permitted reliance on information recorded by the guards or interrogators or other officials, particularly on the cover sheets of documents containing confessions, or annotations written by such persons on the text of the confession, it has rejected any attempt to rely on the text of the confession statement itself.[58] However, some ECCC organs' rulings have been ambiguous, such as allowing 'the use of torture-tainted statements for the limited purpose of determining what action resulted based on the fact that a statement was made'.[59] ECCC rulings have also sometimes included asides, not necessary to the particular decision, that seem needlessly to risk undermining the authority of the exclusionary rule.[60] Such elements make it difficult to ascertain from the judgments themselves, whether such rulings may in practice be failing to prevent use of evidence in ways that are inconsistent with international law and standards.

PHYSICAL AND OTHER FORMS OF DERIVATIVE EVIDENCE

The UN Special Rapporteur on Torture has firmly concluded that as a matter of general international law, the exclusionary rule extends to all pieces of evidence obtained as a result of any act of torture or other ill-treatment, including physical evidence, and is not restricted to a confession or statement.[61] The Human Rights Committee has also stated that 'no statements or confessions *or, in principle, other evidence*' (emphasis added) obtained in violation of Article 7 of the ICCPR may be relied upon in proceedings covered by Article 14 of the ICCPR.[62]

The Committee against Torture has not often addressed the use of forms of evidence derived from torture (or ill-treatment) other than statements. This may be because the issue has not arisen on the facts of the individual cases brought before it, or it may be due to the fact that the Committee's mandate is to interpret and apply the Convention against Torture, and Article 15 refers specifically to 'statements'. Nevertheless, in its Concluding Observations the Committee has expressed concern where national laws in one State 'permit[ted] the admission of derivative evidence even if the confession is excluded'.[63] In its review of another State it concluded that, 'The judicial practice of admitting objective evidence derived from an inadmissible confession is of concern to the Committee', and accordingly recommended that,

---

[57] *Nuon Chea and Khieu Samphan, Decision on Objections to Document Lists* (n 14 above), para 47.

[58] *Ibid*, para 49. However, see ECCC Pre-Trial Chamber, *Case No 003/07-09-2009-ECCC/OCIJ (PTC 34)*, D257/1/8 (24 July 2018), paras 19, 21, 28–35, and *Case No 003/07-09-2009-ECCC-OCIJ, Closing Order*, D267 (28 November 2018), footnote 265, where lower-instance ECCC organs seek to make 'investigative lead' use of information from within the confessions or statements themselves (see further discussion below).

[59] *Nuon Chea and Khieu Samphan, Decision on Evidence Obtained Through Torture* (n 14 above), paras 74–78.

[60] *Nuon Chea and Khieu Samphan, Decision on Objections to Document Lists* (n 14 above), para 65: 'The Supreme Court Chamber cannot categorically exclude that there may be rare and extreme cases where departing from the exclusionary rule is thinkable, the case at hand is certainly not one of them.'

[61] Special Rapporteur on Torture (Juan E. Méndez), SR Torture Report 2014 (n 1 above), paras 29, 66, 82(e).

[62] HRC General Comment 32 (n 5 above), para 6.

[63] Concluding Observations on the United Kingdom, UN Doc A/54/44(Supp.) (1999), para 76(d).

'Such legislative measures as are necessary should be taken to ensure the exclusion of not merely a confession extorted by torture, but also any evidence derived from such confession.'[64]

The European Court has held that admission of statements obtained by any form of torture or other ill-treatment, or admission of real evidence obtained as a direct result of torture, always automatically renders a trial unfair, whether or not the evidence can be shown to have had an impact on the defendant's conviction or sentence.[65] The Court has also held that real evidence obtained as a result of inhuman or degrading treatment other than torture will always violate the right to fair trial if it is shown to have 'had a bearing on the outcome of the proceedings against the defendant, that is, had an impact on his or her conviction or sentence'.[66] However, it appears that the European Court will not automatically find a trial unfair on the basis of admission of real evidence obtained by such other ill-treatment, in the absence of proof of impact on the conviction or sentence (though this does not necessarily mean that simple admission of such evidence, taken together with other factors, could not contribute to an overall assessment that the trial was unfair).[67] Similar reasoning may also lie behind the Human Rights Committee's insertion of the qualifier 'in principle', before its reference to derivative evidence in the passage cited above.[68]

The Inter-American Court, on the other hand, has more categorically stated that, 'the absolute nature of the exclusionary rule is reflected in the prohibition on granting probative value not only to evidence obtained directly by coercion, but also to evidence derived from such action'.[69]

The ECCC has addressed 'derivative evidence' in several decisions. In one decision, after reviewing several international and national sources, the Trial Chamber opined that, 'In the absence of consistent international jurisprudence ... an international standard concerning the use of evidence derived from torture has not yet been established' and that, 'free admissibility of evidence' under civil law systems 'militates in favour of accepting derivative evidence so long as the proposed use does not circumvent the prohibition against invoking the contents of torture-tainted confessions to establish their truth'.[70] Strangely, though the Chamber cited several significant European Court cases, it referred only to the more conditional rule for real evidence derived from ill-treatment *other* than torture, and not the more absolute rule applicable to real evidence located as a result of torture *per se*.[71] The ECCC's conclusion in fact seems at odds with other international sources properly considered, and alongside the other concerns

---

[64] Concluding Observations on Israel, UN Doc A/57/44(Supp.) (2001), paras 52(k) and 53(j).

[65] *Gäfgen v. Germany* (n 26 above), paras 166–167, 173; *El Haski v. Belgium* (n 26 above), para 85; *Ibrahim and Others v. the United Kingdom* [GC], nos 50541/08 and 3 others, 13 September 2016, para 254; ECtHR GC, *Jalloh v. Germany* (n 26 above), para 105.

[66] *Gäfgen v. Germany* (n 26 above), para 178; *El Haski v. Belgium* (n 26 above), para 85.

[67] For criticism of the European Court's approach on this question, see Chedraui, AMT, 'An Analysis of the Exclusion of Evidence Obtained in Violation of Human Rights in Light of the Jurisprudence of the European Court of Human Rights' (2010) 15 *Tilburg Law Review* 205, 216–217.

[68] Viebig (n 11 above), 208–209 suggests that remoteness or proportionality concerns that might factor into decisions about whether to include evidence obtained through other kinds of violations, should have little or no application in respect of evidence obtained as a derivative of torture.

[69] *Cabrera Garcia and Montiel Flores v. Mexico* (n 25 above), para 167.

[70] *Nuon Chea and Khieu Samphan, Decision on Evidence Obtained Through Torture* (n 14 above), paras 69–70.

[71] *Ibid*, para 66.

mentioned earlier, such as seeing itself as bound only by Article 15 and Cambodian law, its conclusion may be of limited or no utility in other settings.

In another ruling, the ECCC Pre-Trial Chamber considered an application by a defendant, who was accused of responsibility for torture at a particular detention centre decades earlier, to have certain witness statements removed from the case file.[72] The ECCC Co-Investigating Judges in the case had examined biographical information found on the cover pages of documents that contained statements that were presumed to have been extracted under torture at the detention centre in question, as part of their efforts to identify and locate witnesses to the torture. The defendant argued that this use itself violated the exclusionary rule, and that the witness statements subsequently obtained by the Co-Investigating Judges were therefore a form of derivative evidence that also had to be excluded. The Chamber rejected both arguments. It found that this use of the cover pages of the historical statements as 'investigative leads' to try to identify and locate victims and witnesses as part of the investigation by the ECCC Co-Investigating Judges did not fall within the scope of Article 15 as it did not constitute 'invocation as evidence', and that 'the degree of causation' was not sufficient to conclude that the witness statements obtained many years later through the interviews of the witnesses by the ECCC Co-Investigating Judges had been 'made as a result of torture' within the meaning of Article 15. However, the Chamber unhelpfully (and seemingly unnecessarily, given its findings), reiterated the view that there was no general prohibition of derivative evidence under international law,[73] and suggested that the fact the defendants were accused of torture might be relevant to the interpretation and application of Article 15, beyond the explicit exception in the text of the Article itself.[74] The criticisms already mentioned above therefore apply to these aspects as well. Of further concern, the ECCC Pre-Trial Chamber and Investigative Judges have more recently sought to push the 'investigative leads' reasoning beyond the 'cover pages' and into use of information contained within the actual confessions or statements themselves.[75]

CONTEXTS OTHER THAN COURT PROCEEDINGS

If there is near consensus that the exclusionary rule applies to criminal and other judicial, quasi-judicial, or administrative proceedings,[76] the lawfulness of use of evidence obtained by torture in other settings, and particularly by the executive branch, remains contested.

---

[72]   *Decision on Request for Annulment of D114/164, D114/167, D114/170, and D114/71* (n 14 above).

[73]   *Ibid*, paras 35–36.

[74]   *Ibid*, para 33.

[75]   See ECCC Pre-Trial Chamber, *Case No 003/07-09-2009-ECCC/OCIJ (PTC 34)*, D257/1/8 (24 July 2018), paras 19, 21, 28–35. Perhaps sensing the danger in expanding the 'investigative leads' rationale to information in the confessions and statements themselves, the ECCC Co-Investigating Judges have again invoked the problematic idea that different rules should apply to investigators depending on whether or not they are 'directly or indirectly connected to the torturing authorities', see *Case No 003/07-09-2009-ECCC-OCIJ, Closing Order*, D267 (28 November 2018), footnote 265.

[76]   E.g. Special Rapporteur on Torture (Juan E. Méndez), SR Torture Report 2014 (n 1 above), para 30; CAT, *G.K. v. Switzerland* (n 46 above), para 6.10; CAT, *Ktiti v. Morocco* (n 32 above), para 8.8; Nowak and McArthur (n 1 above), 504; ECtHR, *Othman (Abu Qatada) v. The United Kingdom* (n 1 above), para 266, citing *P.E. v. France* and *G.K. v. Switzerland* (n 46 above). See also Pollard (n 1

The UN Special Rapporteur on Torture, relying on obligations to prevent torture and other ill-treatment,[77] and the concept of acquiescence and the prohibition of complicity,[78] has concluded that, 'The standards of the exclusionary rule should ... be interpreted in good faith and applied by way of analogy to the collection, sharing and receiving of information tainted by torture, including information obtained by other ill-treatment, even if not used in "proceedings" as narrowly defined.'[79] He has argued that any time there is a 'real risk' that information was obtained by torture, officials of the executive should refrain from use of such information unless further 'due diligence' inquiries are able to dispel the possibility of torture.[80] In situations of systemic torture, in particular, 'the receiving State must presume that the information is a product of torture and therefore refrain from collecting, sharing or receiving such tainted information'.[81] The Special Rapporteur set out detailed recommendations for policies and practices through which executive governments can manage such issues.[82]

Nowak and McArthur affirm that 'nothing in the *travaux préparatoires* suggests that the scope of application of Article 15 was meant to be reduced to judicial proceedings'.[83] However, they consider that 'evidence in any proceedings' in the Article 'only refers to the assessment of evidence before a judicial or administrative authority acting in accordance with certain rules of taking evidence laid down in the respective (*criminal, civil or administrative*) *procedural code*'.[84] They therefore consider that, when executive officials take practical action to for instance prevent a terror attack, Article 15 does not preclude acting on information that may have been obtained through torture. At the same time, they point out that if for instance an executive official detains a suspect to prevent such a suspected attack, the detention will ultimately have to be subject to a proceeding (presumably, for detentions, judicial), in which the executive official will not be able to present the torture-tainted information to justify the detention.[85]

Ernst similarly comes to the conclusion that there is 'no explicit exclusionary rule proscribing the executive use of torture information'.[86] Nevertheless, she appears to accept that restrictions may arise as a result of other obligations concerning complicity and aid and assistance, or prevention, whether under general public international law or other Articles of the UNCAT.[87]

---

above), 358; and Evans (n 1 above), 1134 and 1144. See however Thienel, T, 'Foreign Acts of Torture and the Admissibility of Evidence' (2006) 4 *Journal of International Criminal Justice* 401, who suggests (at 406), relying principally on the Russian version of Article 15, that Article 15 may be restricted to judicial or court proceedings, and, in any event, does not apply to executive use.

[77]   Special Rapporteur on Torture (Juan E. Méndez), SR Torture Report 2014 (n 1 above), paras 40–47, 72–73.

[78]   *Ibid*, paras 48–56, 75, 78.

[79]   *Ibid*, para 74.

[80]   *Ibid*, paras 56, 76, 83(h).

[81]   *Ibid*, para 77, and see paras 54–55.

[82]   *Ibid*, para 83.

[83]   Nowak and McArthur (n 1 above), 530.

[84]   *Ibid*, 531–532 (emphasis in original).

[85]   *Ibid*, 532. See also related discussion in Evans (n 1 above), 1139–1143, and Thienel (n 76 above), 405–406, both discussing the judgment of the United Kingdom House of Lords in *A and Others v. Secretary of State for the Home Department (No 2)*, [2005] UKHL 71; Special Rapporteur on Torture (Juan E. Méndez), SR Torture Report 2014 (n 1 above), para 70.

[86]   Ernst (n 1 above), 212, and see more generally 193–284.

[87]   *Ibid*, 212–287. See for instance Articles on 'Responsibility of States for Internationally Wrongful Acts', UN General Assembly Resolution 56/83 (12 December 2001), Annex, Articles 16, 40 and 41;

The Special Rapporteur has indeed held that these other sources of obligation must restrict executive use,[88] though exactly what forms of knowledge and use by the executive, outside of 'proceedings', are permissible and which are prohibited by international law, remains a matter of some debate. Furthermore, States and other actors would be well-advised to ensure that relevant policy analysis, development and implementation considers ethical, moral and practical reasons that might warrant restrictions or prohibitions on executive use of information that was potentially obtained through torture or other ill-treatment, even in relation to practices or situations where the State does not consider international law and standards to clearly prohibit such use.[89]

TRANSNATIONAL USE AND NON-STATE ACTORS

The UN Special Rapporteur on Torture has emphasised that the exclusionary rule covers 'statements obtained through torture or other ill-treatment of the defendant himself, or of a third party, and evidence obtained in a third State, even if the State seeking to rely on the information had no previous involvement in or connection to the acts of torture or other ill-treatment'.[90]

The Committee against Torture has stated in relation to Article 15, that a State 'should never rely on intelligence material obtained from third countries through the use of torture or other cruel, inhuman or degrading treatment'.[91] In its 2011 decision in *Ktiti v. Morocco*, it found a violation of Article 15 in a case where Morocco admitted information in an extradition proceeding, despite allegations that the information had been obtained from a third party under torture in Algeria by Algerian authorities.[92] In its 2017 decision in *Sarobe v. France*, court proceedings had been brought in France by Spanish authorities pursuant to a European Arrest Warrant that the complaints claimed was based on statements obtained by torture in Spain; having found that the impugned statements had indeed been used in the French proceeding,

---

International Court of Justice, *Legal Consequences of the Construction of a Wall in the Occupied Palestinian Territory, Advisory Opinion, ICJ Reports 2004*, p 136, para 159; *Application of the Convention on the Prevention and Punishment of the Crime of Genocide (Bosnia and Herzegovina v. Serbia and Montenegro), ICJ Reports 2007*, p 43.

[88] Special Rapporteur on Torture (Juan E. Méndez), SR Torture Report 2014 (n 1 above), paras 40–56, 75–78. See also Pollard (n 1 above); Rodley and Pollard (n 1 above), 179–180.

[89] See Association for the Prevention of Torture, 'Beware the Gift of Poison Fruit: Sharing Information with States that Torture' (2012); Special Rapporteur on Torture (Juan E. Méndez), SR Torture Report 2014 (n 1 above), paras 59–62, 83.

[90] Special Rapporteur on Torture (Juan E. Méndez), SR Torture Report 2014 (n 1 above), para 66 and see paras 27–28. See also Ernst (n 1 above); and Ambos (n 10 above), 392–393.

[91] CAT UK 2013 (n 46 above), para 25. See also CAT, Concluding Observations on the United Kingdom, UN Doc CAT/C/CR/33/3 (10 December 2004), para 4(a)(i).

[92] *Ktiti v. Morocco* (n 32 above), para 8.8. *P.E. v. France and G.K. v. Switzerland* (n 46 above) involved similar allegations, with the Committee taking the approach that it was immaterial that the alleged torture had been perpetrated by the State requesting extradition rather than the State where the proceedings were taking place (though as was mentioned earlier, in *P.E.* and *G.K.* the Committee declined to actually find a violation as it considered the allegations not to have been sufficiently proven to the Committee).

the Committee reaffirmed that France had an obligation under Article 15 to verify whether the statements had been obtained by torture.[93]

Regrettably, in *Sarobe*, seemingly influenced by the (perhaps exaggerated) challenges faced by courts of one State in seeking to ascertain the truth about events that occurred in another State, the Committee appeared to apply an extremely deferential standard in evaluating whether the French courts had in fact discharged the obligation under Article 15. The French courts had relied on the outcome of a Spanish investigation, despite the fact that by the time of the ruling of the French appeal court the European Court of Human Rights had already found the Spanish investigations to have been insufficient. The Committee stated that it could not expect French courts to conduct a direct investigation of the events in Spain, being outside French jurisdiction, and held that in the circumstances of the case and based on the evidence before it, the Committee could not conclude that 'la procédure interne ait été caractérisée par un procédé manifestement arbitraire ou par un déni de justice',[94] and ultimately declined to find a violation of Article 15.

The application of such a deferential standard to France's obligation to verify the allegations in the context of Article 15 is difficult to reconcile with the previous case law of the Committee on the burden of proof in national proceedings where evidence is challenged under Article 15 (see above), as well as the Committee's own role. The Committee has occasionally used this phrase before in other contexts, for instance in *Ktiti v. Morocco* in relation to Article 3 of the Convention, on *non-refoulement*; however, in *Ktiti* the Committee went on to scrutinise the State's compliance with Article 15 more strictly without reference to this deferential standard (para 8.8). The Committee has also consistently reaffirmed (including in the face of States seeking to invoke the deferential standard mentioned in *Ktiti*) that under Article 3 while 'it gives considerable weight to findings of fact that are made by the organs of the State party concerned ... at the same time it is not bound by such findings and instead has the power ... of free assessment of the facts based upon the full set of circumstances in each case'.[95] If faced with a similar case in the future, this more usual and less deferential approach by the Committee would seem, even in a transnational setting, more consistent with the object and purpose of Article 15 (being itself an absolute exception to more general rules for admitting and evaluating evidence), and the Committee's own role in securing effective implementation.

At the regional level, the European Court of Human Rights has similarly found a violation of the right to fair trial under Article 6 of the European Convention, in a case where Belgian courts, in the context of criminal proceedings, had admitted statements made in Morocco by third parties, in respect of which there was a real risk they had been obtained using torture or other ill-treatment.[96]

Ernst's detailed consideration of the transnational use of torture evidence concludes that given the extent to which international law already addresses the issue, the remaining difficulty in such cases 'is essentially one of proof'.[97]

---

[93] *Sarobe v. France* (n 46 above), para 10.2.

[94] No official English translation was available at the time of writing, but this could be translated as 'the evidence was assessed in a patently arbitrary manner or one that amounted to a miscarriage of justice'.

[95] Among many other examples, see *T.Z. v. Switzerland*, UN Doc CAT/C/62/D/688/2015 (22 November 2017), para 8.4.

[96] *El Haski v. Belgium* (n 26 above), paras 88–89, 99.

[97] Ernst (n 1 above), 285–288.

Little seems to have been written about international standards on the exclusion of evidence obtained as the result of abuses by non-State actors. Article 1(1) of the UNCAT defines 'torture' for the specific purposes of the treaty, including Article 15, such that the rule would apply only to acts 'by or at the instigation of or with the consent or acquiescence of a public official or other person acting in an official capacity'. Acts by non-State actors performed without such instigation, consent or acquiesce would seem not to fall within the strict terms of Article 15 (though in some cases, subsequent invocation by State authorities of the evidence obtained by the abuse could indicate acquiescence, particularly if the perpetrator goes unpunished). Article 1(2) of the UNCAT, however, explicitly provides that the definition in Article 1(1) 'is without prejudice to any international instrument or national legislation which does or may contain provisions of wider application'; as such the limited scope of application of Article 15 to non-State actors cannot be used as a reason to narrow the application of an exclusionary rule under other provisions of wider application.

The Human Rights Committee has for instance said that while the international legal obligations under the ICCPR apply directly to States and not to private actors,

> the positive obligations on States Parties to ensure Covenant rights will only be fully discharged if individuals are protected by the State, not just against violations of Covenant rights by its agents, but also against acts committed by private persons or entities that would impair the enjoyment of Covenant rights in so far as they are amenable to application between private persons or entities.[98]

It has cited, as an example, that it considers it to be 'implicit in Article 7 that States parties have to take positive measures to ensure that private persons or entities do not inflict torture or cruel, inhuman or degrading treatment or punishment on others within their power'.[99] It would seem logically to flow from this that statements, confessions or other evidence obtained by private persons through such abuse, should be subject to the exclusionary rule in the same manner as if they were obtained by or with approval or acquiescence of State officials.

CONCLUSION

The exclusionary rule is clearly entrenched in international law, with near-universal consensus that evidence obtained by torture may not be used as evidence in criminal or other judicial proceedings. However, beyond this core, certain aspects of the scope or manner of application of the prohibition are, to varying degrees, more contested.

Under most interpretations, the exclusionary rule in international law covers not only torture *per se* but also other forms of cruel, inhuman or degrading treatment; particularly as regards evidence obtained through the deliberate infliction of such ill-treatment, this certainly seems the interpretation the most consonant with the underlying rationale for the exclusionary rule and the broader legal framework of which it is part.

The most prevalent approach to the standard and burden of proof among international sources is that the person who objects to use of certain evidence need only present a plausible

---

[98]   Human Rights Committee, General Comment No 31: The Nature of the General Legal Obligation Imposed on States Parties to the Covenant, UN Doc CCPR/C/21/Rev.1/Add.13 (26 May 2004), para 8.
[99]   *Ibid*.

reason to believe it was obtained by torture or other ill-treatment, at which point the burden falls to the State (or other party seeking to rely on the information) to prove that it was not. At least in criminal and other proceedings where the State seeks to use the information against an individual, if a 'real risk' remains that it was obtained in such manner, it should be excluded.

Apart from the explicit allowance for statements to be used 'against a person accused of torture' for the very limited purpose of 'evidence that the statement was made', international law does not contemplate exceptions to the exclusionary rule. Differences in the procedures of given legal systems, theoretical conjectures about possible conflicts with fair trial rights, or supposedly purposive or inductive reasoning, must not be allowed to result in *de facto* grounds of exception.

International and regional human rights bodies have taken the position that real or other derivative evidence obtained through torture must always be excluded. The position of some of these bodies with respect to real evidence obtained as a result of ill-treatment not constituting torture is perhaps less categorical. However, at minimum it appears that reliance on real evidence obtained by such ill-treatment will be unlawful if it ultimately has 'a bearing on the outcome of the proceedings against the defendant' (in the words of the European Court Grand Chamber in *Gäfgen*). Given that it is difficult to see circumstances in which the prosecution would seek to admit real evidence *without* any intention of it having a bearing on the outcome of the proceeding in which it has been admitted, judges and prosecutors would be well advised simply to adopt a cautionary approach of excluding all evidence tainted in this way.

Clearly the prohibition applies not only to criminal proceedings, but to other judicial proceedings of all kinds. The UN Special Rapporteur has presented compelling legal and policy arguments to apply the prohibition to the use of information by executive actors outside of any legal or other formal proceedings; others, giving a narrower construction to the legal provisions and placing less emphasis on certain moral or policy arguments, find no such general restriction on use by executive officials. Nevertheless, conundrums arise in any approach where members of the executive may act on the basis of such information in respect of actions, such as arrest or search, for which they may later be called upon to present justification in a court proceeding. Furthermore, even if executive actors may not be bound by a total and absolute legal prohibition on use of such information, specific instances of such use could nevertheless constitute violations of particular state obligations or even give rise to individual criminal responsibility, amounting to complicity or breaches of other legal rules. It is therefore essential from both a legal and a policy perspective that executive actors do not view themselves as having an unrestricted scope to receive, solicit or make use of information obtained by torture or other ill-treatment.

The application of the exclusionary rule should not differ in any substantive way when the evidence or information has been obtained by a State other than the State that seeks to rely upon it. Furthermore, statements or other evidence obtained by non-State actors through the infliction of abuse of a similar character to torture or other cruel, inhuman or degrading treatment, should in principle be excluded in the same manner as if the abuse were perpetrated by State actors.

Alongside other obligations to prevent, investigate, ensure prosecution and provide remedy and reparation, the prohibition on the use of evidence obtained by torture and other ill-treatment, in national and international law, is an essential pillar of the overall legal and policy framework against such abuse. The facts of difficult cases, or nuances in the different specific legal frameworks under which particular judicial or other decision-makers operate, may give rise to a temptation to whittle away at the outer edges of the prohibition. The risks to the overall aim of eradicating torture and other ill-treatment posed by any weakening of this pillar must not be ignored; judges, prosecutors, lawyers and other State authorities should always give the prohibition against use of information or evidence obtained through torture or other ill-treatment the broadest and most effective interpretation and application possible.

15. Torture and non-refoulement

Carla Ferstman

INTRODUCTION

This chapter focuses on the right of an individual not to be forcibly expelled, deported, returned, removed or extradited to a country where that person faces a real risk of torture. This non-refoulement principle is *a sine qua non* of States' obligation to prohibit torture. It is set out in, amongst other places, Article 3 of the UN Convention Against Torture (UNCAT),[1] which provides that '[n]o State Party shall expel, return ("refouler") or extradite a person to another State where there are substantial grounds for believing that he would be in danger of being subjected to torture'. It is also the subject of two General Comments adopted by the UN Committee Against Torture,[2] the official interpretive body of that Convention.

Non-refoulement to torture derives from the non-refoulement principle under refugee law, which has been recognised to constitute a peremptory norm of international law.[3] According to Article 33(1) of the Convention Relating to the Status of Refugees (1951 Refugee Convention),[4] 'no Contracting State shall expel or return ("refouler") a refugee in any manner whatsoever to the frontiers of territories where his life or freedom would be threatened on account of his race, religion, nationality, membership of a particular social group or political opinion'. Additionally, the non-refoulement principle is reflected in international humanitarian law; the transfer of detainees and other protected persons in such circumstances is clearly prohibited in times of international armed conflict,[5] and this prohibition arguably extends to non-international armed conflicts.[6]

As will be described, non-refoulement to torture is in some ways more robust than its equivalent under refugee law, given its absolute nature and its application to any person, not

---

[1]   Convention Against Torture and Other Cruel, Inhuman or Degrading Treatment or Punishment (adopted 10 December 1984, entered into force 26 June 1987) 1465 UNTS 85.

[2]   UN Committee Against Torture, General Comment no 1: Implementation of article 3 of the Convention in the context of article 22, UN Doc A/53/44 Annex IX, 16 September 1998; UN Committee Against Torture, General Comment no 4 (2017) on the Implementation of article 3 of the Convention in the context of article 22, UN Doc CAT/C/GC/4, 4 September 2018.

[3]   Allain, J, 'The Jus Cogens Nature of the Nonrefoulement' (2001) 13 *Int'l J Refugee Law* 533; Lauterpacht, E and Bethlehem, D, 'The Scope and Content of the Principle of Non-refoulement' in Feller, E, Türk, V and Nicholson, F (eds), *Refugee Protection in International Law: UNHCR's Global Consultations on International Protection* (Cambridge University Press, 2003), 78.

[4]   Adopted 28 July 1951, entered into force 22 April 1954.

[5]   Geneva Convention (III) relative to the Treatment of Prisoners of War of 12 August 1949 (entered into force 21 October 1950) 75 UNTS 135, Article 12; Geneva Convention (IV) relative to the Protection of Civilian Persons in Time of War of 12 August 1949 (entered into force 21 October 1950) 75 UNTS 287, Article 45(3)–(4). See also, ICTY, *Prosecutor v. Mile Mrkšić (Vukovar Hospital Case)*, IT-95-13/1-A, Judgment (5 May 2009), para 71.

[6]   ICRC, 'Commentary on the First Geneva Convention: Convention (I) for the Amelioration of the Condition of the Wounded and Sick in Armed Forces in the Field' 2nd edn (Geneva, 2016), para 708.

only to refugees. Nevertheless, the principle suffers from some of the same ambiguities that plague the prohibition of torture as a whole. How a State understands, and where it situates the boundaries between, torture and other forms of cruel, inhuman or degrading treatment or punishment, as well as the extent of a State's obligation to respect, protect and fulfil human rights outside its territorial borders, are both questions that have been answered in different ways by States as well as regional and international decision-making bodies. The answers to those questions have impacted on the breadth of individuals recognised as being able to benefit from non-refoulement to torture. But beyond the issue of transfers, the consequence of recognising a person as a refugee, at least in principle if not always in practice, is more significant, in that it requires States to afford that person durable solutions. As will be described, individuals who are not refugees but are nevertheless allowed to remain in a country because they face a real risk of torture if they are forced to leave, can sometimes exist in a state of limbo with few recognised rights in their country of refuge.

This chapter sets out the general scope and content of the principle of non-refoulement to torture, considering, in particular, who is to be granted protection, how the risk of torture is assessed, what type of protection should result and what remedies should flow when the principle is violated. It analyses the differences between the applications of the principle under refugee law and under human rights law and the gaps and occasional synergies these gaps produce in practice. It also considers the techniques used by some States who recognise the validity of the non-refoulement obligation but regularly seek to undermine its application, and analyses the extent to which international human rights law has played or can play in the future a more useful role in securing a more uniform enforcement. The chapter also takes account of the pressures to expand the scope of the principle under both refugee and human rights law and open a space for flexibility in how and when the principle is applied to better reflect the difficulties many individuals face, and the countervailing resolve exhibited by some States to rely on restrictive definitions and narrowly interpret the scope of non-refoulement in order to maintain careful control over borders.

THE PRINCIPLE OF NON-REFOULEMENT: DIFFERENCES BETWEEN REFUGEE AND HUMAN RIGHTS LAW

The non-refoulement principle prohibits States from sending, transferring, expelling, extraditing, deporting or otherwise returning persons to a country or territory where there is a real risk that they would be in danger of being subjected to violations of certain fundamental rights. It also extends to the prohibition against transferring a person to a country where the person would be exposed to a risk of onward removal to another authority or territory in violation of the principle of non-refoulement (chain or indirect refoulement).[7]

---

[7]   UN Committee Against Torture, General Comment no 4 (n 2 above), para 12; UN Human Rights Committee, General Comment no 31, Nature of the General Legal Obligation Imposed on States Parties to the International Covenant on Civil and Political Rights (26 May 2004) UN Doc CCPR/C/21/Rev1/ Add.13, para 12; *Hirsi Jamaa and Others v. Italy* [GC], no 27765/09, ECHR 2012, para 147; *Motumbo v. Switzerland*, UN Doc CAT/C/12/D/013/1993, 27 April 1994.

Non-refoulement has been a guiding principle of refugee law since the 1933 Convention relating to the International Status of Refugees.[8] According to Article 3 of that Convention, parties committed themselves not to return refugees 'across the frontiers of their country of origin ... unless dictated by national security or public order'. Article 33 of the 1951 Refugee Convention incorporated the principle from the 1933 Convention but broadened it, referring not only to the prohibition of returns to the country of origin but also to other countries where the life or freedom of the refugee would be threatened.

The principle of non-refoulement to torture recognises that States have the responsibility not to foster torture or ill-treatment by returning individuals to such harms, or to exacerbate the risks of such treatments through their actions or inactions. It developed from the understanding that States' obligation to prohibit torture extends to situations in which their actions give rise to a real risk of torture outside their territorial jurisdiction. This is reflected in the *Soering* judgment of the European Court of Human Rights (ECtHR), which concerned a German national due to be extradited to the United States, who, if convicted, faced a death penalty and the 'death row phenomenon'.[9] The ECtHR determined that:

> It would hardly be compatible with the underlying values of the Convention, ... were a Contracting State knowingly to surrender a fugitive to another State where there were substantial grounds for believing that he would be in danger of being subjected to torture, however heinous the crime allegedly committed. Extradition in such circumstances, while not explicitly referred to in the brief and general wording of Article 3, would plainly be contrary to the spirit and intendment of the Article, and in the Court's view this inherent obligation not to extradite also extends to cases in which the fugitive would be faced in the receiving State by a real risk of exposure to inhuman or degrading treatment or punishment proscribed by that Article.[10]

The main differences in how the principle is understood under refugee and human rights law are summarised below.

To Whom the Principle Applies

Under refugee law, the principle applies to refugees only – both those who have been recognised formally as such and those who would qualify as refugees but are awaiting a decision confirming their status.[11] The refugee definition is narrow. Refugees are understood to be persons outside the country of their nationality and who cannot benefit from the protection of their State of nationality, that have a well-founded fear of being persecuted for reasons of race, religion, nationality, membership of a particular social group or political opinion.[12] It does not apply to internally displaced persons who may have the same fears as refugees but haven't

---

8   Convention relating to the International Status of Refugees (adopted 28 October 1933), 159 LNTS 3663, Article 3.

9   *Soering v. The United Kingdom*, 7 July 1989, Series A no 161.

10   *Ibid*, para 88.

11   UNHCR, 'Note on International Protection', UN Doc A/AC.96/694, 3 August 1987, para 23. See also, Article 9, Directive 2013/32/EU of the European Parliament and of the Council of 26 June 2013 on common procedures for granting and withdrawing international protection, OJ L 180 (the Asylum Procedures Directive).

12   Article 1 1951 Refugee Convention; Article 1(2) of the Protocol relating to the Status of Refugees (entry into force 4 October 1967).

managed to cross an international border. Nor does it apply to the vast number of persons who are outside their countries of origin because of some other (non-refugee) reasons, such as violence or armed conflict, an environmental or humanitarian catastrophe, a breakdown of the State or the absence of any means of subsistence. Regional conventions and declaratory texts applicable in Africa and the Americas have broadened the scope of persons protected against non-refoulement to those fleeing armed conflict and other situations seriously disturbing public order and mass violations of human rights.[13] However these widened frameworks have not impacted significantly on the narrow framing of the refugee definition applicable in the vast majority of countries worldwide. In the EU, individuals who do not qualify as refugees may be entitled to 'subsidiary protection' which includes '... serious and individual threat to a civilian's life or person by reason of indiscriminate violence in situations of international or internal armed conflict'.[14]

Under human rights law, the principle applies to all persons within a State's jurisdiction, regardless of their citizenship or legal status within that State.[15] In contrast, under international humanitarian law, the principle applies to protected persons such as prisoners of war.[16]

The Absolute Nature of the Prohibition of Non-refoulement to Torture

Exceptions in refugee law: cessation and exclusion clauses

While Article 33 of the 1951 Refugee Convention is not subject to reservation or derogation, there are a number of exceptions built into the provision. Article 33(2) of that Convention makes clear that the non-refoulement obligation does not apply to refugees that pose a risk to national security or a danger to the community, though these exceptions should be interpreted restrictively.[17] Similarly, under Article 32 of that Convention a refugee can be expelled from the territory on grounds of national security or public order, though it is specified that expul-

---

[13]   See, OAU Convention Governing the Specific Aspects of Refugee Problems in Africa (adopted 10 September 1969, entered into force 20 June 1974), Article I(2); Cartagena Declaration on Refugees, Adopted by the Colloquium on the International Protection of Refugees in Central America, Mexico and Panama, Cartagena de Indias, Colombia, 22 November 1984, para III(3).

[14]   'Directive 2011/95/EU of the European Parliament and of the Council of 13 December 2011 on standards for the qualification of third-country nationals or stateless persons as beneficiaries of international protection, for a uniform status for refugees or for persons eligible for subsidiary protection, and for the content of the protection granted (recast)', L 337/9, 20 December 2011, paras 1, 15.

[15]   See, e.g., UNCAT (n 2 above), Article 2(1); Article 2(1) International Covenant on Civil and Political Rights ([ICCRP] adopted 16 December 1966, entered into force 23 March 1976, 999 UNTS 171), Article 2(1); American Convention on Human Rights ([ACHR], adopted 22 November 1969, entered into force 18 July 1978 Treaty no B-32 OAS Treaty Series no 36), Article 1(1); European Convention for the Protection of Human Rights and Fundamental Freedoms ([ECHR] adopted 4 November 1950, entered into force 3 September 1953 ETS no 5), Article 1.

[16]   Geneva Convention IV (above n 5), Articles 45(4), 49. See generally, Droege, C, 'Transfers of Detainees: Legal Framework, Non-Refoulement and Contemporary Challenges' (2008) 90 *Intl Rev Red Cross* 669; Gillard, E-C, 'There's No Place Like Home: States' Obligations in Relation to Transfers of Persons' (2008) 90) *Intl Rev Red Cross* 703.

[17]   The 1951 Refuge Convention, 'The Travaux Préparatoires Analysed with a Commentary by Dr Paul Weis', 1990, available at https://www.unhcr.org/uk/protection/travaux/4ca34be29/refugee-convention-1951-travaux-preparatoires-analysed-commentary-dr-paul.html, Commentary to Article 32, para 2; UNHCR, 'Background Note on the Application of the Exclusion Clauses: Article 1F of the 1951 Convention relating to the Status of Refugees' (4 Sept 2003) 3[4].

sions must be subject to legal process, and prior to carrying out the expulsion the refugee must be given 'a reasonable period within which to seek legal admission into another country'. The commentary to the travaux préparatoires notes the serious consequences of expulsion, and thus, 'the principle of proportionality must be observed, that is, the expulsion must, in the circumstances, be the appropriate measure; the seriousness of the measure has to be weighed against the interests of public order and national security'.[18] Further, it is noted that, 'expulsion to a country where the refugee has a well-founded fear of persecution is excluded, except under the circumstances of Article 33 paragraph 2'.[19]

Also, there are categories of persons who are mandatorily excluded from being recognised as refugees, regardless of the well-founded fear of persecution they may have. Because the non-refoulement obligation in refugee law only applies to refugees, these exclusions constitute significant barriers to protection. In particular, excluded persons consist of

> any person with respect to whom there are serious reasons for considering that: (a) he has committed a crime against peace, a war crime, or a crime against humanity, as defined in the international instruments drawn up to make provision in respect of such crimes; (b) he has committed a serious non-political crime outside the country of refuge prior to his admission to that country as a refugee; (c) he has been guilty of acts contrary to the purposes and principles of the United Nations.[20]

These clauses give the impression that only morally 'worthy' persons are entitled to refugee protection, which stands in contrast to the bulk of international human rights law, which recognises the inherent value and rights of all persons, regardless of what they may be accused or convicted of. That the clauses mandatorily exclude individuals who have not necessarily been subjected to a criminal process but against whom there are 'serious reasons for considering', introduces an ambit for misuse, even though the clauses are supposed to be narrowly construed.[21] The clauses have been said to underscore the humanitarian character of the Convention, and are intended to ensure that refugee status does not promote safe havens for individuals who perpetrate serious crimes or pose related risks.[22]

An absolute principle under human rights law
In contrast, there is no exception to the non-refoulement to torture principle under human rights law; it is an absolute concept, regardless of the legal status of the individuals involved, and irrespective of whether they have been accused, or have been convicted, of any crime. As the UN Special Rapporteur on Torture specified, 'The non-refoulement protection specifically against the risk of torture and ill-treatment is absolute and non-derogable and applies in all

---

[18] The Travaux Préparatoires, *ibid*, Commentary to Article 32, para 1.
[19] *Ibid*, para 3.
[20] 1951 Refugee Convention, Article 1(f). See the similar provision in the OAU Convention Governing the Specific Aspects of Refugee Problems in Africa, Article I(5). See also Statute of the Office of the United Nations High Commissioner for Refugees, UN Doc A/RES/428(V), 14 December 1950, Article 7(d).
[21] See Weis (n 17 above).
[22] UNHCR, Guidelines on International Protection: 'Application of the Exclusion Clauses: Article 1F of the 1951 Convention relating to the Status of Refugees', UN Doc HCR/GIP/03/05, 4 September 2003, para 2.

situations, including war and states of emergency, to all human beings without discrimination of any kind and, in particular, regardless of their entitlement to refugee status.'[23]

Countering the absolute nature of non-refoulement under human rights law: efforts to mitigate the risks

This absolute principle has made it difficult for States to remove from their jurisdiction persons deemed by them to be 'undesirable' because of their alleged links to terrorism, because of the risk of ill-treatment they would face in the destination country. Thus, some States have sought to water down the principle, introducing a balancing exercise or reading in exceptions. For instance, the Canadian Supreme Court determined in *Suresh*, that it was possible to expel a person who faced a real risk of torture, if there are reasonable grounds to believe that the person is a threat to national security of the country of refuge – it was a question of balancing the different interests at stake.[24] Some EU Member States have similarly sought to introduce flexibility or conditionality into the principle of non-refoulement to torture, on the basis that States ought to be entitled to take the danger to the public into account when determining whether to remove a person from the territory.[25]

However, most courts and treaty bodies have rejected such approaches and have remained resolute in their understanding of the absolute nature of the principle. In response to *Suresh*, the UN Committee Against Torture noted as a subject of concern, '[t]he failure of the Supreme Court of Canada ... to recognize at the level of domestic law the absolute nature of the protection of article 3 of the Convention, which is not subject to any exception whatsoever'.[26]

The balancing approach was similarly rejected by the ECtHR.[27] In *Chahal*, which concerned a Sikh separatist leader that British authorities determined was a threat to national security and whose asylum application had been refused, the ECtHR determined that the real risk of ill-treatment he faced if returned to India overrode any other considerations; 'the activities of the individual in question, however undesirable or dangerous, cannot be a material consideration. The protection afforded by Article 3 is thus wider than that provided by Articles 32 and 33 of the United Nations 1951 Convention on the Status of Refugees.'[28] In *Saadi*, the ECtHR Grand Chamber affirmed *Chahal* and made clear that:

---

[23]   UN Human Rights Council, 'Report of the Special Rapporteur on torture and other cruel, inhuman or degrading treatment or punishment', UN Doc A/HRC/37/50, 26 February 2018, para 39. See also UN Committee Against Torture, General Comment no 4 (n 2 above), para 9.

[24]   *Suresh v. Canada* (Minister of Citizenship and Immigration), [2002] 1 SCR 3. See also, *Ahani v. Canada (Minister of Citizenship and Immigration)* [2002] 1 SCR 72, para 22. See in contrast, *Attorney-General v. Zaoui and Ors (Zaoui No 2)* [2005] NZSC 38, 21 June 2005, paras 42, 93.

[25]   Observation of the Governments of Lithuania, Portugal, Slovakia and the United Kingdom Intervening in ECtHR, App No 25424/05 *Ramzy v. the Netherlands* (2005); *Saadi v. Italy* [GC], no 37201/06, ECHR 2008, para 122.

[26]   UNCAT, 'Conclusions and recommendations of the Committee against Torture (Canada)', CAT/C/CR/34/CAN, 7 July 2005, para 4(a). See also, *Gorki Ernesto Tapia Paez v. Sweden*, UN Doc CAT/C/18/D/39/1996, 28 April 1997, para 14.5.

[27]   *Chahal v. The United Kingdom*, 15 November 1996, *Reports of Judgments and Decisions* 1996-V, para 79 et seq.; *Ahmed v. Austria*, 17 December 1996, *Reports of Judgments and Decisions* 1996-VI, para 40 et seq.; *H.L.R. v. France*, 29 April 1997, *Reports of Judgments and Decisions* 1997-III, para 35; *Saadi v. Italy* (n 25 above) para 127; *Sufi and Elmi v. The United Kingdom*, nos 8319/07 and 11449/07, 28 June 2011, para 212.

[28]   *Chahal v. United Kingdom* (n 27 above), para 80.

[T]he argument based on the balancing of the risk of harm if the person is sent back against the dangerousness he or she represents to the community if not sent back is misconceived. ... The prospect that he may pose a serious threat to the community if not returned does not reduce in any way the degree of risk of ill-treatment that the person may be subject to on return. For that reason it would be incorrect to require a higher standard of proof, as submitted by the intervener, where the person is considered to represent a serious danger to the community, since assessment of the level of risk is independent of such a test.[29]

States have also sought to mitigate or lessen the risks to an 'acceptable' level by seeking diplomatic assurances or special agreements from the receiving States that they will refrain from subjecting the returnees to torture or other ill-treatment. These assurances tend to be non-binding political commitments from the receiving State that they will ensure that a particular person who faces a real risk of torture, will not actually be tortured. Occasionally they have been elevated to treaties or other binding forms of undertakings.[30] Some have raised concerns that the practice of seeking assurances has become a 'politically inspired substitute for the principle of non-refoulement',[31] whereas others have argued that such assurances can never serve as adequate mitigation;[32] if a risk exists, it cannot be bypassed by securing unreliable and unenforceable assurances against torture.[33] The UN Committee Against Torture, in a draft of its 2017 General Comment on the principle of non-refoulement, explained that:

[D]iplomatic assurances from a State party to the Convention to which a person is to be deported are contrary to the principle of 'non-refoulement' ... and they should not be used as a loophole to undermine that principle, where there are substantial grounds for believing that he/she would be in danger of being subjected to torture in that State.[34]

The jurisprudence has been more nuanced, however, focusing mainly on an assessment of whether, in the particular circumstances of the case, the assurance may constitute a sufficient reduction of the risk of torture or other prohibited ill-treatment (depending on the treaty framework). The jurisprudence of the UK Special Immigration Appeals Commission (SIAC) makes this clear, noting in the *Abu Qatada* case that

We see no justification for the comments from NGOs that the UK Government's attempt to negotiate and rely on MOUs is an attempt to evade the UK's international obligation; MOUs may or may not succeed in achieving a safe return, but they are rather an attempt to fulfil international obligations when dealing with those who ought to be deported.[35]

---

[29] *Saadi v. Italy* (n 25 above), para 139.

[30] *Othman (Abu Qatada) v. The United Kingdom*, no 8139/09, ECHR 2012 (extracts).

[31] UNGA, 'Report of the Special Rapporteur on torture and other cruel, inhuman or degrading treatment or punishment', UN Doc. A/59/324, 1 September 2004, para 31.

[32] UN Commission on Human Rights, 'Report of the Special Rapporteur on the question of torture, Manfred Nowak', UN Doc. E/CN.4/2006/6, 23 December 2005, para 32.

[33] Human Rights Watch, 'Still at Risk: Diplomatic Assurances No Safeguard against Torture' (April 2005), 6.

[34] UN Committee Against Torture, General Comment no 1 (n 2 above), para 20. Note, however that this text was not ultimately retained in the final version of the General Comment.

[35] *Omar Othman (aka Abu Qatada) v. Secretary of State for the Home Department*, Appeal against the notice of intention to deport, 26 February 2007, para 493. The decision was considered and subsequently quashed (on other grounds) by the Court of Appeal: *Othman (Jordan) v. Secretary of State for the Home Department* [2008] EWCA Civ 290, and reinstated (on other grounds) by the House of Lords:

This case-by-case approach has largely been followed by treaty bodies and human rights courts.[36] Factors taken into account in the assessment include the credibility and reliability of the State issuing the assurance, the likelihood that the assurances will be respected and that mechanisms are in place to enforce them, as well as the adequacy of the assurances as a means to eliminate the risk of mistreatment to the specific person having regard to the nature of the risk that person faces.[37] In *H.Y. v. Switzerland*, the UN Committee Against Torture determined that diplomatic assurances did not eliminate the risk of torture in the case of Turkey:

> [T]he Committee has taken note of the State party's argument that Turkey has provided diplomatic assurances in support of the extradition request, that the Swiss authorities in Turkey would be able to monitor their implementation and that Turkey, as a party to the European Convention on Extradition, has never breached its diplomatic assurances. The Committee has also noted the complainant's contentions that diplomatic assurances are not sufficient or reliable to eliminate the risk of torture in his case due to the political motivation of the extradition request; that the use of torture in places of deprivation of liberty continues to be prevalent in Turkey; that it is difficult to monitor diplomatic assurances as the complainant allegedly did not enjoy the right to legal counsel preceding his conviction; that the Swiss authorities did not deny that the complainant risked persecution after his release; and that there was a heightened risk that he would be apprehended and tortured by members of the secret services before being handed over to the prison authorities due to his affiliation with high-level PKK members in Switzerland. It has taken note of the claim, undisputed by the State party, that the assurances were provided by Turkey only after three unsuccessful attempts, which shows unwillingness on the part of Turkey to comply with them; and that the human rights situation in Turkey has deteriorated significantly since the assurances were issued in 2012, particularly in the light of the 2015 elections and PKK insurgency, the attempted coup and state of emergency in 2016 and the ensuing large-scale arrests, detentions and dismissals of those suspected of subversive activities and the 2017 constitutional amendments.[38]

The final text of the Committee Against Torture's 2017 General Comment on non-refoulement, takes no view on the character of assurances as such. It simply provides that the assurances 'should not be used as a loophole to undermine the principle of non-refoulement ...'.[39]

Potential gaps in protection? The humanitarian crevices between refugee law and human rights law

The absolute nature of the non-refoulement prohibition in human rights law means that individuals who may be ineligible for refugee protection as a result of the application of the cessation or exclusion clauses may nevertheless be entitled to remain in the country, which

---

RB (Algeria) (FC) and Another v. Secretary of State for the Home Department; OO (Jordan) v. Secretary of State for the Home Department [2009] UKHL 10. See also, *MT (Algeria) v. SSHD* [2008] 2 WLR 159 [127].

[36] See, e.g., *Saadi v. Italy* (n 25 above), paras 147–148; *Hanan Ahmed Fouad Abd El Khalek Attia v. Sweden*, UN Doc CAT/C/31/D/199/2002, 24 November 2003; *Mohammed Alzery v. Sweden*, UN Doc CCPR/C/88/D/1416/2005, 10 November 2006.

[37] *Ahmed Hussein Mustafa Kamil Agiza v. Sweden*, UN Doc CAT/C/34/D/233/2003, 24 May 2005, para 13.4; *Alzery v. Sweden* (n 36 above), para 11.5; *Tursunov v. Kazakhstan*, UN Doc CAT/C/54/D/538/2013, 3 July 2015, para 9.10. See also, *Othman (Abu Qatada) v. United Kingdom* (n 30 above), paras 186–205.

[38] *H.Y. v. Switzerland*, UN Doc CAT/C/61/D/747/2016, 7 September 2017, para 10.6.

[39] UN Committee Against Torture, General Comment no 4 (n 2 above), para 20.

has sometimes been referred to as complementary protection.[40] The protections afforded to recognised refugees focus on 'durable solutions', which, assuming voluntary repatriation and resettlement elsewhere are not viable options, focus on local integration. When refugees are locally integrated they are typically granted a progressively wider range of rights and entitlements by the host state, including the right to reside permanently in the host state, the right to work, to free movement, to education and to access medical care and associated social benefits. Even though increasingly, the protections afforded to refugees are more temporary, with the expectation that the persons concerned will return to their countries of origin once the situation evolves sufficiently to allow it,[41] they are usually significantly more extensive than what is afforded to persons with some kind of complementary protection, even though basic human rights protections should apply to all persons within a State's jurisdiction, regardless of legal status.

Some States have put in place hostile environment policies aimed at discouraging individuals from seeking protection as well as encouraging those already on the territory to leave, for example curtailing access to benefits resulting in destitution and using indefinite detention. Such practices have left many individuals in a situation of extreme insecurity, leading to constructive refoulement. The UN Committee Against Torture has underscored in its 2017 General Comment that:

> States parties should not adopt dissuasive measures or policies, such as detention in poor conditions for indefinite periods, refusing to process claims for asylum or prolonging them unduly, or cutting funds for assistance programmes for asylum seekers, which would compel persons in need of protection under article 3 of the Convention to return to their country of origin in spite of their personal risk of being subjected to torture or other cruel, inhuman or degrading treatment or punishment there.[42]

Type of Threat

In refugee law, the non-refoulement obligation focuses on refugees whose life or freedom would be threatened on account of their race, religion, nationality, membership of a particular social group or political opinion.[43] That such persons would face threats to their lives or freedom is insufficient. Additionally, it must be shown that the discrimination such persons face on account of one of the five reasons enumerated above is a relevant factor in the threats to life or freedom that they experience. Article 33(1) of the 1951 Refugee Convention refers to 'threat to life or freedom on account of', whereas Article 1(A)(2) which provides the definition of refugee refers to 'well-founded fear of persecution for reasons of ...'. However, given the similarities and the connection between the two definitions, it can be surmised that a person who is recognised as a refugee under Article 1(A)(2) cannot be refouled in accordance with Article 33(1), but for the exclusions referred to in section II.2, above.

In contrast, human rights law focuses on persons who are at risk of torture, and, unlike refugee law, does not depend on the connection of the threat to any particular discriminatory or other grounds. Depending upon the treaty framework, the principle of non-refoulement to

---

[40]   UNHCR, 'Complementary Forms of Protection', UN Doc EC/GC/01/18, 4 September 2001.
[41]   Crisp, J, 'The Local Integration and Local Settlement of Refugees: A Conceptual and Historical Analysis', UNHCR, New Issues in Refugee Research, Working Paper No 102, April 2004.
[42]   UN Committee Against Torture, General Comment no 4 (n 2 above), para 14.
[43]   1951 Refugee Convention, Article 33(1).

torture may also extend to capture other forms of cruel, inhuman or degrading treatment or punishment.

Cruel, inhuman or degrading treatment or punishment

Article 3 of the UN Convention Against Torture frames the threat narrowly in respect of torture only. This follows on from the general approach of the Convention to separate out 'torture' and other forms of 'cruel, inhuman or degrading treatment or punishment' and to limit some of States' obligations under the Convention to 'torture'. This limitation has been underscored by the UN Committee Against Torture,[44] though in its 2017 General Comment it recognised States parties' duty to prevent acts of cruel, inhuman or degrading treatment or punishment and encourages them to 'consider whether the nature of the other forms of ill-treatment that a person facing deportation is at risk of experiencing could likely change so as to constitute torture, before making an assessment on each case relating to the principle of "non-refoulement"'.[45] In contrast, the ECtHR and UN Human Rights Committee, the respective interpretive bodies of the ECHR and ICCPR which prohibit torture and other forms of ill-treatment in a single article, have interpreted their statutory frameworks as prohibiting refoulement even when the principle of non-refoulement is not mentioned specifically in those treaties, and include in this consideration of non-refoulement both torture and other cruel, inhuman or degrading treatment or punishment.[46] For instance, the ECtHR has found a violation of Article 3 of the ECHR when it 'considers that substantial grounds have been shown for believing that, if expelled at the present time, the applicant would be exposed to a real risk of being subjected to torture *or* to inhuman or degrading treatment or punishment'.[47] The UN Human Rights Committee has clarified that States parties are obliged 'not to extradite, deport, expel or otherwise remove a person from their territory when there are substantial grounds for believing that there is a real risk of irreparable harm, such as that contemplated by article 7 of the Covenant, which prohibits cruel, inhuman or degrading treatment'.[48]

The inclusion by some courts and treaty bodies of cruel, inhuman or degrading treatment or punishment in the non-refoulement obligation has been important for capturing the risks on return posed by deleterious conditions of detention, living conditions or poor access to health or other essential social services. Such circumstances have only been assessed as sufficiently grave to fall within the ill-treatment category[49] when they are adjudged as exceptional. For

---

[44]   *G.R.B. v. Sweden*, UN Doc CAT/C/20/D/83/1997, 15 May 1998, para 6.5. The Committee Against Torture's first General Comment on Article 3 made clear that 'Article 3 is confined in its application to cases where there are substantial grounds for believing that the author would be in danger of being subjected to torture as defined in article 1 of the Convention' ['General Comment on the implementation of article 3 of the Convention in the context of article 22', UN Doc A/53/44, 16 September 1998, Annex IX, para 1].

[45]   UN Committee Against Torture, General Comment no 4 (n 2 above), para 16.

[46]   UN Human Rights Committee, 'General Comment no 20 on Article 7', UN Doc HRI/GEN/1/Rev.9 (Vol. I), 10 March 1992, para 9; UN Human Rights Committee, General Comment no 31 (n 7 above), para 12; *Soering v. United Kingdom* (n 9 above), paras 88–91; *Chahal v United Kingdom* (n 27 above), para 74.

[47]   *Said v. The Netherlands*, no. 2345/02, ECHR 2005-VI, para 54 (emphasis added).

[48]   *Hibaq Said Hashi v. Denmark*, UN Doc CCPR/C/120/D/2470/2014, 28 July 2017, para 9.3.

[49]   In *Babar Ahmad and Others v. The United Kingdom*, nos 24027/07 and 4 others, 10 April 2012, the ECtHR held that extradition to face a mandatory life sentence would not necessarily violate Article 3 of the ECHR, though in *Aswat v. The United Kingdom*, no 17299/12, 16 April 2013, para 49, it recognised

instance, in *M.S.S. v. Belgium and Greece*, the ECtHR Grand Chamber determined that by sending the applicants to Greece under the Dublin Regulation and exposing them to conditions of detention and living conditions that amounted to degrading treatment, Belgium violated Article 3 of the Convention.[50] The UN Committee Against Torture has taken a much stronger stance in making special mention of the situation of survivors of torture or other forms of ill-treatment, who 'suffer physical and psychological harm that may require sustained availability of and access to specialized rehabilitation services. Once such a state of health and the need for treatment have been medically certified, they should not be removed to a State where adequate medical services for their rehabilitation are not available or guaranteed.'[51]

Certain human rights treaties have also been interpreted as recognising the prohibition of refoulement where there is a real risk of arbitrary deprivation of life.[52] Furthermore, several international and regional instruments, regional courts and treaty bodies extend the prohibition against return to other grounds, including the risk of enforced disappearance,[53] being tried by a special or ad hoc court[54] or a flagrant denial of justice.[55]

Non-state actors
Both refugee and human rights law recognise that the threat can emanate from State or non-State actors.[56] In the latter case, it would need to be shown that the State from where the individual fled is unable or unwilling to protect the individual from the threat from non-State

---

that the applicant's extradition would involve prohibited ill-treatment because of the conditions he would face in a maximum security prison which were liable to be aggravated by his condition of paranoid schizophrenia. Equally, the jurisprudence on the impact of sub-standard medical care in the receiving State has been variable. In some cases, the removal of individuals in the advanced stages of terminal illnesses have been held to violate non-refoulement obligations. See, e.g., *D v. The United Kingdom*, 2 May 1997, *Reports of Judgments and Decisions* 1997-III; *M.K.M. v. Australia*, UN Doc CAT/C/60/D/681/2015, 30 June 2017, paras 8.5, 8.6, 8.9. However, such findings have required 'exceptional' circumstances, absent which, no violation has been found. See, e.g., *N. v. the United Kingdom* [GC], no 26565/05, ECHR 2008, paras 49–51; *Bensaid v. the United Kingdom*, no 44599/98, ECHR 2001-I; *Yoh-Ekale Mwanje v. Belgium*, no 10486/10, 20 December 2011, paras 84, 85; *Mohamed M'Bodj v. État belge*, CJEU, C-542/13, [2015] OJ C 65/12. 18 December 2014; *A.S. v. Switzerland*, no 39350/13, 30 June 2015. See also, *R.B. v. Sweden*, UN Doc. CAT/C/20/D/083/1997, 15 May 1998, para 6.7.

[50] *M.S.S. v. Belgium and Greece* [GC], no 30696/09, ECHR 2011, paras 366–367. See similarly, *Tarakhel v. Switzerland* [GC], no 29217/12; *Sufi and Elmi v. United Kingdom* (n 27 above), paras 290–292; *Paposhvili v. Belgium*, no 41738/10, 17 April 2014, para 205.

[51] UN Committee Against Torture, General Comment no 4 (n 2 above), para 22.

[52] Charter of Fundamental Rights of the European Union, [2010] OJ C 83/2 at 389, Article 19(2). See also, UN Human Rights Committee, *Kwok Yin Fong v. Australia*, UN Doc. CCPR/C/97/D/1442/2005, 23 November 2009, paras 9.4, 9.7; *Al-Saadoon and Mufdhi v. The United Kingdom*, no 61498/08, ECHR 2010, para 137.

[53] International Convention for the Protection of All Persons from Enforced Disappearance, 2006, Article 16(1).

[54] Inter-American Convention to Prevent and Punish Torture, 9 December 1985 (entered into force 28 February 1987), Article 13(4).

[55] *Othman (Abu Qatada) v. United Kingdom* (n 30 above), para 258, with references therein.

[56] See, e.g., UNHCR, Guidelines on International Protection No. 12: Claims for Refugee Status Related to Situations of Armed Conflict and Violence under Article 1A(2) of the 1951 Convention and/or 1967 Protocol relating to the Status of Refugees and the Regional Refugee Definitions, UN Doc. HCR/GIP/16/12, 2 December 2016, para 30.

actors.[57] Consideration has also been given as to whether there may be an internal flight alternative or possibility for relocation within the State, which may mitigate the risks from non-state actors associated with return.[58] The UN Committee Against Torture has interpreted narrowly the internal flight alternative in its jurisprudence. In *M.K.M v. Australia*, which concerned a complainant from Afghanistan, the Committee noted that:

> [T]he internal flight or relocation alternative does not represent a reliable and durable alternative, where the lack of protection is generalized and the individual concerned would be exposed to a further risk of persecution or serious harm, in particular when the persecution of the civilian population by anti-government elements is often random in the complainant's country of origin.[59]

In its most recent General Comment, the Committee is more blunt:

> The Committee considers that the so-called 'internal flight alternative', that is, the deportation of a person or a victim of torture to an area of a State where the person would not be exposed to torture, unlike in other areas of the same State, is not reliable or effective.[60]

The standard and burden of proof

While the terminology may differ, the standard and burden of proof associated with the assessment of the risk an individual faces in the country of return has been interpreted somewhat similarly in the associated legal regimes.

In refugee law, the notion of 'well-founded fear' denotes something which has both objective (well-founded) and subjective (fear) elements. Refugee status is thus determined having regard to the state of mind of the person seeking protection, which must be supported by an objective situation.[61]

The burden would usually fall on the person seeking protection,[62] though according to UNHCR, 'the duty to ascertain and evaluate all the relevant facts is shared between the applicant and the examiner'.[63] This follows from the inherent challenges for persons fleeing persecution to take with them or subsequently seek out the necessary documentation to prove their case to a high standard. UNHCR has stressed that '[i]n most cases a person fleeing from persecution will have arrived with the barest necessities and very frequently even without personal documents.'[64] Similarly, The UN Committee Against Torture has underscored that States cannot sit back and wait for vulnerable claimants to put forward incontrovertible proof

---

[57]   *Salah Sheekh v. The Netherlands*, no 1948/04, 11 January 2007, para 137; *M.K.M. v. Australia* (n 49 above), para 8.9.

[58]   See, 'Directive 2011/95/EU of the European Parliament and of the Council of 13 December 2011 on standards for the qualification of third-country nationals or stateless persons as beneficiaries of international protection, for a uniform status for refugees or for persons eligible for subsidiary protection, and for the content of the protection granted (recast)', L 337/9, 20 December 2011, Article 8; *Salah Sheekh v. The Netherlands* (n 57 above), para 141; *Sufi and Elmi v United Kingdom* (n 27 above), para 266.

[59]   *M.K.M. v Australia* (n 49 above), para 8.9.

[60]   UN Committee Against Torture, General Comment no 4 (n 2 above), para 47.

[61]   UNHCR, 'Handbook and Guidelines on Procedures and Criteria for Determining Refugee Status', UN Doc. HCR/1P/4/ENG/REV 3, December 2011, para 38.

[62]   See, e.g., UN Committee Against Torture, General Comment no 4 (n 2 above), para 38.

[63]   UNHCR, 'Handbook and Guidelines on Procedures and Criteria for Determining Refugee Status' UN Doc. HCR/1P/4/ENG/REV 3, December 2011, para 196.

[64]   *Ibid*, para 196.

which they will never be able to access; once a claimant makes a prima facie case, the State is obligated to make sufficient efforts to determine whether there are substantial grounds for believing that the author would be in danger of being subjected to torture.[65] In its 2017 General Comment, the UN Committee Against Torture has gone even further, indicating that:

> [W]hen complainants are in a situation where they cannot elaborate on their case, such as when they have demonstrated that they have no possibility of obtaining documentation relating to their allegation of torture or have been deprived of their liberty, the burden of proof is reversed and the State party concerned must investigate the allegations and verify the information on which the communication is based.[66]

Some States use inferences when assessing the credibility of claims, such as the failure to submit an asylum request within a certain time limit or the inability to recall certain details. Such approaches ignore the impact that trauma has been found to have on refugees' ability to recall with clarity their experiences,[67] and may result in claims being denied inappropriately. The UN Committee Against Torture has held that complete accuracy could not be expected of victims of torture, especially those suffering from trauma, as long as any inconsistencies were of an immaterial nature and did not raise doubts about the general veracity of the author's claims:[68]

> States parties should refrain from following a standardized credibility assessment process to determine the validity of a non-refoulement claim. With regard to potential factual contradictions and inconsistencies in the author's allegations, States parties should appreciate that complete accuracy can seldom be expected from victims of torture.[69]

The necessary degree of risk and the standard of proof depends on how each treaty framework has been interpreted, though there are many similarities in the approaches taken. The ECtHR jurisprudence centres on the need for a 'real risk' of torture or ill-treatment[70] whereas the UN Committee Against Torture has focused on the need for there to be 'substantial grounds for believing that he or she would risk being subjected to torture.'[71] It has specified that its practice has been 'to determine that "substantial grounds" exist whenever the risk of torture is "foreseeable, personal, present and real"'.[72] The UN Human Rights Committee has referred similarly to 'substantial grounds for believing that there is a real risk of irreparable harm',[73] and in some of its jurisprudence, to the need for the complainant to establish that there is a 'a real risk of treatment contrary to article 7 as a necessary and foreseeable consequence of his expulsion'.[74] The jurisprudence is consistent in recognising that all relevant considerations must be taken into account when assessing the risk, such as the existence of a consistent pattern of gross,

---

[65]   See *F.K. v. Denmark*, UN Doc. CAT/C/56/D/580/2014, 9 February 2016, para 7.6.
[66]   UN Committee Against Torture, General Comment no 4 (n 2 above), para 38.
[67]   See e.g., Cummins, ME, 'Post-Traumatic Stress Disorder and Asylum: Why Procedural Safeguards Are Necessary' (2013) 29 *J. Contemp. Health L. & Pol'y* 283, 288.
[68]   *Pauline Muzonzo Paku Kisoki v. Sweden*, UN Doc. CAT/C/16/D/41/1996, 8 May 1996, para 9.3.
[69]   UN Committee Against Torture, General Comment no 4 (n 2 above), para 42.
[70]   *Soering v. United Kingdom* (n 9 above), para 91.
[71]   See e.g., *H.Y. v. Switzerland* (n 38 above), para 10.2.
[72]   UN Committee Against Torture, General Comment no 4 (n 2 above), para 11.
[73]   UN Human Rights Committee, General Comment no 31 (n 7 above), para 12.
[74]   *Hamida v. Canada*, UN Doc CCPR/C/98/D/1544/2007, 11 May 2010, para 8.7.

flagrant or mass violations of human rights, though the absence of such a pattern will not mean that a person might not be subjected to torture in his or her specific circumstances.[75]

The Extraterritorial Reach of the Non-refoulement Principle

Refoulement involves one State taking action within its borders which has extraterritorial consequences for an individual in another State. However, a State's actions taken purely *outside* its territory, may also fall foul of the non-refoulement principle.

Human rights conventions like the ECHR and ICCPR[76] contain jurisdictional clauses which have been interpreted to apply to the conduct of State officials or those acting on behalf of the State operating outside the physical territory of the State to the extent that they have effective control in that location. For instance, Article 2(1) of the ICCPR, which provides that 'Each State Party to the present Covenant undertakes to respect and to ensure to all individuals within its territory and subject to its jurisdiction…' has been interpreted to mean:

> that a State party must respect and ensure the rights laid down in the Covenant to anyone within the power or effective control of that State Party, even if not situated within the territory of the State Party … This principle also applies to those within the power or effective control of the forces of a State Party acting outside its territory, regardless of the circumstances in which such power or effective control was obtained, such as forces constituting a national contingent of a State Party assigned to an international peace-keeping or peace-enforcement operation.[77]

The UN Committee Against Torture, in its 2017 General Comment has specified similarly that 'Each State party must apply the principle of non-refoulement in any territory under its jurisdiction or any area under its control or authority …'.[78]

The extraterritorial reach of the non-refoulement principle has become crucial in respect of the increasingly prevalent practices of certain States to actively impede individuals who may wish to seek protection from accessing their territories, by imposing restrictive visa regimes and air carrier sanctions, erecting physical barriers at borders, summarily rejecting asylum seekers at borders or points of entry, creating international zones, setting up buffer zones or designating safe areas, as well as intercepting asylum seekers and other migrants on the high seas.

Under refugee law, the non-refoulement principle applies specifically to persons who are outside their countries of origin, thus the action by some States to close their borders to avoid the application of the principle to individuals fleeing persecution from neighbouring countries, can be highly problematic. However, UNHCR has made clear that rejection at the frontier is encompassed in the principle of refoulement: '[i]n all cases the fundamental principle of non-refoulement – including non-rejection at the frontier – must be scrupulously observed.'[79] Furthermore, the OAU Convention Governing the Specific Aspects of Refugee Problems in

---

[75]   Summarised in UN Committee Against Torture, General Comment no 4 (n 2 above), para 43 and accompanying footnotes.
[76]   ECHR, Article 1; ICCPR, Article 2(1).
[77]   UN Human Rights Committee, General Comment no 31 (n 7 above), para 10.
[78]   UN Committee Against Torture, General Comment no 4 (n 2 above), para 10; see also, UN Committee Against Torture, General Comment no 2 'Implementation of article 2 by States parties' UN Doc CAT/C/GC/2, 24 January 2008, para 16.
[79]   UNHCR, Executive Committee Conclusions No. 22 (XXXII) – 1981, II(A)(2).

Africa[80] and the Cartagena Declaration on Refugees[81] both explicitly link non-refoulement to non-rejection at the frontier.

For all other purposes, refugee law and international human rights law take much the same approach to States' extraterritorial jurisdiction, which is understood to apply whenever an individual comes under the effective control of the State.[82] For instance, a State's human rights obligations are engaged in respect of individuals who arrive at, but don't quite cross, border zones. As the ECtHR determined in respect of France's detention of asylum seekers at the international zone of a Paris airport:

> The mere fact that it is possible for asylum-seekers to leave voluntarily the country where they wish to take refuge cannot exclude a restriction on liberty ... Furthermore, this possibility becomes theoretical if no other country offering protection comparable to the protection they expect to find in the country where they are seeking asylum is inclined or prepared to take them in.[83]

Connected to the non-refoulement principle under refugee law, is the prohibition of arbitrary[84] or collective expulsion[85] of aliens, which prevents States from expelling persons at a border post without an individual examination of their personal situations or giving them access to an effective remedy to contest their removal. While States have the right to control the entry, residence and expulsion of aliens, denying individuals the opportunity to have their asylum claims adjudicated is contrary to the procedural obligations inherent in the non-refoulement obligation.[86]

Pushbacks at sea

The extraterritorial reach of the non-refoulement principle has regularly arisen in cases concerning pushbacks on the high seas. In *Sale v. Haitian Centers Council*, the US Supreme Court held controversially that Article 33 of the 1951 Refugee Convention had no extraterritorial effect with regard to Haitians rejected on the high seas.[87] In response to the decision, the Inter-American Commission on Human Rights indicated that American pushbacks of Haitians violated Article 27 of the American Declaration of the Rights and Duties of Man, which provides for the right to seek and obtain asylum in foreign territory.[88]

Pushbacks and related non-admission practices have been firmly in place in Australia, with the Human Rights Committee calling on Australia to review 'the policy and practices during interceptions at sea, including on-water assessments, to ensure that all persons under the State

---

[80]   OAU, Convention Governing the Specific Aspects of Refugee Problems in Africa, Article II(3).

[81]   Cartagena Declaration on Refugees, Article III(5).

[82]   UNHCR, 'Advisory Opinion on the Extraterritorial Application of Non-Refoulement Obligations under the 1951 Convention relating to the Status of Refugees and its 1967 Protocol', January 2007, paras 24, 43; UN Human Rights Committee, General Comment no 31 (n 7 above), para 10; *Hirsi Jamaa v. Italy* (n 7 above), paras 72, 74, 136.

[83]   *Amuur v. France*, 25 June 1996, *Reports of Judgments and Decisions* 1996-III, para 48.

[84]   ICCPR, Article 13; ECHR, Protocol No 7, Article 1.

[85]   ECHR, Protocol no 7, Article 4. ECHR. See *N.D. and N.T. v. Spain*, nos 8675/15 and 8697/15, 3 October 2017 [Referred to the Grand Chamber, 29 January 2018].

[86]   UN Committee against Torture, General Comment no 4 (n 2 above), paras 13, 18.

[87]   *Sale v. Haitian Centers Council*, 509 U.S. 155 (1993).

[88]   *Haitian Centre for Human Rights v. United States*, Report No. 51/96, Inter-Am CHR,OEA/ Ser.L/V/II.95 Doc. 7 rev, 550 (1997).

party's jurisdiction who are in need of international protection have access to fair and efficient asylum procedures within the territory of the State, including access to legal representation where appropriate, and to legal remedies'.[89]

The *Hirsi* case was brought to the ECtHR by Somali and Eritrean migrants whose boat was intercepted on the High Seas by an Italian military vessel, and who were then transferred onto that Italian ship and returned to Libya. The ECtHR Grand Chamber held unanimously that pushbacks on the high seas can breach non-refoulement obligations,[90] to the extent that the State carrying out the pushbacks could be said to have jurisdiction over the individuals concerned, and that the State knew or ought to have known at the time of the removal[91] that the individuals lacked protection in Libya and risked persecution in their home countries.[92] Taking migrants on board a government ship was sufficient to establish a jurisdictional link between the ship's flag State and the migrants, and triggered Italy's human rights obligations.[93]

Similarly, in *P.K. v. Spain*, which concerned the towing by Spanish authorities of a boat to Mauritania and the subsequent detention of the passengers in Mauritania at a facility guarded by Spanish forces, the UN Committee Against Torture determined that Spain exercised jurisdiction both during the interception and throughout the detention in Mauritania,[94] because it maintained (de facto) control over the persons on board the boat, even if the events took place in another country's territorial waters.[95]

Cooperation and readmission agreements

States' extraterritorial non-refoulement obligations have also arisen in the context of cooperation and readmission agreements entered into between destination States and their neighbours to prevent individuals from reaching their territories and/or to shift the duty of caring for refugees to neighbouring transit countries. These measures are not *per se* unlawful, though they call into question the meaning of equitable burden sharing and can raise refoulement concerns.[96] A destination State will not exempt itself from its refoulement obligations by simply declaring a cooperating country 'safe'; it must have objective reasons for believing it to be safe. Nor will States avoid their international obligations by using or hiring other States or private actors to exercise their governmental activity.[97] This is without prejudice to the receiving States' own responsibility for any ensuing violations of the human rights of refugees.

Examples of cooperation frameworks include the introduction of 'safe third country' policies[98] or rules to demarcate which country should undertake the human burden of providing refuge, which have ultimately led destination States to transfer or return individuals

---

[89]   HRC, Concluding observations on the sixth periodic report of Australia, UN Doc CCPR/C/AUS/CO/6, 1 December 2017, para 34(b).

[90]   *Hirsi Jamaa v. Italy* (n 7 above)

[91]   *Ibid*, para 121.

[92]   *Ibid*, para 81.

[93]   *Ibid*, para 79.

[94]   *P.K. et al. v. Spain*, UN Doc. CAT/C/41/D/323/2007, 11 November 2008.

[95]   Ibid, para 8.2. Note, however, that the case was declared inadmissible for unrelated reasons [para 8.3].

[96]   See Gammeltoft-Hansen, T and Hathaway, JC, 'Non-Refoulement in a World of Cooperative Deterrence' (2015) 53 *Columbia Journal of Transnational Law* 235.

[97]   Lauterpacht and Bethlehem (n 3 above), para 61.

[98]   See, e.g., EU-Turkey statement, 18 March 2016, summarised at: https://www.consilium.europa.eu/en/press/press-releases/2016/03/18/eu-turkey-statement/

to neighbouring countries deemed by the destination country as 'safe'. Within the European Union, the Dublin Regulation operates so as to prevent refugees from free movement (or forum shopping) within the Union.[99] It requires that the EU Member State where the migrant first enters must assess the individual's status and, where appropriate, afford them protection. The regulation has placed a difficult burden on Italy, Greece and Spain, who are faced with the bulk of arrivals. The regulation has generally been upheld by courts with some notable exceptions.[100] Additionally, the EU has created operational frameworks such as the European Border and Coast Guard Agency (Frontex) to facilitate joint action by States and to provide support to individual States to implement EU border control policies. The institution in its various iterations has been criticised for helping States to deny people the right to seek asylum in connection with the breach of the non-refoulement, and for its role in return operations and work in third countries that do not border the EU.[101] Destination States have also entered into financial, technical and related cooperation agreements with States on migration routes, ostensibly to limit the trade in trafficking in persons but having the clear effect of forestalling the flow of migrants.[102]

The (Intra)territorial Reach of the Non-refoulement Principle

While refoulement is normally associated with the sending or transfer of an individual by one State to another, a State's actions to transfer an individual to another authority *within* its territory, can also raise refoulement concerns.

The issue has arisen in the context of counter-terrorism activities in which the authorities of a State with custody over an individual transfer that individual to foreign security agents operating on their territory with the knowledge that those agents will remove the individual from the territorial jurisdiction of the State. Or, occasionally, State authorities have acquiesced or been wilfully blind to foreign security agents operating on their territory who have detained and removed individuals from their territory outside of any legal process. The *El-Masri* case concerned the role of Macedonia in the rendition, detention and eventual torture of a German national who Macedonian officials had handed over to the CIA at Skopje Airport. Mr El-Masri

---

[99] Regulation (EU) No 604/2013 of the European Parliament and of the Council of 26 June 2013 establishing the criteria and mechanisms for determining the Member State responsible for examining an application for international protection lodged in one of the Member States by a third-country national or a stateless person (recast), L 180/31, 29 June 2013.

[100] See, e.g., *M.S.S. v. Belgium and Greece* (n 50 above); *Tarakhel v. Switzerland* (n 50 above).

[101] See, e.g., ECRE, 'Comments on the Commission Proposal for a Regulation on the European Border and Coast Guard', November 2018; Keller, S, Lunacek, U, Lochbihler, B and Flautre, H, 'Frontex Agency: Which Guarantees for Human Rights? A Study Conducted by Migreurop (www.migreurop.org) on the European External Borders Agency in View of the Revision of its Mandate', 2011.

[102] See, European Commission, 'Communication on establishing a new Partnership Framework with third countries under the European Agenda on Migration', COM(2016) 385 final, 7 June 2016; Memorandum of Understanding between the Government of the Kingdom of Cambodia and the Government of Australia relating to the Settlement of Refugees (MOU), 26 September 2014; Memorandum of understanding on cooperation in the fields of development, the fight against illegal immigration, human trafficking and fuel smuggling and on reinforcing the security of borders between the State of Libya and the Italian Republic, 2 February 2017, unofficial English translation at: http://eumigrationlawblog.eu/wp-content/uploads/2017/10/MEMORANDUM_translation_finalversion.doc.pdf

was flown by CIA officials to Afghanistan where he was arbitrarily detained and subjected to torture. Macedonia was held responsible for the violations which ensued – both those which occurred on Macedonian soil and those perpetrated by the CIA, because they 'knowingly exposed him to a real risk of ill-treatment and to conditions of detention contrary to Article 3'.[103] This reasoning was upheld in the later *Al-Nashiri*[104] and *Abu Zubaydah*[105] cases before the ECtHR concerning Poland, the *Nasr and Ghali* case against Italy,[106] the *Abu Zubaydah* case against Lithuania[107] and the *Al-Nashiri* case against Romania.[108]

A similar problem arises when foreign armed forces or peace-keeping troops operating abroad take custody of individuals in the course of their operations and thereafter wish to transfer them to local law enforcement or military troops, but there is a risk that local authorities may torture these individuals. This problem arose in recent military operations in Afghanistan and Iraq, and has been addressed to an extent in the Copenhagen Process Principles and Guidelines,[109] an international declarative text which sought to identify the baseline of laws applicable to the taking, handling and transfer of civilian detainees in non-international military operations, peace-keeping operations and law enforcement operations. Principle 15 addresses detainee transfers and monitoring:

> A State or international organisation is to only transfer a detainee to another State or authority in compliance with the transferring State's or international organisation's international law obligations. Where the transferring State or international organisation determines it appropriate to request access to transferred detainees or to the detention facilities of the receiving State, the receiving State or authority should facilitate such access for monitoring of the detainee until such time as the detainee has been released, transferred to another detaining authority, or convicted of a crime in accordance with the applicable national law.

What constitutes 'international law obligations' is not spelt out, nor are the circumstances in which it might be appropriate for a State to request access to transferred detainees for the purposes of monitoring the detainee. Nevertheless, it is clear that what is at issue are refoulement-type concerns.

In the *Maya Evans* case,[110] which stemmed from a claim by a British peace activist that Afghan terror detainees transferred by the British Armed Forces to the Afghan National Directorate of Security (NDS) were at risk of being beaten and physically mistreated, thus making the transfers unlawful, the UK courts banned transfers to the NDS detention centre in Kabul as a result of concerns about ill-treatment. Transfers to other facilities were not banned, although the Court imposed a series of 'safeguards' and monitoring arrangements on all future transfers of detainees. In an earlier Canadian case which also concerned transfers in

---

[103] *El-Masri v. The former Yugoslav Republic of Macedonia* [GC], no 39630/09, ECHR 2012, para 220.
[104] *Al Nashiri v. Poland*, no. 28761/11, 24 July 2014, paras 442, 443, 453–459, 517–519.
[105] *Husayn (Abu Zubaydah) v. Poland*, no 7511/13, 24 July 2014, paras 450–456, 512–514.
[106] *Nasr and Ghali v. Italy*, no 44883/09, 23 February 2016, paras 241–247, 284–291.
[107] *Abu Zubaydah v. Lithuania*, no. 46454/11, 31 May 2018, para 643.
[108] *Al Nashiri v. Romania*, no. 33234/12, 31 May 2018, para 678.
[109] Danish Ministry of Foreign Affairs, 'The Copenhagen Process on the Handling of Detainees in International Military Operations: Principles and Guidelines, and Chairman's Commentary' (Copenhagen, 19 October 2012).
[110] *R (Maya Evans) v. Secretary of State for Defence* [2010], EWHC 1445 (Admin) (UK).

Afghanistan, the Canadian Federal Court of Appeal declined to order a stoppage of the transfers on the basis that protection under the Canadian Charter of Rights and Freedoms (the Charter) does not extend to Afghan detainees and did not apply to the conduct of Canadian forces in Afghanistan.[111] However, the Canadian ruling has been criticised; at the least, Canada's human rights obligations (including the prohibition of refoulement to torture) applied to any proposed transfer of detainees to Afghan authorities,[112] and should have been taken into account. These same issues arose in the *Al Saadoon* case,[113] which concerned the transfer to Iraqi custody of Iraqi detainees held by British forces without an assurance on the non-applicability of the death penalty. The ECtHR determined that the transfer violated Aricle 3 of the ECHR:

> [T]hrough the actions and inaction of the United Kingdom authorities the applicants have been subjected, since at least May 2006, to the fear of execution by the Iraqi authorities ... [C]ausing the applicants psychological suffering of this nature and degree constituted inhuman treatment. It follows that there has been a violation of Article 3 of the Convention.[114]

How the Non-refoulement Principle Is Protected and Enforced

There is no international enforcement mechanism under the 1951 Refugee Convention or the 1967 Protocol; it is for each State's judiciary to assess compliance with the Convention in accordance with domestic procedures. The United Nations High Commissioner for Refugees (UNHCR) can provide recommendations to States as to how to improve their compliance with refugee law, however it has no formal supervisory role. This differs from the available procedures under international human rights law, which, in addition to national processes, can be considered by applicable regional human rights courts and/or commissions, some of which can issue decisions which, according to the respective treaty framework, are binding on States. States parties' records can also be reviewed by UN treaty bodies – through individual complaints processes where States have authorised the bodies to consider individual complaints, and through the consideration of States' periodic reports.

REMEDIES FOR REFOULEMENT

When a State violates the prohibition of non-refoulement under human rights law, this constitutes a human rights violation, which, in the normal course of events, should lead to reparation. This cause and effect is underscored by the UN Human Rights Committee in its General Comment 31, paragraph 12 of which explicitly refers to the non-refoulement obligation and paragraph 15 to the State obligation to put in place accessible and effective remedies to vindicate those rights, while paragraph 16 affirms the requirement that States Parties make reparation to individuals whose Covenant rights have been violated.[115] The UN Committee Against

---

[111] *Amnesty International Canada and BCCLA v. Chief of the Defence Staff for the Canadian Forces and Attorney General of Canada* [2009] 4 FCA 149.

[112] See, e.g., Sassoli, M and Tougas, ML, 'International Law Issues Raised by the Transfer of Detainees by Canadian Forces in Afghanistan' (2011) 56 *McGill Law Journal* 959, 991–999.

[113] *Al-Saadoon v. United Kingdom* (n 52 above).

[114] *Ibid*, para 144.

[115] UN Human Rights Committee, General Comment no 31 (n 7 above), paras 12, 15 and 16.

Torture has similarly affirmed in its General Comment 3 on the implementation of Article 14, the obligation of States parties to ensure that victims of torture and other prohibited treatment obtain an effective remedy and reparation, listing restitution, compensation, rehabilitation, satisfaction and guarantees of non-repetition as the full scope of measures required to redress violations under the Convention.[116] The form reparation should take will depend on the breach and must be adequate, effective and comprehensive.[117]

Victims are understood to be 'persons who individually or collectively suffered harm, including physical or mental injury, emotional suffering, economic loss or substantial impairment of their fundamental rights, through acts or omissions that constitute violations of the Convention'.[118] Arguably, this should include victims of refoulement, in that their rights under Article 3 of the Convention Against Torture have been violated, and the treatment they have suffered puts them at a risk of torture. This interpretation would be consistent with the overall approach taken to the principle of non-refoulement, which connects States' actions in subjecting individuals to unacceptable risks of torture with the violation of the prohibition against torture itself.[119] The notion that the breach of the non-refoulement obligation should give rise to reparation is also consistent with much of the jurisprudence.[120] In its *Agiza* decision, the Committee Against Torture underscored that 'the prohibition on refoulement ... should be interpreted the same way to encompass a remedy for its breach, even though it may not contain on its face such a right to remedy for a breach thereof.'[121]

Reparation for the decision to refoul and the consequences of that refoulement should include restitution, which would require the sending State to allow and facilitate the individual to return to the territory of the sending State.[122] The sending State should also guarantee non-repetition,[123] and provide compensation. In the *Alzery* decision, the UN Human Rights Committee indicated that one of the appropriate remedies for refoulement was compensation.[124] Similarly, in *Hirsi Jamaa*, the ECtHR ordered Italy to pay compensatory damages for the non-pecuniary harm the applicants suffered.[125] Despite these findings, however, the Committee Against Torture General Comment 3 (Article 14) is silent on this point, as is its 2017 General Comment on non-refoulement, despite the recommendations made by certain NGOs to address the gap during the drafting process.[126]

---

[116]   UN Committee Against Torture, General Comment no 3: Implementation of article 14 by States parties, UN Doc CAT/C/GC/3 (19 November 2012), paras 1, 2.

[117]   *Ibid*, para 6.

[118]   *Ibid*, para 3.

[119]   *Soering v. United Kingdom* (n 9 above) 7 July 1989.

[120]   *Agiza v. Sweden* (n 37 above), paras 13.6–13.7; *Alzery v. Sweden* (n 36 above), para 13; *Hirsi Jamaa v. Italy* (n 7 above) para 215; *M.S.S. v. Belgium and Greece* (n 50 above), paras 407–411; *Pacheco Tineo Family v. Plurinational State of Bolivia*, Inter-American Court of Human Rights, Judgment of 25 November 2013 Preliminary Objections, Merits, Reparations and Costs, Series C no 272, paras 277–285.

[121]   *Agiza v. Sweden* (n 37 above), para 13.6.

[122]   See, e.g., *Abdussamatov and others v. Kazakhstan*, UN Doc. CAT/C/48/D/444/2010, 11July 2012; *A.H. v. Denmark*, UN Doc CCPR/C/114/D/2370/2014, 7 September 2015.

[123]   *A.H v. Denmark* (n 122 above).

[124]   *Alzery v. Sweden* (n 36 above), para 13.

[125]   *Hirsi Jamaa v. Italy* (n 7 above) para 215. See similarly, *M.S.S. v. Belgium and Greece* (n 50 above), para 410.

[126]   'Joint Observations regarding Revised General Comment No. 1 (2017) on the implementation of article 3 of the Convention against Torture and Other Cruel, Inhuman or Degrading Treatment or

Recognition of the right to reparation is only a part of the challenge, however. Given the nature of pushbacks and other deterrence strategies, once the refugees have been returned or sent to a third country, it will be difficult if not impossible for them to pursue effective complaints and remedies against an offending State or other responsible actor, regardless of the responsibility of that State under domestic or international law. The would-be complainants will typically not have access to lawyers in the offending State after they were forced to leave, and their situation of vulnerability makes such legal remedies illusory in all but a very few cases. At present, remedies are near impossible for potential claimants to pursue from outside the country.

CONCLUSIONS

Non-refoulement is a vital protection which affords important safeguards to individuals facing a real risk of significant harms. Resort to the principle has grown exponentially in recent decades, owing to the failure of States to agree workable humanitarian solutions to the vast displacement of people resulting from mass conflict and insecurity, massive human rights violations, economic disenfranchisement and environmental disasters, even though the principle was not designed to deal with such situations. The non-refoulement principle is narrowly framed, both under refugee law and international human rights law, despite differences in the scope and configuration of the definition in the respective legal regimes.

In general, States have a clear understanding of their obligation to comply with the non-refoulement prohibition. On the whole, few States deny the existence of the principle or its application to their actions. Instead, their efforts have mainly been focused on maintaining the limited framing of the definition, and where possible, seeking to limit it further. Under refugee law, many States have sought to place barriers in the way of individuals to prevent them from being able to claim protection, mainly by limiting access to their territories or by introducing extraterritorial processing and detention zones in agreement with neighbouring countries. This has put many individuals at significant risk, as they are increasingly forced to resort to insecure routes and are at the whim of smugglers and other criminal networks. Under human rights law, States' efforts have mainly been aimed at trying to introduce loopholes to the absolute ban on refoulement – by restricting the types of human rights risks to which non-refoulement applies and, seeking to introduce balancing tests to increase the latitude to deport terror suspects.

On the whole, human rights courts and treaty bodies have played an important role in maintaining a clear jurisprudence on the absolute prohibition against refoulement and providing an important stop-gap for some of the most vulnerable people. However these bodies were never intended, and are not set up to deal with, the high numbers of claims they ultimately receive, many of which relate to humanitarian protection and exceed their narrow mandates. The 'elephant in the room' is States' failure to address politically and sufficiently the causes and consequences of the mass movements of people. There is a tendency to blame the migrants who do not manage to fit within the legal straightjacket of the relevant non-refoulement definitions. Because the refoulement definitions are limited, and the laws technical and procedurally

---

Punishment', March 2017, available at https://www.ohchr.org/Documents/HRBodies/CAT/GCArticle3/JoinNGOSubmission.pdf, paras 43–63.

complicated, ultimately the law is often used as a tool to enforce the unjust absence of policies to deal with major human suffering. It is not sustainable.

16. Universal and extraterritorial jurisdiction for torture

Lutz Oette

INTRODUCTION

In January 2000, seven Chadian victims of torture and a victims' association brought a complaint in Senegal against Chad's former dictator Hissène Habré, then residing in Dakar, Senegal, alleged to be responsible for large-scale, systematic torture and other serious human rights violations during his reign from 1982 to 1990. Thus began a momentous legal struggle, which has arguably become the most important case of criminal universal jurisdiction for torture to date. In 2006, the Committee against Torture (Committee/CAT) found that Senegal had breached its obligations under the Convention against Torture and Other Cruel, Inhuman or Degrading Treatment or Punishment (Convention) by declining to prosecute Habré for lack of jurisdiction, and an African Union (AU) panel called on Senegal to prosecute Habré. In response, Senegal changed its legislation to establish universal jurisdiction over several international crimes, including torture, but did not take further steps to investigate and prosecute Habré. In 2012, the International Court of Justice (ICJ) ruled, in a case brought by Belgium, that the lack of steps taken constituted a breach of Senegal's obligations under the Convention. In the same year, the Extraordinary African Chambers (EAC) was set up within the Senegalese judicial system. Five years on, the EAC's Appeal Court upheld Habré's 2016 conviction for torture, crimes against humanity and war crimes, and sentence of life imprisonment, and ordered him to pay around €123 million in compensation to the victims of these crimes.[1]

The *Habré* case, which played out against the backdrop of major debates and controversies surrounding the exercise of universal jurisdiction for international crimes, suggests that it is premature if not altogether incorrect to talk of the fall of universal jurisdiction.[2] The CAT and ICJ rulings,[3] the United Nations (UN) Secretary General's reports on universal jurisdiction,[4] the International Law Commission's (ILC) study of the obligation *aut dedere aut judicare*

---

[1] *Suleymane Guengueng et al. v. Senegal* (2006) UN Doc CAT/C/36/D/181/2001 (19 May 2006); *Questions relating to the Obligation to Prosecute or Extradite (Belgium v. Senegal)*, Judgment, ICJ Reports 2012, p 442; Extraordinary African Chamber, Appeals Judgment, *The Prosecutor General v. Hissein Habré* (27 April 2017).

[2] Reydams, L, 'The Rise and Fall of Universal Jurisdiction' in Schabas, W and Bernaz, N (eds), *Handbook of International Criminal Law* (Routledge, 2010); and, for a counterpoint, Langer, M, 'Universal Jurisdiction is Not Disappearing: The Shift from "Global Enforcer" to "No Safe Haven" Universal Jurisdiction' (2015) 13 *Journal of International Criminal Law* 245.

[3] See n 1 above.

[4] See reports produced by the United Nations (UN) Secretary-General in relation to General Assembly of the United Nations, Sixth Committee (Legal): The scope and application of the principle of universal jurisdiction (Agenda Item 84).

(extradite or prosecute)[5] and a growing number of prosecutions[6] underscore the critical importance of universal jurisdiction in the architecture of international criminal justice in general,
and of the prohibition of torture in particular. It provides an important avenue of 'transnational' justice where adequate domestic prosecutions for the offence of torture are lacking and
international criminal justice mechanisms either have no jurisdiction, or do not exercise it. Yet,
it is equally clear that it poses multiple challenges.

This chapter examines the legal, practical and political challenges concerning extraterritorial and universal criminal jurisdiction for torture. The rulings of the CAT and the ICJ have
elucidated several aspects of States parties' obligations under the Convention. However,
a number of questions remain to be addressed concerning the types and scope of extraterritorial jurisdiction for torture and its application, and, beyond the Convention, its status under
customary international law. A further pertinent question concerns the applicability of immunities in torture cases, which may, even where jurisdiction is established, frustrate its effective
exercise, and has therefore generated considerable debate.[7]

The objective of depriving perpetrators of torture of safe havens and of holding them
accountable, and thereby to make the struggle against torture more effective worldwide
(preamble) can only be achieved if States put in place a legal and institutional framework
that fosters the effective exercise of extraterritorial jurisdiction. Such a framework includes
implementing legislation, the removal of legal barriers, guaranteeing the rights of victims, and
an adequate institutional set-up. A closer look at relevant practice shows that, notwithstanding
a number of steps taken, many national systems are ill-equipped in this regard. Identifying
the legal and institutional components that foster the effective exercise of extraterritorial
jurisdiction in torture cases has therefore become an important focus. One critical factor in this
context is the significant political opposition to its use, which has also impacted on legislative
and institutional practice.

The debate on extraterritorial and universal civil jurisdiction for torture has largely centred
on the interpretation of Article 14 of the Convention, which obliges States parties to ensure
redress for victims of torture in their legal systems, namely whether it requires, or at least
permits States to establish and exercise such jurisdiction. CAT's position indicates that it
does.[8] However, several courts have ruled that States parties have no such obligation, or
even right, under international law. This chapter subjects this proposition to critical scrutiny,
considers State practice to date, and identifies legal, practical and political challenges to the
exercise of such jurisdiction. It argues that assertions of sovereignty and territoriality conflict
with the objective of making the struggle against torture effective worldwide. Any status quo
denying universal civil jurisdiction for torture remains tentative, as victims of torture and
those advocating their rights continue to probe the system. They thereby expose the denial of

---

[5]   ILC, 'Final Report of the International Law Commission: The obligation to extradite or prosecute
(*aut dedere aut judicare*)' ILC Yearbook (2014) vol II (Part Two).

[6]   Langer, M, 'The Diplomacy of Universal Jurisdiction: The Political Branches and the Transitional
Prosecution of International Crimes' (2011) 105 *American Journal of International Law* 1, 8, identifies
a total of 1051 universal jurisdiction complaints (for all crimes). NGOs have regularly reported on cases,
see for the latest, TRIAL International, REDRESS, FIDH, ECCHR and FIBGAR, Make Way for Justice
#4: Momentum towards accountability, Universal Jurisdiction Annual Review 2018 (2018).

[7]   See further Chapter 17 in this volume.

[8]   'General Comment no 3 of the Committee against Torture: Implementation of article 14 by States
parties' UN Doc CAT/C/GC/3 (19 November 2012), para 22.

justice that such practice entails and challenge the integrity of a legal system that privileges the sovereign rights of States over the rights of individuals who have suffered serious human rights violations such as torture.

UNIVERSAL AND EXTRATERRITORIAL CRIMINAL JURISDICTION FOR TORTURE

Overview

Jurisdiction has been described as 'an aspect of sovereignty: it refers to a state's competence under international law to regulate the conduct of natural and juridical persons'.[9] It comprises prescriptive jurisdiction and adjudicative and/or enforcement jurisdiction, namely the power to establish and to exercise such jurisdiction.[10] Territorial jurisdiction is seen 'as the most fundamental, obvious and undisputed instance of the state exercising its jurisdiction'.[11] While itself 'historically contingent', being linked to the notion of sovereignty,[12] its status is reflected in the 'presumption that jurisdiction (in all its forms) is territorial'.[13] Extraterritorial criminal jurisdiction is therefore viewed as an exception.[14] According to an expansive reading of international law, relying on the *Lotus* case,[15] establishing such jurisdiction is permitted unless it is prohibited; conversely, a more restrictive understanding posits that it needs to be specifically provided for under international law, or at least requires a sufficient connection to the State.[16]

Jurisdiction over torture committed extraterritorially can be based on the notion of 'territory within a State's jurisdiction' in instances where the State exercises 'effective control' over persons or territory abroad, the flag principle, and/or nationality (in respect of the perpetrator or the victim).[17] Universal jurisdiction is the 'assertion of jurisdiction to prescribe in the absence of any other accepted jurisdictional nexus at the time of the relevant conduct'.[18] Such jurisdiction is 'based solely on the nature of the crime, without regard to where the crime was committed, the nationality of the alleged or convicted perpetrator, the nationality of the victim,

---

[9] Crawford, J, *Brownlie's Principles of Public International Law*, 8th edn (Oxford University Press, 2012), 456.

[10] Staker, C, 'Jurisdiction' in Evans, MD (ed), *International Law*, 4th edn (Oxford University Press, 2014), 313–333; O'Keefe, R, 'Universal Jurisdiction – Clarifying the Basic Concept' (2004) 2 *Journal of International Criminal Justice* 735, distinguishes between jurisdiction to prescribe and jurisdiction to enforce.

[11] Orakhelashvili, A, 'State Jurisdiction in International Law: Complexities of a Basic Concept' in Orakhelashvili, A (ed), *Research Handbook on Jurisdiction and Immunities in International Law* (Edward Elgar, 2015), 1, 23.

[12] Ryngaert, C, 'The Concept of Jurisdiction in International Law' in Orakhelashvili (n 11 above), 50–51.

[13] Crawford (n 9 above), 456.

[14] However, see Orakheleshvili (n 11 above), 3, who argues that notions of territory and extraterritoriality become a matter of degree and characterisation.

[15] 'Lotus', *Judgment No 9, 1927, PCIJ, Ser A, No 10*, 19, 20.

[16] See further Ryngaert (n 12 above); O'Keefe (n 10 above).

[17] For an overview of the different types of jurisdiction not covered here, including the protective principle, see Ryngaert (n 12 above), O'Keefe (n 10 above) and Staker (n 10 above).

[18] O'Keefe (n 10 above), 745.

or any other connection to the state exercising such jurisdiction'.[19] It has been recognised in respect of several international crimes, though its scope and the conditions for its exercise remain contested.[20] There has been some debate over whether torture constitutes an international crime (beyond constituting an element of international crimes such as war crimes or crimes against humanity) or a crime subject to universal jurisdiction under international law.[21] Irrespective of the position taken in this regard, it is widely recognised that international law obliges, or at least permits, States to exercise universal jurisdiction over the crime of torture, on account of both its *jus cogens* status and relevant treaty provisions.[22] There is a growing recognition that certain serious offences attacking the integrity of the person are of international concern, and require criminal law responses beyond the territorial State. In the field of human rights, torture has provided the impetus for this development.[23]

Treaty-based Extraterritorial Jurisdiction, with Particular Reference to the Convention against Torture

Travaux préparatoires
The Convention's drafting history is instructive for the contemporary understanding of extraterritorial, particularly universal jurisdiction. It highlights the rationale and support for universal jurisdiction, and opposition thereto, which foreshadowed subsequent challenges to its exercise. The rationale for the obligation *aut dedere aut judicare* eventually adopted in

---

[19]   *The Princeton Principles on Universal Jurisdiction*, Principle 1(1), see Macedo, S and Robinson, M, *Princeton Project on Universal Jurisdiction* (Princeton University, 2001).

[20]   *Arrest Warrant of 11 April 2000 (Democratic Republic of Congo v. Belgium), Preliminary Objections and Merits, Judgment, ICJ Reports 2002*, p 3, Joint Separate Opinion of Judges Higgins, Kooijmans and Buergenthal, para 61; Council of the European Union, The AU-EU Expert Report on the Principle of Universal Jurisdiction, 8672/1/09 (16 April 2009) para 9; UNGA, 'The scope and application of the principle of universal jurisdiction, Report of the Secretary-General prepared on the basis of comments and observations of Governments', UN doc A/65/181 (2010), para 28.

[21]   See e.g. Ambos, K, *Treaties on International Criminal Law, Volume II: The Crimes and Sentencing* (Oxford University Press, 2014) 241ff, particularly at 245, and, on the discussion of 'core crimes' under international law, Kittichaisaree, K, *The Obligation to Extradite or Prosecute* (Oxford University Press, 2018), 99ff.

[22]   Kittichaisaree (n 21 above), particularly at 165. See further *R. v. Bow Street Metropolitan Stipendiary Magistrate and others, ex parte Pinochet Ugarte (Amnesty International and others intervening) (Pinochet No.3)* [1999] 2 All ER 97, Lord Browne-Wilkinson, 109; ICTY, *Prosecutor v. Anton Furundžija* Judgment, Case No IT–95–17/1–T, Trial Chamber (10 December 1998), para 156; IACtHR, *Goiburú et al. v. Paraguay*, Merits, Reparations and Costs, Series C no 153 (22 September 2006), paras 123–132, in the context of extraditions, and CEU Expert Report (n 20 above), para 9. Key treaties effectively require States to establish universal jurisdiction, see UN Convention Against Torture and Other Cruel, Inhuman or Degrading Treatment or Punishment (adopted 10 December 1984, entered into force 26 June 1987) 1465 UNTS 85 Article 5(2); Inter-American Convention to Prevent and Punish Torture (adopted 12 September 1985, entered into force 28 February 1987) OAS Treaty Series no 67, Article 12.

[23]   Nowak, M and McArthur, E, *The United Nations Convention against Torture: A Commentary* (Oxford University Press 2008), 316, note that the Convention was the first human rights treaty, other than the Apartheid Convention 1973, 'incorporating the principle of universal jurisdiction as an international obligation of all States parties without any precondition other than the presence of the alleged torturer'.

Articles 5–7 was to prevent any loopholes and safe havens persisting for suspects of torture.[24] Universal jurisdiction is a prerequisite for effectively discharging this obligation where a State party does not extradite a suspected perpetrator of torture who is present within its jurisdiction. It was viewed as crucial to ensure the effectiveness of the Convention where the territorial State failed to take the requisite action to prosecute perpetrators, particularly in situations where torture was a State policy.[25] The nature of States parties' obligation was modelled on 'other treaties for the suppression of evils which the international community deemed inacceptable'.[26] There is an extensive list of such treaties, such as the Convention for the Suppression of Unlawful Seizure of Aircraft of 1970, though limited use has been made of this in the human rights field.[27] Objections to, and reservations concerning universal jurisdiction centred on its compatibility with domestic legal systems, the risk of adverse consequences for international relations, political friction, difficulties of obtaining evidence, and abuse and lack of guarantees of fair trial rights.[28] Several representatives favoured giving extradition priority over the exercise of universal jurisdiction, effectively making the latter subsidiary.[29] If accepted, this model would have significantly limited the scope of universal jurisdiction under the Convention. Ultimately, opposition receded in light of the persuasive arguments made in favour of universal jurisdiction.[30] The United States (US) representative commented that the final text was the 'product of careful and thorough study of a complex matter and constitute[s] the best compromise of varying points of view [which achieved] the desired result of a workable, effective system of universal criminal jurisdiction'.[31]

Convention against Torture

The nature of offences: Torture and other ill-treatment
Article 5(1) and (2) set out an obligation 'for the State to criminalize torture and to establish its jurisdiction over it'.[32] The ICJ held that '[t]his obligation … has to be implemented by the State concerned as soon as it is bound by the Convention', and stressed its 'preventive and deterrent character, since by equipping themselves with the necessary legal tools to prosecute this type of offence, the States parties ensure that their legal systems will operate to that effect and commit themselves to coordinating their efforts to eliminate any risk of impunity'.[33] A combined reading of the ICJ judgment and CAT's *Guengueng* decision suggests that Article

---

[24]   See for good overviews Burgers, JH and Danelius, H, *The United Nations Convention against Torture: A Handbook on the Convention against Torture and Other Cruel, Inhuman or Degrading Treatment or Punishment*, (Martinus Nijhoff 1988); Nowak and McArthur (n 23 above) 254ff; and reports of the Working Group (travaux préparatoires), UN docs E/CN.4/1367 (5 March 1980) paras 51; E/CN.4/L.1576 (6 March 1981) para 25; E/CN.4/1982/L.40 (5 March 1982) para 22.

[25]   UN Docs E/CN.4/1982/L.40, para 26; E/CN.4/1983/63, para 21; E/CN.4/1984/72, para 29.

[26]   UN Doc E/CN.4/1982/L.40, para 22.

[27]   See further on relevant treaties referred to, Burgers and Danelius (n 24 above) 58, 61, 131–132.

[28]   UN Docs E/CN.4/1367, para 52; E/CN.4/L.1576, para 25; E/CN.4/1982/L.40, para 24; E/CN.4/1983/63, para 22.

[29]   UN Docs E/CN.4/1367, para 50; E/CN.4/1983/63, para 23.

[30]   Burgers and Danelius (n 24 above), 94–95.

[31]   UNGA, 'Report of the Secretary-General' UN Doc A/39/499 (2 October 1984) 20, para 4.

[32]   *Questions relating to the Obligation to Prosecute or Extradite* (n 1 above), para 75.

[33]   *Ibid.*

5 creates an immediate obligation to take the necessary measures to establish the requisite jurisdiction within a 'reasonable time frame'.[34]

States parties have to establish their jurisdiction over offences of torture as referred to in Article 4.[35] Under that article, States parties have to 'ensure that all acts of torture are offences under its criminal law', which, according to CAT, requires them to criminalise torture in line with the elements set out in Article 1.[36] Article 5(1) and (2) seemingly exclude torture by non-State actors, as Article 1 requires the involvement 'of a public official or other person acting in an official capacity'. However, as the *Zardad* case in the United Kingdom (UK) demonstrates, non-state actors, here an Afghan 'warlord' belonging to Hezb-e-Islami, may fall within the definition of Article 1 where they exercise State-like functions, and can be considered to act in an official capacity.[37] Further, the residual clause in Article 5(3), according to which the 'Convention does not exclude any criminal jurisdiction exercised in accordance with internal law', permits States parties to establish universal jurisdiction over non-State actors beyond the definition of torture in Article 1, provided the scope of such jurisdiction is compatible with its international law obligations.

Article 5 expressly applies to acts of torture only. This reflects both the travaux and the international practice that has focused on the suppression of torture as a crime.[38] However, in its General Comment 2, '[t]he Committee [against Torture] considers that articles 3 to 15 are likewise obligatory as applied to both torture and ill-treatment'.[39] Several States have established universal jurisdiction over ordinary crimes that may amount to ill-treatment.[40] While the scope of States parties' obligation remains uncertain in this regard, Article 5(3) can be invoked to establish universal jurisdiction over acts of ill-treatment, particularly where such acts are recognised as entailing criminal responsibility in international law.[41]

Grounds of jurisdiction

Article 5 sets out four grounds of jurisdiction, namely when torture is committed 'in any territory under its [the State party] jurisdiction' or 'on board a ship or aircraft registered in that State', the active nationality principle, the passive nationality principle (discretionary), and universal jurisdiction. The notion of territory in Article 5(1)(a) is clearly broader than

---

[34]   *Suleymane Guengueng v. Senegal* (n 1 above), para 9.5.

[35]   *Questions relating to the Obligation to Prosecute or Extradite* (n 1 above), para 99 held that the obligation does not apply to torture predating the coming into force of the Convention for the State party concerned. Supportive, ILC (n 5 above), para 25. Critical, Separate Opinion of Judge Cançado Trindade, *Questions relating to the Obligation to Prosecute or Extradite* (n 1 above), 132.

[36]   CAT, 'General Comment no 2: Implementation of article 2 by States parties' UN Doc CAT/C/GC/2 (2008) paras 8–11.

[37]   *R v Zardad* [2007] EWCA Crim 279. See also CAT decision, *Elmi v. Australia*, UN Doc CAT/C/22/D/120/1988, 14 May 1999, para 6.5.

[38]   '... the United States believes the Convention should be focused primarily on the prevention and suppression of acts clearly identifiable as torture. Such a focus is necessary in light of the severe penalties, broad jurisdictional provisions, and definitional difficulties embodied in the Convention, and the need for broad international acceptance.' UN Doc E/CN.4/1314 (19 December 1978) para 13.

[39]   CAT, General Comment no 2 (n 36 above), para 6.

[40]   Amnesty International, Universal Jurisdiction: A preliminary survey of legislation around the world – 2012 update, Index: 53/019/2012 (2012), 13-14.

[41]   See in this context principle 2 of the Madrid-Buenos Aires Principles of Universal Jurisdiction (2015).

State territory, as it is not confined to 'its territory'. As held by CAT, foreign territory, such as occupied territory, falls within a State party's jurisdiction where it 'exercises effective control' over persons or territory.[42] This interpretation reflects that of other human rights treaty bodies and courts.[43] The Committee has rejected the position of States parties, particularly the US in respect of the treatment of detainees at Guantanamo Bay and extraordinary renditions, which contested this interpretation.[44] Accordingly, States parties are obliged to exercise jurisdiction that covers alleged acts of torture committed outside their territory in situations where they have effective control, such as during military occupation or renditions. Legislation that explicitly confines jurisdiction to the territory of the State fails to reflect this broader notion of 'territory under its jurisdiction'.[45]

Article 5(1)(b) provides for the active nationality principle where 'the alleged offender is a national of that State'. Several States have established their jurisdiction over their nationals who commit torture abroad.[46] The prosecution of nationals for crimes involving forms of torture or other ill-treatment (frequently as a war crime or terrorism offence) has assumed an important role in relation to offences committed by various actors in Syria, particularly members of Da'esh and other non-State actors.[47] However, States have made limited use of the active nationality principle in cases of torture by public officials, such as in respect of acts of torture committed extraterritorially in the context of armed conflict or counter-terrorism operations.[48]

Article 5(1)(c) provides for the passive personality principle where 'the victim is a national of that State'. Accommodating objections that this jurisdictional ground lacks recognition under international law,[49] it was made discretionary, as reflected in the wording 'if that State considers it appropriate'. Several States have established their jurisdiction over offences of torture committed against their nationals.[50] The passive personality principle has served as

---

[42] CAT, General Comment no 2 (n 36 above), para 16. See already Burgers and Danelius (n 24 above), 131.

[43] See *Al-Skeini and Others v. The United Kingdom* [GC], no 55721/07, ECHR 2011, paras 130–149.

[44] See CAT, 'Conclusions and recommendations: United States of America', UN Doc CAT/C/USA/CO/2 (25 July 2006), para 15, and subsequent concluding observations, namely UN Doc CAT/C.USA/CO/3-5 (19 December 2014), para 10.

[45] Compare s 4 of New Zealand's Crimes of Torture Act of 1989 ('occurred in New Zealand') with s 17(1) of Uganda's Prevention and Prohibition of Torture Act, 2012 ('(a) in Uganda; (b) outside Uganda – (i) in any territory under the control or jurisdiction of Uganda').

[46] See e.g. s 4 of Sri Lanka's Convention against Torture and Other Cruel, Inhuman or Degrading Treatment or Punishment Act of 1994, and s 6(1)(a) of South Africa's Prevention of Combating and Torture of Persons Act, 2013, which, notably, extends South Africa's jurisdiction to a person 'ordinarily resident in the Republic' (ibid s 6(1)(b)). This reflects an 'increasing tendency' in State practice, see Staker (n 10 above), 320.

[47] See Kaleck W and Kroker, P, 'Syrian Torture Investigations in Germany and Beyond: Breathing New Life into Universal Jurisdiction in Europe? (2018) 16 *Journal of International Criminal Justice* 165, 174.

[48] For an example, see the case of Chuckie Taylor, in which the 2008 District Court verdict was upheld on appeal, *United States v. Belfast* 611 F.3d 783 (11th Cir. 2010).

[49] See on the US position, UN Doc E/CN.4/1314 (n 38 above), paras 15, 70.

[50] S 4 of Sri Lanka's Act (n 46 above) and s 6(1)(d) of South Africa's Act (n 46 above) which applies to offences 'against a South African citizen or against a person who is ordinarily resident in the Republic'.

a jurisdictional ground in important cases, such as the trial of Argentine national Adolfo Scilingo in Spain.[51]

In cases with an extraterritorial element, the alleged offender may, and often will be outside the territory of the forum State. This poses limited difficulties in respect of the jurisdiction set out in Article 5(1), with the exception of passive nationality, as the State party will typically either exercise effective control over the territory concerned or be able to demand the extradition of its nationals (Article 5(1)(b)).

Universal jurisdiction
For situations without links such as territory or nationality, Articles 5(2), 6 and 7 establish a system effectively based on universal jurisdiction.[52] The obligations set out in these articles are qualified because they apply, as stipulated in Article 5(2), 'in cases where the alleged offender is *present* in any territory under its jurisdiction' (emphasis added). A State party therefore needs to establish universal jurisdiction over alleged perpetrators of torture present within its jurisdiction. As mere physical presence is sufficient, States may not restrict the scope of such universal jurisdiction by introducing further requirements, such as residence of the alleged perpetrator.[53] States parties may establish wider universal jurisdiction without the presence requirement pursuant to Article 5(3), provided it is compatible with the State's international law obligations.[54] The presence of an alleged offender triggers the obligation of a State party to take him or her into custody, where warranted, undertake a preliminary inquiry, and submit the case to its competent authorities for the purpose of prosecution pursuant to Articles 6 and 7. Article 6(2) 'requires that steps must be taken as soon as the suspect is identified in the territory of the State, in order to conduct an investigation of that case'.[55] A State party therefore needs to open a preliminary inquiry as soon as it knows of the presence of a person suspected of having committed an act of torture, such as in the case of *Habré* where Senegal was found to have breached its obligations under Article 6 for its failure to do so.[56] As highlighted by the ICJ, '[t]he purpose of all these obligations is to enable proceedings to be brought against the suspect, in the absence of his extradition, and to achieve the object and purpose of the Convention, which is to make more effective the struggle against torture by avoiding impunity for the perpetrators of such acts'.[57]

It is less clear whether a State party may open an investigation even in the absence of a suspect. This question can be critical; in practice, many cases do not proceed to an investigation and prosecution because suspects only stay within the State's territory for a limited period of time, within which the authorities may decline to take timely action and/or fail to gather

---

[51]   Spanish Supreme Court, Sentencia no 1362/2004 (18 April 2007) and no 16/2005 (18 April 2007).

[52]   *Questions relating to the Obligation to Prosecute or Extradite* (n 1 above), particularly para 91.

[53]   See concerns raised in 'Concluding observations of the Committee against Torture: France', UN Doc CAT/C/FRA/CO/4-6 (20 May 2010), para 19.

[54]   Such 'absolute universal jurisdiction' remains contested, particularly based on concerns over potential abuse. See further Kluwen, T, 'Universal Jurisdiction in Absentia Before Domestic Courts Prosecuting International Crimes: A Suitable Weapon to Fight Impunity?' (2017) 8 *Goettingen JIL* 7.

[55]   *Questions relating to the Obligation to Prosecute or Extradite* (n 1 above), para 86.

[56]   *Ibid*, paras 79–88.

[57]   *Ibid*, para 74.

sufficient evidence to investigate and detain the suspect to prevent him or her from leaving.[58] A strict presence requirement clearly puts States' authorities at a disadvantage. Opening a 'pre-presence' investigation facilitates an effective investigation and thereby advances the Convention's objective. A pertinent example in recent practice is structural investigations that 'are not (yet) directed against specific persons but … exist for the purpose of investigating (and collecting evidence on) specific structures, within which international crimes have allegedly been committed' even before any specific suspects have been identified.[59] Germany's Federal Prosecutor, for example, has used its discretion to open such an investigation in respect of international crimes committed in Syria.[60] A proactive practice is desirable to make the exercise of universal jurisdiction more effective, while carrying limited risk of inappropriate use where it is of a preliminary nature.[61] This found support in the ruling of South Africa's Constitutional Court on the prosecution of an alleged torturer from Zimbabwe, which held that 'the exercise of universal jurisdiction, for purposes of the investigation of an international crime committed outside our territory, may occur in the absence of a suspect without offending our Constitution or international law'.[62]

A further, related question arises in the reverse scenario. Can a State carry on with investigations and/or prosecutions if the alleged offender leaves the territory after an investigation has formally commenced? The European Court of Human Rights answered in the affirmative in *Ould Dah v. France*.[63] A trial in absentia, however, raises the question of its compatibility with the fair trial rights of the accused, which States parties are duty bound to guarantee under Article 7(3), in addition to their obligations under other human rights treaties guaranteeing the right to a fair trial.

Article 7(1) requires a State party to 'submit the case to its competent authorities for the purpose of prosecution'. As noted by the ICJ, it 'was formulated in such a way as to leave it to the authorities to decide whether or not to initiate proceedings, thus respecting the independence of States parties' judicial systems'.[64] Notably, this 'obligation to prosecute the alleged perpetrator of acts of torture does not depend on the prior existence of a request for his extradition'.[65] The Convention therefore makes prosecution the default obligation.[66] Extradition, in case of a request, merely allows a State 'to relieve itself of its obligation to prosecute'.[67] This obligation must not be circumvented, or even be reinterpreted into one of 'deport or prose-

---

[58]   See on the lack of prosecution of the German authorities in response to complaints brought against former Interior Minister of Uzbekistan Zakir Almatov, and of Austrian authorities in the *Al-Duri* (Iraq) case, Nowak and McArthur (n 23 above) 295–298.

[59]   Kaleck and Kroker (n 47 above), 179.

[60]   *Ibid.* See also on Sweden's practice in this regard, Human Rights Watch, 'These are the Crimes We are Fleeing': Justice for Syria in Swedish and German Courts (3 October 2017).

[61]   See on relevant State practice, REDRESS and FIDH, Extraterritorial jurisdiction in the European Union: A Study of the Laws and Practice in the 27 Member States of the European Union (December 2010), 22–24.

[62]   *National Commissioner of the South African Police Service v. Southern African Human Rights Litigation Centre and Another* [2014] ZACC 30, para 47.

[63]   *Ould Dah v. France* (dec.), no. 13113/03, ECHR 2009, para 16.

[64]   *Questions relating to the Obligation to Prosecute or Extradite* (n 1 above), para 90.

[65]   *Suleymane Guengueng v. Senegal* (n 1 above), para 9.7.

[66]   This priority of prosecution stems from the Hague Convention model followed by the Convention. For a 'typology of provisions in multilateral instruments', see ILC (n 5 above), paras 6–14.

[67]   *Questions relating to the Obligation to Prosecute or Extradite* (n 1 above), para 95.

cute'. Several States screen foreign arrivals, including asylum seekers who may be identified as suspected perpetrators of torture, to determine whether to exclude them under Article 1(F) of the Convention relating to the Status of Refugees of 1951. However, instead of prosecuting persons thus excluded, particularly in the absence of a realistic prospect of extradition, some States have deported them,[68] a practice incompatible with State parties' obligations under Articles 6(2) and 7(1).

Article 7 is silent on what has been referred to as 'subsidiarity'. According to this notion, it is primarily for the territorial State to prosecute acts of torture or other crimes that States are obliged to prosecute as a matter of international law; the exercise of universal jurisdiction is only appropriate where the territorial State is unable or unwilling to do so.[69] The notion appears to enjoy a degree of support among States, some of which have applied subsidiarity considerations in their practice.[70] South Africa's Constitutional Court appears to consider subsidiarity a general principle applicable in universal jurisdiction cases.[71] Subsidiarity may have a limited scope of application in the exercise of judicial discretion.[72] However, reading it into the Convention as a general principle would, besides not having any textual support and having been rejected during the travaux, introduce an unwarranted hierarchy of jurisdictions, and risk undermining universal jurisdiction as an independent avenue. The prospect that an alleged offender is exposed to multiple prosecutions is limited, and can in any case be addressed by applying appropriate criteria.[73]

A number of States, particularly those that are parties to the Convention, have established and exercised universal jurisdiction over acts of torture.[74] Several prosecutions have resulted in convictions on charges of torture, such as that of *Sebastien Nzapali* in the Netherlands, *Faryadi Sarwar Zardad* in the UK, *Ely Ould Dah* and *Khaled Ben Said* in France, *Chuckie Taylor* in the US, and *Hissène Habré* in Senegal.[75] Dozens of other cases were pending in 2018.[76] However, successful prosecutions are easily exceeded by the number of cases that have not led to a conviction or not even resulted in the opening of an investigation or charges being

---

[68]   'Concluding observations of the Committee against Torture: Canada', UN Doc CAT/C/CAN/CO/6 (25 June 2012), para 14: 'The Committee is also concerned about numerous and continuous reports that the State party's policy of resorting to immigration processes to remove or expel perpetrators from its territory rather than subjecting them to the criminal process creates actual or potential loopholes for impunity …'.

[69]   See for a brief overview, Mennecke, M, 'The African Union and Universal Jurisdiction' in Jalloh, CC and Bantekas, I (eds), *The International Criminal Court and Africa* (Oxford University Press, 2017), 33–34.

[70]   UN doc A/65/181 (n 20 above), para 11; REDRESS/FIDH (n 61 above), 25–27.

[71]   *National Commissioner* (n 62 above), para 61.

[72]   REDRESS/FIDH (n 61 above), 27.

[73]   Principle 13 of the Madrid-Buenos Aires Principles (n 41 above).

[74]   See Amnesty International (n 40 above); for EU countries, REDRESS/FIDH (n 61 above), 19ff; and for latest developments, 20 TRIAL International, FIDH, REDRESS, Fibgar and ECCHR, Evidentiary Challenges in Universal Jurisdiction Cases: Universal Jurisdiction Annual Review 2019 #UJAR (2019).

[75]   See for a partial overview, UN doc A/65/181 (n 20 above), paras 94–107, and updates in subsequent reports of the UN Secretary-General on universal jurisdiction, and relevant NGO reports (nn 4 and 6 above).

[76]   TRIAL International (n 6 above).

brought.[77] Yet, such outcomes should not be the sole yardstick for an assessment of universal jurisdiction, which can have a number of impacts, ranging from denying safe havens to raising awareness and triggering justice processes. Nonetheless, it is undeniable that the ultimate lack of accountability constitutes a major, ongoing challenge. Much of the debate on universal jurisdiction has centred on the lack of prosecution of high-profile perpetrators, many of whom were held to benefit from immunity,[78] and purported selectivity.[79] As discussed in further detail in the next section, cases have not succeeded for a range of reasons.

Framework for the Effective Exercise of Universal and Extraterritorial Jurisdiction

As any practitioner can testify, the Convention, and general international law on universal jurisdiction for torture, set out what are rather general legal parameters.[80] The last two decades have been characterised by an intense focus on the components of an effective legislative and institutional framework for the prosecution of extraterritorial torture (and international crimes more generally). Reports by NGOs and practitioners, various bodies, such as the UN Special Rapporteur on Torture, jurisprudence, and studies by the UN Secretary-General and the ILC have produced a wealth of information and analysis.[81] They provide the foundation to identify the key requirements needed to make the Convention and general international law on extraterritorial and universal jurisdiction for torture an 'effective, workable system'.[82]

As demonstrated by the *Habré* case, adequate legislation is typically a prerequisite for the exercise of extraterritorial and universal jurisdiction. In most instances, this will be in the form of legislation implementing, fully or partially, the Convention,[83] or other legislation.[84] According to Amnesty International, as of 2012, at least 85 States provided for universal jurisdiction over torture, and another 40 States for universal jurisdiction over ordinary crimes.[85] Yet, a survey of CAT's concluding observations shows that it has repeatedly raised concerns over the lack of adequate implementing legislation defining torture and/or establishing extraterritorial jurisdiction in conformity with the Convention.[86] A series of factors undermine the

---

[77]   Kaleck, W, 'From Pinochet to Rumsfeld: Universal Jurisdiction in Europe 1998–2008' (2009) 30 *MJIL* 927; Nowak and McArthur (n 23 above), 256: 'In practice, *States parties are extremely reluctant to exercise universal jurisdiction in torture cases*' (emphasis in original).

[78]   See Chapter 17 by McGregor in this volume.

[79]   Kaleck (n 77 above); Langer (n 6 above); Kelly, T, 'Prosecuting Human Rights Violations: Universal Jurisdiction and the Crime of Torture' in Goodale, M (ed), *Human Rights at the Crossroads* (Oxford University Press, 2013). See for a fundamental critique of international criminal justice, Kiyani, A, Reynolds, J and Xavier, S, 'Foreword, Symposium: Third World Approaches to International Criminal Law' (2016) 4 *Journal of International Criminal Justice* 915.

[80]   Ingelse, C, *The UN Committee Against Torture: An Assessment* (Kluwer, 2001), 333, perceptively remarks that 'the Convention is lacking in detail, as a result of which several essential questions remain unanswered'.

[81]   See above nn 4–6.

[82]   See statement by the US representative quoted above (n 31).

[83]   See e.g. s 6 of South Africa's Act (n 46 above); s 17 of Uganda's Act (n 45 above).

[84]   See on the types of legislation, Amnesty International (n 40 above) Chapter 10, and REDRESS/ FIDH (n 61 above) on European practice concerning international crimes.

[85]   Amnesty International (n 40 above), 13–14. The report does not specify to what extent this may cover acts of torture.

[86]   E.g., concluding observations on Congo, UN Doc CAT/C/COG/CO/1 (28 May 2015) para 14; Mexico, UN Doc CAT/C/MEX/CO/5-6 (11 December 2012) para 23. See in respect of African states,

effective exercise of universal jurisdiction. These factors range from shortcomings relating to the definition of relevant crimes, liability and defences; legal barriers, such as statutes of limitation, amnesties, immunities, and non-retroactivity; limited rights of victims; executive control of decision-making; to the lack of effective extradition and mutual legal assistance arrangements.[87]

The rights of victims are increasingly viewed as critical for an effective legal framework governing universal jurisdiction.[88] The ability to complain about torture with a view to triggering criminal investigations, lodge private prosecutions and decisions not to investigate or prosecute allows victims and their representatives to play an active role in proceedings; indeed, many cases have been based on the initiative of victims and those acting on their behalf.[89] Where provided for, joining the prosecution as a civil party gives victims procedural rights and the opportunity to obtain reparation. Protection is also pivotal. Victims play a crucial role in identifying and providing evidence against suspects. Threats and harassment of victims and witnesses may result in their reluctance to testify, and, ultimately, as happened in respect of proceedings against Sri Lanka's Colonel Karuna, the collapse of a case.[90]

An adequate institutional framework has proved critical for the prosecution of torture and other international crimes committed extraterritorially. Such prosecution poses distinctive challenges, particularly the ability to obtain evidence that is capable of being presented to, or relied upon by, domestic courts[91] The political and/or cultural context may be unknown, language barriers need to be overcome, victims, witnesses and others are often located in several countries, and the cooperation of other agencies, such as immigration authorities and various foreign authorities is typically needed.[92] These factors require a concerted focus, and corresponding skills-set, to investigate and prosecute crimes such as torture, which, in turn, requires adequate resources. A number of specialised units tasked with prosecuting international crimes, including torture, have been set up in various countries, with some success.[93] However, practice is inconsistent and may even retrogress where priorities shift, particularly where resources are diverted to areas such as combatting terrorism offences.[94] Immigration authorities also play an important role in identifying suspects and victims. However, as highlighted above, States may use immigration authorities and measures in ways that are incompatible

---

AU-EU Expert Report (n 20 above), para 16: 'most have not enacted legislation to incorporate into national law the Convention's definition of torture or to vest their courts with universal jurisdiction over the offence'.

[87]   See for a brief overview, Amnesty International (n 40 above) 10–11, and detailed discussion of most of these factors in REDRESS/FIDH (n 61 above).

[88]   REDRESS/FIDH (n 61 above), paras 40–55.

[89]   *Ibid*, 42.

[90]   Amnesty International, 'UK: Failure to protect witnesses allows suspected war criminals to avoid prosecution' (3 July 2008).

[91]   See, in particular, TRIAL International et al. (n 74 above), 9–10.

[92]   See for an illustrative case study, including on the use of technology necessitated by the fact that the crime has taken place abroad, Shrestha, S, 'The Curious Case of Colonel Kumar Lama: Its Origins and Impact in Nepal and the United Kingdom, and its Contribution to the Discourse on Universal Jurisdiction', TLT Think! Paper 2/2018.

[93]   REDRESS/FIDH (n 61 above), 69–70.

[94]   See interview with Siri Frigaard, Former Chief Public Prosecutor and Director of the Norwegian National Authority for Prosecution of Organised and Other Serious Crime, in Bantekas, I and Oette, L *International Human Rights Law and Practice*, 3rd edn (Cambridge University Press, 2020), 772–775.

with their obligations under the Convention. Beyond the forum State, the effective exercise of universal jurisdiction requires mutual legal assistance, which is set out as an obligation of States parties under Article 9. The European Union (EU) Genocide network and initiatives to develop a multilateral treaty on mutual legal assistance and extradition for the most serious international crimes signal the collective recognition of the need and endeavour to strengthen cooperation.[95] However, these initiatives do not apply to torture as a separate crime, an area where the framework on mutual legal assistance remains underdeveloped.

The exercise of extraterritorial jurisdiction has generated opposition from various quarters, which has had a considerable influence on State practice.[96] Some of the misgivings evident during the drafting of the Convention came to the fore throughout the 2000s when several States, particularly Belgium and Spain, provided fora for a proactive pursuit of accountability for international crimes on the basis of universal jurisdiction. Victims and human rights NGOs in particular sought to seize the opening provided by the Pinochet precedent,[97] and brought a number of complaints, many of which concerned torture, including against high-ranking US and Israeli officials.[98] This led to political pressure and consequent unease of the authorities in the States concerned, which declined to open prosecutions in certain cases. Eventually, Belgium and Spain significantly narrowed the scope of their universal jurisdiction laws for international crimes,[99] signalling a wider trend to restrict and control the exercise of such jurisdiction.[100] In parallel with cases brought against African leaders before the International Criminal Court, States such as France and Spain initiated proceedings against Rwandan officials for international crimes.[101] The AU responded by denouncing the abuse of universal jurisdiction, which was portrayed as a neo-colonial exercise.[102]

These developments led to a revisiting of universal jurisdiction in various fora. Several States advocated a restrained, 'responsible' exercise of such jurisdiction, stressing the need for respect for sovereignty, subsidiarity and political discretion.[103] The shared policy goal of

---

[95] Cocan, S, 'Fighting against Impunity: The Mutual Legal Assistance Initiative for Domestic Prosecution of the Most Serious Crimes', INTLAWGRRLS (7 December 2017).

[96] Langer (n 6 above).

[97] General Pinochet, Chile's former President, was arrested in the UK in 1998 pursuant to an international arrest warrant by Spain, which sought his extradition for the crimes of murder, genocide and terrorism, as well as, subsequently, further crimes, including torture. The case was heard by the House of Lords, which found, inter alia, that English courts had jurisdiction over offences of torture committed after CAT implementing legislation had come into force. The Pinochet ruling is considered a milestone in the development of international criminal justice, particularly on questions of universal jurisdiction and immunities. See *R. v. Bow Street Metropolitan Stipendiary Magistrate and others, ex parte Pinochet Ugarte (Amnesty International and others intervening) (Pinochet No.3)* (n 22 above). See also Roht-Arriaza, N, *The Pinochet Effect: Transitional Justice in the Age of Human Rights* (University of Pennsylvania Press, 2005).

[98] See the discussion in Kaleck (n 77 above).

[99] See Kaleck (n 77 above), 951–953 and Langer (n 6 above).

[100] See e.g., Concluding Observation on the fifth periodic report of the United Kingdom of Great Britain and Northern Ireland, UN Doc CAT/C/GBR/CO/5 (24 June 2013) para 22.

[101] See further Jalloh, CC, *Universal Jurisdiction, Universal Prescription? A Preliminary Assessment of the African Union Perspective on Universal Jurisdiction*, Pitt Law, Legal Studies Research Paper Series, Working Paper No. 2009-38 (March 2010) 20–21, 31, 42.

[102] AU-EU Expert Report (n 20 above), para 37. See further Mennecke (n 69 above).

[103] See eg Cuba, UNGA, 'Report of the Secretary-General: The scope and application of the principle of universal jurisdiction' UN doc A/69/174 (2014) paras 79–87; Lebanon, UN doc A/66/93 (2011), paras 146–148.

combating impunity for international crimes therefore seemingly gave way to a reassertion of sovereignty and the primacy of State interest. In response, NGOs, like-minded State officials and others have increasingly focused on an evolutionary approach, creating the legislative and institutional enabling environment and pursuing cases against a number of mostly mid-level perpetrators.[104] This strategy has resulted in a steady increase in cases, important precedents and a considerable number of prosecutions. The *Habré* case in Senegal, the *Zimbabwe* case in South Africa and attempts to have suspected Sri Lankan perpetrators of torture prosecuted in Brazil[105] indicate that universal jurisdiction for torture is moving beyond the sphere of European and North American States.[106] The *Habré* case in particular has served an important bridge function in this regard.

Many universal jurisdiction cases do, for various reasons, not result in prosecutions. Yet, the mere threat of being subject to universal jurisdiction has prevented alleged perpetrators from travelling to certain countries; exposure has also resulted in such persons fleeing the country concerned.[107] States who know of individuals alleged to be involved in torture may withdraw invitations, such as to participate in police training programmes, or discontinue existing engagements. Universal jurisdiction, short of prosecutions, has therefore created its own naming and shaming dimension, which increasingly translates into a 'torture suspects not welcome' message, and may even prompt renewed justice debates in the countries concerned, as happened in the Pinochet and Habré cases.[108] Ostracisation may be considered a mere inconvenience, rather than the punishment that the crime of torture merits. Nonetheless, it constitutes an important development which shows the enduring potency of universal jurisdiction as a transnational, collective denunciation of torture.

Assessment

Universal jurisdiction for torture is well established in the Convention and international law. Many pertinent legal questions have been addressed, with some grey areas, particularly concerning the presence element, remaining. A range of actors have identified legislative and institutional prerequisites for the effective exercise of universal jurisdiction, but State practice remains inconsistent. The result is a complex patchwork of practices that are often highly contingent on national approaches, and ultimately do not amount to a coherent system. Further guidance from relevant bodies, such as a CAT general comment on the subject, would prove helpful to highlight and elucidate the legal obligations of States and the practical steps needed to make universal jurisdiction effective.

Ultimately, universal jurisdiction for torture is not an abstract concept but a cornerstone of the absolute prohibition.[109] For all the politicisation that surrounds it, universal jurisdiction epitomises the collective commitment to combat torture by not welcoming, and opposing the

---

[104] Langer (n 6 above).

[105] Cronin-Furman, K, 'Why a Sri Lankan Leader might be Tried for War Crimes in Brazil', *Washington Post* (30 August 2017).

[106] See on Latin America's influence particularly the Congress on Universal Jurisdiction in September 2015, resulting in the adoption of the Madrid-Buenos Aires Principles (n 41 above).

[107] See e.g. n 58 above.

[108] Brody, R, 'Bringing a Dictator to Justice: The Case of Hissène Habré' (2015) 13 *Journal of International Criminal Justice* 209.

[109] Burgers and Danelius (n 24 above) 131.

unperturbed presence of, torturers in one's midst. For victims of torture, universal jurisdiction often remains literally the only hope of seeing their perpetrators being held to account.

UNIVERSAL CIVIL JURISDICTION FOR TORTURE

The Extraterritorial Scope of Article 14 of the Convention

The rationale for criminal universal jurisdiction over torture is to ensure that its perpetrators are denied safe haven and held to account, wherever they are. Its civil counterpart enables victims to seek other forms of reparation from those responsible beyond the State where their torture took place. Similar to the lack of accountability in criminal cases, torture victims are often unable to obtain reparation in the absence of effective domestic and international remedies. The case for universal civil jurisdiction is therefore intuitively compelling, particularly if the effective struggle against torture worldwide is understood to encompass both the accountability of its perpetrators and other forms of reparation for its victims. Yet, neither the Convention, nor the Inter-American Convention to Prevent and Punish Torture, sets out a system for universal civil jurisdiction that mirrors that of criminal jurisdiction, or at least addresses the question of its extraterritorial application.

The lack of detailed focus on reparation during its drafting has led to an ongoing debate concerning the scope of Article 14: does it require States parties to establish and exercise universal civil jurisdiction, and, if there is no such obligation, may States at least do so as a matter of general international law?

The text of Article 14 is silent on the matter: 'Each State Party shall ensure in its legal system that the victim of an act of torture obtains redress and has an enforceable right to fair and adequate compensation, including the means for as full rehabilitation as possible.' This silence has given rise to conflicting interpretations. While some consider Article 14 not to have extraterritorial application,[110] others argue that any geographical restriction of its scope would have to be spelled out.[111] Significantly, during the drafting process, the Working Group removed a proposal on Article 14 by the Netherlands that would have read 'torture committed *in any territory* under its jurisdiction'.[112] The claim made by US lawyers that this restriction had later been left out by mistake has been criticised as being without foundation.[113] While the text remains ambiguous, universal civil jurisdiction can be based on a purposive construction, arguing that it makes the prohibition of torture more effective by preventing those responsible from escaping liability. This is not least because 'civil responsibility would seem to be

---

[110]   See in particular Mora, PD, 'The Legality of Civil Jurisdiction over Torture under the Universal Principle' (2009) 52 *GYBIL* 373. See also Nowak and McArthur (n 23 above), 492–494.

[111]   See in particular Hall, CK, 'The Duty of States Parties to the Convention against Torture to Provide Procedures Permitting Victims to Recover Reparations for Torture Committed Abroad' (2007) 18 *EJIL* 957. See for a succinct overview of the debate and literature, Larocque, F, 'Torture, Jurisdiction and Immunity: Theories and Practices in Search of Each Other' in Orakhelashvili (n 11 above) 424 and Ryngaert, C, 'From Universal Civil Jurisdiction to Forum of Necessity: Reflections on the Judgment of the European Court of Human Rights in Nait-Liman' (2017) 3 *RivDirInt* 782.

[112]   Emphasis added.

[113]   Hall (n 111 above), 932–935.

a natural corollary of criminal responsibility' as has been argued in respect of international crimes.[114]

Several developments lend support to a broad interpretation of Article 14. In 2005, CAT began expressing its concern at '[t]he absence of effective measures to provide civil compensation to victims of torture in all cases'.[115] It made its position explicit in its General Comment 3 on Article 14:

> ... the application of article 14 is not limited to victims who were harmed in the territory of the State party or by or against nationals of the State party. The Committee has commended the efforts of States parties for providing civil remedies for victims who were subjected to torture or ill-treatment outside their territory. This is particularly important when a victim is unable to exercise the rights guaranteed under article 14 in the territory where the violation took place. Indeed, article 14 requires States parties to ensure that all victims of torture and ill-treatment are able to access remedy and obtain redress.[116]

Some States expressed support for universal civil jurisdiction in the draft Hague Convention on Jurisdiction and Foreign Judgments in Civil and Commercial Matters, which envisaged an exception to the general rule requiring a 'substantial connection' to the forum state in cases of genocide, crimes against humanity, a serious crime under international law and a grave violation, such as torture.[117] However, the two latter exceptions 'apply only if the party seeking relief is exposed to a risk of a denial of justice because proceedings in another State are not possible or cannot reasonably be required'.[118]

There is also some, albeit limited, State practice to support universal civil jurisdiction for torture.[119] In the US, victims of torture have been able to bring claims under the Alien Torts Claim Act (ATCA) and the Victim Torture Protection Act,[120] particularly following the landmark judgment in the case of *Filartiga v. Pena-Irala*.[121] However, the *Kiobel* judgment, which postulated a presumption against extraterritoriality, has significantly curtailed ATCA's scope.[122] In other countries, victims of torture have been able to bring claims as civil parties where provided for, including in the *Habré* case,[123] although this avenue is dependent on the existence and exercise of extraterritorial criminal jurisdiction.

---

[114] Tomuschat, C, 'Reparation for Victims of Grave Human Rights Violations' (2002) 10 *Tulane Journal of International and Comparative Law* 157, 181–182.

[115] 'Conclusions and recommendations of the Committee against Torture: Canada', UN Doc CAT/C/CR/34/CAN (7 July 2005), para 4(g).

[116] General Comment no 3 of the Committee against Torture (n 8 above), para 22.

[117] Article 18(3) Variant One; Variant Two refers to 'a serious crime under international law, provided that this State has established its criminal jurisdiction over that crime in accordance with an international treaty to which it is a party', which would apply to the Convention. Variant Two further limits the exception to claims 'for civil compensatory damages for death or serious bodily injury arising from that crime'. See further Beth van Schaack, B, 'In Defense of Civil Redress: The Domestic Enforcement of Human Rights Norms in the Context of the Proposed Hague Judgments Convention' (2001) 42 *HILJ* 141.

[118] Article 18(3) Variant One, *ibid*.

[119] See overview in *Naït-Liman v. Switzerland* [GC], no 51357/07, 15 March 2018, paras 67–83.

[120] Alien Tort Statute, 28 USC § 1350 of 1789 and Torture Victim Protection Act of 1991, 28 USC § 1350.

[121] *Filartiga v Pena-Irala*, 630 F.2d 876, 878 (2d Cir. 1980).

[122] *Kiobel v Royal Dutch Petroleum Co.*, 133 S. Ct. 1659 (2013).

[123] *The Prosecutor General v Hissein Habré* (n 1 above).

Invoking the *jus cogens* status of the prohibition of torture as a basis for universal civil jurisdiction,[124] the position of CAT, and other relevant developments charted above, has not gained traction with several courts and States. The Supreme Court of Canada,[125] the UK House of Lords[126] and the New Zealand High Court[127] rejected CAT's broad interpretation of Article 14. CAT's response to these challenges has largely failed to persuade courts. Already in 2006, Lord Bingham had been dismissive of CAT's recommendation to provide remedies to all victims of torture, stating that 'the Committee did not, in making this recommendation, advance any analysis or interpretation of Article 14 of the Convention ... Whatever its value in influencing the trend of international thinking, the legal authority of this recommendation is slight.'[128] In light of such criticism, the Committee's lack of a detailed analysis of the territorial scope of Article 14 constitutes a missed opportunity to engage with its critics and the challenge they pose. Its 2014 inadmissibility decision in *Z v. Australia* did not help to clarify matters. In that case, the complainant had claimed that Australia's lack of exercise of its jurisdiction over claims relating to torture in China constituted a violation of Article 14, referring to and relying on CAT's position. The Committee, without further discussion, stated, after referring to its General Comment no 3, that 'in the specific circumstances of this case, the State party is unable to establish jurisdiction over officials of another State for alleged acts committed outside the State party's territory'.[129]

Parallel to the controversy surrounding the scope of Article 14(1), several States protested against the exercise of universal civil jurisdiction by US courts, particularly in the *Sosa* and *Kiobel* cases, arguing that such practice was contrary to international law in the absence of a nexus to the forum.[130] They argued that the practice interferes with the sovereignty of States 'by subjecting their nationals and enterprises to (i) the risk of conflicting legal commands and proceedings, and (ii) the costs and uncertainties of defending themselves against private lawsuits under ambiguous and unacceptable rules of law in a foreign forum'.[131] An initiative to establish universal civil jurisdiction through the Torture Damages Bill was opposed by the UK Government as being contrary to its international law obligations.[132]

The European Court of Human Rights' Grand Chamber held in *Naït-Liman v. Switzerland* that there had been no violation of the right of access to a court under Article 6 of the European Convention on Human Rights since 'the Swiss courts' refusal ... to accept jurisdiction to

---

[124] *Prosecutor v. Furundžija* (n 22 above), para 155. See van Schaack, B, 'Justice Without Borders: Universal Civil Jurisdiction' in *Proceedings of the Ninety-Ninth Annual Meeting of ASIL: Universal Civil Jurisdiction – The Next Frontier* (2005), 120; McGregor, L, 'The Need to Resolve the Paradoxes of the Civil Dimension of Universal Jurisdiction', in *ibid*, 125; and discussion of Bucher's *erga omnes* argument by Ryngaert (n 111 above), 789–793.

[125] *Kazemi Estate v. Islamic Republic of Iran* [2014] 3 S.C.R., paras 135–148.

[126] *Jones v. Ministry of the Interior of the Kingdom of Saudi Arabia* [2006] UKHL 26, para 25.

[127] *Fang v. Jiang* [2007] NZAR 420, para 64 (endorsing the House of Lords ruling in the *Jones* case].

[128] *Jones v. Ministry of Interior* (n 126 above), para 23. See in support of CAT, and critical of the courts' position, Larocque (n 111 above) 451–452; Orakhelashvili (n 11), 44–45.

[129] *Z v. Australia*, Communication no 511/2012 (26 November 2014), para 6.3.

[130] See e.g., Brief of the Governments of the Commonwealth of Australia, the Swiss Confederation and the United Kingdom of Great Britain and Northern Ireland in Support of the Petitioner, *Sosa v. Alvarez-Machain*, 542 U.S. 692 (2004) (Nos. 03-339, 03-485).

[131] *Ibid*, 2.

[132] Human Rights Joint Committee, 'Closing the Impunity Gap: UK law on genocide and related crimes' Twenty-Fourth Report (2009), paras 87–88.

examine the applicant's action seeking redress for the acts of torture to which he was allegedly subjected [committed in Tunisia] pursued legitimate aims and was not disproportionate to them'.[133] The Court found that Article 14 of the Convention against Torture was inconclusive, and that 'international law did not oblige the Swiss authorities to open their courts to the applicant pursuant to universal civil jurisdiction for acts of torture'.[134] The dissenting opinion of Judge Dedov echoed a highly critical joint dissenting opinion to the initial Chamber judgment (which had equally found no violation of Article 6) by Judges Karakaş, Vučinić and Kūris, who emphasised that:

> The interpretation and application of Article 6 § 1 of the [European] Convention in this case ought to have built on the significant developments in recent years seeking to combat the impunity of the perpetrators of acts of torture, to the effect of enabling an action for reparation to be brought before a foreign court.[135]

If Article 14(1) is interpreted as not requiring States parties to establish universal civil jurisdiction, the question arises whether they are permitted to do so under Article 14(2): 'Nothing in this Article shall affect any right of the victim or other persons to compensation which may exist under national law.' The Court of Appeal of England and Wales found in the *Jones* case that the provision of redress on the basis of universal civil jurisdiction remains permissible.[136] The US Restatement of Law espouses a similar position,[137] as does the Institute of International Law (IIL).[138] Several commentators agree that States are free to establish such universal civil jurisdiction.[139] Others do not, claiming that 'unilateral assertions of universal civil jurisdiction … are contrary to customary international law'[140] if they cannot be based on a recognised ground.[141] Interpretations of Article 14 therefore cover the whole spectrum concerning universal civil jurisdiction, ranging from making it obligatory for States parties, or at least permissive, to ruling it out altogether.

Irrespective of the position taken on the interpretation of Article 14, it is clear that efforts to promote, or establish universal civil jurisdiction have suffered setbacks. Transnational litigation and law reform efforts have prompted resistance if not hostility, reflecting a very different zeitgeist compared to 2001, when Al Adsani lost his case by the narrowest of margins.[142] Courts have been reluctant to depart from established rules of jurisdiction without an unequiv-

---

[133]   *Naït-Liman v. Switzerland* (n 119 above), para 217.
[134]   *Ibid*, para 198.
[135]   *Naït-Liman v. Switzerland*, App no 51357/07 (ECtHR, 21 June 2016) Joint Dissenting Opinion of Judges Karakaş, Vučinić and Kūris, para 19.
[136]   *Jones v. The Ministry of the Interior of the Kingdom of Saudi Arabia* [2004] EWCA Civ 1394, Mance LJ, para 21.
[137]   Restatement Third, The Foreign Relations Law of the United States, §404. See also ALI, Restatement of the Law Fourth, The Foreign Relations Law of the United States Jurisdiction, Tentative Draft No. 2 (22 March 2016) §217.
[138]   IIL, Resolution 'Universal Civil Jurisdiction with regard to Reparation for International Crimes' (30 August 2015), art 2.
[139]   Nowak and McArthur (n 23 above) 494–501; Parlett, K, 'Universal Civil Jurisdiction for Torture' (2007) 4 *EHRLR* 385, 398–399; Donovan, DF and Roberts, R 'The Emerging Recognition of Universal Civil Jurisdiction', (2006) 100 *American Journal of International Law* 142, 149–155.
[140]   Mora (n 110 above), 402.
[141]   Wallach, W, 'The Irrationality of Universal Civil Jurisdiction' (2015/2016) 46 *GJIL* 803.
[142]   *Al-Adsani v. The United Kingdom* [GC], no 35763/97, ECHR 2001-XI 34 EHRR 11.

ocal mandate, and States have reasserted their sovereignty. This can partly be explained by a closing of ranks, where States are concerned about the adverse repercussions of such litigation for their nationals, themselves and international relations, a development closely tied up with the debate concerning the scope of State and individual immunity.[143] It would nonetheless be premature to declare the end of universal civil jurisdiction for torture. The lack of recognition of such jurisdiction constitutes an anomaly that is at odds with several developments in the field of international human rights law and international justice. As the prohibition of torture is considered to be of a *jus cogens* nature with *erga omnes* application, and the 'international community' has a shared interest in making the prohibition more effective worldwide,[144] it is difficult to see why such an approach should be limited to criminal measures, and not equally extend to civil jurisdiction.[145] Such a restrictive view also runs counter to the increasing recognition of the rights of victims of serious violations.[146] The doctrinal position that denies recognition of universal civil jurisdiction must, ultimately, accept that it leaves torture victims without an effective remedy, and that it endorses an abdication of responsibility on the part of third States. This is not a purely theoretical consideration. In the absence of other available avenues, there will be ongoing demand for universal civil jurisdiction. Further litigation is to be expected which will probe the status quo and explore alternative avenues. One notable development in the UK and France has been the focus on suing companies registered in the forum State for their responsibility for extraterritorial torture, such as in the context of mining projects.[147] Presence, if not residence of victims and/or perpetrators in the forum State, which is becoming more common in a globalised world, is also likely to act as a driver for litigation. This quest for justice in third States will invariably raise the issue of universal civil jurisdiction, particularly where, in the absence of other jurisdictional grounds, such as forum of necessity, victims of egregious violations such as torture are left without a remedy.

The Future of Universal Civil Jurisdiction for Torture

Achieving wider recognition of universal civil jurisdiction for torture has been a history of trials and tribulations. Strategies may not have been particularly effective to date but leave a legacy to build on. CAT, US jurisprudence, civil party cases, the recognised exception in the Hague Convention, considerable support for the Torture Damages Bill in the UK, and a range of voices making the case for such jurisdiction provide a sound foundation. Legal instruments and recognition in national legislation and/or jurisprudence present potential openings to develop practice. In addition, the increasing recognition of domicile or habitual residence or

---

[143] See Chapter 17 in this volume.

[144] *Questions relating to the Obligation to Prosecute or Extradite* (n 1 above), para 74.

[145] Larocque (n 111 above), 452.

[146] Bassiouni, MC, 'International Recognition of Victims' Rights' (2006) 2 *Human Rights Law Review* 203.

[147] See 'Peruvian torture claimants compensated by UK mining company', Leigh Day (20 July 2011); 'Landmark High Court case begins over alleged abuses by UK-based mining company in Sierra Leone', Leigh Day (26 January 2018), and cases pending against the French company Amesys for 'allegedly aiding and abetting crimes of torture committed in Libya during the Muammar Gaddafi regime', TRIAL International (n 6 above), 33–34.

citizenship of plaintiffs, at least in EU member States, as providing the required connection, opens the jurisdiction of the forum State to refugees and others who have settled there.[148]

A pivotal issue will be whether the court concerned is considered a suitable forum.[149] The position of States and courts signal a reluctance to exercise jurisdiction beyond recognised connections to the forum State, connections that are typically 'material' in terms of a territorial or nationality link rather than 'idealistic' in terms of a universal need for justice. Reservations and concerns that persist in this regard can be overcome by applying, effectively, an 'exhaustion of domestic remedies' test.[150] Where, in the words of the Torture Damages Bill, 'no adequate and effective remedy for damages is available in the State in which the torture is alleged to have been committed,'[151] the courts of the forum State become the appropriate forum. This is recognised in the European context in what has been termed '"emergency" jurisdiction … (where the ordinary jurisdictional connecting factors are not present but no other forum is available)'.[152] Courts that exercise jurisdiction in these circumstances do so with a view to the enforcement of an internationally recognised norm, and to providing victims of 'an enemy of all mankind'[153] with an avenue for justice that they would otherwise not have.

CONCLUSION

Universal and extraterritorial criminal jurisdiction is an integral part of the absolute prohibition of torture, and pivotal for the effectiveness of its international justice component. Accountability and the prevention of safe havens for perpetrators of torture are highly relevant in a world where millions of persons move in and out of, and operate in, various jurisdictions. This includes both victims and perpetrators of torture, who increasingly face the prospect of being present in the same territory away from home. It is also a world in which States increasingly engage in extraterritorial operations, be it fighting wars or combating terrorism. This loosening of boundaries reflects growing interconnectedness. The universalisation of justice for acts of torture would seem to flow naturally from this. Yet, these developments have not taken place in a political vacuum. The exercise of universal jurisdiction, though initially driven by a small number of largely European States, is, notwithstanding the scope for potential abuse and double standards, typically not a tool of the powerful against the weak. On the contrary, it often threatens powerful interests, as the backlash from various actors demonstrates. Even if support for such jurisdiction can be generated and maintained, the extraterritorial nature of events poses considerable challenges to its effective application. It is clear that States and other international actors have not adequately risen to this challenge. The case for the effective exercise of universal jurisdiction seemingly needs to be made again and again, even though

---

[148]   *Naït-Liman v. Switzerland* (n 119 above); Written Comments by REDRESS and the World Organisation against Torture (2011), para 23.

[149]   See in this context also discussion of forum of necessity in *Naït-Liman v. Switzerland* (n 119 above), paras 84–93.

[150]   Brief of the European Commission on Behalf of the European Union as Amicus Curiae in Support of Neither Party, *Kiobel v. Royal Dutch Petroleum*, 133 S. CT. 1659 (2013) (No.10-1491) 30; art 2 IIL Resolution (n 138 above).

[151]   Article 1(2) Torture (Damages) Bill [HL] 2007–2008.

[152]   Written Comments (n 14 above), para 23.

[153]   *Filartiga v. Pena-Irala* (n 121 above), at 890.

the debates of the working group on the Convention already provided a compelling case for it that has lost none of its validity. Victims, activists and like-minded States therefore have had to undertake an enormous effort to make such jurisdiction work. It is largely to their credit that considerable progress has been made in creating an enabling environment for the effective exercise of universal jurisdiction, with some, albeit still limited, success. The pragmatism of this approach might yet prove to be the most effective strategy to deny perpetrators of torture the enjoyment of refuge or foreign comforts with impunity. Universal civil jurisdiction as an avenue for victims of torture to obtain reparation faces an even bigger challenge, largely due to the lack of an unequivocal and uncontested recognition of such obligation, or even right, on the part of States. The case for such jurisdiction, or the availability of courts as forum of necessity, can be expected to be made repeatedly in the course of litigation and beyond. The application of universal and extraterritorial jurisdiction will in light of these developments continue to constitute a litmus test for the extent to which States take the combatting of impunity and the rights of victims seriously as a cornerstone of the prohibition of torture.

17. Foreign state immunities as a barrier to accessing remedies

Lorna McGregor

INTRODUCTION

The prohibition of torture and other cruel, inhuman or degrading treatment or punishment under international law is well established.[1] The International Covenant on Civil and Political Rights and the regional human rights treaties all provide for a right to a remedy or a right of access to justice, including for torture and other cruel, inhuman or degrading treatment or punishment. While the prohibition of torture and other cruel, inhuman or degrading treatment or punishment is treated as one prohibition under international law, the jurisprudence on the nature and scope of the rights to a remedy and to access justice has developed asymmetrically as a result of attempts to bring criminal and civil complaints outside of the state in which the torture was alleged to have taken place. Faced with procedural barriers to access justice, such as foreign state immunities, in these cases litigants typically focused narrowly on the status of the prohibition of torture under international law, for example, as a *jus cogens* norm and an international crime, to try to overcome these procedural barriers.

As the focus of this chapter is on foreign state immunities, it examines the right to a remedy for torture survivors as the particular focus of litigation in national and regional courts, without prejudice to the right to a remedy for survivors of cruel, inhuman or degrading treatment or punishment.

The right to a remedy for torture is both procedural and substantive.[2] Procedurally, international law provides claimants with a right of access to justice. In order to effectively exercise such a right, states are under an obligation to put in place adequate, available and effective remedies so that claimants can present their claim. The second dimension to the right to an effective remedy is the right to adequate and effective reparation, where a claim is upheld. Under international law, reparation primarily takes the form of restitution. As this is rarely possible in cases of torture, given the nature of physical and psychological injuries it usually entails, other forms of reparation such as compensation, rehabilitation, satisfaction and guarantees of non-repetition are critical. While an independent obligation of the state, the undertaking of a full, thorough and effective investigation, capable of identifying and punishing those responsible, also forms a key part of the right to a remedy.

In practice, torture survivors often face many challenges and obstacles to exercising their right to a remedy. In the state allegedly responsible for the torture, political pressures and a lack

---

[1] All of the major human rights instruments contain provisions on the prohibition of torture as does common Article 3 of the four Geneva Conventions.

[2] United Nations Basic Principles and Guidelines on the Right to a Remedy and Reparation for Victims of Gross Violations of International Human Rights Law and Serious Violations of International Humanitarian Law, UNGA Res 60/147, 16 December 2005.

of independence on the part of the police and prosecuting authorities may mean that a criminal investigation is not initiated or where it is, there is political interference and constraints to its independence. Torture survivors, witnesses and their representatives (whether lawyers or civil society) may face intimidation, threats and actual violence. Domestic amnesties, immunities and restrictive limitation periods may also be in place presenting procedural barriers to bringing a claim. For these and other reasons, remedies may be unavailable or ineffective in the state allegedly responsible for the torture.

In such situations, many torture survivors are unable to exercise their right to a remedy. This can have an adverse impact on their ability to rehabilitate and go on with their lives, due to the lack of official acknowledgment of what happened to them and the persistence of impunity. Where available, some torture survivors have taken their claims to a regional human rights court or a UN treaty body. While these are key forums for torture survivors to access remedies, they take many years, and even when a judgment is rendered in a torture survivor's favour, challenges can arise in implementation, particularly in relation to forms of reparation beyond compensation.

In other situations, torture survivors have attempted to bring claims in the domestic courts of other states. In civil cases, this most typically has occurred where the torture survivor is a citizen or resident of the state concerned. In criminal cases, it has most often arisen where the individual alleged to have committed, known or ordered the alleged torture has been visiting the state concerned. However, as torture is often carried out 'by or at the instigation of or with the consent or acquiescence of a public official or other person acting in an official capacity',[3] foreign state immunities have presented a barrier to the successful litigation of many of these claims.

As the courts of a foreign state often present the only forum in which a torture survivor can try to exercise their right to a remedy, during the 1990s and 2000s attempts were made to overcome the barriers of foreign state immunities, with varying degrees of success. This chapter discusses the different approaches adopted in theory and in practice to overcome the barrier of each immunity in torture cases. It argues that international law appears to have settled on the continuing availability of foreign state immunity, changes to which only seem likely through international agreement. While theoretically possible, such a development seems currently unlikely politically at the current time. Similarly, the personal immunity available to high ranking officials (such as the head of state) while in office as well as diplomatic immunity also continue to apply in cases of alleged torture. However, the availability of functional immunities to foreign state officials is less stable, particularly in criminal cases, meaning that claims may still be possible against such officials.

THE CURRENT POSITION ON THE AVAILABILITY OF FOREIGN STATE IMMUNITY WHERE TORTURE IS ALLEGED

States can claim immunity at two points in a case. The first is immunity from jurisdiction and the second is immunity from enforcement or execution. The focus of this chapter is on immu-

---

[3]   Convention against Torture and Other Cruel, Inhuman or Degrading Treatment or Punishment (adopted 10 December 1984, entered into force 26 June 1987) 1465 UNTS 85, Article 1(1).

nity from jurisdiction as this is the relevant point at which a state may claim that a criminal investigation or civil suit against the state or its officials may not proceed.

Under international law, foreign states enjoy immunity from the jurisdiction of national courts, subject to specific exceptions, such as in relation to their commercial activities. Within the literature, there has been debate over whether, under customary international law,[4] immunity is an exception to jurisdiction or whether a general rule of immunity exists subject to certain exceptions.[5] The latter is the framing of many national statutes as well as the UN Convention on the Jurisdictional Immunities of States and their Property 2004 (which is not yet in force).[6]

As noted above, while states have been amenable to the introduction of exceptions to immunity in relation to torts committed on their territory and commercial activities, attempts to secure an exception to state immunity for torture and other crimes under international law have been much more difficult. The exception to this has been in the US, where the Anti-Terrorism and Effective Death Penalty Act of 1996 amended the Foreign Sovereign Immunities Act 1976 which provides for exceptions to a general rule of immunity, although an exception for torture does not feature. The Anti-Terrorism and Effective Death Penalty Act emulates traditional international law, whereby national courts often recognised immunity in relation to states with which the state had friendly relations but denied claims of immunity by enemy states.[7] In this regard, the Anti-Terrorism and Effective Death Penalty Act sets out that immunity will not be available to 'state sponsors' of terrorism as designated by the US State Department, where the underlying claim for 'money damages' involves allegations of a range of crimes, including torture.[8]

Beyond this specific example, efforts to establish a general exception to state immunity for torture have been through advocacy efforts for a human rights protocol to the UN Convention on Jurisdictional Immunities[9] and litigation in national courts, typically in the state in which the claimant is a citizen or resident.[10]

In relation to the Convention, six years prior to its adoption, the International Law Commission's Working Group determined that whether a *jus cogens* exception to immunity exists 'did not seem to be ripe enough for the Working Group to engage in a codification exercise over it'.[11] It did so on the grounds that in adopting a Convention it was undertaking a cod-

---

[4]   See, for example, Trooboff, PD, 'Foreign State Immunity: Emerging Consensus of Principles' (1986) 200 *Recueil Des Cours* 235; Caplan, L, 'State Immunity, Human Rights and *Jus Cogens*: A Critique of the Normative Hierarchy Theory' (2003) 97 *American Journal of International Law* 741.

[5]   Garnett, G, 'Should Foreign State Immunity Be Abolished?' (1999) 20 *Australian Yearbook of International Law* 175.

[6]   UN Convention on the Jurisdictional Immunities of States and their Property (adopted 2 December 2004, not yet in force 26, UN Doc A/59/505), Article 5.

[7]   Hill, H, 'A Policy Analysis of the American Law of Foreign State Immunity' (1981–82) 50 *Fordham Law Review* 155, 170.

[8]   Anti-Terrorism and Effective Death Penalty Act 1996, Pub.L. 104–132, Section 221.

[9]   Hall, CK, 'The UN Convention on State Immunity: The Need for a Human Rights Protocol' (2006) 55 *International and Comparative Law Quarterly* 411.

[10]   For example, in the *Bouzari v. Iran* case, Mr Bouzari had refugee status in Canada; in *Al-Adsani v. Kuwait*, Mr Al-Adsani was a dual national of Kuwait and the UK; and the claimants in *Jones and others v. United Kingdom* were British nationals or dual nationals. These cases are discussed below.

[11]   UN General Assembly, Convention on Jurisdictional Immunities of States and their Property: Report of the Chairman of the Working Group, A/C.6/54/L.12 (12 November 1999), para 47.

ification exercise to determine the current state of international law. At the time, I observed that in theory this exclusion was appropriate as the 'interaction between State immunity and *jus cogens* norms reflects an area of international law in a state of flux'.[12] Equally, I expressed concern that the construction of the treaty as providing a general rule of immunity subject to specific exceptions risked ossifying the development of international law in this area or could even 'result in regressive development of international law'.[13] No further opportunities have opened up to explore the possibility of a human rights protocol, although theoretically, it is still possible.

In this part of the chapter, I discuss the two main lines of argument advanced in the litigation at the national, regional and international level on the relationship between allegations of torture and state immunity within customary international law. These are first, that a *jus cogens* exception to immunity exists and second, that immunity is a disproportionate restriction on the right of access to justice, particularly where no other forum exists within which to bring a claim.

The *Jus Cogens* Argument

One of the dominant arguments pursued to establish an exception to state immunity has been that the *jus cogens* status of the prohibition of torture under international law means that state immunity (not enjoying a similar status) could not apply. This is known as the 'hierarchy of norms' doctrine in international law.[14] This argument was drawn from an oft-cited paragraph from the *Furundžija* decision of the International Criminal Tribunal for the former Yugoslavia, in which the Tribunal held that:

> Because of the importance of the values it protects, [the prohibition of torture] has evolved into a peremptory norm or *jus cogens*, that is a norm that enjoys a higher rank in the international hierarchy than treaty law and even 'ordinary' customary rules …
>
> Clearly the *jus cogens* nature of the prohibition has now become one of the most fundamental standards of the international community. Furthermore, this prohibition is designed to produce a deterrent effect, in that it signals to all members of the international community and the individuals over whom they wield authority that the prohibition of torture is an absolute value from which nobody must deviate.[15]

The argument garnered significant support in academic literature.[16] While it was not followed by the majority in the earlier and closely divided case of *Al-Adsani v. The United Kingdom* before the European Court of Human Rights, the minority was persuaded by the hierarchy of norms argument, finding that 'the procedural bar of State immunity is automatically lifted, because those roles, as they conflict with a hierarchically higher rule [such as the prohibition],

---

[12] McGregor, L, 'State Immunity and *Jus Cogens*' (2006) 55 *International and Comparative Law Quarterly* 437, 437.

[13] *Ibid.*

[14] Caplan (n 4 above).

[15] *Prosecutor v. Furundžija*, Judgment, Case No IT-95-17/1-T, Trial Chamber (10 December 1998), paras 153–154.

[16] Orakhelashvili, A, 'State Immunity and Hierarchy of Norms: Why the House of Lords Got it Wrong' (2007) 18 *European Journal of International Law* 955; Orakhelashvili, A, 'State Immunity and International Public Order Revisited' (2006) 49 *German Yearbook of International Law* 327.

do not produce any legal effect'.[17] It was also successfully argued in some national cases, such as the case of *Ferrini v. The Federal Republic of Germany* in Italy. This case concerned allegations of forcible deportation and forced labour during World War II. In this case, Mr Ferrini had brought a case before the German courts, but the courts found that they did not have jurisdiction as the claim did not meet the terms of the domestic reparations law. The Italian Court found that as the prohibition of forced labour constitutes a *jus cogens* norm under international law, it 'trumped' the claim of state immunity. The Court found that a *jus cogens* norm is absolute, whereas the availability of state immunity is increasingly restricted and that crimes such as forced labour, 'take on the gravest connotations, and ... figure in customary international law as *international crimes*, since they undermine *universal values* which transcend the interest of single States'.[18] The Court held that to grant immunity 'would *hinder* the protection of values whose safeguard is to be considered ... essential to the whole community'.[19]

As a variation to this argument, others argued that the status of the prohibition of torture and other crimes under international law meant that states had implicitly waived earlier rules of international law, such as state immunity, as the two were incompatible.[20] For example, in *Prefecture of Voiotia v. The Federal Republic of Germany*, the Greek court found that the acts of the German military during World War II could not be considered sovereign acts since they were 'in breach of peremptory international law'.[21] It employed the theory of implied waiver rather than the hierarchy of norms doctrine, to find that Germany had implicitly waived any immunity that may have otherwise been available to it.[22] However, the theory of implied waiver did not garner favour before other national courts.[23]

The *jus cogens* or peremptory norm argument was also advanced in other cases. However, other national courts, most notably in dualist countries, such as Canada and England and Wales, rejected these arguments.[24] For example, in *Bouzari v. The Islamic Republic of Iran,* Mr Bouzari alleged that he had been tortured in Iran. While recognising the peremptory status of the prohibition of torture under international law, the Ontario Court of Appeal held that it could not read in an exception to the State Immunity Act due to the absence of express language to that effect and established state practice.[25]

Academics also challenged the use of *jus cogens* norms in this way, questioning whether the *jus cogens* status attaches to the right of access to justice flowing from the prohibition

---

[17]   *Al-Adsani v. The United Kingdom* [GC], no. 35763/97, ECHR 2001-XI, Joint Dissenting Opinion of Judges Rozakis and Caflisch, Joined by Judges Wildhaber, Costa, Cabral Barreto and Vajic, para 3.

[18]   de Sena, P and de Vittor, F, 'State Immunity and Human Rights: The Italian Supreme Court Decision on the Ferrini Case' (2005) 16 *European Journal of International Law* 89, 98 (translation of the judgment, emphasis in the original).

[19]   *Ibid*, 102.

[20]   Belsky, AC, Merva, M and Roht–Arriaza, N, Comment, 'Implied Waiver Under the FSIA: A Proposed Exception to Immunity for Violations of Peremptory Norms of International Law' (1989) 77 *California Law Review* 365.

[21]   Gavouneli, M and Bantekas, I, '*Prefecture of Voiotia v. Federal Republic of Germany*' (2001) 95 *American Journal of International Law* 198.

[22]   Belsky et al. (n 20 above).

[23]   For example, it was rejected in *Ferrini v. Italy*, see de Sena and de Vittor (n 18 above), 101.

[24]   See, for example, *Jones v. Saudi Arabia* [2006] UKHL 26.

[25]   *Bouzari v. Islamic Republic of Iran* 71 OR (3d) 675 (Ont CA), 30 June 2004, paras 90–95.

of torture, or only to the negative obligation not to torture itself.[26] Some scholars questioned whether a substantive rule, such as the prohibition of torture, could have a relationship to a procedural rule such as state immunity. For example, Lady Hazel Fox, argued that:

> State immunity is a procedural rule going to the jurisdiction of a national court. It does not go to substantive law; it does not contradict a prohibition contained in a *jus cogens* norm but merely diverts any breach of it to a different method of settlement. Arguably, then, there is no substantive content in the procedural plea of State immunity upon which a *jus cogens* norm can bite.[27]

The claim that a *jus cogens* exception to state immunity exists was ultimately defeated in two international decisions, first by the International Court of Justice in *Germany v. Italy*[28] and then by the European Court of Human Rights in *Jones v. The United Kingdom*.[29] In this regard, the European Court referred to a number of national court decisions on whether a *jus cogens* exception to immunity exists, but found that:

> it is not necessary for the Court to examine all of these developments in detail since the recent judgment of the ICJ in Germany v. Italy ... which must be considered by this Court as authoritative as regards the content of customary international law – clearly establishes that, by February 2012, no jus cogens exception to State immunity had yet crystallised.[30]

In a recent article reflecting on the anniversary of the UK State Immunity Act, Lord Lloyd-Jones argued that, 'the notion that a rule of jus cogens can override an immunity in international law has now been widely discredited'.[31] As discussed further below, it now seems unlikely that a plea of state immunity in torture cases can be successfully overcome in judicial cases using arguments of *jus cogens* or implied waiver, in the absence of clear international agreement.

The Access to Justice Argument

The second way in which practitioners and scholars have sought to establish an exception to state immunity in cases in which torture is alleged is through an assessment of its impact on the right of access to justice. This challenge has a wide and a narrow form. In its wider form, claimants have argued that Article 14 of the UN Convention against Torture provides a right to a civil remedy which would be undercut if a plea of foreign state immunity was upheld. Since Article 14 does not clarify its territorial reach, the question arises whether the provision only extends to the courts of the state in which the torture was alleged to have been committed or

---

[26] Voyiakis, E, 'Access to Court v State Immunity' (2003) 52 *International and Comparative Law Quarterly* 297, 322.

[27] Fox, H, *The Law of State Immunity* (Oxford University Press, 2002), 525. See also, Zimmerman, A, 'Sovereign Immunity and Violations of International *Jus Cogens* – Some Critical Remarks' (1994) 16 *Michigan Journal of International Law* 433, 438.

[28] *Jurisdictional Immunities of the State (Germany v Italy: Greece Intervening), Judgment of 3 February 2012, ICJ Reports 2012*, p 99, para 96.

[29] *Jones and Others v. The United Kingdom*, nos 34356/06 and 40528/06, ECHR 2014.

[30] *Ibid*, para 198.

[31] The Rt Hon Lord Lloyd-Jones, 'Forty Years On: The State Immunity Act 1978' (2019) 68 *International and Comparative Law Quarterly* 247, 264.

whether it has a broader reach. In this regard, scholars have questioned whether international law recognises an obligation to provide universal civil jurisdiction, and if not, whether such an obligation is emerging.[32]

The establishment of universal civil jurisdiction has encountered resistance due to the lack of clarity in the text or the travaux préparatoires of the Convention on whether states have an obligation to provide redress for torture alleged to have been committed extraterritorially. In *Bouzari,* the Ontario Court of Appeal rejected the argument, finding that Article 14(1) provides 'no clear guidance' on a civil remedy for torture committed extraterritorially.[33]

In cases brought before the European Court of Human Rights, claimants have argued that the right of access to justice under Article 6(1) of the European Convention on Human Rights would be frustrated by a claim of immunity. In both *Al-Adsani v. The United Kingdom* and *Jones and Other v. The United Kingdom*, the respondent state challenged the applicability of Article 6(1) as the underlying acts of torture were alleged to have taken place extraterritorially. The Court rejected this argument, finding that Article 6(1) is engaged in such cases. As a qualified right, the Court assessed whether a grant of foreign state immunity pursued a legitimate aim and whether the restriction on the exercise of the right of access to justice under Article 6(1) was proportionate to that aim. In both *Al-Adsani v. The United Kingdom* and *Jones and Others v. The United Kingdom*, the European Court found that the grant of immunity pursues the legitimate aim of 'complying with international law to promote comity and good relations between States through the respect of another's sovereignty'.[34] In making a proportionality assessment, however, the Court in *Al-Adsani,* accorded the United Kingdom a wide margin of appreciation, and as I have previously observed, did not carry out 'a detailed assessment of how the provision of State immunity fulfilled a legitimate aim or met the requirements of proportionality'.[35] In *Jones*, the Court again did not carry out an assessment of proportionality but rather deferred to the International Court of Justice's decision, as noted above.

Beyond the claim that Article 14 of the UN Convention against Torture indicates a requirement of universal civil jurisdiction, a narrower way in which to assess the proportionality of a restriction on access to justice is available. This narrower approach does not rest on the status of the prohibition of torture or a claim of universal civil jurisdiction. Rather, it engages with Lady Fox's analysis set out above that the provision of state immunity merely diverts the claim to another forum and the International Court of Justice's finding in the *Arrest Warrant* case that,

> immunity from jurisdiction enjoyed by incumbent Ministers for Foreign Affairs does not mean that they may enjoy impunity in respect of any crimes that they may have committed, irrespective of their gravity. Immunity from criminal jurisdiction and individual criminal responsibility are quite separate concepts. While jurisdictional immunity is procedural in nature, criminal responsibility is a question of substantive law. Jurisdictional immunity may well bar criminal prosecution for a certain period or for certain offences; it cannot exonerate the person to whom it applies from all criminal responsibility.[36]

---

[32]   Donovan, D and Roberts, A, 'The Emerging Recognition of Universal Civil Jurisdiction' (2006) 100 *American Journal of International Law* 142.

[33]   *Bouzari v. Islamic Republic of Iran* (n 25 above), para 76.

[34]   *Jones v. United Kingdom* (n 29 above), para 88.

[35]   McGregor (n 12 above).

[36]   *Arrest Warrant of 11 April 2000 (Democratic Republic of Congo v. Belgium), Preliminary Objections and Merits, Judgment, ICJ Reports 2002,* p 3, para 60. See also *Al-Adsani v United Kingdom* (n 17 above), para 48.

As I have previously argued, this proposition only holds if there is another forum to which to divert the claim.[37] For torture survivors, the reason for seeking to bring a claim before a foreign national court is that there is not another forum in which to bring the claim. In such circumstances – namely where the claimant can establish that remedies are unavailable or ineffective in the state allegedly responsible for the torture and that no regional human rights court exists or has jurisdiction to hear the claim – I have argued that it would constitute a disproportionate restriction on the right of access to justice if immunity was upheld. This accords with the view of Judge van den Wyngaert in her dissenting opinion in the *Arrest Warrant* case, where she observed that in such circumstances, immunity would, in practice, lead to impunity.[38] Such an exception is tightly drawn and introduces a high threshold to establish disproportionality, placing an onerous burden on claimants to prove the lack of an alternative forum.

However, in the *Jurisdictional Immunities* case, the International Court of Justice rejected this argument, finding that:

> The Court can find no basis in the State practice from which customary international law is derived that international law makes the entitlement of a State to immunity dependent upon the existence of effective alternative means of securing redress. Neither in the national legislation on the subject, nor in the jurisprudence of the national courts which have been faced with objections based on immunity, is there any evidence that entitlement to immunity is subjected to such a precondition.[39]

Where Now?

Given the decisions by a regional court and particularly the International Court of Justice, it appears unlikely that courts offer a forum in which to challenge the availability of state immunity in cases in which torture is alleged. For change to happen, it appears that it will have to emanate from an agreement between states. As already noted above, during the negotiations on the UN Convention on the Jurisdictional Immunities of States and their Property, the Working Group of the International Law Commission decided that it could not consider the relationship between state immunity and *jus cogens* as it was not 'ripe' for codification and the proposal for a human rights protocol was not discussed, although scholar-practitioners such as the late Christopher Keith Hall of Amnesty International made the case for one at the time.[40] However, given the current foreclosure of judicial routes to access justice, which contributes to a de facto situation in which torture survivors cannot exercise their right to a remedy, it may be timely to assess the parameters within which a human rights exception to state immunity could be introduced. In this regard, I have previously argued that a 'hard or soft law instrument' may be appropriate as a means to reach agreement on the denial of immunity in cases in which no alternative forum in which to bring the claim exists and in doing so, 'to flesh out how national judiciaries should assess the availability of alternative avenues for dispute resolution'.[41]

---

[37] McGregor, L, 'Torture and State Immunity: Deflecting Impunity, Distorting Sovereignty' (2007) 18 *European Journal of International Law* 903.

[38] *Arrest Warrant* case (n 36 above), Dissenting Opinion of Judge van der Wyngaert, para 34.

[39] *Jurisdictional Immunities* case (n 28 above), para 101.

[40] Hall (n 9 above).

[41] McGregor, L, 'State Immunity and Human Rights: Is There a Future After *Germany v. Italy*' (2013) 11 *Journal of International Criminal Justice* 125, 136.

THE IMMUNITIES OF FOREIGN STATE OFFICIALS

The availability of immunity to foreign state officials is more complex and appears to be less settled than the current position within international law on state immunity. In this regard, depending on their rank and position, three forms of immunity are potentially available to foreign state officials.

The first form of immunity is immunity *ratione materiae*, often referred to as functional or subject matter immunity. This is the immunity that attaches to the acts or omissions of foreign state officials, when carried out in an official capacity. The justification for this type of immunity is that these acts are deemed to constitute the acts of the foreign state. Immunity therefore extends to both current and former state officials in order to prevent the circumvention of state immunity by claimants bringing cases against foreign state officials when barred from proceeding against the state itself, due to state immunity. As the immunity essentially belongs to the state, the state can waive it, thus subjecting the official to a civil or criminal law suit, although this rarely happens in practice.

The second form of immunity is immunity *ratione personae* or personal immunity. This only attaches to certain high-level officials, such as heads of state and government and ministers of foreign affairs,[42] for so long as they are in office (thereafter functional immunity applies), in order to enable them to carry out their functions, and travel abroad, without fear of arrest.

The third form of immunity is diplomatic immunity. In contrast to functional and personal immunities, diplomatic immunity derives from treaty law rather than custom and is justified on the basis that a necessary part of a diplomatic role is being posted in other states.[43] Accordingly, immunity is necessary in order to carry out diplomatic functions without the risk of legal proceedings (including potentially spurious actions) being lodged against the diplomat, particularly in situations in which the bilateral relationship between the host and sending state are tense. Like personal immunity, this form of immunity lasts for the duration of the office. Thereafter, a form of functional immunity applies.

In this part of the chapter, I examine the challenges that have been made to the availability of immunity, particularly with regard to functional immunity in criminal and civil cases.

The Availability of Personal Immunity

For officials to whom personal immunity is available, the possibilities of challenging a plea of immunity have been limited. As noted above, the justification for this type of immunity is practical in that it focuses on the need for certain high-ranking officials to be able to carry out the business of the state, particularly through travel to other states. If such officials were at risk of being subject to litigation every time they travelled, significant disorder could emerge as well as creating opportunities for states to bring spurious claims against high-ranking officials of other states, which could have a destabilising effect. Dapo Akande and Sangeeta Shah argue that 'these immunities are necessary for the maintenance of a system of peaceful cooperation

---

[42]   *Arrest Warrant* case (n 36 above).
[43]   Vienna Convention on Diplomatic Relations (adopted 18 April 1961, entered into force 24 April 1961 500 UNTS 95).

and co-existence among states. Increased global cooperation means that this immunity is especially important'.[44]

This immunity does not deny possibilities for criminal investigation or civil claims for redress as in theory, at least, these officials will not hold office forever and once they leave, personal immunity will no longer attach. While there has been some debate around the officials to whom personal immunity extends, both the International Court of Justice and the International Law Commission have settled on the view that customary international law provides that it covers heads of state, heads of government and ministers of foreign affairs.[45]

The Availability of Functional Immunity in Criminal Cases

The denial of functional immunity in criminal cases in which torture is alleged reflects the area in which there has been the most traction in the literature and in practice. However, as discussed further below, whether state practice establishes that functional immunity no longer applies in cases of torture and other international crimes or is indicative of the future direction of international law, remains contentious. The *Pinochet* case before the UK House of Lords generated significant interest in the literature and in practice on whether functional immunity was available in criminal proceedings against a former head of state (meaning that personal immunity did not apply) for alleged torture.[46] In this case, two lines of reasoning can be identified within the separate opinions of the five judges. The first relates to the *jus cogens* or peremptory norms argument. However, as already noted, the strength of this argument has weakened over time, in state immunity cases at least, and will therefore not be rehearsed here.

The second line of reasoning focuses on the state obligation to extradite or prosecute individuals alleged to have been involved in torture, as set out in Article 5 of the UN Convention against Torture. In this regard, the House of Lords found that the UK could not simultaneously meet this obligation while upholding a plea of subject matter immunity. It therefore found that the 'later in time' rule (Article 5 of the Convention against Torture) within international law displaced the earlier one (functional immunity). Interestingly, in comparison to state immunity, the implied waiver argument has been more favourably received in relation to functional immunity in criminal proceedings.

Following the *Pinochet* case, state practice and academic analysis on universal jurisdiction then grew – albeit not always consistently – resulting in an increasing recognition of the incompatibility of functional immunity with a requirement to provide universal jurisdiction. This led scholars such as Dapo Akande and Sangeeta Shah to argue that 'the principle of universal jurisdiction over certain international crimes is inconsistent with immunity *ratione materiae*; it follows that that type of immunity does not exist in relation to those crimes'.[47] In

---

[44]   Akande, D and Shah, S, 'Immunities of State Officials, International Crimes, and Foreign Domestic Courts' (2011) 21 *European Journal of International Law* 815, 818.

[45]   *Arrest Warrant* case (n 37 above). Articles 3 and 4, Draft Articles on Immunity of State Officials from Foreign Criminal Jurisdiction Provisionally Adopted So Far by the Commission, International Law Commission, Report of the International Law Commission, A/72/10 (2017), ch VII.

[46]   *R v. Bow St Metropolitan Stipendiary Magistrate ex parte Pinochet Ugarte (No. 3)* [1999] UKHL 17.

[47]   Akande and Shah (n 44 above), 849.

their view this includes torture, as the provision of functional immunity would be 'contrary to the object and purpose' of Article 5 of the Convention against Torture.[48]

The International Law Commission then took up the question of the immunities of foreign state officials in criminal cases, arriving at a set of draft articles in 2018. Draft Article 7(1) provides that:

> Immunity *ratione materiae* from the exercise of foreign criminal jurisdiction shall not apply in respect of the following crimes under international law:

> (a)   crimes of genocide;
> (b)   crimes against humanity;
> (c)   war crimes;
> (d)   crime of *apartheid*
> (e)   torture;
> (f)   enforced disappearance.

On its face, this appears to provide an authoritative interpretation of the current position under existing international law, with 21 members voting in favour of the article, eight against and one abstaining.[49] However, within the academic literature, the draft article has received criticism and debate has emerged on whether the article reflects established customary international law (*lex lata*) or is an exercise in the progressive development of the law and therefore representative of emerging international law. For example, Rosanne van Alebeek questions whether the members voting in favour of the draft article did so on the basis of an understanding that international law already establishes an exception to immunity or whether it indicates a move in the direction of an exception.[50] However, Dire Tladi (a member of the ILC) points out that 'the Commission has not generally identified individual provisions as either progressive development or codification'.[51]

Others, including the members of the International Law Commission that voted against the draft article, have questioned whether state practice exists to support even a claim of an emerging state practice denying the availability of functional immunity in cases of torture and other international crimes. In her report, the Rapporteur identified some state practice supporting an exception to functional immunity in criminal cases.[52] However, some of the members of the Commission and academic commentators have questioned the strength of these sources. For example, Sean Murphy (a member of the Commission) is doubtful of the sufficiency of state practice, asking whether it is 'widespread, representative or consistent'.[53] Philippa Webb also criticised the report for 'cross-pollinat[ing]' different forms of immunity, for example, by using cases involving state immunity, diplomatic immunity and functional immunity in

---

[48]   *Ibid*, 842.

[49]   See International Law Commission 2017 Report (n 45 above).

[50]   van Alebeek, R, 'The "International Crime" Exception in the ILC Draft Articles on the Immunity of State Officials from Foreign Criminal Jurisdiction: Two Steps Back?' (2018) 112 *AJIL Unbound* 28.

[51]   Tladi, D, 'The International Law Commission's Recent Work on Exceptions to Immunity: Charting the Course for a Brave New World in International Law?' (2019) 32 *Leiden Journal of International Law* 169.

[52]   See International Law Commission, 2017 Report (n 45 above).

[53]   Murphy, SD, 'Immunity *Ratione Materiae* of State Officials from Foreign Criminal Jurisdiction: Where is the State Practice in Support of Exceptions?' (2018) 112 *AJIL Unbound* 4, 8.

civil cases as evidence of the emergence of an exception to functional immunity in criminal proceedings.[54] Interestingly, Tladi (also a member of the Commission) notes that the members of the Commission who did not support the recognition of an exception to functional immunity argued that there should be no distinction between the availability of such immunity in civil or criminal cases. He observes that part of the rationale for this argument appeared to rest with the number of civil cases in which a plea of functional immunity has been upheld by national courts.[55] A final criticism of the draft article was the decision of the Special Rapporteur not to include procedural safeguards, such as protection against frivolous or abusive prosecutions, within the draft articles.[56]

From a customary international law perspective, the question of functional immunity is likely to continue to be challenged in national courts, potentially with varying results, depending on whether the courts follow the Commission's majority or the minority critiques.[57] For claimants seeking to access justice through criminal cases, the fact that as authoritative a body as the International Law Commission has recognised the inapplicability of functional immunity where torture or other international crimes are alleged may provide impetus for confirmatory state practice.

The Availability of Functional Immunity in Civil Cases

While there is greater recognition of the inapplicability of functional immunity in criminal cases, it has been more challenging to make the case for the denial of this form of immunity in civil cases. Many of the same types of arguments that have been advanced in cases against foreign states and foreign officials in criminal proceedings have also been used in civil cases against foreign state officials, such as the *jus cogens* argument.

One approach adopted by claimants and scholars has been to argue that if functional immunity is not available in criminal cases, it should also not be available in civil cases. This argument has faced difficulties due to the difference in the language of Articles 5 and 14 of the UN Convention against Torture, where Article 5 provides a binary obligation to extradite or prosecute, whereas, as already discussed, Article 14 does not explicitly clarify its territorial scope. Thus, for the same reasons as in state immunity cases, the argument that functional immunity is incompatible with Article 14 or a doctrine of universal civil jurisdiction has not yet been successful.

The other challenge in cases against foreign officials has been the argument by states that the foreign state would be impleaded in a case against a foreign official, thus becoming vicariously liable, with the result that state immunity would be circumvented in practice.[58] This argument derives from the traditional rationale for the provision of functional immunity, namely that officials have no separate responsibility in international law but are the 'mere

---

[54] Webb, P, 'How Far Does the Systemic Approach to Immunities Take Us?' (2018) 112 *AJIL Unbound* 16, 17 See also Tladi (n 51 above), 176.

[55] Tladi (n 51 above), 177.

[56] See Forteau, M, 'Immunities and International Crimes before the ILC: Looking for Innovative Solutions' (2018) 112 *AJIL Unbound* 22, 24 (discussing this point).

[57] *Ibid*, 24 (noting that more states were critical of the draft article in the Sixth Committee of the General Assembly, particularly as the International Law Commission did not adopt the article by consensus).

[58] *Jones v. Saudi Arabia* (n 24 above), para 10.

instruments of the state',[59] meaning that, 'a suit against an individual acting in his official capacity is the practical equivalent of a suit against the sovereign directly'.[60]

Even if this is the general position within international law, where allegations of torture are made, the situation may be different. This is because of the increasing recognition of the dual responsibility of the state and individuals for crimes such as torture under international law, which may mean there is scope for the emergence of an exception to functional immunity where torture is alleged in the future. Chimene Keitner explains the different situations in which individuals act for the state and the consequences for allocation of responsibility under international law:

1) Acts attributable solely to the state and for which such attribution discharges the individual from personal responsibility, such as signing a treaty or entering into a commercial transaction on behalf of the state ('Category One').
2) Acts attributable to the state and for which such attribution does not discharge the individual from personal responsibility under domestic and/or international law, such as ordering torture ('Category Two').
3) Acts not attributable to the state and for which the individual bears sole responsibility, such as vandalizing a neighbor's property without actual or apparent state authority ('Category Three').[61]

In this regard, I have argued, as has Keitner, that the dual responsibility of the state and individual attaches to her second category.[62] In such circumstances, insistence that individual officials enjoy subject-matter immunity because of state immunity and the desire to avoid impleading the state would result in an overreaching of state immunity by covering the responsibility of the individual as well as the state. In an earlier article, I suggested that:

> It would therefore appear difficult to sustain the argument that immunity *ratione materiae* could continue to apply in civil proceedings expressly aimed at achieving the personal accountability of the official, particularly where it has already been removed in criminal proceedings and civil proceedings brought in the course of a criminal action.[63]

On this argument, this would mean that even where state immunity continues to be available, state officials could be sued in foreign courts for allegations of torture, in order to establish whether they are individually responsible for the allegations under international law.

In *Jones v. The United Kingdom*, the European Court did not find that the grant of immunity to the foreign state officials was a disproportionate restriction on the right of access to justice. It noted that:

> Since an act cannot be carried out by a State itself but only by individuals acting on the State's behalf, where immunity can be invoked by the State then the starting-point must be that immunity *ratione*

---

[59]   *Judgment on the Request of the Republic of Croatia for Review of the Decision of Trial Chamber II of 18 July1997, Blaskic (IT-95-14)*, Appeals Chamber, 29 October 1997, para 38.

[60]   Court of Appeals for the Ninth Circuit, *Chuidian v. Philippine National Bank* (1990) 912 F.2d1095, Ninth Circuit, 1101.

[61]   Keitner, C, 'Categorizing Acts by State Officials: Attribution and Responsibility in the Law of Foreign Official Immunity' (2016) 26 *Duke Journal of Comparative & International Law* 451, 453.

[62]   McGregor (n 41 above), 141.

[63]   *Ibid*, 144.

materiae applies to the acts of State officials. If it were otherwise, State immunity could always be circumvented by suing named officials.[64]

However, it also recognised the possible future development of an exception to functional immunity in civil cases based on dual responsibility. It recognised that, '[t]here is no doubt that individuals may in certain circumstances also be personally liable for wrongful acts which engage the State's responsibility, and that this personal liability exists alongside the State's liability for the same acts'.[65] It found that such dual responsibility is clearly demonstrated in criminal cases.[66] In relation to civil cases, it found that there is 'some emerging support in favour of a special rule or exception' but that 'State practice on the question is in a state of flux, with evidence of both the grant and the refusal of immunity *ratione materiae* in such cases'.[67] It concluded that, '[i]nternational opinion on the question may be said to be beginning to evolve, as demonstrated recently by the discussions around the work of the ILC in the criminal sphere. This work is ongoing and further developments can be expected'.[68] Accordingly, like functional immunity in criminal cases, this may be a dimension to immunity that could move more clearly in the direction of an exception to functional immunity where torture is alleged.

CONCLUSION: THE FUTURE DEVELOPMENT OF FOREIGN STATE IMMUNITIES

This chapter has established that current international law has now settled on the availability of state immunity in cases in which torture is alleged. It therefore appears unlikely that claimants will have success in overcoming the barrier of state immunity in judicial cases, particularly given the pronouncements by the European Court of Human Rights and critically, the International Court of Justice. The only route left appears to be through international agreement, which currently appears remote.

The prospects of the development of international law to recognise an exception to functional immunity in both criminal and civil proceedings appear better. While Article 7 of the Draft Articles on Immunity of State Officials from Foreign Criminal Jurisdiction, recognising that functional immunity does not apply in criminal cases concerning torture, has received some criticism in the academic literature, it nonetheless received majority support in the International Law Commission and therefore either establishes the current state of international law or indicates its future progression. Similarly, in *Jones v. The United Kingdom*, the European Court left the door open for further development of international law in civil cases. As the recognition of dual responsibility of states and individuals for crimes such as torture crystallises, courts may be willing to reject pleas of functional immunity in civil cases involving torture, thus potentially meaning that judicial routes may still be open to bring civil claims for compensation against foreign state officials, where they are not diplomats or sitting heads of state, government or foreign affairs.

---

64   *Jones v. United Kingdom* (n 29 above), para 202.
65   *Ibid*, para 207.
66   *Ibid*.
67   *Ibid*, para 213.
68   *Ibid*.

As argued throughout this chapter, the most important policy justification for overcoming state immunity and functional immunities is the lack of an alternative forum in which to bring a claim. In this regard, the focus of organisations and practitioners seeking to secure justice for torture survivors should be multidimensional and not only focus on foreign state immunities. As such, the central focus must still be overcoming the inadequacy, unavailability and ineffectiveness of remedies within the state alleged to have carried out the torture. This is a complex and challenging project which is beyond the scope of this chapter, but needs to be at the centre of strategies to secure justice for torture survivors.

An additional strand that is often neglected in discourse on access to justice is the need for improvements within international law on diplomatic protection. Diplomatic protection currently cannot be considered to constitute a route to a remedy. While it is recognised as a right in some jurisdictions and in others a decision not to take up a claim can be reviewed, international law still recognises the decision to provide diplomatic protection as at the discretion of the state concerned. Moreover, it typically does not extend to non-nationals, even if stateless, and when espoused becomes a claim of the state rather than the individual affected.[69]

The more other routes to access to justice can be opened, the easier it may be to convince states that a denial of state immunity and functional immunities would be relatively rare and only be required in situations in which no other avenue to access justice is available. As already noted, this would still be a particularly onerous task for claimants and would therefore be unlikely to result in a flood of claims in foreign courts.

While there are currently no clear openings or developments suggesting that states are ready to start tackling the significant barriers torture survivors face at the national, regional and international level or moves to revisit the question of the immunities of states and their officials, in other areas, such as the immunity of state officials in relation to their employees, there has been movement, thus suggesting that immunities are not static or necessarily stable in international law, particularly in cases involving human rights.[70]

---

[69]   McGregor (n 37 above), 908–911 for a fuller discussion.
[70]   Webb, P and Garciandia, R, 'State Responsibility for Modern Slavery: Uncovering and Bridging the Gap' (2019) 68 *International and Comparative Law Quarterly* 539; Ziegler, K, 'Immunity *Versus* Human Rights: The Right to a Remedy after *Benkharbouche*' (2017) 17 *Human Rights Law Review* 127.

18. Torture and international medical ethics standards

Vivienne Nathanson

INTRODUCTION

Health care professionals have long recognised that they have a unique and important role in the prevention and detection of instances of torture. While the basic root of health care provision is a commitment by providers to help those in need this has not historically prevented health care professionals from abusing their patients, or from becoming involved in and, at times, leading the abuse of vulnerable persons.

Medical ethics standards, often written as codes, have developed over centuries to delineate acceptable behaviour by medical professionals. They establish a series of rules that assure patients and the public of the behaviours and standards they can expect from doctors, nurses and other health care professionals. They limit the freedoms of health care professionals to act as they wish by establishing an acceptable set of principled rules, protecting the public from possible abuse. Ethical standards can have real power, protecting people and patients from abuse, but their power only exists where health professionals know the standards and believe that they are binding upon them.

While most of the examples given below are of physicians many different health care professionals have taken similar stances – and may be included in the roll of human rights protectors and of human rights abusers. The International Council of Nurses has, for example, been an early adopter of a principled stand and has supported nurses globally following its lead.

Standards Versus Codes

Physicians and other health care professionals have long been associated with codes of ethics or with other standard-setting documents and guidance. Physicians in particular have agreed to be bound by codes. In many countries there are national examples of such codes, that all physicians may swear or otherwise avow, often at the time of qualifying or commencing work in medicine.

In many countries formal swearing of ethical codes no longer takes place on a systematic basis, but physicians continue to be bound by the ethical concepts. Courts and other legal bodies regard physicians as bound by these codes regardless of whether they individually swore them; many regulatory systems will incorporate the concepts into the rules that they impose upon their physicians and to which they bind physicians. The codes will vary – they may be the historic codes of Hippocrates or Maimonides, the Geneva Declaration or a local, regional or national example.

In some countries ethical standards are set by the regulatory bodies. In all countries where there are such regulatory bodies the standards that are applied to regulatory investigation of a practitioners' behaviour or professional practice will refer back to some sort of standards document or professional code.

In some countries there has been recent interest in establishing ethical codes for other professionals, such as research scientists, to replicate the perceived success of the codes within the health care sector.[1] This has especially related to scientists who work with technologies that could be used in the development of biological and chemical weapons. Important questions, such as the limits that might apply to research that could be carried out within an ethical framework, or the publication of knowledge related to research where that knowledge might have weaponisable components, have caused significant concern and debate. An example was the publication of research on the production and development of a new form of small-pox, resistant to current existing vaccines. Could this have led to the development of a new bio-weapon? Is this type of research legitimate given its potential for abuse? Should the results of such research be published when the publication puts the results into the public domain, and increases the risk of weaponisation of the technology and techniques described?

There is much debate about whether standards or codes have more value; in practice what matters is knowledge and understanding of them, as well as the voluntary adherence to them. The most brilliantly constructed code or standards document has no value if those supposed to be bound by it do not know its contents, do not understand it or do not believe it to be relevant to them and to their work. Most codes are attempts to put the body of ethical thought into a brief form that is readily remembered by physicians; understanding is essential. Experience from those teaching is that codes can open up as many questions as they answer, and that there can be many varying interpretations of the meaning of the contents of the code.[2] The authors seek to write a document that is clear, concise and easy to understand, but as with all such attempts, no such document is immune to misunderstanding. Codes and standard-setting documents therefore, in common with laws, become the subject of discussion, debate and legal or quasi-legal judgements. These interpret their meaning and should add to understanding.

Codes such as those of Maimonides and Hippocrates

Historic oaths and prayers have value as foundations to ethical thinking in medicine. The specific language is often inappropriate; physicians in the 21st century would not swear by ancient gods, nor would they agree with Hippocrates to abstain from "cutting for stone" – attempts at the surgical removal of kidney or bladder stones that would have been inevitably fatal in the time of Hippocrates but that are safe and routine today. Other elements such as the call to abstain from performing abortions remain contentious in some parts of the world. Elements such as the requirements to ensure confidentiality of medical information and to teach others remain cornerstones of medical practice. Modern practice is ruled by requirements that are more complex, but the fundamentals come back to concepts such as respect, self-determination, confidentiality and consideration of others.

Ancient codes are often written as prayers – the Hippocratic Oath commences with a plea to Apollo and to others. The Prayer of Maimonides is a traditional Jewish prayer. Given the

---

[1]   See, for example, work undertaken by a group of scientific bodies in the UK, organised by the Department of Peace Studies at the University of Bradford.

[2]   For example, early in the 21st century a number of explanatory notes to parts of the Declaration of Helsinki (considered below) were published by the WMA.

diversity of belief systems worldwide, such prayers are thought to be unacceptable and are gradually being replaced in rewritten versions by promises.

The Hippocratic Oath starts, in one of many translations, with the following promise

> I swear by Apollo the Healer, by Aslepius, by Hygieia, by Panacea, and by all the gods and goddesses, making them my witnesses, that I will carry out, according to my ability and judgement, this oath and this indenture.

This is clearly difficult for those of faith, as it would mean swearing by a group of gods and goddesses that are not part of their belief system. The archaic language elsewhere is also problematic – which is largely why the in 1940s the Declaration of Geneva was created.

The 1948 version of the Declaration of Geneva[3] states, inter alia, that:

> I SOLEMNLY PLEDGE myself to consecrate my life to the service of humanity …
> I MAKE THESE PROMISES solemnly, freely and upon my honour.

In 2017, after a two-year review process, a number of changes were made to the Declaration.[4] The opening line changed to

> I SOLEMNLY PLEDGE to dedicate my life to the service of humanity.

This reflected an understanding that pledges, or oaths, are acceptable globally if they do not include quasi-religious words such as consecrate, which exclude those of some faiths or of no faith. The concept of dedicating one's life is universally acceptable.

The revised oath also includes amongst other new language the following three new clauses:

> I WILL RESPECT the autonomy and dignity of my patient;
> I WILL ATTEND TO my own health, well-being, and abilities in order to provide care of the highest standard;
> I WILL NOT USE my medical knowledge to violate human rights and civil liberties, even under threat;

The first of these reflects modern views of patient/physician relationships, and the concept in both ethics and law that individuals are autonomous and nothing, including medical investigations, examinations or treatment, can be carried out without their freely given and valid consent. The second of these clauses discusses the ability of physicians to care for their patients without limitations caused by their own poor physical or mental health. It seeks to abolish practices such as presentee-ism (in which individuals continue to work despite being unwell) because of the imperative to protect patients. The third of these for the first time explicitly includes a promise of respect for human rights within the oath. This reflects the contents of many other World Medical Association (WMA) Declarations, including the Tokyo, Hamburg and Malta Declarations (described below), as well as making it clear in the "over-arching" Geneva Declaration that physicians are bound to specific behaviours in

---

[3]   For the text of the 1948 Declaration of Geneva see https://www.wma.net/wp-content/uploads/2018/07/Decl-of-Geneva-v1948-1.pdf

[4]   The current version of the Declaration is available at https://www.wma.net/policies-post/wma-declaration-of-geneva/

these areas. This assists in refuting the concept that physicians can be persuaded or coerced into breaching the rights and liberties of patients and the public. It reinforces other specific Declarations which are cited below.

The Prayer and Oath of Maimonides are traditional Jewish statements. Written in Hebrew and translated variously over the years the Prayer is too long to be useful as a succinct statement of ethical principles and the Oath arguably too short. In both cases the swearing according to faith raises concerns for those of other, or no, faiths.

The Oath ends:

> Oh, God, Thou has appointed me to watch over the life and death of Thy creatures: here am I ready for my vocation and I turn unto my calling.

BREACHES OF CODES DURING WORLD WAR II

During World War II there were well-documented systematic abuses of human rights. The mass human experimentation perpetrated in Germany by Mengele and mirrored in Mongolia and China involving Japanese physicians, most notoriously by Unit 731, were low points in the behaviour of doctors. Both have been extensively studied.

In Germany, physicians were governed by ethical standards for medical research that were among the best in the world, with extensive protections of the rights of patients. German physicians were generally aware of the ethical standards and felt bound by them. But by defining people such as Jews, Homosexuals and Gypsies as 'less-that-human' they were excluded from the protections established by ethical codes. The research carried out by Robert Jay Lifton[5] defined the concept of *malignant normality* to describe the process by which the perpetration of almost indescribable abuses of human rights became normal. Support from peers was part of the process for many.

No similar studies were carried out on physicians and others involved in the extensive and systematic abuse of civilians in Mongolia in the 1930s by Japanese military forces. The systematic abuse was extensively detailed[6] but as there were no full war crimes trials or similar investigations, no complete analyses were performed on those involved in the abuses.

In both cases medical personnel were extensively involved in experimenting upon people, causing extreme suffering and very many deaths. The information from the treatment meted out was recorded and its results analysed – some of the information from Japanese experiments to investigate the results of prolonged exposure to cold or to high atmospheric pressure were later used in the space race to inform those designing methods of managing the physiological stresses that would be experienced by astronauts, as well as more direct use of the results of the biological experimentation for those involved in offensive and defensive bio-warfare research.

Research from this experimentation is still on occasion being cited in medical research and may find its way through this into contemporary medical literature. There is a general consensus amongst publishers that it should not be used because of the grossly unethical manner of

---

[5]   Lifton, R, *The Nazi Doctors: Medical Killing and the Psychology of Genocide*, 2nd revised edn (Basic Books, 2017).

[6]   See, for example, Harris, SH, *Factories of Death: Japanese Biological Warfare 1932–45 and the American Cover-Up*, 2nd edn (Routledge, 2002).

its collection. In an editorial in the journal *Anaesthesia* the Editor in Chief, Bogod described the use of data from the Dachau Hypothermia experiments by Richter and went on to describe the consensus and the dissenting views on the use of such data.[7] It is perhaps inevitable that so long after the events in World War II many of the current generation of health care professionals and researchers are unaware of the levels of abuse perpetrated.

ESTABLISHMENT OF TREATMENT BODIES AND STANDARD SETTING

After World War II a formal war crimes trial took place in Nuremberg. This included consideration of the atrocities carried out by Josef Mengele. Part of the outcome of the trials was the writing of a formal code to establish in law the restrictions upon the actions of doctors and other health care workers.

The Nuremberg Code of Ethics[8] was written by lawyers and based upon the findings of the trials. Adherence to it would mean that the actions of Mengele and other physicians could and would never be repeated.

It has ten major points in relation to experimentation:

- Required is the voluntary, well-informed understanding and consent of a human subject with appropriate legal capacity.
- The experiment should aim at positive results for society that cannot be procured in some other way.
- It should be based upon previous knowledge that justifies the experiment
- The experiment should be set up in a way as to avoid unnecessary physical and mental suffering and injuries.
- It should not be conducted when there is any reason to believe that it implies a risk of death or disabling injury.
- The risks of the experiment should be in proportion to the expected humanitarian benefits.
- Preparations and facilities must be provided that adequately protect the subjects against the experiments' risks.
- The staff who conduct or take part in the experiment must be fully trained and scientifically qualified.
- The human subjects must be free to immediately quit the experiment at any point when they feel physically or mentally unable to go on.
- Likewise, the medical staff must stop the experiment at any point when the observe that continuation would be dangerous.

These points outline the key areas of ethical research in legal terms. They remain silent on some of the most ethically challenging areas, which include issues related to the acceptability of double-blind trials (the so-called gold standard of medical research) and in relation to research on children or on mentally incapacitated adults.

---

[7]   Bogod, D, 'The Nazi Hypothermia Experiments: Forbidden Data?' (2004) 59 *Anaesthesia* 1155–1159.

[8]   See 'Permissible Medical Experiments' in *Trials of War Criminals before the Nuremberg Military Tribunals under Control Council Law No 10*, Vol 2, 181–182. This is widely reproduced elsewhere.

Development of the Declaration of Helsinki

The Nuremberg Code followed the trials and concentrated upon the need to protect the subjects of research and experimentation from abuse. While this is a major area of potential abuse it is far from the only area, weakening the utility of the Nuremberg Code. At the same time that it was being published medical associations around the world were getting together to form a new body – the World Medical Association (WMA) (see below) – and were discussing and publishing an agreed code of ethics meant to be applicable to all doctors.

This would lead after a long period of development and debate to the writing of the Declaration of Helsinki on research and experimentation on human subjects. The first version was eventually published in 1964.[9] This document establishes standards of research based upon the views of doctors. Over the next fifty years it was subject to many amendments and significantly extended. While it is wholly coherent with the Nuremberg Code it also considers matters such as the nature of valid consent, the standards that apply to ensuring that double-blind and placebo controlled trials are ethical, and the availability of any new treatment to research subjects once the trial has been completed. Matters such as the necessity for publishing results, so that they can be used by others and subjected to rigorous peer review are also included in the latest version, adopted in 2013 and published on the WMA website,[10] itself a completely new rewrite based on a process lasting several years and involving physicians, other health care professionals, research scientists and the public.

Establishment of the WMA

The WMA was established in 1947, after the Nuremberg trials, at least in part as a response to the abuses performed during the war by doctors. Its avowed intent was to ensure a high standard of ethics and medical education and training globally. Ethics remains a cornerstone of its work with a related commitment to human rights, especially where there is some medical involvement.

During World War II there had been a series of meetings in London of medical associations of the allied nations to consider problems in medical practice during peacetime and the state of medical education. As the Nuremberg trials progressed, the focus of discussions in the nascent Association also focused on the state of medical ethics, including education on this subject.

In the immediate post-war period it became clear that there were specific concerns that needed to be addressed, but the group of founders also believed it was important to work with all physicians, including those from countries that had been enemies during the war. In addition to addressing the issues of research and experimentation, the founders also considered the quality of medical education and training, recognising the inherent link between this and the ethical standards applying to medical practice.

The Association studied the adoption of ethical standards, associated with the swearing of an oath on qualification. Looking at examples submitted by members led to the development

---

9   For the text of the now superseded 1964 version of the Declaration see www.wma.net/wp-content/uploads/2018/07/DoH-Jun1964.pdf
10   See https://www.wma.net/policies-post/wma-declaration-of-helsinki-ethical-principles-for-med ical-research-involving-human-subjects/

of the International Code of Medical Ethics[11] at the 1949 Assembly. This took what members felt to be the best examples of oaths from around the world and was designed to be sworn at the time of qualifying as a physician, or of starting first employment.

The organisation itself is a grouping of physicians' associations from around the world. Member associations must be independent of their governments, represent physicians and should be the largest or otherwise pre-eminent association from their country. There is wide variety between the different member associations, with some being essentially regulatory bodies, some trades union, and others falling into areas in between, and they thus concentrate on different elements of the representation of physicians.

The founders of the WMA established a set of ethical principles, and eventually a series of codes, declarations and other guidance to all doctors. The aim was to ensure a global reach for its standard setting and to work with the medical associations within different countries to spread understanding of the standards and adherence to them.

WMA Codes

From its inception the World Medical Association (WMA) debated and adopted guidelines, declarations and codes that were meant to apply to all their member associations, and to their individual physician members. Given both the root cause of its foundation and its timing, it was inevitable that the first such piece of work was the development of the Declaration of Geneva with its synergistic International Code of Medical Ethics.

The WMA process is based upon an idea being initiated by a constituent member, and then debated and discussed by individual members before amendment and adoption first by the standing committees and council of the Association and then formally by the General Assembly of all members making it formal policy. This process can take less than a year or many years depending in part on the complexity of the issues involved, the general agreement already existing on those issues, and upon linguistic clarity and simplicity. All WMA documents are formally translated into all three of the Association's working languages (English, French and Spanish). These agreed translations are the formal, adopted versions of the documents and are all available on the WMA website.[12]

The Geneva Declaration
The Geneva Declaration is a simple declaration, essentially restating in more modern terms the basic tenets of the Hippocratic Oath, without those elements that were clearly inappropriate, such as the requirement not to cut for stone as mentioned above. The Declaration remained largely unchanged over decades until 2017 when a complete rewrite was agreed, again updating the language and ensuring that the basic concepts were expressed in a manner that reflected contemporary attitudes.[13]

The Geneva Declaration is far from the only ethical code established by the WMA, which has formulated specific agreements on many different matters. These include in addition to the Declaration of Helsinki mentioned above the Declarations of Tokyo, Hamburg and Malta.

---

[11]   For the text see https://www.wma.net/policies-post/wma-international-code-of-medical-ethics/
[12]   https://www.wma.net/; policies are listed alphabetically and by subject under the policy section.
[13]   See n 4 above.

It should be noted that major documents are often named after the cities in which the General Assembly that adopted them took place.

The Declaration of Tokyo

The WMA Declaration of Tokyo[14] constitutes guidelines for physicians concerning torture and other cruel, inhuman or degrading treatment or punishment in relation to detention and imprisonment. The current version was adopted in October 2016. This document dates originally from 1975 and reflects the WMA's concerns about the involvement of physicians in human rights abuses in relation to prisoners. At the time the majority of the reports came from Latin America but there was also concern in relation to the abuse of psychiatry in the Soviet Union and emerging concerns about the involvement of physicians in the management of hunger strikes in prisons around the world.

The Declaration opens by providing:

> 1. The physician shall not countenance, condone or participate in the practice of torture or other forms of cruel, inhuman or degrading procedures, whatever the offense of which the victim of such procedures is suspected, accused or guilty, and whatever the victim's beliefs or motives, and in all situations, including armed conflict and civil strife.

This makes it abundantly clear that the Tokyo Declaration adopts an absolutist view of physician involvement in abuses. It also provides that:

> 6. The physician shall not use or allow to be used, as far as he or she can, medical knowledge or skills, or health information specific to individuals, to facilitate or otherwise aid any interrogation, legal or illegal, of those individuals.

The Tokyo Declaration therefore is broad in the areas covered. It also specifically references both the Hamburg and the Malta Declarations with their additional details on the roles of physicians.

In 2001 a 'checking mechanism' was agreed so that the activities medical associations undertake to investigate allegations of medical involvement in torture within their countries could be listed.[15] It was recognised that National Medical Associations (NMAs) do not have the power to compel testimony and rarely have the wherewithal to carry out full investigations. But the policy expects them to do what they can to investigate, and to act to protect any members or non-members who seek to protect their patients against the use of cruel, inhuman and degrading treatment or torture. This is meant to encourage engagement at National Medical Associations with the concept of human rights, and engagement with supportive activities.

---

[14] For the text see https://www.wma.net/policies-post/wma-declaration-of-tokyo-guidelines-for-physicians-concerning-torture-and-other-cruel-inhuman-or-degrading-treatment-or-punishment-in-relation-to-detention-and-imprisonment/

[15] See WMA Recommendation on the Development of a Monitoring and Reporting Mechanism to Permit Audit of Adherence of States to the Declaration of Tokyo, October 2011, available at https://www.wma.net/policies-post/wma-recommendation-on-the-development-of-a-monitoring-and-reporting-mechanism-to-permit-audit-of-adherence-of-states-to-the-declaration-of-tokyo/

The Declaration of Hamburg

The WMA Declaration of Hamburg[16] concerning support for medical doctors refusing to participate in, or to condone, the use of torture and other cruel, inhuman or degrading treatment was adopted October 1997 and reaffirmed 2007 and 2017. This explicitly recognises the continued use of inhuman and degrading treatment around the world, and the pressures brought to bear on physicians to cooperate with these practices. It requires National Medical Associations to support physicians refusing to be involved and also calls upon its membership to support actions locally, regionally, nationally and internationally to support refusals to participate in torture and attempts to denounce such practices.

Amongst other clauses are the following:

5.1 To protest internationally against any involvement of, or any pressure to involve, physicians in acts of torture and or other forms of cruel, inhuman or degrading treatment or punishment;

5.2 To support and protect, and to call upon its constituent member NMAs to support and protect physicians who are resisting involvement in such inhuman procedures or who are documenting and reporting these procedures or who are working to treat and rehabilitate victims thereof, as well as to secure the right to uphold the highest ethical principles including medical confidentiality;

The essential elements in this part of the Declaration are the requirements that the medical associations themselves, representing their physician members, seek to protect those who are trying to protect their patients from abuse. It recognises that there is an inherent power in organisations and that this power can be used for public good.

The Declaration of Malta

The Malta Declaration (Declaration of Malta on Hunger Strikers, adopted 1991, current version revised 2017)[17] is extensively used around the world, especially by doctors and others from the International Committee of the Red Cross's detention medicine section. Hunger strikes are common around the world and physicians can protect those on hunger strike from being subject to torturous treatment. The response to hunger strikes is considered in more detail in the concluding section of this chapter as an example of the way in which the various issues which it addresses can combine to address torture and ill-treatment.

Resolution on Prohibition of Forced Anal Examinations

In addition to major documents of the type presented above, there are many others that either cover less major areas or relate less obviously to torture and inhuman and degrading treatment. One example that clearly relates closely to attempts to force doctors to engage in actions which fall squarely under such prohibited areas of activity is the WMA Resolution on Prohibition of Forced Anal Examinations to Substantiate Same-Sex Sexual Activity, adopted October 2017.[18] This reflects a growing awareness that in at least eight countries doctors were being asked to perform such examinations on the flawed premise that examination of anal sphincter

---

[16]   For the text see https://www.wma.net/policies-post/wma-declaration-of-hamburg-concerning-support-for-medical-doctors-refusing-to-participate-in-or-to-condone-the-use-of-torture-or-other-forms-of-cruel-inhuman-or-degrading-treatment/

[17]   For the text see https://www.wma.net/policies-post/wma-declaration-of-malta-on-hunger-strikers/

[18]   For the text see https://www.wma.net/policies-post/wma-resolution-on-prohibition-of-forced-anal-examinations-to-substantiate-same-sex-sexual-activity/

tone would identify those engaging in anal intercourse. In addition to the flawed science it was clear to the WMA that such examinations ignored the medical evidence that homosexuality is a normal variant of human sexuality and, if involving consenting partners above the legal age of consent, should never be criminalised.

Updates of Codes

The World Medical Association formally considers all policies on a rolling basis, so that currently documents are reviewed every 10 years. During this process they can be rescinded and archived, subject to minor or major revision, or simply reaffirmed. This process allows small changes to language – particularly reflecting the need to remain appropriate to current practice and linguistics.

Major rewrites can be based upon a change in understanding of the issues covered by the code, or by a change in the scientific or legal basis. WMA codes that relate primarily to public health need updating as the science of medicine changes and the epidemiology of a medical condition evolves or is altered by interventions. Changes to ethical codes more often reflect changes in the relevant legislation, including international humanitarian law and human rights law, or observed trends in the issues that the code was designed to manage.

For example, the Declaration of Tokyo establishes guidance for physicians working with the management of prisoners and relates particularly to preserving and protecting their human rights. While human rights are protected legally by the UN Declaration of Human Rights, the Tokyo Declaration establishes a set of principles under which the specific duties of physicians are made clear. From time to time this Declaration has been changed and updated reflecting conditions in different parts of the world. Challenges to the neutrality of physicians in conflict situations and to domestic laws seeking to involve physicians in the force feeding of detainees on hunger strike have required amendments to ensure these are clearly established and defined as unacceptable.

Another change to the Tokyo Declaration was the creation of the reporting mechanism, previously mentioned. This calls upon National Medical Associations made aware of breeches of human rights within their country to take action. Recognising that they have no legal or quasi-legal authority, the guidance requires NMAs to take such action as they can, including investigating complaints against individuals and seeking to ensure that physicians are not persuaded or coerced into unethical behaviours.

The UN Principles of Medical Ethics

In 1982 the UN General Assembly adopted the 'Principles of Medical Ethics relevant to the Role of Health Personnel, particularly Physicians, in the Protection of Prisoners and Detainees against Torture and Other Cruel, Inhuman or Degrading Treatment or Punishment'.[19] This short set of principles makes it clear that involvement in such practices is both a breach of ethics and of international human rights law. The Principles set out the importance of understanding that general medical knowledge as well as knowledge relating to an individual cannot ever be used to assist in interrogation, and that the certification of the 'fitness' of prisoners

---

[19]   See UN Doc UNGA Res 37/194, adopted 18 December 1982.

or detainees to undergo treatments or punishments that might affect their mental or physical health is also prohibited.

Breaches of Codes since 1948

Breaches of codes are common. Many countries continued to inflict corporal punishment – and under Shari'a law this continues today. Often physicians may be called upon to certify individuals fit for punishments such as flogging, to resuscitate them during the punishment or to deal with the aftermath – including of judicial amputations. All of these are clear breaches of the UN Principles and of WMA Codes. The on-going involvement of physicians in some countries in force feeding hunger strikers is another example which is considered further below, as is the certification by doctors of fitness for prolonged solitary confinement or of fitness for punishment. The commonest abuse is that of failing to act against conditions in prisons and other places of detention that endanger the life and health of the prisoner or detainee.

While ethical codes proscribing medical involvement in human rights abuses, independent of the law that has the same effect, are not new, the involvement of clinical professionals remains common. Some of the activities below are not only ethical breaches but also contrary to international human rights law.

For example, there is compelling evidence of the involvement of health care professionals in several areas of abuse at Guantanamo Bay. While the names of some so involved are known, the positioning of the prison off-shore and specific legal manoeuvres by the US government has so-far prevented effective legal or regulatory action against those involved. The "protection" offered by a legal advice issued in Washington DC that stated that enhanced interrogation was not torture may have reassured some participants, but legal advice never overrides ethical requirements.

More worryingly there is compelling evidence from many current and ex-prisoners that persons with health care training participated in so-called enhanced interrogation, specifically water-boarding. Interventions by such health care professionals led to the resuscitation of victims, or the, often temporary, suspension of the practice giving the prisoner time to recover.

The American Psychological Association (a membership body of psychologists) stated that its members could justifiably aid and assist in interrogations, using their professional knowledge and expertise. This led both to the use of detailed psychological knowledge and theory but also to the use of patient notes and specific psychological information in designing individual interrogation regimens. This is clearly in breach of ethical principles and has been condemned globally. As the UN Principles on Medical Ethics make clear:[20]

> It is a contravention of medical ethics for health personnel, particularly physicians:
> To apply their knowledge and skills in order to assist in the interrogation of prisoners and detainees in a manner that may adversely affect the physical or mental health or condition of such prisoners or detainees and which is not in accordance with the relevant international instruments …

Given that included at Principle 6 is the statement that there may be no derogation from the foregoing principles, the position of those advising psychologists is puzzling, and could be said to be encouraging and condoning unethical practice and probably also breach of law.

---

[20]   *Ibid*, Principle 4.

PATTERNS OF MEDICAL ABUSE

Medical involvement in human rights abuses falls into a number of categories. These include active involvement as perpetrators of torture, assisting torture perpetrated by others, for example by treating victims allowing them to be tortured again, devising torture methods to be used by others, covering up torture, for example by falsifying death certificates or by writing medical reports omitting mention of signs of torture, and by remaining silent in the community when seeing released detainees with signs and symptoms of torture. One final and important area of involvement can be failure to take note of or act on evidence of torture or of other systematised abuse.

There have been many reports, especially from South America, in the 1970s and 1980s of "men in white coats" being involved in the perpetration of torture. It was not always clear whether those wearing the white coats, or otherwise advising on the medical treatment of victims of torture, were actually physicians, or other health care professionals, but there can be little doubt that at least some were qualified health care professionals. It seems likely that they were engaged in the same process of malignant normalisation as the Nazi doctors examined by Lifton. The health professionals involved may not be physicians but nurses, psychologists, paramedics or others.

The activities of apparent physicians are varied. There have been cases where they would examine individuals who had been tortured or abused and provide some forms of first aid. In other cases it became clear that physicians were involved in designing forms of torture, either by using medical or other related knowledge, including specific medical information related to the detainee to aid abusers in designing and delivering the abuse. In some cases, such as Guantanamo Bay, health care professionals have provided specific medical information on detainees, helped to design forms of 'enhanced interrogation' (torture), assessed whether the detainees life is at risk from the interrogation – controlling the level of abuse, resuscitating detainees especially after so-called water-boarding, and force feeding hunger strikers. Each of these activities is a breach of ethical codes – many are also activities that are contrary to international human rights law. In the case of Guantanamo Bay, immunity from prosecution was granted by the federal government, and at least one professional association gave its blessing to involvement in enhanced interrogation.

Specific Circumstances of Medical Involvement as Abusers

The public Inquiry into the murder of Baha Mousa by the British military in Iraq during the second Gulf War considered evidence in relation to the recognition and reporting of that abuse by medical personnel. As with some trials around the world, the Inquiry made it clear that physicians were expected to consider the possibility of torture or of systematised abuse when they saw prisoners with bruises and other stigmata.

The Inquiry recommended that all those newly taken prisoner during war should be examined as soon as possible after first detention to detail obvious signs of prior injury. Where the prisoner refuses to be examined an external review should be undertaken and recorded. In the absence of qualified physicians another health care professional should undertake the documentation.

Evidence given to the tribunal relied upon World Medical Association documentation and codes to describe what should be expected of physicians involved in managing the prisoners.

Before the end of the Inquiry a meeting between military authorities and expert witnesses led to an agreed statement detailing the matters set out above, and the reissuing of the Ministry of Defence guidance to physicians on their roles relating to prisoners of war.

It was also emphasised that physicians should be expected to make regular visits to the places of detention to inspect the conditions in which prisoners were kept. This would give information that might be essential to an understanding of the possible and probable health consequences of detention, as well as make evidence of abuse clearer. Examples given in evidence related to the importance of regular inspections, including inspection to ensure that the living conditions of prisoners are conducive to good health, as well as looking for evidence of abuse.

Systematic Abuse of Psychiatry

In the mid-20th century reports began to emerge of Russian psychiatrists classifying those protesting against communism or the Soviet state as mentally ill. These "patients" were forced into treatment to change their behaviour and views, despite those views being political and not evidence of mental disease.

Some brave psychiatrists, such as Semyon Gluzman, refused to take part in this abuse of their profession and were themselves sent to Siberian Gulags. Information on the practice got out of Russia and the World Psychiatric Association condemned the practice that eventually dwindled. It should also be recognised that some of the psychiatrists active during the 1960–1990 era, and their pupils, continue to "recognise" sluggish schizophrenia and to regard any dissent from the majority view as a sign of mental impairment.[21]

Despite this success, doctors in many countries continue to act as instruments of the state and may follow political will rather than medical evidence. Attitudes to homosexuality in some countries have been supported by doctors, including psychiatrists, despite its removal from the Diagnostic Manual as "disease" and the more modern understanding of it as a normal variant of human sexuality. These attitudes allow for the continuation of "treatment regimes" intended to change the expressed sexuality of people, and may support public and political hostility. Treatment for something that is not a disease or other medical abnormality is a clear breach of ethical standards.

SPECIFIC EXAMPLES OF MEDICAL INVOLVEMENT AS PROTECTORS

Wendy Orr was a young District Surgeon in Port Elizabeth in the Eastern Cape in 1985, after the death and related legal cases following the death of Steve Biko. Examining newly admitted prisoners she recognised the signs of recent abuse on almost every new inmate, all giving the same cause – abuse by the police. In seeking to report these findings and stopping the abuse Dr Orr faced a complete lack of support from her senior colleagues and her medical association. Support that was forthcoming included from doctors in other countries. Despite the lack of local support, she took a principled stand and eventually went to the Supreme Court for an

---

[21] "Sluggish schizophrenia" is not recognised by most psychiatrists. It was used in the Soviet era to classify political dissidents as mentally ill.

interdict against the abuse. While this led to a dramatic reduction in abuses against prisoners it also led to Dr Orr being sidelined and marginalised, and to her changing the direction of her medical career. She had graphically proven that one person of courage can make a difference; despite working in a notorious centre, she produced a dramatic change. But her conclusions included the need for an organisational support network, and for better education of young physicians so that they are more aware of the ethical challenges they may face.

For decades the Turkish Medical Association (TMA), often working with the Human Rights Foundation in Turkey, have resisted abuses of human rights. They have campaigned for a torture-free society, and supported prisoners demonstrating signs of abuse upon release from detention. While taking this principled stand the Association itself, its officers and the active members taking part in this work have been threatened and often charged with crimes. Aiding and assisting the ill, even as physicians caring for sick and injured people, the TMA has found the state classifying its action as crimes, effectively of giving aid to enemies of the state.

At a meeting in Izmir to discuss the advantages and disadvantages of a potential move towards small cell incarceration (holding prisoners in individual cells as opposed to large group cells) the "secret" police arrived to record speakers on film. The meeting could not start to preserve the safety of those wishing to take part. Only the arrival of a BBC film crew (notified of the event by a speaker) led to the departure of the police and the meeting being able to proceed. This was a minor example of coercion and intimidation.

More recently, rendering first aid or help to the injured without a prior permit has been criminalised so that physicians aiding the injured after public protests have been arrested. Trials of senior physicians have been a running sore in Turkey for a number of decades, but the TMA continues to provide help, support and documentation of injuries to all, including those harmed by the state. When doctors are brought to trial, international observers from the World Medical Association and its members ensure that local authorities are in no doubt as to the support the doctors have.

Prison Doctors

Prison doctors around the world continue to see evidence of human rights abuses. Reporting these abuses is an important element of improving human rights and of the move to end torture. It is frequently rejected by the authorities – for example, in a case in Barlinnie Prison in Glasgow, Scotland, in the 1990s, the first response of the prison management was to dismiss the doctor's concerns, and it was only persistence in the face of harassment that led to a full investigation and charges being brought against abusive prison guards.

The International Committee of the Red Cross (ICRC) seeks to ensure that prison doctors are aware of their duties in respect of human rights generally, and of the management of hunger strikers particularly. They also teach about more general issues such as public health in prisons and matters such as not certifying individuals fit for punishment, or for solitary confinement.

It is clear that in many countries a career in prison medicine is regarded as having a low professional status. Committed and caring physicians practising in this environment may receive little support from their medical associations, who are often ignorant of the difficulties being faced.

In one ICRC conference offering instruction to such physicians this author was told by a group of prison doctors that they faced assault and even murder by the prison guards if they acted in the interests of prisoners who were being systematically abused, and assault and murder by prisoners for failing to support them. They felt that their medical association offered little support.

In other countries the abuses that are perpetrated include prolonged solitary confinement, punishment beatings, reduced food offerings, force feeding of hunger strikers, forms of corporal punishment and the death penalty.

In some prisons conditions are conducive to illness; this may follow malnourishment or environmental conditions that lead to the spread of infectious disease. The ability of prison doctors to take action on these elements of abuse may be significant in limiting the harm to prisoners. The awareness of prison physicians of the conditions prevalent within the prisons remains an ethical requirement.

Letter Writing and Other Action

The majority of medical associations around the world have limited staff and other resources. They find taking coordinated action difficult and may find their members under threat. One common example is when physicians who offer help, including first aid and more complex medical support, to those injured during political protests are then charged with aiding and abetting the rebel or protest groups. These physicians are following the Hippocratic tradition and helping those in need, and then need support themselves.

The international medical community has undertaken a number of supportive initiatives in relation to physicians under threat. These are based upon letter writing to the government of the country, associated with letters for publication in the international and national media.

These campaigns are based upon compelling evidence, usually from at least two sources, and spell out the role of physicians in difficult circumstances. After the so-called Arab Spring, physicians in Bahrain were imprisoned and subjected to military trials with inadequate opportunities to be properly represented. A campaign involving, amongst others, the World Medical Association and the British Medical Association led to retrials and the freeing of the majority of the physicians originally sentenced to imprisonment.

While such letter-writing campaigns are generally low in risk to those outside the country the writers may find themselves threatened, harassed and subject to some attempts at intimidation. The success of the campaigns makes their continuation inevitable; and the active associations are gradually increasing in number.

Observation of trials, as in Turkey, is part of the same process. The WMA policy development process has also contributed by producing either brief immediate Emergency Resolutions or more formally debated Declarations and Statements that cover the issues that have led to the targeting of physicians. These WMA policies make it clear that their actions relate to the ethical duties that bind all physicians.

HUNGER STRIKES: A CONCLUDING EXAMPLE

The involvement of physicians in human rights abuses can be the subject of domestic legislation. The commonest example in recent years has been the requirement on physicians to intervene in hunger strikes by force feeding those on such strikes.

The WMA is quite clear that force feeding is never acceptable. Its position is based upon both fundamental ethical principles and upon an understanding of the medical implications of such feeding. As has been seen, force feeding is mentioned in the Tokyo Declaration and the Malta Declaration. This last declaration was written after the hunger strikes in the Maze prison in Northern Ireland and has been updated adding in information gleaned from other examples globally. Most recently there was a major rewrite, reflecting common patterns of hunger strikes and of government responses to them.

Governments seeking to legitimise force feeding often do so on the basis that these are attempts at suicide that may be itself criminalised. Aiding and abetting a suicide may be a criminal activity, even when suicide itself has been decriminalised. In addition, suicide may be condemned by religious views and therefore its avoidance or prevention considered especially important within theocracies. The reality is that hunger strikes are not an attempt at suicide; they are an attempt to take the only action that may be open to prisoners and detainees to protest or to achieve change. While those undertaking them accept the risk of death or permanent incapacity it is not one of the reasons for their action.

The physicians working in the Detainee Health Unit of the International Committee of the Red Cross have the widest possible experience of hunger strikes and have been important collaborators for those editing the Malta Declaration. They have used the Declaration in a wide variety of countries. They have also provided support for physicians resisting involvement – working for example with the Israel Medical Association in its principled opposition to a new law that would have required physicians to force feed hunger strikers to prevent them from dying due to the effects of the hunger strike. At the same time the ICRC teaches medical associations, Ministries of Justice and of Home Affairs, and prison doctors and management, about the rules that apply to the management of hunger strikes by doctors.

The history of hunger strikes, and of the force feeding associated with them goes back over a hundred years. The well-documented cases of members of the womens' suffrage movement who were force fed in the early years of the 20th century demonstrate clearly that this is a painful "treatment" and that it can be lethal. Both remain true in the 21st century.

Hunger strikes are common globally. Strikes can be by one individual protesting his/her prison conditions or some other matter related to their detention or may be organised by a group of prisoners with similar aims and intentions. Teaching by the ICRC, based upon their experience in many different countries, makes it clear that detainees do not want to die, they are not committing suicide, but are taking action in one of the few areas open to them. The issues that they use hunger strikes to protest about could include prison conditions that amount to cruel and inhuman treatment, or the presence of routine torture.

Recent examples include the force feeding of prisoners in the US prison in Guantanamo Bay. It is clear that health care professionals were involved in the establishment of the force-feeding regime at the prison, at least in training custody officers to pass nasogastric feeding tubes and devising feeding regimens.[22] Both of these actions are a breach of the Declarations of Tokyo and of Malta and of the UN Principles. As with other mass protests, including the Maze protests of the 1970s, these are actions carried out by detainees who feel they have no other route to achieving a change to their living and detention conditions, or to achieving some sort of recognition of their grievances, including protests about unfair or arbitrary detention.

It is clear that force feeding is the imposition of a so-called medical treatment without the consent of the individual – itself a major breach of medical ethics. The discomfort, often

---

[22]   The standard operating procedures for force feeding at Guantanamo Bay can be accessed at https://www.documentcloud.org/documents/4106101-Gitmo-force-feeding-2013-standard-operating.html

amounting to severe pain, fits this so-called treatment into at the very least inhumane treatment and in the view of most observers, to torture. In Guantanamo Bay prisoners were strapped into specially designed restraint chairs, demonstrating an institutionalised and systematised approach to this abusive treatment in addition to reinforcing the, at least, painful and humiliating nature of the process.

While hunger strikes occur on a regular basis in prisons around the world, on occasion they become systematic and pervasive. At the time of writing this is clearly the case in Israel, where Israeli Arabs have been undertaking hunger strikes in large numbers. This led to the Israeli government passing a law to require doctors to force feed these prisoners when the hunger strike had proceeded for certain a period of time. The Israel Medical Association (IMA) took a principled stand and opposed this law, and publically told its members to refuse to take part in these actions. This has effectively stopped the law from being effective, keeping doctors working in line with the provisions of the Declaration of Malta. The IMA was supported in this resistance by the ICRC Health in Detention team.

Physicians involved in this process are breaching ethical codes; but not all health care professionals feel they are bound by such codes. Some will use this as an excuse for participating in unethical treatment, others may feel that having not sworn an ethical code enables them to participate in matters that are condemned by such codes. In practice courts, tribunals and related bodies have generally found that medical ethics applies equally to all regardless of whether they have or have not sworn to uphold such principles.

19. Torture methods and their health impact

José Quiroga and Jens Modvig

INTRODUCTION

Torture involves the infliction of severe pain or suffering on another human being. This can obviously be obtained by means of numerous different techniques, and the range of methods of torture developed by perpetrators from ancient to modern times is enormous and varies according to region and country. To facilitate an overview of torture methods, different ways of categorization have been used. This chapter describes the most common health consequences associated with torture in general as well as with some specific categories of torture methods.

Categorization of Torture Methods

Torture methods may be categorized based on different criteria: (1) the tools or instruments used to inflict pain or suffering (e.g. picana electrode, beatings with cables or batons, cigarette burns, musical torture); (2) the mechanism for the infliction of pain or suffering (e.g. systematic beatings, suspension, asphyxiation or threats of execution); (3) the name ('nick-name') of the torture method (e.g. 'submarino', the 'grilled chicken', the 'baby elephant' or the 'parrot perch'); (4) the anatomic location of the torture (e.g. dental torture, pulling out of nails); and (5) the pathological injury created (blunt trauma, crush lesion, fracture).

Several categorizations of torture methods can be found: during the dictatorship of Augusto Pinochet, the network of information of human rights organizations of Chile developed a thesaurus of methods of torture (FASIC, 1988) which comprises 17 categories. The Istanbul Protocol system describes eight categories of torture methods, and Huridocs has developed the most complete thesaurus of methods, which is used worldwide (Dueck and Guzman, 2001) and comprises 33 categories of torture methods.

The categorization used in this chapter is based on the mechanical ways of inflicting pain and suffering, that is, a modified version of the system of the Istanbul Protocol, which comprises:

- Beatings
- Suspension
- Positional torture
- Electrical torture
- Asphyxiation
- Stabs, cuts, bites and amputations
- Burns, freezes, corrosion
- Exposure to infectious and infesting agents
- Forced ingestion, infusion or injection
- Sexual torture

- Deprivation
- Humiliations
- Threats

BEATINGS

Unsystematic Beatings

Beatings can be both unsystematic or systematic (focused). In unsystematic beatings, perpetrators slap, kick or punch all over the prisoner's body during detention and interrogation. To inflict more pain the perpetrator may use rifle butts, whips, straps or heavy wooden, metal or plastic sticks, stones, etc. To avoid skin marks, perpetrators might use sandbags, or beat a person whilst they are wearing some clothes. Beatings are often manifested by injuries to the skin. The skin is the first protective barrier against physical torture taking the form of mechanical injuries such as beatings, chemical hazards and exposure to extreme heat or cold. When an injury resulting from a torture method extends through the epidermis, such as cuts, lacerations, or second or third degree burns to the dermis, bleeding occurs, and an inflammatory response will begin. Most often, a scar will result from the injury.

Acute skin lesions after beatings

Abrasions happen when the epidermis of the detainee's skin is scraped off as a result of rubbing against a rough surface. Abrasions can occur when the victim has fallen or has been pushed against a rough surface such as a rock or a concrete wall. They can be very painful because sensitive nerve endings are involved.

Bruises are patches of discolored skin areas caused by broken blood vessels that bleed into the tissue under the skin. They appear as black, blue and red patches and change color during the healing process to green, then later to yellow. The skin will look normal after a week or two, depending on the extent of the bruising. Frequently, the shape of the bruise follows the contour of the instrument used, for instance, a chain, a belt, or the sole of the military boot on the back of the detainee when they jump on the backs of victims. *Tramline bruises* (two parallel lines of bruises) with normal skin in between them are the typical shape of bruises resulting from being hit by cylindrical objects such as a police baton, a stick or a cable.

Hematoma is a collection of blood caused by the rupture of a venous or arterial blood vessel bleeding into surrounding tissue or body cavity as a result of a severe trauma such as having been beaten with any type of instrument. If a hematoma is superficial in subcutaneous tissue, it will be visible as a red or blue colored tender mass. A deeper intramuscular hematoma may be visible and palpable during a physical examination as a tender mass. Most hematomas resolve spontaneously over time. Surgical removal or evacuation (drainage) of the blood in a hematoma may be undertaken, depending on the symptoms or its location.

Lacerations are skin lesions caused by tissue tearing. They may develop when a blunt object is applied with force against a bony segment of a victim's the body. The skin-tearing may be deep with irregular borders and may require stitches. Lacerations – contrary to abrasions and bruises – often leave scars which may last for years.

Chronic skin lesions after beatings

Scars are fibrous tissue resulting from the natural repair of skin wounds. Scars are formed when the healing process exceeds 3–4 weeks, whereas wounds which heal quickly may leave the skin unchanged. The fibrous scar tissue which replaces the original skin tissue does not contain hair or sweat glands. If scars appear in the scalp area of the head, hairless areas will result (cicatricial alopecia).

Post-inflammatory hyperpigmentation may develop after beatings. The color of the human skin depends on the distribution of melanin pigment. An inflammatory response of the skin, for instance after beatings or other injury, may increase melanization and hyperpigmentation of the inflamed area. The hyperpigmented area follows the original inflammatory response. Such skin lesions can help in the assessment of torture months or even years after the traumatic event (Peel, 2003).

Fractures

Forceful beatings may result in bone fractures. Unless the fracture is severely dislocated, it will heal itself after a number of weeks or months, leaving no evidence. However, diagnostic imaging including bone scintigraphy (the use of radioisotopes to detect inflammatory processes) may identify late bone healing processes resulting from fractures (Ozkalipci et al., 2013).

Traumatic head and brain injuries

Severe blunt force trauma to the head, such as being struck with a baton, hammer or rock or kicked on the head, can cause damage to the head and the brain (traumatic brain injury/ TBI). Such damage can be focal, confined to one area of the brain, or diffuse, involving more than one area (National Institute of Neurological Disorders and Stroke, 2015). Concussion is the most common and most frequent type of traumatic head injury (THI), resulting in a loss of consciousness for a short period. A severe injury could fracture the bone. The author (Dr Quiroga) has seen cracks or breaks in the external surface of the skull, and also victims with epidural (above the epidural membrane) and subdural (below the epidural membrane) hematomas resulting from THI. Some victims develop epileptic seizures as well as dementia.

Keatley et al. (2013) studied self-reported torture among 488 refugees being treated in a center in the USA and found that 335 people (69%) reported suffering a blow to the head, 185 (55%) of whom also reported loss of consciousness (LOC). The high rates of head injury and LOC indicate the need for the further study of TBI.

There are also psychiatric effects: from a self-reported sample of 967 Cambodian refugees living in a Thai refugee camp, THI comprised 4 percent of total traumatic events and there was a strong association with depression and PTSD (Mollica et al., 2002). Out of a community sample of 337 South Vietnamese former political detainees, 90.6 percent were also found to have THI. This compared to a rate of 3.6 percent of a sample of 82 South Vietnamese non-detainees who had had some trauma event but not THI. Depression and PTSD were also higher in the former detainee cohort (40.9% vs 23.2% and 13.4% vs 0% respectively) (Mollica et al., 2014). A sample of 42 South Vietnamese political detainees with head injuries were also studied by magnetic resonance imaging. They showed a high rate of depression. Cortical thickness measurements showed thinning in left prefrontal and temporal cortical regions. The left and right amygdala volume was smaller in the severe trauma group. Pre-frontotemporal deficit may affect higher cortical functions including judgment, memory and emotional regulation (Mollica, 2009).

Rhabdomyolysis and renal failure
A severe complication resulting from beating (and other torture methods such as suspension) is the destruction of muscle tissue (rhabdomyolysis). Myoglobin is a protein component of the muscle cells which – when muscle tissue is destroyed – is released into the blood. When the myoglobin in the blood is filtrated in the kidneys it may cause acute renal failure, possibly leading to death.

Rhabdomyolysis resulting from torture has been well documented in India. Malik gave medical care to 34 victims who presented acute renal failure secondary to rhabdomyolysis due to severe beatings involving muscles. These victims would all have died without emergency dialysis and, despite their treatment, five did so, a lethality of 15 percent (Malik et al., 1993; Malik et al., 1995). Two other victims with similar medical problems were diagnosed in Israel (Bloom et al., 1995). A fatal case of rhabdomyolysis resulting from Palestinian hanging (for which see below) was reported due to extensive necrosis of the pectoralis major, biceps and deltoid muscles and glenohumeral joint hemorrhage (Pollanen, 2016). A diagnosis of rhabdomyolysis is confirmed by detecting elevated muscle enzymes including creatinine kinase in a blood sample test.

Dental injuries
According to the findings of the study by Arge, Hansen and Lynnerup (2014), the most frequent injuries were teeth which had been damaged and then later extracted, teeth that had been fractured and, less frequently, jaw fractures, discoloration or sensitive teeth. Most dental injuries were the result of the victim being beaten or kicked all over their bodies, including their heads and faces. Only the extraction of teeth with pliers without anesthesia could be considered direct dental torture. The forensic evaluation concluded that all cases were consistent with the method of torture described by the victim (Arge et al., 2014).

Peripheral neuropathies
Moreno and Grodin (2002) reviewed the neurological sequelae of torture. For example, beatings (especially blunt trauma), the most common form of physical torture, and crushing may produce intracranial and spinal cord bleeding, intracranial edema, CSF fistulas and seizures. Shaking may cause retinal and subdural hemorrhages and axonal injury. Bone fractures may affect peripheral nerves, whilst gunshots and stab wounds may destroy a large amount of nerve tissue. The authors found that seizures following head trauma were associated with brain lesions, such as subdural and intracranial hemorrhages, and intracranial edema. Cervical spine fractures with spinal cord compression may result in quadriplegia.

Specific Types of Systematic Beatings

Systematic beatings are focused, that is, they involve repeated beatings on the same part of the body in order to increase pain. As described in the following paragraphs, this may occur on the ears, the soles of the feet, the buttocks or any other part of the body.

'Telephone'

'Telephone' is the nickname used for simultaneous repeated beatings on both ears. Ruth Sinding (1999) reviewed her experience with 63 torture survivors who had been referred to ear, nose and throat specialists because of their symptoms, the most common of which were tinnitus (75%), decreased hearing (46%), impaired air passage through the nose (41), and dizziness (40%). There was a significant association between 'telephone' torture and tinnitus.

Falanga

Falanga (also known as falaka or bastinado) refers to beatings on the soles of the feet with a wooden, plastic or metallic baton or any form of blunt instrument. It is one of the few methods of torture where the health consequences have been studied extensively.

Victims complain of chronic, dull, cramping pain, which intensifies with weight-bearing and muscle activity in the soles of the feet and lower extremities. They also experience a burning, stinging pain. Structural changes show a flat, wide heel, reduced elasticity and thickening of the fascia plantaris at examination (plantar fasciitis). The pain and sensory dysfunction in the feet and lower legs are related to neuropathic changes (Prip and Persson, 2008; Prip et al., 2012; Amris et al., 2009). A case-control study was conducted using magnetic resonance of the foot, showing a significant thickness in the central portion of the plantar aponeurosis (Savnik et al., 2000).

Other types of beatings

In some countries individuals are executed by *stoning* to death (lapidation), usually carried out by a group and often implemented as a punishment for adultery. This can be considered as a form of beating.

Shaking involves grabbing the clothing or grasping the shoulder of the detainee and a severe, rapid and repetitive backward and forward movement of the head. Shaking produces an angular acceleration and deceleration of the head. The Shin Bet or General Security Service (GSS) in Israel had special permits authorizing the use of shaking during the interrogation of detainees. Abd Al-Samad Harizat died in official custody after being interrogated and tortured by shaking on several occasions until he lost consciousness. The autopsy showed bruising of the upper chest and shoulders, with the cause of death being a marked edema (swelling) of the brain, as well as a right parietal subdural hematoma (Physicians for Human Rights, 1995).

SUSPENSION

Suspension involves hanging the victim by the hands, feet, shoulders or even fingers in order to make the bodyweight create pain by pulling the limbs. Historically, suspension has been a frequently used method of torture that has been documented at least since the time of the Spanish Inquisition, through the two world wars, including times of genocide and in Nazi concentration camps, and continues today. Several distinct methods have been documented. Suspension is almost always combined with other psychological and physical methods of torture, mostly beatings (Rejali, 2007; Peel and Iacopino, 2002).

Specific Types of Suspension

Palestinian hanging, also called *reverse hanging* or *strappado*, means that the victim's hands are tied together behind his or her back, and the individual is then raised from the ground by their wrists with a rope. The rope may be abruptly released causing a painful jerk. Palestinian hanging produces immediate and severe pain due to the overstretching of the major muscles and frequent dislocation of the shoulder joints. Fractures of the shoulder due to prolonged hanging are possible as well as damage to the brachial nerve plexus, causing permanent neurological symptoms (sensory or motor dysfunctions in the arms).

Crucifixion is a mode of suspension, where the arms are abducted and tied to a horizontal bar.

Reverse hanging or *upside-down hanging* was commonly employed in Japan during the 17th century. The victim is hung upside down by the feet, causing blood to flow to the head. Prolonged suspension in this manner can result in loss of consciousness or even death.

Horseman is suspension, where a naked prisoner with their arms tied behind their back is straddling a long horizontal metallic bar with his feet in the air (Rejali, 2007). Amnesty International has published photographs of prisoners from Uruguay in this position.

The parrot perch or *poulet roti* ('grilled chicken') – names originating from Brazil and Northern Africa, respectively – is a suspension where the wrists are tied, knees are put between the arms, and a stick is put through the knees.

As with Palestinian hanging, these other forms of suspension may induce damage to peripheral nerves and dislocation of joints. Peripheral neuropathies in arms have been documented in prisoners who have been suspended by their arms during disciplinary punishment in jails. A winged scapula, a consequence of a brachial plexus injury, was found in a torture survivor who was suspended by the arms (Moreno and Grodin, 2002; Pollanen, 2016).

POSITIONAL TORTURE

Positional torture restrains movement in different manners. These methods are generally intended to initially produce pain but leave few or no physical marks. The body positions imposed on the detainees concentrates their weight on a few muscles creating an intense demand on those parts of the body. For example, victims may be forced to squat while having a board tied between their arms behind them. The pain is derived from muscle fatigue. Stress positions are often used in combination with other enhanced interrogation techniques.

Specific Types of Positional Torture

The 'banana' is intended to inflict pain on the detainee by hyperextension of the spine backwards towards the floor while his or her weight is held up by a backless chair. The feet and arms are bound together beneath the chair. The position is maintained for extended periods of time.

In *forced standing (plantón* in Latin America), the tortured individual is compelled to stand on a single foot or on both feet without moving for several hours to days. A small circle is drawn with chalk around the victim who is beaten if they move beyond the marked area. Prisoners during the Uruguayan dictatorship were tortured in this manner and were often not allowed bathroom breaks, forcing them to urinate and defecate on themselves. Forced standing, including *wall standing* as described in Box 19.1 below, may be combined with other torture methods, such as hooding and electrical torture.

Long-term standing may lead to lower limb tenderness and erythema, in addition to an ascending edema, which may reflect progressive cellulitis or venous thrombosis.

BOX 19.1 CIA GUIDELINES FOR STRESS POSITIONS

Stress positionings are detailed in the Central Intelligence Agency's (CIA) manuals as part of enhanced interrogation techniques and used during the interrogation of suspected terrorists (JFT GTMO, 2002). The authorized positions are the following:

(1) Head rest/index finger position – Detainee is placed with forehead or fingers against the wall, then the detainee's legs are backed out to the point that the detainee's leaning weight is brought to bear on fingers or head.
(2) Kneeling position – Administered by placing detainee on knees and having him lean backward on heels and hold hands extended to the sides or front, palms upward. Light weights such as small rocks, may be placed in the detainee's upturned palms. The detainee will not be placed in a position facing the sun or floodlights
(3) Worship-the-Gods – The detainee is placed on knees with head and torso arched back, with arms either folded across the chest or extended to the side or front. The detainee will not be placed in a position facing the sun or floodlights.
(4) Sitting position – The detainee is placed with his back against a wall, tree or post; thighs are horizontal, lower legs are vertical with feet flat on floor or ground as though sitting in a chair. Arms may be extended to sides horizontally, palms up and boots on.
(5) Standing position – While standing, the detainee is required to extend arms either to the sides or front with palms up. Light weights such as small rocks may be placed in upturned palms. The Standing position is allowed by CIA guidelines for up to 48 hours.

In *cramped confinement (confinement boxes* – sometimes called the 'tortoise'), the victims are placed in a confined space intended to limit the individual's movement. Detainees are placed in boxes of limited dimensions, specifically constructed for this purpose. These confined spaces are usually without light, thus producing sensory deprivation.

Physical Restraints

Methods of physical restraints include those which can be used lawfully by the police and other law enforcement agencies (for example, handcuffs and placement in *total appendage restraint position (TARP)*). The use of such methods may, however, be excessive and, if so, their use may be considered ill-treatment or even torture. Other means of legitimate restraint can be a violation of international standards when used for the purposes of punishment, for instance, *shackling*. Shackling is used on the ankles of a prisoner to restrict walking and to prevent running and physical resistance. Such restraints are often used in conjunction with stress positions and sleep deprivation.

Handcuff neuropathy

There is usually policy guidance concerning the use of handcuffs and other forms of restraint during detention and arrest. Metallic, nylon or plastic cuffs may be used only to restrain a person's hands and only for as long as is reasonably necessary to ensure the safety of the detaining officers or others. Metallic handcuffs should be double locked to prevent tightening. Most handcuffs should be applied with hands behind the person's back.

If handcuffs are overtight for prolonged periods, they can cause significant local damage, such as acute superficial abrasions, lacerations or chronic scars. Superficial handcuff radial neuropathy is most common, but it can also affect the median and ulnar nerves (Scott et al., 1989; Haddad et al., 1999; Cook, 1993).

Eight cases of tight handcuffing were presented at a poster session during the Torture Symposium of the International Rehabilitation Council for Torture Victims (IRCT) in Mexico in 2016. The victims complained of shoulder and wrist pain and numbness of fingers. Neuropathy was documented with electromyography (Dokudan et al., 2016).

Interrogation chairs

Interrogation chairs – sometimes called *tiger chairs* – are used in China for interrogating those suspected of criminal offences. The metal chairs are fixed to the floor and have straps to restrain the legs and hands.

ELECTRIC TORTURE

The application of electricity to sensitive parts of the body is a frequently used torture method. The injury depends on the voltage, the current and the tissue involved. Due to resistance of the tissue, the energy will produce heat, which again will cause electrothermal burn injury. The current may produce acute lesions and, depending on instrument and voltage, these may appear as reddish areas following the route of the current (Danielsen and Rasmussen, 2006). Chronic lesions will reflect the tissue necrosis and scar healing, often appearing as pale, well-demarcated scars (Pollanen, 2018).

Specific Methods of Electrical Torture

A Picana or *parrilla* is a hand-cranked magneto generator. A picture of this machine was first published in a Turkish newspaper called *Democrat* in May 1980 and was reproduced by Amnesty International (Amnesty International, 1984). The victim is lying down on his back over a metal bed frame. The electric current is applied using an electric wire from a generator. The typical electric injury is a burn crust 1–5 mm round. This lesion is the entrance of the electric current.

Electrical discharge weapons (stun guns and taser guns) can legally be used by law enforcement agencies in many countries. These weapons deliver a series of electrical pulses intended to temporarily incapacitate subjects through infliction of pain and involuntary muscle contractions. The electrical energy can be delivered either through direct contact ('drive-stun') or through metal probes fired from a distance of up to 10 meters delivering electricity through two wires.

Electric dental torture comprises any stimulus in the crown of a tooth, such as cold, heat or electricity, that is strong enough to trigger a nervous response that will produce pain. The sensitive part of a tooth is the pulp. Dentists themselves practiced dental torture during the Pinochet dictatorship in Chile in 1973, involving the application of electrical currents in the first premolar of the mandible, producing severe throbbing pains, acute inflammation of the pulp and damage to the enamel and dentine of the tooth, resulting in the need for extraction (Abd-Elmeguid, 2009; Arge et al., 2014).

ASPHYXIATION

Asphyxiation is defined as the deprivation of oxygen, either partial (hypoxia) or total (anoxia). It is a brutal torture method because the victim experiences an intense sensation of panic because of the imminence of death. The torturer can cut off the victim's oxygen supply in a number of different ways. Some of the more common methods will be discussed below.

Dry Submarine

In this method, a plastic bag is placed over the victim's head and is tied around the neck. Air cannot penetrate and the victim experiences hypoxia or anoxia until the bag is removed or the individual passes out. Another variation of this torture method is to use a textile bag containing an irritant powder such as chili or lime (calcium oxide). The perpetrator interrupts the victim's breathing by taping the mouth and manually clasping the nose of the victim. Once allowed to breath after prolonged asphyxiation, the victim takes a deep inspiration often inhaling a substantial amount of powder resulting in severe inflammation of the mucous membranes of nose, throat and bronchial system.

Wet Submarine

This method involves forcibly immersing the head of the victim in a container filled with water, urine or sometimes feces. The victim is allowed to breathe air only after struggling to avoid aspirating liquid into the lungs or drowning. A variation of this method is to restrain the victim by the ankles and repeatedly plunge them into a barrel or large container full of water or other liquid. This technique requires several offenders and/or specialized equipment (UN OHCHR, 2001; Peel and Iacopino, 2002).

Waterboarding

Waterboarding involves binding the victim to a bench with their feet elevated above their head. The victim's head is immobilized, and a cloth is placed over the detainee's mouth and nose while water is poured onto the cloth in a controlled manner. Airflow is restricted for 20 to 40 seconds. The technique produces the sensation of drowning and suffocation (Central Intelligence Agency, 2004a). The CIA's Office of Medical Services (OMS) Guidelines authorized a maximum of six applications per session, with a maximum of two sessions per day, and five sessions per months, and required that a physician should be present (OMS Guidelines, 2004).

Strangulation

Strangulation is the compression of the neck by a ligature, with or without suspension of the victim. The neck's constriction can also be accomplished by the perpetrator applying hand or arm pressure over the neck. This technique produces a reduction, or a complete stoppage, of air movement past the trachea, as well as a reduction of blood flow through the carotid arteries to the brain. If the anoxia persists beyond three to four minutes brain damage is permanent. The victims can also die of anoxia. Traumatic bruising (ecchymosis in the skin of the neck as well as hemorrhages of the neck muscles) and pharyngeal and laryngeal cartilage fractures are common findings in strangulation victims (Rao, n.d.; Beal and Martin, 1998).

Head Restraining or Chokeholds

In these maneuvers, the forearm of the offender is placed across the front of the subject's neck while positioned behind the victim. The procedure is used to subdue a person and prevent any physical resistance or aggression, including harming themselves or others. The procedure can be applied while in standing, kneeling or in the prone position. There are two types of choke-holds employed. A vascular or *blood choke*, known as the *carotid sleeper*, applies bilateral pressure over the carotid arteries on the neck. This pressure is accomplished by firmly gripping the neck from behind with the arm flexed in a v-shape. Force from the forearm and arm results in bilateral compression of the carotid arteries, its baroreceptors and the jugular veins of the neck, leading to a decrease in blood circulation to the brain and possible loss of consciousness.

The second type of neck restraint is a respiratory or *air choke*. In this form of chokehold, mechanical compression of the anterior structures of the neck impede airflow to the lungs. In this method, the perpetrator collapses the airway by placing his/her forearm across the neck of the victim while positioned behind. More pressure is generated by pulling back on the arm with the free hand. Chokeholds are very dangerous procedures and have caused many deaths. For this reason, chokeholds have been outlawed in many jurisdictions in the US for use by the police (Baker and Goodman, 2015; Panzar, 2014; Peel and Iacopino, 2002; UN OHCHR, 2001).

STABS, CUTS, BITES AND AMPUTATIONS

The use of sharp instruments such as knifes, bayonets, swords, daggers, machetes, razors, pieces of broken glass and scissors to inflict skin cuts has been a common method of torture throughout history. The sharp instrument can be a single or a doubled edged blade. Inflicted lacerations, flesh wounds and stab injuries are frequent methods of torture. The incised wounds can be produced in any part of the body but are most commonly found on the face, scalp, neck, arms and hands of the victims. The effects that these wounds produce an immediate painful impact and, may also cause frequent long-lasting disfigurement and psychological trauma to the victim.

Stab, Penetrating, or Puncture Wounds

Stab wounds are penetrating injuries that are characteristically deeper than they are wide. Stab wounds are usually produced with sharp pointed instruments such as a knife that penetrates the skin and underlying tissue. Careful wound examinations that includes measurements of the size, depth, angle and location are helpful in determining forensic evidence. Most fatal wounds involve the left chest area and often affect the heart and the great vessels. Suturing and other more extensive examinations like exploratory laparotomies may be necessary when appropriately evaluating a stabbing victim.

Puncture wounds are generally small. The instrument used is usually slender sharp instrument like an ice pick that penetrates the skin and underlying tissue. The wounds are often deep and may involve a variety of vital organs and body spaces like the thorax and abdomen. The visible bleeding may be deceptively small. Other times, the wound may bleed profusely, requiring compression, vessel repair, stitches, dressings and medical follow up. Sutures could be needed when the cut is deep, more than two centimeters in length, when bleeding persistently, or when located in an area of the body that bends such knee or elbow joints. When necrotic or foreign material is present in a wound, sharp or surgical debridement is necessary to reduce the risk of wound infection, cellulitis and sepsis. It also can aid in wound healing (Kirschner and Peel, 2002; Payne-James et al., 2018).

Dismemberment

Dismemberment is the act of cutting parts or whole extremities – arms and legs – as a torturous method of killing a prisoner. This barbaric torture method was practiced during the Colombian Civil War by the paramilitary forces (Morcillo-Mendez and Campos, 2012).

Animal Bites

Animal bites can cause significant physical injury to the skin and soft tissues. A dog's teeth and jaws are very powerful and the wounds they inflict can crush or tear muscles and skin. Dog bites are more commonly found in the lower extremities of tortured victims. The ferocity of a dog's attack is also intended to intimidate victims. These torture elements are well illustrated by photographs from Abu Ghraib prison in Iraq published by CBS news in 2004, showing a terrorized naked prisoner intimidated by a ferocious unmuzzled guard dog. Prisoners had been bitten, as evidenced by pictures showing wound lacerations consistent with bites. Dog bites can be infectious and can include the rabies virus. Therefore, victims need close medical care and follow up.

Nail Extractions

Nail extraction is a classic form of torture. Denailing involves the extraction of the nails from fingers and/or toes and sometimes involves introducing metallic needles under the nails. It is one of the most cruel and painful methods of torture. Denailing generally is done using metal forceps or pliers. Physical examinations can show stripped, thin, deformed nails or overgrowths tissue, and x-rays can show fractures, as chronic sequela (UN OHCHR, 2001, p 36; Kerrigan, 2001; Peel and Iacopino, 2002).

   Historically, during the Spanish Inquisition for example, thumbscrews and special metallic instruments were used to crush knuckles phalanges and nails, as often seen in exhibitions and books concerning medieval torture (Held, 1983; Langbein, 1976).

BURNS AND CORROSION

Burns are a common method of torture. Frequently, they are easy to inflict and can be produced with a wide variety of ubiquitous instruments. The pain produced is intense and can last a significant amount of time. Depending the extent of the burns, the impact can be anywhere from fleeting to life-threatening. Burns are considered serious injuries and are caused by a multitude of factors among the physical methods of torture. Burns are classified in levels of severity. First degree burns affect only the epidermis (outer layer) usually causing pain and, only rarely, requiring medical care. Second degree burns affect the dermis (subcutaneous tissues) causing intense pain, producing blisters, and swelling and requiring medical care. Depending of the extent of the burns, life-threatening infections may ensue, and medical care becomes necessary. Lastly, third degree burns, ones that extend into the muscle and bones are always life threatening. Victims need admission to specialized burn care centers.

Cigarette Burns

Perhaps the most common type of burn in victims of torture, cigarette burns are typically 5–10 mm circular lesions. Once healed, the center is hypo-pigmented and the areas around the borders appear usually hyper-pigmented. The classic shape of the cigarette burn can change when more than one burn was inflicted in the same area or depending of the position of the cigarette (round or triangular). Cigarette burns have been frequently employed in torture in Latin American countries.

Hot Metal Burns

Burns produced by the application of a hot metal instrument against the skin of victims has been a common method of torture for many centuries. The practice is found in the annals of history through different civilizations. The metal instruments used to produce the burns vary from metal rods and old metallic to modern electric irons. The shape of the scars created can often help to identify the instruments used to produce the burns.

Hot Fluid Burns

Generally, this involves boiling water or hot oil being thrown over the torture victim. These burns can acutely be first, second or third-degree burns. Although the location of the burns can be localized anywhere in the body, the burning of genital areas is a common occurrence among torture victims who suffer burns.

Sunburn

Sunburn occurs as a result of prolonged exposure of the skin to ultraviolet rays, usually from the sun. In the context of torture, it often happens when a prisoner is left unprotected from the hot sun while partially or completely naked for excessive periods of time. Sunburn is at a minimum painful but can be life threatening in extreme cases. As a method of torture, detainees have been made to stand for days exposed to the sun.

Death by Burning

Death by burning as a form of capital punishment has a long history in various civilizations throughout history. Many societies have used burning to death as an execution method. A common manner to accomplish the burning is by tying the condemned person to a large stake (burning at the stake). At public protests, demonstrators frequently burn tires to disrupt street traffic. Police who detain them have then sat those detained in these burning tires. The victims could suffer first, second or third degree burns to their buttocks. There are documented cases of demonstrators being burned to death in Chile, described in the section on being tortured to death, below.

Acid or Vitriol Attack

This involves throwing corrosive acid onto the body of another person with the intention of disfiguring or maiming the victim. Such attacks are often perpetrated against women with the intention of disfiguring the face and/or maiming the victim and are most commonly reported in the Middle East and Africa. The corrosive acid will damage the skin and subcutaneous tissues, sometime even reaching the bone. The most frequent acid used is sulphuric or hydrochloride acid.

This leaves permanent scaring and blindness if the acid reaches the eyes. Victims need highly specialized medical and ophthalmological care in addition to psychological and social support (Danielsen and Rasmussen, 2006; UN OHCHR, 2001; Kirschner and Peel 2002; CDC, 2015; Payne-James et al., 2018).

INFECTIOUS AND INFESTING AGENTS

Any method of torture that produces a skin rupture, such as cuts, scrapes and lacerations, can lead to an infection and, as has been seen, animal bites, such as dog bites, also carry the risk of infection, such as rabies. Moreover, one of the most significant consequences of a sexual assault and of rape is the risk of pregnancy and of acquiring a sexually transmitted disease, such as gonorrhea, chlamydia, genital herpes, hepatitis, HIV/AIDS, syphilis, trichomoniasis, etc. (Koss and Kilpatrick, 2001). The Center for Disease Control (CDC) in the US has published guidelines for the treatment of persons who have been or who are at risk from sexually transmitted diseases (STDs) (CDC, 2015).

FORCED INGESTION, INFUSION OR INJECTION

The introduction of different substances into the body may take place as forced ingestion (for instance of food, drink, medicine, feces or amputated body parts) or as injections (glucose, 'truth serum', contagious bio-agents, etc.).

BOX 19.2 CIA MIND CONTROL OF DETAINEES

Since the Second World War, the US Central Intelligence Agency (CIA) has sought to develop techniques of mind control. This includes hypnotizing prisoners prior to interrogation without their knowledge or consent and having responses suggested to them, resulting in a form of brain washing. After several years of research, mind control projects were centralized in the MKUltra project. Multiple studies were conducted in an attempt to find effective procedures to extract confessions through mind control. A number of citizens were unwittingly exposed to mind altering substances, including hallucinogenic drugs such as LSD, to manipulate their mental state and make them more likely to confess. A combination of hypnosis, LSD and pentothal (truth serum) were used with this purpose. The program was officially halted in 1973, after having begun in 1953 as a part of the Special Operations Division of the US Army's Chemical Corps. Recent research in the field has emphasized sensory deprivation as a behavioral component of the interrogation of detainees (McCoy, 2006).

Mefloquine, an FDA approved anti-malarial drug, was developed by the US military, initially for its neuro-psychochemical effects. The drug is associated with severe neuropsychiatric adverse effects when taken in larger doses and further research is needed into its consequences (Nevin, 2012). The CIA has also published detailed guidelines concerning the use of pharmaceutical agents during interrogations (CIA, 2004b).

Hunger Strikes and Force Feeding

The decision of a competent prisoner to stage a hunger strike has to be respected. Any unwanted ingestion or infusion of nutrients or water is a violation of medical ethics and should be considered ill-treatment or even torture, depending on the methods and circumstances, as reflected in the World Medical Association's Malta Declaration (WMA, 1991; Physicians for Human Rights, 2013).

The standard operation procedure for the force feeding of hunger striking detainees in Guantanamo Bay has been made public and involved the use of a restraint chair while nutrients were infused via a feeding tube (Physicians for Human Rights, 2013; Reprieve, 2013). According to the Senate Select Committee Study of the CIA's Detention and Interrogation Program, at least five detainees were subjected to *rectal feeding*, that is, infusing nutrients, fluids or even pureed food through a tube inserted into the rectum. This is a procedure which serves no medical purpose and should be considered torture masquerading as medicine (Senate Select Committee on Intelligence, 2014; Standard operating procedure, 2013).

SEXUAL AND GENDER-BASED TORTURE

Virginity Testing

Virginity testing is a gynecological examination of the hymen to determine if the woman has had sexual intercourse. Occasionally the examiner introduces one or two fingers in the woman's vagina. The test has no scientific value and the hymen has no correlation with previous sexual intercourse. Virginity examinations are frequently undertaken forcibly, without the consent of the victim. Forcible virginity examinations can have physical and always have psychological consequences, victims experiencing severe emotional pain, humiliation and a sense of worthlessness as a result of the violation of physical integrity and human dignity.

Several international organizations consider virginity testing to be a form of sexual violence and the Independent Forensic Expert Group (IFEG) has concluded that 'this examination constitutes inhuman and degrading treatment and may amount to torture depending on the individual circumstances' (IFEG, 2015).

Rectal Examination in Cases of Alleged Homosexuality

Anal visual and digital examinations are often forcibly conducted, by medical personal, in countries where consensual anal intercourse is a criminal act. These examinations are based on the false assumption that anal sphincter laxity is a sign of homosexuality and rectal intercourse. However, there are no scientific studies that support this view. Anal examination can be intentionally painful and humiliating, particularly if in public and in a condition of enforced nudity and without consent. The IFEG, after an extensive analysis of international jurisprudence, concluded that forcible anal examination should be considered a form of sexual assault and rape and may amount to torture (IFEG, 2016). The General Assembly of the World Medical Association (WMA) adopted a similar resolution in 2017 (WMA, 2017).

DEPRIVATION

Deprivation may include deprivation of food and water, deprivation of light or dark, quiet or sound, deprivation of necessary medicine, and deprivation of social interaction.

Sensorial Deprivation and Solitary Confinement

These methods are also called 'no touch torture' or non-lethal methods because they do not leave physical marks. Sensory deprivation has been used throughout history, in different geographical areas, and in combination with other methods of torture.

Hooding, blindness
Human beings are conscious of the external world from information received by brain from sensory receptors strategically located in our bodies, including our eyes, ears, nose, tongue, skin and so on. These five senses are specialized sensory cell organs that transform environmental information into electrical signals that are then transmitted to the brain. The information that the brain receives provides us with awareness of the universe and the environment

that surround us. The information is sent as digital sensory outputs in neurochemical form to different centers in the brain.

Hooding and Blindness is a type of sensory deprivation. The hood, which completely covers the victim's head, and goggles serve to create a feeling of disorientation causing a loss of perception of the sequence of day and night, and, thus, the notion of time.

After being detained, most individuals are usually blindfolded during transportation to detention centers, often during interrogations and at many other times for indefinite periods. Whilst hooded, other forms of torture are often applied. The Independent Forensic Expert Group (IFEG) has concluded that 'When hooding is practiced in conjunction with other acts that may be considered inhumane and degrading treatment, it may constitute torture' (IFEG, 2011).

Solitary confinement
The International Psychological Trauma Symposium approved a Statement on solitary confinement which was published in the journal *Torture* in 2008. Solitary confinement is defined as the physical isolation of individuals who are confined to their cells for between 22 and 24 hours a day, with perhaps one hour of solitary exercise. Contact with other people is reduced to a minimum, insufficient to maintain health and wellbeing. When solitary confinement is additionally associated with restrictions on access to the radio, television and reading materials this increases further the sensory deprivation of the prisoner (International Psychological Trauma Symposium, 2008). The United Nations Standard Minimum Rules for the Treatment of Prisoners (the Nelson Mandela Rules) represent universally acknowledged standards – Rules 43, 44 and 45 of which also define and restrict solitary confinement (United Nations, 2015).

Solitary confinement produces serious psychological and physiological consequences, including:

- Anxiety
- Hyper-responsivity to external stimuli
- Perceptual distortions and fearful hallucinations (auditory, visual, olfactory)
- Difficulty with concentration and memory
- Acute confusion, at times associated with dissociative features, mutism, and subsequent amnesia
- Ego-dystonic aggressive fantasies
- Motor excitement, associated with sudden, violent distractive outbursts
- Psychosis with persecutory delusions
- Rapid subsidence of symptoms upon termination of isolation

(International Psychological Trauma Symposium, 2008; Smith, 2008; Grassian, 1983; Grassian and Friedman, 1986).

Loud white noise or loud music
Hyperstimulation and torture has resulted from exposure to loud, constant and unpleasant sound levels. The systematic use of music has been used for many years as a weapon of war and of torture. Recently, loud music has been utilized as part of the 'Enhanced Interrogation Techniques' deployed against terrorists (Cusick, 2006; *Torture Journal*, 2013).

Torture survivors from Latin America, Guantanamo Bay and Iraq all describe having been forced to listen to extremely loud and unchanging popular music for several hours per day for days on end, sometimes whilst being subjected to other methods of torture. Victims expressed feelings of powerless, of being humiliated, deprived of sleep, severely anxious, and being unable to offer further resistance. A specific example includes the playing of a specific song immediately before periods of interrogation and torture, causing victims to associate it with ill-treatment and to react with fear and feelings of helplessness on hearing it, making them more vulnerable (Senate Select Committee on Intelligence, 2014, p 429).

Sleep deprivation

Sleep deprivation may be total (no sleep at all) or take the form of sleep reduction (that is, disrupting periods of sleep). Sleep deprivation results in:

- Reduced cognitive performance
- Increased anxiety
- Reductions in pain thresholds, so that pain is perceived to be stronger
- Increased emotional reactions to stimuli.

All of these effects make victims more vulnerable to interrogation and torture. As stated by the CIA:

> Sleep deprivation (with or without associated stress positions) is among the most effective adjuncts to interrogation and is the only technique with a demonstrably cumulative effect – the longer the deprivation (to a point), the more effective the impact. (CIA OMS, 2004)

HUMILIATION

Margalit defines humiliation as 'any sort of behavior or condition that constitutes a sound reason for a person to consider his or her self-respect injured' (cited by Neuhäuser, 2011, p 22).

Pérez-Sales (2017, p 83) describes humiliation as 'the feeling associated with being deprived of dignity by others'. The feeling is associated with a sense of shame and guilt. Shame results from the inability to effectively oppose the stronger aggressor or defend one's values, ideology, culture and loved ones. These negative and painful views of oneself also arise in part from an inability to adhere to deeply held moral principles, such as by naming a comrade when tortured or helping the aggressor in some manner in order to survive (Mollica, 2004; Mollica, 2006; Pérez-Sales, 2017; Neuhäuser, 2011). Humiliation can occur when a person is interrogated standing naked, depersonalized by being called a number instead of a name or treated as an animal, and by being forced to violate taboos or general human standards.

THREATS

Fear of being detained and tortured is a constant concern of every political activist during periods of political unrest and martial law in any society. Activists are normally expected to maintain silence usually for no less than 24 hours after being detained to allow sufficient time for other members of the group to take cover in the prospect of an arrest. One of the principle purposes of torture, particularly at first, is the exploitation of the detainee's weaknesses in order to increase the effectiveness of a detention.

Death Threats and Mock Executions

Death threats and other threats of significant harm to the individual or their family, friends or colleagues are frequently employed as forms of psychological torture. Death threats include mock executions where a person is told that they will be executed, for example by a firing squad, which is realistically presented. Sometimes, the victim is even made to dig their own grave. Detainees are blindfolded and then lined up facing the firing squad. At the officer's command, the squad fires in a different direction. Alternatively, the torture victim may be threatened by having a gun pointed at their head. After intimidating demands are made, the trigger is pulled in order to increase the level of fear.

Many torture victims consider mock executions to be more emotionally damaging than any physical torture that they experienced. Persistent symptoms of anxiety, PTSD, and major depression are commonly seen for extended periods of time in individuals that have undergone death threats or mock executions during their time of torture.

Witnessing Torture

Forced witnessing of the execution, torture, rape or other forms of significant harm to a family member, friend, or other prisoner has been used as a form of psychological torture. It is intended to increase the level of fear in the victim, usually in order to coerce their behavior and often to make some form of confession. Research has shown that those exposed to such forms of torture are particularly prone to PTSD and chronic depression (Başoğlu et al., 2007).

Learned Helplessness

Detention and torture are very painful experiences for the victims. They are designed to produce a sense fear, uncertainty and loss of control which are magnified by the perpetrators. A further consequence of torture is that victims often experience cognitive dissociation resulting in a feeling of complete hopelessness and helplessness.

TORTURE, DEATH AND THE PUNISHMENT OF DETAINEES

Dismemberment

Dismemberment is one of the cruelest methods of torture and killing. Examples of its systematic use include the 60-year civil war in Colombia where there were examples of living prisoners having arms and legs removed with chain saws, a machete or an axe. Death might result from hypovolemic shock due to massive bleeding (Morcillo-Mendez and Campos, 2012).

Torture to Death of Detainees in US Custody in the War against Terrorism

Following the release of 23 death certificates by the Armed Forces Office of Medical Examiners (AFME) of detainees who had died in US custody in Afghanistan and Iraq, studies suggested that 17 of those concerned had been tortured to death – six in Afghanistan and 11 in Iraq (Miles, 2005).

Other researchers examined deaths in the custody of US forces between 2002 to 2005 and concluded that of the 43 (out of 112) cases classed as homicide, only 12 had autopsy reports, all of which were suggestive of gun shots (four) or torture (eight) (Allen et al., 2006). A similar study by Human Rights First reached similar conclusions, meaning that the cause of death of many others remains unknown (Human Rights First, 2006). What is clear is that torture results in death in numerous instances.

Burning to Death: A Case in Chile

A further example of torturous death concerns a group protesting against the Pinochet dictatorship in Chile, where a military patrol seized two of the protesters. Having beaten them, they were doused in petrol and wrapped in blankets which were set on fire, resulting in second and third degree burns, then left in a ditch. One died, another was rescued and ultimately treated in Canada. In 2017 criminal charges were finally brought in relation to this act of punishment and torture (Bonnefoy, 2015).

REFERENCES

Abd-Elmeguid, A, Yu, D C (2009) 'Dental Pulp Neurophysiology: Part 1. Clinical and Diagnostic Implications', *JCDA*, 75(1), 55–59.

Allen, SA, Rich, JD, Bux, RC, Faberblum, B, Berns, M and Rubenstein, L (2006), 'Deaths of Detainees in the Custody of US Forces in Iraq and Afghanistan from 2002 to 2005', *MedGenMed*, 8(4), 46.

Amnesty International (2016), 'Sobrevivir la muerte. La tortura por policías y fuerzas armadas en México' (Amnesty International).

Amris, K, Torp-Pedersen, S, Rassmussen, OV (2009), 'Long-term Consequences of Falanga Torture', *Torture*, 19(1), 33–40.

Arge, SO, Hansen, SH and Lynnerup, N (2014), 'Forensic Odonatological Examinations of Alleged Torture Victims at the University of Copenhagen 1997–2011', *Torture*, 24(1), 17–24.

Baker, A and Goodman, D (2015), 'Police Keep Using Chokeholds Despite Bans and Scrutiny', *The New York Times* (12 January 2015) http://www.nytimes.com/2015/01/13/nyregion/police-keep -using-chokeholds-despite-bans-and-scrutiny.html?&hp&action=click&pgtype=Homepage&module =photo-spot-region&region=top-news&WT.nav=top-news

Başoğlu, M, Livanou M and Crnobarić, C (2007), 'Torture vs Other Cruel, Inhuman, and Degrading Treatment: Is the Distinction Real or Apparent?', *Arch. of Gen. Psychiatry*, 64(3), 277–285.

Beal, F and Martin, JB (1998), 'Anoxia-Ischemia' in Fauci, AS et al. (eds), *Harrison's Principles of Internal Medicine*, 14th edn (McGraw-Hill Education), 2452.

Bloom, AI, Zamir, G, Muggia, M, Friedlaender, M, Gimmon, Z and Rivkind, A (1995), 'Torture Rhabdomyolysis: A Pseudo Crush Syndrome', *J Trauma*, 38, 252–254.

Bonnefoy, P (2015), 'Officers Arrested in 1986 Burning Death of US Student in Chile', *The New York Times* (21 July 2015) https://www.nytimes.com/2015/07/22/world/americas/officers-ordered-arrested -in-1986-burning-death-of-us-student-in-chile.html

Center for Disease Control (CDC) (2015), 'Sexually Transmitted Diseases Treatment Guidelines, 2015', *Morbidity and Mortality Weekly Report* (5 June 2015) https://www.cdc.gov/mmwr/index.html

Central Intelligence Agency (CIA) (2004a), 'Counterterrorism Detention and Interrogation Activities (September 2001–October 2003)', released 7 May 2004 https://fas.org/irp/cia/product/ig-interrog.pdf

Central Intelligence Agency (CIA) (2004b), 'OMS Guidelines on Medical and Psychological Support to Detainee Rendition, Interrogation, and Detention', released 10 June 2016 https://www.cia.gov/library/readingroom/document/6541536.

Cook, AA (1993), 'Handcuff Neuropathy among US Prisoners of War from Operation Desert Storm', *Military Medicine*, 158, 253–254.

Cusick, SG (2006), 'Music as Torture/Music as Weapon', *Transcultural Music Review*, 10, 1–12.

Danielsen, L and Rasmussen, OV (2006), 'Dermatological Findings after Alleged Torture', *Torture*, 16(2), 108–127.

Dokudan, E, Kormaz, C, Unuvar, U, Sirin, G and Fincanci, SK (2016), 'Recent Torture Method: Handcuffed Behind', *10th International Scientific Symposium, IRCT, Mexico City 4–9 December*, 2016 Book of Abstracts.

Dueck, J and Guzman, M (2001), '"Verstappen Bert. Micro-Thesauri": A Tool for Documenting Human Rights Violations' (Huridocs Publication).

Fundación de Ayuda Social de las Iglesias Cristianas (FASIC) (1988), 'Glosario de Definiciones operacionales de las violaciones de los derechos humanos de Chile', *Publicación FASIC Colección Documentos 19.*

Grassian, S (1983), 'Psychopathological Effects of Solitary Confinement', *Am. J. Psychiatry*, 140, 1450–1454.

Grassian, S and Friedman, N (1986), 'Effects of Sensory Deprivation in Psychiatric Seclusion and Solitary Confinement', *International Journal of Law and Psychiatry*, 8, 49–65.

Haddad, FS, Goddard, NJ, Kanvinde, RN and Burke, FR (1999), 'Complaints of Pain after Use of Handcuffs should not be Dismissed', *BMJ*, 318, 55.

Held, R (1983), 'Bilingual Guide to the Exhibition in Various Cities of the World of "Torture Instruments from the Middle Ages to the Industrial Era. The Thumbscrews"', 92–93 (Marlborough Books).

Human Rights First (2006), 'Human Rights First Release, First Comprehensive Report on Detainee Deaths in US Custody' https://www.humanrightsfirst.org/2006/02/22/human-rights-first-releases-first-comprehensive-report-on-detainee-deaths-in-u-s-custody

Independent Forensic Expert Group (IFEG) (2015), 'Statement on Virginity Testing', *Torture*, 25(1), 62–68.

Independent Forensic Expert Group (IFEG) (2016), 'Statement on Anal Examination in Cases of Alleged Homosexuality', *Torture*, 26(2), 85–91.

International Forensic Expert Group (IFEG) (2011), 'Statement on Hooding', *Torture*, 21(2), 186–189.

International Psychological Trauma Symposium (2008), 'The Istanbul Statement on the Use and Effects of Solitary Confinement, Adopted on 9 December 2007', *Torture*, 18(1), 63–66.

JFT GTMO (2002), 'SERE Interrogation Standard Operating Procedure, Subj: Guidelines for Employing "SERE" Techniques During Detainee Interrogation, 10 December 2002' http://humanrights.ucdavis.edu/projects/the-guantanamo-testimonials-project/testimonies/testimonies-of-standard-operating-procedures/gtmo_sere_interrogation_sop.pdf

Keatley, E, Ashman, TA, Im, B and Rasmussen, A (2013), 'Self-Reported Head Injury Among Refugee Survivors of Torture', *J. Head Trauma Rehabil.*, 28(6), E8–E13.

Kerrigan, M (2001), *The Instruments of Torture* (The Lyons Press).

Kirschner, R and Peel, M (2002), 'Physical Examination for Late Signs of Torture' in Peel, M and Iacopino, V (eds), *The Medical Documentation of Torture* (Cambridge University Press), 149–158.

Koss, MP and Kilpatrick, DG (2001), 'Rape and Sexual Assault' in Gerrity, E, Keane, TM and Tuma, F (eds), *The Mental Health Consequences of Torture* (Kluwer Academic/Plenum Publisher), 177–187.

Langbein, JH (1976), *Torture and the Law of Proof* (University of Chicago Press).

Malik, GH, Reshi, AR, Najar, MS, Ahmad, A and Massod, T (1995), 'Further Observation on Acute Renal Failure Following Physical Torture', *Nephrol Dial Transplant*, 10, 198–202.

Malik, GH, Sirwal, IA, Reshi, AR, Najar, MS, Tanvir, M and Altaf, M (1993), 'Acute Renal Failure Following Physical Torture', *Nephron* 63, 434–437.

McCoy, AW (2006), *A Question of Torture: CIA Interrogation, from the Cold War to the War on Terror* (Henry Holt and Co), 21–59.

Miles, SH (2005), 'Medical Investigations of Homicides of Prisoners of War in Iraq and Afghanistan', *MedGenMed*, 7(3), 4.

Mollica, RF (2004), 'Surviving Torture', *N. Engl J. Med*, 351(1), 5–7.

Mollica, RF (2006), *Healing Invisible Wounds: Paths to Hope and Recovery in a Violent World* (Vanderbilt University Press), 62–87.

Mollica, RF (2009), 'Brain Structural Abnormalities and Mental Health Sequelae in South Vietnamese Ex-Political Detainees Who Survive Traumatic Brain Injury and Torture', *Arch. Gen. Psychiatry*, 66(111), 1221–1232.

Mollica, RF, Anderson, DC and Tor, S (2002), 'Psychiatric Effects of Traumatic Brain Injury Events in Cambodian Survivors of Mass Violence', *British Journal of Psychiatry*, 181, 339–347.

Mollica, RF, Chernoff, MC, Berthold, M, Lavelle, J, Lyoo, IK and Renshaw, P (2014), 'The Mental Health Sequelae of Traumatic Head Injury in South Vietnamese Ex-Political Detainees Who Survive Torture', *Comp. Psychiatry*, 55(7), 1626–1638.

Morcillo-Mendez, MD and Campos, IY (2012), 'Dismemberment: Cause of Death in the Colombian Armed Conflict', *Torture*, 22(1), 5–13.

Moreno, A and Grondin, MA (2002), 'Torture and its Neurological Sequelae', *Spinal Cord*, 40, 213–223.

National Institute of Neurological Disorders and Stroke (2015), 'Traumatic Brain Injury: Hope through Research' https://www.ninds.nih.gov/Disorders/Patient-Caregiver-Education/Hope-Through -Research/Traumatic-Brain-Injury-Hope-Through

Neuhäuser, C (2011), 'Humiliation: The Collective Dimension' in Kaufmann, P, Kuch, H, Neuhäuser, C and Webster, E (eds), *Humiliation, Degradation, Dehumanization* (Springer Netherlands), 21–36.

Nevin, RL (2012), 'Mass Administration of the Antimalarial Drug Mefloquine to Guantanamo Detainees: A Critical Analysis', *Tropical Medicine and International Health*, 17(10), 1281–1288.

OMS Guidelines (2004), OMS Guidelines on Medical and Psychological Support to Detainee Rendition, Interrogation, and Detention, https://www.thetorturedatabase.org/files/foia_subsite/pdfs/ DOJOLC001145.pdf

Ozkalipci, O, Unuvar, U, Sahin, U, Irencin, S and Fincanci, SK (2013), 'A Significant Diagnostic Method in Torture Investigation: Bone Scintigraphy', *Forensic Science International*, 226, 142–145

Panzar, J (2014), 'Police Wrestle with Definition of Chokehold', *Los Angeles Times* (9 December 2014) http://www.latimes.com/nation/la-na-chokehold-20141210-story.html

Payne-James, J, Beynon, J and Vieira, DN (2018), 'Assessment of Physical Evidence of Torture or Cruel, Inhuman and Degrading Treatment during Visits to Places of Detention' in Payne-James, J, Beynon, J and Vieira, DN (eds), *Monitoring Detention, Custody, Torture and Ill Treatment: A Practical Approach to Prevention and Documentation* (CRC Press), 85–126.

Peel, M (2003), 'Postinflamatory Hyperpigmentation Following Torture', *J. Clin. Forensic Medicine*, 10(2), 193–196.

Peel, M and Iacopino, V (2002), *The Medical Documentation of Torture* (Cambridge University Press).

Pérez-Sales, P (2017), 'From Dignity to Identity: Humiliation as Paradigm of the Differences between Legal and Mental Perspectives' in Pérez-Sales, P (ed), *Psychological Torture Definition, Evaluation and Measurement* (Routledge), 81–89.

Physicians for Human Rights (1995), *A Medico Legal Report. Israel and the Occupied Territories. Shaking as a Form of Torture. Death in Custody of Abd Al-Salam Harizat* (PHR Publication).

Physicians for Human Rights (2013), 'Hunger Strikers and the Practice of Force-Feeding', https://phr .org/resources/hunger-strikes-and-the-practice-of-force-feeding/

Pollanen, MS (2016), 'Fatal Rhabdomyolysis after Torture by Reverse Hanging', *Forensic Sci. Med. Pathol*, 12(2), 170–173.

Pollanen, MS (2018), 'The Pathology of Torture', *Forensic Science International*, 284, 85–96.

Prip, K and Persson, AL (2008), 'Clinical Findings in Men with Chronic Pain After Falanga Torture', *Clin. J. Pain*, 24, 135–141.

Prip, K, Persson, AL and Sjolund, BH (2012), 'Pain when Walking: Individual Sensory Profiles in the Foot Sole of Torture Victims – a Controlled Study using Quantitative Sensory Testing', *BMC*, 1–10.

Rao, D (n.d.), 'Ligature Strangulation', Forensic Pathology Online http://www.forensicpathologyonline .com/e-book/asphyxia/ligature-strangulation (accessed 18 January 2018).

Rejali, D (2007), *Torture and Democracy* (Princeton University Press).

Reprieve (2013), 'Down the Tubes: The 2013 Hunger Strike at Guantanamo Bay' Reprieve Report https://reprieve.org.uk/press/2013_07_10_guantanamo_hunger_strike_violence_obama/

Savnik, A, Amris, K, Rogind, H, Prip, K, Danneskiold-Samsoe, B, Bojsen-Moller, F, Bartels, EM, Bliddal, H, Boesen, J and Egund, N (2000), 'MRI of the Plantar Structures of the Foot after Falanga Torture', *Eur.Radiol.* 10, 1655–1659.

Scott, TF, Yaeger, JG, Gross, JA (1989), 'Handcuff Neuropathy Revisited', *Muscle and Nerve*, 12, 219–220.

Senate Select Committee on Intelligence (2014), Committee Study of the Central Intelligence Agency's Detention and Interrogation Program, 9 December 2014, 113th Congress, 2nd session Senate Report, 113–288 https://www.intelligence.senate.gov/press/committee-releases-study-cias-detention-and -interrogation-program

Sinding, R and Smidt-Nielsen, K (1999), 'The Late Ear, Nose, and Throat Region Sequelae of Torture', *Torture*, 9(1), 21–22.

Smith, PS (2008), 'Solitary Confinement: An Introduction to the Istanbul Statement on the Use and Effects of Solitary Confinement', *Torture*, 18(1), 56–62.

Standard Operating Procedure: Medical Management of Detainees on Hunger Strike. Joint Task Force, Guantanamo Bay, Cuba, Joint Medical Group, 5, March, 2013 www.aele.org/law/gitmo-force-feed .pdf

Torture Journal (2013), 'Thematic Issue on Music in Detention', *Torture*, 23(2), 1–68.

United Nations (2015), Standard Minimum Rules for the Treatment of Prisoners (the Nelson Mandela Rules), UN Doc A/RES/70/175 (17 December 2015).

United Nations OHCHR (2001), *Manual on the Effective Investigation and Documentation of Torture and Other Cruel, Inhuman or Degrading Treatment or Punishment (The Istanbul Protocol)* (United Nations Publications, Professional Training Series No 8).

World Medical Association (WMA) (1991), Declaration of Malta on Hunger Strikers, Adopted by the 43rd World Medical Assembly, November 1991: latest revision, 68th WMA General Assembly, October 2017.

World Medical Association (WMA) (2017), Resolution on Prohibition of Forced Anal Examinations to Substantiate Same-Sex Sexual Activity, Adopted by the 68th WMA General Assembly, October 2017.

20. Psychological torture

Pau Pérez-Sales

DOES 'PSYCHOLOGICAL' TORTURE EXIST? MAPPING THE SEMANTIC FIELD

Psychological torture is part of our folk language, part of the experience of survivors, appears in court rulings and news and it is incorporated in our daily life. Society imposes the concept because it is a *common-sense* concept. But for a survivor, a researcher or a therapist there is a mind-body unity that makes it fallacious to distinguish purely physical or purely psychological methods or impacts.

The term – and many other versions connected to the idea – is, however, used and there are different meanings associated with it. Box 20.1 summarizes the broad semantic field of psychological torture.

BOX 20.1 DEFINITIONS OF PSYCHOLOGICAL TORTURE AND CONNECTED TERMS

Emphasis on Target and Purpose

- Methods used to break down a detainee psychologically (Kramer, 2010).
- Methods aimed at profoundly disrupting the senses or the personality (PHR, 2005).
- The use of methods upon a person intended to obliterate the personality of the victim or to diminish his physical or mental capacities, even if they do not cause physical pain or mental anguish (extracted from the definition in the Inter-American Convention for Prevention and Sanction of Torture).

Emphasis on Method

- Methods which cause aversive stimuli not based on producing physical pain or that do not physically attack the body (Quiroga and Jaranson, 2008; Reyes, 2008).
- No touch-torture (Cunniffe, 2013).
- A set of practices to inflict pain or suffering without resorting to direct physical violence, thus including those techniques in which there is no 'aggression' but there is physical pain (like being held in stress positions) (CSHRA, 2005).

Emphasis on Impact

- Brain torture: Physical torture that targets the brain (i.e. blows to the head, anoxia, chemicals or drugs) (Panayiotou, Jackson and Crowe, 2010).
- Mental torture: Actions producing severe mental pain or suffering. This suffering can be described in non-clinical terms (e.g. despair, loneliness, disorientation, terror, depres-

---

sion, confusion, claustrophobia, anxiety or loss of personality) or it may take the form of clinically recognized psychiatric conditions, although it need not (Luban and Shue, 2012).

Connected terms

- *White torture*: Torture based on the use of sensory deprivation techniques leading to disintegration of personality and psychotic-like symptoms (Suedfeld, 1990).
- *No-touch torture*: Techniques developed in MK-Ultra and other CIA-sponsored research programs aimed, as reflected in the Kubark manual 'to induce psychological regression in the subject by bringing a superior outside force to bear on his will to resist'. McCoy (2006, 2012) groups these techniques into two categories: 'sensory disorientation' and 'self-inflicted pain'.
- *Clean torture*: Torture, either physical or psychological, that leaves no marks. Although such torture may involve intense physical pain, it leaves almost no marks visible to an observer (Rejali, 2007).
- *Lite torture*: Low-intensity torture that uses coercive methods (e.g. sleep deprivation, stress positions) to a level that might not provoke enough suffering be judged to violate the prohibition against torture. A special case in the US context are the so-called 'Enhanced Interrogation Techniques'. The concept purposively ignores the subjective nature of suffering and its cumulative effect (Wolfendale, 2009).
- *Non-violent torture*: Use of coercive methods that do not imply physical violence (specially applied to the use of music and unbearable noise). It hides the fact that all torture methods entail a form of violence.
- *Moral injury*: Being forced to act in a way that transgresses deeply held moral beliefs and expectations, or to witness such acts. This is often associated with lasting psychological, biological, spiritual, behavioral and social impacts (Nickerson et al., 2015).

Source: CSHRA, 2005; Cunniffe, 2013; Kramer, 2010; Luban and Shue, 2012; McCoy, 2006; Nickerson et al., 2015; Panayiotou, Jackson and Crowe, 2010; Physicians for Human Rights, 2005; Quiroga and Jaranson, 2008; Rejali, 2007; Reyes, 2008; Suedfeld, 1990; Wolfendale, 2009.

An extensive definition of psychological torture (i.e. defining it by the methods usually considered as constituting it) would include, as the most cited examples, solitary confinement; confinement in spaces where the environment is inhuman; deprivation of food, water or clothes; sleep-deprivation; prolonged stress positions or strenuous exercises; continuous interrogation; manipulation of the senses (blindfolding, hooding, the use of lights, loud noise, music or shouting); forced nakedness and other unacceptable sexual behaviours; the use of phobias; breaking moral taboos or sacrilege; arbitrary rules and random punishments; ambivalent behaviours with alternate affection and hate; threats of physical torture or death, including dry and wet asphyxia and mock executions; threats to relatives and loved ones or forced witnessing of torture; among many others. The list is endless.

Three Categories in One Term

The review in Box 20.1 leads us, in fact, to three different conceptions of psychological torture in the interplay between the physical and psychological elements of distress:

Type 1: Situations where the person is submitted to *pure cognitive and emotional suffering*, with two nuclear elements:

- Threats and fear
- Questioning the core self through emotions (humiliation, shame and guilt)

Type 2: Situations where the person is submitted to cognitive and emotional attacks through no-touch physical manipulation of the body. This includes, for instance, solitary confinement, music or painful sounds, hunger or sleep deprivation. This does not necessarily mean that there is no physical pain (hunger can be very painful) but there is a 'hands-off' policy.

Type 3: Situations where the person is submitted to a physical attack that in fact is transactional to a critical psychological attack. The body is used as a means to critically target the mind. Examples would include asphyxia or prolonged stress positions. In dry asphyxia (use of plastic bags) or wet asphyxia (such as the 'tacho', the 'bañera' or waterboarding), the breathlessness produces critical anguish due to being confronted with the survival instinct, uncontrollability and feeling physically close to an imminent death (Başoğlu, 2017b).

All these three patterns can be combined in the model shown in Figure 20.1.

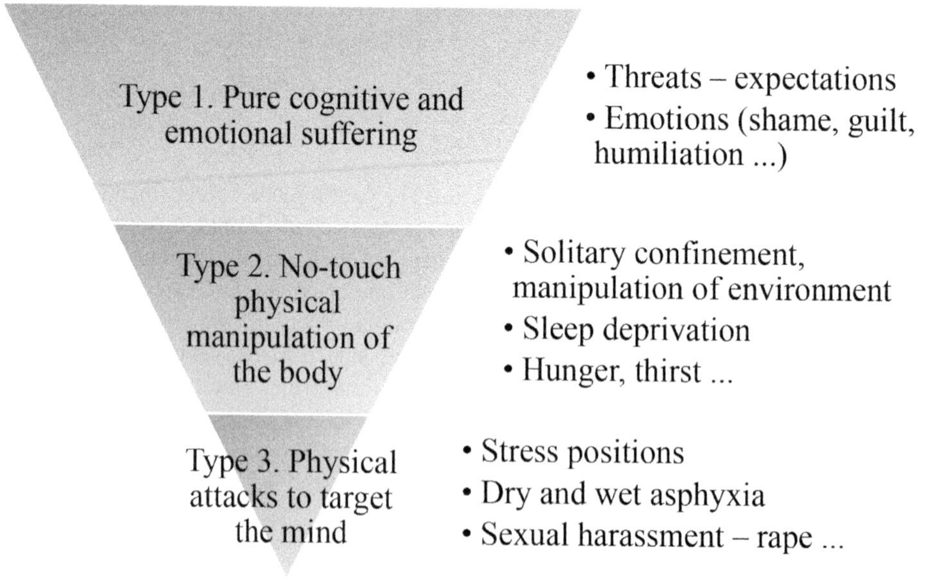

Figure 20.1   Patterns of psychological torture

Pragmatic and Pedagogical Reasons for Using the Notion of Psychological Torture

It is unclear whether this medical and psychological classification and the mixture of concepts in the semantic field of psychological torture have practical implications in terms of legal claims, diagnosis and treatment. But there is a strong pragmatical and pedagogical reason to reflect on it. It is the same kind of debate as to whether the distinction between torture and cruel, inhuman and degrading treatment (CIDT) must be maintained. From a medical and psychological point of view, surely not: there is no correlation between the severity of the acts perpetrated to a person, the level of physical and especially emotional suffering and the short- and long-term damage associated with these acts. Apparently less severe actions from the point of view of physical pain (like being kept naked in public) would be considered degrading treatment by most western courts although they can produce extreme psychological distress and permanent identity damage to many survivors. However, from a legal point of view the distinction is necessary as a way to scale the severity of the wrongdoing and the responsibility and associated punishment of it. Not every act against others can be sanctioned at the same level.

Furthermore, when we speak of psychological torture, we want to make a change in outlook. What we want to indicate is that the ultimate battlefield of torture is not the body in pain (which is the primary one) but the 'I', the self, the identity.[1] The ultimate target of torture is the human being, understood as a consciousness that feels. When talking about psychological torture, what we do is, from an epistemological, pragmatic and pedagogical point of view, (a) break the myth of wrecked bodies as the defining nucleus of torture and (b) focus our reflection on the psychological processes associated with the breaking of will that torture implies. Physical pain and broken bodies are usually the main source of suffering in the short term. But, in the long term, torture is about submission, dignity and will, and this is what, in most cases, defines damage and healing.

From a practical point of view, the term has gained acceptance in the medical, legal, social and folk domains, and, what is most important and is the reason that justifies this chapter: while not denying the unity of mind and body, it simply puts the focus on the process of attacking the sentient consciousness that we call a 'human being'. This is why it deserves being a topic on its own.

CHARACTERIZING TORTURE AND PSYCHOLOGICAL TORTURE FROM A MEDICAL AND PSYCHOLOGICAL POINT OF VIEW

The Old Idea of Regression

The situations that are nowadays included as potentially violating the United Nations Convention against Torture (UNCAT) include contexts that do not fit into the classical interrogational model of torture on which most reflections are still based.

---

[1]   In some legal definitions, such as that in the *Inter-American Convention to Prevent and Punish Torture* (IACPPT) the 'personality' is included, which medical professionals would consider to be a different concept. Identity refers to who are you; personality refers to how you normally react in life.

The origin of the idea of psychological torture is usually given as rooted in notions from the 1950s and summarized in the 1963 CIA Kubark manual. According to this, physical torture often creates resistance while psychological torture destroys it (pp. 90–91). The purpose of contemporary torture was allegedly defined in the *Human Resource Exploitation Training Manual* as to progressively reduce the victim to an infantile regressive state where the person will surrender to the will of the perpetrator, while not letting the person enter into apathy and passive avoidance (CIA, 1963, 1983). This idea has been developed extensively, including contextual, interactional and cognitive elements, into different comprehensive models of torture (Pérez-Sales, 2017; Başoğlu, 2017a).

Some contexts involving long-term coercion and damage clearly reproduce the model (i.e. trafficking or detention centres for migrants), while others pursue a temporary breakdown of the person (e.g. torture in demonstrations, obtaining a confession in a short-term detention center). These are not clear-cut categories, but there is a continuum. Some studies show, for instance, that permanent identity breakdown can result from brief incommunicado detentions (Pérez-Sales, Navarro-Lashayas and Plaza, 2016).

Definition of Torture and Psychological Torture

There is a legal definition of torture that analyses four elements: three related to the act perpetrated (purpose, intent and state involvement) and one related to impact (severity of pain or suffering). This is the definition intended to be used by governments, institutions and courts. For the purpose of research and work with survivors it can be useful to conceptualize torture as 'the use of techniques of physical, cognitive, emotional or sensory attacks that target the conscious mind aiming to coerce, break the will and ultimately produce an identity breakdown of the person'. This is associated with physical and psychological suffering and damage in most of the persons exposed to such techniques. The methods or techniques may be used alone or together with other methods to produce a cumulative effect. From this point of view, torture and psychological torture are indistinguishable. In a restricted definition, involving only Type 1 and Type 2, Psychological Torture (PT) (Figure 20.1), 'involves attacking or manipulating the inputs and processes of the conscious mind that allow the person to stay oriented in the surrounding world, retain control and have the adequate conditions to judge, understand and freely make decisions which are the essential constitutive ingredients of an unharmed self' (Pérez-Sales, 2017, p. 8).

Figure 20.2 shows the relationship between coercion, will and identity and torture. In the following sections, we will go through the process involved in each one of them.

This definition implies an important change in outlook. Over the years there have been many efforts to classify torture methods (Rejali, 2007). But the experience of survivors shows that the list of torture methods is as infinite as the imagination, circumstances and tools available to the perpetrator, and that the torture method itself, as horrible as it can be, represents the symbolic space in which the interaction between the torturer and the tortured takes place. What torture means is an attempt to subdue a human being and the method represents the specific way in which the self is attacked. We will go back to this idea later in this chapter.

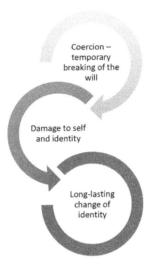

Figure 20.2   Torture, coercion and will

Comparing Medical, Ethical, Sociological and Legal Definitions of Torture

The well-known legal definition of torture reflected in UNCAT Article 1, discussed elsewhere in this book, considers torture as essentially the intentional infliction of (or omission of protection from) physical or mental pain or suffering by State agents for one of the purposes stated in the Convention (information or confession, punishment, intimidation or discrimination being the most well-known examples). As already said, the definition emphasizes the acts that one person exercises over another. This does not necessarily reflect the medical and psychological aspects stated above that emphasize the ultimate goal of the torturing process: coercing, breaking and submitting a human being (Viñar, 1993). From a neurobiological point of view, this is achieved by building contexts (including pain, but not reduced to only that) which induce overwhelming primary emotions[2] (helplessness, loss of control and fear) and unbearable secondary emotions (humiliation, shame and guilt) that leave indelible marks on most people subjected to such processes. The legal definition of a certain phenomenon is the practical expression of political agreements that try to protect essential values, defining what are to be considered duties and transgressions and the consequences of both. Its adequacy to medical knowledge and science might be only partial.

From an ethical and philosophical point of view, torture would be defined as an imposed relationship between two or more human beings characterized by a violation of dignity (understood as the lack of recognition and respect) and a violation of autonomy (expressed in

---

[2]   Primary emotions are those innate to human beings: joy, fear, sadness, disgust and anger. Secondary emotions or self-conscious emotions are interpersonal emotions acquired during the first years of life in interactions with others: shame, pride, guilt, among others.

the absolute power, control and imposing of the will of the perpetrator and the absolute lack of control, powerlessness and suppression of free will of the victim) (Luban and Shue, 2012; Maier, 2011; Pollmann, 2011; Sussman, 2005). In philosophy and ethics, free will means free choice in the likeness of absolute agency. This is a complex and ambiguous concept for a health professional that can be reframed in terms of independence of choice and integrity of cognitive and emotional mechanisms (Bandura, 2008).

Additionally, from a socio-political point of view, torture is a method of social control that instils fear and helplessness in individuals and society as a whole. Torture takes places because there is a machinery (a torturing system) that crosscut all different levels of a State and a society, from those who design, those who order or protect, those who decide not to know, and those that are direct immediate perpetrators, to a society at large that suffers, tolerates or even supports it.

HOW DOES PSYCHOLOGICAL TORTURE WORK? AN INTEGRATIVE VIEW

In contemporary torture the victim is often forced to play an active role in his or her own suffering by displacing the focus from the external infliction of pain by the torturer to subtle no-touch methods of pitting the person against his own body and mind, leading, through these battles, to a process of cognitive and emotional exhaustion (Pérez-Sales, 2017). Examples are wall-standing for hours instead of beatings, or creating scenarios that foster expectations of unsurmountable pain, instead of the use of the pain itself. In contemporary torture, pain is not the only and core element of torture, but one more, and often not the most important, of a set of different components of a global process of breaking the self.

Table 20.1 offers a layered, integrative picture of torture from a teleological (purpose it serves) point of view. If the purpose of torture is breaking the self, the table proposes to understand methods of torture not in a classical way, through their *modus operandi*, but through their *target*. The table considers a map of basic human needs and the way torturing methods act in the overall process of demolishing the self. Level 1 shows how torture is the result of a combination of methods that act upon different targets including a combined and cumulative effect. Of course, one torture method can act upon more than one target. Sexual harassment is an attack on at least three basic needs: safety and sense of security; physical integrity and body boundaries; and identity linked to gender and sexuality. Importantly enough, Level 1 also puts at the same level fear, manipulation of hope or humiliation, with environment manipulation or pain. All of them are part of the same process and none can be understood without the other. This is the basis of the idea of a 'torturing environment' that we will develop below.

To group methods according to the basic needs of a human being means abandoning classifications based on which technique (among almost infinite possible methods) is used to produce pain or suffering, and focusing instead on the aim that the perpetrator seeks to achieve with the technique. While the list of torture methods is limited only by human imagination, all methods seek to impact on a short range of basic human functions.

Table 20.1   *Torture – an integrative view from the point of view of attacks on human needs*

Level 1 A MAP OF HUMAN NEEDS AND POTENTIAL ATTACKS	*1. Basic physiological functions [primary needs]:* Size and cell conditions, sleep/waking disruptions, food and water intake, heat/cold, humidity, urination/defecation… *2. Relation to the environment:* Sensory deprivation (hooding, earmuffs …), handling time, sounds, noises, music, light conditions, mind-altering methods *3. Need for safety:* Fear/panic (witnessing, threats to person/family, use of phobias), manipulation of hope/pain, expectations/terror (waiting time, ruminations on past, present and future), near-death (dry and wet asphyxia, mock executions …) *4. Physical integrity:* Pain inflicted by others (beatings, blunt trauma), self-inflicted forced pain (stress positions, positional torture), exhaustion exercises, extreme pain (electric, chemical mechanical pain devices …), mutilations, brain injury… *5. Reproduction/sexual integrity:* Forced nakedness, forced sex, sexual assaults, rape *6. Need for belonging, acceptance and care:* Blocking human contact (isolation, solitary confinement, incommunicado detention), breaking social identity networks (family, social, political, religious networks), manipulation of affect (forced traumatic bonding with the torturer, love/hate manipulations, random rewards …)
Level 2 NEUROBIOLOGICAL IMPACTS	*1. Conscience system. Arousal system (tension – control):* Confusion, unreality, emotional exhaustion *2. System of fight and defense (primary emotions):* Fear, anxiety, hyperarousal, rage, hopelessness *3. System of secondary emotions (social emotions):* Humiliation, guilt, shame *4. Higher functions:* Impaired reasoning, impairment of the capacity for reflection, reasoned judgment and decision making *5. Ego functions (metacognitive functions):* Questioning the self/identity, submissive pseudo-self, identity loss, submissive attitudes
Level 3 MEDICAL AND PSYCHOLOGICAL SYNDROMES	*1. Brain:* Brain damage, neuropsychological alterations *2. Affect and anxiety circuits:* Acute and chronic PTSD, panic attacks and other anxiety symptoms, permanent fear – phobias, chronic depression, dysthymia, chronic guilt, learned helplessness. *3. Higher functions (mind) – identity:* Lasting personality changes, lasting changes in belief systems and worldviews, complex PTSD, modified/changed/grafted identity, identification with aggressor/perpetrator

Torturing Environments

We define a torturing environment 'as a set of conditions or practices that obliterate the control and will of a detainee and that compromise the self' (Pérez-Sales, 2017). A torturing environment is formed by a set of cumulative or sequential attacks to basic needs, creating physical, cognitive and emotional exhaustion and confusion, and the interconnection of the expectations of pain with actual physical pain and actions targeted to the self. Its final purpose is to break the will of the person. The Torturing Environment Scale (TES) (Pérez-Sales, 2017), now in its second version, is a tool specifically designed to profile torture methods, adopting a new outlook that gathers them together according to which human function is under attack.

The role of pain in torture
Pain has been and is considered the core element of torture. The very definition of the Convention itself speaks of inflicting severe pain or suffering. In her indispensable book

The Body in Pain, Elaine Scarry (1985) takes up her analysis of torture in the idea that pain is inexpressible and indescribable, and in this very nature of its inexpressibility is where the possibility of connection between the victim and others is broken, the victim becomes isolated and her world of meanings and relationships is mostly destroyed. The experience of the body boundaries being violated, of the lack of empathy and compassion in the process of destroying the body, the breaking of limits in consideration for dignity and care among human beings and the profound incommunicability of the experience of pain constitute the core of the alienating disruption of torture. The production of pain is finally the exhibition of power. Whoever can inflict this pain is the one who holds absolute power over the body. Not necessarily over the mind.

Through extreme and unbearable pain, the human being is reduced to an animal state. Unable to think or feel anything other than pain or terror. There is an obliteration of consciousness, focused in a desperate attempt to survive. Inhuman pain confronts the person with cruelty, brutality, viciousness, defencelessness, uncontrollability and inescapability, all of them elements that leave a permanent mark both in the body (as unspecific pains or chronic insomnia that lasts for decades) and the mind (as scripted memories of fear). The attempt to preserve life often forces the person into breaking her own moral rules and into submission, which finally ends the circle of humiliation and shame.

No doubt this classical analysis around pain is accurate. But this analysis can be kept the same without the need for extreme physical pain. As we know from the testimonies of survivors of torture, it is often the waiting time, the expectations of pain that feed the fear and terror that destroy the person. The terror and ruminations associated with expectations of pain and the anguish in the face of the unknown are, in the experience of many survivors, more destructive than the pain itself, which, paradoxical as it may seem, has sometimes been described as a relief. Physical pain and suffering are, increasingly, a certain possibility that leads the person to terror, but not the core element of torture in itself. It is part of a more global architecture of breaking the self.

Fear and threats

The prospect of pain and unending waiting time becomes more devastating than pain itself when it is unavoidably associated with ruminations and manipulation of expectations. This potentially adds to an oppressive atmosphere, lack of rules and arbitrariness of the situation; the feeling of the unreal; the need for hope and the destructiveness of each thwarted hope. In an atmosphere of physical exhaustion, there is a cognitive and emotional battle that debilitates the person: time ('we have unlimited time, and at the end, everybody talks'); the omnipotence and control of the torturer ('everything is possible – we can do whatever we want with you', 'we are in absolute control'); pain and death as a clear possibility; uncertainty (isolation, blindfolding, changing time and norms …); loneliness; absurdity and lack of meaning, etc. The person is physically and emotionally overwhelmed and confronted with a set of impossible dilemmas: one's own body is both one's own enemy but at the same time one's only support. The mind is both a source of anguish, rumination and shame, and of one's inner self and identity. The torturer is both the cause of all pain and the key to relief.

Identity

Finally, there is consciousness and identity. Denigration and disgust lead to questioning the self. Elements that foster this are being treated as an animal and not a human being, feeling clumsy, childish, blocked, simple, foul-smelling, or dirty, being stripped or abused, not being able to think clearly and being confronted with unsolvable ethical dilemmas and ambivalent situations in an atmosphere of increasing physical, psychological and emotional exhaustion. We will discuss this process in detail in the following sections.

Case Studies

Type 1 Psychological Torture: cognitive and emotional suffering – humiliation

In the legal world, humiliation is equated to degrading treatment and considered in the lowest rank of the gradation of torture. This is anchored in the strong association between torture and physical pain. But secondary emotions (humiliation, shame and guilt) leave long-lasting marks, and for most survivors these marks are permanent. Studying secondary emotions provides a good example of how neglected psychological torture is in the legal world, something we will review later.

Humiliation is an interaction between human beings that deprives one party of their dignity, understood as the basic right to be respected by others. Humiliation is the aversive feeling of perceiving one's identity being degraded, ridiculed, demeaned or devalued – of being treated like a non-human being.

Shame and humiliation (as guilt) are determined by culture, experiences in childhood, ego characteristics and cognitive traits and are thus extremely painful individual answers to a certain situation and interaction (including the characteristics of the perpetrators). Humiliation is for some people an extremely painful irreversible stain that entails an imbalance between an offender and an offended that needs some kind of restoring action. Forgiving is possible but requires the contribution of the offender and his/her wish to restore equilibrium. When this is not possible, the mental suffering of humiliation finds alleviation in real or imaginary justice or revenge. In therapy, the patients with the worst prognosis are those that feel so deeply ashamed that there is no way to restore equilibrium (Baer, Vorbrügeen and Vorbrüggen, 2007). This can happen because the perpetrator is not accessible, impunity prevails and forgiveness is unacceptable. Even justice is sometimes not enough because justice is done in the name of society while the harm of humiliation is perpetrated on an interpersonal basis.

As humiliation is associated with a lessening of one's valued identity or status, humiliation can be experienced collectively, and a person can feel humiliated by feeling an attack to his or her group identity.

How painful is the pain of humiliation?

It can be helpful to see the intensity of the pain associated with humiliation in neurophysiology experiments. For instance, Otten and Jonas (2014) have compared parameters of the overall intensity of cortical activation in different emotions by recording the participant's EEG while they read a potentially emotional scenario and think about how they would feel in that situation. They found out that humiliation was the negative emotion that aroused the highest activation pattern, even more than happiness, anger or shame, and that it was a long-lasting increase. A series of experimental studies have shown that physical and social pain share a common phenomenological and neural basis (Eisenberger, 2012a, 2012b; Kross et al., 2011). Social pain – the profound distress experienced when social ties are absent, threatened, damaged, or lost – is elaborated by the same neural and neurochemical substrates involved in processing physical pain, including both the affective and somato-sensorial components of pain. This opens new avenues of research in understanding the deep emotional *and physical* suffering associated with negative social emotions, the 'embodiment' of emotional suffering and the way that extreme emotions have biological consequences. Both biological pain and the impact of emotions that target identity can be traced and can leave long-lasting damage. A recent review has shown the deep interconnections between acute and chronic shame and the risk of medical diseases (Dolezal and Lyons, 2017).

Is humiliation a form of psychological pain?
Why is being criticized by others so painful? Embarrassment, humiliation, shame and guilt are painful self-conscious emotions (Leary and Tangney, 2012) that are markers of emotional suffering in a similar way to how physical pain is a marker of suffering in a component of the physical body. We built identity in early infancy by being progressively aware of the impact we have on the world that surrounds us, and as we grow up, by contrasting expectations and outcomes. The self has, thus, a 'nuclear identity' resulting from the reflection on oneself, an 'experiential identity', the fruit of successes or failures in daily interaction with the environment, and a 'relational identity' stemming from experience with others and the feedback that they give us. One single overloading negative experience of threat to physical integrity has deeper and longer-lasting effects than many non-negative experiences. An attack by a mad dog or the loss of all control during a car accident will have a deeper impact on one's sense of security and emotional trauma than many previous non-negative experiences.

In a similar way, torture is an overloading negative experience of attack to the inner self. The person faces situations for which they can hardly ever be prepared and are attacked on their nuclear identity and who they are (execrable, weak, nasty, stupid, ridiculous …), their experiential identity and what they do (blocked, without memory, confused, incapable of thinking, hasty, saying precisely what they should not say, stupid ...) and their relational identity and how others treat them (vulnerable, helpless, submissive, at the mercy of others that are repulsive, deprived of dignity, humiliated …). All this happens along with overwhelming emotions and loss of control.

As with physical torture, the impact of the attacks on self and identity greatly depends on individual and vulnerability factors. Besides a neurobiological proneness to embarrassment and shame shown in image studies (Müller-Pinzler et al., 2015), we might hypothesize vulnerabilities linked to a personal life history and previous negative underlying assumptions on self that torture somehow confirms (Platt and Freyd, 2012), a cognitive style linked to self-critical thinking (Harman and Lee, 2009) and rumination, ego strength (Gregg and Sedikides, 2010), value priorities in life (universalism versus self-direction) (Silfver, Helkama, Lönnqvist and Verkasalo, 2008), shameful identities (Leary and Tangney, 2012) and stigma and the personal meaning of humiliations and shame (Leeming and Boyle, 2004).

Type 2 Psychological torture: no-touch physical manipulation – sleep regulation
Sleep deprivation alters most aspects of the cognitive and emotional functioning of the human brain. Some of these functions are necessary for understanding context, using memory,

processing information and for proper assessment, judgement and decision making. Sleep deprivation also affects emotion regulation and impulse control. In sleep deprivation:

a. Working memory is altered. Both retrieval of old information, that is blurred and blocked, and consolidation of new memories. Thus, memory is more vulnerable to being changed, mixed, distorted or manipulated (Poe, 2017).
b. Recognition of emotions is affected and a tendancy emerges for negative emotional labelling of neutral stimuli (Killgore, Balkin, Yarnell and Capaldi, 2017; Tempesta et al., 2010).
c. Cognitive functioning can be impaired, including executive attention and higher cognitive functions. In long-term chronic partial sleep deprivation, profound neurocognitive deficits accumulate over time, in spite of subjective adaptation to the sensation of sleepiness. Studies show that individual vulnerability to sleep loss plays a critical role in the affects produced (Dinges, 2005; Lim and Dinges, 2010).
d. One can become less morally aware and less able to recognize morality in others, although results are inconclusive (Barnes, Gunia, and Wagner, 2015; Killgore et al, 2007; Tempesta et al., 2012).
e. Regulatory-inhibitory systems are impaired leading to short-term impulsive decisions and wrongful assessment of risk-taking behaviours (McKenna, Dickinson, and Orff, 2007).

All these elements imply that in the creation of a torturing environment, sleep deprivation is a cue in provoking the following phenomena:

- The unreal can be confused with the real
- The environment can be perceived as more menacing and strong emotions are elicited that overflow the person
- Memory and reasoning are more vulnerable to distortion through suggestive influences
- The rational analysis and evaluation of incoming information and decision making are impaired, and the person is less able to resist coercive pressures and persuasion influences
- Moral decisions are impaired.

Type 3 Psychological torture: physical attack targeting the mind – wet asphyxia
In dry and wet asphyxia, survivors describe the anguish of a near death experience. In the debate on whether waterboarding was considered torture, Christian Correa, a Chilean attorney and Secretary of the National Commission on Political Imprisonment and Torture explained the effects of torture by 'submarine': 'Besides the physical pain, torture also provoked a near-death experience that made victims feel helpless. Most victims reported feeling deep humiliation and that [during "submarine"] their lives were entirely at the mercy of their torturers'. According to the Valech report (2005), this is precisely why torture is used: to destroy prisoners' will, dignity, and moral, psychological and physical resolve, so that they reveal the desired information. The Commission report describes the deep psychological trauma suffered by torture victims not only at the time of their torture but, significantly, even thirty years later. Most victims reported having some or all of the symptoms of post-traumatic stress disorder, including feelings of insecurity or fear, humiliation, worthlessness, shame, guilt, depression, anxiety and hopelessness. A man tortured at age 22 in 1980 and interviewed 24 years later in 2004 said, 'Even today I wake up because of having nightmares of dying from drowning' (Correa, 2007).

From Coercion to Identity Change

There is a progression from breaking the will in short-term coercion to causing permanent damage and changes through prolonged torture (Figure 20.2).

Short-term torture: coercion and breaking the will

Defining the breaking point
In short-term torture the objective is a temporary attack to produce emotional pain and suffering for any of two kinds of purposes: (a) punishment, humiliation, instilling fear or intimidating, or (b) coercing the person to act against his wish and will.

We define the breaking point as being when in the subjective experience of the survivor, the perpetrator achieves their goal by either making an indelible mark of humiliation or fear in the person that will determine their future actions (e.g. refraining from being involved again in political activities) or by obtaining from the survivor what the perpetrator wanted (e.g. confession, information, accusation).

It is important to bear in mind that it is the subjective experience of the survivor that defines the breaking point. For instance, a Basque survivor recalled in therapy how he endured three days of very harsh physical torture without even answering the initial question about his name until a last day when after a seemingly endless session of dry asphyxia he was submitted to credible menaces to his family and in his words, he broke. This means he gave his name and some basic, useless contextual information already known to the police. The shame was deep and prolonged. A Palestinian survivor of torture recalled in therapy how he endured three days of harsh torture by the Israeli intelligence services until a day when after four hours of extremely painful positions ('banana') and credible immediate menaces to his family he admitted to some of the things attributed to him. He was proud of himself as he had resisted three days of unbearable physical and psychological pain and never considered that he had been 'broken'. The definition is not based on what the perpetrator *gets* but on what the survivor *thinks and feels.* This distinction is, obviously, of utmost importance in therapy.

The IRRD model as an example
Davis and Leo (2012b) have applied these principles to the specific case of interrogational torture and have proposed the 'Interrogation-related regulatory decline (IRRD) model' for induced confessions. According to their model, self-regulation is the process by which individuals control their thoughts, emotions and behaviours in service of the pursuit of one or more goals. In interrogation the person must avoid the impulse to accept what the interrogator asserts in order to stop suffering. This means a balance between short-term objectives (stop suffering) and long-term objectives (stating innocence). But the energy for self-regulation is limited and there is an ego-depletion process that affects tasks requiring cognitive and emotional resources. What they call the 'perfect storm' of a false confession is the combination of 'the Big Three': high levels of emotions – emotional distress, due to the events that triggered or justified detention or to the interrogation itself; fatigue and sleep deprivation; and low food and water intake and especially glucose depletion (Davis and Leo, 2012a). This is usually associated with lengthy interrogations (more than four continuous hours with alternating interrogators) using coercive interrogation techniques. In an expanded version of their model they

add environments that foster fear, actions that question self-esteem and identity and coercive styles of questioning.

Prolonged attacks to self and identity

Interrogational torture seeks a temporary break in the person's will, and in some cases achieve permanent submission and collaboration. The well known cases of Marcia Merino (1993) or Luz Arce (1993), in Chile, are examples of people who, after torture, collaborated for years with the intelligence services of the dictatorship, even identifying with it, although later, when circumstances changed, they became partially self-critical. Similar transient changes in identity can be observed in child soldiers, chronically sexually abused children, victims of trafficking who 'choose' to continue with their captors, members of religious sects, members of extremist paramilitary groups or people who have been in totalitarian institutions such as prisons or concentration camps for a long time. In that case, there is prolonged torture that, as an effect, goes beyond the temporary breaking of the will to provoke identity changes, which in some aspects will be reversible and in others will be permanent and already part of the future identity of the person.

Identity is constructed in a dialectical way with the environment and especially in interaction with the different groups we belong to. Many mechanisms operate in the evolution of identity under a torturing environment, but it is important to highlight the following factors:

1. *Isolation.* In order to change a natural person's identity through torture, the first necessary element is to isolate him or her from the influence of other identities. This may involve physical isolation incorporating violence or psychological isolation, or controlling sources of information and learning.
2. *Breaking with the past.* Everything that belongs to the subjects' previous identities must be eliminated. Family, community groups, world view or ideology are all remnants of a past that must be eradicated.
3. *Stimulus control.* Regulations, rituals, codes, structures and planning prevent the person from developing and exercising his free will by accustoming him to a planned and submissive life. The person finds in the absence of will, affective anaesthesia and compliance with rules a source of stimulus and pleasure. Continuous and controlled action prevents reflection by creating situations where reversal will be virtually impossible.
4. *Fear, panic and terror.* Caused by threats of pain or actual pain (e.g. trafficking, child soldiers) or by the psychological internalization of fear, for example through the use of humiliation, threats of rejection (e.g. child abuse, gender violence, sects).
5. *Lack of control.* Fully-controlled environments where there is a control of noise, lights, temperature, and the organisation of time including any seemingly banal element in which the person can try to exercise control (e.g. concentration camps, prolonged kidnappings).
6. *Helplessness and arbitrariness.* The institution or the perpetrator is the ultimate decision maker without necessarily having to be logical in these decisions. The hierarchy is more important than the instruction itself. Any discussion or search for logic is punishable.
7. *Use of the body.* Breaking or dissolution of bodily limits and intimacy. The body can be stripped, beaten, used or transgressed, as an expression that nothing escapes the power of the other, that there are rules that break the unquestionable and as a way of annulling intimate and essential aspects of the core personal identity. If this is possible, everything is now possible.

8. *Affective and emotional manipulation.* The person is involved in overwhelming emotions that progressively lead to confusion or exhaustion. In this context, the person is highly susceptible to messages that alleviate distress or fear, that provide emotional attachments or love and that the person wishes to see as sincere. This generates emotional ambivalence towards the perpetrator who becomes the one who handles the emotions of affection and pain, creating a deep dependency.

9. *Breaking cognitive patterns, beliefs and worldviews.* Forcing experiences that produce irreversible changes in the way human beings are perceived, in the principles of trust, kindness and reciprocity, breaking personal ideological values and the principles of security, justice and order. Forcing to suppress or minimize reflective processes as an adaptive survival strategy, which in the long run will allow the adoption of new principles.

10. *Questioning of moral principles.* The person experiences how the differences between right and wrong, between good and evil, are blurred, subject to ethical dilemmas in which survival is at stake. Human, ideological and commitment values are questioned and broken through situations that generate contradictions and insoluble dilemmas. In any case, such circumstances will generate guilt, shame and the need to avoid and distance oneself from the past and to flee forward by clinging to more or less utilitarian explanations that preserve a minimum sense of dignity.

11. *Group pressure.* Human beings have a deep need for belonging, and in contexts of isolation and fear seek shared elements of identity with others to feel protected and experience the strength of the group. This includes multiple elements: seeing other groups as enemies, making it very difficult to be admitted to a group and costly to leave, collective actions of perpetrating harm with dilution of responsibility in the group, rituals and symbolic practices, emphasis on loyalty as a value even above life itself, rules of reciprocity and debt, and the creation of mythologies with positive values or with ideas of collective power, among others.

12. *New paradigms.* Models of understanding reality that involve new values and meanings, and which are transmitted through readings, group discussions, re-education, control of behaviour and attitudes by supervisors or leaders and internal control systems, the achievement of objectives, reinforcement of progress in the right direction and punishment of deviations.

All these methods do not work in isolation, but in different combinations and sequences. Moreover, depending on the torturing environment and the ultimate goal of the break and identity modification there will be more emphasis on one technique or another.

Sometimes, the changes may lead to the creation of a pseudo-self. That means one or more dissociated identities that coexist or overlap with the former self, which may in part reappear when the conditions of torture cease. At other times, the changes will be progressive and will imply a more or less permanent transformation of the person who will find in this new identity elements that are definitively incorporated into his or her previous identity.

PSYCHOLOGICAL CONSEQUENCES

Understanding Suffering and Damage

The breaking point is a temporary submission through fear, suffering, manipulation or confusion. Sometimes it leaves no marks. It is a transitory process. But sometimes it affects the way the person understands himself, others or the surrounding world (Figure 20.3). In dimensions related to the self, it can lead to loss of self-confidence and a deteriorated image of self, loss of sense of control and agency and feelings of vulnerability and helplessness, lack of tolerance to uncertainty and ambiguity and the need to be re-assured in front of minor problems, internal attributions of responsibility, leading to remorse or guilt, the inability to make sense of the experience (why me?), difficulties in finding a purpose and meaning in life (including spirituality and ideological convictions), a perception of a lack of future and a lack of a sense of wholeness associated with the life project.

In relation to others, the psychological impact of torture relates to changes in the basic belief in the kindness of human beings, to the capacity for having trust and confidence in others, broken expectations of empathy and compassion and eventually losing one's own's capacity for feeling empathy or compassion, along with a loss of the capacity to express the experience, either through words, art or movement, the incommunicability of the experience of torture and the associated experience of alienation from those that did not undergo a similar experience and might not understand what it means.

Finally, there is a lack of a sense of security and fears are now part of the daily emotions. Some of those fears are known and rational, while others are unknown and apparently irrational. The disturbing idea that our life can depend on randomness and everything can change in a moment can take root. Furthermore, survivors may have a sense of loss of an old world of order and a predictable universe where there is justice for those who have been wronged and punishment for those responsible for wrongdoing.

All these complex elements are the expression of damage to the identity, understood as the way the person sees herself from an individual and a collective dimension. The consciousness of what we call a human being is transformed and torture can be part of a new identity.

The VIVO scale was created in an attempt to measure this complex network of phenomena as an aid for forensic documentation and especially for psychotherapy (Pérez-Sales et al., 2012). It is a 116-item measure that offers a profile of the impact of experience of trauma, crisis and loss in ten conceptual blocks (Worldviews, Attitude towards the World, View of Human Beings, Coping, Impact of Past Situations, Emotions, Telling the Experience, Consequences, Social Support and Identity) and 35 subscales.

Epidemiological Data on the Devastating Impact of Psychological Torture

Although the above concepts reflect the experience of most survivors, clinical research is largely based on the concept of post-traumatic stress disorder. It is beyond the scope of this chapter to review the studies that have compared the prevalence of psychological disorders linked to physical and psychological torture. Furthermore, there are strong methodological problems: (a) studies are mostly based on ad-hoc definitions from a list of torture methods of what is considered 'psychological torture', and (b) most persons have been subjected to both physical and psychological torture and it is quite difficult to isolate the effect of one or

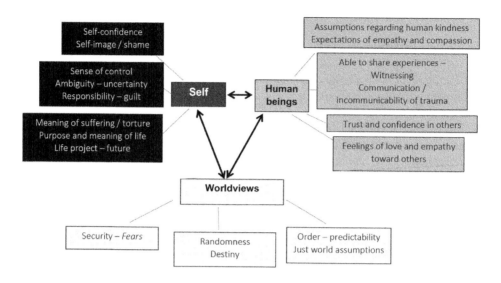

Figure 20.3   Conscious and unconscious beliefs and assumptions about the world, others and self challenged by torture as an extreme traumatic experience

the other. Table 20.2 collects a selection of studies from different contexts and cultural backgrounds that compare the impacts of physical versus psychological torture. This cross-cultural narrative review shows the equal or greater impact and sequels of psychological over physical torture.

CONTRASTING THE MEDICAL AND LEGAL DEFINITIONS OF TORTURE

Psychological torture has been progressively recognized in the international legal sphere through the statements and hearings of multiple international bodies. We will not present or summarize those finding here, since they are explored at length in earlier chapters of this book, save to say that they embrace a broad range of practices and experiences.

The purpose of this section is limited to highlighting some relevant aspects in which the legal and medical models of understanding torture diverge.

Torture is not equivalent to physical pain: although the UNCAT definition includes physical or mental pain or suffering, in the folk conception, torture is associated with producing extreme physical pain. However physical pain is only one of many elements (although an extremely important one) employed in the process of breaking the self.

Fear and threats are not only critical elements in breaking the will of the survivor, but they leave indelible marks and can turn into deep, permanent anguish over time. Research shows that this anguish is a biological imprint of extreme and insurmountable feelings of vulnerability, unpredictability and loss of control.

Table 20.2   Long-term psychiatric consequences of physical versus psychological torture

Author	Sample	Findings
Somnier and Genefke (1986)	200 VoT resettled in Denmark. Qualitative in-depth interviews	Psychological torture was associated with more severe and lasting clinical symptoms.
Momartin, Silove, Manicavasagar and Steel (2003)	126 Bosnian Muslim refugees resettled in Australia	PTSD was predicted by threat to life but not physical torture. Threat to life and traumatic loss also contributed to symptom severity and disability associated with PTSD.
Bauer, Priebe, Häring and Adamczak (1993)	55 former German Democratic Republic political prisoners	Psychological torture produced enduring depression, anxiety and psychosomatic disorders that persisted over time without improvement.
Hooberman, Rosenfeld, Lhewa, Rasmussen and Keller (2007)	325 VoT resettled in the US	PTSD, anxiety and depression symptoms were significantly correlated with rape/sexual assault but not to psychological torture (witnessing the torture of others, torture of family members, deprivation/passive torture) nor physical torture (beating).
De Zoysa and Fernando (2007)	90 survivors – Sri Lanka	No differences found. Results indicated that in most cases survivors suffered both physical and psychological torture.
Başoğlu, Livanou, and Crnobaric (2007)	279 VoT – Balkans	Psychological torture (sham executions, threats of rape, sexual advances, threats against self or family, witnessing the torture of others, humiliating treatment, isolation, deprivation of urination/defecation, blindfolding, sleep deprivation) was as distressing as physical torture. Physical pain per se was not the most important determinant of traumatic stress in survivors of torture.
Başoğlu (2009)	432 torture survivors in former Yugoslavia and Turkey	Post-traumatic stress disorder was related to psychological torture (war-related captivity, deprivation of basic needs, sexual torture, exposure to extreme temperatures, isolation and forced stress positions) but not to physical torture.
Punamäki, Qouta, and Sarraj (2010)	275 Palestinian men	Both physical and psychological torture methods were associated with increased PTSD symptoms, especially when combined. Psychological torture was also associated with increased somatic symptoms.
Kira, Ashby, Odenat and Lewandowsky (2013)	326 VoT from 30 countries (mainly Burma, Butan) resettled in the US	Torture predicts Cumulative Trauma Disorder (CTD) but not PTSD. Witnessing and being subjected to sexual tortures were significant predictors of PTSD and Cumulative Trauma Disorder.
Choi, Lee and Lee (2017)	206 Korean VoT tortured between 1970 and 2000	Psychological torture and deprivation but not physical damage explained post-traumatic stress disorder (PTSD).

Questioning the self through humiliation, or the use of methods that induce shame or guilt is not a minor form of ill-treatment but probably one of the most severe. The suffering and psychological pain associated with self-conscious emotions often leaves permanent scars and damage which are even more severe in the long term than physical pain. The category *inhuman or degrading treatment* as an indicator of severity is misleading as it entails the idea of less-severe torture or torture-lite, thus hiding the devastating nature of psychological torture.

Emphasising the **severity of suffering** as a criterion to distinguish ill-treatment and torture is not consistent with medical and psychological scientific evidence. It is impossible to medically define a limit for 'extreme suffering' or 'extreme psychological suffering' because that limit depends on the subjective experience of each survivor. It assumes a linear relationship between the torture experience, the severity of suffering and psychological impacts which in fact does not occur. There are different profiles of torturing environments that produce different types of suffering (affective, emotional, somatosensorial …), which are impossible to quantify and can affect individuals in very particular ways. The impact of torture depends on the physical and psychological characteristics of the detainee and his or her physical and psychological vulnerability and resilience.

From the point of view of perpetrators, torture is the 'art' of finding the limits of physical and psychological endurance to reach a breaking point of temporary or permanent submission. The torturer seeks the 'limits' of the tortured person. But what are the limits? The only true limit is death. It is impossible to assess psychological damage or severe psychological suffering during the act of torture, whether interrogational or not. The only possible way is to state clear regulations in any situation liable to turn into torture, taking as a reference what science shows are the limits that guarantee not harming another human being.

The methods employed are relevant, but they should not be the central criteria. Torture methods cannot be conceptualized as more or less humane – 'rough' or 'lite' or amounting, by themselves, to ill-treatment or torture according to the supposed level of suffering they entail. Each torture method causes a different type of physical or psychological pain and awakens different personal dreads. Each method or set of methods challenges different psychological and physical limits, but in the end, all methods are strategies within the broader game of domination and subjugation. The most banal technique can destroy a victim if applied to a person vulnerable to it. Finding the solution to what can be considered torture in a list of *authorised methods* is, thus, erroneous from a medical and psychological point of view and confers a false sense of protection. It makes more sense to assess the aims and targets of torture, and the different pathways involved in breaking the individual. And, accordingly, protect human beings from these situations or environments.

Time and reiteration are partially relevant criteria to assess torture. They are not necessarily a signal of more severe suffering or consequences, because even very short ill-treatment periods can have long-lasting effects. But both can be criteria to support intentionality. It is misleading to distinguish ill-treatment from torture using length of detention or reiteration of abuses as a primary criterion.

All the above leads to the conclusion that in defining torture and distinguishing it from ill-treatment, the emphasis should be placed on the purpose, not the method. The legal world should move towards sentences, resolutions and statements where intentionality, motivation and purposes are put at the centre, while the severity of suffering is considered a secondary element.

PROFILING TORTURE FOR SCIENTIFIC STUDIES

Trying to produce academic research from across all these complex worlds requires tools that allow the profiling of torture. Torture has traditionally been measured through checklists. There have been various attempts to create such checklists, including, to name a few, the Exposure to Torture Scale (Başoğlu, 1999), the Allodi Torture Scale (Allodi, 1991) and the Torture Checklist (Rasmussen, Crager, Keatley, Keller and Rosenfeld, 2011). A review collected up to 48 different checklists of war-related events (including torture), ranging in length from 8 to 164 items (Green, Rasmussen and Rosenfeld, 2010). They are mostly designed in terms of semi-structured interviews for use in rapid assessments with displaced populations or in refugee camps, as an aid to elaborate clinical histories in rehabilitation centres, or for forensic assessments of legal claims. None of these checklists has been validated (Green et al., 2010; Hollifield et al., 2002), nor have their psychometric properties been published; they are useful insofar as they provide a structured listing of methods. Torture severity measurements are somewhat more refined versions of a checklist. Half of the studies in Green's review derived scores by simply summing the number of different types of abuse suffered (whether or not they were considered to be torture). A small number of studies also took into account the frequency and duration of techniques. None of these measures includes the subjective perception of the impact of each torture method. Only the Semi-Structured Interview for Survivors of War (SISOW) (Başoğlu, 1999) operationalizes torture severity by calculating the total number of types of torture (from a list of 44 events), frequency of exposure to torture, duration of detention and perceived severity of each type of experienced torture (i.e. distress) rated along a 5-point Likert scale. The SISOW was designed for use in the Balkans and the list of torture methods was derived from the testimony of survivors. Its applicability in other countries or cultures might be limited.

Checklists, in summary, are rough and inaccurate measures of torture that can incorporate neither the infinite methods of producing suffering that the human imagination of perpetrators can create nor the subjective experience of the combination of methods that happens in actual torture. According to what we called earlier in this chapter the *teleological approach*, although the number of torture methods is infinite, the final targets (coercion or breaking of the self) are limited. A more parsimonious node of research is to focus not on the method of producing suffering, but on the profile of attacks on the different physical and psychological systems of a human being and the purpose of using the method in this overall process of breaking the person (see Table 20.1). We need to understand torture methods framed in the overall picture of the torturing process. This connects with the idea that the impact of torture is not related to a single technique but to a cumulative effect or a combination of techniques that if used alone would not produce the same effects (Koenig, Stover and Fletcher, 2009; Reyes, 2008).

This, among other reasons, suggests shifting academic research from defining and measuring torture methods, to defining and measuring *torturing environments*. We define a torturing environment as a milieu that creates the conditions for torture. It is made up of a group of contextual elements, conditions and practices that obliterate the will and control of the victim, compromising the self. This environment will amount to cruel, inhuman or degrading treatment or torture when it has been generated for any of the purposes stated in the United Nations definition. The creation of a torturing environment can include one or more of the following: attacks to primary needs and relation to the environment; attacks to the need for safety and physical integrity, including pain, threats and fear; and attacks to the self and identity, including individual, group and collective dimensions of identity (Table 20.1).

The Torturing Environment Scale (TES) (Pérez-Sales, 2017) was designed as an alternative that adopts this new outlook by gathering torture methods which attack human functioning using a purposive approach to offer a profile of a torture interaction (if used on an individual basis) or a torture milieu (if used as a tool for monitoring detention centres). It can also be used for forensic reports as a complementary tool to the Istanbul Protocol (IP) to better define the experience of the alleged survivor. The TES is a measure of the complex and multidimensional elements that can target a human being submitted to torture.[3] We hope more measures will emerge that open up the field of research on how torture targets the self and the mind.

REFERENCES

Allodi, FF (1991), 'Assessment and treatment of torture victims: a critical review', *Journal of Nervous and Mental Disease*, 179, 4–11.

Arce, L (1993), *El infierno [Hell]* (Editorial Océano).

Baer, HU, Vorbrügeen, M and Vorbrüggen, M (2007), 'Humiliation: the lasting effect of torture', *Military Medicine*, 172, 12–29.

Bandura, A (2008), 'The reconstrual of "free will" from the agentic perspective of social cognitive theory' in Baer, J, Kaufman, J and Baumeister, R (eds), *Are we free? Psychology and free will* (Oxford University Press).

Barnes, CM, Gunia, BC and Wagner, DT (2015), 'Sleep and moral awareness', *Journal of Sleep Research*, 24(2), 181–188.

Başoğlu, M (1999), Semi-Structured Interview for Survivors of War (SISOW) (personal communication).

Başoğlu, M (2009), 'A multivariate contextual analysis of torture and cruel, inhuman, and degrading treatments: implications for an evidence-based definition of torture', *American Journal of Orthopsychiatry*, 79(2), 135–145.

Başoğlu, M (2017a), *Torture and its definition in international law* (Oxford University Press).

Başoğlu, M (2017b), 'Effective management of breathlessness: a review of potential human rights issues', *European Respiratory Journal*, 49(5), 1602099.

Başoğlu, M, Livanou, M and Crnobaric, C (2007), 'Torture vs other cruel, inhuman, and degrading treatment', *Archives of General Psychiatry*, 64, 277–285.

Bauer, M, Priebe, S, Häring, B and Adamczak, K (1993), 'Long-term mental sequelae of political imprisonment in East Germany', *The Journal of Nervous and Mental Disease*, 181, 257–262.

Choi, H, Lee, H-J and Lee, H-Y (2017), 'The effects of torture-related stressors on long-term complex post-traumatic symptoms in South Korean torture survivors', *International Journal of Psychology*, 52, 57–66.

CIA (1963), *Kubark counterintelligence interrogation of resistance sources*, USA Declassified Document.

Comisión Nacional sobre Prisión Política y Tortura (2005), *Informe de la Comisión Nacional sobre Prisión Política y Tortura (Valech I)* [Report of the National Commission on Political Imprisonment and Torture (Valech I)], Ed. La Nacion, Santiago de Chile, Chile.

CIA (1983), *Human resource exploitation training manual*.

Correa, C (2007), 'Waterboarding prisoners and justifying torture: lessons for the U.S. from the Chilean experience', *Human Rights Brief*, 14(2), 21–25.

CSHRA (2005), 'The neurobiology of psychological torture', retrieved from http://humanrights.ucdavis.edu/projects/the-neurobiology-of-psychological-torture-1/

Cunniffe, D (2013), 'The worst scars are in the mind: deconstructing psychological torture', *ICL Journal*, 7(1), 1–61.

Davis, D and Leo, RA (2012a), 'Acute suggestibility in police interrogation' in Ridley, AM, Gabert, F and La Rooy, D (eds), *Suggestibility in legal contexts* (Wiley-Blackwell), 171–195.

Davis, D and Leo, RA (2012b), 'Interrogation-related regulatory decline: ego depletion, failures of self-regulation, and the decision to confess', *Psychology, Public Policy, and Law*, 18(4), 673–704.

de Zoysa, P and Fernando, R (2007), 'Methods and sequelae of torture: a study in Sri Lanka', *Torture*, 17(1), 53–56.

Dinges, D (2005), 'Neurocognitive consequences of sleep deprivation', *Seminars in Neurology*, 25(1), 117–129.

---

[3]   The TES can be freely accessed in English, Spanish and French through the website of the Project (www.psicosocial.info).

Dolezal, L and Lyons, B (2017), 'Health-related shame: an affective determinant of health?' *Medical Humanities*, 43(4), 257–263.

Eisenberger, NI (2012a), 'The neural bases of social pain: evidence for shared representations with physical pain', *Psychosomatic Medicine*, 74(2), 126–135.

Eisenberger, NI (2012b), 'The pain of social disconnection: examining the shared neural underpinnings of physical and social pain', *Nature Reviews Neuroscience*, 13(6), 421–434.

Green, D, Rasmussen, A and Rosenfeld, B (2010), 'Defining torture: a review of 40 years of health science research', *Journal of Traumatic Stress*, 23(4), 528–531.

Gregg, AP and Sedikides, C (2010), 'Narcissistic fragility: rethinking its links to explicit and implicit self-esteem', *Self and Identity*, 9(2), 142–161.

Harman, R and Lee, D (2009), 'The role of shame and self-critical thinking in the development and maintenance of current threat in post-traumatic stress disorder', *Clinical Psychology & Psychotherapy*, 17(1), 13–24.

Hollifield, M, Warner, TD, Lian, N, Jenkins, JH, Kesler, J and Stevenson, J (2002), 'Measuring trauma and health status in refugees', *JAMA*, 288(5), 611–621.

Hooberman, JB, Rosenfeld, B, Lhewa, D, Rasmussen, A and Keller, A (2007), 'Classifying the torture experiences of refugees living in the United States', *Journal of Interpersonal Violence*, 22(1), 108–123.

Killgore, WDS, Balkin, TJ, Yarnell, AM and Capaldi, VF (2017), 'Sleep deprivation impairs recognition of specific emotions', *Neurobiology of Sleep and Circadian Rhythms*, 3 (December 2016), 10–16.

Killgore, WDS, Killgore, DB, Day, LM, Li, C, Kamimori, GH and Balkin, TJ (2007), 'The effects of 53 hours of sleep deprivation on moral judgment', *Sleep*, 30(3), 345–352.

Kira, IA, Ashby, JS, Odenat, L and Lewandowsky, L (2013), 'The mental health effects of torture trauma and its severity: a replication and extension', *Psychology*, 4(5), 472–482.

Koenig, KA, Stover, E and Fletcher, LE (2009), 'The cumulative effect: a medico-legal approach to United States torture law and policy', *Essex Human Rights Review*, 6(1), 145–168.

Kramer, D (2010), 'The effects of psychological torture', *Berkeley Law*, June, 1–9.

Kross, E, Berman, MG, Mischel, W, Smith, EE and Wager, TD (2011), 'Social rejection shares somatosensory representations with physical pain', *Proceedings of the National Academy of Sciences*, 108(15), 6270–6275.

Leary, MR and Tangney, JP (2012), *Handbook of self and identity* (Guilford Press).

Leeming, D and Boyle, M (2004), 'Shame as a social phenomenon: a critical analysis of the concept of dispositional shame', *Psychology and Psychotherapy*, 77(Pt 3), 375–396.

Lim, J and Dinges, DF (2010), 'A meta-analysis of the impact of short-term sleep deprivation on cognitive variables', *Psychological Bulletin*, 136(3), 375–389.

Luban, D and Shue, H (2012), 'Mental torture: a critique of erasures in U.S. law', *The Georgetown Law Journal*, 100, 823–863.

Maier, A (2011), 'Torture: how denying moral standing violates human dignity' in Kaufmann, P, Kuch, H, Neuhäuser, C and Webster, E (eds), *Humiliation, degradation, dehumanization* (Springer Netherlands), 101–118.

McCoy, AW (2006), *A short history of psychological torture: its discovery, propagation, perfection, and legalization* (University of California Press).

McCoy, AW (2012), *Torture and impunity: the U.S. doctrine of coercive interrogation* (University of Wisconsin Press).

McKenna, BS, Dickinson, DL and Orff, HJ (2007), 'The effects of one night of sleep deprivation on known-risk and ambiguous-risk decisions', *J Sleep Research*, 16, 245–252.

Merino, MA (1993), *Mi verdad: mas allá del horror, yo acuso [My truth: beyond the horror, I accuse]* (Merino Vega).

Momartin, S, Silove, D, Manicavasagar, V and Steel, Z (2003), 'Dimensions of trauma associated with posttraumatic stress disorder (PTSD) caseness, severity and functional impairment: a study of Bosnian refugees resettled in Australia', *Social Science & Medicine*, 57(5), 775–781.

Müller-Pinzler, L, Gazzola, V, Keysers, C, Sommer, J, Jansen, A, Frässle, S, … Krach, S (2015), 'Neural pathways of embarrassment and their modulation by social anxiety', *NeuroImage*, 119, 252–261.

Nickerson, A, Schnyder, U, Bryant, RA, Schick, M, Mueller, J and Morina, N (2015), 'Moral injury in traumatized refugees', *Psychotherapy and Psychosomatics*, 84(2), 122–123.

Otten, M and Jonas, K J (2014), 'Humiliation as an intense emotional experience: Evidence from the electro-encephalogram', *Social Neuroscience*, 9(1), 23–35.

Panayiotou, A, Jackson, M and Crowe, SF (2010), 'A meta-analytic review of the emotional symptoms associated with mild traumatic brain injury', *Journal of Clinical and Experimental Neuropsychology*, 32(5), 463–473.

Pérez-Sales, P (2017), *Psychological torture: definition, evaluation and measurement* (Routledge Books).

Pérez-Sales, P, Eiroa-Orosa, FJ, Olivos, P, Barbero-Val, E, Fernández-Liria, A and Vergara, M (2012), 'Vivo questionnaire: a measure of human worldviews and identity in trauma, crisis, and loss – validation and preliminary findings', *Journal of Loss and Trauma*, 17(3), 236–259.

Pérez-Sales, P, Navarro-Lashayas, MA and Plaza, A (2016), 'Incommunicado detention and torture in Spain, Part III: "five days is enough": the concept of torturing environments', *Torture*, 26(3), 21–33.

Physicians for Human Rights (2005), *Break them down: systematic use of psychological torture by US forces* (PHR).

Platt, M and Freyd, J (2012), 'Trauma and negative underlying assumptions in feelings of shame: an exploratory study', *Psychological Trauma: Theory, Research, Practice, and Policy*, 4(4), 370–378.

Poe, GR (2017), 'Sleep is for forgetting', *The Journal of Neuroscience*, 37(3), 464–473.

Pollmann, A (2011), 'Embodied self-respect and the fragility of human dignity: a human rights approach', in Kaufmann, P, Kuch, H, Neuhäuser, C and Webster, E (eds), *Humiliation, Degradation, Dehumanization* (Springer Netherlands), 243–261.

Punamäki, R-L, Qouta, SR and El Sarraj, E (2010), 'Nature of torture, PTSD, and somatic symptoms among political ex-prisoners', *Journal of Traumatic Stress*, 23(4), 532–536.

Quiroga, J and Jaranson, J (2008), 'Torture', in *Encyclopedia of Psychological Trauma* (Wiley), 1–6.

Rasmussen, A, Crager, M, Keatley, E, Keller, AS and Rosenfeld, B (2011), 'A narrative checklist comparing legal definitions in a torture treatment clinic', *Zeitschrift für Psychologie/Journal of Psychology*, 219(3), 143–149.

Rejali, D (2007), *Torture and democracy* (Princeton University Press).

Reyes, H (2008), 'The worst scars are in the mind: psychological torture', *International Review of the Red Cross*, 89(867), 591–617.

Scarry, E (1985), *The body in pain* (Oxford University Press).

Silfver, M, Helkama, K, Lönnqvist, J-E and Verkasalo, M (2008), 'The relation between value priorities and proneness to guilt, shame, and empathy', *Motivation and Emotion*, 32(2), 69–80.

Somnier, FE and Genefke, IK (1986), 'Psychotherapy for victims of torture', *The British Journal of Psychiatry*, 149(3), 323–329.

Suedfeld, P (1990), *Psychology and torture* (Hemisphere Publishing Corp.).

Sussman, D (2005), 'What's wrong with torture?', *Philosophy and Public Affairs*, 33(1), 1–33.

Tempesta, D, Couyoumdjian, A, Curcio, G, Moroni, F, Marzano, C, De Gennaro, L and Ferrara, M (2010), 'Lack of sleep affects the evaluation of emotional stimuli', *Brain Research Bulletin*, 82(1–2), 104–108.

Tempesta, D, Couyoumdjian, A, Moroni, F, Marzano, C, De Gennaro, L and Ferrara, M (2012), 'The impact of one night of sleep deprivation on moral judgments', *Social Neuroscience*, 7(3), 292–300.

UN General Assembly (1984), The Convention Against Torture and Other Forms of Cruel, Inhuman and Degrading Treatment or Punishment (adopted 10 December 1984, entered into force 26 June 1987) 1465 UNTS 85.

Viñar, M (1993), *Fracturas de la memoria* (Trilce).

Wolfendale, J (2009), 'The myth of "torture lite"', *Ethics & International Affairs*, 23, 47–61.

21. Medico-legal documentation of torture and ill treatment

Vincent Iacopino

INTRODUCTION

Torture[1] is one of the most heinous crimes known to humanity, not only because it involves the intentional infliction of severe physical and/or mental pain, but because it is committed by or with the acquiescence of State officials and often effectively concealed to prevent justice and accountability. Consequently, torture victims suffer profound and enduring physical and mental pain and the reality of their pain and the crimes committed against them are often dismissed by the State in judicial and administrative proceedings.

In countries where torture and other cruel, inhuman and degrading treatment or punishment (ill treatment) is widespread, inadequate legal investigation of crimes fosters a legal system that depends on 'confessions' obtained through torture and ill treatment. Under such circumstances, torture is often viewed as the only means of achieving 'successful' prosecution of crimes; impunity becomes the norm and sustains a 'confession-based' legal system.[2] Police and other law enforcement officials torture with impunity because prosecutors and judges effectively turn a blind eye to evidence of torture, and victims remain silent for fear of reprisals by law enforcement officials. Impunity for torture not only undermines the rule of law; it creates a permissive environment within law enforcement for predatory police practices of extorting money in exchange for dropping or mitigating fabricated charges.

Given the State's power to commit and conceal the crime of torture, especially in countries where torture is widespread and systematic, the prospect of ending torture is extremely challenging. Ending torture and ill treatment requires effectively addressing a number of factors that facilitate torture *including*, inter alia:

- Inadequate safeguards during arrest and detention;
- Inadequate legal investigations of torture and ill treatment;
- Inadequate medico-legal evaluations of alleged victims;
- Inadequate police investigations of torture and ill treatment;
- Inadequate legal defense of alleged victims;

---

[1]   Torture in this chapter is defined in accordance with Article 1 of the UN Convention against Torture. See Convention against Torture and Other Cruel, Inhuman or Degrading Treatment or Punishment (adopted 10 December 1984, entered into force 26 June 1987) 1465 UNTS 85.

[2]   See Iacopino, V and Moreno, A, *Ending Impunity: The Use of Forensic Medical Evaluations to Document Torture and Ill Treatment in Kyrgyzstan* (Physicians for Human Rights, 2012). Available at: http://physiciansforhumanrights.org/library/reports/ending-impunity-forensic-medical-evaluations-in -kyrgyzstan.html; see also Moreno, A, Crosby, S, Xenakis, S and Iacopino V, 'Implementing Istanbul Protocol Standards for Forensic Evidence of Torture in Kyrgyzstan' (2015) 30 Journal of Forensic and Legal Medicine 39. Available at: http://dx.doi.org/10.1016/j.jflm.2014.12.009

- Allowing confessions obtained under torture into judicial and administrative proceedings;
- Inadequate sanctions against perpetrators and those who are complicit;
- Lack of systematic monitoring of torture and ill treatment practices;
- Fear of reprisals;
- Inadequate redress for victims of torture and ill treatment;
- Corruption of government officials.

While many factors contribute to torture practices, effective medico-legal documentation represents one of the most powerful ways to corroborate allegations of torture and ill treatment and achieve prevention, accountability, and redress for such crimes. This chapter reviews the international norms of medico-legal documentation of torture and ill treatment known as the Istanbul Protocol, as well as the challenges of applying these norms in everyday practice. In this chapter the term 'medico-legal evaluation' refers to clinical assessments of possible physical and psychological evidence of torture and/or ill treatment in legal contexts.[3] Although the term 'forensic evaluation' includes probative material clinical evidence in legal and non-legal contexts, the use of this term is limited to official State examinations by experts with formal forensic training.[4]

THE ISTANBUL PROTOCOL: UNITED NATIONS STANDARDS FOR THE EFFECTIVE INVESTIGATION AND DOCUMENTATION OF TORTURE AND ILL TREATMENT

Development, Recognition and Applications

Before the development of international norms for the effective investigation and documentation of torture and ill treatment there was no standard by which to judge the quality and adequacy of medico-legal evaluations, whether conducted by State forensic officials or clinical experts[5] in civil society. Consequently, high-quality medico-legal evaluations conducted by clinical experts in civil society were often excluded from judicial and administrative proceedings, while, at the same time, inadequate and inaccurate State forensic evaluations were routinely admitted into evidence. For example, in Turkey comprehensive evaluations of physical and psychological evidence conducted by clinical experts, so-called 'alternative reports,' were rejected by courts while State forensic evaluations simply stating 'no sign of injury or lesion' were routinely accepted in the adjudication of cases of alleged torture.[6]

---

[3]   The term 'forensic' is defined as, 'relating to or denoting the application of scientific methods and techniques to the investigation of a crime'. See Oxford Online Dictionary, available at: https://en.oxforddictionaries.com/definition/forensic

[4]   Such evaluations may be conducted by clinicians who are employed by both State and non-State institutions

[5]   The term 'clinical experts' refers to health professionals who document physical and/or psychological evidence of torture and ill treatment.

[6]   See Iacopino, V, Heisler, M, Pishever, S et al., 'Physician Complicity in Misrepresentation and Omission of Medical Evidence in Post-Detention Medical Examinations in Turkey' (1996) 276 *Journal of the American Medical Association* 396–402; and Iacopino, V, Heisler, M and Rosoff, R, *Torture in Turkey and its Unwilling Accomplices* (Physicians for Human Rights, 1996), 221–241.

This state of affairs changed in 1999 when members of civil society, together with United Nations (UN) bodies, including the Office of the High Commissioner for Human Rights (OHCHR), the UN Special Rapporteur on Torture (SRT), the UN Committee against Torture (CAT) and the UN Voluntary Fund for Victims of Torture (UNVFVT) developed international standards for effective investigation and documentation of torture and ill treatment, known as *the 'Istanbul Protocol', or United Nations Manual on Effective Investigation and Documentation of Torture and Other Cruel, Inhuman or Degrading Treatment or Punishment*.[7] The Istanbul Protocol served to bridge the gap between the treaty-based duties of States to investigate and document torture and ill treatment and the lack of normative guidance, particularly medico-legal investigation and documentation of torture.

The Istanbul Protocol outlines international legal standards on protection against torture and sets out specific guidelines on how effective legal and clinical[8] investigations into allegations of torture and ill treatment should be conducted. The Istanbul Protocol also contains a series of 'Istanbul Principles' which represent minimum standards for State adherence to ensure the effective investigation and documentation of torture and ill treatment.

Many procedures for a legal investigation are included in the Istanbul Protocol manual, such as how to interview the alleged victim and other witnesses, selection of the investigator, the safety of witnesses, how to collect the alleged perpetrator's statement, how to secure and obtain physical evidence, and detailed guidelines on how to establish a special independent commission of inquiry to investigate alleged torture and ill treatment. The manual also includes comprehensive guidelines for clinical evaluations to detect physical and psychological evidence of torture and ill treatment. According to the Istanbul Protocol, clinical evaluations must include detailed assessments and documentation of both physical and psychological evidence by one or more qualified experts. Clinical experts correlate the degree of consistency between individual allegations of abuse and physical and psychological evidence. They must also provide an opinion on the possibility of torture and/or ill treatment based on their interpretations of physical and psychological evidence and communicate their opinions to adjudicators.

The Istanbul Protocol was the result of three years of analysis, research, and drafting undertaken by more than 75 forensic experts, physicians, psychologists, human rights monitors, and lawyers who represented 40 organizations and institutions from 15 countries. The development of the Istanbul Protocol was initiated and coordinated by Physicians for Human Rights (PHR), the Human Rights foundation of Turkey (HRFT), and Action for Torture Survivors (HRFT-Geneva).

It is no coincidence that health professionals played a key role in initiating the Istanbul Protocol. Health professionals are often the first to observe and witness the health consequences of torture and ill treatment.[9] Furthermore, in countries where torture and ill treatment

---

[7] See Iacopino, V, Özkapıçı, O, Schlar, C et al., Manual on the Effective Investigation and Documentation of Torture and Other Cruel, Inhuman or Degrading Treatment or Punishment (The Istanbul Protocol) (United Nations Publications, 2001). See UN Doc HR/P/PT/8/Rev.a (2004), also available at: http://www.ohchr.org/Documents/Publications/training8Rev1en.pdf. See also Iacopino, V, Özkapıçı, O, Schlar, C, (1999). 'The Istanbul Protocol: International Standards for the Effective Investigation and Documentation of Torture and Ill-treatment' (1999) 354 The Lancet 1117.

[8] While the 2004 edition of the Istanbul Protocol uses the term 'medical' when referring to physical and psychological evaluations and the experts who conduct them, a soon to be published edition of the Istanbul Protocol and this chapter use the terms 'clinical' and 'medico-legal' instead.

[9] Iacopino, Özkapıçı and Schlar (n 7 above).

are common, coercion of health professionals to misrepresent, neglect, or falsify clinical evidence of torture and ill treatment is an important element of States' denials of the existence of these abuses.[10] The development of the Istanbul Protocol represented more than a set of guidelines and standards; it was for many health professionals in civil society, a means of empowerment, a statement of purpose and responsibility, and a remedy to the silence and complicity of health professionals in the crime of torture.

The Istanbul Protocol was officially recognized by the UN High Commissioner for Human Rights in 1999 and included in the Office of the High Commissioner for Human Rights (OHCHR) Professional Training Series first in 2001 and later updated in 2004. The 'Istanbul Principles' have been adopted in UN General Assembly and UN Commission on Human Rights (renamed the UN Human Rights Council in 2006) resolutions. These Principles, together with the Istanbul Protocol guidelines have served as international standards for conducting the clinical and legal investigation and documentation of torture and ill treatment in national and international judicial proceedings. The Istanbul Protocol has also been recognized as providing normative standards by regional human rights bodies including the Inter-American Commission on Human Rights, the African Commission on Human and Peoples' Rights, and the European Court of Human Rights, as well as a number of national human rights institutions. In addition, the Istanbul Principles are routinely used as a point of reference for measuring the effectiveness of torture investigations by the UN Committee against Torture, the UN Special Rapporteur on Torture, and the UN Subcommittee for the Prevention of Torture.

In his annual report to the UN General Assembly in October 2014, the then UN Special Rapporteur on Torture, Mr Juan Mendez, recognized the critical the role of forensic and medical sciences in the investigation and prevention of torture and other ill treatment. Mr Mendez stated that, 'The Istanbul Protocol serves as a standard for medical evidence given by experts, for benchmarking the effectiveness of the evidence, and for establishing redress for victims' and that 'Quality forensic reports are revolutionizing investigations of torture'.[11]

Such recognition represents a significant factor in the widespread use and acceptance of Istanbul Protocol standards in medico-legal and other contexts. The Istanbul Protocol and its Principles are now routinely used by clinical experts in court cases in which torture and/or ill treatment is alleged. Recognizing its importance, a number of countries have taken steps to incorporate the Istanbul Protocol as part of its legal framework.

Istanbul Protocol standards have been used in a wide range of anti-torture activities including:

- Legal investigation and documentation of torture and ill treatment;
- Medical evaluations of alleged torture and ill treatment in criminal, civil, and administrative cases;
- Psychological evaluation of alleged torture and ill treatment in criminal, civil, and administrative cases;
- Human rights investigations;

---

[10]   Iacopino, Özkapıçı, Schlar et al. (n 7 above).
[11]   Interim report of the Special Rapporteur on torture and other cruel, inhuman or degrading treatment or punishment: 'Role of forensic and medical sciences in the investigation and prevention of torture and other ill-treatment', UN Doc A/69/387 (23 September 2014).

- Torture prevention and international human rights monitoring (UN anti-torture bodies, national preventive mechanisms, national human rights institutions, the European Committee for the Prevention of Torture, the International Committee of the Red Cross, etc.);
- Capacity building for relevant target groups in civil society and State actors;
- Advocacy for torture prevention, accountability and redress;
- Accountability of State officials and State investigation and documentation practices;
- Development of training materials;
- Implementation of conditions necessary for the effective investigation and documentation of torture and ill treatment; and
- As an intake tool for rehabilitation services.

Clinical Evaluations of Alleged Torture

The guidelines contained in the Istanbul Protocol manual are not designed to be fixed, rather they represent an elaboration of the minimum standards contained in the Istanbul Principles and should be applied in accordance with a reasonable assessment of available resources. The Istanbul Protocol requires that all clinical evaluations in which torture or ill treatment is alleged must be in accordance with the following Istanbul Principles:[12]

- Clinical evaluators should behave in conformity with the highest ethical standards and obtain informed consent before any examination is conducted.
- Clinical evaluations must:

    – Conform to established standards of clinical practice;
    – Be under the control of clinical experts, not security personnel; and
    – Be conducted promptly.

- Written reports must be accurate and include the following:

    – Identification of the alleged victim and conditions of the evaluation;
    – A detailed account of allegations including torture or ill treatment methods and physical and psychological symptoms;
    – A record of physical and psychological findings;
    – Interpretation of all findings, an opinion on the possibility of torture and/or ill treatment, and clinical recommendations; and
    – Identification and the signature of the clinical expert(s).

While these minimum standards apply to all clinical evaluations of alleged or suspected torture and ill treatment, comprehensive clinical evaluations of torture and ill treatment typically involve the application of the detailed guidelines set forth in the 83-page Istanbul Protocol

---

[12]   See Iacopino, Ozkalipci, Schlar et al, 2001 (n 7 above), Annex I.

manual. Such comprehensive evaluations include the following components (see Istanbul Protocol, Annex IV):[13]

1. Relevant case information;
2. Clinician's qualifications;
3. Statement regarding veracity of testimony;
4. Background information;
5. Allegations of torture and ill treatment;
6. Physical symptoms and disabilities;
7. Physical examination;
8. Psychological evaluation;
   - Methods of assessment;
   - Current psychological complaints;
   - Post-torture history;
   - Pre-torture history;
   - Past psychological/psychiatric history;
   - Substance use and abuse history;
   - Mental status examination;
   - Assessment of social functioning;
   - [Psychological testing – optional];
   - [Neuropsychological assessment – optional];
9. Photographs and diagrams;
10. Diagnostic test results;
11. Consultations;
12. Interpretation of physical and psychological findings;
13. Conclusions and recommendations;
14. Statement of truthfulness;
15. Statement of restrictions on the clinical evaluation/investigation;
16. Clinician's signature, date, place;
17. Relevant appendices.

It is important to understand that comprehensive Istanbul Protocol clinical evaluations typically take two to four hours, or longer, to conduct and that medico-legal affidavits may be 10 or 20 pages in length. This often represents a significant departure from normative practice and requires considerable efforts to reform. Also, it takes considerable time for clinicians to become proficient in conducting these evaluations. It may take several years for medico-legal experts to achieve high-quality Istanbul Protocol medico-legal evaluations. In addition, comprehensive evaluations of alleged torture and ill treatment often require the expertise of more than one expert including medical and psychological expertise, but also subspecialists in medicine and surgery and neuropsychologists. In legal cases, it is important, where possible, to integrate the findings of multiple evaluations into one comprehensive evaluation. Some have argued that comprehensive medico-legal evaluations of alleged torture and ill treatment

---

[13]   *Ibid*, Annex IV; Note: These categories for clinical evaluations may be useful in assessing the consistency of medico-legal evaluations with the Istanbul Protocol and its Principles, but assessing the accuracy of a clinical evaluation requires clinical expertise to assess the extent to which physical and psychological findings support an expert's interpretations and conclusions.

are not practical in low-income countries, but the Istanbul Protocol does not require complex diagnostic equipment; it requires knowledge, practical training and adequate time to conduct an evaluation, regardless of the income status of the country in which the evaluation is conducted.[14] All clinicians should do their utmost to fulfill their ethical obligation to document and report torture and ill treatment in all settings. The Istanbul Protocol and its Principles should be considered the principal framework to fulfill this obligation.

Since torture and ill treatment, by definition, are crimes committed by State officials and typically involve assessments of severely traumatized individuals, clinical evaluators need to be aware of important interview considerations, procedural safeguards and the emotional reactions of victims as well as clinical evaluators.

Interview considerations

Clinicians should be aware of a number of interview considerations that are essential in conducting an effective evaluation. The Istanbul Protocol provides specific guidance on: (1) obtaining informed consent; (2) maintaining confidentiality; (3) ensuring the safety of the alleged victim; (4) allowing the alleged victim control over some elements of the interview (e.g. taking breaks and asking questions); (5) earning trust with active listening, meticulous communication, courtesy, and genuine empathy and honesty; (6) preparing for the interview by reviewing relevant material; (7) using effective interview techniques (open-ended questions followed by more specific questions); and (8) pursuit of inconsistencies and potential reasons for them.

Procedural safeguards

Persons deprived of their liberty are often at risk of additional harm if they complain of abuse to clinical evaluators. The Istanbul Protocol provides guidance on procedural safeguards for all clinicians who conduct evaluations of alleged torture and ill treatment in custody, which include:

- State forensic medical evaluations of detainees should be conducted in response to official written requests by public prosecutors or other appropriate officials;
- Requests for medical evaluations by law enforcement officials are to be considered invalid unless they are requested by written orders of a public prosecutor;
- Detainees themselves, their lawyer, or relatives have the right to request a clinical evaluation to assess possible evidence of torture and ill treatment;
- The detainee should be taken to the clinical examination by officials other than soldiers and police since torture and ill treatment may have occurred in the custody of these officials;
- The officials who supervise the transportation of the detainee should be responsible to the public prosecutors and not to law enforcement officials;
- The detainee's lawyer should be present during the request for examination and post-examination transport of the detainee;
- Detainees have the right to obtain a second or alternative clinical evaluation by a qualified clinician during and after the period of detention;

---

[14] See Beriashvili, R and Iacopino, V, 'Istanbul Protocol in Low-Income Countries – A Reply' (2016) 26(3) *Torture* 74–76.

- Each detainee must be examined in private. Police or other law enforcement officials should never be present in the examination room;
- Clinical evaluation of detainees should be conducted at a location that the clinician deems most suitable;
- The presence of police officers, soldiers, prison officers or other law enforcement officials in the examination room, for whatever reason, should be noted in the clinician's official medico-legal report as it may serve as legal grounds for disregarding a negative medico-legal report;
- The identity and titles of others who are present in the examination room during the clinical evaluations should be indicated in the report;
- Medico-legal evaluations of detainees by State forensic officials should include the use of a standardized clinical report form;
- The original, completed evaluation should be transmitted directly to the person requesting the report, generally the public prosecutor;
- When a detainee or a lawyer acting on his or her behalf requests a medico-legal report, they must be provided with the report;
- Copies of all medico-legal reports should be retained by the examining clinician;
- A national medical association or a commission of inquiry may choose to audit medico-legal reports to ensure that adequate procedural safeguards and documentation standards are adhered to, particularly by forensic experts and clinicians employed by the State;
- Under no circumstances should a copy of the medico-legal report be transferred to law enforcement officials;
- It is mandatory that a detainee undergo a clinical examination at the time of detention and an examination and evaluation upon release;
- Access to a lawyer should be provided at the time of the clinical examination;
- Evaluators working with prisoners must respect medical ethics and be capable of carrying out their professional duties independently of any third-party influence; and
- If a medico-legal evaluation supports allegations of torture, the detainee should not be returned to the place of detention, but rather should appear before the prosecutor or judge to determine the detainee's legal disposition.

These procedural safeguards supplement the Istanbul Principles that provide for prompt clinical evaluations of alleged torture and ill treatment by qualified, independent clinicians.

Transference and countertransference reactions

Clinicians who conduct evaluations should also be aware of the potential emotional reactions that evaluations of trauma may elicit in the interviewee and interviewer. These emotional reactions are known as transference and countertransference respectively. For example, mistrust, fear, shame, rage, and guilt are among the typical transference reactions that torture victims experience, particularly when asked to recall and recount details of their trauma history. In addition, the clinician's emotional responses to the torture victim, known as countertransference (e.g., horror, disbelief, depression, anger, over-identification, nightmares, avoidance, emotional numbing, and feelings of helplessness and hopelessness), may affect the clinical evaluation. Considering victims' extreme vulnerability and propensity to re-experience their trauma when it is either recognized or treated, it is critical that health professionals maintain a clear perspective of a healing relationship. Such vicarious or secondary trauma to the clinician can be minimized by discussions with other colleagues after the interview. Effective documentation of torture and other forms of ill treatment requires significant understanding of the motivations for working in this area. It is important that a clinician not use a traumatized population to work out unresolved issues in himself or herself, inasmuch as these issues can clearly hamper effectiveness.

Clinical evaluations
Clinical evaluations of alleged torture require a careful and thorough clinical history and examination of physical and psychological evidence by clinicians who are sensitive to cross-cultural issues and interpersonal dynamics between traumatized individuals and persons in positions of authority.

Clinicians must be knowledgeable about the physical and psychosocial consequences of torture and the established Istanbul Protocol and its Principles for effective documentation. While torture can have devastating health consequences, it is important to recognize that there is individual variability in physical and psychological findings. Individuals respond to and recover from traumatic events, including torture, in a variety of ways. In some cases, torture may not result in physical findings, for example in a 'mock execution.' Also, physical evidence may not be detectable when clinical evaluations are conducted after the resolution of acute signs and symptoms of physical injuries. Psychological symptoms, on the other hand, are often enduring in nature and also can play a critical role in documenting evidence of torture.

Physical manifestations of torture may involve all organ systems. Some effects are typically acute while others may be chronic. Symptoms and physical findings will vary in a given organ system over time, though psychosomatic and neurologic symptoms are typically chronic findings. Musculoskeletal symptoms are commonly present in both acute and chronic phases. A particular method of torture, its severity, and the anatomical location of injury often indicate the likelihood of specific physical findings. Some forms of torture may not produce physical findings, but are strongly associated with other conditions. For example, a history of head trauma with loss of consciousness is particularly important to the clinical diagnosis of traumatic brain injury as is a history of genital trauma and subsequent sexual dysfunction. The clinician should note all pertinent positive and negative findings using photographs and/ or body diagrams to record the location and nature of all injuries. Torture victims may display injuries that are substantially different from other forms of trauma. Although acute lesions may be characteristic of the alleged injuries, most lesions heal within about six weeks of torture leaving no scars or nonspecific scars.

Although there may be considerable variability in psychological effects, torture and ill treatment often result in profound, long-term psychological trauma. According to the Istanbul Protocol, the most common psychological problems are posttraumatic stress disorder (PTSD) and major depression, but may include others such as: acute stress disorder, complex PTSD, damaged self-concept, depersonalization/derealization syndrome, somatic symptom disorder, sexual dysfunction, substance abuse, neuropsychological impairment, and psychosis, among others.

Such psychological symptoms and disabilities can last many years or even a lifetime. It is important to realize that the severity of psychological reactions depends on the unique cultural, social, and political meanings that torture and ill treatment have for each individual, and significant adverse effects do not require extreme physical harm. Seemingly benign forms of ill treatment can and do have marked, long-term psychological effects. Moreover, psychological symptoms and disabilities often change over time based on both external stressors and individual mitigation factors.

In some countries where psychological experts and expertise is lacking, the duty of the psychological evaluation often falls on physicians and other medical personnel. While this may be less than ideal, physicians are trained in psychiatry and physicians in primary care are often in the position of diagnosing common psychological disorders such as major depression and anxiety disorders. Such circumstances underscore the need for a national plan of action to develop the capacity for effective clinical evaluations of torture and ill treatment, including both the physical and psychological components of the evaluation.

The Istanbul Protocol requires clinicians to correlate allegations of abuse with the findings of the clinical evaluation and indicate his or her level of confidence in the correlations (e.g. Not consistent with/Consistent with/Highly consistent with/Typical of/Diagnostic of). A final statement of opinion regarding all sources of evidence (physical and psychological findings, historical information, photographic findings, diagnostic test results, knowledge of regional practices of torture, consultation reports, etc.) and the possibility of torture should be included. The clinician also should provide any referrals or recommendations for further evaluation and care for the alleged victim.

Limitations and Misuse of the Istanbul Protocol

It is important to recognize limitations and potential misuse of the Istanbul Protocol. The Istanbul Protocol and its Principles aid medico-legal evaluators in their efforts to correlate specific allegations of abuse with physical and/or psychological evidence. The absence of physical and/or psychological evidence of torture, however, does not mean that it did not take place. Many factors may account for the absence of physical and/or psychological findings and documenting these factors can be useful in corroborating specific claims of abuse. Unfortunately, in some instances, the Istanbul Protocol has been misused to exonerate police who are accused of abuses on the basis of the absence of physical and/or psychological findings, for example in the absence of diagnostic criteria for PTSD. Such misuse of the Istanbul Protocol should never be tolerated.

In other circumstances, prosecutors have disqualified non-governmental expert testimony on the basis of omission of a minor component of a comprehensive clinical evaluation. Prosecutors have also attempted to assert that all clinical evaluations of alleged torture and ill treatment must include assessments of possible self-infliction (or self-infliction by proxy) of injuries and possible simulation of psychological symptoms and disabilities. The Istanbul Protocol and its Principles indicate that these possibilities should be considered when there is a foundation to suspect self-infliction and/or simulation. Efforts to establish a burden of proof to exclude the possibility of self-infliction and/or simulation in all cases is not consistent with the primary purpose of the Istanbul Protocol and likely represents a bias in legal systems against the recognition of torture and ill treatment.

In addition, courts have attempted to exclude clinical opinions of the possibility of torture and ill treatment and also sought to reject the Istanbul Protocol as authoritative guidance for medico-legal assessments of alleged torture and ill treatment. In a recent decision[15] by the Supreme Court of the United Kingdom, the Court recognized the Istanbul Protocol as forming authoritative standards for medico-legal assessments of alleged torture including the role of clinicians in opining on the possibility of torture and ill treatment as a cause of the physical and psychological findings that they document.

Current Efforts to Strengthen Istanbul Protocol Standards

While the Istanbul Protocol provides critical norms for legal and clinical investigation and documentation of torture and ill treatment, it does not provide specific documentation guidance to health professionals working in 'non-legal' settings; nor does it provide guidance on how States should implement Istanbul Protocol norms.

During the past several years, there has been increasing recognition of the need to strengthen the Istanbul Protocol standards and prevent misuse and weaponization of Istanbul Protocol norms. A project to update the Istanbul Protocol was initiated in January, 2018 to strengthen the Istanbul Protocol with updates and clarifications based on practical experience and the needs of Istanbul Protocol stakeholders involving more than 180 participants from 51 countries and led by Physicians for Human Rights, the International Rehabilitation Council for Torture Victims, the Human Rights Foundation of Turkey, REDRESS, the UN Committee against Torture, the UN Subcommittee for the Prevention of Torture, the UN Special Rapporteur on Torture, and the UN Voluntary Fund for Victims of Torture, with the support of DIGNITY – the Danish Institute against Torture and the UN Voluntary Fund for Victims of Torture. On May 11, 2018 the United Nations High Commissioner for Human Rights, Zeid Ra'ad Al Hussein, endorsed the project saying:[16]

> I would like to express my support to the IPS Project, in particular because it is being set in motion at a time when there is a growing need for strengthening international norms and preventive tools in the face of the pervasive use of torture across the globe. It is without any doubt that efforts, such as yours, to prevent occurrence of acts of torture and ill-treatment, to identify and effectively investigate such acts and to assist the victims of torture and ill-treatment are essential.

The development of updates to and clarifications of the Istanbul Protocol are based on a large-scale assessment during the past two years, including international meetings in Bishkek, Mexico City, and Copenhagen and a survey of more than 200 Istanbul Protocol stakeholders.[17] The project to strengthen Istanbul Protocol standards will include specific guidance to health professionals working in 'non-legal' settings and guidance to States on how to implement Istanbul Protocol norms. In an effort to contribute to the development of emerging international guidance on these issues, a review of relevant considerations is presented below.

---

[15]   *KV (Sri Lanka) v Secretary of State for the Home Department* [2019] UKSC 10.
[16]   Statement by UN High Commissioner for Human Rights, Zeid Ra'ad Al Hussein, 18 April 2018.
[17]   Haar, R, Lin, J, Modvig, J, Nee, J and Iacopino, V, 'The Istanbul Protocol: A Global Stakeholder Survey on Past Experiences, Current Practices and Additional Norm Setting' (2019) 29(1) *Torture* 70–84.

The Role of Health Professionals in Different Settings

Documentation of torture by health professionals is not limited to comprehensive evaluations for medico-legal purposes. Alleged victims of torture frequently encounter health professionals in other 'non-legal' settings for the primary purpose of evaluating health status rather than an allegation or suspicion of possible torture or ill treatment. The information collected in such settings is of critical probative value for medico-legal cases since the evaluations often occur soon after the alleged abuse and physical and psychological evidence is pronounced at that time. The need for clinicians to document and report clinical evidence of torture and ill treatment is not unlike other forms of violence that they encounter in their healthcare practices such as domestic abuse, sexual assault, and child and elder abuse.

The extent to which documentation in primary health encounters may differ from documentation for medico-legal purposes is not directly addressed by the 2004 edition of the Istanbul Protocol. Efforts to provide additional guidance to health professionals on torture documentation in primary healthcare encounters should be based on relevant international legal obligations and ethical duties as well as the potential benefits and risks of such guidance.

STATE OBLIGATIONS AND ETHICAL DUTIES

States have the duty to respect, protect, and fulfill everyone's right of freedom from torture. This includes the duty to investigate and document incidents of torture and other forms of ill treatment and to hold perpetrators accountable at national and international levels in order to eradicate torture and ill treatment and to provide reparation to victims.[18] States also have the duty to ensure education regarding the prohibition of torture to relevant personnel including clinical personnel.[19]

The UN Standard Minimum Rules for the Treatment of Prisoners (the Nelson Mandela Rules)[20] articulate the duty of health professionals to document *any signs of torture or ill treatment and to report their findings to appropriate authorities in Rule 34. In addition, the World Medical Associa*tion (WMA) Resolution on the Responsibility of Physicians in the Documentation and Denunciation of Acts of Torture or Cruel or Inhuman or Degrading Treatment establishes the duty of physicians to document and denounce acts of torture and ill treatment, and that a failure to do so constitutes complicity in such abuse.[21] It is worth noting that the complicity of physicians and other health professionals in United States (US) torture practices was enabled, in part, by the US Department of Defense policy of exempting clinicians working in 'non-clinical' settings, such as assisting in interrogations, from international medical ethical norms.[22] The European Committee for the Prevention of Torture and Inhuman

---

[18] UN Convention against Torture (n 1 above), Article 12.

[19] *Ibid*, Article 10.

[20] United Nations Standard Minimum Rules for the Treatment of Prisoners (the Nelson Mandela Rules), UN Doc A/RES/70/175 (17 December 2015).

[21] Adopted October 2007. For text see: www.wma.net/policies-post/wma-resolution-on-the-responsibility-of-physicians-in-the-documentation-and-denunciation-of-acts-of-torture-or-cruel-or-inhuman-or-degrading-treatment

[22] Assistant Secretary of Defense for Health Affairs, 'Medical program principles and procedures for the protection and treatment of detainees in the custody of the armed forces of the United States'

or Degrading Treatment or Punishment (CPT) also requires health professionals to document and report clinical evidence of torture and ill treatment, even when in conflict with the ethical duty of maintaining patient confidentiality.[23] The obligation of States to investigate and document torture and ill treatment should ultimately be codified in criminal statutes, forensic and health law, administrative regulations, and other legal standards, but are often absent or inadequate with respect to international legal standards in countries where torture and ill treatment are practiced with impunity.

As previously stated, the Istanbul Principles provide authoritative guidance to States on their duty to effectively investigate and document torture. These minimum standards refer to 'clinical experts involved in the investigation of torture or ill treatment …', however, not health professionals in other settings where the primary purpose is healthcare, rather than investigation or documentation of torture or ill treatment.

Alleged or Suspected Torture

When an individual alleges the crime of torture or ill treatment, the State has a duty to investigate the possibility of torture, which includes clinical assessments of both physical and psychological evidence in accordance with the Istanbul Protocol and its Principles. Regardless of the type of legal case (criminal, civil, administrative, or other) or the setting in which it is alleged (custodial or extra-custodial), the State is obliged to conduct timely assessments by qualified experts. It is important to note that the Istanbul Principles require health professionals to provide 'an interpretation of all findings, and an opinion on the possibility of torture and/or ill-treatment."[24] While non-governmental health professionals do not conduct evaluations on behalf of the State's duty, it is reasonable to assert that, when they opine on torture and ill treatment in legal cases, their evaluations should conform to the minimum standards contained in the Istanbul Principles.

As previously stated, the Istanbul Protocol guidelines are not fixed. So, the content of medico-legal evaluations can vary as long as the evaluations follow the Istanbul Principles. Non-governmental health professionals, therefore, should not be required to use a standardized evaluation form that may be required of State health professionals. On the other hand, since torture and ill treatment are crimes committed by or with the acquiescence of State officials, and forensic experts and clinicians who are employed by the State often lack professional independence and have well-founded fears of reprisals, States should establish policies and procedures for State-employed health professionals. Such policies would likely include compulsory evaluations in accordance with the Istanbul Protocol and its Principles and requiring the use of standardized forms to ensure the quality, accuracy, and accountability of official forensic evaluations.

In all cases of alleged or suspected torture and ill treatment, the duty of health professionals to investigate and document torture and ill treatment supersedes any limitations that may be

---

[Memorandum for the Secretaries of the military departments, June 3, 2005]. See also Rubenstein, L, Pross, C, Davidoff, F and Iacopino, V, 'Coercive US Interrogation Policies: A Challenge to Medical Ethics' (2005) 294 *Journal of the American Medical Association* 1544–1549.

[23]   23rd General Report on the CPT's Activities (2012-13), CPT/Inf (2013) 29.

[24]   The term 'torture' in the Istanbul Protocol is defined in accordance with the definition found in UN Convention against Torture (n 1 above), Article 1.

imposed by statutory considerations, the scope of a legal inquiry, and/or specific questions that prosecutors and judges may ask of clinical and forensic experts.

It should be noted that clinicians who conduct any health assessments of persons deprived of their liberty, for example in the case of routine health assessments of detainees, healthcare delivery of prisoners, and detention monitoring visits, should be trained and have the capacity to conduct clinical evaluations in accordance with the Istanbul Protocol and its Principles given the high likelihood of possible torture and ill treatment in these settings.

When non-governmental health professionals conduct evaluations of alleged or suspected torture and ill treatment in other, non-legal settings such as human rights field investigations, rehabilitation, advocacy, and other settings, they do not have the same evidentiary requirements as those conducted in legal settings. In such cases, it would be reasonable for clinicians to follow the Istanbul Principles and note any departures from their required elements. For example, some human rights field investigations may not permit sufficient time to conduct psychological evaluations and, therefore, would need to be noted.

Primary Healthcare Encounters

In settings where health professionals encounter individuals for the primary purpose of assessing their health status, such as in hospitals and clinics, health professionals should understand that their health evaluations have probative value and may be the only source of material clinical evidence in cases of alleged torture and ill treatment, and that the failure to document clinical evidence of torture may constitute a form of complicity. If, in the course of a primary healthcare encounter, injuries and/or psychological stress is observed, the clinician should consider the following guidance to ensure compliance with their ethical and legal duties.

- Obtain informed consent, if not already done, before proceeding with further evaluation and disclose any mandatory reporting requirements. If the individual does not provide consent to proceed with an assessment of possibile torture or ill treatment, this should be respected and the evaluation suspended.
- Exclude any third parties from the evaluation room to ensure privacy.
- Inquire about the cause of such injuries or psychological distress and whether the individual has been in the custody of any State officials including law enforcement.
- Record any symptoms or disabilities related to the alleged abuse.
- Conduct a directed physical examination of all organ systems that are relevant to the allegations of abuse.
- Document the presence of injuries associated with alleged or suspected abuse with photographs if at all possible.
- State the level of consistency between clinical findings and the alleged method(s) of injury (e.g. Not consistent with/Consistent with /Highly consistent with /Typical of/Diagnostic of).
- If ill treatment is alleged or suspected on the basis of clinical findings and the individual provides consent to document and report clinical findings, the clinician should:

  - Refer the individual for a comprehensive forensic evaluation by one or more qualified experts including a psychological evaluation;
  - Notify legal authorities as required by law; and
  - Inform the individual of his/her right to clinical evaluations by independent,

non-governmental clinical experts.
- Make appropriate referrals for treatment of medical and/or mental health conditions.
- Provide a copy of the evaluation to appropiate legal authorities and the patient, if requested, but not to law enforcement officials.

The question of whether health professionals in primary healthcare settings have a duty to provide interpretations and conclusions with respect to the possibility of torture and ill treatment as indicated in the Istanbul Principles or not should take into consideration the potential benefits and risks. Requiring health professionals in primary healthcare settings to provide interpretations and conclusions with respect to the possibility of torture and ill treatment would likely result in the benefit of empowering health professionals to relate their findings to the most likely cause or causes of presenting signs and symptoms, as is the case in clinical medicine. Also, since primary healthcare encounters often take place closer in time to the alleged abuse than subsequent more comprehensive evaluations, the opportunity to make appropriate interpretations and conclusions are critical, as clinical evidence, particularly physical findings, may resolve over time.

On the other hand, requiring health professionals in primary healthcare settings to provide interpretations and conclusions on the possibility of torture and ill treatment would likely be associated with a number of significant risks. Clinicians who conduct initial evaluations of possible victims of torture and ill treatment would be empowered as gatekeepers to subsequent more comprehensive clinical evaluations and be in a position to deny individual victims appropriate referral to legal investigation and prosecution of those responsible for crimes committed against them. Clinicians who have not received training in Istanbul Protocol documentation standards may not have adequate knowledge or experience to make accurate interpretations and conclusions regarding the possibility of torture and ill treatment. In addition, clinicians may fear reprisals for making conclusions regarding the possibility of torture and ill treatment, which would likely bias interpretations and conclusions in the direction of failing to recognize torture and ill treatment and subsequently create an evidentiary conflict with later clinical evaluations, thus precluding the accurate adjudication of legal cases.

In ongoing efforts to update and strengthen Istanbul Protocol standards, it will be important to weigh these potential benefits and risks. Whether health professionals in primary healthcare settings are advised to provide interpretations of clinical findings and a conclusion on the possibility of torture and ill treatment or not, the guidance they receive should include automatic triggers for appropriate referral for timely evaluation by qualified clinicians, including non-governmental clinicians, and appropriate legal referral to ensure effective legal and judicial proceedings.

Physicians for Human Rights (PHR) has considerable experience in implementing Istanbul Protocol standards in both legal and non-legal settings and has developed standardized evaluation forms for clinicians working in these settings. Standardized clinical evaluation forms developed for medico-legal settings are based on the Istanbul Principles, the comprehensive guidelines included in the 83-page Istanbul Protocol manual, and Annex IV of the Istanbul Protocol. More recently, PHR has developed a standardized form for use by clinicians in primary healthcare settings based on the considerations mentioned above and included in Annex 21.1. Regarding the duty of health professionals to provide interpretations of clinical findings and a conclusion on the possibility of torture and ill treatment, this form balances potential benefits and risks by requiring clinicians to assess the level of consistency between their clinical findings and the allegations of abuse, but does not require them to provide a conclusion on the possibility of torture and ill treatment. Such guidance may represent a reasonable minimum standard for clinicians working in primary healthcare settings.

IMPLEMENTATION OF ISTANBUL PROTOCOL STANDARDS

As previously stated, effective documentation of torture and ill treatment can serve as powerful material clinical evidence to corroborate the allegations of alleged victims, but such documentation requires a wide range of conditions in order for the evaluations to be undertaken promptly by qualified and independent clinicians who have adequate legal representation and before judges who will take such information into account in their judicial decisions. While the Istanbul Protocol provides critical norms for legal and clinical investigation and documentation of torture and ill treatment, it does not provide guidance on how States should implement Istanbul Protocol standards. In their efforts to conduct effective evaluations of torture and ill treatment during the past 20 years, clinicians have learned that their evaluations can be meaningless in the face of inadequate and corrupt forensic, legal, and judicial practices unless they also work to realize the necessary conditions for effective implementation of Istanbul Protocol standards.

Since 1999, the primary authors and principal organizers of the Istanbul Protocol have worked to implement Istanbul Protocol standards in approximately 40 countries. This extensive practical experience has provided insight into the needs and challenges associated with State implementation of the Istanbul Protocol. In 2012, four partner organizations (Physicians for Human Rights, the International Council for the Rehabilitation of Torture Victims, the Human Rights Foundation of Turkey, and REDRESS) developed as series of practical guidelines – known as the 'Istanbul Protocol Plan of Action' – for State implementation of the Istanbul Protocol. The Istanbul Protocol Plan of Action was recognized and supported by the UN High Commissioner for Human Rights in 2012[25] and includes the following categories of guidelines:

- Conditions necessary for implementation such as ratification and implementation of primary human rights treaties including the UN Convention Against Torture, the International Covenant on Civil and Political Rights and the Optional Protocol to the Convention Against Torture, sustained political will to eradicate torture, official, State recognition of the Istanbul Protocol, and active civil society participation, among other conditions;
- Legal, administrative and judicial reforms for effective criminalization of torture and ill treatment, safeguards for persons deprived of their liberty, complaints procedures, investigation and prosecution, adjudication, redress, and forensic medical evaluations;

---

[25]   Statement by UN High Commissioner for Human Rights, Navanethem Pillay, 24 February 2012. The Istanbul Protocol Plan of Action guidelines are largely based on Physicians for Human Rights' Istanbul Protocol implementation experience in Central Asia and will be incorporated in the updated edition of the Istanbul Protocol. See: Iacopino, V, Haar, RJ, Heisler, M, Beriashvili, R, 'Istanbul Protocol Implementation in Central Asia: Bending the Arc of the Moral Universe' (2020) 69 *Journal of Forensic and Legal Medicine* 101886. Available at https://doi.org/10.1016/j.jflm.2019.101886.

- Establishing and enforcing forensic rules and regulations to ensure timely evaluations of alleged torture and ill treatment by qualified State and non-governmental clinical experts including mental health experts;
- Instituting compulsory Istanbul Protocol training and continuing education for all relevant target groups; and
- Establishing effective mechanisms of monitoring of and accountability for Istanbul Protocol implementation.

The Istanbul Protocol Plan of Action guidelines have been applied in a number of countries and have been instrumental in improving torture investigation and documentation practices. These experience-based guidelines will be considered in the current efforts to update and strengthen Istanbul Protocol standards. Such guidance will not only provide States with a detailed roadmap for policy reform, comprehensive capacity building, and monitoring, but the guidelines also will serve as a framework for accountability for State implementation of effective torture investigation and documentation practices.

CONCLUSION

Torture and ill treatment are heinous crimes committed by State officials and are often concealed to effectively preclude justice, accountability, and redress. The Istanbul Protocol is a tool that empowers civil society to prevent torture and ill treatment, hold perpetrators accountable, and afford victims the redress and rehabilitation that they deserve. The strength of the Istanbul Protocol lies in the global consensus that it represents and the power of medico-legal evidence that it employs.

ANNEX 21.1

Assessment of Possible Torture and Ill Treatment in Primary Healthcare Settings
Physicians for Human Rights

1. This form should be used by health professionals in primary healthcare settings if, in the course of a primary healthcare encounter, injuries and/or psychological stress is observed.
2. Informed consent must be obtained before proceeding with any clinical evaluation and any mandatory reporting requirements disclosed to the individual.
3. Evaluations must be conducted in private. No third parties (i.e. investigators, prosecutors, judges) should be present during the evaluation.
4. Clinicians must inquire about the possibility of ill treatment, including sexual assault, in all healthcare settings when injuries and/or psychological stress is observed and document whether the individual has been in the custody of any State officials.
5. Neglect, misrepresentation and/or falsification of clinical evidence of torture and ill treatment are punishable crimes under the law in many countries.
6. All symptoms and disabilities related to the alleged abuse should be reported and the clinician must conduct a directed physical examination of all organ systems that are relevant to the allegations of abuse.
7. The presence or absence of injuries associated with alleged or suspected abuse should be documented photographically.
8. State the level of consistency between clinical findings and the alleged method(s) of injury (e.g. Not consistent/Consistent/Highly Consistent/Virtually Diagnostic).
9. If ill treatment is alleged or suspected on the basis of clinical findings and the individual provides consent to document and report clinical findings, the clinician should:
    a. Refer the individual for a comprehensive forensic evaluation by one or more qualified experts including a psychological evaluation;
    b. Notify legal authorities as required by law; and
    c. Inform the individual of his/her right to clinical evaluations by independent, non-governmental clinical experts.
    d. Make appropriate referrals for treatment of medical and/or mental health conditions.
    e. Provide a copy of their evaluation to appropiate legal authorities and the patient, if requested, but NOT to law enforcement officials.
10. Clinicians who conduct medico-legal evaluations of alleged torture and ill treatment should do so in accordance with the Istanbul Protocol and its Principles.

I.	Case Information

Clinical Examination   Date:_____,   Place: _____,   Time: _____

Patient/Detainee Name: _____   Patient/Detainee ID #: _____

Gender: ☐ Male   ☐ Female   Age: _____   Date of Birth (dd/mm/yy): ____ / ____ / _____

Informed Consent Obtained: ☐ Yes   ☐ No   If "No" explain: _____

[Identify yourself, the purpose and nature of your examination, potential benefit and risks and any limits on confidentiality including any mandatory reporting requirements. Inform the individual of their right to refuse the evaluation and the option to request an evaluation by a clinical expert of his/her choice. Do not conduct the evaluation if the individual does not consent.]

Person Requesting Clinical Evaluation:

    State Official Name: _____   Position: _____   ID #: _____

    Detainee: ☐ Yes   ☐ No

Reason For Request:	Routine medical check	☐ Yes
	Medical complaint	☐ Yes
	"Accident/Injury"	☐ Yes
	Physical harm	☐ Yes
	Psychological harm	☐ Yes
	Other (Specify) _____	☐ Yes

Time Elapsed From Allegations of Abuse by State Officials: _____ (Hours)   _____ (Days)

Interpreter Needed?   ☐ Yes   ☐ No   Interpreter provided: ☐ Yes   ☐ No

Police/Others Present During Examination: ☐ Yes   ☐ No

Name	Position/Institution	ID Number	Asked to Leave by Clinician
1.	/		☐ Yes ☐ No
2.	/		☐ Yes ☐ No
3.	/		☐ Yes ☐ No

Note any of the following limitations on the clinical evaluation:

Patient/Detainee Restrained (Describe): _____   ☐ Yes

Inadequate Time For Evaluation: _____   ☐ Yes

Lack of Privacy (Expain): _____   ☐ Yes

Other (Specify): _____   ☐ Yes

II.	Relevant Clinical History

Chief Clinical Complaint(s): ☐ Yes ☐ No

1. _____

2. _____

3. _____

History of Present Illness/Clinical Complaint(s):

_____

_____

Clinical Records/Foresic Report Available for Review: ☐ Yes ☐ No

_____

Medications: _____

Past Medical History: _____

Past Psychiatric History: ☐ Yes _____ ☐ No

III.	If Injuries and/or Psychological Stress is Observed, Inquire About the Possibility of Ill Treatment, Including Sexual Assault and Ask the Following Question:

"Have you experienced any form of ill treatment while in custody? If so please explain – when, where, what and by whom this happened."

Individual's Response ☐ Yes ☐ No [If "Yes," conduct open-ended, chronological inquiry followed by direct questions as indicated. Be sure to ask about the possibility of sexual assault.]

_____

_____

Sexual Assault: ☐ Yes (describe details above) ☐ No

Summary of Alleged Abuse(s) and Perpetrators:

Date (dd/mm/yy)	Place	Alleged Abuse	Alleged Perpetrator(s) (name, position & institution)
1.			
2.			
3.			
4.			

IV.	Physical Symptoms and/or Disabilities Related to Alleged Abuse (Describe the development of acute and chronic symptoms and disabilities, frequency, location, intensity, duration, potentiating and alleviating factors, and subsequent healing processes)

1. _____

2. _____

3. _____

4. _____

V.	Psychological Symptoms Related to Alleged Abuse

Ask the following:

"Do you feel that your mental state (thoughts and emotions) has been significantly affected by the abuse that you alleged?"

Patient/Detainee Response   ☐ Yes   ☐ No   [If "Yes," refer for psychological assessment]

"To what extent has the change in your mental state affected your life or your ability to function?"

Patient/Detainee Response   ☐ None   ☐ Mild   ☐ Moderate   ☐ Extreme

What psychological symptoms have you experienced: _____

_____

_____

VI.	Examination of Physical Evidence (Include all pertinent positive and negative findings; complete neurologic and mental status exam for alleged head trauma, loss of consciousness or asphyxiation; for acute vaginal or anal rape, use of rape kit and collect physical evidence for analysis.)

General Appearance & vital signs: _____

Skin: _____

Face/Head: _____

Eyes/Ears/Nose/Throat _____

Oral Cavity/Teeth: _____

Chest/Abdomen (including vital signs) _____

Genitourinary System _____

Musculoskeletal System _____

Nervous System (including Mental Status Exam): _____

VII.	Assessment of Clinical Problems and Plan

Clinical Problem	Plan (including diagnostic tests and/or referrals)
1.	
2.	
3.	

VIII. Assessment of Observed Injuries and/or Psychological Distress (Provide correlations between each physical finding and the alleged method of injury)

Physical Finding(s)	Alleged Method of Injury	Correlation (Circle One)	Photograph #s
1.		Not consistent/Consistent/Highly Consistent/Virtually Diagnostic	☐ Yes #____ ☐ No
2.		Not consistent/Consistent/Highly Consistent/Virtually Diagnostic	☐ Yes #____ ☐ No
3.		Not consistent/Consistent/Highly Consistent/Virtually Diagnostic	☐ Yes #____ ☐ No
4.		Not consistent/Consistent/Highly Consistent/Virtually Diagnostic	☐ Yes #____ ☐ No

Overall Conclusion: Based on my qualifications, knowledge and experience, it is my opinion that the individual's allegations of abuse are (CIRCLE ONE):

Not Consistent With

Consistent With

Highly Consistent With

Virtually Diagnostic Of

the alleged victim's physical findings.

Not consistent with: *the lesion could not have been caused by the trauma described*

Consistent with: *the lesion could have been caused by the trauma described, but it is non-specific and there are many other possible causes*

Highly consistent with: *the lesion could have been caused by the trauma described, and there are few other possible causes*

Virtually Diagnostic of: *this appearance could not have been caused in any way other than that described*

Diagnostic Test Ordered:	☐ Yes	☐ No

1. _____

2. _____

3. _____

Referrals/Consultations Requested:

Official Forensic Medical Expert	☐ Yes (name)_____	☐ No
Official Forensic Mental Health Expert	☐ Yes (name)_____	☐ No
Official Legal Authority	☐ Yes (name)_____	☐ No
Non-Gov Clinician for Medico Legal Eval	☐ Yes (name)_____	☐ No
Clinical Rehabilitation Services	☐ Yes (name)_____	☐ No
Other	☐ Yes (name)_____	☐ No

IX.	**Clinician's Declaration**

I declare that the information provided above is true and complete to the best of my knowledge and belief.

_____   _____   _____

Clinician's Signature   *Clinician's Printed Name*   *Date*

22. Rehabilitation in Article 14 of the Convention Against Torture and Other Cruel, Inhuman, or Degrading Treatment or Punishment

Nora Sveaass, Felice Gaer, and Claudio Grossman[1]

INTRODUCTION

Persons exposed to torture have suffered serious attacks on their lives, relationships, health, and sense of dignity. The torture they experienced will remain a part of them even if they manage to move ahead and work through the pain. The destructive power of torture affects life on so many levels: mind and body, values and relationships, and the capacity for work and leisure. Providing opportunities to reconstruct lives after torture should be a priority in the international effort to prevent and prohibit torture.

International recognition of the right to redress, including rehabilitation for all victims of torture and other cruel, inhuman, or degrading treatment, as provided in Article 14 of the Convention against Torture and Other Cruel, Inhuman or Degrading Treatment or Punishment (UNCAT),[2] is an important step in countering the negative effects of torture. Recognition of this right will shed light on the many aspects of rehabilitation and the different initiatives that States must undertake to comply with their obligation under Article 14. As such, the Committee Against Torture (Committee) developed General Comment 3 on Article 14,[3] which 'clarifies that the right to redress under [UNCAT] extends both to victims of torture and victims of … "ill-treatment."'[4] This 'reflects long-standing committee jurisprudence, which argues, *inter alia*, that ill-treatment as outlined in [A]rticle 16 also violates [UNCAT] and requires redress.'[5] In adopting the General Comment, the Committee constantly referenced the United Nations' 'Basic Principles and Guidelines on the Right to a Remedy and Reparation for Victims of Gross Violations of International Human Rights Law and Serious Violations of International Humanitarian Law' (Basic Principles), which 'identify mechanisms, modalities, procedures

---

[1] This chapter was first published as an article in (2018) 51(1) *The International Lawyer* 1–25. It is reprinted with the permission of *The International Lawyer*.

[2] Convention against Torture and Other Cruel, Inhuman or Degrading Treatment or Punishment (adopted 10 December 1984, entered into force 26 June 1987) 1465 UNTS 85 [hereinafter Convention against Torture, or UNCAT].

[3] CAT General Comment No 3: Implementation of Article 14 by States Parties, (2012) UN Doc CAT/C/GC/3, para 1.

[4] See Gaer, F, 'The Treatment of Torture Victims: What Are a Government's Obligations?' (Chatham House, 2013), available at https://www.chathamhouse.org/sites/default/files/public/Research/International%20Law/210113summary.pdf.

[5] Gaer (n 4 above). See also *Sonko v. Spain*, UN Doc CAT/C/47/D/368/2008 (20 February 2012) paras 10.4 and 10.8; *Keremedchiev v. Bulgaria*, UN Doc CAT/C/41/D/257/2004 (21 November 2008), paras 3, 9.2 and 9.3; *Dzemajl v. Serbia and Montenegro*, UN Doc CAT/C/29/D/161/2000 (21 November 2002), para 9.6.

and methods for the implementation of existing legal obligations under international human rights law and international humanitarian law …'[6] The Basic Principles establish five forms of redress for such violations: 'restitution, compensation, rehabilitation, satisfaction and guarantees of non-repetition'.[7] Rehabilitation is defined in the Basic Principles as including 'medical and psychological care as well as legal and social services'.[8] This definition of rehabilitation may sound like a medical term with a narrow scope, but the Committee has interpreted it to include the many aspects involved in the reconstruction of the lives of victims of torture and not exclusively as a medical undertaking.

Studies show that there is a wide range of reactions to torture, and not all victims of torture need rehabilitation in the form of special care or treatment.[9] This underpins the importance of identifying individual victim's needs and claims. Furthermore, rehabilitation is not an action that is 'done' or 'given to' someone but a series of measures that must be based on close collaboration and planning between the person who is in need of such care and the service provider. Giving voice to and respecting the decisions and agency of torture survivors are vital components of a process of recovering life and dignity. Failure to take victim participation into account in this process not only violates important ethical principles but also risks continued humiliation of victims of torture. The lack of specificity with regard to rehabilitation and the lack of State engagement as to planning, implementing, and evaluating rehabilitation programs has called for a more in-depth approach to the obligation of States.

In the following pages, the scope of the obligation to provide rehabilitation as a form of reparation for victims of torture in accordance with the requirements of Article 14 of UNCAT will be outlined and discussed using General Comment 3 as a framework for reference. The right to rehabilitation, as defined in other international human rights documents and treaties, will also be addressed as applicable. The right to redress under Article 14 of UNCAT specifies:

> Each State Party shall ensure in its legal system that the victim of an act of torture obtains redress and has an enforceable right to fair and adequate compensation, including the means for as full rehabilitation as possible. In the event of the death of the victim as a result of an act of torture, his dependents shall be entitled to compensation.[10]

Article 14 requires States to establish a legal provision ensuring redress for victims of torture that includes compensation for the victims. Rehabilitation or rehabilitative services must be provided to victims in need. Article 14 states that the means for 'as full rehabilitation as possible' must be ensured. 'As full as possible' refers to possible limitations in restoring the person after torture, not to limitations of the State party's capacity to provide redress.[11] Redress, according to Article 14, refers to legal redress and compensation, which may include rehabilitation of both mental and physical health, rehabilitation in relation to training and social

---

6   UN Doc GA Res 60/147 (16 December 2005), para 7.

7   *Ibid*, para 18.

8   *Ibid*, para 21.

9   Başoğlu, M, 'Prevention of Torture and Rehabilitation of Survivors – Review of the UN Committee Against Torture Working Document on Article 14: Convention Against Torture and other Cruel, Inhuman or Degrading Treatment or Punishment', *Mass Trauma, Mental Health & Human Rights* (July 29, 2011), https://metinbasoglu.wordpress.com/2011/07/29/200/

10   Convention against Torture (n 2 above), Article 14(1).

11   General Comment 3 (n 3 above), para 12.

integration, and economic compensation to victims.[12] General Comment 3 emphasizes that the term 'redress' covers all five forms of reparation as outlined in the Basic Principles.[13] All such forms of redress provided by the State 'must be adequate, effective and comprehensive.'[14] General Comment 3 further specifies that all victims of torture have a right to obtain redress, not only to seek it.[15]

THE RIGHT TO REHABILITATION UNDER INTERNATIONAL LAW

An overview of how the right to rehabilitation has been dealt with in other international law contexts is presented in this section. The right to rehabilitation has been established in human rights treaties,[16] General Comments, and reports of United Nations special procedures, but references to rehabilitation are not always presented in the context of the right to reparation.

According to the treaties recognizing a right to rehabilitation, States have a duty to provide defined groups or persons with certain characteristics or experiences with some form of rehabilitation, such as: the right to social rehabilitation in the penitentiary system, particularly for juvenile offenders, as stated in the International Covenant on Civil and Political Rights (ICCPR);[17] the right to rehabilitation for disabled children and the right to health for children generally, as stated in the Convention on the Rights of the Child (CRC);[18] and the right to habilitation and rehabilitation for persons with disabilities, as stated in the Convention on the Rights of Persons with Disabilities (CRPD).[19]

The right to rehabilitation after torture exists as a component of the right to redress for victims of torture.[20] The right to rehabilitation after torture could in principle be regarded as a right to all persons subjected to torture, that is, without reference to the right to reparation. Being a torture victim or survivor would, in itself bestow the person with a right to rehabilitation. This would be considered a free-standing right to those exposed to torture *and* in need of rehabilitation services.[21]

---

[12]   *Ibid*, para 10.
[13]   *Ibid*, para 6.
[14]   *Ibid*.
[15]   *Ibid*, para 20.
[16]   International Convention for the Protection of All Persons from Enforced Disappearance (adopted 20 December 2006, entered into force 23 December 2010) 2716 UNTS 3, Article 24 (5); Convention on the Rights of Persons with Disabilities (adopted 13 December 2006, entered into force 3 May 2008) 2515 UNTS 3, Articles 16 (4), 22 (2), 25 and 26(1)–(3); International Convention on the Protection of the Rights of All Migrant Workers and Members of their Families (adopted 18 December 1990, entered into force 1 July 2003) 2220 UNTS 3, Articles 17(4) and 18(4); Convention on the Rights of the Child (adopted 20 November 1989, entered into force 2 September 1990) 1577 UNTS 3, Articles 23(3) and 24(1); International Covenant on Civil and Political Rights (adopted 16 December 1966, entered into force 23 March 1976) 999 UNTS 171, Articles 10(3) and 14(4).
[17]   International Covenant on Civil and Political Rights (n 16 above).
[18]   Convention on the Rights of the Child (n 16 above).
[19]   Convention on the Rights of Persons with Disabilities (n 16 above), Articles 26(1)–(3).
[20]   General Comment 3 (n 3 above) para 6.
[21]   Sveaass, N, 'Gross Human Rights Violations and Reparation Under International Law: Approaching Rehabilitation as a Form of Reparation' (2013) 4 *Eur. J. of Psychotraumatology* 5.

It may be argued that it is unsettled, whether the right to rehabilitation after torture exists as a freestanding right to all victims of torture regardless of claims of reparation, such as under the CRPD, [22] or whether it is primarily linked to a reparation scheme.[23]

The question of whether victims of torture and ill-treatment should be entitled to rehabilitation, regardless of where they are and who tortured them, has been frequently raised.[24] General Comment 3 establishes that it should be a universal duty to provide torture victims with health care and re-integrative services, without consideration as to whether formal complaints or court decisions have been made or to the question of who was responsible for the torture or where it happened.[25] This obligation to provide services regardless of location underlies the argument that rehabilitation facilities for torture victims should be established in all countries.[26] In practice, 'this would mean that an Iraqi refugee [tortured in his or her home country] coming to Switzerland should be entitled not only to general health care, but also be given the option of a fuller rehabilitation directly related to the health damage suffered,' including medical, psychological, social, and legal services.[27] In most scenarios, 'this would imply something beyond what would usually be considered basic and necessary health care' and may include, for example, 'complicated dental treatment, long-term physiotherapy and/or psychotherapy, [o]r surgery.'[28]

Some argue that 'in order to strengthen this free-standing right to rehabilitation for victims of torture and other gross human rights violations one could directly invoke the rights entailed in the [CRPD]'.[29] The basis for this argument is that many victims of torture may in fact be considered as persons with disabilities, given the serious psychological and physical problems they often encounter. The focus in the CRPD on measures to 'enable persons with disabilities to attain and maintain maximum independence, full physical, mental, social and vocational ability, and full inclusion and participation in all aspects of life' and the obligation of State parties to 'organize, strengthen and extend comprehensive habilitation and rehabilitation services and programs, particularly in the areas of health, employment, education and social services' are highly relevant for victims of torture and cruel, inhuman or degrading treatment or punishment.[30]

Unfortunately, there is a significant gap between the establishment of rights and their implementation. Moreover, defining the rights of victims does not mean that victims will necessarily have access to, be able to seek, or be able to realize these rights. This is true for most of the disabled people in the world, including those in countries that have ratified the CRPD, and it is certainly true for most of those who have been exposed to torture.

---

[22] Tokle, HK, *Seeking a Free-Standing Right to Rehabilitation for Torture Survivors* (Dignity: Danish Inst. Against Torture, 2010).
[23] Convention on the Rights of Persons with Disabilities (n 16 above), Article 26.
[24] Sandoval Villalba, C, *Rehabilitation as a Form of Reparation Under International Law* (REDRESS, 2009), 58–63.
[25] General Comment 3 (n 3 above), paras 3, 23 and 27.
[26] Report of the Special Rapporteur on Torture and Other Cruel, Inhuman or Degrading Treatment or Punishment (Juan Méndez), UN Doc A/HRC/16/52 (3 February 2011), para 33.
[27] Sveaass (n 21 above).
[28] *Ibid*, p. 5.
[29] *Ibid.*
[30] Convention on the Rights of Persons with Disabilities (n 16 above), Article 26(1).

DEFINING THE SCOPE AND OBLIGATION OF THE RIGHT TO REDRESS UNDER ARTICLE 14

The importance of defining and clarifying the content and scope of the obligations under Article 14 of UNCAT has long been a concern raised in the Committee. The need for full implementation of the obligation to ensure redress for persons who have been subjected to torture, who often live in situations of prolonged injustice, denial, insecurity, and lack of assistance, makes the need for clarifications even more pressing. As previously stated, General Comment 3 was an important step in this direction. General Comments are a useful tool for interpreting and implementing treaties and can:

(1)   focus each state party on the inadequacies, lacunae and recurring violations of the treaty as found in the reports submitted by each of the state parties, or through the interactive dialogue between representatives of the state party and members of the committee;
(2)   inform states parties on the experiences gained by the members of the treaty body which can assist them in implementing the treaty;
(3)   guide states parties in their general implementation of the treaty and possible improved reporting procedures to the committee;
(4)   identify future preventive measures that states parties can take to realize the rights in the relevant treaties; and
(5)   provide victims with information of their rights under the Convention.[31]

State parties must also provide victims with information of their rights under UNCAT.[32]

In November 2009, the Committee began the process of drafting a General Comment on Article 14 after the Chair of the Committee (and co-author of this chapter), Professor Claudio Grossman, presented a draft. Based on discussion of this draft, the Committee created a working group consisting of four Committee members: Claudio Grossman, Felice Gaer (Vice-chairperson), Abdul Gaye (member), and Nora Sveaass (Rapporteur).[33] The working group emphasized that the draft should adequately reflect the Committee's own jurisprudence, and therefore, it postponed further discussion until May 2011 so that the Committee's jurisprudence and practice on this issue could be summarized and studied. Committee members were also encouraged to submit alternative draft language for discussion. Another draft was submitted by two of the working group members (Gaer and Sveaass), and the working group sought to merge these two drafts into one.

During the May 2011 session, the working group presented a merged draft, which the Committee discussed and, in June, decided to post on the Committee website. The Committee invited State parties, civil society members, stakeholders, experts, and academics to submit their comments and feedback by September 15, 2011. This represented the first round of consultations on General Comment 3. The feedback was generally very positive and the General Comment was widely supported. At the same time, observers offered substantial comments and suggestions, including some criticism. A large number of civil society organizations pre-

---

[31]   Gaer (n 4 above).
[32]   General Comment 3 (n 3 above), para 29.
[33]   The authors of this chapter were involved in the drafting process of General Comment 3. As such, some of what is said in this section is based on their recollection of how General Comment 3 came about.

sented valuable comments, and a number of UN bodies submitted constructive observations. Although few States commented in the first round, more engaged when the draft was presented a second time for further discussion. Two open meetings were held during the UNCAT sessions in May and November 2012 – one invited NGOs and one invited States. Both meetings were well attended and generated helpful feedback evidencing strong agreement on the need for the General Comment. General Comment 3 was adopted by the Committee in November 2012.[34]

In its more than twenty-five years of work, the Committee has adopted very few General Comments. For the Committee, the workload has always been very heavy and time allocated for the development of General Comments has been limited.[35] For more than a decade, the Committee had only General Comment 1 on the implementation of Article 3 (1997).[36] After extensive efforts, General Comment 2 on Article 2, which discusses State party obligations to prevent torture, was adopted in 2008.[37] General Comment 3 builds on principles from General Comment 2 and addresses additional matters not covered by it.

There is a close relationship, both legally and psychologically, between rehabilitation and the other forms of reparation, such as restitution, compensation, satisfaction, and guarantees of non-repetition, which reflect the full scope of measures required to redress violations under UNCAT.[38] One may ask whether it is possible for rehabilitation to take place if there is still fear that the violence may be repeated, or, in situations where there is no truth or justice, if attempts to provide fair compensation or other measures to ensure satisfaction have not been addressed.

General Comment 3 takes 'an explicitly holistic and victim-oriented approach, remind[ing] states to take into account the specifics of each case and that redress should be proportionate to the "gravity of the violations committed"'.[39] It 'further emphasizes the "inherent preventive and deterrent effect" of providing reparation to victims.'[40] The following pages provide analysis of the necessary components and contextual conditions that make rehabilitation an adequate form of redress.

---

[34] The adoption of General Comment 3, referred to as a 'key document' regarding States' obligations under Article 14, was hailed as a 'significant development' and 'one of the most encouraging highlights of the year' REDRESS, *Annual Report 2012–13* (REDRESS, 2013), 3, 24. Amnesty International referred to General Comment 3 as a 'landmark General Comment' that would 'provide excellent guidance to states when implementing the Convention,' 'United Nations Committee Against Torture Adopts Landmark General Comment on the Right to Reparation' (Amnesty International, 2012), 1, available at https://www.amnesty.org/en/documents/ior51/005/2012/en/

[35] UN High Commissioner for Human Rights (Navanethem Pillay), *Report on Strengthening the United Nations Human Rights Treaty Body System*, UN Doc A/66/860 (June 2012), 23.

[36] UN Committee Against Torture, General Comment no 1: Implementation of Article 3 of the Convention in the Context of Article 22, UN Doc A/53/54, annex IX (1997).

[37] UN Committee Against Torture, General Comment no 2, Implementation of Article 2 by States parties, UN Doc CAT/C/GG /2 (24 January 2008).

[38] General Comment 3 (n 3 above), para 6.

[39] Gaer (n 4 above), 7 (quoting General Comment 3 (n 3 above), para 6).

[40] *Ibid.*

Procedural and Substantive Obligations Are Essential Components of the Right to Redress

General Comment 3 'identifies both procedural and substantive obligations to provide redress.'[41] It extensively outlines procedural elements, such as the enactment of legislation and the establishment of complaints mechanisms, investigative bodies, and other judicial bodies that enable victims of torture or ill-treatment to seek and obtain redress.[42] It also 'addresses substantive requirements that provide the victim with "full and effective redress" in response to each claim.'[43] The 'establishment of "effective" and "accessible" bodies is central to meeting' these procedural and substantive obligations.[44]

Concerning the substantive aspects of the right, 'by identifying the five components of redress outlined above, [General Comment] 3 clarifies that the concept of redress is substantially broader than compensation and rehabilitation, the two forms of redress mentioned by name in [A]rticle 14.'[45] General Comment 3 thus also offers an important elaboration of the concept of rehabilitation for victims of torture and ill-treatment, emphasizing it must be 'holistic and include medical and psychological care as well as legal and social services.'[46] It specifies that rehabilitative services should be provided 'as soon as possible following an assessment by qualified independent medical professionals' and should not depend on the victim's pursuit of judicial remedies.[47] General Comment 3 'takes a victim-oriented approach with regard to participation and selection of services, in keeping with the approach encouraged by the former UN Special Rapporteur on Torture, Juan Mendez.'[48]

Defining Victims

General Comment 3 uses the term 'victim' when referring to persons who have suffered and survived torture.[49] The term 'survivor' may also be appropriate, as the term 'victim' may be construed by some as indicating that the person is victimized, permanently harmed, and/or in lesser charge of his or her own life.[50] This may not necessarily be the case, as many people demonstrate strong resilience even when faced with torture. Nevertheless, their experiences as persons subjected to torture entitle them to redress and compensation or other forms of reparative measures, regardless of whether they seek out rehabilitative services.

Victims of torture entitled to redress have 'individually or collectively suffered harm, including physical or mental injury, emotional suffering, economic loss or substantial impairment of their fundamental rights, through acts or omissions that constitute violations' of UNCAT.[51] This concept is flexible and has a wide scope. Victims also include 'affected

---

41   *Ibid.* See also General Comment 3 (n 3 above), para 5.
42   General Comment 3 (n 3 above), para 5.
43   Gaer (n 3 above), 7 (quoting General Comment 3 (n 3 above), para 5).
44   *Ibid.*
45   *Ibid.*
46   *Ibid* (quoting General Comment 3 (n 3 above), para 11).
47   *Ibid* (quoting General Comment 3 (n 3 above), para 15).
48   *Ibid*; Gaer (n 4 above), 7.
49   General Comment 3 (n 3 above), para 3.
50   *Ibid.*
51   *Ibid.*

immediate family or dependents of the victim as well as persons who have suffered harm in intervening to assist victims or to prevent victimization'.[52] This definition reflects the Committee's view that 'family members and dependents of disappeared persons are entitled to redress and not merely to compensation'.[53] The Committee has recommended compensation, including in the form of rehabilitation, to family members of persons who have disappeared. In 2008, the Committee made recommendations to Algeria and asked the State to guarantee the right of families of disappeared persons to redress and to pay fair compensation, 'including by giving them the necessary psychological, social and financial support ....'[54] This 'tracks definitions developed in such multilateral instruments as the 1985 United Nations Declaration of Basic Principles of Justice for Victims of Crime and Abuse of Power.'[55] It also follows the 1999 Declaration on the Right to Restitution for Victims of Gross Human Rights Violations, adopted by the UN Commission on Human Rights,[56] and the Basic Principles and Guidelines on the Right to a Remedy and Reparation.[57] The Committee's definition reflects ways to 'ensure the maximum protection of a person who has suffered harm as a result of torture or ill-treatment'.[58] Furthermore, General Comment 3 provides that 'a person should be considered a victim regardless of whether the perpetrator of the violation is identified, apprehended, prosecuted or convicted'.[59]

Torture affects not only the tortured person but also those confronted with the fact that a loved one is being subjected to or threatened with pain. Torture of a family member may alter the lives of relatives when the victim returns or, alternatively, if the victim dies as a result of the torture. Reconstructing family life after torture or death can be a long and hard process, as is the reconstruction of the family following a member's brutal death. The right of dependents to receive assistance, such as rehabilitation, is thus formulated in General Comment 3 and represents an important step toward positive change from a psychological, social, and legal point of view.

Victims of torture with a right to redress also include those who suffer because of a lack of protection against torture and ill-treatment by non-State actors.[60] Noncompliance by a State with an obligation to exercise due diligence to intervene in, stop, or sanction acts of torture and ill-treatment 'enables non-State actors to commit such acts impermissible under the Convention with impunity, [and] the State's indifference or inaction provides a form of encouragement and/or de facto permission.'[61] Persons who have been victimized by such acts and by a lack of protection or due diligence exercised by the State, whether in homes, institutions, schools, etc., are entitled to redress, including rehabilitation.

---

[52]   *Ibid.*
[53]   Gaer (n 4 above), 6.
[54]   Consideration of Reports Submitted by States Parties Under Article 19 of the Convention: Concluding Observations: Algeria, UN Doc CAT/C/DZA/CO/3 (2008), para 13.
[55]   Gaer (n 4 above), 6.
[56]   *Ibid.*
[57]   *Ibid*, 7.
[58]   *Ibid*, 6.
[59]   General Comment 3 (n 3 above), para 3.
[60]   *Ibid*, para 7, citing General Comment 2 (n 37 above).
[61]   General Comment 2 (n 37 above), para 18.

Right to Redress as an Individual Right

General Comment 3 'emphasizes that legislation providing a remedy and the right to redress "must allow individuals to exercise this right" and States parties must "ensure that all victims have access to judicial remedies."'[62] The Committee acknowledges that, '[w]hile collective reparation and administrative reparation programs may be acceptable as a form of redress, such programs may not render ineffective the individual right to a remedy and to obtain redress.'[63] The Committee has addressed this issue. For example, in its concluding observations and recommendations on Cambodia in 2010, the Committee noted that 'the Internal Rules of the ECCC only provide for moral and collective reparation, precluding individual financial compensation.'[64] Consequently, the Committee recommended that 'the ECCC [should] amend its Internal Rules to permit reparation to victims consistent with article 14 of the Convention, including, as appropriate, individual financial compensation.'[65] General Comment 3 'also stipulates that development projects and humanitarian aid programs are not a substitute for an individual victim's right to redress.'[66] It specifies further that '[c]ulturally sensitive collective reparation measures shall be available for groups with shared identity, such as minority groups, indigenous groups, and others', while reiterating that 'collective measures do not exclude the individual right to redress.'[67]

Gender Sensitivity and Non-Discriminatory Measures

General Comment 3 emphasizes that effective implementation of the right to redress requires a gender-sensitive approach. In this regard, it states:

> The Committee considers that complaints mechanisms and investigations require specific positive measures which take into account gender aspects in order to ensure that victims of abuses such as sexual violence and abuse, rape, marital rape, domestic violence, female genital mutilation, and trafficking are able to come forward and seek and obtain redress.[68]

Furthermore, such measures should apply to any marginalized or vulnerable person.[69] Both in judicial and non-judicial proceedings, as well as in all circumstances where redress – particularly in the form of rehabilitation – is provided, sensitivity and specific training on the impact of torture and ill-treatment on victims from marginalized and vulnerable groups are essential.[70, 71] Such training must include 'how to exercise sensitivity towards victims of torture

---

[62]   Gaer (n 4 above), 8 (quoting General Comment 3 (n 3 above), para 20).

[63]   General Comment 3 (n 3 above), para 20.

[64]   Consideration of Reports Submitted by States Parties Under Article 19 of the Convention: Concluding Observations: Cambodia, UN Doc CAT/C/KHM/CO/2 (2011), para 27.

[65]   *Ibid.*

[66]   Gaer (n 4 above), 8.

[67]   General Comment 3 (n 3 above), para 32.

[68]   *Ibid*, para 33.

[69]   *Ibid*, para 34.

[70]   *Ibid.*

[71]   See also, Sveaass, N, 'The UN Convention Against Torture and other Cruel, Inhuman or Degrading Treatment or Punishment: The Absolute Prohibition and the Obligation to Prevent' in Başoğlu, M (ed),

and ill-treatment, including in the form of sexual- or gender-based discrimination, in order to prevent re-victimization and stigmatization'.[72]

THE RIGHT TO REHABILITATION UNDER ARTICLE 14

Rehabilitation is explicitly identified as part of the State's obligation to redress all victims of torture in Article 14 of UNCAT.[73] State responsibility in relation to rehabilitation is also closely linked to obligations defined in other provisions of UNCAT, such as Article 10 (on training), Article 12 (on investigation), and Article 13 (on the right to complain),[74] which should be read together with Article 14. In practice, a prerequisite for rehabilitation is good and thorough training of professionals in different capacities in society. Such training includes training on UNCAT with a special reference to 'law enforcement personnel, civil or military, medical personnel, public officials and other persons who may be involved in the custody, interrogation or treatment of any individual subjected to any form of arrest, detention or imprisonment'.[75]

This obligation to educate and provide information on the prohibition of torture also implies that the State must ensure that medical and other relevant personnel have the necessary professional knowledge and capacity to detect, investigate, refer, and treat the consequences of torture. Thus, in the reporting process under UNCAT, States are frequently asked about available programs to train medical personnel, not only to identify and document torture, but also to provide rehabilitation services.[76] Article 10 specifies the obligation to include information about the prohibition of torture in education and training programs.[77] In its recommendations, the Committee has frequently referred to the need, not only to provide information about prohibition to a wide range of relevant personnel, but also to develop education programs related to the identification of torture and ill-treatment and to the provision of rehabilitation services.[78] The importance of training as a condition for ensuring the right to rehabilitation is illustrated in

---

Torture and Its Definition in International Law: An Interdisciplinary Approach (Oxford University Press, 2017), 247–271.

[72]   General Comment 3 (n 3 above), para 34.

[73]   Convention against Torture (n 2 above).

[74]   *Ibid*, Articles 10, 12 and 13.

[75]   *Ibid*, Article 10(1).

[76]   Committee against Torture, List of Issues to be Considered During the Examination of the Initial Report of Montenegro, UN Doc CAT/C/MNE/1 (9 September 2008); List of Issues to be Taken up in Connection With the Consideration of the Second Periodic Report of Belgium, UN Doc CAT/C/BEL/2 (9 September 2008; List of Issues to be Considered During the Examination of the Fourth Periodic Report of Hong Kong, UN Doc CAT/C/HKG/4 (4 August2008).

[77]   Convention against Torture (n 2 above), Article 10(1).

[78]   See, e.g., Concluding Observations: Cambodia (n 64 above), para 25.

the Committee's recommendations to Serbia and Spain.[79] Finally, complaints mechanisms and investigations must be in place, as required under Articles 12 and 13 of UNCAT.[80]

The right to rehabilitation is defined as part of the right to redress and compensation.[81] UNCAT was the first human rights treaty to refer to rehabilitation in the context of redress and to specify that the right to be provided was defined within a framework of redress or compensation for harm done.[82] The right holders are those who have been subjected to torture or ill-treatment (mental and/or physical) and those dependent on the victim.[83]

Based on Article 14, many questions are posed by members of the Committee to representatives of States concerning the monitoring of State compliance with their obligations under UNCAT. Most States include information as to legal measures taken, outlining the established laws, and, sometimes, the mechanisms relating to the right to redress.[84] The Committee also enquires about monetary compensation provided, including information on how much was paid, to whom, and for what reasons.[85] Some States also report on procedural aspects regarding how individuals can obtain redress.[86] Less information has been provided to the Committee about rehabilitative measures, including how such measures are implemented, to whom rehabilitation is provided, who provides it, and where it takes place. Information about existing services provided in a context of rehabilitation to torture victims has been scant.[87] States sometimes provide limited information on the monitoring and evaluation of the training programs

---

[79]   Consideration of Reports Submitted by States Parties Under Article 19 of the Convention: Concluding Observations: Serbia, UN Doc CAT/C/SRB/CO/1 (2009), para 14 ('However, it is concerned that the training is not targeted at education and information regarding the prohibition of torture and that training programs for medical personnel for the identification and documentation of cases of torture in accordance with the Istanbul Protocol, is insufficient, as is the rehabilitation of victims'); Concluding Observations on the Sixth Periodic Report of Spain, UN Doc CAT/C/ESP/CO/6 (2015), para 23.

[80]   Convention against Torture (n 2 above), Articles 12 and 13.

[81]   *Ibid*, Article 14(1).

[82]   McKay, F, 'What Outcomes for Victims?' in Shelton, D (ed), *Oxford Handbook of International Human Rights Law* (Oxford University Press, 2013), 930 n 41.

[83]   Convention against Torture (n 2 above), Article 14(1).

[84]   Consideration of Reports Submitted by States Parties Under Article 19 of the Convention: Concluding Observations: Azerbaijan, UN Doc. CAT/C/AZE/CO/3 (2009), paras 4–6; Consideration of Reports Submitted by States Parties Under Article 19 of the Convention Pursuant to the Optional Reporting Procedure: United States, UN Doc CAT/C/USA/3-5 (2013), para 147.

[85]   See e.g., Consideration of Reports Submitted by States Parties Under Article 19 of the Convention: Concluding Observations: Slovakia, UN Doc. CAT/C/SVK/CO/2 (2009), para 16 (The State 'should [...] collect data on the number of victims who have received compensation and other forms of assistance'); List of Issues to be Taken Up During the Consideration of the Fourth Periodic Report of Cameroon, Article 14, UN Doc CAT/C/CMR/Q/4 (2010), para 27 ('Please indicate whether there have been cases where persons have received compensation following cases of torture or ill-treatment. If so, please indicate the amount that they received and the number of such cases and describe the type of violence to which the persons in question were subjected').

[86]   See, e.g., Consideration of Reports Submitted by States Parties Under Article 19 of the Convention Pursuant to the Optional Reporting Procedure: United States (n 84 above).

[87]   Smith, S et al., *A Remedy for Torture Survivors in International Law: Interpreting Rehabilitation* (Freedom from Torture, 2010), 18, explaining that 'the assessment of whether a [...] State fulfils its obligation to provide as full rehabilitation as possible is . . . extremely difficult due to the paucity of available information relating to clinical provision for torture survivors'.

for personnel in charge of such services.[88] As a result, there has been little available statistical data on existing rehabilitation services and beneficiaries and little information on any assessment or evaluation as to the outcome or effectiveness of rehabilitation-related services. The absence of this information, which is both unfortunate and unacceptable, shows a prima facie lack of compliance with the Committee's mandate to comply fully with Article 14. When services exist but information is not provided, the Committee cannot assess the situation and/or provide proper guidance to the State on the full satisfaction of its obligations under UNCAT.

General Comment 3 elaborates on rehabilitation as part of the right to redress under Article 14.[89] In the following section, this chapter presents the main aspects of rehabilitation as a wide-ranging service provided to victims of torture and ill-treatment.

Rehabilitation Entails Holistic and Multidisciplinary Services

General Comment 3 affirms the importance of rehabilitation, which is holistic and multidisciplinary in nature and includes medical and psychological care as well as legal and social services. According to General Comment 3, rehabilitation refers to:

> [T]he restoration of function or the acquisition of new skills required by the changed circumstances of a victim in the aftermath of torture or ill-treatment. It seeks to enable the maximum possible self-sufficiency and function for the individual concerned, and may involve adjustments to the person's physical and social environment. Rehabilitation for victims should aim to restore, as far as possible, their independence, physical, mental, social and vocational ability; and full inclusion and participation in society.[90]

Given the short-term and long-term emotional, social, and cognitive effects of torture, 'a holistic and integrative concept of rehabilitation is vital.'[91]

Torture aims to break down the body and mind and may result in the 'disintegration of the personality.'[92] Systematic humiliation, lack of control, and a sense of helplessness resulting from torture can be serious impediments to any form of regular social, vocational, or personal life, which underscores the importance of a broad concept of rehabilitation.[93] But rehabilitation may often be insufficient for restitution, as the effects of torture may be too pervasive to allow full recovery to take place. Thus, the term 'as full rehabilitation as possible' refers to 'the need to restore and repair the harm suffered by a victim whose life situation, including dignity, health, and self-sufficiency may never be fully recovered as a result of the pervasive effect of torture.'[94] A lack of resources, including limited available professionals to deal with these issues, does not eliminate the requirement to fulfill these obligations.

---

[88]   See, e.g., Concluding Observations: Azerbaijan (n 84 above), para 23.
[89]   General Comment 3 (n 3 above), para 2.
[90]   *Ibid*, para 11.
[91]   Ilangamuwa, N, 'Why Torture is Wrong', *Counter Punch* (11 October 2013), available at https://www.counterpunch.org/2013/10/11/why-torture-is-wrong/
[92]   See Interim Report of the Special Rapporteur on Torture and Other Cruel, Inhuman or Degrading Treatment or Punishment (Manfred Nowak), UN Doc A/65/273 (10 August 2010), para 63.
[93]   *Ibid.*
[94]   General Comment 3 (n 3 above), para 12.

Rehabilitation Services Should Be Appropriate, Available and Accessible

Under General Comment 3, States should develop and adopt a 'long-term, integrated approach and ensure that specialized services for victims of torture or ill-treatment are available, appropriate and readily accessible'.[95] Rehabilitation services should be professional, effective, and accessible.[96] This means that those in need of rehabilitative services and their dependents or others supporting them should know where services are, how to contact providers of services, how to obtain information, and how to access such services. Rehabilitation services must furthermore be predictable, safe, and stable.[97] Services should be offered that, in practice, take care of the multi-professional and multi-dimensional aspects of rehabilitation after torture, and are available to those who need them. This also means that they must be free of charge for those who need the care. The '[m]ere availability of general healthcare' does not necessarily mean that the services are appropriate.[98] A victim's ability to receive good care depends on the circumstances in which this occurs. For assistance to be beneficial, it is vital to offer a context where safety, confidence, and trust can be established. Also, given the experiences of torture victims, the risk of re-traumatization is always present, especially in situations that may remind them of the torture or ill-treatment they experienced.[99]

For rehabilitation to be effective, it must be based on professionally-sound assessments of a victim's needs and the mental and physical sequelae caused by the torture.[100] 'Procedure[s] for assessment and evaluation' must be established, including procedures for the documentation of torture, 'based on, among others, the Manual on the Effective Investigation and Documentation of Torture and Other Cruel, Inhuman or Degrading Treatment or Punishment (The Istanbul Protocol).'[101] Furthermore, an individual's therapeutic needs must be assessed, as well as needs related to areas such as social functioning, work, economy, and training. This encompasses 'a wide range of inter-disciplinary measures, such as medical, physical and psychological rehabilitative services; re-integrative and social services; community and family-oriented assistance and services; vocational training; [and] education.'[102]

Victims of torture have been exposed to severe human rights violations, and their rehabilitation must provide, in practice, a wide range of assistance depending on their actual needs. All therapy and assistance, particularly for survivors of gross human rights violations, must emphasize the strength and resilience of those affected.[103] Active victim participation is one

---

[95]   *Ibid*, para 13.

[96]   Patel, N and C de C Williams, A, *Monitoring and Evaluation of Rehabilitation Services for Torture Survivors* (International Centre for Health and Human Rights, 2014), 17–24, available at http://nebrastunisie.org/pdf/ICHHR+Handbook+for+Service+Providers+MandE+of+Torture+Rehabilitat ion+Services+2014+Final.pdf; see also Smith et al. (n 87 above), 28–29.

[97]   Smith et al., *ibid*.

[98]   *Ibid*, 28.

[99]   General Comment 3 (n 3 above), para 13.

[100]   Grossman, C, 'The Normative Value of the Istanbul Protocol' in Susanne Kjær, S and Kjærum, A (eds), *Shedding Light on a Dark Practice: Using the Istanbul Protocol to Document Torture* (IRCT, 2009), 11–12.

[101]   General Comment 3 (n 3 above), para 13; Istanbul Protocol: Manual on the Effective Investigation and Documentation of Torture and Other Cruel, Inhuman or Degrading Treatment or Punishment, UN Doc HR/P/PT/8/Rev.1, (2004).

[102]   General Comment 3 (n 3 above), para 13.

[103]   Başoğlu (n 9 above).

way in which victims' own self-awareness about their needs and reactions can be utilized for the good of the individual and as a way to reengage with life and the world. Because torture often means destruction of a victim's personality, agency, and meaning in life, the victim must play an active role in the subsequent process of care and support in order to enable the process to be one of re-empowerment and of bringing back a sense of life, meaning, and dignity.[104]

Rehabilitation and Legal Remedies

General Comment 3 addresses the important issue of whether rehabilitation depends on the victim first pressing legal charges against those responsible for torture and ill-treatment or if this can be provided without such charges. Two aspects merit consideration: first, whether there is a demand for judicial remedies, and/or second, whether the perpetrator is identified. General Comment 3 is very clear with regard to these two points: '[a]ccess to rehabilitation programs should not depend on the victim pursuing judicial remedies', and 'a person should be considered a victim regardless of whether the perpetrator of the violation is identified, apprehended, prosecuted or convicted, and regardless of any familial or other relationship between the perpetrator and the victim.'[105]

States Are Responsible for Providing Rehabilitation to Victims of Torture or Ill-treatment

General Comment 3 explains that State parties to UNCAT are required to ensure that all victims of torture and ill-treatment are able to access remedies and obtain redress.[106] The Committee 'considers that the application of [A]rticle 14 is not limited to victims harmed on the territory of the State party' or by or against its nationals.[107] The Committee explicitly notes and values when State parties 'provide civil remedies to victims tortured or ill-treated outside the territory of the state party,' such as in the case of the United States Alien Tort Claims Act.[108]

General Comment 3 reflects the Committee's view that refugees, asylum-seekers, stateless persons, and other victims of torture are entitled to protection and rights under UNCAT once they enter a State party.[109]

> An analysis of the *traveaux préparatoires* of [UNCAT], which explicitly dropped all reference to the nationality of the perpetrator of torture for which the victim is seeking redress, shows that the state party's obligations under [UNCAT] are not limited by nationality or the territory where the abusive act took place.[110]

The fact that the United States felt the need to lodge a reservation arguing that acts under Article 14 should be limited to acts on its territory reveals that Article 14, when adopted, was

---

[104] General Comment 3 (n 3 above), para 4 (emphasizing the importance of the victim's participation in the redress process).
[105] *Ibid*, paras 3 and 15.
[106] *Ibid* (citing Convention against Torture (n 2 above), Article 14(1)).
[107] *Ibid*, para 22.
[108] Gaer (n 4 above), 10.
[109] General Comment 3 (n 3 above), para 32.
[110] Gaer (n 4 above), 10.

not, in fact, understood by its drafters to be limited to violations within the territory of the State.[111]

In practice, States can be asked about services available for refugees and asylum-seekers who have suffered torture elsewhere, and the Committee has called for redress, including compensation and rehabilitation, to be ensured for all victims including refugees.[112] Indeed, Article 14 requires State parties to ensure that all victims of torture and ill-treatment are able to access remedies and obtain redress.[113] General Comment 3 further underscores that rehabilitation services shall be accessible to all victims 'without discrimination and regardless of a victim's identity or status within a marginalized or vulnerable group ... including asylum seekers and refugees'.[114]

In instances where rehabilitation is provided – not by those responsible for the torture but by others – one question that may arise is whether it is regarded as redress or rather as necessary health care provided to victims after extreme violence. Rehabilitation provided by States unrelated to torture violations, such as in refugee-receiving countries, may be understood as ways of complying with refugee law through protection or as part of the humanitarian support provided to victims of torture and ill-treatment who have sought protection in the country. It may also be understood as complying with the obligation to provide international cooperation and assistance to fulfil economic, social, and cultural rights.

REHABILITATION IN PRACTICE

Providing as full rehabilitation as possible requires States to set up a system of effective rehabilitation services and programs able to meet the individual needs of persons with different backgrounds and requirements regarding rehabilitation.[115] These services must be provided under circumstances that are as safe and stable as possible for the person involved. When rehabilitation is offered in the country or region where torture has occurred, special considerations must be taken, and those responsible for the redress may need to ensure rehabilitation by services other than the public health services. In this regard, General Comment 3 indicates:

> [T]he obligation in [A]rticle 14 to provide for the means for as full rehabilitation as possible can be fulfilled through the direct provision of rehabilitative services by the State, or through the funding of private medical, legal and other facilities, including those administered by NGOs in which case the State shall ensure that no reprisals or intimidation are directed to them.[116]

This means that rehabilitation can be offered and organized by civil society organizations or groups of professionals not directly affiliated with the public system with services funded by

---

[111] Senate Resolution of Advice and Consent to Ratification, 100th Congress (1990), available at https://www.congress.gov/treaty-document/100th-congress/20/resolution-text
[112] Sveaass (n 21 above), 7; General Comment 3 (n 3 above), para 15.
[113] Convention against Torture (n 2 above), Article 14(1).
[114] General Comment 3 (n 3 above), para 15.
[115] *Ibid.*
[116] *Ibid.*

the State.[117] Again, it is important to emphasize the importance of victim participation when deciding upon service providers.[118]

An important part of developing rehabilitation services is the inclusion of 'systems for assessing the effective implementation of rehabilitation programs and services' as well as the outcomes of such services.[119] These components should be firmly based on relevant research in the area and on 'appropriate indicators and benchmarks' developed for such purposes.[120] General Comment 3 requires State parties to carry out assessments and evaluations of the effectiveness of rehabilitation services as part of their reporting obligations.[121]

General Comment 3 further emphasizes the importance of 'ensuring that victims and their families are adequately informed of their right to pursue redress'.[122] Such instruction must cover information about rights and ways in which those rights can be enjoyed. This means that there must be available, professional, and confidential procedures and mechanisms to allow redress and rehabilitation to occur without imposing economic burdens on those subjected to torture.[123] Both judicial procedures should be available for those whose rights have been abused, but rehabilitation must neither rest nor be contingent upon legal decisions.[124] General Comment 3 reiterates and expands upon a list of impermissible discriminatory elements first identified in General Comment 2, including:

> race, color, ethnicity, age, religious belief or affiliation, political or other opinion, national or social origin, gender, sexual orientation, transgender identity, mental or other disability, health status, economic or indigenous status, reason for which the person is detained, including persons accused of political offences or terrorist acts, asylum-seekers, refugees or others under international protection, or any other status or adverse distinction.[125]

General Comment 3 further emphasizes that complaints mechanisms should 'avoid re-victimization and stigmatization' of 'person[s] marginalized or made vulnerable on the basis of identities and [membership of] groups,' such as those noted above, and it requires that States support victims who are members of these or other marginalized groups in seeking and obtaining redress.[126]

Seeking redress and rehabilitation may entail a number of social and emotional hardships on the part of the exposed persons. Many will avoid entering into such processes out of fear of threats and reprisals, further shaming, and risk to the security of family, friends, and those who have provided assistance to the victims.[127] For these reasons, some will attempt to obtain their rights in secrecy. While some who attempt to obtain their rights will have support from those in their surroundings, others may encounter resistance from their social networks. Regardless of the social support available, there should be sufficient support in the system providing redress

---

[117] Sveaass (n 21 above), 9.
[118] General Comment 3 (n 3 above), para 15.
[119] *Ibid.* See also Patel and Williams (n 96 above) 86–103 and 105–29.
[120] General Comment 3 (n 3 above), para 15.
[121] *Ibid*, para 13.
[122] *Ibid*, para 29.
[123] *Ibid.*
[124] *Ibid*, paras 15 and 30.
[125] *Ibid*, para 32.
[126] *Ibid*, paras 15, 33 and 34.
[127] Smith et al (n 87 above), 29.

and rehabilitation to allow victims to feel protected and that their needs are being respected and taken seriously. For many victims, the process may bring back very painful memories, and in some cases, it can be an active re-traumatizing event.[128] In rehabilitation, assessment and mapping will be vital, and they will require going back, referring, and talking to strangers about painful events. When redress also entails legal processes – which many will feel is both right and necessary – it may mean confronting the perpetrator, listening to the defenses of persons who have committed atrocities, and possibly having to live with legal decisions that do not seem fair or just.[129] As a result, there is a psychological and social necessity to provide victims and witnesses with support and assistance as part of the individual right to redress, or possibly even as a prerequisite for redress.[130]

General Comment 3 refers to assessment and evaluation of needs as important parts of what States should provide.[131] Nevertheless, in many cases there may not be a need for lengthy assessment and documentation in order to determine that a person is a torture victim and, as such, entitled to rehabilitation. A person's ability to document having been present or held in places where torture has been known to take place in a systematic manner (e.g., concentration camps, prisons during authoritarian rule, etc.) can be regarded as sufficient evidence of torture without requiring detailed evidence of how many times electric shocks, beatings, immersion in water, etc. occurred. For example, documentation showing that an individual was held in one of the detention centers run by General Pinochet during the military dictatorship in Chile, such as Tejas Verdes or Tres Alamos, should be sufficient in itself to prove that individual's status as a victim of torture and no further documentation or assessment should be required. This approach, in contrast to presenting claims and making determinations on an individual basis, will facilitate broader realization of the right to reparation and rehabilitation. This approach is significant not only from a human rights perspective but also from a psychological perspective – it represents an acknowledgement of suffering and survival after atrocities. This may amount to a powerful public statement and recognition of the broad injustice that has been done, in contrast to requiring detailed and re-traumatizing individual findings and determinations as to whether the individuals detained were victimized in a particular way.

A final issue to be raised regarding rehabilitation is identification of the models, best practices, and existing empirical research in the field of rehabilitation of torture survivors. This chapter outlines the guidelines and specifications regarding rehabilitation contained in the UNCAT and General Comment 3. With regard to monitoring and reporting, General Comment 3 refers to the need to employ 'methods available for assessing the effectiveness of rehabilitation programs and services, including the application of appropriate indicators and benchmarks, and the result of such assessment.'[132] Furthermore, States shall report on the 'rehabilitation facilities available to victims of torture or ill-treatment and their accessibility as well as the budget allocation for rehabilitation programs.'[133]

There is a need for further systematization and research on rehabilitation services in a broader sense on medical, social, psychological, legal, and training measures, among

---

[128] Istanbul Protocol (n 101 above), paras 94, 147 and 149.
[129] Sveaass (n 21 above), 3.
[130] Istanbul Protocol (n 101 above), para 94.
[131] General Comment 3 (n 3 above), para 13.
[132] *Ibid*, para 46(d).
[133] *Ibid*, para 46(c).

others.[134] *Monitoring and Evaluation of Rehabilitation for Torture Victims*, a handbook for service providers, suggests relevant standards and benchmarks in relation to rehabilitation from both clinical health and human rights perspectives, and it may be a valuable tool in this process.[135] Because of the specialized nature of these matters, professionals and practitioners in the fields of health, education, social integration, and law have a critical role to play. They are faced with the important challenge of developing strategies and best practices. In addition, they are tasked with systematizing knowledge aiming to provide the most effective form of rehabilitative care and services based on research and outcome studies of interventions made 'to ensure … access to the highest quality of care and rehabilitation to torture survivors, which is their right, not a privilege.'[136] Professionals involved in this work must continually monitor, adapt, and update their approaches, and they should also 'examine the usefulness of various components of their rehabilitation program' in order to develop the best possible program.[137] This work will benefit the individuals whom it strives to assist.

OBSTACLES TO REHABILITATION

There are numerous obstacles to enforcing the right to redress and, in particular, to providing effective rehabilitation.[138] Some of these obstacles relate to situations where torture and ill-treatment have rendered a person unable to stand up for him or herself. Others relate to the fear of being re-traumatized and re-encountering the pain suffered. The best way to address this is to create ways of dealing with the system-related obstacles frequently encountered, thereby heightening the State's obligation to ensure that people obtain redress.

General Comment 3 'presents a lengthy list of measures that constitute obstacles to the realization of the right to redress, as set forth in [UNCAT].'[139] The list begins with the need for 'clear acknowledgement' that the redress is awarded for violations of UNCAT 'by action or omission.'[140] The Committee is concerned about a lack of due diligence by State parties in many circumstances, which may give rise to State responsibility, hence the reference to 'omission.'[141]

Among the many other items cited as obstacles are ineffective mechanisms and courts; 'discrimination in accessing complaints and investigation mechanisms;' State secrecy laws; and 'evidential burdens and procedural requirements' that may unduly delay access to the right

---

[134] See, e.g., Montgomery, E and Patel, N, 'Torture Rehabilitation: Reflections on Treatment Outcome Studies', (2011) 21 *Torture* 141, 142 explaining that evidence is limited because 'whilst outcome research is valued and recognised as crucial to the delivery of quality services, it is not seen as a priority.'

[135] Patel and Williams (n 96 above), 17–24.

[136] Montgomery and Patel (n 134 above), 145.

[137] Başoğlu (n 9 above).

[138] General Comment 3 (n 3 above), paras 37–43.

[139] Gaer (n 4 above), 9 (citing General Comment 3 (n 3 above), paras 37–43).

[140] General Comment 3 (n 3 above), para 37.

[141] *Ibid.*

to redress.[142] Failure to ensure protection of victims and witnesses from reprisals for bringing claims is also cited as an obstacle to the right to redress.[143]

Noting the 'continuous nature' of the effects of torture, General Comment 3 proscribes statutes of limitations for torture or ill-treatment, pointing out, for example, that post-traumatic stress may actually increase over time, requiring 'medical, psychological and social support.'[144] Similarly, General Comment 3 recalls its consistent position that 'amnesties for torture and ill-treatment pose impermissible obstacles to a victim in his or her efforts to obtain redress,' and it calls on State parties to remove these.[145] General Comment 3 further notes that 'granting immunity in violation of international law ... is in direct conflict with the obligation of providing redress to victims,' identifying de facto impunity as yet another obstacle.[146]

CONCLUSIONS

Rehabilitation after torture is a complex and potentially long-term process. It may include support and assistance on many different levels, including social, medical, and psychological care, work-training, and often economic and judicial assistance.[147] Special attention must be given to interventions dealing with traumatic stress-related problems, as these may frequently be the main source of disruption of normal life activities and may debilitate effective reintegration into society after torture.[148] For rehabilitation to fulfill any of its objectives, the person being rehabilitated should be a close collaborator in the process. The victim should experience the care, interventions, and assistance as something that engages and re-vitalizes them and also as something that provides a tool with respect to dealing with trauma-related stress reactions. Accordingly, rehabilitation must take place in a secure, reliable, trustworthy, and predictable context.

Rehabilitation should be provided by professionals, in special training or rehabilitation centers, if possible. Providers should include personnel specially prepared to deal with all aspects of sequelae after torture and the complexities involved in this work, particularly in relation to ways of dealing with traumatic memories, avoidance reactions, painful triggers, etc. Rehabilitation must be accessible and available to the person seeking assistance. The care system providing rehabilitation needs to be able to convey professionalism, a high level of competency with regard to listening, and the capacity to adapt to the variety of needs involved. Furthermore, the process and the care providers should establish trust, stability, confidentiality, and a sense of safety. The capacity to assess needs and develop plans for rehabilitation, together with a system for ongoing monitoring and evaluation during the process, all aiming to improve rehabilitation services, is required.[149] To be as effective as possible, the rehabilitation programs and services must build upon systematic clinical knowledge, taking into account the

---

[142] *Ibid*, para 38.
[143] *Ibid*.
[144] *Ibid*, para 40.
[145] *Ibid*, para 41.
[146] *Ibid*, para 42.
[147] *Ibid*, para 11; Başoğlu (n 9 above).
[148] Başoğlu (n 9 above), maintaining that 'the greatest obstacle to a survivor's meaningful re-integration into society is the debilitating problems of traumatic stress.'
[149] Patel and Williams (n 96 above), 89.

complex social and cultural situations in which services are provided.[150] The need for more outcome studies on rehabilitation programs is highlighted in overview studies by Jaranson and Quiroga.[151] In particular, Jaranson and Quiroga emphasize that in order to improve the quality of care, studies on '[t]reatment efficacy (or clinical impact) … [t]reatment effectiveness (or economic impact) … [and] [e]fficiency (or cost/benefit analysis of the program]' must be undertaken.[152] Additionally, there is a need to focus on studies that include a variety of different approaches to rehabilitation as well as studies that cover work done with children and adolescents.[153]

Confidentiality and trust are vital to the process of providing and receiving rehabilitation. There may be serious issues related to lack of trust for many victims of torture, especially with regard to those who will provide services and assistance.[154] Health professionals in countries where torture has taken place may have been involved or complicit in torture and ill-treatment and those governing the health services may have engaged in or been part of the oppressing system. Even if time has passed and the system has changed, the person in need of rehabilitation may feel unsafe and vulnerable in such systems. This problem reinforces the importance of involving non-state actors in the rehabilitation process. Such non-state actors include different organizations involved in human rights monitoring and assistance, many of which are affiliated with qualified professionals whose competency and experience should be used in post-conflict rehabilitation. As indicated in General Comment 3:

> The obligation in [A]rticle 14 to provide for the means for as full rehabilitation as possible can be fulfilled through the direct provision of rehabilitative services by the State, or through the funding of private medical, legal and other facilities, including those administered by non-governmental organizations (NGOs), in which case the State shall ensure that no reprisals or intimidation are directed at them.[155]

The requirements (or obligations) listed in General Comment 3 may seem complex to some, but General Comment 3 sets forth, in its richness, what is required to provide full redress and rehabilitation when possible in accordance with the legal requirements of UNCAT. It is extremely important that any system of redress avoid the doubling of efforts and repeated and protracted processes in order for victims to obtain necessary assistance. This is true in all stages of the rehabilitation process, including the initial determination as to whether one is entitled to redress and determinations related to health care and other measures.

All of these aspects must be considered when human beings have been subjected to torture or ill-treatment. Such considerations also provide useful guidance for the process of developing and adopting programs of redress and rehabilitation, including situations where groups of individuals have been affected and knowledge of violations has been established.

By elaborating on the concepts of redress, rehabilitation, and the enforceable right to rehabilitation after torture, the Committee, through General Comment 3, has taken a long-needed

---

[150] *Ibid*, 79.
[151] *Ibid*, 106.
[152] Jaranson, J M, and Quiroga, J, 'Evaluating the Services of Torture Rehabilitation Programmes: History and Recommendations' (2011) 21 *Torture* 98, 105.
[153] Montgomery and Patel (n 134 above), 143.
[154] Istanbul Protocol (n 101 above), para 142(c).
[155] General Comment 3 (n 3 above), para 15.

and important step forward. The obligations under UNCAT have been specified and clarified, and ways in which redress, including rehabilitation, can be ensured and realized, have been explicitly outlined. But the contribution has not been only in relation to the meaning of Article 14 of UNCAT. Indeed, General Comment 3 has also contributed to our understanding of the right to redress and rehabilitation under international law. Realizing what General Comment 3 has outlined helps to ensure that care is given to, and new options in life are, in fact, made possible for victims of torture through prompt, adequate, and effective reparation and rehabilitation for harm suffered.

23. Psychological care for torture survivors, their families and communities

Nimisha Patel

You are like a shell. Even if I try to smile. Say hello. Look into my eyes – there is nothing left. I am dead ...

We argue a lot, he was tortured too, sometimes he loses his temper and beats me, hits the children ... the children are always scared. They crushed the life in us all. No hope. No future.

You learn to look at no one. Everyone in the community knows what happens. You learn that the only way to stay alive, to protect your family is look at no one talk to no one. Trust no one. What does this do to our children, their future? What will they teach their children? That life is about fear? About mistrust? About inhumanity? About silence? This is not a society I want my grandchildren and their children to grow up in. This must not be our legacy to them.

(Survivor of torture)

INTRODUCTION

At the most fundamental level, torture brutalises the essence of being human and the social bonds of humanity. The essence of being human is a philosophical, health/well-being, theological and political question, raising further questions of whose definition of being human, and of well-being, is salient, and in which particular context. These questions become more than an abstract notion when we consider the harm of torture. However, torture as a political tool, is potent precisely because the dynamics of torture embedded as a political and ideological strategy in societal institutions, and its harm, can reverberate in every human system built on human bonds: intimate relationships, families, peers, neighbourhoods, communities. The impacts of torture are multidimensional (physical, psychological, social, existential, spiritual, interpersonal, functional); profound; potentially long-term; and beyond the individual level: in other words, torture is 'the catastrophe of a bond' (Arestivo, 2018, p. 7). The ripples of harm from torture reach beyond the physical and psychological impacts on the individual torture survivor to their social worlds – their families, social networks and communities. In so doing, torture can achieve the purpose of destroying the survivor's relational bonds – the very bonds which validate one's humanity, dignity and worth, affirm social identities, sustain human relationships and enable individual and social agency. In effect, the ripples of the harm of torture dehumanise and can fragment, silence, isolate, alienate and annihilate the torture survivor, their families and communities – whilst also dehumanising the perpetrators.

This chapter considers the language and some problematic assumptions in the psychological literature before outlining the ripples of harm of torture, at the individual, family and community levels and the psychological literature on addressing these harms. The limitations of the empirical literature are summarised and key recommendations for future research are highlighted.

499

THE RIPPLES OF HARM

Torture has physical and mental health impacts (see Chapters 24 and 25), regardless of whether the methods are artificially defined as physical or psychological. The psychological impacts of torture are extremely varied, complex and often interlinked, and at the individual level they are intertwined with physical, emotional, cognitive, spiritual, interpersonal and familial well-being. In the psychological literature, these impacts of harm are commonly conceptualised as 'sequelae', 'consequences', 'symptoms' and 'psychiatric disorders'. Psychological difficulties are described by survivors in their diverse and kaleidoscopic ways. Each person's experience of torture, its impacts, how they make sense of them and express these difficulties, is unique and mediated by a multitude of personal and contextual factors. These include the economic, legal and political context of the torture and the survivor; the gender, sexuality, age, culture, beliefs and language in which meaning is made of these experiences; and the wider, social and cultural context. The ripples of harm and impact on families of survivors and communities affected by torture is also varied, shaped by culture, social norms, taboos and dominant discourses, and the economic, political and legal context of torture and impunity.

'PSYCHOLOGICAL TREATMENT' OR 'REHABILITATION' FOR TORTURE SURVIVORS?

Given the multidimensional and multi-level impact of torture and the pervasive and enduring ripples of harm arising from torture, to speak of psychological impacts of torture as symptoms or disorders renders the destruction caused by torture somewhat simplistic, reductionist and essentialist. Another important consideration is whether the language of 'psychological treatment' is appropriate as a response to such deliberate harm and suffering. Yet, there is a burgeoning literature on psychological treatment for torture survivors (reviewed subsequently) in the Global North. In many countries in the Global South, and in regions such as Latin America, the language of psychological 'treatment' for psychological 'disorders' is vehemently rejected in the context of torture, although the psychological *suffering* caused by torture is not dismissed, minimised or underestimated. This rejection is echoed by challenges to the dominant discourses of trauma (e.g. Bracken et al., 1997; Summerfield, 1999, 2001; Silove, 1999; Patel, 2003, 2010). Some of the pivotal and problematic assumptions underpinning the existing literature are now considered.

First is the assumption that psychological treatments constitute rehabilitation, by targeting specific psychological symptoms, understood as universally meaningful, with interventions aimed at symptom-reduction and change in psychiatric caseness, as constructed in Western nosologies. Yet, globally, many torture survivors will suffer immense and severe suffering and pain, not always manifest in shared symptomatology, and without reaching the diagnostic thresholds of psychiatric diagnoses. Also, many will experience, manifest and make sense of their suffering and pain not using Western language and constructions of mental health or psychological problems or psychiatric disorders. Psychological treatments then narrowly focus on and target only those survivors who are able to access formal psychological or psychiatric services and whose suffering is deemed to reach (Western) normative standards for 'abnormality' or 'illness'. This essentially minimises or disregards those survivors who do not construct or present their experiences of suffering in language and expressions recognised by clinicians as reaching psychiatric diagnostic thresholds.

Second, the language of treatment, and focus on the individual's symptoms, assumes that suffering and pain is to be primarily understood in medical illness terms; and locates the site of assumed pathology within the individual – specifically, within their psyche. This obscures both the structural causes of harm (or 'structural pathologies' – significant disparities in wealth, corruption, discrimination, social inequalities, armed conflict etc.), which may lead to and maintain the systematic practices of torture and impunity) as well as the ripples of harm from torture which exceed psychological difficulties and possible symptoms, extending to many other physical, emotional, existential, social, interpersonal, welfare and other domains of profound suffering. It also obscures the impact on family members, including intergenerationally, and on communities and society at large. One could argue that focusing on psychological symptom-reduction does not mean other aspects cannot be addressed, or that they would not improve as a result (such as social functioning). Indeed, psychological distress may interact in many ways with other aspects of suffering, and improvements in one aspect can lead to improvements in others. However, most often, the literature is at odds with the clinical consensus that holistic care by a multidisciplinary team of doctors, psychologists, psychotherapists, social workers, arts therapists, family therapists, community workers, educational and vocational support professionals and lawyers, etc. is ideal to meet the diverse and multiple impacts of torture. A focus on psychological treatment alone, or as a discrete component of care, obscures the possible gains and improvements in well-being more generally (not just psychological functioning) of more holistic care, where social, medical, legal, welfare and individual, family and community-based psychological support may, in combination, provide relevant care to address the insidious ripples of the harm of torture.

Third, another problematic assumption underpinning the discourse of psychological treatments for torture is that context is only tangentially relevant. The multiple experiences of torture, ill-treatment, persecution, violent losses, etc. are homogenised and simplified as 'trauma events' and the harm of torture is decontextualised and depoliticised; context is backgrounded, or erased and torture as a grave human rights violation and an international crime, sanctioned by the State charged with the protection of its nationals, is rendered invisible, or given a cursory glance. The social, economic, legal and political context of torture, including the context of stigma, disbelief, denial and impunity, is at best acknowledged tokenistically, and at worse, simply ignored.

Inevitably, as the experiences of torture, their impacts and trajectories of suffering and survival are highly heterogeneous, complex and unique to each survivor and their family and community, there can be no one single method, intervention or psychological method which can work for all or most survivors in all contexts. In other words, there can be no 'one size fits all' approach to psychological care for torture survivors (Montgomery and Patel, 2010).

General Comment 3 of the United Nations Committee on the Convention against Torture and other Cruel, Inhuman or Degrading Treatment or Punishment (UNCAT, 2012) emphasises that rehabilitation for torture survivors should be holistic (paras 11 and 13), specific to the needs of each survivor, and 'may include a wide range of inter-disciplinary measures, such as medical, physical and psychological rehabilitative services; re-integrative and social services; community and family-oriented assistance and services; vocational training; education etc.' (para. 13). Hence, psychological care may include specific, specialist psychological interventions – for individuals and groups of survivors and their families, as part of holistic rehabilitation. Psychological care, as a significant aspect of advocacy and prevention activities, community-based network-building and activities, as well as welfare, educational, vocational and legal support, can also contribute to rehabilitation.

However, rehabilitation is more than particular activities or interventions (see Sveaass et al., Chapter 22 in this volume), and psychological care, as part of a range of rehabilitation activities, can also be hindered by factors beyond the nature and quality of the care – such as ongoing conflict and conditions of threat, insecurity and lack of safety, unemployment, income poverty, food insecurity, homelessness, impunity, immigration detention, xenophobia, social stigma, discrimination, intimidation, etc. – all of which can lead to repeated and multiple harms. The protection of other civil, political, social and economic rights of survivors are highly relevant, alongside the protection and realisation of the right to rehabilitation (Patel, 2019a); and any rehabilitation gains or lack of, cannot be reliably attributed only to specific psychological interventions.

WHAT IS PSYCHOLOGICAL CARE?

The term psychological care is used deliberately here to acknowledge that such care is not limited to traditional, Western notions of 'treatment', and that it can encompass a range of activities and interventions. These include generic psychosocial care and support, symptom-specific psychological interventions and a range of model-specific or integrative psychological therapies or cultural practices. These forms of psychological care can be offered in a variety of ways and settings to torture survivors, to individuals and groups of survivors (adults, children or young people), or to families or couples, or as community-based activities.

Individual-based Psychological Care

The commonest forms of psychological care for torture survivors reported in the literature include psychosocial support, generic psychological counselling, trauma-focused psychological interventions and different forms of psychological therapy.

Psychosocial support addresses the psychological and social dimensions of well-being and suffering, and may include generic counselling which considers the emotional, social, political and economic realities of survivors. Psychosocial support is often offered alongside other social, welfare, legal and other forms of support. It does not target specific psychological symptoms, but is generally premised on the notion that suffering is multidimensional and that generic psychosocial support can help mobilise the individual's resources, strengths and capacities to cope and function in everyday life as a survivor. Psychosocial support can be offered to all ages, and individually or groups, in formal settings (e.g. rehabilitation services, clinics), within schools; and within the local community.

Psychological counselling may be specific to a particular theoretical model, time-limited and goal-focused. Supportive, general counselling may be a component of psychosocial support, though specific counselling, from a theoretical base (e.g. psychodynamic, humanistic) can also be aimed at specific difficulties experienced by an individual survivor, for example psychological counselling for a woman who has been raped and who is struggling with depressive feelings and difficulties in trusting others and maintaining an intimate relationship with her partner, or for a person who has experienced bereavement or a traumatic loss of a family member as a result of torture or during armed conflict, or for a parent who is struggling to cope with supporting and caring for a child who has been tortured.

Psychological therapy is a generic term which encompasses a range of therapeutic methods that are usually based on one theoretical model (e.g. psychodynamic, humanistic, cognitive-behavioural, narrative exposure and systemic), or on an integration of different theoretical models. Psychological therapies tend to be more specific, some with specific interventions targeting specific symptoms or emotional, behavioural, cognitive, relational and communication patterns. Psychological therapies can be more exploratory and in-depth than generic psychological counselling, although the distinctions are arbitrary, particularly in working with torture survivors where psychological care may involve a combination of specific therapy interventions with supportive counselling, used in combination, simultaneously or at different stages of the rehabilitative process. Psychological therapies and interventions specific to different therapies may focus on a range or one of the following psychological difficulties: anxiety, excessive fear, guilt, shame, feelings of helplessness, hopelessness, despair, suicidality, depression, sleep difficulties, chronic pain, trauma memories, cognitive difficulties, interpersonal and relationship difficulties, sexual difficulties, social withdrawal and isolation, social functioning at home, work or in everyday life, etc. Psychological therapies may also use different mediums – verbal, visual art, dance and movement and music, for example.

Trauma-focused psychological interventions or therapy target specific symptoms and difficulties understood to be a specific feature of a trauma response that can be experienced by torture survivors. The understanding of trauma responses underpinning these interventions is invariably derivative of theoretical models of post-traumatic stress disorder (PTSD) (not models of trauma – which vary), and focus primarily on two key trauma responses: intrusive phenomena (involuntary re-experiencing of trauma-related memories, which can be visual and/or auditory); and avoidance behaviour (avoiding places, people, situations which remind the person of the original trauma(s)). Trauma-focused interventions include Eye Movement Desensitization and Reprocessing (EMDR), Narrative Exposure Therapy (NET) and trauma-focused Cognitive-Behavioural Therapy (CBT). All typically include exposure techniques (exposing the person to specific or non-specific memories or cues related to the traumatic experience(s)) and cognitive-processing methods (challenging unhelpful thinking patterns related to the traumatic experience(s), developing more helpful thinking patterns and related behaviours) and facilitate (whether explicitly stated or not) emotional expression and processing of psychological distress.

Testimonial Therapy, is an adaptation of Testimonial Method, which was originally developed as a human rights-based method, but was adapted as a therapeutic approach (see later).

Despite a plethora of approaches to individual-based support, counselling and therapy, including multidisciplinary and multimodal approaches for torture survivors applied in practice within specialist rehabilitation services over three decades, there has been a breadth of literature but to date, limited, quality evidence on their impacts and effectiveness. A broader range of literature exists but the majority of studies and reviews of psychological interventions focus on refugees, or people living in or affected by war, with far fewer specifically focusing on torture survivors.

Over the last decade, there have been around ten literature reviews of psychological and other mental health interventions for refugees, but they vary enormously in their focus (e.g. including studies only on adults, only on children or youth, or a mixture of all, or including studies only on individual-based interventions to groups and families) and in their inclusion criteria (e.g. whether asylum seekers are included, the types of studies reviewed). They invariably do not specify the number of torture survivors across studies reviewed, most include only refugees with symptoms which meet caseness for PTSD, and they vary in the interventions reviewed. Systematic reviews specifically and explicitly on the psychological care of torture survivors are far fewer in number. Inevitably, the studies included overlap across all reviews.

Evidence for psychological care for refugee people

Murray et al.'s (2010) review focused on studies on a range of mental health interventions (including CBT, EMDR, pharmacotherapy, expressive, exposure and testimonial therapies, multi-family and empowerment groups, individual psychodynamic therapy) for refugee children, adults and families, conducted in resettlement countries. Most studies reviewed used CBT (for adults or children), which was found to be very effective for reducing symptoms of traumatic stress; similarly, strong effects were found for EMDR and for exposure therapy (though based on only one study for each intervention method at the time of the review).

Other literature reviews on 'refugees and asylum seekers' (Crumlish and O'Rourke, 2010), refugees diagnosed with PTSD (Nickerson et al., 2011), 'traumatized asylum seekers and refugees' (Slobodin and De Jong, 2015) and a systematic review and meta-analysis of psychological interventions for asylum seekers and refugees diagnosed with PTSD (Thompson et al., 2018), all indicate positive outcomes for trauma-focused psychological interventions in terms of reducing trauma-related symptoms in those diagnosed with PTSD. All the reviews highlight methodological problems in many studies reviewed, noting the limited evidence for treatments reviewed and cautioning against definitive conclusions. The review by Nickerson et al. (2011) focused on interventions for PTSD versus multimodal interventions seeking to address psychological, social, health-related and cultural adaptation issues, and the studies evaluating multimodal interventions reviewed reported positive outcomes, though not significant improvements. Palic and Elklit's (2011) systematic review included cognitive behavioural therapies (including CBT, NET, Exposure therapy), multidisciplinary treatments (including counselling, psychotherapy, medication, physiotherapy) and 'alternative treatments' (including music therapy, short-term psychodynamic therapy and Thought-Field Therapy – which combined psychotherapy with acupuncture and chiropractic) for adult refugees, and found very large effect sizes reported in some CBT studies, in treating core symptoms of PTSD, although, again, they emphasise the tentativeness of interpretations of treatment results, noting the diversity of the methods and refugee populations studied.

A meta-analysis assessing 12 controlled trials on trauma-focused psychological interventions (including EMDR, CBT and NET) for 'traumatised adult refugees' also indicated positive impacts on PTSD and depression symptoms, with overall large effect sizes, for trauma-focused interventions (Lambert and Alhassoon, 2015). A review of 14 randomised and non-randomised studies and a meta-analysis on 12 of those studies on psychosocial interventions for PTSD in refugees and asylum seekers in high-income countries showed the efficacy of psychosocial interventions (including mainly NET, CBT and trauma-focused psychotherapy) in decreasing PTSD symptoms (Nosè et al., 2017). The Tribe et al. (2017) systematic review on the effectiveness of multi- and uni-modal psychological interventions for 'traumatised refugees and/or asylum seekers' echoes findings of earlier reviews. They report evidence of medium to high quality supporting NET for refugee populations; evidence for studies described as using 'culturally-sensitive CBT'; and mixed evidence found supporting standard CBT and EMDR. In the six studies reviewed, the evidence for multidisciplinary treatments (with differing durations – 3–24 months – and methodologies and various combinations of social care, psychotherapy, social counselling, physiotherapy and pharmacotherapy) was mixed, but most studies reviewed showed improvements in psychological symptoms with small to medium effect sizes. As with earlier reviews, they note a number of limitations of the studies reviewed, including small sample sizes, insufficient follow-up periods, heterogeneous populations studied, poor data reporting and bias. A recent systematic review and meta-analysis of randomised controlled trials on the efficacy and acceptability of psychosocial interventions for asylum seekers and refugees found moderate quality evidence of the beneficial effect on PTSD, depression and anxiety symptoms, and no difference between psychosocial interventions and control conditions in terms of effect on functioning and quality of life (measured in only four studies) (Turrini et al., 2019). The authors recommend CBT, whilst suggesting that EMDR needed further study for this population, since the four studies reviewed did not show significant effects on PTSD symptoms. Unlike findings reported in other systematic reviews (e.g. Nosè et al., 2017; Tribe et al., 2017), Turrini et al. found that NET failed to show a beneficial impact for PTSD and depression symptoms at post-intervention. Of the 26 studies reviewed most were related to adults or mixed populations of adults and children, with one study on NET with children (Ruf et al., 2010) that had poor data. Again, the limited participant numbers, the heterogeneity, high risk of bias in most studies reviewed and their moderate to low quality were highlighted as limitations by the authors.

Evidence for individual psychological care for adults

The aforementioned reviews did not focus on, nor state explicitly how many study participants were torture survivors, though some studies reviewed likely included torture survivors. Early desk reviews (Gurr and Quiroga, 2001; Quiroga and Jaranson, 2005) surveyed the burgeoning literature on the impact of torture and care of torture survivors, constructing the latter as rehabilitation, within an explicitly political, not 'treatment' context. To date, only two systematic meta-analyses of randomised controlled trials (Patel et al., 2014; Hamid et al., 2019) of interventions for torture survivors exist. Patel et al. (2014) assessed the beneficial and adverse effects of psychological, social and welfare interventions for torture survivors, comparing these effects with those reported by active and inactive controls. Of the nine randomised controlled studies reviewed all included psychological interventions (NET, CBT and mixed methods for trauma symptoms) for adults; none included social and welfare interventions, which in practice in specialist torture rehabilitation services, are commonly provided alongside psychological interventions for torture survivors. No benefits at the end of psychological therapy were noted in comparison with controls in terms of psychological distress (usually depression), nor for PTSD symptoms, PTSD caseness, or quality of life, and surprisingly, at six-month follow-up, three NET and one CBT study showed moderate effect sizes for intervention over control in reduction of psychological depression, although these effects may not have been attributed six months after treatment end to the treatment, and the evidence was very low quality. Hamid et al. (2019) updated this review, including six new studies, reviewing in total 15 eligible studies. They conclude that the overall results were comparable to the previous review, with small positive effects of psychological interventions (based on CBT, NET or Testimony Method (TM) and relative to comparator arms) in reducing PTSD symptoms and improving functioning at the end of interventions (though the latter were not sustained at follow up), and no significant effects were found for reducing depression at end of treatment and follow-up. Notwithstanding the slight improvement in the quality of evidence, the number of eligible trials and sample sizes were small, precluding firm conclusions about the efficacy of psychological interventions for torture survivors.

McFarlane and Kaplan's (2012) literature review of 40 studies of different research designs, over a 30-year period, included psychosocial interventions (including multicomponent rehabilitation, psychological interventions – individual and group-based) for adult torture survivors, as well as for other refugees, asylum seekers or displaced survivors of trauma (undefined). In 90 per cent of the studies reviewed, significant improvements were found on at least one outcome indicator (e.g. symptoms of PTSD, depression, anxiety) post-intervention, with studies biased in their focus on symptoms of PTSD over depression and anxiety. The review did not identify any effects related to the specific amount, type or length of the interventions; and treatment effects were shown to vary between 3 and 18 months. Moderate and cautious support was found for NET and CBT, although these studies were not exclusively with torture survivors.

A subsequent narrative literature review (Weiss et al., 2016) identified 88 studies (including those reviewed previously by McFarlane and Kaplan (2012), and single case studies) of various mental health interventions with survivors of torture or of 'systematic violence by organized groups' (p. 19) (undefined but including 'refugees from war' (p. 19)). CBT with exposure components (not including studies on NET) was concluded as having sufficient evidence for reducing symptoms associated with PTSD, depression and anxiety in adult torture survivors. Other methods, including multidisciplinary and multi-therapy type interventions (including components of pharmacotherapy, general counselling, CBT, testimonial therapy and physiotherapy) also showed promise in improving some symptoms of trauma, although their individual impact or continuation to symptom reduction cannot be established based on the available evidence. Multidisciplinary and multi-therapy types of interventions (e.g. general counselling, CBT with and without exposure, EMDR, physiotherapy and pharmacotherapy) focusing on anxiety symptoms showed some impact. Salo and Bray (2016) in their systematic literature review of 22 articles from 13 studies on interventions for majority survivors of torture (in country of resettlement) also include studies with youth and adults, or families with adults. They note that whilst torture survivors' difficulties are best understood from an ecological perspective (difficulties within different levels of the survivor's microsystem, mesosystem, exosystem and macrosystem), all interventions reported in the studies reviewed targeted individual-level change with effectiveness operationalised as symptom reduction, and only 11 interventions addressed other ecological needs and life domains (e.g. family, occupational).

Studies evaluating the efficacy of multimodal interventions are rare, with some exceptions. Dix-Peek and Werbeloff's (2018) study found that following a three-month counselling intervention based on a multimodal framework of interventions, compared to a waiting-list group, there were improvements in coping, PTSD, depression, anxiety symptoms and in functioning. They note that there was a high level of attrition (with refugee torture survivors moving to seek employment, accommodation or safety) during longer therapeutic interventions, compromising the quality of the findings. Whilst not being a controlled trial, this study is particularly significant for a number of reasons: (a) the psychosocial approach it evaluates most closely resembles the nature of multimodal approaches, tailored according to the needs of individual torture survivors, offered in many multidisciplinary rehabilitation services for torture survivors, but insufficiently evaluated; (b) it addresses the range of needs of refugee and 'in-country' torture survivors with multiple past traumas and living in contexts of environmental stressors, lack of safety and continuing traumatic experiences; and (c) it is an evaluation of an approach offered within a developing-country context where torture is ongoing.

Arts-based therapy (visual art, music, dance and movement-based) is also often used in rehabilitation services for torture survivors, alongside other psychological, social, family and welfare interventions. However, there are few studies on such methods and most did not meet inclusion criteria in the available reviews. A review by Longacre et al. (2012) suggests that certain complementary and alternative medicine modalities may prove effective as part of an integrated care plan for torture survivors, but further research is warranted. Practice-based evidence suggests that dance and movement therapies for torture survivors improve depression (Callaghan, 1993; Gray, 2001; Koch and Weidinger-von der Recke, 2009); and that Qigong and T'ai Chi provide relief for psychological and physical difficulties experienced by torture survivors. Art therapy with mindfulness meditation with adult refugees (not specifically torture survivors) is described as contributing to self-awareness, expression of anxiety and loss, an internal sense of safety, calming, emotional regulation and catharsis, and helps them connect with others (Kalmanowitz and Ho, 2016). Thought Field Therapy, a brief therapy method based on energy psychology (drawing on the Chinese Meridian system and applied kinesiology) has also been shown to improve symptoms of PTSD in refugees in the US (Folkes, 2002), in adult (Connolly and Sakai, 2011; Connolly et al., 2013) and adolescent (Sakai et al., 2010) survivors of the Rwandan genocide, and in survivors of conflict in Uganda (Robson et al., 2016).

Evidence for individual psychological care for minors
The literature on psychological care for children and young people subjected or exposed to torture or conflict is predominantly centred on traditional psychological therapy (mainly trauma-focused interventions) or psychosocial interventions, either individual-based or group-based (including in schools).

Gillies et al.'s (2016) systematic review, a meta-analysis of 51 randomised controlled trials of psychological interventions for minors, included only ten studies with children and adolescents exposed to 'war or community violence' – torture unspecified. Interventions included CBT, EMDR, supportive therapy, play therapy and family therapy with children and adolescents who had experienced traumatic events found that those who received psychological therapies were less likely to be diagnosed with PTSD, and had fewer symptoms up to a month, than those who received no treatment, treatment as usual or were on a waiting list, although the quality of the evidence was considered low. There was moderate quality evidence favouring CBT over EMDR, play therapy and supportive therapy, as effective in reducing PTSD symptoms for up to a month. As with reviews of studies with adults, the positive outcomes identified in this review were not apparent in the long term. A subsequent narrative review and meta-analysis of 23 studies focusing on psychosocial interventions in 'war-traumatized refugee and internally displaced minors' (Nocon et al., 2017) found evidence for trauma-focused psychological interventions reducing PTSD symptoms and that CBT and interpersonal therapy (IPT) showed promising results (although many of the studies were also of low methodological quality).

Beyond pure efficacy and effectiveness research, Brown et al. (2017) emphasise the need to focus on identifying necessary and active treatment components for effective interventions for children and young people affected by war, in order to develop interventions for delivery by non-specialists. To identify common practice elements in effective psychosocial interventions, Brown et al. (2017) conducted a systematic review of 28 randomised controlled trials and controlled trials conducted in conflict☐affected settings, and 25 efficacious treatments, using psychosocial interventions (including group, individual, self-help, family-based or community-based interventions – offered by non-specialist providers in 54 per cent of studies) in LMICs, addressing the needs of children and young people (up to age 24). The review found that the most common practice elements in treatments showing a positive treatment effect in at least one outcome included: accessibility promotion – strategies to enhance the accessibility of services to improve treatment participation; psychoeducation for the child and caregiver; insight-building; relationship/rapport-building; cognitive strategies; narratives; exposure; and strategies for relapse prevention/maintenance. Several practice elements were found across more than 50 per cent of the intervention protocols of these treatments. These were access promotion, psychoeducation for children and parents, insight building, rapport-building techniques, cognitive strategies, use of narratives, exposure techniques and relapse prevention.

Evidence for focused psychosocial interventions for children in low-resource humanitarian settings (including in Uganda, Kosovo, Sierra Leone, Democratic Republic of Congo, Sri Lanka, Burundi and Rwanda) was noted by a systematic review which included a meta-analysis of individual participant data of over 3,100 children exposed to traumatic events, from 11 randomised controlled trials, to explore which children were most likely to benefit (Purgato et al., 2018). Focused psychosocial interventions (including creative play, class-based interventions, sport, teaching recovery techniques, emotional writing) were found to have a small beneficial effect in reducing PTSD symptoms (with stronger improvements in older children aged 15–18, in non-displaced children, and children living in smaller households), as well as in reducing functional impairment and in increasing hope, coping and social support. Notwithstanding the methodological limitations of the study, including heterogeneity in approaches and in sociocultural contexts of studies reviewed and potential investigator bias, this review focused on strengths. Its findings are consistent with, and go beyond, a meta-analytic systematic review evaluating a broad range of psychological interventions for PTSD and depression in young survivors of mass violence in low- and middle-income countries (Morina et al., 2017), while other systematic reviews of children and adolescents affected by war indicate promising effects, particularly with trauma-focused CBT (Jordans et al. 2009; O'Sullivan et al., 2016). That said, it is unclear how many of the participants in any of these reviews would be considered torture survivors, and which psychosocial interventions are effective for them.

Studies of other types of psychological or integrative interventions also suggest promising outcomes, for example, Thought Field Therapy has been shown to improve symptoms of PTSD in adolescent survivors of Rwandan genocide (Sakai et al., 2010). One study (Ugurlu et al., 2016) with Syrian refugee children (aged 7–12) settled in Turkey involved a five-day workshop with three separate creative arts therapy groups (visual art aimed at emotional expression, stress reduction, increasing self-esteem and improving problem-solving skills; music therapy aimed at learning musical skills, leadership skills, promoting social interaction and team work; and dance and movement therapy aimed at increasing self-awareness, mindfulness and enhancing relaxation and grounding). All 63 study participants attended all the sessions, with a significant decrease in PTSD and depression symptoms at the end of the therapy interventions, but no significant change in anxiety. Similarly, an art therapy programme for Burmese adolescent refugees in the US (16 sessions over the school year, school-based), tailored to each young person's needs, to allow emotional expression related to trauma memories was evaluated with a pre-post design (Rowe et al., 2017). Findings include a reduction in anxiety and improvements in self-concept, although the authors note that one limitation was the use of measures which may not adequately capture post-traumatic growth and measures which presented cultural and language barriers.

In summary, a number of reviews exist for psychological or psychosocial interventions for refugees, asylum seekers and displaced people resettled or living in low to medium resources countries and those affected by war; although very few systematic reviews and only two meta-analyses exist on psychological interventions for adult survivors of torture, and none specifically with children survivors of torture. Some reviews include studies with individual interventions only for adults, others include studies with families and groups; some include minors. Hence, the reviews vary considerably in their focus, design, quality and in the considerable methodological limitations (considered later) and variance in the quality of the studies reviewed, which means that no clear conclusions can be made about the effectiveness of different psychological interventions for torture survivors.

Overall, the empirical evidence base for individual-based psychological care is insufficient and interpretations must be considered tentative.

Broadly, the findings for adults indicate:

- No to moderate effects of evidence for NET in reducing symptoms of PTSD and depression;
- Significant effects of trauma-focused CBT in reducing symptoms of PTSD, while the evidence for impact in reducing symptoms of depression varies from no effects to moderate effects;
- No to strong effects of evidence for EMDR in reducing PTSD;
- Some promising improvements from arts-based therapies;
- Positive outcomes but not statistically significant for a multidisciplinary approach, with small to medium effects.

For children and young people, the findings are even more tentative, suggesting:

- some evidence of psychological treatments (over waiting-list/treatment as usual/no treatment) leading to improvements in psychological presentations;
- Small effects of evidence for trauma-focused therapies (CBT, EMDR) and focused psychosocial interventions (e.g. creative play, class-based interventions, sport, teaching recovery techniques, emotional writing) in reducing PTSD symptoms. CBT was found to be no more or less effective than EMDR and supportive therapy for reducing the diagnosis of PTSD in the short term;
- Positive outcomes for CBT, IPT, supportive counselling and Thought-Field therapy, showing improvements in reducing PTSD and depression symptoms.

Group-based Psychological Care for Torture Survivors

Group-based psychological care for torture survivors can be varied, depending on its theoretical basis, the composition of the groups, methods used and intended outcomes. Groups may offer generic psychosocial support, psychological counselling, psychological therapy or specific psychological interventions targeting trauma-specific responses to torture or particular health problems. Some types of groups may use a combination of verbal therapies and arts-based therapies, including movement, music and art. They may also include activities which are not explicitly driven by a psychological model, nor regarded as therapy, but nonetheless are seen to have beneficial psychological and social impacts. For example, groups can focus on horticultural activities (with or without psychological counselling or therapy as an element), relaxation and leisure activities, literary, musical, creative, arts-based or social activities, etc.

Group-based psychological care for children, particularly in the context of refugees and communities affected by war, can be provided in schools. Group-based psychological care for adult torture survivors can be constructed around their specific difficulties (e.g. traumatic loss and bereavement, interpersonal difficulties, social functioning); by the nature of the torture (e.g. sexual torture); or by a psychiatric diagnosis (e.g. depression, PTSD); as well as by a combination of a range of other factors, including gender, nationality, ethnicity, language, or cultural or faith background. Groups may be time-limited (short-term or long-term) or open-ended; some may be highly structured, others fluid and flexible according to what group members bring to the group. Groups for torture survivors are offered through different organisations and services by qualified psychologists or psychotherapists, other mental health professionals, physiotherapists, or community or case-workers; and in community settings groups may be offered by health professionals, therapists, lay counsellors or community workers.

The assumptions which underpin group-based psychological care, such as those regarding what constitutes support or care, what is beneficial and how, the optimal size of a group, who can benefit or is suitable for a group or not, and how groups should be facilitated or structured, etc. vary according to the nature of the group, the theoretical preferences and work experience of group facilitators, the philosophy and approach of the service or organisation, the identified needs of survivors and the service context – whether it takes place in conditions of safety and security, in resettlement contexts, refugee camps, during ongoing conflict, etc. As with individual psychological care, group-based psychological care is highly heterogeneous and there is no 'one size fits all' approach to torture survivors.

Evidence for group-based psychological care for adults
A review of non-specialised, group-based mental health and psychosocial interventions in displaced populations yielded 11 publications (Wood and Kallestrup, 2018), of which only three were randomised trials. The marked heterogeneity of group interventions and their effects, and the methodological issues in the interventions reviewed, precluded any firm conclusions. Whilst the studies on group-based psychological interventions (including trauma-focused interventions, nonverbal and psychotherapy groups) for adult asylum seekers and refugees show some positive effects, they focus on symptom reduction for adults diagnosed as suffering from PTSD (e.g. Droždek and Bolwerk, 2010a; Droždek et al., 2012, 2014; Robertson et al., 2013).

There is a dearth of studies evaluating other approaches to group work specifically for refugees and for torture survivors, although a range of improvements (including emotional processing of traumatic experiences, sharing, building trust, emotional intimacy and networks of social support) are described in the literature on group psychotherapy approaches for adult refugee torture survivors (e.g. Tucker and Price, 2007; Woodcock, 1997), storytelling for refugee children and adolescents (Schwartz and Melzak, 2005), groups based on empowerment and multicultural frameworks for LGBT asylum seekers (Reading and Rubin, 2011), and social support groups for LGBTQ African and Caribbean refugees (Logie et al., 2016). Group approaches described by the authors as culture-sensitive, including peer groups for Chechnyan refugees (Renner et al., 2011) and groups combining psychological counselling with a traditional spiritual and psychological healing Kaffa intervention (coffee ceremony) with refugee women (Loewy, Williams and Keleta, 2002), report positive effects. A collaboratively designed and culturally relevant group for refugee women using health literacy intervention has also been used to help women develop supportive networks to prevent social isolation and mental health problems (Felsman, 2016).

There is limited literature on group-based psychological care specifically for torture survivors (and studies on group interventions offered in the community, typically described as community-based interventions, are considered subsequently). A literature review by Bunn et al. (2015), based on 36 articles and chapters describing group interventions for torture survivors, concluded that there is insufficient conceptual rationale for using group treatment and that there is very limited empirical literature presently. One study suggests that attending a psychological therapy group is related to torture survivors' clinical engagement with other adjunct services, and that they sought out more mental health services, though there was no significant difference in engagement with social or legal services (Smith, Keatley and Min, 2019). Whilst most group-based psychological care addresses the individual and group dimension, one model of group therapy with torture survivors is seen as also extending to community healing, for example by survivors leaving a therapy group and going on to join social clubs and organisations and contributing to the continuation of group and community support (Kira et al., 2012).

Evidence for group-based psychological care for minors
Literature on group-based, preventive and early interventions, specifically for the psychological well-being of children and their families who have been subjected to torture, are notably lacking. Studies offering group-based interventions to refugee children or children living in armed conflict are of some relevance, in that they may include minors subjected to or who have witnessed torture.

One study evaluating group-based, brief (six session) CBT to refugee children showed a significant decrease in post-trauma symptoms (though not sustained on follow up after two months) and significant improvements in behavioural difficulties (Ehntholt et al., 2005). Studies evaluating psychosocial interventions for minors exposed to conflict have yielded limited evidence, due in part to the low quality of studies (Jordans et al., 2009; Persson and Rousseau, 2009), with some exceptions (e.g. Tol et al., 2008; Layne et al., 2008). Several reviews conclude that psychosocial interventions for children affected by conflict show promising results for some in reducing mental health difficulties (Jordans et al., 2009; Persson and Rousseau, 2009; Peltonen and Punamaki, 2010).

Psychosocial and psychological interventions within schools can be useful, where the educational system can become a critical partner (Betancourt and Williams, 2008) and enable access and support for children's families and communities. However, the evidence is mixed. Sullivan and Simonson (2016) in their systematic review of school-based interventions for refugee and 'war-traumatized youth' indicate that whilst some psychological interventions have positive effects, multiple others have null or negative effects. Similarly, another review of school-based interventions implemented in war-exposed countries for children and adolescents with reported higher levels of psychological symptoms than their peers, indicated mixed results, with the authors suggesting that school-based group crisis interventions may not be sufficient to reduce mental distress and sometimes may increase it (Persson and Rousseau, 2009). In contrast, Tyrer and Fazel's (2014) review of studies with refugee and asylum-seeking children concludes that school-based psychological interventions (in high-income countries), using both individual and group-based interventions (including creativity and arts, supportive counselling, verbal processing using trauma-focused therapies) led to significant change in the reduction of PTSD, anxiety and depression symptomatology, functioning and peer problems, though they highlight methodological problems and variance in the studies reviewed, leading to limited conclusions. Others have found that using school-based interventions for children living in armed conflict had no impact on decreasing psychological symptoms but was effective only in limiting the deterioration of friendships and prosocial behaviour (Peltonen et al., 2012).

A study using Teaching Recovery Techniques intervention in schools for children living in war-affected settings indicated gender differences, with a significant reduction of post-trauma stress symptoms amongst boys, and to a lesser extent, in girls (Qouta et al., 2012), and a reduction in loneliness amongst boys and a reduction in sibling rivalry amongst girls (Diab et al., 2012); although another study with war-affected refugee children using the same group and school-based method found positive outcomes in depression symptoms but not in PTSD and psychosocial functioning outcomes (Ooi et al., 2016). Arts-based interventions (e.g. Yohani, 2008), for example in the form of school-based interventions integrating drama and language awareness (Rousseau et al., 2007, 2011), have also been shown to have positive impacts, and a reduction in emotional distress symptoms and behavioural difficulties has been noted (Quinlan et al., 2015). A culturally-relevant, community-based three-day camp for African refugee children, designed specifically as a psychosocial intervention to instil cultural pride, increase self-esteem, decrease isolation and support the children's adjustment, whilst including family and community resources and drawing on African traditions, offered over ten years to many children and families, is an innovative, though unfortunately not formally evaluated, approach to group work with children (Akinsulure-Smith et al., 2013).

In summary, there is very little evidence of group-based interventions specifically with children and youth torture survivors. On the whole, whilst school-based interventions have the advantage of reaching large numbers of children (particularly group-based interventions) in normalised environments and settings accessible to children and their families, there is an insufficient evidence base for school-based interventions for children exposed to war, including refugees, or community-based interventions for children still living in conflict or emergency settings; and it is unclear from existing studies as to which particular group-based interventions, or which ingredient(s) of the intervention or activity, are most effective.

Family and Couple-based Psychological Care

By destroying the capacity to trust, torture ruptures existing relational bonds and depletes the capacity to form and maintain new relationships. In so doing, torture attacks the essence of humanness – that we are social beings who thrive on relational bonds – thereby impacting on the survivor's family. For survivors, the difficulties in trusting others, loss of control over their life, inability to communicate to others their depth of pain, despair and suffering, fearing not being believed, or valued as a human being, and ongoing chronic ill-health, disability, pain and other psychological difficulties can all contribute to poor social functioning. This can impact on family relationships, as well as relationships with friends, peers or colleagues. For many, these difficulties can adversely impact the ability to work again (thereby impacting on the economic stability of the family and dependents within their extended families), or to continue education or follow previously held aspirations and ambitions.

Torture can also impact on family relationships and limit the quality of family life. Family patterns of communication can become characterised by conflict, silence, secrets, shame and blame, while relationships can become fraught, severed or contorted, such that every member of the family is affected and family dynamics and trust are markedly changed, which in turn may impair the potential for family support and resilience. Torture can lead to a breakdown in family relationships, rupture interpersonal and intimate couple relations and sometimes lead to violence towards their children and intimate partners. Torture can also lead to, and entail multiple losses – of health, functioning, livelihoods, relationships – as well as separations and deaths. Grief as a result of torture can impact entire families, and in itself become privatised or silenced, such that family functioning is severely disrupted, affecting all. Families enduring the disappearances of family members can face prolonged, traumatic grief – a process with no end in the absence of knowledge of the whereabouts, safety or fate of their loved ones. For refugee families of torture survivors there are the added challenges of multiple losses and traumatic experiences arising from the process of fleeing and seeking safety, the ongoing fear, helplessness, uncertainty, insecurity and threats, prolonged separations and multiple losses of family members, coping with deprivation and navigating the legal, social welfare, educational and health systems and structures in their country of asylum, adjusting to a new language, climate, diet and cultures etc., coping with xenophobia and racism, coping with social stigma and negative social discourses of refugees and torture survivors as unwanted 'economic migrants' or terrorists, establishing new social networks, seeking economic security in the face of loss of work and livelihoods and managing challenges to cultural identity and intergenerational conflicts where children are more immersed in the dominant social cultures and values in society than their parents.

Psychological care for families (including minors) and couples affected by torture can take various forms. It may include psychosocial support or counselling aimed at one or more members of a family, or a couple, where one or more person has been tortured. It can also entail couple counselling or therapy (e.g. systemic, psychodynamic), or family therapy (e.g. systemic family therapy), and be provided simultaneously or sequentially with individual psychological care for more than one member of the family. Methods used vary according to the theoretical foundations of the particular counselling or therapy approach. Psychological care for families where one or more member has been tortured is an extremely complex endeavour, bearing in mind simultaneously the needs and strengths of the family's capacity to adjust, function and support one another, the unique needs of each of the family members who were tortured, and the impact of the external socio-political, legal and economic context, alongside the impact of the internal dynamics, conflicts, secrets on all family members and on the family system as a whole.

Family-based psychological care may involve supporting children, youth and their families to address these challenges, stresses, conflicts and dilemmas which families confront. These can involve coping with the shifts and ruptures which families experience in their couple, parenting and sibling relationships as a result of torture; changes in family communication patterns, roles, responsibilities and positions within the family and related power differentials and shifts; and changes in their relationships and connectedness or isolation from the local and their own faith-based, nationality or ethnicity-based communities.

Couple-based psychological care can be used to address the impact of torture, including sexual violence and rape, on couple relationships. Couples where one or both have been subjected to torture may also experience intense and enduring interpersonal, emotional and sexual difficulties, compounded by mistrust, secrets, shame, guilt, fears of being unable to fulfil the other's needs or expectations, fears of being judged, seen as 'less than' and fears of betrayal. Couple difficulties as a result of torture can manifest as conflicts, poor or no communication, rage, blame, sexual difficulties or cessation of sexual intimacy, and intimate partner violence. The ruptures in the couple relationship can profoundly impact both individuals, depleting their individual and couple emotional resources, as well as disrupting their ability as a couple to manage the emotional, physical, financial and other strains on each other, and on their family. Breakdown in couple relations then can also affect the couple's parenting relationship and their parenting behaviour, and compromise their capacity to attend to the emotional, developmental and physical needs of their children.

Adults may find it difficult to carry out previously held parenting responsibilities, or the birth of children after the experience of torture may raise intense ambivalent feelings about parenting and about the child(ren), and fears for their safety and the capacity of the parent to protect them from harm in life. Parenting difficulties can include role reversals whereby children become emotional caretakers (and caring for their daily needs) of one or both parents, with adverse impacts on children's emotional, physical, social and educational development. Where torture affects the parenting of children, including where children have been left behind, separated or where there is a risk of or actual emotional, sexual or physical harm towards children from one or both parents or guardians, family-based psychological care can be a very complex and delicate endeavour, aimed at addressing the protection needs, as well as the emotional, developmental, physical, educational and other needs, of each child in the family. Children and young people may have been imprisoned and subjected to torture themselves, witnessed their parents or other family or community members being tortured or killed and have been forced to torture or harm others. Family-based psychological care for children will depend on the children's ages, the age (and duration of years) when and how they were tortured, when they were displaced/exiled, their developmental stages, gender, culture, disabilities, physical health, educational and social welfare needs and many other factors. Where one or both parents are absent, deceased or separated from the child(ren), psychological care may be provided to siblings, or to the individual unaccompanied minor, with their current carer or guardian, where possible. Family-based psychological care in this sense, can be with individuals, whilst adopting a systemic approach, holding the whole family in mind, including absent family members.

The transgenerational transmission from parent(s) to their children, and potentially subsequent generations, of values and beliefs as well as memories and some of the impacts of traumatic experiences (e.g. Harkness, 1993; Danieli, 1998; Coetzer, 2007; Schwab, 2010), including torture (Daud et al., 2005), also constitute a significant consideration in psychological care. The extent to which torture per se, or other related traumatic events and daily stresses arising from living in conflict, account for trauma responses in parents and then on future generations is unclear. The exact mechanisms by which the impact of torture, and related traumatic experiences and stresses, can manifest across generations, for example in children's distress, behaviour and development, or if this is the case for all torture survivors and their families, is also not fully understood. Explanations can range from psychological to social and epigenetic.

Psychologically, many factors and multiple mechanisms may be at play. Where families are exposed to prolonged violence and conflict, the developmental trajectory of children can be affected (Villamor et al., 2009), perhaps shaped partly by psychological impacts on both parents (e.g. Zerach et al., 2016), which can influence their parenting and their children's adjustment (East et al., 2017). Parental trauma-related grief, anger and disappointments may be externalised and trauma-related anxieties and fears projected onto children, affecting the parenting relationship with children, caregiving interactions and parenting behaviour. The communication style regarding refugee parents' trauma experiences has also been shown to be associated with disruptions in their children's attachment styles (Dalgaard et al., 2016). Relationships between parents/parental figures and children may also be further compounded by the parental modelling of inadequate coping skills for children. The impact of torture on an individual's physical, social and psychological health and functioning, can in turn lead to changes in family structure, relationships, communication and dynamics and family life, as well as the family environment in which their children are raised. This may be a family environment where the isolation, grief, fear, pain, despair, shame, guilt, conflict, secrets, traumatic memories and historical legacies of political insecurity, discrimination, persecution and violence that the family has endured become part of the tapestry of ongoing survival, suffering and struggle. Similarly, the wider environmental, social, political and economic conditions and the cultural context of a family, and their changes over time, may also impact on family life and relationships, affecting parents and children. Also, families across many generations may have experienced historical marginalisation, persecution and torture. The collective memory across generations may contribute to the family and community milieu and be riddled with competing narratives of strengths, survival, pain and suffering. Parent(s) who have been tortured may also actively or unintentionally shape the cultural and social environment in which children develop their own world views and scripts for managing conflicts, hurts and traumas in life. Some of those children, as adults, may then suffer from their own psychological difficulties, potentially affecting future generations.

Social explanations emphasise the impact of torture on poor social functioning and related unemployment, chronic social deprivation and economic insecurity impacting on the family. These factors can also interact with an inability to access material resources to satisfy basic needs of the family and adequate housing, as well as an inability to access health services, education, legal support, etc., which can exacerbate the psychological difficulties for torture survivors and their families.

Intergenerational ecological mechanisms have also been proposed (Devakumar et al., 2014), whereby the environment, such as exposure to conflict, malnutrition, infectious diseases, mental health difficulties and harms (including other traumatic experiences, such as torture), may lead to adverse effects in maternal health and in intergenerational effects, including congenital malformations, low birth weight, perinatal morbidity and mortality, premature birth, altered physical and mental development, impaired growth, neuroendocrine and immune system modulation, mental health problems and poor social functioning. Others propose that epigenetic changes to the DNA expression of the mother affected by traumatic experiences can also contribute to transgenerational epigenetic effects (Youngson and Whitelaw, 2008).

Evidence for family and couple-based psychological care
There are no literature reviews of family-based and couple-based psychological care for torture survivors. There are a few studies and some narrative descriptions of family-based and

couple-based care for torture survivors, predominantly focused on refugee people (not all of whom may be torture survivors) (e.g. Sveaass and Reichelt, 2001; Björn et al., 2013; Utrzan and Northwood, 2017). One longitudinal study with refugee families suggests that family separation creates a sense of ambiguous loss and uncertainty, and memory work in the recalling and sharing of family memories, within family work, can help alleviate the suffering related to such losses and absences of family members (Rousseau et al., 2004).

Some qualitative studies, although not on psychological care nor specifically for torture survivors and their families, are of potential relevance. Björn et al. (2013) studied a family systems and narrative approach with refugee families and suggest that reconstructing trauma narratives in therapy enables opportunities for new meanings to be created within families. The importance of family relationships to how individuals within a family make sense of their loss and construct meaning of their suffering, including reconciling their need to remember and preserve their heritage and also wishing to forget the traumatic experiences they suffered, is also emphasised by some (Gangamma, 2018). A study on family strategies for managing family life after the experience of political violence (Weine et al., 2004) also has implications for psychological care services. An exploration into family beliefs related to young people highlighted how these beliefs were affected by the interplay of war-related traumatic memories and familial transitions, which the authors suggest should be addressed to ensure that work with refugee youth and their families is socially and culturally specific (Weine et al., 2006).

One approach to family work, which entails the provision of support within the Coffee and Family Education and Support (CAFES) (Weine et al., 2004) and Tea and Families Education and Support (TAFES) (Weine et al., 2003), is described as a collaborative approach to community-building by creating groups of families who come together in a 'family-friendly space' to learn, share and support one another. Morgan et al. (2017) also describe positive impacts of a group-based model for couple therapy for couples who are torture survivors. The model seeks the reconstruction of the couple's narratives and re-visions about their past, present and future lives together, and aims to strengthen the couple's reconnection with each other to enable mutual support, using methods including normalisation and processing grief and trauma via role plays and discussion.

Whilst psychological care (e.g. systemic family therapy, individual psychodynamic psychotherapy) for children, parents or primary caregivers and families may be important to address any transgenerational effects of torture, and to prevent adverse impacts on future generations, there are no empirical studies to assess the impact of individual or family-based psychological care, interdisciplinary interventions, or parenting or community-based programmes, specifically on mediating such effects in torture survivors' children and subsequent generations.

Community-based Approaches

The systematic means of torture ensure that the ripples of harm radiate beyond individuals and their families, particularly where significant proportions of society or particular communities are targeted. Dominant discourses of blame and demonising torture survivors as 'terrorists', 'criminals' or as 'deserving' (of harm) can obscure the criminality of torture and its perpetrators, thereby fuelling social stigma, social exclusion and discrimination and reprisals against survivors and their families. The absence of justice and resultant impunity then further exacerbates the public denial of torture and the marginalisation of survivors who feel repeatedly betrayed, silenced and erased from history. The individual isolation and alienation of the survivor is then systematised by the fragmentation and marginalisation of communities and the isolation of families, even from their own communities and from society – which in turn can increase the risks of further discrimination, exploitation and harm. The rupturing of social bonds, including long-standing friendships and relationships with relatives, neighbours and friends, along with the duality of a personal sense of isolation and the active social denigration and marginalisation of survivors and their families, can together engender and compound the pervasive and chronic fear, mistrust, mutual suspiciousness, despair, helplessness and hope-lessness within communities. Historically, this may contribute to social fragmentation and breakdown, and prevent survivors from any meaningful integration into society or any sense of healing. It can also give birth to new wounds and exacerbate existing social wounds and rifts, as well as intensifying the marginalisation and dehumanisation of different communities with further entrenched divisions and conflicts. Thus, torture can lead to a breakdown in social cohesion, both within and between communities, and within society.

The term community-based approaches is a loose description of a wide range of interven-tions and activities (not exclusively psychological in focus), with differing conceptions of the community. Community-based approaches may address the impacts of torture, historical persecution and conflict on different communities; the interrelations within communities and between different communities; and the relations to wider social, economic, political and cul-tural context and macro systems. These approaches, often externally driven by professionals or organisations, may echo an ecological framework (Bronfenbrenner, 1979), directing attention at factors and processes within different micro, meso and macro levels which are impacting on the community under focus. Interestingly, the notion of community 'interventions' implies an external, professional interjection and interventions led from those outside the community, which risk being glorified as expert solutions and experienced by the communities 'receiving' them as voyeuristic, intrusive and alien, context-stripped, problem-focused and culturally naïve, patronising and inappropriate.

Many culturally diverse approaches, including practical, social welfare, physical, psycho-logical and spiritual, as well as informal care by extended families, neighbours and community and spiritual leaders, likely have existed historically in different communities, some with longstanding experiences of surviving persecution, conflict and violence. Methods evolved by and used within different communities, in effect, are not 'interventions', and often have profound and diverse cultural and religious traditions, their focus being on strengthening cultural, faith and social bonds, utilising community strengths and resources and serving the functions of internal regulation, healing and social cohesion. These methods and traditions may be disrupted by widespread torture, conflict and external interventions. Nevertheless, they are rarely recognised, understood, valued or legitimised as a form of psychosocial care as apprehended in the West, or are likely to be published in the literature as 'community-based care/interventions' for torture survivors, unless, usually Western, professionals and academics engage in or endorse such methods in their publications. Activities offered by non-governmen-tal rehabilitation services, some in conjunction with local community groups and leaders, may include and adapt some of these community methods. For example, there may be variations of testimony-giving and collective memory-building using group/community-based story-telling, music, arts, drama and spiritual practices; the development of collectives for educational, social and vocational support for community members; and policy advocacy initiatives in col-laboration with other non-governmental organisations, local community groups and activists.

Community-based activities as 'interventions', whatever the theoretical approach, may seek one or more of the following as outcomes: (a) improved social functioning of individuals within their social context and current environment – within both their families and communities; (b) improved social connectedness, social networks and informal care and support systems from within the community; (c) strengthened community resources, social capital and social bonds between and within communities; (d) collective trust-building; (e) community identity-building, emphasising shared histories, values, hopes and aspirations for people's collective future; (f) establishment of a physical environment conducive to community life, including the re-establishment of communal safe spaces, places for leisure, social interaction and worship; (g) security and peace-building; (h) changes in social and political structures, social and legal policies (or their absence) and social or governmental practices which have adverse impacts on the community(ies); (i) awareness-building of relevant political processes and legal avenues for redress and reparation to increase participation in those processes, etc.

Community-based activities for torture survivors and their communities are often offered by non-governmental organisations and community-based grassroots groups. They may include training lay counsellors or community workers and torture survivors to support other survivors; activities to raise awareness of torture and its impact; activities to combat stigma, social marginalisation and discrimination against survivors and their families; activities to address social isolation and the loss of spaces to build social connection and social networks; and activities and programmes to support survivors and their families to build their vocational and livelihood capacities. In contrast to individual psychological care, community-based activities can be seen as further supporting and facilitating social well-being. Broadly speaking, social well-being can be characterised by social connectedness, social interaction and participation within the community, social cohesion, social harmony/peace, collective identity which acknowledges and accepts within group and between group differences, social networks which enable social support, cohesion and community functioning, social agency and collective investment in the community's wider social context and environment, shared values, etc. Thus, community-based care has the potential to facilitate social rehabilitation for torture survivors, their families and communities, and community-based activities. However, the relative benefits and advantages of community-based care which is derived from within natural, informal care systems in the community and community/cultural traditions and rituals, compared to community-based 'interventions' which are conceived, designed and initiated by external agencies, professionals or academics, is unknown. Similarly, the immediate and long-term harms, or adverse impacts, from such externally-driven interventions on communities has received no attention in the empirical literature.

The conceptualisation of what constitutes community-based interventions for communities affected by torture is rarely articulated in studies, and the theoretical underpinnings of the interventions tend to draw on psychological constructs of individual trauma, not collective suffering and social well-being. This, despite ample literature theorising the collective trauma which results from war and human rights violations (e.g. Ajdukovic, 2004, 2005; Somasundaram, 2007; Arestivo, 2018); post-conflict memory in communities (Kevers et al., 2016); and the importance of community-based interventions in creating 'the healing community' (Ajdukovic, 2006) and addressing the betrayals and breakdown in trust within communities ravaged by war (Ajdukovic and Corkalo, 2004). Innovative approaches to community-based interventions post-war, developed by those living in conflict situations (Ajdukovic and Ajdukovic, 2000, 2003) have been incorporated, though not acknowledged, in international guidelines (IASC, 2007), and not evaluated in terms of impact on torture survivors, their families and communities.

Evidence on community-based approaches

Where community-based care or interventions are noted in the literature, their focus is mostly on communities defined as refugees, internally displaced and war-affected people, not as torture survivors. Existing literature highlights informal care for refugee communities provided by their social networks of families, friends and neighbours (Chase and Sapkota, 2017); sociotherapy with Rwandan survivors in their communities (Jansen et al., 2017); capacity-building by training refugee community members to provide mental health services as peer counsellors to their community (Binta and Pearson, 2004); community day centres for asylum seekers (Chase and Rousseau, 2018); community gardens for refugees (Hartwig and Mason, 2016); psychological services based within the community of asylum seekers (Khawaja and Stein, 2016); and education, awareness-building and community mediation to address disputes, which it is suggested, helps provide social justice and avert torture and ill-treatment by preventing disputes entering formal judicial systems (Dinesh, 2004). A study evaluating the Refugee Well-being Project Model community interventions (Learning Circles to facilitate cultural exchange and paired work to build advocacy skills to increase access to healthcare, affordable housing, etc.) with resettled refugees in the US indicates positive impacts. It is also rare in its mixed methods assessment of community-based interventions using a range of outcome indicators, including psychological distress and well-being, quality of life, access to resources (education, healthcare, housing, employment, child care, material goods and resources, etc.), language proficiency, social support and 'enculturation' (identification and engagement with traditional cultural practices) (Goodkind et al., 2014).

Studies assessing community-based interventions for communities affected by war and torture vary in terms of their conceptual underpinnings, the nature and focus of their activities, participants (rarely do they note how many are torture survivors) and their intended outcomes. These studies and approaches to community-based interventions fall into one of three broad categories.

One category of community-based approaches focuses on *individuals and individual psychological distress*, engaging and supporting individuals within their communities, not in clinics or formal services, seeking as key outcomes the reduction of psychological symptoms (e.g. of PTSD, anxiety, depression) in individuals. In other words, activities which are exclusively, or predominantly framed as individual psychological therapy, but provided in the community, sometimes by training lay counsellors/facilitators in Western methods of individual psychological counselling/therapy. Schulz et al.'s (2006) study of a community mental health programme in the US for refugees (66% torture survivors) in their homes using manualised Cognitive Processing Therapy by trained therapists, demonstrated that this was a highly effective method in reducing symptoms of PTSD. An effectiveness study evaluating the impact of a CBT-based intervention (the EMPOWER programme) for internally displaced people in camps in Uganda reported significantly lower scores on the 'depression-like syndromes' and 'the anxiety-like syndrome' and significantly more 'prosocial behaviours', than participants in the control condition (Sonderegger et al., 2011). Other controlled trials using Narrative Exposure Therapy (NET) with refugees in settlements demonstrated that NET was superior to supportive counselling (with a problem-solving focus avoiding the discussion of traumatic events) and psychoeducation with respect to long-term changes in PTSD symptoms (Neuner et al., 2004), while another study indicated that there was a statistically significant reduction in symptoms of PTSD in groups receiving both NET and trauma counselling, compared to the control group (Neuner et al., 2008).

Another category of community-based approaches focuses on *psychosocial programmes* conceived, designed and initiated by external, often Western professionals, and provided to conflict-affected communities, with or without community collaboration. One large-scale study evaluating a community-based psychosocial programme offered by multidisciplinary teams during and post-conflict in Bosnia-Herzegovina, included 10–15 sessions of individual and group counselling interventions, relaxation, guided meditation and communication, systematic desensitisation and behaviour modification (Mooren et al., 2003). While scores on psychological distress and health symptoms after counselling were still high, there was a marked improvement in functioning, indices of general health and reduced post-trauma psychological symptoms. Similarly, other community-based psychosocial programmes have included a combination of brief psychological interventions (offered for individuals and in groups) and psychoeducation for adults (e.g. de Jong et al., 2000; de Jong and Kleber, 2007). Fewer studies exist which focus on children and young people, and those that do have mixed results. A study of brief trauma-focused therapy with children showed a very high dropout rate, but most of those who stayed in the programme showed self-reported improvement in their presenting complaint (Lokuge et al., 2013). Interventions for adolescents affected by war and living in camps for internally displaced people involved group interpersonal psychotherapy and creative play, compared in a controlled trial (Bolton et al., 2007). Results highlighted gender differences, with girls receiving group interpersonal psychotherapy showing substantial and statistically significant improvement in depression symptoms compared with controls, though no statistically significant change was noted for boys, and no effect for creative play on depression severity.

One study evaluating a psychosocial programme for Liberian and Sierra Leone survivors of torture and war in refugee camps, alongside community awareness of the effects of torture and war, described significant reductions in psychological trauma symptoms and increases in daily functioning and social support (Stepakoff et al., 2006); whilst another assessing the effectiveness of psychosocial programmes in Jordan and Lebanon indicated that the majority of adult and children refugee people offered basic counselling showed an improvement in their levels of distress, 'general well-being', 'adjustment skills' and 'social skills difficulties' (Le Roch et al., 2010). A controlled study assessing the impact of treatment with and without psychoeducation workshops showed a significant reduction in PTSD symptoms in both groups at follow-up compared to the waiting-list control group (Yeomans et al., 2010), while another controlled trial assessing the efficacy of Culture-Sensitive Resource-Oriented Peer (CROP) group, compared with CBT and EMDR offered in the community reported significant reductions in symptoms of trauma, depression and anxiety post intervention in both the CROP and CBT groups, greater than the EMDR and waiting list control group (Renner et al., 2011). Whilst some of these approaches combined or adapted traditional community rituals with their psychological interventions (e.g. de Jong and Kleber, 2007; Stepakoff et al., 2006; Yeomans et al., 2010), the outcomes assessed were awareness of psychosocial well-being and improved individual general and psychological health and social support networks.

Few studies focus explicitly on torture survivors, and while they bridge individual and community-based approaches to psychological care, their focus in terms of outcomes is also largely confined to individual psychological distress markers (e.g. Stepakoff et al., 2006).

A study comparing two interventions, the community-based method of Tree of Life (described as a method of 'trauma healing') and psychoeducation and coping skills workshops for torture survivors, showed that both interventions led to significant reduction in individual psychological distress and significant increase in community engagement of the survivors (Reeler et al., 2009), although the impact on the wider community, or social well-being was not assessed.

The Testimony Method, developed originally in Chile by Cienfuegos and Monelli (1983) as a human-rights-based therapeutic tool, not as a form of therapy for individuals' psychological symptoms, has also been adapted and described subsequently as a psychological 'treatment' or psychotherapy method (e.g. Agger and Jensen, 1990; Weine et al., 1998; van Dijk et al., 2003; Lustig et al., 2004). The method of narrating a testimony, verbally, or through movement/dance, and the public telling of truth and of individuals' and families' stories of injustice and harm, sometimes combined with prayers, religious rituals, music, dance/movement and the sharing of food, is not new to many communities seeking social healing, social justice and the building of collective memories. In contrast, the potential of individual, private, testimony-telling (to a therapist/lay counsellor), which is subsequently publicly acknowledged, as a route to individual healing and well-being and the social condemnation of atrocities is underlined in the Testimony Method.

Significant improvements are reported in overall well-being following the use of the Testimony Method within communities, as a brief (four session) psychosocial intervention supplemented with what are described as culture-specific coping strategies (meditation and a 'delivery ceremony' – whereby torture survivors receive their written testimony as a route to social recognition and re-connecting the survivor to their community) (Agger et al., 2009). Few controlled trials have been carried out, the first controlled trial with Mozambican war survivors (Igreja et al., 2004) evaluated the Testimony Method, described as a community-based intervention, though the intervention was with individuals, living within one rural community. The results suggest no significant effects but there was a significant reduction of individuals' psychological symptoms in both the control and interventions groups, though not attributed to the intervention, raising questions of what are potentially ameliorative and contextual factors of relevance and whether the application of the method within a community led to additional interactions within the community, reported as 'uncontrolled interaction and communication' (p.255), with a sense of their collective suffering being recognised, acknowledged and heard and shared benefits for both study groups within the community. Notably, outcome effectiveness focused solely on individual symptoms of post-trauma stress. Subsequent controlled trials report significant improvement over a two- to three-month period in psychosocial functioning in Sri Lankan torture survivors following 'testimonial therapy' (Puvimanasinghe and Price, 2016), and significantly reduced symptoms of PTSD, anxiety and depression, from baseline to three months, from a culturally-adapted 'testimony therapy plus ceremony' in a sample of Khmer Rouge torture survivors in Cambodia (Esala and Taing, 2017). Whilst the advantages of Testimony Method are typically seen as the brevity of the method, its amenability to cultural and local adaptations, and its applicability by trained lay counsellors and within a community setting, the benefits to the community and social well-being are at best implied, while the outcomes measured focus almost exclusively on individual psychological symptoms and functioning, not on wider understandings of individual well-being, and show uncertain benefits in the long-term (e.g. Esala and Taing, 2017).

On the whole, findings from a limited number of studies focused on refugee and war-affected communities suggest some impact of community-based psychological interventions (including those incorporating limited elements of cultural traditions and rituals) in reducing psychological symptoms, though none mentions or assesses wider indicators of social well-being. The inadequate reporting on what proportion of study participants were torture survivors prevents any conclusions from being made in terms of the effectiveness of such community-based psychosocial interventions for torture survivors and their communities.

The third category of community-based approaches for communities affected by torture, more common in post-conflict, transitional justice settings and in societies plagued by ongoing torture and other human rights violations, focus on a *rights-based approach*. This category of community-based approaches includes activities to raise awareness of torture and its impact, to challenge negative social discourses of torture survivors and discrimination against survivors and their families, to facilitate social connection and a collective sense of safety and security, to enable and mobilise communities towards social action and activism in order to challenge macro systems and policies, and their adverse impacts on communities, and to engage in legal processes to seek justice and reparation. No studies exist which evaluate the effectiveness of such community-based approaches, or specific activities, for torture survivors and their communities. These approaches are more closely aligned to human rights advocacy and prevention activities within communities, and are also aimed at awareness-raising, but with a view to challenging, via social activism and judicial means, harmful or obstructive State practices, legal structures and policies. Poignantly, and importantly, they do not take individual psychology as their starting, or end point; their intended overarching outcomes may include an end to impunity, justice, prevention, peace and security. Although there is potential for such activities and justice mechanisms to contribute to social recovery and rehabilitation (Patel, 2019) and healing (Doru, 2008; Danieli, 2009), and the pursuit of justice for crimes of torture within communities is essential to combat impunity and ensure accountability and reparation for survivors, the extent to which retributive or restorative justice is 'healing' for individuals, and/or for communities, is unclear in the literature (see Patel, 2011; Mendlehoff, 2009; Fletcher and Weinstein, 2002).

In summary, a wide range of interventions and activities with torture survivors fall under the umbrella of community-based approaches. Yet, studies on their effectiveness for torture survivors are rare; the theoretical or conceptual models for community-based interventions in existing studies are lacking; and these studies do not evaluate the impact of the full range of community activities and interventions; nor do they assess impact beyond individual psychological symptoms (mainly post trauma symptoms) and functioning. The evidence of effectiveness of some of these individual-focused psychological interventions (offered within a community, but not community interventions), is promising, but as yet very limited. The evidence of effectiveness for community-based activities or interventions, for communities affected by torture and their social well-being, is absent.

LIMITATIONS OF RESEARCH ON PSYCHOLOGICAL CARE FOR TORTURE SURVIVORS

The limitations of the empirical studies, and of the interpretations within the literature, have been discussed by study/review authors and others (e.g. Montgomery and Patel, 2010; Jaranson and Quiroga, 2011; Patel et al., 2016; Carlsson et al., 2014). They require detailed consideration, beyond the scope of this chapter, but since these limitations significantly con-strain what can be gleaned from the literature to inform rehabilitation practice with torture survivors, they are summarised here.

Conceptual Limitations

Most studies and literature/systematic reviews:

- Do not define 'torture survivor', and while this may not affect practitioners working with torture survivors who are unaware of existing definitions, this may be difficult for researchers as empirical studies are constrained by a lack of reporting on the numbers of torture survivors within their sample and by the lack of specificity and transparency of the definitions used, making interpretations on what is beneficial or not for torture survivors and the reasons why, at best, speculative.
- Conflate refugees with asylum seekers, and some with internally displaced people. The experiences of all groups may overlap, although there are some very distinct experiences and external, ongoing stressors which each group may face, depending on their context (e.g. resettlement country, refugee camp) and the rights, privileges and restrictions they face within specific legal, economic and political contexts, or the cultural context and the cultural proximity or distance from those in the host country and therapists/counsellors.
- Do not consider or report on the heterogeneity of refugee/asylum seeking/internally displaced/'war-affected' populations referred to in the studies, noting demographic and other basic data, without examining what these mean and not just if, but *how* they interact with interventions offered – in other words, what helps or not, for whom, in which settings. The poor quality of many studies and of reporting largely accounts for this tendency to overlook or to make tentative conclusions, without a nuanced and intersectional analysis. Further, torture survivors may be amongst all of those groups, but may face additional socioeconomic stressors, lack of access to justice, absence of justice and reparations, multiple losses and ongoing traumas, physical injury and debility from torture, all potentially impacting on their psychological well-being and recovery and response to any psychological interventions.
- Fail to conceptualise 'psychological interventions' both as one component of holistic rehabilitation and as one aspect which pervades and *interacts* with other forms of rehabilitation (including social, legal, educational). In other words, interventions are constructed narrowly as psychological, and despite the lack of feasibility in conducting truly randomised controlled trials with torture survivors, and the paucity of such studies, the effectiveness of the interventions is understood without adequate consideration of other contextual factors and resources (or lack of).

Theoretical Limitations

Almost all studies:

- Provide little by way of rationale for the interventions and their applicability, their relevance and cultural acceptability to the population in question, and for why and how they were prioritised for the study population.
- De-contextualise distress and suffering as a result of torture, ignore the wider environment of survivors which may maintain or ameliorate suffering, and individualise and psycholo-

gise suffering from torture (Patel, 2011). For example, studies invariably use psychological interventions based on theoretical models developed in the West (e.g. NET, CBT, EMDR), by those predominantly from Western backgrounds, and constructed within the Cartesian dualist philosophy of health (mind-body). They focus on improving symptoms mainly of PTSD, and to a lesser extent depression and anxiety, as defined in Western psychiatric nosologies. As such, interventions, even those that are group- and community-based, offer interventions aimed at symptom-reduction at the individual level. Such Eurocentric understandings of health ignore the wider construction of health (including spiritual) and well-being (including familial and social), and their complex interactions – crucial especially for torture survivors whose well-being can be intimately connected with their familial and social well-being, community responses, the legal, economic, political and social contexts in which they live and their wider recovery environment (Patel, 2019a).

- Fail to report the economic, cultural and political context in which the theories underpinning the interventions studied were developed, and fail to note their inherent gender and cultural biases and their limitations.
- Which report 'cultural adaptations' describe the adaptations as add-ons to Western theoretical models, with no detail or evidence provided by studies of how these methods were scrutinised for their cultural biases and how adaptations were made, by whom and why.
- Fail to theorise the interactions of the 'ripples of harm' of torture; and fail to take an intersectional analysis of the multiple processes of power (gender, ethnicity, culture, sexuality, faith, etc.) and oppression (e.g. sexist, racist, economic, homophobic) faced by study participants – all of which are relevant to the impact, experience and effectiveness of psychological interventions.

Epistemological Limitations

All studies reviewed:

- Do not make their epistemological stance explicit, or the related limitations of the study. As a result, claims about the nature of evidence presented fail to consider the philosophical basis of what is valued (and devalued) as evidence. Typically, research on psychological care for torture survivors has adopted a positivist epistemology and privileged evidence which is deemed least biased (despite numerous biases, considered later) and assumed to be more generalisable to other populations. One serious implication is that survivor-based and practice-based evidence (from practitioners with extensive experience of multidisciplinary rehabilitation including psychological aspects) is diminished and devalued as apparently the most biased and as not good quality evidence. The complexity of change processes, in specific and diverse contexts, not just what has changed or not but how and why, and the meanings survivors give to their experiences of torture and suffering, and how they overcome this, is absolutely crucial to understanding what is rehabilitative and enabling for whom, when, how and in which situations. The perspectives and experiences of survivors and practitioners thus afford invaluable insights into what helps, and a wider range of research epistemologies beyond positivism, and methodologies, may yield a wider range of evidence which can inform practice, services and community programmes.

Methodological Limitations

Studies vary in their methodological limitations, and hence study quality:

Samples

- Samples are typically small and therefore underpowered to show change or difference.
- Samples are mostly heterogeneous and highly variable, including in their experiences of torture (if specified) and other traumatic events, environmental, socioeconomic and political stressors and support structures; in the period of resettlement (if refugees or asylum seekers); and in the country, cultural, ethnic, linguistic and other backgrounds. Along with other limitations, the findings of studies are rarely generalisable to other populations or settings.
- There may be a lack of detail on attrition rates during study interventions, and at follow-up, and possible reasons why.
- Generally, there can be a lack of detail on how participants were selected for the studies. Most studies recruited their sample based on the severity of symptoms, psychiatric diagnoses or care-seeking behaviour. High symptom levels at baseline may be expected, and may decline even without treatment but with time; where there is symptom reduction after treatment, this may not seem significant, particularly in the context of other ongoing stressors and factors related to the family, community or societal environment.
- Many studies defined the sample by a diagnosis (PTSD) and/or nationality, and/or their legal status as asylum seekers, internally displaced or refugee people; few by their experiences of torture. There was no evidence of whether participants acknowledged or accepted the diagnoses applied as inclusion criteria – in other words, their suffering may have been severe, and comparable to others not included in studies.

Procedural

- The diversity of, and lack of detail on, the therapists/counsellors, may be a problem, including a lack of information on the duration and level of their training, their qualifications and experience in working therapeutically with the study population (not just in the method, as applied in Western contexts and with Western populations), as well as on their primary language, gender, ethnicity and cultural backgrounds.
- The quality of interventions, even if manualised and supervised, can vary and interact with the quality of the therapeutic relationship (a skill acquired with clinical experience), in influencing the outcome.
- There may be a lack of sufficient detail in some studies on the methods used.
- There may be a lack of sufficient detail on the nature and quantum of supervision for therapists/lay counsellors in the study, as well as on the experience of the supervisor(s) in therapeutic work with the study population (not just in the intervention method, as applied in Western contexts, with Western populations). Underlying assumptions may include that a method, 'purely' applied (however decontextualised or culturally inappropriate) can be tested for its efficacy with populations other than those it was originally designed for, and by, in the West.

- Most randomised controlled trials had more than one intervention arm, and the control group was typically a waiting-list group or no treatment group, which does not allow comparisons to other interventions. Where baseline symptoms were reported as severe, improvement can be with time even with no intervention (as in PTSD), such that any reported improvement at treatment end, without a control group, provides lower level of evidence of effectiveness than true randomised controlled trials, instead giving a pre and post measure of impact.
- There can be a lack of detail on the specific interventions used in the studies, and if adapted, why and how.
- Limited reporting of the length and frequency of intervention (with variability across studies), and the levels of severity of distress across different domains, at baseline (variable within and across studies) can be a problem.
- There can be a lack of detail on whether, and which, interventions were used to target specific symptoms, or if offered as a part of general psychological care or alongside or close to other individual, group- or community-based activities or interventions.
- Lack of assessment at follow-up, and mostly less than 12 months – sustainability of any improvements could then not be established or adequately interpreted in the absence of an assessment of the specific context and other factors which may contribute to or inhibit improvements (e.g. safety and security, refugee status, adequate housing and welfare to address basic needs, employment and social networks).
- There may be a lack of detail on the specific socioeconomic, cultural and political context and setting of the research, as well as on the possible additional external adverse factors (e.g. post-migration, poverty, xenophobia, impunity, social stigma and marginalisation of survivors) and the mediating and ameliorative factors (e.g. personal and social resources, access to justice mechanisms, reparations) in terms of study outcomes. Similarly, for studies with children, any changes at the end of intervention, or at follow-up, could be related to other social activities and support in schools or at home.
- There may be an absence of evidence of the acceptability of study interventions to study populations.

Measures/instruments

- Almost all studies use psychiatric diagnosis-specific symptom measurement in individuals, some alongside general health assessment, precluding a broader assessment of potential change in individual distress across different domains and in coping, personal and social resources, functioning, quality of life. The focus on individual symptom-reduction also ignores ripples of harm and potential changes in social well-being and within families, groups and participants' community(ies).
- There can be limited validity (including cultural validity) and reliability of measures used in studies, with very limited, if any, discussion of the ethical implications of using lay interpreters/translators, or translated, but not culturally-validated measures for the specific population studied. Where validity is asserted by authors, there is an absence of information on methodologies for validating the tools for the relevant population, by culture, language and other factors deemed significant to the study population. Understandings of well-being can vary across cultures and communities, and particular presentations or difficulties may

be misinterpreted by researchers, or simply ignored as the measures used do not capture culturally-specific understandings of distress and well-being.
- There can be a problem with the heterogeneity of outcome measures used, with variability in the information provided on all measures and outcome indicators used, as well as their administration (by researcher, self-report, interpreter, etc.).

Bias

- Effectiveness studies mostly had very low compliance with the CONSORT and TREND checklists, suggesting a high risk of bias in the estimated treatment effects.
- Although therapist or participant blinding in psychological intervention studies is notoriously difficult to achieve, its absence can lead to bias. Blinding was mostly poorly reported or not reported in both randomised controlled trails and effectiveness studies.
- Most trials provided no information on power, raising the risk of bias from underpowered trials, or sample size decisions.
- In some studies (particularly of NET), evidence for reduction in PTSD symptoms came mainly from one group of investigators, or interventions were designed by one or more of the investigators, raising the issue of investigator bias.
- Almost all reviews only included studies in English (excluding those in other languages, such as Spanish, French, Arabic), and only some reviews were explicit in stating that most studies reviewed were in English (e.g. Weiss et al., 2016; Bunn et al., 2015), and from Europe (44%) or the USA (32%) (Weiss et al., 2016) – leading to a bias towards studies conceived, designed, led and published predominantly by Western researchers, even if conducted in a range of countries, ostensibly about 'other' populations.
- Similarly, studies (or researchers) were likely funded in the West and predominantly published by Global North publishers, which can lead to bias, and also deter or exclude practitioners and researchers from the Global South working with torture survivors from disseminating their work in formal (Western) academic journals and fora. The privileging and imposition of Eurocentric knowledge and methods as apparently universal, a form of epistemic violence, in the literature in the rehabilitation and psychological care of torture survivors is resonant with general psychological literature and practice (see Patel and Keval, 2018), with most psychological research published by scholars from Western, Educated, Industrialised, Rich, and Democratic ('WEIRD') societies (Henrich et al., 2010), with its applicability to the 'neglected 95%' of the rest of the world (Arnett, 2008) remaining largely unquestioned.

Reporting

- In the literature reviewed there is an enormous variation in the quality of reporting in individual studies and in reviews of: the conceptual, theoretical and epistemological bases of studies; study samples; power analysis; inclusion and exclusion criteria; intervention methods; measures used (and their cultural validity); drop-outs and reasons why; methods for handling missing data; study setting and socioeconomic, cultural, legal and political context and related adverse events; data results/outcomes; different forms of bias; deterioration or adverse impacts of the psychological interventions; and other study limitations.

Poor reporting of study details and quality, and the variations in focus, design and definitions used in reviews also make interpretations highly tentative.

Ethical Limitations

- Most studies do not specify the processes of seeking informed consent from participants, and to what extent this was fully informed, i.e. sought in the language of the participant, without any deception, coercion or implied benefit/lack of adverse or distressing impact of participation – all standard ethical considerations.
- Most studies do not specify issues of confidentiality or the safety and security of participants, and how participation in the study may compromise any of these.
- Almost all studies fail to explicitly acknowledge and explain the power differentials between the researchers, their funding and institutional bodies, and the study participants, as well as the implications for the cultural appropriateness and acceptability of the interventions to the participants, study adherence, implementation and dissemination. These ethical issues have far-reaching implications for how findings can be used to inform clinical practice, often in diverse settings and contexts (e.g. country context and resettlement, refugee camp, post-conflict and transitional contexts).

RECOMMENDATIONS

The considerable limitations of available studies, and the fact that the majority of empirical studies are not specifically focused on torture survivors, but refugees, asylum seekers and those affected by war, undoubtedly prevents any convincing conclusions or recommendations to be made for practices, rehabilitation services and programmes for torture survivors. Nevertheless, several recommendations can be made, each bringing a set of philosophical, theoretical and methodological challenges, and requiring a critical interrogation of unexamined assumptions underlying the existing literature.

The default conclusion might be that 'more empirical research, of better quality, addressing the limitations of previous studies, is needed'. Of course, all research should seek to improve on, not emulate and reproduce, the shortcomings of previous research. Yet, the pressing question is *what kind of research is really needed, valued, by whom, for whom and to what end?* The end, for which there is consensus in the field, is better psychological care as part of holistic rehabilitation, for all, or as many torture survivors as possible. The question of 'for whom' is absolutely fundamental: torture survivors, their families and communities. The purpose of any research that purports to improve care for torture survivors is not to serve academia and research teams, but to serve torture survivors and to facilitate their access to appropriate and effective care, in recognition of their right to rehabilitation as a form of reparation.

Recommendations for future research include:

- *Embedding human rights principles in all research:* Ensure ethical and human rights principles are adhered to in all types of psychological research and evidence-gathering – since torture survivors are not mere participants in an empirical experiment, but human beings subjected to gross human rights violations. There are numerous human rights principles established in human rights instruments, and a synthesis of those considered particularly relevant to psychological practice, including in research (see Patel, 2019b) include, amongst others:

– Ensuring the safety of torture survivors (preventing and monitoring harm to participants, including iatrogenic impacts of research interventions, and harm to family members and their communities);
– Ensuring equality and fairness in all research activities (including evaluating study methods for inadvertent or deliberate discrimination with negative consequences) and in deciding exclusion criteria;
– Respecting and upholding dignity;
– Ensuring the gender and culture appropriateness of research activities and interventions.

• *Participation:* Ensure meaningful, not tokenistic, participation from survivors and collaboration with their communities to establish what their priorities are (which may include, in different settings and different communities, security, social, welfare, medical, psychological, vocational and educational support). Meaningful participation should include genuine participant-action research to better inform rehabilitation services.
• *Examine the ripples of care:* Focus not just on individual psychological interventions centred on psychological trauma symptoms, or measurement of psychological symptoms, but also on the wider and interacting needs and suffering of survivors, their families and communities, as well as on the ripples of care: the strengths, resources and coping abilities of survivors, families and their communities, and what can be supported and augmented to enable them in the rehabilitation process. Holistic care is much more than psychological interventions, and very rarely can one intervention or method, in isolation, repair the ripples of the harm of torture.
• *Ensure quality of rehabilitation services:* Establish how to improve the overall quality of rehabilitation services for torture survivors, which includes exploring not just effectiveness, but also safety, impact, appropriateness, timeliness, cost-effectiveness and the sustainability of services and interventions and activities which together constitute multidisciplinary rehabilitation (Patel and Williams, 2014). Research should focus on developing improved programmes which involve staff in high-quality research and involve an iterative process of intervention development and evaluation within specialist services (Carlsson et al., 2014). Research can also focus on evaluating multidisciplinary interventions to establish what approaches, whether offered in particular combinations, simultaneously or consecutively, are most effective for whom, when, in which settings and why. Indeed, there is an urgent need for transparency and rigour in routine outcome monitoring and service quality evaluations, as there is for research, and both require us to address the many and complex challenges of conducting such research with torture survivors, their families, communities and services.
• *Ensure a diversity of epistemologies, methods and evidence:* Ensure a diversity in research epistemologies and methods (including survivor- and practitioner-based evidence, case studies, and qualitative and mixed methods) to contribute to a diverse evidence base which is meaningful, valid and useful in practice. Ensure a diversity of evidence is explored, including evidence from survivors and practitioners, and in naturalistic settings. Future research could examine the full range of impacts of psychological care in individual psychological distress domains (not naïvely relying on psychiatric diagnoses), as well

as family well-being and collective/social well-being and impact in the longer-term, for individuals, their families and communities. Research should not only focus on psychological outcomes (as defined by researchers) and use a range of social, welfare and community-based approaches to assess related outcomes, but it should also consider the wider contextual factors which may enable or impede rehabilitation. Studies should also explore the processes and possible mechanisms of change, in different survivor populations – what helps who, how and why. Since no single research method provides the range of evidence and understandings, relevant to all unique and diverse settings and populations, required by practitioners and services to best serve torture survivors, a common components approach to future research with torture survivors, whatever type of evidence is pursued, holds promise.

- *Address power:* Ensure that power dynamics characterised by a domination of Eurocentric ideologies and theories on the suffering and psychological 'treatment' of 'others' are not reproduced in psychological care and in the wider rehabilitation of torture survivors who have already endured multiple impresses and abuses of power: in torture itself and through societal denial of torture, impunity, social marginalisation, xenophobia, institutional discrimination, etc. Researchers need to be aware of power dynamics and processes of intersectional oppression and discrimination in research. Research methods, and the interventions they seek to assess, should not be oppressive or harmful (very few studies report the harm or iatrogenic effects of the study or interventions); they should be appropriate and acceptable to those for whom they are intended and applied to, and minimise and name power differentials explicitly – to study participants, funders and professional peers, and in publications.

CONCLUSIONS

The more research we do, the less it seems we understand what torture survivors from diverse backgrounds and experiences actually want, what they need and what they may benefit from, within their own contexts and settings. The psychological care methods we design and offer, like the research to assess them, are not for our fame or gain. The worth of our methods and research lies in the extent to which they are meaningful and acceptable to, and experienced as helpful by, torture survivors, as well as the extent to which they minimise oppressive practices and the subjugation of survivors' own world views and ways of understanding and addressing psychological distress within their own cultural, social and political contexts. The true worth of research on and of the practice of psychological care for torture survivors, then, can be ascertained from the extent to which survivors find methods offered (or imposed on them) acceptable, meaningful, relevant, appropriate and useful. The rehabilitation of torture survivors can advance only if we, as clinicians and researchers, practice humility and allow ourselves to be led by, and accompany torture survivors, in understanding what exactly the recovery process is for them, their families and their communities – from *their* world views and perspectives.

REFERENCES

Agger, J and Jensen, S (1990), 'Testimony as ritual and evidence in psychotherapy for political refugees', *Journal of Traumatic Stress*, 3, 115–130.

Ajdukovic, D (2004), 'Social contexts of traumatization and healing', *Medicine, Conflict and Survival*, 20(2), 120–135.

Ajdukovic, D (2005), 'Social (re)construction of a local community after massive traumatization' in Friedman, MJ and Mikus-Kos, A (eds), *Promoting the psychosocial wellbeing of children following war and terrorism* (IOS Press), 3–9.

Ajdukovic, D and Ajdukovic, M (2000), 'Community based programme in meeting the psychosocial needs of children in resettlement process' in van Willigen, L (ed), *Health hazards of organized violence in children* (II) (Pharos), 169–177.

Ajdukovic, D and Ajdukovic, M (2003), 'Systemic approaches to early interventions in a community affected by organized violence' in Orner, R and Schnyder, U (eds), *Reconstructing early interventions after trauma* (Oxford University Press), 82–92.

Ajdukovic, D and Corkalo, D (2004), 'Trust and betrayal in war' in Stover, E and Weinstein, H (eds), *My neighbor, my enemy: Justice and community in the aftermath of mass atrocity* (Cambridge University Press), 287–302.

Akinsulure-Smith, A, Dachos, N and Jones, W (2013), 'Nah We Yone's De Fambul Camp: Facilitating resilience in displaced African children', *Journal of Immigrant & Refugee Studies*, 11(3), 221–240.

Arestivo, C (2018), 'Torture: The catastrophe of a bond' in Moore, AS and Swanson, E (eds), *Witnessing torture* (Palgrave Macmillan), 17–19.

Arnett, J (2008), 'The neglected 95%: Why American psychology needs to become less American', *American Psychologist*, 63(7), 602–614.

Betancourt, T and Williams, T (2008), 'Building an evidence base on mental health interventions for children affected by armed conflict', *Intervention*, 6, 39–56.

Binta, B and Pearson, L (2004), 'Rebuilding communities: Training trauma survivors to help communities heal after atrocities. New Tactics Project of the Center for Victims of Torture', accessed 12 May 2019 at https://www.newtactics.org/sites/default/files/resources/Rebuilding-Communities- EN.pdf

Björn, GJ, Gustafsson, PA, Sydsjö, G and Berterö, C (2013), 'Family therapy sessions with refugee families: A qualitative study', *Conflict and Health*, 7(1), 1.

Bolton, P, Bass, J, Betancourt, T, Speelman, L, Onyango, G, Clougherty, K, Neubauer, R, Murray, L and Verdeli, H (2007), 'Interventions for depression symptoms among adolescent survivors of war and displacement in Northern Uganda: A randomized controlled trial', *JAMA*, 298(5), 519–527.

Bracken, P, Giller, J and Summerfield, D (1997), 'Rethinking mental health work with survivors of wartime violence and refugees', *Journal of Refugee Studies*, 10(4), 431–442.

Bronfenbrenner, U (1979), *The ecology of human development: Experiments by nature and design* (Harvard University Press).

Bunn, M, Goesel, C, Kinet, M and Ray, F (2015), 'Group treatment for survivors of torture and severe violence: A literature review', *Torture*, 26(1), 45–67.

Callaghan, K (1993), 'Movement psychotherapy with adult survivors of political torture and organized violence', *The Arts in Psychotherapy*, 20(5), 411–421.

Carlsson, J, Sonne, C and Silove, D (2014), 'From pioneers to scientists: Challenges in establishing evidence-gathering models in torture and trauma mental health services for refugees', *Journal of Nervous and Mental Disease*, 202(9), 630–637.

Chase, LE and Rousseau, C (2018), 'Ethnographic case study of a community day center for asylum seekers as early stage mental health intervention', *American Journal of Orthopsychiatry*, 88(1), 48–58.

Cienfuegos, A and Monelli, C (1983), 'The testimony of political repression as a therapeutic instrument', *American Journal of Orthopsychiatry*, 53, 43–51.

Coetzer, W (2007), 'The impact of intergenerational trauma. Explorative perspectives and some pastoral notes', *Acta Theologica*, 2, 2–22.

Connolly, S and Sakai, C (2011), 'Brief trauma symptom intervention with Rwandan genocide survivors using Thought Field Therapy', *International Journal of Emergency Mental Health*, 13(3), 161–172.

Connolly, S, Roe-Sepowitz, D, Sakai, C and Edwards, J (2013), 'Utilizing community resources to treat PTSD: A randomized controlled study using Thought Field Therapy', *African Journal of Traumatic Stress*, 3(1), 24–32.

Crumlish, N and O'Rourke, K (2010), 'A systematic review of treatments for post-traumatic stress disorder among refugees and asylum-seekers', *The Journal of Nervous and Mental Disease*, 198(4), 237–251.

Dalgaard, NT, Todd, BK, Daniel, SIF and Montgomery, E (2016), 'The transmission of trauma in refugee families: Associations between intra-family trauma communication style, children's attachment security and psychosocial adjustment', *Attachment and Human Development*, 18(1), 69–89.

Danieli, Y (1998), 'Introduction: History and conceptual foundations' in Danieli, Y (ed), *International handbook of multigenerational legacies of trauma* (Plenum Press), 1–17.

Danieli, Y (2009), 'Massive trauma and the healing role of reparative justice', *Journal of Traumatic Stress*, 22(5), 351–357.

Daud A, Skoglund E and Rydelius, PA (2005), 'Children in families of torture victims: Transgenerational transmission of parents' traumatic experiences to their children', *International Journal of Social Welfare*, 14(1), 23–3.

De Jong, K and Kleber, R (2007), 'Emergency conflict-related psychosocial interventions in Sierra Leone and Uganda: Lessons from Médecins Sans Frontières', *Journal of Health Psychology*, 12(3), 485–497.

De Jong, K, Kleber, R and Puratic, V (2000), 'Mental health programmes in areas of armed conflict: The Médicins Sans Frontières counselling centres in Bosnia-Herzegovina', *International Journal of Mental Health, Psychosocial Work and Counselling in Areas of Armed Conflict*, 1(1), 14–32.

Devakumar, D, Birch, M, Osrin, D, Sondorp, E and Wells, JC (2014), 'The intergenerational effects of war on the health of children', *BMC Medicine*, 12(57), accessed 4 April 2018 at https://bmcmedicine.biomedcentral.com/articles/10.1186/1741-7015-12-57#citeas

Dinesh, S (2004), 'Access to justice: Creating local level, citizen action mediation bodies to ensure human rights. New Tactics Project of the Center for Victims of Torture', accessed 5 May 2019 at https://www.newtactics.org/sites/default/files/resources/Access-Justice-EN.pdf

Dix-Peek, D and Werbeloff, M (2018), 'Evaluation of the efficacy of a South African psychosocial framework for the rehabilitation of torture survivors', *Torture*, 28(1), 34–57.

Doru, C (2008), *Healing the wounds, correcting injustice: The road to national reconciliation*. Paper presented to the International Seminar on National Reconciliation, 26 September 2008, Bucharest, Romania.

Droždek, B and Bolwerk, N (2010a), 'Evaluation of group therapy with traumatised asylum seekers and refugees: The Den Bosch Model', *Traumatology*, 16(4), 117–127.

Droždek, B and Bolwerk, N (2010b), 'Group therapy with traumatised asylum seekers and refugees: For whom it works and for whom it does not?', *Traumatology*, 16(4), 160–167.

Droždek, B, Kamperman, AM, Tol, WA, Knipscheer, JW and Kleber, R (2014), 'Seven☐year follow☐up study of symptoms in asylum seekers and refugees with PTSD treated with trauma☐focused groups', *Journal of Clinical Psychology*, 70(4), 376–387.

East, P, Gahagan, S and Delaimy, WK (2017), 'The impact of refugee mothers' trauma, posttraumatic stress, and depression on their children's adjustment', *Journal of Immigrant and Minority Health*, 20(2), 1–12.

Ehntholt, KA, Smith PA and Yule, W (2005), 'School-based cognitive-behavioural therapy group. Intervention for refugee children who have experienced war-related trauma', *Clinical Child Psychology and Psychiatry*, 10, 235–250.

Esala, JJ and Taing, S (2017), 'Testimony therapy with ritual: A pilot randomized controlled trial', *Journal of Traumatic Stress*, 30, 94–98.

Felsman, IC (2016), 'Supporting health and well-being for resettled refugee women: The global women's group', *Creative Nursing*, 22(4), 226–232.

Folkes, C (2002), 'Thought field therapy and trauma recovery', *International Journal of Emergency Mental Health*, 4, 99–103.

Gangamma, R (2018), 'A phenomenological study of family experiences of resettled Iraqi refugees', *Journal of Marital and Family Therapy*, 44(2), 323–335.

Gillies, D, Maiocchi, L, Bhandari, AP, Taylor, F, Gray, C and O'Brien, L (2016), 'Psychological therapies for children and adolescents exposed to trauma. The Cochrane Database of Systematic Reviews', 10, CD012371.

Goodkind, J, Hess, J, Isakson, B, LaNoue, M, Githinji, A, Roche, N, Vadnais, K and Parker, D (2014), 'Reducing refugee mental health disparities: A community-based intervention to address post-migration stressors with African adults', *Psychological Services*, 11(3), 333–346.

Gray, A (2001), 'The body remembers: dance/movement therapy with an adult survivor of torture', *American Journal of Dance Therapy*, 23(1), 29–43.

Gurr, R and Quiroga, J (2001), 'Approaches to torture rehabilitation: A desk study covering effects, cost-effectiveness, participation and sustainability', *Torture*, 11(1), 1–35.

Hamid, A, Patel, N, Williams, A C d C (2019), 'Psychological, social, and welfare interventions for torture survivors: A systematic review and meta-analysis of randomised controlled trials', *PLoS Med* 16(9): e1002919.

Harkness, LL (1993), 'Transgenerational transmission of war-related trauma' in Wilson, JP and Raphael, B (eds), *International handbook of traumatic stress syndromes* (Plenum Press), 635–643.

Hartwig, KA and Mason, M (2016), 'Community gardens for refugee and immigrant communities as a means of health promotion', *Journal of Community Health*, 41(6), 1153–1159.

Henrich, J, Heine, S and Norenzayan, A (2010), 'The weirdest people in the world?', *Behavioural and Brain Sciences*, 33, 61–83.

Inter-Agency Standing Committee (IASC) (2007), 'IASC guidelines on mental health and psychosocial support in emergency settings' (IASC).

Jansen, S, White, R, Hogwood, J, Jansen, A, Gishoma, D, Mukamana, D and Richters, A (2015), 'The "treatment gap" in global mental health reconsidered: Sociotherapy for collective trauma in Rwanda', *European Journal of Psychotraumatology*, 6, 28706, doi:10.3402/ejpt.v6.28706.

Jordans, MJ, Tol, WA, Komproe, IH and De Jong, JV (2009), 'Systematic review of evidence and treatment approaches: Psychosocial and mental health care for children in war', *Journal of Child and Adolescent Mental Health*, 14, 2–14.

Kalmanowitz, D and Ho, RTH (2016), 'Out of our mind: Art therapy and mindfulness with refugees, political violence and trauma', *Arts in Psychotherapy*, 49, 57–65.

Kira, IA, Ahmed, A, Wasim, F, Mahmoud, V, Colrain, J and Rai, D (2012), 'Group therapy for refugees and torture survivors: Treatment model innovations', *International Journal of Group Psychotherapy*, 62(1), 69–88.

Kevers, R, Rober, P, Derluyn, I and De Haene, L (2016), 'Remembering collective violence: Broadening the notion of traumatic memory in post-conflict rehabilitation', *Culture, Medicine and Psychiatry*, 40(4), 620–640.

Khawaja, NG and Stein, G (2016), 'Psychological services for asylum seekers in the community: Challenges and solutions', *Australian Psychologist*, 51(6), 463–471.

Koch, S and Weidinger-von der Recke, B (2009), 'Traumatised refugees: An integrated dance and verbal therapy approach', *Arts in Psychotherapy*, 36(5), 289–296.

Lambert, JE and Alhassoon, OM (2015), 'Trauma-focused therapy for refugees: Meta-analytic findings', *Journal of Counseling Psychology*, 62(1), 28–37.

Layne, CM, Saltzman, WR, Poppleton, L, Burlingame, GM, Pašalic, A and Duraković, E (2008), 'Effectiveness of a school-based group psychotherapy program for war-exposed adolescents: A randomized controlled trial', *Journal of the American Academy of Child and Adolescent Psychiatry*, 47, 1048–1062.

Logie, CH, Lacombe-Duncan, A, Lee-Foon, N, Ryan, S and Ramsay, H (2016), '"It's for us – newcomers, LGBTQ persons, and HIV-positive persons. You feel free to be": A qualitative study exploring social support group participation among African and Caribbean lesbian, gay, bisexual and transgender newcomers and refugees in Toronto, Canada', *BMC International Health and Human Rights*, 16(1), 18, doi: 10.3402/ejpt.v4i0.21407.

Lokuge, K, Shah, T, Pintaldi, G, Thurber, K, Martinez-Viciana, C, Cristobal, M, Palacios, L, Dear, K and Banks, E (2013), 'Mental health services for children exposed to armed conflict: Médecins Sans Frontières' experience in the Democratic Republic of Congo, Iraq and the occupied Palestinian territory', *Paediatric International Child Health*, 33(4), 259–272.

Longacre, M, Silver-Highfield, E, Lama, P and Grodin, M (2012), 'Complementary and alternative medicine in the treatment of refugees and survivors of torture: A review and proposal for action', *Torture*, 22(1), 38–57.

Lustig SL, Weine SM, Saxe GN and Beardslee WR (2004), 'Testimonial psychotherapy for adolescent refugees: A case series', *Transcultural Psychiatry*, 41, 31–45.

McFarlane, C and Kaplan, I (2012) 'Evidence-based psychological interventions for adult survivors of torture and trauma: A 30-year review', *Transcultural Psychiatry*, 49(3–4), 539–567.

Mendlehoff, D (2009), 'Trauma and vengeance: Assessing the psychological and emotional effects of post-conflict justice', *Human Rights Quarterly*, 31, 592–623.

Montgomery, E and Patel, N (2011), 'Reflections on treatment outcome studies in torture rehabilitation field', *Torture*, 21(2), 141–145.

Mooren, T, Kelber, R and De Jong, K (2003), 'The efficacy of a mental health programme in Bosnia-Herzegovina: Impact on coping and general health', *Journal of Clinical Psychology*, 59(1), 57–69.

Morgan, E, Hubbard, J and Kraus, E (2017), 'The development and implementation of a multi-couple therapy model with torture survivors in the Democratic Republic of Congo', *Journal of Marital and Family Therapy*, 44(2), 235–247.

Morina, N, Malek, M, Nickerson, A and Bryant, R (2017), 'Psychological interventions for post-traumatic stress disorder and depression in young survivors of mass violence in low- and middle-income countries: meta-analysis', *British Journal of Psychiatry*, 210, 247–254.

Mpande, E, Higson-Smith, C, Chimatira, RJ, Kadaira, A, Mashonganyika, J, Ncube, QM and Ziwoni, N (2013), 'Community intervention during ongoing political violence: What is possible? What works?' Peace and Conflict: Journal of Peace Psychology, 19(2), 196–208.

Murray, K, Davidson, G and Schweitzer, R (2010), 'Review of refugee mental health interventions following resettlement: Best practices and recommendations', *American Journal of Orthopsychiatry*, 80(4), 576–585.

Neuner, F, Onyut, P, Ertl, V, Odenwald, M, Schauer, E and Elbert, T (2008), 'Treatment of posttraumatic stress disorder by trained lay counselors in an African refugee settlement: A randomized controlled trial', *Journal of Consulting and Clinical Psychology*, 76(4), 686–694.

Neuner, F, Schauer, M, Klashik, C, Karunkara, U and Elbert, T (2004), 'A comparison of narrative exposure therapy, supportive counselling and psychoeducation for treating posttraumatic stress disorder in an African refugee settlement', *Journal of Consulting and Clinical Psychology*, 72(4), 579–587.

Nicholl, C and Thompson, A (2004), 'The psychological treatment of post-traumatic stress disorder (PTSD) in adult refugees: A review of the current state of psychological therapies', *Journal of Mental Health*, 13(4), 351–362.

Nickerson, A, Bryant, R, Silove, D and Steel, Z (2011), 'A critical review of psychological treatments of posttraumatic stress disorder in refugees', *Clinical Psychology Review*, 31(3), 399–417.

Nocon, A, Eberle-Sejari, R, Unterhitzenberger, J and Rosner, R (2017), 'The effectiveness of psychosocial interventions in war-traumatized refugee and internally displaced minors: Systematic review and meta-analysis', *European Journal of Psychotraumatology*, 8(2), 1–15.

Nosè, M, Ballette, F, Bighelli, I, Turrini, G, Purgato, M, Tol, W, Priebe, S and Barbui, C (2017), 'Psychosocial interventions for post-traumatic stress disorder in refugees and asylum seekers resettled in high-income countries: Systematic review and meta-analysis', *PLoS ONE*, 12, 1–16.

Ooi, CS, Rooney, RM, Roberts, C, Kane, RT, Wright, B and Chatzisarantis, N (2016), 'The efficacy of a group cognitive behavioral therapy for war-affected young migrants living in Australia: A cluster randomized controlled trial', *Frontiers in Psychology*, 7, 1641.

O'Sullivan, C, Bosqui, T and Shannon, C (2016), 'Psychological interventions for children and young people affected by armed conflict or political violence: A systematic literature review', *Intervention*, 1, 142–164.

Palic, S and Elklit, A (2011), 'Psychosocial treatment of posttraumatic stress disorder in adult refugees: A systematic review of prospective treatment outcome studies and a critique', *Journal of Affective Disorders*, 131(1–3), 8–23.

Patel, N (2003), 'Clinical psychology: Reinforcing inequalities or facilitating empowerment?', *International Journal of Human Rights*, 7(1), 16–39.

Patel, N (2011a), 'The psychologisation of torture' in Rapley, M, Moncrieff, J and Dillon, J (eds), *De-medicalising misery: Psychiatry, psychology and the human condition* (Palgrave Macmillan), 239–255.

Patel, N (2011b), 'Justice and reparation for torture survivors', *Journal of Critical Psychology, Counselling and Psychotherapy*, 11(3), 135–147.

Patel, N (2019a), 'Conceptualising rehabilitation as reparation for torture survivors: A clinical perspective', *International Journal of Human Rights*, 23(9), 1546–1568. DOI: 10.1080/13642987.2019.1612373

Patel, N (2019b), 'Human rights-based approach to applied psychology', *European Psychologist*, 24, 113–124.

Patel, N and Keval, H (2018), 'Fifty ways to leave … your racism', *Journal of Critical Psychology, Counselling and Psychotherapy*, 18(2), 61–79.

Patel, N and Williams, A (2014), *Conducting monitoring and evaluation for torture rehabilitation services: A handbook for service providers* (ICHHR).

Patel, N, Kellezi, B and Williams, A C de C (2014), 'Psychological, social and welfare interventions for psychological health and well-being of torture survivors', *Cochrane Database of Systematic Reviews*, Issue 10, Art No: CD009317.

Patel, N, Williams, A C de C, and Kellezi, B (2016), 'Reviewing outcomes of psychological interventions with torture survivors: Conceptual, methodological and ethical issues', *Torture*, 26(1), 2–16.

Peltonen, K and Punamaki, RL (2010), 'Preventive interventions among children exposed to trauma of armed conflict: A literature review', *Aggressive Behavior*, 36, 95–116.

Peltonen, K, Qouta, S, El Sarraj, E and Punamäki, R-L (2012), 'Effectiveness of school-based intervention in enhancing mental health and social functioning among war-affected children', *Traumatology*, 18(4), 37–46.

Persson, T and Rousseau, C (2009), 'School-based interventions for minors in war-exposed countries: A review of targeted and general programmes', *Torture*, 19(2), 88–101.

Purgato, M, Gross, A, Betancourt, T, Bolton, P, Bonetto. C, Gastaldon, C, Gordon, J, O'Callaghan, P, Papola, D, Peltronen, K, Punamaki, R, Richards, J, Staples, J, Unterhitzenberger, J, van Ommeren, M, de Jong, J, Jordans, M, Tol, W and Barbui, C (2018), 'Focused psychosocial interventions for children in low-resource humanitarian settings: A systematic review and individual participant data meta-analysis', *The Lancet Global Health*, 6, e390–e400.

Puvimanasinghe, TS and Price, IR (2016), 'Healing through giving testimony: An empirical study with Sri Lankan torture survivors', *Transcultural Psychiatry*, 53(5), 531–550.

Qouta, S, Palosaari, E, Diab, M and Punamaki, R-L (2012), 'Intervention effectiveness among war-affected children: A cluster randomized controlled trial on improving mental health', *Journal of Traumatic Stress*, 25, 288–298.

Quinlan, R, Schweitzer, RD, Khawaja, N and Griffin, J (2015), 'Evaluation of a school-based creative arts therapy program for adolescents from refugee backgrounds', *Arts in Psychotherapy*, 47, 72–78.

Quiroga, J and Jaranson, J (2005), 'Politically-motivated torture and its survivors: A desk study of the literature', *Torture*, 15(2–3), 1–111.

Reading, R and Rubin, L (2011), 'Advocacy and empowerment: group therapy for LGBT asylum seekers', *Traumatology*, 17(2), 86–98.

Reeler, T, Chirsike, K, Maizva, F and Reeler, B (2009), 'The tree of life: A community approach to empowering and healing survivors of torture in Zimbabwe', *Torture*, 19(3), 180–193.

Renner, W, Bänninger-Huber, E and Peltzer, K (2011), 'Culture-sensitive and resource oriented peer (CROP)-groups as a community based intervention for trauma survivors: A randomized controlled pilot study with refugees and asylum seekers from Chechnya', *Australasian Journal of Disaster and Trauma Studies*, 1, 1–13.

Robertson, ME, Blumberg, JM, Gratton, JL, Walsh, EG and Kaval, H (2013), 'A group-based approach to stabilisation and symptom management in a phased treatment model for refugees and asylum seekers', European Journal of Psychotraumatology, 4, 10.3402/ejpt.v4i0.21407.

Robson, R, Robson, P, Ludwig, R, Mitabu, C and Phillips, C (2016), 'Effectiveness of Thought Field Therapy provided by newly instructed community workers to a traumatized population in Uganda: A randomised trial', *Current Research in Psychology*, 7(1), 1–11.

Rooze, M, De Ruyter, A, Ajdukovic, D, Fundter, N and Hövels, J (2006), 'The healing community: The importance of community-based interventions' in Griffiths, J and Ingleton, T (eds), *Real risk* (Tudor Rose), 103–106.

Rousseau, C, Armand, F, Laurin-Lamothe, A, Gauthier, M and Saboundjian, R (2011), 'Innovations in practice: A pilot project of school-based intervention integrating drama and language awareness', *Child and Adolescent Mental Health*, 17(3), 187–190.

Rousseau, C, Benoit, M, Gauthier, M-F, Lacroix, L, Alain N, Viger Rojas, M et al. (2007), 'Classroom drama therapy program for immigrant and refugee adolescents: A pilot study', *Clinical Child Psychology and Psychiatry*, 12, 451–465.

Rousseau, C, Rufagari, MC, Bagilishya, D and Measham, T (2004), 'Remaking family life: Strategies for re-establishing continuity among Congolese refugees during the family reunification process', *Social Science & Medicine*, 59(5), 1095–1108.

Rowe, C, Watson-Ormond, R, English, L, Rubesin, H, Marshall, A, Linton, K, Amolegbe, A, Agnew-Brune, C and Eng, E (2017), 'Evaluating art therapy to heal the effects of trauma among refugee youth', *Health Promotion Practice*, 18(1), 26–33.

Ruf, M, Schauer, M, Neuner, F, Catani, C, Schauer, E, and Elbert, T (2010), 'Narrative exposure therapy for 7- to 16-year-olds: A randomized controlled trial with traumatized refugee children', *Journal of Traumatic Stress*, 23, 437–445.

Sakai, C, Connolly, S and Oas, P (2010), 'Treatment of PTSD in Rwanda genocide survivors using Thought Field Therapy', *International Journal of Emergency Mental Health*, 12(1), 41–49.

Schulz, P, Resick, P, Huber, L and Griffin, M (2006), 'The effectiveness of cognitive processing therapy for PTSD with refugees in a community setting', *Cognitive Behavioural Practice*, 13, 322–331.

Schwab, G (2010), *Haunting legacies: Violent histories and transgenerational trauma* (Columbia University Press).

Schwartz, S and Melzak, S (2005), 'Using story telling in psychotherapeutic group work with young refugees', *Group Analysis*, 38(2), 293–306.

Silove, D (1999), 'The psychological effects of torture, mass human rights violations, and refugee trauma. Toward a conceptual framework', *Journal of Nervous & Mental Disease*, 187, 200–207.

Slobodin, O and de Jong, JT (2015), 'Mental health interventions for traumatized asylum seekers and refugees: What do we know about their efficacy?', *International Journal of Social Psychiatry*, 61(1), 17–26.

Smith, H, Keatley, E and Min, M (2019), 'Group treatment with French-speaking African survivors of torture and its effects on clinical engagement: Can hope be operationalized?', *International Journal of Group Psychotherapy*, 69(2), 240–252.

Somasundaram, D (2007), 'Collective trauma in northern Sri Lanka: A qualitative psychosocial-ecological study', *International Journal of Mental Health Systems*, 1, 1–27.

Sonderegger, R, Rombouts, S, Ocean, B and McKeever, R (2011), 'Trauma rehabilitation for war affected persons in northern Uganda: A pilot evaluation of the EMPOWER programme', *British Journal of Clinical Psychology*, 50, 234–248.

Stepakoff, S, Hubbard, J, Katoh, M, Falk, E, Mikulu, J, Nkhoma, P and Omagwa, Y (2006), 'Trauma healing in refugee camps in Guinea: A psychosocial program for Liberian and Sierra Leonean survivors of torture and war', *American Psychologist*, 921–932.

Sullivan, A and Simonson, G (2016), 'A systematic review of school-based social-emotional interventions for refugee and war-traumatized youth', *Review of Educational Research*, 86(2), 503–530.

Summerfield, D (1999), 'A critique of seven assumptions behind psychological trauma programmes in war-affected areas', *Social Science and Medicine*, 48(10), 1449–1462.

Summerfield, D (2001), 'The invention of post-traumatic stress disorder and the social usefulness of a psychiatric category', *British Medical Journal*, 322, 95–98.

Sveaass, N and Reichelt, S (2001), 'Engaging refugee families in therapy: Exploring the benefits of including referring professionals in first family interviews', *Family Process*, 40(1), 95–114.

Thompson, C, Vidgen, A and Roberts, N (2018), 'Psychological interventions for post-traumatic stress disorder in refugees and asylum seekers: A systematic review and meta-analysis', *Clinical Psychology Review*, 63, 66–79.

Tol, WA, Komproe, IH, Susanty, D, Jordans, MJ, Macy, RD and De Jong, JT (2008), 'School-based mental health intervention for children affected by political violence in Indonesia: A cluster randomized trial', *JAMA*, 300, 655–662.

Tribe, R, Sendt, K and Tracy, D (2017), 'A systematic review of psychosocial interventions for adult refugees and asylum seekers', *Journal of Mental Health*, 28(6), 662–676.

Tucker, S and Price, D (2007), 'Finding a home: Group psychotherapy for traumatised refugees and asylum seekers', *European Journal of Psychotherapy & Counselling*, 9(3) 277–287.

Turrini, G, Purgato, M, Acarturk, C, Antitila, M, Au, T, Ballete, F et al. (2019), 'Efficacy and acceptability of psychosocial interventions in asylum seekers and refugees: A systematic review and meta-analysis', *Epidemiology and Psychiatric Sciences*, 28(4), 376–388.

Tyrer, R and Fazel, M (2014), 'School and community-based interventions for refugee and asylum seeking children: A systematic review', *PLoS ONE*, 9(2): e89359, doi:10.1371/journal.pone.0089359

Ugurlu, N, Akca, L and Acarturk, C (2016), 'An art therapy intervention for symptoms of posttraumatic stress, depression and anxiety among Syrian refugee children', *Vulnerable Children and Youth Studies*, 11(2), 89–102.

United Nations Committee Against Torture (2012), General Comment No. 3: Convention against Torture and Other Cruel, Inhuman or Degrading Treatment or Punishment: implementation of Article 14 by States parties, 19 November 2012, CAT/C/GC/3.

Van Dijk, J, Schoutrop, M and Spinhoven, P (2003), 'Testimony therapy: Treatment method for traumatized victims of organized violence', *American Journal of Psychotherapy*, 57(3), 361–373.

Villamor, E, Chavarro, JE and Caro, LE (2009), 'Growing up under generalized violence: An ecological study of homicide rates and secular trends in age at Menarche in Colombia, 1940s–1980s', *Journal of Economics and Human Biology*, 7, 238–245.

Weine, S, Feetham, S, Kulauzovic, Y, Knafl, K, Besic, S, Klebic, A et al. (2006), 'A family beliefs framework for socially and culturally specific preventive interventions with refugee youths and families', *American Journal of Orthopsychiatry*, 76(1), 1–9.

Weine, S, Kulenovic, A, Pavkovic, I et al. (1998), 'Testimony psychotherapy in Bosnian refugees: A pilot study', *American Journal of Psychiatry*, 155(12), 1720–1726.

Weine, S, Muzurovic, N, Kulauzovic, Y, Besic, S, Lezic, A, Mujagic, A et al. (2004), 'Family consequences of refugee trauma', *Family Process*, 43(2), 147–160.

Weine, SM, Raina, D, Zhubi, M, Delesi, M, Huseni, D, Feetham, S, et al. (2003), 'The TAFES multi-family group intervention for Kosovar refugees: A feasibility study', *The Journal of Nervous and Mental Disease*, 191(2), 100–107.

Weiss, W, Ugueto, A, Mahmooth, Z, Murray, L, Hall, B, Nadison, M, Rasmussen, A, Lee, J, Vazzano, A, Bass, J and Bolton, P (2016), 'Mental health interventions and priorities for research for adult survivors of torture and systematic violence: A review of the literature', *Torture*, 26(1), 17–44.

Wood, B and Kallestrup, P (2018), 'A review of non-specialised, group-based mental health and psychosocial interventions in displaced populations', *International Journal of Migration, Health and Social Care*, 14(3), 347–359.

Woodcock, J (1997), 'Group work with refugees and asylum seekers' in Mistry, T and Brown, A (eds), *Race & Group Work* (Whiting and Birch), 254–277.

Yeomans, P, Forman, E, Herbert, J and Yuen, E (2010), 'A randomized trial of a reconciliation workshop with and without PTSD psychoeducation in Burundian sample', *Journal of Traumatic Stress*, 23(3), 305–312.

Yohani, SC (2008), 'Creating an ecology of hope: Arts-based interventions with refugee children', *Child and Adolescent Social Work Journal*, 25, 309–323.

Youngson, NA and Whitelaw, E (2008), 'Transgenerational epigenetic effects', *Annual Review of Genomics Human Genetics*, 9, 233–257.

Zerach, G, Kanat-Maymon, Y, Aloni, R and Solomon, Z (2016), 'The role of fathers' psychopathology in the intergenerational transmission of captivity trauma: A twenty three-year longitudinal study', *Journal of Affective Disorders*, 190, 84–92.

24. Treating pain after torture

Kirstine Amris, Lester E Jones and Amanda Williams

INTRODUCTION

Torture is associated with a wide range of health-related consequences, of which pain and pain-related disability have long been recognised as defining features (Amris and Williams, 2007; Burnett and Peel, 2001; Edston, 2005; Olsen et al., 2006a; Rasmussen, 1990). The central role of pain means that health professionals engaged in the care of torture survivors need to be knowledgeable and up to date with pain theory and conceptual models, pain mechanisms, barriers to effective pain control, variables that influence the experience of and response to pain, reliable and meaningful methods of clinical pain assessment, and best evidence-based practice in managing pain.

Recent advances in basic and clinical neuroscience suggest that the central nervous system (CNS), in particular the brain, plays a pivotal role in the development of persistent pain. Uncontrolled and prolonged pain can alter multiple aspects of brain function, so that chronic pain should be viewed as a complex CNS state in which patterns of sensory system activation are integrated with descending modulatory activity from various brain systems including emotional and cognitive processes. CNS changes across the lifespan, particularly those related to adverse life events, can contribute to the development of a disabling pain condition (Denk et al., 2014; Generaal et al., 2016; Grace et al., 2014).

The biopsychosocial model of pain (Turk and Okifuji, 2002) emphasises pain as multidimensional and complex, with many components in addition to nociceptive signalling. These include emotional, cognitive, behavioural, existential and cultural components, all of which influence pain experience and response. Furthermore, persistent pain adversely affects all aspects of functioning: physical, emotional, interpersonal and vocational. Pain assessment should, therefore, be as comprehensive as possible, representing the biopsychosocial nature of the phenomenon and serving as a guide to a diverse therapeutic intervention. Given that no single intervention is likely to address all domains of pain, multiple approaches are required, best implemented in an integrated or coordinated manner. Modern pain management therefore integrates several treatment modalities: education about the nature of persistent pain; physical exercise and recovery of valued activities, by gradual steps; cognitive therapeutic methods to address unhelpful beliefs and thinking processes around pain and low mood; guiding changes in behaviour in the person with pain and those around him or her to maximise autonomy and confidence in managing the pain (Williams et al., 2012). Importantly, these skills can be learned and maintained for long-term self-management of pain.

Survivors of torture are likely to present with complex and multiple, long-lasting pains, often accompanied by moderate to severe symptoms of depression, anxiety and traumatic stress (Berliner et al., 2004; el Serraj, 1996). Unfortunately, both in specialist psychologically oriented torture services and in mainstream health systems, such pain is often misunderstood and dismissed as a non-specific symptom related to, or in some way produced by, psychological disturbance. The effect of this is that, although multidisciplinary team contribution approach to psychosocial rehabilitation has long been the gold standard in torture services (Jaranson and Quiroga, 2011), in the field of torture survivor care, pain continues to be misunderstood, under-assessed and undertreated, or subsumed under nonspecific psychological symptoms. Regrettably, the research literature on rehabilitation for survivors of torture is predominantly targeted at mental health problems without specific reference to pain and pain as a significant cause of distress and disability (Patel et al., 2014; Williams and Amris, 2017).

Torture survivors have a right to have their pain adequately addressed, particularly when it is one of their foremost concerns, and this chapter discusses the imperative for the recognition and management of pain in survivors of torture. We first describe persistent (chronic) pain and pain mechanisms in general and then pain from torture. We summarise issues of clinical pain assessment and address the treatment and rehabilitation of acute and chronic pain after torture. We close with clinical and research implications.

PAIN MODELS, PAIN MECHANISMS AND PERSISTENT PAIN

Pain may be associated with an acute tissue event or become persistent (chronic) without ongoing tissue pathology. Explanations of pain need to accommodate both these states. Acute pain is best explained as playing a protective role as it motivates the individual to withdraw from threatening situations, to protect a damaged body part while it is vulnerable, and to avoid similar experiences in the future. Acute pain is usually brief and self-limiting, induced by tissue injury and inflammation. In its simplest form, pain arises from activation of sensory receptors in peripheral tissues, specialised to detect actual or impending tissue damage (i.e. nociceptors). However, pain is always complex. We need only to look at placebo and nocebo research that demonstrates that activity in nociceptors is insufficient to explain pain. The human pain experience involves the integration of neural, immune and endocrine functions to detect, evaluate and respond to internal and external threats. In this way it may be better to consider pain not as simply having a protective role, but as being the most overt part of a highly evolved and complex body protection system.

In the acute situation, the conscious emergence of pain involves a system of mechanisms that encode and transmit danger signals along the ascending (incoming) pathways, from the point of noxious stimulation in the periphery to the spinal dorsal horn neurons and higher centres in the brain. Ascending nociceptive information is not conveyed passively to the higher brain areas. Pain is continuously subject to *descending modulation* controlled by the state of the organism, including past history, context (threat, safety) and other ongoing demands. Brain and brainstem structures involved in descending pain modulation, which plays a crucial role for homeostasis and pain control, directly project to and modify the responses of spinal and medullary dorsal horn neurons to incoming sensory stimulation. Engagement of these 'top-down' modulatory pathways can enhance, as well as inhibit nociceptive traffic, changing the experience of pain.

The mechanisms when pain persists involve altered central pain processing, the phenomenon of central sensitisation. *Central sensitisation* refers to enhanced function of neurons and circuits in the CNS caused by increased excitation and/or decreased inhibition driven by various brain circuits, including those representing learned responses and earlier adverse experiences (Katz and Seltzer, 2009; Woolf, 2011). Changes in brain activity that are also associated with neuroimmune plasticity. Indeed, some authors describe a state of pain vulnerability (Denk et al., 2014) – an overapplied protective response with pain hypersensitivity that amplifies the sensory response elicited by normal inputs, including those that usually evoke innocuous sensations such as touch. Thus central sensitisation represents a major functional shift in the sensory system from high-threshold nociception to low-threshold pain hypersensitivity (Woolf, 2011).

Clinically, *pain hypersensitivity* is characterised by increased responsiveness to noxious stimuli, producing an amplified and prolonged pain (*hyperalgesia*), and lowered receptor thresholds, with pain elicited by normally non-painful stimuli (*allodynia*). Increased responsiveness of peripheral and central neurons (pain hypersensitivity) in the presence of tissue injury and inflammation is a normal adaptive response (neuroplasticity) that ensures healing.

However, pain hypersensitivity may persist long after an injury has healed or occur in the absence of any injury. In this case, pain provides no benefits, and is a manifestation of maladaptive changes in the nervous system (Woolf, 2011). Persistent pain is processed differently in the brain from acute pain, findings from which cannot be directly extrapolated. In persistent pain, processing is far more widespread, and involves emotional meaning (Apkarian et al., 2009); there is no fixed 'network' or 'pain matrix' but a characteristic set of connections activated by and integrating the various dimensions of pain: a connectome (Jensen et al., 2016; Kucyi and Davis, 2015). Thus, the current understanding is that persistent pain is not a symptom or manifestation of underlying tissue damage, but results from altered nociceptive function and might be considered a disease in its own right (Tracey and Bushnell, 2009).

In spite of this understanding of chronic pain, it is frequently included in the category of 'medically unexplained symptoms' or 'functional disorders', based on the lack of identifiable tissue-based pathology (Williams and Cella, 2012). This view arises from a simplistic, *unidimensional biomedical model of pain*, in which the experience of pain is equated with peripheral stimulation and physiological processing of noxious stimuli (nociception) and the pain experience is assumed to be directly proportional to the extent of observable tissue damage. Alternatively, the psychogenic view suggests that pain is a physical manifestation of psychological problems in the absence of any apparent tissue-based explanation, a model with no supporting evidence (Crombez et al., 2009). Pain is never a purely sensory or purely psychological phenomenon but is *multidimensional*, integrating motivational-affective and cognitive-evaluative components with sensory-physiological ones. Accordingly, the International Association for the Study of Pain (IASP) defines pain as 'an unpleasant sensory and emotional experience associated with actual or potential tissue damage or described in terms of such damage'. This definition emphasises the inherent subjectivity of pain, with both sensory and affective dimensions, that are usually, but not necessarily, associated with tissue damage. Further, the influence of culture and social context on pain expression or suppression can be considerable (Brady et al., 2016), so not only is there no 'right' or 'wrong' amount of pain for a given injury or disease, there is also no 'right' or 'wrong' way to express that pain.

THE PROBLEM OF PAIN IN TORTURE POPULATIONS – PAIN EPIDEMIOLOGY

Prevalence of post-torture pain cannot be studied by standard epidemiological methods: populations studied are usually selected on some clinical grounds, or are accessible through some chance circumstances that tend to reduce representativeness. Data are derived mainly from descriptive studies in selected populations, and rarely specifically focus on pain experience. Nevertheless, studies of torture survivors attending specialised documentation and/or rehabilitation centres are consistent in reporting an extremely high prevalence of persistent pain, with overall estimates as high as 83 per cent (Olsen et al., 2006a; Olsen et al, 2006b; Williams et al., 2010). Although one study comparing survivors seen within two weeks of torture with those seen later indicated some spontaneous resolution of pain (Dülgeroglu, 2000), a follow-up study of survivors in Denmark showed increased prevalence of chronic pain over the intervening ten years (Olsen et al., 2007), an unusual and concerning finding. Studies of multiply traumatised refugees also produce high prevalence estimates, and it is often difficult to distinguish torture survivors from survivors of other trauma (Teodorescu et al., 2015).

Commonest is headache (Amris, 2005; Musisi et al., 2000) and musculoskeletal pain, pain related to the spine (Dülgeroglu, 2000; Musisi et al., 2000; Rasmussen, 1990), joint pain (Moisander and Edston, 2003), foot pain (Edston, 2005; Moisander and Edston, 2003; Olsen et al., 2007) and pelvic pain (Musisi et al., 2000). Regional and widespread muscular pain is frequent (Moisander and Edston, 2003). Several forms of physical torture (e.g. beatings, strapping, suspension by the extremities, forced positions, electrical torture) may cause injuries in the musculoskeletal system, mainly soft tissue lesions, but the best described pain problems arising from specific torture methods are foot pain from falanga (Edston, 2005; Prip and Persson, 2008; Prip et al., 2011) and shoulder and upper limb pain from suspension by the arms (Rasmussen et al., 2005). There are rather less well-developed associations of pelvic pain in women from sexual assault and sexual torture (Rasmussen et al., 2005; Williams et al., 2010), and of anal pain and urological problems in men after sexual torture (Norredam et al., 2005; Williams et al., 2010). While pain is sometimes noted in studies with a focus on mental health (e.g. Morina et al., 2017), pain is inadequately assessed or combined with diverse other symptoms, so the data are of limited value in understanding the specific relationships of pain with torture history or with current psychological status.

In populations whose members have not been subject to torture or major trauma, pain persistence is predicted primarily by pain severity in the acute or onset phase, particularly where there is nerve injury (many studies are of postsurgical pain), and by psychological and social factors, effectively distress in some form (Katz and Seltzer, 2009; Kehlet et al., 2006; McBeth et al., 2001). Pain is inflicted in torture often under conditions of extreme and prolonged stress that may have profound effects on neurophysiology and the processing of pain. Anxiety about the cause of pain, about its persistence, and about a future disabled by pain all impinge on the experience of it and capacity to cope with it (Turk and Okifuji, 2002). All these risk factors are highly represented in the torture situation, with no reliable access to protective factors such as social support or healthcare including analgesia. On this basis, the very high prevalence figures for persistent pain, in a mostly young adult population, are more explicable.

POSSIBLE PAIN MECHANISMS INVOLVED IN POST-TORTURE PAIN

Most literature on the long-term consequences of torture is descriptive, listing symptoms or clusters of symptoms, so the aetiology and pathophysiology of persistent pain after torture are incompletely understood. The interactive models of pain emphasise the neurophysiological as well as environmental circumstances as an explanation for the development of chronic pain states. These models are tailored towards explanations for chronic and musculoskeletal pain problems that develop long after apparent injury. The concepts of pain syndromes evolving over time, predicted by the severity, extent and repetition of the original trauma, are therefore presumed to apply to post-torture pain, but studies are lacking. Careful documentation and studies of torture survivors are, however, beginning to establish connections between some forms of torture and persistent pain, better described by mechanism than by pain location.

Mechanism-based pain classification refers to the classification of pain according to the pathophysiological mechanism presumed to be responsible for its initiation and/or maintenance (Woolf et al., 1998). This concept is used in clinical settings to provide a way of examining and classifying patients that may inform better treatment. Nociceptive pain, neuropathic pain, and pain originating from altered nociceptive function (nociplastic pain) have been suggested as clinically meaningful mechanistic terms or descriptors of putative contributors to the experience of pain (Kosek et al., 2016).

Nociceptive pain is pain that can predominantly be explained by physiological activation of nociceptors in response to potential or actual tissue injury (inflammation, ischaemia and/or mechanical trauma). Typically, nociceptive pain is described as intermittent and localised to the area of injury or dysfunction, and has a clear, proportionate mechanical/anatomical relationship with aggravating and easing factors. In the torture survivor, nociceptive pain may be caused by acute injury or permanent deformity in in the musculoskeletal system, such as lesion of the shoulder joint after suspension by the upper extremities, lesion of the knees caused by direct blows or prolonged knee-loading positions, or lesions of plantar structures after falanga, and/or strain in the musculoskeletal system secondary to overload and disuse, for instance compensatory altered posture, movement or gait. Magnetic resonance imaging (MRI) (Savnik et al., 2000) have identified thickening of the plantar aponeurosis in torture survivors exposed to falanga, and distorted gait with abnormal unwinding of the foot are typical findings at clinical examination.

Neuropathic pain is defined as 'pain arising as a direct consequence of a lesion or disease affecting the somatosensory system'. As such, neuropathic pain involves a history of nerve injury or pathology of somatosensory pathways. The mechanisms underlying neuropathic pain are complex and not yet fully understood. It is clear that the nervous system is capable of significant plasticity, with various peripheral and central changes occurring in response to nerve injury, altering both structure and function. Injured primary sensory neurons and their immediate non-injured neighbours begin to fire action potentials spontaneously as a result of increased or novel expression of sodium channels. This ectopic pacemaker-like activity contributes to spontaneous pain and, by inducing central sensitisation, further heightens pain sensitivity. Additionally, there are changes in the expression of synaptic transmitters and receptors and many other genes that modify transmission and responsiveness (Dickenson et al., 2002).

Clinical experience has highlighted a number of features that are common in neuropathic pain syndromes, including symptoms and signs of spontaneous and evoked pains. None are pathognomonic but their presence may point to a diagnosis of neuropathic pain. Spontaneous pains can be continuous or paroxysmal and occur with no apparent stimulation. Examples of spontaneous pains that are continuous in nature include unpleasant or abnormal sensations felt in the skin (dysesthesias) described as burning, tingling, itching or pins and needles. Some describe 'insects crawling' or 'water running' over skin. Deeper pains may be described as aching, gnawing, cramping or crushing. Paroxysmal elements are often described as stabbing, shooting or electric-shock-like pains. Evoked pains where an ordinary physical stimulus produces an unusual or exaggerated sensation of pain include allodynia or hyperalgesia. Allodynia describes pain that is experienced from a stimulus that would normally go unnoticed, such as skin contact with clothing or a cold breeze. Hyperalgesia is an exaggerated painful sensation after a painful stimulus. Other symptoms that may support a diagnosis of neuropathic pain include descriptions of areas of numbness or symptoms of concurrent motor or autonomic nerve involvement.

Traumatic nerve lesions caused by blows, strangulation, traction and other forces are probably common in survivors of torture, and neuropathic pain is therefore a very likely contributing mechanism. Neuropathic pain syndromes have been described in torture survivors based on clinical presentation: neuropathic pain due to partial lesion of the brachial plexus after suspension by the upper extremities; partial lesion of the lumbosacral plexus after suspension by the lower extremities; segmental, radiating pain after forced, back-loading positions; trigeminal neuralgia after head trauma; and peripheral neuropathy after tight binding of wrists or ankles (Amris and Williams, 2007; Moreno and Grodin, 2002; Rasmussen et al., 2005; Thomsen et al., 2000). Involvement of a neuropathic pain component in the typical pain syndrome seen after falanga is supported by quantitative sensory testing indicating small fibre neuropathy (Prip et al., 2012a; Prip et al., 2012b).

Central sensitisation and dysfunction of descending pain modulating systems are implicated in several chronic muscular pain syndromes, variously diagnosed in other settings as chronic widespread pain and fibromyalgia. A marker of pain caused by altered nociceptive function is the occurrence of regional or widespread pain in conjunction with hypersensitivity in apparently normal tissues, often associated with other centrally mediated symptoms, such as fatigue, sleep disruption, cognitive difficulties, visceral symptoms and emotional distress – a symptom constellation not unlike the one seen in many torture survivors. Despite obvious differences, including the spatial distribution of pain, there are striking phenotypic similarities between neuropathic pain and pain in disorders of central processing, namely how persons express their abnormal sensory perceptions and in particular the quality of their pain. Besides spontaneous pain in the muscle and joints, individuals with widespread muscular pain syndromes often report hypersensitivity of the skin to mechanical or thermal stimuli, and burning or prickling sensations as well as neuralgic pain attacks. Unsuccessful attempts among healthcare professionals to match subjective pain reports to objective findings, in the context of unfamiliarity with chronic pain mechanisms and evident psychological distress in the survivor, are erroneously used to support psychosomatic theories of pain, even when torture has been disclosed and documented. Evidence supports understanding this type of pain in terms of changes in pain signalling in the CNS in the context of the changes described above (Amris, 2005; Amris and Williams, 2007).

As the different pain mechanisms may coexist and contribute to the overall experience of pain, clinicians should try to identify different pain components and treat each of them according to the best available evidence (see Box 24.1 and Figure 24.1).

BOX 24.1 THE PAIN AND MOVEMENT REASONING MODEL

The Pain and Movement Reasoning Model shows promise as a tool to help practitioners capture the complexity of pain in their clinical reasoning, including physiotherapists working with survivors of torture. A premise of the model is that pain is complex and, even in acute presentations, central processes will play a role (Jones and O'Shaughnessy, 2014). It is presented as a gridded triangle where each corner represents a different category of pain mechanisms – local stimulation, regional influences, central modulation (see Figure 24.1). The subjective component of assessment, and the physical examination, can be facilitated by the assessor attending to each category. Using assessment findings, the practitioner uses clinical judgement to plot a point on the central grid that indicates the relative contributions of each category. This promotes consideration by clinicians of all potential mechanisms of pain when making decisions about treatment. By structuring the model around pain mechanisms and integrating a biopsychosocial approach, this reasoning tool supports the comprehensive assessment and management of pain that is crucial for effectively helping survivors of torture.

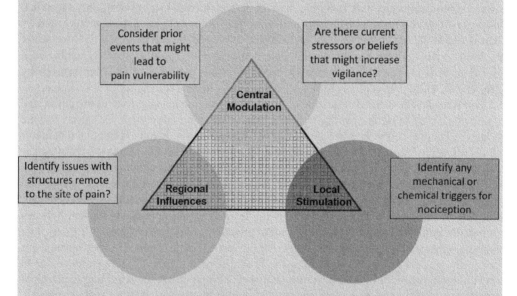

Note: The Pain and Movement Reasoning Model was created to facilitate the integration of the range of pain mechanisms into clinical decision making.
Source: Des O'Shaughnessy and Lester Jones, Creative Commons Attribution-NonCommercial-Share Alike 4.0 International (CC BY-NC-SA 4.0) License.

Figure 24.1   Pain and Movement Reasoning Model

CLINICAL ASSESSMENT FROM A PAIN PERSPECTIVE

Clinical assessment of a torture survivor can be done in order to document findings consistent with allegations of torture or to plan intervention and rehabilitation. In documenting torture, the focus will be on the description of symptoms and signs that provide evidence to support the account of torture. When the assessment is for the purpose of intervention and rehabilitation, the assessment should inform clinical decision making and focus not only on the biological basis of symptoms but also on the range of factors that modulate nociception and moderate the pain experience and related disability. Pain rehabilitation in a biopsychosocial paradigm is concerned with limitations of functioning and disability associated with pain, and with the complex interaction with personal factors and the environment, hence the wider social and political context is very relevant: these give meaning to the pain and values to activities.

However, a standard clinical pain assessment, with thorough examination of the musculoskeletal system and neurological evaluation, is essential to identify potentially treatable musculoskeletal injuries and dysfunction and, where possible, to identify the mechanisms generating or maintaining pain. Most torture survivors have been exposed to multiple forms of torture and may present with numerous pains and physical impairments, so proper examination is time-consuming and may take several sessions. Knowledge of common torture methods and of the likely mechanisms by which they produce pain is required for a systematic and effective examination, but since the underlying mechanisms in chronic pain states are more likely to be central than peripheral in origin, prolonged and unproductive investigations and referrals seeking tissue-based explanations for the persistence of pain should be avoided.

The pain history should include questions about the location, intensity, quality and temporal profile of the pain, along with possible exacerbating and easing factors. Most torture survivors attribute the start of the pain to the torture, and describe continuing pain, albeit with varying intensity; others describe remission of initial pain only for it to reappear later at high intensity and with a different quality. It is also important to ask the survivors about their beliefs about pain, about damage done, and about the causes and implications of their pain. If pain is believed by the survivor to signal ongoing tissue damage, then an explanation of persistent pain without damage enables reframing of pessimistic beliefs about the possibility of improved functioning and discussion of changes in behaviour towards rehabilitation. Since the main objective of pain rehabilitation programmes is not to cure pain, but to promote self-management of symptoms in order to return to desired activities and lifestyle, the survivor will be required to try new and perhaps counter-intuitive ways of managing pain. Individuals vary in their readiness to accept assurance that they do not have undetected and remediable damage as the cause of pain, and to adopt a self-management approach, so it is important at all stages to address beliefs about pain and how the pain should be managed.

Assessment of Neuropathic Pain

Neurological examination in suspected neuropathic pain should include assessment of motor, sensory and autonomic phenomena in order to identify all signs of neurological dysfunction. Proper assessment requires a clear understanding of the possible types of negative (e.g., sensory loss) and positive (e.g., pain and paraesthesia) symptoms and signs. In addition to sensory loss, which is a universal response to nerve damage, there can be so-called positive phenomena; spontaneous pain, dysesthesia and hypersensitivity, including allodynia and hyperalgesia. Sensory disturbances, including pain, should be recorded in detail, preferably on body maps (schematic charts of the body front and back). Although difficult for the non-specialist and time-consuming for everybody, drawing the sensory abnormality provides valuable information. Tactile sense is best assessed with a piece of cotton wool, pinprick sense with a needle or wooden cocktail stick, thermal sense with warm and cold objects (e.g., metal thermorollers), and vibration sense with a 128-Hz tuning fork. Hyperalgesia and allodynia can be confirmed by testing for disproportionate patterns of pain provocation in response to movement, mechanical testing, or non-painful stimuli. Guidelines on assessment of neuropathic pain may be helpful (Haanpaa et al., 2011). Widespread pain and deep tissue hyperalgesia (e.g. multiple tender points), for which no apparent tissue-based pathology can be identified, is the hallmark of disorders of central processing such as fibromyalgia and suggestive of central sensitisation mechanisms.

A number of tools have been developed, among which are neuropathic pain descriptors. These include the neuropathic pain scale, the Leeds Assessment of Neuropathic Symptoms and Signs (LANSS) (Bennett, 2001), Pain DETECT (Freynhagen et al., 2006), and the Neuropathic Pain Symptom Inventory (NPSI) (Bouhassira et al., 2004). The LANSS has been shown to be suitable for assessing neuropathic pain in a range of clinical contexts, including chronic pain populations, and has shown good validity and reliability. It comprises five symptoms and two examination items (allodynia and pin-prick testing). It has also been developed into a patient self-report tool (S-LANSS). Screening tools are not designed as diagnostic tools but they can be useful in alerting the clinician to the possibility of a neuropathic pain component.

Assessment of the Musculoskeletal System

Before beginning the assessment of the musculoskeletal system, it is important to prepare the environment so that the person feels safe. This will often mean a private and quiet space. It sometimes means the gender of the assessor and how s/he dresses might be important. However, it is best to check with the person for any preferences and how to maximise her or his sense of safety. A trusting therapeutic alliance is essential for any assessment process and this might take time to build. When working with survivors of torture it should be anticipated that the musculoskeletal assessment will be slower to complete and may take several sessions.

Other modifications in the approach to musculoskeletal assessment are required. Normally a comprehensive history is taken to determine mechanism of injury and subsequent management and to understand a person's prior level of activity and function, as well as the impact of the injury or pain on current activity and function. However, when working with survivors of torture there may be a risk of triggering unwanted flashbacks and re-experiencing of the torture event. While it will always be valuable to obtain information about the person to make decisions about diagnosis and treatment, this needs to be tempered by the harm that might be done. Giving the survivor a clear rationale for why information is sought and giving her or him the control of disclosure will help facilitate the best outcome.

Often when survivors present for assessment of their pain, they will have had time for tissues to heal from the initial injury. However, it is important not to assume that healing is complete and no local tissue mechanisms are at play. It should also be recognised that any injury that is sustained during torture is likely to have been managed poorly and so delayed tissue healing, deformity and movement restrictions are likely.

The assessing practitioner should always rule out new injury or re-injury. A key part of this is to identify if there are any mechanical loads – compression or traction – on tissue, or changes in the chemical milieu of tissue at the site of pain, caused for example by inflammation or poor oxygenation of muscle tissue (i.e. local stimulation). With regard to the latter, resettled survivors can find themselves in occupations for which they are not physically conditioned, so some pain may be explained by persistent novel postures (McGill et al., 2000). Notably, there is a likelihood that thresholds of response in nociceptors are lowered and so the assessor needs to adjust for this sensitivity, as the level of mechanical and chemical stimuli required to trigger a nociceptive response will be less than in an unsensitised state.

It is essential that the practitioner assesses for musculoskeletal contributors to the pain away from the site of pain (i.e. regional influences). This includes pathology that is linked to the site of pain by convergence of the nervous system (e.g. referred pain from spinal nerve roots that is felt in the legs) and may lead to evaluation of adjacent joints, muscles and fascia but also investigation of relevant visceral structures. This category also includes the role of biomechanical factors. For example, someone's foot pain could be explained by weakness and therefore lack of control at the hip, putting excessive and abnormal loads through the foot in weight bearing. Antalgic or guarding postures and movements can especially lead to excessive and abnormal forces on the body, if they persist and have not been corrected by appropriate rehabilitation. Survivors of torture often hold themselves in a protective way that may be due to pain but equally be due to emotional vulnerability. Alternatively, they may find themselves significantly less physically active than previously and in more static postures in home or study. No matter the cause of this postural variation it needs to be addressed to prevent secondary musculoskeletal symptoms developing.

Where the person is holding her or himself in a protective way, it is important to assess the breathing pattern (Smith and Rowley, 2011). It can be useful to consider the three dimensions of chest movement in assessment – frontal, sagittal, transverse. Commonly, the activity during breathing is limited to the upper chest and involves constant shoulder activity. The muscles of the neck and shoulder girdle often display over-activity and have the potential to contribute to a restricted breathing pattern.

When assessing the musculoskeletal system it is important to be aware of the vast influences on sensitivity and learning associated with pain. As mentioned previously, modification of transmission and processing of nociception (i.e. danger signals) is apparent at the dorsal horn of the spinal cord. The presence of diseased or damaged nerves, and persistent intense peripheral input, seem to contribute to these changes in processing. Other adverse experiences, including pre-injury or pre-pain, and long episodes of poor health, can prime the neuroimmune system. While it is almost certainly not just these experiences but the person's psychological and physiological responses to the experiences that is important, adverse experiences need to be considered in making sense of the assessment findings. Pain may not mean pathology in the musculoskeletal system but reflect sensitivity. The assessing practitioner needs to be very clear about this to avoid making a clinical reasoning error. That is, to assume there is tissue pathology when there is pain, and equally, to assume there is no tissue pathology because the torture happened a long time ago.

Finally, stress, mood, sleep and thoughts and beliefs and the social safety of the person can all modulate the pain experience by central mechanisms. There is considerable evidence that psychological distress amplifies pain, compromises adaptation to pain, and acts as a stressor, thereby worsening distress (Crombez et al., 2012; Eccleston and Crombez, 2007). In considering the pain reported by a survivor of torture, issues relating to re-settlement, loss of role, worries about missing or distant loved ones and rumination over adverse events could all be relevant. The practitioner can optimise the musculoskeletal assessment by taking care to reduce or avoid any stress-provoking expectations or actions. This will include checking regularly with the survivor of torture as to the appropriateness of touch, state of undress, the level, type of and repetition of movements and the duration of the assessment process.

Standardised Scales Used in Multidimensional Pain Assessment

Routine audit and evaluation may require standardised scales, but some critical considerations and caution is needed when extending the use of any measures, even well-established ones, to populations that differ substantially from those in which the scales were developed. Most scales used in the assessment of core outcome domains of pain are developed and validated for use in particular patient populations, and none has been validated for torture survivors with chronic pain. Reliability, validity, responsiveness and interpretability (the psychometric properties of an instrument) can be condition- or context-specific, and are not invariant properties of an assessment tool. The context of assessment is important, and standardised scales have limited use in documentation where the agenda is likely to bias survivor and clinician responses. A final concern is that instruments developed on native language speakers may not be transferable to second language speakers, unless carefully translated and conceptually and linguistically validated. Thus, many standard instruments may not be adequate to capture and quantify problems of torture survivors or desired outcomes.

Assessing pain

Since pain is a subjective experience, the person with pain is the only source of information about location, intensity, duration, quality and other characteristics. Pain may also be expressed in a range of behaviours, some more reflexive and others at least partially under voluntary control, but the inferences made by an observer are subject to many biases, particularly from the observer (Tait et al., 2009), and cannot be a substitute for self-report where available. For those who cannot speak or write, behavioural scales and observations are possible, but this is a very specialised area which does not occur often in the field of torture survivors so is not addressed here.

   Pain is multidimensional, and assessing only one dimension, or an unquantifiable combination of dimensions in a single metric, provides little useful information for evaluating treatment or change over time. Characteristics such as quality, duration, whether pain is episodic or constant, and its location(s) are usually assessed informally. It is particularly important to note all the sites of pain, since the more sites of pain the individual has, the more disabled she or he tends to be. It is common to describe research participants or clinical populations only by the main site of pain, but this may be a serious misrepresentation. Multiple sites of pain also have implications for treatment, in that pains in different sites may have different mechanisms that respond to different treatments.

   Pain assessment consistent with the definition above would quantify both intensity (sensory dimension) and distress (emotional dimension), the simplest dimensional representation of pain, but pain is usually quantified in a single score. Assessment can be done directly using numbers, in a numerical rating scale (NRS), by a spatial scale (visual analogue scale: VAS), or by words (verbal rating scale: VRS) that are then converted to numbers (Jensen and Karoly, 2011). There are also face scales, suitable only for young children. Given diversity of language and problems of scaling, verbal rating scales are not recommended for torture survivors. Nor does the VAS have any advantage over NRSs, and the instructions can be hard for people unused to rating experiences to follow.

   A common NRS consists of an instruction such as 'Rate your pain on average between 0 for no pain and 10 for extreme pain', followed by the numbers 0 to 10 with the anchors 'no pain' and 'extreme pain' at the left and right hand ends respectively. The instruction can be varied:

rating pain at its worst, or at this moment, etc., so long as suitable (clear and consistent) anchor values for the end points are used. This is relatively easy to translate, including reversing the direction of the scale (for several examples see https://www.britishpainsociety.org/british-pain-society-publications/pain-scales-in-multiple-languages/). It can also be used for momentary ratings that are then averaged, and easily represented on smartphone applications or similar. Assigning meaning to scores can be more difficult, and even comparisons across time within an individual is not entirely reliable, particularly where a single score is used to represent all pain, but there is a convention that 1–3 is represented as mild pain, 4–6 as moderate pain, and 7–10 as severe pain, usefully linked to the proposal that no more than mild pain should be the universal outcome for all pain interventions (Moore et al., 2013). Similar scales can be used to represent other dimensions of pain than intensity or severity, such as asking about distress associated with pain, or interference by pain with everyday life (Wood et al., 2010). One of the widely used pain assessments, available in the very many languages in which it has been standardised, the Brief Pain Inventory (BPI) uses four NRSs for pain (current, average, least and worst), and seven NRSs for interference by pain, including one on emotional effects of pain. The BPI is one of the best short and reasonably comprehensive scales available, and effectively assesses disability as well as pain (see next section).

Assessing functioning and disability

Although functioning is considered a core outcome domain in pain management and clinical pain trials, there are different understandings of the term functioning and no consensus on how it should be assessed. However, it is recommended to include measures of physical functioning that provide evaluations of meaningful aspects of an individual's life and that assessment should be based on a clear conceptual model of functioning (Taylor et al., 2016). The WHO International Classification of Functioning, Disability and Health (ICF) (2001) provides one conceptual framework that can be used to describe and classify aspects of functioning and disability. As a classification, the ICF systematically groups different domains for a person in a given health condition. These domains are described from the perspective of the body, the individual and society in two basic lists: (1) body functions and structures; and (2) activity (execution of tasks) and participation (involvement in life situations). Functioning is an umbrella term covering all body functions, activities and participation; similarly, disability serves as an umbrella term for impairments at the body level, activity limitations and participation restrictions. This means that the broad construct of functioning can be assessed in some or all the different domains of human functioning classified by the ICF: the body functions and structures of people (functioning at the level of the body, for example muscle strength, muscle endurance, joint mobility) and impairments thereof; the activities of people (functioning at the level of the individual, for example mobility, activities of daily living (ADL) such as household chores and self-care) and the activity limitations they experience; the participation or involvement of people in life situations (functioning of a person as a member of society, for example interpersonal relationships, fulfilment of social roles) and the restrictions in participation they experience.

A number of studies indicate that different interventions for chronic pain may have differential effects on body level impairments, activity limitation and restriction in participation (Taylor et al., 2016). Assessment of functioning should therefore be appropriate for the population being studied and directed at the specific level of functioning that is of interest;

measures of functioning obtained at the body level or measures of mobility are no substitute, for instance, for assessment of ADL ability or social participation.

There is a plethora of methods that can be used to assess functioning, each providing information on a certain aspect of the concept. These can range from direct observation and monitoring devices, to patient reported outcomes (PROs). PROs can be generic or condition/pain and pain-site specific; some questionnaires focus solely on physical functioning, whereas others include multiple domains in which physical functioning is only one component or sub-scale of the assessment tool. Most of the commonly applied generic self-report tools used to assess functioning are composed of a mixture of activity and mobility task items. For example, the physical functioning subscale of the MOS SF-36 (Ware and Sherbourne, 1992), a generic Health-related Quality of Life instrument, is a ten-item scale that contains five items related to mobility and five items related to ADL ability. It enquires as to how much 'your health now limits you in these activities'. The SF-36 has been widely used to assess health status, including functional ability in subjects with chronic pain.

Participation in work, within and outside the home, and family, social, and leisure activities are important aspects of functioning that are most often assessed by self-report questionnaires. The WHO Disability Assessment Schedule 2.0 (WHODAS 2.0) is a generic instrument developed for the assessment of health and disability, aligning with the ICF levels of functioning. The instrument provides a global disability score as well as six domain scores: cognition, mobility, self-care, getting along with others, participation in society, and life activities (Üstün, 2010). However, there are no established thresholds for interpreting the global or domain-specific scores in relation to a criterion of clinically significant impairment, and the instructions for the WHODAS 2.0 require respondents to make attributions about the source of their disability. These attributions may be inaccurate, particularly in the context of complex health problems with co-occurring disorders (Konecky et al., 2014). Several of the pain-specific self-report questionnaires, for example the Pain Disability Index (Pollard, 1984; Tait et al., 1990) and the Brief Pain Inventory (Cleeland and Ryan, 1994), have been developed as more global measures of the degree to which chronic pain interferes with various life domains, including family/home responsibilities, recreation, social activity, work, and self-care and domestic activities.

It is important to remember that a range of personal, health, social, political and environmental factors influence physical functioning and disability. Patients' reporting of functional ability may be related to other issues associated with the pain problem, including patients' pain-related beliefs and ability to adjust to chronic pain, and it is generally agreed that self-report and performance-based measures of functioning seem to provide different, but complementary information.

Currently, there are few performance-based tests that are widely used for any specific pain condition. Most approaches target a particular body function (e.g. muscle and joint functions) or particular physical functions; for example, mobility and activity tests such as the six-minute walk test, timed-up-and-go test, and stair climb test. Performance-based tests like these, however, may not be relevant to the particular needs of individuals or capture disability affecting daily life activities, a primary concern for patients. Only a few studies have evaluated ADL ability in chronic pain patients, based on observation. The Assessment of Motor and Process Skills (AMPS) is an observation-based evaluation of functioning, developed to establish the extent of an individual's ability to perform and complete familiar and relevant activities of daily living (Fisher, 2006). The AMPS has been validated and used to assess ADL ability in patients with chronic widespread pain and fibromyalgia (Waehrens et al., 2010) and applied in a single study of traumatised refugees, demonstrating considerable ADL performance difficulties in these populations (Morville et al., 2014; Morville et al., 2015).

Assessing distress associated with pain

Distress – emotion – is part of the pain experience (see 'Assessing pain', above). It is also a consequence of pain and the problems it creates in everyday life, and a common effect of torture. The standard mental health categories of anxiety and depression apply, but the widely used and standardised scales for these include somatic symptoms (such as sleep problems, fatigue, restlessness) that overlap with the problems of persistent pain. This means that a straight score without considering the overlap can overestimate the extent of anxiety or depression. But there is also a risk of overlooking psychological problems during the search for a diagnosis and attempts to treat.

There are several pain-specific scales related to anxiety, but the most widely established (although not available in many languages other than European ones) is the Pain Catastrophizing Scale (PCS) (Sullivan et al., 2001; Sullivan et al., 1995). This captures the tendency to over-interpret physical symptoms as threatening, to anticipate severe problems, and to feel unable to cope with those problems, with or without help. It has 13 items, statements which the respondent rates according to how often s/he thinks like that. Clinically, it is quite demanding to include such scales (particularly when they require translation). Instead, asking what the survivor believes to be the cause of the pain, and how worrying s/he finds that, is often very helpful, uncovering fears about irreparable damage, unhealed fractures, foreign objects retained, and similar. It is important to recognise that while such problems are very rare in most clinical populations, they are more possible in torture survivors, and working with anxiety about them means being able to give convincing evidence that they are not the case.

There are no pain-specific scales for depression, and all commonly used scales in this field contain a substantial proportion of somatic items, with the risks described. It may be better to use a brief scale (e.g. PHQ-9, http://www.phqscreeners.com/select-screener; PHQ-2, Kroenke et al., 2003): the two-item version asks about recent feelings of depression and having little interest or pleasure in activities, the core symptoms in DSM and ICD taxonomies. If a generic scale is used (given that psychological screening may be done for a variety of reasons other than pain), the survivor should be asked about somatic items: does s/he have disturbed sleep because of worry, or pain, or early waking feeling low, for instance. This will help to interpret the score more accurately (see, for instance, Morley et al. (2002) on the Beck Depression Inventory (BDI)). The Hospital Anxiety and Depression Scale (HADS) (Zigmond and Snaith, 1983) is widely used in pain but is no longer recommended for separate scales of anxiety and depression, since these are unstable (Cosco et al., 2012): it provides a combined score for distress.

It is relatively common for multi-component scales to be used that combine pain with other symptoms (e.g. Symptom Checklist 90, SCL-90), and this usually arises from a model of somatisation that is entirely inappropriate in relation to pain (Williams and Johnson, 2011), based as it is on an anachronistic and dualistic conception of pain rather than the evidence-based model described above.

MANAGING POST-TORTURE PAIN

It is rare in specialised care centres/western recipient countries to see people sufficiently soon after torture that damage-specific, causal treatment with a higher likelihood of pain relief are possible. The associated acute signs and symptoms are, however, similar to those following other acute traumas causing lesions in soft tissues, joints and skeleton. While there is no a priori reason why evidence-based treatments for acute pain should not be offered with expectation of benefit to survivors of torture, considerable care should be taken not to underestimate pain and the likelihood of it becoming chronic. A recent systematic review of treatment for persistent pain from torture (Baird et al., 2017) found only three randomised controlled trials: two of psychological treatment and one physiotherapeutic, none with much benefit. There were no pharmacological trials or other medical interventions. This reflects the low level of awareness of pain in the torture rehabilitation field, as described above. Given this dearth, the best course is to provide the highest quality pain treatment, as appropriate after assessment and discussion of options with the patient, and to monitor progress, preferably with standardised tools so that outcomes can be benchmarked against published and/or local results, using N of 1 methods (Morley, 2017). It is an open question whether pain from torture responds identically in terms of treatment attempts to pain from other causes.

As is recommended for chronic pain in general, an interdisciplinary, multimodal approach to pain management in survivors of torture is optimal, with a focus on agreed goals of improved understanding, functioning and participation. A structured approach to rehabilitation therefore involves the following: identification of the problems and needs most relevant to the torture survivor; relating the problems to modifiable impairments, personal and environmental factors; and multimodal therapy delivered in a coordinated, problem-solving and individual-centred process with defined intervention targets for each professional member of the interdisciplinary team. Thus, in order to provide relevant interventions and outcomes, it is necessary to explore how the torture survivor with persistent pain experiences and prioritises activities and social participation. Interdisciplinary pain rehabilitation generally integrates education about the nature of pain, psychological interventions targeting cognitive and behavioural aspects of adaptation to pain, physical therapy with the principal goal of enhancing overall physical functioning and reducing musculoskeletal impairment caused by the torture, and pharmacological pain treatment. The torture survivor, as a refugee or as a persecuted person within his or her own country, may have considerable psychological and social problems in addition to pain and other health concerns, with uncertain accommodation and social status, as well as separation from family, friends, culture, and usual means of support and access to work. These can all interact with goals, with the resources that the survivor is able to devote to working on pain management, and affect the rate and extent of progress. Given these difficulties, language gaps and the uniqueness of the survivor's history, it can be hard to fit survivors into existing treatment regimens, and at least the initial part of treatment needs to be individualised.

It is often difficult for torture survivors to accept that the pain inflicted by torture is a permanent condition for which there is no cure, and to understand that realistic rehabilitation goals are reduction but not elimination of pain, as well as improvement in activity and societal level functioning through physical, practical and psychological skills development. It is therefore essential, before rehabilitation begins, to address the torture survivors' expectations. If negotiating a shared model of pain (as outlined above) through discussion proves very difficult, behavioural experiments may be a more helpful way forward. For some survivors, the pain they feel has an important part to play in their sense of self – as a survivor, or as a punishment for letting down those who did not survive or who have been left behind, or as a representation of the experience they and their community have been through. In such cases, pain relief may not be beneficial until some reconceptualisation has been achieved.

Psychological intervention consists of behavioural and cognitive methods, often including acceptance and mindfulness, and is best combined with physiotherapeutic guidance (rather than hands-on treatments) to help restore activities and movement despite continuing pain. All interventions aim to enable the individual with chronic pain to reverse habits of caution and avoidance that over time become the major disability. It is not asking people to 'override' pain, more to circumvent its toxic effects, particularly worry about ongoing or worsening pain that discourages activity (Crombez et al., 2012; Eccleston and Crombez, 2007; Osborn and Smith, 2006). The intervention is often delivered as a package of interventions: education and information on chronic pain and the treatment rationale; cognitive techniques to identify and change or dismiss unhelpful and often fearful ways of thinking about pain (such as that severe pain must mean something is severely wrong, and increased pain implies worsening of the condition); goal setting and steady (not pain-contingent) progress towards goals, including challenging negative predictions about activity exacerbating pain; often relaxation and stress management; and developing better awareness of the body and of unhelpful habits of move-ment. Staff (the minimum is a psychologist and a physiotherapist) are trained in working with chronic pain, and liaise closely and/or work jointly.

Evidence for efficacy is good in the sense of being consistent across many systematic reviews and meta-analyses (Williams et al., 2012), to the point where it would take a very improbable number of trials to overturn the findings (Morley et al., 2013). However, the size of change in the main outcomes of disability and distress, and to a lesser extent pain, is small, although no smaller than other conventional treatments for chronic pain. It is unclear how to increase the benefits of these methods, but simple suggestions such as discovering univariate predictors are misguided. Nor is it likely that adding more components will bring bigger changes, and they risk reducing the benefits of other components: despite its popularity in northern Europe, it may be that biofeedback results rely on equipment that when withdrawn leaves the patient with no maintainable skills (Newton-John et al., 1995). We need far more studies of how patients change during and after intervention, and probably much smarter use of electronic devices to support the maintenance and extension of treatment gains. Many torture survivors present pain problems of greater severity and often in a complex context that may undermine attempts at treatment.

Physiotherapy Informed by Modern Neuroscience

A growing number of physiotherapists are adopting contemporary pain science in their man-agement of clients with pain. In some cases this involves employing new approaches for which the evidence is still being consolidated. For other approaches to management it requires the physiotherapist to re-appraise, re-interpret and in some instances re-label strategies that had been developed and appraised with a focus on peripheral tissues only, for example graded exercise versus graded exposure, mobilisation versus body awareness.

Tactile acuity, or the ability to accurately discriminate the location of one stimulus to an adjacent other, has been found to be important in phantom limb pain. In studies examining cor-tical representations of the body, it was found there was an asymmetry in the representation of the amputated body part that corresponded to a discrepancy in tactile acuity and pain. Tactile acuity training apparently corrected the asymmetry and reduced pain by more than 60 per cent (Flor et al., 2006). The assumption is this brain retraining approach normalises or perhaps harmonises the natural order of relative symmetry in cortical representation and so central pain processing is less alarmed by the missing limb. Unfortunately the clinical utility for this treatment in other types of pain is yet to be established, in particular the duration and intensity of acuity training that is required (Moseley and Flor, 2012).

Graded Motor Imagery (GMI) adopts a graded exposure paradigm and features a process involving imagined, virtual and actual experiences that allow the central processing of danger signals to accommodate to normal movement, rather than be activated by it. An interpretation of this approach is that it involves a person working at or below the threshold point of a painful movement or activity – ensuring the person feels safe. For some people this point may be performing part of the activity. For others, performing part of the activity might be too much and so they might start with imagining a movement. GMI seeks to be more sophisticated by considering the process in terms of brain plasticity and the creators promote a sequence involving implicit motor imagery – for example right and left discrimination using images of the affected body part – explicit motor imagery – imagining movement – and mirror therapy – where a reflected image of an unaffected body part appears as the affected body part (Moseley and Flor, 2012; Wallwork et al., 2016).

While evidence for GMI is still building, the employment of psychological constructs and paradigms shows a growing trend. A special issue of the American Physical Therapy Association journal presented a series of papers on psychologically informed physiotherapy introduced by an editorial as a 'convincing case for the psychologically informed physical therapist' (Craik, 2011). While this message had been presented years earlier (Harding et al., 1994), the re-interpretation of traditional physiotherapy practice – such as graded exercise to incorporate not just graded tissue loading but graded exposure to fears about movement – along with an understanding of the neuroimmune and endocrine influences on pain, has provided the context for change in practice.

More traditional forms of manual therapy are also appropriate for treating pain in survivors of torture and, increasingly, the multimodal effects of treatments presumed to be targeting peripheral tissues are realised (Bialosky et al., 2009). Best outcomes are likely to be achieved when the practitioner is not just considering local tissue changes but also the central impacts of touch, movement and sense of safety and the impact on the body's protection systems.

This extends into movement and exercise. Prescribing movement tasks that have meaning and enjoyment rather than limited outcomes, such as improved joint movement or muscle strength, is likely to help the survivor build confidence and find her or his motivation to increase participation in life (Sullivan and Vowles, 2017; Williams, 2017). The benefits extend to the circulation of stress-buffering substances such as oxytocin and endorphin, re-oxygenation of muscles that might be normally operating in a protective pattern, and increases in movement capacity and variability.

Pharmacological Treatment

Pharmacological pain treatment is often neglected in the management of post-torture pain, and currently there are no systematic studies in this population to suggest variation from best practice. As in other pain conditions, pharmacological treatment should be based on a thorough pain assessment and identification of underlying pain mechanisms.

Pain from tissue damage (inflammatory pain) will respond to, for example, non-steroidal-anti-inflammatory-drugs (NSAIDs) whereas neuropathic pain (resulting from a lesion or disease of sensory nerves) will respond to drugs that target the altered ion channels within the nerves. Thus, peripherally targeted treatments must reflect the type of pain mechanism. However, signalling and controlling systems in the CNS appear to use common mechanisms, so that centrally acting agents have broader effects. Whatever the cause of pain, the next key stage in communication between peripheral nerves and CNS neurons is the release of transmitter into the spinal cord. Tissue and nerve trauma cause abnormal impulse propagation towards the spinal cord causing the release of more transmitter, thereby favouring central spinal hypersensitivity. Calcium channels are required for transmitter release and calcium channel levels and function are altered in different pain states. This is the target for certain anticonvulsants, more specifically those acting on α2δ subunits of calcium channels. These drugs are active in certain physiopathological states, which may be generated peripherally by neuropathic mechanisms or intense stimuli, but also in disorders of central processing such as fibromyalgia.

Blocking the generation of excitability is one approach to pain control, and this can be achieved by targeting the periphery or spinal cord, but increasing pain inhibition may also provide control of pain. Descending pain modulatory pathways influence spinal sensory processing. These projections originate from the midbrain and brainstem in predominantly monoamine systems (noradrenaline, serotonin). The actions for anti-depressant drugs in pain therefore link to these systems.

Opioids both increase descending inhibitions and reduce descending facilitations by CNS actions. All of these mechanisms are altered as pain shifts from acute to chronic. Opioids can be useful in pain control, although this is less clear for chronic non-malignant pain where there are issues with side effects, abuse potential and overdose risk from the opioid load and potential paradoxical hyperalgesia as the inhibited spinal neuronal systems compensate.

Thus, a mechanism-based approach to pharmacological intervention supports the use of centrally acting drugs in neuropathic pain and disorders of central pain processing. Guidelines on the pharmacological treatment of neuropathic pain and fibromyalgia have been proposed by several groups in recent years (Dworkin et al., 2010; Finnerup et al., 2007; Macfarlane et al., 2017). In these, certain antidepressants (including tricyclic antidepressants (TCAs) and serotonin-noradrenaline reuptake inhibitors (NSRIs) such as Duloxetine) and certain anticonvulsants (Gabapentin and Pregabalin, anticonvulsants that block calcium channels) are recommended as potential first-line treatment options. Dual acting agents (Tramadol and Tapentadol) and opioids are proposed as general second- and third-line treatment. Tramadol has been referred to as an atypical centrally acting analgesic based on its dual effects on dorsal horn neurons and descending pathways. Clinical studies support the use of Tramadol for neuropathic pain and fibromyalgia. Tapentadol is a centrally acting analgesic that demonstrates μ opioid receptor agonism and noradrenaline reuptake inhibition that may address both nociceptive and neuropathic pain mechanisms. The clinical relevance of selective serotonin inhibitors (SSRIs) in pain treatment is questionable.

The absence of a gold standard in the treatment of neuropathic pain and disorders of central processing such as fibromyalgia that is effective in all patients should be taken into account. Adherence to medical treatment is often low, and accurate information especially about side effects is therefore essential. Particular attention should be paid to the possibility that the survivor has been forcibly medicated during torture.

CONCLUSION AND SUGGESTIONS FOR FUTURE RESEARCH

There is an urgent need for better evidence on outcomes of treatment of pain in torture survivors. Their diversity and complexity make it hard to use trial methodologies that require homogeneous groups of patients, and it would be unrealistic to suggest re-testing every treatment for pain in torture survivors. It makes much better sense to use best practice according to the evidence, to assess broadly, and to analyse as single cases (Morley, 2017) that can be benchmarked against outcomes in non-tortured populations.

But a broader concern is for pain to be taken seriously by researchers in the field, recognised, assessed and treated as a problem in its own right. Left unaddressed, persistent pain may not only undermine attempts to treat other common problems such as distress and sleep disturbance, but also hinder the acquisition of self-management skills that are essential for improvement in activity and societal level functioning in order for the survivor to reach his or her potential.

REFERENCES

Amris, K (2005), 'Chronic pain in survivors of torture – psych or soma?' in Berliner, P, Arenas J and Haagensen, J (eds), *Torture and organised violence: contributions to a professional human rights response* (Dansk Psykologisk Forlag), 31–69.

Amris, K and Williams, A (2007), 'Pain Clinical Update: chronic pain in survivors of torture', *Pain Clinical Update*, 15 (7).

Apkarian, AV, Baliki, MN and Geha, PY (2009), 'Towards a theory of chronic pain', *Prog.Neurobiol.*, 87, 81–97.

Baird, E, Williams, A, C de C, Hearn, L and Amris, K (2017), 'Interventions for treating persistent pain in survivors of torture', *Cochrane.Database.Syst.Rev.*, 8, CD012051.

Bennett, M (2001), 'The LANSS Pain Scale: the Leeds assessment of neuropathic symptoms and signs', *Pain*, 92, 147–157.

Berliner, P, Mikkelsen, E, Bovbjerg, A and Wiking, M (2004), 'Psychotherapy treatment of torture survivors', *Journal of Psychosocial Rehabilitation*, 8, 85–96.

Bialosky, JE, Bishop, MD, Price, DD, Robinson, ME and George, SZ (2009), 'The mechanisms of manual therapy in the treatment of musculoskeletal pain: a comprehensive model', *Man.Ther.*, 14, 531–538.

Bouhassira, D, Attal, N, Fermanian, J, Alchaar, H, Gautron, M, Masquelier, E et al. (2004), 'Development and validation of the Neuropathic Pain Symptom Inventory', *Pain*, 108, 248–257.

Brady, B, Veljanova, I and Chipchase, L (2016), 'Are multidisciplinary interventions multicultural? A topical review of the pain literature as it relates to culturally diverse patient groups', *Pain*, 157, 321–328.

Burnett, A and Peel, M (2001), 'Asylum seekers and refugees in Britain: the health of survivors of torture and organised violence', *BMJ*, 322, 606–609.

Cleeland, CS and Ryan, KM (1994), 'Pain assessment: global use of the Brief Pain Inventory', *Ann.Acad. Med.Singapore*, 23, 129–138.

Cosco, TD, Doyle, F, Ward, M and McGee, H (2012), 'Latent structure of the Hospital Anxiety and Depression Scale: a 10-year systematic review', *J.Psychosom.Res.*, 72, 180–184.

Craik, RL (2011), 'A convincing case – for the psychologically informed physical therapist', *Phys.Ther.*, 91, 606–608.

Crombez, G, Beirens, K, Van Damme, S, Eccleston, C and Fontaine, J (2009), 'The unbearable lightness of somatization: a systematic review of the concept of somatization in empirical studies of pain', *Pain*, 145, 31–35.

Crombez, G, Eccleston, C, Van Damme, S, Vlaeyen, JW, and Karoly, P (2012), 'Fear-avoidance model of chronic pain: the next generation', *Clin.J.Pain*, 28, 475–483.

Denk, F, McMahon, SB, and Tracey, I (2014), 'Pain vulnerability: a neurobiological perspective', *Nat. Neurosci.*, 17, 192–200.

Dickenson, AH, Matthews, EA and Suzuki, R (2002), 'Neurobiology of neuropathic pain: mode of action of anticonvulsants', *Eur.J.Pain*, 6 Suppl A, 51–60.

Dülgeroglu, D (2000), *Pathology of the musculoskeletal system occurring after torture* (Rep. No. Annual Report 2000 of Humans Right Foundation of Turkey) (HRFT Publications).

Dworkin, RH, O'Connor, AB, Audette, J, Baron, R, Gourlay, GK, Haanpaa, ML et al. (2010), 'Recommendations for the pharmacological management of neuropathic pain: an overview and literature update', *Mayo Clin.Proc.*, 85, S3–14.

Eccleston, C and Crombez, G (2007), 'Worry and chronic pain: a misdirected problem solving model', Pain, 132, 233–236.

Edston, E (2005), 'Police torture in Bangladesh – allegations by refugees in Sweden', *Torture*, 15, 16–24.

El Serraj, E (1996), 'Experiences of torture and ill-treatment and posttraumatic stress disorder symptoms among Palestinian political prisoners', *Journal of Trauma and Stress*, 9, 595–606.

Finnerup, NB, Otto, M, Jensen, TS and Sindrup, SH (2007), 'An evidence-based algorithm for the treatment of neuropathic pain', *MedGenMed.*, 9, 36.

Fisher, AG (2006), *Assessment of motor and process skills: development, standardization, and administration manual*, 6th edn (vol 1) (Three Star Press).

Flor, H, Nikolajsen, L and Staehelin, J T (2006), 'Phantom limb pain: a case of maladaptive CNS plasticity?', *Nat.Rev.Neurosci.*, 7, 873–881.

Freynhagen, R, Baron, R, Gockel, U and Tolle, TR (2006), 'painDETECT: a new screening questionnaire to identify neuropathic components in patients with back pain', *Curr.Med.Res.Opin.*, 22, 1911–1920.

Generaal, E, Vogelzangs, N, Macfarlane, GJ, Geenen, R, Smit, JH, de Geus, EJ et al. (2016), 'Biological stress systems, adverse life events and the onset of chronic multisite musculoskeletal pain: a 6-year cohort study', Ann.Rheum.Dis., 75, 847–854.

Grace, PM, Hutchinson, MR, Maier, SF and Watkins, LR (2014), 'Pathological pain and the neuroimmune interface', *Nat.Rev.Immunol.*, 14, 217–231.

Haanpaa, M, Attal, N, Backonja, M, Baron, R, Bennett, M, Bouhassira, D et al. (2011), 'NeuPSIG guidelines on neuropathic pain assessment', *Pain*, 152, 14–27.

Harding, VR, Williams, AC, Richardson, PH, Nicholas, MK, Jackson, JL, Richardson, IH et al. (1994), 'The development of a battery of measures for assessing physical functioning of chronic pain patients', *Pain*, 58, 367–375.

ICF (2001), *International Classification of Functioning, Disability and Health: ICF (2001)*, 2nd edn (World Health Organization).

Jaranson, J and Quiroga, J (2011), 'Evaluating the series of torture rehabilitation programmes: history and recommendations', *Torture*, 21, 98–140.

Jensen, KB and Karoly, P (2011), 'Self-report scales and procedures for assessing pain in adults' in Turk, DC and Melzak, R (eds), *Handbook of pain assessment*, 3rd edn (Guilford Press), 19–44.

Jensen, KB, Regenbogen, C, Ohse, MC, Frasnelli, J, Freiherr, J and Lundstrom, JN (2016), 'Brain activations during pain: a neuroimaging meta-analysis of patients with pain and healthy controls', *Pain*, 157, 1279–1286.

Jones, LE and O'Shaughnessy, DF (2014), 'The pain and movement reasoning model: introduction to a simple tool for integrated pain assessment', *Man.Ther.*, 19, 270–276.

Katz, J and Seltzer, Z (2009), 'Transition from acute to chronic postsurgical pain: risk factors and protective factors', *Expert.Rev.Neurother.*, 9, 723–744.

Kehlet, H, Jensen, TS and Woolf, CJ (2006), 'Persistent postsurgical pain: risk factors and prevention', *Lancet*, 367, 1618–1625.

Konecky, B, Meyer, EC, Marx, BP, Kimbrel, NA and Morissette SB (2014), 'Using the WHODAS 2.0 to assess functional disability associated with mental disorders', *Am J Psychiatry*, 171, 818–820.

Kosek, E, Cohen, M, Baron, R, Gebhart, GF, Mico, JA, Rice, AS et al. (2016), 'Do we need a third mechanistic descriptor for chronic pain states?', *Pain*, 157, 1382–1386.

Kroenke, K, Spitzer, RL and Williams, JB (2003), 'The Patient Health Questionnaire-2: validity of a two-item depression screener', *Med.Care*, 41, 1284–1292.

Kucyi, A and Davis, KD (2015), 'The dynamic pain connectome', *Trends Neurosci.*, 38, 86–95.

Macfarlane, GJ, Kronisch, C, Dean, LE, Atzeni, F, Hauser, W, Fluss, E et al. (2017), 'EULAR revised recommendations for the management of fibromyalgia', *Ann.Rheum.Dis.*, 76, 318–328.

McBeth, J, Macfarlane, GJ, Hunt, IM and Silman, AJ (2001), 'Risk factors for persistent chronic wide-spread pain: a community-based study', *Rheumatology (Oxford)*, 40, 95–101.

McGill, SM, Hughson, RL and Parks, K (2000), 'Lumbar erector spinae oxygenation during prolonged contractions: implications for prolonged work', *Ergonomics*, 43, 486–493.

Moisander, P and Edston, E (2003), 'Torture and its sequel: a comparison between victims from six countries', *Forensic Science International*, 137, 133–140.

Moore, RA, Straube, S and Aldington, D (2013), 'Pain measures and cut-offs – "no worse than mild pain" as a simple, universal outcome', *Anaesthesia*, 68, 400–412.

Moreno, A and Grodin, M (2002), 'Torture and its neurological sequelae', *Spinal Cord*, 40, 213–223.

Morina, N, Kuenberg, A, Schnyder, U, Bryant, R, Nickerson, A and Schick, M (2017), 'The association of post-traumatic and other post-migration stress with pain and other somatic symptoms: an explorative analysis in traumatized refugees and asylum seekers', *Pain Medicine*, 19(1).

Morley, S (2017), *Single case methods in clinical psychology: a practical guide* (Oxford University Press).

Morley, S, Williams, AC and Black, S (2002), 'A confirmatory factor analysis of the Beck Depression Inventory in chronic pain', *Pain*, 99, 289–298.

Morley, S, Williams, A and Eccleston, C (2013), 'Examining the evidence about psychological treat-ments for chronic pain: time for a paradigm shift?', *Pain*, 154, 1929–1931.

Morville, AL, Amris, K, Eklund, M, Danneskiold-Samsoe, B and Erlandsson, LK (2015), 'A longitudi-nal study of changes in asylum seekers ability regarding activities of daily living during their stay in the asylum center', *J.Immigr.Minor.Health*, 17, 852–859.

Morville, A L, Erlandsson, LK, Eklund, M, Danneskiold-Samsoe, B, Christensen, R and Amris, K (2014), 'Activity of daily living performance amongst Danish asylum seekers: a cross-sectional study', *Torture*, 24, 49–64.

Moseley, GL and Flor, H (2012), 'Targeting cortical representations in the treatment of chronic pain: a review', *Neurorehabil.Neural Repair*, 26, 646–652.

Musisi, S, Kinyanda, E, Liebling, H and Mayengo-Kiziri, R (2000), 'Post-traumatic torture disorders in Uganda', *Torture*, 10, 81–87.

Newton-John, TR, Spence, SH and Schotte, D (1995), 'Cognitive-behavioural therapy versus EMG biofeedback in the treatment of chronic low back pain', *Behav.Res.Ther.*, 33, 691–697.

Norredam, M, Crosby, S, Munarriz, R, Piwowarczyk, L and Grodin, M (2005), 'Urologic complications of sexual trauma among male survivors of torture', *J Urology*, 65, 28–32.

Olsen, D, Montgomery, E, Bøjholm, S and Foldspang, S (2006a) 'Prevalent musculoskeletal pain as a correlate of previous exposure to torture', *Scand J Public Health*, 34, 496–503.

Olsen, D, Montgomery, E, Carlsson, J and Foldspang, S (2006b), 'Prevalent pain and pain level among torture survivors', *Dan Med Bull*, 53, 210–214.

Olsen, D, Montgomery, E, Bøjholm, S and Foldspang, S (2007), 'Prevalence of pain in the head, back and feet in refugees previously exposed to torture: a ten-year follow-up study', *Disability and Rehabilitation*, 29, 163–171.

Osborn, M and Smith, JA (2006), 'Living with a body separate from the self: the experience of the body in chronic benign low back pain: an interpretative phenomenological analysis', *Scand.J.Caring.Sci.*, 20, 216–222.

Patel, N, Kellezi, B and Williams, AC (2014), 'Psychological, social and welfare interventions for psychological health and well-being of torture survivors', *Cochrane.Database.Syst.Rev.*, CD009317.

Pollard, CA (1984), 'Preliminary validity study of the pain disability index', *Percept.Mot.Skills*, 59, 974.

Prip, K and Persson, A (2008), 'Clinical findings in men with chronic pain after falanga torture', *Clin J Pain*, 24, 135–141.

Prip, K, Persson, AL and Sjolund, BH (2011), 'Self-reported activity in tortured refugees with long-term sequelae including pain and the impact of foot pain from falanga – a cross-sectional study', *Disabil. Rehabil.*, 33, 569–578.

Prip, K, Persson, AL and Sjolund, BH (2012a), 'Pain when walking: individual sensory profiles in the foot soles of torture victims – a controlled study using quantitative sensory testing', *BMC.Int.Health Hum.Rights*, 12, 40.

Prip, K, Persson, AL and Sjolund, BH (2012b), 'Sensory functions in the foot soles in victims of gener-alized torture, in victims also beaten under the feet (falanga) and in healthy controls – a blinded study using quantitative sensory testing', *BMC.Int.Health Hum.Rights*, 12, 39.

Rasmussen, O (1990), 'Medical aspects of torture', *Dan Med Bull*, 37, 1–88.

Rasmussen, O, Amris, S, Blaauw, M and Danielsen, L (2005), 'Medical physical examination in connec-tion with torture: section II', *Torture*, 15, 37–45.

Savnik, A, Amris, K, Rogind, H, Prip, K, Danneskiold-Samsoe, B, Bojsen-Moller, F et al. (2000), 'MRI of the plantar structures of the foot after falanga torture', *Eur.Radiol.*, 10, 1655–1659.

Smith, C and Rowley, J (2011), 'Breathing pattern disorders and physiotherapy: inspiration for our profession', *Physical Therapy Reviews*, 16, 75–86.

Sullivan, MD and Vowles, KE (2017), 'Patient action: as means and end for chronic pain care', *Pain*, 158, 1405–1407.

Sullivan, M, Bishop, S and Pivik, J (1995), 'The pain catastrophizing scale: development and validation', *Psychological Assessment*, 7, 524–532.

Sullivan, MJ, Thorn, B, Haythornthwaite, JA, Keefe, F, Martin, M, Bradley, LA et al. (2001), 'Theoretical perspectives on the relation between catastrophizing and pain', *Clin.J.Pain*, 17, 52–64.

Tait, RC, Chibnall, JT and Kalauokalani, D (2009), 'Provider judgments of patients in pain: seeking symptom certainty', *Pain Med.*, 10, 11–34.

Tait, RC, Chibnall, JT and Krause, S (1990), 'The Pain Disability Index: psychometric properties', *Pain*, 40, 171–182.

Taylor, AM, Phillips, K, Patel, KV, Turk, DC, Dworkin, RH, Beaton, D et al. (2016), 'Assessment of physical function and participation in chronic pain clinical trials: IMMPACT/OMERACT recommen-dations', *Pain*, 157, 1836–1850.

Teodorescu, DS, Heir, T, Siqveland, J, Hauff, E, Wentzel-Larsen, T and Lien, L (2015), 'Chronic pain in multi-traumatized outpatients with a refugee background resettled in Norway: a cross-sectional study', *BMC.Psychol.*, 3, 7.

Thomsen, A, Eriksen, J and Scmidt-Nielsen, K (2000) 'Chronic pain in torture survivors', *Forensic Science International*, 108, 155–163.

Tracey, I and Bushnell, MC (2009), 'How neuroimaging studies have challenged us to rethink: is chronic pain a disease?', *J.Pain*, 10, 1113–1120.

Turk, DC and Okifuji, A (2002), 'Psychological factors in chronic pain: evolution and revolution', *J.Consult Clin Psychol.*, 70, 678–690.

Üstün, TB (2010), *Measuring health and disability: Manual for WHO disability assessment schedule WHODAS 2.0* (World Health Organization).

Waehrens, EE, Amris, K and Fisher, AG (2010), 'Performance-based assessment of activities of daily living (ADL) ability among women with chronic widespread pain', *Pain*, 150, 535–541.

Wallwork, SB, Bellan, V, Catley, MJ and Moseley, GL (2016), 'Neural representations and the cortical body matrix: implications for sports medicine and future directions', *Br.J.Sports Med.*, 50, 990–996.

Ware, JE Jr. and Sherbourne, CD (1992), 'The MOS 36-item short-form health survey (SF-36). I. Conceptual framework and item selection', *Med.Care*, 30, 473–483.

Williams, ACC (2017), 'Patient action as means and end of chronic pain care: risks and routes to mean-ingful action', *Pain*, 158, 1403–1404.

Williams, ACC and Amris, K (2017), 'Treatment of persistent pain from torture: review and commen-tary', *Med.Confl.Surviv.*, 33, 60–81.

Williams, A and Cella, M (2012), 'Medically unexplained symptoms and pain: misunderstanding and myth', *Curr.Opin.Support.Palliat.Care*, 6, 201–206.

Williams, AC and Johnson, M (2011), 'Persistent pain: not a medically unexplained symptom', *Br.J.Gen.Pract.*, 61, 638–639.

Williams, AC, Eccleston, C and Morley, S (2012), 'Psychological therapies for the management of chronic pain (excluding headache) in adults', *Cochrane.Database.Syst.Rev.*, 11, CD007407.

Williams, AC, Pena, CR, and Rice, AS (2010), 'Persistent pain in survivors of torture: a cohort study', *J.Pain Symptom.Manage.*, 40, 715–722.

Wood, BM, Nicholas, MK, Blyth, F, Asghari, A and Gibson, S (2010), 'Assessing pain in older people with persistent pain: the NRS is valid but only provides part of the picture', *J.Pain*, 11, 1259–1266.

Woolf, CJ (2011), 'Central sensitization: implications for the diagnosis and treatment of pain', *Pain*, 152, S2–15.

Woolf, CJ, Bennett, GJ, Doherty, M, Dubner, R, Kidd, B, Koltzenburg, M et al. (1998), 'Towards a mechanism-based classification of pain?', *Pain*, 77, 227–229.

Zigmond, A and Snaith, R (1983), 'The Hospital Anxiety and Depression Scale' *Acta Psychiatrica Scandinavica*, 67, 361–370.

25. Torture in the 21st century: three stories, three lessons

Yuval Ginbar

In all honesty, even Amnesty International cannot provide a reliable statistical or even overall factual assessment of torture worldwide.[1] This is because the practice of torture is too far mired in secrecy, and the extent to which it is exposed varies too widely from state to state for an attempt at such an assessment to succeed. I have therefore abandoned that original mission. Instead, the bulk of this short chapter will consist of three individual stories of torture in this century, followed by a few lessons of a more general nature that we may learn from these stories.

THE STORY OF ABU GHOSH

As'ad Abu Gosh, a resident of the Balata refugee camp in Nablus in the occupied Palestinian West Bank, was interrogated by the Israeli Security Agency (ISA), also known as Shabak, in September–October 2007. He was held incommunicado for several weeks, deprived of sleep and subjected to threats and verbal abuse. The following are excerpts from his affidavit, providing a very partial description of other interrogation methods used against him:[2]

> Several interrogators entered; the Major who I believe is known as Segal sat next to me and began to ask questions. When I did not answer he began to hit me. At first he slapped me, then with his hand clenched to a fist he punched me in the chest.
>   They returned about half an hour later. They told me that I would be subjected to a military interrogation for which they had received special permission from the Supreme Court.
>   Segal grabbed me by the front of my shirt and threw my body, my back, against the wall. This continued for some minutes and then he would throw me sideways to another interrogator, who would fling me back to Segal. They played with me like this; every time they threw me it hurt greatly. This continued for 20–30 minutes.
>   Then they seated me on a chair so that the backrest was on my left and my back was in the air. My hands were still shackled behind my back. One of them grabbed my legs and wrapped my feet around

---

[1] For a detailed description and analysis of torture and other ill-treatment under international law and standards, as well as Amnesty International's campaigning and positions on this subject see Amnesty International, *Combating torture and other ill-treatment: a manual for action*, AI Index: Index: POL 30/4036/2016 (2016), www.amnesty.org/ctm. Amnesty International's reports on the subject are too numerous to list here.
[2] Affidavit taken by Attorney Taghreed Shbeita at Sharon Prison on 18 October 2007. English translation by PCATI (with minor adjustments). Numbering omitted and footnote added.

the legs of the chair. Yoel pushed and bent my body backwards at a certain angle. He told me I must sustain this position, and that if I moved in any direction I would be beaten.[3]

I didn't last long. [...] I have back pain and suffer from disc problems; every time I moved or wanted to sit up normally, to straighten up on the chair, Segal struck my neck, arm (shoulder) and side opposite the kidneys, with his hand.

They worked with a stopwatch, looking at the watch to decide whether to change the torture methods. They explained that each method was limited to a set amount of time.

When I fell backwards sometimes, Herzl would grab my hands from behind by the handcuffs and pull them back, throwing them powerfully against the chair. So I received strong blows through the handcuffs and sometimes the hands themselves struck the chair.

They stood me up against the wall again and made me slip down so that my legs became bent at a certain angle. Once my body reached the position he decided upon, he told me that I must hold this position without moving or standing up.

Every time I moved he kneed me in the stomach.

Every time I fell down I was beaten and they would stand me up again, until the time they had allotted for this method was reached – about half an hour.

He sat me down in the chair once again and they repeated the torture method of backward bending and beating. [...]

Beating, bending backwards on the chair, standing and sliding down against the wall, crouching on the toes and blows when I fell – this continued for hours and hours until the evening.

[...] At 1a.m. they decided to put me through some new techniques:

They [Herzl and Doron] brought handcuffs. They cuffed each hand separately. Each one grabbed a hand and a handcuff and pushed with all his strength the hand he had a hold of [causing the handcuff to tighten]. Several times they tightened and pressed, each time for 5–10 minutes.

Between every backwards cuffing they would put me through the techniques I spoke about earlier. My hands became swollen and took on a blue colour.

Abu Gosh was tried in a military court, sentenced to five years' imprisonment, and released in 2012. He still suffers from, *inter alia*, anxiety, depression, apathy, difficulties falling asleep, outbursts of rage, flashbacks, memory impairment and difficulties with day-to-day functioning.[4]

When the Public Committee Against Torture in Israel brought the case to Israel's Supreme Court, the State did not deny having used what it described as 'pressure methods' and as 'violent methods'[5] – it only claimed that using those was lawful. Under a 1999 Supreme Court ruling, ISA interrogators are not authorised to use 'physical interrogation methods'. However, if they do use such methods in what the Court called 'ticking time-bomb' situations, then after the fact the Attorney-General could decide that the interrogators would not face trial, or even be subjected to a criminal investigation.[6]

Ruling on the case in 2017, the Supreme Court accepted that this was indeed a 'ticking time-bomb' situation. Moreover, setting aside an opinion by four of the world's leading

---

[3]   This method is often described as the 'banana position' and is not unique to the ISA.

[4]   See forensic evaluation report on Mr Abu Gosh by Dr Revital Arbel, Dr Bettina Birmanns and Dr Maya Mukamel, 4 July 2013, 16–17. I met Abu Gosh in the summer of 2017 and he had similar complaints.

[5]   *HCJ 5722/12 As'ad Abu Gosh et al. v. the Attorney-General et al.*, Preliminary Response on Behalf of Respondents, paras 10–11, 21–22, 41.

[6]   *HCJ 5100/94 Public Committee Against Torture in Israel v. the Government of Israel, PD 73(4) 817 (1999)*, paras 34–38.

experts on torture,[7] the Court ruled that these methods, even in combination, did not constitute torture.[8]

Not a single ISA interrogator has been criminally investigated (let alone prosecuted) for using any 'pressure methods' since the 1999 ruling. In more recent decisions, in 2019, the Court clarified further – and more honestly than in the *Abu Gosh* case, to my mind – that under current Israeli law, 'torture is prohibited, other than in very exceptional cases'.[9]

THE STORY OF 'MAINUMBY'

In 2015, Mainumby (not her real name), a girl from a poor family who had become pregnant aged 10 as a result of rape by a relative, was refused an abortion by the authorities in Paraguay. The case was described at the time by Debbie Sharnak, Amnesty International's Argentina-Paraguay country specialist.[10] I am reproducing this description with minor adjustments and additions:

> A ten-year-old girl and her mother arrived at a hospital in Asunción, Paraguay on 21 April 2015 with stomach pains. The doctors quickly discovered the cause of the discomfort – the girl was 21-weeks pregnant, the result of having been raped by her stepfather. The girl's mother had reported the rape in 2014.
>
> At such a young age, the pregnancy is considered high risk by the World Health Organization – child pregnancies are extremely dangerous for the health of the pregnant girl and may lead to complications and even death, because the bodies of young girls are not fully developed to carry a baby. In Latin America, the risk of maternal death is four times higher among adolescents younger than 16-years old.
>
> The girl's mother submitted an administrative plea to request an abortion. Paraguay, however, has some of the world's strictest abortion laws, permitting the procedure only when the mother's life is in danger. No other exceptions are allowed, even for cases of rape, incest, or an unviable foetus. Yet, even with the risk to the health and life of the girl, the Paraguayan authorities denied the girl access to a safe and therapeutic abortion. Instead, the girl was transported to a center for young mothers.
>
> UN human rights experts issued a statement condemning the conduct of the Paraguayan authorities and declaring, among other things, that 'the Paraguayan authorities' decision results in grave viola-

---

[7]   Expert opinion on the interrogation of Mr As'ad Abu Gosh in the case of *HCJ 5722/12 As'ad Abu Gosh et al. v. the Attorney-General et al.* before the Israeli Supreme Court, sitting as High Court of Justice. By Professor Sir Nigel Rodley, Professor Peter Burns, Professor Malcolm Evans and Professor Manfred Nowak. Submitted 10 February 2014, http://www.stoptorture.org.il/files/Expert%20opinion %20on%20the%20interrogation% 20of%20Mr%20As'ad%20Abu%20Gosh.pdf. I took part (working for the Public Committee Against Torture in Israel) in drafting this opinion.

[8]   HCJ 5572/12 *Abu Gosh v. the Attorney-General*, ruling of 12 December 2017.

[9]   *HCJ 9018/17 Tbeish et al v. the Attorney-General et al., Ruling of 26 November 2018*, [Concurring] Opinion of Justice David Minz, para 3. This view of Israeli law was later confirmed by the Court's Chief Justice, see *HCJ/AH 9105/18 Firas Tbeish et al. v. the Attorney-General et al.*, Decision of 25 February 2019, para 14. For a short discussion see Ben-Natan, S, 'Revise your syllabi: Israeli Supreme Court upholds authorization for torture and ill-treatment' (2019) 10(1) *J Int' Hum Legal St* 41 and Ginbar, Y, 'It's now (even more) official: torture is legal in Israel', OMCT website, 19 March 2019, http://blog.omct .org/its-now-even-more-official-torture-is-legal-in-israel/

[10]   Amnesty International USA, *Raped, pregnant and denied a life-saving abortion – all at 10 years old*, 14 May 2015, https://www.amnestyusa.org/raped-pregnant-and-denied-a-life-saving-abortion-all-at -10-years-old/

tions of the rights to life, to health, and to physical and mental integrity of the girl as well as her right to education, jeopardizing her economic and social opportunities.'[11]

The Paraguayan government resisted all pressure and forced the girl to carry her pregnancy to term, luckily surviving the birth.[12]

One legal aspect of the Paraguayan government's action was not covered by the UN experts, but was unequivocally stated in an open letter sent by Amnesty International's Secretary-General to Paraguay's President. I believe this short legal explanation warrants no further elaboration:

> The combination of the girl's powerlessness and absence of choice; her total reliance on the goodwill of the authorities; the severe pain she will suffer if she is forced to carry her pregnancy to term; and the intentional act by the authorities to coerce her into childbirth by denying her the option of abortion – based clearly on reasons of gender discrimination – *would make the girl a victim of torture*, a serious human rights violation and a crime under international law.[13] [emphasis added]

Three years later, Mainumby's mother, 'Rosana', told *The Guardian* that her daughter suffers chronic pain in her hips and waist, was self-harming, on anti-depressants, and had attempted suicide. The mother summed it up thus: 'They destroyed the girl that she was'. Her case is, unfortunately, far from unique.[14]

THE STORY OF 'RUJ'

Ruj (not his real name), a man in his twenties, was conscripted into the Thai army sometime during the late 2010s, under the country's mandatory conscription laws. The following are excerpts from his testimony, given to Amnesty International in October 2019.[15] In it Ruj describes the way he and other new recruits were treated during their basic training. The description here is very partial.

---

[11]   Office of the UN High Commissioner for Human Rights, 'Human rights: Paraguay has failed to protect a 10-year old girl child who became pregnant after being raped, say UN experts', 11 May 2015, https://www.ohchr.org/EN/NewsEvents/Pages/DisplayNews.aspx?NewsID=15944&LangID=E

[12]   Amnesty International, '11-year-old rape survivor gives birth as Paraguay upholds draconian anti-abortion law', 13 August 2015, https://www.amnesty.org/en/latest/news/2015/08/11-year-old-rape-survivor-gives-birth-as-paraguay-upholds-draconian-anti-abortion-law/

[13]   Open letter from Amnesty International's Secretary General, Salil Shetty, to the President of the Republic of Paraguay, Horacio Cartes: Urgently protect the human rights of a pregnant 10 year old girl, 15 May 2015, https://www.amnesty.org/download/Documents/Submitted%20after%202015-05-11T11%2024%2035/AMR4516582015ENGLISH.pdf

[14]   Blair, L and Carneri, S, "'It destroyed the girl she was": the toll of pregnancy on Paraguay's children', *The Guardian*, 13 July 2018, https://www.theguardian.com/global-development/2018/jul/13/destroyed-girl-she-was-toll-pregnancy-paraguay-children

[15]   And more precisely to this author (with the help of a translator, name withheld). Ruj's testimony forms part of research leading to a short Amnesty International report on the treatment of new conscripts in the Thai military.

Everything was punishments. There were two types: One to make us tired, the other to hurt us. The first was in the shape of physical exercises, the second was beatings.

Punishment exercises included 'iron fists' – where you stay in a push-up position, arms bent at an angle on bare fists. We had to do this everywhere, including on concrete floor. Once they ordered us to do this on the hot road, and we all had burns, blisters and grazes.

[…] if we stared at them, or if they envied us for any reason, they would accuse us of incitement. We'd often be divided into four groups. So they'd call an individual, or everyone in one of the groups, to strip naked. If you turned out the light it's very dark and they used it to beat people up. They would kick us, punch us. Their first rule was: not in the face or limbs – only on the torso. They don't want anything to be seen. I personally was beaten in this way, while naked. It happened a lot.

In the bathing area, before we washed [while naked] they ordered us to lie down behind each other, so your nose would be between the butt-cheeks of the next person. Then the trainer[16] told us to inhale through our noses on his command and repeated this time and time again – it was entertainment for them […] this happened several times.

They also made us do the 'train' – to hold each other's penis[17] and walk around the water container. We needed to put our hand under the butt of the person before us to reach his penis … It happened maybe 3–4 times a week.

If two conscripts were caught fighting they would be told to kiss each other, stick out their tongues and rub them together. Sometimes when people fought they were told to roll in the bath area together, naked.

When we take lessons at night most of the people would be in the dorm areas, four of us would be assigned to guard the two dorm areas. One time I was guarding with another person, and a senior asked me: do you like even or odd numbers? I gave the wrong answer. He ordered me to enter an empty room. Then he asked: do you like Japanese porn or Western porn? Then he forced me to masturbate. That was the first time – they did this to us constantly.

Every soldier was given a small box of condoms, to prevent STDs. One day the senior was asking me questions in front of the dorm that I was guarding. Then he took my condoms from me. I was confused – I was picked in the draw as I gave the 'wrong' answer to the question but instead of being taken to a room and having to masturbate he just took my condom. But then he took a conscript who was a ladyboy and went inside a room to have sex with the him. I'm not sure where the ladyboy was called from.

Some of the conscripts were gay, but there was a power dynamic. Even if the trainer or sergeant asks for sex there's no way to say no to them. Whatever they told us we had to do.

Ruj is now a civilian. He has moved on. But at times he found it hard to tell us his story – his voice would shake or stop altogether, he stared into space, he needed breaks, but he insisted on telling everything.

All these types of torture and other ill-treatment described by Ruj, were reported consistently by other conscripts who spoke to us, having undergone basic training in a variety of bases serving a variety of military units during different periods between 2016 and 2019.

LESSONS

It would be futile to claim that the three torture stories above encapsulate everything there is to know about torture in the 21st century. And yet I believe they do carry some general lessons

---

[16]   'Trainer' and 'senior' refer to longer-serving conscripts who served as low-level commanders. Under the UN Convention against Torture's definition they would clearly qualify as 'officials'.

[17]   Meaning, each held the penis of the conscript in front of him and that of the one behind – as clarified from other testimonies.

for our approach to, and fight against, torture and other ill-treatment as this century enters its second decade.

The first lesson is that while we must continue exploring innovative ways of understanding, interpreting and preventing torture, we should be careful not to focus solely on the new. Rather, we would be wise to bear in mind the continued validity of these longstanding truths:

- That torture prevails in 'classic' contexts such as punishment or the interrogation of detainees, as do efforts to legitimise and legalise it.
- That the most prevalent form of torture is not sophisticated 'enhanced interrogation' methods using hi-tech gear or advanced psychology. Rather, it is the simple, straightforward, often ignored or downplayed method of beatings, where officials use either their hands and feet or sticks, batons or whatever is available to inflict intolerable pain. Such beatings constitute torture either on their own (when severe) or in combination with other forms, such as in the ISA's interrogation centres, or in the basic military training camps of Thailand.
- That those who bear the brunt of torture and other ill-treatment are neither dangerous terrorists nor famous opposition politicians. Most victims are tortured for being poor. A rich 'Rosana' would have taken her daughter abroad to undergo a safe, discrete, humane abortion and then resume her life as a child. And in the Thai army – we've learned – as well as practically everywhere in the world, the richer you are the less likely you are to be tortured.

The second lesson is that, the above notwithstanding, it is thanks to our expanding understanding of the gender dimensions of torture that we can firmly place within the torture legal framework not only Mainumby's treatment by officials but also (due to failure to exercise due diligence) her rape, as well as the rape and other sexual torture that Ruj and fellow new conscripts in Thailand's military have suffered.

The third lesson is about prevention, a crucial topic which so far I have appeared to ignore. Amnesty International often speaks about the need for states to implement changes 'in law, policy and practice'. But at the root of practices of torture and other ill-treatment lies, I believe, a problem of culture. Torture remains – as it has always been – inextricably linked to dehumanisation within societies, in its myriad forms. These include, among many others, racism, sexism, misogyny, homophobia, contempt for persons with disabilities, hatred and fear of minorities, and the many ways of dehumanising others that almost invariably accompany poverty as well as other human-made ills such as war and occupation. Officials torturing a detainee, a pregnant girl, a new army conscript or anyone else, represent a culture that nullifies certain people, and in doing so legitimises turning their bodies and minds, their pain and suffering, into tools for bringing about some other purpose, whether couched in terms of the fight against terrorism, the perceived right to life of a foetus or the need to turn civilians into soldiers.

It is virtually impossible to torture someone you consider your equal, your fellow human. So alongside the extremely useful and detailed means of preventing torture developed by UN bodies, NGOs and other experts, this reflection suggests that we firmly place listening to, sharing, and magnifying victims' and survivors' voices and stories as an essential method, not only of documenting or reporting torture but of torture prevention itself. I believe these voices and stories are indispensable if we are to 'rehumanise' torture victims, and together with them erect a truly human shield against future inhumanity.

26. Torture today

Tom Porteous

The prohibition against torture is a fundamental principle of international law. Unlike most other human rights, it is non-derogable and absolute: it allows no exceptions whatsoever. It remains valid in armed conflict as well as in peacetime. No national or public emergency or imminent terrorism threat, however acute, justifies the use of torture. The prohibition not only requires states to prohibit and criminalize torture, it also includes other important provisions intended to strengthen the prohibition in practice.

Despite the prohibition, in over forty years of monitoring human rights abuses around the world, Human Rights Watch has documented thousands of cases of torture in myriad situations in both authoritarian and democratic states. While international treaties and mechanisms against torture may have increased in this period, torture remains an all-too-shameful blot on humanity.

The motivation for torture and its circumstances vary. Some perpetrators, in authoritarian states, use torture routinely and flagrantly as a tool of repression, punishment and deterrence. Others, particularly in democracies, hide it behind legal euphemisms and denials, or when caught out claim that it is the work of rogue officials. In some contexts, perpetrators justify torture as necessary to obtain intelligence required to prevent the enemy from carrying out atrocities. In others, law enforcement personnel use it as a routine means of extracting confessions and securing convictions.

Torture is often likely to be found where there is acute political crisis, repression, or armed conflict, or some combination of these. For years, Human Rights Watch had documented widespread torture in Syria under the repressive governments of both President Bashar al-Assad and his father Hafiz al-Assad. But after armed conflict broke out in 2011, triggered by the violent suppression of protests against police brutality, there was an explosion of torture at the hands of almost all parties to the conflict, including government forces and anti-government armed groups. Tens of thousands of individuals, including children as young as 13, have passed through Syrian government detention facilities, a kind of torture archipelago where extreme ill-treatment is almost inevitable. Many have died as a result of the torture and inhumane conditions inside these facilities.[1]

In Egypt, torture and police brutality were also among the underlying grievances of the protesters who took to the streets in January 2011. Torture, including forced virginity tests for women detained at protests, was also a key part of the government's response. The protests led to the removal of President Hosni Mubarak and elections that brought the Muslim Brotherhood to power. But that brief democratic interlude was swiftly overthrown in a violent military coup that returned Egypt to an even greater political repression than Mubarak's.

---

[1] *Torture Archipelago: Arbitrary Arrests, Torture and Enforced Disappearances in Syria's Underground Prisons since March 2011* (Human Rights Watch, 2012).

Torture and ill-treatment in Egypt's prisons, police stations and unofficial detention sites is on such a scale that it may amount to a crime against humanity.[2]

Turkey is another country with a historical record of torture, including the torture of children, especially in the context of the period after the September 12, 1980 military coup d'état and the long-running armed conflict with the Kurdistan Workers Party (PKK). President Recep Tayyip Erdogan's crackdown following the failed coup against him in 2016, which the government blamed on the influential Fethullah Gülen movement, was accompanied by an increase in incidents of torture.[3]

The escalation of the violent crisis in Cameroon's Anglophone regions since late 2016 has led to an increase in the use of torture by both government forces and armed separatist groups. Human Rights Watch research has found that government forces tortured hundreds of suspected separatists and other detainees in several detention facilities, including the State Defense Secretariat (SED), the Headquarters of the National Gendarmerie in the capital, Yaoundé. Armed separatists have also tortured scores of civilians across the Anglophone regions and some of these abuses have been caught on camera.[4]

Marginalized groups are often at greatest risk of torture. Migrants and refugees are particularly vulnerable. In Libya, traffickers, smugglers, armed groups and detention centre guards have used torture to control, manipulate and extort money from migrants and refugees seeking to reach Europe. Human Rights Watch researchers who visited detention centres for migrants in Libya in 2018 found that almost all those they interviewed, including children, said they had experienced some form of ill-treatment or torture.[5]

Besides migrants and refugees, other marginalized groups vulnerable to torture include religious and ethnic minorities such as the Uyghurs in China, the Kurds in Turkey, Shi'a Muslims in Saudi Arabia, and the Rohingya in Myanmar, as well as LGBT people in countries such as Uganda, Zimbabwe, and Lebanon and in the Republic of Chechnya in Russia.

Sexual and gender-based violence remains endemic across the world and is perpetrated by both state actors (a recent example is the alleged torture and sexual abuse of detained women's rights activists in Saudi Arabia) and private individuals. Domestic violence is a particularly grave and pervasive problem worldwide: where it does not lead to outright murder or suicide, it often rises to the level of torture. Human Rights Watch has extensively documented governments' failures to adequately prevent such violence, protect survivors, and prosecute abusers.

Law enforcement officials in many states practice torture routinely within the criminal justice system as a means of obtaining confessions for prosecutions. Victims are most vulnerable in the period immediately after arrest when detainees may not have access to lawyers, independent medical examiners, or family members who can raise the alarm about potential ill-treatment. In some cases, authorities at first often deliberately hold suspects incommunicado, perhaps in unofficial detention facilities, specifically in order to circumvent protections

---

[2]   'Egypt: Torture Epidemic May Be Crime Against Humanity', Human Rights Watch news release, 6th September 2017.

[3]   *In Custody: Police Torture and Abductions in Turkey* (Human Rights Watch, 2017).

[4]   'Cameroon: Routine Torture, Incommunicado Detention', Human Rights Watch news release, 6th May 2019.

[5]   *'No Escape from Hell': EU Policies Contribute to Abuse of Migrants in Libya* (Human Rights Watch, 2019).

against torture that may exist and give police interrogators time to extract confessions and information under torture.

In Mexico according to a survey of more than 64,000 people incarcerated in 338 prisons located throughout the country in 2016, 64 percent of the prison population reported having suffered some type of physical violence at the time of their arrest: 19 percent reported receiving electrical shocks; 36 percent being choked, held underwater, or smothered; and 59 percent being hit or kicked. In addition, 28 percent reported that they were threatened that their family would be harmed.[6]

In India, despite the rapid economic modernization of recent years, police continue to use antiquated and often brutal methods, including torture, as part of their daily law enforcement routine. According to the government's own figures, almost 600 people died in police custody between 2010 and 2015. While the official record states that only six of these deaths were due to physical assault by the police, evidence collected by Human Rights Watch and others suggests that many of these deaths were in fact the result of torture, as is alleged by the families of victims.[7]

If regional powers – and democratic ones at that – like India and Mexico are setting a poor example when it comes to torture, the big powers are not doing much better. Torture has long been a key tool in China's authoritarian toolbox and the China's economic success and ascent to superpower status has done nothing to change that. Whether the Chinese authorities are stepping up the repression of 13 million Turkic Muslims in the northwestern region of Xinjiang, continuing decades-old repression in Tibet, or persecuting human rights defenders and other civil society actors, torture remains a constant feature of China's iron-fisted approach to maintaining the Communist Party's political control.

In Russia, the Communist Party may have lost power with the fall of the Soviet Union, but torture and other ill-treatment remain widespread, especially in pre-trial detention and prisons. In 2018, a leaked video of penitentiary officials viciously beating a prisoner in a penal colony in Yaroslavl, 266 kilometers from Moscow, sparked a wave of public indignation so strong that in an unprecedented move, the leadership of the country's penitentiary service publicly apologized and promised full accountability for all the staff involved. Over a dozen staff are currently standing trial for abuse of official powers. However, in many other cases authorities continue to deny ill-treatment and refuse to prosecute and hold the perpetrators accountable.[8]

As for the United States, it subverted the image it once sought to project as a global champion of human rights when, after the attacks on the World Trade Center and Pentagon on September 11, 2001, the Bush administration secretly opted to use 'enhanced interrogation techniques' on terrorist suspects in US custody. Many of these techniques, including waterboarding, long-term standing, sleep deprivation, and stress positions, were clear acts of torture. US officials used such methods against hundreds of suspects at Guantanamo and other detention facilities around the world. As part of the US government's secret rendition program they also frequently delivered terrorism suspects into the custody of officials of other states for the express purpose of extracting information from them under torture. The failure of the sub-

[6] *Human Rights Watch World Report 2019: Mexico* (Human Rights Watch, 2019).
[7] *'Bound by Brotherhood': India's Failure to End Killings in Police Custody* (Human Rights Watch, 2016).
[8] Lokshina, T, 'A Torture Scandal Makes Russia Pay Attention', *Open Democracy*, 16th August 2018.

sequent Obama administration to criminally investigate anyone for the CIA's torture program was not only a dereliction of the US's obligations under international law, it also effectively signaled that torture remains a policy option for the US.[9]

Donald Trump, both during his campaign and after he entered the White House as president, indicated not only that he thinks torture works but that he would authorize it were he advised to do so by his subordinates. He has failed to criticize dictators with whom he has become friendly for their abusive practices, including torture, which sends the message that the US has no serious objections to the practice. Trump underlined this same message with the appointment of Gina Haspel as director of the CIA in 2018. Haspel ran a CIA detention center in Thailand where she oversaw torture, and in 2005 helped to destroy videotaped evidence of CIA torture.[10]

If only we could say with confidence that the European Union remained the staunch champion of the prohibition on torture that it once claimed to be. Unfortunately, we cannot. Many EU states were complicit in the CIA's rendition program. Some of the 'black sites' where US officials interrogated terrorism suspects were even located in the territory of EU member states. Efforts to establish the full truth about the extent of complicity or who authorized it have been frustrated across the region. One area of relief though is the European Court of Human Rights, which has ordered several countries, including Poland, Romania, Italy, Lithuania, and Macedonia to compensate victims of their complicity in US-led torture and secret detention. In the UK, despite inquiries which have established that British troops tortured people in custody in Iraq, investigations have not led to prosecutions. On the contrary, they have fed a right-wing populist press and political agenda claiming that former soldiers are the victims of persecution by lawyers and should not be prosecuted.

The prevalence of torture in the world today presents a bleak outlook. Positive signs are few but nonetheless instructive. In Tunisia, while some of the reforms launched following the democratic revolution of 2011 have stalled, serious if slow progress continues towards securing judicial accountability for human rights abuses, including torture, perpetrated by state officials under the previous authoritarian government. In Ethiopia there have been steps in the right direction since Prime Minister Abiy Ahmed was sworn in in 2018. While no officials have been held accountable for torture, the government has acknowledged its use, closed some detention centers associated with the abuse, and promised to reform repressive laws. Such developments point to a simple truth: that in authoritarian states that rely on torture as a tool of political repression and control the only realistic path to ending torture is the dismantling of the repressive state through political reform, and usually a change of political leadership. International mechanisms can play a supporting role in the lead-up to this process and during the transition, for example through monitoring, maintaining international diplomatic pressure, and on rare occasions bringing the tools of international justice to bear against the worst offenders.

In states which do not rely on torture as a tool of repression but where torture is nonetheless used as a short-cut to criminal prosecutions or is seen as necessary to deal with a national threat, the path to ending torture is different. Here the goal should be to ensure meticulous adherence to all the provisions of the prohibition against torture outlined elsewhere in this

---

[9]   *Letter to President Obama re: CIA torture*, Human Rights Watch, 16th June 2016.
[10]   'US: Haspel Vote Sends Wrong Message on Torture', Human Rights Watch news release, 17th May 2018.

volume. In this endeavor international mechanisms can play a useful role in raising awareness, exerting pressure and providing advice and expertise. But the main burden lies on the shoulders of national actors: the executive and law enforcement agencies to enforce and obey the law; parliaments to scrutinize policies and laws and hold the executive to account; the courts to ensure accountability and fair trials for perpetrators and redress and compensation for victims; national human rights institutions to monitor places of detention and ensure adequate safeguards against torture are in place; and civil society and the media to engage the public, raise awareness, and investigate failures in the political system that allow torture to occur. In other words, to stop torture we need functioning democracies that take human rights seriously. In the face of authoritarian populist movements which explicitly devalue human rights, defending such a vision of democracy is more urgent than ever.

27. Some reflections on torture prevention

Barbara Bernath

Preventing torture and ill-treatment is a legal obligation[1] but 'there is more to torture prevention than compliance with legal commitments'.[2] 'Torture prevention is not asking what happened and how it happened, but asking why it happens and how we can stop it'.[3] The focus is on reducing the likelihood of torture by identifying and addressing factors that increase the risk of torture and ill-treatment. This is why, given that torture happens in secret, the Association for the Prevention of Torture (APT) has promoted and supported the creation of a system of unannounced visits by independent preventive bodies to all places of deprivation of liberty. With the 2002 Optional Protocol to the UN Convention against Torture (OPCAT), this is now a global reality.[4] Going beyond monitoring and visits to places of detention, the first part of this reflection presents some positive contributions made by the preventive approach to the fight against torture, while the second part focuses on the remaining challenges. It shows that preventing torture is more than a series of legal measures; it is a mindset that promotes pragmatism to address risks and root causes, based on a multidisciplinary and cooperative approach.

TORTURE PREVENTION WORKS

Does torture prevention work?[5] is an independent study commissioned by the APT that was published in 2016. It covers a period of 30 years (1984–2014) and 16 countries[6] and is based on a methodology combining qualitative and quantitative analysis. The lead researchers,

---

[1]   Convention against Torture and Other Cruel, Inhuman or Degrading Treatment or Punishment (adopted 10 December 1984, entered into force 26 June 1987) 1465 UNTS 85, Article 2 provides that 'Each State Party shall take effective legislative, administrative, judicial and other measures to prevent acts of torture in any territory under its jurisdiction'. See also UN Committee Against Torture, General Comment no 2, Implementation of Article 2 by States parties, UN Doc CAT/C/GC/2 (24 January 2008).

[2]   'The approach of the Subcommittee on Prevention of Torture to the concept of prevention of torture and other cruel, inhuman or degrading treatment or punishment under the Optional Protocol to the Convention against Torture and Other Cruel, Inhuman or Degrading Treatment or Punishment', CAT/OP/12/6 (2010), para 3.

[3]   Rodriguez, V, in The Global Forum on the OPCAT, *Preventing Torture, Upholding Dignity: From Pledges to Actions. Outcome Report* (Association for the Prevention of Torture, 2012). Rodriguez is a former member and Chairperson of the United Nations Subcommittee for the Prevention of Torture.

[4]   Optional Protocol to the Convention Against Torture and Other Cruel, Inhuman or Degrading Treatment of Punishment (adopted 18 December 2002, in force 22 June 2006) 2375 UNTS 237. There are 90 State Parties to the OPCAT at the time of writing.

[5]   Carver, R and Handley, L, *Does Torture Prevention Work?* (Liverpool University Press, 2016). See also Chapter 3 of this volume.

[6]   These being Argentina, Chile, Ethiopia, Georgia, Hungary, India, Indonesia, Israel, Kyrgyzstan, Norway, Peru, the Philippines, South Africa, United Kingdom, Tunisia and Turkey.

Richard Carver and Lisa Handley, developed an index on the prevalence of torture and measured its correlation with a set of preventive measures, grouped into four clusters: detention,
prosecution, monitoring and complaints. For all these groups, the researchers looked at the
measures both in law and in practice.

The first finding is that a decrease of torture was observed in the countries over the study
period and that 'a general decline in the incidence of torture has probably occurred beyond the
16 countries studied'.[7] This reduction is in itself a positive finding, even if it should not give
rise to complacency, as cases of torture and ill-treatment still occur in many parts of the world.
More importantly, the research provides for the first time academic evidence that torture preventive measures are effective in reducing the risk of torture.

Concrete and Practical Measures Are Effective

The research shows that the highest correlation between preventive measures and the incidence of torture is seen when safeguards are applied in practice from the first hours of deprivation of liberty. The following measures are found to be the most effective in reducing torture:
the prohibition of incommunicado detention; the immediate notification of family about the
arrest; access to a lawyer and their presence during questioning; medical examination by an
independent physician; and video recording interrogations. These procedural safeguards aim
at addressing one of the main causes of torture and ill-treatment: secrecy and isolation, confirming 'that torture happened to people when they were held at the sole mercy of their captors
and interrogators (incommunicado detention). The longer they were denied access to and from
the outside world (i.e., to family, lawyers, doctors, courts) the more they were vulnerable to
abuse by those wishing to obtain information or confessions from them'.[8]

The research also highlights the gap between law and practice. In the majority of countries
studied, safeguards are provided for in the legislation but are not fully implemented in practice.[9] However, some of the safeguards are procedural in nature, not necessarily costly and do
not require complex legal reform but rather a change in practices. Notification of family immediately after arrest is an example of a measure that can be implemented rather easily, at almost
no cost and is effective in reducing the risks of abuse. Another example is the introduction of
a letter of rights, informing those deprived of their liberty of their rights in plain and accessible
language.[10] Such a measure not only empowers the detained persons but also contributes to the
effective exercise of their rights, thus bridging the gap between law and practice.

---

[7]   Carver and Handley (n 5 above), 46.
[8]   Rodley, NS, 'Reflections on Working for the Prevention of Torture' (2009) 6 *Essex Human Rights Law Review* 21, 21.
[9]   Carver and Handley (n 5 above), 52. See also *Yes, Torture Prevention Works – Insights from a Global Research Study on 30 Years of Torture Prevention* (Association for the Prevention of Torture, 2016).
[10]   Directive 2012/13/EU of the European Parliament and of the Council of 22nd May 2012 on the right to information in criminal proceedings, Article 22; African Guidelines on Conditions of Arrest, Police Custody and Pre-Trial Detention in Africa (Luanda Guidelines), Article 5.

Focusing on High-risk Areas: Moving Away from Confession-based Systems

Carver and Handley's research, both the statistical and the country chapters, also shows that one of the major causes of torture and ill-treatment lies in an over-reliance on confessions in the criminal justice system. 'Questioning, in particular of suspects, is inherently associated with risks of intimidation, coercion and mistreatment',[11] but when a premium is placed on confessions, the risk of ill-treatment and coercion is increased.[12]

Accordingly, and following a call by the former Special Rapporteur on Torture,[13] the APT is co-leading, together with the Anti-Torture Initiative and the Norwegian Centre for Human Rights, the development of international guidelines to move away from confession-based systems. The guidelines promote non-coercive police questioning based on investigative interviewing techniques, combined with the implementation of legal and procedural safeguards from the outset of deprivation of liberty.[14] The objective of these guidelines is to provide States, law enforcement agencies, training academies and judicial actors with a policy tool. This will increase the professionalism of law enforcement by providing new means of collecting reliable information, while respecting human rights. Ultimately, it will contribute to better access to justice and safer societies.

A Multidisciplinary Approach to Torture and Ill-treatment

Prevention of torture, in particular monitoring places of detention, requires a multidisciplinary approach and adequate representation from within society in order to enable an inclusive look at detention issues, while accounting for the specific needs of persons in situations of vulnerability. Article 18(2) of the OPCAT mentions the need for National Preventive Mechanisms (NPMs) to strive for 'gender balance and adequate representation of ethnic and minority groups in the country'. In addition, the United Nations Subcommittee on Prevention of Torture (SPT) has underlined the fact that 'Prevention is a multifaceted and interdisciplinary endeavour. It must be informed by the knowledge and experience of those from a wide range of backgrounds – e.g. legal, medical, educational, religious, political, policing and the detention system'.[15] It is positive to see that the majority of NPMs include a diversity of professional expertise in their visiting teams and include at least health professionals in addition to human rights lawyers. Some NPMs go beyond diversity of professional background to include personal experience. In the United Kingdom, the Care Quality Commission includes 'experts by experience' in the visiting team, i.e. persons who have experienced placement in psychiatric institutions. This enables NPMs to take into account the specific needs of persons in situations of vulnerability.

---

[11]   *Report of the Special Rapporteur on Torture and Other Cruel, Inhuman or Degrading Treatment or Punishment*, UN Doc A/HRC/71/298 (2016), para 8.
[12]   *Ibid*, para 11. See also 28th General Report on the CPT's Activities (2018), CPT/Inf (2019) 9, para 73.
[13]   See generally the *Report of the Special Rapporteur on Torture and Other Cruel, Inhuman or Degrading Treatment or Punishment*, UN Doc A/HRC/71/298 (2016).
[14]   See https://www.apt.ch/en
[15]   'The approach of the Subcommittee on Prevention of Torture to the concept of prevention of torture and other cruel, inhuman or degrading treatment or punishment under the Optional Protocol to the Convention against Torture and Other Cruel, Inhuman or Degrading Treatment or Punishment' (n 2 above), para 5(i).

Going beyond a merely legal approach to torture and ill-treatment is also key in other areas. A multidisciplinary approach is at the heart of the drafting of 'Guidelines on Non-Coercive Interviewing and Associated Safeguards' by the APT and others, considered above. The Steering Committee leading the process is composed of experts from different fields: police officers, human rights lawyers, researchers and health professionals including psychiatrists. Such an approach enables the building of bridges among disciplines and experts. More importantly, however, it also enables a blending of positive experiences from law enforcement on investigative interviewing on the one hand and the human rights field regarding safeguards on the other hand.

CHALLENGES TOWARDS A MORE INTEGRATED APPROACH IN THE FIGHT AGAINST TORTURE

Identifying factors that increase the risk of torture and ill-treatment requires on-going analysis, as well as vigilance and the ability to adapt. Torture and ill-treatment are constantly evolving in terms of methods employed, the locations where it takes place and the persons at risk, and over time.[16]

Addressing Risks Beyond Detention

Anti-torture actors and preventive bodies need to be proactive and innovative in looking beyond detention to address the risks of torture and ill-treatment outside custody, in the street or in public places. 'Street vendors, the homeless, sex workers or the unemployed, as well as members of ethnic, sexual or religious minorities, as they go about their everyday lives, routinely experience violent harassment by police officers and other public authorities that easily tip into torture, but never get anywhere near a police station or jail'.[17]

The use of force outside of custody and the use of firearms, including 'less lethal' weapons,[18] constitute 'grey zones' as they are not necessarily illegal per se but come with a risk of passing the acceptable threshold and becoming excessive. From a preventive perspective, the existence of a high risk of torture and ill-treatment is sufficient to take action upstream rather than analyze later whether the principles of 'legality, necessity, proportionality or precaution' have been respected. In some countries, National Preventive Mechanisms (NPMs) have started to implement their mandate creatively to address these issues. In Argentina, the Local Preventive Mechanism of the Province of Salta has decided to focus its efforts on police emergency interventions (911), a high-risk situation for abuse and ill-treatment. Based on an agreement with the police authorities, the mechanism is informed about interventions and is able to be present at random to observe police interventions. This mere presence and observation acts

---

[16]   'Corruption and torture or ill-treatment are best understood as two concurrent effects of the same original cause, namely a failure of the surrounding governance system to prevent the rise and exercise of unchecked powers', *Report of the Special Rapporteur on Torture and Other Cruel, Inhuman or Degrading Treatment or Punishment*, A/HRC/40/59 (2019), para 48.

[17]   Kelly, T, 'The Struggle Against Torture: Challenges, Assumptions and New Directions' (2019) 11 *Journal of Human Rights Practice* 324.

[18]   See Special Rapporteur on Torture, *Report on Extra-custodial Use of Force and the Prohibition of Torture and Other Cruel, Inhuman or Degrading Treatment or Punishment*, A/72/178 (2017).

as a deterrence. The number of complaints against the police during emergency interventions decreased initially by 40 percent and later by 70 percent.[19] In other countries, such as Austria, Chile and Bolivia, NPMs are also monitoring public demonstrations that entail risks of abuse and ill-treatment by law enforcement. Addressing risks beyond detention needs to be strengthened in order to avoid possible 'shifts' of torture and ill-treatment as a response to increased monitoring of places of detention.

Better Analysis of Root Causes

Focusing on factors that increase the risk of torture and ill-treatment is a positive development. There is a need, however, to go further and deepen the capacity to understand and address root causes in terms of social, political contexts and societies' access to justice, equality and respect for non-discrimination. 'It is often the fundamental failure to accord equal dignity that underpins the use of torture'.[20] One way forward is to build bridges with other areas of international work. A positive illustration of this development is the attention given to the interrelations between torture and corruption that 'have long been addressed in both academia and policy circles as two separate domains of knowledge and practice – as examples of gross human rights violations or bad governance respectively'.[21] This is now changing. In 2013 the SPT devoted a section of its Annual Report to torture and corruption;[22] in 2018 Human Rights Council resolution 37/19 considered 'the negative impact of corruption on the right to be free from torture' and the 2019 report of the Special Rapporteur on torture also explored the connections between them.[23] Both address the causal interactions between the two phenomena and the need for effective preventive measures that address torture, as well as corruption. Such a holistic approach aimed at addressing root causes and promoting synergies is at the heart of the 2030 Agenda commitment to peaceful, just and inclusive societies. The roadmap for the implementation of the Sustainable Development Goal 16+ and its transformative strategies to 'invest in prevention', 'transform institutions' and 'include and empower people' represent an opportunity to build stronger synergies among anti-torture actors and within the UN system. In the end, this will help address the root causes of torture and ill-treatment and contribute to societies that are 'free from fear and violence'.[24]

---

[19]   https://www.apt.ch/en/news_on_prevention/torture-prevention-mechanisms-make-headway-in-reducing-the-risks-of-torture-in-the-first-hours-of-detention-in-latin-america

[20]   Munasinghe, V and Celemajer, D, 'Acute and Everyday Violence in Sri Lanka' (2017) 47(4) *Journal of Contemporary Asia* 615.

[21]   Jensen, S and Anderson, MK, *Corruption and Torture: Violent Exchange and the Policing of the Urban Poor* (Aalborg University Press, 2017), 5.

[22]   'Corruption and prevention of torture and other ill-treatment', 7th Annual Report of the Subcommittee on Prevention of Torture and Other Cruel, Inhuman or Degrading Treatment or Punishment, 2013, UN Doc CAT/C/52/2, paras 72–100.

[23]   *Report of the UN Special Rapporteur on Torture*, 2019 (n 16 above). The link between torture and corruption is also included in the Swiss Federal Department of Foreign Affairs Action Plan against Torture and 'Switzerland is committed to ensuring a human-rights based approach to anti-corruption efforts' (2018), 6.

[24]   See *Delivering the 2030 Agenda Commitment to Peaceful, Just and Inclusive Societies – The Roadmap for Peaceful, Just and Inclusive Societies – A Call to Action to Change our World* (Pathfinders, 2019).

Communicating More Creatively to Regain Public Opinion

In the current political environment with the rise of authoritarian regimes, human rights in general and the fight against torture in particular, are under attack. Political discourse, reinforced by TV series and Hollywood movies, are presenting torture as a 'necessary evil' to protect society's security. This worrying trend towards a 'banalization' of this scourge requires a strong, united and creative counter-communication from all anti-torture actors. This is easier said than done. It would require imagination and cooperation with actors in the field of culture. The Malaysian-led campaign 'Cartoonists against torture'[25] is an interesting initiative that could serve as an inspiration for others.

CONCLUSION: HOLISTIC APPROACHES AND JOINED UP FORCES

With the OPCAT system in place, the UN Subcommittee as well as NPMs in all regions of the world are able to have access at any time to any place where persons are or may be deprived of liberty. Access has a deterrent effect and Carver and Handley's research confirms that unannounced visits and the capacity to conduct interviews in private contribute to reducing the risks of torture. Moreover, NPMs – providing they are independent and adequately resourced – have the potential to reduce the risks of torture and ill-treatment and address some of the challenges mentioned above. Thanks to their reports, recommendations and dialogue with the authorities, preventive bodies contribute to changing laws and practices. Further interaction and cooperation with other actors, including with civil society organizations, will strengthen NPMs' capacity as actors for change.

Torture prevention is effective in reducing the risks of torture and ill-treatment. It is worth investing in prevention, which is needed everywhere and at all times. However, only a comprehensive strategy, combining prevention with accountability, redress and rehabilitation, and the complementary efforts of all actors, from the international and regional organizations, as well as civil society organizations, will be effective in realizing the promise of a torture-free world. 'Against the cancer of torture that is attacking our civilisation, there is no panacea, but a series of remedies, all insufficient by themselves but that – far from counteracting each other – shall reinforce each other'.[26]

---

[25] *Cartoonists Against Torture – A Comic and Artwork Collection* (Human Rights Commission of Malaysia, 2019).
[26] See Jean-Jacques Gautier in *La Vie Protestante* (1976) considered in Haenni, C, *20 Ans Consacrés à la realisation d'une Idée* (Association for the Prevention of Torture, 1997).

Index

ticking bomb justification *see* ticking bomb
     scenario
UNCAT prohibition 15
Universal Protocol for Investigative
     Interviewing (UN) 52, 86, 170, 171
by US agents *see* enhanced interrogation
     programme (Bush administration)
investigation of torture complaints 13–14, 52–3,
     56, 65
     complaints mechanisms *see* complaints
          mechanisms
     by doctors *see* Istanbul Protocol
          (medico-legal evidence of torture
          guidelines)
     right to effective remedy *see* right to
          effective remedy
     state obligations 198, 466–8
     universal jurisdiction doctrine *see* universal
          jurisdiction doctrine
     see also prosecution of torture suspects
Iraq 167
     torture by US and British agents in 33–4, 68,
          404, 425–6, 427–8, 570
          Abu Ghraib scandal 24, 36, 420
     transfer of prisoners to Iraqi custody 352,
          353
IRRD (interrogation-related regulatory decline)
     model 444
Israel 48, 136, 414
     force-feeding of hunger strikers 408, 409
     interrogational torture by
          methods used 413, 414, 444, 561–3
          ticking bomb justification 10, 14, 26,
               27–30, 562–3
Istanbul Protocol (medico-legal evidence of
     torture guidelines) 7, 49, 52, 85–6, 160,
     451, 455–6, 467–8
     clinical evaluations of alleged torture
          459–64
          in primary healthcare encounters
               468–70, 472–7
     development, recognition and applications
          456–9, 465
     implementation of 470–71
     limitations and misuse of 464–5
     torture method categories 410–11
     training on 172, 466, 471, 490
     updates to 171, 465–6
     see also medical treatment and ethics
Italy 187, 189, 352, 354, 382, 570
     migration control 123, 192–3, 350, 351
ius cogens see *jus cogens* status of torture
     prohibition

Jamaica 120, 212

Japan 396, 415
Jaranson, James M. 497
Jefferson, Andrew 69
Jensen, Steffen 69
Jonas, Kai J. 441
journalists, harassment of 165, 216, 219, 222
judges, harassment of 165, 219
judicial torture 35
     corporal punishment as criminal sanction
          119, 120, 240, 243, 246, 403
     death penalty *see* death penalty
     non-admissibility of torture evidence *see*
          non-admissibility of torture evidence
     non-admissibility of uncorroborated
          confessions 50–51, 58, 574
     see also police detention
jus cogens status of torture prohibition 1, 294,
     297, 360, 373, 375, 378
     foreign state immunities, *jus cogens* rebuttal
          380–83, 387, 389
justifying torture
     legitimate purpose and proportionality
          assessments 111, 118, 384
     ticking bomb scenario *see* ticking bomb
          scenario
juvenile detention 170, 210, 212, 214–15, 242,
     480

Kambanda, Jean 300
Kathmandu, torture study 71, 72, 73–4
Kaufman-Osborn, Timothy 24
Keatley, Eva 412
Keitner, Chimene 390
Kenya 15, 71–2, 73, 74, 254, 255, 257, 305–6
Khalili, Laleh 24
Kiernan, Victor G. 35
Klein, Naomi 17, 33–4
Kooijmans, Peter 162
Kosovo 508
Kubark manual (CIA, 1963) 433, 436
Kyrgyzstan 48, 49, 50–51, 122–3, 167–8, 172–3

Landau Commission of Inquiry, Israel 27–8
Langbein, John 68
Lauterpacht, Hersch 258
law and practice gap 52–3, 55–6
Lazreg, Marnia 37
Lebanon 142, 143, 146, 273, 568
legal representation of police detainees 48–9, 57,
     152, 573
legitimate purpose assessments 111, 118
Leo, Richard A. 444
Les Centurions (Lartéguy) 23, 41
Lesotho 140, 246, 249
lethal force 112, 117–18, 427–8